W9-BEO-010

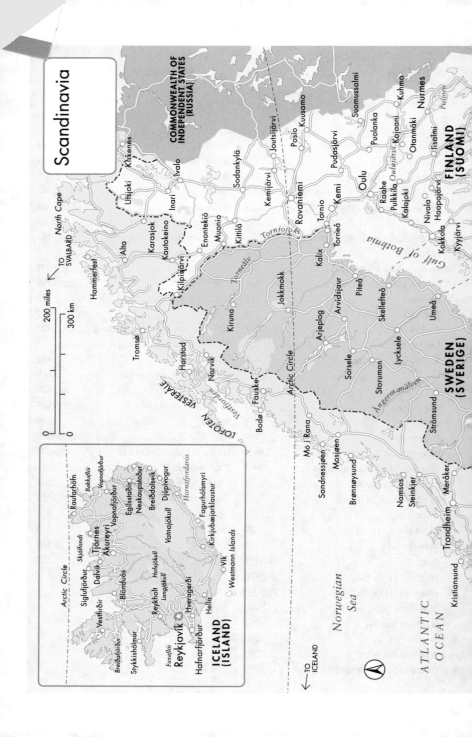

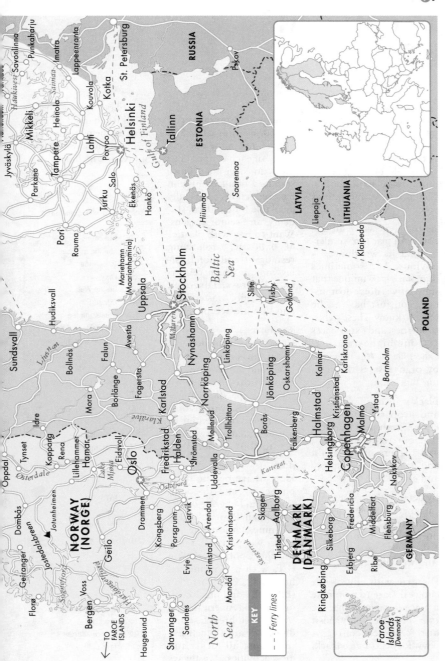

ABOUT THIS BOOK

Our Ratings

Sometimes you find terrific travel experiences and sometimes they just find you. But usually the burden is on you to select the right combination of experiences. That's where our ratings come in.

As travelers we've all discovered a place so wonderful that its worthiness is obvious. And sometimes that place is so unique that superlatives don't do it justice: you just have to be there to know. These sights, properties, and experiences get our highest rating, Fodor's Choice ★, indicated by orange stars throughout this book.

Black stars highlight sights and properties we deem Highly Recommended ★, places that our writers, editors, and readers praise again and again for consistency and excellence.

By default, there's another category: any place we include in this book is by definition worth your time, unless we say otherwise. And we will.

Disagree with any of our choices? Care to nominate a place or suggest that we rate one more highly? Visit our feedback center at www.fodors.com/feedback.

Budget Well

Hotel and restaurant price categories from ¢ to $$$$ are defined in the opening pages of each chapter. For attractions, we always give standard adult admission fees; reductions are usually available for children, students, and senior citizens. Want to pay with plastic? AE, D, DC, MC, V following restaurant and hotel listings indicate whether American Express, Discover, Diner's Club, MasterCard, and Visa are accepted.

Restaurants

Unless we state otherwise, restaurants are open for lunch and dinner daily. We mention dress only when there's a specific requirement and reservations only when they're essential or not accepted—it's always best to book ahead.

Hotels

Hotels have private bath, phone, TV, and air-conditioning and operate on the European Plan (aka EP, meaning without meals), unless we specify that they use the Continental Plan (CP, with a Continental breakfast), Breakfast Plan (BP, with a full breakfast), or Modified American Plan (MAP, with breakfast and dinner) or are all-inclusive (including all meals and most activities). We always

list facilities but not whether you'll be charged an extra fee to use them, so when pricing accommodations, find out what's included.

Many Listings

★	Fodor's Choice
★	Highly recommended
⊠	Physical address
↔	Directions
⌂	Mailing address
☎	Telephone
🖷	Fax
⊕	On the Web
✉	E-mail
🎫	Admission fee
☉	Open/closed times
▶	Start of walk/itinerary
Ⓜ	Metro stations
🖯	Credit cards

Hotels & Restaurants

🏨	Hotel
🛏	Number of rooms
⚘	Facilities
⦿⊖⦿	Meal plans
✕	Restaurant
⚷	Reservations
🏛	Dress code
⚲	Smoking
⟨⟩	BYOB
✕🏨	Hotel with restaurant that warrants a visit

Outdoors

🏌	Golf
⛺	Camping

Other

☺	Family-friendly
🔒	Contact information
⇨	See also
⊠	Branch address
☞	Take note

WHAT'S
WHERE

DENMARK

The Kingdom of Denmark dapples the Baltic Sea in an archipelago of some 450 islands and the arc of one peninsula. Copenhagen is Scandinavia's largest city (population 1.5 million). For almost 600 years Copenhagen has been the seat of the oldest kingdom in the world. Coziness is a Danish trait, and Copenhagen has a lot of it. Bicycles roll alongside cars in the narrow streets, and a handful of skyscrapers are tucked away amid cafés, canals, and quaint old homes. But don't let the low-slung skyline fool you: downtown Copenhagen is a sophisticated cultural hub with a wealth of attractions, such as Tivoli Gardens.

The island of Zealand, the largest of the Danish isles, is the country's most convenient and popular bit of countryside. North of Copenhagen are royal castles (including Helsingør's Kronborg of Hamlet fame), ritzy beach towns, and top-notch museums.

Funen, the smaller of the country's two main islands, is the birthplace of Hans Christian Andersen. It's no wonder this area inspired many fairy tales: coastline and lush stretches of gardens are punctuated by manor houses, beech glades, castles, swan ponds, and thatch-roof houses. In the south is the Egeskov Slot, a well-preserved Renaissance castle that even has a moat. Myriad islands speckle the sea south of Funen, including verdant Ærø. Artists have flocked here for decades, which makes for a more bohemian atmosphere.

Jutland, Denmark's western peninsula, shares its southern border with Germany. South Jutland is pastoral, with smaller, quiet beaches on the eastern side. The hub of central Jutland is Billund, home to Legoland. In North Jutland, Aalborg is the biggest city and one with lots of vitality. At the northernmost point stands Skagen, a luminous, dune-covered site that attracts art lovers, artists, and those seeking a quieter seaside vacation.

The island of Bornholm sits off the coast of Sweden and has a temperate climate that distinguishes it from the rest of Denmark. Its old-fashioned towns and exuberant natural beauty have earned it the title of Pearl of the Baltic. This off-the-beaten-path destination doesn't have as many amenities as Jutland or Zealand.

WHAT'S
WHERE

NORWAY

Norway, roughly 400,000 square km (155,000 square mi), is about the same size as California. Approximately 30% of this long, narrow country is covered with clear lakes, lush forests, and rugged mountains. Western Norway, bordered by the Norwegian Sea and the Atlantic Ocean, is the fabled land of the fjords—few places on Earth can match its power and splendor. Bergen, often hailed as the "Fjord Capital of Norway," is the second-largest city in the country. The cobblestone streets, well-preserved buildings at the Bryggen, and seven mountains that surround the city all add to its storybook charm.

Eastern Norway, bordered by Sweden, and by Finland and Russia to the north, is punctuated by rolling hills, abundant valleys, and fresh lakes—much more subdued than the landscape of the west. Rising from the shores of the Oslofjord is the capital of Norway—Oslo. With a population of about a half million, Oslo is a friendly, manageable city.

If you follow the coast south, you'll come to Kristiansand, one of Sørlandet's (the Southland's) leading cities. Sørlandet is known for its long stretches of unspoiled, uncrowded beach. Stavanger, farther west, is one of the most cosmopolitan cities in Scandinavia—its oil and gas industry draws people from around the globe.

Halfway between Oslo and Bergen lies Hardangervidda (Hardanger Plateau), Norway's largest national park. At the foot of the plateau is Geilo, one of the country's most popular ski resorts. Almost directly north is the bustling city of Trondheim. From here, a thin expanse of land stretches up to the Nordkapp (North Cape). Known as the Land of the Midnight Sun, this region is marked with exquisite landscapes: glaciers, fjords, and rocky coasts.

SWEDEN

In Sweden, ultramodern cities give way to lush forests, and modern western European democracy coexists with strong affection for a monarchy. With 410,934 square km (158,662 square mi; slightly larger than California) for only 9 million residents, almost all have room to live as they choose.

Stockholm, one of Europe's most beautiful capitals, is built on 14 small islands. Bustling, skyscraper-lined boulevards are a short walk from twisting medieval streets here. South of the city, in the densely forested Småland province, you'll find fine crystal glassware by Kosta, Boda, and Orrefors. North of the

capital, the Bothnian Coast is a rugged and windswept finger of land that runs up the eastern side of Sweden. The grand 19th-century towns that form a chain along the coast testify to the wealth that fishing and the paper and wood industries brought to the country.

Sweden's second-largest city, Göteborg, refuses to take its status lying down. Historically Göteborg has used its accessibility to the rest of the world to good effect: a Viking port in the 11th century, today it is Scandinavia's busiest shipping city. Among the ornate 19th-century stone edifices, tree-lined boulevards, and stunning parks are world-class galleries, museums, and cultural venues. Exploring the Göta Canal on Göteborg's outskirts is the perfect way to spend a few days. North of Göteborg, the Bohuslän region has a rocky coastline dotted with attractive fishing villages.

Skåne, the country's southernmost province, along with the other southern provinces, form a different Sweden. Part of Denmark until 1658, the area has its own dialect and is proud of its independent spirit. Lush farmland, coastal headlands, miles of golden beaches, and historic castles abound. If Swedes have a spiritual home, it is Dalarna, the central region of Sweden, and the focal point of most of the country's myth, symbolism, and tradition. Here, among the forests, mountains, lakes, and red-painted wooden farmhouses, you can spend a midsummer feasting on herring. The area is focused around the beautiful Lake Siljan.

In a country known for its wide open spaces, Northern Sweden, one of the least-populated places on Earth, still stands out. A traveler in these parts is more likely to encounter a peacefully munching elk than a fellow human being.

FINLAND

Finland is one of the world's northernmost countries, with its entire Lapland region above the Arctic Circle. It's a country of beautiful scenery and strong, spirited citizens. Sweden and Russia fought over the land for centuries, but the Finns themselves are neither Scandinavian nor Slavic. Finnish, a non–Indo-European language, is closely linked to Estonian and more distantly to Hungarian. Helsinki, the capital since 1812, is built on peninsulas and islands along the Baltic coast. Stunning architecture abounds, from 19th-century neoclassical buildings to sleek, modern high-rises.

WHAT'S
WHERE

In the southwest lies Turku, the former capital. Founded more than 750 years ago, the city remains a busy harbor, from which you can sail for the rugged and fascinating Åland Islands. Encompassing some 6,500 of the more than 30,000 islands that form the magnificent archipelago along Finland's coastline, the Ålands are home to many families that fish or run small farms.

Eastern and central Finland are dimpled with nearly 200,000 lakes, most fringed with tiny cabins—Finnish vacation institutions. Amid the many delightful small towns of the Lakelands, Savonlinna is hugged by gigantic Lake Saimaa and is worth a visit for its water-bound scenery and cultural life—especially the Savonlinna Opera festival in July.

Tampere, the largest city in the region, was famous for its textile industry, but now it's a busy university city, with a variety of festivals throughout the year, including an international short film festival in March. Lapland, north of the Arctic Circle, remains unspoiled wilderness. The area has become more accessible, but nature is the star attraction: reindeer, great forests, crystal-clear streams, and the midnight sun's reflection on a lake's dark water.

ICELAND

Iceland is Europe's westernmost outpost, 800 km (500 mi) from Scotland, its nearest European neighbor. More than 80% of its 103,000 square km (40,000 square mi) remains uninhabited and uninhabitable. It is home to Europe's largest glacier, Vatnajökull, and the namesake of all spouting hot springs, Geysir. The thundering Dettifoss is also Europe's most powerful waterfall.

In this isolated land, nature is inextricably linked to the Icelandic psyche. Well over half of the population will cheerfully tell you of their belief in the Huldufólk (Hidden People)—elves and other creatures that live in the rocks and hills around the country. At the same time, however, Iceland is one of the world's most modern societies, with almost ubiquitous use of the Internet and mobile phones and a 100% literacy rate.

Reykjavík, the world's northernmost capital, is home to half the nation's 290,000 citizens. Along with most of the island, it enjoys pollution-free warmth from geothermal hot springs, which also heat many popular swimming pools. These hot springs gave Reykjavík its name, which means "smoky bay."

There's a thriving arts scene, and Reykjavík's vibrant nightlife is legendary in Europe and North America. Þingvellir, a national park and, as site of the original Alþingi (the world's oldest functioning parliament, founded in AD 930), is only an hour's drive from Reykjavík. The eerie waters of the Blue Lagoon are also only a short trip from the capital. In the north, Akureyri, Iceland's second-largest city, makes a great base to visit other attractions like Dettifoss waterfall. In the south you'll find black-sand beaches, glaciers, and an ice lagoon, Jökulsárlón.

QUINTESSENTIAL SCANDINAVIA

Beer & Aquavit

Aquavit is a Scandinavian liquor of about 40% alcohol by volume. Its name comes from aqua vitae (Latin for "water of life"). Like other liquors made in Scandinavia, it is distilled from potatoes or grains and is flavored with herbs such as caraway seeds, cumin, dill, fennel, or coriander. Aquavit, or akvavit, is an acquired taste. It's usually drunk as a shot, or as the Danes say, a "snaps," during meals—especially during the appetizer course—along with a chaser of beer.

There's a renewed interest in the Danish national drink: beer (or øl in Danish). Danes are rarely short of an excuse for a beer celebration, and Christmas and Easter are no exceptions, when both Carlsberg and Tuborg breweries release special holiday beers. Microbreweries have popped up all over the country, and even in Copenhagen, where Carlsberg beer was founded in the early 19th century, loyalty for that stalwart

is wavering in favor of newer flavors and brands. Independent microbreweries in Copenhagen alone include Nørrebro Bryghus, Bryggeriet Apollo, Brøckhouse, and Færgekroen (in Tivoli). Denmark now has more breweries per capita than any other European country.

Design

If there's one word associated with Sweden around the world, it is *design*. Even the most unobservant of visitors can't fail to notice a design sensibility that seems to pervade every corner of the nation; from the airport you land in to the furnishings in your hotel room to the table setting in the restaurant, most things Swedish have an air of the simply fabulous. Focused product design started early in Sweden with the graceful curves of the Viking ships. The 20th-century Swedish utilitarian vision of society cemented the nation's

aesthetic approach. As Sweden prospered, and as more homes were built, Swedish designers made objects in which functionality was blended with a guarded, well-planned modern aesthetic. The rest of Sweden quickly followed suit, and the Swedish consumer was bombarded with practical but seductive objects, from Ericsson phones and Electrolux refrigerators to SAAB cars and affordable IKEA practicality. Design also encompasses many facets of Danish life, like lighting, electronics, and everyday household items. The Danish design aesthetic itself is simple and inventive, marked by clean lines. Even the local grocery store will impress you with "Made in Denmark" kitchen items that somehow look so much better than the fare sold back home.

Saunas

An authentic Finnish sauna is an obligatory experience, and not hard to find: there are 1.6 million saunas in this country of just over 5 million people—even the parliament has its own sauna. The traditional Finnish sauna—which involves relaxing on wooden benches, pouring water onto hot coals, and swatting your neighbor's back with birch branches—is an integral part of cabin life and now city life, as apartments are outfitted with small saunas in their bathrooms. Almost every hotel has at least one sauna available free of charge, usually at standard times in the morning or evening for men and women to use separately. Larger hotels offer a private sauna in the higher-class rooms and suites. Public saunas (with swimsuits required) are becoming increasingly popular, even in winter, when sauna goers jump into the water through a large hole in the ice (called *avantouinti*). Public swimming pools are also equipped with saunas that can be used at no extra charge. For information, contact the Finnish Sauna Society.

GREAT ITINERARY

SAND, SURF & SHIPS, SCANDINAVIA-STYLE

Scandinavia is defined by water. Glaciers, rivers, and sea tides determine the geography; oceans shape the history and culture. Tiny Denmark, for example, would probably not exist as a country today, except for the way it sticks up like a cork in the bottleneck entrance to the Baltic Sea. Its shape makes it strategically important for such major shipping and trading countries as England, which has both attacked and defended the country over trading issues during the past 400 years. What better way, then, to see the land of the Vikings than by water?

Denmark: 3 days

Fly to Copenhagen. Explore the city and its waterways: Nyhavn's tall ships and myriad restaurants; Christianshavn, with its encircling moat and canals reflecting colorful old buildings; and the canal-ringed palace of Christiansborg, where you can visit the Danish Parliament and the royal reception rooms. Enjoy the twinkling lights and happy atmosphere of Tivoli from mid-April through mid-September and its frostier but less-crowded attributes several weeks before Christmas. Take a harbor cruise, passing *Den Lille Havfrue* (*The Little Mermaid*), perched on her rock. Sun on the beaches north of town or sail the Øresund—maybe even all the way around Sjælland. You'll love the castle of Frederiksborg, set in its lake a little less than an hour north of Copenhagen, and the Karen Blixen Museum at Rungstedlund. Continue by air to Stockholm.

Sweden: 6 Days

Beautiful Stockholm is made up of 14 islands surrounded by sparkling water, clean enough for fishing and swimming even in

the city center. You can take ferries all around town and out into the enchanting archipelago, with its 24,000 islands. Don't miss the picturesque Old Town; the museum for the salvaged 17th-century warship *Vasa*; or Skansen, the world's oldest open-air museum.

From Stockholm, take the train across Sweden to Göteborg, where you can explore the west-coast beaches warmed by the Gulf Stream. Try sea fishing or windsurfing, and visit the 17th-century fortress of Elfsborg, which guards the harbor entrance. Take a ferry to Oslo.

Norway: 5 days

In Oslo, visit the Viking Ship and Kon-Tiki museums and the fabulous Vigeland sculpture park. The Bergen Railway will carry you across the roof of Norway in 6½ dramatic hours. If you can spare an extra day, stop in Myrdal for a side trip on the Flåm Railway and a short cruise on the beautiful Aurland Fjord before continuing to Bergen. Here you can explore Bryggen, a collection of reconstructed houses dating from the Hansa period in the 14th century, the famous fish market, and the funicular. View the magnificent, ever-changing Norwegian coastline aboard a Coastal Express ship to Trondheim, where you can fly to Oslo or Copenhagen, then home.

Bornholm & Gotland

Alternate days. If you already know Copenhagen and Stockholm, consider visiting the beautiful islands of Bornholm in Denmark or Sweden's Gotland. Bornholm is graced by beaches perfect for surfing and

sailing; excellent golf courses; one of the largest castle ruins in Scandinavia; and some memorable architecture, including the famous round churches from the 12th and 13th centuries. You can reach it by ferry from Copenhagen or from Ystad, in southern Sweden, bringing your car if you like. Alternatively, you can fly to Rønne, the capital of Bornholm, directly from Copenhagen in about 30 minutes.

Gotland is the largest island in the Baltic, with peaceful little towns and fishing villages, and a striking capital, Visby, with a medieval flavor and a well-preserved city wall dating from the 14th and 15th centuries. "Medieval Week" in early August is celebrated with mummers, knights, tournaments, and lots of other special attractions. Ferries sail from Stockholm and several other Swedish ports.

WHEN TO GO

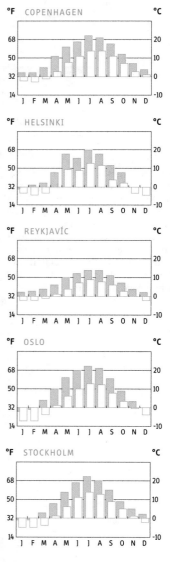

The Scandinavian tourist season peaks in June, July, and August, when daytime temperatures are often in the 70s (21°C to 26°C) and sometimes rise into the 80s (27°C to 32°C). Detailed temperature charts are below. In general, the weather is not overly warm, and a brisk breeze and brief rainstorms are possible anytime. Nights can be chilly, even in summer.

Visit in summer if you want to experience the delightfully long summer days. In June, the sun rises in Copenhagen at 4 AM and sets at 11 PM. Daylight lasts even longer farther north, making it possible to continue your sightseeing into the balmy evening. Many attractions extend their hours in summer, and many shut down altogether when summer ends. Fall, spring, and even winter are pleasant, despite the area's reputation for gloom. The days become shorter quickly, but the sun casts a golden light not seen farther south. On dark days, fires and candlelight will warm you indoors.

The Gulf Stream warms Denmark, the western coast of Norway, and Iceland, making winters in these areas similar to those in London. Even the harbor of Narvik, far to the north in Norway, remains ice-free year-round. Away from the protection of the Gulf Stream, however, northern Norway, Sweden, and Finland experience very cold, clear weather that attracts skiers; even Stockholm's harbor, well south in Sweden but facing the Baltic Sea, freezes over completely.

Climate

Below are average daily maximum and minimum temperatures for major Scandinavian cities.

F Forecasts **Weather Channel Connection** ⊕ www.weather. com.

SMART TRAVEL TIPS

Finding out about your destination before you leave home means you won't spend time organizing everyday minutiae once you've arrived. You'll be more streetwise when you hit the ground as well, better prepared to explore the aspects of Scandinavia that drew you here in the first place. The organizations in this section can provide information to supplement this guide; contact them for up-to-the-minute details, and consult the A to Z sections that end each chapter for facts on the various topics as they relate to the countries of Scandinavia. Happy landings!

AIR TRAVEL

CARRIERS

🛪 Major Airlines **Air France** ☎ 800/237-2747 🌐 www.airfrance.com to Copenhagen, Helsinki, Oslo, and Stockholm. **American** ☎ 800/433-7300 🌐 www.aa.com to Copenhagen, Helsinki, Oslo, and Stockholm. **British Airways** ☎ 800/247-9297 🌐 www.ba.com to Copenhagen, Helsinki, Oslo, and Stockholm. **Delta** ☎ 800/221-1212 🌐 www.delta.com to Copenhagen, Oslo, and Stockholm. **Finnair** ☎ 800/950-5000 🌐 www.finnair.com to Helsinki, Stockholm, Copenhagen, and Oslo. **Icelandair** ☎ 800/223-5500 🌐 www.icelandair.com. **Lufthansa** ☎ 800/399-5838 🌐 www.lufthansa.comto Copenhagen, Helsinki, Oslo, and Stockholm. **SAS** ☎ 800/221-2350 🌐 www.scandinavian.net.

CUTTING COSTS

The **SAS Visit Scandinavia/Europe Air Pass** offers up to eight flight coupons for one-way travel within and between Scandinavian cities (and participating European, Baltic, and Russian cities such as Barcelona, Frankfurt, Paris, St. Petersburg, Tallin, and London). Most one-way tickets for domestic travel within each Scandinavian country cost $65; one-way fares between Scandinavian countries are usually $75, unless you are venturing into northern Lapland (these flights range from $115 to $200). These passes can only be bought in conjunction with a round-trip ticket between North America and Europe on SAS and must be used within three months of arrival. Contact SAS for information.

The least expensive airfares to Scandinavia are often priced for round-trip travel and must usually be purchased in advance. Airlines generally allow you to change your return date for a fee; most low-fare tickets, however, are nonrefundable. It's smart to call a number of airlines and check the Internet; when you are quoted a good price, book it on the spot—the same fare may not be available the next day, or even the next hour. Always check different routings and look into using alternate airports. Also, price off-peak and red-eye flights, which may be significantly less expensive than others. Travel agents, especially low-fare specialists (⇨ Travel Agencies), are helpful.

Consolidators are another good source. They buy tickets for scheduled flights at reduced rates from the airlines, then sell them at prices that beat the best fare available directly from the airlines. (Many also offer reduced car-rental and hotel rates.) Sometimes you can even get your money back if you need to return the ticket. Carefully read the fine print detailing penalties for changes and cancellations, purchase the ticket with a credit card, and confirm your consolidator reservation with the airline.

🛪 Consolidators **AirlineConsolidator.com** ☎ 888/468-5385 ⊕ www.airlineconsolidator.com; for international tickets. **Best Fares** ☎ 800/880-1234 ⊕ www.bestfares.com; $59.90 annual membership. **Cheap Tickets** ☎ 800/377-1000 or 800/652-4327 ⊕ www.cheaptickets.com. **Expedia** ☎ 800/397-3342 or 404/728-8787 ⊕ www.expedia.com. **Hotwire** ☎ 866/468-9473 or 920/330-9418 ⊕ www.hotwire.com. **Now Voyager Travel** ☎ 212/459-1616 ⊕ www.nowvoyagertravel.com. **Onetravel.com** ⊕ www.onetravel.com. **Orbitz** ☎ 888/656-4546 ⊕ www.orbitz.com. **Priceline.com** ⊕ www.priceline.com. **Travelocity** ☎ 888/709-5983, 877/282-2925 in Canada, 0870/111-7061 in the U.K. ⊕ www.travelocity.com.

🛪 Courier Resources **Air Courier Association/Cheaptrips.com** ☎ 800/211-5119 ⊕ www.aircourier.org or www.cheaptrips.com; $20 annual membership. **Courier Travel** ☎ 303/570-7586 🖷 313/625-6106 ⊕ www.couriertravel.org; $50 annual membership. **International Association of Air Travel Couriers** ☎ 308/632-3273 🖷 308/632-8267 ⊕ www.courier.org; $45 annual membership. **Now Voyager Travel** ✉ 1717 Avenue M, Brooklyn, NY 11230 ☎ 212/459-1616 🖷 718/504-4762 ⊕ www.nowvoyagertravel.com.

🛪 Discount Passes **FlightPass**, EuropebyAir, ☎ 888/387-2479 ⊕ www.europebyair.com. **SAS Air Passes**, Scandinavian Airlines, ☎ 800/221-2350, 0870/6072-7727 in the U.K., 1300/727-707 in Australia ⊕ www.scandinavian.net.

FLYING TIMES

Flying time from New York to Reykjavìk is 5½ hours; to Copenhagen, 7¾ hours; to Stockholm, 8 hours; to Oslo, 7½ hours; to Helsinki, 8 hours. From Los Angeles to Copenhagen, flying time is 9¾ hours; to Helsinki, 11¼ hours. From London's Heathrow Airport, flying time to Helsinki is 3 hours; to Stockholm, 2¼ hours; to Reykjavìk, 3 hours. From Sydney and major cities in New Zealand, the flight to any Scandinavian country will be more than 20 hours, and will require at least one transfer.

HOW TO COMPLAIN

If your baggage goes astray or your flight goes awry, complain right away. Most carriers require that you **file a claim immediately.** The Aviation Consumer Protection Division of the Department of Transportation publishes *Fly-Rights*, which discusses airlines and consumer issues and is available online. You can also find articles and information on mytravelrights.com, the Web site of the nonprofit Consumer Travel Rights Center.

🛪 Airline Complaints **Aviation Consumer Protection Division** ✉ U.S. Department of Transportation, Office of Aviation Enforcement and Proceedings, C-75, Room 4107, 400 7th St. SW, Washington, DC 20590 ☎ 202/366-2220 ⊕ airconsumer.ost.dot.gov. **Federal Aviation Administration Consumer Hotline** ✉ For inquiries: FAA, 800 Independence Ave. SW, Washington, DC 20591 ☎ 800/322-7873 ⊕ www.faa.gov.

WITHIN SCANDINAVIA

Scandinavia is larger than it looks on a map, and many native travelers choose to fly between the capital cities, using trains and buses for domestic travel. Flying times between Copenhagen, Helsinki, Oslo, and Stockholm range between one and two hours; a direct flight from Copenhagen or Stockholm to Reykjavìk is approximately three hours.

If you are traveling from south to north in Norway, Sweden, or Finland, flying is often a necessity: Stavanger in southern Norway is as close to Rome, Italy, as it is to the northern tip of Norway.

For international travelers, one or two stopovers can often be purchased more cheaply along with an international ticket. Icelandair, which connects all of the Scandinavian capitals with North America, gives the option to extend a layover in Reykjavík for up to three days at no extra charge; Icelandair also arranges Fly and Drive specials, which offer discounts on car rental and hotel fees if booking a flight to one of the Scandinavian capitals.

The cheapest tickets that SAS sells are round-trip, include a Saturday-night layover, and must be bought within Scandinavia three weeks ahead of time. Low-price round-trip weekend excursions from one Scandinavian capital to another (minimum three-day stay) can be bought one day in advance from SAS.

AIRPORTS

Major gateways to Scandinavia include Denmark's **Kastrup International Airport,** 8 km (5 mi) southeast of Copenhagen; Finland's **Helsinki-Vantaa International Airport,** 20 km (14 mi) north of Helsinki; Iceland's **Keflavík International Airport,** 50 km (31 mi) southwest of Reykjavík; Norway's **Gardermoen Airport,** about 53 km (33 mi) northeast of Oslo; and Sweden's **Arlanda International Airport,** 42 km (26 mi) north of Stockholm.

🛪 Airport Information **Arlanda International Airport** ☎ 46/87976100 ⊕ www.lfv.se. **Gardermoen Airport** ☎ 47/815-50-250 ⊕ www.osl.no. **Helsinki-Vantaa International Airport** ☎ 358/200-14636, €0.57 per min ⊕ www.ilmailulaitos.com. **Kastrup International Airport** ☎ 45/32-31-24-47 ⊕ www.cph.dk. **Keflavík International Airport** ☎ 354/425-0600 for airport information, 011-354-425-0200 for flight information (Icelandair) ⊕ www.keflavikairport.com.

BOAT & FERRY TRAVEL

Taking a ferry isn't only fun, it's often necessary in Scandinavia. Many companies arrange package trips, some offering a rental car and hotel accommodations as part of the deal. The word "ferry" can be deceptive; generally, the ferries are more like small-scale cruise ships, with several dining rooms, sleeping quarters, shopping, pool and sauna, and entertainment.

Ferry crossings often last overnight. The trip between Copenhagen and Oslo, for example, takes approximately 16 hours; most lines leave at about 5 PM and arrive about 9 the next morning. The direct cruise between Stockholm and Helsinki takes 12 hours, usually leaving at about 6 PM and arriving the next morning at 9. Trips from Germany to Oslo and Helsinki generally take about 20 hours; crossings to Reykjavík from Bergen tend to last about two days (25 hours to the Faroe Islands, and another 24 hours to Iceland). The shortest ferry route runs between Helsingør, Denmark, and Helsingborg, Sweden; it takes only 20 minutes.

CAR FERRIES

Travel by car in Scandinavia often necessitates travel by ferry. Some well-known vehicle and passenger ferries run between Helsingør, Denmark, and Helsingborg, Sweden; between Copenhagen and Göteborg, Sweden; and between Stockholm, Sweden, and Helsinki, Finland. Taking a car on the Helsingør/Helsingborg ferry costs about SKr 290 (about $37 or £21) one-way.

Transporting a car between Stockholm and Helsinki costs about € 75 during high season and € 55 during low season (about $90 and $66 or £52 and £37). Round-trip fares are cheaper, or look for packages that combine a cabin, and car and passenger transport, in one price. The Øresund Runt pass (for crossing between the Copenhagen-Malmö bridge one way, and passage on the Helsingborg and Helsingør ferry the other way) costs only SKr 450 (about $57 or £32). The pass is available through ScandLines.

FARES & SCHEDULES

🛥 Boat & Ferry Information **Color Line AS** ✉ Box 1422 Vika, N-0115 Oslo, Norway ☎ 47/810-00-811 🖷 47/22-83-07-76 ⊕ www.colorline.no. **Scand-Lines** 🖪 Scandlines Danmark AS, Færgestationsvej 8, DK-3000 Helsingør, Denmark ☎ 45/33-15-15-15

🚂 45/33-15-10-20 ✉ Knutpunkten 43, S-252 78 Helsingborg, Sweden ☎ 46/42186100 🚂 46/42186049 🌐 www.scandlines.com.

FERRIES FROM ENGLAND

The chief operator between England and many points within Scandinavia, Holland, and Germany is DFDS Seaways, with ships connecting Harwich to Esbjerg, Denmark; and Newcastle to Kristiansand, Norway, and Amsterdam. Fjord Line offers the only direct service from England to Bergen and northern Norway.

🗺 Major Operators **DFDS Seaways** ✉ Sundkrogsgade 11, DK-2100 Copenhagen, Denmark ☎ 45/33-42-33-42 🚂 45/33-42-33-41 ✉ DFDS Seaways Travel Centre, Scandinavia House, Parkeston Quay, Harwich, Essex, U.K. CO12 4QG ☎ 44/8705-333-000 🚂 44/1255-244-382 ✉ DFDS Seaways USA Inc., c/o SeaEurope 6801 Lake Work Rd., Suite 107, Lake Worth, FL 333467 ☎ 800/533-3755 🚂 561/432-2550 ✉ Box 8895, Scandiahamnen, S-402 72 Göteborg, Sweden ☎ 46/31650610 🌐 www.dfdsseaways.com or www.seaeurope.com. **Fjord Line** 🏠 Skoltegrunnskaien, Box 7250, N-5020 Bergen, Norway ☎ 47/55-54-87-00 🚂 47/55-54-87-01 ✉ International Ferry Terminal, Royal Quays, North Shields, Tyne & Wear, NE29 6EE, Newcastle, U.K. ☎ 44/191-296-1313 🚂 44/191-296-1540 🌐 www.fjordline.co.uk or www.fjordline.com.

PLYING SCANDINAVIAN WATERS

Connections from Denmark to Norway and Sweden are available through DFDS and the Stena Line. Fjord Line sails along the magnificent west coast of Norway. Connections to the Faroe Islands and Iceland from Norway and Denmark are available through the Smyril Line. Silja Line and Viking Line offer a variety of cruises to Finland, with departures from Stockholm to Mariehamn in the Åland archipelago, Turku (Åbo), and Helsinki (Helsingfors), and crossings from Helsinki to Talinn, Estonia, and St. Petersburg, Russia.

🗺 Major Operators **DFDS Seaways** (➪ Ferries from England). **Fjord Line** (➪ Ferries from England). **Silja Line** ✉ Mannerheimintie 2, 00100 Helsinki, Finland ☎ 358/9-18041 🚂 358/9-1804279 ✉ Kungsgatan 2, S-111 43 Stockholm, Sweden ☎ 46/86663512 or 46/8222140 🚂 46/86119162 or 46/

92316066 ✉ C/o DFDS Seaways, Scandinavia House, Parkeston Quay, Harwich, Essex, U.K. England CO12 4QG ☎ 44/1255-240-240 🚂 44/255-244-382 ✉ c/o SeaEurope Holidays, 6801 Lake Worth Rd., Suite 107, Lake Worth, FL 33467 ☎ 561/432-4100 or 800/533-3755, ext. 114 🚂 561/432-2550 🌐 www.silja.com. **Smyril Line** ✉ J. Brockgøta 37, Box 370, FO-110 Tùrshavn, Faroe Islands ☎ 298/34-59-00 🚂 298/34-59-50 ✉ Slottsgaten 1, Box 4135 Dreggen, N-5835 Bergen, Norway ☎ 47/55-59-65-20 🚂 47/55-59-65-30 🌐 www.smyril-line.com. **Stena Line** ✉ Trafikhamnen, DK-9900 Frederikshavn, Denmark ☎ 45/96-20-02-00 🚂 45/96-20-02-80 ✉ PB 764, Sentrum, N-0106 Oslo, Norway ☎ 47/23-17-91-00 🚂 47/23-17-90-60 ✉ Stena Line AB, S-405 19 Göteborg, Sweden ☎ 46/317040000 🚂 46/31858595 🌐 www.stenaline.com. **Viking Line** ✉ Mannerheimintie 14, 00100 Helsinki, Finland ☎ 358/9-12351 🚂 358/9-647075 🌐 www.vikingline.fi.

BUS TRAVEL

Bus tours can be effective for smaller regions within Norway, Sweden, Finland, and Denmark, but all have excellent train systems, which offer much greater coverage in less time than buses. Buses do, however, tend to be a less-expensive mode of transport in Scandinavia, and are necessary if you're traveling without a car between smaller towns in Lapland, the Danish islands, and Iceland. Detailed information on bus routes is available through local tourist offices.

CUTTING COSTS

Eurolines (🌐 www.eurolines.com) offers 15-, 30-, and 60-day passes for unlimited travel between Gothenburg, Sweden, Copenhagen, and Oslo, and more than 20 destinations throughout Europe.

CAR RENTAL

Rates in Stockholm begin at $70 a day and $275 a week for a manual economy car without air-conditioning and with unlimited mileage. Rates in Oslo begin at $70 a day and $350 a week. Rates in Helsinki begin at $80 a day and $350 a week, and in Copenhagen, car rentals can begin at $80 a day and $350 a week. This does not include tax, which is 25% in Sweden and Denmark, 24% in Norway and Iceland,

and 22% in Finland. A service charge is usually added, which ranges $15–$25.

🚗 Major Agencies Alamo ☎ 800/522-9696 ⊕ www.alamo.com. **Avis** ☎ 800/331-1084, 800/879-2847 in Canada, 0870/606-0100 in the U.K., 02/9353-9000 in Australia, 09/526-2847 in New Zealand ⊕ www.avis.com. **Budget** ☎ 800/472-3325, 800/268-8900 in Canada, 1300/794-344 in Australia, 0800/283-438 in New Zealand ⊕ www.budget.com. **Dollar** ☎ 800/800-6000, 0800/085-4578 in the U.K. ⊕ www.dollar.com. **Hertz** ☎ 800/654-3001, 800/263-0600 in Canada, 0870/844-8844 in the U.K., 02/9669-2444 in Australia, 09/256-8690 in New Zealand ⊕ www.hertz.com. **National Car Rental** ☎ 800/227-7368 ⊕ www.nationalcar.com.

CUTTING COSTS

For a good deal, book through a travel agent who will shop around. Do look into wholesalers, companies that do not own fleets but rent in bulk from those that do and often offer better rates than traditional car-rental operations. Prices are best during off-peak periods. Rentals booked through wholesalers often must be paid for before you leave home.

🚗 Wholesalers Auto Europe ☎ 207/842-2000 or 800/223-5555 🖷 207/842-2222 ⊕ www.autoeurope.com. **Destination Europe Resources** (DER) ✉ 9501 W. Devon Ave., Rosemont, IL 60018 ☎ 800/782-2424 🖷 800/282-7474. **Europe by Car** ☎ 212/581-3040 or 800/223-1516 🖷 212/246-1458 ⊕ www.europebycar.com. **Kemwel** ☎ 877/820-0668 or 800/678-0678 🖷 207/842-2124 or 866/726-6726 ⊕ www.kemwel.com.

INSURANCE

When driving a rented car you are generally responsible for any damage to or loss of the vehicle. Collision policies that car-rental companies sell for European rentals typically do not cover stolen vehicles. Before you rent—and purchase collision or theft coverage—see what coverage you already have under the terms of your personal auto-insurance policy and credit cards.

REQUIREMENTS & RESTRICTIONS

Ask about age requirements: Several countries require drivers to be over 20 years old, but some car-rental companies require that drivers be at least 25. In Scandinavia

your own driver's license is acceptable for a limited time; check with the country's tourist board before you go. An International Driver's Permit is a good idea; it's available from the American or Canadian Automobile Association, or, in the United Kingdom, from the Automobile Association or Royal Automobile Club.

SURCHARGES

Before you pick up a car in one city and leave it in another, ask about drop-off charges or one-way service fees, which can be substantial. Also inquire about early-return policies; some rental agencies charge extra if you return the car before the time specified in your contract while others give you a refund for the days not used. Most agencies note the tank's fuel level on your contract; to avoid a hefty refueling fee, return the car with the same tank level. If the tank was full, refill it just before you turn in the car, but be aware that gas stations near the rental outlet may overcharge. It's almost never a deal to buy a tank of gas with the car when you rent it; the understanding is that you'll return it empty, but some fuel usually remains.

CAR TRAVEL

Excellent, well-marked roads make driving a great way to explore Scandinavia, but it can be an expensive choice as gasoline in Scandinavia costs roughly four times the typical U.S. price. Ferry costs can be steep, and reservations are vital. Tolls on some major roads add to the expense, as do the high fees for city parking; tickets for illegal parking are painfully costly.

International driving permits (IDPs) are available from the American and Canadian automobile associations and, in the United Kingdom, from the Automobile Association and Royal Automobile Club. These international permits, valid only in conjunction with your regular driver's license, are universally recognized; having one may save you a problem with local authorities.

Also be aware that there are relatively low legal blood-alcohol limits and tough penalties for driving while intoxicated in Scandinavia; Iceland, Finland and Sweden have zero-tolerance laws. Penalties include suspension of the driver's license and fines or imprisonment and are enforced by random police roadblocks in urban areas. In addition, an accident involving a driver with an illegal blood-alcohol level usually voids all insurance agreements, so the driver becomes responsible for his own medical bills and damage to the cars.

In a few remote areas, especially in Iceland and northern Norway, Sweden, and Finland, road conditions can be unpredictable, and careful planning is required for safety's sake. Several mountain and highland roads in these areas close during winter—when driving in remote areas like these, especially in winter, it is best to let someone know your travel plans. It is also wise to **use a four-wheel-drive vehicle** and to **travel with at least one other car** in these areas.

Keep your headlights on at all times; this is required by law in most of Scandinavia. Also by Scandinavian law, everyone, including infants, must **wear seat belts.**

AUTO CLUBS

◪ In Australia **Australian Automobile Association** ☎ 02/6247-7311 ⊕ www.aaa.asn.au.
◪ In Canada **Canadian Automobile Association (CAA)** ☎ 613/247-0117 ⊕ www.caa.ca.
◪ In New Zealand **New Zealand Automobile Association** ☎ 09/377-4660 ⊕ www.aa.co.nz.
◪ In the U.K. **Automobile Association (AA)** ☎ 0870/550-0600 or 0161/495-8945 ⊕ www.theaa.com. **Royal Automobile Club** (RAC) ☎ 0870/5722-722 membership, 0845/3000-775 insurance ⊕ www.rac.co.uk.
◪ In the U.S. **American Automobile Association** ☎ 800/564-6222 ⊕ www.aaa.com.

CHILDREN IN SCANDINAVIA

In Scandinavia children are to be seen *and* heard and are genuinely welcome in most public places.

If you are renting a car, don't forget to arrange for a car seat when you reserve. For general advice about traveling with children, consult *Fodor's FYI: Travel with Your Baby* (available in bookstores everywhere).

DISCOUNTS

Children are entitled to discount tickets (often as much as 50% off) on buses, trains, and ferries throughout Scandinavia, as well as reductions on special City Cards. Children under age 12 pay 75% of the adult fare and children under age 2 pay 10% on SAS round-trips. There are no restrictions on the children's fares when booked in economy class.

With the Scanrail Pass (⇨ Train Travel)— good for rail journeys throughout Scandinavia—children under age 4 (on lap) travel free; those ages 4–11 pay half fare and those ages 12–25 can get a Scanrail Youth Pass, providing a 25% discount off the adult fare.

FLYING

If your children are two or older, ask about children's airfares. As a general rule, infants under two not occupying a seat fly at greatly reduced fares or even for free. But if you want to guarantee a seat for an infant, you have to pay full fare. Consider flying during off-peak days and times; most airlines will grant an infant a seat without a ticket if there are available seats. When booking, confirm carry-on allowances if you're traveling with infants. In general, for babies charged 10% to 50% of the adult fare you are allowed one carry-on bag and a collapsible stroller; if the flight is full, the stroller may have to be checked or you may be limited to less.

Experts agree that it's a good idea to use safety seats aloft for children weighing less than 40 pounds. Airlines set their own policies: if you use a safety seat, U.S. carriers usually require that the child be ticketed, even if he or she is young enough to ride free, because the seats must be strapped into regular seats. And even if you pay the full adult fare for the seat, it may be worth it, especially on longer trips. Do **check your airline's policy about using safety seats during takeoff and landing.** Safety seats are not allowed everywhere in the plane, so get your seat assignments as early as possible.

When reserving, request children's meals or a freestanding bassinet (not available at all airlines) if you need them. But note that bulkhead seats, where you must sit to use the bassinet, may lack an overhead bin or storage space on the floor.

For all airlines servicing Scandinavia, it is necessary to reserve children's and baby meals at least 24 hours in advance; travel of an unaccompanied minor should be confirmed at least three days prior to the flight.

LODGING
Most hotels in Scandinavia allow children under a certain age to stay in their parents' room at no extra charge, but others charge for them as extra adults; be sure to find out the cutoff age for children's discounts.

SIGHTS & ATTRACTIONS
Places that are especially appealing to children are indicated by a rubber-duckie icon (🐥) in the margin.

CRUISE TRAVEL
To learn how to plan, choose, and book a cruise-ship voyage, consult *Fodor's FYI: Plan & Enjoy Your Cruise* (available in bookstores everywhere).

🚢 Cruise Lines **DFDS Seaways** ✉ Sundkrogsgade 11, DK-2100 Copenhagen, Denmark ☎ 45/33-42-33-42 🖷 45/33-42-33-41 ✉ DFDS Seaways Travel Centre, Scandinavia House, Parkeston Quay, Harwich, Essex, U.K. CO12 4QG ☎ 44/8705-333-000 🖷 44/1255-244-382 ✉ DFDS Seaways USA Inc., c/o SeaEurope 6801 Lake Work Rd., Suite 107, Lake Worth, FL 333467 ☎ 800/533-3755 🖷 561/432-2550 ✉ Box 8895, Scandiahamnen, S-402 72 Göteborg, Sweden ☎ 46/31650610 ⊕ www.seaeurope.com. **Fjord Line** ⚓ Skoltegrunnskaien, Box 7250, N-5020 Bergen, Norway ☎ 47/55-54-87-00 🖷 47/55-54-87-01 ✉ International Ferry Terminal, Royal Quays, North Shields, Tyne & Wear, NE29 6EE, Newcastle, U.K. ☎ 44/191-296-1313 🖷 44/191-296-1540 ⊕ www.fjordline.co.uk or www.fjordline.com.

CUSTOMS & DUTIES
When shopping abroad, keep receipts for all purchases. Upon reentering the country, **be ready to show customs officials what you've bought.** Pack purchases together in an easily accessible place. If you think a duty is incorrect, appeal the assessment. If you object to the way your clearance was handled, note the inspec-

tor's badge number. In either case, first ask to see a supervisor. If the problem isn't resolved, write to the appropriate authorities, beginning with the port director at your point of entry.

IN CANADA
Canadian residents who have been out of Canada for at least seven days may bring in C$750 worth of goods duty-free. If you've been away fewer than seven days but more than 48 hours, the duty-free allowance drops to C$200. If your trip lasts 24 to 48 hours, the allowance is C$50; if the goods are worth more than C$50, you must pay full duty on all of the goods. You may not pool allowances with family members. Goods claimed under the C$750 exemption may follow you by mail; those claimed under the lesser exemptions must accompany you. Alcohol and tobacco products may be included in the seven-day and 48-hour exemptions but not in the 24-hour exemption. If you meet the age requirements of the province or territory through which you reenter Canada, you may bring in, duty-free, 1.5 liters of wine *or* 1.14 liters (40 imperial ounces) of liquor *or* 24 12-ounce cans or bottles of beer or ale. Also, if you meet the local age requirement for tobacco products, you may bring in, duty-free, 200 cigarettes, 50 cigars or cigarillos, and 200 grams of tobacco. You may have to pay a minimum duty on tobacco products, regardless of whether or not you exceed your personal exemption. Check ahead of time with the Canada Border Services Agency or the Department of Agriculture for policies regarding meat products, seeds, plants, and fruits.

You may send an unlimited number of gifts (only one gift per recipient, however) worth up to C$60 each duty-free to Canada. Label the package UNSOLICITED GIFT—VALUE UNDER $60. Alcohol and tobacco are excluded.

📋 **Canada Border Services Agency** ✉ Customs Information Services, 191 Laurier Ave. W, 15th fl., Ottawa, Ontario K1A 0L5 ☎ 800/461-9999 in Canada, 204/983-3500, 506/636-5064 ⊕ www.cbsa.gc.ca.

IN SCANDINAVIA

Limits on what you can bring in duty-free vary from country to country. **Check with individual country tourist boards for limits on alcohol, cigarettes, and other items.** Also be careful to check before bringing food of any kind into Iceland: uncooked meat and uncooked milk and egg products are all prohibited.

IN THE U.K.

If you are a U.K. resident and your journey was wholly within the European Union, you probably won't have to pass through customs when you return to the United Kingdom. If you plan to bring back large quantities of alcohol or tobacco, check EU limits beforehand. In most cases, if you bring back more than 200 cigars, 3,200 cigarettes, 400 cigarillos, 3 kilograms of tobacco, 10 liters of spirits, 110 liters of beer, 20 liters of fortified wine, and/or 90 liters of wine, you have to declare the goods upon return.

From countries outside the European Union, including Iceland and Norway, you may bring home, duty-free, 200 cigarettes, 50 cigars, 100 cigarillos, or 250 grams of tobacco; 1 liter of spirits or 2 liters of fortified or sparkling wine or liqueurs; 2 liters of still table wine; 60 ml of perfume; 250 ml of toilet water; plus £145 worth of other goods, including gifts and souvenirs. Prohibited items include meat and dairy products, seeds, plants, and fruits.

🔢 **HM Customs and Excise** ⊠ Portcullis House, 21 Cowbridge Rd. E, Cardiff CF11 9SS ☎ 0845/010–9000 or 0208/929–0152 advice service, 0208/929–6731 or 0208/910–3602 complaints ⊕ www.hmce. gov.uk.

IN THE U.S.

U.S. residents who have been out of the country for at least 48 hours may bring home, for personal use, $800 worth of foreign goods duty-free, as long as they haven't used the $800 allowance or any part of it in the past 30 days. This exemption may include 1 liter of alcohol (for travelers 21 and older), 200 cigarettes, and 100 non-Cuban cigars. Family members from the same household who are traveling together may pool their $800 personal exemptions. For fewer than 48 hours, the duty-free allowance drops to $200, which may include 50 cigarettes, 10 non-Cuban cigars, and 150 ml of alcohol (or 150 ml of perfume containing alcohol). The $200 allowance cannot be combined with other individuals' exemptions, and if you exceed it, the full value of all the goods will be taxed. Antiques, which U.S. Customs and Border Protection defines as objects more than 100 years old, enter duty-free, as do original works of art done entirely by hand, including paintings, drawings, and sculptures. This doesn't apply to folk art or handicrafts, which are in general dutiable.

You may also send packages home duty-free, with a limit of one parcel per addressee per day (except alcohol or tobacco products or perfume worth more than $5). You can mail up to $200 worth of goods for personal use; label the package PERSONAL USE and attach a list of its contents and their retail value. If the package contains your used personal belongings, mark it AMERICAN GOODS RETURNED to avoid paying duties. You may send up to $100 worth of goods as a gift; mark the package UNSOLICITED GIFT. Mailed items do not affect your duty-free allowance on your return.

To avoid paying duty on foreign-made high-ticket items you already own and will take on your trip, register them with a local customs office before you leave the country. Consider filing a Certificate of Registration for laptops, cameras, watches, and other digital devices identified with serial numbers or other permanent markings; you can keep the certificate for other trips. Otherwise, bring a sales receipt or insurance form to show that you owned the item before you left the United States.

For more about duties, restricted items, and other information about international travel, check out U.S. Customs and Border Protection's online brochure, *Know Before You Go*. You can also file complaints on the U.S. Customs and Border Protection Web site, listed below.

🔢 **U.S. Customs and Border Protection** ⊠ For inquiries and complaints, 1300 Pennsylvania Ave. NW,

Washington, DC 20229 ⊕ www.cbp.gov ☏ 877/227-5551, 202/354-1000.

DISABILITIES & ACCESSIBILITY

Facilities for travelers with disabilities in Scandinavia are generally good, and most of the major tourist offices offer special booklets and brochures on travel and accommodations. Most Scandinavian countries have organizations that offer advice to travelers with disabilities, and can give information on public and local transportation, sights and museums, hotels, and special interest tours. Notify and make all local and public transportation and hotel reservations in advance to ensure a smooth trip.

🖪 Local Resources **DHR De Handikappades Riksförbund** ⌂ Box 47305, Katrinebergsvägen 6, 100 74 Stockholm, Sweden ☏ 46/86858000 ⊕ www.dhr.se. **Norwegian Association of the Disabled** ⌂ Box 9217 Grønland, N-0134 Oslo, Norway ☏ 47/24-10-24-00 🖷 47/24-10-24-99 ⊕ www.nhf.no. **Rullaten ry** ✉ Pajutie 7, FIN-02770 Espoo, Finland ☏ 358/9-805-7393 ⊕ www.rullaten.fi.

LODGING

Best Western offers properties with wheelchair-accessible rooms in Helsinki, Oslo, Stockholm, and just outside Copenhagen. If wheelchair-accessible rooms on other floors are not available, ground-floor rooms are provided.

🖪 Wheelchair-Friendly Chain **Best Western** ☏ 800/528-1234.

SIGHTS & ATTRACTIONS

Although most major attractions in the Scandinavian capitals present no problems, winding cobblestone streets in the older sections of cities may be challenging for travelers with disabilities, especially in Stockholm's hilly Gamla Stan (Old Town), and on some of the smaller cobblestone streets in Helsinki's Kruunuhaka district, near Senaatintori.

TRAVEL AGENCIES

In the United States, the Americans with Disabilities Act requires that travel firms serve the needs of all travelers. Some agencies specialize in working with people with disabilities.

🖪 Travelers with Mobility Problems **Access Adventures/B. Roberts Travel** ✉ 1876 East Ave.,

Rochester, NY 14610 ☏ 800/444-6540 ⊕ www.brobertstravel.com, run by a former physical-rehabilitation counselor. **CareVacations** ✉ No. 5, 5110-50 Ave., Leduc, Alberta, Canada, T9E 6V4 ☏ 780/986-6404 or 877/478-7827 🖷 780/986-8332 ⊕ www.carevacations.com, for group tours and cruise vacations. **Flying Wheels Travel** ✉ 143 W. Bridge St., Box 382, Owatonna, MN 55060 ☏ 507/451-5005 🖷 507/451-1685 ⊕ www.flyingwheelstravel.com.

EATING & DRINKING

Scandinavia's major cities offer a full range of dining choices, from traditional to international restaurants. The restaurants we list are the cream of the crop in each price category. Properties indicated by an ✕ are lodging establishments whose restaurant warrants a special trip.

Restaurant meals are a big-ticket item throughout Scandinavia, but there are ways to keep the cost of eating down. Take full advantage of the large buffet breakfast often included in the cost of a hotel room. At lunch, look for the "menu" that offers a set two- or three-course meal for a set price, or limit yourself to a hearty appetizer. Some restaurants now include a trip to the salad bar in the dinner price. At dinner, pay careful attention to the price of wine and drinks, since the high tax on alcohol raises these costs considerably. For more information on affordable eating, *see* Money Matters.

MEALS & SPECIALTIES

The surrounding oceans and plentiful inland lakes and streams provide Scandinavian countries with an abundance of fresh fish and seafood: salmon, herring, trout, and seafood delicacies are mainstays, and are prepared in countless ways. Elk, deer, reindeer, and lamb feed in relatively unspoiled areas in Iceland and northern Norway, Sweden, and Finland, and have the succulent taste of wild game. Berries (including such delicacies as lingonberries and cloudberries) and mushrooms are still harvested from the forests; sausage appears in a thousand forms, as do potatoes and other root vegetables such as beets, turnips, radishes, rutabaga, and carrots. Some particular northern tastes can seem unusual, such as the fondness for pickled and fermented fish—to be sampled carefully at first—and a universal obsession with sweet pastries, ice cream, and chocolate.

Other novelties for the visitor might be the use of fruit in main dishes and soups, or sour milk on breakfast cereal, or preserved fish paste as a spread for crackers, or the prevalence of tasty, whole-grain crisp breads and hearty rye breads. The Swedish *smörgåsbord* (a kind of buffet meal) and its Scandinavian cousins are less common these days, but are still the traveling diner's best bet for breakfast. A smörgåsbord usually comes with a wide range of cheeses, fresh fish, and vegetables alongside meat and breads and other starches.

MEALTIMES
Unless otherwise noted, the restaurants listed in this guide are open daily for lunch and dinner.

Meals in Scandinavia are taken early and many restaurants, particularly in rural areas, will close mid-evening.

RESERVATIONS & DRESS
Reservations are always a good idea; we mention them only when they're essential or not accepted. Book as far ahead as you can, and reconfirm as soon as you arrive. (Large parties should always call ahead to check the reservations policy.) We mention dress only when men are required to wear a jacket or a jacket and tie.

WINE, BEER & SPIRITS
Restaurants' markups on alcoholic beverages are often very high in Scandinavia: as much as four times that of a standard retail price.

ELECTRICITY
To use electric-powered equipment purchased in the U.S. or Canada, **bring a converter and adapter.** The electrical current in Scandinavia is 220 volts, 50 cycles alternating current (AC); wall outlets take Continental-type plugs, with two round prongs.

If your appliances are dual-voltage, you'll need only an adapter. Don't use 110-volt outlets marked FOR SHAVERS ONLY for high-wattage appliances such as blow-dryers.

Most laptops operate equally well on 110 and 220 volts and so require only an adapter.

EMERGENCIES
Ambulance, fire, and police assistance is available 24 hours.
◼ Denmark, Finland, Iceland, Norway, Sweden 📞 112.

GAY & LESBIAN TRAVEL
Just as many Scandinavian countries were at the forefront of women's rights at the turn of the 20th century (Finland, for instance, was the first European country to grant women the right to vote, in 1906), Scandinavia has also had a liberal attitude toward gays and lesbians. The governments of Denmark, Sweden, Finland, and Norway grant to same-sex couples the same, or nearly the same, rights as their heterosexual counterparts, and Iceland allows gay couples joint custody of a child.

Reykjavík, Copenhagen, and Stockholm in particular have active, although not large, gay communities and nightlife.
◼ Gay- & Lesbian-Friendly Travel Agencies Different Roads Travel ✉ 1017 N. LaCienega Blvd., Suite 308, West Hollywood, CA 90069 📞 310/289–6000 or 800/429–8747 (Ext. 14 for both) 🖷 310/855–0323 ✍ lgernert@tzell.com. **Kennedy Travel** ✉ 130 W. 42nd St., Suite 401, New York, NY 10036 📞 800/237–7433 or 212/840–8659 🖷 212/730–2269 🌐 www.kennedytravel.com. **Now, Voyager** ✉ 4406 18th St., San Francisco, CA 94114 📞 415/626–1169 or 800/255–6951 🖷 415/626–8626 🌐 www.nowvoyager.com. **Skylink Travel and Tour/Flying Dutchmen Travel** ✉ 1455 N. Dutton Ave., Suite A, Santa Rosa, CA 95401 📞 707/546–9888 or 800/225–5759 🖷 707/636–0951; serving lesbian travelers.

HOLIDAYS
In general, all Scandinavian countries celebrate New Year's Eve and Day, Good Friday, Easter and Easter Monday, May Day (May 1; celebrated as Labor Day for many of the countries), Midsummer Eve and Day (although its date varies by country), Christmas (as well as Christmas Eve and Boxing Day, the day after Christmas).

On major holidays such as Christmas, most shops close or operate on a Sunday schedule. On the eves of such holidays, many shops are also closed all day or are open with reduced hours.

On May Day, the city centers are usually full of people, celebrations, and parades. During Midsummer, at the end of June, locals flock to the lakes and countryside to celebrate the beginning of long summer days with bonfires and other festivities.

The following holidays are not celebrated throughout Scandinavia entirely, only in particular countries.

Denmark: Maundy Thursday; First Day of Summer (observed mid-April); Ascension; Pentecost; Common Prayer Day (fourth Friday after Easter); Constitution Day, June 5.

Finland: Epiphany, Jan. 6; May Day Eve, Apr. 30; All Saints' Day, Nov. 1; Independence Day, Dec. 6.

Iceland: Maundy Thursday; First Day of Summer (observed mid-April); Ascension; Pentecost Independence Day, June 17; Commerce Day (first Mon. in August).

Norway: Maundy Thursday; Ascension; Constitution Day, May 17; Pentecost; St. Olav's Day, July 29.

Sweden: Epiphany, Jan. 6; Ascension; Pentecost Monday, Valbourg's Eve, Apr. 30; National Day, June 6; All Saints' Day (observed the first Sat. after Oct. 30).

INSURANCE

The most useful travel-insurance plan is a comprehensive policy that includes coverage for trip cancellation and interruption, default, trip delay, and medical expenses (with a waiver for preexisting conditions).

Without insurance you'll lose all or most of your money if you cancel your trip, regardless of the reason. Default insurance covers you if your tour operator, airline, or cruise line goes out of business—the chances of which have been increasing. Trip-delay covers expenses that arise because of bad weather or mechanical delays. Study the fine print when comparing policies.

If you're traveling internationally, a key component of travel insurance is coverage for medical bills incurred if you get sick on the road. Such expenses aren't generally covered by Medicare or private policies. U.K. residents can buy a travel-insurance policy valid for most vacations taken during the year in which it's purchased (but check preexisting-condition coverage). British and Australian citizens need extra medical coverage when traveling overseas.

Always **buy travel policies directly from the insurance company**; if you buy them from a cruise line, airline, or tour operator that goes out of business you probably won't be covered for the agency or operator's default, a major risk. Before making any purchase, review your existing health and home-owner's policies to find what they cover away from home.

🔒 Travel Insurers In the U.S.: **Access America** ✉ 2805 N. Parham Rd., Richmond, VA 23294 ☎ 800/284-8300 🖷 804/673-1469 or 800/346-9265 ⊕ www.accessamerica.com. **Travel Guard International** ✉ 1145 Clark St., Stevens Point, WI 54481 ☎ 800/826-1300 or 715/345-1041 🖷 800/955-8785 or 715/345-1990 ⊕ www.travelguard.com.

🔒 Insurance Information In the U.K.: **Association of British Insurers** ✉ 51 Gresham St., London EC2V 7HQ ☎ 020/7600-3333 🖷 020/7696-8999 ⊕ www.abi.org.uk. In Canada: **RBC Insurance** ✉ 6880 Financial Dr., Mississauga, Ontario L5N 7Y5 ☎ 800/387-4357 or 905/816-2559 🖷 888/298-6458 ⊕ www.rbcinsurance.com. In Australia: **Insurance Council of Australia** ✉ Level 3, 56 Pitt St. Sydney, NSW 2000 ☎ 02/9253-5100 🖷 02/9253-5111 ⊕ www.ica.com.au. In New Zealand: **Insurance Council of New Zealand** ✉ Level 7, 111-115 Customhouse Quay, Box 474, Wellington ☎ 04/472-5230 🖷 04/473-3011 ⊕ www.icnz.org.nz.

LANGUAGE

Despite the fact that four of the five Scandinavian tongues are in the Germanic family of languages, it is a myth that someone who speaks German can understand Danish, Icelandic, Swedish, and Norwegian. Fortunately, English is widely spoken in Scandinavia. German is the most common third language. English becomes rarer outside major cities, and it's a good idea to **take along a dictionary or phrase book.** Even here, however, anyone under the age of 50 is likely to have studied English in school.

Danish, Norwegian, and Swedish are similar, and fluent Norwegian and Swedish speakers can generally understand each other. While Finns must study Swedish (the second national language) in school, they much prefer to speak English with their Scandinavian counterparts.

Characters special to these three languages are the Danish "ø" and the Swedish "ö," pronounced a bit like a very short "er," similar to the French "eu"; "æ" or "ä," which sounds like the "a" in "ape" but with a glottal stop, or the "a" in "cat," depending on the region, and the "å" (also written "aa"), which sounds like "or." The "ä" and the "ö" are also found in the Finnish alphabet, with similar pronunciations. The important thing about these characters isn't that you pronounce them correctly—foreigners usually can't—but that you know to look for them in the phone book at the very end. Mr. Søren Åstrup, for example, will be found after "Z." Æ or Ä and Ø or Ö follow. The Swedish letter "K" softens to a "sh" sound next to certain vowels such as the Ö—beware when pronouncing place-names such as Enköping (sounds like "Enshöping").

Icelandic, because of its island isolation, is the language closest to what the Vikings spoke 1,000 years ago. Although Norwegian, Danish, and Swedish have clearly evolved away from the roots common to all four languages, Icelandic retains a surprising amount of its ancient heritage, and Icelanders want to keep it that way: a governmental committee in Iceland has the express task of coming up with Icelandic versions of more modern words such as *computer*. Two characters are unique to Icelandic and Faroese: the "Þ," which is pronounced like the "th" in "thing"; and the "ð," which is pronounced like the "th" in "the."

Finnish is Finno-Ugric, a non-Germanic language more closely related to Estonian and Hungarian than to the other Scandinavian languages. A visitor isn't likely to recognize anything on the average newspaper's front page. A linguistic cousin to Finnish is still spoken by the Sami (Lapps), who inhabit the northernmost parts of Norway, Sweden, Finland, and Russia.

LODGING

The lodgings we list are the cream of the crop in each price category. We always list the facilities that are available—but we don't specify whether they cost extra: When pricing accommodations, always ask what's included and what costs extra.

In the larger cities, lodging ranges from first-class business hotels run by Radisson SAS, Hilton, and Scandic to good-quality tourist-class hotels, such as Best Western and Choice (Comfort, Clarion, or Quality), found throughout Scandinavia, to a wide variety of single-entrepreneur hotels. In the countryside, look for independently run inns and motels. In Denmark they're called *kroer;* in Norway, *fjellstuer* or *pensjonat;* in Finland, *kievari;* and elsewhere, guesthouses. "Mökki" holidays, in summer cottages or farmhouses, have become popular with foreign visitors to Finland; farm holidays have also become increasingly available to tourists in the other Scandinavian countries, all of which have organizations that can help organize stays in the countryside.

Before you leave home, **ask your travel agent about discounts,** including summer hotel checks for Best Western, Scandic, and Choice hotels, a summer Fjord pass in Norway, a Finncheque Hotels pass in Finland, and the Skanplus Hotel Pass that works throughout Scandinavia. Discounts of up to 25% can be found at Radisson SAS hotels for travelers over 65.

Two things about hotels usually surprise North Americans: the relatively limited dimensions of Scandinavian beds and the generous size of Scandinavian breakfasts. Scandinavian double beds are often about 60 inches wide or slightly less, close in size to the U.S. queen size; in local hotels a double bed often consists of two twin-size beds pushed together. King-size beds (72 inches wide) are difficult to find and, if available, require special reservations.

Older hotels may have some rooms described as "double," which in fact have one double bed plus one foldout sofa big enough for two people. This arrangement is occasionally called a combi-room but is being phased out.

Many older hotels, particularly the country inns and independently run smaller hotels in the cities, do not have private bathrooms. Ask ahead if this is important to you.

Scandinavian breakfasts resemble what many people would call lunch, usually including breads, cheeses, marmalade, hams, lunch meats, eggs, juice, cereal, milk, and coffee. Generally, the farther north you go, the larger the breakfasts become. Breakfast is usually included in hotel rates.

Make reservations whenever possible. Even countryside inns, which usually have space, are sometimes packed with vacationing Europeans.

Ask about high and low seasons when making reservations, since different countries define their tourist seasons differently. Some hotels lower prices during tourist season, whereas others raise them during the same period.

Assume that hotels operate on the European Plan (EP, with no meals) unless we specify that they use the Continental Plan (CP, with a Continental breakfast), Breakfast Plan (BP, with a full breakfast), Modified American Plan (MAP, with breakfast and dinner), or the Full American Plan (FAP, with all meals).

APARTMENT & HOUSE RENTALS

If you want a home base that's roomy enough for a family and comes with cooking facilities, consider a furnished rental. These can save you money, especially if you're traveling with a group. Home-exchange directories sometimes list rentals as well as exchanges.

🎲 International Agents **Hideaways International** ✉ 767 Islington St., Portsmouth, NH 03801 ☎ 603/

430-4433 or 800/843-4433 🖷 603/430-4444 ⊕ www.hideaways.com, annual membership $185.

CAMPING

Campsites are plentiful in the Scandinavian countries, and are often near a lake or by the sea. Central Iceland and Lapland hold some of the most pristine forests and highland areas in Europe, with exceptional camping for those wanting to make the extra effort to find less-inhabited, backcountry areas. The Finnish archipelago, off Finland's southwest, offers seaside and island camping. Contact the local tourist boards for details.

FARM & COTTAGE HOLIDAYS

The old-fashioned farm or countryside holiday, long a staple for Scandinavian city dwellers, is becoming increasingly available to tourists. In general, you can choose to stay on the farm itself, and even participate in daily activities, or you can opt to rent a private housekeeping cottage. In Finland, lakeside cottages, where many Finns spend their summers, are as common as the sauna; in Norway, seaside fisherman's cabins or *rorbuer* are available, particularly in the Lofoten Islands (most Scandinavian cottages will be near a lake or by the sea). Contact the local tourist board, or one of the organizations specializing in farm and cottage holidays, for details.

🎲 **Icelandic Farm Holidays** ✉ Síðumúli 13, IS-108 Reykjavík, Iceland ☎ 354/570-2700 🖷 354/570-2799 ⊕ www.farmholidays.is. **Landsforeningen for Landboturisme** ✉ Føllevej 5, Foelle, DK-8410 Rønde, Denmark ☎ 45/87-91-20-00 ⊕ www.bondegaardsferie.dk. **Lomarengas-Finnish Country Holidays** ✉ Eteläesplanadi 22 C, 3rd fl., 00130 Helsinki, Finland ☎ 358/9-5766-3350 🖷 358/9-5766-3366 ⊕ www.lomarengas.fi. **Swedish Farm Holidays** ⊕ www.bopalantgard.org.

HOSTELS

No matter what your age, you can save on lodging costs by staying at hostels. In some 4,500 locations in more than 70 countries around the world, Hostelling International (HI), the umbrella group for a number of national youth-hostel associations, offers single-sex, dorm-style beds and, at many hostels, rooms for couples and family accommodations. Membership in any HI national hostel association, open to travelers of all ages, allows you to stay in HI-affiliated hostels at member rates; one-year membership is about $28 for adults (C$35 for a two-year minimum membership in Canada, £15 in the U.K., A$52 in Australia, and NZ$40 in New Zealand); hostels charge about $10–$30 per night. Members have priority if the hostel is full; they're also eligible for discounts around the world, even on rail and bus travel in some countries.

🚪 **Organizations Hostelling International–USA** ✉ 8401 Colesville Rd., Suite 600, Silver Spring, MD 20910 ☎ 301/495-1240 🖷 301/495-6697 ⊕ www. hiusa.org. **Hostelling International–Canada** ✉ 205 Catherine St., Suite 400, Ottawa, Ontario K2P 1C3 ☎ 613/237-7884 or 800/663-5777 🖷 613/237-7868 ⊕ www.hihostels.ca. **YHA England and Wales** ✉ Trevelyan House, Dimple Rd., Matlock, Derbyshire DE4 3YH, U.K. ☎ 0870/870-8808, 0870/770-8868, 0162/959-2600 🖷 0870/770-6127 ⊕ www.yha.org.uk. **YHA Australia** ✉ 422 Kent St., Sydney, NSW 2001 ☎ 02/9261-1111 🖷 02/9261-1969 ⊕ www.yha.com.au. **YHA New Zealand** ✉ Level 1, Moorhouse City, 166 Moorhouse Ave., Box 436, Christchurch ☎ 03/379-9970 or 0800/278-299 🖷 03/365-4476 ⊕ www.yha.org.nz.

HOTELS

All hotels listed have private bath unless otherwise noted.

Most of the Scandinavian countries offer Inn Checks, or prepaid hotel vouchers, for accommodations ranging from first-class hotels to country cottages. These vouchers, which can be purchased from participating travel agents, tourist or hotel offices in the destination country, or directly off the Web site of each hotel voucher company, are sold as unlimited use cards or in packets for as many nights as needed and offer savings of up to 50%. Most countries also offer summer bargains for foreign tourists; winter bargains can be even greater. For further information about Scandinavian hotel vouchers, contact the Scandinavian

Tourist Board. You can also order hotel vouchers for most Scandinavian countries from Nordic Saga Tours.

Skanplus Hotel Passes can be used in more than 185 hotels across Scandinavia for savings of up to 50%. The pass costs about €12; it's valid for one summer and for weekends and holidays throughout that year. Every sixth night is free. Advance reservations should be made with the central reservations offices listed on the card. The pass can be bought at cooperating travel agencies, at participating hotels, or ordered online from Skanplus. Skanplus also offers the 60-plus Hotel Pass for senior citizens.

🚪 **Hotel Passes** In Sweden: **Countryside Hotels Summer Cheques** ☎ 46/8590-32732 ⊕ www. countrysidehotels.se. In Finland: **Finncheque** ⊕ www.visitfinland.com/finncheque. In Norway and Sweden: **Fjord Pass** ☎ 47/55-55-76-60 ⊕ www. fjord-pass.com. Throughout Scandinavia: **Nordic Hotel Pass and Choice Hotel Cheque–Choice Hotels** ⊕ www.choicehotels.se. **Nordic Saga Tours** ☎ 800/848-6449 ⊕ www.nordicsaga.com. **Skanplus** ⊕ www.skanplus.com.

🚪 **Toll-Free Numbers Best Western** ☎ 800/528-1234 ⊕ www.bestwestern.com. **Choice** ☎ 800/424-6423 ⊕ www.choicehotels.com. **Clarion** ☎ 800/424-6423 ⊕ www.choicehotels.com. **Comfort Inn** ☎ 800/424-6423 ⊕ www.choicehotels.com. **Hilton** ☎ 800/445-8667 ⊕ www.hilton.com. **Holiday Inn** ☎ 800/465-4329 ⊕ www.ichotelsgroup.com. **Quality Inn** ☎ 800/424-6423 ⊕ www.choicehotels.com. **Radisson** ☎ 800/333-3333 ⊕ www.radisson.com.

MONEY MATTERS

Prices throughout this guide are given for adults. Substantially reduced fees are almost always available for children, students, and senior citizens. For information on taxes, *see* Taxes.

Costs are high in Denmark, Norway, and Sweden, higher still in Finland, and highest in Iceland, where so many things must be imported. Basic sample prices are listed in the Country A to Z section at the end of each chapter. Throughout the region, be aware that sales taxes can be very high, but foreigners can get some refunds by shopping at tax-free stores (⇨ Taxes). City cards can save you transportation and entrance fees in many of the larger cities.

You can **reduce the cost of food by planning.** Breakfast is often included in your hotel bill; if not, you may wish to buy fruit, sweet rolls, and a beverage for a picnic breakfast. **Opt for a restaurant lunch instead of dinner,** since the latter tends to be significantly more expensive. Instead of beer or wine, drink tap water—liquor can cost four times the price of the same brand in a store—but do specify tap water, as the term "water" can refer to soft drinks and bottled water, which are also expensive. Throughout Scandinavia, the tip is included in the cost of your meal; however, a little extra is always appreciated and is becoming more expected in the larger cities.

In most of Scandinavia, liquor and strong beer (over 3% alcohol) can be purchased only in state-owned shops, at very high prices, during weekday business hours, usually 9:30 to 6 and in some areas on Saturday until mid-afternoon. A midsize bottle of whiskey in Sweden, for example, can easily cost SKr 250 (about $35). Denmark takes a less-restrictive approach, with liquor and beer available in the smallest of grocery stores, open weekdays and Saturday morning—but Danish prices, too, are high. (When you visit friends or relatives in Scandinavia, a bottle of liquor or fine wine bought duty-free on the trip over is often much appreciated.) Weaker beers and ciders are usually available in grocery stores in Scandinavia.

🚩 ATM Locations **Cirrus** ☎ 800/424-7787.

CREDIT CARDS

Throughout this guide, the following abbreviations are used: **AE,** American Express; **DC,** Diners Club; **MC,** MasterCard; and **V,** Visa.

CURRENCY

Finland is the only Scandinavian country that has switched to the euro. The FM (Finnish mark) is no longer accepted as currency. Denmark and Sweden, both EU countries like Finland, are still using their currencies, the DKr (Danish kroner) and SKr (Swedish kronor). Norway and Iceland, non-EU countries, are keeping their currencies, the NKr (Norwegian kroner) and the IKr (Icelandic kroner). In individ-

ual countries you may see prices indicated with Kr only, and you may see exchange rates in banks quoted for DKK, EUR, ISK, NOK, and SEK. Currency-exchange rates at press time are listed in the Country A to Z sections at the end of each chapter, but **since rates fluctuate daily, you should check them at the time of your departure.**

CURRENCY EXCHANGE

For the most favorable rates, **change money through banks.** Although ATM transaction fees may be higher abroad than at home, ATM rates are excellent because they're based on wholesale rates offered only by major banks. You won't do as well at exchange booths in airports or rail and bus stations, in hotels, in restaurants, or in stores. To avoid lines at airport exchange booths, get a bit of local currency before you leave home.

🚩 Exchange Services **International Currency Express** ✉ 427 N. Camden Dr., Suite F, Beverly Hills, CA 90210 ☎ 888/278-6628 orders 🖷 310/278-6410 ⊕ www.foreignmoney.com. **Travel Ex Currency Services** ☎ 800/287-7362 orders and retail locations ⊕ www.travelex.com.

TRAVELER'S CHECKS

Do you need traveler's checks? It depends on where you're headed. If you're going to rural areas and small towns, go with cash; traveler's checks are best used in cities. Lost or stolen checks can usually be replaced within 24 hours. To ensure a speedy refund, buy your own traveler's checks—don't let someone else pay for them: irregularities like this can cause delays. The person who bought the checks should make the call to request a refund.

PACKING

Bring a folding umbrella and a lightweight raincoat, as it is common for the sky to be clear at 9 AM, rainy at 11 AM, and clear again in time for lunch. **Pack casual clothes,** as Scandinavians tend to dress more casually than their Continental brethren. If you have trouble sleeping when it is light or are sensitive to strong sun, **bring an eye mask and dark sunglasses;** the sun rises as early as 4 AM in some areas, and the far-northern latitude causes it to slant at angles unseen elsewhere on the globe. **Bring bug repellent** if you plan to venture away from the capital cities; large mosquitoes can be a real nuisance on summer evenings throughout Scandinavia.

In your carry-on luggage, pack an extra pair of eyeglasses or contact lenses and enough of any medication you take to last a few days longer than the entire trip. You may also ask your doctor to write a spare prescription using the drug's generic name, as brand names may vary from country to country. In luggage to be checked, **never pack prescription drugs, valuables, or undeveloped film.** And don't forget to carry with you the addresses of offices that handle refunds of lost traveler's checks. Check *Fodor's How to Pack* (available at online retailers and bookstores everywhere) for more tips.

To avoid customs and security delays, carry medications in their original packaging. Don't pack any sharp objects in your carry-on luggage, including knives of any size or material, scissors, nail clippers, and corkscrews, or anything else that might arouse suspicion.

To avoid having your checked luggage chosen for hand inspection, don't cram bags full. The U.S. Transportation Security Administration suggests packing shoes on top and placing personal items you don't want touched in clear plastic bags.

CHECKING LUGGAGE

You're allowed to carry aboard one bag and one personal article, such as a purse or a laptop computer. Make sure what you carry on fits under your seat or in the overhead bin. Get to the gate early, so you can board as soon as possible, before the overhead bins fill up.

Baggage allowances vary by carrier, destination, and ticket class. On international flights, you're usually allowed to check two bags weighing up to 70 pounds (32 kilograms) each, although a few airlines allow checked bags of up to 88 pounds (40 kilograms) in first class. Some international carriers don't allow more than 66 pounds (30 kilograms) per bag in business class and 44 pounds (20 kilograms) in economy. In general, carry-on bags shouldn't exceed 40 pounds (18 kilograms). Most airlines won't accept bags that weigh more than 100 pounds (45 kilograms) on domestic or international flights. Expect to pay a fee for baggage that exceeds weight limits. Check baggage restrictions with your carrier before you pack.

Airline liability for baggage is limited to $2,500 per person on flights within the United States. On international flights it amounts to $9.07 per pound or $20 per kilogram for checked baggage (roughly $640 per 70-pound bag), with a maximum of $634.90 per piece, and $400 per passenger for unchecked baggage. You can buy additional coverage at check-in for about $10 per $1,000 of coverage, but it often excludes a rather extensive list of items, shown on your airline ticket.

Before departure, itemize your bags' contents and their worth, and label the bags with your name, address, and phone number. (If you use your home address, cover it so potential thieves can't see it readily.) Include a label inside each bag and **pack a copy of your itinerary.** At check-in, make sure each bag is correctly tagged with the destination airport's three-letter code. Because some checked bags will be opened for hand inspection, the U.S. Transportation Security Administration recommends that you leave luggage unlocked or use the plastic locks offered at check-in. TSA screeners place an inspection notice inside searched bags, which are resealed with a special lock.

If your bag has been searched and contents are missing or damaged, file a claim with the TSA Consumer Response Center as soon as possible. If your bags arrive damaged or fail to arrive at all, file a written report with the airline before leaving the airport.

🚩 Complaints **U.S. Transportation Security Administration Contact Center** ☎ 866/289–9673 ⊕ www.tsa.gov.

PASSPORTS & VISAS

When traveling internationally, carry your passport even if you don't need one. Not only is it the best form of ID, but it's also being required more and more. **Make two photocopies of the data page** (one for someone at home and another for you, carried separately from your passport). If you lose your passport, promptly call the nearest embassy or consulate and the local police.

U.S. passport applications for children under age 14 require consent from both parents or legal guardians; both parents must appear together to sign the application. If only one parent appears, he or she must submit a written statement from the other parent authorizing passport issuance for the child. A parent with sole authority must present evidence of it when applying; acceptable documentation includes the child's certified birth certificate listing only the applying parent, a court order specifically permitting this parent's travel with the child, or a death certificate for the nonapplying parent. Application forms and instructions are available on the Web site of the U.S. State Department's Bureau of Consular Affairs (⊕ travel.state.gov).

ENTERING SCANDINAVIA
All U.S. citizens, even infants, need only a valid passport to enter any Scandinavian country for stays of up to three months.

PASSPORT OFFICES
The best time to apply for a passport or to renew is in fall and winter. Before any trip, check your passport's expiration date, and, if necessary, renew it as soon as possible.

🛃 Australian Citizens **Passports Australia** Australian Department of Foreign Affairs and Trade ☎ 131-232 ⊕ www.passports.gov.au.

🛃 Canadian Citizens **Passport Office** ✉ To mail in applications: 70 Cremazie St., Gatineau, Québec J8Y 3P2 ☎ 819/994-3500 or 800/567-6868 ⊕ www.ppt.gc.ca.

🛃 New Zealand Citizens **New Zealand Passports Office** ☎ 0800/22-5050 or 04/474-8100 ⊕ www.passports.govt.nz.

🛃 U.K. Citizens **U.K. Passport Service** ☎ 0870/521-0410 ⊕ www.passport.gov.uk.

🛃 U.S. Citizens **National Passport Information Center** ☎ 877/487-2778, 888/874-7793 TDD/TTY ⊕ travel.state.gov.

SAFETY
Don't wear a money belt or a waist pack, both of which peg you as a tourist. Distribute your cash and any valuables (in-cluding your credit cards and passport) between a deep front pocket, an inside jacket or vest pocket, and a hidden money pouch. Do not reach for the money pouch once you're in public.

WOMEN IN SCANDINVIA
If you carry a purse, choose one with a zipper and a thick strap that you can drape across your body; adjust the length so that the purse sits in front of you at or above hip level. (Don't wear a money belt or a waist pack.) Store only enough money in the purse to cover casual spending. Distribute the rest of your cash and any valuables between deep front pockets, inside jacket or vest pockets, and a concealed money pouch.

SENIOR-CITIZEN TRAVEL
To qualify for age-related discounts, mention your senior-citizen status up front when booking hotel reservations (not when checking out) and before you're seated in restaurants (not when paying the bill). Be sure to have identification on hand. When renting a car, ask about promotional car-rental discounts, which can be cheaper than senior-citizen rates.

Several larger chains (Choice Hotels, Radisson SAS), as well as Skanplus, offer significant hotel discounts for travelers 60 to 65 and over (⇨ Lodging).

TRAIN TRAVEL
Seniors over 60 are entitled to discount tickets (often as much as 50% off) on buses, trains, and ferries throughout Scandinavia, as well as reductions on special City Cards. Eurail offers discounts on Scanrail and Eurail train passes (⇨ Train Travel).

🛃 Educational Programs **Elderhostel** ✉ 11 Ave. de Lafayette, Boston, MA 02111 ☎ 877/426-8056, 978/323-4141 international callers, 877/426-2167 TTY 🖷 877/426-2166 ⊕ www.elderhostel.org. **Interhostel** ✉ University of New Hampshire, 6 Garrison Ave., Durham, NH 03824 ☎ 603/862-1147 or 800/733-9753 🖷 603/862-1113 ⊕ www.learn.unh.edu.

STUDENTS IN SCANDINAVIA
🛃 I.D.s & Services **STA Travel** ✉ 10 Downing St., New York, NY 10014 ☎ 212/627-3111, 800/777-0112

24-hr service center ☎ 212/627–3387 ⊕ www.sta. com. **Travel Cuts** ✉ 187 College St., Toronto, Ontario M5T 1P7, Canada ☎ 800/592–2887 in the U.S., 416/979–2406 or 866/246–9762 in Canada ⛀ 416/979–8167 ⊕ www.travelcuts.com.

TAXES

VALUE-ADDED TAX

Specific information on V.A.T. (value-added taxes) can be found in the Country A to Z section at the end of each chapter.

One way to beat high prices is to **take advantage of tax-free shopping.** Throughout Scandinavia, you can make major purchases free of tax if you have a foreign passport. Ask about tax-free shopping when you make a purchase for $50 (about £32) or more. When your purchases exceed a specified limit (which varies from country to country), you receive a special check for the V.A.T. refund (or ask the staff to provide you with one if you think you may have exceeded the limits). Keep the parcels intact and take them out of the country within 30 days of purchase.

You can claim a V.A.T. refund from Finland, Sweden, and Denmark when you leave the last EU country visited; the V.A.T. refund (called *moms* all over Scandinavia) can be obtained in cash from a special office at the airport, or, upon arriving home, you can send your receipts to an office in the country of purchase to receive your refund by mail. Citizens of EU countries are not eligible for the refund.

In Sweden, for non-EU citizens, the refund is about 18%; in Finland, 10% to 16%; in Norway, 11% to 18%; in Denmark, about 18%; in Iceland, up to 15% for purchases over IKr 4,000.

Note: Tax-free sales of alcohol, cigarettes, and other luxury goods have been abolished within EU countries, with Sweden, Finland, and Denmark among the last to adopt these regulations. Finland's Åland Islands have some special rights under the EU and therefore allow tax-free sales for ferries in transit through its ports. All Sweden–Finland ferry routes now pass through the islands, de facto continuing the extremely popular tax-free sales for tourists. Air travel to the Scandinavia EU member states (Sweden, Finland, Denmark), as well as Norway, no longer allows tax-free sales.

Global Refund is a V.A.T. refund service that makes getting your money back hassle-free. The service is available Europe-wide at 275,000 affiliated stores. In participating stores, **ask for the Global Refund form** (called a Shopping Cheque). Have it stamped like any customs form by customs officials when you leave the European Union (be ready to show customs officials what you've bought). Then take the form to one of the more than 700 Global Refund counters—conveniently located at every major airport and border crossing—and your money will be refunded on the spot in the form of cash, check, or a refund to your credit-card account (minus a small percentage for processing).

🗗 V.A.T. Refunds **Global Refund** ✉ Montreal Eaton Centre 705, Ste-Catherine St. W, Suite 4-121, Montreal, Quebec H3B 4G5 ☎ 800/566–9828 ⊕ www.globalrefund.com.

TELEPHONES

AREA & COUNTRY CODES

The country code for Denmark is 45; for Finland, 358; for Iceland, 354; for Norway, 47; and for Sweden, 46. In this chapter, phone numbers outside the United States and Canada include country codes; in all other chapters only the area codes are listed.

The country code is 1 for the United States and Canada, 61 for Australia, 64 for New Zealand, and 44 for the United Kingdom.

INTERNATIONAL CALLS

When dialing from outside the country you're trying to reach, drop the initial 0 from the local area code.

LONG-DISTANCE SERVICES

AT&T, MCI, and Sprint access codes make calling long-distance relatively convenient, but you may find the local access number blocked in many hotel rooms. First ask the hotel operator to connect you. If the hotel operator balks, ask for an international operator, or dial the international operator yourself. One way to improve your odds of getting connected to your long-distance carrier is to travel with more than one company's calling card (a hotel may block Sprint, for example, but not MCI). If all else fails, call from a pay phone. If you are traveling for a longer period of time, consider renting a cell phone from a local company.

F Access Codes **AT&T Direct** ☎ 8001/0010 Denmark, 9800/10010 Finland, 800/9001 Iceland, 800/19011 Norway, 020/795611 Sweden. **MCI WorldPhone** ☎ 8001/0022 Denmark, 9800/10280 Finland, 800/9002 Iceland, 800/19912 Norway, 020/795922 Sweden. **Sprint International Access** ☎ 800/10877 Denmark, 9800/10284 Finland, 800/9003 Iceland, 800/19877 Norway, 020/799011 Sweden.

MOBILE PHONES

Scandinavia has been one of the world leaders in mobile phone development; almost 90% of the population in Scandinavia owns a mobile phone. Most standard North American cellular phones will not work in Scandinavia unless they support a GSM (Global System for Mobile) network in a foreign country; check with your carrier to see if you have capabilities for service abroad or if you can insert an international card into your phone. If not, most Scandinavian capitals have several companies that rent cellular phones to tourists. Contact the local tourist offices for details.

TIME

Scandinavia falls into two time zones. Denmark, Norway, and Sweden are one hour ahead of Greenwich Mean Time (GMT) and six hours ahead of Eastern Standard Time (EST). Since Iceland does not observe Daylight Savings Times, the country is one hour ahead of GMT and five hours ahead of EST in the summer but in the same time zone as Denmark, Norway, and Sweden the rest of the year.

Finland is two hours ahead of GMT and seven hours ahead of EST.

TIPPING

When taking a taxi, a 10% tip is appreciated but not essential.

TRAIN TRAVEL

Consider a Scanrail Pass, available for travel in Denmark, Sweden, Norway, and Finland for second-class train travel only: you may have 5 days of unlimited travel in any two-month period ($291 second-class); 10 days of unlimited travel in two months ($390); or 21 days of consecutive days of unlimited train travel ($453). With the Scanrail Pass, you also enjoy travel bonuses, including free or discounted ferry and boat travel.

Passengers ages 12–25 can **buy Scanrail Youth Passes** ($203 second-class, 5 travel days in two months; $273 for 10 travel days in two months; $316 for 21 days of unlimited travel).

Those over age 60 can **take advantage of the Scanrail Senior Pass,** which offers the travel bonuses of the Scanrail Pass and discounted travel ($258 second-class, 5 days; $348 10 days; $400 for 21 consecutive days). Buy Scanrail passes through Rail Europe and travel agents.

For car and train travel, price the Scanrail'n Drive Pass: Within a two-month span you can get five days of unlimited train travel and two days of car rental (choice of three car categories) with unlimited mileage in Denmark, Finland, Norway, and Sweden. You can purchase extra car rental days and choose from first- or second-class train travel. Individual rates for two adults traveling together (compact car $359 per person second-class) are considerably lower (about 25%) than for single adults; the third or fourth person sharing the car only needs to purchase a Scanrail pass.

In Scandinavia, you can **use EurailPasses,** which provide unlimited first-class rail travel, in all of the participating countries, for the duration of the pass. If you plan to rack up the miles, get a standard pass. These are available for 15 days ($588), 21 days ($762), one month ($946), two months ($1,338), and three months ($1,654). Eurail- and EuroPasses are available through travel agents and Rail Europe.

If you are an adult traveling with a youth under age 26 and/or a senior, consider buying a **EurailSaver Pass**; this entitles you to second-class train travel at the discount youth or senior fare, provided that you are traveling with the youth or senior at all times. A Saver pass is available for $498 (15 days), $648 (21 days), and $804 (one month); two- and three-month fares are also available.

In addition to standard EurailPasses, **ask about special rail-pass plans.** Among these are the Eurail YouthPass (for those under age 26), a Eurail FlexiPass (which allows a certain number of travel days within a set period), the Euraildrive Pass, and the EuroPass Drive (which combines travel by train and rental car).

Whichever pass you choose, remember that you must **purchase your pass before you leave** for Europe.

Many travelers assume that rail passes guarantee them seats on the trains they wish to ride. Not so. You need to **book seats ahead even if you are using a rail pass**; seat reservations are required on some European trains, particularly high-speed trains, and are a good idea on trains that may be crowded—particularly in summer on popular routes. You will also need a reservation if you purchase sleeping accommodations.

🎫 Where to Buy Rail Passes **DER Travel Services** 🖉 9501 W. Devon Ave., Rosemont, IL 60018 ☎ 800/782–2424 🖷 800/282–7474 ⊕ www. raileurope.com. **Rail Europe** ✉ Westchester One, 44 S. Broadway, White Plains, NY 10601 ☎ 800/438–7245 or 888/382–7245 in the U.S., 800/361–7245 in Canada ✉ 2087 Dundas E, Suite 105, Mississauga, Ontario L4X 1M2, Canada ☎ 800/438–7245 or 888/382–7245 in the U.S., 800/361–7245 in Canada ⊕ www.raileurope.com.

CUTTING COSTS

To save money, **look into rail passes.** But be aware that if you don't plan to cover many miles, you may come out ahead by buying individual tickets.

TRANSPORTATION AROUND SCANDINAVIA

Vast distances between cities and towns make air transportation a cost-efficient mode of travel in Scandinavia. SAS is Scandinavia's major air carrier; it also operates domestic lines in Norway, Sweden, and Denmark. SAS offers discount packages for travel among the Scandinavian

capitals, as well as reduced domestic fares in summer. Finnair is also expanding its routes in Scandinavia.

Trains—comfortable, clean, and fast—are also good for covering the large distances here. Remember to specify a smoking or no-smoking seat or compartment. You should inquire with your travel agent about Scanrail Passes, or individual country passes, for travel within the region.

Another means of getting around Scandinavia's countries is to go by ferry. Some of the larger vessels offer a combination of efficient travel (you sleep aboard and wake up in your destination the next morning) and amenities approaching what you might expect on a cruise ship: luxury dining, gambling, a sauna and pool, and entertainment. Travelers should beware, however, that the noise level may be high and the crowd is usually very lively.

If you prefer the freedom of planning an itinerary and traveling at your own pace, a rental car is a good, albeit expensive, alternative. Most major car-rental companies operate in Scandinavia. Roads are generally good, but allow plenty of time for navigating the region's winding highway network. Scandinavia enforces some of the most strict drinking-and-driving laws in the world—a drunk driver could end up in jail after one offense.

Public transportation in Scandinavia's cities is safe, fast, and inexpensive. Some cities, including the capitals, offer day passes reducing the cost of buses and train travel.

Taxis in Scandinavia are safe, clean, *and* expensive. All taxis should be clearly marked and have a meter inside; unmarked taxis—usually operated illegally by unlicensed drivers—are not recommended. A 10% tip is a friendly gesture, but by no means necessary. Most taxis accept major credit cards and cash.

TRAVEL AGENCIES

A good travel agent puts your needs first. Look for an agency that has been in business at least five years, emphasizes customer service, and has someone on staff who specializes in your destination. In addition, **make sure the agency belongs to a professional trade organization.** The American Society of Travel Agents (ASTA) has more than 10,000 members in some 140 countries, enforces a strict code of ethics, and will step in to mediate agent-client disputes involving ASTA members. ASTA also maintains a directory of agents on its Web site; ASTA's TravelSense.org, a trip planning and travel advice site, can also help to locate a travel agent who caters to your needs.

🔁 Local Agent Referrals **American Society of Travel Agents (ASTA)** ✉ 1101 King St., Suite 200, Alexandria, VA 22314 ☎ 703/739-2782 or 800/965-2782 24-hr hotline 🖷 703/684-8319 ⊕ www.astanet.com and www.travelsense.org. **Association of British Travel Agents** ✉ 68-71 Newman St., London W1T 3AH ☎ 020/7637-2444 🖷 020/7637-0713 ⊕ www.abta.com. **Association of Canadian Travel Agencies** ✉ 130 Albert St., Suite 1705, Ottawa, Ontario K1P 5G4 ☎ 613/237-3657 🖷 613/237-7052 ⊕ www.acta.ca. **Australian Federation of Travel Agents** ✉ Level 3, 309 Pitt St., Sydney, NSW 2000 ☎ 02/9264-3299 or 1300/363-416 🖷 02/9264-1085 ⊕ www.afta.com.au. **Travel Agents' Association of New Zealand** ✉ Level 5, Tourism and Travel House, 79 Boulcott St., Box 1888, Wellington 6001 ☎ 04/499-0104 🖷 04/499-0786 ⊕ www.taanz.org.nz.

VISITOR INFORMATION
Learn more about foreign destinations by checking government-issued travel advisories and country information. For a broader picture, consider information from more than one country.

🔁 Scandinavian Tourist Board In the U.S.: **Scandinavian Tourist Board** ✉ 655 3rd Ave., New York, NY 10017 ☎ 212/885-9700 🖷 212/885-9710 ⊕ www.goscandinavia.com.

In the U.K.: **VisitDenmark** ✉ 55 Sloan St., London SW1X 9SY ☎ 44/20-7259-5959 🖷 44/20-7259-5955 ⊕ www.visitdenmark.com. **Finnish Tourist Board** ✉ 177-179 Hammersmith Rd., London W6 8BS ☎ 44/20-7365-2512. **Iceland Tourist Board** ✉ Laekgargata 3, Reykjavìk 101 ☎ 354/535-5500 🖷 354/535-5501. **Norwegian Tourist Board** ✉ Charles House, 5 [Lower] Regent St., London SW1Y 4LR ☎ 44/207-389-8800 🖷 44/207-

839-6014. **Swedish Travel and Tourism Council** ☎ 0207/108-6168 🖷 46/620-150-11 ⊕ www.visitsweden.com.

🔁 Government Advisories **U.S. Department of State** ✉ Bureau of Consular Affairs, Overseas Citizens Services Office, 2201 C St. NW Washington, DC 20520 ☎ 202/647-5225, 888/407-4747 or 317/472-2328 for interactive hotline ⊕ www.travel.state.gov. **Consular Affairs Bureau of Canada** ☎ 800/267-6788 or 613/944-6788 ⊕ www.voyage.gc.ca. **U.K. Foreign and Commonwealth Office** ✉ Travel Advice Unit, Consular Directorate, Old Admiralty Bldg., London SW1A 2PA ☎ 0870/606-0290 or 020/7008-1500 ⊕ www.fco.gov.uk/travel. **Australian Department of Foreign Affairs and Trade** ☎ 300/139-281 travel advisories, 02/6261-1299 Consular Travel Advice ⊕ www.smartraveller.gov.au or www.dfat.gov.au. **New Zealand Ministry of Foreign Affairs and Trade** ☎ 04/439-8000 ⊕ www.mft.govt.nz.

WEB SITES
Be sure to visit Fodors.com (⊕ www.fodors.com), a complete travel-planning site.

DANISH RESOURCES
Danish Tourist Board (general ⊕ www.dt.dk ✉ For North Americans ⊕ www.visitdenmark.com ✉ For those in Ireland and the U.K. ⊕ www.dtb.dt.dk). **Wonderful CopenhagenCopenhangen** (Copenhagen Tourist Board; ⊕ www.visitcopenhagen.com). **Danish Meteorological Institute** (includes weather forecasts; ⊕ www.dmi.dk).

FINNISH RESOURCES
Finland Tourist Board (⊕ www.visitfinland.com or www.gofinland.org); **Virtual Finland** (Ministry for Foreign Affairs of Finland; ⊕ virtual.finland.fi). **City of Helsinki** (⊕ www.hel.fi/tourism). **King's Road Information** (⊕ www.finlandkingsroad.com or www.kuninkaantie.net).

ICELANDIC RESOURCES
Tourist Boards (North Atlantic ⊕ www.goiceland.org ✉ Iceland ⊕ www.visiticeland.com). **What's on in Iceland** (entertainment and cultural events

⊕ www.whatson.is). **Reykjavík Tourism and Events** (⊕ www.visitreykjavik.is).

NORWEGIAN RESOURCES

Norwegian Tourist Board (⊕ www.visitnorway.com). **Visit Oslo** (⊕ www.visitoslo.com). **Royal Norwegian Embassy in the United States** (⊕ www.norway.org).

SWEDISH RESOURCES

Swedish Travel & Tourism Council (⊕ www.visitsweden.com). **Stockholm Visitors Board** (⊕ www.stockholmtown.com). **City of Stockholm** (⊕ www.stockholm.se/english).

Denmark

WORD OF MOUTH

"I'll always love Copenhagen. Wander up and down the Strøget. Eat dinner at one of the many alfresco restaurants on Greyfriars Square. Watch the changing of the guard at Amalienborg at noon. Have a beer (best draft beer in the world) at '90 Vin Stue on Gammel Kongevej."

—Snoopy

"Tivoli Gardens are only semi-impressive by day, but at night, all lit up, it's a magical place, with some of the world's best people-watching."

—Annam

Updated by
Charles Ferro
and Eduardo
López de
Luzuriaga

THE KINGDOM OF DENMARK dapples the Baltic Sea in an archipelago of some 450 islands and the crescent of one peninsula. Measuring 43,069 square km (17,028 square mi) and with a population of 5 million, it is the geographical link between Scandinavia and Europe. Half-timber villages and tidy agriculture rub shoulders with provincial towns and a handful of cities, where pedestrians set the pace, not traffic. Mothers safely park baby carriages outside bakeries while outdoor cafés fill with cappuccino-sippers, and lanky Danes pedal to work in lanes thick with bicycle traffic. Clearly this is a land where the process of life is the greatest reward.

While in Denmark, visitors pinch themselves in disbelief and make long lists of resolutions to emulate the natives. The Danes' lifestyle is certainly enviable, not yet the pressure-cooked life of some other Western countries. Long one of the world's most liberal nations, Denmark has a highly developed social-welfare system. Hefty taxes are the subject of grumbles and jokes, but Danes are proud of their state-funded medical and educational systems and high standard of living. Educated, patriotic, and keenly aware of their tiny international position, most Danes travel extensively and have a balanced perspective of their nation's benefits and shortfalls.

The history of this little country stretches back 250,000 years, when Jutland was inhabited by nomadic hunters, but it wasn't until AD 500 that a tribe from Sweden, called the Danes, migrated south and christened the land Denmark. The Viking expansion that followed was based on the country's strategic position in the north. Struggles for control of the North Sea with England and western Europe; of the Skagerrak (the strait between Denmark and Norway) with Norway and Sweden; and of the Baltic Sea with Germany, Poland, and Russia ensued. With high-speed ships and fine-tuned warriors, intrepid navies navigated to Europe and Canada, invading and often pillaging, until, under King Knud (Canute) the Great (995–1035), they captured England by 1018.

After the British conquest, Viking supremacy declined as feudal Europe learned to defend itself. Internally, the pagan way of life was threatened by the expansion of Christianity, introduced under Harald Bluetooth, who in AD 980 "baptized" the country, essentially to avoid war with Germany. For the next several hundred years, the country tried to maintain its Baltic power with the influence of the German Hanseatic League. Under the leadership of Valdemar IV (1340–75), Sweden, Norway, Iceland, Greenland, and the Faroe Islands became a part of Denmark. Sweden broke away by the mid-15th century and battled Denmark for much of the next several hundred years, whereas Norway remained under Danish rule until 1814, Iceland until 1943. Greenland and the Faroe Islands are still self-governing Danish provinces.

Denmark prospered again in the 16th century, thanks to the Sound Dues, a levy charged to ships crossing the Øresund. Under King Christian IV, a construction boom crowned the land with what remain architectural gems today, but his fantasy spires and castles, compounded with the Thirty Years' War in the 17th century, led to state bankruptcy.

Denmark is divided into three regions: the two major islands of Zealand and Funen, and the peninsula of Jutland. To the east, Zealand is Denmark's largest and most populated island, with Copenhagen its focal point. Denmark's second largest island, Funen, is a pastoral, undulating land dotted with farms and summerhouse beach villages, with Odense as its one major town. To the west, the relatively vast Jutland connects Denmark to the European continent; here you find the towns of Århus and Aalborg.

1

If you have **3 days**

Take at least two days to explore and enjoy **Copenhagen.** The third day, head north of the city, first to **Rungsted** to see Karen Blixen's manor house and the lush garden surrounding it, then to the Louisiana modern-art museum in **Humlebæk.**

If you have **5 days**

After two days and nights in **Copenhagen,** head north to **Rungsted** and **Humlebæk**; then spend the third night in **Helsingør.** The next day, visit the castles of Helsingør and **Hillerød,** and spend the night in medieval **Roskilde.** Day 5, venture southeast to enjoy the dramatic nature and history of **Møn** and the villages and beaches of Lolland and Falster. An alternative last-day tour is to head west to Hans Christian Andersen's birthplace of **Odense,** on Funen.

If you have **7 days**

In a week you can see Copenhagen and environs and explore Funen and Jutland. Rent a car for the latter—it's the quickest way to make it from the historic cities of **Århus** and **Aalborg** to the blond beaches of **Skagen,** with time left over to meander through a couple of smaller villages.

By the 18th century, absolute monarchy had given way to representative democracy, and culture flourished. Then—in a fatal mistake—Denmark sided with France and refused to surrender its navy to the English during the Napoleonic Wars. In a less than valiant episode of British history, Lord Nelson turned his famous blind eye to the destruction and bombed Copenhagen to bits. The defeated King Frederik VI handed Norway to Sweden. Denmark's days of glory were over.

Though Denmark was unaligned during World War II, the Nazis invaded in 1940. Against them, the Danes used the only weapons they had: a cold shoulder and massive underground resistance. After the war, Denmark focused inward, refining its welfare system and concentrating on its main industries of agriculture, shipping, and financial and technical services. It is an outspoken member of the European Union (EU), championing environmental responsibility and supporting development in emerging economies. And, expensive as it is, Denmark is in many ways less pricey than the rest of Scandinavia.

Copenhagen fidgets with its modern identity as both a Scandinavian–European link and cozy capital. The center of Danish politics, culture, and finance, it copes through balance and a sense of humor with a taste for the absurd. Stroll the streets and you'll pass classic architecture painted in candy colors, and businessmen clad in jeans and T-shirts.

The surrounding countryside in the rest of Zealand is not to be missed. Less than an hour from Copenhagen, fields and half-timber cottages checker the land. Roskilde, to the east, has a 12th-century cathedral, and in the north, the Kronborg Castle of *Hamlet* fame crowns Helsingør. Beaches, some chic, some deserted, are powdered with fine white sand.

Funen rightly earned its storybook reputation by making cuteness a local passion. The city of Odense, Hans Christian Andersen's birthplace, is cobbled with crooked old streets and Lilliputian cottages. Jutland's landscape is the most severe, with Ice Age–chiseled fjords and hills, sheepishly called mountains by the Danes. In the cities of Århus and Aalborg, you can find museums and nightlife rivaling Copenhagen's.

The best way to discover more of Denmark is to strike up a conversation with an affable and hospitable Dane. *Hyggelig* defies definition but comes close to meaning a cozy and charming hospitality. A summertime beach picnic can be as hyggelig as tea on a cold winter's night. The only requirement is the company of a Dane.

Exploring Denmark

Denmark is divided into three regions: the two major islands of Zealand and Funen, and the peninsula of Jutland. To the east, Zealand is Denmark's largest and most populated island, with Copenhagen its focal point. Denmark's second-largest island, Funen, is a pastoral, undulating land dotted with farms and summerhouse beach villages, with Odense as its one major town. To the west, the relatively vast Jutland connects Denmark to the European continent; here you find the towns of Århus and Aalborg.

Numbers in the text correspond to numbers in the margin and on the maps.

About the Restaurants

Denmark's major cities have a good selection of restaurants serving both traditional Danish and international cuisines. The restaurants we list are the cream of the crop in each price category. Properties indicated by an ✕⊡ are lodging establishments whose restaurant warrants a special trip.

You can reduce the cost of food by planning. Breakfast is often included in your hotel bill; if not, you may wish to buy fruit, sweet rolls, and a beverage for a picnic breakfast. Bakeries abound and offer all the fixings for breakfast, except coffee or tea. In recent years many corner convenience stores have begun to sell hot drinks. Opt for a restaurant lunch instead of dinner, since the latter tends to be significantly more expensive. Instead of beer or wine, drink tap water—liquor can cost four times the price of the same brand in a store—but do specify tap water, as the term "water" can refer to soft drinks and bottled water, which are also expensive.

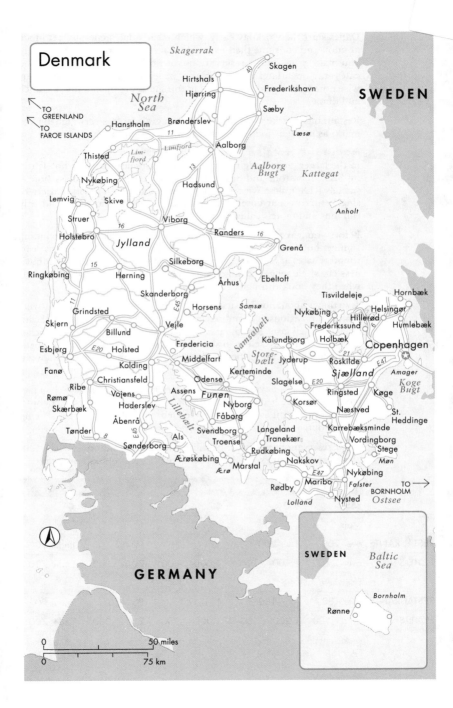

Danes start the workday early, which means they generally eat lunch at noon and consume their evening meal on the early side. Make sure you make your dinner reservations for no later than 9 PM. Bars and cafés stay open later, and most offer at least light fare. Unless otherwise noted, the restaurants listed in this guide are open daily for lunch and dinner.

Restaurants' markups on alcoholic beverages are often very high in Denmark: as much as four times that of a standard retail price.

About the Hotels

In the larger cities, lodging ranges from first-class business hotels run by SAS, Sheraton, and Scandic; to good-quality tourist-class hotels, such as RESO, Best Western, and Scandic Budget; to a wide variety of single-entrepreneur hotels. In the countryside, look for independently run inns and motels called *kroer.*

Before you leave home, **ask your travel agent about discounts,** including summer hotel checks for Best Western and Scandic, and enormous year-round rebates at SAS hotels for travelers over 65. All EuroClass (business class) passengers can get discounts of at least 10% at SAS hotels when they book through SAS.

Two things about hotels usually surprise North Americans: the relatively limited dimensions of Scandinavian beds and the generous size of Scandinavian breakfasts. Scandinavian double beds are often about 60 inches wide or slightly less, close in size to the U.S. queen size. King-size beds (72 inches wide) are difficult to find and, if available, require special reservations.

Older hotels may have some rooms described as "double," which in fact have one double bed plus one foldout sofa big enough for two people. This arrangement is occasionally called a combi-room but is being phased out.

Make reservations whenever possible. Even countryside inns, which usually have space, are sometimes packed with vacationing Europeans.

WHAT IT COSTS In Danish Kroner					
	$$$$	$$$	$$	$	¢
	Main Cities				
RESTAURANTS	over 200	151–200	121–150	90–120	under 90
HOTELS	over 1,700	1,400–1,700	1,000–1,400	700–1,000	under 700
	Elsewhere				
RESTAURANTS	over 180	141–180	121–140	90–120	under 90
HOTELS	over 1,500	1,200–1,500	1,000–1,200	700–1,000	under 700

Restaurant prices are for a main course at dinner, excluding tip. Hotel prices are for two people in a standard double room in high season.

Timing

Summertime—when the lingering sun of June, July, and August brings out the best in the climate and the Danes—is the best time to visit. In July most Danes flee to their summer homes or go abroad. If you do go in winter, the weeks preceding Christmas are a prime time to explore Tivoli. Although the experience is radically different from the flower-filled summertime park, the winter park has a charm all its own. Much of Tivoli is closed during these weeks, but you can still experience some of the shops, restaurants, a handful of rides, an "elf house," and some Danish theater.

Mainland Denmark and its surrounding islands have a cool maritime climate with mild to warm summers and cold (but not frigid) winters. Late summer and early fall is the rainiest season, but even then, precipitation is rarely heavy. In summer, Bornholm tends to stay warmer and sunnier longer than elsewhere. Winter is dark and misty, but it's a great time to visit museums, libraries, and the countless atmospheric meeting places in which the Danes take refuge.

COPENHAGEN

Copenhagen—København in Danish—has no glittering skylines, few killer views, and only a handful of meager skyscrapers. Bicycles glide alongside manageable traffic at a pace that's utterly human. The early-morning air in the pedestrian streets of the city's core, Strøget, is redolent of freshly baked bread and soap-scrubbed storefronts. If there's such a thing as a cozy city, this is it.

The town was a fishing colony until 1157, when Valdemar the Great gave it to Bishop Absalon, who built a castle on what is now Christiansborg. It grew as a center on the Baltic trade route and became known as *købmændenes havn* (merchants' harbor) and eventually København. In the 15th century it became the royal residence and the capital of Norway and Sweden. A hundred years later, Christian IV, a Renaissance king obsessed with fine architecture, began a building boom that crowned the city with towers and castles, many of which still stand. They are almost all that remain of the city's 800-year history; much of Copenhagen was destroyed by two major fires in the 18th century and by British bombing during the Napoleonic Wars.

Despite a tumultuous history, Copenhagen survives as the liveliest Scandinavian capital. With its backdrop of copper towers and crooked rooftops, the venerable city is amused by playful street musicians and performers, soothed by one of the highest standards of living in the world, and spangled by the thousand lights and gardens of Tivoli.

Exploring Copenhagen

The sites in Copenhagen rarely jump out at you; the city's elegant spires and tangle of cobbled one-way streets are best sought out on foot at an unhurried pace. Excellent bus and train systems can come to the rescue of weary legs. The city is not divided into single-purpose districts; people work, play, shop, and live throughout the central core of this multilayered, densely populated capital.

Be it sea or canal, water surrounds Copenhagen. A network of bridges and drawbridges connects the two main islands—Zealand and Amager—on which Copenhagen is built. The seafaring atmosphere is indelible, especially around Nyhavn and Christianshavn.

Some Copenhagen sights, especially churches, keep short hours, particularly in fall and winter. It's a good idea to call directly or check with the tourist offices to confirm opening times.

Rådhus Pladsen, Christiansborg Slot & Strøget

In 1728 and again in 1795, fires broke out in central Copenhagen with devastating effect. Disaster struck again in 1807, when the British fleet, under the command of Admiral Gambier, unleashed a heavy bombardment on the city and destroyed many of its oldest and most beautiful buildings. The attack also inflicted hundreds of civilian casualties. These events still shape modern Copenhagen, which was rebuilt with wide, curved-corner streets—making it easier for fire trucks to turn—and large, rectangular apartment buildings centered on courtyards. Arguably the liveliest area of the city, central Copenhagen is packed with shops, restaurants, businesses, and apartment buildings, as well as the crowning architectural achievements of Christian IV—all of it overflowing with Danes and visitors. Copenhagen's central spine consists of the five consecutive pedestrian strands known as Strøget and the surrounding tangle of roads and courtyards—less than a mile square in total. Across the capital's main harbor is the smaller, 17th-century Christianshavn. In the early 1600s this area was mostly a series of shallows between land, which were eventually dammed. Today Christianshavn's colorful boats and postcard maritime character make it one of the toniest parts of town.

a good walk

The city's heart is the Rådhus Pladsen, home to the baroque-style **Rådhus** ❶ ⊩ and its clock tower. On the east side of the square is the landmark **Lurblæserne** ❷. Off the square's northeastern corner is Frederiksberggade, the first of the five pedestrian streets making up **Strøget** ❸, Copenhagen's shopping district. Walk northeast past the cafés and trendy boutiques to the double square of Gammeltorv and Nytorv.

Down Rådhusstræde toward Frederiksholms Kanal, the **Nationalmuseet** ❹ contains an amazing collection of Viking artifacts. Cross Frederiksholms Kanal to Christiansborg Slotsplads, a small atoll divided by the canal and dominated by the burly **Christiansborg Slot** ❺. North of the castle is **Thorvaldsens Museum** ❻, devoted to the works of one of Denmark's most important sculptors, Bertel Thorvaldsen. On the south end of Downtown is the three-story Romanesque **Kongelige Bibliotek** ❼, edged by carefully tended gardens and tree-lined avenues. To the south, on the harbor side of the royal library, is its glass-and-granite annex, nicknamed the "Black Diamond." The newest addition to the library complex is the **Dansk Jødisk Museum** ❽. Back on the south face of Christiansborg are the **Teatermuseet** ❾ and the **Kongelige Stald** ❿.

On the street that bears its name is the **Tøjhusmuseet** ⑪, and a few steps away are the architecturally marvelous **Børsen** ⑫ and the **Holmens Kirke** ⑬. To the southeast is **Christianshavn,** connected to downtown by the drawbridge Knippelsbro. Farther north, the former Holmen shipyard houses major institutions, several departments of Københavns Universitet, and the new Opera House, which opened in January 2005.

From nearly anywhere in the area you can see the green-and-gold spire of **Vor Frelsers Kirken** ⑭. Northwest of the church, the **Dansk Arkitektur Center** ⑮ occupies a hulking old warehouse on Strandgade. Back across the Knippels Torvegade Bridge, about 1½ km (less than a mile) down Børgsgade through Højbroplads, is Amagertorv, one of Strøget's five streets. Farther west down the street is the 18th-century **Helligaandskirken** ⑯. On Strøget's Østergade, the massive spire of **Nikolaj Kirken** ⑰ looks many sizes too large for the tiny cobblestone streets below.

TIMING   The walk itself takes about 2 hours. Typically, Christiansborg Slot and its ruins and the Nationalmuseet both take at least 1½ hours to see—even more for Viking fans. The hundreds of shops along Strøget are enticing, so plan extra shopping and café time—at least as much as your wallet can spare. Note that many attractions on this walk are closed Sunday or Monday, and some have odd hours; always call ahead or check with the tourist information office.

WHAT TO SEE   **Børsen** (Stock Exchange). This masterpiece of fantasy and architecture
⑫   is the oldest stock exchange in Europe. The Børsen was built between 1619 and 1640, with the majority of the construction in the 1620s. Christian IV commissioned the building in large part because he wanted to make Denmark the economic superpower and crossroads of Europe. Rumor has it that when it was being built he was the one who twisted the dragons' tails on the spire that tops the building. When it was first opened, it was used as a sort of medieval mall, filled with shopping stalls. Though parts of the Børsen still operate as a stock exchange, the bulk of the building houses the Chamber of Commerce, and therefore it's open only to accredited members and brokers. ✉ *Christiansborg Slotspl., Downtown.*

off the beaten path

★

CHRISTIANIA – If you are nostalgic for 1960s counterculture, head to this anarchists' commune on Christianshavn. Founded in 1971, when students occupied army barracks, it is now a peaceful community of nonconformists who run a number of businesses, including a bike shop, bakery, rock-music club, and communal bathhouse. Wall cartoons preach drugs and peace, but the inhabitants are less fond of cameras—picture-taking is forbidden. ✉ *Prinsesseg. and Bådsmandsstr., Christianshavn* ☎ *32/57–60–05 guided tours* ⊕ *www.christiania.org/folderus.*

❺   **Christiansborg Slot** (Christiansborg Castle). Surrounded by canals on
Fodor'sChoice   three sides, the massive granite castle is where the queen officially re-
★   ceives guests. From 1441 until the fire of 1795, it was used as the royal residence. Even though the first two castles on the site were burned, Christiansborg remains an impressive baroque compound, even by European

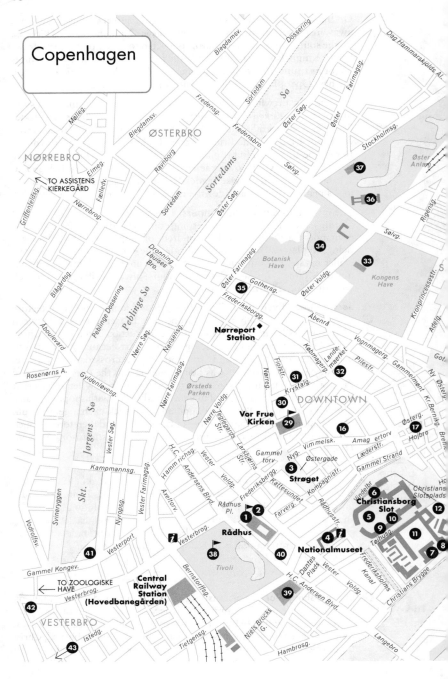

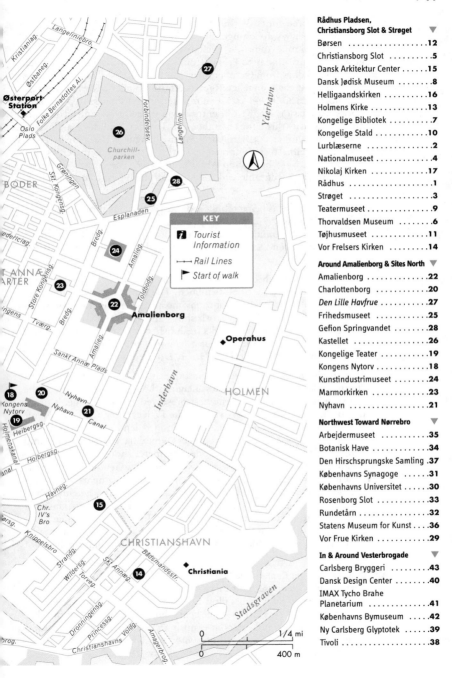

standards. Free tours of the **Folketinget** (Parliament House; ☎ 33/ 37–55–00 ⊕ www.folketinget.dk) are given Monday through Saturday from June to mid-August, as well as on Sunday from July to mid-August; tours run Sunday to Friday from mid-August through September, and on weekdays from October through April. English-language groups begin at 2. At the **Kongelige Repræsantationlokaler** (Royal Reception Chambers; ☎ 33/92–64–92), you're asked to don slippers to protect the floors. Admission is DKr 60; entry is via guided tour only. Tours are given daily May through September, and Tuesday, Thursday, and weekends from October through April; English-language tours are at 11, 1, and 3. The **Højesteret** (Supreme Court), on the site of the city's first fortress, was built by Bishop Absalon in 1167. The guards at the entrance are knowledgeable and friendly; call them first to double-check the court's complicated opening hours.

While the castle was being rebuilt around 1900, the Nationalmuseet excavated the **ruins** (☎ 33/92–64–92) beneath it. The resulting dark, subterranean maze contains fascinating models and architectural relics. The ruins are open October through April, daily 10–4, and admission is DKr 25.

Wander around **Højbro Plads** and the delightful row of houses that borders the northern edge of Slotsholmen. The quays here were long ago Copenhagen's fish market, but today most fresh fish is transported directly from boats to the city's fish shops and supermarkets. However, one lone fisherwoman still hawks fresh fish, marinated herring, and eel in the early morning. She is the last fishmonger you'll see carrying on the tradition. ☒ *Prins Jørgens Gård 1, Downtown.*

Christianshavn. Cobbled avenues, antique street lamps, and Left Bank charm make up one of the oldest neighborhoods in the city. Even the old system of earthworks—the best preserved of Copenhagen's original fortification walls—still exists. In the 17th century, Christian IV offered what were patches of partially flooded land for free, and with additional tax benefits; in return, takers would have to fill them in and construct sturdy buildings for trade, commerce, housing for the shipbuilding workers, and defense against sea attacks. Gentrified today, the area harbors restaurants, cafés, and shops, and its ramparts are edged with green areas and walking paths, making it the perfect neighborhood for an afternoon or evening amble. The central square, Christianshavn Torv, is where all activity emanates from, and Torvegade, a bustling shopping street, is the main thoroughfare. For a pleasant break, relax at one of the cafés along Wilders Canal, which streams through the heart of town.

⑮ Dansk Arkitektur Center. The Danish Architecture Center occupies an old wharf-side warehouse built in 1880. The hulking structure fell into a state of disrepair after lying fallow for many years, but was rescued, renovated, and reopened in 1986. The center hosts rotating exhibitions that cover trends and trendsetters in Danish architecture and architectural design. ☒ *Strandg. 27B, Christianshavn* ☎ *32/57–19–30* ⊕ *www.dac. dk* ☒ *DKr 40; exhibitions vary* ☉ *Weekdays 10–5.*

⑧ Dansk Jødisk Museum (Danish Jewish Museum). In a wing of the Royal Library, this national center of Jewish culture, art, and history opened in June 2004. Objects of both secular and religious interest are on display, including paintings, prints, jewelry, scrapbooks, films, and much more. The site was designed by Daniel Libeskind, the architect behind the winning design proposal for the World Trade Center memorial in New York City. The museum also gives extensive coverage to the Danish resistance movement, whose work during World War II helped bring nearly all of Denmark's 7,000 Jews to safety in Sweden. The museum is the first minority museum in the country. ⊠ *Proviantpassegen. 6, Downtown* ☏ *33/11–22–18* ⊕ *www.jewmus.dk* 🖅 *DKr 40* ☉ *June–Aug., Tues.–Sun. 10–5; Sept.–May., Tues.–Fri. 1–4, weekends 11–5.*

⑯ Helligaandskirken (Church of the Holy Ghost). This 18th-century church was founded by an abbey of the Holy Ghost and is still one of the city's oldest places of worship. Its choir contains a font by the sculptor Thorvaldsen, and more modern art is found in the large exhibition room—once a hospital—that faces Strøget. ⊠ *Niels Hemmingsensg. 5, Amagertorv section, Downtown* ☏ *33/18–16–45* ⊕ *www. helligaandskirken.dk* 🖅 *Free* ☉ *Weekdays 9–1, Sat. 10–noon.*

off the beaten path

HOLMEN – Previously isolated from central Copenhagen, this former navy base just north of Christianshavn produced ships and ammunition until the 1980s. It was formally opened as the site of the 1995 United Nations Summit on Human Development and played an important role as a cultural area during Copenhagen's 1996 reign as the Cultural Capital of Europe. Today, among its several cultural venues is the city's biggest performance space, the Torpedo Hall, where torpedoes were actually assembled. You'll also find the Danish Art Academy's Architecture School, the National Theater School, the Rhythmic Music Conservatory, and the Danish Film School, all of which host special activities. The most famous new resident is, of course, the new Opera House, that opened in 2005 at a cost of DKr 2.5 billion.

⑬ Holmens Kirke (Islet's Church). Two of the country's most revered naval heroes are buried here: Niels Juel crushed the Swedish fleet at Køge in 1677, and Peder Tordenskjold defeated Charles XII of Sweden during the Great Northern War in the early 18th century. ⊠ *Holmenskanal, Christianshavn* ☏ *33/11–37–40* ⊕ *www.holmenskirke.dk* 🖅 *Free* ☉ *Weekdays 9–2, Sat. 9–noon, Sun. during services.*

need a break?

Øieblikket Espresso Bar m.m (⊠ Søren Kierkegaards Pl. 1, Downtown ☏ 33/47–49–50) operates out of a prime corner on the ground floor of the Royal Library's Black Diamond. The "m.m" in the name means "and more." It's named after a literary journal to which philosopher Søren Kierkegaard once contributed—and you, too, may be inspired to wax poetic as you gaze out over the harbor and bask in the sunlight streaming through the soaring glass walls. In summer the café sets up outdoor tables. When summer days turn nippy you can stay snug indoors, while enjoying the illusion of being outside, thanks to the natural light that floods in at all angles. The simple fare includes croissants, brownies, and sandwiches made on fluffy round buns.

❼ Kongelige Bibliotek (Royal Library). The Royal Library houses the country's largest collection of books, newspapers, and manuscripts. Among the more than 2 million volumes are accounts of Viking journeys to America and Greenland and original manuscripts by Hans Christian Andersen and Karen Blixen (Isak Dinesen). If you happen to be in the area, ramble around the statue of philosopher Søren Kierkegaard (1813–55), the formal gardens, and tree-lined avenues surrounding the building. The library's massive glass-and-granite annex, called the Black Diamond, looms between the main building and the waterfront. The Black Diamond hosts temporary historical exhibits that often feature books, manuscripts, and artifacts culled from the library's extensive holdings. The **National Museum of Photography,** also housed in the Black Diamond, contains a far-reaching collection of more than 25,000 Danish and international photographs, from which temporary exhibits display selections. ⊠ *Søren Kierkegaards Pl. 1, Downtown* ☎ *33/47–47–47* ⊕ *www.kb.dk* ▣ *Library free, temporary exhibits DKr 30* ☉ *Library and museum Mon.–Sat. 10–7.*

❿ Kongelige Stald (Royal Stables). Between 9 and noon, time seems to stand still while riders, elegantly clad in breeches and jackets, exercise the horses. The vehicles, including coaches and carriages, and harnesses on display have been used by the Danish monarchy from 1778 to the present. ⊠ *Christiansborg Ridebane 12, Downtown* ☎ *33/40–10–10* ▣ *DKr 20* ☉ *May–Sept., Fri.–Sun. 2–4; Oct.–Apr., weekends 2–4.*

❷ Lurblæserne (Lur Blower Column). Topped by two Vikings blowing an ancient trumpet called a *lur,* this column displays a good deal of artistic license—the lur dates from the Bronze Age, 1500 BC, whereas the Vikings lived a mere 1,000 years ago. City tours often start at this important landmark, which was erected in 1914. ⊠ *East side of Rådhus Pl., Downtown.*

★ ☺ ❹ Nationalmuseet (National Museum). An 18th-century royal residence, peaked by massive overhead windows, has contained—since the 1930s—what is regarded as one of the best national museums in Europe. Extensive permanent exhibits chronicle Danish cultural history from prehistoric to modern times—included is one of the largest collections of Stone Age tools in the world—and Egyptian, Greek, and Roman antiquities are on display. The children's museum, with replicas of period clothing and all sorts of touchable items, transforms history into something to which children under age 12 can relate. ⊠ *Ny Vesterg. 10, Downtown* ☎ *33/13–44–11* ⊕ *www.natmus.dk* ▣ *DKr 50, free Wed.* ☉ *Tues.–Sun. 10–5.*

⓱ Nikolaj Kirken (Nicholas Church). Though the green spire of the imposing church—named for the patron saint of seafarers—appears as old as the surrounding medieval streets, it is actually relatively young. The current building was finished in 1914; the previous structure, which dated from the 13th century, was destroyed in the 1795 fire. Today the church is a contemporary art gallery and exhibition center that often shows experimental work. ⊠ *Nikolaj Pl. 10, Downtown* ☎ *33/93–16–26* ⊕ *www. nikolaj-ccac.dk* ☑ *DKr 20, free Wed.* ⊙ *Daily noon—5.*

need a break? | **Café Nikolaj** (⊠ Nikolajpl., Downtown ☎ 33/93–16–26), inside Nikolaj Kirken, is a reliable, inexpensive café with good pastries and light meals. It's open noon to 3 for lunch and until 5 for cakes and drinks. From June through August, you can eat on the open terrace.

▶ ❶ **Rådhus** (City Hall). Completed in 1905, the mock-Renaissance building dominates **Rådhus Pladsen** (City Hall Square), the hub of Copenhagen's commercial district. Architect Martin Nyrop's creation was popular from the start, perhaps because he envisioned that it should give "gaiety to everyday life and spontaneous pleasure to all . . ." A statue of Copenhagen's 12th-century founder, Bishop Absalon, sits atop the main entrance.

Besides being an important ceremonial meeting place for Danish VIPs, the intricately decorated Rådhus contains the first **World Clock.** The multidial, superaccurate astronomical timepiece has a 570,000-year calendar and took inventor Jens Olsen 27 years to complete before it was put into action in 1955. If you're feeling energetic, take a guided tour up the 350-foot bell tower for the panoramic, but not particularly inspiring, view.

The modern glass-and-gray-steel **bus terminal** flanking the square's northwest side has French granite floors, pear-tree-wood shelving, and underground marble bathrooms. The $2.8 million creation proved so architecturally contentious—more for its placement than for its design—that there was serious discussion of moving it.

Look up to see one of the city's most charming bronze sculptures, created by the Danish artist E. Utzon Frank in 1936. Diagonally across Rådhus Pladsen, atop a corner office building, are a **neon thermometer** and a **gilded barometer.** On sunny days there's a golden sculpture of a girl on a bicycle; come rain, a girl with an umbrella appears. ⊠ *Rådhus Pl., Downtown* ☎ *33/66–25–82* ☑ *Tower tours DKr 20* ⊙ *Rådhus weekdays 8–5. Tours Oct.–May, Mon.–Sat. at noon; June–Sept., weekdays at 10, noon, and 2, Sat. at noon.*

need a break? | **Vandkunsten** (⊠ Rådhusstr. 17, Downtown ☎ 33/13–90–40) is a mom-and-pop joint that makes great Italian-inspired sandwiches and salads, and they offer free coffee while you wait. The shop is tiny, but the efficient service keeps customers moving. There is only one table inside and it's usually surrounded by customers; so long as the weather is nice, get something to go and seek out a sunny spot for munching.

★ ❸ **Strøget.** Though it is referred to by one name, the city's pedestrian spine, pronounced *Stroy*-et, is actually a series of five streets: Frederiksberggade,

Nygade, Vimmelskaftet, Amagertorv, and Østergade. By mid-morning, particularly on Saturday, it is congested with people, baby strollers, and street performers. Past the swank and trendy, and sometimes flashy and trashy, boutiques of **Frederiksberggade** is the double square of **Gammeltorv** (Old Square) and **Nytorv** (New Square), in summer often crowded with street vendors selling cheap jewelry.

In 1728 and again in 1795, much of Strøget was heavily damaged by fire. When rebuilding, the city fathers straightened and widened the streets. You can still see buildings from this reconstruction period, as well as a few that survived the fires.

In addition to shopping, you can enjoy Strøget for strolling, as hundreds do. Outside the posh fur and porcelain shops and bustling cafés and restaurants, the sidewalks have a festive street-fair atmosphere.

9 Teatermuseet (Theater Museum). After you brush up on theater and ballet history, wander around the boxes, stage, and dressing rooms of the **Royal Court Theater** of 1767, which King Christian VII had built as the first court theater in Scandinavia. Tours can be arranged. ⊠ *Christiansborg Ridebane 10/18, Downtown* ☎ *33/11–51–76* ⊕ *www.teatermuseet.dk* ⊒ *DKr 30* ⊘ *Tues.–Thurs. 11–3, weekends 1–4.*

6 Thorvaldsens Museum. The 19th-century artist Bertel Thorvaldsen (1770–1844) is buried at the center of this museum in a simple, ivy-covered tomb. Strongly influenced by the statues and reliefs of classical antiquity, he is recognized as one of the world's greatest neoclassical artists, having completed commissions all over Europe. The museum, once a coach house for Christiansborg, now houses Thorvaldsen's interpretations of classical and mythological figures, and an extensive collection of paintings and drawings by other artists that Thorvaldsen assembled while living—for most of his life—in Rome. The outside frieze by Jørgen Sonne depicts the sculptor's triumphant return to Copenhagen after years abroad. ⊠ *Bertel Thorvaldsen Pl. 2, Downtown* ☎ *33/32–15–32* ⊕ *www.thorvaldsensmuseum.dk* ⊒ *DKr 20, free Wed.* ⊘ *Tues.–Sun. 10–5. Guided tours in English Sun. at 3.*

11 Tøjhusmuseet (Royal Danish Arsenal Museum). This Renaissance structure—built by King Christian IV and one of central Copenhagen's oldest—contains impressive displays of uniforms, weapons, and armor in a 600-foot-long arched hall. ⊠ *Tøjhusg. 3, Downtown* ☎ *33/11–60–37* ⊕ *www.thm.dk* ⊒ *DKr 40* ⊘ *Aug.–June, Tues.–Sun. noon–4; July, daily 10–4.*

14 Vor Frelsers Kirken (Church of Our Savior). The green-and-gold spire of this baroque church has dominated the Christianshavn area since it was completed in 1752. Local legend has it that the staircase encircling it was built curling the wrong way around, and that when its architect, Laurids de Thurah, reached the top and realized what he'd done, he jumped. In this case, however, legend is erroneous: de Thurah died in his own bed in 1759. ⊠ *Skt. Annæg. 29, Christianshavn* ☎ *32/57–27–98* ⊕ *www.vorfrelserskirke.dk* ⊘ *Apr.–Aug., daily 11–4:30; Sept.–Mar., daily 11–3:30. Tower closed Nov.–Mar. and in inclement weather.*

Around Amalienborg & Points North

The Sankt Annæ Kvarter district of the city was dubbed New Copenhagen when King Christian IV began to expand the city northeastward in the 17th century, building Sankt Annæ Fort (now the Churchillparken and Kastellet) in the process. The district takes its name from the religious order of St. Anne, which valiantly staffed a 16th-century syphilis ward in the area.

North of Kongens Nytorv the city becomes a fidgety grid of parks and wider boulevards pointing northwest across the canal toward upscale Østerbro—wreathed by manors commissioned by wealthy merchants and blue bloods. In the mid-1700s King Frederik V donated parcels of this land to anyone who agreed to build from the work of architect Niels Eigtved, who also designed the Kongelige Theater. The jewel of this crown remains Amalienborg and its rococo mansions.

a good walk

At the end of Strøget, **Kongens Nytorv** ⑱ ☞ is flanked on its south side by the **Kongelige Teater** ⑲ and backed by **Charlottenborg** ⑳, which contains the Danish Academy of Fine Art (call to see if an exhibition has opened the castle to the public). The street leading southeast from Kongens Nytorv is **Nyhavn** ㉑, a onetime sailors' haunt and now a popular waterfront hub. From the south end of the harbor (and the north end of Havnegade) high-speed craft leave for Malmö, Sweden; farther north, Kvæsthusbroen—at the end of Sankt Annæ Plads—is the quay for boats to Oslo, Norway, and Bornholm, Denmark; farther north still, just before the perch of *The Little Mermaid*, ships depart for Swinoujscie, Poland.

West of the harbor front is the grand square called Sankt Annæ Plads. Perpendicular to the oblong square is Amaliegade, its wooden colonnade bordering the cobbled square of **Amalienborg** ㉒, the royal residence with a pleasant garden on its harbor side. Steps west from the square is Bredgade, where the baroque **Marmorkirken** ㉓ flaunts its Norwegian marble structure. Farther north off Bredgade is the rococo **Kunstindustrimuseet** ㉔. Continuing north on Bredgade (you can also take the more colorful, café-lined Store Kongensgade, just west), turn right onto Esplanaden and you'll see the enormously informative **Frihedsmuseet** ㉕. At the Churchillparken's entrance stands the English church, St. Albans. In the park's center, the **Kastellet** ㉖ serves as a reminder of the city's grim military history. At its eastern perimeter is Langelinie, a waterfront promenade with a view of Denmark's best-known pinup, *Den Lille Havfrue* ㉗. Wending your way back toward Esplanaden and the town center, you'll pass the **Gefion Springvandet** ㉘.

TIMING   This walk amid parks, gardens, canals, and building exteriors should take a full day. If the weather is nice, linger in the parks, especially the Kastellet and Amalienhaven, and plan on a long lunch at Nyhavn. The Kunstindustrimuseet merits about an hour, more if you plan on perusing the design books in the museum's well-stocked library. The Frihedsmuseet may require more time: its evocative portrait of Danish life during World War II intrigues even the most history-weary teens. Avoid taking this tour Monday, when some sites are closed.

WHAT TO SEE
②② **Amalienborg** (Amalia's Castle). The four identical rococo buildings occupying this square have housed the royals since 1784. The Christian VIII palace across from the queen's residence houses the **Amalienborg Museum**, which displays the second part of the Royal Collection (the first is at Rosenborg Slot) and chronicles royal lifestyles between 1863 and 1947. Here you can view the study of King Christian IX (1818–1906) and the drawing room of his wife, Queen Louise. Rooms are packed with family gifts and regal baubles ranging from tacky knickknacks to Fabergé treasures, including a nephrite-and-ruby table clock, and a small costume collection.

In the square's center is a magnificent equestrian statue of King Frederik V by the French sculptor Jacques François Joseph Saly. It reputedly cost as much as all the buildings combined. Every day at noon, the Royal Guard and band march from Rosenborg Slot through the city for the changing of the guard. At noon on Queen Margrethe's birthday, April 16, crowds of Danes gather to cheer their monarch, who stands and waves from her balcony. On Amalienborg's harbor side are the trees, gardens, and fountains of **Amalienhaven**. ⊠ *Christian VIII's Palace–Amalienborg Pl., Sankt Annæ Kvarter* ☎ *33/12–21–86* ⌑ *DKr 75* ☉ *May–Oct., daily 10–4; Nov.–Apr., Tues.–Sun. 11–4. Guided tours in English July–Sept., weekends at 1* PM.

②⓪ **Charlottenborg** (Charlotte's Castle). This Dutch baroque–style castle was built by Frederik III's half brother in 1670. Since 1754 the garden-flanked property has housed the faculty and students of the Danish Academy of Fine Art. It is open only during exhibits, which occur year-round. ⊠ *Nyhavn 2, Downtown* ☎ *33/13–40–22* ⊕ *www.charlottenborg-art.dk* ⌑ *DKr 30* ☉ *During exhibitions, daily 10–5 (Wed. until 7).*

②⑦ ***Den Lille Havfrue*** (*The Little Mermaid*). On the Langelinie promenade, this somewhat overhyped 1913 statue commemorates Hans Christian Andersen's lovelorn creation, and is the subject of hundreds of travel posters. Donated to the city by Carl Jacobsen, the son of the founder of Carlsberg Breweries, the innocent waif has also been the subject of some cruel practical jokes, including decapitation and the loss of an arm, but she is currently in one piece. Especially on a sunny Sunday, the Langelinie promenade is thronged with Danes and visitors making their pilgrimage to see the statue. On this occasion, you may want to read the original Hans Christian Andersen tale; it's a heart-wrenching story that's a far cry from the Disney animated movie. ⊠ *Langelinie promenade, Østerbro.*

①⑨ **Det Kongelige Teater** (The Royal Danish Theater). The stoic, pillared, and gallery-front theater is the country's preeminent venue for music, opera, ballet, and theater. Nearly all theater works performed are in Danish, while operas are in their original language with Danish over-titles on a screen above the stage. The Royal Danish Ballet performs on the older stage in the main building; its repertoire ranges from classical to modern works.

The current building was opened in 1874, though the annex, known as **Stærekassen** (Nesting Box) was not inaugurated until 1931. The Nesting

THE DANISH ROYALS

THE EQUITABLE DANES *may believe that excessive pride is best kept hidden, but ask about their Queen and this philosophy promptly flies out the window. The passion for Queen Margrethe II is infectious, and before long you may find yourself waving the Dannebrog flag along with the rest of them when the Queen passes through. Graceful and gregarious, Queen Margrethe II is the embodiment of the new Danish crown, a monarchy that is steeped in history yet decidedly modern in its outlook.*

Denmark's royal lineage has its roots in the 10th-century Kingdom of Gorm the Old. His son, Harald Bluetooth, established the royal headquarters in Zealand, where it remains to this day. Copenhagen's stately Amalienborg Slot has been the official royal residence since 1784. From here Queen Margrethe reigns in a true Danish style marked by sociability, not stuffiness. Renowned for her informal charm, the Queen has fostered an open, familial relationship between the royal house and the Danish public. Queen Margrethe's nurturing role has evolved naturally in a country of Denmark's petite size and population. Though she lives in Copenhagen, the Queen is far from Zealand-bound.

Margrethe wasn't always destined to be queen. When she was born in 1940, the law of succession was limited to sons, and it wasn't until 1953 that the law was ratified to include female accession of the throne. She was groomed to become queen, and on her 18th birthday stepped into her position as heir apparent to the crown. She studied archaeology and political science both at home and abroad, at the Universities of Copenhagen, Århus, Cambridge, and the Sorbonne. In 1967 Margrethe married the French-born Prince

Henrik, born a count near Cahors, France.

Today's modern monarchy is perhaps best exemplified by what the Queen does when she takes off her crown. An accomplished artist and illustrator, the Queen designed the costumes for an acclaimed television production of Hans Christian Andersen's The Shepherdess and the Chimney Sweep. *She also illustrated an edition of J. R. R. Tolkien's* The Lord of the Rings. *Her paintings have been exhibited in galleries, where they command top prices, all of which she donates to charity.*

If there's anyone in the royal circle who has captured the public's hearts like Queen Margrethe once did, it's Hong Kong–born Princess Alexandra, who married Prince Joachim in 1995, but divorced him in 2004. The Princess not only cuts a gracious figure in her gown and crown, but has also endeared herself forever to the Danes, and to the Queen Mother, by learning to speak flawless Danish and—here's the topper—with hardly a trace of an accent. The birth of two sons, Nikolai and Felix, has not diminished her popularity. Although separated, the couple is friendly and can be seen together at some charitable functions.

Crown Prince Frederik (born in 1968), the future king, married Australian Mary Donaldson in 2004 at Copenhagen Cathedral. Some 180 million people worldwide watched the event. Their first child was born in October 2005.

Box got its name due to an obscure likeness to a birdhouse. Statues of Danish poet Adam Oehlenschläger and author Ludvig Holberg—whose works remain the core of Danish theater—flank the facade. Born in Bergen, Norway, in 1684, Holberg came to Denmark as a student and stayed. Often compared to Molière, he wrote 32 of his comedies in a "poetic frenzy" between 1722 and 1728, and legend has it that he complained of interminable headaches the entire time. He published the works himself, made an enormous fortune, and invested in real estate. In the mid-'90s an annex designed by Norwegian architect Sverre Fehn was planned for construction on the eastern side of the theater, but it has yet to open. The theater closes for the summer months. ⊠ *Tordenskjoldsg. 3, Downtown* ☎ *33/ 69–69–33, 33/69–69–69 for tickets* ⊕ *www.kgl-teater.dk* ⊠ *Guided tours DKr 75* ⊙ *Guided tours Sun. at 11; no tours May 27–Aug. 5.*

㉕ Frihedsmuseet (Resistance Museum). Evocative, sometimes moving displays commemorate the heroic Danish resistance movement, which saved 7,000 Jews from the Nazis by hiding and then smuggling them to Sweden. The homemade tank outside was used to spread the news of the Nazi surrender after World War II. ⊠ *Churchillparken, Sankt Annæ Kvarter* ☎ *33/13–77–14* ⊕ *www.frihedsmuseet.dk* ⊠ *DKr 40, free Wed.* ⊙ *May–mid-Sept., Tues.–Sat. 10–4, Sun. and holidays 10–5; mid-Sept.–Apr., Tues.–Sat. 10–3, Sun. and holidays 10–4.*

㉘ Gefion Springvandet (Gefion Fountain). Not far from *The Little Mermaid* yet another dramatic myth is illustrated. The goddess Gefion was promised as much of Sweden as she could plough in a night. The story goes that she changed her sons to oxen and used them to portion off what is now the island of Zealand. ⊠ *East of Frihedsmuseet, Sankt Annæ Kvarter.*

㉖ Kastellet (Citadel). At Churchill Park's entrance stands the spired Anglican (or Episcopal) church **St. Albans.** From there, walk north on the main path to reach the Citadel. The structure's smooth, peaceful walking paths, marina, and greenery belie its fierce past as a city fortification. Built in the aftermath of the Swedish siege of the city on February 10, 1659, the double moats were among the improvements made to the city's defense. The Citadel served as the city's main fortress into the 18th century; in a grim reversal during World War II, the Germans used it as headquarters during their occupation. ⊠ *Center of Churchill Park, Sankt Annæ Kvarter* ⊠ *Free* ⊙ *Daily 6 AM–dusk.*

▶ **⑱ Kongens Nytorv** (King's New Square). A mounted statue of Christian V dominates the square. Crafted in 1688 by the French sculptor Lamoureux, the subject is conspicuously depicted as a Roman emperor. Every year, at the end of June, graduating high school students arrive in horse-drawn carriages and dance beneath the furrowed brow of the sober statue. ⊠ *Between Gothersg., Holmenskanal, and Tordenskjoldsg., Downtown.*

need a break?   Dozens of restaurants and cafés line Nyhavn. **Cap Horn** (⊠ Nyhavn 21, Downtown ☎ 33/12–85–04) is among the best, with moderately priced and completely organic Danish treats served in a cozy, art-filled dining room that resembles a ship's galley. Try the fried plaice swimming in a sea of parsley butter with boiled potatoes. In summertime try to grab a sidewalk table, the perfect place to enjoy an overstuffed focaccia sandwich and a Carlsberg.

24 **Kunstindustrimuseet** (Museum of Decorative Art). Originally built in the 18th century as a royal hospital, the fine rococo museum houses a large selection of European and Asian crafts. Also on display are ceramics, silverware, tapestries, and special exhibitions that often focus on contemporary design. The museum's excellent library is stocked with design books and magazines. A small café also operates here. ⊠ *Bredg. 68, Sankt Annæ Kvarter* ☎ *33/18–56–56* ⊕ *www.kunstindustrimuseet. dk* ☞ *DKr 40; additional fee for some special exhibits* ⊙ *Permanent collection Tues.–Sun. noon–4, Wed. noon–6; special exhibits Tues.–Fri. 10–4 (Wed. 10–6), weekends noon–4.*

23 **Marmorkirken** (Marble Church). Officially the Frederikskirke, this ponderous baroque sanctuary of precious Norwegian marble was begun in 1749 and remained unworked on from 1770 to 1874 due to budget constraints. It was finally completed and consecrated in 1894. Around the exterior are 16 statues of various religious leaders from Moses to Luther, and below them stand sculptures of outstanding Danish ministers and bishops. The hardy can scale 273 steps to the outdoor balcony. From here you can walk past the exotic gilded onion domes of the **Russiske Ortodoks Kirke** (Russian Orthodox Church), just to the north of the Marmorkirken. ⊠ *Frederiksg. 4, off Bredg., Sankt Annæ Kvarter* ☎ *33/ 12–01–44* ⊕ *www.marmorkirken.dk* ☞ *Church free, tower DKr 20* ⊙ *Mon., Tues., and Thurs. 10–5; Wed. 10–6; weekends noon–5. Guided tours mid-June–Aug., daily 1–3; Sept.–mid-June, weekends 1–3.*

★ **21** **Nyhavn** (New Harbor). This harbor-front neighborhood was built 300 years ago to attract traffic and commerce to the city center. Until 1970 the area was a favorite haunt of sailors. Though restaurants, boutiques, and antiques stores now outnumber tattoo parlors, many old buildings have been well preserved and have retained the harbor's authentic 18th-century maritime character; you can even see a fleet of old-time sailing ships from the quay. Hans Christian Andersen lived at various times in the Nyhavn houses at numbers 18, 20, and 67.

Northwest toward Nørrebro

By the 1880s, many of the buildings that now line Nørrebro were being hastily thrown up as housing for area laborers. Many of these flats—typically decorated with a row of pedimented windows and a portal entrance—have been renovated through a massive urban-renewal program. But to this day, many fall flat of typical modern amenities. Due to the cheaper rents, an influx of young, hip inhabitants have begun to call this neighborhood home. On the Nørrebrogade and Sankt Hans Torv of today you'll discover a fair number of cafés, restaurants, clubs, and shops.

Take the train from Østerport Station, off Oslo Plads, to Nørreport Station on Nørre Voldgade and walk down Fiolstræde to **Vor Frue Kirken** **29** ▶. The church's very tall copper spire and four shorter ones crown the area. Backtrack north on Fiolstræde, to the main building of **Københavns Universitet** **30**; on the corner of Krystalgade is the **Københavns Synagoge** **31**.

Fiolstræde ends at the Nørreport train station. Perpendicular to Nørre Voldgade is Frederiksberggade, which leads northwest to the neighborhood of Nørrebro; to the southeast after the Kultorvet, or Coal Square, Frederiksberggade turns into the pedestrian street Købmagergade. From anywhere in the area, you can see the stout **Rundetårn** ㉜: the round tower stands as one of Copenhagen's most beloved landmarks, with an observatory open on autumn and winter evenings. North from the Rundetårn on Landemærket, Gothersgade gives way to **Rosenborg Slot** ㉝, its Dutch Renaissance design standing out against the vivid green of the well-tended Kongens Have. For a heavier dose of plants and living things, head across Øster Voldgade to the 25-acre **Botanisk Have** ㉞. South of the garden is the **Arbejdermuseet** ㉟, which profiles the lives of workers from the late 1800s to the present.

Leave the garden's north exit to reach the **Statens Museum for Kunst** ㊱, notable for exceptional Matisse works. An adjacent building houses **Den Hirschsprungske Samling** ㊲, with 19th-century Danish art on display. Nearby, on the east side of Øster Voldgade, is **Nyboder,** a neighborhood full of tidy homes built by Christian IV for the city's sailors.

TIMING All of the sites on this tour are relatively close together and can be seen in roughly half a day. Note that some sites close Monday or Tuesday; call ahead. The tour can be easily combined with the one that follows—just head back to Nørreport Station and catch a train to Hovedbanegården.

WHAT TO SEE **Arbejdermuseet** (Workers' Museum). The vastly underrated museum
㉟ chronicles the working class from 1870 to the present, with evocative life-size "day-in-the-life-of" exhibits, including reconstructions of a city street and tram and an original apartment once belonging to a brewery worker, his wife, and eight children. Changing exhibits focusing on Danish and international social issues are often excellent. The museum also has a 19th-century-style restaurant serving old-fashioned Danish specialties and a '50s-style coffee shop. ⊠ *Rømersg. 22, Downtown* ☏ *33/93–25–75* ⊕ *www.arbejdermuseet.dk* ⊡ *DKr 50* ⊙ *Daily 10–4.*

off the beaten path

★ **ASSISTENS KIRKEGÅRD** (Assistens Cemetery) – This peaceful, leafy cemetery in the heart of Nørrebro is the final resting place of numerous great Danes, including Søren Kierkegaard (whose last name means "church garden," or "cemetery"), Hans Christian Andersen, and physicist Niels Bohr. In summer the cemetery takes on a cheerful, city-park air as picnicking families, young couples, and sunbathers relax on the sloping lawns amid the dear departed. ⊠ *Kapelvej 2, Nørrebro* ☏ *35/37–19–17* ⊕ *www.assistens.dk* ⊡ *Free* ⊙ *May–Aug., daily 8–8; Sept., Oct., Mar., and Apr., daily 8–6; Nov.–Feb., daily 8–4.*

need a break?

At the bar-café-restaurant combo **Barstarten** (⊠ *Kapelvej 1, Nørrebro* ☏ *35/24–11–00* ⊕ *www.barstarten.dk*) you can get three squares, snacks, and a dizzying array of beverages. The kitchen whips up simple French-Italian country cooking and a new menu appears every two weeks. A favorite is Barstarten's Menu, a three-course affair with a wine list to accompany the food. DJs liven up the scene late on weekend nights with a soul-and-funk repertoire.

④ Botanisk Have (Botanical Garden). Trees, flowers, ponds, sculptures, and a spectacular 19th-century Palmehuset (Palm House) of tropical and subtropical plants blanket the garden's 25-plus acres. There's also an observatory and a geological museum. Take time to explore the gardens and watch the pensioners feed the birds. Some have been coming here so long that the birds actually alight on their fingers. ⊠ *Gothersg. 128, Sankt Annæ Kvarter* ☎ *35/32–22–40* ⊕ *www.botanic-garden.ku.dk* ⊑ *Free* ☉ *May–Sept., daily 8:30–6; Oct.–Apr., Tues.–Sun. 8:30–4.*

③ Den Hirschsprungske Samling (The Hirschsprung Collection). This museum showcases paintings from the country's Golden Age—Denmark's mid-19th-century school of naturalism—as well as a collection of paintings by the late-19th-century artists of the Skagen School. Their luminous works capture the play of light and water so characteristic of the Danish countryside. ⊠ *Stockholmsg. 20, Østerbro* ☎ *35/ 42–03–36* ⊕ *www.hirschsprung.dk* ⊑ *DKr 35, free Wed.* ☉ *Mon. and Wed.–Sun. 11–4.*

③ Københavns Synagoge (Copenhagen Synagogue). The contemporary architect Gustav Friedrich Hetsch borrowed from the Doric and Egyptian styles in creating this arklike synagogue. ⊠ *Krystalg. 12, Downtown* ☎ *33/12–88–88* ☉ *Daily services 4:15.*

③ Københavns Universitet (Copenhagen University). The main building of Denmark's leading institution for higher learning was constructed in the 19th century on the site of a medieval bishops' palace. The university was founded nearby in 1479. ⊠ *Nørreg. 10, Downtown* ☎ *35/32–26–26* ⊕ *www.ku.dk.*

> **need a break?** Near Copenhagen University is **Sømods Bolcher** (⊠ Nørreg. 24 or 36, Downtown ☎ 33/12–60–46), a Danish confectioner that has been on the scene since the late 19th century. Children and candylovers relish seeing the hard candy pulled and cut by hand.

Nyboder. Tour the neat, mustard-color enclave of Nyboder, a perfectly laid-out compound of flat, long, former sailors' homes built by Christian IV. Like Nyhavn, the area was seedy and boisterous at the beginning of the 1970s, but today has become one of Copenhagen's more fashionable neighborhoods. At **Nyboder Mindestuer** (⊠ Skt. Paulsg. 24, Christianshavn ☎ 33/32–10–05 ⊑ DKr 10) you can view an exhibition of everyday life in Nyboder from its inception in 1631 to the present day. The people at this exhibition center also arrange guided tours of the neighborhood. ⊠ *West of Store Kongensg. and east of Rigensg., Sankt Annæ Kvarter.*

③ Rosenborg Slot (Rosenborg Castle). This Dutch Renaissance castle contains ballrooms, halls, and reception chambers, but for all of its grandeur, there's an intimacy that makes you think the king might return any minute. Thousands of objects are displayed, including beer glasses, gilded clocks,

Fodor's Choice
★

golden swords, family portraits, a pearl-studded saddle, and gem-encrusted tables; an adjacent treasury contains the royal jewels. The castle's setting is equally welcoming: it's in the middle of the **Kongens Have** (King's Garden), amid lawns, park benches, and shady walking paths.

King Christian IV built Rosenborg Castle as a summer residence but loved it so much that he ended up living and dying here. In 1849, when the absolute monarchy was abolished, all the royal castles became state property, except for Rosenborg, which is still passed down from monarch to monarch. Once a year, during the fall holiday, the castle stays open until midnight, and visitors are invited to explore its darkened interior with bicycle lights. ⌧ *Øster Voldg. 4A, Sankt Annæ Kvarter* ☏ *33/ 15-32-86* ✉ *DKr 65* ☉ *Nov.–Apr., Tues.–Sun. 11–2; May and Sept., daily 10–4; June–Aug., daily 10–5; Oct., daily 11–3.*

★ ㉜ **Rundetårn** (Round Tower). Instead of climbing the stout Round Tower's stairs, visitors scale a smooth, 600-foot spiral ramp on which—legend has it—Peter the Great of Russia rode a horse alongside his wife, Catherine, who took a carriage. From its top, you enjoy a panoramic view of the twisted streets and crooked roofs of Copenhagen. The unusual building was constructed as an observatory in 1642 by Christian IV and is still maintained as the oldest such structure in Europe.

The art gallery has changing exhibits, and occasional concerts are held within its massive stone walls. An observatory and telescope are open to the public evenings mid-October through March, and an astronomer is on hand to answer questions. ⌧ *Købmagerg. 52A, Downtown* ☏ *33/ 73-03-73* ⊕ *www.rundetaarn.dk* ✉ *DKr 20* ☉ *Sept.–May, Mon.–Sat. 10–5, Sun. noon–5; June–Aug., Mon.–Sat. 10–8, Sun. noon–8. Observatory mid-Oct.–Mar., Tues. and Wed. 7 PM–10 PM.*

㊱ **Statens Museum for Kunst** (National Art Gallery). Old-master paintings—including works by Rubens, Rembrandt, Titian, El Greco, and Fragonard—as well as a comprehensive array of antique and 20th-century Danish art make up the gallery collection. Also notable is the modern art, which includes pieces by a very small but select group of artists, including Henri Matisse, Edvard Munch, Henri Laurens, Emil Nolde, and Georges Braque. The space also contains a children's museum, an amphitheater, a documentation center and study room, a bookstore, and a restaurant. A sculpture garden filled with classical, modern, and whimsical pieces flanks the building. ⌧ *Sølvg. 48–50, Sankt Annæ Kvarter* ☏ *33/74-84-94* ⊕ *www.smk.dk* ✉ *DKr 50, free Wed.* ☉ *Tues. and Thurs.–Sun. 10–5, Wed. 10–8.*

▶ ㉙ **Vor Frue Kirken** (Church of Our Lady). The site of this cathedral has drawn worshippers since the 13th century, when Bishop Absalon built a chapel here. Today's church is actually a reconstruction: the original church was destroyed during the Napoleonic Wars. Five towers top the neoclassical structure. Inside you can see Thorvaldsen's marble sculptures depicting Christ and the 12 Apostles, and Moses and David cast in bronze. ⌧ *Nørreg. 8, Frue Pl., Downtown* ☏ *33/37-65-40* ⊕ *www.domkirken. dk* ✉ *Free* ☉ *Daily 8–5.*

In & Around Vesterbrogade

To the southwest of the city are the vibrant working-class and immigrant neighborhoods of Vesterbro, where you'll find a good selection of inexpensive ethnic restaurants and shops. Like the area around Nørrebro, the buildings date from the late 1800s and were constructed for workers. From Vesterbro, Vesterbrogade leads farther west to the neighborhood of Frederiksberg. Originally a farming area that supplied the royal households with fresh produce, Frederiksberg is now lined with residences of the well-heeled and home to the zoo and a vibrant theater district.

a good walk

Begin your tour from Copenhagen's main station, Hovedbanegården. When you exit on Vesterbrogade, take a right and you can see the city's best-known attraction, **Tivoli** ㊳ ▶. Just southeast of the gardens, on Hans Christian Andersens Boulevard, the neoclassical **Ny Carlsberg Glyptotek** ㊴ contains one of the most impressive collections of antiquities and sculpture in northern Europe. Just north on Hans Christian Andersens Boulevard, across the street from Tivoli's eastern side, is the sleek **Dansk Design Center** ㊵, with innovative temporary exhibits that showcase Danish and international design. To the west of the main station and tucked between Skt. Jørgens Sø (St. Jørgens Lake) and the main arteries of Vestersøgade and Gammel Kongevej is the **IMAX Tycho Brahe Planetarium** ㊶.

Vesterbro, which resembles New York's Lower East Side for its bohemian vibe and ethnically diverse population, is along Vesterbrogade near Tivoli. Running parallel to the south is **Istedgade,** Copenhagen's halfhearted red-light district.

Farther west on Vesterbrogade is **Københavns Bymuseum** ㊷, its entrance flanked by a miniature model of medieval Copenhagen. Beer enthusiasts can head south on Enghavevej and take a right on Ny Carlsbergvej to see the **Carlsberg Bryggeri** ㊸. The visitor center, nearby on Gamle Carlsbergvej, has exhibits on the brewing process and Carlsberg's rise to fame.

TIMING These sights can be seen in half a day, and could be combined easily with a walk around Nørrebro. Tivoli offers charms throughout the day; visit in the late afternoon, and stay until midnight, when colored lights and fireworks (on Wednesday and weekend nights) illuminate the park. Be sure to call ahead, since some places may be closed Monday or Tuesday.

WHAT TO SEE **Carlsberg Bryggeri** (Carlsberg Brewery). As you approach the world-famous Carlsberg Brewery, the unmistakable smell of fermenting hops greets you, a pungent reminder that this is beer territory. (Indeed, near the brewery is the appealing little neighborhood of Humleby; "humle" means "hops.") Four giant Bornholm-granite elephants guard the brewery's main entrance on Ny Carlsbergvej. Nearby, on Gamle Carslbergvej, is the visitor center, in an old Carlsberg brewery. Colorful displays take you step by step through the brewing process. You can also walk through the draft-horse stalls; at the end of your visit, you're rewarded with a few minutes to quaff a complimentary beer. The free **Carlsberg Museum** (✉ Valby Langgade 1, Vesterbro ☎ 33/21–01–12), open weekdays 10 to 3, offers a further look into the saga of the Carlsberg family, and how it managed to catapult Carlsberg from a local name into one of the most famous beers in the world. ⊠ *Gamle Carlsbergvej 11, Vesterbro* ☎ *33/27–13–14* ⊕ *www.carlsberg.com* ⊒ *Free* ⊙ *Tues.–Sun. 10–4.*

㊵ Dansk Design Center (Danish Design Center). This sleek, glass-panel structure looms in sharp contrast to the old-world ambience of Tivoli just across the street. More of a design showroom than a museum, the center's highlights are the innovative temporary exhibits on the main floor. Past exhibits have included "75 years of Bang & Olufsen," which covered the famed Danish audio-system company, and "Tooltoy," a playful, interactive exhibit of toys over the last century. One-third of the temporary exhibits showcase Danish design; the rest focus on international design. The semipermanent collection on the ground floor (renewed every other year) often includes samples from the greats, including chairs by Arne Jacobsen, several artichoke PH lamps (designed by Poul Henningsen), and Bang & Olufsen radios and stereos. Note how the radios they made in the '50s look more modern than many of the radios today. The center's shop carries a wide range of Danish design items and selected pieces from the temporary exhibits. You can enjoy light meals in the atrium café, sitting amid the current exhibits. ⊠ *H. C. Andersens Blvd. 27, Downtown* ☎ *33/69–33–69* ⊕ *www.ddc.dk* ⊒ *DKr 40* ⊙ *Mon., Tues., Thurs., and Fri. 10–5; Wed. 10–9; weekends 11–4.*

㊶ IMAX Tycho Brahe Planetarium. This modern, cylindrical planetarium, which appears to be sliced at an angle, features astronomy exhibits. It is Denmark's most advanced center for popularizing astronomy and space research and promoting knowledge of natural science. The **IMAX Theater** takes you on visual odysseys as varied as journeys through space and sea, the stages of the Rolling Stones, or Kuwaiti fires from the first Persian Gulf War. These films are not recommended for children under age seven. ⊠ *Gammel Kongevej 10, Vesterbro* ☎ *33/12–12–24* ⊕ *www.tycho. dk/in_english* ⊒ *DKr 90* ⊙ *Thurs.–Tues. 10:30–8:30, Wed. 9:30–8:30.*

Istedgade. In what passes for a red-light district in Copenhagen, mom-and-pop kiosks and ethnic restaurants stand side by side with porn shops and shady outfits aiming to satisfy all proclivities. Istedgade, like neighboring Vesterbrogade, has diversified over the past several years, drawing artists and students. Thanks to the city's urban-renewal projects, cafés and businesses are also moving in, mostly on the southwest end of Istedgade, around Enghave Plads (Enghave Square). Mama Lustra, at No. 96–98, is a laid-back café with comfy armchairs and a mixed crowd of students and older artsy types. Though Istedgade is relatively safe, you may want to avoid the area near Central Station late at night. ⊠ *South of and parallel to Vesterbrogade, running southwest from Central Station, Vesterbro.*

㊷ Københavns Bymuseum (Copenhagen City Museum). For a surprisingly evocative collection detailing Copenhagen's history, head to this 17th-century building in the heart of Vesterbro. A meticulously maintained model of 16th-century Copenhagen is kept outdoors from May through September; inside there is also a memorial room for philosopher Søren

Kierkegaard, the father of existentialism. ⊠ *Vesterbrog. 59, Vesterbro* 🕾 *33/21–07–72* ⊕ *www.kbhbymuseum.dk* 🖙 *DKr 20, free Fri.* ⊙ *May–Sept., Wed.–Mon. 10–4; Oct.–Apr., Wed.–Mon. 1–4.*

㊴ Ny Carlsberg Glyptotek (New Carlsberg Museum). Among Copenhagen's
Fodor'sChoice   most important museums—thanks to its exquisite antiquities and Gau-
★   guins and Rodins—the neoclassical New Carlsberg Museum was donated in 1888 by Carl Jacobsen, son of the founder of the Carlsberg
Brewery. Surrounding its lush indoor garden, a series of nooks and
chambers houses works by Degas and other impressionists, plus an extensive assemblage of Egyptian, Greek, Roman, and French sculpture,
not to mention Europe's finest collection of Roman portraits and the
best collection of Etruscan art outside Italy. A modern wing, designed
as a three-story treasure chest by the acclaimed Danish architect Henning Larsen, houses an impressive pre-impressionist collection that includes works from the Barbizon school; impressionist paintings, including
works by Monet, Alfred Sisley, and Pissarro; and a postimpressionist
section, with 50 Gauguin paintings plus 12 of his very rare sculptures.
Note that extensive rebuilding of this museum will continue during 2006.
Some exhibits remain open. Access to the museum until June 28, 2006,
will be via the temporary entrance at Tietgensgade 25. ⊠ *Dantes Pl. 7,*
Vesterbro 🕾 *33/41–81–41* ⊕ *www.glyptoteket.dk* 🖙 *DKr 40, free*
Wed. and Sun. ⊙ *Tues.–Sun. 10–4.*

Ⓒ ▶ **㊳ Tivoli.** Copenhagen's best-known attraction, conveniently next to its
Fodor'sChoice   main train station, attracts an astounding number of visitors: 4 million
★   people from mid-April to mid-September. Tivoli is more sophisticated
than a mere amusement park: among its attractions are a pantomime
theater, an open-air stage, 38 restaurants (some of them very elegant),
and frequent concerts, which cover the spectrum from classical to rock
to jazz. Fantastic flower exhibits color the lush gardens and float on the
swan-filled ponds.

The park was established in the 1840s, when Danish architect George
Carstensen persuaded a worried King Christian VIII to let him build an
amusement park on the edge of the city's fortifications, rationalizing that
"when people amuse themselves, they forget politics." On Wednesday
and weekend nights, elaborate fireworks are set off, and every day the
Tivoli Guard, a youth version of the Queen's Royal Guard, performs.
Try to see Tivoli at least once by night, when 100,000 colored lanterns
illuminate the Chinese pagoda and the main fountain. Call to double-
check prices, which vary throughout the year and often include family
discounts at various times during the day. Tivoli is also open from late
November to Christmas. ⊠ *Vesterbrog. 3, Vesterbro* 🕾 *33/15–10–01*
⊕ *www.tivoli.dk* 🖙 *Grounds DKr 68, ride pass DKr 195* ⊙ *Mid-*
Apr.–mid-Sept., Sun.–Wed. 11–11, Thurs. 11 AM*–midnight, Fri. 11*
AM*–1* AM*, Sat. 11* AM*–midnight; late Nov.–Dec. 23, Sun.–Wed. 11–9, Fri.*
and Sat. 11–10.

Vesterbro. Students, union workers, and immigrants (who account for 15%
of Vesterbro's population) inhabit this area. It's a great place to find ethnic groceries, discount shops, and cheap international restaurants. The

face of Vesterbro, however, has been gentrified. Due to the city's ongoing urban-renewal and clean-up efforts, the spruced-up Vesterbro is attracting chic eateries, stores, and clubs, along with their arty customers. In the center of it all, a new café square, Halmtorvet, has been constructed. An area where you might not normally go has become a must-go spot to see the latest trends. Nightclubs like headline-grabbing Vega, Ideal Bar, and Byens Lys-Cafe PH have opened, as have the restaurants Carlton and Apropos. The area's best clothing shops, such as Hubsch, Don Ya Doll, Gurlie Hurly, and Designer Zoo are at the western end of Istedgade. ⊠ *At southwestern end of Vesterbrogade, Vesterbro.*

off the beaten path

ZOOLOGISK HAVE – Children love the Zoological Gardens, which are home to 3,300 animals and 264 species. The small petting zoo and playground includes cows, horses, rabbits, goats, and hens. The indoor rain forest has butterflies, sloths, alligators, and other tropical creatures. Sea lions, lions, and elephants are fed in the early afternoon. Be warned: on sunny weekends, the line to enter runs far down Roskildevej; get here early. ⊠ *Roskildevej 32, Frederiksberg* ☎ *70/20–02–00* ⊕ *www.zoo.dk* ⌨ *DKr 95* ☉ *June–Aug., daily 9–6; Sept. and Oct., daily 9–5; Nov.–Feb., daily 9–4; Mar. weekdays 9–4, weekends 9–5; Apr. and May, weekdays 9–5, weekends 9–6.*

Where to Eat

In Copenhagen, with its more than 2,000 restaurants, traditional Danish fare spans all price categories: you can order a light lunch of traditional smørrebrød, munch alfresco from a street-side *pølser* (sausage) cart, or dine out on Limfjord oysters and local plaice. Even the most upscale restaurants have moderately priced fixed menus. Though few Danish restaurants require reservations, it's best to call ahead to avoid a wait. The city's more affordable ethnic restaurants are concentrated in Vesterbro, Nørrebro, and the side streets off Strøget. And for less-expensive, savory noshes in stylish surroundings, consider lingering at a café.

WHAT IT COSTS In Danish kroner				
	$$$$	$$$	$$	$	¢
AT DINNER	over Kr 200	Kr 151–Kr 200	Kr 121–Kr 150	Kr 90–Kr 120	under Kr 90

Prices are for a main course at dinner.

Christianhavn, Holmen & Amager

★ $$$$ ✕ **Era Ora.** Since 1983 this has been the premier Italian restaurant in the city, if not the country. It's known for its changing set menu with many courses that do not use cream or butter, and its climate-controlled wine cellar containing 90,000 bottles of solely Italian vintages. Burnt-umber walls and black, chocolate brown, and white accents predominate in the Ole Tønnesen–designed dining room. You'll be served between 9 and 17 (small) courses, depending on your appetite and time commitment—there is no à la carte menu. The tiny seafood antipasti, including octopus with homemade pasta and a touch of mascarpone cheese, fares well opposite a later main course of St. Peter fish; it's light and delicate in a fresh tomato sauce. This is a full, special night out; prepare to spend at least four hours dining leisurely. ⊠ *Overgaden neden Vandet 33-B, Christianshavn* ☎ *32/54–06–93* ⊕ *www.era-ora.dk* ⌁ *Reservations essential* ⊟ *AE, DC, MC, V* ⊘ *Closed Sun.*

$$–$$$ ╳ **Spiseloppen.** Round out your visit to the Free State of Christiania with a meal at Spiseloppen, a 160-seat warehouse restaurant that was a military storage facility and an army canteen in its former life. Upon entering Christiania, wind your way past shaggy dogs, their shaggy owners, graffiti murals, and wafts of patchouli. (There are few street signs, so just ask; Spiseloppen is the neighborhood's best-known restaurant.) From the outside, this run-down warehouse may seem a bit forbidding, but inside it's a different story. Climb up rickety stairs to the second floor and you're rewarded with a loft-size dining room with low, wood-beam ceilings and candles flickering on the tables. The menu highlights are fresh and inventive vegetarian and fish dishes, which might include artichokes stuffed with eggplant or portobello mushrooms served with squash, mango, and papaya. ⊠ *Bådsmandsstr. 43, Christianshavn* ☎ *32/57–95–58* ⊟ *MC, V* ⊘ *Closed Mon. No lunch.*

$–$$$ ╳ **Krunch.** The motto here is "gastronomy within ecology." Krunch serves natural, organic foods from reliable sources and attempts to integrate an environmentally friendly spirit into every facet of the experience. Within these guiding principles, the objective of the owners is to create authentic French-bistro atmosphere and cuisine. The four-course menu changes seasonally; it typically consists of a choice of a fish, meat, or vegetarian main course and an assortment of side dishes. Krunch is also a fine spot for kids. ⊠ *Øresundsvej 14, Amager* ☎ *32/84–50–50* ⊕ *www.krunch.dk* ⊟ *MC, V* ⊘ *Closed Mon.*

Downtown

★ **$$$$** ╳ **Kommandanten.** Fancifully decorated by master florist Tage Andersen with brushed-iron-and-copper furniture, down pillows, and foliage-flanked lights, this is among the city's most exclusive dinner spots. The adventuresome international fare might include dishes such as rabbit with bouillon-cooked lentils, herbs, and bacon, and marinated salmon with oysters and parsley. Jackets are recommended. ⊠ *Ny Adelg. 7, Downtown* ☎ *33/12–09–90* ⊕ *www.kommandanten.dk* ⊟ *AE, DC, MC, V* ⊘ *Closed Sun.*

★ **$$$$** ╳ **Kong Hans Kælder.** Five centuries ago this was a Nordic vineyard—now it's one of Scandinavia's finest restaurants. Chef Thomas Rode Andersen's French-Danish-Asian–inspired dishes employ the freshest local ingredients and are served in a medieval subterranean space with white-washed walls and vaulted ceilings. Try the foie gras with raspberry-vinegar sauce or the warm oysters in vichyssoise with smoked cheese and lemon. ⊠ *Vingårdstr. 6, Downtown* ☎ *33/11–68–68* ⊕ *www.konghans. dk* ⊟ *AE, D, MC, V* ⊘ *Closed Sun. No lunch.*

$$$$ ╳ **Krogs.** This elegant canal-front restaurant has developed a loyal clientele—both foreign and local—for its old-fashioned atmosphere and its innovative fish dishes. Pale-green walls are simply adorned with paintings of old Copenhagen. The menu includes such specialties as pan-grilled

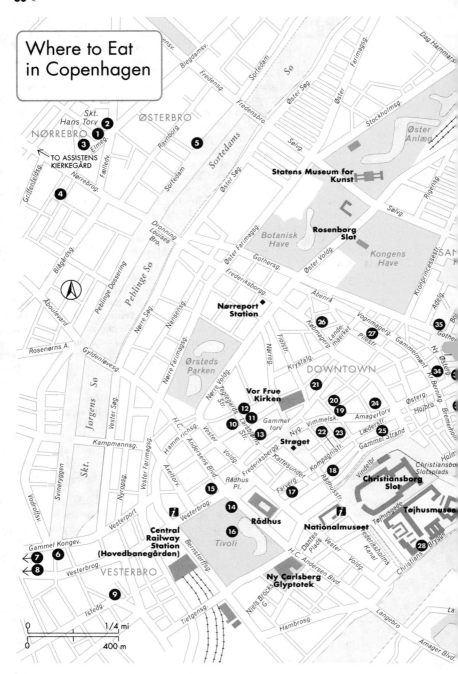

Where to Eat in Copenhagen

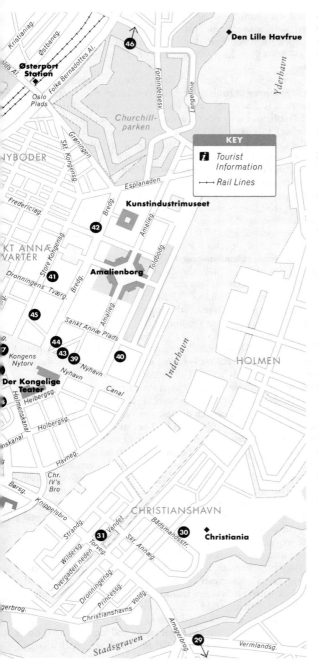

lobster flavored with vanilla oil, and monkfish fillets in a beurre-blanc sauce flavored with arugula and tomato. Jackets are recommended. Krogs is also open for lunch until 4 PM. ⊠ *Gammel Strand 38, Downtown* ☎ *33/15–89–15* ⌗ *Reservations essential* ▤ *AE, DC, MC, V* ☾ *Closed Sun.*

$$$$
Fodor's Choice
★

✕ **The Paul.** From a glass of Bollinger champagne as an aperitif to the very last course at dinner (a rhubarb tart with tea ice cream on caramel), dining at The Paul is a highlight of a visit to Copenhagen. Located in the middle of Tivoli, and only open during the park's season (mid-May to mid-September), this exquisite dining room in a glass-encircled pavilion seems to be favored by everyone in the entertainment world, and it witnesses unannounced visits from members of the Danish royal family. Chef Paul Cunningham takes traditional Danish cuisine and combines influences from other regions; for example, succulent sea bass might be served with Spanish olives and almonds in oil and paired with a crisp Spanish Riesling. The seven-course prix-fixe menu is lovingly prepared from an open kitchen overlooking a chef's table, and service is flawless. ⊠ *Tivoli, Verserbrogade 3.* ☎ *33/75–07–75* ⊕ *www.thepaul.dk* ⌗ *Reservations essential* ▤ *AE, DC, MC, V* ☾ *Closed mid-Sept.–mid-May.*

★ **$$$$**

✕ **Tyvenkokkenhanskoneoghendeselsker.** If you've seen Peter Greenaway's dark and brilliant film *The Cook, the Thief, His Wife, and Her Lover* (with its macabre feast scenes), you may wonder what lies in store at this restaurant with the same name. The same daring humor that inspired the unusual name is exhibited in the innovative seven-course menu, which changes every few weeks. You might be served baked cod in an aromatic coffee sauce or warm rooster simmered in spices and served with horseradish sauce. Desserts include pineapple with mint tortellini. ⊠ *Magstr. 16, Downtown* ☎ *33/16–12–92* ⊕ *www.tyven.dk* ⌗ *Reservations essential* ▤ *DC, MC, V* ☾ *Closed Sun. No lunch.*

$$$–$$$$

✕ **L'Alsace.** Set in the cobbled courtyard of Pistolstræde and hung with paintings by Danish surrealist Wilhelm Freddie, this restaurant is peaceful and quiet, and has attracted such diverse diners as Queen Margrethe, Elton John, and the late Pope John Paul II. The hand-drawn menu lists oysters from Brittany, terrine de foie gras, and *choucrôute à la Strasbourgeoise* (a hearty mélange of cold cabbage, homemade sausage, and pork). Try the superb fresh-fruit tarts and cakes for dessert, and ask to sit in the patio overlooking the courtyard. ⊠ *Ny Østerg. 9, Downtown* ☎ *33/14–57–43* ⊕ *www.alsace.dk* ▤ *AE, DC, MC, V* ☾ *Closed Sun.*

$–$$$$

✕ **Café Ketchup.** You have a choice at this informal, upbeat eatery: for light meals (at light prices), try the lively front café, where you can settle into a red-and-white wicker chair next to the large picture windows and watch the world go by on chic Pilestræde. Try the spring rolls with smoked salmon and cod, flavored with ginger and coriander. The café also serves a tasty brunch from 10 to 1. For more-substantial fare, venture into the restaurant decorated with old French Perrier ads and lighted with white candles. Starters include a potato-and-wasabi soup served with a spicy crab cake, and bruschetta topped with a mango salsa. Main dishes range from halibut stuffed with crabmeat and herbs to marinated duck breast served with sun-dried tomatoes and fennel salad sprinkled with pine nuts. There is also a Café Ketchup in Tivoli, with a large terrace and a similar menu. ⊠ *Pilestr. 19, Downtown* ☎ *33/32–30–30* ⊕ *www.cafeketchup.dk* ▤ *DC, MC, V* ⊘ *Closed Sun.*

$$$ ✕ **Søren K.** Occupying a bright corner of the Royal Library's modern Black Diamond extension, this cool-tone restaurant, with clean lines, blond-wood furnishings, and recessed ceiling lights, serves bold French-Scandinavian concoctions using no cream, butter, or stock. A popular selection is the five-course menu entitled "a couple of hours in the company of fish," which has featured items such as tuna in soy and sesame sauce or mussels drizzled with lemon and thyme. Vegetarian dishes include tofu marinated with red wine and topped with roasted sesame seeds, radishes, and passion fruit. For waterfront views, choose one of the many tables that sit flush up against the Black Diamond's looming glass walls. ⊠ *Søren Kierkegaards Pl. 1 (inside the Black Diamond), Downtown* ☎ *33/47–49–49* ⊕ *www.sorenk.dk* ▤ *DC, MC, V* ⊘ *Closed Sun.*

$$$ ✕ **Sult.** Norwegian author Knut Hamsun's novel *Sult* now shares its moniker with this restaurant on the premises of the Danish Film Institute. The cuisine is Mediterranean, with strong North African and Asian influences. Try the mussels with carrots in a cream sauce or roast guinea fowl with sweet potatoes. The wine list is impressive. ⊠ *Vognmagerg. 8B, Downtown* ☎ *33/74–34–17* ⊕ *www.sult.dk* ▤ *MC, V* ⊘ *Closed Mon.*

$$–$$$ ✕ **El Mesón.** Smoothly worn wooden tables, earthen crockery, and dim lighting characterize the dining room of this Spanish restaurant. The knowledgeable waitstaff serves generous portions of beef spiced with spearmint, lamb with honey sauce, and paella Valenciano—a mixture of rice, chicken, ham, shrimp, lobster, squid, green beans, and peas—for two. ⊠ *Hauser Pl. 12 (behind Kultorvet), Downtown* ☎ *33/11–91–31* ▤ *AE, DC, MC, V* ⊘ *Closed Sun. No lunch.*

★ $$–$$$ ✕ **Reinwalds.** The comfortable black teak chairs with blue upholstery signal the beginning of a series of delightful encounters with comfort and fine food in a pleasant, modern setting. The informative waitstaff ensure that service is far above the norm—they're adept at complementing selected dishes with a fine wine. The three- to five-course menus change monthly, according to the season's harvest. You might find offerings like creamy curry soup with rooster and quail eggs or baked sea bream with almond pesto. ⊠ *Farveg. 15, Downtown* ☎ *33/91–82–80* ⊕ *www. reinwalds.dk* ▤ *AE, DC, MC, V* ⊘ *Closed Sun.*

$–$$$ ✕ **Peder Oxe.** On a 17th-century square, this lively, countrified bistro has rustic tables and 15th-century Portuguese tiles. All entrées—among them grilled steaks, fish, and the best fancy burgers in town—come with an excellent self-service salad bar. Damask-covered tables are set with heavy cutlery and opened bottles of hearty Pyrénées wine. A clever call-light for the waitress is above each table. In spring, when the high northern sun is shining but the warmth still has not kicked in, you won't do badly sitting outside in the Gråbrødretorv (Gray Friars' Square) sipping drinks while wrapped in blankets left thoughtfully for patrons in wicker chairs. ⊠ *Gråbrødretorv 11, Downtown* ☎ *33/11–00–77* ⊕ *www.pederoxe.dk* ▤ *DC, MC, V.*

$–$$ ✕ **Flyvefisken.** Silvery stenciled fish swim along blue-and-yellow walls in this Thai eatery. Spicy dishes include chicken with cashew nuts and herring shark in basil sauce. It's always a busy spot, with media and PR types hanging around, enjoying wet and dry noodles and all manner of typical Thai fare. ⊠ *Larsbjørnsstr. 18, Downtown* ☎ *33/14–95–15* ▤ *DC, MC, V* ☉ *Closed Sun. No lunch.*

$–$$ ✕ **Københavner Caféen.** You know you're in for a real Danish meal when you can smell the vinegary *rød kål* (red cabbage, a Danish staple) upon entering. Dimly lighted and warm, with a dark-wood and burgundy color scheme, this local favorite just oozes with *hygge* (coziness). Choose from a wide range of smørrebrød selections and also a formidable lineup of down-home Danish dishes such as *frikkedeller* (pork meatballs) and butter-fried salmon with boiled potatoes. In summer the kitchen offers a traditional Danish Christmas meal "so that everyone can experience Denmark's Christmas traditions." The meal includes roast pork with red cabbage and the much-loved *ris à l'amande* (rice pudding) for dessert. Hidden inside is an almond, and whoever finds it receives a small present. These Christmas meals are generally offered only to tour groups, but it's worth asking when you reserve. ⊠ *Badstuestr. 10, Downtown* ☎ *33/32–80–81* ♒ *Reservations essential* ▤ *MC, V.*

$–$$ ✕ **Riz Raz.** This Middle Eastern restaurant hops with young locals, families, couples, and anyone who appreciates good value and spicy fare. The inexpensive all-you-can-eat buffet is heaped with lentils, tomatoes, potatoes, olives, hummus, warm pita bread, yogurt and cucumbers, pickled vegetables, and bean salads. The main location is on Kompagnistræde, between Christiansborg Slot and Strøget; there's a second branch behind Vor Frue Kirken. ⊠ *Riz Raz Bla, Kompagnistr. 20, Vesterbro* ☎ *33/15–05–75* ⊠ *Store Kannikestr. 19, Downtown* ☎ *33/32–33–45* ⊕ *www.rizraz.dk* ▤ *DC, MC, V.*

Fodor'sChoice
★

$–$$ ✕ **Victor.** Excellent people-watching and good bistro fare are the calling cards at this French-style corner café. It's best during weekend lunches, when young and old gather for such specialties as rib roast, homemade pâté, and smoked salmon and cheese platters. Come here for one of the best brunches in town. Be warned however that the formal restaurant in the back of the space is quite expensive—order from the front café side for a less expensive meal. ⊠ *Ny Østerg. 8, Downtown* ☎ *33/13–36–13* ⊕ *www.cafevictor.dk* ▤ *AE, DC, MC, V.*

¢–$$ ✕ **Husmanns Vinstue.** If you're looking for old-world Denmark, this is it. Founded in 1888, this warmly lighted basement restaurant is housed in a former stable dating from 1727, which accounts for the low ceilings. Beer mugs dangle above the bar, dark-green lamps shed light onto the heavy wooden tables, and black-and-white photographs of Copenhagen hang on the walls. Until 1981 women were allowed to enter only if accompanied by a male, a rule established by one of the restaurant's female owners. At Husmanns Vinstue you can feast on all types of herring (fried, curried, marinated, and spiced), smoked eel with scrambled eggs, beef tartare with egg yolk, homemade sausage, and roast beef with potato salad, all served on your choice of rye or white bread. ⊠ *Larsbjørnsstr. 2, Downtown* ☎ *33/11–58–86* ⊕ *www.husmannvinstue.dk* ♒ *Reservations essential* ▤ *AE, DC, MC, V* ☉ *No dinner.*

¢–$$ ✕ **Pasta Basta.** This bright, casual eatery just off the Strøget is always crammed with happy diners. Pasta Basta has all the ingredients for its well-deserved success: an all-you-can-eat fresh pasta and salad bar for a refreshingly low price (DKr 79). Main courses on the changing menu may include pasta with prawns, spinach, and chili peppers, or smoked salmon served with pasta in a creamy sauce of scallops, spinach, and herbs. Pasta Basta is one of the city's few restaurants (barring fast-food and shawarma joints) that serves food until 3 AM (and until 5 AM on Friday and Saturday). ☒ *Valkendorfsg. 22, Downtown* ☎ *33/11–21–31* ▭ *DC, MC, V.*

$ ✕ **Atlas Bar.** The health-food café Atlas Bar in the basement of restaurant Flyvefisken serves excellent food to a steady stream of students and hipsters. The snug eatery serves Oriental-inspired and fusion dishes, such as Manila chicken (chicken breasts in a tomato sauce with garlic, ginger, and chili) and medallions of venison. Atlas is also a favorite of vegetarians for its tempting menu of healthful, tasty dishes. ☒ *Larsbjørnsstr. 18, Downtown* ☎ *33/15–03–52* ▭ *DC, MC, V* ⊘ *Closed Sun.*

¢ ✕ **La Galette.** Tucked into a bright little courtyard, this cheery creperie serves an array of savory crepes, including the Asterix, stuffed with ratatouille, egg, and chives, and the Quimper, with spinach, egg, bacon, and cheese. The luscious lineup of sweet crepes includes everything from banana and chocolate to flambéed caramel apples. ☒ *Larsbjørnsstr. 9, Downtown* ☎ *33/32–37–90* ▭ *MC, V* ⊘ *No lunch Sun.*

Nørrebro

$$–$$$$ ✕ **Nørrebro Bryghus.** This microbrewery opened in September 2003 and was an instant hit in this former metal factory. The brewery has 160 seats in a two-story restaurant, and offers a courtyard beer garden in summer. Lunches include tasty salads, sandwiches, and burgers; in the evening you can order three to four courses starting from DKr 298. ☒ *Ryesgade 3 Nørrebro* ☎ *35/30–05–30* ⊕ *www.noerrebrobryghus. dk* ▭ *MC, V.*

$ ✕ **Laundromat Café.** Here's a way to not only wash your clothes (in a soundproofed room), but also enjoy breakfast, lunch, or dinner, or have a coffee or one of a big selection of beers. Best of all is the library containing 4,000 used books. The café serves salads, burgers, steaks, pastas, fish soups, and homemade desserts. ☒ *Elmgade 14, Nørrebro* ☎ *35/35–26–72* ▭ *MC, V.*

$ ✕ **Pussy Galore's Flying Circus.** Done up with a few Arne Jacobsen Swan chairs, naive wall paintings, and tables smashed up against each other, this trendy gathering place frequented by both young families and black-clad poseurs is supposed to be as kitschy as its name. There's surprisingly down-to-earth and affordable fare, with eggs and bacon and other brunch items along with hefty burgers and wok-fried delectables. ☒ *Skt. Hans Torv 30, Nørrebro* ☎ *35/24–53–00* ⊕ *www.pussy-galore.dk* ▭ *DC, MC, V.*

$ ✕ **Sebastopol.** Students and locals crowd this laid-back eatery for brunch and on weekend evenings, but it's a good choice if you want to get off the beaten tourist path. The menu is varied with lots of salads, warm sandwiches, and burgers—and just about the most American-style brunch in the city. ☒ *Skt. Hans Torv 32, Nørrebro* ☎ *35/36–30–02* ⌂ *Reservations not accepted* ▭ *AE, DC, MC, V.*

Sankt Annæ Kvarter & Østerbro

★ **$$$$** ✕ **Godt.** The name says it all: this elegant little two-story restaurant with cool gray walls, silvery curtain partitions, and tulips in clear-glass bottles is *godt* (good). Chef Colin Rice showcases his commitment to fresh, seasonal ingredients in his daily set menu, and you can choose to have three, four, or five courses. Dishes may include a black-bean and crab soup or a fillet of venison drizzled with truffle sauce. ⊠ *Gothersg. 38, Sankt Annæ Kvarter* ☎ *33/15–21–22* ⌳ *Reservations essential* ▤ *DC, MC, V* ⊙ *Closed Sun. and Mon. No lunch.*

$$$ ✕ **Els.** When it opened in 1853, the intimate Els was the place to be seen before the theater, and the painted Muses on the walls still watch diners rush to make an eight o'clock curtain. Antique wooden columns complement the period furniture, including tables inlaid with Royal Copenhagen tile work. The nouvelle French four-course menu changes every two weeks, always incorporating game, fish, and market produce. Jackets are recommended. ⊠ *Store Strandstr. 3, Sankt Annæ Kvarter* ☎ *33/14–13–41* ⊕ *www.restaurant-els.dk* ⌳ *Reservations essential* ▤ *AE, DC, MC, V* ⊙ *No lunch Sun.*

★ **$$$** ✕ **Le Sommelier.** The grande dame of Copenhagen's French restaurants is appropriately named. The cellar boasts more than 800 varieties of wine, and you can order many of them by the glass. Exquisite French dishes are complemented by an elegant interior of pale yellow walls, rough-hewn wooden floors, brass chandeliers, and hanging copper pots. Dishes include guinea fowl in a foie-gras sauce or lamb shank and crispy sweetbreads with parsley and garlic. While waiting for your table, you can sidle up to the burnished dark-wood and brass bar and begin sampling the wine. ⊠ *Bredg. 63–65, Sankt Annæ Kvarter* ☎ *33/11–45–15* ⊕ *www.lesommelier.dk* ▤ *AE, DC, MC, V.*

$$$ ✕ **Zeleste.** This restaurant specializes in inventive fusion cuisine. Outfitted with a short but well-worn bar, a covered and heated atrium, and—upstairs—a U-shape dining room, it serves as a soothing respite to Nyhavn's canal-front party. Although the food is usually excellent, if you're ravenous, ask specifically about portions—otherwise, you could end up with some tiny slivers of fried foie gras or a few tortellini. For lunch, the famished will do well with either the focaccia sandwich or the lobster salad served with toast and an excellent roux dressing; if the latter is not at your table within five minutes, you get a free glass of champagne. ⊠ *Store Strandstr. 6, Sankt Annæ Kvarter* ☎ *33/16–06–06* ⊕ *www.zeleste.dk* ⌳ *Reservations essential* ▤ *DC, MC, V.*

$$–$$$ ✕ **Le Saint Jacques.** The tiny dining room here barely accommodates a dozen tables, but whenever the sun shines, diners spill out from its icon-filled spaces to occupy tables facing busy Østerbrogade. The fare changes according to what is available at the market, but expect fabulous culinary combinations—smoked salmon with crushed eggplant, Canadian scallops with leeks and salmon roe in a beurre blanc sauce, sole with basil sauce and reduced balsamic glaze, and a savory *poussin* (young, small chicken) with sweetbreads scooped into phyllo pastry atop a bed of polenta and lentils. ⊠ *Skt. Jakobs Pl. 1, Østerbro* ☎ *35/42–77–07* ⊕ *www.danielletz.com* ⌳ *Reservations essential* ▤ *DC, MC, V.*

\$\$–\$\$\$ ✕ **Nyhavns Færgekro.** Locals pack into this waterfront café every day at lunchtime, when the staff unveils a buffet with 10 kinds of herring. An unsavory sailors' bar when Nyhavn was the city's port, the butter-yellow building retains a rustic charm. Waiters duck under rough wood beams when they deliver your choice of the delicious dinner specials, which might be salmon with dill sauce or steak with shaved truffles. In summer, sit outside and order an aquavit, the local spirit that tastes like caraway seeds. ⊠ *Nyhavn 5, Sankt Annæ Kvarter* ☎ *33/15–15–88* ⊕ *www.nyhavnsfaergekro.dk* ⊟ *DC, MC, V.*

\$\$ ✕ **Ida Davidsen.** Five generations old, this world-renowned lunch spot is FodorśChoice   synonymous with smørrebrød, and the reputation has brought crowds. ★   The often-packed dining area is dimly lighted, with worn wooden tables and news clippings of famous visitors on the walls. Creative sandwiches include the H. C. Andersen, with liver pâté, bacon, and tomatoes. The terrific smoked duck is smoked by Ida's husband, Adam, and served alongside a horseradish-spiked cabbage salad. ⊠ *Store Kongensg. 70, Sankt Annæ Kvarter* ☎ *33/91–36–55* ⊕ *www.idadavidsen.dk* ⌖ *Reservations essential* ⊟ *AE, DC, MC, V* ☺ *Closed weekends and July. No dinner.*

\$\$ ✕ **Told & Snaps.** This authentic Danish smørrebrød restaurant adheres FodorśChoice   to tradition by offering a long list of Danish delights, and the fare is some- ★   what cheaper than the city's benchmark smørrebrød restaurant Ida Davidsen. The butter-fried sole with rémoulade is a treat, as is the steak tartare. Wine is of course an option, but as this is true Danish cuisine, why not beer and *snaps* (Danish grain alcohol)? ⊠ *Toldbodg. 2, Sankt Annæ Kvarter* ☎ *33/93–83–85* ⊕ *www.toldogsnaps.dk* ⊟ *No credit cards* ☺ *Closed Sun. No dinner.*

\$ ✕ **Lai Hoo.** Denmark's Princess Alexandra, a native of Hong Kong, is known to be a fan of this Chinese restaurant near the city's main square. The lunch specialty is an inspired variety of steamed dumplings (dim sum), and the best bet at dinner is the fixed menu—try the salt-baked prawns in pepper or the luscious lemon duck. ⊠ *Store Kongensg. 18, Sankt Annæ Kvarter* ☎ *33/93–93–19* ⊟ *MC, V* ☺ *No lunch Mon.–Wed.*

Vesterbro & Frederiksberg

\$\$\$\$ ✕ **Formel B.** The name stands for "basic formula," but this French-Danish fusion restaurant is anything but basic. Dishes might include mussel soup flavored with wood sorrel; smoked salmon with dill seeds, spinach, and bacon; or panfried chicken with parsley root and horseradish, accompanied by all its parts—the liver, the heart, the craw, and the red comb—served on an array of small plates. Dessert is a work of art: a collection of individual delicacies is arranged on a large, white eye-shape platter and drizzled with a passion-fruit glaze and pine nuts. ⊠ *Vesterbrog. 182, Frederiksberg* ☎ *33/25–10–66* ⊕ *www.formel-b.dk* ⌖ *Reservations essential* ⊟ *AE, DC, MC, V* ☺ *Closed Sun. No lunch.*

\$\$\$–\$\$\$\$ ✕ **Cofoco.** The name is an acronym for Copenhagen Food Consulting, and its reasonable prices for a three-course meal (DKr 225) in very fashionable surroundings have made it an instant hit in the city. Lamb and fish dishes dominate the menu, and appetizers may include foie gras, crab salad with asparagus, or spinach salad with ricotta. You can reserve a table online, but make sure you do it that way or by phone, as the restaurant fills up frequently on weekends. ⊠ *Abel Cathrines Gade. 7 Vesterbro* ☎ *33/13–60–60* ⊕ *www.cofoco.dk/kontakt.asp* ⌖ *Reservations essential* ▤ *DC, MC, V* ☉ *Closed Sun.*

$–$$ ✕ **Delicatessen.** Happily defying labels, this casual diner-café-bar is done up in Dansk design—silver-gray bucket seats and a stainless-steel-top bar—and serves hearty brunches and global cuisine by day and cocktails and DJ-spun dance tunes by night. Linger over scrambled eggs with bacon and a steaming cup of coffee (served from 11 AM), or tuck into the international cuisine of the month, which runs from North African to Thai to Italian. A trip to the bathroom is good for grins: on your way you pass by two fun-house mirrors; look to one side, and you're squat and fat. Look to the other, and you're slender and tall. ⊠ *Vesterbrog. 120, Vesterbro* ☎ *33/22–16–33* ⊕ *www.delicatessen.dk* ▤ *V.*

¢–$$ ✕ **Yan's Wok.** The former chef of Lai Hoo mans the wok here, serving Hong Kong–style cuisine, as well as peppery dishes from Szechuan province. The theater menu is a great deal and runs from 4 to 6, while a slightly higher-priced card is offered during dinner hours. Regardless of the hour, you can be sure of getting tasty meals at bargain prices. ⊠ *Bagerstr. 9, Vesterbro* ☎ *33/23–73–33* ▤ *DC, MC, V* ☉ *Closed Mon. No lunch.*

Where to Stay

Copenhagen is well served by a wide range of hotels, overall among Europe's most expensive. The hotels around the somewhat run-down red-light district of Istedgade—which looks more dangerous than it is—are the least expensive. Copenhagen is a compact, eminently walkable city, and most of the hotels are in or near the city center, usually within walking distance of most of the major sights and thoroughfares.

Breakfast is almost always included in the room rate, except in some of the pricier American-run hotel chains. Rooms have bath or shower unless otherwise noted. Note that in Copenhagen, as in the rest of Denmark, half (to three-fourths) of the rooms usually have showers only (while the rest have showers and bathtubs), so make sure to state your preference when booking.

WHAT IT COSTS In Danish Kroner				
	$$$$	$$$	$$	$	¢
FOR 2 PEOPLE	over 1,700	1,400–1,700	1,000–1,400	700–1,000	under 700

Prices are for two people in a standard double room, including service charge and tax.

Amager & Kastrup

$$$$ ⊞ **Hilton Copenhagen Airport.** This calm oasis immediately takes the stigma away from common airport hotels that seem to be only brief stopgaps for weary travelers. Executive floors 11 and 12 have special amenities and offer complimentary access to a club room. Rooms have broad windows and are decorated in a modern Scandinavian style with indigenous woods from sustainable forests; the bathrooms are spacious.

Befitting its location, arrival/departure terminals are in the lobby, and the airport's main terminal is just across the street. ⊠ *Ellehammersvej 20, Copenhagen Airport, DK–2770 Kastrup* ☎ *32/50–15–01* 🖷 *32/ 52–85–28* ⊕ *www.hilton.dk* ⤺ *375 rooms, 7 suites* ⚘ *3 restaurants, indoor pool, gym, sauna, bar, meeting rooms, some pets allowed, no-smoking rooms* ▤ *AE, DC, MC, V.*

$$$$ 🖾 **Radisson SAS Scandinavia.** South across the Stadsgraven from Christianshavn, this is one of northern Europe's largest hotels, and Copenhagen's token skyscraper. An immense lobby, with cool, recessed lighting and streamlined furniture, gives access to the city's only casino. Guest rooms are large and somewhat institutional but offer every modern convenience. The hotel's Dining Room restaurant, overlooking Copenhagen's copper towers and skyline, is a fine site for a leisurely lunch, while the dinner menu tempts guests with a changing list of six main courses concocted from fresh seasonal ingredients. ⊠ *Amager Blvd. 70, Amager, DK–2300* ☎*33/96–50–00* 🖷*33/96–55–00* ⊕*www.radissonsas. com* ⤺ *542 rooms, 43 suites* ⚘ *4 restaurants, cable TV, indoor pool, Internet room, meeting rooms* ▤ *AE, DC, MC, V.*

¢ 🖾 **Amager Danhostel.** This simple lodging is 4½ km (3 mi) outside town, close to the airport. The student backpackers and frugal families who stay here have access to the communal kitchen or can buy breakfast and dinner from the restaurant. There are a few rooms with two beds and private baths for a slightly higher price. Before 5 PM on weekdays, take Bus 46 from the main station directly to the hostel. After 5, from Rådhus Pladsen or the main station, take Bus 250 to Sundbyvesterplads, and change to Bus 100. Ask the driver to signal your stop. This hostel is wheelchair-accessible. ⊠ *Vejlands Allé 200, Amager, DK–2300* ☎*32/52–29–08* 🖷 *32/52–27–08* ⊕ *www.copenhagenyouthhostel.dk* ⤺ *64 rooms with 2 beds, 80 family rooms with 5 beds* ⚘ *Restaurant, laundry facilities, Internet room* ▤ *MC, V.*

Downtown

$$$$ 🖾 **D'Angleterre.** The grande dame of Copenhagen welcomes royalty, politi-
Fodor's Choice cians, and rock stars—from Margaret Thatcher to Madonna—in pala-
★ tial surroundings: an imposing New Georgian facade leads into an English-style sitting room. Standard guest rooms are furnished in pastels, with overstuffed chairs and a mix of modern and antique furniture. The spit-and-polish staff accommodates every wish. The elegant Restaurant D'Angleterre serves excellent French cuisine. In winter the square in front of the hotel is converted into a skating rink. ⊠ *Kongens Nytorv 34, Downtown, DK–1021* ☎ *33/12–00–95* 🖷 *33/12–11–18* ⊕ *www.remmen.dk* ⤺ *118 rooms, 19 suites* ⚘ *Restaurant, indoor pool, bar, Internet room, meeting rooms* ▤ *AE, DC, MC, V.*

$$$$ 🖾 **Skt. Petri.** For the better part of a century, a beloved budget department store nicknamed Dalle Valle occupied this site. It has been supplanted by this luxury hotel that screams trendy, designer style, and it's a big hit with interior designers, fashionistas, and (presumably) followers of home-improvement TV shows. From a talking elevator telling you how fabulous the place is, to the model types manning the front desk, you know you're in for a walk on the pretentious side. That said, the individual rooms,

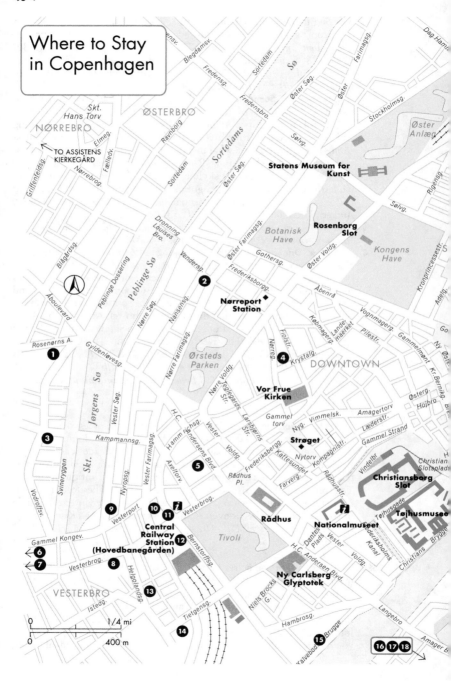

Where to Stay in Copenhagen

NØRREBRO

ØSTERBRO

Skt. Hans Torv

TO ASSISTENS KIERKEGÅRD

Statens Museum for Kunst

Botanisk Have

Rosenborg Slot

Kongens Have

Nørreport Station

Ørsteds Parken

DOWNTOWN

Vor Frue Kirken

Gammel torv

Strøget

Nytorv

Christiansborg Slot

Tøjhusmuseet

Rådhus

Nationalmuseet

Central Railway Station (Hovedbanegården)

Tivoli

Ny Carlsberg Glyptotek

VESTERBRO

Sø Jørgens Sø

Skt. Jørgens Sø

Peblinge Sø

Sortedams Sø

Søer

Øster Søg.

0 — 1/4 mi

0 — 400 m

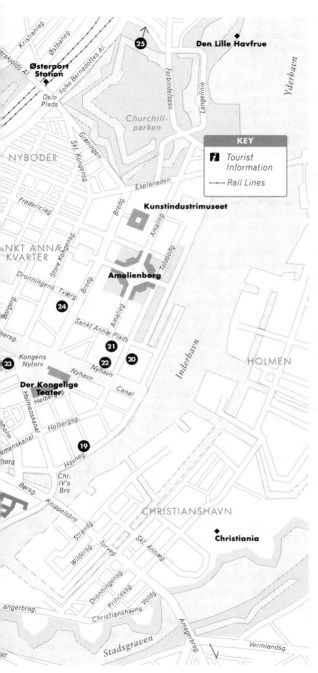

designed by Per Arnoldi, are functional, decorated in a spare, modern aesthetic, with bright and cheery colors. Most units have a terrace or balcony. The breakfast buffet is the best in the city. ⊠ *Krystalg. 22, Downtown, DK–1172* ☎ *33/45–91–00* 📠 *33/45–91–10* ⊕ *www.hotelsktpetri. com* ⟳ *241 rooms, 27 suites* ♨ *Restaurant, café, bar, meeting rooms, no-smoking rooms, parking (free)* ☰ *AE, DC, MC, V.*

$$$–$$$$ 🏨 **Strand.** You can't stay closer to the harbor than here: just a five-minute walk from Nyhavn, this pleasant hotel is housed in a waterfront warehouse dating from 1869. The cozy lobby has brown leather couches and old maritime pictures on the walls. The rooms are small but comfortable, with blue-and-yellow bedspreads and sparkling bathrooms. ⊠ *Havneg. 37, Downtown, DK–1058* ☎ *33/48–99–00* 📠 *33/48–99–01* ⊕ *www. copenhagenstrand.dk* ⟳ *174 rooms, 2 suites* ♨ *Restaurant, bar, meeting rooms, some pets allowed, no-smoking rooms* ☰ *AE, DC, MC, V.*

$$–$$$$ 🏨 **Copenhagen Marriott Hotel.** This large Marriott on the city's waterfront (and the first of its brand in Scandinavia), has great views of Christianshavn, and it's a well-oiled machine, like many well-known chain hotels. Sadly, it lacks any feeling of being in Copenhagen, let alone in Denmark. It has superior business and conference facilities, a great fitness room, and even separate sauna and steam rooms for men and women. Guest rooms are very comfortable and of a good size, but breakfast is not included in the rate. ⊠ *Kalvebod Brygge. 5, DK–1560* ☎ *88/ 33–99–00* 📠 *88/33–12–99* ⊕ *www.marriott.com/cphdk* ⟳ *378 rooms, 17 suites* ♨ *Restaurant, bar, health club, gift shop, meeting rooms, parking (fee), some pets allowed, no-smoking rooms* ☰ *AE, DC, MC, V.*

$$$ 🏨 **Ascot.** This downtown hotel, popular with European businesspeople and group tours, was formerly a public bathhouse designed in 1902 and built by Martin Nyrop, the same architect who did Copenhagen Town Hall. There are a variety of rooms, apartments, and suites, some much better located than others; ask for a street, rather than a courtyard, view. Rooms aren't terribly fancy, but they're clean and comfortable. One big benefit of the Ascot is that it's less than a five-minute walk to Tivoli. ⊠ *Studiestr. 61, Downtown, DK–1554* ☎ *33/12–60–00* 📠 *33/14–60–40* ⊕ *www.ascothotel.dk* ⟳ *171 rooms, 4 suites* ♨ *Cable TV, bar, meeting room, parking (fee), some pets allowed* ☰ *AE, DC, MC, V.*

$$ 🏨 **Ibsens Hotel.** This winsome, family-owned hotel near Nørreport Station has cozy, immaculate rooms and a lovely courtyard. The friendly staff is particularly attentive and goes out of its way to help. The attention to detail is evident in the hotel's decor—each floor has its own theme. The Scandinavian floor showcases cool and modern local designs, while the Bohemian floor is filled with antique furnishings. ⊠ *Vendersg. 23, Downtown, DK–1363* ☎ *33/13–19–13* 📠 *33/13–19–16* ⊕ *www. ibsenshotel.dk* ⟳ *118 rooms, 3 suites* ♨ *Restaurant, bar, some pets allowed, no-smoking rooms* ☰ *AE, DC, MC, V.*

Sankt Annæ Kvarter & North

$$$$ 🏨 **Clarion Neptun.** This elegant central hotel was bought years ago with the intention of making it the bohemian gathering place of Copenhagen, but these days it is more practical than artsy and welcomes business guests, tourists, and even large tour groups. The lobby and lounge are light, with classical furnishings and pale tones, and guest rooms have a tasteful modern decor. Next door is the hotel's Restaurant Gendarmen, run by a group of young restaurateurs who have created a dinner menu on the concept of old-meets-new, marrying traditional Danish dishes (roast pork or cod) with nouveau touches, such as a light truffle or blueberry sauce. ⊠ *Skt. Annæ Pl. 18–20, Sankt Annæ Kvarter, DK–1250* ☎ *33/96–20–00* 🖷 *33/96–20–66* ⊕ *www.choicehotels.dk* ⮡ *133 rooms* ⌂ *Restaurant, bar, babysitting, meeting rooms, free parking, some pets allowed* ▤ *AE, DC, MC, V.*

★ **$$$$** ▥ **Nyhavn 71.** In a 200-year-old warehouse, this quiet, soothing hotel is a good choice for privacy-seekers. It overlooks the old ships of Nyhavn, and its interiors have been preserved with their original thick plaster walls and exposed brick. The rooms are tiny but cozy, with warm woolen spreads, dark woods, soft leather furniture, and crisscrossing timbers. ⊠ *Nyhavn 71, Sankt Annæ Kvarter, DK–1051* ☎ *33/43–62–00* 🖷 *33/43–62–01* ⊕ *www.71nyhavnhotelcopenhagen.dk* ⮡ *150 rooms, 3 suites* ⌂ *Restaurant, bar, meeting rooms, free parking, some pets allowed, no-smoking rooms* ▤ *AE, DC, MC, V.*

$$$$ ▥ **Phoenix.** This luxury hotel has automatic glass doors, crystal chandeliers, and gilt touches everywhere. Originally built in the 1680s, the hotel was then torn down and rebuilt into a plush, Victorian-style hotel in 1847, rising from its rubble just like the mythical Phoenix rose from its ashes, and thus its name. The suites and business-class rooms are adorned with faux antiques and 18-karat-gold-plated bathroom fixtures; the standard rooms are very small, measuring barely 9 feet by 15 feet. It's so convenient to city-center attractions that the hotel gets a fair amount of street noise; light sleepers should ask for rooms above the second floor. Downstairs is Murdoch's Books & Ale, a snug pub done up in mahogany and brass, which serves smørrebrød and light meals. ⊠ *Bredg. 37, Sankt Annæ Kvarter, DK–1260* ☎ *33/95–95–00* 🖷 *33/33–98–33* ⊕ *www.phoenixcopenhagen. dk* ⮡ *206 rooms, 7 suites* ⌂ *Restaurant, bar, meeting rooms, parking (fee), some pets allowed, no-smoking rooms* ▤ *AE, DC, MC, V.*

★ **$$$** ▥ **Admiral.** A five-minute stroll from Nyhavn, overlooking old Copenhagen and Amalienborg, the monolithic Admiral was once a grain warehouse dating from 1787, but now provides travelers with no-nonsense accommodations. It's one of the less-expensive top hotels, cutting frills and prices. Massive stone walls are broken by rows of tiny windows; guest rooms are spare, with jutting beams and modern prints. ⊠ *Toldbodg. 24–28, Sankt Annæ Kvarter, DK–1253* ☎ *33/74–14–14* 🖷 *33/74–14–16* ⊕ *www.admiralhotel.dk* ⮡ *314 rooms, 52 suites* ⌂ *Restaurant, bar, nightclub, meeting room, free parking, some pets allowed, no-smoking rooms* ▤ *AE, DC, V.*

$$ ▥ **Skovshoved.** This delightful, art-filled inn is 8 km (5 mi) north of town,
Fodor's Choice near a few old fishing cottages beside the yacht harbor. Licensed since
★ 1660, it has retained its provincial charm. Larger rooms overlook the sea, smaller ones rim the courtyard; all have both modern and antique furnishings. The best way to get here is to take Bus 6 from Rådhus Pladsen or the S-train to Charlottenlund and walk 10 minutes from the station. ⊠ *Strandvejen 267, DK–2920 Charlottenlund* ☎ *39/64–00–28* 🖷 *39/64–06–72* ⊕ *www.skovshovedhotel.dk* ⮡ *23 rooms, 3 suites* ⌂ *Restaurant, billiards, bar, meeting rooms* ▤ *AE, DC, MC, V.*

Vesterbro & Frederiksberg

$$$$
Fodor's Choice
★
🏨 **Radisson SAS Royal.** Towering over the heart of town, this high-rise hotel was originally designed by Arne Jacobsen in 1960. Recently the owners spent several years—and plenty of kroner—in re-embracing its Jacobsen look, and the result is a paean to the legendary designer. The graceful lobby has blue and white Jacobsen Swan and Egg chairs that are arranged in circles and illuminated by the ceiling's recessed lights. The soothing hotel rooms are paneled in light maple and outfitted with Jacobsen chairs and lamps. Even the heavy door handles, functionally designed to fill the palm, were created by Jacobsen. The most famous room is 606, which looks just like it did in 1960, with all the original furnishings, including a nifty desktop that opens to reveal a lighted makeup mirror. Many of the rooms boast views over Tivoli and the city center's copper-top buildings. The top-floor restaurant, Alberto K, serves top-notch Scandinavian-Italian cuisine. ⊠ *Hammerichsg. 1, Vesterbro, DK–1611* ☎ *33/42–60–00* 🖷 *33/42–61–00* ⊕ *www.radissonsas.com* ⤵ *260 rooms, 6 suites* ⚭ *Restaurant, room service, gym, bar, Internet room, meeting rooms, parking (fee), some pets allowed, no-smoking rooms* ⊟ *AE, DC, MC, V.*

$$$$
🏨 **Scandic Copenhagen.** Rising over Copenhagen's lakes, alongside the cylindrical IMAX Tycho Brahe Planetarium, is this modern high-rise hotel. The comfortable rooms, done up in cool tones and blond-wood furnishings, have splendid views. One side of the hotel overlooks the peaceful lakes, and the other side the bustling heart of Copenhagen, including Tivoli. The higher up you go, the better the view, so inquire about a room on the 17th floor, which is the highest floor that still has standard doubles; it's suites-only on the 18th. ⊠ *Vester Søg. 6, Vesterbro, DK–1601* ☎ *33/14–35–35* 🖷 *33/32–12–23* ⊕ *www.scandic-hotels.com/copenhagen* ⤵ *480 rooms, 6 suites* ⚭ *Restaurant, room service, gym, sauna, bar, concierge, meeting rooms, parking (fee), some pets allowed, no-smoking rooms* ⊟ *AE, DC, MC, V.*

$$$–$$$$
🏨 **First Hotel Vesterbro.** Looming over Vesterbrogade—and just a five-minute walk from Tivoli—this four-star deluxe hotel is Denmark's third largest. The sun-drenched lobby, with floor-to-ceiling windows, has white pillars, blond-wood tables, and gray Dansk design armchairs. The rooms have pale yellow walls, cherrywood furnishings, and contemporary lithographs. Female travelers may want try out the "First Lady" rooms, which include adjustable mirrors and makeup remover in the bathrooms, fluffy bathrobes, an electric kettle, and women's magazines. Complimentary access is offered to a full-service fitness center nearby. ⊠ *Vesterbrog. 23–29, Vesterbro, DK–1620* ☎ *33/78–80–00* 🖷 *33/78–80–80* ⊕ *www.firsthotels.com* ⤵ *403 rooms, 1 suite* ⚭ *Restaurant, gym, bar, meeting rooms, parking (fee), some pets allowed, no-smoking rooms* ⊟ *AE, DC, MC, V.*

$$$–$$$$
🏨 **Grand Hotel.** In operation since the turn of the 20th century, the Grand Hotel went through a soft refurbishment (new carpets, linens, lighting, pictures) of its lobby and all of its guest rooms in the spring of 2005. An Italian restaurant serves good fare, and there's also a café on-site. The old-style lobby is presided over by a crystal chandelier, and this hotel has definite old-world charm. Some guest rooms have tiny bath-

rooms, so inquire about this when booking. ⊠ *Vesterbrog. 9, Vester-bro, DK–1620* ☎ *33/27–69–00* 🖶 *33/27–69–01* ⊕ *www.grandhotelcopenhagen.dk* ↻ *161 rooms, 2 suites* ⚶ *Restaurant, room service, bar, concierge, meeting rooms, parking (fee), no-smoking rooms* ☰ *AE, DC, MC, V.*

$$–$$$$ 🏨 **Sofitel Copenhagen Plaza.** With its convenient location and plush homey atmosphere, this hotel has attracted the likes of Tina Turner and Keith Richards. Close to Tivoli and the main station, the building puts its best foot forward with a stately lobby and the adjacent Plaza Restaurant, which serves haute French-Italian cuisine. The older rooms are scattered with antiques; newer ones are furnished in a more modern style. ⊠ *Bernstorffsg. 4, Vesterbro, DK–1577* ☎ *33/14–92–62* 🖶 *33/93–93–62* ⊕ *www.sofitel.dk* ↻ *87 rooms, 6 suites* ⚶ *Restaurant, room service, bar, concierge, meeting rooms, parking (fee), some pets allowed, no-smoking rooms* ☰ *AE, DC, MC, V.*

$$$ 🏨 **DGI Byen.** "An unusual meeting place" is how the DGI Byen presents itself, and it's a thoroughly apt description. This state-of-the-art recreation and sports center, just behind Central Station, boasts a bowling alley, climbing wall, shooting range, swimming pool, spa, and 104-room hotel. The hotel rooms are an exquisite blend of Danish design. Dark blue furnishings and blond-wood floors are softly illuminated by cylindrical lamps. Though most rooms have doubly insulated windows, you can sometimes hear the distant rumble of trains entering the station. The last train passes by at around 12:30 AM, so ask for a quiet room if you're a light sleeper. The pool is free to hotel guests; nonguests pay DKr 46. You can pamper yourself with a range of soothing treatments at the full-service spa, but it costs extra. Ask about the substantially lower weekend rates. ⊠ *Tietgensg. 65, Vesterbro, DK–1704* ☎ *33/29–80–00* 🖶 *33/29–80–80* ⊕ *www.dgi-byen.dk* ↻ *104 rooms* ⚶ *Restaurant, café, pool, sauna, spa, bowling, meeting rooms, parking (fee), no-smoking rooms* ☰ *AE, DC, MC, V.*

$$–$$$ 🏨 **Guldsmeden.** This family hotel, in a 19th-century Vesterbro building, has rooms decorated and restored in French-colonial style with wood paneling, stucco, and high ceilings. The amenities of the rooms differ; they may have four-poster beds, bathtubs, fireplaces, or furnished balconies. Every room has original art on the walls and hand-picked teak furniture. The owner has a similar, very comfortable property in Århus, with the same name. ⊠ *Vesterbrog. 66, Vesterbro, DK–1620* ☎ *33/22–15–00* 🖶 *33/22–15–55* ⊕ *www.hotelguldsmeden.dk* ↻ *64 rooms, some without bath; 4 suites* ⚶ *Café, some pets allowed* ☰ *AE, D, MC, V.*

$–$$ 🏨 **Saga.** This is one of the newer, refurbished hotels in the vicinity of Central Station. Some rooms have just a sink, while others have full bathrooms. Breakfast is included in the price, and the hotel is good for families. ⊠ *Colbjørnsensg. 18–20, Vesterbro, DK–1652* ☎ *33/24–49–44* 🖶 *33/24–60–33* ⊕ *www.sagahotel.dk* ↻ *79 rooms, 31 with bath* ⚶ *Some pets allowed* ☰ *AE, DC, MC, V* ⦿⍁ *BP.*

¢–$ 🏨 **Sct. Thomas.** Two friends from rural Denmark, Torgut and Rene, run this small and intimate hotel, which is a good value for the money. Among its pluses are its location—a short walk from the center of town in Fredericksberg's theater district—and its new beds (part of 2005 refurbishments). There aren't tons of facilities, but there are bicycle rentals, a sitting room with Internet access, and an included breakfast. Check out the hotel's Web site for a video showing the exterior and interiors of the building. ✉ *Frederiksberg Allé, Vesterbro, DK–1621* ☎ *33/21–64–64* 🖷 *33/25–64–60* ⊕ *www.hotelsctthomas.dk* ⇱ *42 rooms, 26 with bath* ⚴ *Internet room, free parking, no-smoking rooms* ▭ *V.*

¢ ⌸ **Cab–Inn Scandinavia.** This bright hotel is just west of the lakes and Vesterport Station. Its impeccably maintained rooms are very small, but designed with efficiency to include ample showers, fold-away and bunk beds, and even electric kettles. The hotel is popular with business travelers in winter and kroner-pinching backpackers and families in summer. Its sister hotel, the Cab–Inn Copenhagen Express, is just around the corner at Danasvej 32-34, and there is yet another Cab–Inn right behind Tivoli at Mitchellsgade 14. ✉ *Vodroffsvej. 55, Fredericksberg, DK–1900* ☎ *35/36–11–11 Cab–Inn Scandinavia, 33/21–04–00 Cab–Inn Copenhagen Express, 33/46–16–16 Cab–Inn Mitchellsgade* ⊕ *www.cabinn.dk* ⇱ *201 rooms* ⚴ *Bar, meeting rooms, parking (fee)* ▭ *AE, DC, MC, V.*

¢ ⌸ **Euroglobe.** This is a no-frills spot for the traveler who's looking for a comfortable bed with a roof overhead. Rooms are minimal, and guests share two common bathrooms on each floor. There's a little kitchen area on each floor where coffee, tea, or soups can be prepared. With breakfast included, this spot is a fine choice for the frugal. ✉ *Niels Ebbesensvej 20, Frederiksberg, DK–1911* ☎ *33/79–79–54* ⊕ *www.euroglobe.dk* ⇱ *47 rooms without bath* ⚴ *Some pets allowed* ▭ *No credit cards.*

Nightlife & the Arts

Nightlife

Most nightlife is concentrated in the area in and around Strøget, though there are student and "leftist" cafés and bars in Nørrebro and more upscale spots in Østerbro. Vesterbro, whose main drags are Vesterbrogade and Istedgade, has become quite the nightlife neighborhood, with several new bars and cafés. Many restaurants, cafés, bars, and clubs stay open after midnight, a few until 5 AM. Copenhagen used to be famous for jazz, but unfortunately that has changed, with many of the best clubs closing down. However, you can find nightspots catering to almost all musical tastes, from ballroom music to house, rap, and techno, in trendy clubs sound tracked by local DJs. The area around Nikolaj Kirken has the highest concentration of trendy discos and dance spots. Copenhagen's club scene can be fickle—new venues crop up regularly, often replacing last year's red-hot favorites. Call ahead or check out *Copenhagen This Week* (⊕ www.ctw.dk) for current listings. The stylish, biannual magazine *Scandinavian Living* (⊕ www.cphliving.dk) includes informative listings on the latest bars, restaurants, and shops. It also features articles on Danish culture, food, and architecture and is available at stores, hotels, and the tourist office.

BARS & LOUNGES   Copenhagen is peppered with hip restaurants that get even hipper in the evening, when they morph into lively nightspots. **Bang & Jensen** (✉ Istedg. 130, Vesterbro ☎ 33/25–53–18 ⊕ www.bangogjensen.dk), in the way-too-cool Vesterbro neighborhood, is a regular café during the day.

From 9 PM until 2 AM, however, it turns into a cocktail bar jamming with loud music and a disco ambience. The **Café Ketchup** (✉ Pilestr. 19, Downtown ☎ 33/32–30–30), just off the Strøget, draws an informal—though not un-savvy—crowd that gabs and grooves to the sounds of funk, house, hip-hop, and African music. It gets cooking after 11 PM on weekends, once cocktails start replacing coffee. **Charlie's Bar** (✉ Pilestr. 33, Downtown ☎ 33/32–22–89) insists that there are other beers in Copenhagen besides the omnipresent Carlsberg and Tuborg, and serves more than 46 draft and bottled beers to prove it. You can sample a handful of Danish microbreweries or Hoegaarden beer from Belgium. Indeed, there's no better place to enjoy such diversity than at this bar, which calls itself "proudly independent, independently proud" because it doesn't kowtow to the two big Danish brands. The dark room with low ceilings, owned by a transplanted Scotsman, is refreshingly unpretentious, with a laid-back crowd of regulars, both locals and expats. **D'Angleterre Hotel** (✉ Kongens Nytorv 34, Downtown ☎ 33/37–06–64) is home to a tiny English-style bar that's just the place to soak up the posh hotel's ambience without forking over the kroner to stay here. When the hotel restaurant closes at 10 PM, bar guests can sit at tables by windows looking out on Copenhagen's most beautiful square, Kongens Nytorv. Moreover, after a peaceful drink or two, you will be within walking distance of a slew of other, more raucous nighttime spots. It stays open until 1 AM nightly. **Delicatessen** (✉ Vesterbrog. 120, Vesterbro ☎ 33/22–16–33 ⊕ www.delicatessen.dk) serves international cuisine by day, but after 11 PM Thursday through Saturday, it's time for cocktails and dancing to DJ-spun house, hip-hop, and rock.

Hviids Vinstue (✉ Kongens Nytorv 19, Downtown ☎ 33/15–10–64 ⊕ www.hvlidsvinstue.dk) dates from the 1730s and attracts all kinds, young and old, singles and couples, for a glass of wine or cognac. The **Library** (✉ Bernstorffsg. 4, Vesterbro ☎ 33/14–92–62), in the Plaza, is an elegant spot for a quiet but pricey drink. **"90"** ("halvfems" in Danish; ✉ Gammel Kongevej 90, Frederiksberg ☎ 33/31–84–90), which goes only by its street number, is the only watering hole that many Copenhagen old-timers trust for a "real beer." Unfortunately, it can take up to 15 minutes for the harried bartender to pull your draft pint. The small, atmospheric bar with dark orange walls and heavy wooden tables is the second home to a cast of crusty Copenhagen characters and outspoken barflies. At lunch, do as the locals do and buy smørrebrød from around the corner, and then bring it into the bar where you can settle in at one of the tables and enjoy your meal with one of the famous drafts. (There's a DKr 5 charge just to sit at the table.) **Peder Oxe's basement** (✉ Gråbrødretorv 11, Downtown ☎ 33/11–11–93) is casual and young, though nearly impossible to squeeze into on weekends.

CAFÉS Café life appeared in Copenhagen in the 1970s and quickly became a compulsory part of its urban existence. The cheapest sit-down eateries in town (a cappuccino and sandwich often cost less than DKr 60), cafés are lively and relaxed at night. The crowd is usually an interesting mix. Once run-down and neglected, the up-and-coming Istedgade strip is beginning to sprout cheery cafés and restaurants.

Bjørg's (⊠ Vester Voldg. 19, Downtown ☎ 33/14–53–20) has a zinc bar, red seating, and lots of large windows. Guests slouch over huge burgers, club sandwiches, and excellent coffees. **Dan Turrell** (⊠ Store Regneg. 3-5, Downtown ☎ 33/14–10–47), an old café, has become terribly chic lately, partly due to its good food and candlelight. At the fashionable **Europa** (⊠ Amagertorv 1, Downtown ☎ 33/14–28–89), people-watching and coffee naturally go together. **Krasnapolsky** (⊠ Vesterg. 10, Downtown ☎ 33/32–88–00) packs a young, hip, and painfully well-dressed audience at night, while a more mixed group populates its confines on placid afternoons.

Mama Lustra (⊠ Istedg. 96, Vesterbro ☎ 33/25–26–11) looks like it could be a corner of your grandma's attic, with mismatched chairs, old wooden tables, and brass candleholders. Sink into a stuffed chair and sip a coffee or glass of Spanish wine while gazing out over busy Istedgade. The place also serves a simple but tasty brunch with cured ham, Italian sausages, and scrambled eggs, and an assortment of sandwiches including a vegetarian favorite—sun-dried tomatoes, pesto, and arugula. On Sunday, it hosts storytelling and spoken-word sessions. **Norden** (⊠ Østerg. 61, Downtown ☎ 33/11–77–91) resides at the intersection of Købmagergade and Strøget. Substantial portions make up for minimal table space at this art nouveau–style café. **Rust** (⊠ Guldbergsg. 8, Nørrebro ☎ 35/24–52–00) is a constantly crowded all-in-one rock club–restaurant–café on Nørrebro's main square, Skt. Hans Torv. Hearty, fresh dishes are served inside, while grill food is served on the terrace. **Sebastopol** (⊠ Skt. Hans Torv 32, Nørrebro ☎ 35/36–30–02) teems with gussied-up locals in the evening and serves an ample weekend brunch. **Sommersko** (⊠ Kronprinsensg. 6, Downtown ☎ 33/14–81–89) is the granddaddy of Copenhagen cafés, with a surprisingly varied menu (try the delicious french fries with pesto or the wok specialties) and an eclectic crowd. **Victor** (⊠ Ny Østerg. 8, Downtown ☎ 33/13–36–13) is all brass and dark wood, just right for a light lunch.

CASINO The **Casino Copenhagen** (⊠ Amager Blvd. 70, Amager ☎ 33/96–59–65 ⊕ www.casinocopenhagen.dk), at the SAS Scandinavia Hotel, has American and French roulette, blackjack, baccarat, and slot machines. Admission is DKr 80 (you must be 18 years old and show a photo ID), and a dress code (jackets required; no athletic clothing or jeans) is enforced. Outerwear must be left at the wardrobe, for a fee. The dealers and croupiers are not shy about reminding winners that a tip of a certain percentage is customary, even after hitting just one number on the roulette wheel. The casino is open daily 2 PM to 4 AM.

DISCOS, DANCING & LIVE MUSIC Most discos open at 11 PM, charging covers of about DKr 50–DKr 100 and selling drinks at steep prices. **Absalon** (⊠ Frederiksbergg. 38, Downtown ☎ 33/16–16–98 ⊕ www.club-absalon.dk), popular with nearly everyone, has lively live music on the ground floor and a disco above. **Club Mambo** (⊠ Vester Voldg. 85, Downtown ☎ 33/11–97–66 ⊕ www.salsaclub.dk) is the United Nations of discos, with an international crowd dancing to salsa and other Latin rhythms. **Columbus** (⊠ Nørrebrog. 22, Nørrebro ☎ 35/37–00–51) is a lively salsa club where the activity gets hot as a chili pepper on a good night. Excellent salsa lessons are available to the uninitiated and out-of-practice. **Den Røde Pimpernel** (✉ Bernstorffsg. 3, Vesterbro ☎ 33/75–07–60) draws an adult audience for dancing to live orchestras, trios, and old-time music. **Level CPH** (✉ Skinderg. 45, Downtown ☎ 33/13–26–25) pulsates to '80s dance tunes and features a roomy dance floor and a reconstructed airport lounge–like area, outfitted with real airplane seats. **Luft Kastellet** (✉ Strandg. 100-B, Christianshavn ☎ 70/26–26–24) fosters a beachlike atmosphere with its indoor-outdoor layout and harborside location. Guests often dance barefoot on the sand-covered floors to modern jazz, funk, or lounge-inspired chill-out tunes. **Nasa** (✉ Gothersg. 8F, Boltens Gård, Sankt Annæ Kvarter ☎ 33/93–74–15 ⊕ www.nasa.dk) has an exclusive "members only" policy, which has earned it legendary status among Copenhagen's nightclubs. The choosy doorman screens the throngs outside based on his impression of their looks, clothes, and attitude. Luckily, rumor has it that Nasa is relaxing its door policy. Once inside, you get to hobnob in cool, white interiors with the city's chic and moneyed set and local celebrities (Prince Frederik occasionally drops by). Underneath Nasa are two other clubs, Club Bahia and Blue Buddha, with a more casual vibe and much more lax door policies.

Park Café (✉ Østerbrog. 79, Østerbro ☎ 35/42–62–48) offers an old-world café with live music downstairs, a disco upstairs, and a movie theater just next door. The very popular English-style **Rosie McGees** (✉ Vesterbrog. 2A, Vesterbro ☎ 33/33–31–11 ⊕ www.rosiemcgees. dk) pub serves American and Mexican eats and encourages dancing, with DJs performing regularly, and the odd drag show thrown in for good measure. **Sofiekælderen** (✉ Overgaden oven Vandet 32, Christianshavn ☎ 32/57–27–87 ⊕ www.sofiekaelderen.dk) is a veteran of the Copenhagen night scene and serves as a frequent hangout for local musicians. Live music plays on Thursday, a DJ spins on Friday, and live jazz on Saturday afternoons gives way to piano-bar tunes in the evening. The kitchen serves simple fare to accompany cocktails. The **Søpavillionen** (✉ Gyldenløvsg. 24, Vesterbro ☎ 33/15–12–24 ⊕ www.soepavillonen. dk) invariably inspires first-time visitors to ask, "what *is* that building?" The ornate white wooden structure next to Copenhagen's lakes was built in 1894. The pavilion hosts seminars and private events on weekdays and functions as a dance club until 5 AM on weekends, featuring live music and DJs. **Stereo Bar** (✉ Linnésg. 16A, Downtown ☎ 33/13–61–13 ⊕ www.stereobar.dk) has lava lamps and '70s furnishings; plays house, soul, and funk music on Friday and Saturday; and draws an eclectic crowd, from design students to writers, providing your best chance for an interesting conversation in Copenhagen's club scene. **Woodstock** (✉ Vesterg. 12, Downtown ☎ 33/11–20–71) is among the city's most enduring clubs. A mixed audience grooves to music from the '50s to the '80s.

GAY BARS & ESTABLISHMENTS   Given Denmark's longtime liberal attitudes toward homosexuality, it's not surprising that Copenhagen has a thriving and varied gay nightlife scene. In August, Copenhagen celebrates "Mermaid Pride," its boisterous annual gay-pride parade. For more information, call or visit the **Landsforeningen for Bøsser og Lesbiske** (Gay and Lesbian Association;

✉ Teglgårdstr. 13, Boks 1023, Downtown, DK–1007 ☏ 33/13–19–48 ⊕ www.lbl.dk), which has a library and more than 45 years of experience. Check out the free paper *Panbladet* (www.panbladet.dk), or the gay guides *Gayguide* (www.gayguide.dk) and *Copenhagen Gay Life* (www.copenhagen-gay-life.dk) for listings of nightlife events and clubs, and other topical information of special interest to the gay individual.

Amigo Bar (✉ Schønbergsg. 4, Downtown ☏ 33/21–49–15) really gets going after midnight with campy karaoke songs and lots of customers anxious to party. It's popular with men of all ages. For a show-tune showdown, head for the piano bar at **Café Intime** (✉ Allég. 25, Frederiksberg ☏ 38/34–19–58 ⊕ www.cafeintime.dk), where you can sip cocktails. It's easy to meet people at **Can Can** (✉ Mikkel Bryggersg. 11, Downtown ☏ 33/11–50–10), a small place with a friendly bartender and a mostly male clientele.

The small **Central Hjørnet** (✉ Kattesundet 18, Downtown ☏ 33/11–85–49 ⊕ www.centralhjornet.dk) has been around for about 60 years. The dark, casual **Cosy Bar** (✉ Studiestr. 24, Downtown ☏ 33/12–74–27 ⊕ www.cosybar.dk) is the place to go in the wee hours (it usually stays open until 8 AM). **Heaven Café** (✉ Kompagnistr. 18, Downtown ☏ 33/15–19–00 ⊕ www.heaven-copenhagen.dk) is the latest addition to the gay café scene, serving light meals to a casual crowd of locals and foreigners. Meals in the upstairs restaurant are fairly priced and attract a steady clientele. **Jailhouse Event Bar & Restaurant** (✉ Studiestræde. 12, Downtown ☏ 33/15–22–55 ⊕ www.jailhousecph.dk) isn't as odd a place as the name sounds, even if it is decorated like a city jail. Waiters are in varied police uniforms, and overall, it's a fun, convivial atmosphere attracting men in a wide range of age groups. **Jeppes Club** (✉ Allég. 25, Frederiksberg ☏ 38/87–32–48) is patronized mainly by gay women and is open on the first and last Friday of every month. **Masken Bar & Café** (✉ Studiestr. 33, Downtown ☏ 33/91–09–37 ⊕ www.maskenbar.dk) is a relaxed bar welcoming both men and women. **Men's Bar** (✉ Teglgårdstr. 3, Downtown ☏ 33/12–73–03) is men-only with a leather-and-rubber dress code. **Oscar Café & Bar** (✉ Rådhus Pl. 77, Downtown ☏ 33/12–09–99) is a relaxed spot for a drink or a cup of coffee, and a good place to chat with locals. **PAN Club** (✉ Knabrostr. 3, off Strøget, Downtown ☏ 33/11–37–84 ⊕ www.pan-cph.dk) packs men and women into its five levels and two dance areas; there's a total of six bars. It's considered to be one of Europe's biggest gay dance clubs.

JAZZ CLUBS   Hard times have thinned Copenhagen's once-thriving jazz scene. Most of the clubs still open headline local talents, but European and international artists also perform, especially in July, when the Copenhagen Jazz Festival spills over into the clubs. Many jazz clubs host Sunday-afternoon sessions that draw spirited crowds of Danes. **Copenhagen Jazzhouse** (✉ Niels Hemmingsensg. 10, Downtown ☏ 33/15–26–00 ⊕ www.jazzhouse.dk) attracts European and some international names to its chic, modern, barlike interior. **Drop Inn** (✉ Kompagnistr. 34, Downtown ☏ 33/11–24–04) draws a capacity crowd for its popular Sunday-afternoon jazz sessions. The bar was designed with the audience in mind. The stage faces an informal semicircle of chairs and booths so there isn't a bad seat in the house. The eclectic decor includes wrought-iron, wreath-shape candelabras, iron statues of winged bacchanalian figures, and an M. C. Escher–style ceiling fresco. **Jazzhuset Vognporten** (✉ Rådhusstr. 13, Downtown ☎ 33/15–63–53 ⊕ www.swinging-copenhagen.dk), with exposed concrete walls decorated with local art, showcases traditional New Orleans–style jazz acts on Friday and Saturday. (It's closed Sunday.) During the day it functions as a café, in whose sunlit back room you can enjoy coffee, beer, and light sandwiches. An adjoining theater features everything from Shakespeare to experimental plays. **La Fontaine** (✉ Kompagnistr. 11, Downtown ☎ 33/11–60–98) is Copenhagen's quintessential jazz dive, with sagging curtains, impenetrable smoke, and hep cats. This is a must for jazz lovers.

ROCK CLUBS Copenhagen has a good selection of rock clubs, most of which cost less than DKr 50. Almost all are filled with young, fashionable crowds. Clubs tend to open and go out of business with some frequency, but you can get free entertainment newspapers and flyers advertising gigs at almost any café.

Lades Kælder (✉ Kattesundet 6, Downtown ☎ 33/14–00–67 ⊕ www.lades.dk), a local hangout just off Strøget, hosts bands that play good old-fashioned rock and roll. **Loppen** (✉ Bådsmandsstr. 43, Christianshavn ☎ 32/57–84–22 ⊕ www.loppen.dk), in Christiania, is a medium-size concert venue featuring some of the bigger names in Danish music (pop, rock, urban, and jazz) and budding artists from abroad. Cover charges can range from DKr 60 to DKr 80. The **Pumpehuset** (✉ Studiestr. 52, Downtown ☎ 33/93–19–60 ⊕ www.pumpehuset.dk) is the place for soul and rock, and gets some big names. Ticket prices can be steep. **Rust** (✉ Guldbergsg. 8, Nørrebro ☎ 35/24–52–00 ⊕ www.rust.dk) is a smaller club, mainly featuring rock, pop, and urban acts. Live music is available only on Thursday. **Stengade 30** (✉ Steng. 18, Nørrebro ☎ 35/39–09–20 ⊕ www.stengade30.dk), named for an address right down the street from the actual club, is a smallish rock venue doubling as a bar that remains open through the night. **Vega** (✉ Enghavevej 40, Vesterbro ☎ 32/25–70–11 ⊕ www.vega.dk) has evening rock bands, after which the dance club plays house and techno, dragging action into the wee hours.

The Arts

The most complete English calendar of events is listed in the tourist magazine *Copenhagen This Week* (www.ctw.dk), and includes musical and theatrical events as well as films and exhibitions. Copenhagen's main theater and concert season runs from September through May, and tickets can be obtained either directly from theaters and concert halls or from ticket agencies. **Billetnet** (☎ 38/48–11–22 ⊕ www.billetnet.dk), a box-office service available at all post offices, has tickets for most major events. The main phone line is often busy; for information go in person to any post office. There's one on Købmagergade, just off Strøget. Same-day purchases at the box office at **Tivoli** (✉ Vesterbrog. 3, Downtown ☎ 33/15–10–12) are half price if you pick them up after noon; the half-price tickets are for shows all over town, but the ticket center also has full-price tickets for the park's own performances. The box office is open weekdays 11 to 5.

FILM Films open in Copenhagen a few months to a year after their U.S. premieres. There are about 60 cinemas in the greater Copenhagen area. The Danes are avid viewers, willing to pay DKr 70 per ticket, wait in lines for premieres, and read subtitles. Call the theater for reservations, and pick up tickets (with assigned seat numbers) an hour before the movie. Most theaters have a café. **Cinemateket** (✉ Gothersg. 55, Downtown ☎ 33/74–34–12 ⊕ www.dfi.dk), in the Danish Film Institute building, runs art films—often a series with a theme—and houses an excellent gift shop and café. **Grand Teatret** (✉ Mikkel Bryggersg. 8, Downtown ☎ 33/15–16–11 ⊕ www.grandteatret.dk) shows new foreign and art films, and is next door to its sister café. **Vester Vov Vov** (✉ Absalonsg. 5, Vesterbro ☎ 33/24–42–00 ⊕ www.vestervovvov.dk) is an alternative venue for art-house and second-run films.

OPERA, BALLET, Concert and festival information is available from the **Dansk Musik In-**
THEATER & **formation Center** (DMIC; ✉ Gråbrødre Torv 16, Downtown ☎ 33/
MUSIC 11–20–66 ⊕ www.mic.dk).

The **Opera Copenhagen** (Operahurst) (✉ Ekvipagemestervej 10, Dock Island, Holmen ☎ 33/69–69–33 ⊕ www.operahus.dk) is the long-awaited home of the Royal Danish Opera on the southern side of the harbor on Dock Island, Holmen. It opened in January 2005, only three years after construction began. It was funded virtually by one individual, Denmark's wealthiest man, Mærsk McKinney-møller, who bankrolled the project. He chose Henning Larsen, one of Denmark's best architects, to plan and design the Opera House, and its unique location allows it to be seen throughout the entire inner harbor. You approach the Opera House via water taxi or water bus. The interior of the theater hall is being called the "conch." Depending on the orchestra's pit size, the hall contains between 1,400 and 1,700 seats. The building features many roof terraces and a cafeteria with a view over Holmen and Øresunds-broen. In response to its splendid new space, the Royal Danish Opera plans to increase its repertoire in 2006/07 to seven or eight new productions per season. The ticket office opens 90 minutes before performances, and standing-room-only tickets are available from the Royal Theater Tickets Office on Tordenskjoldsgade the same day after 1 PM. Tickets can also be purchased through Billetnet (*above*).

Det Kongelige Teater (The Royal Theater; ✉ Kongens Nytorv, Downtown ✆ Box 2185, 1017 Kobenhavn K ☎ 33/69–69–33 ⊕ www.kgl-teater. dk), where the season runs October to May, is home to the Royal Danish Ballet, one of the premier companies in the world. Plays are exclusively in Danish. For information and reservations, call the theater. Beginning at the end of July, you can order tickets for the next season by writing to the theater.

Dansescenen (✉ Øster Fælled Torv 34, Østerbro ☎ 34/35–83–00 ⊕ www. dansescenen.dk) hosts various modern and experimental dance performances, some of which are put together by their choreographer-in-residence. If you are in search of experimental opera then **Den Anden Opera** (✉ Kronprinsensg. 7, Downtown ☎ 33/32–38–30 ⊕ www.denandenopera. dk) is worth a visit. **Kanonhallen** (✉ Øster Fælled Torv 37, Østerbro ☎ 35/43–20–21 ⊕ www.kanonhallen.net) runs a modern dance troupe in the city. **Nyt Dansk Danseteater** (⊠ Guldbergsg. 29A, Nørrebro ☎ 35/39–87–87 ⊕ www.nddt.dk) has a modern dance company but not a performance space; Copenhagen performances are held at other venues.

Tivoli Concert Hall (⊠ Tietgensg. 20, Downtown ☎ 33/15–10–12) offers more than 150 concerts each summer, presenting a host of Danish and foreign soloists, conductors, and orchestras.

Københavns Internationale Teater (KIT) (Copenhagen International Theatre; ⊠ Vesterg. 5, 3rd fl., Downtown ☎ 33/15–15–64 ⊕ www.kit.dk) offers an interesting lineup of entertainment for all ages between June and August. Under the title "Summerscene," KIT presents international contemporary theater, dance, inventive circus-style shows, and myriad other performances. **London Toast Theatre** (⊠ Kochsvej 18, Frederiksberg ☎ 33/22–86–86 ⊕ www.londontoast.dk) hosts English-language theater productions.

Sports & the Outdoors

Beaches

North of Copenhagen along the old beach road, **Strandvejen** is a string of lovely old seaside towns and beaches. **Bellevue Beach** (⊠ Across street from Klampenborg Station, Klampenborg) is packed with locals and has cafés, kiosks, and surfboard rentals. **Charlottenlund Fort** (Bus 6 from Rådhus Pl.) is a bit more private, but you have to pay (about DKr 20) to swim off the pier. The beaches along the tony town of **Vedbæk,** 18 km (11 mi) north of Copenhagen, are not very crowded as they are not as close to Copenhagen or as easily accessible by public transportation.

Closest to the city, the route along **Amager Strandvej** to and from the airport is a 12-km (7½-mi) stretch of beaches and wooded areas. Helgoland beach, on the north end of this strand, has bathhouses and a long dock and requires a token entrance fee.

Biking

Bike rentals are available throughout the city, and most roads have bike lanes. You might also be lucky and find an advertisement-flanked "city bike," parked at busy points around the city including Kongens Nytorv and the Nørreport train station. Deposit DKr 20 and pedal away; your money is returned when you return the bike. The city bikes are out and about from May to September. The Copenhagen Right Now tourist information office has city bike maps with suggested bike routes including a route of the city's ramparts or of the Copenhagen harbor. Follow all traffic signs and signals; bicycle lights and reflectors must be used at night. The **Danish Cyclist Federation** (⊠ Rømersg. 5, Downtown ☎ 33/32–31–21 ⊕ www.dcf.dk) has information about biking in the city. **Copenhagen Right Now** (⊠ Vesterbrog. 4A, Downtown ☎ 70/22–24–42 ⊕ www.visitcopenhagen.com) can provide information about bike-rental companies and routes throughout the city.

Golf

Although almost all courses in Denmark are run by private clubs, anybody who is a member of a club approved by a recognized authority—such as USPGA or R & A—can play. You will generally be asked to present a handicap card, something many American golfers do not carry around with them. It might be a good idea to have some proof of membership with you when you go to sign in. Otherwise, you will need to convince the staff you are indeed a golfer. It would be wise to call beforehand to find out if and when it is possible to play. Most golf-course staffs are accommodating, especially for visitors. At this writing, there were only three pay-and-play courses within a 30-km (20-mi) radius of Copenhagen, and they tend to be crowded. They also follow varying restrictions that tend to be as strict as those of private clubs. Most courses have handicap limits, normally around 28, for prospective players. Clubs, bags, and handcarts can be rented at virtually all courses, but motorized carts are a rarity. With few exceptions, carts may not be used without a letter from a doctor stating it is necessary. Some clubs do not accept reservations; call for details.

Copenhagen Golf Center (✉ Golfsvinget 16–20, Vallenbæk ☎ 43/64–92–93 ⊕ www.cgc.dk) is one of the publicly accessible courses close to the city center. The 18-hole course is rather flat but challenging; there is a variety of practice facilities, including a driving range. **Copenhagen Indoor Golf Center** (✉ Refshalevej 177-B, Holmen ☎ 32/66–11–00 ⊕ www.cigc. dk) is a newly expanded indoor practice center in what was once the huge B & W shipbuilding plant. Pros are on hand to give lessons at the driving and chipping ranges or the practice green. The 18-hole course at **Københavns Golf Klub** (✉ Dyrehaven 2, Lyngby ☎ 39/63–04–83) is said to be Scandinavia's oldest. It is located on the former royal hunting grounds, which are now a public park, so golfers must yield to people out strolling and to the herds of wild deer who live in the park. Greens fees are about DKr 280; check local rules about obstructions. One of Denmark's best courses, a frequent host of international tournaments, is the 18-hole **Rungsted Golf Klub** (✉ Vestre Stationsvej 16, Rungsted Kyst ☎ 45/86–34–44 ⊕ www.rungstedgolfklub.dk). A 30 handicap for all players is required on weekdays; on weekends and holidays the required handicap is 24 for men and a 29 for women. In 2003 **Simons Golf Club** (✉ Nybovej 5, Kvistgård ☎ 49/19–14–78 ⊕ www.simonsgolf.dk) became the first course in Denmark to host European Tour competition. One of the finest in the country, the course was made even more challenging for the professionals who played there. There are fine practice facilities; call to check about the handicap requirement. A hotel, the Nyborgaard Hotel, is located next to the first green of the golf course.

Horseback Riding

You can ride at the Dyrehavebakken (Deer Forest Hills) at **Fortunens Ponyudlejning** (✉ Ved Fortunen 33, Lyngby ☎ 45/87–60–58). A one-hour session (English saddle), in which both experienced and inexperienced riders go out with a guide, costs about DKr 100.

Axel Mattssons Rideskole (✉ Bellevuevej. 10-12, Klampenborg ☎ 39/64–08–22) is another facility for riding and lessons. It's open weekdays 7 AM–9 PM and weekends 7 AM–5 PM.

Running

The 6-km (4-mi) loop around the three lakes just west of city center—Skt. Jørgens, Peblinge, and Sortedams—is a runner's nirvana. There are also paths at the Rosenborg Have; the Frederiksberg Garden (near Frederiksberg Station, corner of Frederiksberg Allé and Pile Allé); and the Dyrehaven, north of the city near Klampenborg.

Soccer

Danish soccer fans call themselves Rooligans, which loosely translates as well-behaved fans, as opposed to hooligans. These Rooligans idolize the national team's soccer players as superstars. When the rivalry is most intense (especially against Sweden and Norway), fans don face paint, wear head-to-toe red and white, incessantly wave the Dannebrog (Danish flag), and have a good time whether or not they win. The biggest stadium in town for national and international games is **Parken** (⊠ Øster Allé 50, Østerbro ☎ 35/43–31–31). **Billetnet** (☎ 70/15–65–65) sells tickets for all matches. Prices are about DKr 140 for slightly obstructed views at local matches, DKr 220–DKr 320 for unobstructed; international matches are more expensive.

Swimming

Swimming is very popular here, and the pools (all of which are indoor) are crowded but well maintained. Separate bath tickets can also be purchased. Admission to local pools (DKr 20–DKr 50) includes a locker key, but you have to bring your own towel. Most pools are 25 meters long. The **DGI Byen Swim Center** (⊠ Tietgensg. 65, Vesterbro ☎ 33/29–80–00 ⊕ www.dgi-byen.dk) contains a massive oval pool with 100-meter lanes and a nifty platform in the middle that can be raised for parties and conferences. The swim center also has a children's pool and a "mountain pool," with a climbing wall, wet trampoline, and several diving boards. Admission to the swim center is DKr 50. During the popular monthly "spa night," candles are placed around the pool; dinner and wine are served on the raised pool platform; and massages and other spa services are offered. The beautiful **Frederiksberg Svømmehal** (Fredericksberg Swimming Baths; ⊠ Helgesvej 29, Frederiksberg ☎ 38/14–04–00) maintains its old art deco decor of sculptures and decorative tiles. It's open weekdays 7 AM–9 PM and weekends 9 AM–3 PM. The 50-meter **Lyngby Svømmehal** (⊠ Lundtoftevej 53, Lyngby ☎ 45/97–39–60) has a separate diving pool. In the modern concrete **Vesterbro Svømmehal** (⊠ Angelg. 4, Vesterbro ☎ 33/22–05–00), many enjoy swimming next to the large glass windows.

Shopping

A showcase for world-famous Danish design and craftsmanship, Copenhagen seems to have been designed with shoppers in mind. The best buys are such luxury items as crystal, porcelain, silver, and furs. Look for offers and sales (*tilbud* or *udsalg* in Danish) and check antiques and secondhand shops for classics at cut-rate prices. Although prices are inflated by a hefty 25% Value-Added Tax (Danes call it *moms*), non–European Union citizens can receive about an 18% refund. For more details and a list of all tax-free shops, ask at the tourist office for a copy of the *Tax-Free Shopping Guide*.

The **Information Center for Danish Crafts and Design** (⊠ Amagertorv 1, Downtown ☎ 33/12–61–62 ⊕ www.danishcrafts.dk) provides help-

ful information on the city's galleries, shops, and workshops specializing in Danish crafts and design, from jewelry to ceramics to wooden
toys to furniture. Its Web site has listings and reviews of the city's best
crafts shops.

Shopping Districts & Malls

The pedestrian-only **Strøget** and adjacent Købmagergade are *the* shopping streets, but wander down the smaller streets for lower-priced, off-
beat stores. The most exclusive shops are at the end of Strøget, around
Kongens Nytorv, and on Ny Adelgade, Grønnegade, and Pistolstræde.
Kronprinsensgade has become the in-vogue fashion strip, where a number of young Danish clothing designers have opened boutiques. **Bredgade**,
just off Kongens Nytorv, is lined with elegant antiques and silver shops,
furniture stores, and auction houses. A very popular mall in the city is
the gleaming **Fisketorvet Shopping Center** (☏ 33/36–64–00), built in
what was Copenhagen's old fish market. It's near the canal, south of
the city center, within walking distance of Dybbølsbro Station and the
Marriott Hotel. It includes 100 shops, from chain clothing stores (Mang,
Hennes & Mauritz) and shoe shops (including the ubiquitous Ecco) to
a smattering of jewelry, watch, and stereo retailers, such as Swatch and
Bang & Olufsen. Fast-food outlets abound, and there are 10 cinemas.
Field's (✉ Next to the Ørestad Metro Station [or E20 Frakørsel, exit 19]
⊕ www.fields.dk) is the mall of interest for many Danes (and shopping-
crazed Swedes) right now. It's near the Copenhagen Airport and has 130
stores and a full floor devoted to food, entertainment, and leisure pursuits. It's open weekdays 10–8 and Saturday 9–5.

Department Stores

Hennes & Mauritz (✉ Amagertorv 21–24, Downtown ☏ 33/73–70–90),
H & M for short, the Swedish chain, has stores all over town. They offer
reasonably priced clothing and accessories for men, women, and children; best of all are the to-die-for baby clothes. **Illum** (✉ Østerg. 52, Downtown ☏ 33/14–40–02), not to be confused with Illums Bolighus, is
well stocked, with a lovely rooftop café and excellent basement grocery.
Magasin (✉ Kongens Nytorv 13, Downtown ☏ 33/11–44–33 ⊕ www.
magasin.dk), Scandinavia's largest department store, also has a top-quality basement marketplace.

Specialty Stores

ANTIQUES   For silver, porcelain, and crystal, the well-stocked shops on **Bredgade**
are upscale and expensive. **Danborg Gold and Silver** (✉ Holbergsg. 17,
Downtown ☏ 33/32–93–94) is one of the best places for estate jewelry
and silver flatware. **Dansk Møbelkunst** (✉ Bredg. 32, Sankt Annæ Kvarter
☏ 33/32–38–37 ⊕ www.dmk.dk) is spacious and elegant, and home
to one of the city's largest collections of vintage Danish furniture. Some
of the pieces are by Arne Jacobsen, Kaare Klimt, and Finn Juhl, whose
lustrous, rosewood furnishings are some of the finest examples of Danish design. **H. Danielsens** (✉ Læderstr. 11, Downtown ☏ 33/13–02–74)
is a good bet for silver, Christmas plates, and porcelain. **Kaabers Antikvariat** (✉ Skinderg. 34, Downtown ☏ 33/15–41–77) is an emporium
for old and rare books, prints, and maps. The dozens of **Ravnsborggade**
(✉ Nørrebro ☏ 35/37–88–89 ⊕ www.ravnsborggade.dk) stores carry

traditional pine, oak, and mahogany furniture, and smaller items such as lamps and tableware. Some of them sell tax-free items and can arrange shipping. **Royal Copenhagen** (✉ Amagertorv 6, Downtown ☎ 33/13–71–81 ⊕ www.royalcopenhagen.com), along Strøget, carries old and new china, porcelain patterns, and figurines, as well as seconds.

AUDIO EQUIPMENT

For high-tech design and acoustics, **Bang & Olufsen** (✉ Østerg. 3, Downtown ☎ 33/15–04–22 ⊕ www.bang-olufsen.dk) is so renowned that its products are in the permanent design collection of New York's Museum of Modern Art. (Check prices at home first to make sure you are getting a deal.)

CLOTHING

It used to be that Danish clothing design took a backseat to the famous Dansk-designed furniture and silver, but increasingly that's no longer the case. If you're on the prowl for the newest Danish threads, you'll find a burgeoning number of cooperatives and designer-owned stores around town, particularly along Kronprinsensgade, near the Strøget.

Artium (✉ Vesterbrog. 1, Vesterbro ☎ 33/12–34–88) offers an array of colorful, Scandinavian-designed sweaters and clothes alongside useful and artful household gifts. **Bruuns Bazaar** (✉ Kronprinsensg. 8, Downtown ☎ 33/32–19–99 ⊕ www.bruunsbazaar.com) has its items hanging in the closet of almost every stylish Dane. Here you can buy the Bruuns label—inspired designs with a classic, clean-cut Danish look—and other high-end names, including Gucci. **ICCompanys** (✉ Raffinaderivej 10., Downtown ☎ 32/66–77–88 ⊕ www.inwear.dk) carries a trendy, youthful style, typified by the Danish Matinique label. **Mett–Mari** (✉ Vesterg. 11, Downtown ☎ 33/15–87–25) is among the most inventive handmade women's clothing shops. **Munthe plus Simonsen** (✉ Grønneg. 10, Downtown ☎ 33/32–03–12 ⊕ www.muntheplissimon.com/05/) sells innovative and playful—and pricey—Danish designs. **Petitgas Herrehatte** (✉ Købmagerg. 5, Downtown ☎ 33/13–62–70) is a venerable shop for old-fashioned men's hats. The **Sweater Market** (✉ Frederiksbergg. 15, Downtown ☎ 33/15–27–73) specializes in thick, traditional, patterned, and solid Scandinavian sweaters.

CRYSTAL & PORCELAIN

Minus the V.A.T., such Danish classics as Holmegaards crystal and Royal Copenhagen porcelain are usually less expensive than they are back home. Signed art glass is always more expensive, but be on the lookout for seconds as well as secondhand and unsigned pieces. **Bodum Hus** (✉ Østerg. 10, on Strøget, Downtown ☎ 33/36–40–80 ⊕ www.bodum.com) shows off a wide variety of reasonably priced Danish-designed functional, and especially kitchen-oriented, accoutrements; the milk foamers are indispensable for cappuccino lovers. **Rosenthal Studio-Haus** (✉ Frederiksbergg. 21, on Strøget, Downtown ☎ 33/14–21–01 ⊕ www.rosenthal.dk) offers the lead-crystal wildlife reliefs of Mats Johansson as well as the very modern functional and decorative works of many other Italian and Scandinavian artisans. **Royal Copenhagen** (✉ Amagertorv 6, Downtown ☎ 33/13–71–81 ⊕ www.royalcopenhagen.dk) has firsts and seconds of its famous porcelain ware. The **Royal Copenhagen Factory** (✉ Søndre Fasanvej 9, Frederiksberg ☎ 38/34–10–04 ⊕ www.royalcopenhagen.com) offers a look at the goods at their source. The factory runs tours through its facilities on weekdays from 10 to 4. Holmegaards Glass can also be purchased at the Royal Copenhagen store on Amagertorv. Alternatively, you can travel to their dedicated factory **Holmegaards Glasværker** (✉ Glasværkvej 45, Holme-Olstrup ☎ 55/54–50–00), 97 km (60 mi) south of Copenhagen near the town of Næstved.

FUR Denmark, the world's biggest producer of ranched minks, is the place to go for quality furs. Furs are ranked into four grades: Saga Royal (the best), Saga, Quality 1, and Quality 2. **Birger Christensen** (✉ Østerg. 38, Downtown ☎ 33/11–55–55), purveyor to the royal family and Copenhagen's finest furrier, deals only in Saga Royal quality. The store presents a new collection yearly from its in-house design team. Expect to spend about 20% less than in the United States for same-quality furs ($5,000–$10,000 for mink, $3,000 for a fur-lined coat), but as always, it pays to do your homework before you leave home. Birger Christensen is also among the preeminent fashion houses in town, carrying labels like Donna Karan, Chanel, Prada, Kenzo, Jil Sander, and Yves Saint Laurent. **A. C. Bang** (✉ Lyngby Hovedg. 55, Lyngby ☎ 45/88–00–54) carries less expensive furs than Birger Christensen, but has an old-world, old-money aura and very high quality.

FURNITURE & DESIGN **Illums Bolighus** (✉ Amagertorv 10, Downtown ☎ 33/14–19–41) is part gallery, part department store, showing off cutting-edge Danish and international design—art glass, porcelain, silverware, carpets, and loads of grown-up toys. **Lysberg, Hansen & Therp** (✉ Bredg. 75, Sankt Annæ Kvarter ☎ 33/14–47–87 ⊕ www.lysberg.dk), one of the most prestigious interior-design firms in Denmark, has sumptuous showrooms done up in traditional and modern styles. **Paustian** (✉ Kalkbrænderiløbskaj 2, Østerbro ☎ 39/16–65–65 ⊕ www.paustian.dk) offers you the chance to peruse elegant contemporary furniture and accessories in a building designed by Dane Jørn Utzon, the architect of the Sydney Opera House. You can also have a gourmet lunch at the Restaurant Paustian (it's open only for lunch). **Tage Andersen** (✉ Ny Adelg. 12, Downtown ☎ 33/93–09–13) has a fantasy-infused floral gallery-like shop filled with one-of-a-kind gifts and arrangements; browsers (who generally don't purchase the expensive items) are charged a DKr 45 admission.

SILVER Check the silver standard of a piece by its stamp. Three towers and "925S" (which means 925 parts out of 1,000) mark sterling. Two towers are used for silver plate. The "826S" stamp (also denoting sterling, but less pure) was used until the 1920s. Even with shipping charges, you can expect to save 50% versus American prices when buying Danish silver (especially used) at the source. **Danish Silver** (✉ Bredg. 22, Sankt Annæ Kvarter ☎ 33/11–52–52), owned by longtime Jensen collector Gregory Pepin, houses a remarkable collection of classic Jensen designs from holloware and place settings to art deco jewelry. Pepin, an American who has lived in Denmark for over a decade, is a font of information on Danish silver design, so if you're in the market, it's well worth a visit. **Georg Jensen** (✉ Amagertorv 4, Downtown ☎ 33/11–40–80 ⊕ www.georgjensen.com) is one of the most recognized names in international silver, and his elegant, austere shop is aglitter with sterling. Jensen has its own museum next door. **Ira Hartogsohn** (✉ Palæg. 8, Sankt Annæ

Kvarter ☎ 33/15–53–98) carries all sorts of silver knickknacks and settings. **Sølvkælderen** (✉ Kompagnistr. 1, Downtown ☎ 33/13–36–34) is the city's largest (and brightest) silver store, carrying an endless selection of tea services, place settings, and jewelry.

Street Markets

Check with the tourist office or the tourist magazine *Copenhagen This Week* (⊕ www.ctw.dk) for flea markets. Bargaining is expected. When the weather gets warm, it's time for outdoor flea markets in Denmark and the adventure of finding treasure among a vast amount of goods. Throughout summer and into autumn, there are six major flea markets every weekend. Two of the sites are right downtown. Along the walls of the cemetery **Assistens Kirkegård** (✉ Nørrebro), where Hans Christian Andersen and Søren Kierkegaard are buried, there is a flea market on Saturday with vendors who carry cutlery, dishes, clothes, books, and various other wares. At **Gammel Strand** on Friday and Saturday, the "market" is more of an outdoor antiques shop; you might find porcelain and crystal figurines, silver, or even, on occasion, furniture. **Israel Plads** (✉ Near Nørreport Station, Downtown) has a Saturday flea market from May through October, open 8–2. More than 100 professional dealers vend classic Danish porcelain, silver, jewelry, and crystal, plus books, prints, postcards, and more. **Kongens Nytorv** hosts a Saturday flea market in the shadow of the Royal Theater; the pickings are not so regal, but if you arrive early enough, you might nab a piece of jewelry or some Danish porcelain. The side street **Ravnsborggade** (✉ Nørrebro ⊕ www. ravnsborggade.dk) is dotted with antiques shops that move their wares outdoors on Sunday.

Copenhagen A to Z

ADDRESSES

Many of Copenhagen's main neighborhood districts are named after what were once the few points of entry to the city. What can confuse some visitors is that the districts are named after points on the compass, but do not lie in that direction in relation to the city center. For instance, Vesterport means "western bridge" (the bridge was the western entry to Copenhagen), while the district lies southwest of downtown.

Nowadays downtown Copenhagen (indicated by a KBH K in mailing addresses) is concentrated around Strøget, in an area containing lots of stores, cafés, restaurants, office buildings, and galleries, with residential properties on the upper floors. Just over a decade ago the center of town (including its northeastern subdistrict Sankt Annæ Kvarter) was the absolute center of all shopping, dining, and nightlife activity. It still is thriving, but some of the action has moved to neighboring districts.

A couple of centuries ago the districts of Vesterbro (KBH V), Nørrebro (KBH N), and Østerbro (KBH Ø) were once the outskirts of Copenhagen, named after the ports for entering the city. In the past decade nightlife and shops have moved into these districts to make them much sought-after spots to live and play. Halmtorv in Vesterbro was once a haunt for streetwalkers and other urchins, but has become an "in" and increasingly gentrified neighborhood in recent years. The area of Nørre-bro closest to downtown was once the working-class area of the city, but now contains some of the hottest property in town after cafés and shops sprouted in the area. Østerbro was mostly a bourgeois bastion, but has turned into a center for young families with lots of opportunity for shopping and recreation.

The man-made island of Christianshavn (KBH K) was filled and raised between Copenhagen and Amager island by King Christian IV to bol-ster the city's defense installations. Many of the military fortifications can still be seen, such as the Holmen naval base, which has become a thriving spot for creative offices, nightlife, and new residential growth. To the south Amager Island (KBH S) is a main focus of development and expansion plans for the Copenhagen metropolitan region.

Regular mail addressed to Copenhagen should include the street name and number, postal code of the region, and a letter after Copenhagen to signify the neighborhood. For example, Wonderful Copenhagen's of-fice is at Gammel Kongevej 1, DK-1610, Copenhagen V, Denmark. The "V" after Copenhagen stands for Vesterbro neighborhood, and DK-1610 is the country's zip or postal code.

AIRPORTS & TRANSFERS
Copenhagen Airport, 10 km (6 mi) southeast of downtown in Kastrup, is the gateway to Scandinavia and the rest of Europe.
▇ **Copenhagen International Airport** ☎ 32/31-32-31 ⊕ www.cph.dk.

TRANSFERS Although the 10-km (6-mi) drive from the airport to downtown is quick and easy, public transportation is excellent and much cheaper than tak-ing a taxi. The airport's sleek subterranean train system takes about 13 minutes to zip passengers into Copenhagen's main train station. Buy a ticket (DKr 25.50) upstairs in the airport train station at Terminal 3; a free airport bus connects the international terminal with the domes-tic terminal. Three trains an hour leave for Copenhagen, while a fourth travels to Roskilde. Trains also travel from the airport directly to Malmö, Sweden (DKr 60), via the Øresund Bridge, leaving every 20 minutes and taking 35 minutes in transit. Trains run on weekdays from 5 AM to midnight, on Saturday from 6 AM to midnight, and on Sunday from 6 AM to 11 PM.

SAS coach buses leave the international arrivals terminal every 15 min-utes from 5:45 AM to 9:45 PM, cost DKr 50, and take 25 minutes to reach Copenhagen's main train station on Vesterbrogade. Another SAS coach from Christiansborg, on Slotsholmsgade, to the airport runs every 15 minutes between 8:30 AM and noon, and every half hour from noon to 6 PM. HT city buses depart from the international arrivals terminal every 15 minutes from 4:30 AM (Sunday 5:30 AM) to 11:45 PM, but take a long, circuitous route. Take Bus 250S for the Rådhus Pladsen and trans-fer. One-way tickets cost about DKr 22.50.

The 20-minute taxi ride downtown costs around DKr 170, though slightly more after 4 PM and weekends. Lines form at the international arrivals terminal. In the unlikely event there is no taxi available, there are several taxi companies you can call including Københavns Taxa.

🚖 Taxis **Københavns Taxa** ☎ 35/35-35-35.

BIKE TRAVEL

Bikes are delightfully well suited to Copenhagen's flat terrain and are popular among Danes as well as visitors. Bike rental costs DKr 75–DKr 300 a day, with a deposit of DKr 500–DKr 1,000. You may also be lucky enough to find a free city bike chained up at bike racks in various spots throughout the city, including Nørreport and Nyhavn. Insert a DKr 20 coin, which will be returned to you when you return the bike.

🚲 Bike Rentals **Københavns Cykler** ✉ Central Station, Reventlowsg. 11, Vesterbro ☎ 33/33-86-13 ⊕ www.rentabike.dk. **Østerport Cykler** ✉ Oslo Plads 9, Østerbro ☎ 33/33-85-13 ⊕ www.rentabike.dk. **Urania Cykler** ✉ Gammel Kongevej 1, Vesterbro ☎ 33/21-80-88 ⊕ www.urania.dk.

CAR RENTAL

All major international car-rental agencies are represented in Copenhagen; most are at Copenhagen Airport or near Vesterport Station.

🚗 **Avis** ✉ Copenhagen Airport, Kastrup ☎ 32/51-22-99 or 32/51-20-99 ✉ Kampmannsg. 1, Vesterbro ☎ 70/24-77-07 ⊕ www.avis.dk. **Budget** ✉ Copenhagen Airport, Kastrup ☎ 32/52-39-00 ⊕ www.budget.com. **Europcar-Pitzner Auto** ✉ Copenhagen Airport, Kastrup ☎ 32/50-30-90 or 32/50-66-60 ✉ Gammel Kongevej 13A, Vesterbro ☎ 33/55-99-00 ⊕ www.europcar.comdk. **Hertz** ✉ Copenhagen Airport, Kastrup ☎ 32/50-93-00 or 32/50-30-40 ✉ Vester Farimagsg. 1, Vesterbro ☎ 33/17-90-00 ⊕ www.hertzdk.dk.

CAR TRAVEL

The E20 highway, via bridges, connects Fredericia (on Jutland) with Middelfart (on Funen), a distance of 16 km (10 mi), and goes on to Copenhagen, another 180 km (120 mi) east. Farther north, from Århus (in Jutland) you can get direct auto-catamaran service to Kalundborg (on Zealand). From there, Route 23 leads to Roskilde, about 72 km (45 mi) east. Take Route 21 east and follow the signs to Copenhagen, another 40 km (25 mi). Make reservations for the ferry in advance through the Danish State Railways. Since the inauguration of the Øresund Bridge in 2000, Copenhagen is now linked to Malmö, Sweden. The trip takes about 30 minutes, and the steep bridge toll stands at DKr 220 per car at this writing, though prices are likely to decrease to encourage more use. All trips across the Øresund Bridge are paid in Sweden. If you are driving to Sweden, you pay the toll after you have crossed the bridge. If you are headed for Denmark, you pay the toll before you cross the bridge.

If you are planning on seeing the sites of central Copenhagen, a car is not convenient. Parking spaces are at a premium and, when available, are expensive. A maze of one-way streets, relatively aggressive drivers, and bicycle lanes make it even more complicated. If you are going to drive, choose a small car that's easy to parallel park, bring a lot of small change to feed the meters, and be very aware of the cyclists on your right-hand side: they always have the right-of-way. For emergencies, contact Falck.

🚗 **Auto Rescue/Falck** ☎ 70/10-20-30 ⊕ www.falck.dk. **Danish State Railways** (DSB) ✉ Hovedbanegården (main train station), Vesterbro ☎ 70/13-14-15.

EMERGENCIES

Denmark's general emergency number is ☎ 112. Emergency dentists, near Østerport Station, are available weekdays 8 PM–9:30 PM and weekends and holidays 10–noon. The only acceptable payment method is cash. For emergency doctors, look in the phone book under *læge*. After normal business hours, emergency doctors make house calls in the city center and accept cash only; night fees are a minimum of DKr 300–DKr 400. You can also contact the U.S., Canadian, or British embassies for information on English-speaking doctors.

🏥 Doctors & Dentists **Casualty Wards-Skadestuen** ⊠ Italiensvej 1, Amager ☎ 32/34-32-34 ✉ Niels Andersens Vej 65, Hellerup ☎ 39/77-37-64 or 39/77-39-77. **Doctor Emergency Service** ☎ 70/13-00-41, 44/53-44-00 daily 4 PM-8 AM. **Tandlægevagt** (Dental Emergency Service) ⊠ Tandlægevagten. 14, Oslo Plads ☎ 35/38-02-51 ⊕ www.tandvagt.dk.

🏥 Emergency Services **Police, fire, and ambulance** ☎ 112.

🏥 Hospitals **Frederiksberg Hospital** ⊠ Nordre Fasanvej 57, Frederiksberg ☎ 38/16-38-16. **Rigshospitalet** ⊠ Blegdamsvej 9, Østerbro ☎ 35/45-35-45.

🏥 24-Hour Pharmacies **Sønderbro Apotek** ⊠ Amangerbrog. 158, Amager ☎ 32/58-01-40 ⊕ www.apoteket.dk. **Steno Apotek** ⊠ Vesterbrog. 6C, Vesterbro ☎ 33/14-82-66 ⊕ www.apoteket.dk.

ENGLISH-LANGUAGE MEDIA

BOOKS Boghallen, the bookstore of the Politiken publishing house, offers a good selection of English-language books. Arnold Busck has an excellent selection, and also textbooks, CDs, and comic books. Gad Boglader runs shops in various parts of the city, including one on Strøget and another in the new Royal Library, and offers a broad assortment of English-language volumes, fiction and nonfiction, along with other items of interest. Most of these stores have a large section devoted to Denmark and Danish literature. Another option for the bookworm would be to browse the many used-book shops that dot the city.

🏥 **Arnold Busck** ⊠ Kobmagerg. 49, Downtown ☎ 33/73-35-00 ⊕ www.arnoldbusck.dk. **Boghallen** ⊠ Rådhus Pl. 37, Downtown ☎ 33/47-25-60 ⊕ www.boghallen.dk. **Gad Boglader** ⊠ Vimmelskaftet 32, Downtown ☎ 33/15-05-58 ⊕ www.gad.dk.

NEWSPAPERS & *The Copenhagen Post* (www.cphpost.dk) is a weekly newspaper that covMAGAZINES ers Danish news in English. Particularly helpful is its insert, *In & Out*, with reviews and listings of restaurants, bars, nightclubs, concerts, theater, temporary exhibits, flea markets, and festivals in Copenhagen. Anyone planning on staying in Copenhagen for a long period should peruse the classified ads listing apartment-rental agencies and jobs for English-speakers. It's available at select bookstores, some hotels, and tourist offices. The biannual magazine *Scandinavian Living* (⊕ www.scandinavium.comau/scanliving.htm) includes articles on Scandinavian culture, food, and architecture and also lists the latest bars, restaurants, and shops. It's sold at the tourist office, as well as at some stores and hotels.

LODGING

LOCAL AGENTS In summer, reservations are recommended, but should you arrive without one, try the hotel booking desk at the Wonderful Copenhagen tourist information office. The desk offers same-day, last-minute prices (if available) for remaining rooms in hotels and private homes. A fee of DKr 50 is applied to each booking. You can also reserve private-home accommodations at Meet the Danes. The agency Hay4You has a selection of fully furnished apartments for rent to visitors staying in the city for a week or more. Young travelers looking for a room should head for Use It, the student and youth budget travel agency.

Hay4You ✉ Vimmelskaftet 49, Downtown ☎ 33/33-08-05 ⎙ 33/32-08-04 ⊕ www. hay4you.dk. **Hotel booking desk** ✉ Bernstorffsg. 1, Downtown ☎ 70/22-24-32 ⊕ www. visitcopenhagen.dk. **Meet the Danes** ✉ Ravnsborgg. 2, 2nd fl., Nørrebro ☎ 33/46-46-46 ⎙ 33/46-46-47 ⊕ www.meetthedanes.dk. **Use It** ✉ Rådhusstr. 13, Downtown ☎ 33/73-06-20 ⊕ www.useit.dk.

MONEY MATTERS

ATMS ATMs are located around town. Look for the red logos "Kontanten/Dankort Automat." Here you can use Visa, Plus, MasterCard/Eurocard, Eurochequecard, and sometimes JCB cards to withdraw money. Machines are usually open 24 hours, but some are closed at night.

CURRENCY Almost all banks (including the Danske Bank at the airport) exchange EXCHANGE money. Most hotels cash traveler's checks and exchange major foreign currencies, but they charge a substantial fee and give a lower rate. The exception to the rule—if you travel with cash—are the several locations of Forex (including the main train station and close to Nørreport Station). For up to $500, Forex charges only DKr 20 for the entire transaction. Keep your receipt and it will even change any remaining kroner you may still have back to dollars or another currency for free. For traveler's checks, it charges DKr 10 per check. Den Danske Bank exchange is open during and after normal banking hours at the main railway station, daily June through August 7 AM–10 PM, and daily September through May, 7 AM–9 PM. American Express is open weekdays 9–5 and Saturday 9–noon. The Change Group—open April through October, daily 10–8, November through March, daily 10–6—has several locations in the city center. Tivoli also exchanges money; it is open May through September, daily noon–11 PM.

American Express Corporate Travel ✉ Nansensg. 19, Downtown ☎ 70/23-04-60 ⊕ www.nymans.dk. The **Change Group** ✉ Vimmelskaftet 47, Downtown ☎ 33/93-04-18 ✉ Frederiksbergg. 5, Downtown ☎ 33/93-04-15 ✉ Østerg. 61, Østerbro ☎ 33/93-04-55 ✉ Vesterbrog. 9A, Vesterbro ☎ 33/24-04-47. **Den Danske Bank** ✉ Banegård-spl. (main train station), Vesterbro ☎ 33/12-04-11 ✉ Copenhagen Airport, Kastrup ☎ 32/46-02-80 ⊕ www.danskebank.dk. **Forex** ✉ Hovedbanegården 22 (main train station), Vesterbro ☎ 33/11-22-20 ✉ Nørre Voldg. 90, Downtown ☎ 33/32-81-00 ⊕ www.forex-valutaveksling.dk. **Tivoli** ✉ Vesterbrog. 3, Vesterbro ☎ 33/15-10-01 ⊕ www.tivoli.dk.

TAXIS

The shiny computer-metered Mercedes and Volvo cabs are not cheap. The base charge is DKr 23, plus DKr 10 per kilometer (higher after 4 PM). A cab is available when it displays the sign FRI (free); one can be hailed or picked up in front of the main train station or at taxi stands, or by calling the numbers below. Outside the city center, always call for a cab, as your attempts to hail one will be in vain. Try Kobenhavns Taxa or Amager Øbro Taxi. A 40% surcharge applies if you order a cab at night or on the weekend.

🄵 **Amager Øbro Taxi** ☎ 32/52-31-11. **Kobenhavns Taxa** ☎ 35/35-35-35.

TOURS

The tourist office monitors all tours and has brochures and information. Most tours run through summer until September.

BIKE TOURS Basic bicycle tours of Copenhagen with City Safari run around 2½ hours and cover the main sights of the city, while there is a more comprehensive trip (4½ hours) with lunch included. The guides not only point out Copenhagen's main attractions and provide helpful information for travelers, but also give some insight into the daily routines of the Danes. Special theme tours are also available, such as a trip through historic Copenhagen, a tour to and around the Carlsberg brewery, a junket showing modern architecture, a route following the footsteps of Hans Christian Andersen, and an exciting Copenhagen-by-night trip. Prices range from DKr 150 to DKr 350 (lunch included).

If you would prefer that someone else do the peddling, an increasingly popular sightseeing method is provided by Quickshaw, one of the city's many cycle-taxi and -tour companies. Quickshaw bicycle chauffeurs can accommodate two passengers and offer two best-of-Copenhagen sightseeing routes or allow you to dictate your own trip; they will even wait out front while you visit museums or other points of interest. The cyclist-drivers are comfortable and adept as tour guides, narrating as they pedal. The cycle-taxis in service are parked at 18 strategic sites in the inner city.

🄵 **City Safari** ✉ Dansk Arkitektur Center (Gammel Dok), Strandg. 27B, Christianshavn ☎ 33/23-94-90 🌐 www.citysafari.dk. **Quickshaw** ✉ Esplanaden 8D, Downtown ☎ 70/20-13-75.

BOAT TOURS The Harbor and Canal Tour (1 hour) leaves from Gammel Strand and the east side of Kongens Nytorv from May to mid-September. The City and Harbor Tour (2½ hours) includes a short bus trip through town and sails from the Fish Market on Holmens Canal through several more waterways, ending near Strøget. Contact Canal Tours or the tourist office for times and rates. Just south of the embarkation point for the City and Harbor Tour is the equally charming Netto Boats, which also offers hour-long tours for about half the price of its competitors.

🄵 **Canal Tours** ☎ 32/96-30-00 🌐 www.canal-tours.dk. **Netto Boats** ☎ 32/54-41-02 🌐 www.havnerundfart.dk.

BUS TOURS The Grand Tour of Copenhagen (2½ hours) includes Tivoli, the New Carlsberg Museum, Christiansborg Castle, the Stock Exchange, the Danish Royal Theater, Nyhavn, Amalienborg Castle, Gefion Fountain, Grundtvig Church, and Rosenborg Castle. The City Tour (1½ hours) is more general, passing the New Carlsberg Museum, Christiansborg Castle, the Thorvaldsen Museum, the National Museum, the Stock Exchange, the Danish Royal Theater, Rosenborg Castle, the National Art Gallery, the Botanical Gardens, Amalienborg Castle, Gefion Fountain, and *The Little Mermaid*. The Open Top Tours (about 1 hour), which are given on London-style double-decker buses, include stops at

Amalienborg, the Stock Exchange, Christiansborg, *The Little Mermaid,* Louis Tussaud's Wax Museum, the National Museum, the New Carlsberg Museum, Nyhavn, the Thorvaldsen Museum, and Tivoli. This tour gives attendees the option to disembark and embark on a later bus. Only the Grand Tour of Copenhagen, which covers the exteriors of the major sites, and the Open Top Tour, which covers less ground but more quickly, operate year-round. It's always a good idea to call first to confirm availability. Several other sightseeing tours leave from the Lur Blowers Column in Rådhus Pladsen 57, late March through September. For tour information call Copenhagen Excursions or Open Top Tours.

⚑ Copenhagen Excursions ☎ 32/54-06-06 ⊕ www.cex.dk. **Open Top Tours** ☎ 32/66-00-00 ⊕ www.sightseeing.dk.

WALKING TOURS   Due to its manageable size and meandering avenues, Copenhagen is a great city for pedestrians. A number of companies offer walking tours of parts of the city, some catering to Danes and others offering outings in various languages. One of the best companies is Copenhagen Walking Tours, which schedules 10 different English-language guided tours. In addition to tours related to culture and city history, the service offers a Copenhagen shopping primer and a tour of Jewish Copenhagen. The outings begin at the Wonderful Copenhagen tourist information office on weekends—from June through August there are tours from Thursday through Sunday. In addition, there is also a special tour of Rosenborg Castle beginning in front of the palace at 11:30 on Tuesday.

Two-hour walking tours organized by Copenhagen Walks begin in front of the Wonderful Copenhagen office at 10:30 Monday through Saturday from May to September (call to confirm). There are three different routes: uptown on Monday and Thursday, crosstown on Tuesday and Friday, and downtown on Saturday. Richard Karpen, an American who has been living in Denmark for over a decade, leads the tours dressed as Hans Christian Andersen, offering information on both the interiors and exteriors of buildings and giving insight into the lifestyles, society, and politics of the Danes. His tour of Rosenborg Castle, including the treasury, meets at the castle at 1:30 Monday through Thursday from May to September. The Tourist Information Office is located on Vesterbrogade, across from Tivoli Gardens.

⚑ Copenhagen Walking Tours ☎ 40/81-12-17 ⊕ www.copenhagen-walkingtours.dk. **Copenhagen Walks** ☎ 32/84-74-35 ⊕ www.copenhagenwalks.com.

TRAIN TRAVEL

Copenhagen's Hovedbanegården (Central Station) is the hub of the DSB network and is connected to most major cities in Europe. Intercity trains leave every hour, usually on the hour, from 6 AM to 10 PM for principal towns in Funen and Jutland. To find out more, contact the DSB. You can make reservations at Central Station, at most other stations, and through travel agents.

⚑ DSB Information ☎ 70/13-14-15 ⊕ www.dsb.dk. **Hovedbanegården** ✉ Banegårdspl. 1, Downtown ☎ 33/14-17-01 ⊕ www.hovedbanen.dk.

TRANSPORTATION AROUND COPENHAGEN

Copenhagen is small, with most sights within 2½ square km (1 square mi) at its center. Wear comfortable shoes and explore downtown on foot. Or follow the example of the Danes and rent a bike. For those with aching feet, an efficient transit system is available.

The Copenhagen Card offers unlimited travel on buses, harbor buses, and Metro and suburban trains (S-trains), as well as admission to some 60 museums and sights throughout both metropolitan Copenhagen and Malmö, Sweden. They're valid for a limited time, though, and therefore only worthwhile if you're planning a nonstop, intense sightseeing tour. The Card also offers discounts on many other attractions and activities, including car rental and Scandlines' crossing of the Sound (Øresund) between Sweden and Denmark. An adult card also includes passage for two children up to 9 years old. The card costs DKr 199 (24 hours), DKr 429 (72 hours), and is DKr 129 and DKr 249 for children ages 10 to 15. It can be purchased at bus and train stations, tourist offices, and hotels, or from travel agents.

Trains and buses operate from 5 AM (Sunday 6 AM) to midnight. After that, night buses run every half hour from 1 AM to 4:30 AM from the main bus station at Rådhus Pladsen to most areas of the city and surroundings. Trains and buses operate on the same ticket system and divide Copenhagen and surrounding areas into three zones. Tickets are validated on a time basis: on the basic ticket, which costs about DKr 11 per hour, you can travel anywhere in the zone in which you started. A discount *klip kort* (clip card), good for 10 rides, costs DKr 85 and must be stamped in the automatic ticket machines on buses or at stations. (If you don't stamp your clip card, you can be fined up to DKr 500.) Get zone details for S-trains on the information line. The buses have a Danish information line with an automatic answering menu that is not very helpful, but try pressing the number 1 on your phone and wait for a human to pick up. The phone information line operates daily 7 AM–9:30 PM. You might do better by asking a bus driver or stopping by the HT Buses main office (open weekdays 9–7, Saturday 9–3) on the Rådhus Pladsen, where the helpful staff is organized and speaks enough English to adequately explain bus routes and schedules to tourists.

The HT harbor buses are ferries that travel up and down the canal, embarking from outside the Royal Library's Black Diamond, with stops at Knippelsbro, Nyhavn, and Holmen, and then back again, with lovely vistas along the way. The harbor buses run six times an hour, daily from 6 AM to 6:25 PM, and tickets cost around DKr 25. If you have a klip kort, you can use it for a trip on the harbor bus.

The Metro system runs regularly from 5 AM to 1 AM, and all night on weekends. Until the end of 2007 only two Metro lines are in operation linking the northern neighborhood of Vanløse to the beginning of southern Amager through the downtown area.

🚌 **Bus information** ☎ 36/13-14-15 ⊕ www.ht.dk. **Metro information** ☎ 33/11-17-00 ⊕ www.m.dk. **S-train information** ☎ 70/13-14-15 ⊕ www.rejseplan.dk.

TRAVEL AGENCIES

For student and budget travel, try Kilroy Travels Denmark. For charter packages, stick with Spies. Star Tour also handles packages.

🖪 **American Express Corporate Travel** ✉ Nansensg. 19, Downtown ☎ 70/23–04–60 ⊕ www.nymans.dk. **Carlson Wagonlit** ✉ Vester Farimagsg. 7, 2nd fl., Vesterbro ☎ 33/63–78–78 ⊕ www.cwt.dk. **DSB Travel Bureau** ✉ Hovedbanegården (main train station), Vesterbro ☎ 33/13–14–18 ⊕ www.dsb.dk/rejsebureau. **Kilroy Travels Denmark** ✉ Skinderg. 28, Downtown ☎ 70/15–40–15 ⊕ www.kilroytravels.dk. **Spies** ✉ Nyropsg. 41, Vesterbro ☎ 70/10–42–00 ⊕ www.spies.dk. **Star Tour** ✉ H. C. Andersens Blvd. 12, Vesterbro ☎ 70/11–10–50 ⊕ www.startour.dk.

VISITOR INFORMATION

The Wonderful Copenhagen tourist information office is open May through the first two weeks of September, daily 9–8; the rest of September through April, weekdays 9–4:30 and Saturday 9–1:30. Note that the tourist office hours vary slightly from year to year, so you may want to call ahead. Its well-maintained Web site includes extensive listings of sights and events. Youth information in Copenhagen is available from Use It. Listings and reviews of Copenhagen's museums (including temporary exhibits), sights, and shops are included on www.aok.dk. The Visit Denmark Web site has listings on hotels, restaurants, and sights in Copenhagen and around Denmark; AOK also has an excellent Web site on Copenhagen. For more information on the outlying fishing village of Dragør, visit the office or Web site of Dragør Tourist Information.

🖪 **AOK** ⊕ www.aok.dk. **Dragør Tourist Information** ✉ Havnepladsen 2, Dragør ☎ 32/53–41–06 ⊕ www.dragoer-information.dk. **Use It** ✉ Rådhusstr. 13, Downtown ☎ 33/73–06–20 ⊕ www.useit.dk. **Visit Denmark** ⊕ www.visitdenmark.com. **Wonderful Copenhagen** ✉ Vesterbrog. 4C, Vesterbro ☎ 70/22–24–42 ⊕ www.visitcopenhagen.com.

SIDE TRIPS FROM COPENHAGEN

Experimentarium

8 km (5 mi) north of Copenhagen.

In the beachside town of Hellerup is the **Experimentarium,** where more than 300 exhibitions are clustered in various "Discovery Islands," each exploring a different facet of science, technology, and natural phenomena. A dozen body- and hands-on exhibits allow you to take skeleton-revealing bike rides, measure your lung capacity, stir up magnetic goop, play ball on a jet stream, and gyrate to gyroscopes. Once a bottling plant for the Tuborg Brewery, this center organizes one or two special exhibits a year; past installations have included interactive exhibits of the brain and tongue-wagging, life-size dinosaurs. Take Bus 6 or 650S from Rådhus Pladsen or the S-train to Hellerup; transfer to Bus 21 or 650S. Alternatively, take the S-train to Svanemøllen Station, then walk north for 10 minutes. ✉ *Tuborg Havnevej 7, Hellerup* ☎ *39/27–33–33* ⊕ *www.experimentarium.dk* 💶 *DKr 115* ◷ *Mon. and Wed.–Fri. 9:30–5, Tues. 9:30–9, weekends and holidays 11–5.*

Charlottenlund

10 km (6 mi) north of Copenhagen (take Bus 6 from Rådhus Pladsen or S-train to Charlottenlund Station).

Just north of Copenhagen is the leafy, affluent coastal suburb of Charlottenlund, with a small, appealing beach that gets predictably crowded on sunny weekends. A little farther north is Charlottenlund Slot (Charlottenlund Palace), a graceful mansion that has housed various Danish royals since the 17th century. Today, it houses only offices and is not open to the public. The surrounding peaceful palace gardens, however, are open to all, and Copenhageners enjoy coming up here for weekend ambles and picnics.

A favorite with families is the nearby **Danmarks Akvarium** (Danmarks Aquarium), a sizable, well-designed aquarium near the palace with all the usual aquatic suspects, from gliding sharks to brightly colored tropical fish to snapping crocodiles. ⊠ *Kavalergården 1, Charlottenlund* ☎ *39/62–32–83* ⊕ *www.akvarium.dk* ⊠ *DKr 75* ⊗ *Nov.–Jan., daily 10–4; Feb.–Apr., daily 10–5; May–Aug., daily 10–6; Sept. and Oct., daily 10–5.*

Fodor'sChoice ★ While in Charlottenlund, don't miss the remarkable **Ordrupgaard**, one of the largest museum collections of French impressionism in Europe outside France. Most of the great 19th-century French artists are represented, including Manet, Monet, Matisse, Cézanne, Renoir, Degas, Gauguin, Alfred Sisley, Delacroix, and Pissarro. Particularly noteworthy is Delacroix's 1838 painting of George Sand. The original painting depicted Sand listening to her lover Chopin play the piano. For unknown reasons, the painting was divided, and the half portraying Chopin now hangs in the Louvre. The Ordrupgaard also has a superb collection of Danish Golden Age painters, from Christen Købke to Vilhelm Hammershøj, who has been called "the Danish Edward Hopper" because of the deft use of light and space in his haunting, solitary paintings. Perhaps best of all is that much of the magnificent collection is displayed, refreshingly, in a non-museum-like setting. The paintings hang on the walls of what was once the home of museum founder and art collector Wilhelm Hansen. The lovely interior of this graceful manor house dating from 1918 has been left just as it was when Hansen and his wife Henny lived here. The white-and-gold ceiling has intricate flower moldings, and the gleaming dark-wood tables are set with Royal Copenhagen Flora Danica porcelain. Interspersed among the paintings are windows that provide glimpses of the surrounding lush, park-size grounds of beech trees, sloping lawns, a rose garden, and an orchard. ⊠ *Vilvordevej 110, Charlottenlund* ☎ *39/64–11–83* ⊕ *www.ordrupgaard.dk* ⊠ *DKr 65* ⊗ *Tues., Thurs., and Fri. 1–5; Wed. 10–8; weekends 11–5.*

need a break? Before or after your visit to the Ordrupgaard museum, wind down next door at the soothing **Ordrupgaard Café** (⊠ Vilvordevej 110, Charlottenlund ☎ 39/63–00–33 ⊕ www.cafeordrupgaard.dk), housed in the former stable of the manor house–turned–museum. Sink into one of the rustic cane chairs and enjoy the daily changing menu of light Danish–French dishes, such as the smoked salmon drizzled with lime sauce or a fluffy ham quiche served with fresh greens. For an afternoon snack, try a pastry along with a pot of coffee that you can refill as often as you wish. The café is open Tuesday–Sunday, noon–5. Credit cards are not accepted.

Dragør

★ *22 km (14 mi) southeast of Copenhagen (take Bus 30 or 33 from Råd-hus Pladsen).*

On the island of Amager, less than a half hour from Copenhagen, the quaint fishing town of Dragør (pronounced *drah*-wer) feels far away in distance and time. The town is set apart from the rest of the area around Copenhagen because it was settled by Dutch farmers in the 16th century. King Christian II ordered the community to provide fresh produce and flowers for the royal court. Today neat rows of terra-cotta–roof houses trimmed with wandering ivy, roses, and the occasional waddling goose characterize the still meticulously maintained community. If there's one color that characterizes Dragør, it's the lovely pale yellow (called Dragør gul, or Dragør yellow) of its houses. According to local legend, the former town hall's chimney was built with a twist so that meetings couldn't be overheard.

As you're wandering around Dragør, notice that many of the older houses have an angled mirror contraption attached to their street-level windows. This *gade spejl* (street mirror), unique to Scandinavia, was—and perhaps still is—used by the occupants of the house to "spy" on the street activity. Usually positioned at seat level, this is where the curious (often the older ladies of town) could pull up a chair and observe all the comings and goings of the neighborhood from the warmth and privacy of their own homes. You can see these street mirrors all across Denmark's small towns and sometimes in the older neighborhoods of the bigger cities.

The **Dragør Museum,** in one of the oldest houses in town, sits near the water on Dragør's colorful little harbor. The collection includes furniture from old skipper houses, costumes, drawings, and model ships. The museum shop has a good range of books on Dragør's history. ⊠ *Havnepl., Dragør* ☎ *32/53–41–06* ⊕ *www.dragoermuseum.dk* 🎫 *DKr 20* ☉ *May–Sept., Tues.–Sun. noon–4.*

A ticket to the Dragør Museum also affords entrance to the **Mølsted Museum,** which displays paintings by the famous local artist Christian Mølsted, whose colorful canvases capture the maritime ambience of Dragør and its rich natural surroundings. ⊠ *Dr. Dichs Pl. 1, Dragør* ☎ *32/53–41–06* ⊕ *www.dragoermuseum.dk* 🎫 *DKr 20* ☉ *May–Aug., weekends noon–4.*

You can swing by the **Amagermuseet** in the nearby village of Store Magleby, 2 km (1 mi) west of Dragør. The museum is housed in two thatch-roof, whitewashed vintage farmhouses, which were once the homes of the Dutch farmers and their families who settled here in the 16th century. The farmhouses are done up in period interiors, with original furnishings and displays of traditional Dutch costumes. Round out your visit with an outdoor stroll past grazing dairy cows and through well-tended vegetable gardens flourishing with the same vegetables that the settlers grew. ⊠ *Hovedg. 4 and 12, Dragør* ☎ *32/53–93–07* ⊕ *www. amagermuseet.dk* ☜ *DKr 30* ⊙ *May–Sept., Tues.–Sun. noon–4; Oct.–Apr., Wed. and Sun. noon–4.*

Where to Stay & Eat

$$$ ✕ **Restaurant Beghuset.** This handsome restaurant with rustic stone floors and green-and-gold painted doors is named Beghuset (Pitch House), because this is where Dragør's fishermen used to boil the pitch that waterproofed their wooden ships. The creative Danish cuisine includes fried pigeon with mushrooms, grapes, and potatoes drizzled with a thyme-and-balsamic-vinegar dressing. ⊠ *Strandg. 14, Dragør* ☎ *32/53–01–36* ⊕ *www.beghuset.dk* ⊟ *AE, DC, MC, V* ⊙ *Closed Mon.*

$ 🏨 **Dragør Badehotel.** Built in 1907 as a seaside hotel for vacationing Copenhageners, this plain, comfortable hotel is still geared to the summer crowds, yet manages to maintain its wonderfully low prices (you'd easily pay twice the price in Copenhagen). The basic rooms have dark-green carpets and simple furniture; half the rooms include little terraces that face toward the water, so make sure to ask for one when booking. The bathrooms are small and basic, with a shower only (no bathtubs). Breakfast, which is included in the price, is served on the outside terrace in summer. ⊠ *Drogdensvej 43, DK–2791 Dragør* ☎ *32/53–05–00* 🖷 *32/ 53–04–99* ⊕ *www.badehotellet.dk* ↩ *34 rooms* ⚭ *Restaurant, bar, meeting room, some pets allowed* ⊟ *AE, DC, MC, V.*

Klampenborg, Bakken & Dyrehaven

15 km (9 mi) north of Copenhagen (take Bus 6 from Rådhus Pladsen or S-train to Klampenborg Station).

As you follow the coast north of Copenhagen, you'll come upon the wealthy enclave of Klampenborg, whose residents are lucky enough to have the pleasant **Bellevue Beach** nearby. In summer this luck may seem double-edged, when scores of city-weary sun-seekers pile out at the Klampenborg S-train station and head for the sand. The Danes have a perfect word for this: they call Bellevue a *fluepapir* (flypaper) beach. Still and all, Bellevue is an appealing seaside spot to soak up some rays, especially considering that it's just a 20-minute train ride from Copenhagen.

Klampenborg is no stranger to crowds. Just a few kilometers inland, within the peaceful Dyrehaven, is **Bakken,** the world's oldest amusement park—and one of Denmark's most popular attractions. If Tivoli is champagne in a fluted glass, then Bakken is a pint of beer. Bakken's crowd is working-class Danes, and lunch is hot dogs and cotton candy. Of course Tivoli, with its trimmed hedges, dazzling firework displays, and evening concerts, is still Copenhagen's reigning queen, but unpretentious Bakken makes no claims to the throne; instead, it is unabashedly about having a good time—being silly in the bumper cars, screaming at the top of your lungs on the rides, and eating food that's bad for you. There's something comfortable and nostalgic about Bakken's vaguely dilapidated state. Bakken has more than 100 rides, from quaint, rickety roller coasters (refreshingly free of that Disney gloss) to newer, faster rides to little-kid favorites such as Kaffekoppen, the Danish version of twirling teacups, where you sit in traditional Royal Copenhagen–style blue-and-white coffee cups. Bakken opens the last weekend in March, with a festive ride by motorcyclists across Copenhagen to Bakken. It closes in late August, because this is when the Dyrehaven park animals begin to mate, and during their raging hormonal stage the animals can be dangerous around children. ⊠ *Dyrehavevej 62, inside Dyrehaven, Klampenborg, (take S-train to Klampenborg Station)* ☎ *39/63–73–00* ⊕ *www.bakken.dk* ☞ *Free, DKr 239 for a day pass to all rides in peak season (June 27–Aug. 7)* ⊙ *Late Mar.–late Aug., daily 2 PM–midnight.*

★ Bakken sits within the verdant, 2,500-acre **Dyrehaven** (Deer Park), where herds of wild deer roam freely. Once the favored hunting grounds of Danish royals, today Dyrehaven has become a cherished weekend oasis for Copenhageners. Hiking and biking trails traverse the park, and lush fields beckon to nature-seekers and families with picnic hampers. The deer are everywhere; in the less-trafficked regions of the park you may find yourself surrounded by an entire herd of deer delicately stepping through the fields. The park's centerpiece is the copper-top, 17th-century **Eremitagen,** formerly a royal hunting lodge. It is closed to the public. Today, the Royal Hunting Society gathers here for annual lunches and celebrations, most famously on the first Sunday in November, when the society hosts a popular (and televised) steeplechase event in the park. The wet and muddy finale takes place near the Eremitagen when the riders attempt to make it across a small lake. Dyrehaven is a haven for hikers and bikers, but you can also go in for the royal treatment and enjoy it from the high seat of a horse-drawn carriage. The carriages gather at the park entrance near the Klampenborg S-train station. The cost is around DKr 40 for 15 minutes, DKr 60 to Bakken, DKr 250 to the Eremitagen, and DKr 400 for an hour. ⊠ *Park entrance is near Klampenborg S-train station, Klampenborg* ☎ *39/63–39–00.*

Where to Eat

★ **$$$–$$$$** ✕ **Strandmøllekroen.** The 200-year-old beachfront inn is filled with antiques and hunting trophies. The best views are of the Øresund from the back dining room. Elegantly served seafood and steaks are the mainstays, and for a bit of everything try the seafood platter, with lobster, crab claws, and Greenland shrimp. ⊠ *Strandvejen 808, Klampenborg* ☎ *39/63–01–04* ⊕ *www.strandmoellekroen.dk* ▭ *AE, DC, MC, V.*

Frilandsmuseet

16 km (10 mi) northwest of Copenhagen.

North of Copenhagen is Lyngby, its main draw the Frilandsmuseet, an open-air museum. About 50 farmhouses and cottages representing various periods of Danish history have been painstakingly dismantled, moved here, reconstructed, and filled with period furniture and tools.

Trees and gardens surround the museum; bring lunch and plan to spend the day. To get here, take the S-train to the Sorgenfri station, then walk right and follow the signs. ✉ *Kongevejen, Lyngby* ☎ *33/13–44–41* ⊕ *www.frilandsmuseet.dk* 🖾 *DKr 50, free Wed.* ☉ *Easter–Sept., Tues.–Sun. 10–5.*

Museet for Moderne Kunst (Arken)

20 km (12 mi) southwest of Copenhagen (take the S-train in the direction of either Hundige, Solrød Strand, or Køge to Ishøj Station, then pick up Bus 128 to the museum).

Architect Søren Robert Lund was just 25 when awarded the commission for this forward-looking museum, which he designed in metal and white concrete set against the flat coast southwest of Copenhagen. The museum, also known as the Arken, opened in March 1996 to great acclaim, both for its architecture and its collection. Unfortunately, for a couple of years following its opening it was plagued with a string of stranger-than-fiction occurrences, including a director with an allegedly bogus résumé. The situation has greatly improved, and today the museum's massive sculpture room exhibits both modern Danish and international art, as well as experimental works. Dance, theater, film, and multimedia exhibits are additional attractions. ✉ *Skovvej 100, Ishøj* ☎ *43/54–02–22* ⊕ *www.arken.dk* 🖾 *DKr 60* ☉ *Tues.–Sun. 10–5, Wed. 10–9.*

ZEALAND

The goddess Gefion is said to have carved Zealand (Sjælland) from Sweden. If she did, she must have sliced the north deep with a fjord, while she chopped the south to pieces and left the sides bowing west. Though the coasts are deeply serrated, Gefion's myth is more dramatic than the flat, fertile land of rich meadows and beech stands.

Slightly larger than the state of Delaware, Zealand is the largest of the Danish islands. From Copenhagen, almost any point on it can be reached in an hour and a half, making it the most traveled portion of the country—and it is especially easy to explore thanks to the extensive road network. North of the capital, ritzy beach towns line up between Hellerup and Humlebæk. Helsingør's Kronborg, which Shakespeare immortalized in *Hamlet*, and Hillerød's stronghold of Frederiksborg, considered one of the most magnificent Renaissance castles in Europe, also lie to the north. To the west of Copenhagen is Roskilde, medieval Denmark's most important town, with an eclectic cathedral that served as northern Europe's spiritual center 1,000 years ago.

West and south, rural towns and farms edge up to seaside communities and fine white beaches, often surrounded by forests. Beaches with summer cottages, white dunes, and calm waters surround Gilleleje and the neighboring town of Hornbæk. The beach in Tisvildeleje is quieter and close to woods. Even more unspoiled are the Lilliputian islands around southern Zealand, virtually unchanged over the past century.

Rungsted

❶ *21 km (13 mi) north of Copenhagen.*

Between Copenhagen and Helsingør is **Rungstedlund,** the elegant, airy former manor of Baroness Karen Blixen, who wrote *Out of Africa* and several accounts of aristocratic Danish life under the pen name Isak Dinesen. The manor house, where she lived as a child and to which she returned in 1931, is open as a museum and displays manuscripts, photographs, paintings, and memorabilia documenting her years in Africa and Denmark. Leave time to wander around the gardens. ⊠ *Rungsted Strandvej 111, Rungsted Kyst* ☎ *45/57–10–57 for combined train and admission tickets, 70/13–14–16 international, 70/13–14–15 domestic* 🖷 *45/57–10–58* ⊕ *www.karen-blixen.dk* ▱ *DKr 40* ⊙ *May–Sept., Tues.–Sun. 10–5; Oct.–Apr., Wed.–Fri. 1–4, weekends 11–4.*

Where to Eat

★ **$$$–$$$$** ✕ **Nokken.** The terrace, stretching from the base of the harbor to the waters of Øresund, provides a view of the sailboats returning to port as well as a tranquil skyline in the evening. The elegant Italian-style interior pleasantly contradicts the classic French cuisine served. Seafood fresh from the sound is the main attraction but tournedos and other succulent meat dishes are also available. French reserves dominate the wine menu. ⊠ *Rungsted Havn 44, Rungsted Kyst* ☎ *45/57–13–14* ⊕ *www. nokken.dk* ▱ *AE, DC, MC, V.*

Humlebæk

❷ *10 km (6 mi) north of Rungsted, 31 km (19 mi) north of Copenhagen.*

Historically a fishing village, this elegant seaside town with a population of about 6,000 has of late become a suburb of both Copenhagen and Helsingør. In summer the town's many cottages fill with vacationers, and the gardens come alive with vibrant colors. The town takes its name from the plant *humle* (hops), which is abundant in the area.

☪ Humlebæk is home of the must-see **Louisiana,** a modern-art museum as
Fodor's Choice famed for its stunning location and architecture as for its collection. Even
★ if you can't tell a Monet from a Duchamp, you should make the 30-minute trip from Copenhagen to see its elegant rambling structure, surrounded by a large park. Housed in a pearly 19th-century villa surrounded by dramatic views of the Øresund waters, the permanent collection includes modern American paintings and Danish paintings from the COBRA (a trend in northern European painting that took its name from its active locations, Copenhagen, Brussels, and Amsterdam) and deconstructionism movements. Be sure to see the haunting collection of Giacomettis backdropped by picture windows overlooking the sound. The children's wing has pyramid-shape chalkboards, childproof computers, and weekend activities under the guidance of an artist or museum coordinator. To get here from the station, walk north about 10 minutes. ⊠ *Gammel Strandvej 13* ☎ *49/19–07–19* 🖷 *49/19–35–05* ⊕ *www.louisiana.dk* ▱ *DKr 76* ⊙ *Thurs.–Tues. 10–5, Wed. 10–10.*

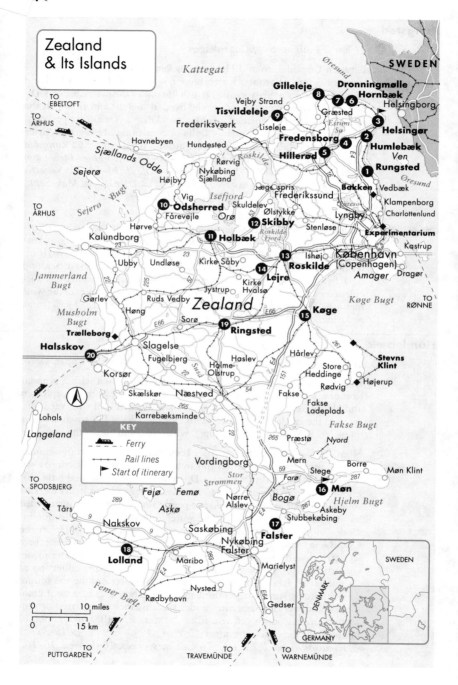

Helsingør

▶ ❸ *14 km (8½ mi) north of Humlebæk, 45 km (28 mi) north of Copenhagen.*

Helsingør dates back to the early 13th century. It wasn't until the 1400s, when Erik of Pomerania established a tariff for all ships passing through the sound, that the town began to prosper. Perhaps Helsingør is best known as the home of Shakespeare's fictional Hamlet. Today more than 55,000 people populate the city.

Fodor'sChoice
★

At the northeastern tip of the island, Helsingør is the departure point for ferries to the Swedish town of Helsingborg, and it's the site of **Kronborg Slot** (Kronborg Castle), which was added to UNESCO's World Heritage List in 2000. William Shakespeare based *Hamlet* on Danish mythology's Amleth, and used this castle as the setting even though he had probably never seen it. Built in the late 16th century, it is 600 years younger than the Elsinore we imagine from the tragedy. It was built as a Renaissance tollbooth: from its cannon-studded bastions, forces collected Erik of Pomerania's much-hated Sound Dues, a tariff charged to all ships crossing the sliver of water between Denmark and Sweden. Coming through the entrance arch decorated in Flemish style, you'll see the castle lawn in front of an octagonal tower, the Trumpeters Tower, whose decoration stands out from the whole.

From the yard there is access to the royal chapel. Still true to its original Renaissance style from 1582, the chapel accommodates the royal throne, which has multicolor carved wood. Among the 27 rooms open to the public are 2 deserving of more attention: the so-called "lille sal" (small room) and the king's bedroom. In the "small room," on the second floor, hang seven tapestries made of silk and wool and created by the Flemish painter Hans Knieper between 1581 and 1586. What makes these tapestries exceptional is not merely their artistic quality but also their subject matter. They portray several Danish kings against backgrounds of stately buildings and luxuriant scenery, with German translations accompanying Danish verses describing their respective achievements. The ceiling of the king's bedroom is worth a couple of extra minutes. If you crane your neck, you can see four scenes of royal life painted by the Dutch artist Gerrit van Honthorst in 1630. Also well worth seeing are the 200-foot-long dining hall and the dungeons, where there is a brooding statue of Holger Danske (Ogier the Dane). According to legend, the Viking chief sleeps, but will awaken to defend Denmark when it is in danger. (The largest Danish resistance group during World War II called itself Holger Danske after its fearless forefather.) ✉ *At the point on the harbor front* ☎ *49/21–30–78* ⊕ *www.ses.dk/kronborgcastle* ◲ *DKr 60* ⊗ *May–Sept., daily 10:30–5; Oct. and Apr., Tues.–Sun. 11–4; Nov.–Mar., Tues.–Sun. 11–3.*

Thanks to the hefty tolls collected by Erik of Pomerania, Helsingør prospered. Stroll past the carefully restored medieval merchants' and ferrymen's houses in the middle of town. On the corner of Stengade and Sankt Annæ gade near the harbor is **Sankt Olai Kirke** (St. Olaf's Church), the country's largest parish church and worth a peek for its elaborately carved wooden altar. ⊠ *Sankt Olai G. 51* ☎ *49/21–04–43 (9–noon)* ⊕ *www. helsingordomkirke.dk* ☞ *Free* ⊙ *May–Sept., daily noon–3; Oct.–Apr., daily noon–2.*

Close to Sankt Olai Kirke is Sankt Marie Kirke with the 15th-century **Carmelite Kloster** (Carmelite Convent), one of the best-preserved examples of medieval architecture in Scandinavia. After the Reformation it was used as a hospital, and by 1630 it had become a poorhouse. ⊠ *Skt. Annæ G. 38* ☎ *49/21–17–74* ☞ *DKr 10* ⊙ *Mid-May–mid-Sept., tour daily at 2; call ahead.*

If you want to know more about Helsingør, right next door to the Carmelite Kloster is the modest **By Museum** (Town Museum), which has exhibits of 19th-century handicrafts, dolls, and a model of the town. ⊠ *Skt. Annæ G. 36* ☎ *49/28–18–00* ☞ *DKr 10* ⊙ *Weekdays noon–4.*

off the beaten path

MARIENLYST SLOT – One kilometer (½ mi) north of Helsingør is the Louis XVI–style Marienlyst Castle. Built in 1587, it provided King Frederik II with a garden, as well as a delicate change of scenery from the militant Kronborg. Today the castle has been renovated and the gardens replanted. Inside are paintings by north Zealand artists and a gallery with changing arts and crafts exhibitions. ⊠ *Marienlyst Allé* ☎ *49/28–37–91* 🖨 *49/21–20–06* ☞ *DKr 25* ⊙ *Daily noon–4.*

Where to Stay & Eat

$$ ✕🏠 **Hotel Hamlet.** A few minutes from the harbor, this overly renovated hotel has lost some of its charm but makes an attempt at character with raw timbers and deep-green walls. The rooms are furnished in rose schemes and dark wood, and all are comfortable, if nondescript. Downstairs, the Ophelia Restaurant serves traditional Danish seafood, steaks, and open-face sandwiches. ⊠ *Bramstr. 5, DK–3000* ☎ *49/21–05–91* 🖨 *49/ 26–01–30* 🛏 *36 rooms* ⚐ *Restaurant, bar, some pets allowed, no-smoking rooms* ⊟ *AE, DC, MC, V.*

★ $$$$ 🏠 **Hotel & Casino Marienlyst.** The rooms in this hotel full of flashy neon lights, bolts of drapery, and glass are all plush and pastel and include plenty of conveniences. The hotel was completely refurbished in August 2002. Rooms on the sound side present a magnificent view of Kronborg Castle and the Swedish coastline. ⊠ *Nordre Strandvej 2, DK–3000* ☎ *49/ 21–40–00* 🖨 *49/21–49–00* ⊕ *www.marienlyst.dk* 🛏 *224 rooms, 17 suites* ⚐ *Restaurant, cafeteria, indoor pool, gym, bar, casino, nightclub, meeting rooms, some pets allowed, no-smoking rooms* ⊟ *AE, DC, MC, V.*

¢ 🏠 **Villa Moltke Vandrerhjem.** This youth hostel faces the sound and has a private beach. It is located 2 km (1 mi) from the city center, but is well served by both bus and train. ⊠ *Nordre Strandvej 24, DK–3000* ☎ *49/ 21–16–40* 🖨 *49/21–13–99* ⊕ *www.helsingorhostel.dk* 🛏 *180 beds* ⚐ *Cafeteria, fishing, badminton, Ping-Pong, soccer, library, laundry facilities* ⊟ *MC, V.*

Nightlife & the Arts

In summer Kronborg Castle is the site of the **Hamlet Festival** (⊠ Havnepl. 1 ☎ 49/28–20–45 ⊕ www.hamletsommer.dk), during which internationally renowned theater companies offer outdoor performances of *Hamlet*. The schedule varies from year to year.

Sports & the Outdoors

GOLF The **Helsingør Golf Klub** (✉ Gamle Hellebækvej 73 ☎ 49/21–29–70 ⊕ www.helsingorgolf.dk) has 18 holes on a lush green course flanked by trees and, on clear days, views across the sound to Sweden. A weekday handicap of 36 for men and women, and a weekend handicap of 24 for men and 36 for women, is expected.

Fredensborg

❹ *15 km (9 mi) southwest of Helsingør, 33 km (20 mi) northwest of Copenhagen.*

Fredensborg means "town of peace," and it was here that the Great Nordic War peace treaty was concluded in 1722. The excellent Fredensborg Castle is a major draw, but the town also accommodates those who come to enjoy the great outdoors.

Commanding the town is the **Fredensborg Slot** (Castle of Peace), built by Frederik IV to commemorate the 1720 peace treaty with Sweden. The castle, with a towering domed hall in the center, was originally inspired by French and Italian castles, but 18th-century reconstructions, concealing the original design, instead serve as a review of domestic architecture. The castle became a favorite of Frederik V, who lined the gardens with marble sculptures of ordinary people. It is now the summer residence of the royal family, and interiors are closed except in July. Queen Margrethe II resides in the castle some months every year, usually in the spring and autumn. When the Queen is present, the Royal Life Guards perform reveille at 8 AM and sound the tattoo (taps) at 10 PM. At noon there is the changing of the guard.

The stately **Slotshave** (castle garden), inspired by the French gardens of Versailles, is Denmark's largest historical garden and well worth a stroll. The garden is open to the public all year with the exception of *den reserverede have* (the reserved garden), which is used privately by the Danish royal family but open to the public in July. The reserved garden includes a flower garden, an herb garden, and the orangerie where Denmark's oldest myrtles, which date back to the 1750s, are preserved. ✉ *Fredensborg* ☎ *33/40–31–87* ⊕ *www.ses.dk/1d70029* 🎟 *Castle DKr 40, reserved gardens DKr 40, combined ticket DKr 60* ☉ *Castle July, daily 1–5 (guided tours of Castle and Chapel every 15 mins); reserved gardens July, daily 9–5.*

Where to Stay & Eat

$$ ✗ **Skipperhuset.** On the grounds of the royal summer residence of Fredensborg Slot, this 18th-century former royal boathouse is on the shore

FodorsChoice

★ of Lake Esrum. When weather permits, an alfresco meal as the sun sets across the lake is pure enchantment. Warm, smoked wild Baltic salmon served with spinach flash-fried in soy sauce and balsamic vinegar is a delightful favorite and a fabulous buy for the money. ✉ *Skipperallé 6* ☎ *48/48–17–17* ⊕ *www.skipperhuset.dk* 🖃 *MC, V* ☉ *Closed mid-Oct.–Easter.*

★ $$$$ ✕⊞ **Hotel Store Kro.** Built by King Frederik IV, this magnificent Renaissance annex to Fredensborg Castle is the archetypal stately inn. Inside are European antiques and paintings; outside, glass gazebos and classical statues overlook a lovely garden. The rooms are equally sumptuous, with delicately patterned wallpapers and antiques. The romantic restaurant, specializing in French fare, has a fireplace and grand piano. ⊠ *Slotsg. 6, DK–3480* ☎ *48/40–01–11* ⊟ *48/48–45–61* ⊕ *www.storekro.dk* ⪡ *49 rooms, 6 suites* ⚭ *Restaurant, minibars, sauna, bar, meeting room* ⊟ *AE, DC, MC, V.*

¢ ⊞ **Fredensborg Vandrerhjem.** This youth and family hostel offers a wide selection of sleeping arrangements. Both shared and private rooms (accommodating up to six people) are available. Breakfast can be ordered for DKr 45. The restaurant serves lunch and dinner for groups only; however, the kitchen is available to all guests. ⊠ *Østrupvej 3, DK–3480* ☎ *48/48–03–15* ⊟ *48/48–16–56* ⊕ *www.fredensborghostel.dk* ⪡ *42 rooms (21 without bath)* ⚭ *Ping-Pong, playground* ⊟ *No credit cards.*

Sports & the Outdoors

Magnificent displays of hawks and eagles in flight can be seen at **Falkonergården.** Located 1 km (½ mi) northeast of Fredensborg, this former farm keeps alive the Danish tradition of hunting with hawks, a method used from the time of the Vikings until early in the 19th century. Falcons swooping at speeds approaching 300 kph (186 mph) can be witnessed in the hour-long shows. ⊠ *Davidsvænge 11* ☎ *48/48–25–83* ⊕ *www.falkonergaarden.dk* ▱ *DKr 65* ⊙ *Showtimes: Apr. and May, Sun. at 2; June, Sept., and Oct., weekends at 2; July, Wed. at 10 and 5, Thurs. at 10, weekends at 5; Aug., Wed. and weekends at 5.*

The **Fredensborg Golf Club** (⊠ Skovsvinget 25 ☎ 48/47–56–59 ⊕ www. fgc.dk) has 18 holes surrounded by woodlands. Men are required to have a handicap of 38 on weekdays and 24 on weekends whereas women need a handicap of 43 and 30, respectively.

Hillerød

❺ *10 km (6 mi) southwest of Fredensborg, 40 km (25 mi) northwest of Copenhagen.*

Hillerød is the main town of Frederiksborg County and appropriately enough is at its center. The town, founded in the 15th century, has developed itself around the Frederiksborg Castle and nowadays is an important industrial area.

★ Hillerød's **Frederiksborg Slot** (Frederiksborg Castle) is probably Denmark's most beautiful royal residence. Acquired in 1560, the castle was rebuilt by King Frederik II, who gave his name to the building. That structure was eventually demolished by his son, king-cum-architect Christian IV, who rebuilt it as one of Scandinavia's most magnificent castles. With three wings and a lower portal entrance, the Dutch Renaissance building is enclosed by a moat, covers three islets, and is peaked with dozens of gables, spires, and turrets. The two-story marble gallery known as the **Great Hall,** with its audacious festooning of drapery, paintings, and reliefs, sits on top of the vaulted chapel where monarchs were crowned for more than 200 years. Devastated by a fire in 1859, the castle was reconstructed with the support of the Carlsberg Foundation and now includes the **Nationalhistoriske Museum** (National History Museum). Frederiksborg Slot has 69 rooms, all of them decorated as they were before the fire. Those works of art that had been destroyed were substituted by other private pieces from the Danish aristocracy. The castle has an admirable Renaissance chapel, **Slotskirke,** with abundant ornamentation. The three-aisle chapel has a wide gallery with large windows. Between them hang Denmark's most important coat of arms, the knights of the Elephant Order, and the Great Cross of Dannebrog. Look for the 17th-century aisle seats as well as the altarpiece and the pulpit made of mahogany with gold and silver panels. The carved organ, made in 1610 and restored in 1988, still proudly carries its original pipes and manual bellows. The lovely **Baroque Gardens,** rebuilt according to J. C. Krieger's layout from 1725, include a series of wide waterfalls that make the neatly trimmed park a lovely place for a stroll. In addition to the Web site listed below, ⊕ www.ses.dk/1d90029 has more information (in English) on the castle. ⊠ *Hillerød* 🕾 *48/26–04–39* ⊕ *www.frederiksborgmuseet. dk* 🖾 *DKr 60; Baroque Gardens free* ☉ *Castle Apr.–Oct., daily 10–5; Nov.–Mar., daily 11–3. Baroque Gardens May–Aug., daily 10–9; Sept., Oct., Mar., and Apr., daily 10–7; Nov.–Feb., daily 10–4.*

Where to Stay & Eat

$$$ ✕ **La Perla.** Simple but good Italian food is served in this beautiful old house in the very center of town. The decor is an interesting mix of Italian and Danish styles, a thoroughly modern twist on the Mediterranean. It opens daily at 11 AM. ⊠ *Torvet 1* 🕾 *48/24–35–33* ⚖ *Reservations essential* ⊟ *AE, DC, MC, V.*

$$$ ✕ **Slotskroen.** Functioning as an inn since 1795, Slotskroen is one of the oldest buildings of this royal town. The restaurant has been completely renovated, but it maintains its antique flavor and stands out for its veal and ox dishes. ⊠ *Slotsg. 67* 🕾 *48/26–01–82* ⊕ *www.slokskroen.dk* ⊟ *AE, DC, MC, V* ☉ *No dinner.*

$–$$ ✕ **Spisestedet Leonora.** In the shadow of Frederiksborg Castle, this family restaurant bustles in what used to be the castle stables. Antique on the outside and bright orange on the inside with hanging prints and paintings of royalty and the castle, it is a popular stopover for castle visitors. The Danish menu ranges from quick open-face sandwiches to savory stews, soups, and steaks. ⊠ *Frederiksborgslot 5* 🕾 *48/26–75–16* ⊕ *www. leonora.dk* ⊟ *DC, MC, V.*

$$ 🏨 **Hotel Hillerød.** In a typically Scandinavian fashion, this hotel's decor is furnished with sensible Danish designs and luxurious lighting accessories. Most rooms have kitchenettes and private terraces. Packages that include greens fees at a local golf course can be arranged. The entire hotel is accessible to wheelchair users. ⊠ *Milnersvej 41, DK–3400* 🕾 *48/ 24–08–00* 🖨 *48/24–08–74* ⊕ *www.hotelhillerod.dk* ➹ *74 rooms* ♨ *Restaurant, some kitchenettes, meeting room, some pets allowed, nosmoking rooms* ⊟ *AE, DC, MC, V.*

Hornbæk

❻ *27 km (17 mi) northeast of Hillerød, 47 km (29 mi) north of Copenhagen.*

Hornbæk is Denmark's answer to France's Riviera. Danish society's upper echelon maintains palatial summer homes here that line the streets closest to the water and are discreetly tucked away behind protective sand dunes. Regardless of your social standing, the bustling town offers lovely shopping opportunities and exciting nightlife year-round. Summer brings the expansive beach alive with parties, volleyball tournaments, and more.

Where to Stay & Eat

★ **$$$$** ✕ **Novo Latino.** The elegant dining room is decorated in light, soft tones, but the terrace takes the cake with its outdoor fireplace. Inspired by classic Latin American cooking, Novo Latino modernizes the cuisine by adding its own touches. This is the ideal place to try innovative dishes such as fish with chocolate sauce. A wide range of excellent wines from the new and old worlds is on hand at prices starting from DKr 300. ⊠ *Nordre Strandvej 154, 5 km (3 mi) east of Hornbæk, Ålsgårde* ☎ *49/70–90–03* 🚪 *AE, DC, MC, V* ☉ *Closed Mon. and Oct.–Mar.*

★ **$$** ✕ **Hansen's Café.** This intimate restaurant, in a National Trust building constructed in 1783, is just a few steps from the harbor. The Danish art hanging from the timber walls provides a cozy ambience for a casual crowd that often lingers for drinks well after dinner. The daily menu is short but provides a taste of what's fresh—especially seafood. Try the lumpfish roe for a tasty local treat. Business hours vary so it's wise to call in advance. ⊠ *Havnevej 19* ☎ *49/70–04–79* ⊕ *www.hansencafe.dk* 🚪 *DC, MC, V.*

$$$$ 🏨 **Havreholm Slot.** A few miles southwest of Hornbæk beach, this small former castle is surrounded by wooded grounds, which hide a couple of fair-size ponds in their midst. The guesthouses' rooms and suites are decorated with Bang & Olufsen televisions and designer furniture; most open onto balconies or terraces. The restaurant produces elaborate French cuisine at dinner and serves smørrebrød and Danish comfort food at lunch. ⊠ *Klosterrisvej 4, Havreholm, DK–3100* ☎ *49/75–86–00* 🖷 *49/75–80–23* ⊕ *www.havreholm.dk* 🛏 *32 rooms, 3 suites* ♧ *Restaurant, 9-hole golf course, indoor-outdoor pool, sauna, fishing, billiards, Ping-Pong, squash, meeting rooms* 🚪 *AE, DC, MC, V.*

$$$ 🏨 **Hotelpension Ewaldsgaarden.** This seaside pension is just a few blocks from the marina and the beach in a residential neighborhood just off one of the town's main (though quiet) streets. An informal family hotel, it is very casual, extremely well kept, and service is provided with commendable pride. ⊠ *Johannes Ewaldsvej 5, DK–3100* ☎ *49/70–00–82* 🖷 *49/70–00–82* ⊕ *www.ewaldsgaarden.dk* 🛏 *12 rooms* ♧ *Restaurant* 🚪 *No credit cards.*

¢ 🏨 **Hornbæk Bed & Breakfast.** Owned by an American-Danish couple, this country villa sits at the edge of the woods only 100 meters from the Danish Riviera. The rooms are a decent size for the reasonable price, all no-smoking, and guests are allowed use of the kitchen. ⊠ *Skovvej 15C, DK–3100* ☎ *49/76–19–10* 🖷 *49/76–19–11* ⊕ *www.hornbaekbandb.dk* 🛏 *7 rooms without bath* ♧ *Kitchen* 🚪 *No credit cards.*

Dronningmølle

❼ *10 km (6 mi) west of Hornbæk, 57 km (35 mi) north of Copenhagen.*

There's little more than a camping ground flanked by a very clean beach and a sculpture museum in Dronningmølle. The beauty of the area lies in the fact that it is largely undiscovered, so it's quite easy to find a spot on the sand away from the crowds.

★ In 1916 Rudolph Tegner (1873–1950) began to buy adjacent parcels of land to realize his dream of a museum and sculpture park dedicated to his own work. The centerpiece of the resultant **Rudolph Tegner Museum** is the 36-foot-high octagonal building in the center of which Tegner is buried. On display here are 191 of his sculptures in plaster, marble, and bronze; works in other media are represented including 12 paintings, many drafts, and several pieces of furniture he constructed. Tegner withstood the pressure toward conformity in Danish society during his era and his best works are both provocative and disquieting. ⊠ *Museumsvej 19* ☎ *49/71–91–77* ⊕ *www.rudolphtegner.dk* ☜ *DKr 25* ◔ *Mid-Apr.–May and Sept.–mid-Oct., Tues.–Sun. noon–5; June–Aug., Tues.–Sun. 9:30–5.*

Where to Stay

¢ ⚠ **Dronningmølle Strandcamping.** Camp right on the sand and enjoy the best of the Danish Riviera without the crowds and high prices of other, better-known coastal towns in north Zealand. The surrounding countryside is a nature conservation area and has trails and bicycle paths. Kitchen facilities are available. ⊠ *Strandkrogen 2B, DK–3120* ☎ *49/71–92–90* 🖷 *49/71–98–93* ⊕ *www.dronningmolle.dk* ☜ *DKr 185* ☖ *Restaurant, cafeteria, miniature golf, sauna, shop, laundry facilities* ▭ *No credit cards* ◔ *Closed mid-Sept.–mid-Apr.*

Gilleleje

❽ *3 km (2 mi) north of Dronningmølle, 58 km (36 mi) northwest of Copenhagen.*

At the northern tip of Zealand, Gilleleje was once a small fishing community. These days the population explodes every summer when northern Europeans take to its woods and fine, sandy beaches. It was a favorite getaway of philosopher Søren Kierkegaard, who wrote: "I often stood there and reflected over my past life. The force of the sea and the struggle of the elements made me realize how unimportant I was." The less existential can go for a swim and visit the philosopher's monument on a nearby hill. The old part of town, with its thatch-roof, colorfully painted houses, is good for a walk.

> off the beaten path

NORDSJÆLLANDS SOMMERPARK – Situated 30 km (18 mi) west of Helsingør, this amusement park mixes water recreation with other attractions such as theater, concerts, and a mini zoo. The Sommerpark bus departs from the Gilleleje or Helsingør train station at 9:30 AM. ⊠ *Kirkevej 33, Græsted* ☎ *48/71–41–41* 🖷 *48/*

71–66–05 ⊕ www.sommerpark.dk 🖾 DKr 50 ☉ Mid-June–mid-Aug., daily 10–8; mid-May–mid-June, daily 10–6.

Tisvildeleje

❾ *28 km (17 mi) west of Gilleleje, 65 km (40 mi) northwest of Copenhagen.*

Tisvildeleje is one of the most popular beaches in north Zealand. There is more than 1 km (½ mi) of sandy beach backed by dunes and woods. The beaches are child-friendly and sandy. Overall, the natural surroundings here are exceptionally clean and charming, open, and unspoiled.

Where to Stay & Eat

$ ✕🖾 **Havgården.** The refurbished old manor house offers comfortable lodging within a typical Danish building. Dinner, served from 6 PM, is primarily Danish—John Dory is the house specialty. The site also rents out vacation cottages, fully furnished with all the comforts of home. Payment with credit card is subject to a 6% surcharge. ⊠ *Strandlyvej 1, DK–3210 Vejby Strand* ☎ *48/70–57–30* 🖷 *48/70–57–72* ⊕ *www.havgaarden.dk* ↩ *13 rooms* ◊ *Restaurant* ▣*MC, V* ☉ *Restaurant closed Sept.–May.*

¢ 🖾 **Skt. Helene Vandrerhjem.** This holiday and conference complex is a 10-minute walk from the beach. The property has 28 chalets accommodating four to five people each; there are also 25 apartments and 40 single rooms, all with varying prices. The whole complex is ecofriendly, with a farm providing organic food on site. Guests are welcome to pitch in with the work. ⊠ *Bygmarken 30, DK–3220* ☎ *48/70–98–50* 🖷 *48/ 70–98–97* ⊕ *www.helene.dk* ↩ *28 chalets, 25 apartments, 40 rooms* ◊ *Restaurant, cafeteria, miniature golf, tennis court, basketball, soccer, volleyball, laundry facilities.*

Odsherred

❿ *45 km (28 mi) southwest of Gilleleje, 80 km (50 mi) northwest of Copenhagen (via Roskilde).*

With steep cliffs, white-sand dunes, and acres of forests to admire, the Odsherred peninsula is a big draw to people who want to relax in beautiful surroundings. The long beaches have silky sand and offer plenty of opportunities to take a refreshing swim in Sejerø Bugt (Sejerø Bay). This hammer-shape peninsula, which curves around Sejerø Bugt, is dotted with hundreds of burial mounds. You can get here either by driving around the fjords to the south and through the town of Holbæk, or by driving to Hundested and catching the 25-minute ferry ride to Rørvig.

If you're a devotee of ecclesiastical art, make a pilgrimage to explore the frescoes of the Romanesque-Gothic-Renaissance **Højby Kirke** (Højby Church) in the town of Højby, near Nykøbing Sjælland. In the town of Fårevejle is the Gothic **Fårevejle Kirke,** with the Earl of Bothwell's chapel.

Fewer than 5 km (3 mi) south of Nykøbing Sjælland, more than 500 ☺ animals of 85 different species can be seen at **Odsherreds Zoo Dyrepark.**

Children love the monkey house. Other inhabitants include raccoons, llamas, reptiles, exotic birds, and the unique black swan. On weekends children can ride ponies. ✉ *Esterhøjvej 94–96, Asnæs* ☎ *59/65–12–31* 🖷 *59/65–12–28* ⊕ *www.odsherreds-zoo.dk* 🎫 *DKr 65* ⊙ *Apr. and Sept.–mid-Oct., daily 10–3:30; May, June, and Aug., daily 10–5; July, daily 10–6.*

Sjællands Odde (Zealand's Tongue), the tiny strip of land north of the Sejerø Bay, offers slightly marshy but secluded beach strands. Inside the bay, the beaches are once again smooth and blond. From here there is access to Århus and Ebeltoft in Jutland by ferry.

🅒 **Sommerland Sjælland,** Zealand's amusement park, caters to visitors of all ages. The dozens of activities include a roller coaster, an aqua park, and a small zoo with pony rides. Children under 10 especially enjoy *Mini-land.* ✉ *Gammel Nykøbingvej 169, Nykøbing Sjælland* ☎ *59/31–21–00* ⊕ *www.sommerlandsj.dk* 🎫 *DKr 130* ⊙ *Mid-May–mid-June and mid-Aug.–Sept., weekends 10–6; mid-June–mid-Aug., daily 10–7.*

Where to Stay & Eat

¢–$$$ ✕ **Den Gyldne Hane.** Built at the beginning of the 19th century by a community of fishermen, Den Gyldne Hane is a family hotel best known for the fish dishes served in its restaurant. The view of the harbor overlooking the fishing boats makes for an enjoyable meal. ✉ *Vestre Havnevej 34, DK–4583 Sjællands Odde* ☎ *59/32–63–86* 🖷 *59/32–65–52* ⊕ *www.dengyldnehane.dk* 🖃 *DC, MC, V* ⊙ *Closed Dec.–Mar. No lunch.*

$$$ 🏨 **Dragsholm Slot.** Ideally located at Nekselø Bay, close to the forest and the beach, Dragsholm Castle, originally built in the 12th century, has been a home since the 18th century. Today the owners cultivate the land and raise their own livestock to provide wholesome ingredients for the restaurant on the premises. ✉ *Dragsholm Allé 1, DK–4534 Hørve* ☎ *59/65–33–00* 🖷 *59/65–30–33* ⊕ *www.dragsholm-slot.dk* 🛏 *28 rooms, 2 suites* ⚭ *Restaurant* 🖃 *AE, DC, MC, V.*

Holbæk

➊ *83 km (51½ mi) southwest of Tisvildeleje (via Odsherred), 67 km (41½ mi) west of Copenhagen.*

Expanding out from the old fortress built in the 13th century by Valdemar II to defend Denmark against its attacking enemies, today Holbæk is an industrial and commercial town.

Situated close to the neo-Gothic Sankt Nicolai Kirke, the **Holbæk Museum** consists of three wooden buildings from the 17th century and another two from the 19th century. The museum collection showcases handicrafts, archaeological artifacts, and objects from the town's more recent history, such as household equipment from typical urban and rural houses of the 17th and 18th centuries. ✉ *Klosterstr. 18* ☎ *59/43–23–53* 🖷 *59/43–24–52* ⊕ *www.holbmus.dk* 🎫 *DKr 30* ⊙ *Tues.–Fri. 10–4, weekends noon–4.*

<table>
<tr><td>

off the
beaten
path

</td><td>

CHURCHES OF HOLBÆK FJORD – A 2-kilometer (1 mi) drive south of Holbæk down the A57 delivers you to **Tveje Merløse,** built in the 13th century and restored at the end of the 19th century. Luckily, you can still see the 13th-century frescoes here. Just 4 km (2½ mi) to the southwest stands the 12th-century **Søstrup Kirke,** with Byzantine-style frescoes. West along road 155 another 4 km (2½ mi) stands **Tuse Kirke,** a typical example of a rural church from the 13th century. Inside the church are Gothic frescoes from the 15th century. North on road A21 is the 12th-century **Hagested Kirke,** which has 13th-century frescoes.

</td></tr>
</table>

Where to Stay & Eat

¢ ✕⊞ **Hotel Orø Kro.** On the tiny island of Orø, this hotel radiates tranquility with the blue of Isefjord on one side and green fields on the other. The restaurant stands out for its simple and tasty fish specialties. ⊠ *Byg. 57, Orø, DK–4300* ☎ *59/47–00–06* 🖷 *59/47–01–99* ⊕ *www.oroe.dk/ kro* ⟳ *21 rooms* ⟁ *Restaurant, some pets allowed* ⊟ *AE, MC, V.*

\$\$ ⊞ **Hotel Strandparken.** Beach and forest are the two views offered from the rooms of this hotel, which has a scenic location in the middle of a park just south of Holbæk Fjord. The pastel rooms are filled with flower prints and landscape paintings. ⊠ *Kalundborgvej 58, DK–4300* ☎ *59/43–06–16* 🖷 *59/43–32–76* ⊕ *www.hotelstrandparken.dk* ⟳ *31 rooms* ⟁ *Restaurant, billiards, meeting room* ⊟ *AE, MC, V.*

Skibby

⑫ *26 km (16 mi) northeast of Holbæk, 65 km (40 mi) northwest of Copenhagen.*

Skibby is the main town of the little peninsula situated between Roskilde Fjord and Isefjord.

Four kilometers (2½ mi) east of Skibby is **Selsø Slot** (Selsø Castle), constructed in 1576 and reworked in 1734. The castle portrays life as it was for the aristocrats and their servants in the 1800s. The museum here displays original 17th-century interiors, as well as Renaissance furniture, weapons, clothes, domestic items, toys, and a collection of drawings. The altarpiece from 1605 and the pulpit from 1637 in the castle church exhibit Renaissance elements. ⊠ *Selsøvej 30A* ☎ *47/52–01–71* ⊕ *www.selsoe.dk* 🎫 *DKr 40* ☉ *May–mid-June and mid-Aug.–Oct., weekends 1–4; mid-June–mid-Aug., daily 11–4.*

<table>
<tr><td>

off the
beaten
path

</td><td>

JÆGERSPRIS SLOT – At the north end of the peninsula stands this medieval castle. The baroque southern wing is from the 17th century, and the rest of the castle, save for the 15th-century northern wing, is from 1722–46. King Frederik VII maintained his residence here in the 19th century and the decor in the southern wing reflects this. The tomb of his wife, the Countess Danner, is in the castle's park. To the north extends Nordskoven, a forest of 100-year-old oaks. To see the castle you must join a guided tour—you can't just wander around on your own. Tours begin at the top of the hour and take 50 minutes.

</td></tr>
</table>

✉ *Slotsgården 15, Jægerspris* ☎ *47/53–10–04* ⊕ *www.museer.fa.dk*
💳 *DKr 35* ⊙ *Apr.–Oct., Tues.–Sun. 11–4.*

Where to Stay & Eat

$$–$$$ ✗ **Sønderby Kro.** This typical countryside inn sits next to the village's duck pond and serves remarkably tasty veal dishes, curried herring, and shrimp. The restaurant is perhaps best known for its smørrebrød. ✉ *Sønderby Bro 2* ☎ *47/52–01–33* ⊕ *www.sonderby-kro.dk* 🚭 *No credit cards* ⊙ *Closed Mon.*

$ 🏨 **Hotel Skuldelev Kro.** In the middle of the countryside, this inn has a peaceful environment in a beautiful location. Rooms are adequate even for families. Some rooms are available for nonsmokers. ✉ *Østerg. 2B, DK–4050 Skuldelev* ☎ *47/52–03–08* 📠 *47/52–08–93* ⊕ *www.hotel-skuldelevkro.dk* ⬐ *32 rooms* ⚲ *Restaurant, pool, sauna, billiards, some pets allowed, no-smoking rooms* 🚭 *AE, DC, MC, V.*

Roskilde

⓭ *31 km (19 mi) southeast of Skibby, 36 km (22 mi) west of Copenhagen (on Rte. 156).*

Roskilde is Zealand's second-largest town and one of its oldest, having been founded in 998. The town is named for Roars Kilde, a Viking king. Today Roskilde has a bustling smelting and machinery industry and two prominent academic institutions, Roskilde University and the Danish Center for Energetic Research of Risø.

FodorśChoice
★

Roskilde was the royal residence in the 10th century and became the spiritual capital of Denmark and northern Europe in 1170, when Bishop Absalon built the **Domkirke** (cathedral) on the site of a church erected 200 years earlier by Harald Bluetooth, the Viking founder of the town. Overwhelming the center of town, the current structure took more than 300 years to complete, and thus provides a one-stop crash course in Danish architecture. Inside are an ornate Dutch altarpiece and the tombs—ranging from opulent to modest—of 38 Danish monarchs. Predictably, Christian IV is interred in a magnificent chapel with a massive painting of himself in combat and a bronze sculpture by Thorvaldsen. In modest contrast is the newest addition, the simple brick chapel of King Frederik IX, who died in 1972, outside the church. In November 2000 his wife Queen Ingrid joined him in his tomb at the foot of the cathedral. On the interior south wall above the entrance is a 16th-century clock depicting St. George charging a dragon, which hisses and howls, echoing throughout the church and causing Peter Døver, "the Deafener," to sound the hour. A squeamish Kirsten Kiemer, "the Chimer," shakes her head in fright but manages to strike the quarter-hours. Around the altar are the Kannikekoret, the wooden choir stalls carved in 1420. Each seat is topped with a panel depicting a Biblical scene. Behind the altarpiece is the alabaster and marble sarcophagus of Queen Margrethe I, who died in 1412. ✉ *Domkirkestr. 10* ☎ *46/35–16–24* ⊕ *www.roskildedomkirke.dk* 💳 *DKr 15* ⊙ *Apr.–Sept., weekdays 9–4:45, Sat. 9–noon, Sun. 12:30–4:45; Oct.–Mar., Tues.–Sat. 10–3:45, Sun. 12:30–3:45.*

Less than 1 km (½ mi) north of the cathedral, on the fjord, is the modern **Vikingeskibshallen** (Viking Ship Museum), containing five Viking ships sunk in the fjord 1,000 years ago. Submerged to block the passage of enemy ships, they were discovered in 1957. The painstaking recovery involved building a watertight dam and then draining the water from that section of the fjord. The splinters of wreckage were then preserved and reassembled. A deep-sea trader, warship, ferry, merchant ship, and fierce 92½-foot man-of-war attest to the Vikings' sophisticated and aesthetic boat-making skills. ⊠ *Vindeboder 12* 🖀 *46/30–02–00* ⊕ *www.vikingeskibsmuseet. dk* 🗐 *May–Sept. DKr 75, Oct.–Apr. DKr 45* ☉ *Daily 10–5.*

Where to Stay & Eat

$$$ ✕ **Svogerslev Kro.** Three kilometers (2 mi) west of Roskilde is the village of Svogerslev, a peaceful location for this traditional thatch-roof Danish inn. Exposed wooden beams make the interior a cozy place to tuck into the hearty Danish fare. The menu includes a vegetarian option as well as some international dishes such as Wiener schnitzel and steak. ⊠ *Hovedg. 45, Svogerslev* 🖀 *46/38–30–05* ⊕ *www.svogerslevkro. dk* 🖃 *AE, DC, MC, V.*

★ **$** ✕ **Club 42.** This popular Danish restaurant spills out onto the sidewalk in summer, while inside the roof opens over the dining room. The fare is typically Danish, including smørrebrød and spareribs, which are simply prepared and served with potato salad. ⊠ *Skomagerg. 42* 🖀 *46/ 35–03–11* 🖃 *MC, V.*

$$$$ 🏨 **Hotel Prindsen.** In downtown Roskilde, this 100-year-old hotel is popular with business guests for its convenient location. The elegant dark-wood lobby leads to the plain but homey and comfortable rooms. ⊠ *Alg. 13, DK–4000* 🖀 *46/30–91–00* 🖷 *46/30–91–50* ⊕ *www.prindsen. dk* 🛏 *76 rooms, 3 suites ⚏ Restaurant, cafeteria, minibars, bar, meeting rooms, some pets allowed, no-smoking rooms* 🖃 *AE, DC, MC, V.*

¢ 🏨 **Roskilde Vandrerhjem.** This youth hostel, perfect for budget travelers, is on Roskilde Fjord, which is close to the town's green areas. Guests have use of the kitchen. ⊠ *Vindeboder 7, DK–4000* 🖀 *46/35–21–84* 🖷 *46/32–66–90* ⊕ *www.rova.dk* 🛏 *152 beds ⚏ Restaurant, laundry facilities* 🖃 *No credit cards.*

Nightlife & the Arts

For one weekend at the end of June, Roskilde holds one of Europe's biggest rock-music gatherings, the **Roskilde Festival** (⊕ www.roskilde-festival.dk). Some 75,000 people show up every year to enjoy the outdoor concerts.

When the town's youth are in the mood for live rock, they head to **Gimle** (⊠ Ringstedg. 30 🖀 46/35–12–13 ⊕ www.gimle.dk) on weekends. At **Bryggergården** (⊠ Alg. 15 🖀 46/35–01–03), or the Draft Horse, adults have a late supper and beer in cozy surroundings. During the summer, **Café Mulle Rudi** (⊠ Djalma Lunds Gård 7 🖀 46/37–03–25) is an arty spot with indoor and outdoor seating and live jazz.

Sports & the Outdoors

GOLF **Roskilde Golf Klub** (⊠ Margrethehåbvej 116 🖀 46/37–01–81 ⊕ www. roskildegolfklub.dk) has an 18-hole golf course with views of the twin-peak Roskilde Cathedral and the surrounding forest.

TOURS   Boat excursions depart from the town's docks for dual-purpose (sight-seeing and transportation) routes on Roskilde Fjord. The boats occasionally make stops at Frederikssund and Frederiksværk, but most passengers are there for a fun and scenic boat ride. Some refreshments can be purchased on board. **Saga Fjord** (☎ 46/75–64–60 ⊕ www. sagafjord.dk) operates more sightseeing-oriented trips.

Shopping

CRAFTS   Between Roskilde and Holbæk is **Galleri Kirke Sonnerup** (✉ Englerupvej 62, Såby ☎ 46/49–26–70), with a good selection of pottery, glass, clothing, and woodwork produced by more than 50 Danish artists.

Lejre

⓮   *10 km (6 mi) west of Roskilde, 40 km (25 mi) west of Copenhagen.*

Archaeological digs unearthing the times of the Vikings show that Lejre has had a glorious past. During the 10th century the town reigned as the kingdom's most sacred place.

Ⓒ   The 50-acre **Lejre Forsøgscenter** (Lejre Archaeological Research Center)
Fodor'sChoice compound contains a reconstructed village dating from the Iron Age and
★ two 19th-century farmhouses. In summer a handful of hardy Danish families live here under the observation of researchers; they go about their daily routine—grinding grain, herding goats, eating with their hands, and wearing furs and skins—providing a clearer picture of ancient ways of life. In Bodalen (Fire Valley), children can try their own hand at such tasks as grinding corn, filing an ax, and sailing in a dugout canoe. ✉ *Slangealleen 2* ☎ *46/48–08–78* ⊕ *www.lejre-center.dk* ⌚ *DKr 75* ⊙ *May–mid-June and mid-Aug.–mid-Sept., Tues.–Fri. 10–4, weekends 10–5; mid-June–mid-Aug., daily 10–5.*

Ledreborg Slot is one of Denmark's finest examples of 18th-century building and landscape architecture. Built in 1742, Ledreborg Castle is now owned by the eighth generation of the Holstein-Ledreborg family. The main building contains a remarkable collection of paintings and furnishings from when it was first built. At the southern part there is an elaborate terraced garden in the 18th-century French style. ✉ *Ledreborg Allé 2* ☎ *46/48–00–38* ⊕ *www.ledreborgslot.dk* ⌚ *DKr 75* ⊙ *May–mid-June and Sept., Sun. 11–5; mid-June–Aug., daily 11–5.*

Køge

⓯   *20 km (13 mi) southeast of Lejre, 47 km (29 mi) southwest of Copenhagen.*

The well-preserved medieval town of Køge began its existence as a fishing village dependent on the herring trade. Køge is also known for the witch hunts that took place in the early 17th century. Today, with about 40,000 inhabitants, this satellite town of Copenhagen exists as a center of trade. It links to the big city by suburban train.

In the 17th century and later during the Napoleonic wars, Køge was witness to many naval battles. The Danish and Swedish fleets clashed repeatedly in order to gain control over the sound, which was the gateway to trade with the Baltic Sea.

Køge Museum is in a centrally located 17th-century merchant's house. On display are mementos and items belonging to Hans Christian Andersen, local costumes, and artifacts including an executioner's sword and a 13th-century stone font. The legend of the font is that it had to be removed from the town church after a crippled woman committed an unsavory act into it, hoping her bizarre behavior would cure her. Also on exhibit are 16th-century silver coins from a buried treasure containing more than 2,000 coins. The stash was found in the courtyard of Langkildes Gård. ⊠ *Nørreg. 4* ☎ *56/63–42–42* ⊕ *www.dmol.dk* ⛫ *DKr 30* ☉ *June–Aug., daily 11–5; Sept.–May, Tues.–Fri. 1–5, Sat. 11–3, and Sun. 1–5.*

Kunstmuseet Køge Skitsesamling (Art Museum Køge Sketches Collection) has changing exhibitions and an extensive permanent collection of sketches, sculpture, and other modern Danish art. The museum features about 7,500 studies and models of paintings and sculptures created for public spaces throughout the country—it's the only museum of its kind in Denmark. Works on permanent loan from private individuals include the studies for *The Little Mermaid* by sculptor Edvard Eriksen. ⊠ *Nørreg. 29* ☎ *56/67–60–20* ⊕ *www.dmol.dk* ⛫ *DKr 30* ☉ *Tues.–Sun. 10–5,* (*Wed. 10–8*).

The old part of Køge is filled with 300 half-timber houses, all protected by the National Trust; it is a lovely area for a stroll. At the end of Kirkestræde is the 15th-century **Sankt Nicolai Kirke** (St. Nicholas Church). Once a lighthouse, its floor is now covered with more than 100 tombs of Køge VIPs. Carved angels line the church's walls, but most have had their noses struck off—a favorite pastime of drunken Swedish soldiers in the 1700s. ⊠ *Kirkestr. 26* ☎ *56/65–13–59* ⛫ *Free* ☉ *Mid-June–Aug., weekdays 10–4, Sat. 10–noon; Sept.–mid-June, weekdays 10–noon. Tower tours mid-June–mid-Aug., weekdays every 30 mins. 10–1:30.*

Where to Stay & Eat

$$$$ ✕ **Horizonten Restaurant.** For a great view, sit on the terrace overlooking the harbor. Horizonten's interior is modern and often decorated with exhibitions of local artists. The food here includes a mixture of Italian, French, Spanish, and Danish cuisine. Any of the grilled-fish dishes on the menu are a good option, but the seafood-and-fish platter is the highlight. Lunch is served only by prior reservation. ⊠ *Havnen 29A* ☎ *56/63–86–28* ⊕ *www.horizonten.dk* ☰ *MC, V* ☉ *Closed Mon.; Closed Sun. in Jan. and Feb.*

$$ ⊡ **Hotel Hvide Hus.** Built in 1966 and overlooking the Bay of Køge, the White House Hotel has fantastic views. The hotel is brightly decorated in a contemporary Danish style. ⊠ *Strandvejen 111, DK–4600* ☎ *56/65–36–90* ⛫ *56/66–33–14* ⊕ *www.hotelhvidehus.dk* ⇆ *127 rooms, 1 suite* ⚶ *Restaurant, cafeteria, sauna, bar, meeting room, some pets allowed, no-smoking rooms* ☰ *AE, DC, MC, V.*

$ ⊡ **Hotel Vallø Slotskro.** Near Vallø Slot and surrounded by the castle's beautifully landscaped grounds, this rural inn is a pleasant place to spend a couple of days. The rooms are charming (some of them have beds with canopies), and the service is personable. ⊠ *Slotsg. 1, DK–4600* ☎ *56/26–70–20* ⛫ *56/26–70–71* ⊕ *www.valloeslotskro.dk* ⇆ *11 rooms, 7*

FodorsChoice
★

with bath �ò *Restaurant, bar, some pets allowed, no-smoking rooms* ▭ *AE, DC, MC, V.*

Nightlife & the Arts

Even if the name suggests another thing, **Hugo's Vinkælder** (Hugo's Winecellar; ✉ Brog. 19, courtyard ☎ 56/65–58–50 ⊕ www.hugos.dk) is an old beer pub, which was opened in 1968 on the ruins of a medieval monastery cellar. It is a favorite gathering spot for locals. There are beers from all over the world and sandwiches to go with them. On Saturday there is live jazz until midnight. It's closed Sunday.

| en route | Twenty-four kilometers (15 mi) south of Køge near Rødvig, the Stevns Klint chalk cliffs make a good stop. The 13th-century **Højerup Kirke** sits on the cliffs. Over time as the cliffs eroded, first the cemetery and then part of the church toppled into the sea. The church has now been restored and the cliffs below have been bolstered by masonry to prevent further damage. ✉ *Højerup Byg., Stevns Klint, Store Heddinge* ☎ *56/50–36–88* ▱ *DKr 15* ☉ *Daily 11–5.* |

Møn

▶ **16** *77 km (47 mi) south of Køge, 122 km (75 mi) south of Copenhagen.*

The island of Møn makes for a wonderful side trip from Copenhagen, especially in summer, and particularly if you like beaches, striking scenery, and orchids—the island has the greatest selection of the flower in all of Denmark. There's also plenty of woodland, ideal for hiking, picnics, and horseback riding. With fewer than 12,000 inhabitants, Møn has a slow, laid-back pace. North of Stege, the main town, is Ulvshale strand, one of the best beaches on the entire island, framed by forest growth with a network of nature trails and hiking tracks. Thanks to the coastal marshlands of Nyord, Møn also offers perfect opportunities for the amateur bird-watcher to pass a fascinating afternoon spotting some local and migratory birds from one of several bird-watching sites placed strategically around the area. You'll see holiday cottages in abundance here; they're very popular among Danes and other Europeans, who like to rent for a week or longer.

The whole island is pocked with nearly 100 Neolithic burial mounds, but it is most famous for its dramatic chalk cliffs, the northern **Møns Klint,** which is three times as large as Stevns Klint. Circled by a beech forest, the milky-white 75-million-year-old bluffs plunge 400 feet to a small, craggy beach—accessible by a path and more than 500 steps. Wear good walking shoes and take care: though a park ranger checks the area for loose rocks, the cliffs can crumble suddenly. Once here, Danish families usually hunt for fossils of cuttlefish, sea urchins, and other sea life. The cliffs are an important navigational marker for ships—an unusual landmark on south Zealand's otherwise flat topography.

Just inland from the northern section of the Møns Klint is **Liselund Slot,** a delightful 18th-century folly. Antoine de la Calmette, the island's sheriff and a royal chamberlain, took his inspiration from Marie-Antoinette's Hameau (Hamlet) at Versailles and built the small Liselund Castle in 1792 for his beloved wife. The thatch-roof palace—the only one of its kind in the world—has landscaping and gardens that were the opposite of the strict, symmetrically cut lines of the baroque garden of the day. A romantic garden of winding paths and hidden views also includes a Swiss house and a Norwegian cottage with elegant Pompeiian interiors. In this lovely setting, Hans Christian Andersen wrote his fairy tale *The Tinder Box*. The palace has been open to the public since 1938, and if you walk behind it you'll find lakes with islands, making the spot ideal for a romantic picnic. This castle is not to be confused with a hotel of the same name. ☒ *Langebjergvej 4, Borre* ☏ *55/81–21–78* ☎ *DKr 20* ☉ *Tours (Danish and German only) May–Oct., Tues.–Fri. 10:30, 11, 1:30, and 2; weekends also 3 and 3:30.*

Møn's capital, **Stege** (population 2,000), received its town charter in 1268. A third of the island's 11,500 inhabitants live here. Stege began as a small fishing village and it expanded slowly around a castle erected in the 12th century. By the 15th century Stege was a commercial center for fishermen, peasants, and merchants. It was in this wealthy period that the town was encircled with moats and ramparts. The fortified town had three entranceways, each of them controlled by a gate tower. One of these gates, **Mølleporten**, raised around 1430, is still standing. You can enjoy a pleasant hour roaming around on Storegade, the main street, stopping for a bite to eat and drink at one of the many cafés and restaurants. Strolling along Søndersti and the ramparts will transport you to medieval times. Many of the plants which grow here are medicinal plants that date back to the Middle Ages.

The **Møns Museum** in Stege showcases antiques and local-history exhibitions and is well worth a stop. ☒*Storeg. 75, Stege* ☏*55/81–40–67* ⊕*www. aabne-samlinger.dk/moens* ☎ *DKr 30* ☉ *May–Oct., daily 10–4.*

One of the island's medieval churches noted for its naive frescoes, **Fanefjord Kirke** may have been completed by a collaborative group of artisans. The whimsical paintings include scholastic and biblical doodlings. The church also maintains an original 13th-century aisle. The Fanefjord church is 12½ km (8 mi) southwest of Stege. Other churches in the area famed for their frescoes include the ones in Elmelunde and Keldby. Note that there are eight other churches in town usually open for a quick visit. ☒ *Fanefjord Kirkevej 51, Askeby* ☏ *55/81–70–05* ☉ *Apr.–Sept., daily 7–4; Oct.–Mar., daily 8–4.*

Ten kilometers (6 mi) west of Stege is **Kong Asgers Høj** (King Asger's Hill), Denmark's biggest passage grave (a collection of upright stones supporting a horizontal stone slab to make a tomb) that dates from the early Stone Age. A 26-foot-long hall precedes the 32-foot grave chamber. During its history, the passage grave has periodically been used as a common grave for locals.

Where to Stay & Eat

$–$$ ✕⊞ **Præstekilde Hotel.** On a small island close to the capital, this hotel has a splendid view of Stege Bay from the middle of the golf course. The service is efficient while maintaining the warmth of rural areas. The restaurant serves good French-inspired Danish food. The small, simply equipped rooms are decorated in light colors, giving a bright impression on sunny days. ⊠ *Klintevej 116, DK–4780 Keldby* ☎ *55/86–87–88* 🖷 *55/ 81–36–34* ⊕ *www.praestekilde.dk* ⇄ *46 rooms, 4 suites* ♨ *Restaurant, minibars, 18-hole golf course, indoor pool, sauna, billiards, meeting rooms, some pets allowed, no-smoking rooms* ▤ *AE, DC, MC, V.*

★ **$$$** 🏨 **Liselund Ny Slot.** In a handsome, pale-yellow grand manor dating from 1887, this modern hotel on an isolated estate offers refined accommodations without being stodgy. The staircase and frescoed ceilings have been preserved and the rooms are fresh and simple, with wicker furnishings and pastel color schemes. Half the rooms overlook the forest and a pond filled with swans. The downstairs restaurant serves Danish cuisine. ⊠ *Langebjergvej 6, DK–4791 Borre* ☎ *55/81–20–81* 🖷 *55/81–21–91* ⇄ *15 rooms* ♨ *Restaurant, meeting room* ▤ *AE, DC, MC, V.*

¢ 🏨 **Pension Bakkegården.** Between the view of the Baltic Sea and the Klinteskov forest, this small hotel farm offers the best qualities of the island. From here it is a simple and relaxing 20-minute stroll through the beech forest to see the cliffs of Møn. Partial board is available upon request. Six of the 12 rooms overlook the sea. If you're traveling with children, they will enjoy the cows, chickens, cats, and a dog. ⊠ *Busenevej 64, Busene, DK–4791 Borre* ☎*55/81–93–01* 🖷*55/81–94–01* ⊕*www.bakkegaarden64. dk* ⇄ *12 rooms without bath* ♨ *Billiards* ▤ *No credit cards.*

Falster

⑰ *3 km (2 mi) south of Bogø; Nykøbing Falster is 49 km (30 mi) southeast of Stege, 134 km (83 mi) south of Copenhagen.*

Accessible by way of the striking Farø Bridge or the parallel Storstrømsbroen (Big Current Bridge) from Fredensborg, Falster is shaped like a tiny South America and has excellent blond beaches to rival those of its continental twin. Among the best are the southeastern Marienlyst and southernmost Gedser. Almost everywhere on the island are cafés, facilities, and water-sports rentals. Falster is also one of the country's major producers of sugar beets.

♻ The **Middelaldercentret** (Center for the Middle Ages or Medieval Center), a reconstructed medieval village, invites school classes to dress up in period costumes and experience life in the late 14th century. Daytime visitors can participate in activities that change weekly—from cooking to medieval knife making to animal herding—and on weekends folk dances and other cultural happenings. A whole marketplace is depicted here, as well as the rougher sides of life back then. There are trebuchet demonstrations (a weapon, or medieval siege engine, made either to batter masonry or to throw projectiles over walls), knight tournaments, archery, and yes, even fireball throwing and bonfires on Midsummer's Day. ⊠ *Ved Hamborgskoven 2, Nykøbing Falster* ☎ *54/86–19–34* ⊕ *www. middelaldercentret.dk* 🎫 *DKr 80* ⊙ *May–Sept., daily 10–4.*

Where to Stay & Eat

$$$–$$$$ ✕**Czarens Hus.** This stylish old inn dates back more than 200 years, when it was a guesthouse and supply store for area farmers and merchants.

Deep-green walls, gold trim, and chandeliers set the backdrop for antique furnishings. The specialty of the house is Continental European–Danish cuisine, which translates as creative beef and fish dishes, often served with cream sauces. Try the Zar Beuf (calf tenderloin in a mushroom-and-onion cream sauce). ⊠ *Langg. 2, Nykøbing Falster* ☎ *54/85–28–29* ☐ *AE, DC, MC, V* ☉ *Closed Sun.*

$$–$$$ ⊡ **Hotel Falster.** This sleek and efficient hotel accommodates conference guests as well as vacationers with its comfortable yet businesslike demeanor. Rustic brick walls and Danish antiques mix with sleek Danish-design lamps and sculpture. Rooms are done in dark wood and modular furniture. ⊠ *Stubbekøbingvej 150, DK–4800 Nykøbing Falster* ☎ *54/ 85–93–93* 🖶 *54/82–21–99* ⊕ *www.hotel-falster.dk* 📮 *68 rooms, 1 suite* ⟋ *Restaurant, gym, bar, meeting room, some pets allowed, no-smoking rooms* ☐ *AE, DC, MC, V.*

Sports & the Outdoors

GOLF   The 18-hole **Sydsjælland Golf Klub** (⊠ Præstø Landevej 39–Mogenstrup, DK–4700 Næstved ☎ 55/76–15–55) is more than 25 years old, and the park course is lined with a number of small lakes and streams. The highest accepted handicap is 36.

Lolland

⑱ *Sakskøbing is 19 km (12 mi) west of Nykøbing Falster and 138 km (85 mi) southwest of Copenhagen.*

The history of Lolland dates back more than 1,000 years, to a man named Saxe who sat at the mouth of the fjord and collected a toll. He later cleared the surrounding land and leased it. It became known as Saxtorp and eventually Sakskøbing, the island's capital. Though most people head straight for the beaches, the area (accessible by bridge from Nykøbing Falster) has a few sights, including a water tower with a smiling face and an excellent car museum near the central 13th-century Ålholm Slot (closed to the public). The **Ålholm Automobile Museum** is northern Europe's largest, with more than 200 vehicles. ⊠ *Ålholm Parkvej 17, Nysted* ☎ *54/87–19–11* ⊕ *www.aalholm.dk* 🖾 *DKr 75* ☉ *Mid-May–Aug., daily 10–5; Sept.–mid-Oct., weekends 10–4.*

🄲   The **Knuthenborg Safari Park,** 8 km (5 mi) west of Sakskøbing and also on Lolland, has a drive-through range where you can rubberneck at tigers, zebras, rhinoceroses, giraffes, and areas where you can mingle with and pet camels, goats, and ponies. Besides seeing 20 species of animals, children can marvel at Småland's to-scale relief map of southern Zealand or play on the jungle gym, minitrain, and other rides. ⊠ *Birketvej 1, Maribo, Bandholm* ☎ *54/78–80–89* ⊕ *www.knuthenborg.dk* 🖾 *DKr 110* ☉ *May, June, Aug., and Sept., daily 9–6; July, daily 9–8; Oct. 15–23, daily 9–6.*

Where to Stay

$$ ⊡ **Lalandia.** This massive water-park hotel has an indoor pool, beach-side view, and lots of happy families. On the southern coast of Lolland, about 27 km (16 mi) southwest of Sakskøbing, the modern white apartments, with full kitchen and bath, accommodate up to eight people. There are three family-style restaurants—a steak house, Italian buffet, and pizzeria. The water park is free and open daily to guests from 10 to 8. ⊠ *Rødbyhavn, DK–4970 Rødby* ☎ *70/30–15–28* 🖷 *54/61–05–01* ⊕ *www.lalandia.dk* ⮑ *636 apartments* ⌕ *3 restaurants, 9-hole golf course, 5 tennis courts, indoor pool, health club, sauna, bar, playground, meeting room* ▤ *AE, DC, MC, V.*

¢ ▥ **Hotel Saxkjøbing.** Behind its yellow half-timber facade, this comfortable hotel is short on character and frills, but the rooms are bright, sunny, and modern, if very simply furnished. In the town center, the hotel is convenient to everything. Its family-style restaurant serves pizzas, steaks, and salads. ⊠ *Torvet 9, DK–4990 Sakskøbing* ☎ *54/70–40–39* 🖷 *54/ 70–53–50* ⊕ *www.hotel-saxkjobing.dk* ⮑ *24 rooms* ⌕ *Restaurant, billiards, bar, meeting room* ▤ *AE, DC, MC.*

Ringsted

⓳ *95 km (59 mi) north of Sakskøbing (Lolland), 68 km (42 mi) southwest of Copenhagen (via Køge).*

During the Middle Ages Ringsted, built around a church and nearby 12th-century Benedictine abbey, became one of the most important Danish towns. The abbey was partially destroyed by a fire in the early 1900s. Nowadays Ringsted is known for being "the town in the middle," the traffic junction of Zealand.

☙ The spirit of fairy tales is tangible at **Eventyrlandet** (Fantasy World), where, among more than 1,000 animated mannequins, a life-size, animated model of Hans Christian Andersen tells his stories via a recorded tape playing in Danish, English, and German. Children enjoy Santa World and Cowboy Land while adults can discover the Adventure Gardens, where Moorish, Japanese, and Roman ornaments dot the well-preserved gardens. ⊠ *Eventyrvej 13, DK–4100* ☎ *57/61–19–30* ⊕ *www.fantasy-world. dk* 🎫 *DKr 75* ☉ *June–Aug. and Oct.–Dec., daily 10–5.*

Sanct Bendts Kirke (St. Benedict's Church) is the only evidence left of the existence of the Benedictine monastery that thrived here in the 12th century. Inside, four Danish kings are buried, including Valdemar I, who died in 1182. ⊠ *Sct. Bendtsg. 3* ☎ *57/61–40–19* ☉ *May–mid-Sept., daily 10–noon and 1–5; mid-Sept.–Apr., daily 1–3.*

off the beaten path

★

SORØ – Eighteen kilometers (11 mi) west of Ringsted is the town of Sorø, known for **Akademiet,** founded in 1623 by King Christian IV. The Academy was established in the abbey built by Bishop Absalon in 1142 and abandoned after the Lutheran reformation. The educational importance of the town increased thanks to the Danish writer Ludvig Holberg, who donated his whole inheritance to the academy on his death in 1754. The academy is on the banks of Sorø Sø (Lake Sorø) inside an extensive park. Not far from here is **Klosterkirke,** a Romanesque church built in the 12th century as a part of a Cistercian abbey. In this church are the remains of Bishop Absalon.

☙ **BONBON-LAND** – Children adore this park in the tiny southern Zealand town of Holme-Olstrup between Rønnede and Næstved, 30 km (19 mi) south of Ringsted. Filled with rides and friendly costumed grown-ups, BonBon-Land is an old-fashioned playland, with a few eating and drinking establishments thrown in for adults. ☒ *Gartnervej 2, DK–4684 Holme-Olstrup* ☎ *55/53–07–00* ⊕ *www. bonbonland.dk* ☜ *DKr 150* ☉ *Mid-May–mid-June and Aug., daily 9:30–5; mid-June–July, daily 9:30–8.*

Where to Stay

$$$–$$$$ 🖼 **Skjoldenæseholm.** Any point of the island can be reached by car within an hour from this luxurious hotel in the very center of Zealand. Luxury prevails, from the Jacuzzis in the suites to the surrounding lush park and forest. Cottages for groups and families, one of them placed by the 15th hole in the nearby golf course, are available to rent. ☒ *Skjold-enæsvej 106, DK–4174 Jystrup Midsjælland* ☎ *57/53–87–50* 🖶 *57/ 53–87–51* ⊕ *www.skj.dk* ⬐ *38 rooms, 5 suites* ⚭ *Restaurant, billiards, bar, meeting room* ▤ *AE, DC, MC, V.*

Halsskov

 48 km (30 mi) west of Ringsted, 110 km (69 mi) southwest of Copenhagen.

Europe's third-longest tunnel-bridge, Storebæltsbro—the entire fixed-link length of which is 18 km (11 mi)—links Halsskov, on west Zealand, to Nyborg, on east Funen. Rail traffic traverses the west bridge and tunnel while auto traffic passes on the east-and-west bridge.

The **Storebæltsbro og Naturcenter** (Great Belt Bridge Center), which details the tunnel-bridge construction process, includes videos and models and makes for an informative stop. There are activities for children and a café on-site. ☒ *Storebæltsvej 88, Halsskov Odde, Korsør* ☎ *58/ 35–01–00* ☜ *Free* ☉ *Mid-Apr.–mid-Oct., daily 10–5.*

> **off the beaten path**

TRÆLLEBORG – Viking enthusiasts will want to head 18 km (11 mi) northeast from Halsskov to Slagelse to see its excavated Viking encampment with a reconstructed army shelter. Harold Bluetooth's gigantic circular fortress from around AD 900 is the best-preserved castle of its kind, and together with the museum and the many activities offered in summer, Trelleborg is definitely worth a visit for the whole family. There are free guided tours in the summer, but they're offered in German and Danish only. ☒ *Trælleborg Allé 4, Hejninge, Slagelse* ☎ *58/54–95–16* ☜ *DKr 50* ☉ *Apr.–mid-Oct., Sat.–Thurs. 10–5.*

Zealand A to Z

AIRPORTS

Kastrup International Airport near Copenhagen is Zealand's only airport. 🛈 **Kastrup International Airport** ☎ *32/31-32-31* ⊕ www.cph.dk.

BIKE TRAVEL

Zealand's flat landscape allows for easy biking, and in summer touring this way can be a delightful experience. Most roads have cycle lanes, and tourist boards stock maps detailing local routes. For more biking information, call the Danish Cycling Association, the Danish Tourist Board, or the bicycle tour operator Bike Denmark.

🚲 **Bike Denmark** ✉Olaf Poulsens Allé 1A, DK-3480 Fredensborg ☎48/48-58-00 🖨48/48-59-00 ⊕ www.bikedenmark.com. **Danmarks Turistråd** (Danish Tourist Board) ✉ Vesterbrog. 6D, Vesterbro, DK-1620 Copenhagen ☎ 33/11-14-15 🖨 33/93-14-16 ⊕www.visitdenmark.com. **Dansk Cyklist Forbund** (Danish Cyclist Federation) ✉Rømersg. 7, Downtown, DK-1362 Copenhagen ☎ 33/32-31-21 🖨 33/32-76-83 ⊕ www.dcf.dk.

BOAT & FERRY TRAVEL

There are several DSB and Scandlines car ferries from Germany. They connect Kiel to Bagenkop, on the island of Langeland (from there, drive north to Spodsbjerg and take another ferry to Lolland, which is connected to Falster and Zealand by bridges); Puttgarden to Rødbyhavn on Lolland; and Travemünde and Warnemünde to Gedser on Falster. If you are driving from Sweden, take a car ferry from Hälsingborg to Helsingør. Molslinien runs routes between Jutland and Zealand, linking Kalundborg and Havnebyen to Århus, and Havnebyen to Ebeltoft.

The ScanRail Pass, for travel anywhere within Scandinavia (Denmark, Sweden, Norway, and Finland), and the Interail and EurailPasses are valid on some ferry crossings. Call the DSB Travel Office for information.

🚢 **DSB** ☎ 70/13-14-16 international, 70/13-14-15 domestic ⊕ www.dsb.dk. **Mols-Linien** ☎70/10-14-18 🖨89/52-52-90 ⊕www.molslinien.dk. **Scandinavian Seaways Ferries** (DFDS) ✉ Skt. Annæ Pl. 30, Sankt Annæ, DK-1295 Copenhagen ☎ 33/42-33-42 🖨 33/42-33-41 ⊕www.dfds.com. **Scandlines** ☎ 33/15-15-15 🖨 35/29-02-01 ⊕ www.scandlines.dk.

BUS TRAVEL

The bus system is cumbersome and not as efficient as the train system; however, the sliver of northwestern peninsula known as Sjællands Odde can only be reached by bus. Trains leave from Holbæk to Højby, where you can bus to the tip of the point. Møn, Falster, and Halsskov are accessible by bus after the train drops you off at the closest station.

On the Web, go to ⊕ www.rejseplanen.dk for information on various transport possibilities, both train and bus connections, in all of Zealand.

CAR TRAVEL

Highways and country roads throughout Zealand are excellent, and traffic—even around Copenhagen—is manageable most of the time. As elsewhere in Denmark, take care to give right-of-way to the bikes driving to the right of the traffic. Zealand is connected to Funen, which is connected to Jutland, by the Storebæltsbroen, and it is connected to Malmö in Sweden by Øresund Bridge, which ends in Copenhagen.

BRIDGES 🌉 **Øresundsbroen** ✉ Vester Søg. 10, Downtown, DK-1601 Copenhagen ☎ 33/41-60-00 🖨 33/93-52-04 ⊕ www.visitoresund.info/us. **Storebæltsbroen** ✉ Storebæltsvej 70, DK-4220 Korsør ☎ 70/15-10-15 🖨 58/30-30-80.

EMERGENCIES

For police, fire, or ambulance assistance anywhere in Denmark, dial 112.

⚑ Major Hospitals Helsingør Sygehus ⊠ Esrumvej 145, Helsingør ☏ 48/29-29-29. **Køge Amts Sygehus** ⊠ Lykkebækvej 1, Køge ☏ 56/63-15-00. **Roskilde Amts Sygehus** ⊠ Køgevej 7-13, Roskilde ☏ 46/32-32-00.

⚑ 24-Hour Pharmacies Hillerød ⊠ Slotsg. 26 ☏ 48/26-56-00 🖷 48/24-23-85. **Roskilde** ⊠ Dom Apotek, Alg. 52 ☏ 46/32-32-77 🖷 46/32-88-22.

SPORTS & THE OUTDOORS

FISHING Zealand's lakes, rivers, and coastline teem with plaice, flounder, cod, and catfish. You can buy a fishing license for one day for DKr 25; for one week for DKr 75; or for one year for DKr 100. Along Zealand's coast it can be bought at any post office. Elsewhere, check with the local tourist office for license requirements. It is illegal to fish within 1,650 feet of the mouth of a stream.

TOURS

The turn-of-the-20th-century *Saga Fjord* gives tours of the waters of the Roskildefjord from April through September. Check with the local tourism boards for general sightseeing tours in the larger towns or for self-guided walking tours. Most tours of Zealand begin in Copenhagen. For information, call Copenhagen Excursions.

⚑ Copenhagen Excursions ⊠ Amager Strandvej 16, DK-2300 Copenhagen ☏ 32/54-06-06 🖷 32/57-49-05 ⊕ www.cex.dk. *Saga Fjord* ⊠ Store Valbyvej 154, DK-4000 Roskilde ☏ 46/75-64-60 🖷 46/75-63-60 ⊕ www.sagafjord.dk.

TRAIN TRAVEL

Zealand's extensive rail network will get you where you need to go in much less time than the cumbersome bus system. Most train routes are directed to and through Copenhagen. Routes to north and south Zealand almost always require a transfer at Copenhagen's main station. Every town in Zealand has a central train station; the only part of the island not connected to the DSB network is the sliver of northwestern peninsula known as Sjællands Odde. For information, call the private railway company Arriva. Two vintage trains dating from the 1880s run from Helsingør and Hillerød to Gilleleje.

The Copenhagen Card, which includes train and bus transport as well as admission to some museums and sites, is valid within the HT bus and rail system, which extends north to Helsingør, west to Roskilde, and south to Køge. However, the Copenhagen Card is valid for a limited time, so it's only worthwhile if you're planning a nonstop, intense sightseeing tour.

⚑ Arriva ☏ 70/27-74-82 ⊕ www.arrivatog.dk. **DSB** ☏ 70/13-14-16 international, 70/13-14-15 domestic ⊕ www.dsb.dk. **HT Bus** ⊠ Gammel Køge Landevej 3, DK-2500 Valby ☏ 36/13-14-15 🖷 36/13-18-97 ⊕ www.ht.dk. **Vintage trains** ☏ 48/30-00-30.

VISITOR INFORMATION

The Fiskeridirektoratet has information about fishing licenses and where to buy them.

⚑ Danmarks Turistråd (Danish Tourist Board) ⊠ Vesterbrog. 6D, Vesterbro, DK-1620 Copenhagen ☏ 33/11-14-15. **Det grønne Sjælland** (Zealand Naturally) ⊕ www.

sjaelland.com. **Fiskeridirektoratet (Danish Directory of Fisheries)** ✉ Stormg. 2, Downtown, DK–1470 Copenhagen ☎ 33/96–30–00 🖷 33/96–39–03 ⊕ www.fd.dk.

FUNEN & THE CENTRAL ISLANDS

CHRISTENED THE GARDEN OF DENMARK by its most famous son, Hans Christian Andersen, Funen (Fyn) is the smaller of the country's two major islands. A patchwork of vegetable fields and flower gardens, the flat-as-a-board countryside is relieved by beech glades and swan ponds. Manor houses and castles pop up from the countryside like magnificent mirages. Some of northern Europe's best-preserved castles are here: the 12th-century Nyborg Slot, travel pinup Egeskov Slot, and the lavish Valdemars Slot. The fairy-tale cliché often attributed to Denmark springs from this provincial isle, where the only place with modern vigor or stress seems to be Odense, its capital. Trimmed with thatch-roof houses and green parks, the city makes the most of the Andersen legacy but surprises with a rich arts community at the Brandts Klædefabrik, a former textile factory turned museum compound.

Towns in Funen are best explored by car. It's even quick and easy to reach the smaller islands of Langeland and Tåsinge—both are connected to Funen by bridges. Slightly more isolated is Ærø, where the town of Ærøskøbing, with its colorfully painted half-timber houses and winding streets, seems caught in a delightful time warp.

Nyborg

▶ ❶ *136 km (85 mi) southwest of Copenhagen (including the bridge across the Great Belt), 30 km (19 mi) southeast of Odense.*

Like most visitors, you should begin your tour of Funen in Nyborg, a 13th-century town that was Denmark's capital during the Middle Ages. The city's major landmark, the moated 12th-century **Nyborg Slot** (Nyborg Castle), was the seat of the Danehof, the Danish parliament from 1200 to 1413. It was here that King Erik Klipping signed the country's first constitution, the Great Charter, in 1282. In addition to geometric wall murals and an armory collection, the castle houses changing art exhibits. ✉ *Slotsg. 34* ☎ *65/31–02–07* ⊕ *www.museer-nyborg.dk* 🎟 *DKr 30, DKr 45 combined ticket with Nyborg Museum* ☽ *Mar.–May and Sept.–mid-Oct., weekdays 10–3; June and Aug., weekdays 10–4; July, weekdays 10–5.*

The **Nyborg Museum** occupies Mads Lerches Gård, a half-timber merchant's house from 1601, and provides an insight into 17th-century life. In addition to furnished period rooms, there's a small brewery. ✉ *Slotspl. 11* ☎ *65/31–02–07* ⊕ *www.museer-nyborg.dk* 🎟 *DKr 30, DKr 45 combined ticket with Nyborg Slot* ☽ *Apr., May, and Sept., weekdays 10–3; June and Aug., weekdays 10–4; July, weekdays 10–5.*

Every Tuesday at 7 PM in July and August, look and listen for the **Nyborg Tappenstreg** (Nyborg Tattoo), a military march accompanied by music that winds through the streets in the center of town. This ceremony dates

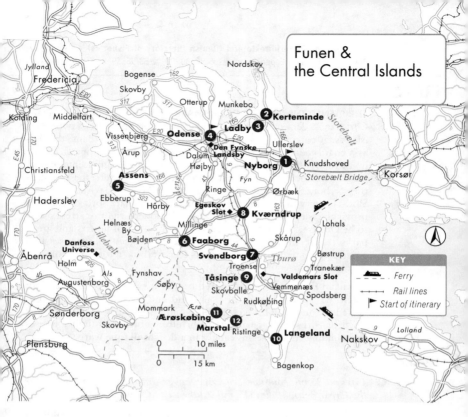

Funen &
the Central Islands

KEY

.🚢. Ferry

Rail lines

▶ Start of itinerary

from the mid-17th century, when officers would march through the streets, rounding up all the soldiers from the bars and beer halls to return them to the barracks. The word "tattoo" has its roots in the old Dutch word "taptoo" (or "taptoe"), which means to close the tap of a barrel; the variant "taps" obviously claims the same etymology.

Where to Stay & Eat

$–$$$ ✕ **Central Cafeen.** In a 200-year-old town house in the center of town, this warm-tone restaurant with velvet seats has been open since 1854. To many a Nyborg native there's nowhere better in town for a Danish smørrebrød lunch or hearty dinner. The menu includes roasted salmon with spinach and boiled potatoes, and fried pork with parsley sauce. Round out the meal with a plate of fresh Funen cheeses served with radishes and chives. ⊠ Nørreg. 6 ☎ 65/31–01–83 ▭ AE, DC, MC, V ⊘ Closed Sun. Oct.–June.

$–$$$ ✕ **Danehofkroen.** Outside Nyborg Slot, this family-run restaurant does a brisk lunch business, serving traditional Danish meals to tourists who enjoy a view of the castle and its tree-lined moat. The menu is basic meat and potatoes, with such dishes as *flæskesteg* (sliced pork served with

the crisp rind). ⊠ *Slotspl.* ☎ *65/31–02–02* ⚐ *Reservations essential* ▭ V
⊙ *Closed Mon. and Oct.–May.*

$$$$ 🏨 **Hesselet.** A modern brick slab outside, this hotel is a refined Anglo-
Fodor'sChoice   Asian sanctuary on the inside. Guest rooms have cushy, contemporary
★   furniture and Bang & Olufsen televisions; most have a splendid view
of the Storebæltsbro suspension bridge. ⊠ *Christianslundsvej 119,*
DK–5800 ☎ *65/31–30–29* 🖷 *65/31–29–58* ⊕ *www.hesselet.dk* 🛏 *43*
rooms, 4 suites ⚒ *Restaurant, indoor pool, bar, meeting room* ▭ AE,
DC, MC, V.

$$$ 🏨 **Nyborg Strand.** This large hotel complex, owned by the Best West-
ern hotel chain, sprawls along the shoreline 1½ km (1 mi) east of Ny-
borg's city center. The Nyborg Strand caters to the conference crowd,
with numerous meeting rooms and an antiseptic lobby that reverber-
ates with the din of noisy groups. However, the seaside location can't
be beat, and the summer rates, particularly for families, are surprisingly
low, especially considering the hotel's lovely location. ⊠ *Østerøvej 2,*
DK–5800 ☎ *65/31–31–31* 🖷 *65/31–37–01* ⊕ *www.nyborgstrand.dk*
🛏 *282 rooms, 2 suites* ⚒ *Restaurant, indoor pool, bar, meeting rooms,*
some pets allowed (fee) ▭ AE, DC, MC, V.

Nightlife & the Arts

★   Take on the Nyborg night at the popular **Café Anthon** (⊠ Mellemg. 25
☎ 65/31–16–64), a laid-back bar in the heart of town, with live jazz,
blues, or rock on Friday and Saturday nights. The walls are hung with
all sorts of instruments, from accordions to cellos to electric guitars, many
of which were gifts from musicians who have played here.

Shopping

ANTIQUES   Many of Funen's manor houses and castles now double as antiques em-
poriums. The largest is **Hindemae** (⊠ Hindemaevej 86, Ullerslev ☎ 65/
35–32–60 ⊕ www.hindemae.dk), which lies 12 km (7 mi) west of Ny-
borg. The site is only open to the public during auctions.

Kerteminde

❷ *21 km (13 mi) north of Nyborg, 20 km (13 mi) northeast of Odense.*

Kerteminde is an important fishing village and popular summer resort.
The pastel paints and red roofs of the town's houses contrast with the
cool blues of the nearby Baltic, which supports recreational fishing, swim-
ming, and other water sports in the summer. On Langegade, walk past
the neat half-timber houses to Møllebakken and the **Johannes Larsen**
Museet, dedicated to the work of the Danish painter (1867–1961).
Across from a strawberry patch and a century-old windmill, the artist
built a large country villa that has been perfectly preserved, right down
to the teacups. In front is a sculpture of a woman done by Kai Nielsen.
Local legend has it that one night, after a particularly wild party in Copen-
hagen, its legs were somehow broken off. An ambulance was called, and
once it arrived, the enraged driver demanded that the artists pay a fine.
A chagrined Larsen paid, and in return kept Nielsen's wounded sculp-

ture. ☒ *Møllebakken 14* ☎ *65/32–37–27* ⊕ *www.kert-mus.dk* ☜ *DKr 60* ⊙ *June–Aug., daily 10–5; Mar.–May, Sept., and Oct., Tues.–Sun. 10–4; Nov.–Feb., Tues.–Sun. 11–4.*

Where to Stay & Eat

★ **$$$$** ✕ **Rudolf Mathis.** This busy harborside restaurant is topped by two chimneys, which are needed to ventilate the open grills where popular fish dishes are broiled. Favorites are catfish with butter, fennel, and Pernod sauce, and grilled turbot in green-pepper–and–lime sauce. ☒ *Dosseringen 13, 13 km (8 mi) northeast of Odense on Rte. 165* ☎ *65/32–32–33* ⊕ *www.rudolfmathis.dk* ☴ *AE, DC, MC, V* ⊙ *Closed Mon. and Jan. and Feb.*

$$$–$$$$ ✕ **Gittes Fiskehus.** Dine to the gentle sounds of lapping water at this friendly fish restaurant that extends out over Kerteminde's small canal amid colorful, bobbing fishing boats. Dishes include shrimp smothered in garlic, cream, rum, and Pernod, or the "Hemingway steak," a plate of blue marlin, the fish protagonist of *The Old Man and the Sea.* An additional dining room is housed inside a permanently moored boat that sits alongside the restaurant. ☒ *Hindsholmvej 5* ☎ *65/32–12–38* ☴ *MC, V* ⊙ *Closed Sun.–Tues. No lunch Sept.–May.*

$ ✕🏠 **Tornøes Hotel.** Steps from Kerteminde's harbor is this comfortable hotel with basic rooms, many of which have partial views of the waterfront. The handsome restaurant has pale yellow walls and matching tablecloths, and serves contemporary Danish fare, including a set "Kerteminde menu" of fried sole as well as crepes with ice cream and strawberries for dessert. ☒ *Strandg. 2, DK–5300* ☎ *65/32–16–05* 🖷 *65/ 32–48–40* ⊕ *www.tornoeshotel.dk* ⇱ *28 rooms, 2 suites* ⊙ *Restaurant, bar, some pets allowed* ☴ *AE, DC, MC, V.*

¢ 🏠 **Danhostel Kerteminde Vandrehjem.** South of Kerteminde, this well-maintained hostel is surrounded by a peaceful patch of woodland and is just a few minutes' walk from the beach. Families flock here in summer, and the rooms are outfitted in typical Danish hostel style, with sturdy wooden bunks and basic showers. An industrial-size kitchen and cafeteria—built to feed the large school groups that come through—serves breakfast. ☒ *Skovvej 46, DK–5300 Kerteminde* ☎ *65/32–39–29* 🖷 *65/ 32–39–24* ⊕ *www.danhostel.dk* ⇱ *30 rooms with shower* ☴ *MC, V.*

Shopping

CERAMICS Just a few miles west of Kerteminde is **Bjørnholt Keramik** (☒ Risingevej 12, Munkebo ☎ 65/97–40–90), where you can watch ceramics being made.

Ladby

❸ *4 km (2½ mi) south of Kerteminde, 16 km (10 mi) east of Odense.*

The village of Ladby is best known as the home of the 1,100-year-old remains of the ***Ladbyskibet.*** This ship belonging to a Viking chieftain was buried along with the hunting dogs and horses he would need for Valhalla—the afterlife. Today you can see a massive hull-shaped indentation in the ground where the excavation took place. All the wooden parts of the ship disintegrated centuries ago, but exhibited at the site are the ship's anchor, and also the remains of the horses and hunting dogs. A replica of the ship (in real size) was in the works until the project stalled because of practical and financial difficulties; if and when it's completed, it will be shown alongside the burial site. ⊠ *Vikingevej 123* ☎ *65/32–16–67* ⊕*www.kert-mus.dk* ⊠*DKr 40* ☉*June–Aug., daily 10–5; Mar.–May, Sept., and Oct., Tues.–Sun. 10–4; Nov.–Feb., Wed.–Sun. 11–3.*

Odense

▶ ❹ *20 km (12 mi) southwest of Ladby on Rte. 165, 144 km (90 mi) west of Copenhagen.*

It's no coincidence that Odense, the capital of Funen and third-largest city in Denmark, is reminiscent of a storybook village—much of its charm is built upon the legend of its most famous son, author Hans Christian Andersen. The town is named after another famous Scandinavian, Odin, the king of the Nordic gods. When you're in town, first see the flourishing Kongens Have (King's Garden) and 18th-century Odense Castle, now a government building. If you walk east on Østre Stationsvej to Thomas B. Thriges Gade and Hans Jensens Stræde, you'll come to ★ the **Hans Christian Andersen Hus** (H. C. Andersen House), which sits amid half-timber houses and cobbled streets. Inside, the storyteller's life is chronicled through his photographs, drawings, letters, and personal belongings. The library has Andersen's works in more than 100 languages, and you can listen to fairy tales on tape. ⊠ *Bangs Boder 29* ☎ *65/51–46–01* ⊕ *www.odmus.dk* ⊠ *DKr 50* ☉ *June–Aug., daily 9–6; Sept.–May, Tues.–Sun. 10–4.*

♺ The **Børnekulturehuset Fyrtøjet** (Children's Culture House, The Tinderbox) museum includes walk-through fairy-tale exhibits as well as studios where children can draw and write their own tales and plays and then dress up and perform them. ⊠ *Hans Jensen Str. 21* ☎ *66/14–44–11* ⊕ *www.fyrtoejet.com* ⊠ *DKr 60* ☉ *Feb.–June, Tues.–Sun. 11–4; July, daily 10–5.*

The sleek **Carl Nielsen Museum** creates multimedia exhibits of the life and work of Denmark's most famous composer (1865–1931) and of his wife, the sculptor Anne Marie Carl-Nielsen (yes, that's the way she took his name). ⊠ *Claus Bergs G. 11* ☎ *65/51–46–01* ⊕ *www.odmus.dk* ⊠ *DKr 25* ☉ *June–Aug., Thurs. and Fri. 2–6, Sun. noon–4; Sept.–May, Thurs. and Fri. 4–6, Sun. noon–4.*

Møntergården, Odense's city museum, occupies four 17th-century row houses adjacent to a shady, cobbled courtyard. Exhibits range from medieval interiors to coverage of Denmark's Nazi occupation to an extensive and impressive collection of ancient coins from all over the world. ⊠ *Overg. 48–50* ☎ *65/51–46–01* ⊕ *www.odmus.dk* ⊠ *DKr 30* ☉ *Tues.–Sun. 10–4.*

The stately **Skt. Knuds Kirke,** built from the 13th to the 15th century, is the only purely Gothic cathedral in Denmark. The intricate wooden altar covered with gold leaf was carved by German sculptor Claus Berg. Beneath the sepulchre are the bones of St. (King) Knud, killed during a farmers' uprising in 1086, and his brother. ✉ *Toward the pedestrian zone of Skt. Knuds Kirkestræde, in front of Andersen Park.*

In the diminutive **Hans Christian Andersens Barndomshjem** (H. C. Andersen's Childhood Home), the young boy and his parents lived in three tiny rooms. The rooms are outfitted with rustic, period furnishings (chairs, lamps, a table) and little else, befitting a humble abode of the early 1800s. ✉ *Munkemøllestr. 3–5* ☎ *66/13–13–72 Ext. 4601* 🎟 *DKr 10* ⊙ *June–Aug., daily 10–4; Sept.–May, Tues.–Sun. 11–3.*

Near the center of town is the elegant **Fyns Kunstmuseum** (Funen Art Museum), which displays a large and varied collection of Danish art from the 18th century to the present. Featured artists include Jens Juel, Vilhelm Hammershøj, P. S. Krøyer, and Robert Jacobsen. The museum's highlight is its comprehensive collection of Funen artists, from Johannes Larsen to Peter Hansen. ✉ *Jernbaneg. 13* ☎ *66/13–13–72 Ext. 4601* ⊕ *www.odmus.dk* 🎟 *DKr 30* ⊙ *Tues.–Sun. 10–4.*

For something completely different, head just west of the center of town to the **Superbowl Odense,** an indoor entertainment center with bowling alleys, a restaurant, and a go-cart track. ✉ *Grønøkken 3* ☎ *66/ 19–16–40.*

Odense River Cruises (☎ 65/95–79–96) operates several boat trips on the Odense Å from Filosofgangen. You can catch a boat (May through mid-August, daily on the hour 10–5, returning 35 minutes later) downriver to the Fruens Bøge (Lady's Beech Forest) and then walk down Erik Bøghs Sti (Erik Bøgh's Footpath) to **Den Fynske Landsby** (the Funen Village). Among the country's largest open-air museums, it includes 25 farm buildings and workshops, a vicarage, a water mill, and a theater, which in summer stages adaptations of Andersen's tales. Afterward, cruise back to the town center or catch Bus 42, and walk down the boutique- and café-lined pedestrian street Vestergade (Kongensgade running perpendicular to the town hall), which in summer is abuzz with street performers, musicians, and brass bands. ✉ *Sejerskovvej 20* ☎ *65/51–46–01* ⊕ *www. odmus.dk* 🎟 *DKr 55* ⊙ *Mid-Apr.–May, Sept., and Oct., Tues.–Sun. 10–5; June–Aug., daily 10–7.*

Occupying a former textile factory, the four-story artist compound **Brandts Klædefabrik** houses the **Museet for Fotokunst** (Museum of Photographic Art), **Danmarks Grafiske Museum** (Danish Graphics Museum), **Dansk Presse Museum** (Danish Press Museum), and **Kunsthallen** (Art Gallery). National and international exhibits shown here vary widely, but the photography museum and the art gallery gravitate toward especially experimental work. The press museum chronicles the history of Denmark's printing trade, and houses lithography, bookbinding, and papermaking workshops. ✉ *Brandts Passage 37 and 43, north of the river and parallel to Kongensgade* ☎ *66/13–78–97* ⊕ *www.brandts.dk* 🎟 *Combined ticket DKr 50; photography museum DKr 25; graphics museum DKr 25; press museum DKr 25; art gallery DKr 30* ⊙ *July and Aug., daily 10–5; Sept.–June, Tues.–Sun. 10–5.*

Where to Eat

$$$$ ✕ **LPC** (La Petite Cuisine). This romantic little restaurant tucked in the Brandts Passage can accommodate about 40 diners. The southern French specialties change every day according to what can be purchased fresh at the market. Typical dishes include Asian-inspired marinated duck breast, grilled skewered salmon or catfish with vegetables, and white mocha parfait for dessert. ⊠ *Brandts Passage 13* ☏ *66/14–11–00* ⊕ *www.lpc. dk* ⌣ *Reservations essential* ▭ *DC, MC, V.*

$$$–$$$$ ✕ **Marie Louise.** Overseen by the illustrious chef Michel Michaud (he now
FodorsChoice lives in Skagen), this is considered one of Funen's—if not Denmark's—
★ finest French restaurants. The elegant whitewashed dining room glitters with crystal and silver. The French-Danish menu typically offers such specialties as scalloped salmon with bordelaise sauce and grilled veal with lobster cream sauce. ⊠ *Lottrups Gaard, Vesterg. 70–72* ☏ *66/17–92–95* ⊕ *www.restaurant-marielouise.dk* ▭ *AE, DC, MC, V* ⊘ *Closed Sun. and Mon.*

$$$–$$$$ ✕ **Restaurant Under Lindetræet.** The snug corner restaurant, situated in the same cozy, cobblestoned neighborhood as the Hans Christian Andersen House, serves homestyle Danish fare, including grilled redfish with boiled potatoes. Burgundy velvet drapes divide parts of the dining room, making dining an intimate experience. ⊠ *Ramsherred 2* ☏ *66/12–92–86* ⌣ *Reservations essential* ▭ *MC, V* ⊘ *Closed Sun. and Mon.*

$$–$$$$ ✕ **Klitgaard.** Named after its young owner-chef, Jacob Klitgaard, this chic, cool-tone restaurant serves a changing menu of innovative French-Italian fusion fare. Stuffed quail is seasoned with rosemary and accompanied by an endive salad; a fricassee of scallops and asparagus is enveloped in a tangy lemon sauce. The fresh cuisine is complemented by a soothing decor of tan walls, hardwood floors, and cane furniture that glow softly under recessed lights. ⊠ *Gravene 4* ☏ *66/13–14–55* ⊕ *www.restaurantklitgaard.dk* ⌣ *Reservations essential* ▭ *DC, MC, V* ⊘ *Closed Sun. and Mon.*

$$$ ✕ **Carlslund.** Ask most any Odense local where to find the best *æggekage* in town, and he'll probably point you in this direction. Cholesterol-watchers, beware: æggekage is a rich dish consisting of a fluffy, cream-whipped, parsley-speckled omelet topped with either bacon strips or pork rinds. Dab on some mustard and scoop it up with hunks of rye bread. It's traditionally washed down with shots of aquavit. Dating from 1860, the cozy, low-ceiling restaurant sits in a wooded park on the outskirts of Odense. In summer Carlslund sets up an outdoor stage and hosts live jazz on the weekends, drawing hundreds. ⊠ *Fruens Bøge Skov 7* ☏ *66/91–11–25* ⊕ *www.restaurant-carlslund.dk* ⌣ *Reservations essential* ▭ *DC, MC, V.*

$–$$$ ✕ **Den Gamle Kro.** Built within the courtyards of several 17th-century homes, this popular restaurant has walls of ancient stone topped by a sliding glass roof. The French-Danish menu includes fillet of sole stuffed with salmon mousse and chateaubriand with garlic potatoes, but there's also inexpensive smørrebrød. ⊠ *Overg. 23* ☏ *66/12–14–33* ⊕ *www. den-gamle-kro.dk* ▭ *DC, MC, V.*

$–$$$ ✕ **Franck A.** Overlooking the pedestrian street, this spacious, stylish café–restaurant–bar with exposed brick walls is Odense's answer to

Copenhagen's trendy venues—minus the pretension. Hipsters and media types mingle over cocktails but, this being Odense, informality prevails. Brunch is served all day; try the salmon–and–cherry-tomato omelet. The lunch and dinner menu of global cuisine runs the gamut from Thai chicken curry to hefty grilled burgers. On Thursday Franck A often hosts a popular '80s music night, with lively cover bands. ✉ *Jernbaneg. 4* ☏ *66/12–27–57* ⊕ *www.francka.dk* ☰ *MC, V.*

★ ¢–$ ✕ **Den Grimme Ælling.** The name of this chain restaurant means "the ugly duckling," but inside it's simply homey, with pine furnishings and a boisterous family ambience. It's extremely popular with tourists and locals alike, thanks to an all-you-can-eat buffet heaped with cold and warm dishes. ✉ *Hans Jensens Str. 1* ☏ *65/91–70–30* ⊕ *www.grimme-aelling.dk* ☰ *DC, MC.*

¢–$ ✕ **Målet.** A lively crowd calls this sports club its neighborhood bar. The schnitzel is served in a dozen creative ways from traditional schnitzel with sautéed potatoes and peas to Indian curry schnitzel with rice, chutney, and pineapple. After the steaming plates of food, watching and discussing soccer are the chief delights of the house. ✉ *Jernbaneg. 17* ☏ *66/17–82–41* ⌲ *Reservations not accepted* ☰ *No credit cards.*

Where to Stay

$$$ ⌯ **Clarion Hotel Plaza.** A five-minute walk from the train station, this stately hotel dates from 1915 and overlooks Odense's leafy central park, Kongens Have. An old-fashioned wooden elevator takes you up to the ample, comfortable rooms outfitted in traditional dark-wood furniture. Adjoining the pale-green lobby is the glass-walled Restaurant Rosenhaven, which serves contemporary Danish fare. ✉ *Østre Stationsvej 24, DK–5000* ☏ *66/11–77–45* ☒ *66/14–41–45* ⊕ *www.hotelplaza.dk* ⇦ *61 rooms, 7 suites* ⌂ *Restaurant, gym, sauna, bar, meeting rooms* ☰ *AE, DC, MC, V.*

$$$ ⌯ **Radisson SAS–Hans Christian Andersen Hotel.** Around the corner from the Hans Christian Andersen House, this blocky brick conference hotel has a plant-filled lobby and ample rooms done up in warm shades of red and yellow. ✉ *Claus Bergs G. 7, DK–5000* ☏ *66/14–78–00 or 800/33–3333* ☒ *66/14–78–90* ⊕ *www.radissonsas.com* ⇦ *145 rooms* ⌂ *Restaurant, gym, sauna, bar, casino* ☰ *AE, DC, MC, V.*

$–$$$ ⌯ **First Hotel Grand Odense.** More than a century old, with renovated fin-de-siècle charm, this imposing four-story, brick-front hotel greets guests with old-fashioned luxury. The original stone floors and chandeliers lead to a wide staircase and upstairs guest rooms that are modern with plush furnishings and sleek marble bathrooms. ✉ *Jernabaneg. 18, DK–5000* ☏ *66/11–71–71* ☒ *66/14–11–71* ⊕ *www.firsthotels.com* ⇦ *138 rooms, 3 suites* ⌂ *Restaurant, room service, sauna, bar, some pets allowed, no-smoking rooms* ☰ *AE, DC, MC, V.*

¢ ⌯ **Hotel Ydes.** This well-kept, bright, and colorful hotel is a good bet for students and budget-conscious travelers tired of barracks-type accommodations. The well-maintained rooms are spotless and comfortable. ✉ *Hans Tausens G. 11, DK–5000* ☏ *66/12–11–31* ☒ *66/12–14–13* ⊕ *www.ydes.dk* ⇦ *25 rooms* ⌂ *Café* ☰ *MC, V.*

Fodor'sChoice
★

Nightlife & the Arts

CAFÉS & BARS   Odense's central arcade is an entertainment mall, with bars, restaurants, and live music ranging from corny sing-alongs to hard rock. For a quiet evening, stop by **Café Biografen** (✉ Brandts Passage ☎ 66/13–16–16) for an espresso, beer, or light snack, or settle in to see one of the films screened here. The **Air Pub** (✉ Kongsg. 41 ☎ 66/14–66–08) is a Danish pub that caters to a thirty- and fortysomething crowd, with meals and a small dance floor. At the **Boogie Dance Café** (✉ Nørreg. 21 ☎ 66/14–00–39), a laid-back crowd grooves to pop, disco, and '60s music. In the heart of town is **Franck A** (✉ Jernbaneg. 4 ☎ 66/12–57–27), a spirited café-restaurant with arched windows overlooking the pedestrian street. Live music on the weekends—from pop to jazz—draws a stylish crowd, as does the popular '80s night on Thursday. The specialty at **Klos Ands** (✉ Vineg. 76 ☎ 66/13–56–00) is malt whiskey.

CASINO   Funen's sole casino is in the slick glass atrium of the **SAS Hans Christian Andersen Hotel** (✉ Claus Bergs G. 7, Odense ☎ 66/14–78–00), where you can play blackjack, roulette, and baccarat.

JAZZ CLUBS   **Dexter's** (✉ Vinderg. 65 ☎ 66/11–27–28) has all kinds of jazz—from Dixieland to fusion—Friday and Saturday nights. **Grøntorvet Café and Bar** (✉ Sortebrødre Torv 9 ☎ 66/14–34–37) presents live jazz at 5 PM Thursday and 2 PM Saturday.

THEATER   **Den Fynske Landsby** stages Hans Christian Andersen plays from mid-July to mid-August. In summer the young members of the **Hans Christian Andersen Parade** present a pastiche of the bard's fairy tales in a couple of different languages at Lotzes Have, an herb garden behind the Hans Christian Andersen Museum.

Sports & the Outdoors

GOLF   **Odense Eventyr Golfklub** (✉ Falen 227 ☎ 66/65–20–15 ⊕ www. eventyrgolf.dk), 4 km (2½ mi) southwest of Odense, has three 9-hole courses, one of which is entirely composed of challenging par-3s. The **Odense Golf Klub** (✉ Hestehaven 200 ☎ 65/95–90–00 ⊕ www. odensegolfklub.dk), 6 km (4 mi) southeast of Odense, has 27 holes on relatively flat ground with some woods. **Blommenlyst** (✉ Vejruplundvej 20, Blommenlyst ☎ 65/96–71–20) is a pleasant 9-hole course with a driving range and putting greens 12 km (7 mi) west of Odense.

Shopping

Odense's compact city center is bustling with clothing, furniture, and shoe stores, and a Magasin department store. The main shopping strips are Vestergade and Kongensgade. Rosengårdcentret, one of northern Europe's largest malls, is 5 km (3 mi) west of Odense. It has more than 125 shops and food outlets, including trendy clothing stores; jewelry, woodwork, and antiques shops; a multiplex cinema; and a post office.

Denmark is well known for its paper mobiles and cutouts, inspired, in part, by Hans Christian Andersen. Using a small pair of scissors and white paper, he would create cutouts to illustrate his fairy tales. Today replicas of Andersen's cutouts are sold at several Odense gift stores. Also popular are mobiles, often depicting Andersen-inspired themes like swans and mermaids. Uniquely Danish—and light on the suitcase—they make great gifts to take home.

Jam-packed with mobiles, cutouts, and Danish flags and dolls, **Klods Hans** (⌂ Hans Jensens Str. 34 ☎ 66/11–09–40) opened just after World War II to cater to all the American soldiers on leave who wanted to bring back Danish gifts. For fine replicas of Scandinavian Viking jewelry, head to **Museums Kopi Smykker** (⌂ Klareg. 3 ☎ 66/12–06–96). Each piece, in either sterling silver or gold, comes with a printed leaflet explaining its Viking origins. Among the offerings are silver bracelets of various weights, once used by the Vikings as currency; pendants of the Nordic god Odin, Odense's namesake; and a Viking "key to Valhalla." A modest selection of antiques is for sale at **Hønnerup Hovgård** (⌂ Hovgårdsvej 6, Hønnerup ☎ 64/49–13–00); take Exit 55 to Route 161 toward Middelfart; follow the signs to Hønnerup.

Assens

⑤ *38 km (24 mi) southwest of Odense.*

★ Near the quiet town of Assens is one of the most extraordinary private gardens in Denmark: Tove Sylvest's sprawling **De 7 Haver** (The Seven Gardens). A privately owned botanical United Nations, the gardens represent the flora of seven European countries, including many plants rare to Denmark. ⌂ Å Strandvej 33, Ebberup ☎ 64/74–12–85 ⊕ www.visit-vestfyn.dk ⌑ DKr 45 ☉ Apr.–Oct., daily 10–5.

On the same street as Seven Gardens is the **Hviids Have,** a 1-acre Japanese garden complete with elegant ponds traversed by rough-plank walkways, as well as stone settings and modest amounts of greenery. ⌂ Å Strandvej 33, Ebberup ☎ 64/74–11–02 ⊕ www.visit-vestfyn.dk ⌑ DKr 40 ☉ May–Oct., daily 10–6.

off the beaten path

TERRARIET – Children may appreciate this detour 18 km (11 mi) northeast to Funen's Terrarium, where they can examine all kinds of slippery and slithery creatures, including snakes, iguanas, alligators, and the nearly extinct blue frog. ⌂ Kirkehelle 5, Vissenbjerg ☎ 64/47–18–50 ⊕ www.reptil-zoo.dk ⌑ DKr 57 ☉ June–Aug., daily 10–6; Sept.–May, daily 10–4.

Faaborg

⑥ *30 km (18 mi) south of Odense (via Rte. 43).*

The beaches surrounding this lovely 13th-century town are invaded by sun-seeking Germans and Danes in summer. Four times a day you can hear the dulcet chiming of a carillon, the island's largest. In the town center is the controversial *Ymerbrønden* sculpture by Kai Nielsen, depicting a naked man drinking from an emaciated cow's udder while it licks a baby.

The 1725 **Den Gamle Gaard** (Old Merchant's House) chronicles the local history of Faaborg through furnished interiors and exhibits of glass and textiles. ☒ *Holkeg. 1* ☏ *63/61–20–00* ⊕ *www.fkm.nu* ☒ *DKr 30* ☉ *Mid-May–Aug., daily 10:30–4:30; Apr.–mid-May, Sept., and Oct., weekends 11–3.*

The **Faaborg Museum for Fynsk Malerkunst** (Funen Painting Museum) has a good collection of turn-of-the-20th-century paintings and sculpture by the Funen Painters, a school of artists whose work captures the dusky light of the Scandinavian sun. ☒ *Grønneg. 75* ☏ *62/61–06–45* ⊕ *www.faaborgmuseum.dk* ☒ *DKr 40* ☉ *Apr.–Oct., daily 10–4; Nov.–Mar., Tues.–Sun. 11–3.*

Where to Stay & Eat

$–$$$ ✕ **Vester Skerninge Kro.** Midway between Faaborg and Svendborg, this traditional inn is cluttered and comfortable. Pine tables are polished from years of serving hot stews and homemade *medister pølse* (mild grilled sausage) and æggekage. ☒ *Krovej 9, Vester Skerninge* ☏ *62/24–10–04* ⊕ *www.vesterskerningekro.dk* ⊟ *AE, MC, V* ☉ *Closed Tues. and Oct.–Mar.*

$$$$ ✕▤ **Falsled Kro.** Once a smuggler's hideaway, the 500-year-old Falsled
Fodor'sChoice Kro is one of Denmark's most elegant inns, and a member of the Re-
★ lais & Chateaux group of hotels. A favorite among well-heeled Euro-peans, it has appointed its cottages sumptuously with European antiques and stone fireplaces. The restaurant combines French and Danish cuisines, using ingredients from markets in Lyon and its own garden. ☒ *Assensvej 513, DK–5642 Millinge, 13 km (8 mi) northwest of Faaborg on Millinge-Assens Hwy.* ☏ *62/68–11–11* ⊟ *62/68–11–62* ⊕ *www.falsledkro.dk* ⚲ *19 rooms, 8 suites* ⟨ *Restaurant, cafeteria, bar, some pets allowed* ⊟ *AE, DC, MC, V.*

$$–$$$$ ✕▤ **Steensgård Herregårdspension.** A long avenue of beeches leads to this 700-year-old moated manor house 7 km (4½ mi) northwest of Faaborg. The rooms are elegant, with antiques, four-poster beds, and yards of silk damask. The fine restaurant serves Danish classics crafted from the wild game from the manor's own reserve. ☒ *Steensgård 4, DK–5642 Millinge* ☏ *62/61–94–90* ⊟ *62/61–78–61* ⊕ *www. herregaardspension.dk* ⚲ *15 rooms, 13 with bath* ⟨ *Restaurant, tennis court, horseback riding* ⊟ *AE, DC, MC, V* ☉ *Closed Feb.*

¢–$ ✕▤ **Hotel Faaborg.** Rising over Faaborg's rustic main square, this small hotel is housed in a brick town house. The rooms are basic and simply furnished. The Danish menu at the spacious restaurant includes baked cod smothered in a tomato ratatouille sauce with oregano, shallots, garlic, and anchovies. Veal is topped with honey-fried apple slices and served with seasonal vegetables. ☒ *Torvet 13–15, DK–5600 Faaborg* ☏ *62/61–02–45* ⊟ *62/61–08–45* ⊕ *www.hotelfaaborg.dk* ⚲ *10 rooms* ⟨ *Restaurant, bar* ⊟ *AE, DC, MC, V.*

★ $ ▤ **Hotel Færgegaarden.** For well over 150 years this spot has been a favorite of budget-conscious tourists and traveling artists, with its traditional dusty yellow and red facade. Newly refurbished, Færgegaarden offers elegantly modern rooms right on the medieval-era harbor front. ☒ *Christian IXs Vej 31, DK–5600 Faaborg* ☏ *62/61–11–15* ⊟ *62/ 61–11–95* ⊕ *www.hotelfg.dk* ⚲ *24 rooms* ⟨ *Restaurant, some pets allowed* ⊟ *AE, DC, MC, V.*

Nightlife & the Arts

Near the waterfront is **Bar Heimdal** (⊠ Havneg. 12 ☎ 62/61–35–35), where Faaborg's fishermen crowd into booths and knock back cold ones after hauling in their nets. An inexpensive menu of simple Danish fare includes fillet of sole with tartar sauce and smoked ham with asparagus. In summer the sunny outdoor terrace draws a mixed crowd of tourists and locals. Just off Faaborg's main square is the homey **Oasen Bodega** (⊠ Strandg. 2 ☎ 62/61–13–15), frequented by regulars who enjoy lingering while imbibing the local brew. Most of the local residents sit by the wooden bar, and this can be a good place to strike up a conversation. Perhaps Faaborg's most hyggelig hangout is the historic **Schankstube** (tap house; ⊠ Havneg. 12 ☎ 62/61–11–15), inside the harborside Hotel Færgegaarden. Housed in a former taproom, this small bar has worn wooden tables, yellow walls hung with richly colored paintings by Faaborg artists, and small windows with views of the harbor. The menu is traditional—smørrebrød and beer. **Tre Kroner** (⊠ Strandg. 1 ☎ 62/ 61–01–50) is a traditional watering hole with varied clientele and the enchantment of an inn from the turn of the 20th century.

Svendborg

❼ *25 km (15 mi) east of Faaborg (via Rte. 44 east), 44 km (28 mi) south of Odense.*

Svendborg is Funen's second-largest town, and one of the country's most important cruise harbors. It celebrates its eight-centuries-old maritime traditions every July, when old Danish wooden ships congregate in the harbor for the circular Funen *rundt*, or regatta. Play your cards right, and you might hitch aboard and shuttle between towns. Contact the tourist board or any agreeable captain. With many charter-boat options and good marinas, Svendborg is an excellent base from which to explore the hundreds of islands of the South Funen archipelago.

On Fruestræde near the market square at the center of town is the black-and-yellow **Anne Hvides Gård**, the oldest secular structure in Svendborg and one of the four branches of Svendborgs Omegns Museum (Svendborg County Museum). This evocative exhibit includes 18th- and 19th-century interiors and glass and silver collections. ⊠ *Fruestr. 3* ☎ *62/21–76–45* ⊕ *www.svendborgmuseum.dk* ☝ *DKr 25* ◷ *Mid-June–Sept., Tues.–Sun. 10–5; Oct.–Dec., Wed.–Sun. 10–4.*

Bagergade (Baker's Street) is lined with some of Svendborg's oldest half-timber houses. At the corner of Grubbemøllevej and Svinget is the **Viebæltegård,** the headquarters of the Svendborg County Museum and a former poorhouse. You can wander through dining halls, washrooms, and the "tipsy clink," where, until 1974, inebriated citizens were left to sober up. ⊠ *Grubbemøllevej 13* ☎ *62/21–02–61* ⊕ *www. svendborgmuseum.dk* ☝ *DKr 40* ◷ *June–Sept., Tues.–Sun. 10–5; Oct.–May, Tues.–Sun. 10–4.*

Changing contemporary-art exhibits are showcased at the two-story **SAK Kunstbygningen** (SAK Art Exhibitions), a skylit gallery-museum just to the west of the city center. The museum's highlight is the small collection of sculptures by Svendborg native Kai Nielsen. One of Denmark's most popular sculptors, Nielsen is best known for his sensual figures of women in languid repose and chubby angelic babies playing together. Nielsen's sculptures are displayed in a sun-drenched octagonal gallery with views over a leafy garden. His works are exhibited all over Denmark, most famously in Copenhagen's Ny Carlsberg Glyptotek. Here, his *Water Mother* fountain sculpture depicts a voluptuous woman reclining atop a lily pond, while a half dozen plump, adorable babies crawl out of the water and over her curves, suckling at her breasts and dozing between her thighs. ⊠ *Vesterg. 27–31* ☎ *62/22–44–70* 🖃 *DKr 25* ⊙ *Tues.–Sun. 11–4.*

> **need a break?**
> In the heart of Svendborg, tucked behind the main street of Brogade, is a small, cobblestone courtyard surrounded by red half-timber houses. Dating from 1650, this charming square used to house Svendborg's general store. **Vintapperiet** (⊠ Brog. 37 ☎ 62/22–34–48), a snug, low-ceiling wine bar and shop, now occupies the square, and here you can taste your way—by the glass or by the bottle—through a range of top-notch French and Italian wines. Wine barrels line the entranceway; the small dining room, with less than a half dozen tables, overlooks the courtyard. They serve a light menu to complement the wines, including pâté and pungent cheese with hunks of bread and olives. It is open for lunch only, and closed on Sunday; in winter it's also closed on Monday.

Where to Stay & Eat

$$$ ✕ **Svendborgsund.** In a harborside building dating from 1682, this warm, maritime-theme restaurant serves traditional Danish cuisine, including pork tenderloin heaped with grilled onions and mushrooms and served with potatoes and pickled cucumbers. The extensive smørrebrød lunch menu includes marinated herring topped with egg yolk and fried fillet of plaice with shrimp, caviar, and asparagus. The summertime terrace is an inviting spot to soak up sun, beer, and the waterfront views. ⊠ *Havnepl. 5* ☎ *62/21–07–19* ⊕ *www.restaurantsvendborgsund.dk* 🖃 *AE, DC, MC, V* ⊙ *Closed Sun. Oct.–Mar.*

¢–$$ ✕ **Hotel Ærø.** A hodgepodge of ship parts and nautical doodads, this dimly lighted restaurant and inn looks like it's always been here. Brusque waitresses take orders from serious local trenchermen. The menu is staunchly old-fashioned, featuring *frikadeller* (fried meatballs), fried *rødspætte* (plaice) with hollandaise sauce, and dozens of smørrebrød options. ⊠ *Brog. 1, Ærøfærgen (at the Ærø ferry), DK–5700* ☎ *62/21–07–60* 🖶 *63/20–30–51* ⊕ *www.hotel-aeroe.dk* 🖃 *DC, MC, V.*

★ $ 🏨 **Missionhotellet Stella Marris.** Southwest of Svendborg, this lovely seaside villa dates from 1904. An old-fashioned English-style drawing room, complete with piano, stuffed chairs, and an elegant chandelier, overlooks the villa's spacious gardens; follow a path through the greenery and you can dive right off the private pier into the sea. Each of the rooms has its own color scheme; one room has flowery wallpaper and white lace curtains, while another has a simple tan-and-rose decor. Bathrooms are basic and include a shower only. The hotel is part of Missionhotel, a Christian hotel chain in operation since the early 1900s. The Stella Marris is one of the few Missionhotels that still maintains an alcohol- and smoke-free environment. ⊠ *Kogtvedvænget 3, DK–5700* 🕾 *62/21–38–91* 🖷 *62/21–41–74* ⊕ *www.stellamaris.dk* ⟟ *25 rooms, 19 with bath* ⚬ *Dining room* ⊟ *AE, DC, MC, V.*

Nightlife & the Arts

BARS & LOUNGES A diverse crowd congregates at **Banjen** (⊠ Klosterpl. 7 🕾 62/22–31–21) to hear live rock and blues. The popular blues shows, usually Friday and Saturday nights, attract all ages. Adjoining the bar is La Tumba nightclub, which throbs with dance music on the weekends. Tucked back from the street, **Barbella Nightclub** (⊠ Vesterg. 10A 🕾 62/22–47–83) is a dimly lighted bar with dark-rose walls and long wooden tables. A casual vibe and friendly staff draws a mixed-age crowd that mingles over cocktails, cheap bar grub (open-face sandwiches and meatballs), and live music in the evenings—jazz on Thursday; rock, pop, or classical on Friday and Saturday nights. On the first Sunday of the month the club has live jazz starting at around noon. (It's closed the other Sundays of the month.)

The beer flows freely at the cavernous pub **Børsen** (⊠ Gerritsg. 31 🕾 62/ 22–41–41), in a building dating from 1620. A young rowdy crowd of tourists and locals packs the place nightly. If this isn't your scene, skip the evening and stop by in the quieter early afternoon instead, when you can better enjoy your beer in the old-style pub atmosphere.

Chess (⊠ Vesterg. 7 🕾 62/22–17–16 ⊕ www.diskotek-chess.dk) is popular with a young crowd that comes for the live bands. **Crazy Daisy** (⊠ Frederiksg. 6 🕾 62/21–67–60 ⊕ www.svendborg.crazydaisy. dk) attracts a casual, over-21 crowd that dances to oldies and rock on Saturday night; a younger crowd pours in on Friday. The restaurant **Oranje** (⊠ Jessens Mole 🕾 62/22–82–92), an old sailing ship moored in the harbor, sometimes has live jazz in summer.

CAFÉS In the heart of town is the spacious **Under Uret Café** (⊠ Gerritsg. 50 🕾 62/21–83–08), playfully decorated with oversize watches on the wall—"Under Uret" means "under watch." For prime people-watching, settle in at one of the outdoor tables. The café menu includes brunch, club sandwiches, burritos, and a range of salads, from Greek to Caesar. Come nightfall, there's live music ranging from soul to rock.

Shopping

Svendborg's **city center** is bustling with shops, particularly on Gerritsgade and Møllergade, which are peppered with clothing stores, gift shops, and jewelers. For colorful, handblown glassworks head to **Glas Blæseriet** (⊠ Brog. 37A 🕾 62/22–83–73), which shares a half-timber courtyard in the center of town with the wine restaurant Vintapperiet. Glassblower Bente Sonne's lovely nature-inspired creations—in pale greens, oranges, and blues—are decorated with seashells, starfish, lizards, fish, and lobsters. You can watch Sonne blowing glass weekdays 10–3:30. On Saturday the shop is open 10–3:30, with no glass-blowing demonstration.

Kværndrup

8 *15 km (9 mi) north of Svendborg, 28 km (18 mi) south of Odense.*

Fodor'sChoice The moated Renaissance **Egeskov Slot**, one of the best-preserved island-
★ castles in Europe, presides over this town. Peaked with copper spires
and surrounded by Renaissance, baroque, English, and peasant gardens,
the castle is still a private home, though visitors can see a few of the
rooms, including the great hall, the hunting room, and the Riborg
Room, where the daughter of the house was locked up from 1599 to
1604 after giving birth to a son out of wedlock. The castle also has an
antique vehicle museum. ⊠ *Kværndrup, 15 km (9 mi) north of Svendborg* ☎ *62/27–10–16* ⊕ *www.egeskov.com* ⊡ *Castle and museum
DKr 145* ☉ *Castle May, June, Aug., and Sept., daily 10–5; July, daily
10–7; Museum June and Aug., daily 10–6; July, daily 10–8 (Wed. open
until 11 PM); May and Sept., daily 10–5.*

Tåsinge

9 *3 km (2 mi) south of Svendborg (via the Svendborg Sound Bridge), 43
km (27 mi) south of Odense.*

Tåsinge Island is known for its local 19th-century drama involving
Elvira Madigan and her married Swedish lover, Sixten Sparre. The
drama is featured in the 1967 Swedish film *Elvira Madigan*. Preferring
heavenly union to earthly separation, they shot themselves and are now
buried in the island's central Landet churchyard. Brides throw their bou-
quets on the lovers' grave.

Troense is Tåsinge's main town, and one of the country's best-preserved maritime villages, with half-timber buildings and their hand-carved
Fodor'sChoice doors. South of town is **Valdemars Slot** (Valdemars Castle), dating from
★ 1610, one of Denmark's oldest privately owned castles, now owned and
run by Caroline Fleming and her husband. You can wander through almost all of the sumptuously furnished rooms, libraries, and the candlelit
church. There's also an X-rated 19th-century cigar box not to be missed.
A yachting museum, with gleamingly restored yachts and skiffs, along
with ship models and historical dioramas, explores Denmark's extensive yachting history. There are also toy and trophy museums within the
castle. ⊠ *Slotsalleen 100, Troense* ☎ *62/22–61–06* ⊕ *www.valdemarsslot.
dk* ⊡ *DKr 110* ☉ *May, June, and Aug., daily 10–5; July, daily 10–6;
Sept., Tues.–Sun. 10–5.*

Where to Stay & Eat

$$$$ ✕ **Lodskroen.** This whitewashed, thatch-roof restaurant opened its doors
in 1774 to serve as an inn for passing sailors. For the past 30 years it
has been run by the husband-and-wife team of Hans and Kirsten Dahl-
gaard, who treat diners as if they were guests in their own home. In fact,
diners are asked to not order more than two main dishes per table because, as a placard explains, "the cook, who is also the hostess, is always alone by the kitchen range and the food is never preprepared."
The French-inspired Danish menu includes fillet of plaice stuffed with

mushrooms, peppers, and herbs. For dessert, try the figs pickled in a sweet sherry and served with whipped cream. A surcharge is applied to credit cards. ☒ *Troense Strandvej 80, Troense* ☎ *62/22–50–44* ☰ *MC, V* ☺ *Closed Mon.–Thurs. Feb., Nov., and Dec.; closed Jan. No lunch weekdays.*

¢–$$ ✕ **Bregninge Mølle.** If you've ever wondered what the inside of a wind-
Fodor'sChoice   mill looks like, this is your chance to find out. Within the Bregninge wind-
★   mill, built in 1805, circular stairs lead to this restaurant's three levels, each with 360-degree views of the surrounding sea and Tåsinge countryside. The traditional Danish menu features *frikadeller* (fried meatballs) served with rice and peas, and ægggekage. ☒ *Kirkebakken 19, Bregninge* ☎ *62/22–52–55* ☰ *MC, V* ☺ *Closed mid-Oct.–Mar.*

$ ✕🏨 **Hotel Troense.** Dating from 1908, this harborside hotel has bright, simply furnished rooms with fringed white bedcovers. The restaurant, with rose walls and a fireplace, serves a Danish menu with such dishes as salmon served with spinach topped with almonds. It also offers a couple of vegetarian dishes, including a pie stuffed with seasonal vegetables. The hotel often has discounted weekend deals that include breakfast and dinner. ☒ *Strandg. 5, DK–5700 Troense* ☎ *62/22–54–12* 🖷 *62/ 22–78–12* ⊕ *www.hoteltroense.dk* ➷ *30 rooms* ⚘ *Restaurant, bar* ☰ *AE, DC, MC, V.*

$ ✕🏨 **Valdemars Slot.** The castle's guest rooms are not enormous, but they are nicely decorated in beige, ochre, light-green, and light-blue tones. Some have a view out to the north; others look out onto the adjacent yard and palace garden. Down below, a domed restaurant is ankle-deep in pink carpet and aglow with candlelight. Fresh French and German ingredients and wild game from the castle's reserve are the menu staples. Venison with cream sauce and duck breast *à l'orange* are typical of the French-inspired cuisine. A second eatery, Æblehaven, serves inexpensive sausages and upscale fast-food. ☒ *Slotsalleen 100, DK–5700 Troense* ☎ *62/22–59–00* 🖷 *62/22–72–67* ⊕ *www.valdemarsslot.dk* ➷ *8 rooms, 1 suite* ⚘ *2 restaurants* ☰ *MC, V.*

¢   🏨 **Det Lille Hotel.** This red half-timber, thatch-roof family house–turned–small hotel has eight snug rooms (none with bath or shower) with pale green walls and flowery curtains. The well-tended back garden blooms brilliantly in summer. A breakfast of homemade bread and jam is included. You can rent a bike for around DKr 50 per day. Note that this is no-smoking hotel. ☒ *Badstuen 15, DK–5700 Troense* ☎ *62/22–53–41* 🖷 *62/22–52–41* ⊕ *www.detlillehotel.dk* ➷ *8 rooms* ⚘ *Dining room* ☰ *MC, V* ☺ *Closed Nov.–Mar.*

Shopping

For delicate handblown glass, visit **Glasmagerne** (☒ Vemmenæsvej 10, Tåsinge ☎ 62/54–14–94).

Langeland

🔟 *16 km (10 mi) southeast of Troense, 64 km (40 mi) southwest of Odense.*

Reached by a causeway bridge from Tåsinge, Langeland is the largest island of the southern archipelago, rich in relics, with smooth, tawny beaches. Bird-watching is excellent on the southern half of the island, where migratory flocks roost before setting off on their cross-Baltic journey. To the south are Ristinge and Bagenkop, two towns with good beaches; at Bagenkop you can catch the ferry to Kiel, Germany.

Sports & the Outdoors

FISHING Langeland has particularly rich waters for fishing, with cod, salmon, flounder, and gar. For package tours, boat rentals, or fishing equipment, contact **Ole Dehn** (⊠ Sønderg. 22, Tranekær ☎ 62/55–17–00).

Ærøskøbing

★ ⓫ *30 km (19 mi) south of Svendborg, 74 km (46 mi) south of Odense, plus a 1-hr ferry ride, either from Svendborg or Langeland.*

The island of Ærø, where country roads wind through fertile fields, is aptly called the Jewel of the Archipelago. About 27 km (16 mi) southeast of Søby on the island's north coast, the storybook town of Ærøskøbing is the port for ferries from Svendborg. Established as a market town in the 13th century, it did not flourish until it became a sailing center during the 1700s. Today Ærøskøbing is a bewitching tangle of cobbled streets lined with immaculately preserved half-timber houses. Stop by the red 17th-century home at the corner of Vestergade and Smedegade, considered to be one of the town's finest examples of its provincial architecture. Ærøskøbing is a bastion of small-town Denmark: every morning the whistling postman, in a red jacket and black-and-gold cap, strides the streets and delivers the mail; the friendly mayor pedals home for lunch and waves to everyone on the way.

As you wander through town, you'll notice that many of the homes display a pair of ceramic dogs on their windowsills. Traditionally, these were used by sailors' wives to signal to outsiders—and, as rumor has it, potential suitors—the whereabouts of their husbands. When the dogs were facing in, it meant that the man of the house was home, and when the dogs were facing out, that he was gone. Ironically, these ceramic dogs were brought home, usually from the Orient, by the sailors themselves, who had received them as "gifts" from prostitutes they had been with. The prostitutes gave these ceramic dogs as a cover-up, so that it appeared that they were selling souvenirs rather than sex.

Ferries provide the only access to Ærø. The ferry from Svendborg to Ærøskøbing takes 1 hour, 15 minutes. In addition, there's a 1-hour ferry from Faaborg to Søby, a town on the northwest end of the island; and a shorter one from Rudkøbing—on the island of Langeland—to Marstal, on the eastern end of Ærø.

History is recorded in miniature at the **Flaske-Peters Samling** (Bottle-Ship Collection), thanks to a former ship's cook known as Peter Bottle, who painstakingly built nearly 2,000 bottle ships in his day. The combination of his life's work and the enthusiastic letters he received from fans and disciples around the world makes for a surprisingly moving collection. ⊠ *Smedeg. 22, Ærøskøbing* ☎ *62/52–29–51* 🕮 *DKr 25* ☉ *May–Oct., daily 10–4; Nov.–Apr., Tues.–Fri. 1–3, weekends 10–noon.*

Ærø Museum houses numerous relics—including some from the Stone Age—culled from archaeological digs on the island. Also displayed are antique domestic furnishings from the homes of skippers on the island. Call ahead or check at the tourist office, because nonsummer hours can vary. ⊠ *Brog. 3–5, Ærøskøbing* ☎ *62/52–29–50* ⊕ *www.arremus.dk* 🖾 *DKr 20* ⊙ *May–mid-Oct., weekdays 10–4, weekends 11–3; mid-Oct.–Apr., weekdays 10–1.*

The two-story half-timber **Hammerichs Hus** (Hammerich's House) was once the home of sculptor Gunnar Hammerich. Today it features reconstructed period interiors of ancient Ærø homes, including antique maritime paintings, furniture, and porcelain pieces. ⊠ *Gyden 22, Ærøskøbing* ☎ *65/52–29–50* 🖾 *DKr 20* ⊙ *Mid-June–mid-Sept., weekdays noon–4.*

Where to Stay & Eat

★ ¢–$$ ✕ **Hos Grethe.** In the heart of town is this amiable restaurant, run by longtime local Grethe. The dining room, with low white ceilings and a black-and-white checkered floor, is nicknamed the *kongelogen* (the royal box) because of the royal portraits, past and present, that line the walls. Grethe is famous for her steaks, thick-cut and juicy, which come with large salads. In summer the outside terrace and beer garden overflow with day-trippers from the mainland. ⊠ *Vesterg. 39* ☎ *62/52–21–43* ⊟ *MC, V* ⊙ *Closed Oct.–May. No lunch Apr.–mid-June and mid-Aug.–Sept.*

¢–$ ✕🖾 **Det Lille Hotel.** Six large, simply furnished rooms make up the second floor of this friendly *lille* (little) hotel. Flowery curtains frame small windows that overlook the garden below. On the bottom floor are a popular restaurant and bar, both of which draw a daily crowd of regulars (reservations are essential for the restaurant). The Danish menu includes fried plaice topped with butter sauce and pork fillet with tomatoes, mushrooms, and a white-wine cream sauce. The snug bar is decorated with a ship's wheel and lanterns. ⊠ *Smedeg. 33, DK–5970* ☎ *62/52–23–00* ⊕ *www.det-lille-hotel.dk* 🖘 *6 rooms without bath* ♨ *Restaurant* ⊟ *MC, V.*

$$$ 🖾 **Hotel Ærøhus.** A half-timber building with a steep red roof, the Ærøhus looks like a rustic cottage on the outside and an old, but overly renovated, aunt's house on the inside. Hanging pots and slanted walls characterize the public areas, and pine furniture and cheerful duvets keep the guest rooms simple and bright. The garden's five cottages have small terraces. ⊠ *Vesterg. 38, DK–5970* ☎ *62/52–31–68* 🖾 *62/52–21–23* ⊕ *www.aeroehus.dk* 🖘 *67 rooms, 56 with bath* ♨ *Restaurant, bar, some pets allowed* ⊟ *V.*

¢ 🖾 **Pension Vestergade 44.** Rising over Ærøskøbing's main street are two superbly maintained patrician homes. Standing side by side, they are mirror images of each other, built by two ship captains, brothers, who wanted to raise their families in identical surroundings. One of the homes has been converted into this small hotel that has been lovingly restored by its owners, a friendly British-German couple, to recapture all of the building's former charms. A claw-foot iron stove heats up the breakfast room that overlooks a sprawling back garden with clucking chickens who lay the eggs for breakfast. White lace curtains frame the windows and an antique wooden plate rack displays blue-and-white English porcelain dishes. The beautifully appointed rooms, each with its own color scheme, have naturally sloping floors and vintage wooden towel racks laden with fluffy, bright-white towels. If you want to pedal around town, they'll lend you a bike. ⊠ *Vesterg. 44, DK 5970* ☎ *62/52–22–98* ↻ *6 rooms without bath* ⚏ *Dining room.*

Nightlife & the Arts

Of Ærøskøbing's few bars, one of the most popular is **Arrebo** (⊠ Vesterg. 4 ☎ 62/52–28–50), with yellow walls, wooden tables, and local art on the walls. On weekends it hosts live music, from blues to rock to jazz. A bell dangles at one end of the bar, and in the sailor tradition, whoever rings it must buy the whole bar a round of drinks.

Shopping

Ærøskøbing is sprinkled with a handful of craft and gift shops. Unfortunately, there are virtually no more bottle-ship makers on the island. Instead, the labor-intensive curiosities are made in Asia and modeled on original Aerø bottle-ship designs. For souvenir bottle-ships, head to **Kolorit** (⊠ Moseager 3 ☎ 62/52–25–21), a small gift shop crammed with Danish mementos.

Marstal

★ *10 km (6 mi) southeast of Ærøskøbing, 40 km (25 mi) south of Svendborg, 84 km (52 mi) south of Odense. From Svendborg it's a 1-hr ferry ride to Ærøskøbing; from Langeland it's a 45-min ferry ride to Marstal.*

Southeast of Ærøskøbing, past a lush landscape of green and yellow hills rolling toward the sea, is the sprightly shipping town of Marstal. From its early fishing days in the 1500s to its impressive rise into a formidable shipping port in the 1700s, Marstal's lifeblood has always been the surrounding sea. At its seafaring height, in the late 1800s, Marstal had a fleet of 300 ships. During this heady time, the Marstal government couldn't expand the harbor fast enough to accommodate the growing fleet, so Marstal's seamen took it upon themselves to extend their port. Working together in the winter season, they built the 1-km (½-mi) stone pier—still in use today—by rolling rocks from the fields, along the ice, and onto the harbor. They began in 1835 and completed the pier in 1841.

Today Marstal is home port to 50 vessels, from tall-masted schooners to massive trawlers. Much of the town's activity—and its cobbled streets—radiates from the bustling port. A nautical school, first established in the 1800s, is still going strong, with more than 150 students. In a nod to its seafaring heritage, the Marstal harbor is one of the few places in the world still constructing wooden ships.

Marstal's winding streets are dotted with well-preserved skippers' homes. **Maren Minors Hjem** (Maren Minor's Home) was once the genteel abode of successful Marstal seaman Rasmus Minor, who eventually settled in the United States. The house has been carefully restored inside and out to look just as it did in the 1700s, including vintage art and furniture. Opening hours vary from year to year, so check with the tourist office. ✉ *Teglg. 9* ☎ *62/53–24–25* 🎟 *Free* ☉ *June–Aug., Tues.–Sun. 11–3.*

Spread out over three buildings, the sprawling **Marstal Søfartsmuseum** (Marstal Maritime Museum) offers a rich and fascinating account of Marstal's formidable shipping days. Thirty-five showrooms are jam-packed with maritime memorabilia, including more than 200 ship models, 100 bottle ships, navigation instruments, and a collection of maritime paintings by artist Carl Rasmussen. He was born in Ærøskøbing and made his name painting Greenland sea- and landscapes. Wandering the museum is like exploring a massive ship: step aboard large-scale decks and hulls and command the gleaming ship's wheels like a Marstal captain. Mind your head as you climb up and down the steep ship stairs that connect many of the rooms. "Back on land," you can duck into the low-ceiling parlors of a skipper's house, meticulously reproduced with period furnishings. Longtime museum director and Marstal historian Erik B. Kromann is a font of maritime information, and will enthusiastically take you on a tour of the museum if you ask. The museum shop is bursting with nifty gifts, including key chains made from maritime rope knots. ✉ *Prinsensg. 1* ☎ *62/53–23–31* ⊕ *www.marmus.dk* 🎟 *DKr 40* ☉ *July, daily 9–8; June and Aug., daily 9–5; May and Sept., daily 10–4; Oct.–Apr., Tues.–Fri. 10–4, Sat. 11–3.*

Where to Stay & Eat

¢ ✕🏨 **Marstal.** Mere paces from the waterfront is this homey locals' favorite, with wooden ceilings, dim lighting, and a ship's wheel on the wall. The homestyle Danish dishes include minced steak with peas, potatoes, and béarnaise sauce, and smoked salmon served with asparagus and scrambled eggs. Another favorite is mussels and bacon on toast. The cozy bar draws a friendly pre- and post-dinner crowd of dockworkers. Above the restaurant are eight very basic rooms, none with bath, and two with partial views of the harbor. ✉ *Dronningestr. 1A, DK–5960* ☎ *62/53–13–52* ⊕ *www.hotelmarstal.dk* 🛏 *8 rooms without bath* ♻ *Restaurant, bar* 🚭 *MC, V* ☉ *Closed Sept.–May.*

$ 🏨 **Ærø Strand.** On the outskirts of Marstal lies this holiday hotel that caters to the island's summer tourists. Blond wood and dark-blue tones adorn the comfortable rooms. In the center of the hotel are a heart-shape pool and, for the after-hours crowd, a popular nightclub disco. ✉ *Egehovedvej 4, DK–5960* ☎ *62/53–33–20* 🖷 *62/53–31–50* ⊕ *www.hotel-aeroestrand.dk* 🛏 *100 rooms, 20 suites* ♻ *Restaurant, tennis court, indoor pool, gym, sauna, nightclub* 🚭 *AE, DC, MC, V.*

Nightlife & the Arts

Marstal's night scene is sedate, but when locals want a beer they head to the informal **Café Victor** (✉ Kirkestr. 15 ☎ 62/53–28–01), with its yellow walls and a brass-lined bar. Here you can also tuck into simple Danish dishes, such as fillet of sole with french fries.

Shopping

The maritime paintings of Marstal artist Rita Lund are popular throughout the island, gracing the walls of several restaurants and decorating the sunny sitting rooms of the ferries that shuttle between Svendborg and Ærø. For a further look, visit Rita Lund's **Galleri Humlehave** (✉ Skoleg. 1 ☎ 62/53–21–73) which, appropriately enough, is near the Marstal harbor. Her extensive collection includes paintings of crashing waves, ships at sea, and Ærø during the four seasons.

Funen & the Central Islands A to Z

BIKE TRAVEL

With level terrain and short distances, Funen and the Central Islands are perfect for cycling. A bike trip around the circumference of the main island, stopping at the series of delightful port towns that ring Funen like a string of pearls, is a wonderful way of spending a few days. The Odense tourist office has a helpful map of cycle routes in and around Odense. You can rent bikes through City Cykler in Odense or at several hotels around the islands. Contact Fyntour for longer cycling tour packages that include bike rental, hotel accommodations, and a half-board (breakfast and one meal) meal plan.

🗾 **City Cykler** ✉ Vesterbro 27, Odense ☎ 66/12–97–93 ⊕ www.citycykler.dk. **Fyntour** ✉ Svendborgvej 83–85, DK-5260 Odense ☎ 66/13–13–37 🖨 66/13–13–38 ⊕ www.fyntour.dk.

BUS TRAVEL

Buses are one of the main public-transportation options in the area. Timetables are posted at all bus stops and central stations. Passengers buy tickets on board and pay according to the distance traveled. If you plan on traveling extensively by bus, ask at any bus station about a 24-hour bus pass, which cuts costs considerably. Contact Fynbus for more information about routes between cities. Odense Bytrafik runs the bus system within Odense.

🗾 **Fynbus** ✉ Odense Bus Station ☎ 63/11–22–33 🖨 63/11–22–99. **Odense Bytrafik** (Odense City Transport) ☎ 65/51–29–29 🖨 66/19–40–27.

CAR TRAVEL

From Copenhagen, take the E20 west to Halsskov, near Korsør, and drive onto the Great Belt bridge, which costs about DKr 250 per car. You'll arrive near Nyborg, which is 30 minutes from either Odense or Svendborg.

The highways of Funen are excellent, and small roads meander beautifully on two lanes through the countryside. A trip around the circumference of the island can be done in a day, but stopping for a night or two at one of the enchanting port towns can be fun, and offers the chance to meet some of the locals. Traffic is light, except during the height of summer in highly populated beach areas.

EMERGENCIES

For fire, police, or ambulance anywhere in Denmark, dial 112. Lægevagten is the service for house calls, but will also dispatch an ambulance in case of emergencies. Trained phone personnel are generally able to judge whether a house call would be sufficient. The doctor's visits are made according to a priority list, with serious illnesses and sick children at the top of the list. Falck is the emergency road service, for towing vehicles in trouble or in case of accidents.

🚺 **Falck** 🖀 70/10-20-30 ⊕ www.falck.dk. **Lægevagten** (Emergency Doctor) 🖀 65/90-60-10 4 PM-7 AM. **Odense University Hospital** ✉ Søndre Blvd. 29, Odense 🖀 66/11-33-33. **Ørnen Apoteket** ✉ Vesterg. 80, Odense 🖀 66/12-29-70.

TOURS

Few towns offer organized tours, but check the local tourist offices for step-by-step walking brochures. The Hans Christian Andersen Tours are full-day tours to Odense that depart from Copenhagen's Rådhus Pladsen. (Six of 11 hours are spent in transit.) Call ahead because departure days and times may vary. The two-hour Odense tour departs from the local tourist office. Contact Fyntour or Odense Tourist Office for details about prices and times of tours. Most itineraries include the exteriors of the Hans Christian Andersen sites and the cathedral and the guides are generally more than willing to answer questions about the area or Denmark as a whole. Odense Tourist Office also offers one-hour tours of the Italian Gothic Odense City Hall. Inside is a long memorial wall commemorating famous Funen citizens. The local calendar of events often presents interesting activities at the city's sites, so it would be wise to call one of the tourist offices to inquire about any events.

🚺**Fyntour** ✉ Svendborgvej 83-85, Odense 🖀 66/13-13-37 ⊕ www.fyntour.dk. **Odense Tourist Office** ✉ Vesterg. 2, Odense 🖀 66/12-75-20 ⊕ www.odenseturist.dk.

TRAIN TRAVEL

Direct trains from Copenhagen's main station depart for the 90-minute trip to Odense's train station about hourly from 5 AM to 10:30 PM every day. The Odense station is central, close to hotels and sites. Large towns in the region are served by intercity trains. The Nyborg–Odense–Middelfart and the Odense–Svendborg routes are among the two most important. You can take the train to Odense direct from Copenhagen Airport.

RESERVATIONS A reservation, which is required during rush hour, costs an additional DKr 20.

🚺 **DSB Train Booking and Information** 🖀 70/13-14-15 ⊕ www.dsb.dk.

VISITOR INFORMATION

For central Odense, the Odense Eventyrpas (Adventure Pass), available at the tourism office and the train station, affords admission to sites and museums and free city bus and train transport. The cost for a 48-hour pass is DKr 150; for a 24-hour pass, DKr 110.

🚺 **Assens Touristbureau** ✉ Tobaksgaarden 7, DK-5610 Assens 🖀 64/71-20-31 🖷 64/71-49-39 ⊕ www.visit-vestfyn.dk. **Egeskov Touristbureau** ✉ Egeskov 1, DK-5772 Kværndrup 🖀 62/27-10-46 🖷 62/27-10-48. **Faaborg Touristbureau** ✉ Banegårdspl. 2A, DK-5600 Faaborg 🖀 62/61-07-07 🖷 62/61-33-37 ⊕ www.visitfaaborg.dk. **Fyntour** ✉ Sivmosevænget 4, DK-5260 Odense 🖀 66/13-13-37 ⊕ www.fyntour.dk. **Kerteminde Touristbureau** ✉ Strandg. 1B, DK-5300 Kerteminde 🖀 65/32-11-21 🖷 65/32-18-17 ⊕ www.kerteminde-turist.dk. **Langeland Touristforeningen** ✉ Torvet 5, DK-5900 Rundkøbing 🖀 62/51-35-05 🖷 62/51-43-35 ⊕ www.langeland.dk. **Marstal Touristbureau** ✉ Havneg. 5, DK-5960 Marstal 🖀 62/52-13-00 🖷 62/53-25-17 ⊕ www.arre.dk. **Nyborg Touristbureau** ✉ Torvet 9, DK-5800 Nyborg 🖀 65/31-02-80 🖷 65/31-03-80 ⊕ www.nyborgturist.dk. **Odense Touristbureau** ✉ Vesterg. 2, DK-5000 Odense 🖀 66/12-75-20 🖷 66/12-75-86

JUTLAND

Jutland (Jylland), Denmark's western peninsula, is the only part of the country naturally connected to mainland Europe; it southern boundry is the frontier with Germany. In contrast to the smooth, postcard-perfect land of Funen and Zealand, the Ice Age–chiseled peninsula is bisected at the north by the craggy Limfjord and spiked below by the Danish "mountains." Himmelbjerget, the zenith of this modest range, peaks at 438 feet. Farther south, the Yding Skovhøj plateau rises 568 feet—modest hills just about anywhere else. The windswept landscapes trace the west coast northward to Skagen, a luminous, dune-covered point. To the east, facing Funen, Jutland is cut by deep fjords rimmed with forests. The center is dotted with castles, parklands, and the famed Legoland. Denmark's oldest and youngest towns, Ribe and Esbjerg, lie in southwest Jutland. In Ribe's medieval town center is the country's earliest church; modern Esjberg, perched on the coast, is the departure point for ferries to nearby Fanø, and island of windswept beaches and traditional villages. Århus and Aalborg, respectively Denmark's second- and fourth-largest cities, face east and have nightlife and sights to rival Copenhagen's. Nearly three times the size of the rest of Denmark, with long distances between towns, the peninsula of Jutland can easily take several days, even weeks, to explore. If you are pressed for time, concentrate on a single tour or a couple of cities, Delightful as they are, the islands are suitable only for those with plenty of time, as many require an overnight stay.

Kolding

❶ *71 km (44 mi) northwest of Odense (via the Little Belt Bridge), 190 km (119 mi) west of Copenhagen.*

Kolding is an interesting world city that screams "design." It's the home of the Danish School of Art & Design, as important to this country as the Parsons School of Design is to the United States, or the Ontario College of Art & Design is to Canada. It's also a link between other Scandinavian cities (Malmö, Sweden, is 250 km [155 mi] away and Hamburg, Germany, is only 240 km [150 mi] away). The city is home to 63,000 residents and is the sixth-largest town in Denmark. It is near the country's second-largest international airport at Billund.

Indeed, Kolding is a place to begin any adventure in Jutland, whether you choose to travel southward on the peninsula or north. The city itself is a pleasing blend of old and new, with a historical center of cobbled streets and brightly painted half-timber houses that give way to industrial suburbs. But what seems to attract many visitors is the Trapholt Museum of modern Danish art, including furniture design and changing exhibits by international artists. Complementing this museum is, oddly, the Koldinghus, an imposing stone structure from the Middle Ages that overlooks the city, and which itself won a couple of international design awards in the 20th century.

Koldinghus, a massive structure that was once a fortress, then a royal residence in the Middle Ages (and the last royal castle in Jutland), is today a historical museum. The wings of the castle are devoted to Romanesque and Gothic church art and sculpture, military history, furniture, ceramics, and silversmithing from 1550 to the present. The building has been used by members of the royal family for exclusive special events. Concerts take place every Thursday night. There is also a popular café, and a gift shop. ⊠ *Rådhusstr.* ☎ *76/33–81–00* ⊕ *www.koldinghus.dk* ▢ *DKr 50* ⊙ *Daily 10–5.*

Fodor'sChoice ★ Just east of town is the **Trapholt Museum for Moderne Kunst** (Trapholt Museum of Modern Art), one of Denmark's largest—and most highly acclaimed—modern-art museums outside Copenhagen. Rising over the banks of the Kolding Fjord, this sprawling white complex has been artfully incorporated into its natural surroundings, affording lovely views of the fjord and parkland from its floor-to-ceiling windows. An extensive collection of 20th-century Danish paintings is displayed in the light-filled galleries; it includes works by Anna Ancher, Ejler Bille, Egill Jakobsen, J. A. Jerichau, Jais Nielsen, Richard Mortensen, Aksel Jørgensen, and Franciska Clausen. A true highlight is the Danish Furniture Museum, inaugurated in 1996, and housed in a specially designed annex that is accessed via a circular ramp topped by a skylight. The superbly displayed collection includes the largest assemblage of Danish-designed chairs in the world, offering a unique historical overview of the birth and popularization of Danish furniture design. There are numerous furnishings by prolific designer Hans J. Wegner, including a rounded, blond-wood chair called "The Chair." The museum keeps its furniture storage room open to the public, so you can peruse the entire collection even when it's not officially on display. The Danish ceramics collection, one of the largest in Denmark, is also well worth a look, featuring works by Thorvald Bindesbøll and one-of-a-kind ceramics by Axel Salto, whose pieces often resemble living organisms. Famous designer Arne Jacobsen's summer cottage was moved to Trapholt and opened on its grounds in the summer of 2005, which garnered much interest from Danes and design aficionados. Café Trapholt serves coffee, beverages, and light meals, including a delicious luncheon plate, Frokosttallerken, for DKr 150. The gift shop also offers nice local and international art and design-related gifts. ⊠ *Æblehaven 23* ☎ *76/30–05–30* ⊕ *www.trapholt.dk* ▢ *DKr 50* ⊙ *Daily 10–5.*

Where to Stay & Eat

★ **$$$$** ✕ **Admiralen.** Across from the harbor is this elegant seafood restaurant, with pale yellow tablecloths, white walls, and blue-suede chairs. It serves excellent fish dishes, including grilled salmon with spinach and steamed lemon sole with scallops. Pigeon with mushrooms, apples, and a basil gravy is another option. ⊠ *Toldbodeg. 14* ☎ *75/52–04–21* ⊕ *www.admiralen.dk* ▭ *AE, DC, MC, V* ⊙ *Closed Sun.*

$$$ ✕▫ **Radisson SAS Hotel Koldingfjord.** This impressive neoclassical hotel has mahogany floors and pyramid skylights. The rooms vary in size (with 39 in a separate annex), but all have pale-wood furnishings and bright prints. The motto of the excellent French-Danish restaurant is "good

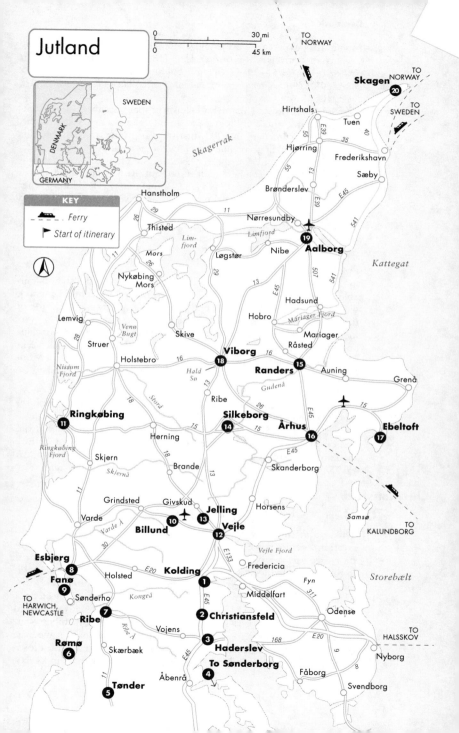

food is art"; expect well-presented seafood dishes, as well as intriguing vegetarian options. ⊠ *Fjordvej 154, DK–6000 Strandhuse* ☎ *75/51–00–00* 🖷 *75/51–00–51* ⊕ *www.koldingfjord.dk* ⤳ *134 rooms, 9 suites* ⚭ *Restaurant, tennis court, indoor pool, sauna, billiards, bar* ▤ *AE, DC, MC, V.*

★ **$$** ✕🖾 **Saxildhus Hotel.** This oh-so-Danish property, with gables, black-painted beams, and clunky antiques in its hallways and guest rooms, celebrated its centenary in 2005. Just steps from the train station, this has long been Kolding's premier hotel. Its rooms come in a range of styles, some with mahogany four-poster beds and others with more contemporary furnishings. The basement restaurant, Restaurant Saxen, serves top-notch Danish dishes, with live music on Sunday. The Hotel's other restaurant, Latin, serves breakfast and dinner (with surprisingly good pizzas, one being ample for two people). ⊠ *Jernbaneg. 39, Banegårdspl., DK–6000* ☎ *75/52–12–00* 🖷 *75/53–53–10* ⊕ *www.saxildhus.dk* ⤳ *80 rooms, 7 suites* ⚭ *Restaurant, bar, Wi-Fi, some pets allowed, no-smoking rooms* ▤ *AE, DC, MC, V.*

Nightlife & the Arts

In the heart of town, on Lilletorv (Little Square), is the stylish and amiable **Den Blå Café** (⊠ Slotsg. 4 ☎ 75/50–65–12 ⊕ www.denblaacafe.dk), with British and American rock and blues music playing to a backdrop of film posters. In the afternoons, locals sidle up to the picture windows overlooking the square and enjoy coffee and warm baguette sandwiches or chips and guacamole. In the evening, beer and cocktails flow freely, and on weekends there's live jazz on the terrace. The café is open until midnight Monday through Wednesday and until 2 AM Thursday through Saturday.

Shopping

Kolding's town center is a jumble of walking streets dotted with clothing and jewelry stores and ice-cream shops. The two-story **Bahne** (⊠ Sønderg. 9 ☎ 75/50–56–22) sells all the big names in Danish design, from Stelton and Georg Jensen tableware to functional wooden furniture made by the Danish design firm Trip Trap. **Furiosa** (⊠ Blæsbjergg. 2A ☎ 75/50–88–87) is the best store in Kolding for interior design.

Christiansfeld

❷ *15 km (9 mi) south of Kolding.*

This unique small town (population: 800) is rural Denmark at its quietest. It deserves more visitors, as its history is unusual and the inhabitants are true survivors, but as it stands, you might be the only tourist in town should you choose to visit. It was founded in 1773 as a Moravian (Brødremenigheden in Danish) community—an evangelical Christian sect from what is now the Czech Republic that can be traced back to the early 1400s. The Moravian people were almost totally destroyed in the religious wars of 1618 to 1648, and the remaining members scattered; over a century later, King Christian VII of Denmark signed the concession that gave the Moravian Church permission to establish a town in what is now South Jutland. The agreement was generous in its day, as although Denmark was officially Lutheran, the Moravians were al-lowed free religious practice, tax concessions, freedom from customs du-ties, their own court, no military service, and cash to help with building projects. Today there are only 385 Moravians in all of Denmark.

A town plan was drawn up along the same lines as Moravian towns in other countries. There would be two parallel streets united by a square, the **Church Square,** around which the most important buildings would be constructed. Today, the Church Square is identical to the way it was built in 1773, lined with linden trees; the straight, austere streets with the broad homes are also the same. The church itself, which has the largest church room without supporting columns in Denmark, has space for approximately 1,000 people, and is striking in its simplicity. The large room is completely white, without an altar, baptismal font, or pictures. The only decorations are the old hand-forged chandeliers, dating from 1776. They are still lowered by rope, and candles are lighted when needed. Besides Sunday service, the church is used for choir and band recitals. ⊠ *Lindeg. at Lysestøbervej* 🖾 *Free* ⊙ *June–Sept., daily 10–1.*

God's Acre, or the Moravian cemetery, is also worth noting. It is in the town's northeastern corner, and the Sisters of the congregation are buried on one side; the Brethren on the other. All grave markers are alike, as a symbol that all members are alike in death. All the graves have been preserved since 1773, and the site is characterized by simplicity and order.

Christiansfeld is also famous in Europe and in culinary circles world-wide for being the home of a very tasty cinnamon-and-honey cake (*hon-ningkager*), first introduced in 1783. The bakery, **Brødremenighedens Bageri,** sells these treats that the Danish royal family orders for its daily teatime. ⊠ *Lindeg. 36* ☎ *74/56–13–43* ⊙ *Weekdays 6 AM–5:30 PM, week-ends 6 AM–4 PM.*

Where to Stay

$–$$$ 🖾 **Tyrstrup Kro.** This inn on the outskirts of Christiansfeld is a rural oasis and is as Danish as you can get. The inn was built in 1655, and much has been done to preserve the original appearance of the building. Rooms are light and airy, with faux 17th-century furnishings and views of the farmlands. The large whirlpool tubs are a welcome surprise in all rooms. The dining room is excellent, serving traditionally Danish and nouvelle cuisine. ⊠ *Tyrstrup Vestervej 6, DK–6070* ☎ *74/56–12–42* 🖨 *74/56–19–70* ⊕ *www.tyrstrupkro.dk* 🗪 *12 rooms, 8 suites* ⚙ *Restau-rant, meeting rooms* ▭ *MC, V* ⦿ *BP.*

¢–$ 🖾 **Brødremenighedens Hotel.** A marble slate outside this hotel lists when every Danish king since 1773 (the year it opened) has visited. Inside, photos and souvenirs from the monarchy abound. The hotel began a slow, extensive renovation in 2005, and once the costly project is com-pleted the place should be a small showpiece. (It's open during renova-tions.) This is a comfortable, clean, and quirky spot. Don't expect five-star service or many in-room amenities, but do expect typical Dan-ish hospitality. The fair-size rooms are comfortable and overlook the main street. ⊠ *Corner of Lindeg. and Kongensg.* ☎ *74/56–17–10* 🗪 *10 rooms* ⚙ *Restaurant, bar* ▭ *No credit cards.*

Haderslev

 27 km (17 mi) south of Kolding, 63 km (39 mi) northeast of Tonder.

This small market city is off the beaten track from the run-of-the-mill tourism centers of the region and therefore doesn't suffer from overwhelming summer crowds. Haderslev would make a good base of operations if you plan on meandering throughout the fjord area, and it has its own attractions as well.

Like many places in this country, Haderslev is old, having been given the rights to become a market town in 1292. In 1525 Duke Christian (later to be King Christian III) introduced the teachings of Martin Luther to Haderslev. As it was the first place in Scandinavia where this happened, the city was called the "Wittenberg of the North" (Wittenberg was the famous university where Luther studied, as did Shakespeare's Hamlet).

Haderslev cathedral, **Our Lady's Church,** became a cathedral in 1920, after being rebuilt several times since the 13th century. The building's beautiful Gothic windows and interiors are worth a visit, and downstairs, behind the altar, are vestments worn by church ministers designed by the current Queen of Denmark, Margrethe. They are on display in glass cases. The steeple towers of the cathedral can be seen far above the roofs in the city. A touching tradition happens every Friday at noon. This is when a music ensemble parades through the town to honor the members of the Haderslev Regiment who were killed in World War II. The parade begins at the barracks at 11:45 and arrives at the cathedral at noon. In the memorial chapel in the cathedral, a page is turned in the regiment's memorial book, and then the parade returns to the barracks.

Walks around the old town are arranged daily from June to August. There are many beautiful gabled homes in the heart of the city from the 16th and 17th centuries that have been preserved, and they continue to be occupied. Contact the Haderslev Tourist Office for times.

The most notable museum in Haderslev, the **Ehlers Collection,** began as a private collection of Danish pottery, and has grown to be the best exhibition of ceramics from the Middle Ages to around 1940 in northern Europe. It's in a house that in itself is noteworthy: it was built in 1557 by a craftsman who was working for Duke Hans the Older, who was commissioning a new castle east of town. In 1976, the house underwent a restoration, and several rooms were found to have painted murals on panels that had been hidden behind 11 layers of wallpaper and 6 layers of paint for 300 years. ⊠ *Slotsg. 20* ☎ *74/53–08–58* ☎ *Free* ☉ *Closed Mon.*

A popular attraction is a ride on the **paddle steamer** *Helene,* with round-trip departures Tuesday through Sunday from May to September. The leisurely sail takes you from Haderslev (right next to the tourist office) to the island of Åro and to Årosund. You can get off in either place, and then take a bus back to the boat. The whole sojourn will occupy four hours of your day, but it's a good way to see the area. Timetables and tickets are available at the Haderslev Tourist Office.

Sønderborg

❹ *90 km south of Kolding, 75 km south of Christiansfeld.*

This town of 30,000 is the center of what is marketed as a "holiday region" of the country—indeed, there are four castles in this area alone. It's deep in southeast Jutland, and has its own airport and train and bus stations. It's the obvious base for a visit to the island of Als, Denmark's seventh largest, which is connected by two bridges from Sønderborg (and a car ferry just north of the town). Southern Jutland was part of Germany between 1864 and 1920, and because of this the art nouveau movement flourished in Sønderborg, whereas in other parts of Denmark the preference was for a traditional Arts and Crafts style. Sønderborg is a wonderful spot for a walking tour, admiring the buildings constructed between 1905 and 1915. A brochure explaining the route is available from the local tourist office.

The **Museum at Sønderborg Castle** is well worth a look, as it offers a wonderful array of artifacts outlining southern Jutland's history and exhibitions on the building's history itself. The castle has the most intact royal chapel preserved from the time of Reformation in Europe. To enjoy the castle in a unique way, take part in the guided Ghost-walking Tours, which take place on Monday and Wednesday nights at 10 PM from June 1 to August 29. Admission is DKr 65 and tickets can be purchased at the Sønderborg Turistbureau. ⊠ *Sønderbro 1* 🕾 *74/42-25-39* ⊕ *www.sonderborgslot.dk* 🖾 *Dkr 30* ۞ *May–Sept., daily 10–5; Oct.–Mar., weekdays 1–4.*

Gråsten Palace Gardens, a summer home of the royal family, isn't quite as sumptuous as you might expect, but it is an enjoyable place for a walk—when the royals aren't in residence. Originally used as the late Queen Mother Ingrid's home between 1935 and her death in 2000, the gardens are a testament to her passion for horticulture and her love for flowers and plants. As far as interiors go, only the chapel of the palace is open to the public; details on opening times (which vary) are available from the local tourist office. ⊠ *Banegården, Kongevej 71, Gråsten* 🕾 *74/65-09-55* ⊕ *www.visitflensborgfjord.com* 🖾 *Free* ۞ *Varies by season; call tourist office for updates.*

Most non-Danes may not be aware of Danfoss, but it has been Denmark's industrial leader in heating and cooling Scandinavian homes and businesses for decades. It's also the benefactor of **Danfoss Universe,** which opened in May 2005, next to the headquarters. Danfoss Universe is a 10-acre park with more than 150 activities for children—and curious adults. The park is built around the Blue Cube, a 75-foot-high pavilion from EXPO 2000 in Hannover, Germany. The Blue Cube is reminiscent of a giant ice cube, especially since water continuously trickles down the cube's outside walls. Inside the cube, there are exhibits on nature's more violent and awe-inspiring phenomena (volcanoes and glaciers, for example). ⊠ *Mads Patent Vej 1, Nordborg, Als* 🕾 *74/88-74-88* ⊕ *www. danfossuniverse.com* 🖾 *DKr 110* ۞ *May–Oct., daily 10–6 (July until 8 PM.*

Where to Stay & Eat

$$$–$$$$ ✕ **Pascal Vinothek & Brasserie.** Black leather chairs are arranged in front of white walls hung with large pop art paintings at this stylish restaurant and wine bar in downtown Søderborg. At dinner you'll get good-size portions of steak, fish, and shellfish, all local and very fresh. ⊠ *Rådhustorvet 5, Sønderborg* ☎ *74/42–38–80* ⊟ *DC, MC, V.*

★ **$$–$$$$** ✕ **Skipperkroen Als.** This restaurant may be the second-most-obvious reason to make a stop in Augustenborg, after seeing the palace. It's on the marina, and you can always stop by for coffee and cake or an icy Danish beer on the terrace if you don't want to commit to a whole meal. The dining room is at once elegant and cozy, with crisp white linens blending in with the modern Danish decor. Pricey prix-fixe meals are featured at dinner (venison in a red currant sauce is a good choice), but you can get a traditional Danish luncheon platter of herring, smoked salmon, prawns, pâté, and cheese, for a very reasonable DKr 125. ⊠ *Langdel 6D, Augustenborg* ☎ *74/47–10–84* ⊟ *AE, DC, MC, V* ☺ *Closed Jan.*

$–$$ ▥ **Ballebro Færgekro.** This inn, overlooking the calm waters of the Als fjord, seems like a location for an Ingmar Bergman film. Mists hover over the water; a gingerbread-style house is surrounded by verdant, broad lawns. The country-inspired guest rooms are very comfortable, with large bathrooms and quality amenities. A traditional Danish breakfast of cold cuts, cheeses, fresh breads, and jellies is served at your table on a three-tiered tray, which is a nice change from the more standard buffets found elsewhere. This inn is a perfect spot for a romantic getaway—and it's steps from the car ferry that takes you on a five-minute ride to Als. ⊠ *Færgevej 5, Blans, Sønderborg, DK–6400* ☎ *74/46–13–03* ⊠ *74/46–13–09* ⊕ *www.ballebro.dk* ↘ *10 rooms, 1 suite* ♦ *Restaurant* ⊟ *AE, DC, MC, V* ⟨○⟩ *BP.*

$ ▥ **Baltic Hotel.** This beautifully restored hotel from the 1800s is in the village of Høruphav, which is a 15-minute drive from Sønderborg. The guest rooms are plush, and most have an easterly ocean view. Meals are well worth having at the hotel's restaurant, with two and three courses. Weekend packages are available in summer. ⊠ *Havbo 29, Sydals, DK–6470* ☎ *74/41–52–00* ⊠ *74/41–53–33* ⊕ *www.hotel-baltic.dk* ↘ *8 rooms, 2 suites* ♦ *Restaurant, bar* ⊟ *DC, MC, V* ⟨○⟩ *BP.*

Tønder

❺ *105 km (66 mi) southwest of Kolding, 195 km (122 mi) southwest of Århus.*

Just 4 km (2½ mi) north of the German border, the historic town of Tønder has long been closely allied with its southern neighbor. In 1864 Tønder was annexed by Germany. After Germany's defeat in World War I, plebiscites were held in the area, and Tønder chose to become reunited with Denmark. Nevertheless, Tønder is still home to a small but important German community, with a German kindergarten, school, gymnasium, newspaper, and library.

The town is surrounded by low-lying marshes, and has been subject to major floods throughout its history. To combat the floods, a series of protective dikes was built in the 16th century. The result was double-edged:

though Tønder was now safe from the sea, it also lost its natural harbor and waterways and, most importantly, its shipping industry. So, the town turned its sights inward, to the Tønder women's sewing rooms, and built itself up as the "lace capital of the world." In the 18th century, lace making became Tønder's most lucrative export. Throughout town are the stately gated homes once owned by successful lace merchants.

Tønder comes vibrantly alive in the last week of August for the **Tønder Folk Music Festival** (☎ 74/72–46–10 ⊕ www.tf.dk), which has been drawing folk music lovers from all over the world since 1974. Big names and local acts perform everything from blues, zydeco, and gospel to the more traditional Irish, Scottish, and American folk tunes. Reserve hotel rooms well in advance, as the town fills up to capacity during this time. Founded in 1923, the **Tønder Museum** has amassed an impressive collection of South Jutland arts and crafts. The extensive lace exhibit includes delicate doilies and baptismal gowns. In another room, intricate silverware is displayed alongside antique furnishings. A highlight is the collection of hand-painted glazed Dutch tiles brought back by sailors during the 17th and 18th centuries. The tiles served as ballast for the ships, and were then used to decorate their homes. Tønder's old water tower, connected to the museum via a glass corridor, houses the world's largest collection of chairs designed by Tønder native Hans J. Wegner, one of Denmark's best-known furniture designers. The 130-foot tower with eight sun-drenched decks is the ideal showroom for Wegner's chairs and furnishings, which range from a rope and ash-wood circle chair to his Y-chair, made of beech wood with a plaited paper yarn seat. The skylit top deck, above which sits the old water-tower lantern, displays a massive circular table designed by Wegner's daughter. Around the table sit 25 of Wegner's most popular chair, a rounded blond-wood design that he called simply "The Chair," which brought Wegner worldwide recognition, particularly in the United States, after both Kennedy and Nixon each sat in one during a television interview. Settle into one and enjoy the 360-degree views of Tønder's red rooftops and surrounding green marshland that unfold to the sea. If you're in the market for some Tønder lace, you can buy some in the small museum store. ⊠ *Kongevej 51* ☎ *74/72–89–89* ⊕ *www.tondermuseum.dk* ⊡ *DKr 20* ⊙ *June–Aug., daily 10–5; Sept.–May, Tues.–Sun. 10–5.*

Lace lovers will be richly rewarded at the **Drøhses Hus,** a well-preserved 1672 town house with exhibits of lace and lace making. In summer, lace makers often work their trade inside the house. ⊠ *Storeg. 14* ☎ *74/72–49–90* ⊡ *DKr 20* ⊙ *Apr.–Dec., weekdays 10–5, Sat. 10–1.*

Where to Stay & Eat

$$$–$$$$ ✕▥ **Schackenborg Slotskro.** Stay at this inn, and you can say that while
Fodor's Choice in Denmark, you were a guest of the Danish royal family. This elegant
★ hotel is the official royal inn of Schackenborg Castle, the next-door residence of Prince Joachim. The prince's former wife, Princess Alexandra, personally decorated the rooms in rich blues, greens, and reds; each has a large, sparkling bathroom and views of the castle. Suites have work areas, living rooms, and hot tubs. The inn's highly acclaimed restaurant

serves superb Danish-French cuisine, including beef tournedos, marsh-land lamb, and an eel appetizer with new potatoes. It's possible in summer to sit outside in the picturesque garden, admiring the Alexandra roses. The castle and inn are 4 km (2½ mi) west of Tønder, in the small village of Møgeltønder. ⊠ *Slotsg. 42, DK–6270 Møgeltønder* ☎ *74/73–83–83* 🖷 *74/73–83–11* ⊕ *www.slotskro.dk* ↩ *25 rooms, 2 suites* ♨ *Restaurant, bar, some pets allowed, no-smoking rooms* ⊟ *AE, DC, MC, V.*

Sports & the Outdoors
Biking trails crisscross Tønder's lush and flat countryside. The tourist office has helpful cycling maps that detail the bike routes in the area. You can rent bikes at **Top Cycler** (⊠ Jernbaneg. 1C ☎ 74/72–18–81).

Shopping
Since 1671 **Det Gamle Apotek** (The Old Pharmacy; ⊠ Østerg. 1 ☎ 74/72–51–11) has dispensed medicine to Tønder's townspeople. In 1989 the pharmacy was converted into a Danish gift and crafts center, but the entire building, both inside and out, was left intact. The beautifully carved front entranceway opens onto a vintage interior lined with pharmaceutical artifacts and medicine jars. Craft items for sale include antique stationery and pens, and handmade candles, glassware, and ceramics. From March to September the cellar bursts with Danish Christmas items, from tree decorations and festive paper cutouts to elves and angels. This is a big import-export company and many items from here are found in Copenhagen stores.

Rømø

❻ *34 km (21 mi) northwest of Tønder, 30 km (19 mi) southwest of Ribe.*

The lush island of Rømø has one of Denmark's widest beaches, which unfurls along the island's sunny western coast and has protected areas for windsurfers, horseback riders, nudists, and dune-buggy riders alike—space for everyone, it seems. Rømø has just 850 permanent residents, but masses of vacationing German and Danish families increase this number tenfold in summer. Indeed, it's a haven for campers, cyclists, and budget vacationers. A causeway crosses green fields and marshy wetlands to connect Rømø to the mainland. Many birds live here, feeding off the seaweed and shellfish washed up by the tides. Summerhouses dot the island; most of Rømø's services and accommodations are in and around the village of Havneby, 8 km (5 mi) south of the causeway, and in the camping and shopping complex of Lakkolk, in the west.

The 18th century was a golden age in Rømø's seafaring history, when more than 50 local sailors were appointed captains of Dutch and German whaling expeditions to Greenland. Upon their return, the newly prosperous captains built lavish farmsteads, such as **Kommandørgård** (Captain's House), in Toftum, 2 km (1 mi) north of the causeway. Part of the Danish National Museum, this stately, thatch-roof–and–brick farmhouse dating from 1874 has been meticulously restored, with opulent period furnishings including brass-lined chests and marble-top tables. Blue-and-white glazed Dutch tiles cover the walls, alongside hand-painted rococo panels and doors. ⊠ *Juvrevej 60, Toftum* ☎ 74/75–52–76 ⊕ *www.natmus.dk* ⊡ *DKr 20* ☉ *May–Sept., Tues.–Sun. 10–6; Oct., Tues.–Sat. 10–3.*

Just north of the Captain's House, in the tiny village of Juvre, is a **whale jawbone fence** built in 1772. Lacking wood and stone, villagers constructed this fence from the whalebones that Rømø captains brought back from Greenland.

Off the main road south of the causeway rises the whitewashed, 18th-century **Rømø Kirke** (Rømø Church), dedicated to St. Clemens, the patron saint of fisherman and sailors. Inside are several hand-painted ship models. The churchyard gravestones, brought back by Rømø captains, are made of Greenlandic stone and carved with depictions of ships. ⊠ *Havnebyvej 152* ☎ *No phone* ☉ *Tues.–Fri. 8–4.*

Where to Stay

$–$$ ⊞ **Hotel Kømmandørgården.** This sprawling resort-style vacation and conference complex gives you the option of a standard hotel room, an apartment, or even a log cabin. The resort is by the Rømø Family and Horse Park, and has great views of the Wadden Sea and the marshland. You certainly won't get bored here: Icelandic horses are available for rides, and the Wellness Center is a fully equipped spa with some unusual features (a "Tepidarium" is a small room incorporating light and sound therapy to presumably rid your mind of toxins). It's a busy, cheery place, filled with families and/or conventioneers. Every unit has a terrace or balcony. ⊠ *Havenybyvej 201, Mølby, DK–6792* ☎ 74/75–51–22 ⊕ *www.kommandoergaarden.dk* ⇄ *40 rooms, 40 apartments and cabins* ⚏ *3 restaurants, 2 pools, spa, billiards, horseback riding, bar, playground, meeting rooms* ⊟ *DC, MC, V* ⦿ *BP.*

Ribe

★ ❼ *60 km (36 mi) southwest of Kolding, 150 km (103 mi) southwest of Århus.*

In the southwestern corner of Jutland, the country's oldest town is well worth the detour for its medieval center preserved by the Danish National Trust. As you stroll around, note the detailed doors and facades of the buildings, and the antique streetlights. From May to mid-September a night watchman circles the town, recalling its history and singing traditional songs. If you want to accompany him, gather at the main square at 10 PM.

The **Ribe Domkirke** (Ribe Cathedral) stands on the site of one of Denmark's earliest churches, built around AD 860. The present structure, which dates from the 12th century, is built of a volcanic tufa stone, transported by boats from quarries in Cologne, France. Note the Cat Head Door, said to be for the exclusive use of the devil. The 14th-century brick bell tower once clanged out flood and fire warnings to Ribe's citizens, and today affords sweeping views of the town's red-slate rooftops and surrounding marshes. ⊠ *Torvet 15* ☎ 75/42–06–19 ⊕ *www.ribe-domkirke.dk* ⊡ *DKr 12* ☉ *Apr. and Oct., Mon.–Sat. 11–4; May–June* *and mid-Aug.–late-Sept., Mon.–Sat. 10–5; July–mid-Aug., Mon.–Sat. 10–5:30; Nov.–Mar., Mon.–Sat. 11–3. Hrs vary Sun. year-round.*

The **Ribes Vikinger** (Ribe Viking Museum) chronicles Viking history with conventional exhibits of household goods, tools, and clothing. There's a multimedia room with an interactive computer screen where you can search for more Viking information in the form of text, pictures, and videos. ⊠ *Odinspl.* ☎ *76/88–11–22* ⊕ *www.ribesvikinger. dk* ⊠ *DKr 55* ☉ *Apr.–June and Sept.–Mar., Tues.–Sun. 10–4; July and Aug., Tues.–Sun. 10–6.*

Take Bus 57 (confirm with the driver) from the railway station across the street from the Ribes Vikinger. The bus travels 2 km (1 mi) south and arrives at the **Viking Center,** an outdoor exhibit detailing how the Vikings lived day-to-day, with demonstrations about homes, food, and crafts. ⊠ *Lustrupvej 4, Lustrupholm* ☎ *75/41–16–11* ⊕ *www. ribevikingecenter.dk* ⊠ *DKr 65* ☉ *May, June, and Sept., weekdays 10–3:30; July and Aug., daily 11–5.*

Where to Stay & Eat

¢–$$ ✕ **Sælhunden.** The 400-year-old canal-side "Seal Tavern" can seat up to 60 people, but it feels smaller, and its coziness draws both wayfarers and locals. The only seal mementos left are a few skins and pictures, but you can still order a "seal's special" of cold shrimp, sautéed potatoes, and scrambled eggs or an old Danish favorite of fat strips of pork served with cream gravy and boiled potatoes (only served on Wednesday in winter). Console yourself in summer with *rød grød med fløde* (red porridge with cream); the pronunciation of this dessert—which defies phonetic spelling—is so difficult that Danes get a kick out of making foreigners try to say it. In summer, you can sit outside by the river or in the courtyard. ⊠ *Skibbroen 13* ☎ *75/42–09–46* ⊕ *www.saelhunden. dk* ▭ *DC, MC, V.*

$$–$$$ ✕▭ **Hotel Dagmar.** The Hotel Dagmar is poised to please the hearts of
Fodor'sChoice those wanting a comfortable trip back in time. The hotel, originally built
★ in 1581 by a city alderman, eventually became an inn by 1800. Although city ordinances prohibit such modern conveniences as an elevator, some contemporary touches are apparent. For a hotel of this vintage, standard rooms are quite comfortable (though not lavish), and some have canopied beds. The cheap amenities in the bathrooms are a bit of a surprise, but shouldn't detract from the hotel's merits overall. The restaurant is fantastic—seasonal menus, where one can choose between two- and six-course set menus (between DKr 325 and DKr 565), or excellent à la carte choices, make this dining room perhaps the best in town. The scallops topped with a sweet-potato crisp and surrounded by vichyssoise is an excellent appetizer, and choosing the North Sea fresh fish of the day in a lobster sauce is a smart idea for the main course. The hotel is next door to the local tourist bureau and across the street from the 900-year old cathedral. ⊠ *Torvet 1, DK–6760* ☎ *75/42–00–33* ☐ *75/ 42–36–52* ⊕ *www.hoteldagmar.dk* ↪ *48 rooms* ♨ *Restaurant, cable TV, Wi-Fi, bar, meeting room, some pets allowed* ▭ *AE, DC, MC, V.*

$ ▭ **Den Gamle Arrest.** Spend the night in the clink at "The Old Jail," a simple yet cozy hotel housed in what was Ribe's main jail from 1893 to 1989. The artist-owner has done a brilliant job of modernizing the cells into comfortably habitable rooms, while preserving all the prison details. The cells, which used to house five prisoners, have been creatively refashioned into single and double rooms with lofts in which the bed can be stored during the day. The tiny windows, once covered with mesh-like gratings so that prisoners couldn't see outside, now offer glimpses of blue sky. The original prison gates, with iron bars and padlocks, still serve as the entrances into the hallways. The prison dungeons have been converted into a sprawling gift shop with handmade Danish crafts, from inventive candles and glassware to hundreds of Christmas decorations. The former guardroom, which opens onto the prison yard–turned–terrace, is now a popular clothing store with exclusive fashions by Danish designers. ⊠ *Torvet 11, DK–6760* ☎ *75/42–37–00* ⊕ *www.dengamlearrest.dk* ↻ *11 rooms, 2 with bath* ⌂ *Café, shop.*

¢ ▦ **Danhostel Ribe.** In the town center, this plain, redbrick hostelry has six- and four-bed family rooms arranged in clusters of two, each with its own private bath and toilet. There are also double rooms with private bath and eight four-bed rooms with completely private facilities. They are functional and childproof, with pine bunks and industrial carpeting. A kitchen is available. ⊠ *Ribehallen, Skt. Pedersg. 16, DK–6760* ☎ *75/42–06–20* 🖷 *75/42–42–88* ⊕ *www.danhostel-ribe.dk* ↻ *152 beds, 38 rooms with bath* ⌂ *Cafeteria* ▭ *No credit cards* ⊘ *Closed Dec. and Jan.*

Shopping

Antikgaarden (⊠ Overdammen 5 ☎ 75/41–00–55) has a varied collection of Danish antiques, including old Royal Copenhagen plates. **Idé Butik Aps** (⊠ Overdammen 4 ☎ 75/42–14–14) sells Danish crafts ranging from paper cutouts and glassware to figurines of Danish *nisser* (elves). For amber jewelry, head to **Rav I Ribe** (⊠ Nedderdammen 32 ☎ 75/42–03–88), one of the largest amber purveyors in town.

Esbjerg

❽ *35 km (22 mi) northwest of Ribe, 145 km (90 mi) southwest of Århus.*

Esbjerg's appropriate motto is "alive and kicking," and for this relatively new Danish city (founded in 1868 as an export harbor for the west coast of the country), it works. It has a performing arts center, **Musikhuset Esbjerg** (⊠ Havneg. 18 ☎ 76/10–90–10 ⊕ www.mhe.dk) designed by Jan Utzon, the son of Jørn Utzon, who won acclaim for designing the Sydney Opera House. Indeed, the same type of ceramic tile that has been used in Australia adorns the exteriors of this light and airy 1,100-seat center. Everything from exhibitions to fashion shows to the musical *Lord of the Dance* (extended into 2006) is showcased here.

There is a pleasant mishmash of architectural styles in town, including stately turn-of-the-20th-century brick government buildings. The fortified **water tower** (⊠ Havneg. 22 ☎ 75/12–78–11) was erected in 1897, and its castlelike appearance was much influenced by the medieval building Haus Nassau in Nuremburg, Germany. Climb to the top (admission is DKr 10) for splendid views of the city and the sea. Standing over the central square is a statue of Christian IX, the reigning monarch when Esbjerg was founded.

The highlight at the **Esbjerg Museum** is its amber collection, one of the largest in Denmark. The west coast of Jutland is well known for being rich in amber. Detailed exhibits trace the history of amber along the Jutland coast over a whopping 10,000-year period. ⊠ *Torveg. 45* ☎ *75/ 12–78–11* ⊕ *www.esbjergmuseum.dk* ⊠ *DKr 30, free Wed.* ☼ *June–Aug., daily 10–4; Sept.–May, Tues.–Sun. 10–4.*

The **Esbjerg Kunstmuseum** (Esbjerg Art Museum) showcases a fine collection of Danish contemporary art starting in 1910, including works by Richard Mortensen. Innovative temporary exhibits feature up-and-coming Danish artists, and have included a retrospective of Danish mobile art and avant-garde sculptures and installations. ⊠ *Havneg. 20* ☎ *75/ 13–02–11* ⊠ *DKr 40* ☼ *June–Dec., daily 10–4.*

One of Esbjerg's most striking sights is the giant whitewashed sculpture by Danish artist Svend Wiig Hansen entitled **Menesket ved Havet** (*Man Meets Sea*), depicting four 19-foot-tall men staring solemnly out to sea. It has been said that it evokes the mood of a temple or acropolis, or, a reminder of the mysterious stone figures on Easter Island. In clear weather the figures can be seen from a distance of 10 km (6 mi).

Where to Stay & Eat

$–$$$$ ✕ **Restaurant Gammelhavn.** This airy pavilion-style restaurant is right on the harbor front, and offers everything from brasserie food (sandwiches start at DKr 65) to gourmet dinners (a four-course meal would be about DKr 400). You can always stop by in mid-afternoon for coffee and cake, as well. ⊠ *Brittaniavej 3* ☎ *76/11–90–00* ▭ *DC, MC, V.*

$$$ ✕ **Sand's Restauration.** Founded in 1907, this warm, dimly lighted restaurant is one of Esbjerg's oldest. The traditional Danish menu of pork dishes and steaks continues to be popular with locals and tourists alike, and there is a new three-course menu every month. The original owners collected more than 50 works of art by west Jutland artists, which cover the walls. ⊠ *Jyllandsg. 32* ☎ *75/12–02–07* ▤ *75/45–47–70* ▭ *AE, MC, V* ☼ *Closed Sun.*

¢–$ ▥ **Palads Cab Inn.** In the heart of Esbjerg is this budget hotel affiliated with the popular Cab—Inn Copenhagen chain. The rooms, though the standard motel type, were refurbished in 2005. Breakfast is served in a colossal, high-ceiling dining room that once served as a ballroom. ⊠ *Skoleg. 14, DK–6700* ☎ *75/18–16–00* ▤ *75/18–16–24* ⊕ *www. cabinn.dk* ⤳ *107 rooms* ⚬ *Cafeteria, cable TV, in-room broadband, bar, no-smoking rooms* ▭ *AE, DC, MC, V* ⟨O⟩ *BP.*

Nightlife & the Arts

Pubs dot Esbjerg's main drag, Skolegade. In the center of town is the friendly restaurant-bar **Dronning Louise** (⊠ Torvet 19 ☎ 75/13–13–44), named after Queen Louise, the wife of Christian IX. The bar has red-leather chairs and a wall lined with bookshelves. In the upstairs club a DJ spins dance tunes on Friday and Saturday nights. Esbjerg locals flock to the live Saturday-afternoon jazz sessions that start at 1 PM.

In summer the jazz is performed on a terrace that faces the main square. The adjoining restaurant serves light lunches (burgers, club sandwiches, and chicken wings) and a Danish dinner menu of meat and fish dishes.

Fanø

❾ *30 km (19 mi) northwest of Ribe, plus 12-min ferry from Esbjerg; 153 km (96 mi) southwest of Århus, plus 12-min ferry from Esbjerg.*

In the 19th century this tiny island had an enormous shipbuilding industry and a fleet second only to Copenhagen's. The shipping industry deteriorated, but the proud maritime heritage remains. Today Fanø is a summer oasis for legions of Danes and other northern Europeans. Silky sand beaches unfold along the west coast, buffered by windswept dunes and green reeds. Cars are allowed on the beach, and it's well worth taking a ride along the flat sandy coast between the ferry port in Nordby, Fanø's capital, and the traditional town of Sønderho, in the south. Spinning along the white sandy expanse is like crossing a desert; only the dark blue sea off in the distance reminds you of your island whereabouts. The beach is so level and wide that the military used to train here. In the off-season, when summer visitors have packed up and returned home, the Fanø shore becomes a tranquil retreat, hauntingly silent save for the rustle of reeds and the far-off squawk of a bird.

The old-fashioned village of Sønderho, 13 km (8 mi) south of Nordby, has tiny winding lanes and thatch-roof cottages decorated with ships' relics, figureheads, painted doors, and brass lanterns. You may even see people wearing the traditional costumes, especially on Sønderhodag, a town festival held on the third Sunday in July.

Where to Stay & Eat

To get an idea of where the locals throw back a few brews, stop by **Hjørnekroen** (⌧ Hovedgaden 14 ☎ 75/16–22–62 ⊕ www.hjoernekroen. dk), which is a true pub with live music, billiards, and darts—it feels a bit like a Danish version of the TV show *Cheers.*

$$$ ✕ **Restaurant Hos Apel.** Located directly behind the Fanø Krogaard hotel, this little restaurant features fish specialties, including the very popular *bakskuld,* a smoked and salted flat fish glazed with butter. ⌧ *Hovedgaden 25* ☎ *75/16–11–44* 🍴 *No credit cards* ☉ *Closed Oct.–Apr.*

★ $–$$ ✕ **Café Nanas Stue.** This half-timber farmhouse restaurant dating from 1854 doubles as the Fanø Flisemuseum (Fanø Tile Museum). The walls and old-fashioned wooden cupboards are lined with glazed Dutch tiles brought back by Danish sailors from the 17th to 19th centuries. The handmade tiles, characteristic of most Fanø homes, are usually blue and white, and depict everything from Bible stories and ships at sea to frolicking children. The restaurant is a favorite among locals, who gather around the wooden tables to tuck into traditional Danish fare, including smørrebrød and pepper steak topped with a cognac sauce. Round out the meal with a taste of their specialty drink, a potent aquavit flavored with orange, vanilla, or coffee beans. In summer, local musicians perform traditional Fanø folk music on the violin, guitar, bagpipe, and harmonica. Inquire at the tourist office for a schedule. ⊠ *Sønderland 1* ☎ *75/16–40–25* ⊕ *www.nanas-stue.dk* ⊟ *AE, MC, V* ⊗ *Closed Mon. Aug.–Sept.; closed Mon.–Thurs. Oct.–May.*

★ $$$ ✕⊡ **Sønderho Kro.** A member of the Relais & Chateaux collection of small hotels, this thatch-roof inn built in 1722 in the heart of Sønderho is one of Jutland's finest. Its charm has been preserved with painted doors and beamed ceilings, and mahogany floors and new carpeting were laid in 2003. Rooms are jazzed up with four-poster beds, elegant tapestries, and gauzy curtains. The French-Danish restaurant serves excellent seafood, with set menus less expensive on weeknights. ⊠ *Kropl. 11, DK–6720 Sønderho* ☎ *75/16–40–09* ☒ *75/16–43–85* ⊕ *www. sonderhokro.dk* ↩ *14 rooms* ♻ *Restaurant, some pets allowed* ⊟ *AE, DC, MC, V* ⊗ *Closed Feb. and weekdays Nov.–Jan.*

Billund

⑩ *101 km (63 mi) southwest of Århus.*

Billund is the site of Denmark's second-biggest tourist attraction outside Copenhagen: Legoland. The son of the founder of the Lego Company, Godtfred Christiansen, invented the Lego toy brick in Billund in 1949; today the Lego Company employs 8,000 people (3,000 of whom work in Billund). Over the years the company has manufactured more than 375 billion Lego bricks, all of which trace back to the modest facilities of the family home which still stands on Main Street here. Billund has grown exponentially with the Lego success, and today boasts its own international airport (constructed by Lego and then given to the community) and a large community center (also donated by Lego). However, outside of Legoland there's not much to keep you here—the bank in town is larger than the town hall, and you're in and out of the little metropolis before you know it.

☾ At the amazing **Legoland** everything is constructed from Lego bricks—
FodorśChoice 45 million of them. Among its incredible structures are scaled-down ver-
★ sions of cities and villages from around the world ("Miniland"), with working harbors and airports; the Statue of Liberty; a statue of Sitting Bull; Mt. Rushmore; a safari park; and Pirate Land. Grown-ups might marvel at toys from pre-Lego days, the most exquisite of which is Titania's Palace, a sumptuous dollhouse built between 1907 and 1922 by Sir Neville Wilkinson for his daughter. The 18 rooms and salons contain hand-carved mahogany furniture, and 3,000 tiny works of art and miniatures from around the world.

Some of the park's newer attractions are more interactive than the impressive constructions. The Falck Fire Brigade, for example, allows a family or group to race eight mini fire engines. The Power Builder Robots allow children and adults to sit inside robots as they program their own ride. ⊠ *Normarksvej 9* ☎ *75/33–13–33* ⊕ *www.legoland. dk* ⊠ *DKr 185* ⊗ *Apr., May, Sept., and Oct., weekdays 10–6, weekends 10–8; June and late Aug., daily 10–8; July–mid-Aug., daily 10–9.*

Sculpturepark Billund is a lovely park, leading from Legoland to the town center, and taking about a half hour to walk. There are 10 permanent sculptures positioned along the path, created by some of Denmark's leading sculptors, and six new and different ones are added each summer. Benches are scattered throughout, making it a nice spot for an impromptu picnic. ⊠ *Across from Legoland Village* 🎫 *Free* ☉ *Daily.*

Where to Stay & Eat

$ ╳ **The Highlander.** If being in a theme park all day puts you in the mood for a good Scotch (or just a beer), head over to this popular pub. The grub is also reminiscent of Scotland's, with U.K. standards such as fish-and-chips. There's live music on Thursday and Saturday. ⊠ *Rådhus-centret 3* ☎ *75/35–44–22* 🍽 *MC, V.*

$$$–$$$$ 🏨 **Hotel Legoland.** It may be a bit pricier than area hotels, but Hotel Legoland is inside Legoland Village, and your room rate includes two days' admission to the park, breakfast, and access to Legoland through the hotel, so you avoid the long lines at the park entrance. The colorful guest rooms overlook all the action. This hotel is beyond kid-friendly: pictograms outside each room help children identify which room they are in, bathrooms are kid-friendly, and rooms include the requisite Legos for kids of all ages to play with. The restaurant serves surprisingly good meals, and, at lunch, a children's buffet is also available. ⊠ *Aastvej 10, DK–7190* ☎ *75/33–12–44* 🖨 *75/35–38–10* ⊕ *www.hotellegoland.dk* 🛏 *176 rooms* ⚴ *Restaurant, bar, pool, gym, meeting rooms* 🍽 *AE, DC, MC, V* ⚬ *BP.*

$$–$$$$ 🏨 **Hotel Propellen.** Very close to the airport (and to Legoland), this stylish hotel is owned by the Danish Air Pilots Union; hence the name. Rooms are tastefully furnished, if not as fun as Hotel Legoland. There is a special summer menu in the restaurant, including an all-you-can-eat ice-cream bar. Note that there's a DKr 30 discount if you pay in cash. ⊠ *Nordmarksvej 3, DK–7190 Billund* ☎ *75/33–81–33* 🖨 *75/35–33–62* ⊕ *www.propellen.dk* 🛏 *91 rooms, 3 suites* ⚴ *Restaurant, indoor pool, sauna, billiards, Ping-Pong, bar, playground, meeting rooms* 🍽 *AE, DC, MC, V* ⚬ *BP.*

Ringkøbing

⑪   *35 km (22 mi) north of Esbjerg, 100 km (62 mi) west of Århus.*

Though it's a pretty medieval town, founded in the 13th century, Ringkøbing's claim to fame is purely thanks to Mother Nature. A thin strip of land, Holmsland, separates the calm waters of the Ringkøbing Fjord with the rough-and-tumble North Sea. If you climb Troldbjerg Hill (by following wheelchair-friendly pathways), you will end up admiring the view over Hvide Sande, Ringkøbing Fjord, and the North Sea, all at the same time.

The shallow waters of the fjord and the best wind statistics in Denmark make it the windsurfing capital of central Jutland. The North Sea's winds are not mild, thereby helping this sport immeasurably, as well as attracting all styles of surfing, including freestyle, free ride, racing, and kite.

Ringkøbing Church is the oldest building in town, dating back to the 14th century. In 1995–96 major renovations of the interior and restoration of all historic furnishings took place. The church elders felt, according to one local historian, that the centuries-old oil painting of Christ with his Apostles was too "dull," so they purchased a new painting—a semiabstract—by artist Arne Hagen Sørensen, which depicts the hand of God cradling civilization. Then, in another bold move they bought a beautiful crystal-and-glass baptismal font designed by the same artist and sculpted by Per Hebesgaard. The organ from 1654 is preserved, but is now used almost exclusively for the summer concerts that are a permanent feature of the town's music life. ⊠ *Town Sq.* ☎ *97/32–02–17* ⊙ *Daily 10–5.*

If you have a penchant for local history and archaeology, stop by the **Ringkøbing Museum,** where you will also find an extensive collection on arctic explorer Mylius Eriksen. ⊠ *Kongevejen 1* ☎ *97/32–16–15* ⊡ *Dkr 30* ⊙ *Mid-June–Aug., daily 11–5; Sept.–mid-June, Mon.–Thurs. 11–4, weekends 1–4.*

Gallery Lodberg is a bit outside town, but here you can get a flavor of a local artist's interpretation of west Jutland and its scenic vistas. In oil paintings and watercolors, Svend Lodberg magically re-creates the beauty of the area. ⊠ *Borkvej 14* ☎ *97/33–00–21* ⊕ *www.s-lodberg. dk* ⊙ *Mon.–Sat. 10–5.*

Where to Stay & Eat

$–$$$
Fodor'sChoice
★

✕⊡ **Hotel Fjordgården.** This friendly hotel, a 10-minute walk from the town square into a residential neighborhood, is probably the best bet for both food and lodging in this area. Built in the mid-1960s, the hotel is remarkably up-to-date with large rooms sleeping up to four; new abstract Danish paintings adorning the public areas and rooms; and a pool complex keeps both kids and adults happy. The restaurant serves a small selection of à la carte dishes and a daily menu with two to four courses and wine pairings. ⊠ *Vesterkær 28* ☎ *97/32–14–00* 🖷 *97/32–47–60* ⊕ *www.hotelfjordgaarden.dk* ⌁ *98 rooms* ⌂ *Restaurant, Wi-Fi, pool, hot tub, sauna, bar, meeting rooms* ▭ *AE, DC, MC, V* ⦿ *BP.*

Vejle

⑫ *40 km (25 mi) east of Billund, 73 km (46 mi) southwest of Århus.*

Vejle is beautifully positioned on a fjord on the east coast, amid forest-clad hills. It's a bustling little city and has its own art museum, a terrific pedestrian street for shopping, and quick access to the countryside. You can hear the time of day chiming on the old **Dominican monastery clock;** the clock remains, but the monastery long ago gave way to the town's imposing 19th-century city hall.

In the town center, at Kirke Torvet, is **Skt. Nikolai Kirke** (St. Nicholas Church). In the left arm of the cross-shape church, lying in a glass Empire-style coffin, is the body of a bog woman found preserved in a peat marsh in 1835; she dates from 500 BC. The church walls contain the skulls of 23 thieves executed in the 17th century. ⊠ *Kirke Torvet* ☎ *75/ 82–41–39* ⊙ *May–Sept., weekdays 9–5, Sat. 9–noon, Sun. 9–11:30.*

Where to Stay

$$$$ 🏨 **Munkebjerg Hotel.** Seven kilometers (4½ mi) southeast of town and sur-rounded by a thick beech forest and majestic views of the Vejle Fjord, this elegant hotel attracts guests who value their privacy. Beyond the rus-tic lobby, rooms furnished in blond pine and soft green overlook the for-est. There are also two top-notch French-Danish restaurants and a swank casino. ✉ *Munkebjergvej 125, DK–7100* ☎ *75/42–85–00* 📠 *75/72–08–86* ⊕ *www.munkebjerg.dk* ➥ *7 rooms, 2 suites ↺ 3 restaurants, cafeteria, tennis court, indoor pool, gym, sauna, bar, casino, meeting room, some pets allowed, no-smoking rooms* ▤ *AE, DC, MC, V.*

$ 🏨 **Park Hotel.** The Park is centrally located and offers very spacious rooms considering its small stature. The pleasant service caps off an overall en-joyable experience, and ensures return visits from its patrons. A boun-tiful breakfast is included in the price, and the restaurant is good though perhaps a bit thin on variety. ✉ *Orla Lehmannsg. 5, DK–7100* ☎ *75/82–24–66* 📠 *75/72–05–39* ⊕ *www.park-hotel.dk* ➥ *32 rooms ↺ Restau-rant, bar, some pets allowed* ▤ *AE, DC, MC, V.*

Jelling

⓭ *10 km (6 mi) northwest of Vejle (via Rte. 18), 83 km (52 mi) southwest of Århus.*

Two 10th-century burial mounds mark the seat of King Gorm and his wife Thyra here. Between the mounds are two **Runestener** (runic stones), one of which is Denmark's certificate of baptism, showing the oldest known figure of Christ in Scandinavia. The inscription explains that the stone was erected by Gorm's son, King Harald Bluetooth, who brought Christianity to the Danes in 960. This is where the power of the Dan-ish king and state developed between A.D. 200 and A.D. 1000.

The most scenic way to get to Jelling is via the **vintage steam train** that runs from Vejle in summer. The journey passes through the striking Gre-jsdal Valley, the longest gorge in Denmark. The train's engine is from a 1920 branch-line train, and the cars are from 1898 to 1916. Call the tourist office for schedules.

Silkeborg

⓮ *60 km (38 mi) north of Jelling, 43 km (27 mi) west of Århus.*

At the banks of the River Gudenå begins Jutland's Lake District. Stretch-ing southeast from Silkeborg to Skanderborg, the area contains some of Denmark's loveliest scenery and most of its meager mountains, includ-ing the 438-foot **Himmelbjerget**, at Julsø (Lake Jul), 15 km (10 mi) south-east of Silkeborg. You can climb the narrow paths through the heather and trees to the top, where an 80-foot tower stands sentinel. It was placed there on Constitution Day in 1875 in memory of King Frederik VII.

In late June, jazz-lovers from all over Europe come to celebrate Silke-borg's **Riverboat Jazz Festival** (☎ 86/80–16–17 ⊕ www.riverboat.dk), with live jazz performed on indoor and outdoor stages over four days. At-tendance is consistent at 40,000–45,000 people, so be sure to reserve lodgings in advance.

The best way to explore the Lake District is by water, as the Gudenå winds its way some 160 km (100 mi) through lakes and wooded hillsides down to the sea. Take one of the excursion boats or the world's last coal-fired paddle steamer, *Hjejlen,* which departs in summer (mid-June through August) from Silkeborg Harbor. Since 1861 it has paddled its way through narrow stretches of fjord, where the treetops meet overhead, to the foot of the Himmelbjerget. ⊠ *Havnen* ☎ *86/82–07–66* ⊕ *www.hjejlen.com* ⊠ *DKr 100.*

The **Silkeborg Museum** is not only the oldest building in the town, dating from 1767, it houses the city's main attractions: the 2,400-year-old Tollund Man and Elling Girl, two bog people preserved by the chemicals in the soil and water. The museum also showcases trades made famous in the area, such as clog and wheel making, and pottery and papermaking. It also has a fine collection of old Danish glass, a café, and a gift shop. ⊠ *Hovedgårdsvej 7* ☎ *86/82–14–99* ⊕ *www. silkeborgmuseum.dk* ⊠ *DKr 40* ⊗ *May–mid-Oct., daily 10–5; mid-Oct.–Apr., Wed. and weekends noon–4.*

Much more eclectic is the **Silkeborg Museum of Art,** which holds Danish artist Asger Jorn's collection of more than 5,000 works by 150 international artists, including Max Ernst, Picabia, Le Corbusier, and many Danish contemporaries, such as Bjerke Petersen, Carl-Henning Pedersen, and Egill Jacobsen. Jorn's own works number around 100, in various mediums (paintings, ceramics, drawings, and graphics). ⊠ *Gudenåvej 7-9* ☎ *86/82–53–88* ⊕ *www.silkeborgkunstmuseum.dk* ⊗ *Apr.–Oct., daily 10–5.*

At the **Aqua Ferskvands Akvarium** (Aqua Aquarium), which is the largest freshwater aquarium in northern Europe, you can see beavers, otters, freshwater fish, and other animals in re-creations of their natural habitat. ⊠ *Vejlsøvej 55* ☎ *89/21–21–89* ⊕ *www.aqua-ferskvandsakvarium. dk* ⊠ *DKr 75* ⊗ *Mid-June.–mid-Sept., daily 10–6.*

Where to Stay & Eat

$$$–$$$$ ✕ **Aalekroen.** Also known as Onkel Peters Hus (Uncle Peter's Place), this spot is noted for its house specialties, fried eel and seafood. The grilled meat dishes are also excellent. This old inn stands at the shore of a scenic lake. ⊠ *Julsøvænget 5* ☎ *86/84–60–33* ⊕ *www.aalekroen.dk* ⚞ *Reservations essential* ⊟ *AE, DC, MC, V* ⊗ *Closed Mon.*

★ **$$$–$$$$** ✕▨ **Radisson SAS Hotel Silkeborg.** This is the newest business-class hotel in the country to open outside Copenhagen, and it's deserving of its rapid, excellent reputation. The hotel has been constructed within the main building of the old paper mill on the bank of the river, and is connected to a convention center (Jysk Musik & Teaterhus). Rooms are soothing, with slate-gray and warm yellow tones and relaxing views of the river. The Riverside Restaurant, also on the main floor, is thought to be Silkeborg's trendiest dining spot, and the food does not disappoint. Note that hotel rates are substantially lower on weekends. ⊠ *Papirfabrikken 12, DK–8600 Silkeborg* ☎ *88/82–22–22* 🖷 *88/82–22–23* ⊕ *www.radisson. dk* ⇌ *86 rooms, 5 suites* ⚘ *Restaurant, in-room broadband, bar, meeting rooms* ⊟ *AE, DC, MC, V.*

Randers

15 *73 km (45 mi) from Silkeborg, 35 km (21 mi) from Århus.*

There's something about Randers that makes you want to return to it, to explore further, to discover what makes its people tick. It's the sixth-largest city in the country, with 60,000 people, and yet it comes across as a bit of a small town—in all the right ways. You may hear people refer to it as Crown Jutland (Kronjylland)—a term used by Danish writers and poets of the 18th century, when they wrote about all the beautiful estates that the king owned in the area.

One of the biggest attractions to be built in Jutland in the past 25 years is located in Randers on the bank of the river Gudenå. The **Randers Regnskov** (Tropical Zoo) opened in 1996 under the patronage of Princess Alexandra. It has three biospheres, or glass domes, under which a complete zoological garden grows and thrives, complete with indigenous animals from the rain forests of Asia, Africa, and South America. It's pretty exceptional to be able to see an aardvark, a sloth, a lemur, a Jaco parrot, a dwarf marmoset, and numerous other members of the animal kingdom, all in one place. Wear light clothing—temperatures inside the domes are exactly that of a real rain forest. The zoo is technically wheelchair accessible, but navigating can be difficult in places. ⊠ *Torvebryggen 11* ☎ *87/10–99–99* ⊕ *www.randers-regnskov.dk* 🖃 *DKr 95* ☉ *Mid-June–mid-Aug., daily 10–6; mid-Aug.–mid-June, weekdays 10–4, weekends 10–5.*

Yes, there really is an **Elvis Unlimited Museum** in Randers. And, it's the largest Elvis memorabilia spectacle outside Graceland. Henrik Knudsen, the owner and fan extraordinaire, says that his interest in Elvis's music began in 1977 (when he was 13), at the time of Presley's death, and he hasn't stopped collecting and selling since. In the actual museum one might feel like it's either very cool or very disturbing to see so much Elvis ephemera all in one place. ⊠ *Undervœrket, Stemannsgade 9C* ☎ *86/42–96–96* ⊕ *www.elvispresley.dk* 🖃 *DKr 20* ☉ *Weekdays 10–5:30, Sat. 10–2.*

The **Randers Kunstmuseum** (Randers Museum of Art) proves that Elvis isn't the end-all, be-all of the city's cultural offerings. Its collection begins with Danish work from 1800 and continues thereafter, including masterpieces from the Danish "golden age" to provocative contemporary pieces. One of the highlights is Icelandic artist Tróndur Patursson's incredible mirror installation, called Cosmic Room, where your image goes on forever. ⊠ *Kulturhuset, Stemannsgade 2* ☎ *86/42–29–22* ⊕ *www.randerskunstmuseum.dk* 🖃 *DKr 30* ☉ *Tues.–Sun. 11–5.*

Where to Stay

$–$$$ 🏨 **Hotel Randers.** Without any doubt, this hotel has become a reason to
Fodor'sChoice   visit Randers in and of itself, because of its history, charm, comfort, and
★   great service. This is the epitome of the great, family-owned and -operated hotel, where tradition, character, and quiet pride have endeared the place to everyone from Danish monarchs to world-weary travelers.

In 1956 Paul Gauguin's son, sculptor and artist Jean René Gauguin, decorated the main dining room and created four ceramic sculptures of mythological figures for the hotel, which are still in the dining room today. All the guest rooms are roomy, and have elegant wall coverings and artwork. The included breakfast in the stunning Banquet Room with its 1927 decor and Venetian chandeliers may be worth the price of the room alone. But what mostly affects the visitor and guest here is the love the owner, Sonja Mathisen, has for the hotel. As she tells visitors, "We do not modernize, but renovate so that we can keep the soul of the hotel." ⊠ *Torvegade 11* ☎ *86/42–34–22* 🖷 *86/40–15–86* ⊕ *www.hotelranders.dk* 🖘 *67 rooms, 12 suites* ⟂ *Restaurant, bar, meeting rooms* 🖃 *AE, MC, V* ⟊ *BP.*

Århus

⓰ *40 km (24 mi) east of Silkeborg.*

Århus is Denmark's second-largest city, and, with its funky arts and college community, one of the country's most pleasant. Cutting through the center of town is a canal called the Århus Å (Århus Creek). It used to run underground, but was uncovered a few years ago. Since then, an amalgam of bars, cafés, and restaurants has sprouted along its banks, creating one of Denmark's most lively thoroughfares. At all hours of the day and night this waterfront strip is abuzz with crowds that hang out on the outdoor terraces and steps that lead down to the creek.

The VisitAarhus tourist office has information about the **Århus Passport,** which includes passage on buses, free or discounted admission to the 12 most popular museums and sites in the city, and tours.

The town comes most alive during the first week of September, when the **Århus Festival** (☎ 89/40–91–91 ⊕ www.aarhusfestuge.dk) begins, combining concerts, theater, and art exhibitions with beer tents and sports. The **Århus International Jazz Festival** bills international and local greats in early or mid-July. In July the **Viking Moot** draws aficionados to the beach below the Museum of Prehistory at Moesgård. Activities and exhibits include market booths, ancient defense techniques, and rides on Viking ships.

The **Rådhus** is probably the most unusual city hall in Denmark. Built in 1941 by noted architects Arne Jacobsen and Erik Møller, the pale Norwegian-marble block building is controversial, but cuts a startling figure when illuminated in the evening. Go to the Kommune Information booth next to the tower entrance to obtain multiride tickets and passport tourist tickets, and to get information on everything connected with traveling by bus in Århus. That office is open from 10 to 5:30 (☎ 89/40–10–10). ⊠ *Park Allé* ☎ *89/40–67–00* 🖃 *City hall DKr 10, tower DKr 5* ⊙ *Guided tours (in Danish only) mid-June–early Sept., weekdays at 11; tower tours weekdays at noon and 2.*

Rising gracefully over the center of town, the **Århus Domkirke** (Århus Cathedral) was originally built in 1201 in a Romanesque style, but was later expanded and redesigned into a Gothic cathedral in the 15th century.

Its soaring, whitewashed nave is one of the longest in Denmark. The cathedral's highlights include its chalk frescoes, in shades of lavender, yellow, red, and black, that grace the high arches and towering walls. Dating from the Middle Ages, the frescoes depict biblical scenes and the valiant St. George slaying a dragon and saving a maiden princess in distress. Also illustrated is the poignant death of St. Clement, who drowned with an anchor tied around his neck. Nonetheless, he became the patron saint of sailors. Climb the tower for bird's-eye views of the rooftops and thronged streets of Århus. ⊠ *Bispetorv* ☎ *86/20–54–00* ⊕ *www. aarhus-domkirke.dk* 🎫 *Tower DKr 10* ⊙ *Jan.–Apr. and Oct.–Dec., Mon.–Sat. 10–3; May–Sept., Mon.–Sat. 9:30–4.*

★ Don't miss the town's open-air museum, known as **Den Gamle By** (Old Town). It's the only three-star museum outside Copenhagen. Its 75 historic buildings, including 70 half-timber houses, a mill, and millstream, were carefully moved from locations throughout Denmark and meticulously re-created, inside and out. ⊠ *Viborgvej 2* ☎ *86/12–31–88* ⊕ *www. dengamleby.dk* 🎫 *DKr 45–DKr 75 depending on season and activities* ⊙ *June–Aug., daily 9–6; Apr., May, Sept., and Oct., daily 10–5; Jan., daily 11–3; Feb., Mar., Nov., and Dec., daily 10–4. Grounds always open.*

ARoS Århus Kunstmuseum, the city's newest art museum, was an immediate hit when it opened in April 2004, and 340,000 people passed through its doors in its first nine months of opening. It may look on the outside like a huge, red, brick cube, but inside it's 19 floors are much more inviting. You're free to wander around in the foyer and go to the café, or browse in the gift shop, or you can buy a ticket to view the four main galleries. On the top floor there is a restaurant as well as a rooftop patio—a photographer's dream. The art, of course, is paramount, and comprises the museum's own collection of more than 9,000 works dating from 1770 to the present, as well as internationally known visiting exhibits. ⊠ *Aros Allé 2* ☎ *87/30–66–00* ⊕ *www.aros.dk* 🎫 *DKr 60* ⊙ *Tues. and Thurs.–Sun. 10–5, Wed. 10–10.*

Just south of the city is **Marselisborg Slot** (Marselisborg Castle), the palatial summer residence of the royal family. The changing of the guard takes place daily at noon when the queen is staying in the palace. When the royal family is away (generally in winter and spring), the palace grounds, including a sumptuous rose garden, are open to the public. Take Bus 1, 8, or 19. ⊠ *Kongevejen 100* ☎ *No phone* ⊕ *www.kongehuset. dk* 🎫 *Free.*

In a 250-acre forest south of Århus is the **Moesgård Forhistorisk Museum** (Prehistoric Museum), with exhibits on ethnography and archaeology, including the famed Grauballe Man, a 2,000-year-old corpse so well preserved in a bog that scientists could determine his last meal. In fact, when the discoverers of the Grauballe Man stumbled upon him in 1952, they thought he had recently been murdered and called the police. The Forhistorisk vej (Prehistoric Trail) through the forest leads past Stone- and Bronze Age displays to reconstructed houses from Viking times. ⊠ *Moesgård Allé (Bus 6 from center of town)* ☎ *89/42–11–00* ⊕ *www.moesmus.dk* 🎫 *DKr 45* ⊙ *Apr.–Sept., daily 10–5; Oct.–Mar., Tues.–Sun. 10–4.*

If you are in Århus with children, or simply wish to enjoy a young-at-heart activity, visit the provincial **Tivoli Friheden,** with more than 40 rides and activities, attractive gardens, and restaurants. ☒ *Skovbrynet* ☎ *86/14–73–00* ⊕ *www.friheden.dk* ✉ *DKr 55; rides cost extra* ☉ *Call or check Web site as opening times vary greatly throughout summer.*

Where to Stay & Eat

$$$–$$$$ ✕ **Restaurant Margueritten.** Tucked into a cobbled courtyard, this cheery restaurant is housed in former stables, which accounts for the low wood-beam ceiling. Well-worn wooden tables and tan walls round out the warm atmosphere. Contemporary Danish fare includes guinea fowl stuffed with tiger shrimp and marinated in tandoori and yogurt, and chicken breast served with Italian ham. In summer the back garden is open all day. ☒ *Guldsmedg. 20* ☎ *86/19–60–33* ▤ *AE, DC, MC, V* ☉ *No lunch Sun.*

★ **$$–$$$$** ✕ **Bryggeriet Sct. Clemens.** At this popular pub you can sit among copper kettles and quaff the local brew, which is unfiltered and without additives, just like in the old days. Between the spareribs and Australian steaks, you won't go hungry, either. ☒ *Kannikeg. 10–12* ☎ *86/13–80–00* ⊕ *www.bryggeriet.dk* ▤ *AE, DC, MC, V.*

$$–$$$$ ✕ **Seafood.** Just south of town is Marselis Harbor, a bustling little sailboat cove surrounded by waterfront restaurants and cafés that draw big crowds on sunny summer weekends. Here you'll find Seafood, one of the best seafood restaurants in Århus. Its signature dish, which draws moans of delight from diners, is a seafood bouillabaisse heaped with tiger prawns, squid, Norwegian lobster, and mussels, and served with aioli on the side. Other dishes include oven-baked catfish with asparagus and warm ginger butter. The restful interior has light-blue walls. ☒ *Havnevej 44, Marselisborg* ☎ *86/18–56–55* ▤ *AE, DC, MC, V* ☉ *Closed Sun. Sept.–Apr.*

Fodor'sChoice ★

$$$ ✕ **Prins Ferdinand.** Sitting on the edge of Old Town, and right next to the entrance of Den Gamle By, this premier Danish-French restaurant is named after the colorful Århus-based Prince Frederik (1792–1863), who was much loved despite his fondness for gambling and carousing about town. Here elegant crystal chandeliers hang over large round tables with crisp linen tablecloths and ceramic plates created by a local artist. Vases of sunflowers brighten the front room. Grilled turbot is topped with a cold salsa of radishes, cucumber, and dill. Cabbage, foie gras, and new potatoes accompany a venison dish. A daily vegetarian option is offered, and might include grilled asparagus with potatoes, olives, and herbs. ☒ *Viborgvej 2* ☎ *86/12–52–05* ⊕ *www.prinsferdinand.dk* ▤ *AE, DC, MC, V* ☉ *Closed Sun. and Mon.*

$$$ ✕▨ **Philip.** Occupying a prime spot along the canal, this hotel offers an original—but pricey—concept in lodging. Eight former studio apartments have been converted into luxury suites, each outfitted in its own sumptuous style. Suites have original white wood-beam ceilings, elegant wooden furniture imported from France and Italy, huge gleaming bathrooms, and views of the canal. The plush restaurant, with dark hardwood floors and brass candleholders, serves a blend of cuisines that may include cannelloni stuffed with Serrano ham, Danish feta, and crayfish served with truffles and new potatoes. ☒ *Åboulevarden 28, DK–8000*

87/32–14–44 86/12–69–55 ⊕ *www.hotelphilip.dk* ⊲⊐ 8 suites ♨ *Restaurant, bar* ☰ *DC, MC, V* ⊗ *Closed Sun.*

★ $$$$ **Hotel Royal.** In operation since 1838, Århus's grand hotel has welcomed such greats as musicians Artur Rubinstein and Marian Anderson. Well-heeled guests enter through a stately lobby appointed with sofas, modern paintings, and a winding staircase. Rooms vary in style and decor, but all have velour and brocade furniture and marble bathrooms. ⊠ *Store Torv 4, DK–8100* 86/12–00–11 86/76–04–04 ⊕ *www. hotelroyal.dk* ⊲⊐ *98 rooms, 7 suites* ♨ *Restaurant, cafeteria, sauna, bar, casino, some pets allowed* ☰ *AE, DC, MC, V.*

$ **Hotel Guldsmeden.** Small and intimate, this hotel with a personal touch is housed in a renovated 19th-century town house. The soothing rooms are dressed in cool greens and yellows and have teak shelves; two have claw-foot tubs. The sunny garden blooms with flowers in summer, and the outdoor terrace is just the spot to enjoy the organic breakfast of fruit, muesli, toast, and marmalade. The owners also have a penthouse apartment, fully equipped for four, by the waterfront; it's a short walk away. ⊠ *Guldsmedg. 40, DK–8000* 86/13–45–50 86/ 13–76–76 ⊕ *www.hotelguldsmeden.dk* ⊲⊐ *26 rooms, 20 with bath; 2 suites* ♨ *Bar, some pets allowed* ☰ *AE, DC, MC, V.*

¢ **Danhostel Århus.** As in all Danish youth and family hostels, the rooms here are clean, bright, and functional. The secluded setting in the woods near the fjord is downright beautiful. Unfortunately, the hostel can get a bit noisy. Guests may use the kitchen. ⊠ *Marienlundsvej 10, DK–8100* 86/16–72–98 ⊕ *www.aarhus-danhostel.dk* ⊲⊐ *138 beds in 30 shared rooms, 11 with private shower* ♨ *Dining room* ☰ *AE, MC, V* ⊗ *Closed mid-Dec.–mid-Jan.*

Nightlife & the Arts

There's no better time to visit Århus than during the 10-day **Århus Festival Week** in early September, when jazz, classical, and rock concerts are nonstop, in addition to drama, theater, and dance.

The state-of-the-art **Musikhuset Århus** (Århus Concert Hall; ⊠ Thomas Jensens Allé 2 89/40–40–40) showcases theater, opera, ballet, and concerts of all kinds, from classical music to rock.

BARS & LOUNGES **Café Brasserie Svej** (⊠ Åboulevarden 22 86/12–30–31 ⊕ www.svej. dk), on the canal, is a popular meeting spot for drinks and quiet chats in its Viennese-inspired decor. The friendly **Café Jorden** (⊠ Badstueg. 3 86/19–72–22) has a brass-and-wood bar and a heated outdoor terrace with a red awning. Students and young professionals mix with the chatty bar staff, who like to sing along to the pop and rock classics.

★ The **Café Under Masken** (Under the Mask Café; ⊠ Bispeg. 3 86/ 18–22–66), next door to the Royal Hotel, is the personal creation of Århus artist Hans Krull, who also designed the unique iron sculptures that grace the entrance to the hotel. The surreal bar is crammed with every type of mask imaginable, from grinning Balinese wooden masks to black-and-yellow African visages. Pygmy statues and stuffed tropical birds and fish line the shelves. Everything was collected by Krull and other bar patrons. The back wall is one long aquarium filled with exotic fish. As the bar manager puts it, "Everyone's welcome. This bar is a no-man's-land, a place for all the 'funny fish' of the world." If that's not enough of a draw, consider that the drink prices are the lowest in town, and more than 30 kinds of beer are on offer. It's open nightly until 2 AM.

Carlton (⊠ Rosensg. 23 ☎ 86/20–21–22) is a classy bar and restaurant, presided over by a carousel horse. Sip cocktails in the front bar-café, or dine on contemporary Danish fare in the dining room. The **Cockney Pub** (⊠ Maren Smeds Gyde 8 ☎ 86/19–45–77 ⊕ www.cockneypub.dk) is just that, and a bit more. It offers an exclusive line of beers and a wide selection of whiskeys. It was awarded the Cask Marque medal in 2004, "for pubs which serve the perfect pint." The **Hotel Marselis** (⊠ Strand- vejen 25 ☎ 86/14–44–11) attracts a varied crowd to its two venues: the **Beach Club,** with danceable rock and disco, and the more elegant **Nau- tilus** piano bar. Delighting committed smokers everywhere (it advertises to them specifically), **Ris Ras Filliongongong** (⊠ Mejlg. 24 ☎ 86/18–50–06 ⊙ Daily noon–2 AM), a self-described "sitting-room" with a major se- lection of beers, is never empty. **Sidewalk** (⊠ Åboulevarden 56–58 ☎ 86/ 18–18–66) has a large waterfront terrace that draws crowds on warm nights; in the equally lively interior you can sip cocktails at the long bar or graze on tapas and light meals, including hummus with olives and salad topped with soy-roasted chicken and spinach pasta.

CASINO   The **Royal Hotel** (⊠ Store Torv 4 ☎ 86/12–00–11), the city's casino, of- fers blackjack, roulette, baccarat, and slot machines.

Shopping

With more than 800 shops and many pedestrian streets (Strøget, Fred- ericksgade, Sct. Clemensgade, Store Torv, and Lille Torv), this city is a great place to play havoc with your credit cards. As befits a student town, Århus also has its "Latin Quarter," a jumble of cobbled streets around the cathedral, with boutiques, antiques shops, and glass and ceramic gal- leries that may be a little less expensive. In Vestergade street, you can turn on Grønnengade and stroll along Møllestien to see its charming old homes. At the **Bülow Duus Glassworks** (⊠ Studsg. 14 ☎ 86/12–72–86) you can browse among delicate and colorful glassworks from fishbowls to candleholders. While there, visit Mette Bülow Duus's workshop and witness the creation of beautiful glassware. **Folmer Hansen** (⊠ Sønderg. 43 ☎ 86/12–49–00) is packed with Danish tableware and porcelain, from sleek Arne Jacobsen–designed cheese cutters, ice buckets, and coffeepots to Royal Copenhagen porcelain plates. For the best selection of Georg Jensen designs, head to the official **Georg Jensen** (⊠ Sønderg. 1 ☎ 86/ 12–01–00 ⊕ www.georgjensen.com or www.damask.dk) store. It stocks Jensen-designed and -inspired watches, jewelry, table settings, and art nouveau vases. The textile designs of Georg Jensen Damask, in a sepa- rate department, are truly beautiful.

Ebeltoft

❶⑦ *45 km (28 mi) east of Århus.*

Danes refer to Ebeltoft—a town of crooked streets, sloping row houses, and crafts shops—as Jutland's nose. In the middle of the main square is Ebeltoft's half-timber **Det Gamle Rådhus** (Old Town Hall), said to be the smallest town hall in Denmark. Dating from 1789, it served as the town hall until 1840; today it is an annex of the Ebeltoft Museum, with historical exhibits displayed in its traditionally decorated rooms. The mayor still receives visitors here, and couples come from all over Denmark to be married in the quaint interior.

Near the town hall is the **Ebeltoft Museum**, which holds the Siamesisk Samling (Siamese Exhibit), a motley collection of Thai artifacts—from silks and stuffed lemurs to mounted tropical insects—brought back by explorer and Ebeltoft local Rasmus Havmøller. The museum also encompasses the nearby well-preserved dye-works factory, where the Ebeltoft peasants had their wool dyed until 1925. In summer, dyeing demonstrations are often held. ⊠ *Juulsbakke 1 86/34–55–99* ☎ *DKr 25 (includes town hall)* ☉ *June–Aug., daily 10–5; Sept.–mid-Oct., Apr., and May, Sat.–Thurs. 11–3; mid-Oct.–Dec., Feb., and Mar., weekends 11–3.*

Danish efficiency is on display beside the ferry at the **Vindmølleparken,** one of the largest windmill parks in the world. Sixteen of them on a curved spit of land generate electricity for 600 families. ⊠ Færgehaven ☎ 86/34–12–44 ☎ Free ☉ Daily.

You can't miss the frigate **Jylland,** dry-docked on the town's main harbor. The renovation of the three-masted tall ship was financed by Danish shipping magnate Mærsk McKinney Møller, and it's a testament to Denmark's seafaring days of yore. You can wander through to examine the bridge, gun deck, galley, captain's room, and the 10½-ton pure copper-and-pewter screw. Don't miss the voluptuous Pomeranian pine figurehead. ⊠ Strandvejen 4 ☎ 86/34–10–99 ⊕ www.fregatten-jylland. dk ☎ DKr 70 ☉ Mid-June–Aug., daily 10–7; Apr.–mid-June, Sept., and Oct., daily 10–6; Nov.–Mar., daily 10–5.

The small, light, and airy *Glasmuseet Ebeltoft* is on the Ebeltoft harbor, a perfect setting for the collection, which ranges from the mysterious symbol-laden monoliths of Swedish glass sage Bertil Vallien to the luminous gold pavilions of Japanese artist Kyohei Fujita. The shop sells functional pieces, art, and books. The museum stages six to nine separate exhibitions each year, presenting the latest trends in glassmaking, and from April to October glassblowers can be seen at work in the glassblowing studio. On Wednesday afternoons in July, an event called "Close to Hot Glass" allows you to create your own little work of art (this is an extra DKr 75). ⊠ Strandvejen 8 ☎ 86/34–17–99 ⊕ www. glasmuseet.dk ☎ DKr 40 ☉ Jan.–June and Aug.–Dec., daily 10–5; July, daily 10–7.

Where to Stay & Eat

★ **$$$$** ✕☑ **Molskroen.** Perched on the coast northwest of Ebeltoft, in a sunflower-yellow, half-timber manor house from 1923, is this swanky inn and restaurant. The ample rooms are tastefully decorated in cool tones with four-poster beds and Bang & Olufsen televisions. The large, gleaming bathrooms are done up with designer fixtures and half the rooms overlook the water. Acclaimed young chef Jesper Koch heads the restaurant, which serves fine French fare with an imaginative twist. Roasted duck is stuffed with apricots, figs, and dates and drizzled in a sauce of rum and raisins. Marinated cod sashimi comes with mussels and dill salad. Large picture windows overlook the lush garden, through which a path winds to the private beach. The adjoining sitting room is perfect for a post-dinner brandy and cigar in front of the fireplace. ⊠ *Hovedg. 16, DK–8400* ☎ *86/36–22–00* 🖷 *86/36–23–00* ⊕ *www.molskroen.dk* ⤴ *18 rooms, 3 suites* ⚲ *Restaurant, beach, bar* ☰ *AE, DC, MC, V* ⊘ *Restaurant closed Mon.–Tues. Oct.–Mar.*

Viborg

⓲ *22 km (36 mi) north of Silkeborg, 66 km (41 mi) northwest of Århus.*

Viborg dates back at least to the 8th century, when it was a trading post and site of pagan sacrifice. Later it became a center of Christianity, with monasteries and an episcopal residence. It has no fewer than 16 museums (with interests ranging from psychiatry to cycling) and eight different churches ranging in age from 25 to 900 years old. It's worth a stop if you're looking for a slower-paced town that still has a few attractions.

Built in 1130, Viborg's **Domkirke** (cathedral) was once the largest granite church in the world. Only the crypt remains of the original building, which was restored and reopened in 1876. The dazzling early-20th-century Biblical frescoes are by Danish painter Joakim Skovgard. ⊠ *Sct. Mogensg. 4* ☎ *87/25–52–50* 🖻 *Free* ⊘ *June–Aug., Mon.–Sat. 10–5, Sun. noon–5; Apr., May, and Sept., Mon.–Sat. 11–4, Sun. noon–4; Oct.–Mar., Mon.–Sat. 11–3, Sun. noon–3.*

Where to Stay & Eat

$$$ ✕ **Brygger Bauers Grotter.** A former brewery dating from 1832, this cozy, cavernous underground restaurant has arched wooden ceilings, old paintings depicting Viborg history, and beer barrels lining the back wall. The contemporary Danish menu includes a hearty beef stew served with rice, and chicken breast stuffed with Gorgonzola. ⊠ *Sct. Mathiasg. 61* ☎ *86/61–44–88* ☰ *MC, V.*

$$$ 🏨 **Palads Hotel.** This large hotel near the center of town has ample, simply furnished rooms done up in a rose decor. A third of the rooms are designed for longer stays and have kitchenettes. ⊠ *Sct. Mathiasg. 5, DK–8800* ☎ *86/62–37–00* 🖷 *86/62–40–46* ⊕ *www.hotelpalads.dk* ⤴ *99 rooms, 19 suites* ⚲ *Some kitchenettes, sauna, bar, some pets allowed, no-smoking rooms* ☰ *AE, DC, MC, V.*

Aalborg

⓳ *80 km (50 mi) northeast of Viborg, 112 km (70 mi) north of Århus.*

The gentle waters of the Limfjord cut off the top segment of Jutland completely. Perched on its narrowest point is Aalborg, Denmark's fourth-largest city, which includes the youthful Aalborg University, founded in 1974. Aalborg's began, in 692, as the gateway between north and mid-Jutland. It was granted a municipal charter in 1342, and the Limfjord has been crucial to the city's economy since the heyday of the herring industry. Until 1879 a ferry and pontoon bridge provided the link between the north and south parts of the city; a bridge came in 1933, and then a 1,900-foot-long tunnel was built in 1969. Aalborg's harbor is a busy place, with ships bound for Bornholm, Norway, Iceland, the Faroe Islands, Ireland, and Britain.

In many parts of the world, Aalborg is identified more as a brand—a brand of schnapps, that is: the clear, potent liquor many Danes enjoy with herring. Since **Danish Distillers/De Danske Spritfabrikker** bought Harald Jensen's still in 1883, the city's name has been linked with aquavit, and the world-famous schnapps still carries the name of Aalborg. You can take part in a two-hour guided tour of the plant, with a tasting and a stop at the company store. ⊠ *C. A. Olesens Gade 1* ☎ *98/ 12–42–00* ⊕ *www.aalborgsnaps.dk* ⊠ *DKr 40* ⊙ *Mid-May–Aug., Mon. and Sat. 10 AM and 2 PM.*

The baroque **Budolfi Kirke** (Cathedral Church of St. Botolph) is dedicated to the English saint. Eight cocks crow the hour from four identical clock faces on the tower. The stone church, replacing one made of wood, has been rebuilt several times in its 800-year history. It includes a copy of the original spire of the Rådhus in Copenhagen, which was taken down about a century ago. The money for the construction was donated to the church by a generous local merchant and his sister, both of whom, locals say, had no other family on which to lavish their wealth. ⊠ *Gammel Torv.*

Next to Budolfi Kirke is the 15th-century **Helligåndsklosteret** (Monastery of the Holy Ghost). One of Denmark's best-preserved monasteries— and perhaps the only one that admitted both nuns and monks. It is now a home for the elderly. The building was erected in several stages during the 15th century and the beginning of the 16th century, and coincidentally, the duties of the first nuns and monks were to look after the sick and aged. During World War II the monastery was the meeting place for the Churchill Club, a group of Aalborg schoolboys who became world famous for their sabotage of the Nazis—their schemes were carried out even after the enemy thought they were locked up. ⊠ *C. W. Obels Pl., Gammel Torv* ☎ *98/12–02–05* ⊙ *Guided tours mid- June–mid-Aug. daily at 1:30.*

★ The local favorite landmark is the magnificent 17th-century **Jens Bang Stenhus** (Jens Bang's Stone House), built by the wealthy merchant Jens Bang in 1642. It was rumored that because he was never made a town council member, the cantankerous Bang avenged himself by caricaturing his political enemies in gargoyles all over the building and then adding his own face, its tongue sticking out at the town hall. The five-story building has been the home of Aalborg's oldest pharmacy for more than 300 years. Note that the Aalborg tourist office is directly across the street. ⊠ *Østeråg. 9.*

In the center of the old town is **Jomfru Ane Gade,** named, as the story goes, for an aristocratic maiden accused of being a witch, then beheaded. Now the street's fame is second only to that of Copenhagen's

Strøget. Despite the flashing neon and booming music of about 30 discos, bars, clubs, and eateries, the street attracts a thick stream of pedestrian traffic and appeals to all ages.

The only Fourth of July celebrations outside the United States blast off in nearby **Rebild Park,** a salute to the United States for welcoming some 300,000 Danish immigrants. The tradition dates back to 1912.

Just north of Aalborg at Nørresundby (still considered a part of greater Aalborg) is **Lindholm Høje,** a Viking and Iron Age burial ground where stones placed either in the shape of a ship or in triangles denote where men were buried; oval and circular groups of stones show where women were buried. In total, there are about 682 graves dating from AD 400 to shortly before AD 1000. At the bottom of the hill there is a museum that chronicles Viking civilization.

The **Viking Drama** (☎ 98/17–33–73 ⊕ www.geocities.com/vikingespil ☜ Dkr 70) is a musical and dramatic performance about the daily lives of the Vikings, held on the grounds of Lindholm Høje. It's performed in Danish, but the music, singing, dancing, and costumes don't need any translation. The show is performed mid-June through early July only at 7 PM on weekdays, 4:30 and 11 PM on Saturday, and 4:30 on Sunday. ✉ *Vendilavej 11* ☎ *96/31–04–28* ☜ *Burial ground free, museum DKr 30* ۞ *Easter–mid-Oct., daily 10–5; mid-Oct.–Easter, Tues.–Sun. 10–4.*

The blocky marble-and-glass structure of the **Nordjyllands Kunstmuseum** (North Jutland Museum of Modern Art) was designed by architects Alvar and Elissa Aalto and Jacques Baruël. The gridded interior partition system allows the curators to tailor their space to each exhibition, many of which are drawn from the museum's permanent collection of 20th-century Danish and international art. On the grounds there are also a manicured sculpture park and an amphitheater that hosts occasional concerts. ✉ *Kong Christians Allé 50* ☎ *98/13–80–88* ⊕ *www.nordjyllandskunstmuseum.dk* ☜ *DKr 30* ۞ *Easter–mid-Oct., daily 10–5; mid-Oct.–Easter, Tues.–Sun. 10–4.*

The **Aalborg Historical Museum** contains the well-preserved underground ruins of a medieval Franciscan friary, including a walled cellar and the foundations of the chapel. Enter via the elevator outside the Salling department store. Another favorite attraction is the Renaissance chamber Aalborgstuen, which features furniture and glassware from the 16th and 17th centuries. ✉ *Alg. 48* ☎ *96/31–04–10* ⊕ *www.aahm.dk* ☜ *DKr 30* ۞ *Thurs.–Sun. 10–5.*

۞ **Tivoliland** is a spring and summer amusement park that boasts as its prime attraction the hair-raising Boomerang roller coaster—the biggest roller coaster in Scandinavia—which whips you through narrow bends and loops, both forward and backward. ✉ *Karolinelundsvej 40* ☎ *98/12–33–15* ⊕ *www.tivoliland.dk* ☜ *Admission DKr 50; rides extra* ۞ *May and June, daily noon–8; July, daily 11–9; late-Mar. and Apr., daily noon–7.*

Where to Stay & Eat

$$$$ ✕ **Mortens Kro.** The chef-owner of Mortens Kro, Morten Nielsen, is a celebrity in these parts, and the food here is a delight, both visually and gastronomically. The menu changes monthly, but a starter might be steamed white asparagus with leeks in a mousseline sauce, with herbs and freshly shelled shrimp. A main course could be free-range veal tenderloin from North Jutland, marinated in basil and served with slow-baked small tomatoes and the ubiquitous new potatoes. Every inch of the restaurant is thoughtfully designed, even the washrooms—they're equipped with waterfalls and nature sound effects emanating from invisible speakers. Jackets aren't required, but a "business casual" look is a good way to go. ⊠ *Mølleå Arkaden* ☎ *98/12–48–60* ⊕ *www. mortenskro.com* ⌣ *Reservations essential* ▤ *DC, MC, V* ⊙ *Closed Sun.*

$$$$ ✕ **Rosdahl's Restaurant, Food Market, and Wine Shop.** This one-stop-shopping homage to food and beverage is in an old sugar warehouse just steps from the Limfjord. To pick up picnic items, stop by the fresh-food market every Saturday between 9:30 and 2:30, or, for a more formal repast, the à la carte and prix-fixe menus from the restaurant will be sure to please. The cuisine is definitely French-inspired—even the cheeses sold in the market are from the big Rungis market outside Paris. ⊠ *Strandvejen* ☎ *98/12–05–80* ▤ *DC, MC, V* ⊙ *Closed Sun.*

¢–$$$ ✕ **Søgaards Bryghus.** Microbreweries normally aren't upscale, but this brew house is a cut above the rest. The spotless interior; piping hot food from the kitchen; attractive glassware, brass, and exposed brick; and lots of smiles make this pub special. It serves great food, like barbecued ribs, steaks, and fries; it even has its own in-house butcher shop. Tasting and tours can also be arranged, and if you're in Aalborg for a couple of days you can buy a liter of your favorite homemade brew in a Danish-designed bottle and return for refills. ⊠ *C. W. Obels Pl. 1A* ☎ *98/ 16–11–14* ⊕ *www.soegaardsbryghus.dk* ▤ *MC, V.*

★ ¢–$$ ✕ **Duus Vinkjælder.** Most people come to this cellar—part alchemist's dungeon, part neighborhood bar—for a drink, but you can also get a light bite. In summer enjoy smørrebrød; in winter sup on grilled specialties such as *biksemad* (a meat-and-potato hash), and the restaurant's special liver pâté. ⊠ *Østeråg. 9* ☎ *98/12–50–56* ▤ *DC, V* ⊙ *Closed Sun.*

$$$ 🏨 **Helnan Phønix.** In a central and sumptuous old mansion, this hotel is popular with vacationers as well as business travelers. The rooms are luxuriously furnished with plump chairs and polished, dark-wood furniture; in some the original wooden ceiling beams are still intact. The Brigadier restaurant serves excellent French and Danish food. ⊠ *Vesterbro 77, DK–9000* ☎ *98/12–00–11* 🖷 *98/10–10–20* ⊕ *www.helnan.dk* ⊲ *219 rooms, 2 suites* ⌣ *Restaurant, gym, bar, meeting room, some pets allowed, no-smoking rooms* ▤ *AE, DC, MC, V.*

$–$$$ 🏨 **Hotel Hvide Hus.** This Best Western property is one of the city's few "high-rises," at 15 stories; the bright rooms have balconies overlooking Kildepark. It's a 5-minute walk to the train station diagonally across the park, or a 10-minute walk to the city center. Breakfasts in the top-floor Restaurant Kilden are more than adequate, and it's worth checking out the daily dinner specials in the same room—meals are well presented in a relaxed atmosphere with a wonderful view of the city. Weekend rates are very reasonable. ⊠ *Vesterbro 2, DK–9000* ☎ *98/ 13–84–00* 🖷 *98/13–51–22* ⊕ *www.hotelhvidehus.dk* ⊲ *196 rooms, 2 suites* ⌣ *Restaurant, bar, meeting rooms* ▤ *AE, DC, MC, V* ⊙❙ *BP.*

Nightlife & the Arts

BARS & WINE
CELLARS

Consider a pub crawl along the famed **Jomfru Ane Gade,** wildly popular for its party atmosphere and rock-bottom drink prices, which are much lower than anywhere else in Denmark. Opt for the house drink of the night (usually a Danish beer), and you'll often pay one-third of the normal cost. There's much variety in music and ambience, so if one place doesn't fit your mood, maybe the one next door will.

Dimly lighted and atmospheric, **Duus Vinkjælder** (⊠ Østeråg. 9 ☎ 98/12–50–56) is extremely popular, one of the most classic beer and wine cellars in all of Denmark. It's an obligatory stop for anyone who wants a taste of Aalborg's nightlife. **L. A. Bar** (⊠ Jomfru Ane Gade 7 ☎ 98/11–37–37) is a chatty, American-style bar. **Rendez-Vous** (⊠ Jomfru Ane Gade 5 ☎ 98/16–88–80) has a pleasant outdoor terrace with black and brown wicker chairs. Thursday through Saturday it opens its upstairs dance floor, which attracts 18- to 25-year-olds with standard disco. **Spirit of America** (⊠ Jomfru Ane Gade 16 ☎ 98/12–47–55) is a good spot to catch an international soccer match on the bar's big-screen TV.

CASINO

The city's sole casino is at the **Radisson SAS Limfjord Hotel** (⊠ Ved Stranden 14–16 ☎ 98/16–43–33).

LIVE MUSIC &
DANCE CLUBS

Gaslight (⊠ Jomfru Ane Gade 23 ☎ 98/10–17–50) plays rock and grinding dance music to a young crowd. **Le Bar Bat** (⊠ Jomfru Ane Gade 25 ☎ 98/13–32–41) offers live music Thursday through Saturday. **Pusterummet** (⊠ Jomfru Ane Gade 12 ☎ 98/16–06–39) is open during the day, but turns into a dance club on Friday and Saturday. **Rock Caféen** (⊠ Jomfru Ane Gade 7 ☎ 98/13–66–90) is for serious rock-and-roll lovers, with live music most nights. **Rock Nielsen** (⊠ Jomfru Ane Gade 9-11 ☎ 98/13–99–29) is a rock-and-roll dance club where disco music would most likely never be heard!

Skagen

20 *88 km (55 mi) northeast of Aalborg, 212 km (132 mi) north of Århus.*

For over a century, Skagen (pronounced *skane*), a picturesque area where the North Sea meets the Baltic Sea, has been a favorite destination of well-off travelers, artists, and architects. This 600-year old market town on Jutland's windswept northern tip has long pebbly beaches and huge open skies. Sunsets are tremendous events, so much so that idlers on the beach stop and applaud. Its main industry has traditionally been fishing, but tourism now seems to be eclipsing that.

The 19th-century Danish artist and nationally revered poet Holger Drachmann (1846–1908) and his friends, including the well-known P. S. Krøyer and Michael and Anna Ancher, founded the Skagen School of painting, which sought to capture the special quality of light and idyllic seascapes here. They and their contemporaries mostly enjoyed depicting everyday life in Skagen from the turn of the 20th century until the 1920s, and you can see their efforts on display in the **Skagen Museum.** It's a wonderful homage to this talented group of Danes, and you'll become mesmerized by some of the portraits, which seem more like a

JUL-TIDE IN DENMARK

IT COULD BE THE BLANKET *of snow on thatched roofs, or the dancing flames of candles flickering behind frosted window panes. It might be the pungent aroma of roast goose wafting from the kitchen, or perhaps the giggling group of rosy-cheek children in red clogs catching snowflakes in their mittens. If Denmark is the land of all that's cute and hygellig (the catchall Danish term for cozy), then a Danish Christmas (Jul) just about epitomizes the country's charm.*

It is on December 1 that Danish children are permitted to open the first little window on their advent calendars, a signal that the Christmas season has officially begun. A seasonal staple, the colorful advent calendar (also called Nativity calendar) has 25 windows, behind which lie a Christmas scene and, more importantly, a chocolate. The calendar culminates on December 25th, usually with a depiction of the birth of baby Jesus—and the largest chocolate of the lot.

The Danes' penchant for home decoration blossoms during the holidays. Delicate paper cutouts of snowflakes and reindeer dangle from ceilings. Wreaths heavy with berries hang on front doors, and red and white candles set living rooms aglow.

As any Danish child knows, when you can't find a sock, or if the milk suddenly spills as if an invisible hand pushed it, then it means that the mischievous Christmas nisser (elves) are up to their tricks again. Pranksters at heart, the nimble nisser can wreak havoc on a household—that is, unless they're left a bowl of porridge or some other Christmas goodie, which Danish kids make sure to do. And what goodies to choose from— candy stores and bakeries are bursting with marzipan of all shapes and sizes, drizzled with chocolate and sprinkles in every hue of the rainbow. The windows

are piled high with glistening wienerbrød, Denmark's decadent, flaky pastry—often oozing with creamy fillings—that knows no equal.

Christmas is officially celebrated on the evening of December 24. Families gather 'round the table for a Christmas feast, which may be roast duck or goose stuffed with oranges or prunes, or pork roasted in its own juices. No Danish meal is complete without the omnipresent rød kål, boiled, vinegary red cabbage, and kartoffler (potatoes). The choice for dessert is unanimous: the Christmas meal always ends with riz à l'amande, a thick and creamy rice pudding. Hidden within its fluffy folds is an almond, and whoever finds it receives a gift—and, some believe, good luck for the rest of the year.

A properly decorated Danish Christmas tree is a sight to behold, bedecked in handmade decorations—from gold-paper angels to brightly painted wooden figures—and strung (but of course) with miniature Danish flags. Purists still decorate their trees with white candles, which are lighted for the next phase of the evening. Dancing around the tree, the perfect antidote to falling into a post-feast stupor, is the bonding highlight of the night. Family and guests hold hands and skip and sway around the tree, singing Danish carols. All worries and differences are forgotten as they engage in this refreshingly primary act of sharing, just as generations have before them. The circle breaks when the children can't bear the temptation a moment longer and scamper over to the gifts piled high under the tree. This is when a Danish Christmas ends like any other: kids sitting among reams of ribbons and ripped paper, while the adults sip their spiked eggnog, remembering when happiness was what you got for Christmas.

photographic collection of days gone by. Some of the more famous canvases may be on loan at museums throughout the world, but do try to visit, even if you're only in Skagen for a half day. The museum store offers the best selection in town of posters, postcards, and other souvenirs depicting the Skagen paintings. ⊠ *Brøndumsvej 4* ☎ *98/44–64–44* ⊕ *www.skagensmuseum.dk* 🖻 *DKr 60* ⊙ *June–Aug., daily 10–6; May and Sept., daily 10–5; Apr. and Oct., Tues.–Sun. 11–4; Nov.–Mar., Wed.–Fri. 1–4, Sat. 11–4, Sun. 11–3.*

Michael and Anna Ancher are Skagen's—if not Denmark's—most famous artist couple, and their meticulously restored 1820 home and studio, **Michael og Anna Ancher's Hus** (Michael and Anna Ancher's House), is now a museum. Old oil lamps and lace curtains decorate the parlor; the doors throughout the house were painted by Michael. Anna's studio, complete with easel, is awash in the famed Skagen light. More than 240 paintings by Michael, Anna, and their daughter, Helga, grace the walls. ⊠ *Markvej 2–4* ☎ *98/44–30–09* ⊕ *www.anchershus.dk* 🖻 *DKr 40* ⊙ *May–Sept., daily 10–5 (until 6 late June–mid-Aug.); Apr. and Oct., daily 11–3; Nov.–Mar., weekends 11–3.*

Danes say that in Skagen you can stand with one foot on the Kattegat, the strait between Sweden and eastern Jutland, the other in the Skagerrak, the strait between western Denmark and Norway. It is possible to do this, but by no means go swimming here—it's very dangerous. The point is so thrashed by storms and roiling waters that the 18th-century **Tilsandede Kirke** (Sand-Buried Church), 2 km (1 mi) south of town, is completely covered by dunes.

Fodor'sChoice
★

Even more famed than the Buried Church is the west coast's dramatic **Råbjerg Mile,** a protected migrating dune that moves about 33 feet a year and is accessible on foot from the Kandestederne.

Where to Stay & Eat

$$–$$$$ ✕ **Skagen Fiske Restaurant.** Located on the waterfront, this place at first seems very unassuming, but it actually faces one of the two marinas that dock private yachts—in summer the restaurant's terrace is the place to see and be seen by the denizens of these vessels. On the ground floor a sand floor (over wood) greets you in the restaurant's pub; upstairs, the blue-and-white restaurant might reminder you of a warehouse attic, but this is Danish chic, and that's Russian abstract art on the walls. Upstairs or down, the Pandestegte *fiskefrikadelier* (fish cakes) are a must-try. Made from three Nordic fish and gently creamed with herbs and potatoes, they may be the restaurant's most popular item. Wash them down with a frosty Danish beer or lemon soda. Note that there's no dress code, but you'll want to put on your best casual chic threads. Reservations are recommended. ⊠ *Fiskehuskaj 13* ☎ *98/44–35–44* ⊕ *www.skagen-fiskerestaurant.dk* 🖶 *AE, DC, V* ⊙ *Closed Nov. and Jan.*

$$$–$$$$ ✕🏨 **Ruths Hotel.** This is definitely the grande dame of Old Skagen, originally built by Emma and Hans Christian Ruth. It has been completely rebuilt with modern facilities, and its main restaurant, Ruth's Gourmet, is operated by Chef Michel Michaud, known for heading up the kitchens at such renowned venues as Kong Hans in Copenhagen. (The only drawback is that you have to call ahead at least a month in advance for a reservation!) There is also a brasserie that serves local delicacies prepared by any of Chef Michaud's 17 cooks. Rooms are typically lavish, in an understated way, and all have balconies or terraces and Swedish-made DUX beds; some have hot tubs. The Wellness Centre provides regular spa and beauty treatments, as well as some forms of laser cosmetic surgery. ⊠ *Hans Ruths Vej 1* ☎ *98/44–11–24* 🖷 *98/45–08–75* ⊕ *www. ruths-hotel.dk* ⤶ *14 rooms, 12 suites* ♻ *2 restaurants, in-room broadband, indoor pool, gym, spa, sauna, steam rooms, meeting rooms* ▤ *AE, DC, MC, V.*

$$–$$$ ✕⊡ **Strandhotellet.** Also in Old Skagen, this bright and romantic hotel is the perfect foil to the wild, windy sea- and sandscapes nearby. Built in 1912, it's filled with gently curved wicker furnishings, painted woods, and original art. The guest rooms are painted in pastels, and are reminiscent of those from a country estate—a country estate that just happens to have Bang & Olufsen flat-screen televisions. The staff is friendly and accommodating, though in the off-season they may leave at 10 PM (returning the next morning to prepare a handsome Continental breakfast, of course). ⊠ *Jeckelsvej 2, DK–9990* ☎ *98/44–34–99* 🖷 *98/44–59–19* ⊕ *www.strandhotellet.glskagen.dk* ⤶ *15 rooms, 13 suites, 2 houses* ♻ *Restaurant, café, Wi-Fi, lounge, meeting room* ▤ *AE, DC, MC, V.*

$–$$$ ✕⊡ **Plesner Hotel & Restaurant.** This appealing hotel is just a three-minute walk from the train station. Ulrik Plesner, a famous local architect responsible for many buildings in Skagen, designed this one as well, and his portrait graces the upper landing on the first floor. Rooms are all bright and airy, with nice color schemes of blue, green, or rose. All have a private bath; the newer rooms (21 and 22) have French windows. Rooms in the hotel's annex, although smaller, are charming and have little terraces. There are no phones or elevator, but there are TVs, and the place is spotless. The dining room has popular lunch specials, though note that it's only open from June 16 to August 14. ⊠ *Holstvej 8, DK–9990* ☎ *98/44–68–44* 🖷 *98/44–36–86* ⊕ *www.hotelplesner.dk* ⤶ *24 rooms, 2 suites* ♻ *Restaurant; no room phones* ▤ *MC, V* ⦿❘ *BP.*

Shopping

Skagen's artistic heritage and light-drenched landscapes continue to draw painters and craftspeople, meaning you'll find better-than-average souvenirs in town. The pedestrian street in town has a fascinating and intimate shopping atmosphere with stores as fine as those you'd see in Copenhagen. For colorful, innovative handblown glass, for example, head for **Glaspusterblæser** (⊠ Sct. Laurentii Vej 33 ☎ 98/44–58–75), a large glassblowing workshop housed in what was once Skagen's post office. The amber store and workshop **Ravsliberen I Skagen** (⊠ Sct. Laurentii Vej 6 ☎ 98/44–55–27) sells top-quality amber jewelry, including pieces with insects trapped inside. You can buy miniature replicas of figureheads, ships' "guardian angels," at **Trip Trap** (⊠ Sct. Laurentii Vej 17A ☎ 98/44–63–22), a branch of the popular Danish home-decorating chain.

Jutland A to Z

AIRPORTS & TRANSFERS

Jutland has hubs in Aalborg, Århus and Billund, which handle mainly domestic and European traffic. Billund Airport, 2 km (1 mi) southwest of the city's downtown, is the larger of the two, and the arrival end of flights from major European, Scandinavian, and Danish airports. Århus airport has regular flights to Copenhagen, Gothenburg, Stockholm, Oslo, and London, as well as charters to southern Europe.

🚩 Airports **Aalborg Airport** ☎ 98/17-11-44 ⊕ www.aal.dk. **Århus Airport** ☎ 87/75-70-00 ⊕ www.aar.dk. **Billund Airport** ☎ 76/50-50-50 ⊕ www.billund-airport.dk.

TRANSFERS Hourly buses run between Århus Airport and the train station in town. The trip takes around 45 minutes and costs DKr 80. There is also a scheduled bus service (Bus 212) between Århus Airport and Randers and Ebeltoft. A taxi ride from the airport to central Århus takes 45 minutes and costs well over DKr 300.

From Billund Airport there are buses to Århus (Radisson SAS Hotel, DKr 130), Esbjerg, Kolding, Vejle, Odense, and the Hotel Legoland, near the airport.Taxi and bus routes connect Aalborg Airport with the city. A taxi costs around DKr 175 and takes roughly 20 minutes. Nordjyllands Trafikselskab has buses connecting the airport to towns near Aalborg, and the company Flybusnord runs routes to Sæby and Frederikshavn.

🚩 **Flybusnord** ☎98/43-30-00 ⊕www.flybusnord.dk. **Nordjyllands Trafikselskab** ☎98/11-11-11 ⊕ www.nordjyllandtrafikselskab.dk.

BIKE TRAVEL

The whole peninsula has scores of bike paths, and many highways also have cycle lanes. Keep in mind that distances feel much longer here than elsewhere in the country, and that even a few humble hills are a challenge for children and novice cyclists. The center of this area is distinguished by long subglacial stream trenches, large forests, and lakes; and the southeast has typical fjord landscapes and old market towns. Basically, there is a network of more than 2,500 km (1,550 mi) of bicycling routes, containing over one-fifth of all the bike routes in Denmark.

North Jutland is ideal for a bicycle holiday, and whether you choose to travel along the coastline, go inland, or explore the islands of Mors or Læsø, the area has plenty of quiet roads, disused railway lines, bicycle paths, and signposted routes, which allow you to enjoy the region by bicycle without worrying about cars. The North Jutland tourism Web site can help you choose between 14 different cycling holidays, with packages available from Zig Zag around the Limfjord to Seven Days by the North Sea.

In South Jutland you may want to choose one of the special routes. The newest to open, in May 2005, is along the Danish-German border: 130 km (56 mi) that weave through the varied landscapes and cultural aspects of both countries. Every 3 km (2 mi) you'll pass an information display that has a map and information about the uniqueness of that area. Currently a free guidebook on this route is available in Danish and German only. For more information, go to ⊕ www.graenseruten.dk.

Package holidays for cyclists are offered by the Haderslev Tourism Office and include accommodation, daily breakfast, maps, baggage assistance, and access to a service hotline. Trips last from four nights to seven nights. The costs, which do not include bike rental, are from DKr 2,150 to DKr 3,550 (per person, double occupancy). Bikes usually rent for about DKr 300 per week or DKr 50 per day.

🛈 **Haderslev Tourism Information Office** ⊠ Honnørkajen 1, DK-6100 Haderslev ☎ 74/52-55-50 ⊕ www.cycling.sydjylland.com. **Visit Nord** ☎ 96/96-12-00 ⊕ www. visitnord.dk.

BOAT & FERRY TRAVEL

More than 20 ferry routes still connect the peninsula with the rest of Denmark (including the Faroe Islands), as well as England, Norway, and Sweden, with additional connections to Kiel and Puttgarden, Germany, the Baltics, Poland, and Russia. For most ferries you can get general information and make reservations by calling FDM (Danish Motoring Association). For direct Zealand to Jutland passage, you can take a car-ferry hydrofoil from Zealand's Odden to Ebeltoft (45 minutes) or Århus (1 hour). You can also take the slower, but less expensive, car ferry from Kalundborg (on Zealand) to Århus (2 hours, 40 minutes). Both ferries travel five times daily on weekdays, and slightly less often on weekends. For ferry schedules and information, call Mols-Linien.

🛈 **FDM** ☎ 70/11-60-11. **Mols-Linien** ☎ 70/10-14-18 🖷 89/52-52-90 ⊕ www. molslinien.dk. **Scandinavian Seaways** ☎ 79/17-79-17 Esbjerg, 33/42-30-00 Copenhagen ⊕ www.dfdsseaways.dk. **Stena Line** ☎ 96/20-02-00 ⊕ www.stenaline.com.

BUS TRAVEL

Bus and train travel inside Denmark are made more convenient through Bus/Tog Samarbejde, a comprehensive route and schedule information source. Bus tickets are usually sold on board the buses immediately before departure. Ask about discounts for children, senior citizens, and groups.

Intercity buses are punctual and slightly cheaper but slower than trains. You can buy tickets on the bus and pay according to destination. For schedules and fares, call the local tourist office, as a network of different bus companies covers the peninsula. Should you want to go by bus only to the north, get on one of the Thinggaard buses in Esbjerg, which will take you all the way to Frederikshavn, with stops in Viborg (north-central) and Aalborg (north). A one-way ticket between Esbjerg and Frederikshavn costs around DKr 245.

Long-distance bus routes from Aalborg to Copenhagen (5 hours) are available through Abildskou buses or from Aalborg to Esbjerg (3 hours) through Thinggaard Express.

Schedules for most bus travel within towns are posted at all bus stops and fares are usually about DKr 15.

🛈 **Abildskou** ⊠ Graham Bellsvej 40, Århus ☎ 70/21-08-88 ⊕ www.abildskou.dk. **Bus/ Tog Samarbejde** ⊕ www.rejseplan.dk. **Thinggaard Bus** ☎ 70/10-00-20 ⊕ www.

thinggaard-bus.dk. **Thinggaard Express** ✉ Jyllandsg. 8B, Aalborg ☎ 98/11-66-00 🌐 www.expresbus.dk.

CAR TRAVEL

Although train and bus connections are excellent, sites and towns in Jutland are widely dispersed, and the peninsula is best explored by car. Whether you decide to take speedy, modern highways or winding old roads, traffic is virtually nonexistent.

Getting around Denmark these days is much easier than in the past, thanks to bridges that connect the kingdom to both Sweden and the Continent; that said, it's best to confirm all passage with either a local tourist board or FDM before setting out, to avoid confusion caused by ferry mergers and discontinued routes. Although there are several ferry connections to other parts of Denmark and Europe, most travelers drive north from Germany, or arrive from the islands of Zealand or Funen. Ferry prices can get steep, and vary according to the size of the vehicle and the number of passengers.

From Copenhagen or elsewhere on Zealand, you can drive the approximately 110 km (69 mi) across the island, then cross the world's second-longest suspension bridge, the Storebæltsbro (Great Belt Bridge), to Knudshoved. You then drive the 85 km (53 mi) across Funen and cross from Middelfart to Fredericia, Jutland, over the Lillebæltsbro (Little Belt Bridge). There are more choices, since two bridges link Middelfart to Fredericia. The older, lower bridge (2 km [1 mi]) follows Route 161, whereas the newer suspension bridge (1 km [½ mi]) on E20 is faster.

If you need to rent a car, Europcar/Østergaard Biler is the largest and oldest car-rental business in the country, with 40 outlets nationwide.
🚗 **Europcar** ✉ Sønder Allé 35, 8000 Århus C ☎ 89/33-11-11 🌐 www.europcar.dk. **FDM** ☎ 70/11-60-11.

EMERGENCIES

For ambulance, fire, or police anywhere in Denmark, dial 112. You can contact local pharmacies in Aalborg for information on emergency doctors.
🚗 **Aalborg pharmacy** ✉ Budolfi Apotek, Alg. 60 ☎ 98/12-06-77.

SPORTS & THE OUTDOORS

CANOEING The Silkeborg Turistbureau publishes an excellent brochure on canoeing in that area, on the Gudenå River. It includes information on how to pack a canoe; regulations for canoeing on the river and lakes; and lists of camps and tent sites along the river, including phone numbers and prices. Most important is the description of package trips that are available, including the Family Tour, Pioneer Tour, and the Luxury Tour. After reserving one of the trips (from three to six days), all you need do is show up at the desired starting point, where the canoes and equipment will be waiting for you. The daily distance will have been determined beforehand and accommodation will have been booked.

Tønder and the surrounding area may have the best canoeing in the south. You can rent a canoe for one day or several days and paddle along the scenic river system. Contact Tønder Kanoudlejning for more information; note that at this writing, the Web site is only in Danish.

Silkeborg Turistbureau ☎ 86/82-19-11 🖶 86/81-09-83 ⊕ www.silkeborg.com. **Tønder Kanoudlejning** ☎ 74/72-42-50 ⊕ www.vidaa-kano.dk.

FISHING   The Lake District is a great place for fishing—more than 15 popular species of fish can be found here. License requirements vary, and package tours are also available; contact any local tourist office for details.

TRAIN TRAVEL

DSB makes hourly runs from Copenhagen to Frederikshavn, in northern Jutland, stopping in Aalborg (4¾ hours) along the way. The trip includes train passage across the Storebæltsbro between Korsør, on west Zealand, and Nyborg, on east Funen. A one-way trip from Copenhagen to Frederikshavn is about DKr 320. For long trips, the DSB trains are fast and efficient, with superb views of the countryside. Smaller towns do not have intercity trains, so you have to switch to buses once you arrive.

DSB ☎ 70/13-14-15 ⊕ www.dsb.dk.

VISITOR INFORMATION

At the Århus tourist office, check out the Århus Pass, which includes bus travel, free or discounted admission to museums and sites, and tours.

Aalborg ⊠ Østeråg. 8 ☎ 98/12-60-22 🖶 98/16-69-22 ⊕ www.visitaalborg.com. **Århus** ⊠ Park Allé 2 ☎ 89/40-67-00 ⊕ www.visitaarhus.com. **Ebeltoft** ⊠ Strandvejen 2 ☎ 86/34-14-00 ⊕ www.visitdjursland.com. **Esbjerg** ⊠ Skoleg. 33 ☎ 75/12-55-99 🖶 75/12-27-67 ⊕ www.visitesbjerg.com. **Fanø** ⊠ Færgevej 1, Nordby ☎ 75/16-26-00 🖶 75/16-29-03 ⊕ www.fanoeturistbureau.dk. **Haderslev Tourist Office** ⊠ Honnørkajen 1 ☎ 74/52-55-50 ⊕ www.haderslev-turist.dk. **Jelling** ⊠ Gormsg. 23 ☎ 75/87-13-01 🖶 75/82-10-11 ⊕ www.visitvejle.dk. **Kolding** ⊠ Akseltorv 8 ☎ 76/33-21-00 🖶 76-33-21-20 ⊕ www.visitkolding.dk. **Mid-Jutland** ⊕ www.midtjylland.dk. **North Jutland Tourist Office** ⊕ www.visitnord.dk. **Randers Turistbureau** ⊠ Tørvebryggen 12, DK-8900 ☎ 86/42-44-77 🖶 86/40-60-04 ⊕ www.visitranders.com. **Ribe** ⊠ Torvet 3 ☎ 75/42-15-00 🖶 75/42-40-78 ⊕ www.ribetourist.dk. **Ringkøbing Tourist Association** ⊠ Torvet, Postboks 27 ☎ 70/22-70-01 🖶 97/32-49-00 ⊕ www.ringkobingfjord.dk. **Rømø** ⊠ Havnebyvej 30 ☎ 74/75-51-30 🖶 74/75-50-31 ⊕ www.romo.dk. **Silkeborg** ⊠ Åhavevej 2A ☎ 86/82-19-11 🖶 86/81-09-83 ⊕ www.silkeborg.com. **Skagen** ⊠ Sct. Laurentii Vej 22 ☎ 98/44-13-77 🖶 98/45-02-94 ⊕ www.skagen-tourist.dk. **Sønderborg Turistbureau** ⊠ Rådhustorvet 7 ☎ 74/42-35-55 ⊕ www.visitsonderberg.com. **Tønder** ⊠ Torvet 1 ☎ 74/72-12-20 🖶 74/72-09-00 ⊕ www.visittonder.dk. **Vejle** ⊠ Banegårdspl. 6 ☎ 75/72-31-99 ⊕ www.visitvejle.com. **Viborg** ⊠ Nytorv 9 ☎ 87/25-30-75 🖶 86/60-02-38 ⊕ www.viborg.dk/turisme.

BORNHOLM

Called the Pearl of the Baltic for its natural beauty and winsomely rustic towns, Bornholm, 177 km (110 mi) southeast of Zealand, is geographically unlike the rest of Denmark. A temperate climate has made this 588-square-km (235-square-mi) jumble of granite bluffs, clay soil, and rift valleys an extravagance of nature. Rich plantations of fir bristle beside wide dunes and vast heather fields; lush gardens teem with fig, cherry, chestnut, mulberry, and blue-blooming Chinese Emperor trees; and meadows sprout 12 varieties of orchids. Denmark's third-largest forest, the Almindingen, crowns the center; the southern tip is ringed with some of Europe's whitest beaches.

During the Iron and Bronze ages, Bornholm was inhabited by seafaring and farming cultures that peppered the land with burial dolmens and engravings. From the Middle Ages to the 18th century, the Danes battled the Swedes for ownership of the island, protecting it with strongholds and fortified churches, many of which still loom over the landscape. Bornholm's unique round churches—whitewashed splendors topped with black conical roofs—are a sight to behold. Considered to be some of the finest examples of Scandinavian medieval architecture, the churches imbue the island landscape with a lovely, stylized simplicity.

Today Bornholmers continue to draw their livelihood from the land and sea—and increasingly from tourism. Chalk-white chimneys rise above the rooftops, harbors are abob with painted fishing boats, and in spring and summer fields blaze with amber mustard and grain.

Few people come to Bornholm to stay indoors. Long, silky beaches, gentle hills, and lush forests make this a summer haven for walking, hiking, and swimming—particularly for families, many of whom take their summer vacations by packing provisions and children onto bikes, and cycling throughout the island.

Bornholm is famous throughout Scandinavia for its craftspeople, especially glassblowers and ceramists, whose work is often pricier in Copenhagen and Stockholm. In the center of each town (especially Gudhjem and Svaneke) you can find crafts shops and *værksteder* (workshops). When you're on the road, watch for KERAMIK signs, which direct you to artists selling from home.

Rønne

▶ ❶ *190 km (120 mi) southeast of Copenhagen (7 hrs by ferry from Køge or 3 hrs from Ystad, Sweden).*

Bornholm's capital, port, and largest town is Rønne, a good starting point for exploring northward or eastward. East of Nørrekås Harbor on Laksegade is an enchanting area of rose-clad 17th- and 18th-century houses, among them the tile-roof **Erichsens Gård** (Erichsen's Farm), from 1806. The home of the wealthy Erichsen family, whose daughter married the Danish poet Holger Drachmann, it includes paintings by Danish artist Kristian Zahrtmann, period furnishings, and a lovely garden. ⊠ *Lakseg. 7* ☎ *56/95–87–35* ⊕ *www.bornholmsmuseer.dk/erichs* 💲 *DKr 30* ⊙ *Mid-May–mid-Oct., Mon.–Sat. 10–5.*

Near Store Torv, the main square, is the **Bornholm Museum,** which puts on local geological and archaeological exhibits in addition to regular displays of more than 4,500 pieces of ceramics and glass. The museum

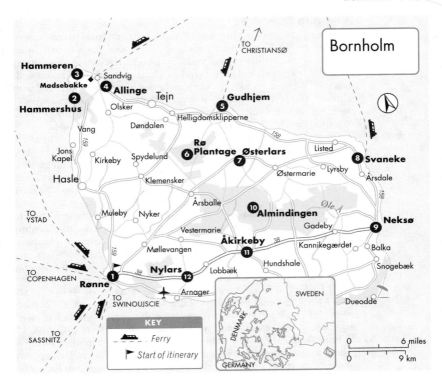

also displays 25 18th-century Bornholmure (Bornholm Clocks), as characteristic of the island as smoked herring. In 1744 a Dutch ship was wrecked on Bornholm, and the English grandfather clocks it carried became the models for the island's clocks. ⊠ *Skt. Mortensg. 29* ☎ *56/95–07–35* ⊕ *www.bornholmsmuseum.dk* ☜ *DKr 35* ☉ *Apr.–June, Sept., and Oct., daily 10–5; July and Aug., daily 10–5.*

Bornholm has long been recognized for its beautiful ceramics. **Hjorths Fabrik** (Hjorth's Factory), founded in 1859 by ceramist Lauritz Hjorth, is one of Bornholm's oldest ceramics factories, and is today a "working ceramics museum." Follow the "route of clay" through the old factory and workshops, from the mixer and the kiln to the painting and decorating rooms. Along the way you see the ceramists at work, casting, glazing, decorating, and firing, and you can observe how a lump of raw clay slowly takes shape on the potter's wheel, blossoming into a lovely vase or bowl. The museum shop sells a wide range of Hjorth ceramics, from its distinctive stoneware to old-fashioned pharmacy jars. ⊠ *Krystalg. 5* ☎ *56/95–01–60* ⊕ *www.bornholmsmuseer.dk/hjorths* ☜ *May–Oct. DKr 30; Nov.–Apr. DKr 10* ☉ *May–Oct., Mon.–Sat. 10–5 (factory closed Sat.); Nov.–Apr., weekdays 1–5, Sat. 10–1 (exhibits and shops only).*

Where to Stay & Eat

★ $$$ ✕ **Fyrtøjet.** Overlooking the Strøget, this bright and spacious restaurant offers an ample dinner buffet with soup, salad, a selection of fish dishes (usually smoked salmon and cod), and beef. The house specialty is *granitbøf*, a hefty slab of beef served on a heated Bornholm granite-and-iron tray. While the beef is cooking on the hot granite, it's flambéed with whiskey. You pour the accompanying cold sauce (usually béarnaise) over the meat when it's suitably done. ⊠ *Store Torveg. 22* ☎ *56/95–30–12* ⊕ *www.fyrtoejet.dk* ▭ *AE, DC, MC, V* ⊗ *No lunch Jan.–Mar.*

★ ¢–$$$ ✕ **Strøgets Spisehûz.** When the hunger pangs hit, Rønne locals head for this friendly, family-owned restaurant at the end of Strøget. The hearty Danish fare includes beef with cognac sauce and potatoes, and smoked salmon sprinkled with lemon. The mood is casual, with hanging plants, little Danish flags, paper napkins, and pink and purple curtains. ⊠ *Store Torveg. 39* ☎ *56/95–81–69* ▭ *MC, V* ⊗ *Closed Mon.*

$$$ ▦ **Radisson SAS Fredensborg.** Along a curve of forest near a small beach, this hotel sets the island's standard for luxury. The glass-and-tile lobby is spare and sunny, the staff pleasant and eager. The dozen ample apartments have full kitchens, and guest rooms have modern furniture and balconies overlooking the sea. The rustic restaurant, De Fem Ståuerne, serves traditional French-Danish food. Guests have use of the pool at Hotel Griffen. ⊠ *Strandvejen 116, DK–3700* ☎ *56/90–44–44* 🖷 *56/ 90–44–43* ⊕ *www.bornholmhotels.dk* ⮑ *72 rooms, 4 suites, 12 apartments* ⌂ *Restaurant, room service, tennis court, hot tub, sauna, bar, meeting room, some pets allowed, no-smoking rooms* ▭ *AE, DC, MC, V.*

$$ ▦ **Hotel Griffen.** One of Bornholm's largest and most modern hotels is just off a busy street near the Rønne harbor. Three stories tall with plenty of windows, it has wonderful views—the sea on one side and Rønne on the other. Rooms have every modern convenience. Guests may use the tennis facilities at the Radisson. ⊠ *Nordre Kystvej 34, DK–3700* ☎ *56/ 90–42–44* 🖷 *56/90–42–45* ⊕ *www.bornholmhotels.dk* ⮑ *142 rooms, 2 suites* ⌂ *Restaurant, room service, cable TV, indoor pool, sauna, bar, dance club, meeting room, some pets allowed, no-smoking rooms* ▭ *AE, DC, MC, V.*

¢ ⚠ **Galløkken Camping.** This site is just a short walk from the Rønne center, near an old military museum. The open grounds are surrounded by a perimeter of trees. The shower and cooking facilities are good. ⊠ *Strandvejen 4, DK–3700 Rønne* ☎ *56/95–23–20* ⊕ *www.gallokken. dk* ⌂ *Kitchen, playground, laundry facilities, flush toilets, drinking water, showers, general store.*

Shopping

Bornholm is famous for its quality ceramics, and Rønne, as the island's capital city, offers the widest variety. The island's history of ceramics starts in 1773 when ceramist Michael Andersen established a factory in Rønne. Today, his legacy lives on at the large factory-turned-shop **Michael Andersen Bornholmsk Keramik** (⊠ Lille Torv 7 ☎ 56/95–00–01 ⊗ Weekdays 10–5:30, Sat. 10–3) on a small square near the center of town. The shop's wide selection includes the distinctive *krakelering* ceramics, where the surface of the ceramics is covered with a web of tiny black lines that give the pieces a cracked look. Ceramists still work in the back studio, and the store sells a range of ceramics.

The distinctive clocks, or Bornholmures, sold on the island are all hand-made and hand-painted with round (or sometimes rectangular) faces. The new-style clocks have a modern touch: on the hour they play classics such as Mozart or Verdi and some even sound the hour with Stephen Sondheim or Andrew Lloyd Webber. Antique versions are the costliest, with prices from DKr 10,000 to DKr 80,000 and up. A handmade custom clock costs DKr 37,000 on average. Reproductions modeled on original clocks are custom-made by **Bornholmerure** (⊠ Torneværksvej 26 ☎ 56/95–31–08).

Hammershus

★ ❷ *8 km (5 mi) north of Jons Kapel, 30 km (19 mi) north of Rønne.*

The **fortress of Hammershus,** now in ruins, was once northern Europe's largest stronghold. The hulking fortress was begun in 1255 by the archbishop of Lund (Sweden), and became the object of centuries of struggle between Denmark and Sweden. In 1658 Danes under Jens Kofoed killed its Swedish governor, and the castle was given back to Denmark. Used until 1743, it was quarried for stone to fortify Christiansø and that island's buildings. The government finally intervened in 1822, and the site is now a mass of snaggle-toothed walls and towers atop a grassy knoll. Occasionally concerts and other performances are held here. 🖾 *Free.*

Hammeren

❸ *5 km (3 mi) north of Hammershus, 36 km (23 mi) north of Rønne.*

This knuckle of land jutting from the island's northern tip is nearly separated from the island by a deep rift valley and the Hammer Sø (Hammer Lake). Despite constant Baltic winds, rare plants and trees grow on the warm, granite-scattered Hammeren (the Hammer), including radiant anemones. Look across the water south of the tip to the stone formation known as the Camel Heads.

> **en route** A little more than 3 km (2 mi) southeast of Hammeren is **Madsebakke,** the largest collection of Bronze Age rock carvings in Denmark. They are presumed to be ceremonial carvings, which ancient fishermen and farmers hoped would bring good weather and bountiful crops. The most interesting of them depicts 11 ships, including one with a sun wheel, an ancient type of sundial.

Allinge

❹ *3 km (2 mi) east of Madsebakke, 21 km (13 mi) north of Rønne.*

In Allinge and its twin town Sandvig you'll find centuries-old neighborhoods and, particularly in Allinge, half-timber houses and herring smokehouses sprouting tall chimneys. Just south is a wood that the islanders call **Trolleskoven** (Trolls' Forest). Legend says that fog comes from the brew in the troll's kitchen and that when the trolls are brewing something they leave their little abodes under the cover of fog to wander the forest looking for trouble. The most mischievous is the littlest troll, Krølle Bølle, who has become a mascot of sorts for Bornholm. His likeness is everywhere—especially in souvenir shops.

Where to Stay

$–$$ ⊞ **Strandhotellet.** Romantic charm is the draw at this venerable hotel,
Fodor'sChoice built in 1895 and refurbished in 1992. It's on a corner across from the
★ harbor. A white arched entry leads into a stone-and-whitewashed lobby. Rooms are furnished in plain beech furniture with woolen covers and pastel colors. ⊠ *Strandpromenaden 7, DK–3770 Sandvig* ☎ *56/48–03–14* 🖷 *56/48–02–09* ⊕ *www.strandhotellet.dk* ⟿ *52 rooms, 1 suite* ⚭ *Restaurant, bar* ⊟ *MC, V.*

¢ ⚠ **Sandvig Familie Camping.** Pleasantly close to the beach, most of the camping sites here have a view of the water. The large kitchen and bathing facilities are well maintained. ⊠ *Sandlinien 5, DK–3770* ☎ *56/48–04–47 or 56/48–00–01* ⚭ *Kitchen, playground, showers* ⊙ *Closed Nov.–Mar.*

Gudhjem

★ ❺ *18 km (11 mi) east of Allinge, 33 km (21 mi) northeast of Rønne.*

At the height of summer, Gudhjem (God's Home) is perhaps the most tourist-packed town on Bornholm. Tiny half-timber houses and gift shops with lace curtains and clay roofs line steep stone streets that loop around the harbor. The island's first smokehouses still produce alder-smoked golden herring.

★ ☪ Walk down Brøddegade, which turns into Melstedvej; here you'll find the **Landsbrugs Museum** (Agricultural Museum) and Melstedgård, a working farm. The farm includes the well-kept house and garden of a 19th-century family who lived here. Notice the surprisingly bright colors used on the interior of the house, and leave time to visit the old shop where you can buy locally produced woolen sweaters, wooden spoons, and even homemade mustard. ⊠ *Melstedvej 25* ☎ *56/48–55–98* ⊕ *www.bornholmsmuseer.dk/melstedg* 🗊 *DKr 35* ⊙ *Mid-May–June and Sept.–Oct. 22, weekdays and Sun. 10–5; July and Aug., daily 10–5.*

Just up the hill from Gudhjem's waterfront is the **Oluf Høst Museet,** with a collection of paintings by Bornholm artist Oluf Høst, including his series of a whitewashed Bornholm farm called Bognemark, which he depicted with glowing splashes of oranges and reds from the setting sun. Høst and other modernist Bornholm artists are well known for their ability to capture Bornholm's natural light. The museum is in Høst's home, which he built in 1929 out of two fisherman's cottages and lived in until his death in 1966. It's easy to see why Høst found artistic inspiration here. At the top of the house's leafy, rock-strewn garden are lovely views over the colorful cottages of Gudhjem. ⊠ *Løkkeg. 35* ☎ *56/48–50–38* ⊕ *www.ohmus.dk* 🗊 *DKr 45* ⊙ *May–mid-June, Tues.–Sun. 11–5; mid-June–Sept., daily 11–5.*

Where to Stay & Eat

¢–$ ✕ **Café Klint.** Locals flock to this red, half-timber harborside restaurant, where the portions of down-home Danish fare are generous and the prices are low. Dishes include smoked salmon with spinach, fillet of sole with rémoulade, or a plate heaped with different kinds of herring. In summer, tables are set out on the terrace. In winter the restaurant changes its name to Vinter Klint (Winter Klint), and you can't get cozier than sitting in the low-ceiling dining room, surrounded by pine-green walls, and perhaps warmed by a glass or two of the house wine. ⊠ *Ejnar Mikkelsensvej 20* ☎ *56/48–56–26* ▭ *MC, V.*

$–$$ ✕▭ **Jantzens Hotel.** Founded in 1872, this bright-yellow building with white shutters and wrought-iron balconies is Gudhjem's oldest hotel. The front windows face the sea, and the backyard gives way to a sunny, idyllic terrace and rose garden. Much of the hotel has been lovingly restored, with an eye to recapturing its turn-of-the-20th-century ambience. Rooms are outfitted with hardwood floors, pale green walls, and rattan furniture. The balconies have views over Gudhjem's yellow and red houses, clustered against a backdrop of the blue Baltic. The bathrooms are small and basic, but all rooms are equipped with a refrigerator. The hotel's interior is still a work in progress; so far half the rooms have been restored, so ask when booking. What was once a pavilion and tea terrace is now utilized by the restaurant, Andi's Kokken, which includes on its French-Danish menu such dishes as mussels in a mild curry sauce with capers, and venison with shallots and mushrooms. Dessert might be fresh blueberries, hand-picked by the chef from the nearby fields. The restaurant is closed Monday and November through April. ⊠ *Brøddeg. 33, DK–3760* ☎ *56/48–50–17* ▭ *56/48–57–15* ⊕ *www.jantzenshotel.dk* ↰ *18 rooms* ⌂ *Restaurant, some pets allowed (fee)* ▭ *MC, V* ☉ *Closed Nov.–Apr.*

¢ ▭ **Danhostel Gudhjem.** In a half-timber 100-year-old former manor house, this hostel in the middle of Gudhjem offers single- to eight-bed rooms of standard pine bunks and industrial carpeting. There are six kitchens available for use. The hostel also has rooms in several houses within the village (with common kitchens and baths), which tend to be quieter than the main house. ⊠ *Løkkeg. 7, DK–3760* ☎ *56/48–50–35* ▭ *56/48–56–35* ⊕ *www.danhostel-gudhjem.dk* ↰ *50 rooms without bath* ⌂ *Restaurant, laundry facilities* ▭ *MC, V.*

Shopping

Baltic Sea Glass (⊠ Melstedvej 47 ☎ 56/48–56–41), on the main road just on the outskirts of town, offers high-quality, bright, and imaginative decanters, glasses, candlesticks, and one-of-a-kind pieces, including an old-fashioned contraption to catch flies. In town, see the delicate porcelain bowls of **Per Rehfeldt** (⊠ Salenevej 1 ☎ 56/48–54–13). Unique, hand-thrown ceramic work is available from and by **Julia Manitius** (⊠ Holkavej 12 ☎ 56/48–55–99).

Rø Plantage

❻ *6 km (4 mi) southwest of Gudhjem, 24 km (15 mi) northeast of Rønne.*

Rø Plantation is dense forest that serves as a quiet foil to the hubbub of Gudhjem. A century ago it was a heather-covered grazing area, but after stone dikes were erected to keep the cattle out, spruce, pine, larch, and birch were cultivated. The cool refuge now consists largely of saplings and new growth—the result of devastating storms in the late '50s and '60s.

Rø Golfbane (⊠ Spellingevej 3 ☎ 56/48–40–50) has won various European and Scandinavian awards for its natural beauty—and challenges. Its 18 holes are set close to the coastal cliffs and have views of the sea. It has a pro shop and a restaurant.

Østerlars

❼ *5 km (3 mi) east of Rø Plantage, 22 km (14 mi) northeast of Rønne.*

FodorśChoice   The standout attraction here is the **Østerlars Kirke.** The largest of the is-
★   land's four round churches, it was built in about 1150; extensions, in-
cluding the buttresses, were added later. Constructed from boulders and slabs of limestone, the whitewashed church was part spiritual sanctu-ary, part fortification, affording protection from enemy armies and pi-rates. Inside is the island's only painted tympanum, with a faded image of a cross and decorative foliage. Several Gothic wall paintings—including depictions of the Annunciation and Nativity—have survived from the 1300s. ⊠ *Gudhjemsvej 28* ☎ *56/49–82–64* 🎫 *DKr 10* ☉ *May–mid-Oct., Mon.–Sat. 9–5; in July, also open Sun. 1–5.*

Svaneke

❽ *21 km (13 mi) east of Østerlars, 49 km (31 mi) northeast of Rønne.*

The coastal town of Svaneke, Denmark's easternmost settlement, is an enchanting hamlet of 17th- and 18th-century houses, winding cobbled streets, and a harbor sliced from the rocky earth. Once a fishing village, it is now immaculately preserved and the site of a thriving artists' com-munity.

Bornholm's smoked herring is famous throughout Scandinavia, and no visit to the island is complete without sampling it for yourself—preferably in the manner of the Danes, who eat it outside on a sunny terrace, with a cold Carlsberg in hand. For more than 35 years, Hjorth Hansen has been smoking herring at **Hjorths Røgeri** (Hjorth's Smoke-house), 2 km (1 mi) south of Svaneke. Every morning at 6 AM, Hjorth hauls in big baskets of elm wood, lights a fire, and begins smoking the fresh herring, tending to the fire with a long pole wrapped with rags at one end. Five hours later, he serves up plates of warm, smoked herring in the adjoining terrace. Hjorth works from late April to Oc-tober. The best time to watch him in action is around 10 AM, in the last hour of the smoking process. ⊠ *Brugsebakken 18, Årsdale* ☎ *56/49–61–10* ☉ *Late Apr.–Oct.*

Where to Stay & Eat

¢–$$ ✕ **Bryghuset.** Microbreweries are a new concept in the land of Carls-berg, but the idea is catching on, and Svaneke's Bryghuset (Brew House) is one of the first. All the beer is brewed on the premises, in a massive copper brew kettle linked by piping to the kitchen. The menu is based on the concept that food should compliment the beer. The house specialty is Bryggerben ("Brewer's bone"), a messy, finger-licking plate of spareribs smothered in barbecue sauce, which can be enjoyed at one of the long wooden tables set under the beam ceilings or on the large summer terrace. Also on offer is a platter of Christiansø herring served with egg, rye bread, and butter. At Easter and Christmas, try the stronger festive brew. ⊠ *Torvet 5* ☎ *56/49–73–21* ☰ *MC, V* ⊗ *Closed Jan.*

$$ ✕▥ **Siemsens Gaard.** Built in a 270-year-old merchant house, this U-shape hotel with a gravel-courtyard café overlooks the harbor. The inside is cushy with sofas below severe black-and-white prints and antiques. The rooms are varied, but all have stripped pine and soft colors, and all are no-smoking. The bright, modern restaurant serves French-Danish food, with a menu of 75 dishes—from club sandwiches to smoked Baltic salmon to smørrebrød. The restaurant is closed from November to May. ⊠ *Havnebryggen 9, DK–3740* ☎ *56/49–61–49* ⊕ *www. siemsens.dk* ⤴ *51 rooms* ⅋ *Restaurant, café, some pets allowed, no-smoking rooms* ☰ *AE, DC, MC, V.*

Shopping

Stroll through the boutiques in the central Glastorvet in Svaneke. Among them is the studio of **Pernille Bülow** (⊠ Glastorvet, Brænderigænget 8 ☎ 56/49–66–72), one of Denmark's most famous glassblowers. Her work is sold in Copenhagen's best design shops. Even if you buy directly from her studio, don't expect bargains, but do expect colorful, experimental work.

Neksø

❾ *9 km (5½ mi) south of Svaneke, 48 km (30 mi) northeast of Rønne.*

Neksø (or Nexø) bustles with tourists and locals who shop and live around its busy harbor, lined with fishing boats from throughout the Baltics and Eastern Europe. It might seem like a typical 17th-century town, but it was rebuilt almost completely after World War II, when the Russians bombed it to dislodge stubborn German troops who refused to surrender—three days after the rest of Denmark had been liberated. The Russians lingered on the island until April 1946.

Wander down to the harbor to find the **Neksø Museum**, housed in a mustard-yellow building that was once the town's courthouse. The museum has a fine collection of fishing and local history exhibits and maritime memorabilia. ⊠ *Havnen* ☎ *56/49–25–56* ⊕ *www.bornholmsmuseer. dk* ▧ *DKr 35* ⊗ *May–Oct., Tues.–Sun. 10–4.*

The **Andersen Nexøs Hus** contains photographs and mementos of Danish author Martin Andersen Hansen (1909–55), who changed his last name to Nexø after his beloved town. A complicated man and vehement socialist, he wrote, among other works, *Pelle the Conqueror,* set in Bornholm at the turn of the 20th century, when Swedish immigrants were exploited by Danish landowners. The story was turned into an Academy Award–winning film. ⊠ *Ferskesøstr. 36* ☎ *56/49–45–42*

⊕ *www.bornholmsmuseer.dk/manexo* 🎫 *DKr 20* ⊙ *Mid-May–Oct., weekdays 10–4, Sat. 10–2.*

Where to Eat

$$–$$$ ✕ **Tre Søstre.** Facing Nexø's bustling harbor, this spacious restaurant, housed in a converted storage warehouse, is named after a 19th-century Danish ship *The Three Sisters,* a model of which hangs on the wall. The creatively decorated interior (right down to the plates and the candlesticks) pays tribute to Bornholm's artists. The lavender, pale-orange, and sea-green vases of Svaneke glassblower Pernille Bülow grace the window sills, providing a bright and delicate contrast to the restaurant's rustic furnishings. Hanging from the ceiling is a playful, blue-and-green ceramic fish, created by long-time Bornholmer Kirsten Clemann. The Danish menu includes grilled salmon with spinach and hollandaise sauce, and fried scampi flavored with cognac, garlic, and curry. Occasionally, jazz concerts are performed here. ⊠ *Havnen 5* ☎ *56/49–33–93* 🍽 *AE, DC, MC, V* ⊙ *Closed Sept.–May.*

Shopping

For exquisite woodwork see **Bernard Romain** (⊠ Rønnevej 54 ☎ 56/48–86–66).

Almindingen

❿ *23 km (14 mi) west of Neksø, 27 km (17 mi) northeast of Rønne.*

The lush Almindingen, Denmark's third-largest forest, is filled with ponds, lakes, evergreens, and well-marked trails, and it blooms with lily of the valley in spring. Within it, the oak-lined **Ekkodalen** (Echo Valley)—where children love to hear their shouts resound—is networked by trails leading to smooth rock faces that soar 72 feet high. At the northern edge, near the road to Østermarie, once stood one of Bornholm's most famous sights: seven evergreens growing from a single trunk. The plant succumbed to old age in 1995, but you may still be able to see the remains of its curious trunk.

Sports & the Outdoors

HIKING   Check with the tourist board for a map showing three 4-km (2½-mi) hikes through the Almindingen Forest and several more through its Echo Valley. The *Bornholm Green Guide,* available in shops and tourism offices, offers walking and hiking routes.

Åkirkeby

⓫ *5 km (3 mi) south of Almindingen, 16 km (9 mi) east of Rønne.*

Åkirkeby is the oldest town on the island, with a municipal charter from 1346. The town's church, the **Åkirke,** is Bornholm's oldest and largest, dating from the mid-12th century. Though it is not one of the more typical round churches, its walls and tower were well suited for defense. The altarpiece and pulpit are Dutch Renaissance pieces from about 1600, but the carved sandstone font is as old as the church itself. ⊠ *Torvet* ☎ *56/97–41–03* 🎫 *DKr 10* ⊙ *Mon.–Sat. 10–4.*

Nylars

12 *8 km (5 mi) west of Åkirkeby, 9 km (6 mi) east of Rønne.*

Like the Østerlars church, the round **Nylars Kirke** dates from 1150. The chalk paintings from the Old Testament on its central pillar are the oldest on the island, possibly dating from 1250. Even older are the runic stones on the church's porch. Both are of Viking origin. ⊠ *Kirkevej* ☎ *56/ 97–20–13* 🎫 *Free* ☉ *Mid-May–mid-Sept., weekdays 9–5.*

Bornholm A to Z

AIRPORTS
Bornholm's airport is 5 km (3 mi) south of Rønne at the island's southwestern tip.

Cimber Air has six flights a day to Copenhagen (three per day on weekends); the trip lasts 35 minutes and costs about DKr 750.
🗂 **Bornholms Lufthavn** ☎ 56/95-26-26 ⊕ www.slv.dk/bornholm. **Cimber Air** ☎ 56/ 95-11-11 ⊕ www.cimber.dk.

BIKE TRAVEL
Biking is eminently feasible and pleasant on Bornholm, thanks to a network of more than 200 km (125 mi) of cycle roads, including an old railway converted to a cross-island path. The network is made up of paths, forest tracks, quiet roads, and marked cycle lanes on main roads. The cycle routes are marked by green and blue signs. Today Bornholm has one of the best and most beautiful cycle networks in northern Europe.

Rentals of sturdy two-speeds and tandems are available for about DKr 50 a day at more than 20 different establishments all over the island—near the ferry; at the airport; and in Allinge, Gudhjem, Hasle, Pedersker (near Åkirkeby), Rønne, Svaneke, and most other towns.
🗂 Bike Rentals **Bornholms Cykeludlejning** ⊠ Nordre Kystvej 5, Rønne ☎ 56/ 95-13-59. **Cykel-Centret** ⊠ Sønderg. 7, Rønne ☎ 56/95-06-04.

BOAT & FERRY TRAVEL
The Bornholmstrafikken car ferry is Bornholm's "lifeline" to the rest of Denmark, with the Køge–Rønne service, which allows you to travel from Køge to the island overnight (travel time is 6½ hours). There is one departure nightly.

With the opening of the Øresund Bridge between Copenhagen and Malmö, *Bornholmstrafikken* has increased its ferry departures from Ystad, which lies 57 km (36 mi) southeast of Malmö. There are two to four departures from Ystad to Rønne daily, on either the high-speed ferry (1 hour, 20 minutes), or the conventional ferry (2½ hours). There are up to nine departures a day during the peak season.

Nordbornholms Turistbureau (North Bornholm Tourist Board) is the agent for a summer ferry that links Neu Mukran and Fährhafen Sassnitz on the island of Rügen in Germany. Scandlines, a competing company, offers passage aboard the ferry to Fährhafen Sassnitz. Prices vary according to the number of people traveling and the size of the vehicle. There is also a boat between Swinoujscie, Poland and Rønne (7 hours); call Polferries in Poland.

◪ **Bornholmstrafikken** ☏ 56/95-18-66 ⊕ www.bornholmferries.dk. **Nordbornholms Turistbureau** ☏ 56/48-00-01 ⊕ www.bornholmsbooking center.dk. **Polferries** ✉ Norgesvej 2 Rønne ☏ 56/95-10-69, 48/943-552-102 in Poland ⊕ www.polferries. com. **Scandlines** ☏ 33/15-15-15 ⊕ www.scandlines.dk.

BUS TRAVEL

The *Bornholmerbussen* (Bornholm Bus) No. 866 runs from Copenhagen's main station, travels across the Øresund Bridge to Malmö, in Sweden, and then continues to Ystad, where it connects with a ferry to Rønne. The trip takes around three hours. Buses depart two to four times daily, usually once in the morning and several times in the afternoon and evening. Call Bornholmerbussen for more details.

Though bus service is certainly not as frequent as in major cities, there are regular connections (with BAT, *see below*) between Bornholm towns. Schedules are posted at all stations, and you can usually pick one up on board. The major bus routes have an hourly service, and all buses depart from Rønne. In peak season an additional service also operates around the coast. The timetable is coordinated with ferry arrivals and departures.

◪ **BAT** (Bornholm Municipality Traffic Company) ☏ 56/95-21-21 ⊕ www.bat.dk. **Bornholmerbussen** ✉ Yderholmen 18, DK-2750 Ballerup ☏ 44/68-44-00 ⊕ www.bornholmerbussen.dk.

CAR RENTAL

Rønne's Hertz agency is near the ferry arrivals and departures area. The Avis branch is also nearby.

◪ **Avis** ✉ Snellemark 19, Rønne ☏ 56/95-22-08. **Hertz** ✉ Munch Petersens Vej 1, Rønne ☏ 56/91-00-12.

EMERGENCIES

The general emergency number for ambulance, accident, or fire anywhere in Denmark is 112.

◪ **Bornholm's Central Hospital** ✉ Sygehusvej, Rønne ☏ 56/95-11-65. **Rønne Apotek** (Rønne Pharmacy) ✉ Store Torveg. 12, Rønne ☏ 56/95-01-30.

SPORTS & THE OUTDOORS

FISHING Cod, salmon, and herring fishing are excellent in season, though better from a boat than from shore. There are unique experiences in autumn, winter, and spring: massive releases of salmon fry from the Salmon Hatchery in Nexø and the deep water around the island provide perfect conditions and ensure good salmon fishing in the Baltic. Licenses cost DKr 25 per day, DKr 75 per week, and DKr 100 per year. Contact the tourist office for details and information on charter trips.

TOURS

Klippefly can arrange a 20- to 40-minute aerial tour in a Cessna or Piper plane that covers either the entire coast or the northern tip.

The BAT (Bornholm Municipality Traffic Company) offers some inventive summer tours. All are available Tuesday through Friday, from mid-July until early August. All begin at the red bus terminal at Snellemark 30 in Rønne at 10 AM and cost DKr 110. (You can also buy a 24-hour bus card for DKr 110, or a five- or seven-day card for DKr 390, good for both the regional buses and the tours.) Tour prices do not include some DKr 5–DKr 10 admissions or lunch at a herring smokehouse. The five-hour tour aboard the Kunsthåndværkbussen (Arts and Crafts Bus) includes stops at glass, pottery, textile, and silver studios. In summer, different studios are visited each day. The Havebussen (Garden Bus) visits sights that illustrate the ways in which the island's exquisite flora and fauna are being preserved. The Veteranbussen (Veteran Bus), a circa–World War II Bedford, connects some of Bornholm's oldest industries, including a clockmaker, water mill, and Denmark's last windmill used for making flour.

From mid-June to mid-September, boats to the Helligdomsklipperne (Sanctuary Cliffs) leave Gudhjem at 10:30, 1:30, and 2:30, with extra sailings from mid-June to mid-August. Call Thor Båd.

You can visit the Ertholmene archipelago near Bornholm, which is better known as Christiansø, the name of the biggest island in the group. King Christian V's old fortress stands on Christiansø today almost as it did when the fortress was built in 1684, and offers an exciting historical experience. Boats to Christiansø depart from Svaneke at 10 AM daily year-round; May to September daily at 10:20 from Gudhjem, and at 1 from Allinge; and between mid-June and August an additional boat leaves Gudhjem weekdays at 9:40 and 12:15. The cost is DKr. 160. Call Christiansø Farten for additional information.

🚌**BAT** (Bornholm Municipality Traffic Company) ☎ 56/95-21-21 ⊕ www.bat.dk. **Christiansø Farten** ✉ Ejnar Mikkelsensvej 25, Gudhjem ☎ 56/48-51-76 ⊕ www.christiansoefarten.dk. **Klippefly** ✉ Søndre Landevej 2, Rønne ☎ 56/95-35-73 ⊕ www.bornholmerguiden.dk/klippefly. **Thor Båd** ✉ Melstedvej 17, Gudhjem ☎ 56/48-51-65.

TRAIN TRAVEL
A DSB Intercity train travels two to five times a day from Copenhagen's main station, across the Øresund Bridge to Malmö, and then to Ystad, where it connects with a ferry to Rønne.

🚂 **DSB** ☎ 70/13-14-15 ⊕ www.dsb.dk.

VISITOR INFORMATION
The main tourist office in Rønne operates a Web site with area listings.

🚂 **Allinge-Nordbornholms Turistbureau** ✉ Kirkeg. 4, DK-3770 Allinge ☎ 56/48-00-01 🖷 56/48-00-20 ⊕ www.bornholmsbookingcenter.dk. **Åkirkeby** ✉ Torvet 2, DK-3720 Åkirkeby ☎ 56/97-45-20 🖷 56/97-58-90 ⊕ www.sydborn.dk. **Bornholm Tourist Office** ✉ Nordre Kystvej 3, DK-3700 Rønne ☎ 56/95-95-00 🖷 56/95-95-68 ⊕www.bornholminfo.dk. **Gudhjem** ✉Åbog. 9 DK-3760 Gudhjem ☎56/48-52-10 🖷56/48-52-74. **Hasle** ✉ Havneg. 1 DK-3790 Hasle ☎ 56/96-44-81 🖷 56/96-41-06 ⊕ www.hasle-turistbureau.dk. **Nexø** ✉Søndre Hammer 2A DK-3730 Nexø ☎56/49-70-79 🖷56/49-70-10 ⊕ www.nexoe-dueodde.dk. **Svaneke** ✉ Storeg. 24, DK-3740 Svaneke ☎ 56/49-70-79 🖷 56/49-70-10 ⊕ www.nexoe-dueodde.dk.

DENMARK A TO Z

Air Travel

CARRIERS Nearly all international air service to Denmark flies into Copenhagen Airport. SAS, the main carrier, makes nonstop flights to the capital from Chicago, Newark, and Seattle. British Airways offers connecting flights via London from Atlanta, Baltimore, Boston, Charlotte, Chicago, Dallas, Denver, Detroit, Houston, Los Angeles, Miami, New York, Orlando, Philadelphia, Phoenix, Pittsburgh, San Diego, San Francisco, Seattle, Tampa, and Washington, D.C. Icelandair has connecting flights to Copenhagen via Reykjavík from Baltimore, Fort Lauderdale, New York, and Orlando. Finnair has service through Helsinki from Miami, New York, and—from May to September—San Francisco and Toronto.

British Airways flies nonstop to Copenhagen from London (Heathrow and Gatwick), Birmingham, and Manchester. SAS Scandinavian Airlines flies nonstop from London, Manchester, and Glasgow, and also from London to Århus. Aer Lingus flies from Dublin, connecting in London; the flights are operated by British Airways. Mærsk Air flies nonstop from Gatwick to Billund and Copenhagen. Easyjet has cheap flights between London's Stansted airport and Copenhagen. Virgin Airlines is also inexpensive and flies between London's Gatwick and Stansted airports via Brussels to Copenhagen. Air France also flies out of Copenhagen.

In Jutland, Billund Airport is Denmark's second-largest airport. Mærsk Air flies to Billund from Amsterdam, Bergen, Brussels, the Faroe Islands, Frankfurt, London, Manchester, Nice, Oslo, Stockholm, and Paris. Sunair serves Århus, Billund, Göteborg, Oslo, and Stockholm. Several domestic airports, including Aalborg, Århus, and Esbjerg, are served by Mærsk and SAS, both of which have good connections to Copenhagen. Cimber Air links Sønderborg, just north of the German border, with Copenhagen.

Cimber Air makes several daily flights to Bornholm from Copenhagen, and flies also from Berlin. Lufthansa flies to Bornholm from Berlin and Hamburg.

▶ **Air France** ☎ 800/237-2747 in North America, 82/33-27-01 in Denmark ⊕ www.airfrance.com/dk. **Air Greenland** ☎ 299/34-34-34 in Greenland, 32/31-40-88 in Denmark ⊕ www.airgreenland.gl. **Aer Lingus** ☎ 800/474-7424 in North America, 0161/832-5771 in Ireland ⊕ www.aerlingus.com. **British Airways** ☎ 0207/491-4989 in the U.K., 800/247-9297 in North America, 80/20-80-22 in Denmark ⊕ www.britishairways.com. **Cimber Air** ☎ 74/42-22-77, 56/95-11-11 in Bornholm ⊕ www.cimber.dk. **Easyjet** ☎ 0870/600-0000 in the U.K., 70/12-43-21 in Denmark ⊕ www.easyjet.com. **Finnair** ☎ 800/950-5000 in North America, 32/50-45-10 in Denmark ⊕ www.finnair.fi. **Icelandair** ☎ 354/505-0300 in Iceland, 0207/874-1000 in the U.K., 800/223-5500 in North America, 33/70-22-00 in Denmark ⊕ www.icelandair.com. **Lufthansa** ☎ 33/37-73-33 ⊕ www.lufthansa.com. **Mærsk Air** ☎ 0207/333-0066 in the U.K., 32/31-44-44 or 70/10-74-74 in Denmark ⊕ www.maersk-air.dk. **SAS Scandinavian Airlines** ☎ 0207/706-8832 in the U.K., 800/221-2350 in North America, 32/32-00-00 in Denmark ⊕ www.scandinavian.net. **Sunair** ☎ 75/33-16-11 ⊕ www.sunair.dk/uk/html/index1.html. **Vir-**

gin Airlines ☎ 01293/450-150 in the U.K., 800/862-8621 in North America ⊕ www. virgin-atlantic.com.

CUTTING COSTS Intra-Scandinavian air travel is usually expensive. If you want to economize, look into the **SAS Visit Scandinavia/Europe Air Pass** offered by SAS. One coupon costs between $84 and $97, but they vary depending on routing and destination. The coupons are valid for destinations within Denmark, Norway, and Sweden, and also to Finland (for $97). They are sold only in the United States and only to non-Scandinavians. Coupons can be used year-round for a maximum of three months and must be purchased in conjunction with transatlantic flights. SAS also provides family fares—children between 2 and 17 and a spouse can receive 50% off the full fare of business-class tickets with the purchase of one full-fare business-class ticket. Contact SAS for information.

The least expensive airfares to Denmark are often priced for round-trip travel and must usually be purchased in advance. Airlines generally allow you to change your return date for a fee; most low-fare tickets, however, are nonrefundable. It's smart to call a number of airlines and check the Internet; when you are quoted a good price, book it on the spot—the same fare may not be available the next day, or even the next hour. Always check different routings and look into using alternate airports. Also, price off-peak flights and red-eye, which may be significantly less expensive than others. Travel agents, especially low-fare specialists, are helpful.

Consolidators are another good source. They buy tickets for scheduled flights at reduced rates from the airlines, then sell them at prices that beat the best fare available directly from the airlines. (Many also offer reduced car-rental and hotel rates.) Sometimes you can even get your money back if you need to return the ticket. Carefully read the fine print detailing penalties for changes and cancellations, purchase the ticket with a credit card, and confirm your consolidator reservation with the airline.

🛂 Consolidators **Airline Consolidator.com** ☎ 888/468-5385 ⊕ www.airlineconsolidator. com; for international tickets. **Best Fares** ☎ 800/880-1234 ⊕ www.bestfares.com; $59.90 annual membership. **Cheap Tickets** ☎ 800/377-1000 or 800/652-4327 ⊕ www. cheaptickets.com. **Expedia** ☎ 800/397-3342 or 404/728-8787 ⊕ www.expedia.com. **Hotwire** ☎ 866/468-9473 or 920/330-9418 ⊕ www.hotwire.com. **Now Voyager Travel** ☎ 212/459-1616 ⊕ www.nowvoyagertravel.com. **Onetravel.com** ⊕ www.onetravel. com. **Orbitz** ☎ 888/656-4546 ⊕ www.orbitz.com. **Priceline.com** ⊕ www.priceline.com. **Travelocity** ☎ 888/709-5983, 877/282-2925 in Canada, 0870/111-7061 in the U.K. ⊕ www.travelocity.com.

FLYING TIMES The flight from London to Copenhagen takes 1 hour, 55 minutes. From New York, flights to Copenhagen take 7 hours, 40 minutes. From Chicago, they take 9 hours, 30 minutes. From Seattle and Los Angeles the flight time is about 10 hours, 55 minutes. Flight times within the country are all less than 1 hour.

Airports

Kastrup International Airport (CPH) is the hub of Scandinavian and international air travel in Denmark, 10 km (6 mi) from the center of Copenhagen. Jutland has regional hubs in Aalborg (AAL), Århus (AAR), and

Billund (BLL), which handle mainly domestic and some European traffic. Rønne (RNN) is the main airport in Bornholm.

🚩 Airport Information **Kastrup International Airport** ☎ 32/31-32-31 ⊕ www.cph.dk.

Bike Travel

Biking is a way of life in Denmark, with more people biking to work than driving. Biking vacations in Denmark are popular and they are easy for all ages due to the flat landscape and about 9,600 km (6,000 mi) of mapped and signposted bike paths throughout the country. Most towns have rentals, but check with local tourism offices for referrals.

"Inclusive" cycling trips, offered by many organizations in Denmark, are just that—these trips include everything from bike rental to ferry tickets to maps to overnight accommodations. Note that bikes are the standard Danish variety; you can bring your own bike, which will also reduce the price of the trip. Routes are determined by local experts, ensuring that less-trafficked, more scenic roads are chosen.

If you want to do it yourself, there is a nationwide labeling scheme for cyclists which allows you to find the best offers and experiences during your vacation. The national quality logo—a white silhouette of a bike with an orange star in the background—indicates accommodations that are amenable to cyclists, fulfilling their extra needs (such as toolboxes, places to dry clothing, secure bike parking, and hearty breakfasts). For more information, contact the Danish Cyclist Federation. The Danish Tourist Board publishes helpful bicycle maps and brochures.

Danish State Railways (DSB) allows cyclists to check their bikes as luggage on most of their train routes, but only if there is room. S-trains that serve the suburbs of Copenhagen don't permit bikes during rush hour (7 AM–8:30 AM and 3:30 PM–5 PM). Bicycles can also be carried onto most trains and ferries; contact the DSB travel office for information; a bicycle ticket usually costs from DKr 10 to DKr 60, depending on the distance traveled. Taxis are required to take bikes and are equipped with racks, though they add a modest fee of DKr 10.

From May to October, you'll also see *bycykler* (city bikes) parked at special bike stands placed around the center of Copenhagen and Århus. Deposit DKr 20 and pedal away. The bikes are often dinged and dented, but they do function. Your deposit will be returned when you return the bike.

🚩 **Danmarks Turistråd** (Danish Tourist Board) ⊠ Vesterbrog. 6D, Vesterbro, DK-1620 Copenhagen ☎ 33/11-14-15 🖷 33/93-14-16 ⊕ www.visitdenmark.com. **Dansk Cyklist Forbund** (Danish Cyclist Federation) ⊠ Rømersg. 7, Downtown, DK-1362 Copenhagen ☎ 33/32-31-21 🖷 33/32-76-83 ⊕ www.dcf.dk. **DSB** ☎ 70/13-14-15 ⊕ www.dsb.dk.

Boat & Ferry Travel

Once upon a time, ferries were an indispensable mode of transport in and around the many islands of Denmark. This is changing as more people drive or take trains over new bridges spanning the waters. However, ferries are still a good way to explore Denmark and Scandinavia, especially if you have a rail pass.

Scandinavian Seaways Ferries (DFDS) sail from Harwich in the United Kingdom to Esbjerg (20 hours) on Jutland's west coast. Schedules in both summer and winter are highly irregular. DFDS also connects Denmark with the Baltic States, Belgium, Germany, the Netherlands, Norway, Poland, Sweden, and the Faroe Islands. There are many discounts, including 20% for senior citizens and travelers with disabilities, and 50% for children between the ages of 4 and 16.

Mols-Linien links up Jutland and Zealand, while Scandlines services the southern islands as well as Germany, Sweden, and the Baltic countries. The island of Bornholm, Denmark's farthest outpost to the East and a popular domestic tourist destination, is reachable with Bornholms Trafikken.

The ScanRail Pass, for travel anywhere within Scandinavia (Denmark, Sweden, Norway, and Finland), and the Interail and Eurail passes are valid on some ferry crossings. Call the DSB Travel Office for information.

CAR FERRIES Vehicle-bearing hydrofoils operate between Funen's Ebeltoft or Århus to Odden on Zealand; the trip takes about 1 hour. You can also take the slower (2 hours, 40 minutes), but less expensive, car ferry from Århus to Kalundborg on Zealand. From there, Route 23 leads to Copenhagen. Make reservations for the ferry in advance through Mols-Linien. Scandlines services the southern islands. (*Note:* During the busy summer months, passengers without reservations for their vehicles can wait hours.)

Some well-known international vehicle and passenger ferries run between Helsingør, Denmark, and Helsingborg, Sweden, and between Copenhagen and Göteborg, Sweden. The Helsingør/Helsingborg ferry (Scandlines) takes only 20 minutes; taking a car costs between €32 and €67 (about $39–$81) one-way.

🚢 Boat & Ferry Information **Bornholms Trafikken** ✉ Havnen, DK-3700 Rønne ☎ 56/95-18-66 🖷 56/91-07-66 ⊕ www.bornholmstrafikken.dk. **DSB** ☎ 70/13-14-15 ⊕ www.dsb.dk. **Mols-Linien** ☎ 70/10-14-18 🖷 89/52-52-90 ⊕ www.molslinien.dk. **Scandinavian Seaways Ferries** (DFDS) ✉ Skt. Annæ Pl. 30, DK-1295 Copenhagen ☎ 33/42-33-42 🖷 33/42-33-41 ⊕ www.dfds.com. **Scandlines** ☎ 33/15-15-15 🖷 35/29-02-01 ⊕ www.scandlines.dk.

Bus Travel

Although not particularly comfortable or fast, bus travel is inexpensive. Eurolines departs from London's Victoria Station on Saturday at 2:30 PM, crossing the North Sea on the Dover–Calais ferry, and arrives in Copenhagen about 22 hours later. With its many other routes, Eurolines links the principal Danish cities to a network of service that includes major European cities. Säfflebussen is the other main bus company with international routes to Denmark. The company offers regular trips between Copenhagen and Berlin, Göteborg, Karlstad, Stockholm, and Oslo.

To encourage travelers to make full use of Denmark's domestic transportation services, private bus operators and Danish State Railways (DSB) have collaborated to create Bus/Tog Samarbejde. This useful resource consolidates schedule and route information for the country's trains and buses.

Domestic bus companies include Thinggaard, which has regular routes between Zealand and Jutland, and Abildskou, which offers service from Århus to Copenhagen and Ebeltoft, as well as between Roskilde and the Copenhagen airport. Bus tickets are usually sold on board the buses immediately before departure. Ask about discounts for children, senior citizens, and groups.

🚌 **Abildskou** ✉ Graham Bellsvej 40, DK-8200 Århus ☎ 70/21-08-88 ⊕ www. abildskou.dk. **Bus/Tog Samarbejde** ⊕ www.rejseplan.dk. **Eurolines** ✉ 52 Grosvenor Gardens, SW1 London ☎ 0207/730-8235 ✉ Reventlowsg. 8, DK-1651 Copenhagen ☎ 70/10-00-30 ⊕ www.eurolines.com. **Säfflebussen** ✉ Halmtorvet 5, DK-1700 Copenhagen ☎33/23-54-20 ⊕www.safflebussen.se. **Thinggaard Ekspres** ✉Jyllandsg. 6, DK-9000 Aalborg ☎ 70/10-00-20 ⊕ www.thinggaard-bus.dk.

Business Hours

BANKS & OFFICES   Banks in Copenhagen are open weekdays 9:30 to 4 and Thursdays until 6. Several *bureaux de change,* including the ones at Copenhagen's central station and airport, stay open until 10 PM. Outside Copenhagen, banking hours vary.

MUSEUMS &   A number of Copenhagen's museums hold confounding hours, so al-
SIGHTS   ways call first to confirm. As a rule, however, most museums are open 10 to 3 or 11 to 4 and are closed Monday. In winter, opening hours are shorter, and some museums close for the season, especially on the smaller islands, including Bornholm, Ærø, and Fanø. Check the local papers or ask at tourist offices for current schedules.

SHOPS   Though many Danish stores are expanding their hours, sometimes even staying open on Sunday, most shops still keep the traditional hours: weekdays 10 to 5:30, until 7 or 8 on Friday, and until 1 or 2 on Saturday—though the larger department stores stay open until 5. Everything except bakeries, kiosks, flower shops, and a handful of grocers are closed Sunday. The first Saturday of every month is a Long Saturday, when even the smaller shops, especially in large cities, stay open until 4 or 5. Grocery stores stay open until 8 on weekdays, and kiosks until much later.

Car Rental

Rental rates in Copenhagen begin at DKr 550 a day and DKr 2,220 a week. This does not include an additional per-kilometer fee and any insurance you choose to purchase; there is also a 25% tax on car rentals.

🚗 Major Agencies **Alamo** ☎ 800/522-9696 ⊕ www.alamo.com. **Avis** ☎ 800/331-1084, 800/879-2847 in Canada, 0870/606-0100 in the U.K., 02/9353-9000 in Australia, 09/526-2847 in New Zealand ⊕www.avis.com. **Budget** ☎800/527-0700 ⊕www.budget. com. **Dollar** ☎ 800/800-6000, 0800/085-4578 in the U.K. ⊕ www.dollar.com. **Hertz** ☎ 800/654-3001, 800/263-0600 in Canada, 0870/844-8844 in the U.K., 02/9669-2444 in Australia, 09/256-8690 in New Zealand ⊕ www.hertz.com. **National Car Rental** ☎ 800/227-7368 ⊕ www.nationalcar.com.

Car Travel

The only part of Denmark that is connected to the European continent is Jutland, via the E45 highway from Germany. The E20 highway then leads to Middelfart on Funen and east to Nyborg. The Storebæltsbro bridge connects Funen and Zealand via the E20 highway; the E20 then continues east, over the Lillebæltsbro bridge, to Copenhagen. The bridges have greatly reduced the driving time between the islands. You can reach many of the smaller islands via toll bridges. In some locations car ferries are still in service; for ferry information, *see* Boat & Ferry Travel.

In Scandinavia your own driver's license is acceptable for a limited time; check with the Danish Tourist Board before you go. International driving permits (IDPs) are available from the American and Canadian automobile associations and, in the United Kingdom, from the Automobile Association and Royal Automobile Club. These international permits, valid only in conjunction with your regular driver's license, are universally recognized; having one may save you a problem with local authorities.

EMERGENCY SERVICES
Members of organizations affiliated with Alliance International de Tourisme (AIT) can get technical and legal advice from the Danish Motoring Organization, open 10–4 weekdays. All highways have emergency phones, and you can call the rental company for help. If you cannot drive your car to a garage for repairs, the rescue corps Falck can help anywhere, anytime. In most cases they do charge for assistance. In the event of an emergency, call 112.

Falck ✉ Polititorvet, DK–1780 Copenhagen ☎ 70/10–20–30 for emergencies, 70/33–33–11 for headquarters 🖷 33/14–41–73 ⊕ www.falck.dk. **Forenede Danske Motorejere (Danish Motoring Organization)** ✉ Firskovvej 32, DK–2800 Lyngby ☎ 70/13–30–40 🖷 45/27–09–93 ⊕ www.fdm.dk.

GASOLINE
Gasoline costs about DKr 10 per liter (¼ gallon). Stations are mostly self-service and open from 6 or 7 AM to 9 PM or later.

PARKING
You can usually park on the right-hand side of the road, though not on main roads and highways. Signs reading PARKERING/STANDSNING FORBUNDT mean no parking or stopping, though you are allowed a three-minute grace period for loading and unloading. In town, parking disks are used where there are no automated ticket-vending machines. Get disks from gas stations, post offices, police stations, or tourist offices, and set them to show your time of arrival. For most downtown parking you must buy a ticket from an automatic vending machine and display it on the dash. Parking costs about DKr 10 or more per hour.

ROAD CONDITIONS
Roads in Denmark are in good condition and largely traffic-free (except for the manageable traffic around Copenhagen).

RULES OF THE ROAD
To drive in Denmark you need a valid adult driver's license, and if you're using your own car it must have a certificate of registration and national plates. A triangular hazard-warning sign is compulsory in every car and is provided with rentals. No matter where you sit in a car, you must wear a seat belt, and cars must have low beams on at all times. Motorcyclists must wear helmets and use low-beam lights as well. Talking on the phone while operating a car, bicycle, or any other kind of vehicle is illegal.

Bicyclists have equal rights on the road, and a duty to signal moves and observe all traffic regulations. Be especially careful when making turns. Check for bicyclists, who have the right of way if they are going straight and a car is turning.

Drive on the right and give way to traffic—*especially to bicyclists*—on the right. A red-and-white YIELD sign or a line of white triangles across the road means you must yield to traffic on the road you are entering. Do not turn right on red unless there is a green arrow indicating that this is allowed. Speed limits are 50 kph (30 mph) in built-up areas; 100 kph (60 mph) on highways; and 80 kph (50 mph) on other roads. If you are towing a trailer, you must not exceed 70 kph (40 mph). Speeding and, especially, drinking and driving are punished severely, even if no damage is caused. The consumption of one or two beers might lead to a violation, and motorists traveling across the Øresund Bridge must remember that Sweden has an even lower legal limit for blood-alcohol levels. It is therefore possible to drive legally out of Denmark and illegally into Sweden. Americans and other foreign tourists must pay all fines on the spot.

Customs & Duties

If you are 16 or older, have purchased goods in a country that is a member of the European Union (EU), and pay that country's value-added tax (V.A.T.) on those goods, you may import duty-free 1½ liters of liquor and 300 cigarettes or 150 cigarillos or 75 cigars or 400 grams of tobacco. If you are entering Denmark from a non-EU country or if you have purchased your goods on a ferryboat or in an airport not taxed in the EU, you must pay Danish taxes on any amount of alcoholic beverages greater than 1 liter of liquor or 2 liters of strong wine, plus 2 liters of table wine. For tobacco, the limit is 200 cigarettes or 100 cigarillos or 50 cigars or 250 grams of tobacco. You are also allowed 50 grams of perfume. Other articles (including beer) are allowed up to a maximum of DKr 1,350.

Non-EU citizens can save 20% (less a handling fee) off the purchase price if they shop in one of the hundreds of stores throughout Denmark displaying the TAX-FREE SHOPPING sign. The purchased merchandise must value more than DKr 300 and the taxes will be refunded after submitting the application with customs authorities at their final destination before leaving the EU.

🗐 **Told og Skat** (Toll and Taxes) ✉ Tagensvej 135, DK-2200 Copenhagen ☎ 35/ 87-73-00 🖷 35/85-90-94 ⊕ www.toldskat.dk.

Embassies

New Zealanders should contact the U.K. embassy for assistance.

🗐 Australia ✉ Dampfærgevej 26, 2nd. fl., Østerbro, DK-2100 Copenhagen ☎ 70/ 26-36-76 🖷 70/26-36-86 ⊕ www.denmark.embassy.gov.au.

🗐 Canada ✉ Kristen Bernikows G. 1, Downtown, DK-1105 Copenhagen ☎ 33/48-32-00 🖷 33/48-32-20 ⊕ www.canada.dk.

🗐 Ireland ✉ Østbaneg. 21, Østerbro, DK-2100 Copenhagen ☎ 35/42-32-33 🖷 35/ 43-18-58.

🗐 South Africa ✉ Gammel Vartov Vej 8, DK-2900 Hellerup ☎ 39/18-01-55 🖷 39/ 18-40-06 ⊕ www.southafrica.dk.

🗐 U. K. ✉ Kastelsvej 36-40, Østerbro, DK-2100 Copenhagen ☎ 35/44-52-00 🖷 35/ 44-52-93 ⊕ www.britishembassy.dk.

🗐 U. S. ✉ Dag Hammarskjölds Allé 24, Østerbro, DK-2100 Copenhagen ☎ 33/41-71-00 🖷 35/43-02-23 ⊕ www.usembassy.dk.

Emergencies
The general 24-hour emergency number throughout Denmark is 112.

Language
Danish is a difficult tongue for foreigners—except those from Norway and Sweden—to understand, let alone speak. Danes are good linguists, however, and almost everyone, except perhaps elderly people in rural areas, speaks English. In Sønderjylland, the southern region of Jutland, most people speak or understand German. If you are planning to visit the countryside or the small islands, it would be a good idea to bring a phrase book.

Difficult-to-pronounce Danish characters include the "ø," pronounced a bit like a very short "er," similar to the French "eu"; "æ," which sounds like the "a" in "ape" but with a glottal stop, or the "a" in "cat," depending on the region; and the "å" (also written "aa"), which sounds like "or." The important thing about these characters isn't that you pronounce them correctly—foreigners usually can't—but that you know to look for them in the phone book at the very end. Mr. Søren Åstrup, for example, will be found after "Z;" Æ and Ø follow.

Lodging
The lodgings we list are the cream of the crop in each price category. We always list the facilities that are available—but we don't specify whether they cost extra. When pricing accommodations, always ask what's included and what costs extra.

APARTMENT & VILLA RENTALS Each year many Danes choose to rent out their summer homes in the verdant countryside and along the coast. Typically, a simple house accommodating four persons costs from DKr 1,000 weekly up to 10 times that amount in summer. You should book well in advance. A group of Danes who regularly rent out their holiday houses have formed the Association of Danish Holiday House Letters (ADHHL). You can also contact DanCenter and Lejrskolebureauet for information. Homes for You lists fully furnished homes and apartments.

⚑ International Agents **Hideaways International** ✉ 767 Islington St., Portsmouth, NH 03801 ☎ 800/843–4433 or 603/430–4433 🖷 603/430–4444 ⊕ www.hideaways.com, annual membership $185.

⚑ Local Agents **DanCenter** ✉ Lyngbyvej 20, Østerbro, DK-2100 Copenhagen ☎ 70/13–16–16 🖷 70/13–70–73 ⊕ www.dancenter.com. **Feriehusudlejernes Brancheforeningen (ADHHL)** ✉ Obels Have 32, DK-9000 Aalborg ☎ 96/30–22–44 🖷 96/30–22–45 ⊕ www.fbnet.dk. **Homes for You** ✉ Vimmelskaftet 49, Downtown, DK-1161 Copenhagen ☎ 33/33–08–05 🖷 33/32–08–04 ⊕ www.hay4you.dk. **Lejrskolebureauet (LSB)** ✉ Nordlævej 13, DK-3250 Gilleleje ☎ 48/30–14–88 🖷 48/30–14–66.

BED & BREAKFASTS Contact Dansk Bed & Breakfast to order their B&B catalog for the whole of Denmark. Odense Tourist Bureau maintains its own list for the Funen and the Central Islands region.

⚑ Reservation Services **Dansk Bed & Breakfast** ✉ Bernstorffsvej 71a, DK-2900 Hellerup ☎ 39/61–04–05 🖷 39/61–05–25 ⊕ www.bedandbreakfast.dk. **Odense Tourist Bureau** ✉ Rådhuset, DK-5000 Odense ☎ 66/12–75–20 🖷 66/12–75–86 ⊕ www.bed-breakfast-fyn.dk.

CAMPING   If you plan to camp in one of Denmark's 500-plus approved campsites, you'll need an International Camping Carnet or Danish Camping Pass (available at any campsite and valid for one year). Call Campingrådet for information.

🚩 **Campingrådet** ✉ Mosedalsvej 15, DK-2500 Valby ☎ 39/27-88-44 🖷 39/27-80-44 ⊕ www.campingraadet.dk.

FARM VACATIONS & HOMESTAYS   A farm vacation is perhaps the best way to experience the Danish countryside, sharing meals with your host family and perhaps helping with the chores. Bed-and-breakfast packages are about DKr 200, whereas half board—an overnight with breakfast and one hot meal—runs around DKr 280. Full board, including an overnight with three square meals, can also be arranged. The minimum stay is three nights. Contact Landboferie for details.

If you aren't necessarily looking for a pastoral experience but would still like to get an insider's view of Danish society, you might want to consider a homestay. Meet the Danes helps travelers find accommodation in Danish homes. The informative local hosts can give you invaluable tips regarding sightseeing, shopping, dining, and nightlife.

🚩 **Landboferie** (Holiday in the Country) ✉ Ceresvej 2, DK 8410 Rønde ☎ 86/37-39-00 🖷 86/37-35-50 ⊕ www.bondegaardsferie.dk. **Meet the Danes** ✉ Ravnsborgg. 2, 2nd fl., Nørrebro DK-2200 Copenhagen ☎ 33/46-46-46 🖷 33/46-46-47 ⊕ www.meetthedanes.dk.

HOME EXCHANGES   If you would like to exchange your home for someone else's, join a home-exchange organization, which will send you its updated listings of available exchanges for a year and will include your own listing in at least one of them. It's up to you to make specific arrangements.

🚩 **Exchange Clubs HomeLink USA** ✉ 2937 N.W. 9th Terr., Wilton Manors, FL 33311 ☎ 800/638-3841 or 954/566-2687 🖷 954/566-2783 ⊕ www.homelink.org; $75 yearly for a listing and online access; $45 additional to receive directories. **Intervac U.S.** ✉ 30 Corte San Fernando, Tiburon, CA 94920 ☎ 800/756-4663 🖷 415/435-7440 ⊕ www.intervacus.com; $128 yearly for a listing, online access, and a catalog; $68 without catalog.

HOSTELS   No matter what your age, you can save on lodging costs by staying at hostels. In some 4,500 locations in more than 70 countries around the world, Hostelling International (HI), the umbrella group for a number of national youth-hostel associations, offers single-sex, dorm-style beds and, at many hostels, rooms for couples and family accommodations. Membership in any HI national hostel association, open to travelers of all ages, allows you to stay in HI-affiliated hostels at member rates; one-year membership is about $28 for adults (A$52 in Australia, C$35 for a two-year minimum membership in Canada, NZ$40 in New Zealand, £15 in the United Kingdom); hostels charge about $10–$30 per night. Members have priority if the hostel is full; they're also eligible for discounts around the world, even on rail and bus travel in some countries.

Youth hostels in Denmark are open to everyone regardless of age. If you have an International Youth Hostels Association card (it costs DKr 160 to obtain in Denmark), the rate is roughly DKr 115 for a single bed, DKr 150–DKr 575 for a private room accommodating up to four people. Without the card, there's a surcharge of about DKr 30 per person. Prices don't include breakfast.

The hostels fill up quickly in summer, so make your reservations early. Most hostels are sympathetic to students and will usually find them at least a place on the floor. Bring your own linens or sleep sheet, though these can usually be rented at the hostel. Sleeping bags are not allowed. Contact Danhostel Danmarks Vandrerhjem—the organization charges for information, but you can get a free brochure, *Camping/Youth and Family Hostels,* from the Danish Tourist Board.

🚩 Organizations **Danhostel Danmarks Vandrerhjem** ⊠ Vesterbrog. 39, Vesterbro, DK-1620 Copenhagen ☎ 33/31-36-12 🖷 33/31-36-26 ⊕ www.danhostel.dk. **Hostelling International–Canada** ⊠ 205 Catherine St., Suite 400, Ottawa, Ontario K2P 1C3 ☎ 800/663-5777 or 613/237-7884 🖷 613/237-7868 ⊕ www.hihostels.ca. **Hostelling International–USA** ⊠ 8401 Colesville Rd., Suite 600, Silver Spring, MD 20910 ☎ 301/495-1240 🖷 301/495-6697 ⊕ www.hiusa.org. **YHA Australia** ⊠ 422 Kent St., Sydney, NSW 2001 ☎ 02/9261-1111 🖷 02/9261-1969 ⊕ www.yha.com.au. **YHA England and Wales** ⊠ Trevelyan House, Dimple Rd., Matlock, Derbyshire DE4 3YH, U.K. ☎ 0870/870-8808, 0870/770-8868, 0162/959-2600 🖷 0870/770-6127 ⊕ www.yha.org.uk. **YHA New Zealand** ⊠ Level 1, Moorhouse City, 166 Moorhouse Ave., Box 436, Christchurch ☎ 0800/278-299 or 03/379-9970 🖷 03/365-4476 ⊕ www.yha.org.nz.

HOTELS All hotels listed have private bath unless otherwise noted. Many Danes prefer a shower to a bath, so if you particularly want a bath, ask for it, but be prepared to pay more. Taxes are usually included in prices, but check when making a reservation. As time goes on, it appears that an increasing number of hotels are eliminating breakfast from their room rates; even if it is not included, breakfast is usually well worth its price. Many of Denmark's larger hotels, particularly those that cater to the conference crowd, offer discounted rates on weekends, so inquire when booking. (Oddly, these are the hotels where breakfast is usually not included in the price of the room.) Try www.danishhotels.dk for listings not included in this book.

The Scandinavian countries offer Inn Checks, or prepaid hotel vouchers, for accommodations ranging from first-class hotels to country cottages. These vouchers, which must be purchased from travel agents or from the Scandinavian Tourist Board (⊕ www.goscandinavia.com) before departure, are sold individually and in packets for as many nights as needed and offer savings of up to 50%. Most countries also offer summer bargains for foreign tourists; winter bargains can be even greater. For further information about Scandinavian hotel vouchers, contact the Scandinavian Tourist Board.

ProSkandinavia checks can be used in 400 hotels across Scandinavia for savings up to 50%, for reservations made usually no earlier than 24 hours before arrival, although some hotels allow earlier bookings. One check costs about $40. Two checks will pay for a double room at a hotel, one check for a room in a cottage. The checks can be bought at many travel agencies in Scandinavia or directly from ProSkandinavia.

The old stagecoach *kroer* (inns) scattered throughout Denmark can be cheap yet charming alternatives to standard hotel rooms. You can cut your costs by contacting Danske Kroer & Hoteller to invest in a book of Inn Checks, valid at 83 participating inns and hotels throughout the country. Each check costs about DKr 690 per couple and entitles you to an overnight stay in a double room including breakfast. Family checks for three (DKr 790) and four (DKr 890) are also available. Order a free catalog from Danske Kroer & Hoteller, but choose carefully; the organization includes a few chain hotels bereft of the charm you might be expecting. Some of the participating establishments tack on a DKr 150 surcharge.

🗹 Reservation Services **Danske Kroer & Hoteller** ✉ Vejlevej 16, DK-8700 Horsens ☎ 75/64-87-00 🖷 75/64-87-20 ⊕ www.krohotel.dk. **ProSkandinavia** ✉ Akersgt. 11, N-0158 Oslo, Norway ☎ 47/22-41-13-13 ⊕ www.proskandinavia.no.

RESERVING A
ROOM
Make your reservations well in advance, especially in resort areas near the coasts. Many places offer summer reductions to compensate for the slowdown in business travel and conferences. The very friendly staff at the hotel booking desk at Wonderful Copenhagen can help find rooms in hotels, hostels, and private homes, or even campsites in advance of a trip. If you find yourself in Copenhagen without a reservation, head for the tourist office's hotel booking desk, which is open May through August, Monday to Saturday 9–8 and Sunday 10–8; September through April, weekdays 10–4:30 and Saturday 10–1:30. Note that hours of the hotel booking desk can be fickle, and change from year to year depending on staff availability; in the low season they are often closed weekends. Young travelers looking for a room should head for Use It, the student and youth budget travel agency.

Reservations should be made two months in advance, but last-minute (as in same-day) hotel rooms booked at the tourist office can save you 50% off the normal price.

🗹 Local Reservation Services **Hotel booking desk** ✉ Bernstorffsg. 1, Vesterbro, DK-1577 Copenhagen ☎ 70/22-24-42 ⊕ www.visitcopenhagen.com. **Use It** ✉ Råd-husstr. 13, Downtown, DK-1466 Copenhagen ☎ 33/73-06-20 🖷 33/73-06-49 ⊕ www.useit.dk.

🗹 Toll-Free Numbers **Best Western** ☎ 800/528-1234 ⊕ www.bestwestern.com. **Choice** ☎ 800/424-6423 ⊕ www.choicehotels.com. **Clarion** ☎ 800/424-6423 ⊕ www.choicehotels.com. **Comfort Inn** ☎ 800/424-6423 ⊕ www.choicehotels.com. **Hilton** ☎ 800/445-8667 ⊕ www.hilton.com. **Holiday Inn** ☎ 800/465-4329 ⊕ www.ichotelsgroup.com. **Quality Inn** ☎ 800/424-6423 ⊕ www.choicehotels.com. **Radisson** ☎ 800/333-3333 ⊕ www.radisson.com.

Mail & Shipping

POSTAL RATES
Airmail letters and postcards to non-EU countries cost DKr 6.50 for 50 grams. Airmail letters and postcards within the EU cost DKr 5.50. Length, width, and thickness all influence the postage price. Letters must be marked with an "A." Contact Copenhagen's main post office for more information. You can buy stamps at post offices or from shops selling postcards.

RECEIVING MAIL
You can arrange to have your mail sent general delivery, marked *poste restante,* to any post office, hotel, or inn. If no post office is specified, the letter or package is automatically sent to the main post office in Copenhagen.

🗹 **Copenhagen Main Post Office** ✉ Tietgensg. 37, Vesterbro, DK-1566 Copenhagen ☎ 80/20-70-30 ⊕ www.postdanmark.dk.

Money Matters

Denmark's economy is stable, and inflation remains reasonably low. On the other hand, the Danish cost of living is quite high, even for Europe. In some areas prices are comparable to other European capitals, while other goods or services tend to be higher. As in all of Scandinavia, prices for alcoholic beverages and tobacco products are steep due to heavy taxation. Prices are highest in Copenhagen, lower elsewhere in the country. Some sample prices: cup of coffee, DKr 20–DKr 30; bottle of beer, DKr 30–DKr 35; soda, DKr 20–DKr 25; ham sandwich, DKr 35–DKr 45; 1½-km (1-mi) taxi ride, about DKr 55.

Prices throughout this guide are given for adults. Substantially reduced fees are almost always available for children, students, and senior citizens. For information on taxes, *see* Taxes.

ATMS   Automatic Teller Machines/ATMs are located around most towns and cities. Look for the red signs for KONTANTEN/DANKORT AUTOMAT. You can use Visa, Plus, MasterCard/Eurocard, Eurochequecard, and sometimes JCB cards to withdraw cash. Many, but not all, machines are open 24 hours. Check with your bank about daily withdrawal limits before you go.

⧉ ATM Locations **MasterCard/Cirrus** ☎ 800/424-7787 ⊕ www.mastercard.com.

CREDIT CARDS   Most major credit cards are accepted in Denmark, though it's wise to inquire about American Express and Diners Club beforehand. Throughout this guide, the following abbreviations are used: **AE**, American Express; **DC**, Diners Club; **MC**, MasterCard; and **V**, Visa.

⧉ Reporting Lost Cards **American Express** ✉ Amagertorv 18, DK-1146 Copenhagen ☎ 33/11-50-05. **Diners Club** ✉ H. J. Holst Vej 5, DK-2605 Brøndby ☎ 36/73-73-73. **MasterCard** ☎ 44/89-27-50. **Visa** ☎ 44/89-29-29.

CURRENCY   The monetary unit in Denmark is the krone (DKr), divided into 100 øre. Even though Denmark has not adopted the euro, the Danish krone is firmly bound to it at about DKr 7.5 to 1€, with only minimal fluctuations in exchange rates.

At this writing, the krone stood at 7.46 to the euro, 4.71 to the Australian dollar, 11.07 to the British pound, 5.26 to the Canadian dollar, 4.31 to the New Zealand dollar, 0.96 to the South African rand, and 6.14 to the U.S. dollar.

Sports & the Outdoors

FISHING   Licenses are required for fishing along the coasts; requirements vary from one area to another for fishing in lakes, streams, and the ocean. Licenses cost about DKr 100 for a year, DKr 75 for a week, and DKr 25 for a day, and you can buy them at any post office. Remember—it is illegal to fish within 1,650 feet of the mouth of a stream. Contact the Danish Tourist Board for more information.

⧉ **Danish Tourist Board** ✉ Vesterbrog. 6D, Vesterbro, DK-1620 Copenhagen ☎ 33/11-14-15 🖷 33/93-14-16 ⊕ www.visitdenmark.dk.

GOLF   Danish golf courses can be a real challenge, with plenty of water, roughs that live up to their name, and wind that is often a factor. Due to environmental controls, chemical fertilization is prohibited, so greens tend to be flatter with fewer breaks. Motorized riding carts are prohibited for general use, though most courses have one on hand for anyone with (documented) ambulatory problems.

Danish golf courses are open to any player who is a member of a certified golf club or has a valid handicap card. When entering a clubhouse to pay a greens fee, you will be asked to present documentation of membership in a club or a card stating your handicap. This can present a problem for Americans, many of whom are unfamiliar with this system and can produce no such evidence. The Danes are generally flexible when a golfer doesn't have a card, but it's wise to have some sort of documentation handy just in case.

🚩 **Dansk Golf Union** ✉ Brøndby Stadium 20, DK-2605 Brøndby ☎ 43/26-27-00 📠 43/26-27-01 ⊕ www.dgu.org/danishgolffederation/.

Taxes

All hotel, restaurant, and departure taxes and V.A.T. (what the Danes call *moms*) are automatically included in prices.

VALUE-ADDED   V.A.T. is 25%; non-EU citizens can obtain an 18% refund. The more
TAX   than 1,500 shops that participate in the tax-free scheme have a white TAX FREE sticker on their windows. Purchases must be at least DKr 300 per store and must be sealed and unused in Denmark. At the shop you'll be asked to fill out a form and show your passport. The form can then be turned in at any airport or ferry customs desk, where you can choose a cash or charge-card credit. Keep all your receipts and tags; occasionally customs authorities do ask to see purchases, so pack them where they will be accessible.

Telephones

Telephone exchanges throughout Denmark were changed over the past couple of years. If you hear a recorded message or three loud beeps, chances are the number you are trying to reach has been changed. Contact the main Danish operator, TDC, for current numbers.

Denmark, like most European countries, has a different cellular-phone switching system from the one used in North America. Newer phones can handle both technologies; check with the dealer where you purchased your phone to see if it can work on the European system. If all else fails, several companies rent cellular phones to tourists. Contact local tourist offices for details.

COUNTRY CODES   The country code for Denmark is 45.

DIRECTORY &   Most operators speak English. For national directory assistance, dial 118;
OPERATOR   for an international operator, dial 113; for a directory-assisted interna-
ASSISTANCE   tional call, dial 115. You can reach U.S. operators by dialing local access codes.

INTERNATIONAL   Dial 00, then the country code (1 for the United States and Canada, 44
CALLS   for Great Britain), the area code, and the number. It's very expensive to call or fax from hotels, although the regional phone companies offer a

discount after 7:30 PM. You can save a lot on the price of calls by purchasing a country-specific telephone card from any post office or one of the many kiosks and groceries in Copenhagen's Vesterbro and Nørrebro neighborhoods.

LOCAL CALLS Phones accept 1-, 2-, 5-, 10-, and 20-kroner coins. Pick up the receiver, dial the number, always including the area code, and wait until the party answers; then deposit the coins. You have roughly a minute per krone; on some phones you can make another call on the same payment if your time has not run out. When it does, you will hear a beep and your call will be disconnected unless you deposit another coin. Coin-operated phones are becoming increasingly rare; it is cheaper and less frustrating to buy a local phone card from a kiosk.

Dial the eight-digit number for calls anywhere within the country. For calls to the Faroe Islands (298) and Greenland (299), dial 00, then the three-digit code, then the five-digit number.

LONG-DISTANCE SERVICES AT&T, MCI, and Sprint access codes make calling long-distance relatively convenient, but you may find the local access number blocked in many hotel rooms. First ask the hotel operator to connect you. If the hotel operator balks, ask for an international operator, or dial the international operator yourself. One way to improve your odds of getting connected to your long-distance carrier is to travel with more than one company's calling card (a hotel may block Sprint, for example, but not MCI). If all else fails, call from a pay phone. If you are traveling for a longer period of time, consider renting a cell-phone from a local company.

⚡ Access Codes AT&T USADirect ☎ 800/10010 ⊕ www.travel.att.com. **Sprint Global One** ☎ 800/10877 ⊕ www.sprint.com. **World Phone** ☎ 800/10022 ⊕ www.mci.com.

Tipping

It has long been held that the egalitarian Danes do not expect to be tipped. This is often the case, but most people do tip and those who receive tips appreciate them. Service is included in hotel bills. Many restaurants frequented by tourists have started adding a gratuity to bills, although you should check your bill to see if a service charge has already been included. If not, a token tip at bars or restaurants is the general rule of thumb.

The same holds true for taxis—if a bill comes to DKr 58, most people will give the driver DKr 60. If the driver is extremely friendly or helpful, tip more at your own discretion. Hotel porters expect about DKr 5 per bag.

Tours

For information on excursions and tours, call the Danish Tourist Board, Copenhagen Excursions, or Auto–Paaske.

⚡ Copenhagen Excursions ✉ Rådhuspl. 57, Downtown, DK-1550 Copenhagen ☎ 32/54-06-06 🖶 32/57-49-05 ⊕ www.cex.dk. **Danish Tourist Board** ✉ Vesterbrog. 6D, Vesterbro, DK-1620 Copenhagen ☎ 33/11-14-15 🖶 33/93-14-16 ⊕ www.visitdenmark.dk.

BIKE TOURS Copenhagen-based BikeDenmark combines the flexibility of individual tours with the security of an organized outing. Choose from seven pre-planned 5- to 10-day tours, which include bikes, maps, two fine meals per day, hotel accommodations, and hotel-to-hotel baggage transfers.

BikeDenmark tours can be booked directly by fax, via their Web site, or through any travel agency below. Many U.S. tour companies can arrange booking. Try Borton Oversees, Nordique Tours Norvista, ScanAm World Tours, or Gerhard's Bicycle Odysseys.

Bike and Sea also leads biking tours through southern Jutland, Funen, and southern Zealand.

🚲 **Bike and Sea** ⊠ Svendborgvej 83–85, DK-5260 Odense ☎ 66/13-13-37 🖷 66/13-13-38 ⊕ www.bikeandsea-denmark.com. **BikeDenmark** ⊠ Olaf Poulsens Allé 1A, DK-3480 Fredensborg ☎ 48/48-58-00 🖷 48/48-59-00 ⊕ www.bikedenmark.com. **Borton Overseas** ⊠ 5412 Lyndale Ave. S, Minneapolis, MN 55419 ☎ 800/843-0602 or 612/822-4640 🖷 612/822-4755 ⊕ www.bortonoverseas.com. **Gerhard's Bicycle Odysseys** 🖅 Box 757, Portland, OR 97207 ☎ 800/966-2402 🖷 503/223-5901 ⊕ www.since1974.com. **Nordique Tours Norvista** ☎ 800/995-7997 or 310/645-7527 🖷 310/645-1071 ⊕ www.nordiquetours.com. **ScanAm World Tours** ⊠ 108 N. Main St., Cranbury, NJ 08512 ☎ 800/545-2204 (toll-free) 🖷 609/655-1622 ⊕ www.scandinaviantravel.com.

Train Travel

Trains within Europe are well connected to Denmark, with Copenhagen serving as the main hub; however, it's often not much cheaper than flying, especially if you make your arrangements from the United States. A ScanRail Pass offers discounts on train, ferry, and car transportation in Denmark, Finland, Sweden, and Norway. The EurailPass, purchased only in the United States, is accepted by the Danish State Railways and on some ferries operated by DSB.

DSB and a few private companies cover the country with a dense network of services, supplemented by buses in remote areas. Hourly intercity trains connect the main towns in Jutland and Funen with Copenhagen and Zealand, using high-speed diesels, called IC-3s, on the most important stretches. All these trains make 1-hour crossings of the Great Belt Bridge. You can reserve seats (for an extra DKr 15) on intercity trains, and you *must* have a reservation if you plan to cross the Great Belt. Buy tickets at stations. From London, the transit takes 18 hours, including ferry. Call the British Rail European Travel Center or Wasteels for information.

CUTTING COSTS   The ScanRail Pass, which affords unlimited train travel throughout Denmark, Finland, Norway, and Sweden and restricted ferry passage in and beyond Scandinavia, comes in various denominations. It is much better to buy the ScanRail Pass before you leave home, as you will have more flexibility to use it. You can order 5 days of travel within 60 days ($291); 10 days within 60 days ($390); or 21 days consecutive use ($453). All prices given are for second-class travel. In Denmark you will still be able to reserve a seat for DKr 20 with your pass, and you will be given the option of a no-smoking or smoking car.

A ScanRail Pass will also allow you free or discounted travel on selected ferries, boats, and buses. Most ferries offer 50% discount (e.g. Frederikshavn-Goteborg on the Stena Line). There is a 25% discount on railway museums (there is a large one in Odense, Funen, and a few very small ones in other areas) in Denmark, and a 50% discount on the private railway lines Frederikshavn-Skagen (Skagensbanan) and Hjorring-Hirtshals (Hjorring Privatbaner). You can also receive a discounted price on the following hotel chains: Best Western, Sokos Hotels, Choice Hotels, and VIP Backpackers Resorts.

With a ScanRail 'n Drive Pass, you get any five days of unlimited train travel, along with two days car rental with unlimited mileage in Denmark, Finland, Norway, and/or Sweden; you have two months to complete your travel. Train passage is second class. The car rental is chosen from three car categories with manual transmission. Local tax is included with the rental, and the same bonuses apply as above on ferries. You can purchase extra travel days of Avis car rental for Denmark, Finland, Norway, and Sweden and the third and fourth person sharing the car need only purchase a ScanRail Pass. For two adults traveling, the price ranges from $678 to $738.

In the United States, call Rail Europe, Nordic Saga Tours, ScanAm World Tours, Passage Tours, or DER Travel Services for rail passes. In Canada, contact Rail Europe. You can also buy the ScanRail Pass at the train stations in most major cities, including Copenhagen, Odense, and Århus, but you will not have as much of a time frame in which to use the pass. The ScanRail Pass and Interail and Eurail passes are also valid on all DSB trains.

Call Arriva for train travel in central and northern Jutland, or the DSB Travel Office for the rest of the country.

⛭ Train Information **Arriva** ☎ 72/13-96-00 ⊕ www.arriva.dk. **DSB Travel Office** ☎ 70/13-14-15 ⊕ www.dsb.dk.

⛭ Rail Passes **DER Travel Services** ✉ 9501 W. Devon Ave., Rosemont, IL 60018 ☎ 800/782-2424 🖷 888/712-5727 ⊕ www.der.com. **Nordic Saga Tours** ✉ 303 5th Ave. S, Suite 109, Edmonds, WA 98020 ☎ 800/840-6449 or 425/673-4800 🖷 425/673-2600 ⊕ www.nordicsaga.com. **Passage Tours** ✉ 239 Commercial Blvd., Fort Lauderdale, FL 33308 ☎ 954/776-7188 🖷 954/776-7070 ⊕ www.passagetours.com. **Rail Europe** ☎ 888/382-7245 in the U.S., 800/361-7245 in Canada ⊕ www.raileurope.com in the U.S., www.raileurope.ca in Canada. **ScanAm World Tours** ✉ 108 N. Main St., Cranbury, NJ 08512 ☎ 800/545-2204 🖷 609/655-1622 ⊕ www.scandinaviantravel.com. **Wasteels** ✉ Skoubog. 6, Downtown, DK-1158 Copenhagen ☎ 33/14-46-33 🖷 33/14-08-65 ⊕ www.wasteels.dk.

Visitor Information

⛭ Tourist Information Danish Tourist Board ✉ 655 3rd Ave., New York, NY 10017 ☎ 212/885-9700 🖷 212/885-9726 ✉ 55 Sloane St., London SWIX 9SY ☎ 44/20-7259-5959 🖷 44/20-7259-5955 ✉ Level 4, 81 York St., Sydney NSW 2000 ☎ 61/2-9262-5832 🖷 61/2-9290-1981 ⊕ www.visitdenmark.com. **Danmarks Turistråd (Danish Tourist Board)** ✉ Vesterbrog. 6D, Vesterbro, DK-1620 Copenhagen ☎ 33/11-14-15 🖷 33/93-14-16 ⊕ www.visitdenmark.com.

Norway

WORD OF MOUTH

"You must visit Vigeland Park in Oslo to see the sculptures of Gustav Vigeland—absolutely amazing depictions of people throughout the life cycle."

—Barb

"Bergen is fantastic. You can see it in two days, but if you like an unhurried pace, stopping to read every sign and post as we do, take three days. Hanging around the market at the marina is great fun."

–joegri

Revised by
Daniel Cash
and Lars Ursin

NORWEGIANS HAVE A STRONG ATTACHMENT to the natural beauty of their mountainous homeland. Whether in the verdant dales of the interior, the brooding mountains of the north, or the fjords and archipelagoes of the coast, Norwegians' *hytter* (mountain cabins) dot even the harshest landscapes.In almost any kind of weather, blasting or balmy, large numbers of Norwegians are outdoors, fishing, biking, skiing, hiking, or playing soccer. Everybody—from cherubic children to hardy, knapsack-toting seniors—bundles up for just one more ski trip or hike in the mountains. In one recent research poll, 70% of Norwegian respondents said that they wanted to spend even more time in nature. Although Norway is a modern, highly industrialized nation, vast areas of the country (up to 95%) remain forested or fallow. When discussing the size of their country, Norwegians like to say that if Oslo remained fixed and the northern part of the country were swung south, it would reach all the way to Rome. Perched at the very top of the globe, this northern land is long and rangy, 2,750 km (1,705 mi) in length, with only 4.5 million people scattered over it—making it the least densely populated country in Europe, after Iceland.

Exploring Norway

Norway is long and narrow with a jagged coastline carved by deep, dramatic fjords. Oslo, Norway's capital, is in the east, only a few hours from the Swedish border. The coast, from Oslo around the southern tip of the country up to Stavanger, is filled with wide beaches and seaside communities. North of here, in Norway's central interior, the country is blanketed with mountains, creating dramatic valleys and plateaus. Bergen, on the west coast, is considered the gateway to fjord country. Moving north, the land becomes wild and untouched. Outside the north's two main cities, Trondheim and Tromsø, the land stretches for miles into the Arctic Circle and up to the Russian border. We describe each of these regions in its own section below.

About the Hotels & Restaurants

Major cities like Oslo, Bergen, and Stavanger offer a full range of restaurants, from traditional to international. Although restaurant meals in Norway are quite expensive, there are ways of cutting costs. For lunch, do as the Norwegians on the road do and pack your own. Enjoy exploring Norwegian groceries and trying different sandwich ingredients, such as traditional breads and cheeses.

Norwegian hotels have high standards in cleanliness and comfort and prices to match. Even the simplest youth hostels provide good mattresses with fluffy down comforters and clean showers or baths. Breakfast, usually served buffet style, is often included in the room price at hotels. Special summer and weekend rates may save you money. Through the Thon and Norlandia hotels, you can purchase their money-saving Scan+ Hotel Pass. The pass entitles you to receive up to a 50% discount and a fifth night free at 200 of their hotels in Scandinavia.

The Farmer's Association operates simple hotels in most towns and cities. These reasonably priced accommodations usually have *heimen* as part of the name, such as Bondeheimen in Oslo. The same organization also runs cafeterias serving traditional Norwegian food, usually called Kaffistova. All of these hotels and restaurants are alcohol-free. Rustic cabins and campsites are also available all over the countryside, as are independent hotels.

WHAT IT COSTS In Norwegian Kroner				
$$$$	**$$$**	**$$**	**$**	**¢**
Oslo and Bergen				
RESTAURANTS over 270	230–270	180–230	110–180	under 110
HOTELS over 2,000	1,600–2,000	1,200–1,600	800–1,200	under 800
Other Areas				
RESTAURANTS over 230	190–230	150–190	90–150	under 90
HOTELS over 1,500	1,000–1,500	800–1,000	400–800	under 400

Restaurant prices are for a main course at dinner, excluding tip. Hotel prices are for two people in a standard double room in high season.

Timing

The tourist season peaks in June, July, and August, when daytime temperatures are often in the 70s (21°C to 26°C) and sometimes rise into the 80s (27°C to 32°C). In general, the weather is not overly warm, and a brisk breeze and brief rainstorms are possible anytime. Nights can be chilly, even in summer.

Visit in summer if you want to experience the endless days of the midnight sun; the best time to visit is mid-May to late July. Hotels, museums, and sights have longer opening hours and the modes of transportation run on more frequent schedules. If you decide to travel in May, try to be in the country on the 17th, or *Syttende Mai*, Norway's Constitution Day, when flag-waving Norwegians bedecked in national costumes, or *bunader*, fill the streets. Fall, spring, and even winter are pleasant, despite the Nordic reputation for gloom. The days become shorter quickly, but the sun casts a golden light not seen farther south. On dark days, fires and candlelight will warm you indoors.

Winter Norway is a wonderland of snow-covered mountains glowing under the northern lights, and few tourists are around to get in your way (although many tourist attractions are also closed). The days may seem perpetually dark, and November through February can be especially dreary. If it's skiing you're interested in, plan your trip for March or April, as there's usually still plenty of snow left. Take note that during Easter Week, many Norwegians head for the mountains, so it's hard to get accommodations—cities are virtually shut down, and even grocery stores close.

OSLO

What sets Oslo apart from other European cities is not so much its cultural traditions or its internationally renowned museums as its

2

The famous Norway in a Nutshell tour was devised by Norwegian State Railways (⊕ www.nsb.no), or NSB, in the 1960s, and has since become the most popular way to see Norway, both for independent travelers and those taking part in a guided trip. Tickets can be purchased through myriad agencies, including NSB's own tour company, **Fjord Tours AS** (⊕ www.norwaynutshell. com), and tourist information offices throughout the country.

Essentially a highlights tour, you can complete the trip in one whirlwind day, but we suggest taking at least three. You can start from either Oslo or Bergen and do a one-way or round-trip tour. Below we've outlined the most popular route, one way from Oslo to Bergen.

Day 1: Oslo

Norway's capital makes a good starting point since most flights to Norway arrive here. Spend your first day exploring the city. Meander on Karl Johans Gate, see Akershus Castle and the Kvadraturen, and walk through Vigelands (Frogner) Park. In the afternoon, head out to Bygdøy and visit the area's museums—the Folkemuseum is a must.

Day 2: The Flåm Railway

Plan to stay the night either in Flåm, Voss, or at the Stalheim Hotel. Start early from Oslo and take the Bergen train line to Myrdal. When you reach Myrdal, transfer to the Flåm railway. The five-hour trip across Norway's interior between Oslo and Bergen passes over the Hardangervidda plateau and is considered one of the most spectacular train rides in the world. It only gets better on the Flåm railway, which winds between towering mountains and immense fjords, passing cascading waterfalls and tiny villages. The trip from Myrdal to Flåm covers 20 km (12 mi) and takes 53 minutes. From Flåm the tour continues with a boat ride through Aurlandsfjord and into the Nærøyfjord, the narrowest fjord in Europe. Both inlets are part of the larger Sognefjord, one of Norway's most famous fjords and, at 204 km (127 mi), its longest. The ride lasts two hours and ends at Gudvangen, at which point you board a bus for the one-hour trip to Voss up the Nærøyfjord Valley and along the old Stalheimskleivane Road with its dramatic hairpin bends. You'll pass the 18th-century Stalheim Hotel along the way.

Day 3: Bergen

From Voss, the train to Bergen takes one hour. When you get to Bergen, check into your hotel and head to Bryggen, the wharf, where you'll find some of the city's oldest and best-preserved buildings. If you have time, visit Troldhaugen, which was composer Edvard Grieg's house for 22 years; it's a half-day trip from Bergen's center.

---

simply stunning natural beauty. How many world capitals have subway service to the forest, or lakes and hiking trails within city limits? But Norwegians will be quick to remind you that Oslo is a cosmopolitan metropolis with prosperous businesses and a thriving nightlife.

Once overlooked by travelers to Scandinavia, Oslo is now a major tourist destination and the gateway to what many believe is Scandinavia's most scenic country. That's just one more change for this town of 500,000—a place that has become good at survival and rebirth throughout its nearly 1,000-year history. In 1348 a plague wiped out half the city's population. In 1624 a fire burned almost the whole of Oslo to the ground. It was redesigned and renamed Christiania by Denmark's royal builder, King Christian IV. After that it slowly gained prominence as the largest and most economically significant city in Norway.

During the mid-19th century, Norway and Sweden were ruled as one kingdom, under Karl Johan. It was then that the grand main street that's his namesake was built, and Karl Johans Gate has been at the center of city life ever since. In 1905 the country separated from Sweden, and in 1925 an act of Parliament finally changed the city's name back to Oslo. Today, Oslo is Norway's political, economic, industrial, and cultural capital.

Exploring Oslo

Karl Johans Gate, starting at Oslo Sentralstasjon (Oslo Central Station, also called Oslo S Station and simply *Jernbanetorget,* or "railway station" in Norwegian) and ending at the Royal Palace, forms the backbone of downtown Oslo. Many of Oslo's major museums and historic buildings lie between the parallel streets of Grensen and Rådhusgata. To the southeast of the center of town is **Gamlebyen,** a historic district with a medieval church. West of downtown are **Frogner** and **Majorstuen,** residential areas known for their fine restaurants, shopping, cafés, galleries, and the Vigeland sculpture park. Southwest is the **Bygdøy Peninsula,** with a castle and five interesting museums that honor aspects of Norway's taste for exploration. Northwest of town is **Holmenkollen,** with its stunning bird's-eye view of the city and the surrounding fjords, a world-famous ski jump and museum, and three historic restaurants. On the more multicultural east side, where a diverse immigrant population lives alongside native Norwegians, are the Munch Museum and the Botanisk Hage og Museum (Botanical Gardens and Museum). The trendy neighborhood of **Grünerløkka,** with lots of cafés and shops, is northeast of the center.

Downtown: The Royal Palace to City Hall

Although the city region is huge (454 square km [175 square mi]), downtown Oslo is compact, with shops, museums, historic buildings, restaurants, and clubs concentrated in a small, walkable center that's brightly illuminated at night.

a good walk

From the **Royal Palace (Kongelige Slottet)** ❶ ⌐, walk east along Karl Johans Gate, Oslo's main promenade. To your right is a large courtyard and three yellow buildings, which were part of the old **Universitet** ❷—today they are used only by the law school. Murals painted by Munch decorate the interior walls of these buildings. Around the corner from the university on Universitetsgata is the **Nasjonalgalleriet** ❸. You can enter to see a few of the hundreds of Norwegian, Scandinavian, and other European works. To the rear of the National Gallery, across a parking lot,

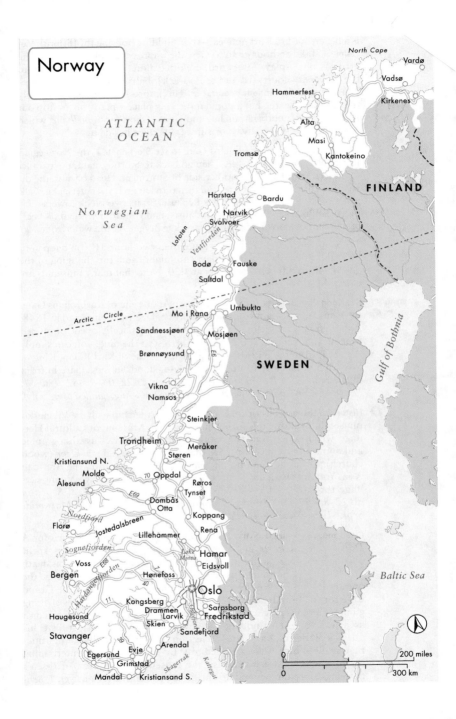

is a big cream-brick art nouveau–style building housing the **Historisk Museum** ❹. Take an hour or so to view the impressive collection of Viking artifacts on display. Afterward, continue along Frederiksgate back to the university courtyard and cross Karl Johans Gate to Studenterlunden Park and the **Nationaltheatret** ❺. This impressive building is not only the national theater, but a popular meeting place—many buses stop out front, and the suburban train line and T-bane (short for *tunnelbane,* which is an underground railway, or subway) is right beside it.

Walk farther down Karl Johans Gate to see **Stortinget** ❻, the Norwegian Parliament, facing the castle. Then go back to Stortingsgata, the parallel street to Karl Johan on the other side of Stortinget. Head back in the direction of the Nationaltheatret and then turn left on Universitetsgata. Walk just a block to reach the redbrick **Rådhuset** ❼, its two block towers a familiar landmark. After visiting Rådhuset, end your tour with an *øl* (beer) at one of the many outdoor cafés at Aker Brygge on the waterfront.

TIMING   The walk alone should take no more than two hours. If you happen to be at the Royal Palace at midday, you might catch the changing of the guard, which happens every day at 1:30. Note that many museums are closed Monday.

WHAT TO SEE   **Det Kongelige Slottet** (The Royal Palace). At one end of Karl Johans Gate,
▶ ❶   the vanilla-and-cream-color neoclassical palace was completed in 1848. Although generally closed to the public, the palace is open for guided tours in summer at 2 and 2:20 PM. The rest of the time, you can simply admire it from the outside. An equestrian statue of Karl Johan, King of Sweden and Norway from 1818 to 1844, stands in the square in front of the palace. ✉ *Drammensvn. 1, Sentrum* ☎ *22–04–89–52* ⊕ *www. kongehuset.no* 🖹 *Tour NKr 90* ☉ *Mid-June–mid-Aug. (guided tours only).*

❹   **Historisk Museum** (Historical Museum). In partnership with the Vikingskiphuset (in Bygdøy), this forms the University Museum of Cultural Heritage, which concentrates on national antiquities as well as ethnographic and numismatic collections. See the intricately carved *stavkirke* (wood church) portals and exhibitions on subjects ranging from the Arctic to Asia. You can also gain a deeper understanding of Norway's Viking heritage through artifacts on display here. ✉ *Frederiksgt. 2, Sentrum* ☎ *22–85–99–00* ⊕ *www.ukm.uio.no* 🖹 *NKr 40* ☉ *Mid-May–mid-Sept., Tues.–Sun. 10–4; mid-Sept.–mid-May, Tues.–Sun. 11–4.*

Ibsen-museet. Famed Norwegian dramatist Henrik Ibsen, known for *A Doll's House, Ghosts,* and *Peer Gynt,* among other classic plays, spent his final years here, in the apartment on the second floor, until his death in 1906. Every morning, Ibsen's wife, Suzannah, would encourage the literary legend to write before allowing him to head off to the Grand Café for his brandy and foreign newspapers. His study gives striking glimpses into his psyche. Huge, intense portraits of Ibsen and his Swedish archrival, August Strindberg, face each other. On his desk still sits his "devil's orchestra," a playful collection of frog and troll-like figurines that inspired him. Take a guided tour by well-versed and entertaining Ibsen scholars. Afterward, visit the museum's exhibition of Ibsen's drawings and paintings and first magazine writings. ✉ *Arbiensgt. 1, Sen-*

trum, Across Drammensvn. from Royal Palace 🕾 *22–12–35–50* ⊕ *www. ibsenmuseet.no* 🖾 *NKr 50* ⊗ *Tues.–Sun., guided tours at noon, 1, and 2; June–Aug., additional guided tours at 11 and 3.*

★ ❸ **Nasjonalgalleriet** (National Gallery.) The gallery was recently amalgamated with the former National Museum of Art, Architecture, and Design. It houses Norway's largest collection of art created before 1945. The deep-red Edvard Munch room holds such major paintings as *The Dance of Life* and several self-portraits (*The Scream* was stolen in 2004). Classic landscapes by Hans Gude and Adolph Tidemand—including *Bridal Voyage on the Hardangerfjord*—share space in galleries with other works by major Norwegian artists. The museum also has works by Monet, Renoir, Van Gogh, and Gauguin. ⊠ *Universitetsgt. 13, Sentrum* 🕾 *22–20–04–04* ⊕ *www.nasjonalgalleriet.no* 🖾 *Free* ⊗ *Tues., Wed., and Fri. 10–6; Thurs. 10–8; weekends 10–5.*

❺ **Nationaltheatret** (National Theater). In front of this neoclassical theater, built in 1899, are statues of Norway's great playwrights, Bjørnstjerne Bjørnson, who also composed the national anthem, and Henrik Ibsen. Most performances are in Norwegian, so you may just want to take a guided tour of the interior, which can be arranged by appointment. Some summer performances are in English. ⊠ *Stortingsgt. 15, Sentrum* 🕾 *22–00–14–00* ⊕ *www.nationaltheatret.no.*

❼ **Rådhuset** (City Hall). This redbrick building is best known today for the awarding of the Nobel peace prize, which takes place here every December.

Fodor'sChoice In 1915, the mayor of Oslo made plans for a new City Hall, and ordered
★ the clearing of slums that stood on the site. The building was finally completed in 1950. Inside, many museum-quality masterpieces are on the walls. After viewing the frescoes in the Main Hall, walk upstairs to the Banquet Hall to see the royal portraits. In the East Gallery, Per Krogh's mosaic of a pastoral scene covers all four walls, making you feel like you're part of the painting. On festive occasions, the Central Hall is illuminated from outside by 60 large spotlights that simulate daylight. ⊠ *Rådhuspl., Sentrum* 🕾 *23–46–16–00* ⊕ *www.rft.oslo.kommune.no* 🖾 *NKr 40* ⊗ *May–Aug., daily 9–5; Sept.–Apr., daily 9–4.*

Stenersen-museet. Named for art collector Rolf E. Stenersen, this city-owned museum opened in 1994 displays highly regarded and sometimes provocative temporary exhibitions. It also houses three private art collections—including works by Edvard Munch—donated to the city at various times by Rolf E. Stenersen, Amaldus Nielsen, and Ludvig Ravensberg. ⊠ *Munkedamsvn. 15, Sentrum* 🕾 *23–49–36–00* ⊕ *www.stenersen.museum.no* 🖾 *NKr 45* ⊗ *Tues. and Thurs. 11–7; Wed., Fri., and weekends 11–5.*

❻ **Stortinget** (Norwegian Parliament). Informative guided tours of this classic 1866 building are conducted daily in summer, and on Saturday the rest of the year. In front of the Parliament building, the park benches of Eidsvolls plass are a popular meeting and gathering place. ⊠ *Munkedamsvn. 15, Sentrum* 🕾 *23–49–36–00* ⊕ *www.stortinget. no* 🖾 *Free* ⊗ *Guided tours July–mid-Aug., weekdays at 10, 11:30, and 1; mid-Aug.–June, Sat. at 10, 11:30, and 1.*

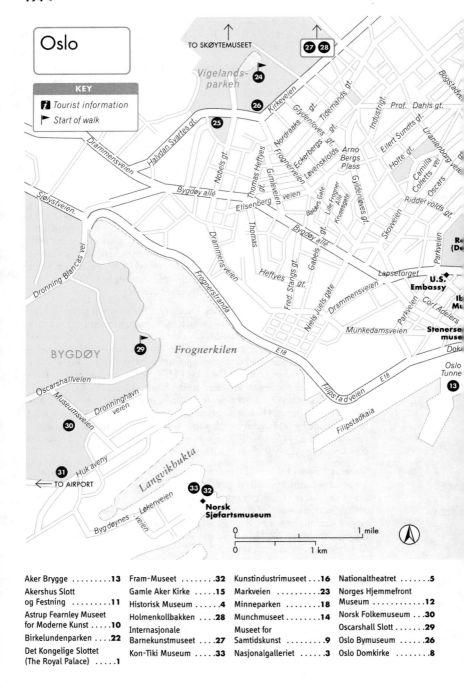

Oslo

KEY

i Tourist information

▶ Start of walk

TO SKØYTEMUSEET

Vigelands-parken

BYGDØY

Frognerkilen

Langvikbukta

TO AIRPORT

Norsk Sjøfartsmuseum

U.S. Embassy

Lapsetorget

Munkedamsveien

Stenerse muse

Oslo Tunne

Filipstadkaia

0 ____ 1 mile
0 ____ 1 km

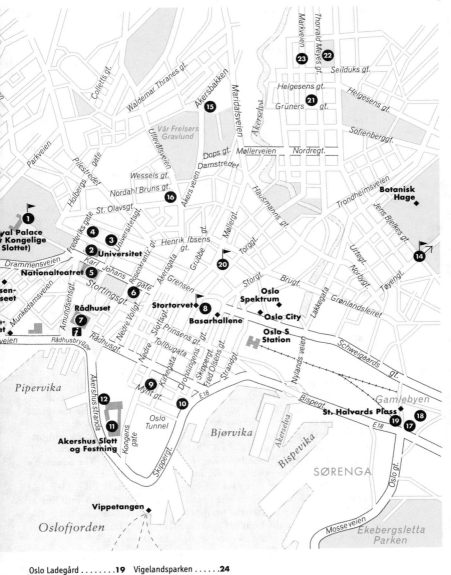

② Universitet (The University). The great hall in the middle building (there are three in all) is decorated with murals by Edvard Munch. Look for *The Sun,* which shows penetrating rays falling over a fjord. This building was the site of the Nobel peace prize award ceremony until 1989, when it was moved to the City Hall. ✉ *Aulaen, Karl Johans gt. 47, Sentrum* ☎ *22–85–97–11* 🖃 *Free* ⊙ *July, weekdays 10–2.*

Kvadraturen, Akershus Castle & Aker Brygge

The Kvadraturen is the oldest part of Oslo still standing. In 1624, after the town burned down for the 14th time, King Christian IV renamed the city Christiania and moved it from the area that is southeast of Oslo S Station, called Gamlebyen, rebuilding it adjacent to the Akershus fortress. In order to prevent future fires, the king decreed that houses were to be built of stone or brick instead of wood. He also built a stone wall around the rebuilt city to protect it from his enemies, the Swedes.

a good walk

The Kvadraturen area, which includes Akershus Slott, is bound on the east side of the fortress by Skippergata and on the north side by Karl Johans Gate between Oslo Domkirke and Stortorvet. The boundary follows Øvre Vollgata around to the other side of the fortress. Kvadraturen translates roughly as "square township," which refers to the area's geometrically ordered streets. Be aware that the streets around Skippergata and Myntgata are a bit seedy and known as a mini red-light district at night.

Start at Stortorvet, the small market square outside the store GlasMagasinet. To the east of the square is **Oslo Domkirke ⑨**, the city's landmark cathedral. Artists have been contributing to the cathedral's richly decorated interior since the 18th century.

From the cathedral, follow Kirkegata left past Karl Johans Gate to the **Museet for Samtidskunst ⑨**, inside the 1906 Bank of Norway building. Spend time wandering through the museum's halls to admire both its art nouveau architecture and contemporary art. From the museum, take the side street Revierstredet to Dronningensgate, where there's a building that does not seem to fit in with its 17th-century neighbors. Designed and built in the early 1990s, this brick-and-steel office building houses the **Astrup Fearnley Museet for Moderne Kunst ⑩**. The museum's permanent and temporary exhibitions emphasize modern art. Make a left into Dronningensgate and head up to Rådhusgata. Take a left and walk down the street. Keep an eye out for the 17th-century building at Rådhusgata 11. It houses the Statholdergaarden restaurant, in a building that was once the home of the *statholder,* the official representative from Copenhagen when Norway was under Danish rule.

Continue on Rådhusgata until you reach the corner of Nedre Slottsgate. The yellow building you see was originally the City Hall (1641), but since the 1800s has been Det Gamle Rådhus restaurant. Diagonally across Rådhusgata in two 17th-century buildings are an art gallery and a trendy, artsy café. The building that houses Kafé Celsius was one of the first buildings erected in Christian IV's town. Directly ahead is Christiana Torv—a re-creation of Christian IV's finger as he points to where the "new Oslo" was be built.

Turn left on Akersgata and walk alongside the grassy hill to the entrance of **Akershus Slott og Festning** ⑪, the center of Christian IV's Kvadraturen. It's a worthwhile stroll to the top for its incredible Oslo harbor-front and fjord views, especially at sunset. The castle became the German headquarters during the occupation of Norway in World War II, and many members of the Resistance were executed on the castle grounds. In a building next to the castle, at the top of the hill, is the **Norges Hjemmefront Museum** ⑫, which tells the gripping story of German occupation and Norwegian resistance.

For a break from history and architecture, walk over to **Aker Brygge** ⑬, the harbor in front of Akershus Castle. Aker Brygge is probably the most popular place in Oslo to enjoy a refreshing beer and a snack of shrimp during the long daylight hours of summer. You can sit at tables on the deck of one of the ships permanently docked in the bay, and window-shop in the boutiques surrounding the harbor.

TIMING   The walk alone will take at least three hours. Combined with museum visits and breaks, the itinerary could take the better part of a day. Akershus Slott will take at least half an hour. Try to do this tour during daylight hours, catching late-afternoon sun from atop the Akershus grounds. Finish the tour with a late lunch or early dinner at Aker Brygge.

WHAT TO SEE   **Aker Brygge.** This area was the site of a disused shipbuilding yard until
⑬   redevelopment saw the addition of residential town houses and a commercial sector. Postmodern steel and glass buildings dominate the sky-
Fodor'sChoice   line now. The area has more than 40 restaurants and 60 shops, including
★   upmarket fashion boutiques, as well as pubs, cinemas, theaters, and an indoor shopping mall. There is outdoor dining capacity of 2,500 as well as an open boulevard for strolling. Service facilities include banks, drugstores, and a parking lot for 1,600. ⊠ *Aker Brygge* ☎ *22–83–26–80* ⌷ *Free* ⊙ *Shopping hrs weekdays 10–8, Sat. 10–6.*

⑪   **Akershus Slott og Festning** (Akershus Castle and Fortress). Dating to 1299, this stone medieval castle and royal residence was developed into a fortress armed with cannons by 1592. After that time, it withstood a number of sieges and then fell into decay. It was finally restored in 1899. Summer tours take you through its magnificent halls, the castle church, the royal mausoleum, reception rooms, and banqueting halls. ⊠ *Akershus Slott, Festningspl., Sentrum* ☎ *22–41–25–21* ⌷ *Grounds and concerts free, castle NKr 40* ⊙ *Grounds: daily 6 AM–9 PM. Castle: May–mid-Sept., Mon.–Sat. 10–6, Sun. 12:30–4; mid-Sept.–Apr., Thurs. tours at 1. Guided tours: May–mid-Sept., daily at 11, 1, and 3; mid-Sept.–Apr., Thurs. at 1.*

⑩   **Astrup Fearnley Museet for Moderne Kunst** (Astrup Fearnley Museum for Modern Art). This privately funded museum opened in 1993 and earned an international reputation for its collections of postwar Norwegian and international art. In its smaller gallery, British artist Damien Hirst's controversial installation *Mother and Child Divided* is on display. The museum's permanent collection includes works by international artists, such as Yoko Ono and Jeff Koons, as well as Norwegians like Odd Nerdrum and Olav Christopher Jenssen. There's also a glassed-in sculpture garden with Niki de St. Phalle's sparrow and several other oversize 20th-century figures. ☒ *Dronningensgt. 4, Sentrum* ☎ *22–93–60–60* ⊕ *www. af-moma.no* ☜ *Free* ☉ *Tues., Wed., and Fri. 11–5; Thurs. 11–7; weekends noon–5. Guided tours weekends at 1.*

❾ **Museet for Samtidskunst** (National Museum of Contemporary Art). A stunning granite-and-marble example of art nouveau architecture, this 1906 former bank building is the largest museum of postwar Norwegian and international art. Its ornate gilded interior contrasts with the modern and contemporary art shown in its permanent and temporary exhibitions. The permanent collection of 4,700 works spans the genres of graphic art, drawing, photography, sculpture, decorative arts, installations, and video. Take time to ponder the two fascinating permanent installations: Ilya Kabakov's *The Garbage Man* and Per Inge Bjoørlo's *Inner Room V.* ☒ *Bankpl. 4, Sentrum* ☎ *22–86–22–10* ⊕ *www.museumsnett.no/ mfs* ☜ *Free* ☉ *Tues., Wed., and Fri. 10–5; Thurs. 10–8; Sat. 11–4; Sun. 11–5. Guided tours by appointment only.*

⓬ **Norges Hjemmefront Museum** (Norwegian Resistance Museum). Striped prison uniforms, underground news sheets, and homemade weapons tell the history of the resistance movement that arose before and during Norway's occupation by Nazi Germany. A gray, winding path leads to two underground stone vaults in which models, pictures, writings, and recordings trace the times between Germany's first attack in 1940 to Norway's liberation on May 8, 1945. Every year, on the anniversaries of these dates, Norwegian resistance veterans gather here to commemorate Norway's dark days and honor those who lost their lives. The former ammunitions depot and the memorial lie at the exact spot where Norwegian patriots were executed by the Germans. ☒ *Akershus Slott, Sentrum* ☎ *23–09–31–38* ⊕ *www.nhm.mil.no* ☜ *NKr 30* ☉ *Mid-Apr.–mid-June, Mon.–Sat. 10–4, Sun. 11–4; mid-June–Aug., Mon., Wed., Fri., and Sat. 10–5, Tues. and Thurs. 10–6, Sun. 11–5; Sept., Mon.–Sat. 10–4, Sun. 11–4; Oct.–mid-Apr., weekdays 10–3, weekends 11–4.*

❽ **Oslo Domkirke** (Oslo Cathedral). Consecrated in 1697 as Oslo's third cathedral, this dark-brown brick structure has been Oslo's main church ever since. The original pulpit, altarpiece, and organ front with acanthus carvings still stand. Take a look at the endless ceiling murals made between 1936 to 1950 and stained-glass windows by Emanuel Vigeland. In the 19th century the fire department operated a lookout from the bell tower, which you can visit. ☒ *Stortorvet 1, Sentrum* ☎ *23–31–46–00* ☜ *Free* ☉ *Daily 10–4.*

need a break? **Pascal Konditori** (☒ Tollbugt. 11, Sentrum ☎ 22–42–11–19), a trendy, Parisian-style patisserie inside an old-fashioned Norwegian *konditori* (café), is known for its French coffee, homemade pastries, and ice cream. It's a place to see and be seen.

Munch Museum & Damstredet

The Munch Museum is east of the city center in Tøyen, an area in which Edvard Munch spent many of his years in Oslo. The Tøyen district has a much different feel than Oslo's cushy west side—it's ethnic and more industrial.

West of Tøyen, north of the city center near Vår Frelsers Gravlund, is the quiet, old-fashioned district of Damstredet, one of the few areas with original, 18th-century wooden houses.

a good walk

Start by taking any T-bane from the city center (Sentrum) to Tøyen, where **Munchmuseet** 🔟 ▶ sits on a hill near the Botanisk Hage, a quiet oasis of plants and flowers. After visiting the museum, head back to town center. Take the T-bane and get off at Stortinget.

Head down Karl Johans Gate and take a right onto Akersgata. Follow it past the offices of *Aftenposten,* Norway's leading daily paper. As you head up the hill, you can see a huge rotund building, Deichmanske Bibliotek, the city's library, to your right. Continue along Akersveien and veer to your right as you pass Saint Olav's Church. Next head down Dops Gate and Damstredet—they are some of the city's oldest streets, with well-preserved houses dating from the 18th century when this area was a shantytown. Today the neighborhood has developed into an artist community. On your left is Vår Frelsers Gravlund (Our Savior's Graveyard), where you can seek out the gravestones of many famous Norwegians, including Ibsen and Munch. At the graveyard's northeastern corner is **Gamle Aker Kirke** 🔟, the city's only remaining medieval church.

After visiting the church, walk along the north side of the cemetery and then take a left onto Ullevålsveien. Take the road down the hill to the corner of St. Olavs Gate and Akersgata, where you'll find the **Kunstindustrimuseet** 🔟, one of Europe's oldest museums of decorative arts and design.

TIMING The Munch Museum will take up most of the morning, especially if you take a guided tour. The second half of the tour, through Damstredet, is a perfect way to spend a summer Sunday afternoon. Things are quiet, and locals tend to stroll around this area when the weather is nice. You can see the rest of the sights in a couple of hours.

WHAT TO SEE **Gamle Aker Kirke** (Old Aker Church). Dating to 1100, this medieval stone ★ 🔟 basilica is Oslo's oldest church—it's still in use as a parish church. Inside, the acoustics are outstanding, so inquire about upcoming concerts. ✉ *Akersbakken 26, Bislett* ☎ *22–69–35–82* ⊕ *www.orgnett.no/kor/gak* 🎫 *Free* ⊙ *Mon.–Sat. noon–2, Sun. 9 AM–11 AM.*

🔟 **Kunstindustrimuseet** (Museum of Decorative Arts and Design). Rich Baldishol tapestries from 1100, Norwegian dragon-style furniture, and royal apparel (including Queen Sonja's wedding gown from 1968) make this a must-see museum. Founded in 1876, it also has exquisite collections of Norwegian 18th-century silver, glass, and faience. A contemporary Scandinavian section follows the history of design and crafts in the region. ✉ *St. Olavs gt. 1, Sentrum* ☎ *22–03–65–40* 🎫 *NKr 25, special exhibits NKr 65* ⊙ *Tues., Wed., and Fri. 11–4; Thurs. 11–7; weekends 11–4.*

▶ 🔟 **Munchmuseet** (Munch Museum). Edvard Munch, Norway's most famous FodorśChoice artist, bequeathed his enormous collection of works (about 1,100 paint- ★ ings, 3,000 drawings, and 18,000 graphic works) to the city when he

STEALING MUNCH

ON AUGUST 22, 2004, *Norway lost a national icon when armed robbers stole Edvard Munch's painting, The Scream from the Munch Museum in the Tøyen neighborhood of Oslo. Two masked thieves entered the museum in broad daylight, pulled the work and another painting, The Madonna, off the wall as guards and visitors watched, and sped away in a waiting vehicle. The car was later recovered outside some nearby tennis courts, along with the gun that was used to threaten museum staff during the robbery. Neither the paintings nor the thieves have been found, however, and the crime has left Norway and the art world wondering how security at a major museum could have failed to protect some of Norway's most important national treasures. Museum security has since been beefed up, but is it enough? Norwegian paintings have been the target of art thieves in the past.*

On the opening day of the 1994 Winter Olympic Games in Lillehammer, another Scream painting—Munch painted four versions altogether—was stolen from the Norwegian National Gallery. The painting was later discovered undamaged in a hotel room, and three suspects were arrested.

In an incident in 1988, The Vampire was stolen from the Munch Museum but was later recovered. And most recently, in March 2005 three Munch paintings were taken from a hotel in Moss, in southern Norway. These were also recovered, three days after the theft.

Despite this series of thefts, Norway is known for being a very safe country where people often leave their doors unlocked and where public parks and monuments, such as the Royal Palace, don't have gates. Until the late 1990s Norway continually recorded insignificant crime rates. Police numbers, even in the capital of Oslo, were considered low compared to other European cities, and armed robbery continues to be rare. As the country moves toward modernization, however, one side effect has been an increase in unemployment, inner-city drug problems, disfranchised ethnic groups, and crime.

While officials in Oslo work toward keeping the general crime rate low, investigators are still looking for The Scream and The Madonna, which are worth an estimated $19 million together. In April 2005, three men were arrested for the crime but the paintings are still missing.

As was expected, the Munch Museum revealed that the stolen paintings were not insured against theft. Indeed, many international galleries and collectors do not insure their art, either because they cannot afford to pay for insurance or they don't think they will need it. Theft continues to plague the art world, however, at least in galleries where security is minimal. Thousands of famous paintings and works of art are displayed uninsured across galleries worldwide, and an estimated $8 billion worth of art is stolen each year.

A year after The Scream disappeared, the Munch Museum announced the completion of a $6 million security upgrade that took 10 months to put into place. Visitors to the museum can expect to find metal detectors and bulletproof glass in front of some much safer paintings.

died in 1944. The museum is a monument to his artistic genius, housing the largest collection of his works and changing exhibitions. Munch actually painted several different versions of *The Scream,* the image for which he known best. An important one of his Scream paintings, as well as another painting, *The Madonna,* were stolen from the Munch Museum in an armed robbery in 2004 and have yet to be recovered. While most of the Munch legend focuses on the artist as a troubled, angst-ridden man, he moved away from that pessimistic and dark approach to more optimistic themes later in his career. ✉ *Tøyengt. 53, Tøyen* ☎ *23–49–35–00* ⊕ *www.munch.museum.no* ✉ *NKr 60* ⊙ *June–mid-Sept., daily 10–6; mid-Sept.–May, weekdays 10–6, weekends 11–5.*

Gamlebyen & Grønland

If you've got a yen for history and archaeology, visit Gamlebyen (the Old Town), to the southeast of the center. Sometimes referred to as the "Pompeii of Scandinavia," Gamlebyen contains the last remains of medieval Oslo. Self-guided tour brochures for Gamlebyen can be picked up at the tourist office in Sentrum. North of Gamlebyen is the hip and multicultural neighborhood of Grønland. If Oslo has broken your budget, you may be glad to discover Grønland—it has the cheapest dining, drinking, and shopping in the city. If your time is limited, however, you need not plan to spend much time in either neighborhood. Gamlebyen is somewhat off the beaten track, and some of the ruins are barely discernible. Grønland can be sampled at night with dinner at an ethnic restaurant preceded or followed by a drink in a pub.

a good walk

To get to Gamlebyen, you can take trikk (cable car) 18 or 19 from beside Oslo S Station and get off at St. Halvard's plass, or walk for about 40 minutes through Grønland. To walk, head down Storgata, just north of Oslo S Station, and take a right down Brugata. Walk east down Brugata to find Vietnamese grocers alongside Middle-Eastern take-out stores and African silk and textile traders. Grønland has a number of what Norwegians call *brun* (brown) pubs. These small, often dingy establishments serve the cheapest beer in town and are popular with local students.

Brugata becomes Grønlandsleiret. Next, go over Schweigaards Gate to St. Halvards plass. During the 13th century, this area was the city's ecclesiastical center. Also here are the intact foundations of **St. Halvards Kirke** ⓱, which dates from the early 12th century. Other ruins, including Korskirke and Olavs Kloster, lie in **Minneparken** ⓲. Nearby on Bispegata is **Oslo Ladegård** ⓳, a restored baroque-style mansion that sits on foundations of a 13th-century bishop's palace.

If you continue south, you'll find the oldest traces of human habitation in Oslo: the 5,000-year-old carvings on the runic stones near Ekebergsletta Park. They are across the road from the park on Karlsborgveien and are marked by a sign reading FORTIDSMINNE. To reach the park, walk south on Oslo Gate until it becomes Mosseveien. The stones will be on your right. The park is a good spot to rest your feet and end your tour.

TIMING You can walk through Grønland in 40 minutes and see the Gamlebyen sights in an hour. It's a 20- to 25-minute walk from Gamlebyen to the runic stones at Ekebergslettaparken. You can also take Tram 19 from St. Halvards plass for 10 stops to Ljabrua.

WHAT TO SEE **Minneparken.** Oslo was founded by Harald Hardråde ("Hard Ruler") **18** in 1048, and the earliest settlements were near what is now Bispegata, a few blocks behind Oslo S Station. Ruins are all that's left of the city's former religious center: the **Korskirke** (Cross Church; ✉ Egedesgt. 2), a small stone church dating from the end of the 13th century; **Olavs Kloster** (Olav's Cloister; ✉ St. Halvards pl. 3), built around 1240 by Dominican monks; and **Olavskirken** (Olav's Church; ✉ Egedesgt. 4), remnants of a 13th-century stone church. ✉ *Entrance at Oslogt. and Bispegt, Gamlebyen* ▣ *Free* ☉ *Sun. noon–2.*

19 **Oslo Ladegård.** The original building, the 13th-century Bispegård (Bishop's Palace), burned down in the famous 1624 fire, but its vaulted cellar survived. The present mansion was restored and rebuilt in 1725; it now belongs to the city council and contains scale models of 16th- to 18th-century Oslo. ✉ *St. Halvards pl., Oslogt. 13, Gamlebyen* ☎ 22–19–44–68 ▣ *NKr 40* ☉ *Late May–mid-Sept., Tues., Thurs., and Fri. 2–4; Wed. 2–6; guided tours Sun. at 4.*

17 **St. Halvards Kirke** (St. Halvard's Church). This medieval church, named for the patron saint of Oslo, remained the city's cathedral until 1660. ✉ *Minneparken, entrance at Oslogt. and Bispegt, Gamlebyen.*

Grünerløkka

Once a simple working-class neighborhood north of the center, Grünerløkka has undergone a revival since the '90s and now hosts a number of trendy bars, cafés, eateries, eclectic galleries, and gift stores. Popular with young people, the area is now known as Oslo's little Greenwich Village. Take a shopping tour here during the day or come for dinner and a drink at night.

a good walk

Begin your tour just north of the city center at **Youngstorget** **20** ⌐, the market square on Torggata, just north of Karl Johans Gate. The headquarters of Oslo's main political parties, as well as national union and employee organizations, surround this square.

Walk north along Torggata past Henrik Ibsen's Gate and note Rockefeller Music Hall on your left. Oslo's best medium-size live-music venue also hosts film and quiz nights midweek. Continue for three blocks to cross Akerbrua (Aker Bridge), where artist Dyre Vaa's bronze figures bring to life traditional Norwegian fairy tales, such as *Peer Gynt*. Across the bridge, veer to your right past a restaurant called Delicatessen. In summer you'll find its wall of windows open to the sidewalk. This is a great place to stop for a tapas lunch.

Turn left at Thorvald Meyers Gate and continue for three blocks. This street has several popular bars and is quite busy at night. You'll see a grassy square called Olaf Ryes plass on your left, and near that, on Gruners Gate, the **Parkteatret** **21**, an old movie house converted into a hip café/bar. Back on Thorvald Meyers Gate, continue north to explore the shops, such as Boa, at No. 50, Probat at No. 24, and Rebella at No. 52.

Farther on to your right, stop for lunch at Fru Hagen Café and admire its classical-looking chandeliers and elegant velvet-furnished sofas. Alternatively, try the Mexican eatery Mucho Mas next door, or Hotel Havana, a Cuban-inspired delicatessen that also sells Norwegian fish products. Rest your feet at **Birkelundenparken** ㉒ at the next block. In summer, hundreds of locals sit in the park grilling Norwegian hot dogs on portable barbecues. Oslo council even has special garbage bins designed to hold the smoldering remains of *en-gang griller* (single-use grills).

At the top of the park, turn left down Schleppegrells Gate, then left again down **Markveien** ㉓ to begin the return leg of your journey. The Markveien strip of Grünerløkka hosts fewer restaurants but more galleries and gift stores.

TIMING   The walking tour around Grünerløkka will take around two hours, not including shopping time. To skip the 15-minute walk from the center to Grünerløkka, catch Tram 12 from Oslo S Station for six stops and get off at Olav Ryes plass.

WHAT TO SEE

㉒ **Birkelundenparken.** This green lung and center of Grünerløkka features concerts, fairs, weekend markets, and political rallies in summer, as well as the usual host of stripped-down sun worshippers. The square and fountain were built in the late 19th century by merchant Thorvald Meyer and city planner G. A. Bull. ⊠ *Off Thorvald Meyers gt., Grünerløkka.*

㉓ **Markveien.** This street hosts fewer restaurants but more galleries and gift stores than Thorvald Meyers Gate. **Galleri Markveien**, at No. 26, displays the work of the commercially successful artist Tone Granberg, who uses the same abstract motif in every one of her paintings. Visit **Lene Middelthon** next door, a glassblower with a distinctively Scandinavian style. Farther along Markveien, other shopping highlights include **Panda** for Asian pottery, silks, and furniture; and the **Ceramo Sculpture Gallery,** which sells African artifacts that are functional as well as aesthetically pleasing. **Den Kule Mage** (The Round Stomach) at No. 55 has every maternal item a mother could need and features Norway's only baby café, smartly decorated as a nursery. **Markveien Mat og Vinhus** is a highly recommended restaurant where you can sample delicacies such as giant Russian crab or Norwegian quail. ⊠ *Off Schleppegrells gt., Grünerløkka.*

㉑ **Parkteatret.** This atmospheric art deco–style movie house (built in 1907) has been converted into a funky bar, café, restaurant, and venue. Live music gigs, literary evenings, films, and theater are held in the converted cinema room inside, which has seating for 250. To get a sense of the laid-back Grünerløkka lifestyle, chill out here with a cocktail. Free jazz is held on weekends in the front bar. ⊠ *Olaf Reyes pl. 11, Grünerløkka* ☎ *22–35–63–00* ⊕ *www.parkteatret.no* 🎫 *Free* ⊙ *Daily, noon until performances end (around 1 AM).*

⑳ **Youngstorget.** Cafés, eateries, and shops line the bazaar at the rear of this square, which has been used as an active marketplace on weekends to sell food and other wares since 1850. Large-scale exhibitions showcasing art, sport, fashion, and street culture are held here in summer and autumn. The square is also a starting point for political demonstrations. ⊠ *Torggata, Sentrum* ☎ *23–48–33–10* ⊕ *www.youngstorget.com.*

Frogner, Majorstuen & Holmenkollen

Among the city's most stylish neighborhoods, Frogner and Majorstuen combine classic Scandinavian elegance with contemporary European chic. Hip boutiques and galleries coexist with embassies and ambassadors' residences on the streets near and around Bygdøy Allé. Holmenkollen, the hill past Frogner Park, has the famous ski jump and miles of ski trails.

a good walk

Catch the No. 15 Majorstuen *trikk* (cable car) from Nationaltheatret on the Drammensveien side of the Royal Palace grounds. You can also take the No. 15 from Aker Brygge.

Opposite the southwest end of the palace grounds is the triangular U.S. Embassy, designed by Finnish-American architect Eero Saarinen and built in 1959. Look to the right at the corner of Drammensveien and Parkveien for a glimpse of the venerable Nobel Institute. Since 1905 these stately yellow buildings have been the secluded setting where the five-member Norwegian Nobel Committee decides who will win the Nobel peace prize. The library is open to the public.

To walk from the southwest end of the palace grounds to Frognerparken, head east away from the city to the roundabout intersecting four roads and turn right down Frognerveien. This road winds through the pleasant, leafy district of Frogner, passing cafés, a bar, a cinema, and some impressive houses. After a 30-minute walk, or about 12 blocks, you will reach the corner of Frognerparken, also called **Vigelandsparken** ㉔ ▶, with the Oslo Bymuseum directly ahead of you.

Walk through the front gates of the park and continue about 100 yards toward the monolith ahead. You'll find yourself in a stunning sculpture garden designed by one of Norway's greatest artists, Gustav Vigeland. You can study the method to Vigeland's madness at **Vigelandsmuseet** ㉕. Cross the street to the **Oslo Bymuseum** ㉖ for a cultural and historical look at the city and its development. After you leave the museum, take a left on Kirkeveien and continue past Frogner Park to the Majorstuen underground station, near the intersection of Bogstadveien. Here you have two options: you can walk down Bogstadveien, look at the shops, explore the Majorstuen area, and then take the Holmenkollen line of the T-bane to Frognerseteren; or you can skip the stroll down Bogstadveien and head right up to Holmenkollen. The train ride up the mountain passes some stunning scenery. If you have children, you may want to make a detour at the first T-bane stop, Frøen, and visit the **Internasjonale Barnekunstmuseet** ㉗.

Continue on the T-bane to the end of the line. This is Frognerseteren—a popular skiing destination on winter weekends. The Tryvann ski center is another kilometer farther up the mountain. The view of the city here is spectacular. The restaurant Frognerseteren also has a great view of Oslo. Downhill is **Holmenkollbakken** ㉘, where Norway's most intrepid skiers prove themselves every March during the Holmenkollen Ski Festival.

TIMING This is a good tour for Monday, since the museums mentioned are open, unlike most others in Oslo. You will need a whole day for Frogner and Majorstuen since there is some travel time involved. The trikk ride

TOURS IN & AROUND OSLO

TICKETS FOR ALL TOURS are available at both **Oslo tourist offices** (☎ 24–14–77–00), in Oslo S Station and in Sentrum. All tours, except HMK's Oslo Highlights tour, operate in summer only.

Starting at noon and continuing at 45-minute intervals until 10 PM, the **Oslo Train**, which looks like a chain of dune buggies, leaves Aker Brygge for a 30-minute ride around the town center. The train runs daily in summer. Contact a tourist center for departure times.

Boat Tours

Taking a boat tour in and around the Oslo fjords is a memorable way to see the capital. **Cruise-Båtene** (✉ Rosenkrantz gt. 22, Sentrum ☎ 22–42–36–98) organizes fjord excursions for all occasions on modern luxury or older restored vessels. The **Norway Yacht Charter** (✉ Rådhusbrygge 3, Sentrum ☎ 23–35–68–90) arranges lunch or evening tours or dinner cruises for anywhere from 12 to 600 passengers. **Viking Cruise** (✉ Skogfaret 20 B, Ullern ☎ 22–73–31–21) offers chartered tours on sailing yachts or replica Viking ships that serve traditional viking fare.

Bus Tours

Båtservice Sightseeing (✉ Rådhusbryggen 3, Sentrum ☎ 23–35–68–90) has a bus tour, five cruises, and one combination tour. Tickets for bus tours can be purchased on the buses. **HMK Sightseeing** (✉ Hegdehaugsvn. 4, Majorstuen ☎ 23–15–73–00) offers several bus tours in and around Oslo. Tours leave from the Tourist Information Center at Vestbanen; combination boat-bus tours depart from Rådhusbrygge 3, the wharf in front of City Hall.

Private Guides

Guideservice (✉ Akershusstranda 35, Sentrum ☎ 22–42–70–20) caters to large groups in and around Oslo, and prices start at NKr 1,150 for a two-hour tour. **Oslo Guidebureau** (✉ Nedre Slottsgt. 13, Sentrum ☎ 22–42–28–18) specializes in guiding VIP clients and business delegations, and prices start at NKr 1,050 for two hours. **OsloTaxi** (☎ 02323) gives private car tours from NKr 250 per hour.

Special-Interest Tours

For an exhilarating experience, tour the forests surrounding Oslo (the marka) by dogsled. Both lunch and evening winter tours are available through **Norske Sledehundturer** (✉ Einar Kristen Aas, 1514 Moss ☎ 69–27–56–40 ☎ 69–27–37–86). The tourist information center can arrange four- to eight-hour motor safaris through the marka, and in winter **Vangen Skistue** (✉ Laila and Jon Hamre, Fjell, 1404 Siggerud ☎ 64–86–54–81) can arrange an old-fashioned sleigh ride (in summer, they switch to carriages).

Walking Tours

Organized walking tours are available through **Oslo City and Nature Walks** (✉ Elgefaret 70B, 1362 Hosle ☎ 41–31–87–40 ⊕ www.oslowalks.no). Authorized city guides with acting experience lead you on themed walks, including a ghost walk through the old Kvadraturen area, exploring the creepier parts of Oslo's history. Contact **Oslo Byantikvar** (☎ 23–46–02–50), at the Antiquities Department of Oslo, for information on guided tours of Gamlebyen.

from the city center to Frogner Park takes about 15 minutes; the T-bane to Frognerseteren takes about 20 minutes. You're no longer in the compact city center, so distances between sights are greater. The walk from Frognerseteren to Holmenkollbakken is about 15 minutes and is indicated with signposts. Try to save Holmenkollen, with its magnificent views, for a clear day.

28 **Holmenkollbakken** (Holmenkollen Ski Museum and Ski Jump). A distinctive
Fodor'sChoice part of the city's skyline, Oslo's ski jump holds a special place in the
★ hearts of Norwegians. Originally built in 1892, it was reconstructed for the 1952 Winter Olympics, and is still a popular site for international competitions; it also attracts a million visitors every year. Take the elevator and walk to the top for the view that skiers have in the moment before they take off. Back down at the base of the jump, turn right, past the statue of King Olav V on skis, to enter the oldest ski museum in the world. A hands-on exhibition awaits you, with alpine and cross-country skis, poles, and bindings that have been used through the ages. See the earliest skis, from AD 600; explorer Fridtjof Nansen's wooden skis from his 1888 Greenland crossing; and the autographed specimens used by retired champion Bjørn Daehlie. Then, head to the ski simulator outside for the thrilling sensation of a ski jump. ⊠ *Kongevn. 5, Holmenkollen* ☎ *22–92–32–00* ⊕ *www.skiforeningen.no* ⊠ *NKr 50* ☉ *Jan.–Apr. and Oct.–Dec., daily 10–4; May and Sept., daily 10–5; June–Aug., daily 9–8.*

WHAT TO SEE **Internasjonale Barnekunstmuseet** (International Museum of Children's Art).
☾ **27** A brainchild of Rafael Goldin, a Russian immigrant, the museum showcases her collection of children's drawings from more than 150 countries. You can see the world though the eyes of a child in its exhibitions of textiles; drawings; paintings; sculptures; and children's music, dancing, and other activities. ⊠ *Lille Frøens vei 4, Blindern* ☎ *22–46–85–73* ⊕ *www.childrensart.com* ⊠ *NKr 50* ☉ *Late June–early Aug., Tues.–Thurs. and Sun. 11–4; mid-Sept.–mid-Dec. and late Jan.–late June, Tues.–Thurs. 9:30–2, Sun. 11–4.*

26 **Oslo Bymuseum** (Oslo City Museum). One of the world's largest cities, Oslo has changed and evolved greatly over its thousand years. A two-floor, meandering exhibition covers Oslo's prominence in 1050, the Black Death that came in 1348, the great fire of 1624 and subsequent rebuilding, and the urban development of the 20th century. Among the more interesting relics are the red coats that the first Oslo police, the watchmen, wore in 1700, and the first fire wagon in town, which appeared in 1765. Plan to visit the museum near the beginning of your stay for a more informed understanding of the Norwegian capital. ⊠ *Frognervn. 67, Frogner* ☎ *23–28–41–70* ⊕ *www.oslobymuseum.no* ⊠ *NKr 50* ☉ *Wed.–Sun. noon–4, Tues. 10–7.*

Skøytemuseet (Ice Skating Museum). Tucked away in Frogner Stadium, this is Norway's only museum devoted to ice skates and ice-skaters. Gleaming trophies, Olympic medals, and skates, skates, and more skates serve to celebrate the sport. Photographs of skating legends such as Johan Olav Koss, Hjalmar Andersen, and Oscar Mathisen line the walls. Take a look at ways that skates have evolved—compare the bone skates from 2000 BC to the wooden skates that came later. ⊠ *Frogner Park, Middelthunsgt. 26, Majorstuen* ☎ *22–43–49–20* ⊕ *www.oslosk.no/museet.htm* ⊠ *NKr 20* ☉ *Tues. and Thurs. 10–2:30, Sun. 11–2.*

need a break?

Generations of families have warmed themselves by the open fires of **21 Frognerseteren** (⊠ Holmenkollen 200 ☎ 22–92–40–40) with a cup of hot chocolate after a long day skiing on the slopes. This restaurant and lookout occupies a special place in the hearts of Norwegians. The two-story log cabin has earthy wooden tables decked with iron candelabras, and traditional rose paintings and taxidermied animals adorning the walls. Try to get a seat on the upper floor to enjoy the view over the Oslo fjord, or use the telescopes on the terrace.

㉕ Vigelandsmuseet. "I am anchored to my work so that I cannot move. If I walk down the street one day a thousand hands from work hold on to me. I am tied to the studio and the road is never long," said Gustav Vigeland in 1912. This museum was the Norwegian sculptor's studio and residence. It houses models of almost all his works as well as sculptures, drawings, woodcuts, and the original molds and plans for Vigeland Park. Wander through this intense world of enormous, snowy-white plaster, clustered nudes, and busts of such famous Norwegians as Henrik Ibsen and Edvard Grieg. ⊠ *Nobelsgt. 32, Frogner* ☎ *23–49–37–00* ⊕ *www.vigeland.museum.no* ⊠ *NKr 45* ☉ *Sept.–May, Tues.–Sun. noon–4; June–Aug., Tues.–Sun. 11–5.*

㉔ Vigelandsparken (Vigeland's Park). Also known as Frogner Park, Vigelandsparken has 212 bronze, granite, and wrought-iron sculptures by **Fodor'sChoice** Gustav Vigeland (1869–1943). Most of the stunning park sculptures are ★ placed on a nearly 1-km-long (½ mi-long) axis and depict the stages of life: birth to death, one generation to the next. See the park's 56-foot-high granite *Monolith Plateau,* a column of 121 upward-striving nude figures surrounded by 36 groups on circular stairs. The most beloved sculpture is a bronze of an enraged baby boy stamping his foot and scrunching his face in fury. Known as *Sinnataggen* (The Angry Boy), this famous statue has been filmed, parodied, painted red, and even stolen from the park. It is based on a 1901 sketch Vigeland made of a little boy in London. ⊠ *Kirkevn., Frogner* ☎ *23–49–37–00* ⊕ *www.vigeland. museum.no* ⊠ *Free* ☉ *Daily.*

Bygdøy

Several of Oslo's best-known historic sights are concentrated on the Bygdøy Peninsula (west of the city center), as are several beaches, jogging paths, and the royal family's summer residence.

a good walk

The most pleasant way to get to Bygdøy—available from May to September—is to catch Ferry 91 from the rear of the Rådhuset on Pier 3. Times vary, so check with Trafikanten (☎ 177) for schedules. Another alternative is to take Bus 30, marked "Bygdøy," from Stortingsgata at Nationaltheatret along Drammensveien to Bygdøy Allé, a wide avenue lined with chestnut trees. The bus passes Frogner Church and several embassies on its way to Olav Kyrres plass, where it turns left, and soon left again, onto the peninsula. The royal family's summer residence, actually just a big white frame house, is on the right. Get off at the next stop, Norsk Folkemuseum. The pink castle nestled in the trees is **Oscarshall Slott** ㉙ ⌐, once a royal summer palace.

The **Norsk Folkemuseum** ㉚ consists of an open-air museum as well as some indoor exhibits of folk art. Around the corner from the museum, to the right, is the **Vikingskiphuset** ㉛, one of Norway's most popular attractions; it houses some of the best-preserved Viking-era remains yet discovered.

Follow signs on the road to the **Fram-Museet** ㉜, a pyramid-shape structure resembling a Viking boathouse. After viewing the exhibitions, you can watch a panoramic movie about Norway's maritime past at the Norsk Sjøfartsmuseum. Across the parking lot is the older **Kon-Tiki Museum** ㉝, with Thor Heyerdahl's famous raft, along with the papyrus boat *Ra II*. You can get a ferry back to the City Hall docks from the dock in front of the Fram-Museet.

TIMING Block out a day for Bygdøy. You could spend at least half a day at the Folkemuseum alone. Note that the museums on Bygdøy tend to be open daily, but close early.

WHAT TO SEE **Fram-Museet.** Once known as the strongest vessel in the world, the enor-
★ ☾ ㉜ mous, legendary Norwegian polar ship *Fram* has advanced farther north and south than any other surface vessel. Built in 1892, it made three arctic voyages conducted by Fridtjof Nansen (1893–96), Otto Sverdrup (1898–1902), and Roald Amundsen (1910–12). Climb on board and peer inside the captain's quarters, which has explorers' sealskin jackets and other relics on display. Surrounding the ship are many expedition artifacts. ✉ *Bygdøynes, Bygdøy* ☎ *23–28–29–50* ⊕ *www.fram.museum.no* ☑ *NKr 40* ☾ *Jan.–Apr., daily 10–3:45; May–mid-June, daily 10–5:45; mid-June–Aug., daily 9–6:45; Sept., daily 10–4:45; Oct.–Dec, daily 10–3:45.*

★ ☾ ㉝ **Kon-Tiki Museum.** The museum celebrates Norway's most famous 20th-century explorer. Thor Heyerdahl made a voyage in 1947 from Peru to Polynesia on the *Kon-Tiki,* a balsa raft, to lend weight to his theory that the first Polynesians came from the Americas. His second craft, the *Ra II,* was used to test his theory that this sort of boat could have reached the West Indies before Columbus. The museum also has a film room and artifacts from Peru, Polynesia, and the Easter Islands. ✉ *Bygdøynesvn. 36, Bygdøy* ☎ *23–08–67–67* ⊕ *www.kon-tiki.no* ☑ *NKr 45* ☾ *Apr., May, and Sept., daily 10:30–5; June–Aug., daily 9:30–5:45; Oct.–Mar., daily 10:30–4.*

☾ ㉚ **Norsk Folkemuseum** (Norwegian Folk Museum). One of the largest open-
Fodor'sChoice air museums in Europe, this is a perfect way to see Norway in a day.
★ From the stoic stave church to farmers' houses made of sod, the old buildings here span Norway's regions and history as far back as the 14th century. Indoors, there's a fascinating display of folk costumes. The displays of richly embroidered, colorful *bunader* (national costumes) from every region includes one set at a Telemark country wedding. The museum

also has stunning dragon-style wood carvings from 1550 and some beautiful rosemaling. The traditional costumes of the Sami (Lapp) people of northern Norway are exhibited around one of their tents. If you're visiting in summer, inquire about Norwegian Evening, a summer program of folk dancing, guided tours, and food tastings. On Sunday in December, the museum holds Oslo's largest Christmas market. ☒ *Museumsvn. 10, Bygdøy* ☎ *22–12–37–00* ⊕ *www.norskfolke.museum. no* ☒ *NKr 90* ☉ *Mid-Sept.–mid-May, weekdays 11–3, weekends 11–4; mid-May–mid-Sept., daily 10–6.*

☼ **Norsk Sjøfartsmuseum** (Norwegian Maritime Museum). Norwegian fishing boats, paintings of fishermen braving rough seas, and intricate ship models are all on display here. The arctic vessel *Gjøa* is docked outside. The breathtaking, panoramic movie *The Ocean: A Way of Life* delves into Norway's unique coastal and maritime past. Also on display is the model of the Kvaldor boat (AD 600), a 19th-century armed wooden warship (*Kong Sverre*), and a modern-day tanker. ☒ *Bygdøynesvn. 37, Bygdøy* ☎ *22–43–82–40* ⊕ *www.norsk-sjofartsmuseum.no* ☒ *NKr 40* ☉ *Mid-May–Aug., daily 10–6; Sept.–mid-May, Mon–Wed. and Fri.–Sun. 10:30–4, Thurs. 10:30–6.*

㉙ **Oscarshall Slott.** This small country palace was built (1847–52) in eccentric English Gothic style for King Oscar I. There's a park, pavilion, fountain, and stage on the grounds. The original interior has works by the Norwegian artists Adolph Tidemand and Hans Gude. ☒ *Oscarshallvn., Bygdøy* ☎ *22–56–15–39* ☒ *NKr 20* ☉ *Late May–mid-Sept., Tues., Thurs., and Sun. noon–4.*

㉛ **Vikingskiphuset** (Viking Ship Museum). The Viking legacy in all its glory lives on at this classic Oslo museum. Chances are you'll come away fascinated by the three blackened wooden Viking ships *Gokstad, Oseberg,* and *Tune,* which date to AD 800. Discovered in Viking tombs around the Oslo fjords between 1860 and 1904, the boats are the best-preserved Viking ships ever found and have been exhibited since the museum's 1957 opening. In Viking times, it was customary to bury the dead with food, drink, useful and decorative objects, and even their horses and dogs. Many of the well-preserved tapestries, household utensils, dragon-style wood carvings, and sledges were found aboard ships. The museum's rounded white walls give the feeling of a burial mound. Avoid summertime crowds by visiting at lunchtime. ☒ *Huk Aveny 35, Bygdøy* ☎ *22–13–52–80* ⊕ *www.ukm.uio.no* ☒ *NKr 40* ☉ *May–Sept., daily 9–6; Oct.–Apr., daily 11–4.*

Fodor'sChoice
★

Where to Eat

Many Oslo chefs have developed menus based on classic Norwegian recipes but with exciting variations, like Asian or Mediterranean cooking styles and ingredients. You may read about "New Scandinavian" cuisine on some menus—a culinary style that combines seafood and game from Scandinavia with spices and sauces from any other country.

Spend at least one sunny summer afternoon harborside at Aker Brygge eating shrimp and watching the world go by. Floating restaurants serve

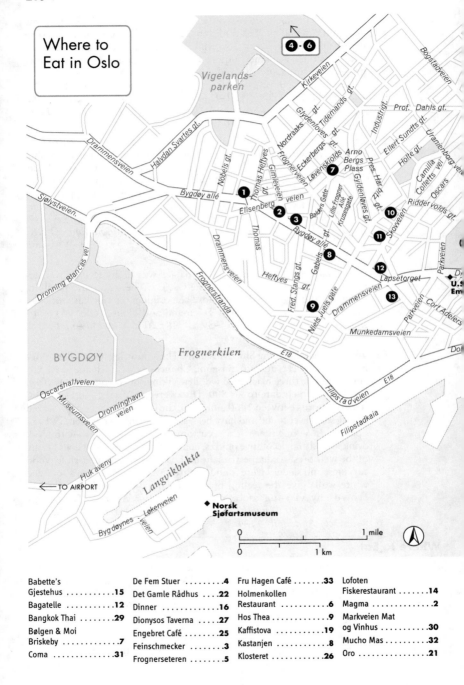

Where to Eat in Oslo

Vigelands-parken

BYGDØY

Frognerkilen

Langvikbukta

← TO AIRPORT

◆ Norsk Sjøfartsmuseum

0   1 mile
0   1 km

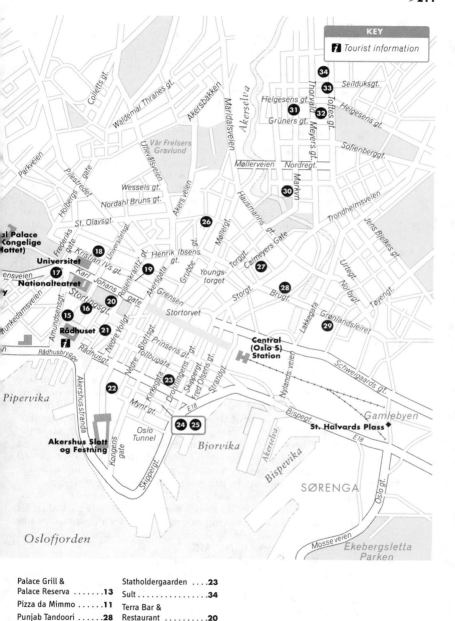

KEY

🛈 Tourist information

Palace Grill &
Palace Reserva **13**
Pizza da Mimmo **11**
Punjab Tandoori **28**
Restaurant Eik **18**
Restaurant
Le Canard **10**

Statholdergaarden **23**
Sult **34**
Terra Bar &
Restaurant **20**
A Touch of France **24**
Vegeta Vertshus **17**
Village Tandoori **1**

shrimp in bowls with baguettes and mayonnaise. Or better still, buy steamed shrimp off the nearby docked fishing boats and plan a picnic in the Oslo fjords or Vigeland or another of the city's parks. Note that some restaurants close for a week around Easter, in July, and during the Christmas holiday season.

Downtown: Royal Palace to the Parliament

Restaurants downtown along Karl Johans Gate cater to tourists and offer a range of cuisines, including Indian, Chinese, and traditional Norwegian. Many are high-quality restaurants, and prices are generally steep.

$$$$ ✗ **Restaurant Eik.** This is Norway's first smoke-free restaurant, although cigar smoke would not be out of place here, among the plush chairs, deep-red sofa, somber artwork, and soft music. The food, in contrast, is thoroughly up-to-date. Three- and five-course prix-fixe menus change daily but might include lightly smoked wild salmon served with pasta and asparagus or chicken served with tarragon and corn puree. ⊠ *Hotel Savoy, Universitetsgt. 11, Sentrum* ☎ *23–33–54–50* ▭ *AE, DC, MC, V* ☉ *Closed Sun., Mon., and July.*

$$$–$$$$ ✗ **Babette's Gjestehus.** Near City Hall, this restaurant's dark-blue walls and lace curtains make it resemble an old-fashioned Norwegian living room. French chef Dominique Choquet serves Scandinavian and international dishes with flair. Try the reindeer fillet in port sauce, lamb with apricots, or monkfish. The staff is friendly and welcoming. ⊠ *Rådhuspassasjen, Fridtjof Nansens pl. 2, Sentrum* ☎ *22–41–64–64* ▭ *AE, DC, MC, V* ☉ *Closed Sun. and July. No lunch.*

$$–$$$
Fodor'sChoice
★
✗ **Oro.** One of the city's hottest restaurants, Oro ("gold" in Spanish) was opened by celebrity chef Terje Ness in 2000. Ness has since resigned following a fallout with the restaurant's investors, but Oro's unique Mediterranean menu and cool airy design remains. Large chandeliers hang over tables surrounded by slip-covered chairs. Contemporary art hangs on the walls and a fireplace burns at eye level. You can order à la carte or try the Taste of Oro prix-fixe menu (a 7- or 12-course dinner). Specialties include steak, game, and fowl. For dessert, savor the delicious Chocolate Oro—chocolate mousse with passion fruit, topped with gold leaf. ⊠ *Tordenskjolds gt. 6, Sentrum* ☎ *23–01–02–40* ⇔ *Reservations essential* ▭ *AE, DC, MC, V* ☉ *Closed Sun. No lunch.*

$$–$$$ ✗ **A Touch of France.** As its name suggests, this wine bar near the Parliament building is straight out of Paris. The waiters' long, white aprons; the art nouveau interior; old French posters; and closely packed tables all add to the illusion. The tempting menu includes a delicious, steaming-hot bouillabaisse and duck confit. ⊠ *Øvre Slottsgt. 16, Sentrum* ☎ *23–10–01–65* ▭ *AE, DC, MC, V.*

$–$$$ ✗ **Terra Bar & Restaurant.** Spanish pottery and earth tones hint at the Mediterranean-inspired dishes served here. Across the street from the Parliament building, it attracts its share of politicians. Half the menu is fish, such as oven-baked salmon stuffed with sea scallops and baked cod with lobster sauce. A special treat is the Tired of Everything dessert: homemade vanilla ice cream topped with warm espresso syrup. ⊠ *Stortingsgt. 2, Sentrum* ☎ *22–40–55–20* ▭ *AE, DC, MC, V* ☉ *No lunch July–mid-Aug.*

$-$$ ✕ **Dinner.** The simple name belies the fact that this is one of the best places
Fodor'sChoice in Oslo for Chinese food, as well as dishes that combine Norwegian and
★ Cantonese styles. Peking duck is a speciality here, or, for a lighter meal,
try the delectable platter of seafood in chili-pepper sauce. ⊠ *Stortingsgt. 22, Sentrum* ☎ *23–10–04–66* ⊟ *AE, DC, MC, V* ⊗ *No lunch.*

¢-$ ✕ **Vegeta Vertshus.** This innovative buffet-style vegetarian restaurant
opposite the national theater was established in 1938. Vegeta Vertshus
is a godsend for vegetarians in a town with meat- and fish-centric
menus. A wide variety of meals are on offer here, including vegetarian
pasta dishes, pizza, curries, and quiches. ⊠ *Munkedamsvn. 3B, Sentrum*
☎ *22–83–42–32* ⊟ *AE, DC, MC, V.*

¢ ✕ **Kaffistova.** Norwegian home cooking is served cafeteria-style at this
downtown restaurant on the first floor of the Hotell Bondeheimen.
Daily specials come in generous portions and include soup and a selection of entrées. There is always at least one vegetarian dish, as well as
fish and, usually, homemade meatballs. ⊠ *Hotell Bondeheimen,
Rosenkrantz gt. 8, Sentrum* ☎ *23–21–42–10* ⊟ *AE, DC, MC, V.*

Kvadraturen & Aker Brygge

If you're after typical Norwegian dining, try the restaurants around
Kvadraturen in Sentrum (the center), which offer very traditional meals
in typical Norwegian settings. The patrons are mostly locals and the food
is usually quite simple, based on seasonal fish and game. Aker Brygge
caters to tourists and young professionals with pricier restaurants that
have a more international flavor, without being too daring or trendy.

$$$$ ✕ **Statholdergaarden.** Onetime Bocuse d'Or champion Bent Stiansen's
Asian-inspired French dishes have long been popular with locals. The
six-course gastronomic menu changes daily; you can also order from
the à la carte menu. Try his sesame-roasted duck breast with ginger sauce
or the panfried perch with tomato cannelloni. More than 400 years old,
the rococo dining room is one of Norway's largest and seats 75 people.
⊠ *Rådhusgt. 11, Sentrum* ☎ *22–41–88–00* ⌖ *Reservations essential*
⌂ *Jacket and tie* ⊟ *AE, DC, MC, V* ⊗ *Closed Sun. and 3 wks in July.*

★ **$$$-$$$$** ✕ **Lofoten Fiskerestaurant.** Named for the Lofoten Islands off the north-
west coast, this Aker Brygge restaurant is considered one of Oslo's best
for fish, from salmon to cod to monkfish. It has a bright, fresh, mini-
malistic interior with harbor views and a summertime patio. From Jan-
uary through March, try the cod served with its own liver and roe; April
through September, the shellfish; and from October through December,
the lutefisk. Call ahead, since sometimes only large groups are served.
⊠ *Stranden 75, Aker Brygge* ☎ *22–83–08–08* ⊟ *AE, DC, MC, V.*

$$-$$$$ ✕ **Engebret Café.** This somber old-fashioned restaurant at Bankplassen
was a haunt for bohemian literati at the turn of the 20th century and
the building itself dates from the 17th century. The formal, French-tinged
Norwegian dinner menu includes traditional seasonal fare around *Jule-
tide* (Christmastime), including lutefisk and *pinnekjøtt* (sticks of meat),
which is lamb steamed over branches of birch. For a real taste of Norway, try the *smalahove* (a whole sheep's head). Many Norwegian families consider it a treat to visit the restaurant around Christmas, so book
early if that's your plan, too. During the rest of the year, try the rein-

deer in cream sauce or the poached catfish. ✉ *Bankpl. 1, Sentrum* ☎ *22–82–25–25* ▭ *AE, DC, MC, V.*

$–$$$ ✕ **Det Gamle Rådhus.** Inside Oslo's City Hall, built in 1641, this is the city's oldest restaurant. Its reputation is based mostly on traditional fish and game dishes. An absolute must, if you're lucky enough to be visiting at the right time, is the house specialty, the pre-Christmas lutefisk platter. The backyard has a charming outdoor area for dining in summer. ✉ *Nedre Slottsgt. 1, Sentrum* ☎ *22–42–01–07* ▭ *AE, DC, MC, V* ☺ *Closed Sun.*

Tøyen & Grønland

The most internationally diverse group of restaurants can be found east of downtown, particularly in multicultural Tøyen and Grønland. This area also has the most reasonable dining prices in Oslo.

$$$–$$$$ ✕ **Klosteret.** The name of this popular east-side restaurant means "the cloisters." Its not-very-medieval, informal dining room is in a spacious, candlelit, rounded brick cellar. Pictures of saints and other religious figures adorn the walls, and Gregorian chants play in the background. The handwoven menus, bound to look like hymnals, contain a list of appealing meat and fish dishes, plus a daily vegetarian option. Consider the baked cod with puree of Jerusalem artichoke and marinated beet. Three-course dinners cost NKr 425. ✉ *Fredensborgvn. 13, Sentrum* ☎ *23–35–49–00* ▭ *AE, DC, MC, V* ☺ *Closed Sun. and July.*

$ ✕ **Bangkok Thai.** Some of the best Thai food in Oslo can be had here, including *tom yum,* a hot-and-sour seafood-based soup; Thai beef salads; and all varieties of curry. Spacious and carefully decorated with Thai paintings and artifacts, this restaurant is a bit more upmarket than other eateries in this neighborhood. Sharp service here makes for pleasant dining. ✉ *Grønlandsleiret 27, Grønland* ☎ *22–17–70–03* ▭ *MC, V* ☺ *Closed Mon.*

★ $ ✕ **Dionysos Taverna.** Owner Charalambos Eracleous imports fresh fish, wine, and ouzo from Greece to serve at his cobalt-blue-and-white-washed restaurant. The *tzatziki* (yogurt and cucumber salad), souvlaki, and moussaka are authentically prepared, as are the more unusual casseroles, such as *exohiko* (lamb baked with red wine, tomatoes, and onions). For a taste of everything, order *mezes,* Greek-style tapas. A bouzouki trio accompanies your dining experience on Thursday, Friday, and Saturday nights. ✉ *Calmeyersgt. 11, Sentrum* ☎ *22–60–78–64* ▭ *MC, V* ☺ *No lunch.*

¢ ✕ **Punjab Tandoori.** Plastic tables, a kitschy decor, and a refrigerator that hums will not suit picky diners. However, the homemade tandoori is a treat here, and prices go as low as NKr 60 for a main course. You may have to wait for a table as local Indians also recognize the value of Punjab Tandoori—always a good sign. ✉ *Grønland 24, Grønland* ☎ *22–17–20–86* ▭ *MC, V.*

Grünerløkka

Grünerløkka, just north of the center, is Oslo's up-and-coming artsy neighborhood. Most of its restaurants serve modern versions of Norwegian fare and international dishes.

$$ ✕ **Mucho Mas.** Large servings are the order of the day here but a table may be hard to find, such is Mucho Mas's popularity. Burritos, nachos, and quesadillas are served as spicy as you like in a simple setting decorated with cool pastel colors. ✉ *Thorvald Meyers gt. 36, Grünerløkka* ☎ *22–37–16–09* ▭ *AE, DC, MC, V.*

$–$$ ✕ **Coma.** This eccentric but very hip restaurant has white, blue, green, and purple ceiling lights, striped walls, and comfy pillows to create a dreamy mood. Tongue-in-cheek signs over the door are there to let you know when you are entering and when you are leaving the coma. Try one of the fish dishes on the French-inspired menu. ✉ *Helgesensgt. 16, Grünerløkka* ☎ *22–35–32–22* ▭ *AE, DC, MC, V.*

$–$$ ✕ **Markveien Mat og Vinhus.** This restaurant in the heart of the Grünerløkka district serves fresh French-inspired cuisine. It's a relaxed, artsy place with a bohemian clientele. Paintings cover the yellow walls, and the tables are laid with white linen. The menu lists delicacies such as giant Russian crab and Norwegian quail. For a special treat, try the homemade cheesecake. ✉ *Torvbakkgt. 12, entrance on Markvn. 57, Grünerløkka* ☎ *22–37–22–97* ▭ *AE, DC, MC, V* ☺ *Closed Sun.*

$–$$ ✕ **Sult.** Trendy, Norwegian, bohemian informality is the essence of this small restaurant, whose name means "hunger." Large windows, small square tables, and a simple homemade look attracts students and writers. Try one of the fish or pasta specials. Next door, the bar-lounge, appropriately named *Tørst* (thirst), has it own unique blended drinks, including Raspberry Parade, a blend of raspberry juice, champagne, and vodka. ✉ *Thorvald Meyers gt. 26, Grünerløkka* ☎ *22–87–04–67* ▭ *AE, DC, MC, V.*

$ ✕ **Fru Hagen Café.** Classic chandeliers and elegant velvet sofas decorate this old-fashioned café and restaurant. The fare is light and inexpensive—American-style hamburgers, pastas, and spicy chicken salads, for example. At night, Fru Hagen doubles as a bar with a DJ. ✉ *Thorvald Meyers gt. 40, Grünerløkka* ☎ *22–35–67–87* ▭ *AE, DC, MC, V.*

Frogner & Majorstuen

Some of Oslo's best restaurants are here in the wealthier western side of the city. The upmarket international dining scene includes many French-inspired kitchens.

$$$$ ✕ **Bagatelle.** Chef and owner Eyvind Hellstrøm has established an international reputation for his modern Norwegian cuisine and superb service. Bagatelle attracts the who's who of Oslo society, and is widely recognized as one of the city's best restaurants. Paintings by contemporary Norwegian artists accent the understated, elegant dining room. The three-, five-, and seven-course menus change daily. The lobster is always a standout. ✉ *Bygdøy Allé 3, Frogner* ☎ *22–12–14–40* ▭ *AE, DC, MC, V* ☺ *Closed Sun. mid-July–mid-Aug. No lunch.*

Fodor'sChoice ★

$$$$ ✕ **Feinschmecker.** The name is German, but the food is international and Scandinavian. Modern and stylish, the dining room's warm, earthy tones give it a cozy look. Owners Lars Erik Underthun, one of Oslo's foremost chefs, and Bengt Wilson, a leading food stylist, make sure the food looks as good as it tastes. Feinschmecker is a haven for vegetarians with a three-course menu of local produce that changes according

MEALTIMES IN NORWAY

FOR CENTURIES, Norwegians regarded food as fuel, and their dining habits still bear traces of this. Frokost (breakfast) is a fairly big meal, usually with a selection of crusty bread, jams, herring, cold meat, and cheese. Norway's famous brown goat cheese, Geitost (a sweet, caramel-flavor whey cheese made from goat and cow milk) and Norvegia (a Norwegian Gouda-like cheese) are on virtually every table. They are eaten in thin slices, cut with a cheese plane or slicer—a Norwegian invention—on buttered wheat or rye bread.

Lunsj (lunch) is simple and usually consists of smørrbrød (open-face sandwiches). Most businesses have only a 30-minute lunch break, so unless there's a company cafeteria, people bring their lunch from home.

Middag (dinner), the only hot meal of the day, is early—from 1 to 4 in the country,

3 to 7 in the city—so many cafeterias serving home-style food close by 6 or 7. In Oslo it's possible to get dinner as late as midnight, especially in summer. Most restaurants in Oslo stop serving dinner around 10.

to the season. ⊠ *Balchensgt. 5, Frogner* ☎ *22–12–93–80* ⌑ *Reservations essential* ▤ *AE, DC, MC, V* ☉ *Closed Sun. and last 3 wks July. No lunch.*

$$$$ ✕ **Restaurant Le Canard.** Behind the Royal Castle, this elegant restaurant is in what looks like a brick manor house. Inside are such antique furnishings as a stained-glass window by Maria Vigeland, the wife of Emanuel. Chef Trond Andresen shows off his simple, French-inspired compositions in a menu that changes weekly. The wine cellar of 30,000 bottles includes rare champagne from 1928. In summer you can dine in special style on Le Canard's stunning garden terrace. ⊠ *Pres. Harbitz gt. 4, Frogner* ☎ *22–54–34–00* ⌑ *Reservations essential* ▤ *AE, DC, MC, V* ☉ *Closed Sun. No lunch.*

$$–$$$ ✕ **Bølgen & Moi Briskeby.** Restaurateurs Toralf Bølgen and Trond Moi

Fodor'sChoice have a winner in this minimalistic restaurant. If you're tired of eating
★ breakfast in your hotel, rise and shine here instead. Housed in a former power station, the restaurant incorporates the past with a long, eye-catching, cement dining table and open fires. Well-known Norwegian artists such as photographer Knut Bry showcase their work in the restaurant's bar, brasserie, and formal dining room. Try the oversize Thorenfeldt burger,

or the three-course set menu, which changes daily. Most dishes are cooked in the wood-burning oven in the corner. ⊠ *Løvenskioldsgt. 26, Frogner* ☎ *24–11–53–53* ⊟ *AE, DC, MC, V* ⊗ *Closed Sun. and Mon.*

★ **$$–$$$** ✕ **Hos Thea.** An intimate yet lively dining experience awaits in this white-and-blue restaurant with a fleur-de-lis motif. From the open kitchen, owner Sergio Barcilon and the other chefs often serve the French and Spanish food themselves. The small menu lists four or five choices for each course, but every dish is superbly prepared. Noise and smoke levels can be high late at night. ⊠ *Gabelsgt. 11, entrance on Drammensvn., Skillebekk* ☎ *22–44–68–74* ⌂ *Reservations essential* ⊟ *AE, DC, MC, V* ⊗ *No lunch.*

$$–$$$ ✕ **Magma.** Vibrant, warm, and intense, the orange- and yellow-splashed interior captures the character of this Mediterranean restaurant-bar and its celebrity chef, Sonja Lee. It has become one of the city's hottest restaurants, attracting everyone from businesspeople to artists. The changing menu is based on seasonal ingredients and follows the owners' philosophy of rough-hewn simplicity. Consider the ricotta ravioli and the spit-roasted veal with macaroni gratin. There is also live jazz on Sunday starting at 11 AM. ⊠ *Bygdøy Allé 53, Frogner* ☎ *23–08–58–10* ⊟ *AE, DC, MC, V.*

Fodor'sChoice ★

$$–$$$ ✕ **Palace Grill & Palace Reserva.** A tiny, eight-table restaurant near the Royal Palace, the Palace Grill is one of the most fashionable spots on the Oslo dining scene. Don't let the "grill" part fool you: it may be relaxed, but its French-inspired cuisine is certainly not fast food. The original Palace Grill doesn't take reservations and is usually full, so try to get here before 5 PM for a table. Alternatively, reserve a table at its new sister restaurant, the more spacious and slightly less expensive Palace Reserva. ⊠ *Solligt. 2, off Drammensvn., Frogner* ☎ *22–56–14–02* ⊟ *AE, DC, MC, V* ⊗ *Closed Sun. and Mon.*

★ **$$** ✕ **Kastanjen.** This rustic, laid-back Frogner bistro, named after the chestnut trees that line the street, is the kind every neighborhood needs. Try the Norwegian white fish *kveite* with bacon as a main course and the homemade sorbet for dessert. The warmly lighted downstairs lounge serves drinks and light snacks. ⊠ *Bygdøy Allé 18, Frogner* ☎ *22–43–44–67* ⊟ *AE, DC, MC, V* ⊗ *Closed Sun. and July.*

$ ✕ **Village Tandoori.** Walking through this restaurant feels like a nighttime wander through an Indian or Pakistani village, about a hundred years ago. Pakistani owner Mobashar Hussain has collected antique rugs, including vibrant silk ones with embroidery and beadwork. The chicken and lamb curries and tandooris are delicious. ⊠ *Bygdøy Allé 65, Frogner* ☎ *22–56–10–25* ⊟ *AE, DC, MC, V* ⊗ *No lunch.*

¢–$ ✕ **Pizza da Mimmo.** Named for owner Domenico Giardina, aka Mimmo, this is Oslo's best pizzeria. In 1993, Mimmo, who's originally from Calabria, was the first to bring thin-crust Italian pizza to the city. Taste his perennially popular panna and prosciutto pizza, and the Pizza Calabrigella. The casual restaurant is on the basement level in a white-brick building; earthy colors, hanging rugs, and small cellar windows give it a cavelike appearance. ⊠ *Behrensgt. 2, Frogner* ☎ *22–44–40–20* ⌂ *Reservations essential* ⊟ *AE, DC, MC, V.*

Fodor'sChoice ★

Holmenkollen

This small wealthy neighborhood is a 15-minute drive northwest of the center, halfway into the forest. It's a popular place for downhill and Nordic skiing, and the few restaurants here are popular in winter and serve hearty, traditional, Norwegian meals.

$$$-$$$$
Fodor's Choice
★

✕ **De Fem Stuer.** Near the famous Holmenkollen ski jump, in the historic Holmenkollen Park Hotel, this restaurant has first-rate views and food. Chef Jørn Dahl's modern Norwegian dishes have strong classic roots. The fish dishes, particularly those made with salmon, cod, and wolffish, are his specialty. Try the four-course menu called A Taste of Norway to get exactly that. ✉ *Holmenkollen Park Hotel, Kongevn. 26, Holmenkollen* ☎ *22-92-27-34* 🍴 *Jacket and tie* ▭ *AE, DC, MC, V.*

$$-$$$$
✕ **Holmenkollen Restaurant.** An old-fashioned, luxury mountain cabin café, restaurant, and banquet hall, this Oslo institution dates to 1892. The spacious café is perfect for an afternoon coffee and cake after walking or skiing. In the smaller, formal restaurant, dishes come from the hands of well-known chef Harald Osa. The menu focuses on Norwegian fish and game dishes served with innovative sauces. ✉ *Holmenkollvn. 119, Holmenkollen* ☎ *22-13-92-00* ▭ *AE, DC, MC, V.*

$-$$
✕ **Frognerseteren.** Just above the Holmenkollen ski jump and therefore with sweeping mountain views, this is possibly Oslo's most famous restaurant. Popular with locals and travelers, it specializes in fish and game. The scrumptious apple cake is legendary, and perfect for dessert or for an afternoon treat with coffee. Eating reindeer in brown sauce with local *tittebær* (red berries) at Frognerseteren would have to be the ultimate Norwegian experience. Take the Holmenkollbanen to the end station and then follow the signs downhill to the restaurant. ✉ *Holmenkollvn. 200, Holmenkollen* ☎ *22-92-40-40* ▭ *DC, MC, V.*

Where to Stay

Most lodgings are central, just a short walk from Karl Johans Gate. Many are between the Royal Palace and Oslo S Station, with the newer ones closer to the station. For a quiet stay, choose a hotel in either Frogner or Majorstuen, elegant residential neighborhoods behind the Royal Palace and within walking distance of downtown. Television and phones can be expected in most Oslo hotel rooms. Typical Oslo hotels operate on the European Plan, that is, rates are for a double room without breakfast.

Downtown: Royal Palace to the Parliament

Downtown has many traditional Norwegian hotels dating from the 19th and early-20th centuries. These establishments are pricey, but they cater to travelers with the best service and amenities.

$$-$$$$
🏨 **Grand Hotel.** In the center of town on Karl Johans Gate, the Grand opened in 1874. The hotel is the choice of visiting heads of state, and there is even a Nobel suite. Ibsen used to drink brandy at the Grand Café in the company of journalists. Munch was also a regular guest; you can see him with his contemporaries in Per Krohg's painting on the café's far wall. Norwegians book several years in advance for National Day, May 17, in order to have a room overlooking the parades below. ✉ *Karl*

Johans gt. 31, Sentrum, 0101 ☎ *23–21–20–00* 🖷 *23–21–21–00* 🌐 *www. grand.no* 📞 *288 rooms, 51 suites* 🍴 *2 restaurants, indoor pool, health club, sauna, bar, meeting room* 🟰 *AE, DC, MC, V.*

★ **$$–$$$$** 🏨 **Hotel Continental.** With its elegant early-20th-century facade, the Continental is an Oslo landmark that continues to attract with gracious service and wonderful restaurants. Near Nationaltheatret, and close to many cafés, clubs, and movie theaters, the hotel is ideal for leisure as well as business travelers. The hotel's Theatercafeen restaurant is an Oslo landmark, and the nightspot Lipp is a trendy hangout for the well-to-do. Dagligstuen (The Sitting Room) is a popular meeting place for drinks and quiet conversation. ✉ *Stortingsgt. 24–26, Sentrum, 0161* ☎ *22–82–40–00* 🖷 *22–42–96–89* 🌐 *www.hotel-continental.no* 📞 *159 rooms, 23 suites* 🍴 *3 restaurants, cable TV, in-room data ports, 2 bars* 🟰 *AE, DC, MC, V.*

$$$ 🏨 **Hotel Bristol.** With its interior design inspired by Edwardian England, the Bristol has a dignity and class all its own. Rooms are elegant and understated. The lounge and bar were decorated in the 1920s with an intricate Moorish theme and recall Fez more than Scandinavia. Josephine Baker performed in the piano bar in the 1920s. Today, the library and bar, with their red, burnished leather sofas, are among Oslo's places to see and be seen. ✉ *Kristian IVs gt. 7, Sentrum, 0130* ☎ *22–82–60–00* 🖷 *22–82–60–01* 🌐 *www.bristol.no* 📞 *252 rooms, 10 suites* 🍴 *3 restaurants, health club, sauna, 3 bars, nightclub, convention center* 🟰 *AE, DC, MC, V.*

$–$$$ 🏨 **Radisson SAS Scandinavia Hotel.** Popular with business travelers, this 1974 hotel has a winning combination of service and classic style. Simple, elegant rooms come in different designs: art deco, Italian, Asian, Continental, Scandinavian, and—predictably, for a hotel run by an airline—69 high-tech business-class rooms. The Summit 21 Bar has a stunning, panoramic view of Oslo—it's a great place for an evening cocktail. ✉ *Holbergsgt. 30, Sentrum, 0166* ☎ *23–29–30–00* 🖷 *23–29–30–01* 🌐 *www.radissonsas.com* 📞 *488 rooms, 4 suites* 🍴 *Restaurant, cable TV, pool, health club, 2 bars, business services* 🟰 *AE, DC, MC, V.*

$$ 🏨 **Rica Victoria.** This modern business hotel occupies one of the city center's taller buildings, giving some top-floor rooms views of Oslo's rooftops. The rooms, built around a center atrium, are elegant and stylish: they're furnished with Biedermeier reproductions, brass lamps, and paisley fabrics in bold reds and dark blues. ✉ *Rosenkrantz gt. 13, Sentrum, 0121* ☎ *24–14–70–00* 🖷 *24–14–70–01* 🌐 *www.rica.no* 📞 *199 rooms, 5 suites* 🍴 *Restaurant, cable TV, in-room data ports, bar, convention center, meeting rooms, no-smoking rooms* 🟰 *AE, DC, MC, V.*

$$ 🏨 **Thon Hotel Stefan.** A home away from home, this hotel tries hard to make guests feel well looked after. Hot drinks are served to late arrivals, and breakfast tables come with juice boxes and plastic bags for packing a lunch (request this service in advance). The top-floor lounge has magazines in English, and the restaurant serves one of the best buffet lunches in town. ✉ *Rosenkrantz gt. 1, Sentrum, 0159* ☎ *23–31–55–00* 🖷 *23–31–55–55* 🌐 *www.thonhotels.no/stefan* 📞 *150 rooms, 11 suites*

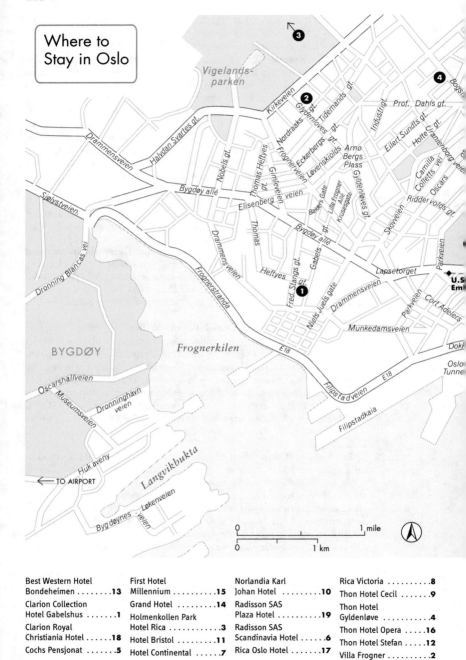

Where to Stay in Oslo

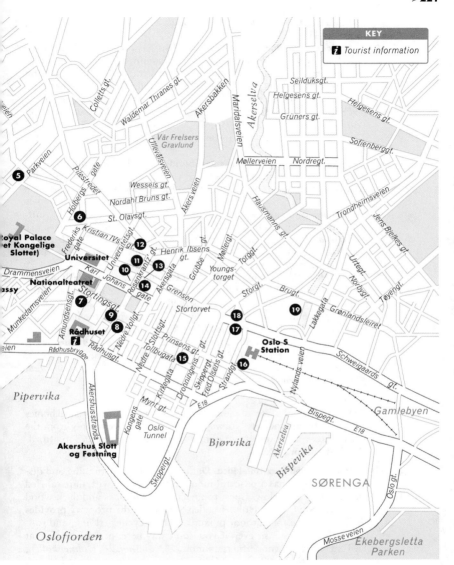

KEY

i *Tourist information*

♿ *Restaurant, cable TV, in-room broadband, lounge, library, meeting room* 🗐 *AE, DC, MC, V.*

$–$$ 🖭 **Norlandia Karl Johan Hotel.** The late-19th-century Karl Johan Hotel, once known as the Nobel, is elegant, with stained-glass windows that line the circular staircase, bringing to mind 19th-century Paris. During a renovation in 2004, rooms were painted and given new carpets and furnishings. Most rooms also have Norwegian antique pieces, giving the place an air of sophisticated luxury. ✉ *Karl Johans gt. 33, Sentrum, 0162* 📞 *23–16–17–00* 🖶 *22–42–05–19* ⊕ *www.norlandia.no* 🛏 *112 rooms, 1 suite* ♿ *Restaurant, bar, meeting room, business services* 🗐 *AE, DC, MC, V.*

$ 🖭 **Best Western Hotell Bondeheimen.** Founded in 1913 for country folk visiting the city, Bondeheimen, which means "farmers' home," still gives discounts to members of Norwegian agricultural associations. Rooms have a minimalistic look, in dark greens and earthy reds. This is a good choice for families. If you are looking for quiet, ask for a room in back. The Kaffistova restaurant is in the same building. ✉ *Rosenkrantz gt. 8, entrance on Kristian IVs gt., Sentrum, 0159* 📞 *23–21–41–00* 🖶 *23–21–41–01* ⊕ *www.bondeheimen.com* 🛏 *127 rooms, 5 suites* ♿ *Cafeteria, in-room broadband, shop, meeting rooms* 🗐 *AE, DC, MC, V.*

$ 🖭 **Thon Hotel Cecil.** A short walk from Parliament, this modern hotel is
Fodor'sChoice a relatively inexpensive option in the center of town. Although the
★ rooms are basic, they are perfectly suited to the active, on-the-go traveler. The second floor opens onto a plant-filled atrium, the hotel's "activity center." In the morning it's a breakfast room, but in the afternoon it becomes a lounge, serving coffee, juice, and fresh fruit. ✉ *Stortingsgt. 8, Sentrum, 0130* 📞 *23–31–48–00* 🖶 *23–31–48–50* ⊕ *www.thonhotels. no/cecil* 🛏 *111 rooms, 2 suites* ♿ *Lounge, cable TV, in-room data ports, no-smoking rooms* 🗐 *AE, DC, MC, V.*

Frogner, Majorstuen & Holmenkollen

These leafy suburbs west of the center are known for large beautiful homes inhabited by prosperous Norwegians. The hotels are mainly from the 19th century and range from upmarket boutique properties to affordable bed-and-breakfasts.

$$–$$$ 🖭 **Holmenkollen Park Hotel Rica.** Dating to 1894, this stunning and distinguished hotel has a peaceful mountaintop setting with unparalleled views of the city below. Guest rooms have earth tones and dark-wood furniture. Next to the Holmenkollen Ski Arena, the property provides the perfect base for outdoor pursuits such as cycling, skiing, and running. It's worth a visit even if you don't stay here, perhaps to dine at De Fem Stuer, the wonderful restaurant. ✉ *Kongevn. 26, Holmenkollen, 0787* 📞 *22–92–20–00* 🖶 *22–14–61–92* ⊕ *www.holmenkollenparkhotel. no* 🛏 *220 rooms* ♿ *2 restaurants, cable TV, in-room broadband, pool, gym, sauna, spa, cross-country skiing, bar, cinema, convention center, meeting rooms* 🗐 *AE, DC, MC, V.*

$$ 🖭 **Clarion Collection Hotel Gabelshus.** In a blending of old and new styles, the Gabelshus became part of the Choice Hotels Scandinavia Group in 2005 when it literally joined together with a neighboring hotel, formerly the Oslo Ritz. The original building of the Gabelshus retains its old-world

English charm, while its newer counterpart offers rooms with a modern, minimalistic, Scandinavian style. ⊠ *Gabelsgt. 16, Frogner, 0272* ☎ *22–55–22–60* 🖷 *23–27–65–60* ⊕ *www.gabelshus.no* ⤢ *114 rooms* ⌂ *In-room broadband, sauna, steam room, lounge, meeting rooms* ⊟ *AE, DC, MC, V.*

¢–$ ▦ **Thon Hotel Gyldenløve.** Nestled among the many shops and cafés on Bogstadveien, this hotel is a very good value for its location. Rooms are light and airy and have stylish Scandinavian furniture. It is within walking distance of Vigelandparken, and the trikk stops just outside the door. ⊠ *Bogstadvn. 20, Majorstuen, 0355* ☎ *23–33–23–00* 🖷 *22–60–33–90* ⊕ *www.thonhotels.no/gyldenlove* ⤢ *168 rooms* ⌂ *Coffee shop, cable TV with movies, some in-room data ports* ⊟ *AE, DC, MC, V.*

¢ ▦ **Cochs Pensjonat.** A stone's throw from the Royal Palace, this no-frills guesthouse has reasonably priced, comfortable, but rather spartan rooms. Most of the 88 rooms have private bathrooms, but check when you make your reservation; some also have kitchenettes. ⊠ *Parkvn. 25, Majorstuen, 0350* ☎ *23–33–24–00* 🖷 *23–33–24–10* ⊕ *www.virtualoslo. com/cochs_pensjonat/* ⤢ *88 rooms* ⌂ *No room phones, no TV in some rooms* ⊟ *MC, V.*

★ ¢ ▦ **Villa Frogner.** In a white 19th-century villa close to Vigelandparken, this elegant bed-and-breakfast will appeal to anyone who appreciates charming individually decorated rooms and homemade breakfasts. With hardwood floors, Persian rugs, antique furniture, and long drapes, the rooms are cozy and inviting, but the proximity of the park and Bogstadveien, a major shopping street, with make you want to explore. The villa was first owned by Norwegian shipowners and in the late 1980s became the Indonesian embassy for a brief period. ⊠ *Nordraaks gt. 26, Frogner 0260* ☎ *22–56–19–60* 🖷 *22–56–07–42* ⊕ *www.bedandbreakfast.no* ⤢ *7 rooms, 7 apartments* ⌂ *Some kitchens, sauna, lounge* ⊟ *AE, DC, MC, V* ⦿ *CP.*

Near Oslo Airport & Oslo S Station

The hotels near Oslo Airport have all been built since the late 1990s, like the airport itself, and offer modern facilities. Most are part of a large chain and cater to business travelers. The hotels near Oslo S Station vary more in age and style and are closer to the center, but they're also more expensive than hotels near the airport. A taxi ride from the airport to Karl Johans Gate will cost you around NKr 500.

$$$ ▦ **Thon Hotel Opera.** Named after the Opera building under construction next door which is scheduled to open in 2007, this is arguably Oslo's most conveniently located hotel. It's just 110 yards from Karl Johans Gate, and a stone's throw from the Oslo S railway station. Rooms are elegant and well equipped, although slightly plain. Views from most of the rooms aren't special, but the two grand suites, the gym, and the Scala restaurant offer sweeping views of the Oslo fjord. ⊠ *Christian Frederiks pl. 5, 0103* ☎ *24–10–30–00* 🖷 *24–10–30–10* ⊕ *www.thonhotels. no/opera* ⤢ *434 rooms, 2 suites* ⌂ *Restaurant, in-room broadband, gym, sauna, bar, convention center* ⊟ *AE, DC, MC, V.*

★ $–$$$ ▦ **Clarion Royal Christiania Hotel.** What was once bare-bones housing for 1952 Olympians is now a luxury hotel. Although the original plain exterior remains, the interior is more recent, designed using feng shui principles. Rooms have white walls and mahogany furniture. ⊠ *Biskop Gunnerus gt. 3, 0106* ☎ *23–10–80–00* 🖶 *23–10–80–80* ⊕ *www.royalchristiania.no* 🖘 *412 rooms, 91 suites* ⚿ *Restaurant, indoor pool, health club, sauna, bar, business services, convention center* ▭ *AE, DC, MC, V.*

★ **$–$$$** 🏨 **Radisson SAS Plaza Hotel.** Standing out from other buildings on the city's skyline, northern Europe's largest hotel is the jewel of the Radisson SAS chain. The understated, elegant rooms have gilded fixtures and marble, and many have spectacular views. The Plaza SkyBar on the top floor, the fit-for-a-king breakfast buffets, and luxuriously grand bathtubs all make a stay in this 37-floor glass extravaganza memorable. Since it's next to Oslo S Station, buses and other local transit are convenient. ⊠ *Sonja Henies pl. 3, 0134* ☎ *22–05–80–00* 🖶 *22–05–80–10* ⊕ *www.radissonsas.com* 🖘 *673 rooms, 20 suites* ⚿ *2 restaurants, in-room data ports, indoor pool, health club, sauna, 2 bars, convention center* ▭ *AE, DC, MC, V* ⑩ *CP.*

$–$$ 🏨 **Rica Oslo Hotel.** Close to Oslo S Station, this former office building calls itself an art hotel. There are paintings by Norwegian artists throughout, and many prints of works that are in the National Gallery. Rooms are painted cream and have red-painted wood furnishings. The Rica is popular with business travelers because it's central and has a convention center on the premises. ⊠ *Europarådetspl. 1, 0105* ☎ *23–10–42–00* 🖶 *23–10–42–10* ⊕ *www.rica.no* 🖘 *174 rooms, 2 suites* ⚿ *Restaurant, cable TV, in-room data ports, gym, sauna, bar, convention center* ▭ *AE, DC, MC, V.*

$ 🏨 **First Hotel Millennium.** This boutique hotel is comfortable, with an understated, downtown chic. Guest rooms are simple, with a dark-blue, green, and yellow color theme; all have bathtubs. Several rooms are geared toward women and come with a bathrobe, skin products, and women's magazines. The main-floor lounge has games, a music room, Internet access, and a library. The restaurant-bar, Primo, serves an impressive international menu, which includes quail and swordfish. ⊠ *Tollbugt. 25, 0157* ☎ *21/02–28–00* 🖶 *21/02–28–30* ⊕ *www.firsthotels.com* 🖘 *112 rooms, 10 suites* ⚿ *Restaurant, cable TV, in-room data ports, bar, lounge, meeting rooms* ▭ *AE, DC, MC, V.*

Cafés & Nightlife

More than ever, the Oslo nightlife scene is vibrant and varied. Cafés, restaurant-bars, and jazz clubs are laid-back and mellow. But if you're ready to party, there are many pulsating, live-rock and dance clubs to choose from. Day or night, people are usually out on Karl Johans Gate, and many clubs and restaurants in the central area stay open until the early hours. Aker Brygge, the wharf area, has many bars and some nightclubs, attracting mostly tourists, couples on first dates, and other people willing to spend extra for the waterfront location. Grünerløkka and Grønland have even more bars, pubs, and cafés catering to a younger crowd. A more mature upmarket crowd ventures out to the less-busy west side of Oslo, to Frogner and Bygdøy.

Drinking out is very expensive in Oslo, starting at around NKr 50 for a beer or a mixed drink. Many Norwegians save money by having drinks at friends' houses—called a *forschpiel*—before heading out on the town. Some bars in town remain quiet until 11 PM or midnight when the first groups of forschpiel partyers arrive.

For nightlife listings, pick up a copy of the free monthly paper *Natt og Dag* or Friday's edition of *Avis 1*.

BARS & LOUNGES With its 1970s theme, **Café Con Bar** (✉ Brugt. 11, Grønland ☎ 22–05–02–00), is one of Oslo's trendy crowd pleasers. The kitchen closes at 10 and guest DJs spin on weekends. For cheap beer and an informal crowd, visit the popular student hangout **Stargate Pub** (✉ Grønlandsleiret 33, Grønland ☎ 22–04–13–77) at Brugata, just alongside the bridge. **Choice Bar** (✉ Grønlandsleiret 38, Grønland ☎ 22–12–23–00) opposite Stargate Pub, is another low-key dive bar. Down the street from Choice and Stargate, try **Olympen** (✉ Grønlandsleiret 15, Grønland ☎ 22–17–28–08) to experience 1950s deco and Bulgarian folk bands in a large barnlike setting. The clientele is friendly and the atmosphere always relaxed. **Parkteatret** (✉ Olaf Ryes pl. 11, Grünerløkka ☎ 22–35–63–00), set in a converted art deco theater, has either theater, film, live music, or DJs every night of the week.

If you're more partial to lounging than drinking, try an English-style pub **Bristol** (✉Kristian IVs gt. 7, Sentrum ☎22–82–60–00). **Onkel Donald** (✉Universitetsgt. 26, Sentrum ☎ 23–35–63–10) is the trendiest meeting place in the center and has a capacity for hundreds. For a change of pace, try **Lorrys** (✉Parkvn. 12, Sentrum ☎22–69–69–04), behind the Royal Palace grounds. It has stuffed wildlife and early-20th-century sketches of famous Norwegians adorning the walls. It also advertises 180 different types of beer, but don't be surprised if not all of them are in stock.

Serious beer drinkers may find **Oslo Mikrobryggeriet** (✉ Bogstadvn. 6, Majorstuen ☎ 22–56–97–76) worth a stop. Eight different beers are brewed on the premises, including the increasingly popular Oslo Pils. The **Underwater Bar** (✉ Dalsbergstein 4, St. Hans Haugen ☎ 22–46–05–26) is a pub with an undersea theme, complete with fish tanks and scuba gear, and live opera on Tuesday and Thursday at 9 PM.

CAFÉS As a mark of Oslo's growing cosmopolitanism, the city now has a Continental café culture, with bohemian coffeehouses and chic cafés dotting the sidewalks. Grünerløkka especially has lots of cafés to suit every taste; they're great for people-watching and whiling away warm summer afternoons.

Café Bacchus (✉ Dronningensgt. 27, Sentrum ☎ 22–33–34–30), in the old Basarhall at the rear of Oslo Domkirke, is tiny but serves a mean brownie. Background music is classical during the day, jazz at the night. With its mulitcolor furniture, oversize coffee mugs, and children's play area, **Clodion Art Café** (✉ Bygdøy Allé 63, Frogner ☎ 22–44–97–26) is popular with families.

For a slightly bohemian experience, head to **Fru Hagen** (✉ Thorvald Meyers gt. 40, Grünerløkka ☎22–35–68–71), with its classical-looking chandeliers and elegant velvet-furnished sofas. Aim for a window seat to check out the passing traffic. **Glazed & Amused** (⊠ Vestheimgt. 4B, Frogner ☎ 22–56–25–18) offers a twist on a normal coffee shop, since you can paint your own ceramic mug here. A cup of coffee to go takes on new meaning.

Kaffebrenneriet (⊠ Storgt. 2, Sentrum) is Oslo's answer to Starbucks, with good coffee and shops throughout town. Head to the **Tea Lounge** (⊠ Thorvald Meyers gt. 33B, Grünerløkka ☎ 22–37–07–07) for alcoholic and nonalcoholic tea drinks. It's very stylish, with mellow music, a mosaic tile bar, picture windows, and high-backed plush red sofas, and it attracts a trendy crowd.

FESTIVALS The popular outdoor music festival **Norwegian Wood** (☎ 67/10–34–50 ⊕ www.norwegianwood.no) is held at the Frognerbadet (Frogner Swimming Pool) in June. Begun in the early '90s, the festival hosts performers such as Iggy Pop and Bob Dylan as well as fledgling Norwegian bands. The large **Øya Music Festival** (⊕ www.oyafestivalen.com) is held at Middelalderparken in Gamlebyen August 10–13 and features well-known bands, such as Franz Ferdinand and Sissy Wish.

GAY BARS For information about gay and lesbian clubs and bars in Oslo, you can read *Blikk*, the gay newsletter; check out www.gaysir.no; or call **LLH** (Landsforening for Lesbisk og Homofil Frigjøring; ☎ 22–41–11–33), the national gay and lesbian liberation association. A fixture on Oslo's gay scene since the 1970s, **London Pub** (⊠ C. J. Hambros pl. 5, Sentrum ☎ 22–70–87–00) has a piano bar on the top floor and Sunday theme parties. A younger breed of clientele frequents the bar **Chairs** on the ground floor. A popular spot is **Soho** (⊠ Kirkegt. 34, Sentrum ☎ 22–42–91–00), a large venue with nightclub, lounge, and bar areas, and a separate stage with live shows or DJs spinning the decks.

JAZZ CLUBS Norwegians take their jazz seriously. Every August, the **Oslo Jazz Festival** (⊠ Tollbugt. 28, Sentrum ☎ 22–42–91–20) brings in major international artists and attracts big crowds. **Blå** (⊠ Brennerivn. 9C, Grünerløkka ☎ 22–20–91–81), on the Akers River, is considered the leading club for jazz and related sounds in the Nordic countries. The riverside patio is popular in summer. At **Herr Nilsen** (⊠ C. J. Hambros pl. 5, Sentrum ☎ 22–33–54–05), some of Norway's most celebrated jazz artists perform in a stylish space. There's live music three nights a week and jazz on Saturday and Sunday afternoon. **Stortorvets Gjæstgiveri** (⊠ Grensen 1, Sentrum ☎ 23–35–63–60) often presents New Orleans–style jazz on Thursday and Saturday afternoon from 1:30 to 5 PM.

MUSIC CLUBS At Oslo's numerous rock clubs, the cover charges are low, the crowds young and boisterous, and the music loud. **Oslo Spektrum** (⊠ Sonia Henies pl. 2, Sentrum ☎ 22–05–29–00), one of Norway's largest live-music venues, is just behind the Oslo City shopping center. Past acts have included big names such as Radiohead and Britney Spears. The lineup at **Rockefeller/John Dee** (⊠ Torggt. 16, Sentrum ☎ 22–20–32–32) features everything from hard-rock to alternative and hip-hop acts, including Nick Cave, Blondie, and Ashe.

NIGHTCLUBS Most dance clubs open late, so the beat doesn't really start until midnight. Many establishments have a minimum age for entry, which can be as high as 25. There's also usually a cover of around NKr 50–NKr 100. **Cosmopolite** (✉ Møllergt. 26, Sentrum ☏ 22–20–78–76) has a big dance floor and plays music from all over the world, especially Latin America. **Galleriet** (✉ Kristian IVs gt. 12, Sentrum ☏ 22–42–29–46), a hot spot in town, has a live jazz club, a disco, and a bar spread over its four art-bedecked floors. Oslo's beautiful people congregate at **Lille** (✉ Bygdøy allé 5, Bygdøy ☏ 22–44–80–44) on the west side of Oslo. **Lipp** (✉ Olav Vs gt. 2, Sentrum ☏ 22–82–40–60) is an upscale nightclub, bar, and restaurant. Serious clubbers should try **Skansen** (✉ Rådhusgt. 25, Sentrum ☏ 22–42–28–88) for house and techno music. It has a good dance floor and DJs on weekends.

Most of the big hotels have discos that appeal to the over-30 crowd. **Smuget** (✉ Rosenkrantz gt. 22, Sentrum ☏ 22–42–52–62) is an institution: it hosts live rock and blues bands every night except Sunday, when crowds flock to the in-house discotheque.

Sports & the Outdoors

Oslo's natural surroundings and climate make it ideally suited to outdoor pursuits. The Oslo fjord and its islands, the forested woodlands called the *marka,* and as many as 18 hours of daylight in summer all make the Norwegian capital an irresistible place for outdoor activities. Just 15 minutes north of the city center by tram is the **Oslomarka**, where locals ski in winter and swim in the lakes or hike in summer. The area contains 27 small *hytter* (cabins), which are often available free of charge for backpackers on foot or on skis. These can be reserved through the **Den Norske Turistforening** (✉ Storgt. 3, Sentrum ☏ 22–82–28–00), which has maps of the marka surrounding Oslo as well as equipment for rent, and other information; it also organizes events. The **Villmarkshuset** (✉ Christian Krohgs gt. 16, Sentrum ☏ 22–05–05–22) is an equipment, activities, and excursion center specializing in hiking, climbing, hunting, fishing, cycling, and canoeing. You can rent a canoe from here, drop it into the Akers River at the rear of the store, and paddle out into the Oslo fjord. There's also an indoor climbing wall, a pistol range, and a diving center and swimming pool. Books and maps are also available. The **Oslo Archipelago** is a favorite destination for sunbathing urbanites, who hop ferries to their favorite isles.

Beaches

Beaches are scattered throughout the archipelago. Sun-loving Scandinavians pack every patch of sand during the long summer days to make up for lack of light in winter. The most popular beach is at Huk (on the Bygdøy peninsula), one portion of which is for nude bathing. A family beach is located nearby at Paradisbukta. To get to the beach, follow signs along Huk Aveny from the Folk and Viking Ship museums. You can also take Bus 30A, marked "Bygdøy," to its final stop. To get to the archipelago of island beaches on the Oslo fjord alongside Aker Brygge, take a ferry leaving from the southern pier of Vippetangen in summer. To get to Vippetangen, take Bus 60 from town or walk to the Forsvarsmuseet (Armed Forces Museum) on Akershusstranda and look for the signs. These islands are great for bathing and relaxing, and one of them, Hovedøya, has monastery ruins dating from 1100.

Biking

Oslo is a great biking city. One scenic ride starts at Aker Brygge and takes you along the harbor to the Bygdøy peninsula, where you can visit the museums or cut across the fields next to the royal family's summerhouse. **Syklistenes Landsforening** (National Organization of Cyclists; ✉ Storgata 23D, Sentrum ☎ 22–47–30–30) sells books and maps for cycling holidays in Norway and abroad and gives friendly, free advice.

Glåmdal Cycledepot (✉ Waldemar Thranes gt. 51, Grünerløkka ☎ 22–83–52–08), rents bikes and equipment, including helmets. The store also offers five different sightseeing tours and has maps of the area for those braving it on their own. If you feel like roughing the terrain of the Holmenkollen marka, you can rent mountain bikes from **Tomm Murstad** (✉ Tryvannsvn. 2, Holmenkollen ☎ 22–13–95–00) in summer. Just take T-bane line 1 to Frognerseteren and get off at Voksenkollen Station.

Hiking & Running

Head for the woods surrounding Oslo, the marka, for jogging or walking; there's an abundance of trails, and many are lighted. Frogner Park has many paths, and you can jog or hike along the Aker River, but take extra care late at night or early in the morning. Or you can take the Sognsvann trikk to the end of the line and walk or jog along Sognsvann Lake.

Sailing

Spend a sunny summer afternoon at Oslo's harbor, Aker Brygge, admiring the docked boats; or venture out into the fjords on a charter or tour. Sky-high masts and billowing white sails give the **Christian Radich** (☎ 22–47–82–70) a majestic, old-fashioned style. This tall ship makes nine different sailing trips, varying from a three-day voyage to an autumn sail across the Atlantic. Although you aren't required to have prior sailing experience, do expect rough seas, high waves, lots of rain, and being asked to participate in crew-members' tasks. For general information on boating, call, the Royal Norwegian Sailing Association, **Kongelig Norsk Seilforening** (☎ 23–27–56–00).

Skiing

Cross-country, downhill, telemarking, and snowboarding—whatever your snow-sport pleasure, Oslo has miles of easily accessible outdoor areas minutes from the center of town. Nine alpine ski areas have activities until late at night. More than 2,600 km (1,600 mi) of prepared cross-country ski trails run deep into the forest, of which 90 km (50 mi) are lighted for special evening tours.

The **Skiforeningen** (✉ Kongevn. 5, 0787 ☎ 22–92–32–00) provides national snow-condition reports and can give tips on cross-country trails. They also offer cross-country classes for young children (3- to 7-year-olds), downhill classes for older children (7- to 12-year-olds), and both kinds of classes, as well as instruction in telemark-style racing and snowboarding techniques, for adults.

Among the **flood-lighted trails in the Oslomarka** are the **Bogstad** (3½ km [2 mi]), marked for the disabled and blind; the **Lillomarka** (25 km [15½ mi]); and the **Østmarka** (33 km [20½ mi]).

You can rent downhill and cross-country skis from **Tomm Murstad Skiservice** (⊠ Tryvannsvn. 2, Holmenkollen ☎ 22–13–95–00) at the Tryvann T-bane station. This is a good starting point for skiing; although there are few downhill slopes in this area, a plethora of cross-country trails exist for every level of skill. Oslo's most accessible ski center is the **Tryvann Winter Park** (⊠ Tryvannsveien 64, Holmenkollen ☎ 40/46–27–00 ⊕ www.tryvann.no). It has 11 downhill slopes, six lifts, and a terrain park with a half-pipe for snowboarders. It's open weekdays until 10 PM.

Shopping

Oslo is the best place in the country for buying anything Norwegian. Popular souvenirs include knitwear, wood and ceramic trolls, wood spoons, boxes with rosemaling, gold and silver jewelry, items make from pewter, smoked salmon, caviar, *akvavit* (a white spirit), chocolate, and goat cheese.

Established Norwegian brands include Porsgrund porcelain, Hadeland and Magnor glass, David Andersen jewelry, and Husfliden handicrafts. You may also want to look for popular, classical, or folk music CDs; English translations of Norwegian books; or clothing by a Norwegian designer.

Prices in Norway, as in all of Scandinavia, are generally much higher than in other European countries. Prices of handmade articles, such as knitwear, are controlled, making comparison shopping useless. Otherwise, shops have both sales and specials—look for the words *salg* and *tilbud*. In addition, if you are a resident of a country other than Norway, Sweden, Finland, or Denmark, you can have the Norwegian Value Added Tax (*moms*) refunded at the airport when you leave the country. When you make a purchase, you must clearly state your country of residence in order to have the necessary export document filled in by store staff.

Department Stores

GlasMagasinet (⊠ Stortorvet 8, Sentrum ☎ 22–90–87–00), opposite Oslo Komkirke, is more accurately an amalgam of shops under one roof rather than a true department store. Many of its stores sell handcrafted items made with glass, silver, and pewter. Traditionally, families visit GlasMagasinet at Christmastime, so the store is usually open on Sunday in December. **Steen & Strøm** (⊠ Kongensgt. 23, Sentrum ☎ 22–00–40–45), one of Oslo's first department stores, sells the usual: cosmetics, clothing, books, and accessories. It also has a well-stocked floor of accoutrements for outdoor activities.

Shopping Centers

Aker Brygge, Norway's first major shopping center, is right on the water across from the Tourist Information Center at Vestbanen. Shops are open until 8 most days, and some open on Sunday. **ByPorten** (✉ Jernbanetorget 6, Sentrum ☎ 23–36–21–60) is a shopping center with about 30 fashion, food, and gift stores next to Oslo S Station. **Gunerius Shopping Center** (✉ Storgata 32, Grønland ☎ 22–17–10–97) is set on three levels and caters to the more price-conscious shopper with budget stores for shoes, clothing, and books as well as a large supermarket. **Oslo City** (✉ Stenersgt. 1, Sentrum ☎ 815/44–033), at the other end of downtown, with access to the street from Oslo S Station, is the city's largest indoor mall, but the shops are run-of-the-mill, and the restaurants mostly serve fast food. The elegant **Paleet** (✉ Karl Johans gt. 39–41, between Universitetsgt. and Rosenkrantz gt., Sentrum ☎ 22–03–38–88) opens up into a grand, marbled atrium and has many clothing, accessories, and food stores, including a basement food court.

Shopping Neighborhoods

Basarhallene, the arcade behind the cathedral, is worth a browse for glass and crystal and handicrafts made in Norway. Walk 15 minutes west of the city center and you can wander up the tree-lined Bygdøy Allé and browse the fashionable **Frogner** and **Bygdøy** areas, which are brimming with modern and antique-furniture stores, interior design shops, food shops, art galleries, haute couture, and Oslo's beautiful people. The streets downtown around **Karl Johans Gate** draw many of Oslo's shoppers. The concentration of department stores is especially high in this part of town. **Majorstuen** starts at the T-bane station with the same name and proceeds down Bogstadveien to the Royal Palace. There's a flower market on Stortorget in front of the Oslo Cathedral, and a fruit-and-vegetable market at Youngstorget. Every Saturday, a flea market is open at **Vestkanttorget,** at Amaldus Nilsens plass near Frognerparken. **Grünerløkka,** a 15-minute walk north of the center, is blooming with trendy new and bohemian fashion boutiques.

Specialty Stores

ANTIQUES Norwegian rustic antiques (those objects considered of high artistic and historic value) cannot be taken out of the country, but just about anything else can with no problem. The Frogner district has many antiques shops, especially on Skovveien and Thomas Heftyes Gate between Bygdøy Allé and Frogner plass. Deeper in the heart of Majorstuen, Industrigate is famous for its good selection of shops. The rare volumes at **Damms Antiqvariat** (✉ Tollbugt. 25, Sentrum ☎ 22–41–04–02) will catch the eye of any antiquarian book buff, with volumes in English as well as Norwegian. **Esaias Solberg** (✉ Kirkeristen, Sentrum ☎ 22–86–24–80), behind Oslo Cathedral, has exceptional small antiques. **Kaare Berntsen** (✉ Universitetsgt. 12, Sentrum ☎ 22–99–10–10) sells paintings, furniture, and small antique items. **Marsjandisen** (✉ Fridtjof Nansens pl. 2, Sentrum ☎ 22–42–71–68), specializes in Hadeland glass, silver, cups, and mugs. **West Sølv og Mynt** (✉ Niels Juels gt. 27, Frogner ☎ 22–55–75–83) has the largest selection of antique silver in town.

ART GALLERIES The **Ceramo Sculpture Gallery** (✉ Olaf Ryes pl. 3, Grünerløkka ☎ 22–38–14–26) sells African artifacts that are functional as well as aesthetically pleasing. **Galleri Elenor** (✉ Kirkevn. 50, Frogner ☎ 22–46–16–90), near Frognerparken west of the center, displays modern Norwegian and international art. **Galleri Markveien** (✉ Markveien 30, Grünerløkka ☎ 93/42–10–65) displays the work of the commercially successful artist Tone Granberg, who uses the same abstract motif in every one of her paintings. **Kunstnernes Hus** (The Artists' House; ✉ Wergelandsvn. 17, Sentrum ☎ 22–85–34–10 🖷 22–85–34–11 ⊕ www.kunstnerneshus.no) exhibits contemporary art, and hosts an art show every fall. The gallery also has a bar/restaurant that is a weekend hot spot for artists and local celebrities.

BOOKS In Oslo bookshops, you can always find some English-language books. You may want to pick up some classic works by Henrik Ibsen and Knut Hamsun in translation, as well as some by contemporary writers such as Jostein Gaarder, Linn Ullmann, and Nikolaj Frobenius.

ARK Qvist (✉ Drammensvn. 16, Sentrum ☎ 22–54–26–00), considered Oslo's "English bookshop," specializes in fiction, crime, and Norwegian-Scandinavian translations. **Avalon** (✉ Paleet, Karl Johans gt. 39–41, Sentrum ☎ 22–33–33–08) has Norway's largest selection of science fiction and fantasy (all in English) as well as comics and board, computer, and card games. **Bjørn Ringstrøms Antikvariat** (✉ Ullevålsvn. 1, Sentrum ☎ 22–20–78–05), carries a wide selection of used books and records.

Bokkilden Interbok (✉ Akersgt. 34, Sentrum ☎ 23–31–77–00) stocks an amazing 6,000 maps as well as two walls of travel books. Head to **Nomaden** (✉ Uranienborgvn. 4, Frogner ☎ 22–56–25–30), behind the Royal Palace, for travel-related books and guidebooks as well as photography books and equipment. **Norli** (✉ Universitetsgt. 24, Sentrum ☎ 22–00–43–00) is a bookstore chain that has the largest number of titles in Norway. This store keep a substantial number of Scandinavian-language fiction and travel books on hand. **Tanum** (✉ Karl Johans gt. 43, Sentrum ☎ 22–41–11–00) is strong in the arts, health and healing, and travel. **Tronsmo** (✉ Kristian Augusts gt. 19, Sentrum ☎ 22–99–03–99) carries books on such topics as politics, feminism, gay and lesbian interests, and movies, as well as mainstream fiction and nonfiction. There are English-language books, plus a comic-book section in the basement.

EMBROIDERY **Husfliden** (✉ Møllergt. 4, Sentrum ☎ 24–14–12–80) sells embroidery kits, including do-it-yourself bunader, the national costumes of Norway.

FASHION & **H & M** (Hennes & Mauritz; ✉ Oslo City and other locations, Sentrum
SPORTSWEAR ☎ 22–17–13–90) carries fresh, up-to-date looks at reasonable prices. **Kamikaze** (✉ Hegdehaugsvn. 24, Majorstuen ☎ 22–60–20–25) and the nearby **Kamikaze Donna** (✉ Hegdehaugsvn. 27, Majorstuen ☎ 22–59–38–45) specialize in men's and women's designer fashions, mainly from France and Italy. **Soul** (✉ Vognhallene, Karenlyst Allé 18, Skøyen ☎ 22–55–00–13) carries Norwegian and international labels from major London, Milan, and Paris fashion houses; shoes and accessories; and home products.

Grünerløkka, north of the city center, is becoming a major shopping district filled with hip little boutiques. **Den Kule Mage** (The Round Stomach ✉ Markveien 55, Grünerløkka ☎ 22–35–76–90) has every maternal item a mother could need and features Norway's only baby café, smartly decorated as a nursery. **Probat** (✉ Thorvald Meyers gt. 54, Grünerløkka ☎ 22–35–20–70) sells just hip T-shirts from all around the world. **Rebella** (✉ Thorvald Meyers gt. 52, Grünerløkka ☎ 22–37–94–22), next door to Probat, showcases edgier clothes by young Norwegian fashion designers.

Norwegian sportswear chain stores are easy to spot in the city's malls and on Karl Johans Gate, but also consider checking out some specialty shops. **Peak Performance** (✉ Bogstadvn. 13, Majorstuen ☎ 22–96–00–91) is a top choice for fashionable sportswear. **Skandinavisk Høyfjellutstyr** (✉ Bogstadvn. 1, Majorstuen ☎ 23–33–43–80) has a great selection of traditional mountain sportswear.

FOOD Throughout Oslo, there are bakeries, delis, fishmongers, and gourmet food shops to tempt all tastes. **Åpent Bakeri** (✉ Inkognito Terrasse 1, Frogner ☎ 22–44–94–70) bakes the city's best-tasting bread for devoted locals and top restaurants. **Fjelberg Fisk og Vilt** (✉ Bygdøy Allé 56, Frogner ☎ 22–44–60–41) has a reputation for its high-quality fish and seafood, including salmon (smoked, tartar, fresh, and cured), lobster, shrimp, and fish soup. A good restaurant is also on the premises. **Hotel Havana** (✉ Thorvald Meyers gt. 36, Grünerløkka ☎ 23–23–03–23) is a hip delicatessen with cheeses, Cuban coffee and cigars, tapas plates, and fresh fish. **Skafferiet** (✉ Elisenbergvn. 7, Frogner ☎ 22–44–52–96), open daily from 10 to 10, is popular with sophisticated Oslo residents for its gourmet foods and fresh flowers.

GLASS, CHINA, The shops at **Basarhallene,** behind the cathedral, sell glass and ceram-
CERAMICS & ics. **Gastronaut** (✉ Bygdøy Allé 56, Frogner ☎ 22–44–60–90) sells top-
PEWTER quality china, cutlery, linen, and glass, as well as spices and condiments from Spain and Italy.

If there's no time to visit a glass factory outside of town, department stores are the best option: **GlasMagasinet** (✉ Stortorvet 8, Sentrum ☎ 22–90–87–00) stocks both European and Norwegian designs in glass, pewter, and silver. **Lenes Glass** (✉ Markveien 30, Grünerløkka ☎ 22–35–47–15) is a glassblower producing modern vases, glasses, and gifts with distinctive blue and gray tones. **Norway Designs** (✉ Stortingsgt. 28, Sentrum ☎ 23–11–45–10) showcases Scandinavian art glass, kitchenware, ceramics, silver, and other household items.

HANDICRAFTS **Basarhallene,** the arcade behind the cathedral, is worth a browse for handicrafts made in Norway. **Heimen Husflid A/S** (✉ Rosenkrantz gt. 8, enter at Kristian IVs gt., Sentrum ☎ 23–21–42–00) has small souvenir items and a department dedicated to traditional Norwegian costumes. **Husfliden** (✉ Møllergt. 4, Sentrum ☎ 22–14–12–80), one of the finest stores for handmade goods in the country, has an even larger selection than that at Heimen Husflid. You can find pewter, ceramics, knits, and Norwegian handmade textiles, furniture, felt boots and slippers, loafers, sweaters, traditional costumes, wrought-iron accessories, Christmas ornaments, and wooden kitchen accessories. **Norsk Kunsthandverkeri** (✉ Munkedamsvn. 57, Sentrum ☎ 22–94–40–80) has beautiful, colorful pieces.

JEWELRY   Gold and precious stones are no bargain, but silver and enamel jewelry and Viking period productions can be. Some silver pieces are made with Norwegian stones, particularly pink thulite. **David-Andersen** (✉ Karl Johans gt. 20, Sentrum ☎ 24–14–88–00 ✉ Bogstadvn. 23, Majorstuen ☎ 22–59–50–00) is Norway's best-known goldsmith. He makes stunning silver and gold designs. The **ExpoArte** (✉ Drammensvn. 40, Frogner ☎ 22–55–93–90) gallery specializes in custom pieces and displays the work of avant-garde Scandinavian jewelers. **Heyerdahl** (✉ Roald Amundsensgt. 6, Sentrum ☎ 22–41–59–18), near City Hall, is a good dependable jeweler.

KNITWEAR   Norway is famous for its hand-knit, colorful wool sweaters, and even mass-produced (machine-knit) models are of top quality. Prices are regulated and they are always lower than buying a Norwegian sweater abroad.

Boa (✉ Thorvald Meyers gt. 50, Grünerløkka ☎ 22–38–04–91) produces innovative and modern knitwear designs. **Maurtua Husflid** (✉ Akershusstranda, Sentrum ☎ 22–41–31–64), on the waterfront beneath Akershus Castle, has a large selection of sweaters and blanket coats. The designer at **Oleana** (✉ Stortingsgt. 8, Sentrum ☎ 22–33–31–63), Solveig Hisdahl, takes traditional women's sweater patterns and updates them in elegant ways. **Oslo Sweater Shop** (✉ SAS Scandinavia Hotel, Tullinsgt. 5, Sentrum ☎ 22–11–29–22) is known for having one of the widest selections in the city. **Rein og Rose** (✉ Ruseløkkvn. 3, Sentrum ☎ 22–83–21–39), in the Vika shopping district, has friendly salespeople and a good selection of knitwear, yarn, and textiles. **William Schmidt** (✉ Fridtjof Nansens pl. 9, Sentrum ☎ 22–42–02–88), founded in 1853, is Oslo's oldest shop. The firm specializes in sweaters and souvenirs.

Oslo A to Z

To research prices, get advice from other travelers, and book travel arrangements, visit www.fodors.com

AIR TRAVEL TO & FROM OSLO

CARRIERS   SAS Scandinavian Airlines is the main carrier, with both international and domestic flights. Norwegian Air Shuttle operates from eight cities in Norway and has flights from southern Europe and London. Other major airlines serving Oslo Airport include British Airways, Air France, Aeroflot, Finnair, KLM, and Lufthansa. *See* the Smart Travel Tips chapter for airline phone numbers and Web sites.

AIRPORTS & TRANSFERS

Oslo Airport is 45 km (28 mi) north of the city. The spacious airport has huge windows that give excellent views of the landscape and the Nordic light. State-of-the-art weather systems have decreased the number of delayed flights, but always check with your airline regarding the status of your flight.

🛪 **Oslo Airport** ☎ 64–81–20–00, 815/50–250 flight information ⊕ www.osl.no.

AIRPORT   Oslo Airport is a 50-minute car ride via the E6 from Oslo's city center.
TRANSFERS   From Oslo S Station, it's a 19-minute ride by Flytoget (express train,

NKr 150 one-way), with trains scheduled every 10 minutes (4:40 AM–1:16 AM).

Flybussen buses depart from Oslo Bussterminalen Galleriet every 20 minutes and reach Oslo Airport approximately 45 minutes later (NKr 100 one-way, NKr 150 round-trip). Going to the airport, they operate daily from 6 AM to 9:40 PM (7:40 on Saturay night). Going from the airport to Oslo, the buses operate daily from 7:30 AM to 11:30 PM (11 on Saturday night).

Flybussekspressen can be picked up at any one of 114 stops, including Oslo S Station, Stortinget, Nationaltheatret, and Aker Brygge on its way to the airport. There are two bus lines following two different routes to the airport. One traverses the inner city, while the other follows the ring roads. Passengers simply hail the bus from bus stops on the street. Buses leave twice per hour and the trip costs NKr 100–NKr 140 depending on where you get on. Call the information number for details of the routes.

There is a taxi line at the front of the airport. By taxi the trip into town takes about 50 minutes and is extremely expensive—upward of NKr 600—so try to catch the Flytoget. All taxi reservations should be made through the Oslo Airport Taxi no later than 20 minutes before pickup time.

For Ryan Air flights from Oslo's second airport, Torp at Sandefjord, take the Torp Express Buss from the main bus terminal at the rear of Galleri Oslo. Buses depart every hour and the journey takes two hours.

🚏 Taxis, Shuttles & Trains **Flybussekspressen** ☎ 820/21-300 departure information, 820/54-301 recorded information. **Flybussen** ☎ 22-80-49-71. **Flytoget** ☎ 815/00-777. **Oslo Airport Taxi** ☎ 23-23-23-23 dial 1 for direct reservation. **Torp Express Buss** ☎ 23-00-24-00.

BOAT & FERRY TRAVEL

Several ferry lines connect Oslo with the United Kingdom, Denmark, Sweden, and Germany. Color Line sails to Kiel, Germany, and to Hirtshals, Denmark; DFDS Scandinavian Seaways to Copenhagen via Helsingborg, Sweden; and Stena Line to Frederikshavn, Denmark.

A ferry to Hovedøya and other islands in the harbor basin leaves from Aker Brygge (take Bus 60 from Jernbanetorget). These are great spots for picnics and short hikes. From April through September, ferries run between Rådhusbrygge 3, in front of City Hall, and Bygdøy, the western peninsula, where many of Oslo's major museums are located. There is also ferry service from Aker Brygge to the town of Nesodden, as well as to popular summer beach towns along the fjord's coast, including Drøbak.

FARES & SCHEDULES 🚏 **Bygdøfergene Skibs A/S** ☎ 23–35–68–90. **Color Line** ☎ 810/00–811. **DFDS Scandinavian Seaways** ☎ 23–10–68–00 ⊕ www.dfds.no. **Nesodden Bunnefjord Dampskibsselskap** ☎ 23–11–52–20. **Stena Line** ☎ 23–17–91–00.

BUS TRAVEL TO & FROM OSLO

The main bus station, Oslo Bussterminalen, is across from the Oslo S Station. You can buy local bus tickets at the terminal or on the bus. Tickets for long-distance routes on Nor-Way Bussekspress can be purchased here or at travel agencies. Trafikanten provides transit information.

📋 **Nor-Way Bussekspress** ✉ Oslo Bussterminalen Galleriet, Sentrum ☎ 820/21-300, 177 within Oslo 🖶 22-17-59-22 ⊕ www.nor-way.no. **Oslo Bussterminalen** ☎ 23-00-24-00. **Trafikanten** ☎ 815/00-176, 177 within Oslo ⊕ www.trafikanten.no.

BUS TRAVEL WITHIN OSLO

About 50 bus lines, including 16 night buses on weekends, serve the city. Most stop at Jernbanetorget opposite Oslo S Station. Tickets can be purchased from the driver.

CAR RENTAL

📋 Major Agencies in Oslo **Avis** ☎ 64-81-06-60 at Oslo Airport, 815/33-044 downtown. **Europcar** ☎ 64-81-05-60 Oslo Airport, 22-83-12-42 downtown. **Hertz** ☎ 67/16-80-00 at Oslo Airport, 22-21-00-00 downtown.

CAR TRAVEL

The E18 connects Oslo with Göteborg, Sweden (by ferry between Sandefjord and Strömstad, Sweden); Copenhagen, Denmark (by ferry between Kristiansand and Hirtshals, Denmark); and Stockholm directly overland. The land route from Oslo to Göteborg is the E6. All streets and roads leading into Oslo have tollbooths a certain distance from the city center, forming an "electronic ring." The toll is NKr 20 and was implemented to finance road development in and around Oslo. If you have the correct amount in change, drive through one of the lanes marked "Mynt." If you don't, or if you need a receipt, use the "Manuell" lane. Car rentals can be made directly at Oslo Airport or downtown.

If you plan to do any amount of driving in Oslo, buy a copy of the *Stor Oslo* map, available at bookstores and gasoline stations. It may be a small city, but one-way streets and few exit ramps on the expressway make it very easy to get lost.

EMERGENCY SERVICES 📋 **Falken** ☎ 02468. **NAF Car Rescue** (Norwegian Automobile Association) ☎ 810/00-505.

PARKING Oslo Card holders can park for free in city-run street spots or at reduced rates in lots run by the city (P-lots), but pay careful attention to time limits and be sure to ask at the information office exactly where the card is valid. Parking is very difficult in the city—many spaces have one-hour limits and can cost more than NKr 25 per hour. Instead of individual parking meters in P-lots, a machine dispenses validated parking tickets to display in your car windshield. Travelers with disabilities who have valid parking permits from their home country are allowed to park free and with no time limit in specially reserved spaces.

EMBASSIES & CONSULATES

📋 Canada ✉ Wergelandsvn. 7, Sentrum ☎ 22-99-53-00.
📋 New Zealand ✉ Billengstadsletta 19, Billingstad ☎ 66/77-53-30.
📋 U.K. ✉ Thomas Heftyes gt. 8, Frogner ☎ 23-13-27-00 ⊕ www.britain.no.
📋 U.S. ✉ Drammensvn. 18, Sentrum ☎ 22-44-85-50 ⊕ www.usa.no.

INTERNET SERVICE
🚹 **Arctic Internet** ✉ Oslo S Station, Sentrum ☎ 22-17-19-40. **Studenten Nett-Café** ✉ Karl Johans gt. 45, Sentrum ☎ 22-42-56-80.

SUBWAY TRAVEL
Oslo has seven T-bane (subway) lines, which converge at Stortinget Station. The four eastern lines all stop at Tøyen before branching off, whereas the four western lines run through Majorstuen before emerging aboveground for the rest of their routes to the northwestern suburbs. Tickets can be purchased at the stations.
🚹 **Trafikanten** (public transportation information) ✉ Jernbanetorget, Sentrum ☎ 815/00-176, 177 within Oslo ⊕ www.trafikanten.no ⊙ Weekdays 7 AM-8 PM, weekends 8-6.

TAXIS
Taxis are radio dispatched from a central office, and it can take up to 30 minutes to get one during peak hours. Cabs can be ordered from 20 minutes to 24 hours in advance. (If you leave a cab waiting after you've sent for one, there is an additional fee added to your fare.) Special transport, including vans and cabs equipped for people with disabilities, can be ordered. Taxi stands are located all over town, usually near Narvesen newsstands and kiosks. In the center, there are taxi stands at Stortinget in Karl Johans Gate, at Stortorget by the cathedral, at Youngstorget, and at Oslo Central Station. If there are no available taxis after midnight, take a night bus leaving from outside Oslo S Station.

It is possible to hail a cab on the street, but cabs are not allowed to pick up passengers within 100 yards of a stand. It is not unheard of to wait for more than an hour at a taxi stand in the wee hours of the morning, after everyone has left the bars. Never take pirate taxis; all registered taxis should have their roof lights on when they're available. Rates start at NKr 30 for hailed or rank cabs, and NKr 49 for ordered taxis, depending on the time of day.
🚹 **Norgestaxi** ☎ 08000. **Oslo Taxi** ☎ 02323. **Taxi 2** ☎ 02202.

TRAIN TRAVEL
Norway's state railway, NSB (Norges Statsbaner), has two train stations downtown—Oslo Sentralstasjon (Oslo S), and a station at Nationaltheatret. Long-distance domestic and international trains arrive at and leave from Oslo S Station. Suburban commuter trains use one or the other station. Commuter cars reserved for monthly-pass holders are marked with a large black "M" on a yellow circle. Trains marked "C," or InterCity, offer such upgraded services as breakfast and office cars—with phones and power outlets—for an added fee.
🚹 **NSB Customer Service** ☎ 815/00-888.

TRANSPORTATION AROUND OSLO
The subways and most buses and trikken start running at 5:30 AM, with the last run after midnight. On weekends, there's night service on certain routes. Trips on all public transportation within Oslo cost NKr 30, with a one-hour free transfer; tickets that cross municipal boundaries have different rates. It often pays to buy a pass or multiple-travel card,

which includes transfers. A day card *(dagskort)* costs NKr 55 and a seven-day pass costs NKr 190. Tickets can be used on subway, bus, or trikk.

A *flexikort* for NKr 150 is available at Narvesen newsstands, 7-Eleven stores, tourist information offices, T-bane stations, and on some routes; it is valid for eight trips by subway, bus, or trikk. The **Oslo Card** offers unlimited travel on all public transport in greater Oslo. A one-day Oslo Card costs NKr 190, a two-day card NKr 285, and a three-day card NKr 375. Children's cards cost NKr 75, NKr 95, and NKr 125 and a family card costs NKr 395. The cards can be purchased at tourist information offices and hotels. The Oslo Card also includes free admission to museums and sightseeing attractions; free parking in certain public spaces; a miniboat cruise; admission to public swimming pools; discounts on car, ski, and skate rentals; and discounts at specified restaurants and theaters.

VISITOR INFORMATION

The tourist information office in Sentrum is open weekdays 9 to 7 in July, 9 to 5 the rest of the year.

🔢 In Oslo **Oslo Sentralstasjonen (Oslo S Station)** ✉ Jernbanetorget, Sentrum 📠 No phone 🕐 Daily 8 AM–11 PM. **Tourist Information Center in Oslo** ✉ Fridtjof Nansens pl. 5, entrance from Roald Amundsens gt., Sentrum 📞 24-14-77-00 📠 22-42-92-22 🌐 www.visitoslo.com.

SIDE TRIPS FROM OSLO

Drøbak

❶ *35 km (21 mi) south of Oslo off Route E18.*

Drøbak's pretty collection of white wooden houses and small winding streets gives the impression of a typical Sørlander (southern) town, yet it is only one hour's drive from the capital. Oslovians often take day trips to Drøbak to sit by the beach and eat fresh shrimp. During World War II Norwegian forces sunk the German cruiser *Blucher* here. From May to September you can take the scenic one-hour ferry ride from Oslo's Aker Brygge to Drøbak on the **M/S *Prinsessen*** (📞 23/11–52–20).

More than 1,000 species of fish and marine life from the Oslo Fjord are exhibited in the **Drøbak Akvarium** (aquarium). There's a children's area where kids can handle a variety of shellfish, and a special exhibit explains how you can make lutefisk, the Norwegian fish delicacy popular at Christmastime. ✉ *Havnegata* 📞 *64–98–87–80* 🌐 *www.akvarium. net* 💰 *NKr 30* 🕐 *May–Aug., daily 11–5; Sept.–Apr., daily 11–4.*

> **need a break?**
>
> On the main square, stop in **Det Gamle Bageri Ost & Vinstue** (The Old Bakery Wine and Cheese Room; 📞 64–93–21–05) for salads, pies, and hearty fare such as salmon in a mouthwatering sweet-mustard sauce. The wood interior dates from 1740, and classical music soirees are held on weekends.

Jegstad Gård farm, a traditional Norwegian dairy, has animals to visit and horse carriages to ride. Wander along the nature trail or visit the

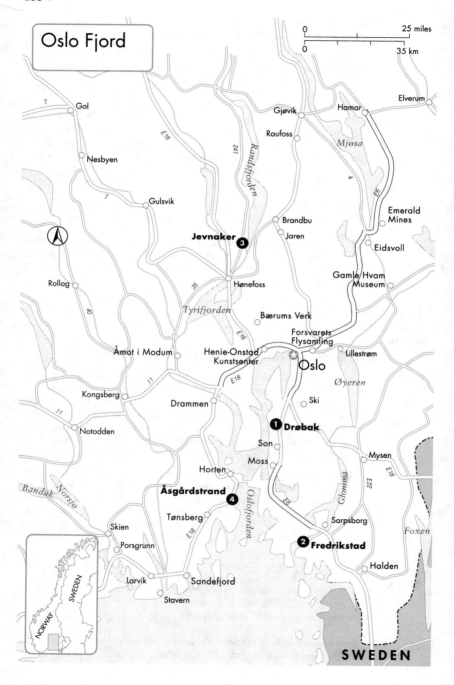

Oslo Fjord

0 25 miles

0 35 km

Elverum

Gol

7

Gjøvik Hamar

E16

Nesbyen

Raufoss

Mjøsa

241

Randsfjorden

4

E6

7

Gulsvik

Brandbu

Emerald
Mines

Jevnaker ❸

Jaren

Eidsvoll

35

Hønefoss

Gamle Hvam
Museum

Rollag

Tyrifjorden

Bærums Verk

40

E16

Forsvarets
Flysamling

Lillestrøm

Åmot i Modum

Henie-Onstad
Kunstsenter

⭐ Oslo

Øyeren

11

E18

Kongsberg

Drammen

Ski

11

❶ **Drøbak**

Notodden

Son

Mysen

Moss

E18

Horten

E6

Glomma

E22

Åsgårdstrand ❹

Oslofjorden

Bandak *Norsjø*

Tønsberg

E18

Sarpsborg

Foxen

Skien

❷ **Fredrikstad**

Porsgrunn

Halden

Larvik Sandefjord

Stavern

NORWAY SWEDEN

SWEDEN

stable, farm museum, and Viking burial mounds. You can play sports or relax on the large lawn. The farm is between Drøbak and Vestby, to the south. ⊠ *Rte. E6, Vestby* ☎ *64–95–00–58* ⊞ *NKr 50* ☉ *Apr.–Aug., Sun. noon–4 (July, daily); by special arrangement rest of yr.*

☺ The inviting **Tregaardens Julehus** (Christmas House) dominates the town's central square. Just around the corner from the post office, this 1876 building was once a mission for seafarers unable to reach Oslo because the fjord was frozen over. Now it's a retail store that sells Christmas wares and gifts such as wooden dolls and mice made of cloth—all handmade by Eva Johansen, the store's creator and owner. Many Norwegian children believe Father Christmas resides in Drøbak because there's a Santa's post office in this store. ⊠ *Main Sq.* ☎ *64–93–41–78.*

Where to Stay

$ ⊞ **Reenskaug Hotel.** Old-fashioned, wooden, and whitewashed, this early-20th-century hotel is on Drøbak's main road. With its traditional Norwegian country-style interior, it is a very Scandinavian place to stay. Ask for Room 213; in 1904 Norway's Nobel Prize for Literature winner Knut Hamsun wrote here. ⊠ *Storgt. 32, 1440* ☎ *64–93–33–60* 🖷 *64–93–36–66* ⊕ *www.reenskaug.no* ➢ *30 rooms* ⚙ *Restaurant, in-room data ports, bar, meeting rooms* ⊟ *AE, DC MC, V.*

Fredrikstad

❷ *34 km (20 mi) south of Moss.*

Norway's oldest fortified city lies peacefully at the mouth of the Glomma, the country's longest river. Its bastions and moat date from the 1600s. After spending time in town browsing the shops and museum, take the ferry to the little island of Hvaler, a popular vacation spot.

In the center of town is ★ **Fredrikstad Domkirke** (Fredrikstad Cathedral). Built in 1860 in a flamboyant neo-Gothic style, it contains stained-glass decorations by Emanuel Vigeland, whose work also adorns Oslo Cathedral. ☎ *69–30–02–80* ⊞ *Free* ☉ *Tues.–Fri. 11–3.*

The **Fredrikstad Museum** documents the town's history in two separate exhibitions and locations. The first focuses on the town's maritime and shipping heritage and has period commercial vessels and sailing boats. The second tells the story of the development of the town and city from 1860 to 1960 through objects related to its industrial, commercial, hospital, and day-to-day life. ☎ *69–95–85–00* ⊞ *NKr 40* ☉ *June–Sept., weekdays 9–4.30, weekends noon–5.*

Fodor'sChoice **Gamlebyen** (Old Town) has been preserved and has museums, art galleries, cafés, artisans' workshops, antiques shops, and old bookstores.
★

Where to Stay

$–$$ ⊞ **Hotel City.** This comfortable, stylish hotel is in the center of downtown, but is still quiet and peaceful. The restaurant serves a mixture of Norwegian and Italian dishes. ⊠ *Nygaardsgt. 44–46, 1607* ☎ *69–38–56–00* 🖷 *69–38–56–01* ➢ *110 rooms* ⚙ *Restaurant, cable TV, sauna, bar, nightclub, convention center, meeting rooms* ⊟ *MC, V.*

Shopping

Glashytte (✉ Torsnesvn. 1 ☎ 69–32–28–12) is a well-known glass-blowing studio and shop; its glassware is exhibited and sold in galleries throughout Norway. You can watch glassblowers perform their magic, creating everything from schnapps glasses to vases in primary colors. If you're in the area, you can place a special order and go see your glass object blown. You can pick it up a few days later after it's been cooled slowly in a kiln, which makes it less fragile.

Jevnaker

❸ *Follow E16 toward Hønefoss, then follow Rte. 241 to Jevnaker, which is about 70 km (42 mi) northwest of Oslo; it's about a 2-hr drive.*

A day trip to Jevnaker combines a drive along the Tyrifjord, where you can see some of the best fjord views in eastern Norway, with a visit to Norway's oldest glassworks, in operation since 1762.

☾ At **Hadeland Glassverk** you can watch artisans blowing glass, or, if you get there early enough, you can blow your own for NKr 75. Both practical table crystal and one-of-a-kind art glass are produced here, and you can buy first-quality pieces as well as seconds in the gift shop. Learn the history of glass at the Glass Museum. For children, there's a Honey House of bees and a Children's House that celebrates Christmas every weekend from April through December. There is also a bakery and a restaurant, Kokkestua, which serves traditional Norwegian meals. ⌖ *Rte. 241, Postboks 85* ☎ *61–31–66–00* ⊕ *www.hadeland-glassverk.no* ▨ *Glass museum NKr 30* ☉ *Weekdays 10–5, Sat. 10–4, Sun. 11–5.*

Åsgårdstrand

❹ *10 km (6 mi) south of Horten.*

Since 1920 the coastal town of Åsgårdstrand has been a popular vacation and bathing spot. A couple of decades before that, it was known as an artists' colony for outdoor painting, attracting Edvard Munch, Fritz Thaulow, and others. In summer the local tourist office can arrange guided history tours of the area, led by well-versed guides.

Fodor'sChoice ★ **Munchs lille hus** (Munch's little house) was the summerhouse and studio in which the artist spent seven summers. Now a museum, it was here that he painted *Girls on the Bridge* and earned a reputation as a ladies' man. ✉ *Munchsgt.* ☎ *33–08–21–31* ▨ *NKr 40* ☉ *May and Sept., weekends 11–7; June–Aug., Tues.–Sun. 11–7.*

Where to Stay

$ ▥ **Åsgårdstrand Hotell.** Steps away from the harbor, the Åsgårdstrand has large, airy rooms, some with spectacular ocean views. Perfect for those who want to be part of the town's active sailing culture, it even has a harbor that guests can use. ✉ *Havnegt. 6, 3167* ☎ *33–08–10–40* ▤ *33–08–10–77* ⊕ *www.asgardstrand-hotell.no* ⚓ *73 rooms, 5 suites* ⚒ *Restaurant, cable TV, bar, sauna* ▣ *AE, DC, MC, V.*

Side Trips from Oslo A to Z

BOAT & FERRY TRAVEL

The most luxurious and scenic way to see the region around the Oslo Fjord is by boat. There are guest marinas at just about every port. An underground tunnel links Drøbak, on the east side of the fjord, with Hurum, on the west side, just north of Horten. The tunnel toll is NKr 55. Contact Drøbak Turistinformasjon for schedule information. You can also take a ferry, the M/S *Prinsessen,* from Aker Brygge in Oslo to Drøbak for NKr 50.

M/S *Prinsessen* ⊠ Stranden 1 ☎ 23/11-52-20 ⊕ www.nbds.no.

BUS TRAVEL

The trip on Bus 541 or 542 from Strandgata at the corner of Prinsensgata in Oslo to Drøbak affords great glimpses of the fjord (and bathers in summer). The trip takes an hour, and buses depart hourly at 15 minutes to and 15 minutes past the hour during the week, with reduced service on weekends. Bus 100 (E6 Ekspress) departs during the day at 7:15 AM, 12:15 PM, and 3:15 PM, stopping at Svindsen, where you can catch a local bus to Halden.

Nor-Way Bussekspress ☎ 815/44-444 ⊕ www.nor-way.no.

CAR TRAVEL

Follow Route E18 southeast from Oslo to Route E6. Follow signs to Drøbak and Son. Continue through Moss, following signs to Halden, farther south on E6. The road then takes you north to Sarpsborg, where you can turn left to Fredrikstad.

TRAIN TRAVEL

Trains for Halden leave from Oslo S Station and take two hours to make the 136-km (85-mi) trip, with stops in Moss, Fredrikstad, and Sarpsborg.

VISITOR INFORMATION

Drøbak Drøbak Turistinformasjon ☎ 64-93-50-87 ⊕ www.drobakguiden.no. **Fredrikstad** Fredrikstad Turistkontor ⊠ Turistsentret vøstre Brohode ⊠ 1632 Gamle Fredrikstad ☎ 69-30-60-00 ⊕ www.fredrikstad.kommune.no. **Horten and Åsgårdstrand** Horten Turist Kontor ⊠ Tollbugt. 1A, 3187 Horten ☎ 33-03-17-08.

SOUTHERN NORWAY

In summer, many of Oslo's residents migrate to the forests of Telemark and the sunny southern coast. Southern Norway is an ideal area for those who want to get close to nature, with a mild summer climate and terrain varying from inland mountains and forests to coastal flatland.

South of Telemark, you reach the famed beaches and fjords of the coast. Many splendid points mark the route of the North Sea Road. Beginning in the relaxed resort town of Kristiansand, the road winds west along the major section of Norway's southern coast, Sørlandet. Wide, sun-kissed, inviting beaches have their blue waters warmed by the Gulf

Stream. Sandy terrain turns to coastal flatlands, inland mountain peaks and green forests ideal for cycling, hiking, and mountaineering. Freshwater lakes and rivers, and this section of the ocean, are some of the best places to go salmon fishing—they're also superb for canoeing, kayaking, and rafting. The region is the perfect habitat for such wildlife as beavers, deer, foxes, and many birds. When the North Sea Road reaches its final destination, it's in a landscape of fjords, islands, mountains, and valleys. Stavanger, Norway's oil capital, is here; a cosmopolitan city yet with small-town charm, it has some of the country's best restaurants, hotels, and cultural life.

Numbers in the margin correspond to points of interest on the Southern Norway map

Skien

❶ *88 km (55 mi) south of Kongsberg on Rtes. 32 and 36.*

Best known as the birthplace of playwright Henrik Ibsen, Skien, with a population of 50,000, is the capital of the Telemark region. Skien celebrates its favorite son every summer with the **Ibsen-Kultur-festival** (☎ 35–90–55–20), which includes concerts as well as plays.

The **Telemark Museum at Brekkeparken,** housed in a 1780 manor house, displays folk art from the 18th and 19th centuries. Brekkeparken is one of northern Europe's largest tulip parks, with more than 25,000 tulips. The exhibit "90 Years of Scouting" chronicles the activities of Norwegian boy scouts in the Skien area. ⊠ *Øvregt. 41* ☎ *35–54–45–00* ⊕ *www. telemark.museum.no* ⊠ *NKr 50* ☉ *Mid-May–Aug., daily 10–6.*

Now the Henrik Ibsen Museum, **Venstøp** looks just as it did when the Ibsen family lived here from 1835 to 1843. The dark attic was the inspiration for the *Wild Duck*. This house, part of Skien's County Museum, is 5 km (3 mi) northwest of the city. ⊠ *Venstøphøgda 74* ☎ *35–52–57–49* ⊠ *NKr 50* ☉ *Mid-May–Aug., daily 10–6; otherwise by appointment.*

Where to Stay & Eat

★ **$$$$** ✕ **Boden Spiseri.** The consistently excellent kitchen here serves French-influenced Norwegian dishes. The fillet of reindeer is rich and delicious. For dessert, try the strawberry ice cream or the passion-fruit cake. ⊠ *Landbrygga 5* ☎ *35–52–61–70* ☰ *AE, DC, MC, V* ☉ *No lunch.*

$$ 🏨 **Thon Hotel Høyers.** This venerable hotel in the center of town has style and sophistication. The exterior, with its cornices and pedimented windows, is reflected in the hotel's lobby, in an incongruous mixture of old and new. The large rooms are bright, thanks to big windows, and have modern furnishings. ⊠ *Kongensgt. 6, 3700* ☎ *35–90–58–00* 🖷 *35–90–58–05* ⊕ *www. thonhotels.no/hoyers* ⇄ *73 rooms, 8 suites* ₺ *Restaurant, in-room data ports, bar, meeting rooms* ☰ *AE, DC, MC, V.*

Sports & the Outdoors

BIKING The Coastal Route goes along the Telemark coastline and is part of the North Sea Cycle Route, which passes through six other countries. There's also a 115-km (71-mi) path along the Telemark Canal from Ule-

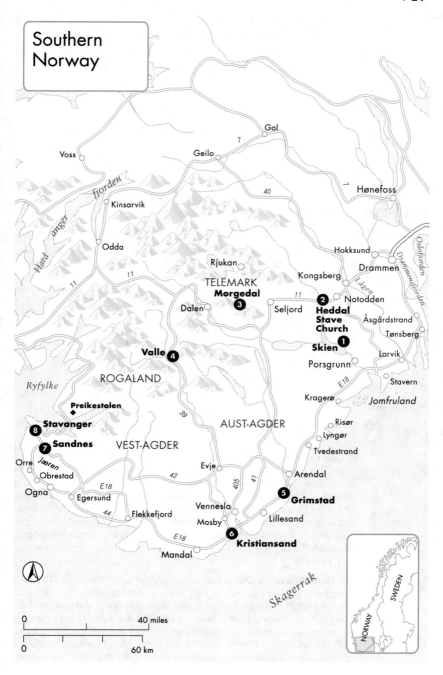

Southern Norway

Voss
Gol
Geilo
7
Hønefoss
40
Kinsarvik
7
Odda
Hokksund
Drammen
Rjukan
Kongsberg
Notodden
TELEMARK
11
Morgedal ❸
Dalen
Seljord
Heddal Stave Church ❶
Åsgårdstrand
Tønsberg
Skien ❶
Valle ❹
Porsgrunn
Larvik
ROGALAND
E18
Stavern
Ryfylke
Kragerø
Jomfruland
Preikestolen ◆
AUST-AGDER
Risør
❽ **Stavanger**
Lyngør
❼ **Sandnes**
Tvedestrand
VEST-AGDER
Jæren
Orre
Evje
Arendal
Obrestad
E18
405
41
Ogna
42
❺ **Grimstad**
Egersund
Vennesla
44
Flekkefjord
Mosby
Lillesand
E18
❻ **Kristiansand**
Mandal

Skagerrak

| 0 | | 40 miles |
| 0 | | 60 km |

NORWAY SWEDEN

foss to Dalen. **Telemark Reiser** (☎ 35–90–00–30) has cycling maps, and bicycle package trips that include accommodation and transport.

GOLF   About 7 km (4½ mi) north of Skien is **Jønnevald** (☎ 35–59–07–03), an 18-hole championship golf course. It costs NKr 400 to play.

> en route   Running 105 km (65 mi) from Skien to Dalen with a detour to Notodden, **Telemarkskanalen** (Telemark Canal; ☎ 35–90–00–30 ⊕ www.telemarkskanalen.com) was carved into the mountains more than 100 years ago. It took 500 men 5 years to blast through the mountains to create 28 locks. The canal became "the fast route" between east and west Norway and upper and lower Telemark. Telemarkskanalen still has its original stone walls, locks, and closing mechanism.

Heddal Stave Church

★ **❷**   *68 km (42 mi) northwest of Skien, 35 km (21 mi) west of Kongsberg.*

Today the town of Notodden, just south of Kongsberg, is not much more than a small industrial town. However, it's believed that the area was prosperous in the Middle Ages because of the size of the town's *stavkirke* (stave church). At 85 feet high and 65 feet long, the Heddal Stave Church is Norway's largest still in use, and it dates back to the 12th century. The structure is resplendent with rosemaling (decorative flower painting from the 17th century), a bishop's chair, and incense vessels from the Middle Ages. Look out for the stylized animal ornamentation and the grotesque human heads on the portals. ☎ 35–02–04–00 🖾 *NKr 35* ☉ *Mid-May–mid-June and mid-Aug.–mid-Sept., daily 10–5; mid-June–mid-Aug., daily 9–7.*

Morgedal

❸   *77 km (46 mi) southwest of Rjukan via Åmot.*

In the heart of Telemark is Morgedal, the birthplace of modern skiing, thanks to the persistent Sondre Norheim, who in the 19th century perfected his skis and bindings and practiced jumping from his roof. His innovations included bindings that close behind the heel and skis that narrow in the middle to facilitate turning. In 1868, he took off for a 185-km (115-mi) trek to Oslo just to prove it could be done. A hundred years ago skiers used one long pole, held diagonally, much like high-wire artists. Eventually the use of two short poles became widespread, although purists still feel that the one-pole method is the "authentic" way to ski.

★ ☾   The **Norsk Skieventyr** (Norwegian Skiing Adventure Center) in Morgedal guides you through the 4,000-year history of the winter sport with life-size exhibits of typical ski cottages and authentic skis and costumes. Displays include the inside of Norway's original and last ski-wax factory, where specialists melted a variety of secret ingredients, including cheese, to make uphill and downhill slides smoother. Visit Norheim's cottage, Øvrebø, above the edge of the forest, where the Olympic flame was lighted.

Several action-packed skiing films can be seen here. ✉ *Rte. 11 between Brunkeberg and Høydalsmo* ☎ *35–05–42–50* 🎫 *NKr 55* ☉ *Late May–mid-June, daily 11–5; mid-June–mid-Aug., daily 9–7; mid-Aug.–late Aug., daily 11–5; Sept.–mid-Dec. and mid-Jan–late May, Sat. 11–4.*

Valle

❹ *56 km (35 mi) southwest of Dalen.*

Near Valle sits **Sylvartun,** a clump of grass-roof cottages that house a silversmith's workshop, a jewelry shop, and an art gallery. It's also a cultural center that hosts concerts and displays local crafts, including many Hardanger fiddles. Every summer during the "Setesdal Evenings," professional musicians and folk dancers perform while a traditional Norwegian dinner is served. ✉ *Rte. 19 near Valle, Nomeland* ☎ *37–93–63–06* ☉ *Silversmith's shop: May–Oct., Mon.–Sat. 10–6, Sun. 11–6. Call for program schedules.*

Grimstad

❺ *15 km (9 mi) south of Arendal.*

Grimstad is a pretty coastal town with a charming wharf. In the mid to late 19th century, the town was famous as a shipbuilding center, and from 1844 to 1850 the teenage Henrik Ibsen worked as an apprentice at the local apothecary shop. Later, in the early 20th century, author Knut Hamsun, winner of the Nobel Prize for Literature yet infamous for his support of Nazi Germany, lived here. Today Grimstad is called the "Town of Poets," and is still home to many artists. A popular Norwegian short-film festival is held here in early summer.

★ Grimstad Apotek is now a part of **Ibsenhuset–Grimstad Bymuseum** (the Ibsen House) and has been preserved with its 1837 interior intact. Ibsen wrote his first play, *Catlina,* here. Every summer Grimstad holds an Ibsen festival celebrating the famous playwright. The museum also has a maritime department and a section honoring Terje Vigen, a folk hero who was the subject of a poem by Ibsen. He is credited with riding to Denmark to bring back food for the starving Norwegians. ✉ *Henrik Ibsens gt. 14, 4890* ☎ *37–04–04–90* ⊕ *www.ibsen.net* 🎫 *NKr 35* ☉ *May–Sept. 11–5.*

Kristiansand

❻ *55 km (34 mi) south of Grimstad on E18.*

Nicknamed "Sommerbyen" ("Summer City"), Norway's fifth-largest city has 75,000 inhabitants. Norwegians come here for its sun-soaked beaches and beautiful harbor. Kristiansand has also become known internationally for the outdoor **Quart Festival** (☎ *38–14–69–69* ⊕ *www.quart.no*), which hosts local and international rock bands every July.

According to legend, in 1641 King Christian IV marked the four corners of Kristiansand with his walking stick, and within that framework the grid of wide streets was laid down. The center of town, called the

Kvadraturen, still retains the grid, even after numerous fires. In the northeast corner is **Posebyen,** one of northern Europe's largest collections of low, connected wooden house settlements, and there's a market here every Saturday in summer. Kristiansand's **Fisketorvet** (fish market) is near the south corner of the town's grid, right on the sea. **Christiansholm Festning** (⊙ Mid-May–Aug., daily 9–9) is a fortress on a promontory opposite Festningsgata. Completed in 1674, the circular building with 16-foot-thick walls has played more a decorative role than a defensive one; it was used once, in 1807 during the Napoleonic Wars, to defend the city against British invasion. Now it contains art exhibits.

The **Agder naturmuseum og botaniske hage** (Agder Nature Museum and Botanical Gardens) takes on Sørlandet's natural history from the Ice Age to the present, examining the coast and moving on to the high mountains. There's a rainbow of minerals on display, as well as a rose garden with varieties from 1850. There's even the country's largest collection of cacti. ⊠ *Gimlevn. 23, 4630* ☎ *38–09–23–88* ⊕ *www.museumsnett. no/naturmuseum* 🎫 *NKr 45* ⊙ *Mid-June–mid-Aug., Tues.–Fri. 10–6, Sat.–Mon. noon–6; mid-Aug.–mid-June, Tues.–Fri. 10–3, Sun. noon–5.*

A wealthy merchant-shipowner built **Gimle Gård** (Gimle Manor) around 1800 in the Empire style. Inside are furnishings from that period, including paintings, silver, and hand-printed wallpaper. To get there from the city center, head north across the Otra River on Bus 22 or drive to Route E18 and cross the bridge over the Otra to Parkveien. Turn left onto Ryttergangen and drive to Gimleveien; take a right. ⊠ *Gimlevn. 23, 4630* ☎ *38–09–02–28* 🎫 *NKr 45* ⊙ *Mid-June–mid-Aug., weekdays noon–4, Sun. noon–6; May–mid-June and mid-Aug.–early Jan., Sun. noon–5.*

The Gothic Revival **Kristiansand Domkirke** (Kristiansand Cathedral) from 1885 is the third-largest church in Norway. It often hosts summer concerts in addition to the weeklong **International Church Music Festival** (☎ 38–12–09–40) in mid-May. Organ, chamber, and gospel music are on the bill. ⊠ *Kirkegt., 4610* ☎ *38–10–77–50* 🎫 *Free* ⊙ *June–Aug., daily 9–2.*

★ ℭ One of Norway's most popular attractions, **Kristiansand Dyreparken** is actually five separate parks, including a water park (bring bathing suits and towels); a forested park; an entertainment park; a theme park; and a zoo, which contains an enclosure for Scandinavian animals such as wolves and elk, and a large breeding ground for Bactrian camels. The theme park, **Kardemomme By** (Cardamom Town), is named for a book by Norwegian illustrator and writer Thorbjørn Egner. In the zoo the "My Africa" exhibition allows you to move along a bridge observing native savanna animals such as giraffes and zebras. The park is 11 km (6 mi) east of town. ⊠ *Kristiansand Dyreparken, Kardemomme By* ☎ *38–04–97–25* ⊕ *www.dyreparken.no* 🎫 *NKr 225, includes admission to all parks and rides; discounts offered off-season* ⊙ *June–Aug., daily 10–7; Sept.–May, weekdays 10–3, weekends 10–5.*

At the **Kristiansand Kanonmuseum** (Cannon Museum) you can see the cannon that the occupying Germans rigged up during World War II. With

A BRIEF HISTORY OF NORWAY

NORWEGIANS ARE JUSTIFIABLY PROUD of their ability to survive the elements. The first people to appear on the land were reindeer hunters and fisherfolk who migrated north, following the path of the retreating ice. By the Bronze Age, settlements began to appear, and, as rock carvings show, Norwegians first began to ski—purely as a form of locomotion—some 4,000 years ago.

The Viking Age has perhaps left the most indelible mark on the country. The Vikings' travels and conquests took them west to Iceland, England, Ireland (they founded Dublin in the 840s), and North America, and east to Kiev and as far as the Black Sea. Though they were famed as plunderers, their craftsmanship, fearlessness, and ingenuity have always been respected by Norwegians.

Harald I, better known as Harald the Fairhaired, swore he would not cut his hair until he united Norway, and in the 9th century he succeeded in doing both. But a millennium passed between that great era and Norwegian independence. Between the Middle Ages and 1905, Norway remained under the rule of either Denmark or Sweden, even after the constitution was written in 1814.

The 19th century saw the establishment of the Norwegian identity and a blossoming of culture. This Romantic period produced some of the nation's most famous individuals, among them composer Edvard Grieg, dramatist Henrik Ibsen, expressionist painter Edvard Munch, polar explorer Roald Amundsen, and explorer-humanitarian Fridtjof Nansen. Vestiges of nationalist lyricism, including Viking dragonheads and scrollwork, spangle the buildings of the era, symbolizing the rebirth of the Viking spirit.

Faithful to their democratic nature, Norwegians held a referendum to choose a king in 1905, when independence from Sweden became reality. Prince Carl of Denmark became King Haakon VII. His baby's name was changed from Alexander to Olav, and he, and later his son, presided over the kingdom for more than 85 years. When King Olav V died in January 1991, normally reserved Norwegians stood in line for hours to write in the condolence book at the Royal Palace. Rather than simply sign their names, they wrote personal letters of devotion to the man they called "the people's king."

Harald V, Olav's son, is now king, with continuity assured by his popular son, Crown Prince Haakon Magnus, who married in 2001. Norwegians continue to salute the royal family with flag-waving and parades on May 17, Constitution Day, a spirited holiday of independence that transforms Oslo's main boulevard, Karl Johans Gate, into a massive street party.

The 1968 discovery of oil in the North Sea dramatically changed Norway from an outpost for fishing, subsistence farming, and shipping to a highly developed industrial nation. Norway has emerged as a wealthy country, with a per capita income, standard of living, and life expectancy that are among the world's highest.

Domestically, great emphasis has been placed on social welfare programs. Internationally, Norway is known for the annual awarding of the Nobel peace prize and participating in peace talks about the Middle East and other areas.

Unlike its Nordic siblings, Norway has resisted the temptation to join the European Union (EU). However, Norwegians are warming to the EU as it expands its membership across Europe.

calibers of 15 inches, the cannon was said to be capable of shooting a projectile halfway to Denmark. In the bunkers, related military materials are on display. ☒ *Møvik* ☎ *38–08–50–90* 🖾 *NKr 50* ☉ *May–Sept., daily 11–6; prebooked tours available all yr.*

The striking rune stone in the cemetery of **Oddernes Kirke** (Oddernes Church) tells that Øyvind, godson of Saint Olav, built this church in 1040 on property he inherited from his father. One of the oldest churches in Norway, it has a baroque pulpit from 1704 and is dedicated to Saint Ola. ☒ *Oddernesvn., 6430* ☎ *38–09–01–87* 🖾 *Free* ☉ *May–Aug., Sun.–Fri. 9–2.*

FodorśChoice ★ A favorite with hikers and strolling nannies, **Ravnedalen** (Raven Valley) is a lush park that's filled with flowers in springtime. Wear comfortable shoes to hike the narrow, winding paths up the hills and climb the 200 steps up to a 304-foot lookout. ☒ *Northwest of Kristiansand.*

🐾 **Vest-Agder Fylkesmuseum** (County Museum), the region's largest cultural museum, has more than 40 old buildings on display. The structures, transported from other locations in the area, include two *tun*—farm buildings traditionally set in clusters around a common area—which suited the extended families. If you have children with you, check out the old-fashioned toys, which can still be played with. The museum is 4 km (2½ mi) east of Kristiansand on Route E18. ☒ *Kongsgård* ☎ *38–09–02–28* ⊕ *www.museumsnett.no/vafymuseum* 🖾 *NKr 30* ☉ *Mid-June–mid-Aug., Tues.–Fri. 10–6, Sat.–Mon. noon–6; mid-Aug.–mid-June, Sun. noon–5.*

Where to Stay & Eat

$$$–$$$$ ✕ **Luihn.** In the center of town, Luihn is an elegant, intimate restaurant, perfect for a quiet dinner. Fish dishes are a specialty, and the menu varies according to season. Don't hesitate to call in advance if you have any special cravings—providing they can get hold of it, the chefs can prepare just about anything for you. The wine selection is impressive. ☒ *Rådhusgt. 15* ☎ *38–10–66–50* 🖃 *AE, DC, MC, V.*

★ **$$$–$$$$** ✕ **Sjøhuset Restaurant.** Considered one of the city's best restaurants, Sjøhuset was built in 1892 as a salt warehouse—a white-trimmed red building. The specialty is seafood. Take a seat on the sunny patio and dine on fresh lobster, or try the baked fillet of monkfish with pancetta, served with artichoke risotto. ☒ *Østre Strandgt. 12A* ☎ *38–02–62–60* 🖃 *AE, DC, MC, V.*

$$–$$$$ ✕ **Bølgen & Moi.** Toralf Bølgen and Trond Moi, Norway's most celebrated restaurateurs, opened this southernmost addition to their chain of high-profile restaurants. Near the old fishing pier, the scene is more chic than rustic, with artwork and even dinnerware designed by local artist Kjell Nupen. Norwegian game and fish are cooked in an international style. ☒ *Sjølystvn. 1A* ☎ *38–17–83–00* 🖃 *AE, DC, MC, V.*

$$$ 🏨 **Quality Hotel Kristiansand.** Nicknamed "the children's hotel," this chain hotel is perfect for young families on the go. Inside, there are a huge playroom, activity leaders, child care, and a children's buffet. Even more toys are outdoors. Rooms are comfortable, with cheerful pastel walls and wood furniture. ☒ *Sørlandsparken, 4696* ☎ *38–17–77–77* 🖷 *38–17–77–80* ⊕ *www.quality-kristiansand.no* 🛏 *210 rooms*

♿ *Restaurant, pool, babysitting, children's programs (ages 3–12), playground, Internet room; no a/c in some rooms* ▤ *AE, DC, MC, V.*

$$–$$$ 🏨 **Clarion Ernst Park Hotel.** Convenience is the main reason to stay at this rather traditional city hotel. It is central, and close to the city beach and main shopping street, Markens. The staff at the reception desk will gladly tell you about local attractions and help you purchase tickets to Dyreparken. You can get connected online at a nearby Internet café. ✉ *Rådhusgt. 2, 4601* ☎ *38–12–86–00* 🖷 *38–02–03–07* 🌐 *www.ernst. no* 🛏 *136 rooms, 5 suites* ♿ *Restaurant, 2 bars, meeting rooms; no a/c in some rooms* ▤ *AE, DC, MC, V.*

$$–$$$ 🏨 **Rica Dyreparken Hotel.** Built like Noah's Ark, this modern hotel is designed to appeal to children of all ages. Inspired by the Kristiansand Dyreparken, many of the rooms go a little wild, with tiger-stripe chairs and paw prints on walls. Children have their own playroom and cinema on board this ark. ✉ *Dyreparken, 4609* ☎ *38–14–64–00* 🖷 *38–14–64–01* 🌐 *www.rica.no* 🛏 *160 rooms* ♿ *Restaurant, bar, children's programs (ages 3–12)* ▤ *AE, DC, MC, V.*

Nightlife & the Arts

Markens gate, the city's main street, is the place for clubbing, pubbing, and live music.

Dr. Fjeld (✉ Rådhusgt. 2 ☎ 38–12–86–00) at Clarion Ernst Park Hotel is a popular place to dance the night away. Party types in their late twenties and thirties head to **Lobbybaren** (✉ Vestre Strandgt. 7 ☎ 38–11–21–00) at Radisson SAS Caledonien Hotel. A younger crowd flocks to **Club Etcetera** (✉ Vestre Strandgt. 23 ☎ 38–02–96–66) for up-to-date beats.

Sports & the Outdoors

Troll Mountain (✉ Setesdal Rafting og Aktivitetssenter, Rte. 9, Evje ☎ 37–93–11–77), about one hour's drive from Kristiansand, organizes many activities. Be it mountain climbing, sailing, biking, rafting, paintball, or even beaver or deer safaris, this is the place for outdoorsy types.

BIKING   Kristiansand has 70 km (42 mi) of bike trails around the city. The tourist office can recommend routes and rentals. **Kristiansand Sykkelsenter** (✉ Grim Torv ☎ 38–02–68–35) rents bicycles and off-road vehicles.

CLIMBING   Whether you're an experienced pro or just a gung-ho beginner, you can rent climbing equipment or learn more about the sport from **Samsen Kulturhus** (✉ Vestervn. 2 ☎ 38–00–64–00).

FISHING   Just north of Kristiansand there's excellent trout, perch, and eel fishing at Lillesand's **Vestre Grimevann** lake. You can get a permit at any sports store or at the **Lillesand Tourist Office** (☎ 37–40–19–10).

HIKING   In addition to the gardens and steep hills of Ravnedalen, the **Baneheia Skog** (Baneheia Forest) is full of evergreens, small lakes, and paths that are ideal for a lazy walk or a challenging run. It's just a 15-minute walk north from the city center.

RIDING   If you're at home in the saddle, then head to **Islandshestsenteret** (The Icelandic Horse Center; ✉ Søgne ☎ 38–16–98–82). Specializing in the Icelandic horse breed, this center offers courses, trips, and camping for children and adults.

Shopping

There are many shops next to Dyreparken in Kristiansand. **Kvadraturen** (☎ 38–02–44–11) has 300 stores and eating spots. **Sørlands Senteret Steen and Strom** (☎ 38–04–91–00) is one of the region's larger shopping centers, with 100 stores, a pharmacy, and a post office.

Sandnes

❼ *25 km (16 mi) south of Stavanger, 52 km (32 mi) north of Orre.*

For good reason, this city of 53,000 is called Bicycle Town. Local company Øglænd DBS, founded in 1898, has manufactured nearly 2 million bicycles here. Sandnes has 200 free city bicycles, miles of bicycle paths, a bicycle museum, the Bicycle Blues Festival, a bicycle library, and an active racing club. Besides bicycles, brickworks, pottery, and textiles have been the traditional industries. Eleven factory outlets and art galleries sell historic and modern Sandnes crafts and products at reduced prices.

The Sandnes, Øglænd, and Krossens Havremølle (Krossen's Oatmeal) museums have been combined as part of the larger Jærmuseet to form the **Sandnes Museum**. The museum documents the town's development, with special attention to the oat-milling and bicycle-manufacturing industries. Photographs, and cultural and industrial artifacts, including a working model of an oat mill, are on display. ✉ *Storgt. 26* ☎ *51–97–25–40* ⊕ *www.museumsnett.no/jaermuseet/avd_sandn.htm* 🎫*NKr 40* 🕐 *Mid-June–mid-Aug., weekdays noon–5, weekends noon–4; mid-Aug–mid-Dec. and mid-Mar.–mid-June, Sun noon–3.*

Where to Stay & Eat

$$–$$$ ✕🏨 **Hotel GamlaVærket Gjæstgiveri og Tracteringsted.** A former brick-and-pottery works, this intimate hotel has a warm, old-fashioned charm. Simple white-wall rooms have slanted ceilings and dark-wood furniture. The well-regarded restaurant has a menu that ranges from sandwiches to delicious seven-course meals. ✉ *St. Olavs gt. 38, 4306* ☎ *51–68–51–70* 🖷 *51–68–51–71* ⊕ *www.gamlavaerket.no* 🛏 *26 rooms* ♿ *Restaurant, bar, meeting rooms; no a/c in some rooms* ▭ *AE, DC, MC, V.*

Sports & the Outdoors

BICYCLING Can you actually visit Norway's bicycle town and not spin a few wheels yourself? If the cycling mood strikes, borrow one of the 200 that are available for free downtown. The tourist office has bicycle maps of the area. **Scan One Tours** (☎ 51–89–39–00) organizes and sells packaged bicycle trips. You can rent a bike at **Spinn Sykkelshop** (☎ 51–68–62–65) or **Naboen** (☎ 51–57–07–10).

Stavanger

❽ *256 km (123 mi) northwest of Kristiansand, 4½ hrs southeast of Bergen by car and ferry, 8–9 hrs southwest of Oslo by car.*

Stavanger has always prospered from the riches of the sea. During the 19th century huge harvests of brisling and herring established it as the sardine capital of the world. Some people claim the locals are called

Siddis, from S (tavanger) plus *iddis,* which means "sardine label," although linguists argue it's actually a mispronunciation of the English word "citizen."

During the past three decades a different product from the sea has been Stavanger's lifeblood—oil. Since its discovery in the late 1960s, North Sea oil hasn't just transformed the economy, Stavanger has emerged as cosmopolitan and vibrant, more bustling than other cities with a population of only 110,000. Norway's most international city, it has attracted residents from more than 90 nations. Roam its cobblestone streets or wander the harbor front and you're likely to see many cafés, fine restaurants, and lively pubs. For many visitors, Stavanger is a place to be entertained. As you tour the city, keep an eye out for 23 rusty figures, sculptures created by British artist Antony Gormley.

Designed to help children learn about the prehistoric past, the **Arkeologisk Museum** (Museum of Archaeology) has changing exhibitions, instructive models, open archives, and movies designed to make learning history fun. Children can research their ancestors in computer games, treasure hunts, and other activities. In summer children can look through stones in search of fossils and other signs of life. There are also old-fashioned games and toys, which have become popular attractions. ⊠ *Peder Klowsgt. 30A* ☏ *51–84–60–00* 💲 *NKr 20* ⊙ *June–Aug., Tues.–Sun. 11–5; Sept.–May, Tues. 11–8, Wed.–Sat. 11–3, Sun. 11–4.*

Take a scented stroll in Stavanger's wild rose garden. At the **Botanisk Hage** (Botanical Gardens), you can find some 2,000 varieties of herbs and perennials. ⊠ *Rektor Natvig Pedersensv. 40* ☏ *51–50–78–61* 💲 *Free* ⊙ *Apr.–Sept., weekdays 7 AM–8 PM, weekends 10–8; Oct.–Mar., weekdays 7–5, weekends 10–5.*

★ **Breidablikk** manor house has a perfectly preserved interior and exterior and feels as if the owner has only momentarily slipped away. The building is an outstanding example of what the Norwegians call "Swiss-style" architecture, and also has some elements of the Norwegian National Romantic style. It was built in 1882 by the Norwegian merchant and shipowner Lars Berentsen. ⊠ *Eiganesvn. 40A* ☏ *51–84–27–00* ⊕ *www. stavanger.museum.no* 💲 *NKr 50* ⊙ *Mid-June–mid-Aug., daily 11–4; mid-Aug.–mid-June, Sun. 11–4 or by appointment.*

If you have a Norwegian branch on your family tree, trace your roots at **Det Norske Utvandresenteret,** in a harborside wharf house from the early 1700s. The Norwegian Emigration Center has passenger lists, parish registers, census records, and a comprehensive collection of books on Norway's rural past. Bring along any information you have, especially the dates and places from which your ancestors left Norway. The center organizes the annual Norwegian Emigration Festival in October, with exhibitions, concerts, and excursions to historical sites. ⊠ *Strandkaien 31* ☏ *51–53–88–60* 🖷 *51–53–88–63* ⊕ *www.emigrationcenter.com* 💲 *NKr 35* ⊙ *Mon. and Wed.–Fri. 9–3, Tues. 9–7.*

More than 35 military and civilian planes make up the collection at the **Flyhistorisk Museum Sola** (History of Flying Museum, Sola municipality), which emphasizes aviation history from World War II on. Besides checking out changing exhibitions, you can sit in a passenger seat of a 1950s Metropolitan plane and see the changing designs through the years of the Norwegian Air Force's jet fighters. ☒ *Sjøflyhaven, Stavanger Lufthavn* ☎ *51–65–56–57* 🖅 *NKr 40* ☉ *Late June–mid-Aug., daily noon–4; May–late June and mid-Aug.–Nov., Sun. noon–4.*

Although it's a reconstruction, the **Jernaldergarden** late Iron Age farm complex from the Migration Period (AD 350–550) feels like the real thing. The reconstructed historical buildings have been positioned on original foundations. Relics such as a Bronze Age gravestone have been discovered here. Research is still underway. Taste some mead, the Vikings' favorite drink, or have breakfast or lunch on wooden benches before fireplaces. ☒ *Ullandhaugvn. 165* ☎ *51–84–60–00* 🖅 *NKr 40* ☉ *Mid-June–mid-Aug., daily 11–4; mid-Aug.–mid-June, by appointment.*

☾ **Kongeparken** amusement park has go-carts, radio cars, bumper boats, Norway's longest bobsled run, and its largest merry-go-round. In the Chocolate Factory children can make their own Freia-brand milk chocolate. ☒ *4330 Ålgård* ☎ *51–61–26–66* ⊕ *www.kongeparken.no* 🖅 *NKr 140* ☉ *May–Aug., daily 10–6; Sept., weekends 10–6; mid-Nov.–mid-Dec., daily 10–6.*

Ledaal, the royal family's Stavanger residence, is a mansion museum and is used for receptions by the Stavanger Council. It was built for shipping magnate Gabriel Schanche Kielland, and completed in 1803. The building is a prime example of the Norwegian neoclassical style, and it's decorated with rococo furnishings and details, as well as pieces in the Empire, and Biedermeier styles. The second-floor library is dedicated to writer Alexander Kielland, a social critic and satirist. ☒ *Eiganesvn. 45* ☎ *51–84–27–00* ⊕ *www.stavanger.museum.no* 🖅 *NKr 50* ☉ *Mid-June–mid-Aug., daily 11–4; mid-Aug.–mid-June, Sun. 11–4 or by appointment.*

Lysefjordsenteret. Lysefjord Center has a slanting roof that mimics the mountains. An exhibition shows how a trickling brook created this sliver of a fjord. You'll also learn about the geology and culture of Lysefjord. A ferry to the bottom of Pulpit Rock drops off passengers midway. For more information, call **Rogaland Traffik** (☎ 51–86–87–00) or **Clipper Fjord Sightseeing** (☎ 51–89–52–70). The center has a café and can help with finding accommodations. ☒ *Oanes, Forsand* ☎ *51–70–31–23* ☉ *May–Aug., weekdays 11–6, Sat. 11–6, Sun. noon–8.*

☾ The **Norsk Barnemuseum** (Norwegian Children's Museum) has Norway's largest collection of children's toys. Storytelling, dramatic performances, and other activities focus on the country's culture and history. ☒ *Sølvberget (Stavanger Culture Center)* ☎ *51–91–23–93* ⊕ *www.norskbarne.museum.no* 🖅 *NKr 65* ☉ *Wed.–Fri. 1–7, Sat. noon–5, Sun. 1–5.*

The fascinating **Norsk Hermetikkmuseum** (Norwegian Canning Museum) is in a former canning factory. From the 1890s to the 1960s, canning fish products like brisling, fish balls, and sardines was Stavanger's main industry. On special activity days the public can take part in the production process, sometimes tasting newly smoked brisling—on the first Sunday of every month and Tuesday and Thursday in summer, the ovens used for smoking fish are stoked up once again. ⊠ *Øvre Strandgt. 88A* ☎ *51–84–27–00* ⊕ *www.stavanger.museum.no* ⊠ *NKr 50* ⊗ *Mid-June–mid-Aug., daily 11–4; early June and late Aug., Mon.–Thurs. 11–3, Sun. 11–4; Sept.–May, Sun. 11–4 or by appointment.*

FodorśChoice
★
Resembling a shiny offshore oil platform, the dynamic **Norsk Oljemuseum** (Norwegian Petroleum Museum) is an absolute must-see. In 1969 oil was discovered off the coast of Norway. The museum explains how oil forms, how it's found and produced, its many uses, and its impact on Norway. Interactive multimedia exhibits accompany original artifacts, models, and films. A reconstructed offshore platform includes oil workers' living quarters—as well as the sound of drilling and the smell of oil. The highly recommended museum café, by restaurateurs Bølgen & Moi, serves dinners as well as lighter fare. ⊠ *Kjeringholmen, Stavanger Havn* ☎ *51–93–93–00* ⊕ *www.norskolje.museum.no* ⊠ *NKr 80* ⊗ *Sept.–May, Mon.–Sat. 10–4, Sun. 10–6; June–Aug., daily 10–7.*

FodorśChoice
★
The charm of the city's past is on view in **Old Stavanger,** northern Europe's largest and best-preserved wooden house settlement. The 150 houses here were built in the late 1700s and early 1800s. Wind down the narrow, cobblestone streets past small, white houses and craft shops with many-paned windows and terra-cotta roof tiles.

★ **Preikestolen** (Pulpit Rock). A huge cube with a vertical drop of 2,000 feet, the Pulpit Rock is not a good destination if you suffer from vertigo—it has a heart-stopping view. The clifflike rock sits on the banks of the finger-shape Lysefjord. You can join a tour to get to the region's best-known attraction, or you can do it on your own from early June to early September by taking the bus—it costs NKr 50 one-way from the town of Tau to the Pulpit Rock. The buses are paired with morning ferry departures from Stavanger at 8:20 and 9:15. Then you can hike the two-hour walk on a marked trail. The ferry and bus take a total of about 40 minutes from Stavanger.

Rogaland Kunstmuseum (Rogaland Museum of Fine Arts) has the country's largest collection of works by Lars Hertervig (1830–1902), the greatest Romantic painter of Norwegian landscapes. With Norwegian paintings, drawings, and sculptures, the museum's permanent collection covers the early 19th century to the present. The Halvdan Haftsten Collection has paintings and drawings done between the world wars. There's also a collection of works by Kitty Kielland. The museum is near Mosvannet (Mos Lake), which is just off highway E18 at the northern end of downtown. ⊠ *Tjensvoll 6, Mosvannsparken* ☎ *51–53–09–00* ⊠ *NKr 50* ⊗ *Tues.–Sun. 11–4.*

Along Strandkaien, warehouses face the wharf; the shops, offices, and apartments face the street on the other side. Housed in the only two shipping merchants' houses that remain completely intact is the **Sjøfartsmuseet** (Stavanger Maritime Museum). Built between 1770 and 1840, the restored buildings trace the past 200 years of trade, sea traffic, and shipbuilding. Visit a turn-of-the-20th-century general store, an early-1900s merchant's apartment, and a sailmaker's loft. A reconstruction of a shipowner's office and a memorial are here, as are two 19th-century ships, *Anna af Sand* and *Wyvern*, moored at the pier. ⊠ *Nedre Strandgt. 17–19* ☎ *51–84–27–00* ⊕ *www.stavanger.museum.no* 🎟 *NKr 50* ⊘ *Early–mid June and mid–late Aug., Mon.–Thurs. 11–3, Sun. 11–4; mid-June–mid-Aug., daily 11–4; Sept.–Nov. and Jan.–May, Sun. 11–4 or by appointment.*

Legend has it that Bishop Reinald of Winchester ordered the construction of **Stavanger Domkirke** (Stavanger Cathedral) in 1125, so that the king could marry his third wife there, after his divorce from Queen Malmfrid. The church was built in Anglo-Norman style, probably with the aid of English craftsmen. Patron saint St. Svithun's arm is believed to be among the original relics. Largely destroyed by fire in 1272, the church was rebuilt to include a Gothic chancel. The result: its once elegant lines are now festooned with macabre death symbols and airborne putti. Next to the cathedral is **Kongsgård,** formerly a residence of bishops and kings but now a school and not open to visitors. ⊠ *Near Torget* 🎟 *Free* ⊘ *Mid-May–mid-Sept., Mon. and Tues. 11–6, Wed.–Sat. 10–6, Sun. 11–6; mid-Sept.–mid-May, Wed.–Sat. 10–3.*

The **Stavanger Museum** is made up of five smaller museums, including a former smaller version of the Stavanger Museum, Stavanger Sjøfartsmuseum, Norsk Hermetikkmuseum, Ledaal, and Breidablikk. In the zoological department you'll find a collection of preserved birds and animals from around the world. In the Department of Cultural History there are reenactments of church and school life and artisans at work. It traces Stavanger's growth from its 12th-century beginnings to the oil city it is today. Buy a ticket to one of the museums and you get free admission to the other four on the same day. ⊠ *Muségt. 16* ☎ *51–84–27–00* ⊕ *www.stavanger.museum.no* 🎟 *NKr 50* ⊘ *Mid-June–mid-Aug., daily 11–4; early June and late Aug., Mon.–Thurs. 11–3, Sun. 11–4; Sept.–Nov. and Jan.–May, Sun. 11–4 or by appointment.*

The site where Norway was founded has been memorialized by the **Sverd i fjell** (Swords in the Mountain). The three huge bronze swords were unveiled by King Olav in 1983 and done by artist Fritz Røed. The memorial is dedicated to King Harald Hårfagre (Harald the Fairhaired), who through an 872 battle at Hafrsfjord managed to unite Norway into one kingdom. The Viking swords' sheaths were modeled on ones found throughout the country; the crowns atop the swords represent the different Norwegian districts that took part in the battle. ⊠ *Hafrsfjord, on Grannesveien to Sola, 6 km (4 mi) south of Stavanger.*

off the
beaten
path

UTSTEIN KLOSTER – Originally the palace of Norway's first king, Harald Hårfagre, and later the residence of King Magnus VI, Utstein was used as a monastery from 1265 until 1537, when it reverted to the royal family. Just one bus departs for Utstein from Stavanger weekdays at 9 AM, and it doesn't return from the monastery until 4:05 PM, so its best to hire a car. By bus or car it's about a half-hour trip to the palace, north of Stavanger on coastal Highway 1, through the world's second-longest undersea car tunnel. If you rent a car to get to Utstein Kloster, you can also take in the medieval ruins nearby on **Åmøy Island** as well as the lighthouse, **Fjøløy Fyr.** Turn left after the tunnel and look for the tourist information sign before the bridge. ☎ *51–72–47–05.*

As Stavanger grew into an important town in the Middle Ages, watchmen were hired to look out for fires, crime, and anything else out of the ordinary. The **Vektermuseet i Valbergtårnet** (Watchman's Museum in the Valberg Tower) examines the role the watchmen played in keeping the town safe. The Valbergtårnet was built in the 1850s to give a panoramic view of the town below. With so many wooden houses, an early warning was essential. The view remains as incredible as ever. ⌧ *Valbergtårnet* ☎ *90/72–63–94* ⌑ *NKr 10* ☉ *Mon.–Wed. and Fri. 10–4, Thurs. 10–6, Sat. 10–2.*

Where to Eat

Stavanger has established a reputation for culinary excellence. In fact, the city has the distinction of having the most bars and restaurants per capita in Norway. Many restaurant menus burst with sumptuous international dishes. The city is home to the Culinary Institute of Norway, and hosts many food and wine festivals every year, including the Gladmat Festival, Garlic Week, Stavanger Wine Festival, Chili Festival, and Creole Week.

$$$$ ✕ **Cartellet Restaurant.** The elegant dining room reflects the timelessness of this classic restaurant that was founded in 1890 in Stavanger's first hotel. It has gold accents, stone walls hung with richly colored paintings, a dark-wood interior, and leather furniture. Based on fresh, seasonal ingredients from Norway's fjords and mountains, the menu changes every day. ⌧ *Øvre Holmegt. 8* ☎ *51–89–60–22* ✍ *Reservations essential* ⊟ *AE, DC, MC, V.*

$$$$ ✕ **Straen Fiskerestaurant.** Right on the quay, this esteemed fish restaurant claims it's "world famous throughout Norway." The nostalgic interior filled with memorabilia and the white-clothed tables make the restaurant comforting and homey. If you're traveling with a group, reserve the bookshelf-lined library dining room. Try the famous fish soup of salmon and cream of shellfish, or the grilled monkfish, or lutefisk. The three-course meal of the day is always the best value. The aquavit bar carries more than 30 varieties. ⌧ *Nedre Strandgt. 15* ☎ *51–84–37–00* ⊟ *AE, DC, MC, V.*

$$$–$$$$ ✕ **Craigs Kjøkken & Bar.** Oklahoman Craig Whitson's café-restaurant is a great place for wining as well as dining. Stylish glass cabinets house the collection of more than 600 bottles of wine, with a focus on Italy and the Rhone and Alsace regions of France. The food is seasonal, experimental, and eclectic, its influences ranging from Mediterranean to Asian. Try the popular spring lamb burger or the huge, juicy Babe burger. The café hosts annual events such as chili and wine festivals. Whitson's offbeat sense of humor comes through in the "12 disciples" that sit against one wall—a dozen smoked, salted, and dried pigs' heads. ⌧ *Breitorget* ☎ *51–93–95–90* ⊟ *AE, DC, MC, V.*

$$$–$$$$ ✕ **Timbuktu Bar and Restaurant.** This is one of the Stavanger's trendiest restaurants. Within its airy interior of blond wood and yellow and black accessories, enthusiastic chefs serve Asian-inspired cuisine with African ingredients such as tuna fish from Madagascar. Known for its NKr 350 three-course dinners and its sushi, the restaurant often has visiting celebrity chefs, and hosts special events such as salsa parties and nights of Spanish tapas. ⊠ *Nedre Strandgt. 15* ☎ *51–84–37–40* ▤ *AE, DC, MC, V.*

$$$–$$$$ ✕ **Vertshuset Mat & Vin.** The style of this restaurant matches the traditional Norwegian dishes served up by the kitchen. Amid wood walls, white lace curtains, and traditional paintings, you can enjoy popular dishes such as monkfish with saffron and *komler* (dumplings) with salted meats. ⊠ *Skagen 10* ☎ *51–89–51–12* ▤ *AE, DC, MC, V.*

$$–$$$$ ✕ **Saken er Biff.** A Norwegian country-style steak house, this restaurant has a whole lot more than beef on its menu. Be daring and try venison, reindeer, or moose, prepared rare, medium, or well done. ⊠ *Skagenkaien 28* ☎ *51–89–60–80* ▤ *AE, DC, MC, V.*

$$–$$$$ ✕ **Sjøhuset Skagen.** A sort of museum, this 18th-century former boathouse is filled with wooden beams, ship models, lobster traps, and other sea relics. The Norwegian and international menu has such dishes as halibut, monkfish, and grilled medallions of reindeer, plus potatoes and vegetables. ⊠ *Skagenkaien 16* ☎ *51–89–51–80* ▤ *AE, DC, MC, V.*

$–$$$$ ✕ **N. B. Sørensen's Dampskibsexpedition.** Norwegian emigrants waited
Fodor's Choice   here before boarding steamships crossing the Atlantic to North America 150 years ago. Restored in 1990, the historic wharf house is now a
★   popular waterfront restaurant and bar. Emigrants' tickets, weathered wood, nautical ropes, old maps, photographs, and gaslights set the scene. At street level is an informal brasserie where you can get barbecued spareribs. Upstairs is an elegant and more expensive dining room with prix-fixe menus including such entrées as a delicious grilled entrecôte with garlic. ⊠ *Skagen 26* ☎ *51–84–38–20* ▤ *AE, DC, MC, V.*

$$–$$$ ✕ **Harry Pepper.** Norway's first Tex-Mex restaurant is still considered one of the country's best. Earth tones, cacti, and tacky souvenirs combine to make the joint lighthearted and playful. Try the sizzling fajitas or the lime-grilled fish kebab served with triple pesto. Have a tequila shot or two at the lively bar. ⊠ *Øvre Holmegt. 15* ☎ *51–56–79–67* ▤ *AE, DC, V.*

Where to Stay

$$–$$$$ ▦ **Radisson SAS Atlantic Hotel Stavanger.** In the heart of downtown, the Atlantic overlooks Breiavatnet pond. All rooms are elegantly decorated in understated yellows, beiges, and reds, with plush furniture. The King Oscar lobby bar, Alexander Pub, and Café Ajax are popular with Stavanger's residents. ⊠ *Olav Vs gt. 3, 4001* ☎ *51–76–10–00* 🖶 *51–53–48–69* ⊕ *www.radisson.com* ↘ *350 rooms, 4 suites* ⌂ *Restaurant, café, cable TV with movies, in-room data ports, sauna, bar, lounge, pub, dance club, nightclub, meeting rooms* ▤ *AE, DC, MC, V.*

$$–$$$$ ▦ **Victoria Hotel.** Stavanger's oldest hotel was built at the turn of the 20th century and retains a clubby Victorian style, with elegant carved furniture and floral patterns. Ask for a room overlooking the harbor. Stavanger's museums, Gamle Stavanger, and shopping are all within short walking distances. ⊠ *Skansegt. 1, Postboks 279, 4001* ☎ *51–86–70–00*

🖥 *51–86–70–10* ⊕ *www.victoria-hotel.no* 📞 *107 rooms, 3 suites* 🍴 *Restaurant, bar, meeting rooms* ☰ *AE, DC, MC, V* ⑩⑪ *BP.*

$$–$$$ 🖥 **Clarion Hotel Stavanger.** This downtown business hotel has an up-to-the-minute design. Famed local artist Kjell Pahr Iversen's vibrant paintings hang on the hotel's walls. The light, simple interior is punctuated by the clean lines of Phillipe Starck lamps and Erik Jørgensen chairs. The rooms are also bright and simply furnished. ☒ *Ny Olavskleiv 8, 4008* 🖥 *51–91–00–00* 🖨 *51–91–00–10* ⊕ *www.clhs.no* 📞 *250 rooms, 23 suites* 🍴 *Restaurant, café, cable TV, in-room data ports, gym, hot tub, sauna, bar, meeting rooms* ☰ *AE, DC, MC, V.*

★ $$–$$$ 🖥 **Skagen Brygge Hotell.** A symbol of Stavanger, this classic hotel's white wooden wharf houses are common subjects for city postcards and photographs. It has a well-deserved reputation for superb service. The blue-accented, wood-beam rooms tend to have somewhat irregular shapes. Half the rooms face the harbor, and half face the street. Have a coffee anytime at the fourth floor's relaxing Kaffekroken lounge. On weekends Hovemesteren Bar is a popular nightspot. The hotel has an arrangement with 14 area restaurants whereby when you dine at any of them, you can arrange for the tab to be added to your hotel bill. ☒ *Skagenkaien 30, Postboks 793, 4004* 🖥 *51–85–00–00* 🖨 *51–85–00–01* ⊕ *www.skagenbryggehotell.no* 📞 *110 rooms, 2 suites* 🍴 *Restaurant, minibars, in-room data ports, sauna, steam room, bar, convention center* ☰ *AE, DC, MC, V.*

Festivals

Stavanger has earned the title "Festivalbyen" (festival city) for its year-round celebrations. More than 20 official festivals are held throughout the year—comedy, garlic, chili, food, chamber music, jazz, literature, beach volleyball, wine, belly dancing, vintage boats, emigrants, immigrants. There are probably just as many unofficial events, since locals love any reason to have a party. Contact **Destination Stavanger** (🖥 51–85–92–00 ⊕ www.visitstavanger.com) for a listing.

Cafés & Nightlife

CAFÉS   Stavanger has its share of cozy and hip locations to have a drink, read the papers, listen to live music, or just hang out. **Amys Coffeebar** (☒ Salvågergt. 7 🖥 51–86–07–65) is a sweet little spot for an afternoon coffee or takeaway lunch. At **Café Italia** (☒ Skagen 8 🖥 51–56–33–88), there's an Italian coffee bar, a restaurant, and even a boutique selling Italy's top fashion names. **Café Sting** (☒ Valberget 3 🖥 51–89–38–78), a combination restaurant, nightclub, art gallery, and performance venue, is an institution. News junkies head to Norway's first news café, **Newsman** (☒ Skagen 14 🖥 51–84–38–80), for CNN on the TV and for Norwegian and foreign periodicals. For a quick snack or a glass of freshly squeezed fruit juice, stop by **Sitrus Sandwichbar** (☒ Bakkegt. 7, entrance from Salvågergt. 🖥 51–89–15–90); the smoothies are delicious.

CLUBS & PUBS   Stavanger clubs and pubs can show you a good time year-round. Walk along **Skagenkaien** and **Strandkaien** streets for a choice of pubs and nightclubs. In summer, harborside places with patios don't usually close until dawn. **Checkpoint Charlie** (☒ Lars Hertevig gt. 5 🖥 51–53–22–45) is popular with the twentysomethings, and sometimes doubles as a concert venue. Step into the stylish wine cellar **Flaskehalsen** (⊠ Øvre Holmegt. 20 ☎ 51–86–41–58) if you're seeking quiet, romantic moments. College kids hang out at **Folken** (⊠ Ny Olavskleiv 16 ☎ 51–56–44–44), an independent student club that frequently holds rock concerts. Sun-kissed **Hansen Hjørnet** (⊠ Skagenkaien 18 ☎ 51–89–52–80 ☉ Mid-May–mid-Sept.) is a bar and restaurant that always attracts a crowd. With its open fireplace and stone walls, **Nåloyet** (⊠ Nedre Strandgt. 13 ☎ 51–84–37–60) is Stavanger's answer to the London pub. Dance the night away to pulsating sounds at the lively **Taket Nattklubb** (⊠ Nedre Strandgt. 15 ☎ 51–84–37–20), popular with those in their twenties and thirties.

Sports & the Outdoors

FISHING Angling for saltwater fish doesn't require a license or a fee of any kind. The local tourist office can help you get the permits required for other types of fishing.

North of Stavanger is the longest salmon river in western Norway, the Suldalslågen, made popular 100 years ago by a Scottish aristocrat who built a fishing lodge there. **Lakseslottet Lindum** (⊠ 4240 Suldalsosen ☎ 52/79–91–61) still has rooms, cabins, and camping facilities, as well as an upscale restaurant. The main salmon season is July through September. Wear diving gear and you can go on a **Salmon Safari** (⊠ Mo Laksegard ☎ 52/79–76–90), floating in the river 2 km (1 mi) to study wild salmon in their natural environment.

On the island of Kvitsøy, in the archipelago just west of Stavanger, you can rent an apartment, complete with fish-smoking and -freezing facilities, and arrange to use a small sailboat or motorboat. **Kvitsøy Kurs & Konferanse** (✆ Box 35, 4090 Kvitsøy ☎ 51–73–51–88) can help with arrangements.

HIKING Specialized books and maps are available through **Stavanger Turist-forening** (✆ Postboks 239, 4001 ☎ 51–84–02–00 ⊕ www.stavanger-turistforening.no). The office can help you plan a hike through the area, particularly in the rolling Setesdalsheiene and the thousands of islands and skerries of the Ryfylke Archipelago. The tourist board oversees 33 cabins for members (you can join on the spot) for overnighting along the way.

HORSEBACK **Fossanmoen** (☎ 51–70–37–61 ⊕ www.fossanmoen.no) organizes riding RIDING camps and trips on Iceland ponies that go through scenic surroundings. They can last anywhere from an hour to all day.

ICE-SKATING From November through March you can skate outdoors at **Kunstisbanen** (⊠ Åsen, Sørmarka ☎ 51–58–06–44). **Stavanger Ishall** (⊠ Siddishallen ☎ 51–53–74–50) has ice-skating from mid-September to mid-April.

SKIING Skiing in the Sirdal area, 2½ hours from Stavanger, is possible from January to April. Special ski buses leave Stavanger on weekends at 8:30 AM during the season. Especially recommended is **Sinnes** (☎ 38–37–12–02) for its non-hair-raising cross-country terrain. Downhill skiing is available at **Ålsheia,** which is on the same bus route. Other places to ski include **Gullingen skisenter, Suldal** (☎ 52/79–99–01), **Sandalen skisenter, Sauda**

(☎ 52/78–56–56), and **Stavtjørn alpinsenter** (☎ 51–45–17–17). Contact **Connex Vest** (✉ Treskevn. 5, Hafrsfjord, Stavanger ☎ 51–59–90–00) for transportation information.

WATER SPORTS Diving is excellent all along the coast—although Norwegian law requires all foreigners to dive with a Norwegian as a way of ensuring that wrecks are left undisturbed. If you just want to take a swim, plan a trip to **local beaches** such as **Møllebukta** and **Madia**, which are both deep inside the Hafrsfjord. **Solastranden** has 2⅓ km (1½ mi) of sandy beach ideal for windsurfing and beach volleyball. Other prime beach spots are Vaulen badeplass, Godalen badeplass, Viste Stranden, and Sande Stranden. The World Tour Beach Volleyball tournament is held downtown on a temporary beach volleyball court at the end of June.

The local swimming pool is **Stavanger Svømmehall** (☎ 51–50–74–51). **Gamlingen Friluftsbad** (✉ Tjodolfsgt. 53 ☎ 51–52–74–49) is an outdoor heated swimming pool that's open year-round.

Shopping

Kvadrat Steen & Strøm (✉ Forus between Stavanger and Sandnes ☎ 51–96–00–00) is Norway's biggest shopping center, with 160 shops, restaurants, a pharmacy, a post office, a state wine store, and a tourist information office. Bookworms might find literary treasures in the aptly titled **Odd Book Shop** (✉ Kirkegt. 30 ☎ 51–89–47–66). Reindeer hides, sheepskin, and other souvenirs are sold at **Olaf Pettersen & Co.** (✉ Kirkegt. 31 ☎ 51–89–48–04). If jewelry's your passion, head to the city's best shop: **Sølvsmeden på Sølvberget** (✉ Sølvberggt. 5 ☎ 51–89–42–24). **Stavanger Storsenter Steen & Strøm** (✉ Klubbgt. 5 ☎ 51–93–80–00) is a centrally located shopping center.

In an early-17th-century wharf house, **Straen Handel** (✉ Strandkaien 31 ☎ 51–52–52–02) has an impressive collection of knitted items, rosemaling, Norwegian dolls, trolls, books, and postcards.

Southern Norway A to Z

To research prices, get advice from other travelers, and book travel arrangements, visit www.fodors.com.

AIR TRAVEL

Kristiansand and Stavanger are served by SAS Braathens, with nonstop flights from Oslo, Bergen, Trondheim, and Newcastle, as well as Copenhagen, Aberdeen, Göteborg, and London. MUK Air serves Aalborg, Denmark; Agder Fly serves Göteborg, Sweden, and Billund, Denmark. Tickets on the last two airlines can be booked through SAS Braathens. The low-cost Norwegian Air Shuttle has flights from Oslo to Stavanger. Widerøe flyveselskap specializes in flights within Norway.

🔢 Airlines & Contacts **Norwegian Air Shuttle** ☎ 815–21–815. **Widerøe** ☎ 810–01–200. **SAS Braathens** ☎ 05400.

AIRPORTS

Kristiansand's Kjevik Airport is about 16 km (10 mi) outside town. The airport bus departs from the Braathens office approximately one hour before every departure and proceeds to Kjevik, stopping at downtown hotels along the way. A similar bus makes the return trip from the airport.

In Stavanger, Sola Airport is 14 km (11 mi) south of downtown. The Flybussen (airport bus) leaves the airport every 20 minutes. It stops at hotels and outside the railroad station in Stavanger. It then heads back to the airport.

🚌 **Flybussen** ☎ 51–52–26–00.

BOAT & FERRY TRAVEL

Color Line has four ships weekly on the Stavanger–Newcastle route. High-speed boats to Bergen are operated by Flaggruten. Fjord Line offers car ferries that go from Stavanger to Newcastle, England, and from Egersund to Hanstholm, in northern Denmark. Another line connects Larvik to Frederikshavn, on Denmark's west coast. For information about this crossing, contact DSB in Denmark, or Color Line or DFDS Scandinavian Seaways in Norway.

🚢 **Color Line A/S** ✉ Nygt. 13, 4006 Stavanger ☎ 810–00–811 ⊕ www.colorline.no. **DFDS Scandinavian Seaways** ☎ 38–17–17–60 ⊕ www.seaeurope.com. **DSB** ☎ 33–14–17–01, 42–52–92–22 in Denmark ⊕ www.dsb.dk. **Fjord Line** ☎ 815–33–500 ⊕ www.fjordline.com. **Flaggruten** ☎ 51–86–87–80.

BUS TRAVEL

Aust-Agder Trafikkselskap, based in Arendal, has one departure daily in each direction for the 5½- to 6-hour journey between Oslo and Kristiansand. Nor-Way Bussekspress runs between Oslo and Stavanger, which is about a 10-hour trip. Sørlandsruta, based in Mandal, has two departures in each direction for the 4½-hour trip from Kristiansand bus terminal to Stavanger. The main bus terminal is outside the train station.

Bus connections in Sørlandet are infrequent; the tourist office can provide a comprehensive schedule. HAGA Reiser operates buses between Stavanger and Hamburg.

🚌 **Aust-Agder Trafikkselskap** ☎ 37–02–65–00. **HAGA Reiser** ☎ 51–67–65–00 or 38–12–33–12. **Kristiansand Bus Information** ✉ Strandgt. 33 ☎ 38–00–28–00. **Ruteservice Stavanger, Nor-Way Bussekspress** ☎ 820/53–300 or 815–44–444. **Sørlandsruta** ☎ 38–03–83–00.

CAR TRAVEL

From Oslo it is 320 km (199 mi) to Kristiansand and 452 km (281 mi) to Stavanger. Route E18 parallels the coastline but stays slightly inland on the eastern side of the country and farther inland in the western part. Although seldom wider than two lanes, it is easy driving because it is so flat. Driving from Bergen to Stavanger along the jagged western coastline is difficult and requires a detour of 150 km (93 mi).

Sørlandet is also flat, so it's easy driving throughout. The area around the Kulturhus in the Stavanger city center is closed to car traffic, and one-way traffic is the norm in the rest of the downtown area.

CAR RENTALS 🚗 Major Agencies **Avis Bilutleie** ☎ 815–33–044. **Budget** ☎ 815–60–600. **Hertz Bilutleie** ☎ 67/16–80–00.

TAXIS

All Kristiansand and Stavanger taxis are connected with a central dispatching office. Journeys within Stavanger are charged by the meter, elsewhere strictly by distance.

🔢 Taxi Information **Norgestaxi Stavanger** ☎ 08000. **Stavanger Taxisentral** ☎ 51-90-90-90. **Taxi Sør** ☎ 38-02-80-00 Kristiansand.

TOURS

Tours of Kristiansand are offered only in summer. The City Train is a 15-minute tour of the center part of town. The MS *Maarten* gives two-hour tours of the eastern archipelago and a three-hour tour of the western archipelago daily at 10 AM, from early June until August 8.

In Stavanger a two-hour bus tour leaves from the marina at Vågen daily at 1 between June and August. Rødne Clipper Fjord Sightseeing offers three different tours. FjordTours operates sightseeing and charter tours by boat.

🔢 Fees & Schedules **City Train** ✉ Nedre Torv ☎ 38-03-05-24. **FjordTours** ☎ 51-53-73-40. **MS Maarten** ✉ Pier 6 by Fiskebrygga ☎ 38-10-83-84. **Rødne Clipper Fjord Sightseeing** ✉ Skagenkaien 18, 4006 ☎ 51-89-52-70.

TRAIN TRAVEL

The Sørlandsbanen leaves Oslo S Station four times daily for the 5-hour journey to Kristiansand and five times daily for the 8½- to 9-hour journey to Stavanger. Two more trains travel the 3½-hour Kristiansand–Stavanger route. Kristiansand's train station is at Vestre Strandgata. For information on trains from Stavanger, call Stavanger Jernbanestasjon.

🔢 Train Information **Kristiansand Train Station** ☎ 38-07-75-32. **NSB** (Norwegian State Railways) ☎ 815-00-888. **Stavanger Jernbanestasjon** (Stavanger Train Station) ☎ 51-56-96-10.

VISITOR INFORMATION

🔢 Tourist Information **Destinasjon Sørlandet: Kristiansand** ✉ Vestre Torv, Vestre Strandgt. 32, Box 592, 4665 ☎ 38-12-13-14 ⊕ www.sorlandet.com. **Destinasjon Sørlandet: Lillesand** ✉ Strandgt. 14, 4790 ☎ 37-26-16-80. **Destinasjon Sørlandet: Vennesla** ✉ Vennesla stasjon, 4700 ☎ 38-13-72-00. **Destinasjon Stavanger** ✉ Rosenkildetorget ☎ 51-85-92-00 ⊕ www.regionstavanger.com. **Notodden** ✉ Teatergt. 3 ☎ 35-01-50-00. **Sandnes Tourist Board** ✉ Våsgt. 22 ☎ 51-97-55-55. **Setesdal** ✉ 4735 Evje ☎ 37-93-14-00. **Skien** ✉ Reiselivets Hus, N. Hjellegt. 18 ☎ 35-90-55-20. **Telemarkreiser** (Telemark Canal tourist organization) ✉ Nedre Hjellegt. 18, 3702 Skien ☎ 35-90-00-20 🖷 35-90-00-21 ⊕ www.telemarkreiser.no.

BERGEN

Many fall in love with Bergen, Norway's second-largest city, at first sight. Seven rounded lush mountains, pastel-color wooden houses, historic Bryggen, winding cobblestone streets, and Hanseatic relics all make it a place of enchantment. Its many epithets include "Trebyen" (Wooden City; it has many wooden houses), "Regnbyen" (Rainy City, due to its 200 days of rain a year), and "Fjordbyen" (Gateway to the fjords). Surrounded by forested mountains and fjords, it's only natural that most Bergensers feel at home either on the mountains (skiing, hiking, walking, or at their cabins) or at sea (fishing and boating). As for the rainy weather, most visitors quickly learn the necessity of rain jackets and umbrellas. Bergen is even the site of the world's first umbrella vending machine.

Residents take legendary pride in their city and its luminaries. The composer Edvard Grieg, the violinist Ole Bull, and Ludvig Holberg, Scandinavia's answer to Molière, all made great contributions to Norwegian culture. Today their legacy lives on in nationally acclaimed theater, music, film, dance, and art. The singer Sondre Lerche, pianist Leif Ove Andsnes, choreographer Jo Strømgren, and author Gunnar Staalesen all live in Bergen. Every year a host of lively festivals attracts national and international artists.

This harbor city has played a vital role in the Norwegian economy. Before the discovery of North Sea oil and Bergen's subsequent rise as the capital of Norway's oil industry, the city was long a major center of fishing and shipping. In fact, Bergen was founded in 1070 by Olav Kyrre as a commercial center. In the 14th century, Hanseatic merchants settled in Bergen and made it one of their four major overseas trading centers. The surviving Hanseatic wooden buildings on Bryggen (the quay) are topped with triangular cookie-cutter roofs and painted in red, blue, yellow, and green. Monuments in themselves (they are on the UNESCO World Heritage List), the buildings tempt travelers and locals to the shops, restaurants, and museums inside. In the evening, when the Bryggen is illuminated, these modest buildings, together with the stocky Rosenkrantz Tower, the Fløyen, and the yachts lining the pier, are reflected in the waters of the harbor—and provide one of the loveliest cityscapes in northern Europe.

Exploring Bergen

The heart of Bergen is Torgallmenningen, the city's central square, which runs from Ole Bulls plass to Fisketorget on the harbor, facing Bryggen. From here, the rest of Bergen spreads up the sides of the seven mountains that surround it, with some sights concentrated near the university and others near a small lake called Lille Lungegårdsvann. Fløyen, the mountain to the east of the harbor, is the most accessible for daytrippers. Before you begin your walking tour, you can take the funicular (cable car) up to the top of it for a particularly fabulous overview of the city.

Numbers in the text correspond to numbers in the margin and on the Bergen map.

Historic Bergen: Bryggen to Fløyen

a good walk

Start your tour in the center of town at Torget, also called **Fisketorget** ❶ ► or the fish market, where fishermen and farmers sell their goods. Next, walk over to **Bryggen** ❷, the wharf on the northeast side of Bergen's harbor. The gabled wood warehouses lining the docks mark the site of the city's original settlement. Take time to walk the narrow passageways between buildings; shops and galleries are hidden among the wooden facades. Follow the pier to the **Hanseatisk Museum** ❸ at

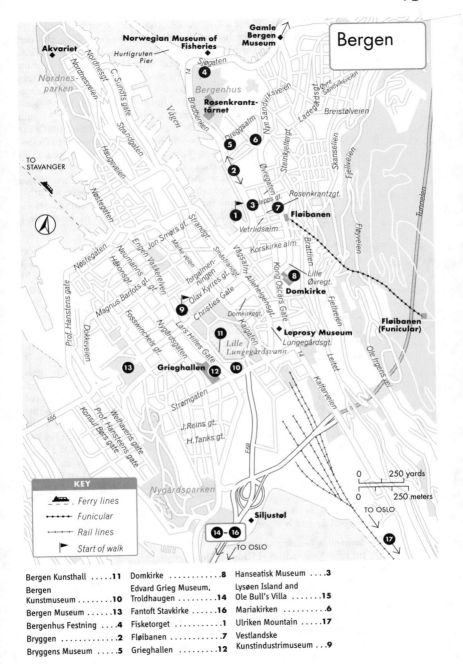

Bergen

Akvariet

Norwegian Museum of Fisheries

Hurtigruten Pier

Gamle Bergen Museum

Nordnes-parken

Sjøgaten

Bergenhus

Rosenkrantz-tärnet

TO STAVANGER

Fløibanen

Vetrlidsalm

Korskirke alm

Lille Øvregt.

Domkirke

Fløibanen (Funicular)

Leprosy Museum

Grieghallen

Lille Lungegårdsvann

Strømgaten

J.Reins gt.

H.Tanks gt.

Nygårdsparken

KEY

- 🚢 Ferry lines
- •—•—• Funicular
- ┼—┼—┼ Rail lines
- ▶ Start of walk

0 ———— 250 yards

0 ———— 250 meters

TO OSLO

Siljustøl

14 – 16

TO OSLO

Finnegårdsgaten and have a look inside. Afterward, continue your walk down the wharf, past the historic buildings, to the end of the Holmen promontory and to **Bergenhus Festning** ❹ (Bergenhus Fort), which dates from the 13th century; the nearby Rosenkrantztårnet is a 16th-century tower residence. After you've spent some time out here, retrace your steps back to the Radisson SAS Royal Hotel. Beside the hotel is **Bryggens Museum** ❺, which houses magnificent archaeological finds. Just behind the museum is the 12th-century church called **Mariakirken** ❻. Around the back of the church up the small hill is Øvregaten, a street that's the back boundary of Bryggen. Walk down Øvregaten four blocks to **Fløibanen** ❼, the funicular that runs up and down Fløyen, one of the city's most popular hiking mountains. Don't miss a trip to the top, whether you hike or take the funicular—the view is like no other. When you've returned, walk south on Øvregaten to the **Domkirke** ❽ (Bergen Cathedral). It's on your left, at the intersection with Kong Oscars Gate. Finally, head back to Torgallmenningen in the center of town for a late-afternoon snack at one of the nearby cafés.

TIMING This tour will take a good portion of a day. Be sure to get to the Fisketorget early in the morning, since many days it may close as early as 1 or 2. Also, try to plan your trip up Fløyen for a sunny day. It may be difficult, as Bergen is renowned for rain, but you may want to wait a day or two and see if the skies clear up.

WHAT TO SEE **Akvariet.** Here you will see one of the largest collections of North Sea fish and invertebrates in Europe, as well as tropical saltwater and freshwater fish. The aquarium has 60 tanks and three outdoor pools of seals, carp, and penguins. On a realistic nesting cliff, adorable penguins rest, waddle by, and stare back curiously at onlookers. Watch the seals, Kobbe-Lars, Amalie, and their companions, as they zoom by like swimming torpedoes. Tanks inside are filled with schools of brilliantly colored tropical fish as well as Norwegian salmon and common eels, which tend to wrap around each other. *The Aquarium: Bergen and the Local Coastline*—a 360-degree video directed by one of Norway's most beloved animators, the late Ivo Caprino—is shown every hour, as is *SOS Planet*, a 3-D film that you watch with special glasses. The aquarium is on Nordnes Peninsula, a 20-minute walk from the fish market. You can also get to it by taking Bus 11 or the ferry from the fish market. ✉ *Nordnesbakken 4, Nordnes* ☎ *55–55–71–71* ⊕ *www.akvariet.com* 🖅 *NKr 100* ☉ *May–Aug., daily 9–8; Sept.–Apr., daily 10–6. Feeding times: May–Aug., daily noon, 3, and 6; Sept.–Apr., daily noon and 3.*

❹ **Bergenhus Festning** (Bergenhus Fortress). The buildings here date from the mid-13th century. **Håkonshallen,** a royal ceremonial hall erected during the reign of Håkon Håkonsson between 1247 and 1261, was badly damaged by the explosion of a German ammunition ship in 1944, but was restored by 1961. Erected in the 1560s by the governor of Bergen Castle (Bergenhus), Erik Rosenkrantz, **Rosenkrantztårnet** (Rosenkrantz Tower) served as a combined residence and fortified tower. ✉ *Bergenhus, Bryggen* ☎ *55–58–80–10* 🖅 *NKr 25* ☉ *Mid-May–mid-Aug., daily 10–4; mid-Aug.–mid-May, Sun. noon–3. Closed during Bergen International Music Festival.*

② **Bryggen** (The Wharf). A trip to Bergen is incomplete without a trip to
Fodor'sChoice Bryggen. A row of mostly reconstructed 14th-century wooden buildings
★ that face the harbor makes this one of the most charming walkways in
Europe, especially on a sunny day. The originals were built by Hansa
merchants, while the oldest reconstruction dates from 1702. Several fires,
the latest in 1955, destroyed the original structures.

⑤ **Bryggens Museum.** This museum contains archaeological finds from the
Middle Ages. An exhibit on Bergen circa 1300 shows the town at the
zenith of its importance, and has reconstructed living quarters as well
as artifacts such as old tools and shoes. Back then, Bergen was the
largest town in Norway, a cosmopolitan trading center and the national
capital. ⊠ *Dreggsalmenning 3* ☎ *55–58–80–10* ⊕ *www.uib.no/bmu*
⌨ *NKr 40* ⊘ *May–Aug., daily 10–5; Sept.–Apr., weekdays 11–3, Sat.
noon–3, Sun. noon–4.*

⑧ **Domkirke** (Bergen Cathedral). The cathedral's long, turbulent history has
shaped the eclectic architecture of the current structure. The Gothic-style
choir and the lower towers are the oldest, dating from the 13th century.
Note the cannonball lodged in the tower wall—it dates from a battle
between English and Dutch ships in Bergen harbor in 1665. From June
through August, a Sunday service is held in English at 9:30 AM in the
Chapter House, an organ recital is held Thursday at noon, and there is
a concert in the church every Sunday at 7:30 PM. September through
May the Sunday concerts are held at 6 PM. ⊠ *Kong Oscars gt. and
Domkirke gt.* ☎ *55–59–32–73* ⊘ *June–Aug., Mon.–Sat. 11–4; Sept.–May,
Tues.–Fri. 11–12:30.*

▶ **①** **Fisketorget** (Fish Market). Turn-of-the-20th-century photographs of this
pungent square show fishermen in Wellington boots and raincoats and
women in long aprons. Now the fishmongers wear bright-orange rubber overalls as they look over the catches of the day. In summer the selection is mostly limited to shrimp, salmon, and monkfish. There is much
greater variety and more locals shop here the rest of the year. There are
also fruit, vegetable, and flower stalls, and some handicrafts and souvenir vendors at this lively market. You'll also find the world's first umbrella vending machine. Have a classic lunch of smoked shrimp or
salmon on a baguette with mayonnaise and cucumber. ⊠ *Zacharias-
bryggen* ☎ *55–31–56–17* ⊕ *www.torgetibergen.no* ⊘ *June–Aug., daily
7–7; Sept.–May, Mon.–Sat. 7–4.*

★ **⑦** **Fløibanen** (Fløyen Funicular). A magnificent view of Bergen and its suburbs can be taken in from the top of **Mt. Fløyen,** the most popular of
the city's seven mountains. The eight-minute ride on the funicular takes
you to the top, 1,050 feet above the sea. A car departs every half hour.
Take a break at the restaurant and café (open daily in summer and weekends the rest of the year), the gift shop, or the children's playground.
Stroll down the walking path back to downtown or explore the mountains that lead to Ulriken, the highest of the mountains surrounding Bergen.
⊠ *Vetrlidsalmenning 21, Bryggen* ☎ *55–33–68–00* ⊕ *www.floibanen.
no* ⌨ *NKr 60* ⊘ *Sept.–Apr., Mon.–Thurs. 7:30 AM–11 PM, Fri. 7:30
AM–11:30 PM, Sat. 8 AM–11:30 PM, Sun. 9 AM–11 PM; May–Aug., same
start times, runs until midnight.*

★ ❸ **Hanseatisk Museum.** One of the best-preserved buildings in Bergen, the Hanseatic Museum was the 16th-century office and home of an affluent German merchant. The apprentices lived upstairs, in boxed-in beds with windows cut into the wall. Although claustrophobic, the snug rooms had the benefit of being relatively warm—a blessing in the unheated building. ⊠ *Finnegårdsgaten 1A* ☎ *55–54–46–90* ⊕ *www. hanseatisk.museum.no* 🎟*NKr 45, off-season NKr 25* ☉ *May, daily 11–2; June–Aug., daily 9–5; early–mid Sept., daily 10–3; late Sept. daily 11–2; Oct.–Apr., Tues.–Sat. 11–2, Sun. noon–5.*

❻ **Mariakirken** (St. Mary's Church). Considered one of the most outstanding Romanesque churches in Norway, this is the oldest building in Bergen used for its original purpose. It began as a church in the 12th century but gained a Gothic choir, richly decorated portals, and a splendid baroque pulpit, much of it added by the Hanseatic merchants who owned it from 1408 to 1766. See the gilded triptych at the high altar that dates from the late Middle Ages. Organ recitals are held every Tuesday at 7:30 PM from late June through August. ⊠ *Dreggen, Bryggen* ☎ *55–59–32–73* 🎟 *NKr 20* ☉ *Late June–Aug., weekdays 9:30–11:30 and 1–4; Sept.–early June, Tues.–Fri. 11–12:30.*

Fodor'sChoice
★

Rasmus Meyers Allé & Grieghallen

a good walk

From Torgallmenningen, walk to Nordahl Bruns Gate and turn left for the **Vestlandske Kunstindustrimuseum** ❾ ▶, the West Norway Museum of Decorative Art. After you've had your fill of the museum's elaborately crafted works, head out for Christies Gate. Follow it along the park and turn left on Rasmus Meyers Allé, which runs along the small lake, Lille Lungegårdsvann, to reach the **Bergen Kunstmuseum** ❿ (Bergen Art Museum), which encompasses the **City Art Collection,** the **Stenersen Collection,** and the **Rasmus Meyer Collection,** all housed next to each other. Nudged in between is the bright green building housing the **Bergen Kunsthall** ⓫ (Bergen Art Hall), a gallery featuring contemporary art. Near these galleries, right on Lars Hilles Gate, is **Grieghallen** ⓬, Bergen's famous music hall.

Behind the hall, on Nygårdsgaten, walk up Herman Foss Gate to Muséplass to the **Bergen Museum** ⓭. Heading back into the center of the city, walk down Nygårdsgaten to Strømgaten to Kong Oscars Gate to the **Leprosy Museum.**

TIMING   The museums on this tour are quite small and very near each other, so you will be able to view most of them on a single outing if you want to, and you probably won't need more than half a day to go around them.

WHAT TO SEE   **Bergen Kunsthall** (Bergen Art Hall). Nestled snuggly between its more established cousins, this small museum focuses solely on contemporary art, usually Norwegian. It features two art galleries and a café, **Landmark,** which is popular among local art students and sometimes also doubles as an extra showroom, theater, or concert hall. ⊠ *Rasmus Meyers Allé 5, City Center* ☎ *55–55–93–10* ⊕ *www.kunsthall.no* 🎟 *NKr 50* ☉ *Tues.–Sun. noon–5.*

❿ **Bergen Kunstmuseum** (Bergen Art Museum). This important Bergen institution, one of the largest museums in Norway, is made up of the Lysver-

TOURS IN & AROUND BERGEN

BERGEN IS THE GUIDED-TOUR capital of Norway because it is the starting point for most fjord tours. Tickets for all tours are available from the **tourist office** (✉ Vågsalmenningen 1 ☎ 55–55–20–00 ⊕ www.visitbergen.com).

The ambitious all-day Norway-in-a-Nutshell bus-train-boat tour (you can book through the tourist office) goes through Voss, Flåm, Myrdal, and Gudvangen— truly a breathtaking trip—and is the best way to see a lot of the area in a short amount of time. The ticket is valid for weeks, so it is possible to break the trip up into more manageable chunks and stay a night or two at hotels along the way. If you choose to do that, the tourist office can assist with bookings.

Boat Tours

Traveling by boat is an advantage because the contrasts between the fjords and mountains are greatest at water level. The vessels are comfortable and stable (the water is practically still), so seasickness is rare. Stops are frequent, and all sights are explained. **Bergen Fjord Sightseeing** (☎ 55–25–90–00) offers several local fjord tours. **Fjord1 Fylkesbaatane** (☎ 55–90–70–70 ⊕ www.fjord1.no) has several combination tours. Tickets are sold at the tourist office and at the quay.

Norway's largest and oldest tall sailing ship, **Statsraad Lehmkuhl,** (☎ 55–30–17–00 ⊕ www.lehmkuhl.no) is the pride of Bergen. Sailing cruises, short skerry cruises, and charters are available. The **TMSY Weller** (☎ 55–19–13–03 or 40–82–58–28 ⊕ www.weller.no) can be booked for charter and fishing tours.

Bus & Walking Tours

Bergens-Expressen (☎ 55–53–11–50), a "train on tires," leaves from Torgallmenningen for a one-hour ride around the center of town (summer only).

Bergen Guide Service (☎ 55–30–10–60 ⊕ www.bergenguideservice.no) has about 100 authorized guides who give different city walking tours such as Unknown Bergen and Bergen Past and Present.

ket, Rasmus Meyer, and Stenersen collections. They are housed in buildings along the Lille Lungegårdsvann lake. The large, neoclassicist Lysverket building used to house the municipal power company, but was bought by the city council and reopened as an art museum in 2003. The permanent exhibit showcases both medieval icons and Dutch Renaissance masters, but there's also a large collection of classic and contemporary Norwegian art on display. The changing exhibits usually feature contemporary art. ⊠ *Bergen Art Museum, Rasmus Meyers Allé 3 and 7, Lars Hilles gt. 10, City Center* ☎ *55–56–80–00* ⊕ *www. bergenartmuseum.no* 🎫 *NKr 50* ⊗ *Daily 11–5.*

⓭ Bergen Museum. Part of the University of Bergen, this museum has two collections. The **Cultural History Department** has a fascinating collection of archaeological artifacts and furniture and folk art from western Norway. Some of the titles of the displays are "Inherited from Europe," "Viking Times," "Village Life in the Solomon Islands," and "Ibsen in Bergen"; the latter focuses on the famous playwright's six years in Bergen working with the local theater. The **Natural History Department** is perfect for lovers of the outdoors, since it includes botanical gardens. Exhibits include "The Ice Age," "Oil Geology," "Fossils," "Mineral Collections," and "The Evolution of Man." ⊠ *Haakon Sheteligs pl. 10 and Musépl. 3, City Center* ☎ *55–58–81–72 or 55–58–29–05* ⊕ *www. museum.uib.no* 🎫 *NKr 40* ⊗ *June–Aug., Tues.–Fri. 10–4, weekends 11–4; Sept.–May, Tues.–Fri. 10–2, weekends 11–3.*

off the beaten path

GAMLE BERGEN MUSEUM (Old Bergen Museum) – This family-friendly open-air museum transports you to 18th- and 19th-century Bergen. Streets and narrow alleys with 40 period wooden houses show town life as it used to be. A baker, dentist, photographer, jeweler, shopkeeper, and sailor are represented. Local artists often hold exhibitions here. The grounds and park are open free of charge year-round. ⊠ *Nyhavnsveien 4, Sandviken* ☎ *55–39–43–00* ⊕ *www.gamlebergen.museum.no* 🎫 *NKr 60* ⊗ *May 8–Sept. 4; guided tours every hr 10–5.*

⓬ Grieghallen. Home of the Bergen Philharmonic Orchestra and stage for the annual International Festival, this music hall is a conspicuous slab of glass and concrete. The acoustics are marvelous. Built in 1978, the hall was named for the city's famous son, composer Edvard Grieg (1843–1907). From September to May, every Thursday and some Fridays and Saturdays at 7:30 PM, the orchestra gives concerts. Throughout the year, the hall is a popular venue for cultural events. ⊠ *Edvard Griegs pl. 1* ☎ *55–21–61–00* ⊕ *www.grieghallen.no.*

Leprosy Museum. St. George's Hospital houses the Bergen Collection of the History of Medicine, which includes this museum. Although the current buildings date from the early 1700s, St. George's was a hospital for lepers for more than 500 years. This unusual museum profiles Norway's contribution to leprosy research. Many Norwegian doctors have been recognized for their efforts against leprosy, particularly Armauer Hansen, after whom "Hansen's disease" is named. ⊠ *St. George's Hos-*

pital, Kong Oscars gt. 59 ☎ *55–96–11–55* ⊕ *www.lepra.no* ✉ *NKr 30* ⊗ *Mid-May–Aug., daily 11–3.*

off the beaten path

NORWEGIAN MUSEUM OF FISHERIES – The sea and its resources, territorial waters, management and research, boats and equipment, whaling and sealing, and fish farming are all covered in the exhibits here. There are also substantial book, video, and photography collections. ✉ *Bontelabo 2* ☎ *55–32–27–10* ⊕ *www.fiskerimuseum. no* ✉ *NKr 30* ⊗ *June–Aug., daily 10–6; Sept.–May, Sun.–Fri. 11–4.*

Fodor'sChoice
★
Rasmus Meyer Collection. When the businessman Rasmus Meyer (1858–1916) was assembling his superb collection of works by what would become world-famous artists, most of them were unknowns. On display are the best Edvard Munch paintings outside Oslo, as well as major works by J. C. Dahl, Adolph Tidemand, Hans Gude, Harriet Backer, and Per Krogh. Head to the Blumenthal Room to see a fine 18th-century interior and some incredible frescoes. ✉ *Bergen Art Museum, Rasmus Meyers Allé 3 and 7, Lars Hilles gt. 10, City Center* ☎ *55–56–80–00* ⊕ *www.bergenartmuseum.no* ✉ *NKr 50* ⊗ *Mid-May–mid-Sept., daily 11–5; mid-Sept.–mid-May, Tues.–Sun. 11–5.*

★ **Stenersen Collection.** This is an extremely impressive collection of modern art for a town the size of Bergen. Modern artists represented include Max Ernst, Paul Klee, Vassily Kandinsky, Pablo Picasso, and Joan Miró, as well as Edvard Munch. There's also a large focus here on Norwegian art since the mid-18th century. ✉ *Bergen Art Museum, Rasmus Meyers Allé 3 and 7, Lars Hilles gt. 10, City Center* ☎ *55–56–80–00* ⊕ *www.bergenartmuseum.no* ✉ *NKr 50* ⊗ *Mid-May–mid-Sept., daily 11–5; mid-Sept.–mid-May, Tues.–Sun. 11–5.*

▶ ❾ **Vestlandske Kunstindustrimuseum** (West Norway Museum of Decorative Art). One of Norway's best museums, this eclectic collection contains many exquisite art and design pieces. Its permanent "People and Possessions" exhibit spans 500 years and has everything from Bergen silverware to Ole Bull's violin, which was made in 1562 by the Italian master Saló. Bull's violin has a head of an angel on it, carved by Benvenuto Cellini. A fine collection traces the history of chair design. "The Art of China," the other permanent exhibition, presents one of Europe's largest collections of Buddhist marble sculptures alongside porcelain, jade, bronzes, textiles, and paintings. The silk robes embroidered with dragons and other ceremonial garments are stunning. Changing exhibitions focus on painting, decorative art, and design. ✉ *Permanenten, Nordahl Bruns gt. 9, City Center* ☎ *55–33–66–33* ⊕ *www.vk.museum. no* ✉ *NKr 50* ⊗ *Mid-May–mid-Sept., daily 11–5; mid-Sept.–mid-May, Tues.–Sun. noon–4.*

Troldhaugen, Fantoft, Lysøen & Ulriken

a good drive

Once you've gotten your fill of Bergen's city life, you can head out to the countryside to tour some of the area's interesting, and lesser-known, low-key attractions. Follow Route 580 or the E39 (toward Stavanger) out of town about 6 km (4 mi) to **Edvard Grieg Museum, Troldhaugen** ⑩, the villa where Grieg lived for 22 years. After you've wandered the grounds, head for **Lysøen Island and Ole Bull's Villa** ⑮, the Victorian dream castle of Norwegian violinist Ole Bull. Getting here is a 30-minute trek by car and ferry, but it's well worth the effort. From Troldhaugen, get back on Route 580 and drive south toward the airport. At Rådal make a left onto Route 546 (toward Fana). When you reach Fana Kirke, a beautiful 12th-century stone church, Route 546 branches off to the right. Continue straight ahead, leaving Route 546, and drive over Fanafjell to Sørestraumen. Follow signs to Buena Kai. From here, take the ferry to Lysøen. On your way back to Bergen, you can see the **Fantoft Stavkirke** ⑯, which was badly damaged in a fire in 1992 but has been completely rebuilt. End your day with a hike up **Ulriken Mountain** ⑰, the tallest of Bergen's seven mountains. If you're worn out from your sightseeing, but still want take in the view from the top, you can take the Ulriken cable car up the mountain.

About 12 km (7 mi) from Bergen city center, following Route 580 to the airport, is **Siljustøl,** the former home of composer Harald Sæverud. His home is now a music school and museum.

TIMING   Driving and visiting time (or bus time) will consume at least a day or several days, depending on your pace and interest. Visiting these sights is a pleasant way to explore Bergen's environs.

WHAT TO SEE   **Edvard Grieg Museum, Troldhaugen** (Hill of the Trolls). Built in 1885, this
⑭   was the home of Norway's most famous composer, Edvard Grieg. In the little garden hut by the shore of Lake Nordås, he composed many of his best-known works. In 1867 he married his cousin Nina, a Danish soprano. They lived in the white clapboard house with green gingerbread trim for 22 years beginning in about 1885. A salon and gathering place for many Scandinavian artists then, it now houses mementos—a piano, paintings, prints—of the composer's life. Its 1907 interior shows it the way that Grieg knew it. At Troldsalen, a concert hall seating 200, chamber music is performed. Summer concerts are held on Wednesday and weekends, and daily during the Bergen International Festival. To get here, catch a bus from Platform 19, 20, or 21 at the bus station, and get off at Hopsbroen. Turn right, walk 200 yards, turn left on Troldhaugsveien, and follow the signs for roughly 2 km (1 mi). ⊠ *Troldhaugv. 65* ☎ *55–92–29–92* ⊕ *www.troldhaugen.com* ⊠ *NKr 60* ⊙ *May–Sept., daily 9–6; Oct., Nov., and Apr., weekdays 10–2, weekends noon–6; mid-Jan.–Mar., weekdays 10–2.*

⑯   **Fantoft Stavkirke** (Fantoft Stave Church). During the Middle Ages, when
Fodor's Choice   European cathedrals were built in stone, Norway used wood to create
★   unique stave churches. These cultural symbols stand out for their dragon heads, carved doorways, and walls of staves (vertical planks). Though as many as 750 stave churches may have once existed, only 30 remain standing. The original stave church here, built in Fortun in Sogn in 1150 and moved to Fantoft in 1883, burned down in 1992. Since then, the church has been reconstructed to resemble the original structure. From the main bus station next to the railway station, take any bus leaving from Platform 19, 20, or 21. ⊠ *Paradis* ☎ *55–28–07–10* ⊠ *NKr 30* ⊙ *Mid-May–mid-Sept., daily 10:30–2 and 2:30–6.*

🅸 **Lysøen Island and Ole Bull's Villa.** The beautiful villa of Norwegian violin virtuoso Ole Bull (1810–80) is on Lysøen, which means "island of light." Bull was a musician and patron of great vision. In 1850, after failing to establish a "New Norwegian Theater" in America, he founded the National Theater in Norway. He then chose the young playwright Henrik Ibsen to write full time for the theater, and later encouraged and promoted another neophyte—15-year-old Edvard Grieg.

Built in 1873, this villa, with an onion dome, gingerbread gables, curved staircase, and cutwork trim just about everywhere, has to be seen to be believed. Stroll along the 13 km (8 mi) of pathways Bull created, picnic or swim in secluded spots, or rent a rowboat. In summer (the only season that Bull lived here), concerts are performed in the villa.

To get here by bus (Monday–Saturday), take the Lysefjordruta bus from Platform 19 or 20 at the main bus station to Buena Kai, where the *Ole Bull* ferry will take you across the fjord to the island. By car, it's a 25-km (15-mi) trip from Bergen to the ferry. Take road E39 south out of the city. Fork left onto Route 546, signposted FANA; continue straight over Fanafjell Mountain to Sørestraumen and follow signs to Buena Kai from there. ☎ *56–30–90–77* ⊕ *www.lysoen.no* 🎫 *NKr 25* ☼ *May 18–Aug., Mon.–Sat. noon–4, Sun. 11–5; Sept., Sun. noon–4.*

┌──────────┐
│ **off the** │
│ **beaten** │
│ **path** │
└──────────┘

SILJUSTØL – Norway's most important composer of the 20th century, Harald Sæverud (1897–1992), called this unusual house home. He built it in 1939 of wood and stone and followed old Norwegian construction methods. Concerts are occasionally held here on Sunday at 3 PM (admission NKr 150). Take Bus 23 from the Bergen bus station, Platform 19. By car, drive 12 km (7 mi) from Bergen center to Route 580 heading toward the airport. ⊠ *Siljustølsvegen 50* ☎ *55–92–29–92* ⊕ *www.siljustol.no* 🎫 *NKr 50* ☼ *Mid-June–mid-Oct., Sun. noon–4.*

🅸 **Ulriken Mountain.** There are great views of the city, fjords, islands, and coast from the top of the highest of the seven Bergen mountains. The famous Ulriken cable car, running every seven minutes, transports you here. Bring a lunch and hike on well-marked trails in unspoiled mountain wilderness. Or take a break at Ulriken Restaurant and Bar. To get here from downtown, take the Bergen in a Nutshell sightseeing bus along the harbor and Bryggen, through the town center. The same bus returns you to town afterward. ⊠ *Ulriken 1, 5009* ⊕ *www.ulriken.no* ☎ *55–20–20–20* 🎫 *Round-trip, including bus and cable car, NKr 130* ☼ *June–Aug., daily 9 AM–10 PM; May and Sept., daily 9 AM–7 PM; Oct.–Apr., sunny days only 10 AM–5 PM.*

Where to Eat

"Bergen is the city with the ocean and sea completely in its stomach," someone once said. Bergensers love their seafood dishes: *Fiskepudding* (fish pudding), *fiskekaker* (fish cakes), *fiskeboller* (fish balls), and *Bergensk fiskesuppe* (Bergen fish soup)—delicious renditions of such classic dishes show up on local menus with great regularity.

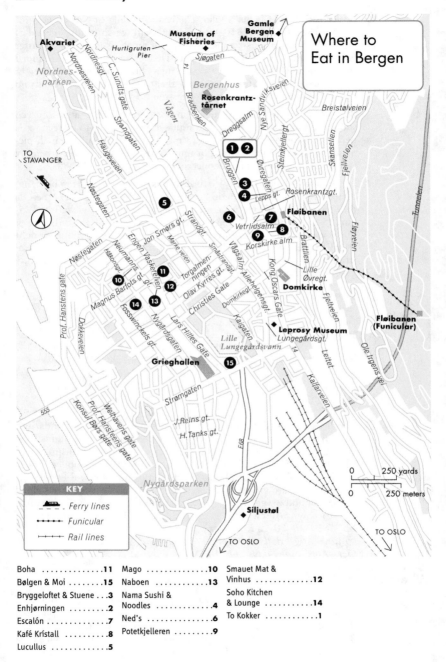

Where to Eat in Bergen

Any Bergen dining experience should start at *Fisketorget,* the fish market. Rain or shine, fresh catches go on sale here in shiny, stainless-steel stalls. The fishmongers dole out shrimp, salmon, monkfish, and friendly advice. Usually, they have steamed *reker* (shrimp), or smoked *laks* (salmon), served on a baguette with mayonnaise and cucumber—a perfect quick lunch. As for desserts, *skillingsbolle,* a big cinnamon roll, or *sommerbolle,* the same with a custard center, are both popular. *Lefse* is a round flat cake of oatmeal or barley that has a sugar or cream filling. Like other major Norwegian cities, Bergen has international cuisines from Tex-Mex, tapas, and Mediterranean to Japanese sushi restaurants. Some Oslo celebrity chefs—for example Bølgen & Moi—have also opened restaurants here.

$$$$ ╳ **Lucullus.** Although the eclectic interior—modern art matched with lace doilies and boardroom chairs—seems a bit out of kilter with the classic French menu here, don't be alarmed; the food is consistently good. The trout with savoy cabbage is excellent. For a meatier treat, try the duck breast with pistachios and orange. The five-course meal is particularly indulgent. ⊠ *Hotel Neptun, Walckendorfsgt. 8* ☎ *55–30–68–20* 👔 *Jacket and tie* ⊟ *DC, MC, V* ⊘ *Closed Sun. No lunch.*

★ **$$$$** ╳ **To Kokker.** Ranked among Bergen's best restaurants by many, To Kokker is on Bryggen wharf. The 300-year-old building has crooked floors and slanted moldings. The seafood and game are excellent. Try the Jerusalem artichoke soup with smoked reindeer heart—a great starter that combines two traditional Norwegian staples. The halibut au gratin with Parmesan sits in a delicate beetroot sauce, a very tasty combination. ⊠ *Bryggen 29* ☎ *55–30–69–55* 🍴 *Reservations essential* ⊟ *AE, DC, MC, V* ⊘ *Closed Sun. No lunch.*

$$$–$$$$ ╳ **Enhjørningen.** This restaurant is named after the unicorn that adorns
Fodor's Choice the doorway of the old wooden building in which it is housed. En-
★ hjørningen has traditions dating back to the Middle Ages, but there's nothing medieval about the menu—it's contemporary Norwegian and it changes according to the day's catch. Try the herb-fried anglerfish served with morel mushroom sauce. If you have trouble deciding, just go for the classic fish platter: salmon, anglerfish, and catfish, steamed and served with two sauces. Enhjørningen is in the running for best seafood restaurant in Bergen. ⊠ *Bryggen 29* ☎ *55–32–79–19* ⊟ *AE, DC, MC, V.*

$$$–$$$$ ╳ **Ned's.** Right at the fish market, Ned's, formerly Fiskekrogen (or the Fishhook), is a quintessential seafood restaurant. The market's last original fish tank from 1888 holds the fresh lobster, codfish, and crab on offer here. The blue-and-white interior and open kitchen make the place feel rustic, as does the stuffed brown bear that still growls. Although Ned's also serves game, stick to seafood dishes such as the grilled salmon with caviar buerre blanc. ⊠ *Zachariasbryggen* ☎ *55–55–96–60* 🍴 *Reservations essential* ⊟ *AE, DC, MC, V.*

$$$–$$$$ ╳ **Potetkjelleren.** A popular contemporary restaurant in very old sur-
Fodor's Choice roundings, Potetkjelleren literally means "potato cellar," and the restau-
★ rant's two main dining rooms are in fact old brick-walled storage rooms in the basement. Everything but the menu seems slightly off balance here: the chairs and tables have a rickety feel, mostly due to the uneven stone-tile floor. What the restaurant lacks in comfort it more than makes up

for in quality and atmosphere. The cozy cellar is perfect for a romantic candlelight dinner, the service is friendly and efficient, and the kitchen turns out such dishes as It's no wonder Potetkjelleren gets rave reviews from local media. ⊠ *Kong Oscars gt. 1 A* ☎ *55–32–00–70* ▤ *AE, DC, MC, V.*

$$$ ✕ **Kafé Krystall.** This small, intimate restaurant is one of the most fashionable in town. The chef combines his own eclectic contemporary style with traditional Norwegian ingredients in lavish set menus. Try the duck breast with Gorgonzola polenta and foie gras or the three kinds of fish soup with clear mussel sauce. ⊠ *Kong Oscars gt. 16* ☎ *55–32–10–84* ⌂ *Reservations essential* ▤ *AE, DC, MC, V* ☉ *Closed Sat. No lunch.*

FodorśChoice
★

$$–$$$ ✕ **Boha.** This modern Italian-inspired restaurant is popular both for business dinners and romantic candlelight suppers. The chef does a particularly good job with seafood. Try the fresh trout with creamy mussels, or the red snapper with pureed celery and garlic. ⊠ *Vaskerelven 6* ☎ *55–31–31–60* ▤ *AE, DC, MC, V.*

★ **$$–$$$** ✕ **Bølgen & Moi.** In the same building as the Bergen Art Museum, this local outlet of Norway's fast-expanding Bølgen & Moi restaurant franchise is the perfect place for a break from the galleries. The lunch menu offers excellent value for money, but the brasserie is well worth a visit later in the evening. Try the fried mackerel with creamed summer cabbage, a modern take on a Norwegian classic. For a hearty lunch, try one of the burgers, such as the Gorgonzola burger with chili mayonnaise. The well-stocked bar is a trendy meeting place for local businesspeople. ⊠ *Rasmus Meyers Allé 9* ☎ *55–59–77–00* ▤ *AE, DC, MC, V.*

$$–$$$ ✕ **Bryggeloftet & Stuene.** Dining here on lutefisk in fall and at Christmastime is a time-honored tradition for many Bergensers. Also consider the *pinnekjøtt* (lumpfish) or the reindeer fillets. The hearty Norwegian country fare suits the somber, wooden dining room, with its fireplace and old oil paintings on the walls. ⊠ *Bryggen 11* ☎ *55–31–06–30* ▤ *AE, DC, MC, V.*

$$–$$$ ✕ **Smauet Mat & Vinhus.** Inside a cozy blue cottage is one of Bergen's least-expensive fine restaurants. Hidden away in a small alley near Ole Bulls plass, this cozy restaurant has a reputation for being innovative with Mediterranean and Norwegian cuisine. Try the glazed guinea hen or one of the seafood dishes. ⊠ *Vaskerelvssmauet 1* ☎ *55–21–07–10* ⌂ *Reservations essential* ▤ *AE, DC, MC, V.*

$$ ✕ **Mago.** The menu here offers modern Mediterranean takes on classic Norwegian ingredients, such as scallops with pureed cauliflower and beetroot. For a main course, try the chicken stuffed with foie gras. Mago used to be a health-food restaurant, and appliances once used to make fiber-laced fruit shakes have now come to better use, for making homemade ice cream. Mago (which means "magician" in Norwegian) also has one of Bergen's best selections of wine by the glass. If you find one you like, you can take your glass downstairs to get cozy in front of a huge fireplace in the wine bar. ⊠ *Neumanns Gate 5* ☎ *55–96–29–80* ▤ *AE, DC, MC, V.*

$$ ✕ **Nama Sushi & Noodles.** The city's most popular sushi bar ("nama" means "fresh and raw" in Japanese) has garnered good reviews for its minimalist, aquatic-inspired interior, and half-sushi, half-noodles menu.

Their fish comes fresh from the market nearby, and there are daily happy hour sushi specials. The sashimi *moriawase* (assortment), the breast of duck, and the banana mousse dessert are delicious. The café/bar is perfect for an afternoon coffee break. ⊠ *Lodin Lepps gt. 2 B* ☎ *55–32–20–10* ⊟ *AE, DC, MC, V.*

$$ ✕ **Soho Kitchen & Lounge.** Perhaps the owners of Soho couldn't decide whether to start a sushi bar or a modern Mediterranean-inspired place, as this restaurant has elements of both. It's an eclectic, interesting restaurant in a suitably schizoid environment that's either minimalist or excessive and flashy, depending on which way you're facing. The bento box is a pricey but tasty lunch deal with miso soup, sushi, and the dessert of the day. If you're hungry for more European flavors, try the succulent roasted chicken breast stuffed with Brie and spinach. ⊠ *Håkon-sgt. 27* ☎ *55–90–19–60* ⊟ *AE, DC, MC, V.*

¢–$$ ✕ **Naboen.** Although many Norwegian restaurants specialize in more traditional dishes, this Swedish restaurant offers delicious, modern variations on Scandinavian classics. Naboen has two menus, an à la carte menu with contemporary styled Swedish and Norwegian specialties, and a moderately priced Swedish menu. Try the popular *Køttbullar* (Swedish meatballs) from the Swedish menu, or if you are feeling more adventurous, the tasty *ristet gravlaks* (roasted cured salmon) from the à la carte menu. ⊠ *Neumanns gt. 20* ☎ *55–90–02–90* ⊟ *AE, DC, MC, V.*

¢ ✕ **Escalón.** Near the Fløibanen, this tiny tapas restaurant and bar is a trendy place to go for a bite or a drink. Taste the *gambas al ajillo* (scampi in wine and garlic) or the *albódigas en salsa de tomate* (meatballs in tomato sauce). ⊠ *Vetrlidsalmenningen 21* ☎ *55–32–90–99* ⊟ *AE, DC, MC, V.*

Where to Stay

From the elegance of the Radisson SAS hotels to the no-frills Crowded House, Bergen has a good selection of accommodation options for every traveler's budget and style. Most Bergen hotels are within walking distance of the city's shopping, restaurants, entertainment, and other attractions. Many hotels offer favorable summer and weekend rates depending on vacancies. Last-minute summer rates may be booked 48 hours prior to arrival June 16–August 31. Off-season (September–May) there are often weekend specials. Bergen Tourist Information Office will assist you in booking your accommodations for a fee of NKr 30, make a reservation for NKr 50, and process a cancellation for NKr 50.

$$$ ▦ **Clarion Hotel Admiral.** Known as "the hotel with the sea on three sides," the Clarion has stunning views of the wharf, the fish market, and Mt. Fløien. Book well in advance for the rooms with the best harbor views. Most rooms have upscale chain-hotel-style furnishings. Some of the suites, however, are decorated with hardwood antique reproductions. Sjøtonnen, the à la carte restaurant, specializes in seafood. After dinner, have a nightcap in the hotel's cognac-and-cigar lounge, which has burnished red-leather sofas. ⊠ *C. Sundtsgt. 9–13 5004* ☎ *55–23–64–00* 🖷 *55–23–64–64* ⊕ *www.admiral.no* ↪ *210 rooms, 2 suites* ♨ *Restaurant, cable TV, bar, lounge, business services, meeting rooms, no-smoking rooms* ⊟ *AE, DC, MC, V.*

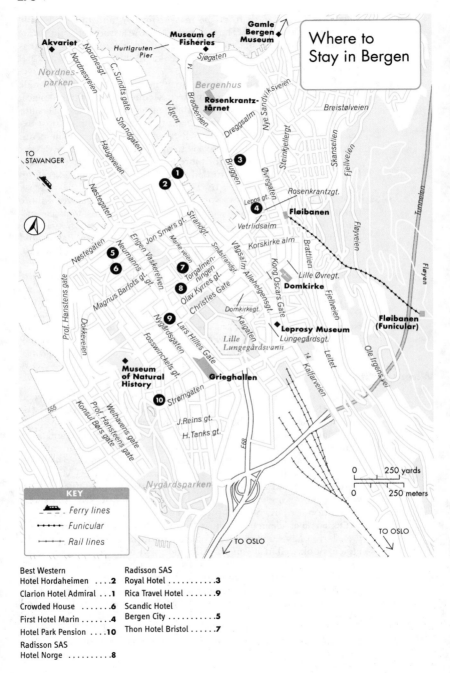

Where to Stay in Bergen

KEY

🚢 Ferry lines
•••••• Funicular
┼┼┼┼ Rail lines

Best Western
Hotel Hordaheimen **2**

Clarion Hotel Admiral ...**1**

Crowded House **6**

First Hotel Marin **4**

Hotel Park Pension **10**

Radisson SAS
Hotel Norge **8**

Radisson SAS
Royal Hotel **3**

Rica Travel Hotel **9**

Scandic Hotel
Bergen City **5**

Thon Hotel Bristol **7**

★ $$$ ⌂ **First Hotel Marin.** On the harborside near Bryggen, in an elegant brick building that once housed one of Bergen's largest print shops, this business hotel is within walking distance of the city's buses, ferries, and trains. Every room has a bathtub and is decorated in yellows and blues, with oak furniture and hardwood floors. Some rooms feature original artwork from local artists. The penthouse suites have magnificent views of Bergen. ⊠ *Rosenkrantzgt. 8, 5003* ☎ *53–05–15–00* 🖶 *53–05–15–01* ⊕ *www.firsthotels.com* ⌁ *122 rooms, 28 suites* ⌂ *2 restaurants, café, cable TV, gym, sauna, Turkish bath, meeting rooms, no-smoking rooms* ⊟ *AE, DC, MC, V.*

$$–$$$ ⌂ **Radisson SAS Hotel Norge.** A Bergen classic, this hotel attracts important people, from prime ministers to musicians. The architecture is modern, with large salmon-color, dark-wood rooms that blend contemporary Scandinavian comfort with traditional warmth. The restaurant T. G. I. Fridays has American-style fare, and the Contra Bar and Library Bar are popular with locals and visitors alike. The Metro nightclub is packed on weekends. The hotel's fresh smorgasbord breakfast is the perfect way to start your day. Ask for a room facing Lille Lungegårdsvann for a scenic view. Rooms facing Ole Bulls plass can be noisy at night. ⊠ *Ole Bulls pl. 4, 5012* ☎ *55–57–30–00* 🖶 *55–57–30–01* ⊕ *www.radissonsas.com* ⌁ *347 rooms, 12 suites* ⌂ *Restaurant, cable TV, indoor pool, health club, 2 bars, nightclub, meeting room* ⊟ *AE, DC, MC, V.*

$$–$$$ ⌂ **Radisson SAS Royal Hotel.** Behind Bryggen, this hotel stands where old warehouses used to be. Ravaged by nine fires since 1170, the warehouses were repeatedly rebuilt in the same style, which has been carried over into the Radisson's facade. The small but comfortable rooms have light gold walls and wood accents. Under a glass ceiling, the Café Royal Restaurant serves Scandinavian and international dishes as well as light snacks. The Madam Felle pub and bar on the waterfront is known for its live jazz and rock music, as well as its whiskeys. Engelen nightclub keeps people dancing until the early hours. ⊠ *Bryggen, 5003* ☎ *55–54–30–00* 🖶 *55–32–48–08* ⊕ *www.radissonsas.com* ⌁ *273 rooms, 10 suites* ⌂ *2 restaurants, cable TV, indoor pool, health club, sauna, bar, pub, dance club, nightclub, convention center* ⊟ *AE, DC, MC, V.*

$$ ⌂ **Best Western Hotel Hordaheimen.** Dating from 1913, one of the city's oldest and most distinctive hotels is on a quiet, central street. The lobby has a memorable collection of painted Norwegian furniture by Lars Kinsarvik. The hotel's café-restaurant, Hordastova, is well known for its traditional fare, especially *klippfisk* (salted and sun-dried cod), fried mackerel, and smoked cod. Rooms are small but nicely decorated with simple Scandinavian-style furniture in solid colors like beige and plum. ⊠ *C. Sundtsgt. 18, 5004* ☎ *55–33–50–00* 🖶 *55–23–49–50* ⊕ *www.hordaheimen.no* ⌁ *64 rooms, 8 suites* ⌂ *Restaurant* ⊟ *AE, DC, MC, V.*

$–$$ ⌂ **Rica Travel Hotel.** Popular with business travelers, this hotel is steps away from Torgallmenningen. The rooms are stylish and the location is ideal, but there are few facilities. A public swimming pool and a popular fitness center are nearby. ⊠ *Christiesgt. 5–7, 5808* ☎ *55–36–29–00* 🖶 *55–31–32–50* ⊕ *www.rica.no* ⌁ *144 rooms* ⌂ *Restaurant, cable TV, bar, meeting rooms, parking (fee)* ⊟ *AE, DC, MC, V.*

$–$$ ⌂ **Thon Hotel Bristol.** The Bristol is within walking distance of many pop-
ular attractions. Built in the 1930s but redecorated in 2001, its rooms
★ are small but comfortable, with cheerful yellow and maroon furnishings. They offer excellent value for money, and several are wheelchair-
accessible. ⌂ *Torgallmenningen 11, 5014* ☎ *55–55–10–00*
🖷 *55–23–23–19* ⊕ *www.thonhotels.no/bristolbergen* ⇥ *134 rooms, 1
suite* ⌂ *Restaurant, cable TV, bar* ⊟ *AE, DC, MC, V.*

★ **$** ⌂ **Hotel Park Pension.** Near the university, this intimate family-run hotel,
one of Norway's historic hotels, is in a well-kept Victorian structure built
in the 1890s. Both the public rooms and the guest rooms are furnished
with antiques. It's a short distance to Grieghallen, downtown, and the
bus and railway stations. ⌂ *Harald Hårfagres gt. 35, 5007*
☎ *55–54–44–00* 🖷 *55–54–44–44* ⊕ *www.parkhotel.no* ⇥ *21 rooms*
⌂ *Dining room, cable TV* ⊟ *AE, DC, MC, V.*

$ ⌂ **Scandic Hotel Bergen City.** This business hotel runs Bergen Congress
Center, the city's largest convention center, and has warm, stylish, comfortable rooms. Take a seat in a wicker chair in the spacious lobby bar
to meet people or relax. The hotel is right between Bergen Kino, two
cinema multiplexes, and it's a short walk to Den Nationale Scene theater, Grieghallen, and restaurants. ⌂ *Håkonsgt. 2–7, 5015*
☎ *55–30–90–80* 🖷 *55–23–49–20* ⊕ *www.scandic-hotels.com* ⇥ *171
rooms, 4 suites* ⌂ *Restaurant, cable TV, bar, business services, convention
center* ⊟ *AE, DC, MC, V.*

¢ ⌂ **Crowded House.** Named after an Australian band that was popular
in the 1980s, this no-frills lodge is perfect for students and budget travelers. It's a short walk from shopping, restaurants, entertainment, and
other attractions, as well as train, bus, and ferry connections. Most of
the spartan rooms have good beds, telephones, and washbasins. Showers and toilets are in the corridor. ⌂ *Håkonsgt. 27, 5015* ☎ *55–90–72–00*
🖷 *55–23–13–30* ⊕ *www.crowded-house.com* ⇥ *34 rooms without
bath* ⌂ *Café* ⊟ *AE, DC, MC, V.*

Nightlife & the Arts

Nightlife

Bergen is a university town, and the many thousand students who live
and study here all year round contribute to making the city's nightlife
livelier than you might expect of a small town. Most nightspots center
around Ole Bulls plass, the plaza at one end of Torgallmenningen.
Within a stone's throw of the plaza you can find dozens of relaxing bars,
lively pubs, dancing, live music, and trendy cafés.

If you prefer a quiet glass of wine in peaceful historic surroundings, try
Altona (⌂ Strandgaten 81 ☎ 55–30–40–72), a bar in a 400-year-old wine
cellar neighboring the Augustin Hotel. **Kamelon** (⌂ Vågsalmenning 16
☎ 91–87–07–23), next door to the nightclub Mood, caters to a more
relaxed crowd. Here you will often find live music, ranging from contemporary pop to folk, mostly by local artists. If you prefer conversation over dancing, try **Logen Bar** (⌂ Øvre Ole Bulls pl. 6 ☎ 55–23–20–15),
a popular meeting place with live acoustic music every Sunday. **Metro**
(⌂ Nedre Ole Bulls pl. 4 ☎ 55–96–02–92) is right in front of the Ole
Bull statue, and is a nightclub popular among local twentysomethings.

It features pulsating dance music, minimalist decor, and serious crowds on weekends. **Mood** (✉ Vågsalmenning 16 ☎ 55–55–96–55) is one of Bergen's largest nightclubs, but is still usually packed weekends with local clubbers in their twenties and thirties.

CAFÉS **Café Opera** (✉ Engen 18 ☎ 55–23–03–15) is a classic, both sumptuous and stylish. It's often crowded on Friday and Saturday nights. **Jonsvoll** (✉ Engen 10 ☎ 55–90–03–84), just across the street from Café Opera, is another popular hangout, both for the sensible food served during the day and for the hip crowd sipping cocktails and beer at night. **Kafe Kippers** (✉ Georgernes Verft 12 ☎ 55–31–00–60), Bergen's largest outdoor café, has cozy wool blankets and a spectacular view of the water at sunset.

Pygmalion (✉ Nedre Korskirke Allmenning 4 ☎ 55–32–33–60) serves tasty organic food and has contemporary art on the walls. Just up the road from Pygmalion is **Godt Brød** (✉ Nedre Korskirke Allmenning 12 ☎ 55–32–80–00), a popular organic bakery that makes scrumptious cinnamon rolls and delicious open-faced sandwiches and subs to order. A second location near the theater has more seating space and is often even busier. **Vågen Fetevare** (✉ Kong Oscars gt. 10 ☎ 55–31–65–13) is a homey and bohemian coffeehouse. Books are sold and readings are held here.

GAY BARS Bergen has an active gay community. Call Wednesday from 7 to 9 PM or check the Web site of **Landsforeningen for Lesbisk og Homofil Frigjøring** (✉ Nygårdsgt. 2A ☎ 55–31–21–39), the National Association for Lesbian and Gay Liberation, to ask about events in the city. In the same building as the Landsforeningen, there's the popular gay bar **Fincken** (✉ Nygårdsgt. 2A ☎ 55–32–13–16), which is open daily until 1 AM.

LIVE MUSIC Bergensers love jazz. The **Bergen Jazz Forum** (✉ Kulturhuset USF, Georgernes Verft 3 ☎ 55–30–72–50 ⊕ www.usf.no) is *the* place to find it—there are concerts every Friday from September to May. The international **Nattjazz** festival offers more than 60 concerts in late May and early June. Since the mid-'90s, Bergen has become a haven for up-and-coming pop and rock bands. A lot of them have their concert debut at **Garage** (✉ Christies gt. 14 ☎ 55–32–19–80), a hangout popular with local musicians.

Bergenfest (☎ 55–21–50–60 ⊕ www.bergenfest.no), formerly known as Ole Blues, runs from late April to early May and features several internationally known rock and blues artists. **Det Akademiske Kvarter** (✉ Olav Kyrres gt. 49–53 ☎ 55–30–28–00) is run by students from Bergen University, and there are pop, rock, and jazz concerts here on a weekly basis most of the year. During the university semester, the rock club **Hulen** (✉ Olaf Ryes vei 48 ☎ 55–33–38–38) attracts college students and other music enthusiasts to weekly rock concerts in a rebuilt air-raid shelter.

The Arts

Bergen is known for its **Festspillene** (International Music Festival), held each year during the last week of May and the beginning of June. Famous names in classical music, jazz, ballet, the arts, and theater perform. Tickets are available at Grieghallen from the **festival office** (✉ Lars Hilles gt. 3, 5015 ☎ 55–21–61–50 ⊕ www.fib.no). Tickets can also be ordered from **Billettservice** (☎ 815–33–133 ⊕ www.ticketmaster.no).

CLASSICAL MUSIC   Recitals are held at **Troldhaugen** (☎ 55–92–29–92 ⊕ www.troldhaugen. com), home of composer Edvard Grieg, all summer. Tickets are sold at the tourist office and at the door. Performances are given from late June through August, Wednesday and Sunday at 7:30 and Saturday at 2; and from September through November, Sunday at 2. A special concert series, **Grieg in Bergen** (✉ Gamle Norges Bank, Vågsalmenning ☎ 55–31–04–45 ⊕ www.musicanord.no), is held every evening from mid-June to late August. The venue is easy to find, in the old bank building at Vågsalmenning, across the plaza from the tourist office.

FOLK MUSIC   Twice a week in summer the **Bergen Folklore Dance Group** performs a one-hour program of traditional dances and music from rural Norway at the Bryggens Museum. Tickets are sold by the tourist office and at the door. ✉ *Dreggsalmenning 3* ☎ *55–55–20–06* 🎟 *NKr 95.*

The extensive **Fana Folklore** program is an evening of traditional wedding food, dances, and folk music, plus a concert—at the 800-year-old Fana Church. Tickets are also available from the tourist office. ✉ *Flølo, Torgalmenning 9* ☎ *55–91–52–40* 🎟 *NKr 300, includes dinner and return bus transportation* ☉ *June–Sept., Thurs. and Fri. at 7 PM. Catch the bus from Festplassen in the center of Bergen and return by 10:30 PM.*

Sports & the Outdoors

Bergen is literally wedged between the mountains and the sea, and there are plenty of opportunities to enjoy the outdoors. Bergensers are quick to do so on sunny days. In summer, don't be surprised to see many Bergensers leaving work early to enjoy sports and activities outdoors, or just relax in the parks.

Fishing

With so much water around, it's no wonder sport fishing is a popular pastime in Bergen. Angling along the coast around Bergen is possible all year, although it is unquestionably more pleasant in summer. In late summer many prefer to move up the area rivers to catch spawning salmon and trout. Whether you prefer fishing in streams, fjords, or the open sea, there are several charter services and fishing tours available. Most can also provide all the fishing gear you need, but be sure to bring warm and waterproof clothes, even in summer.

The **Bergen Angling Association** (✉ Fosswinckelsgt. 37 ☎ 55–32–11–64 ⊕ www.bergen.sportsfiskere.no) has information and fishing permits. A local fishing supply store, **Campelen** (✉ Strandgt. 17 ☎ 93–41–29–58 ⊕ www.campelen.no) also arranges fjord fishing, deep-sea fishing, and charter tours, all departing from central Bergen. **Norwegian Sportsfishing Adventures** (☎ 91–10–72–48) specializes in guided tours for small groups. **Sotra Rorbusenter** (✉ Spildepollen ☎ 56–31–79–76 ⊕ www. rorbusenter.com) offers boat rental, guided tours, and chartered tours from Sotra outside Bergen.

Hiking

Like most Norwegians, Bergensers love to go hiking, especially on one or more of the seven mountains that surround the city. **Bergen Turlag**

(Bergen Hiking Association; ⊠ Tverrgt. 4–6, 5017 ☎ 55–33–58–10 ⊕ www.bergen-turlag.no) is a touring club that arranges hikes and maintains cabins for hikers. You can pick up maps of many self-guided walking tours around Bergen from the office, as well as from bookstores around Bergen. Bergen Turlag stages the **7-fjellsturen,** or Seven-Mountain Hike, an event that attracts thousands of hikers for the one-day trek across seven nearby mountains.

Take the funicular up **Mt. Fløyen** (⊠ Vetrlidsallmenningen 21, 5014 ☎ 55–33–68–00 ⊕ www.floibanen.no), and minutes later you'll be in the midst of a forest. From the nearby gift shop and restaurant, well-marked paths fan out over the mountains. Follow Fløysvingene Road down for an easy stroll with great views of the city and harbor.

Mt. Ulriken (⊠ Ulriken 1 5009 ☎ 55–20–20–20 ⊕ www.ulriken.no) is popular with walkers and hikers of all levels. The easiest way to reach the summit is via the cable car from Haukeland University Hospital. (To get there, take the double-decker bus that leaves from Torget.) Once you get off the cable car, you'll find trails leading across the mountain plateau, **Vidden,** which is above the tree line. The plateau connects the Fløyen and Ulriken mountains, and you can hike between them in four to six hours. Views from the alpine trail are spectacular. Be advised that foggy and rainy weather, even in the summer months, can make hiking here dangerous. Consult the tourist information center or Bergen Turlag for maps and general advice.

Shopping

Shopping Centers

Bergen has several cobblestoned pedestrian shopping streets, including Gamle Strandgaten, (Gågaten), Torgallmenningen, Hollendergaten, and Marken. Stores selling Norwegian handicrafts are concentrated along the Bryggen boardwalk. Near the cathedral, the tiny Skostredet has become popular with young shoppers. The small, independent speciality stores here sell everything from army surplus gear to tailored suits and designer trinkets. Most Bergen shops are open Monday–Wednesday and Friday from 9 to 5; Thursday from 9 to 7; and Saturday from 10 to 3. Bergen's shopping centers—Galleriet, Kløverhuset, and Bergen Storsenter—are open weekdays from 9 to 8 and Saturday from 9 to 6.

Sundt (⊠ Torgallmenningen 14) is the closest thing Norway has to a traditional department store, with everything from fashion to interior furnishings. But you can get better value for your kroner if you shop around for souvenirs and sweaters. **Kløverhuset** (⊠ Strandkaien 10), between Strandgaten and the fish market, has 40 shops under one roof, including outlets for the ever-so-popular Dale knitwear, souvenirs, leathers, and fur. **Galleriet,** on Torgallmenningen, is the best of the downtown shopping malls. Here you will find **GlasMagasinet** and more exclusive small shops along with all the chains, including **H & M (Hennes & Mauritz). Bergen Storsenter,** by the bus terminal near the train station, is a newer shopping center.

Fishing Supplies

Campelen (⊠ Strandkaien 2A and 18 ☎ 55–32–34–72 or 55–23–07–30 ⊕ www.campelen.no) has fishing equipment. Its staff also arranges fishing trips that leave from Bergen Harbor. **Finn de Lange** (⊠ Marken 32 ☎ 55–32–34–44) sells fishing gear as well as outdoor clothing.

Food

Kjøttbasaren (⊠ Vetrlidsalmenning 2 ☎ 55–55–22–23) is in a restored 1877 meat market. The Meat Bazaar sells everything from venison to sweets. **Kvamme kolonial og fetevarer** (⊠ Strandkaien 18 ☎ 55–23–14–25) is a fine-foods store, selling rare Norwegian products like cured leg of indigenous wild mutton, as well as the usual dairy products and smoked and cured meats. Famous all over Norway, **Søstrene Hagelin** (⊠ Olav Kyrres gt. 33 ☎ 55–32–69–49) is a Bergen institution, a delicatessen that sells traditional fish balls, fish pudding, and other seafood products made following its secret recipes.

Glass, Ceramics, Pewter

Hjertholm (⊠ Olav Kyrres gt. 7 ☎ 55–31–70–27) is the ideal shop for gifts; most everything is of Scandinavian design. The pottery and glassware are of the highest quality—much of it made by local artisans. **Tilbords, Bergens Glasmagasin** (⊠ Olav Kyrres gt. 9 ☎ 55–31–69–67) claims to have the town's largest selection of glass and china, in both Scandinavian and European designs.

Handicrafts

Amerie (⊠ Finnegårdsgt. 6 ☎ 55–31–18–20) has traditional and modern knitwear, jewelry, souvenirs, leather goods, china, and crystal. **Berle Bryggen** (⊠ Bryggen 5 ☎ 55–10–95–00) has the complete Dale of Norway collection in stock and other traditional knitwear and souvenir items—don't miss the troll cave. **Husfliden** (⊠ Vågsalmenning 3 ☎ 55–54–47–70) caters to all your handicrafts needs, including a department for Norwegian national costumes. This is one of the best places to pick up handmade Norwegian goods, especially handwoven textiles and hand-carved wood items.

Juhls' Silver Gallery (⊠ Bryggen 39 ☎ 55–32–47–40) has its own exclusive jewelry called "Tundra," which is inspired by the Norwegian north. **Oleana** (⊠ Strandkaien 2A, Bryggen ☎ 55–31–05–20) sells Norwegian wool sweaters, silk scarves from Tyrihans, and Norwegian silver. **Theodor Olsens** (⊠ Torgallmenningen 15 ☎ 55–55–14–80) stocks silver jewelry of distinctive Norwegian and Scandinavian design.

Toys

Take a stroll through **Troll** (⊠ Bryggen ☎ 55–21–51–00) for adorable, mean-looking trolls of all shapes and sizes. The same complex that holds Troll also has an all-year **Julehuset** (⊠ Bryggen ☎ 55–21–51–00 ⊕ www.goshopNorway.com), or Christmas House, full of cheery Norwegian *Nisser* (gnomes).

Bergen A to Z

To research prices, get advice from other travelers, and book travel arrangements, visit www.fodors.com.

AIR TRAVEL TO & FROM BERGEN

CARRIERS SAS Braathens, KLM, Norwegian, Widerøe and Sterling are the major airlines flying into Bergen.

🛫 **KLM** ☎ 22-64-37-52 ⊕ www. klm.com. **Norwegian** ☎ 815-21-815 ⊕ www. norwegian.no. **SAS Braathens** ☎05400 ⊕www.sasbraathens.no. **Sterling** ☎815-58-810 ⊕ www.sterlingticket.com. **Widerøe** ☎ 810-01-200 ⊕ www.wideroe.no.

AIRPORT Flesland is a 30-minute bus ride from the center of Bergen at off-peak
TRANSFERS hours. The Flybussen (Airport Bus) departs every 15 minutes (less frequently on weekends) from the SAS Royal Hotel, the Radisson SAS Hotel Norge, and the bus station.

Driving from Flesland to Bergen is simple, and the road is well marked. Bergen has an electronic toll ring surrounding it, so any vehicle entering the city weekdays between 6 AM and 10 PM has to pay NKr 15. There is no toll in the other direction.

A taxi stand is outside the Arrivals exit. The trip into the city costs about NKr 250.

🛫 Taxis & Shuttles **Bergen Taxi** ☎ 07000. **Norgestaxi** ☎ 08000.

BOAT & FERRY TRAVEL

Boats have always been Bergen's lifeline to the world.

Fjord Line serves North Norway, Stavanger and Haugesund, and Hardangerfjord and Sunnhordland. There's also service to Sognefjord, Nordfjord, and Sunnfjord.

The Smyril Line has a ferry that departs once a week in summer to the Shetland Islands, the Faroe Islands, and Iceland. Smyril also has service between Bergen and Scotland.

Hurtigruten (the Coastal Steamer) departs daily from Frielenes Quay, Dock H, for the 11-day round-trip to Kirkenes in the far north.

HSD express boats (to Hardangerfjord, Sunnhordland, Stavanger, and Haugesund) and Fylkesbaatane express boats (to Sognefjord, Nordfjord, and Sunnfjord) depart from Strandkai Terminalen.

International ferries depart from Skoltegrunnskaien.

🛥 **Fjord Line** ☎ 815-33-500 ⊕ www.fjordline.com. **Fjord1 Fylkesbaatane** ☎ 55-90-70-70 ⊕ www.fjord1.no. **HSD** ☎ 55-23-87-80 ⊕ www.hsd.no. *Hurtigruten* ☎ 810-30-000 ⊕ www.hurtigruten.com. **Smyril Line** ☎ 55-59-65-20 ⊕ www. smyril-line.com. **Strandkai Terminalen** ☎ 55-90-70-70.

BUS TRAVEL TO & FROM BERGEN

The summer-only bus from Oslo to Bergen, Geiteryggekspressen (literally, "Goat-Back Express," referring to the tunnel through Geiteryggen Mountain, which looks like a goat's back, between Hol and Aurland) leaves the Nor-Way bus terminal at 8 AM and arrives in Bergen 12½ hours later. Buses also connect Bergen with Trondheim and Ålesund. Western Norway is served by several bus companies, which use the station at Strømgaten 8.

⚑ Central Bus Station ✉ Strømgt. 8 ☎ 177.

CAR TRAVEL

Bergen is 478 km (290 mi) from Oslo. Route 7 is good most of the way, at least until the ferry crossing at Hardangerfjord. The ferry, from Brimnes to Bruravik, runs from 5 AM to midnight and takes 10 minutes. From Granvin, 12 km (7 mi) farther north, to Bergen, Route 7 hugs the fjord part of the way, making for spectacular scenery, but the quality of the road deteriorates considerably. A quicker, better but less scenic drive is to follow Route 13 from Granvin to Voss, and take E16, an alternative route to Oslo, from Voss to Bergen. In winter, several mountain passes are prone to closing at short notice. The Public Roads Administration's **road information line** can give you the status of most roads.

Driving from Stavanger to Bergen involves two to four ferries and a long journey packed with stunning scenery. The Stavanger tourist information office can help plan the trip and reserve ferry space.

Downtown Bergen is enclosed by an inner ring road. The area within is divided into three zones, which are separated by ONE WAY and DO NOT ENTER signs. To get from one zone to another, return to the ring road and drive to an entry point for the desired zone. It's best to leave your car at a parking garage (the cheapest and most accessible is the ByGarasjen near the train station) and walk. You pay a NKr 15 toll every time you drive into the city—but driving out is free.

⚑ Car Emergencies Norsk Automobil Forbund (NAF) ☎ 810-00-505 operates 24 hours a day.

⚑ Road Information Public Roads Administration ☎ 175 ⊕ www.vegvesen.no.

⚑ Car Rental Agencies Avis ✉ Lars Hilles gt. 20B ☎ 815-33-044. **Budget** ✉ Lars Hilles gt. 120A ☎ 815-60-600. **Europcar** ☎ 55-36-70-00. **Hertz** ✉ Nygårdsgt. 89 ☎ 55-96-40-70. **National** ✉ Minde Allé 30 ☎ 55-59-97-15.

INTERNET SERVICE

⚑ Accezzo ✉ Galleriet, Torgallm. 8 ☎ 55-31-11-60. **Cyberhouse** ✉ Hollendergt. 3 ☎ No phone.

MONEY MATTERS

Most Bergen banks in downtown are open Monday, Tuesday, Wednesday, and Friday from 8:15 to 3:30, and Thursday from 8:15 to 6. Some are open on Saturday from 10 to 1. From mid-May through September, most close a half hour earlier. The 24-hour **Bergen Card**, which costs NKr 165 (NKr 245 for 48 hours), gives admission to most museums, as well as Fantoft Stave Church, St. Mary's Church, Banco Rotto, and Bergen Trotting Park; unlimited bus travel in central Bergen; parking at public meters and outdoor automatic ticket machines; unlimited funicular rides; and discounts at Akvariet aquarium, Troldhaugen, Vannkanten, and selected restaurants, and on car rentals, concerts, theater, and selected souvenirs. The card is available at the tourist office and in most

hotels. The Fjord Pass gives considerable discounts on hotel rooms, and can be purchased at the railway station.
🗷 **Fjord Pass** ☎ 55-55-76-60 ⊕ www.fjordpass.no.

TAXIS

Taxi stands are in strategic locations downtown. Taxis are dispatched by the Bergen Taxi central office and can be booked in advance. Bergen Taxi runs the largest and most reliable service.
🗷 **Bergen Taxi** ☎ 07000 ⊕ www.bergentaxi.no. **Norgestaxi** ☎ 08000. **Taxi1** ☎ 55-50-00-37.

TRAIN TRAVEL

The Bergensbanen has several departures daily in both directions on the Oslo–Bergen route; it's widely acknowledged to be one of the most beautiful train rides in the world. Trains leave from Oslo S Station for the 7½- to 8½-hour journey.
🗷 **NSB** (Norwegian state railways) ☎ 55-96-69-00 or 815-00-888.

VISITOR INFORMATION

Bergen's Tourist Information Office is in the Fresco Hall in Vågsalmenning Square opposite the fish market. The office's staff sells the Bergen Card, brochures, and maps, arranges accommodations and sightseeing, and exchanges currency.
🗷 **Tourist Information Office** ✉ Vågsalmenningen 1 ☎ 55-55-20-00 ⊕ www.visitbergen.com.

THE WEST COAST: FJORD COUNTRY

Revised by Lars Ursin

The intricate outline of the fjords makes Norway's coastline of 21,347 km (13,264 mi) longer than the distance between the north and south poles. Majestic and magical, the fjords can take any traveler's breath away in a moment. Among the world's most spectacular geological formations, a typical fjord consists of a long, narrow, and deep inlet of the sea, with steep mountainsides stretching into mountain massifs. Fjords were created by glacier erosion during the ice ages. In spectacular inlets like Sognefjord, Geirangerfjord, and Hardangerfjord, walls of water shoot up the mountainsides, jagged snowcapped peaks blot out the sky, and water tumbles down the mountains in an endless variety of colors. Lush green farmlands edge up the rounded mountainsides and the chiseled, cragged, steep peaks of the Jotunheimen mountains, Norway's tallest, seem to touch the blue skies.

The farther north you travel, the more rugged and wild the landscape. The still, peaceful Sognefjord is the longest inlet, snaking 190 km (110 mi) inland. At the top of Sogn og Fjordane county is a group of fjords referred to as Nordfjord, with the massive Jostedalsbreen, mainland Europe's largest glacier, to the south. In the county of Møre og Romsdal, you'll see mountains that would seem more natural on the moon—all gray rock—as well as cliffs hanging over the water below. Geirangerfjord is Norway's best-known fjord. In the south, the Hardangerfjord, Norway's fruit basket, is best seen in early summer when it's in full blossom.

Boat cruises are the classic way of exploring this region, but there's much to be gained by more up-close-and-personal experiences. You can walk or climb on one of Norway's 1,630 glaciers, remnants of the 30 ice ages that carved the fjords. Head to Eid and ride one of the ponylike Fjord horses, originally bred for farmwork.

Numbers in the margin correspond to points of interest on the West Coast map.

Åndalsnes

❶ *495 km (307 mi) north of Bergen, 354 km (219 mi) south of Trondheim.*

Åndalsnes is an industrial alpine village of 3,000 people that is best known for three things: its position as the last stop on the railway, making it a gateway to fjord country; the Trollstigveien (Troll Path); and the Trollveggen (Troll Wall). The tourist office has special maps and guides outlining the popular trails and paths. The tourist office can also make arrangements for you to join a fishing trip to the fjords. Trips last four hours, and leave three times a day; the cost is NKr 250. Six or seven species of mostly whitefish, such as cod, live in the waters.

★ From **Horgheimseidet,** which used to have a hotel for elegant tourists—often European royalty—you can view **Trollveggen** (Troll Wall), Europe's highest vertical rock face at 3,300 feet. The birthplace of mountain-climbing sports in Scandinavia, this rock face draws elite climbers from all over.

FodorśChoice **Trollstigveien,** Norway's most popular tourist road, starts in Åndalsnes.
★ The road took 100 men 20 summers (1916–36) to build, in a constant struggle against the forces of rock and water. Often described as a masterpiece of construction, the road snakes its way through 11 hairpin bends up the mountain to the peaks named **Bispen** (the Bishop), **Kongen** (the King), and **Dronningen** (the Queen), which are 2,800 feet above sea level. The roads Trollstigveien and Ørneveien (at the Geiranger end) zigzag over the mountains separating two fjords. Roads are open only in summer. Halfway up, the road crosses a bridge over the waterfall **Stigfossen** (Path Falls), which has a vertical fall of nearly 600 feet. Walk to the lookout point, Stigrøra, by taking the 15-minute return path to the plateau. Signs show the way.

One of Norway's most famous mountaineers, Arne Randers Heen (1905–91), and his wife, Bodil Roland, founded the **Norsk Tindemuseum** (Norwegian Mountain Museum), which is dedicated to mountain climbing. Displays of Heen's equipment and photography follow the development of the sport and Heen's many feats. The mountain nearest to his heart was Romsdalshorn, 5,101 feet·high. He climbed that mountain 233 times, the last time when he was 85. He was the first to climb several mountains, especially in northern Norway. ✉ *2 km (1 mi) south of Åndalsnes center, along E139* ☎ *71–22–36–08* 🖙 *NKr 30* 🕒 *Mid-June–mid-Aug., Tues.–Sun. 1–5.*

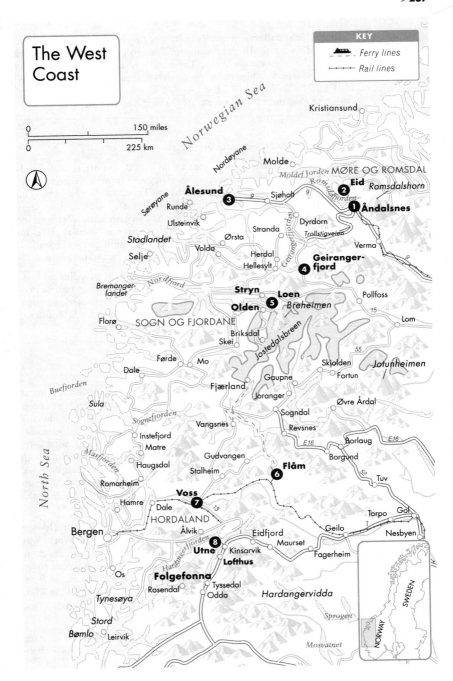

The West Coast

KEY
Ferry lines
Rail lines

0 — 150 miles
0 — 225 km

Norwegian Sea

Kristiansund

Nordøyane

Molde

Moldefjorden MØRE OG ROMSDAL

Romsdalsfjorden

Eid ② *Romsdalshorn*

① **Åndalsnes**

Ålesund ③ Sjøholt

Runde

Ulsteinvik

Stranda Dyrdorn

Trollstigveien

Ørsta

Volda Herdal

Hellesylt

Geiranger-
fjord ④

Verma

Stadlandet

Selje

Bremanger-
landet

Nordfjord

Stryn **Loen**
Olden ⑤ *Breheimen*

Pollfoss

Lom

Florø

SOGN OG FJORDANE

Briksdal

Skei

Jostedalsbreen

Jotunheimen

Førde Mo

Skjolden

Dale

Fjærland

Gaupne

Fortun

Buefjorden

Sula

Sognefjorden

Joranger

Øvre Årdal

Vangsnes

Sogndal

Revsnes

Instefjord

Matre

E16

Borlaug

E16

Gudvangen

Borgund

Haugsdal

Stalheim

Flåm ⑥

Tuv

Romarheim

Voss ⑦

Dale

Torpo

Gol

Hamre

HORDALAND

Ålvik

Geilo

Nesbyen

Bergen

Hardangerfjorden

Utne ⑧

Eidfjord

Kinsarvik Maurset

Lofthus

Fagerheim

Os

Folgefonna

Rosendal Tyssedal

Odda

Hardangervidda

Tynesøya

Sprogen

Stord

Bømlo Leirvik

Mosvatnet

NORWAY SWEDEN

Where to Stay

$$ ⊡ **Grand Hotel Bellevue.** Travelers often begin their exploration of the region at this hotel. All the rooms are done in bright yellow, with old prints of the fjord on the walls. The hotel's restaurant, Trollstua, has delicious seafood dishes, based on fresh, local catches. ⊠ *Åndalsgt. 5, 6301* ☎ *71–22–75–00* 🖷 *71–22–60–38* ⊕ *www.grandhotel.no* ⌕ *86 rooms* ⌂ *Restaurant, bar, meeting room* ☰ *AE, DC, MC, V.*

Eid

❷ *Along E39, near Hornindalsvatnet Lake.*

A small agricultural community of about 6,000, Eid offers such fjord-village attractions as mountain walks, dairy and farm visits, and skiing. It is also near Hornindalsvatnet, northern Europe's deepest lake. The town is best known for the **fjordhest** (fjord horse), which even appears on the official town shield. This historic Norwegian horse was bred for farmwork and played a big role in helping western Norway develop. Every May the community hosts the **Hingsteutstillinga** (State Stallion Show), which attracts horse enthusiasts from Norway and beyond.

The **Norsk Fjordhestsenter** is the official center for the breeding and use of the fjord horse. Open year-round, the center's summer tourist program includes riding camps, riding and horse-drawn carriage trips, cabin rentals, and mountain horseback riding trips. ⊠ *Myroldhaug* ☎ *57–86–48–00* ⊕ *www.norsk-fjordhestsenter.no.*

Ålesund

❸ *240 km (150 mi) west of Åndalsnes.*

On three islands and between two bright-blue fjords is Ålesund, home to 38,000 inhabitants and one of Norway's largest harbors for exporting dried and fresh fish. About two-thirds of its 1,040 wooden houses were destroyed by a fire in 1904. In the rush to shelter the 10,000 homeless victims, Germany's Kaiser Wilhelm II, who often vacationed here, led a swift rebuilding that married German art nouveau (*Jugendstil*) with Viking flourishes. Winding streets are crammed with buildings topped with turrets, spires, gables, dragon heads, and curlicues. Today, it's considered one of the few art nouveau cities in the world. Inquire at the tourism office for one of the insightful walking tours.

Fodor's Choice A little gem, the **Ålesunds Museum** highlights the city's past, including
★ the escape route that the Norwegian Resistance established in World War II—its goal was the Shetland Islands. Handicrafts on display are done in the folk-art style of the area. You can also see the art nouveau room and learn more about the town's unique architecture. ⊠ *Rasmus Rønnebergsgt. 16* ☎ *70–12–31–70* 🖃 *NKr 30* ☉ *July and Aug., Mon.–Sat. 11–4, Sun. noon–4; Sept., Oct., Jan., and Apr.–June, Mon.–Sat. 11–3, Sun. noon–3; Nov., Dec., Feb., and Mar., weekdays 11–3.*

You can drive or take a bus up nearby Aksla Mountain to a vantage point, **Kniven** (the knife), for a splendid view of the city—which absolutely glitters at night. ☎ *70–13–68–00 for bus information.*

TOURS AROUND THE WEST COAST

A 1½-HOUR GUIDED STROLL *through Ålesund, concentrating mostly on the art nouveau buildings, departs from the tourist information center (Rådhuset) Saturday, Tuesday, and Thursday at 1 PM from mid-June to mid-August.* **Aak Fjellsportsenter** *(☎ 71–22–71–00 ⊕ www.aak.no) in Åndalsnes specializes in walking tours of the area.*

From Easter through September, **Jostedalen Breførlag** *(✉ 5828 Gjerde ☎ 57–68–31–11 ⊕ www.jostedalen-breforarlag.no) conducts glacier tours, from an easy 1½-hour family trip on the Nigard branch (equipment is provided) to advanced glacier courses with rock and ice climbing. Besides ice climbing,* **Olden Aktiv Briksdalsbreen** *(✉ Briksdalsbre ☎ 57–87–38–88 ⊕ www.oldenaktiv.no) offers a Blue Ice Excursion of 3–4 hours, and an easier glacier walk.* **Briksdal Breføring** *(Glacier Guiding Association; ✉ 6792 Briksdalsbre ☎ 57–87–68–00*

⊕ www.briksdalsbre.no) leads glacier walks, ice climbing, and other excursions on and around Briksdalsbreen from May to September.

From June through August, the **MS Geirangerfjord** *(✉ Geiranger ☎ 70–26–30–07 ⊕ www.geirangerfjord. no) offers 90-minute guided cruises on the Geirangerfjord. Tickets are sold at the dock in Geiranger.*

"Norway in a Nutshell," Sognefjord & Flåmsbanen railway, and other package tours are available through **Fjord Tours AS** *(☎ 55–55–20–00 ⊕ www.fjord-tours. com).* **Kystopplevelser AS** *(☎ 55–31–59–10) operates several Fjord Explorer tours.*

🌊 **Ålesund Akvarium, Atlanterhavsparken** (Atlantic Sea Park). Teeming with aquatic life, this is one of Scandinavia's largest aquariums. Right on the ocean, 3 km (2 mi) west of town, the park emphasizes aquatic animals of the North Atlantic, including anglers, octopus, and lobster. Nemo, the park's adorable seal mascot, waddles freely throughout the complex. See the daily diving show at which the fish are fed. The divers actually enter a feeding frenzy of huge, and sometimes aggressive, halibut and wolffish. After your visit, have a picnic, hike, or take a refreshing swim at the adjoining Tueneset Park. Bus 18, which leaves from St. Olavs Plass, makes the 15-minute journey to the park once every hour during the day, Monday through Saturday. ✉ *Tueneset* ☎ *70–10–70–60* ⊕ *www. atlanterhavsparken.no* 🎫 *NKr 90* 🕐 *June–Aug., Sun.–Fri. 10–7, Sat. 10–4; Sept.–May, daily 11–4.*

---

off the beaten path

RUNDE – Norway's southernmost major bird rock—one of the largest in Europe—is the breeding ground for some 240 species, including puffins, gannets, and cormorants. The region's wildlife managers maintain many observation posts here. In summer, straying into the bird's nesting areas is strictly forbidden. A catamaran leaves from Skateflua quay in Ålesund for the 25-minute trip to Hareid, where it connects with a bus for the 50-km (31-mi) trip to Runde. A path leads from the bus stop to the nature reserve. Call the Runde tourist office for more information.

Where to Stay & Eat

$–$$ ✕ **Fjellstua.** This mountaintop restaurant has tremendous views over the surrounding peaks, islands, and fjords. The old-fashioned brick building has a stone-and-marine-blue interior, with picture windows. On the menu, try the Norwegian bacalao, salmon, and lamb. ⊠ *Top of Aksla Mountain* ☎ *70–10–74–00* ▤ *AE, DC, MC, V* ☉ *Closed Jan.*

★ $$ 🏨 **Quality Hotel Scandinavia.** Part of the Quality chain, this hotel has impressive towers and arches and dates back to 1905. The modern rooms are beautifully decorated, especially those done in an art nouveau style. ⊠ *Løvenvoldgt. 8, 6002* ☎ *70–15–78–00* 🖷 *70–15–78–05* ⊕ *www. choicehotels.no* ↪ *65 rooms* ♿ *Restaurant, pizzeria, bar, meeting room* ▤ *AE, DC, MC, V.*

Geirangerfjord

★ ❹ *85 km (52½ mi) southwest of Åndalsnes, 413 km (256 mi) from Bergen.*

Geirangerfjord, which made the UNESCO World Heritage List in 2005, is Norway's most spectacular and perhaps best-known fjord. The 16-km-long (10-mi-long), 960-foot-deep Geirangerfjord's most stunning attractions are its roaring waterfalls—the Seven Sisters, the Bridal Veil, and the Suitor. Perched on mountain ledges along the fjord, deserted farms at Skageflå and Knivsflå are being restored and maintained by local enthusiasts.

The village of Geiranger, at the end of the fjord, is home to only 300 year-round residents, but in spring and summer its population swells to 5,000 due to visitors traveling from Hellesylt to the east. In winter, snow on the mountain roads means that the village is often isolated.

The most scenic route to Geiranger is the two-hour drive along Route 63 over Trollstigveien from Åndalsnes. Once you are here, the Ørneveien (Eagles' Road) road to Geiranger, which has 11 hairpin turns and was completed in 1952, leads directly to the fjord.

Where to Stay

$$$ 🏨 **Union Hotel.** One of the biggest hotels in the region, the Union is famous for its location near the fjords. Decked out in rosemaling-decorated wood furniture, the lobby has a country feel, although the rooms are modern. Ask for one of the rooms with good fjord views. ⊠ *Off Rte. 63, 6216 Geiranger* ☎ *70–26–30–00* 🖷 *70–26–31–61* ⊕ *www. union-hotel.no* ↪ *168 rooms, 13 suites* ♿ *Restaurant, miniature golf, 2 pools, sauna, Turkish bath, bar, nightclub, playground* ▤ *AE, DC, MC, V* ☉ *Closed Jan. and Feb.*

Hiking

Trekking through fjord country can occupy a few hours or several days. Trails and paths are marked by signs or cairns with a red T on them. Area tourist offices and bookshops have maps, and of course you can always ask residents for directions or destinations.

Stryn, Loen & Olden

5 *From Geiranger to Stryn, take the ferry across the Geiranger Fjord to Hellesylt, a 55-min ride. It's about 50 km (30 mi) from Hellesylt to Stryn on Rte. 60.*

Stryn, Loen, and Olden, at the eastern end of Nordfjord, were among the first tourist destinations in the region. English salmon fishermen became the first tourists in the 1860s. By the end of the 19th century more hotels had been built, and cruise ships added the area to their routes. Tourism grew into an important industry. The most famous attraction in Stryn is the Briksdal Glacier, which lies between cascading waterfalls and high mountaintops. It's one arm of the Jostedal Glacier.

Covering the mountains between the Sognefjord and Nordfjord, **Jostedalsbreen Glacier** is the largest in Europe. Nearly ¾ km (⅓ mi) wide in parts, it has grown in recent years due to increased snowfall. There are about a hundred known routes for crossing Jostedal Glacier: if you want to hike it, you must have a qualified guide. Contact the Jostedalsbreen Glacier National Park Center or another tourist office. Such hikes should only be attempted in summer; mountain boots and windproof clothing are both essential.

Many of Jostedalsbreen's arms are tourist attractions in their own right. The best-known arm, **Briksdal Glacier**, lies at the end of Oldedal Valley, about 20 km (12 mi) south of Olden. It can be visited by bicycle, by car, or on foot from April to October.

Right outside Stryn, **Jostedalsbreen Nasjonalparksenter** (Jostedalsbreen Glacier National Park Center; ☎ 57–87–72–00 ⊕ www.jostedalsbre. no) covers the glacier and the surrounding region in detail. Landscape models, mineral and photograph collections, films and dioramas describe the region's unique geography, flora, and fauna. There's also a garden of 325 types of wildflowers.

Where to Stay & Eat

$–$$$ ✕ **Kjenndalstova Kafé and Restaurant.** Perhaps western Norway's best-kept secret, this café and restaurant serves up delicious traditional dishes. Close to Kjendal's glacier, towering mountains, cascading waterfalls, and a pristine lake, the scenery from the restaurant alone is well worth a visit. Try the fried fresh trout, the fish stew, and the dessert cakes. ⊠ *Prestestegen 15, Loen* ☎ *94–53–83–85* ▤ *AE, DC, MC, V* ☺ *Closed Oct.–Apr.*

¢–$ ✕ **Briksdalsbre Fjellstove** (Briksdal Glacier Mountain Lodge). The cafeteria at this lodge has a no-frills menu of fresh, hearty country fare. The trout, the fillet of reindeer, and the deep-fried cod's jaws are all worth a try. Accommodation is also available, and as you'd expect from its location, a large gift shop is nearby. ⊠ *Briksdalsbre* ☎ *57–87–68–00* ▤ *AE, DC, MC, V.*

$$$ ✕▦ **Olden Fjordhotel.** Close to the fjord and cruise terminal, this modern hotel has simple, comfortable rooms with standard, chain-hotel-style furniture and balconies overlooking the fjord. Glossy hardwood floors in most common areas and some rooms lend the hotel a degree of so-phistication. An extremely helpful and friendly staff will ensure a pleas-ant stay. Allergen-free rooms and larger rooms for families are also available. ☒ *6788 Olden* 🕾 *57–87–04–00* 🖷 *57–87–04–01* ⊕ *www.olden-hotel.no* ⟿ *60 rooms* ♧ *Restaurant, cable TV, bar, library, night-club* ⊟ *AE, DC, MC, V.*

$$–$$$ ✕🖂**Visnes Hotel.** Dating from 1850, this small hotel has lovely individually decorated rooms filled with pretty antiques. The walls are lined with old-fashioned wallpaper, and most rooms have balconies overlooking the fjord. The hotel is five minutes from Stryn's center. Specialities in the restaurant include smoked salmon and venison. The nearby **Villa Visnes,** a restored 1898 home with classic Norwegian carved-wood dragons arching out from the eaves, now houses an apartment and con-ference center. ☒ *Prestestegen 1, 6781 Stryn* 🕾 *57–87–10–87* 🖷 *57–87–20–75* ⊕ *www.visnes.no* ⟿ *14 rooms, 1 suite* ♧ *Restaurant, convention center* ⊟ *AE, DC, MC, V.*

★ $$–$$$ 🖂 **Alexandra.** This hotel was built in 1884, but has been entirely re-furbished with stone and oak in a modern style. It remains one of the most luxurious hotels in the region. The rooms are spacious and deco-rated in cheerful, light colors. Many offer a spectacular view of either the fjord or the entrance to Lodalen valley. The hotel also has a popu-lar spa, and the friendly staff, some clad in traditional folk costumes, can assist in arranging various outdoor activities in the Nordfjord area. ☒ *6789 Loen* 🕾 *57–87–50–00* 🖷 *57–87–50–51* ⊕ *www.alexandra.no* ⟿ *191 rooms, 9 suites* ♧ *2 restaurants, tennis court, indoor pool, gym, 3 bars, nightclub, convention center* ⊟ *AE, DC, MC, V.*

Sports & the Outdoors

In addition to taking a guided walk on the glaciers, you can follow the many other trails in this area. Ask at the Stryn tourist office for a walk-ing map and hiking suggestions.

SKIING   The **Stryn Sommerskisenter** (Summer Ski Center) has earned a reputation as northern Europe's best summer-skiing resort. Its seasons last from May through September, depending on the weather. The trails run over Tystig Glacier. The center has a ski school, a snowboard park, and a children's tow in June and July. Skis and snowboards are available for rent. ☒ Rte. 258 near Videseter 🕾 57–87–54–74 ⊕ www.stryn-sommerski.no ⊘ May–Aug., daily 10–4.

Flåm

❻ *66 km (41 mi) northeast of Voss.*

One of the most scenic train routes in Europe zooms from Myrdal, high into the mountains and down to the town of Flåm. After the day-trip-pers have departed, it's a wonderful place to extend your tour and spend the night.

The **Flåmsbana** (Flåm Railway) is only 20 km (12 mi) long, but it takes 40 to 55 minutes (one way) to travel the 2,850 feet up the steep moun-tain gorge. The line includes 20 tunnels. From Flåm it's also an easy drive back to Oslo on E16 along the Lærdal River, one of Norway's most famous salmon streams—it was King Harald's favorite. ⊠ *Flåm train station* 🕾 *57–63–21–00* ⊕ *www.flaamsbana.no.*

If you have time to kill before the train departs, make sure you visit the **Flåmsbana Museet** (Flåm Railway Museum). Building the Flåm Railway was a remarkable feat in engineering, and this museum illustrates the challenges the builders faced in detail. You'll find it in the old station building, just 300 feet from the present one. ⊠ *Flåm train station* 🕾 *57–63–23–10* ⊠ *NKr 30, free with ticket to the railway* ☉ *May–Sept., daily 9–5; Oct.–Apr., daily 12–3.*

Where to Stay

$ 🏨 **Fretheim Hotell.** One of western Norway's most beautiful hotels, the Fretheim has a classic, timeless look. Staying true to the Fretheim's 1866 roots, the rooms are furnished simply. Book in advance for a room with a fjord view. Rooms in the new northern wing of the hotel are slightly higher in standard than the older ones, although the price is exactly the same. If you can spring for a suite, you'll have more space and nicer furnishings. There's a spectacular view of the fjord from the restaurant and bar. ⊠ *Flåm Harbor, 5742 Flåm* 🕾 *57–63–63–00* 🖷 *57–63–64–00* ⊕ *www.fretheim-hotel.no* ⤴ *111 rooms, 7 suites* ☖ *Restaurant, bar, business services, convention center* ⊟ *AE, MC, V.*

Shopping

Saga Souvenirs (⊠ Flåm train station 🕾 57–63–19–00 ⊕ www. sagasouvenir.no) is one of the largest gift shops in Norway. The selection of traditional items includes knitwear, wood and ceramic trolls, and jewelry.

Voss

❼ *120 km (75 mi) south of Fjærland, 80 km (50 mi) south of Vangsnes, 80 km (50 mi) north (1 hr by train) from Bergen.*

Set between the Hardanger and Sogne fjords, Voss is in a handy place to begin an exploration of Fjord Norway. Once considered a stopover, Voss now attracts visitors drawn by its concerts, festivals, farms, and other attractions. Norwegians know Voss best for its skiing and Vossajazz, its annual jazz festival. People come from all over Norway for the Sheep's Heads Festival, a celebration of the culinary delicacy of this area.

Galleri Voss shows the works of Norwegian artists in a bright, airy space. ⊠ *Stallgt. 6–8* 🕾 *56–51–90–18* ☉ *Wed., Fri., and Sat. 10–4, Thurs. 10–6, Sun. noon–3.*

Dating from 1277, the enchanting **Voss Kyrkje–Vangskyrkja** (Voss Church) holds services every Sunday. Take a walk through to see the stained glass within. Concerts are occasionally held here. Guided tours are available. ⊠ *Vangsgt. 3* 🕾 *56–51–22–78* ⊕ *voss.kyrkjer.net* ⤴ *Nkr 15* ☉ *June–Aug., weekdays 10–4, Sat. 10–1, Sun. 2–4.*

Perched on the hillside overlooking Voss, **Mølstertunet** is an open-air museum. The 16 farm buildings here were built between 1600 and 1870. Along with handcrafted tools and other items, they reveal much about area farmers' lives and struggles. ⊠ *Mølstervn. 143* ☎ *56–51–15–11* ⊜*NKr 35* ⊙ *Mid-May–mid-Sept., daily 10–5; mid-Sept.–mid-May, weekdays 10–3, Sun. noon–3.*

Where to Stay & Eat

★ **$$$** ╳⊡ **Fleischer's Hotel.** One of Norway's historic wooden hotels, the beautiful, gabled Fleischer looks like a manor from a fairy tale. Its carved wood dragons are fine examples of stave church-style architecture, developed in Hardanger in the late 19th century. First seen in churches, the style became fashionable and eventually was used all over southern Norway to decorate everything from silverware and furniture to prominent buildings like this luxurious hotel. Rooms in the old wing still have some flavor from that era. The restaurant Magdalene serves traditional renditions of sheep's head, grilled venison, fresh mountain trout, and salmon dishes. The hotel is steps away from the railway tracks leading to Bergen. ⊠ *Evangervegen 13, 5700* ☎ *56–52–05–05* ⊟ *56–52–05–01* ⊕ *www.fleischers.no* ⊠ *90 rooms* ◊ *Restaurant, pool, sauna, bar, nightclub, laundry facilities, meeting rooms* ⊟ *AE, DC, MC, V.*

★ **$$$** ╳⊡ **Stalheim Hotel.** Originally a coach station on the old postal route from Oslo to Bergen, this hotel is perched high over the 13 hairpin turns of the dramatic Stalheimskleiva road, halfway between Voss and Flåm. The rooms are comfortable, and an interesting folk museum is on the premises, but it's the view that really makes the Stalheim Hotel worth a visit. To get there by car, follow Route E16. If you're on the Norway in a Nutshell tour, run by Fjord Tours AS, one of the regular stops is just outside the hotel. You can hop off the bus there and pick up the tour again the next day. ⊠ *5715 Stalheim, 32 km (22 mi) north of Voss* ☎ *56–52–01–22* ⊟ *56–52–00–56* ⊕ *www.stalheim.com* ⊠ *124 rooms* ◊ *Restaurant, bar, lounge, shop; no room TVs* ⊟ *AE, DC, MC, V.*

Sports & the Outdoors

FISHING The tourist information office in Voss sells fishing licenses and has a Voss fishing guide to the nearly 500 lakes and rivers in the area where fishing is allowed. Fishing licenses (one-day for NKr 50) are also sold at campsites and the post office.

HIKING Walks and hikes are especially rewarding in this region, with spectacular mountain and water views everywhere. Be prepared for abrupt weather changes in spring and fall. Voss is a starting point for mountain hikes in Slølsheimen, Vikafjell, and the surrounding mountains. Contact the **Voss Tourist Board** (☎ 56–52–08–00 ⊕ www.voss-promotion. no) for tips. **Hangursheisen** (☎ 56–51–12–12 ⊕ www.voss-fjellheisar.no) is a cable car that runs from the center of Voss to Hanguren mountain. The summit is a good starting point for skiing in winter, and hiking and mountain biking in summer.

PARAGLIDING One of the best places to paraglide in Norway, Voss has easily accessed starting points and constant thermals. The tandem season runs roughly from June to August. To take a tandem paraglider flight (in which an instructor goes with you), you must weigh between 70 and 240 pounds. The flight lasts an hour and costs NKr 1,000. Contact the **Voss Adventure Senter** (☎ 90–68–62–19).

RIVER SPORTS Rivers around Voss are ideal for river paddling, kayaking, and other water sports. **Nordic Ventures** (☎ 56–51–00–17 ⊕ www.nordicventures.com) runs guided sea-kayak tours past the waterfalls and mountains of Sognefjord from April to October; prices start at NKr 400. **Voss Rafting Senter** (☎ 56–51–05–25) offers rafting, river-boarding, and canyoneering at prices beginning around NKr 500. **Voss Ski & Surf** (☎ 56–51–30–43) offers one- to three-day courses in river kayaking for both beginners and experienced kayakers. They also book kayak trips with instructors.

SKIING Voss and its varied mountain terrains are ideal for winter sports. An important alpine skiing center in Norway, **Voss Fjellheisar** (☎ 56–51–12–12 ⊕ www.voss-fjellheisar.no) has 40 km (25 mi) of alpine slopes, one cable car, eight ski lifts, eight illuminated and two marked cross-country trails, a snowboard park, and the Voss School of Skiing.

Utne, Lofthus & Folgefonna

❽ *65 km (41 mi) south of Voss via Rtes. 13 and 7, and the Utne ferry*

In the very heart of Hardanger lies **Utne,** a tiny village that rests at the tip of the peninsula dividing the inlet of Hardangerfjord from the arm that stretches south towards Odda, the Sørfjord. It's an excellent starting point for exploring the area. Going south on both sides of the fjord, you can explore farming communities with traditions dating back to the Middle Ages, or go hiking in the steep mountainsides and the plateaus or glaciers beyond. To get to Utne from Voss, take Route 13 to Granvin, and then Route 7 to Kvanndal where you catch the ferry to Utne. Buses are available from both Bergen (platform 4 on the main bus station) and Voss to Kvanndal several times daily.

Hardanger Folkemuseum is within walking distance of the ferry landing at Utne. Focusing primarily on local heritage, it's one of the largest and best museums of its kind in western Norway. The exhibit on folk costumes is particularly good, and several of the oldest surviving *Hardingfele* (Hardanger fiddles) are on display here. The ornate, usually eight-stringed fiddle was developed in Hardanger and produces a unique sound that inspired great Norwegian composers like Ole Bull and Edvard Grieg. On a little hill overlooking the main building you can sample fresh-baked local delicacies every Tuesday in July. ⊠ *Utne* ☎ *53–67–00–40* 🖷 *53–67–00–41* ⊕ *www.hardanger.museum.no* 🖾 *NKr 50* ☉ *May, daily 10–4; June–Aug., daily 10–5; Sept.–Apr., weekdays 10–3.*

Agatunet is an open-air museum composed of a cluster of old farmhouses— the oldest dating back to the 13th century. Serfdom was not practiced widely in western Norway. In some communities independent farmers clustered their houses together, and divided the pastures and orchards evenly. Although this led to some bizarre situations, like two farmers owning one half of the same apple tree, this semi-communal farming system was practiced until the 19th century. Very few clustered villages remain today, however, and even fewer are in as pristine condition as the Agatunet. The admission covers guided tours and indoor exhibits. Wandering the idyllic grounds is free. ⊠ *Aga, 17 km (11 mi) south of*

Utne ☎ *53/66–22–14 or 53–67–00–40* 🖷 *53–66–30–90* 🎫 *NKr 50* ⊙ *Early May–mid Aug., daily 10–5.*

On the eastern side of the Sørfjord is the village of **Lofthus,** one of the oldest fruit-farming communities in the area, and a spectacular sight in early summer, when its 450,000 fruit trees are in bloom. The last week in July, **Morellfestivalen** (the Morello Festival) celebrates the sweet cherry of the same name, brought here in 1146 by traveling Yorkshire monks. The main event is the Norwegian Championship in Morello Pit Spitting. To get to Lofthus, take the ferry from Utne to Kinsarvik, and follow Route 13 towards Odda, approximately 10 km (6 mi).

The **Folgefonna** glacier straddles the mountain ridge between Rosendal and Sørfjorden. Folgefonna is actually a set of three glaciers, Nordfonna, Midtfonna, and Sørfonna. The latter is the third-largest glacier in Norway. Several hiking paths lead up to the glacier, but you should only attempt to hike on the glacier itself accompanied by a guide. Good footwear and wind- and waterproof clothing are essential, even on sunny days. The easiest way to get up close to the glacier is to drive up to the **Folgefonna Sommarskisenter** (Summer Ski Center) from Jondal, 31 km (19 mi) south of Utne. The drive from Jondal up to the glacier itself is spectacular though bumpy. *Ski center:* ✉ *Jondal* ☎ *57–87–54–74* ⊕ *www.folgefonn.no* ⊙ *May–Aug., daily 9–4.*

<table>
<tr><td>

off the
beaten
path

</td><td>

BARONIET ROSENDAL – In 1658 a wealthy Norwegian heiress, Karen Mowat, wed a Danish nobleman, Ludvig Rosenkrantz, and the two were given a farm at Hattberg, tucked away in a valley west of Folgefonna, as their wedding present. They built a castle on the land, and a few years later the king of Denmark and Norway at the time, Christian V, gave the estate status as a barony, the only one of its kind in Norway. The estate was bequeathed to the University of Oslo in 1927, and today the barony is a combined museum, theater, and gallery with its own bed-and-breakfast on the premises. The castle is in fact a small-ish mansion, decorated in a variety of styles spanning the barony's history over 250 years and surrounded by a rose garden and stunning scenery. In summer there are concerts, lectures, and performances in the mansion or the courtyard. In mid-July the **Theatre Set-Up** company from London performs Shakespeare plays in English. ✉ *Rosendal, From Utne, follow Rte. 550 south toward Odda, then take the Folgefonn tunnel west and follow Rte. 48 to Rosendal* ☎ *53–48–29–99* 🖷 *53–48–29–98* ⊕ *www.baroniet.no* 🎫 *NKr 75, concerts NKr 150–NKr 250* ⊙ *Late June–mid-Aug., weekdays 10–7, weekends 10–5; May–late June and mid -Aug.–early Sept., weekdays 11–3, weekends 11–5; mid–late Sept., Sun. noon–2.*

</td></tr>
</table>

Where to Stay

$$$ ⊞ **Hotel Ullensvang.** This large hotel by the fjord in Lofthus offers comfortable, modern rooms. The restaurant, Zanoni, has a great view of both the fjord and the Folgefonna glacier. Rooms with a fjord and glacier view are about NKr 100 more expensive than those without the views. ✉ *5787 Lofthus* ☎ *53–67–00–00, 53–67–01–00 booking*

🖼 *53–67–00–01* ⊕ *www.hotel-ullensvang.no* ⤴ *157 rooms* ♨ *Restaurant, cable TV, pool, gym, massage, sauna, pub, meeting rooms* ⊟ *AE, DC, MC, V.*

$$$ 🖼 **Utne Hotel.** This small, cozy hotel was built in 1722, and has been
Fodor'sChoice operating continuously since, making it Norway's oldest. The white,
★ wooden main building has a wood-paneled, hand-painted dining room
decorated with copper pans, old china, and paintings. The hotel was
completely renovated and partly modernized in 2003, but still retains
much of its original charm. All 26 rooms have their own distinctive fla-
vor, and several are furnished with unique antiques and artwork from
the area. The rooms can be on the chilly side in winter, but the friendly
staff makes up for that with exceptionally warm service, and extra
wool blankets. Utne Hotel fills up fast in the high season, so book well
in advance. ✉ *5797 Utne* ☎ *53–66–64–00* 🖨 *53–66–69–50* ⊕ *www.
dehistoriske.no/utne_hotel* ⤴ *26 rooms* ♨ *Restaurant, pub, meeting rooms*
⊟ *AE, DC, MC, V.*

Sports

HIKING Steep paths that offer quite literally breathtaking scenery lead from
Lofthus up to the westernmost part of the Hardangervidda plateau. Con-
tact the local tourist office for tips and hiking suggestions. **Folgefonni
Breførarlag** (☎ *55–29–89–21* or *951–17–792* ⊕ www.folgefonni-
breforarlag.no) offers guided tours on the Folgefonna glacier.

The West Coast A to Z

*To research prices, get advice from other travelers, and book travel ar-
rangements, visit www.fodors.com.*

AIR TRAVEL

CARRIERS SAS Braathens has nonstop flights to Ålesund from Oslo, Bergen, Trond-
heim, and Stavanger.
📷 **SAS Braathens** ☎ 05400.

AIRPORTS

Ålesund's Vigra Airport is 15 km (9 mi) from the center of town. It's a
25-minute ride from Vigra to town via Flybussen. Tickets cost NKr 50.
Buses are scheduled according to flights—they leave the airport about
10 minutes after all arrivals and leave town about 60 or 70 minutes be-
fore each departure.
📷 **Flybussen** ☎ 70-13-68-00 ⊕ www.flybussen.no. **Taxi** ☎ 70-10-30-00. **Vigra
Airport information** ☎ 70-11-48-00.

BOAT & FERRY TRAVEL

Car ferries are a way of life in western Norway, but they are often crowded
and don't run as frequently as they should in summer, which causes de-
lays. Considerable hassle can be eliminated by reserving ahead, as cars
with reservations board first. Call the tourist office of the area to which
you're heading for ferry information. Hardanger Sunnhordalandske
Dampskipselskap (HSD) operates fjord express boats from Bergen to
Hardangerfjord and Sunnhordland, and most ferries south and east of
Bergen, including all ferries across Hardangerfjord. Fjord1 express boats

operate on routes between Bergen and Sognefjord, Nordfjord and Sunnfjord, as well as most ferries north of Bergen.

The *Hurtigruten* (coastal steamer) stops at Skansekaia in Ålesund, at noon. It then heads northward at 3. It returns at midnight and heads southward at 1 AM.

A catamaran runs between Ålesund and Molde at least twice daily. In addition to regular ferries to nearby islands, boats connect Ålesund with other points along the coast. Excursions by boat can be booked through the tourist office.

Fjord1 57-75-70-00 ⊕ www.fjord1.no. **Hardanger Sunnhordalandske Dampskipselskap (HSD)** 55-23-87-00 ⊕ www.hsd.no. *Hurtigruten* 810-30-000 ⊕ www.hurtigruten.com.

BUS TRAVEL

In western Norway the bus routes are fairly extensive: there are north–south express routes, like Bergen to Ålesund, and east–west routes like Trondheim to Oslo, all operated by Nor-Way. HSD Buss operates routes in the Bergen–Hardangerfjord region. Fjord1 operates routes in the Sognefjord and Northwest regions, and has glacier buses that run between Stryn and Briksdal.

Fjord1 57-75-70-50 ⊕ www.fjord1.no. **HSD Buss** 815-33-103 ⊕ www.hsd. no. **Nor-Way Bussekspress** 815-44-444 ⊕ www.nor-way.no.

CAR TRAVEL

Traveling around western Norway by car can be both spectacular and frustrating. A good rule of thumb is to stick as much as possible to the routes that qualify as Europavei, the ones that have a capital E in front of the route code, such as Route E16 that runs across the mountains from Oslo to Bergen, or Route E39 that runs along the coastline from Trondheim through Ålesund and Bergen to Stavanger. The road network in Norway is very much a work in progress, however, and not all E-coded routes are up to standard yet. Ask around at your hotel or the nearest tourist office if you're in doubt which route to take.

From Oslo to Ålesund it's 450 km (295 mi) on Route E6 to Dombås and then E136 through Åndalsnes to Ålesund.

From Ålesund to Bergen the E39 is a 381-km (237-mi) drive. It's reasonably well maintained and open most of the year. It involves several ferry crossings and a few tollbooths.

Voss is easily accessible from Bergen via the E16. The 102-km (63-mi) drive takes around 90 minutes. The E16 runs all the way to Oslo. In summer an alternate route is via Route 13 from Voss to Granvin, and from there pick up Route 7, across the Hardangervidda plateau to Oslo.

Route 7 from Oslo to Bergen passes through Eidfjord, and runs to Brimnes, where there's a ferry crossing to Bruravik. The road continues via Granvin to Bergen. At Brimnes Route 13 branches off to the south, past Kinsarvik, where there's a ferry to Utne, and then farther south to Lofthus. Both Route 7 and Route 13 can be very narrow and windy, and especially tricky to negotiate in winter.

Route 5 connects E16 and E39. It branches off E16 at Lærdal, passes through Fjærland through a tunnel beneath the Jostedalsbreen glacier, and joins E39 at Skei, a couple of hours' drive from Stryn. Route 5 has a fairly high standard.

☛ Car-Rental Agencies Avis ✉ Ålesund Vigra Airport ☎ 70-18-34-60. **Budget** ✉ Ålesund Vigra Airport ☎ 70-18-33-07. **Europcar** ✉ Ålesund Vigra Airport ☎ 70-18-23-00. **Hertz** ✉ Ålesund Vigra Airport ☎ 70-18-36-50.

EMERGENCY SERVICES ☛ Car Emergencies **Norsk Automobil Forbund (NAF)** ☎ 810-00-505 operates 24 hours a day.

ROAD CONDITIONS The roads mentioned in this chapter cover some of the most breathtaking scenery in the world. They are narrow two-lane ventures much of the time; passing is difficult, and in summer, traffic can be heavy. Some roads, especially mountain passes, may close at short notice in winter and early spring.

☛ Road Information Statens vegvesen (Public Roads Administration) ☎ 175 ⊕ www.vegvesen.no.

DISCOUNTS & DEALS

Fjord Pass, which costs NKr 100 for two adults and children under 15, is one of Norway's best hotel discount cards. The pass offers substantial discounts on accommodation at approximately 200 hotels, inns, cottages, and apartments all over Norway. Prices can be as low as NKr 225 per person per night.

☛ Fjord Pass ☎ 55-55-76-60 ⊕ www.fjordpass.no.

TRAIN TRAVEL

The *Dovrebanen* and *Raumabanen* between Oslo S Station and Åndalsnes via Dombås run three times daily in each direction. It's a 6½-hour ride. At Åndalsnes, buses wait outside the station to pick up passengers heading to points not served by the train. The 124-km (76-mi) trip to Ålesund takes close to 2 hours.

Voss is accessible via the *Bergensbanen* between Oslo and Bergen. Express trains run several times daily from Oslo and Bergen, all stop at both Voss station and Myrdal. There are also local trains from Bergen that run to Voss. The steep *Flåmsbanen* railway, featured in the "Norway in a Nutshell" tour, runs from Myrdal to Flåm.

☛ Flåmsbana train station ☎ 57-63-21-00 ⊕ www.flaamsbana.no. **NSB** (Norwegian state railways) ☎ 815-00-888 ⊕ www.nsb.no.

VISITOR INFORMATION

Fjord Norway in Bergen is a clearinghouse for information on western Norway. Its Web site and holiday guide are excellent resources for fjord travel planning.

☛ Ålesund ✉ Keiser Wilhelms gt. 11 ☎ 70-15-76-00. **Åndalsnes & Romsdal** ✉ Jernbanegt. 1 ☎ 71-22-16-22. **Eidfjord** ☎ 53-66-59-00. **Fjord Norway** ☎ 815-33-500 ⊕ www.fjordnorway.no. **Flåm** ✉ Railroad station ☎ 57-63-21-06 ⊕ www.visitflam.com. **Geiranger** ✉ Dockside ☎ 70-26-30-99. **Hardangerfjord** ☎ 56-55-38-70 ⊕ www.hardangerfjord.com. **Lofthus** ☎ 53-66-11-90. **Molde** ✉ Torget 4 ☎ 71-20-10-00. **Sognefjorden** ☎ 57-67-23-00 ⊕ www.sfr.no. **Stryn & Nordfjord** ✉ Stryn

☎ 57-87-40-40 ⊕ www.nordfjord.no. **Utne** ☎ 53-66-18-22. **Voss** ☎ 56-52-08-00 ⊕ www.voss-promotion.no.

CENTRAL NORWAY

Revised by
Daniel Cash

Central Norway is dominated by Hardangervidda, one of Europe's largest mountain plateaus. Several mountain areas and valleys—Hallingdal, Numedal, and Hemsedal—surround the plateau. North of Oslo are the famous valleys of Gudbrandsdalen and Valdres, and the mountain regions of Rondane, Dovrefjell, and Jotunheimen. Route 7 crosses Hardangervidda, and the Oslo-to-Bergen railway serves many towns in the region, including some in remote mountain areas that are hard to reach, such as Finse. Traveling by car involves lots of mountain driving, and may be impeded by the occasional avalanche or bad winter weather.

Numbers in the margin correspond to points of interest on the Central Norway map.

Hemsedal

❶ *35 km (21½ mi) north of Torpo.*

The mountains in the area are nicknamed the Scandinavian Alps, and Hemsedal has some of Norway's most stunning high-mountain scenery: you can see mountains and glaciers, numerous lakes, four rivers, as well as fjords and cascading waterfalls. It's the country's most popular skiing town, where Norway's top skiers and snowboarders live and train. The Maifestivalen (May Festival), which takes place on the first weekend of May, marks the end of the ski season; it's a well-attended event. In the summer months you can hike, play golf, and go fishing.

Where to Stay & Eat

★ $ ✕ **Hemsedal Café.** This hip café is a place to see and be seen, or you can just come for the simple dishes like burgers, Thai chicken, or the filling skier's breakfast. Internet usage at the several computers is free. ⊠ *Brustabygge* ☎ *32–05–54–10* ▤ *MC, V.*

★ $$$–$$$$ ✕▦ **Harahorn.** On a mountaintop 3,280 feet above Hemsedal's center, Harahorn is comprised of 11 mountain cabins clustered around the main house. Decorated in deep blues and earthy shades, the luxurious *bonderomantikk*, or "country romantic," pine cabins are filled with antiques and art. You can visit the hotel just to dine at the main house's restaurant, or opt to stay here. There are many outdoor sports and activities available, such as skiing, dogsledding, mountain climbing, and moose safaris. ⊠ *3580 Hemsedal* ☎ *32–06–23–80* ▤ *32–06–23–81* ⊕ *www. harahorn.no* ↵ *22 rooms, 11 cabins* ♨ *Restaurant, café, lounge, meeting room* ▤ *AE, DC, MC, V.*

$$$–$$$$
Fodor's Choice
★

✕▦ **Skarsnuten Hotell.** Perched like an eagle's nest, this mountainside hotel overlooks the village of Skarsnuten Landsby. In 2003 the inn was sold to the Good Life hotel chain. The minimalist interior is dominated by *skifer* (Norwegian stone), gray brushed wool, and wood. Framed mountain-sports photographs line the white walls. Rooms have spectacular views and names like Little Matterhorn. Kids are thoroughly entertained

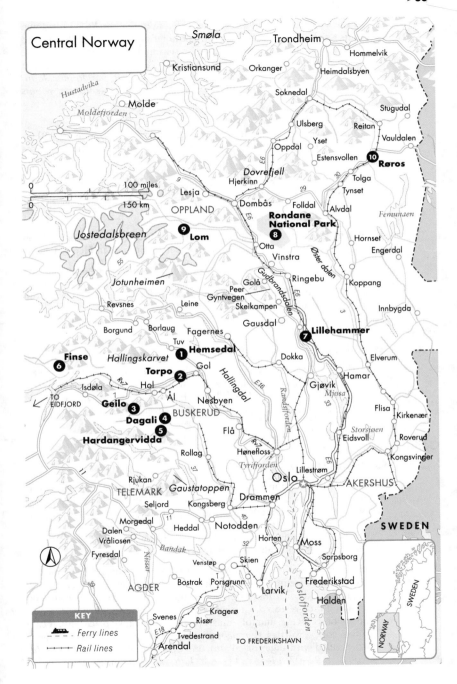

Central Norway

at their own disco and an Internet café. Take the hotel's ski lift down to its resort, Hemsedal Skisenteret. The hotel's restaurant is well regarded for its French-inspired menu based on seasonal Norwegian ingredients. ⊠ *Skarsnuten Landsby, 3560* ☎ *32–06–17–10* 📠 *32–06–17–11* ⊕ *www. skarsnuten.no* 🔄 *35 rooms, 2 suites* ♻ *Restaurant, bar, lounge, laundry facilities, business services, meeting rooms, no-smoking rooms* 🖃 *AE, DC, MC, V.*

Sports & the Outdoors

HIKING & CLIMBING   Experienced guides at **HeimVegen** (⊠ Aalstveit ☎ 32–06–06–20 or 90–65–64–07 ⊕ www.heimvegen.no) offer mountain touring courses year-round.

HORSEBACK RIDING   **Elvestad Fjellridning** (☎ 90–88–45–45 ⊕ www.hemsedal.com) offers half-day riding trips in the forest and mountains for all levels of riders. From late June through August every Tuesday, rides start at 9:30, last 3 to 3½ hours, and cost NKr 380.

PARAGLIDING   Paraglide in tandem with an experienced instructor. **Oslo Paragliding Klubb** (☎ 22–15–08–18 ⊕ www.opk.no) has its main base in Hemsedal.

SKIING   **Hemsedal Skisenteret** (☎ 32–05–53–90 ⊕ www.hemsedal.no) has 34 km (21 mi) of alpine slopes, 175 km (108 mi) of cross-country trails, and 17 ski lifts. The Ski School has superbly run courses for novices from children to adults.

Torpo

❷ *52 km (32 mi) from Hemsedal.*

Although there are seven stave churches in the valley, this tiny village's medieval church is the oldest and best preserved. **Torpo stave church** is the only 12th-century church left in Hallingdal. Its decorative ceiling, which depicts the legend of Saint Margaret, dates back 700 years. ☎ *32–08–31–37* 🖼 *NKr 30* 🕙 *June–Aug., daily 8:30–6.*

Geilo

❸ *35 km (21 mi) west of Torpo.*

More than a million visitors a year head to the slopes and cross-country trails of this *alpeby* (Alpine town) halfway between Oslo and Bergen. Many people ski directly from their hotel or cabin doors. Plan ahead if you want to visit at Easter, since Norwegians flock here for a final ski weekend. The summer season, beginning in June, has such activities as guided mountain walks, horseback riding, and fishing.

In the center of Geilo, the 17th-century farm of **Geilojordet** is a part of Hol Bygdemuseum. The cattle house, storage house, farmer's living quarters, and other buildings were brought here from the surrounding area and then restored. Cultural activities and events, such as rosemaling, wood carving, and folk-music performances, take place here. A café serves coffee, waffles, *rømmebrød* (sour-cream loaf), *lefse* (potato pancakes filled with sugar or cream), and other traditional sweets. ⊠ *Hagafoss* ☎ *32–07–14–85* 🖼 *Free* 🕙 *Late June–mid-Aug., daily 11–5.*

Where to Stay & Eat

Norway's most popular resort town has many hotels, mountain lodges, traditional cabins, apartments, and camping sites. Rooms are booked early for high season: you can contact **Geilo Booking** (☎ 32–09–59–40 ⊕ www.geilo.no) for advice on accommodations.

$$$–$$$$ ✕ **Halling-stuene.** The region's best-known chef, Frode Aga, has become a celebrity through his cookbooks and television appearances. His downtown restaurant has an elegant *bonderomantikk* style. His modern Norwegian cuisine features fish and game with an international influence. Try classic Aga dishes like reindeer fillet with fresh vegetables and mushrooms, or the *bacalao tomat* (dried salt cod with tomato, onion, and paprika). ⊠ *Geilovn. 56* ☎ *32–09–12–50* 🖃 *AE, DC, MC, V* ⊙ *Closed May.*

★ $$$–$$$$ ✕🖾 **Dr. Holms Hotel.** Built in 1909 as a sanitorium for asthma sufferers, the building is now a well-established resort hotel. Resembling a luxury mountain cabin, the hotel has elegantly decorated rooms and panoramic views of the surrounding mountains. Its Galleriet restaurant serves Continental-Norwegian dishes. Have drinks by the fire in the classy Ski bar, one of Norway's most popular après-ski bars. You can read in the peaceful library, which has 2,000 volumes, or watch stand-up comedy at the Recepten pub. Be pampered in the Japanese-style Dr. Holms Spa Klinikk. Make reservations well in advance. ⊠ *Timrehaugvn. 2, 3580* ☎ *32–09–57–00* 🖶 *32–09–16–20* ⊕ *www.drholms.com* ⤻ *124 rooms, 3 suites* ⚭ *Restaurant, cable TV, 2 indoor pools, gym, spa, 3 bars, lounge, pub, library, business services, meeting rooms, no-smoking rooms* 🖃 *AE, DC, MC, V.*

Sports & the Outdoors

BIKING Ask for bike maps at the Geilo tourist information office. Besides Rallarvegen, the Adventure Road, and Numedalsruta, there's excellent cycling in the countryside around Geilo on mountain roads. Bike rentals are available through **Intersport Geilo** (☎ 32–09–55–80 ⊕ www.intersport-geilo.no) for NKr 180 per bike per day.

FISHING Geilo's 90 mountain lakes and river stretches are open to the public from June to September and most are well stocked with trout. Inquire about recreation maps for Geilo and Hallingskarvet at the tourist office. Fishing licenses, which are mandatory, cost NKr 30 for a day and can be purchased at any post office or tourist office. Fishing permits, needed for fishing in certain areas, are available at local shops and the Geilo tourist office for NKr 40 per day. Fishing tackle and boat rentals can be organized through **Geilo Camping** (☎ 32–09–07–33) for NKr 120 a day, while rowboats cost NKr 90 for three hours.

HORSEBACK Many Geilo businesses offer horseback riding and riding lessons and
RIDING lead mountain trips, which can last from several hours to a week. **Eivindsplass Fjellgard** (☎ 32–09–48–45) offers trips only in July. **Geilo Hestesenter** (☎ 32–09–01–81) operates June through October. **Hakkesetstølen** (☎ 32–09–09–20) operates mid-June through late September. **Hallingskarvet Høgfjellshotell** (☎ 32–08–85–25) operates June through August. **Prestholtseter** (☎ 92–03–75–14) operates in July and August. **Ustaoset Hesteridning** (☎ 91–64–82–88) operates July through mid-August.

For independent walking, **Den Norske Turistforening (DNT)** (Norwegian Mountain Touring Association) has marked trails across the Hardangervidda plain and in the countryside around Hallingskarvet. Inquire at the tourist office about DNT routes and the use of their cabins.

Experienced guide Turid Linseth of **Hardangervidda Mountain Guiding** (☎ 97–54–18–60 ⊕ www.fjellguiding.no) has designed guided mountain walks and ski trips for all levels and interests.

Geilo has 38 pistes, three snowboard parks, 20 lifts, and plenty of slopes for children on both sides of the valley. You can purchase a downhill ski pass that allows you to use all the lifts. A free shuttle bus goes between the five ski centers. For cross-country skiers, there are 220 km (137 mi) of groomed and marked cross-country trails through woodland, Hardangervidda's hills and moors, and around Hallingskarvet, which is 6,341 feet above sea level. Snow rafting is the latest winter thrill: participants slide down snowy slopes on rubber rafts.

Geilo Skiheiser (☎ 32–09–59–20) has 24 km (15 mi) of Alpine slopes, 130 km (81 mi) of cross-country trails, 18 lifts, and a ski-board tunnel. **Halstensgård** (☎ 32–09–10–20) and **Slaatta** (☎ 32–09–03–70) have a range of Alpine and cross-country trails. **Havsdalsenteret** (☎ 32–09–17–77) attracts a young crowd to its long Alpine slopes. **Vestlia** (☎ 32–09–55–10), west of the Ustedalsfjord, has easier slopes so it's a good choice for families.

Dagali

❹ *25 km (15 mi) southeast of Geilo, off Rte. 40, on the border of Numedal and Hallingdal.*

The small village of Dagali borders the Hardangervidda National Park and makes a good launching point for mountain hiking, skiing, fishing, and white-water rafting. To replenish expended calories, savor the traditional Norwegian dishes at Dagali Hotell.

The **Dagali Museum** is in the heart of town, in the birch wood below the Fagerlund farm. Teacher Gunnar Stensen lived at Fagerlund from 1870 to 1970. He dedicated his life to the preservation of Norwegian and local culture. The museum houses his collections of agricultural equipment, furniture, and curiosities in 10 houses, an old schoolhouse, and an exhibition hall dating from the 1700s. ⊠ *Dagali center* ☎ *32–09–37–93* 🎫 *NKr 50* ☉ *Mid-June–mid-Aug., daily 10–5.*

Where to Stay & Eat

$–$$$
Fodor's Choice
★
×🖾 **Dagali Hotell.** Ole and Kirsten Halland will make you feel at home in their charming chalet-style hotel 2,870 feet above sea level and overlooking Dagali. The hotel was originally on one of the oldest farms in Dagali—it dates from the 1700s. Rooms are decorated in keeping with the rural Norwegian *bonderomantikk* style of this period. The restaurant is popular with locals for its traditional and seasonal Norwegian dishes. Try Kirsten's mountain trout, which she catches herself in the local lake in September. During the Christmas season, sample *rakfisk,* a salt-cured fish dish, and *lefse* (traditional Norwegian pastry). A short distance away the

Dagali ski center offers downhill skiing and snowboarding, and on the property are 2½ km (1½ mi) of well-lighted cross country ski trails. In summer Kirsten or Ole will give you a tour of the family's private village museum. ⊠ *Off Rte. 40, 3580 Dagali* ☎ *32–09–37–00* 📠 *32–09–38–10* ⊕ *www.dagali.no* ↩ *43 rooms* ♿ *Restaurant, cross-country skiing, bar, lounge, library; no TVs in some rooms* ▤ *AE, DC, MC, V.*

Rafting

Eivind Erik Scharffenberg and his international guides at **Dagali Rafting** (☎ 32–09–38–20 or 90–94–36–12 ⊕ www.dagalirafting.no) lead white-water trips on the Numedal River.

Hardangervidda

❺ *90 km (56 mi) from Geilo to Eidfjord on Rte. 7, the main road that crosses Hardangervidda.*

Norwegians take great pride in their largest national park, which is also Europe's largest mountain plateau—10,000 square km (3,861 square mi). Hardangervidda is home to the largest wild reindeer herds in Europe and is the southernmost outpost of the arctic fox, snowy owl, and other arctic animals and plants. A plateau with a thousand lakes, it has gently rolling hills and wide stretches of level ground. In the west the mountains become more dramatic, the plant life richer, the climate wetter, and temperatures more moderate. In the east the small amount of snow means that it's an almost barren, windswept moorland.

Some 250 Stone Age sites have been found in Hardangervidda. The earliest date from 6,300 BC, which proves that man reached the plateau at the same time as the reindeer. When touring the plateau, either on horseback or on foot, you can find a trail for any level of ability. Den Norske Turistforening (DNT; The Norwegian Mountain Touring Association) has built cabins along the trails. The association organizes tours and activities. All plant and animal life is protected by law. Respect the area to make sure it remains a thing of beauty.

At the foot of Vøringfossen waterfall and Måbødalen valley, the **Hardangervidda Natursenter Eidfjord** (Hardangervidda Nature Center at Eidfjord) focuses on the area's geology, biology, and archaeology. Over half a billion years ago Norway was south of the equator. Twenty-five million years ago glaciers began their descent over Norway. An interactive program explains how glaciers form, grow, and recede. ⊠ *Øvre Eidfjord* ☎ *53–66–59–00* ⊕ *www.hardangervidda.org* 🎫 *NKr 80* ⊙ *June–Aug., daily 9–8; Sept., Oct., Apr,. and May, daily 10–6; Nov.–Mar., by arrangement.*

About an hour's drive north of Geilo is Hardangervidda's highest peak, **Hardangerjøkulen** (Hardanger Glacier), at 6,200 feet. In summer you can join guided glacier walks led by **Jøklagutane** (☎ 95–90–53–53 ⊕ www.finsehytta.no). Near Hardangerjøkulen you can take a guided hike to the archaeological digs of 8,000-year-old Stone Age settlements. Turid Linseth at **Hardangervidda Mountain Guiding** (☎ 97–54–18–60 ⊕www.fjellguiding.no) leads guided walks explaining Hardangervidda's history, flora, and fauna.

Finse

❻ *On the railway line from Oslo to Bergen, in the Hardangervidda plateau.*

The only way to get to car-free Finse is by train, cycling, hiking, or skiing, making a visit there a unique and very remote Norwegian mountain experience, 4,008 feet above sea level. On the Oslo-to-Bergen line, the railway station here is northern Europe's highest. Glistening glaciers, white plateaus, and extreme temperatures and conditions have made Finse a legendary place of pilgrimage for adventurers and outdoors lovers. Some of the oldest traces of Norwegian civilization were found here: the remains of reindeer-hunting settlements dating back 7,000 years. Finse is not a town; its year-round population is fewer than 10 people, and besides the train station there are only a hotel and a few other buildings.

In the 1870s and 1880s, urban-dwelling Norwegian artists and university professors began to hike in the mountains here, and foreign tourists, particularly from Great Britain, started to visit the near-arctic clime. By the early 1900s polar explorers Fridtjof Nansen, Robert F. Scott, and Sir Ernest Shackleton tested their equipment here before setting off on their respective expeditions. In 1979, battle scenes of the second Star Wars film *The Empire Strikes Back* were filmed here.

Long cross-country ski trips, telemarking, ski-sailing, glacier walking on Hardangerjøkulen, dogsledding, hiking, and cycling are still common pastimes. On the last Saturday in April, the traditional end to the ski season, Norwegian skiers gather here for the Skarverennet race.

Every first weekend in February the **Finse Jazz festival** (⊕ www.bergenjazzforum.no) is arranged by Bergen Jazzforum, presenting musicians from all over the world.

Galleri Finse is a small gallery run by Norwegian artist Rannveig Barstad in cooperation with the Bryggen Kunstskole (art school). Changing exhibitions feature Barstad's and regional artists' works. ☎ *56–52–63–57 or 97–56–47–97* 🖾 *NKr 20* ⊙ *Jan.–Sept., daily 9 AM–9 PM.*

Rallarmuseet Finse (Railroaders Museum Finse) recalls the legendary turn-of-the-20th-century construction of the Bergen Railway. One exhibition shows how the railway's high mountain section was built, between 1871 and 1909. Another exhibition, "Kampen mot snøen" ("The Fight Against the Snow"), chronicles man's struggle against fierce winter forces. ⊠ *Østre lokomotivstall, Finse stasjon* ☎ *56–52–69–66* ⊕ *www.rallarmuseet.no* 🖾 *NKr 30* ⊙ *Mid-Jan.–Sept., daily 10 AM–10 PM.*

Where to Stay & Eat

$$$$ ✕🖾 **Finse 1222.** Named for Finse's position 1,222 meters (4,008 feet) above sea level, this 1909 hotel originally served travelers on the Bergen Railway who became snowed in. Despite its remote location, this *villmarkshotell* (wilderness hotel) quickly became a gathering place for Europe's rich and famous. Murals and photographs throughout depict ski scenes and past guests. Guest rooms are spartan, with no televisions,

BIKING THE RALLARVEGEN & EVENTYRVEGEN

THE MOST POPULAR BIKE TREK in Norway is the 80-km (50-mi) **Rallarvegen**, which follows the Bergen Railway, westbound over the Hardangervidda, from Haugastøl to Flå. The route was originally a construction and transportation track used during the building of the railway. (Rallar was the Norwegian name for the railway workmen.) The bikeway was established in 1974, and attracts 20,000 cyclists each year. You can rent a bicycle at Haugastøl, Finse, or nearly every town along the way.

Another popular cycling route is the **Eventyrvegen** (Adventure Trail), a network of bicycle routes that follow the Hallingdal and Hemsil rivers and pass near Krøderen Lake. Eventyrvegen's Route 52, for example, goes from Gol to Hemsedal following the Hemsil River, which is popular with anglers. You can buy an

Adventure Road cycling map at tourist offices or bookshops.

When looking for a place to stay, watch for **Syklist Velkommen** signs. This means that the lodgings are bicycle friendly, welcoming cyclists with bike repair kits, safe parking, and laundry facilities. Not all the cyclists who follow these routes are experienced with mountainous terrain; you can try out some of the less-challenging trails even if you are only a recreational cyclist.

radios, or telephones. The kitchen serves first-class Norwegian fare ($$), including warm smoked salmon and leg of wild lamb. The pub and disco Boggin has authentic railway seating. Summer and winter activities, tours, courses, and ski and bike rentals are available. Make reservations as early as possible, especially for weekends. ⊠ *Next to Finse train station, 5719* ☎ *56–52–71–00* ☎ *56–52–67–17* ⊕ *www.finse1222. no* ⟳ *44 rooms* ♤ *Restaurant, bar, pub, dance club, library, meeting room; no room TVs, no room phones* ☰ *AE, DC, MC, V* ☼ *Closed late Oct.–mid-Jan. and June.*

Sports & the Outdoors

BIKING In summer, cycling enthusiasts flock to **Rallarvegen,** widely considered to be one of the best mountain-biking routes in the world. The ride is on a gentle incline from Haugastøl, at 2,950 feet above sea level, to Finse, at 4,008 feet above sea level. Bike rental is available through **Haugastøl Tourist Center** (☎ 32–08–75–64) or at the Finse 1222 hotel.

HIKING, GLACIER WALKING Finse is an important connection for mountain trips, whether in summer or winter. Several hotels, including Finse 1222 and **Jøklagutane** (☎ 90–84–15–99) have programs and expert guides for mountain hikes and glacier walks.

DNT (☎ 56–52–67–32) arranges mountain trips; maintains well-marked trails south and north of Finse; and operates Finsehytta, a mountain cabin.

SKIING, SKI-SAILING **Finse Skilag** (☎ 55–31–79–56) arranges skiing trips as well as summer mountain activities. **Parmann AS Skiseiling** (☎ 90–56–45–07) offers ski-sailing courses and sells sails.

Lillehammer

❼ *40 km (25 mi) from Gjøvik, 60 km (37 mi) from Hamar, 180 km (111 mi) from Oslo.*

Many Norwegians have great affection for Lillehammer, the winter-sports resort town that hosted the 1994 Winter Olympics. In preparation for the games, the small town built a ski-jumping arena, an ice-hockey arena, a cross-country skiing stadium, and a bobsled and luge track. Lillehammer is known for the slopes on the mountains Nordseter and Sjusjøen; Vinterspillene, its Winter Arts Festival, held in February; and its many old wooden buildings. Lillehammer is a cultural center as well. It hosts the Norwegian Literature Festival in May. Sigrid Undset, who won the Nobel Prize in literature in 1928, lived in the town for 30 years.

> off the beaten path

HUNDERFOSSEN PARK – The world's biggest troll sits atop a cave in this tiny amusement park. The glittering gold Eventyrslottet, or fairy-tale castle, is a must-see. There's a petting zoo for small children; plenty of rides; plus an energy center, with Epcot-like exhibits about oil and gas; and a five-screen theater. The park is 13 km (8 mi) north of Lillehammer. ⊠ *Fåberg* ☎ *61–27–72–22* ⊕ *www.hunderfossen. no* 🎟 *NKr 240* ☉ *Late May–late June, daily 10–5; late June–early-Aug., daily 10–8; early Aug.–late Aug., daily 10–5.*

Fodor'sChoice ★ One of the most important art collections in Norway is housed at the **Lillehammer Kunstmuseum** (Lillehammer Museum of Art), which opened in 1927. The 1,000 works include pieces by Edvard Munch and Adolph Tidemand. The original 1963 building has been remodeled and joined by a new building designed by Snøhetta. Sculptor Bård Breivik created a sculpture garden using stone and water between the two buildings. ⊠ *Stortorgt. 2* ☎ *61–05–44–60* ⊕ *www.lillehammerartmuseum. com* 🎟 *NKr 60* ☉ *Late Aug.–June, Tues.–Sun. 11–4; July–late Aug., daily 11–5.*

★ ☉ Europe's largest open-air museum, **Maihaugen–Sandvigsche Sammlungen,** was founded in 1887. The massive collection of the artifacts of folk life was begun by Anders Sandvik, an itinerant dentist who accepted odds and ends—and eventually entire buildings—from the people of Gud-brandsdalen in exchange for his services. Eventually Sandvik turned the collection over to the city of Lillehammer, which provided land for the museum. The exhibit "We Won the Land" is an inventive meander through Norway's history. It begins in 10,000 BC. After walking past life-size, blue-hue mannequins representing periods like the Black Death and the 400 years of Danish rule, you reach unsettling exhibits about the 20th century. ⊠ *Maihaugvn. 1* ☎ *61–28–89–00* ⊕ *www.maihaugen.*

no ✉ *NKr 90, includes guided tour* ☉ *Oct.–mid-May, daily 11–4; mid-May–Sept., daily 10–5.*

The **Norges Olympiske Museum** (Norwegian Olympic Museum) covers the history of the games from their start in ancient Greece in 776 BC. Multimedia presentations and artifacts like sailboats and skis illustrate Norwegian sporting history in the **Gallery of Honor.** Some of the exhibition captions are in English. ✉ *Håkons Hall, Olympic Park* ☎ *61-25-21-00* ⊕ *www.ol.museum.no* ✉ *NKr 60* ☉ *June–Sept., Tues.–Sun. 10–6; Oct.–May, daily 11–4.*

The **Olympiaparken** has a range of winter as well as summer activities. You can visit the ski-jump tower, take the chairlift, or step inside the bobsled simulator at the **Lysgårdsbakkene Ski Jump Arena,** where the Winter Olympics' opening and closing ceremonies were held. Also in the park are **Håkons Hall,** the main hockey arena, which now holds sporting events and includes simulated, indoor golf-course holes. The **Birkebeineren Ski Stadium** holds cross-country and biathlon events. You can go tobogganing at the **Kanthaugen Freestyle Arena.** And at the **Olympic Bobsleigh and Luge Track** you can bobsled on ice. This involves a rubber bobsled with wooden runners that seats five passengers and can travel as fast as 80 kph (50 mph). ✉ *Elvegt. 19* ☎ *61-25-11-40* ⊕ *www. olympiaparken.no* ✉ *Arena NKr 20; fee varies for athletic events* ☉ *June–Sept., daily 9–5; Oct.–May, daily 11–4.*

Right on the pedestrian street, the tiny café **One Hand Clapping** (✉ Storgata) serves some of the best international coffees to be found between Oslo and Trondheim.

Where to Stay & Eat

$–$$$ ✕ **Blåmann Restaurant & Bar.** Named after a Norwegian folktale about a buck called Blueman, this popular restaurant has a completely blue interior. You'll also find an outdoor café, a bar on the second floor, and a nightclub next door. Try the Mexican tacos, or a reindeer or ostrich steak. ✉ *Lilletorget 1* ☎ *61-26-22-03* ⌖ *Reservations essential* ▭ *AE, DC, MC, V.*

¢–$ ✕ **Nikkers, Svare & Berg.** Nikkers has a rustic, mountain-cabin style, with the predictable moose head. Svare & Berg has a roaring fireplace and caricatures of famous authors hanging on the walls. Next door to each other, these restaurant-bars share the same owner and international cuisine, ranging from nachos to pastas. ✉ *Elvegt. 18* ☎ *61-24-74-30* ▭ *AE, DC, MC, V.*

$$$ ✕⌂ **Rica Victoria Hotel.** Red burnished leather chairs dot the English library–style lobby at this central hotel. Guest rooms are furnished in styles ranging from pure rural romanticism to more classic styles. The hotel has eight "ladies rooms," each with bed alcove and rocking chair. Victoria Stuene and Daily, the hotel's two restaurants, face a pedestrian street. ✉ *Storgt. 84B, 2600* ☎ *61-25-00-49* 🖷 *61-25-24-74* ⊕ *www.rica. no* ⇌ *109 rooms, 17 suites* ⌕ *2 restaurants, cable TV, in-room data ports, bar, nightclub, meeting room* ▭ *AE, DC, MC, V.*

★ $$ ⌂ **Mølla Hotell.** In this converted 1863 mill the small reception area gives the feeling of a private home. The yellow rooms in the former grain silo have rustic pine furniture. At the top of the silo, the Toppen Bar gives you a panoramic view of the Olympic ski jump and Lake Mjøsa. The Egon Restaurant is a beautiful outdoor retreat along the Mesna River. ⊠ *Elvegt. 12, 2600* ☎ *61–26–92–94* 🖶 *61–26–92–95* ⊕ *www. mollahotell.no* 🖾 *58 rooms* ♿ *Restaurant, cable TV, in-room data ports, sauna, bar* ☰ *AE, DC, MC, V.*

$–$$ ☒ **Birkebeineren Hotel/Motel & Apartments.** Ski trails and hiking terrain are steps away from this hotel's doors. The cream-color rooms are understated and country-style. Black-and-white photographs of skiers decorate the walls. ⊠ *Birkebeineren 24, Olympiaparken, 2618* ☎ *61–26–47–00* 🖶 *61–26–47–50* ⊕ *www.birkebeineren.no* 🖾 *75 rooms, 40 apartments* ♿ *Dining room, some in-room data ports, sauna, meeting rooms* ☰ *AE, DC, MC, V.*

Sports & the Outdoors

A highlight of Lillehammer's ski year is the **Birkebeineren cross-country ski race.** The Birkebeiners were a faction in Norway's 13th-century civil war, who got their name because they wrapped their legs in birch bark (hence *birkebeiner*—birch legs). Birch bark was commonly used as footwear by people who couldn't afford wool or leather leggings. The ski race commemorates the trek of two Birkebeiner warriors who carried the heir to the throne, Prince Haakon, to safety from the rival Bagler faction who were pursuing him. The backpack carried by participants during the race is meant to symbolize the young prince being brought to safety through harsh weather conditions.

FISHING   Within Troll Park, the **Gudbrandsdaláen** is touted as one of the best-stocked rivers in the country, and the size and weight of Mjøsa trout (locals claim it's 25 pounds) is legendary. Contact the local tourist board for information about fishing seasons, how to get the required national and local licenses, and other useful tips.

HIKING &   The Nordseter and Sjusjøen tourist centers are good starting points for
BICYCLING   mountain-biking and -hiking excursions. From **Nordseter Aktivitetssenter** (⊠ Off Rte. 6 ☎ 61–26–40–37), about 15 km (9 mi) from the city center, you can hike to Mt. Neverfjell, at 3,573 feet. There you can see the Jotunheimen and Rondane mountain ranges. The center rents mountain bikes, canoes, and other boats. Mt. Lunkefjell (3,320 feet) is a popular hiking destination accessible from **Sjusjøen Sport & Aktiviteter** (⊠ Sjøen ☎ 62–36–30–04). Regular bicycles and mountain bikes can be rented. The center also organizes walks, bicycle and fishing trips, and canoeing.

RAFTING &   The **Sjoa River,** close to Lillehammer, offers some of the most challeng-
CANOEING   ing rapids in the country. Contact **Heidal Rafting** (☎ 61–23–60–37).

SKIING   Lillehammer–Sjusjøen and Nordseter and the four other nearby skiing destinations—Hafjell, Skeikampen, Kvitfjell, and Gålå—are collectively called **Lillehammer Ski Resorts** (⊕ www.lsr). Together, they have 35 lifts, 78 pistes, and more than 1,500 km (932 mi) of cross-country trails. Each destination has its particular charm. A Lillehammer Ski Resorts Pass admits you to all five.

With both high-mountain and forest terrain, **Hafjell** (✉ 10 km [6 mi] north of Lillehammer ☎ 61-27-70-00) is the largest Alpine facility. Snow conditions are generally stable here. The Hunderfossen Familiepark with snowboarding is popular. There's also a child-care center, a ski school, and several after-ski entertainment spots.

Gålå (✉ Near Vinstra, 89 km [40 mi] north from Lillehammer via the E6 ☎ 61-29-76-65) is an all-around ski facility, with spectacular high-mountain terrain and views of Jotunheimen and Rondane national parks. It has cross-country trails and organized activities that include ice fishing, snow rafting, sledding, winter riding, and sleigh riding.

Shopping

Most of Lillehammer's 250-odd shops are on or near Storgata Street. From Lilletorget you can walk to the old industrial area of Mesna Brug, where there's the Mesnasenter (Mesna Center) group of clothing and craft shops. **Husfliden** (✉ Sigrid Undset pl. ☎ 61-26-70-70 ⊕ www. husfliden.no), one of the biggest and oldest home crafts stores in Europe, specializes in hand-knit sweaters and traditional and handmade goods from the Gudbrandsdalen area. Glassblowing is demonstrated at **Lillehammer Kunst Glass** (✉ Elvegt. 17 ☎ 61-25-79-80); you can also buy special glass souvenirs here.

> **en route** The scenic, well-marked Peer Gynt Vegen (Peer Gynt Road) begins in Gausdal. It's named for the real-life man behind Ibsen's character. Just 3 km (2 mi) longer than the main route, the road gives you splendid views of the mountains of Rondane, Dovrefjell, and Jotunheimen as you travel past old farmhouses. It passes two major resorts, Skeikampen/Gausdal and Gålå/Wadahl, before rejoining E6 at Vinstra.

Rondane National Park

❽ *19 km (12 mi) north of Vinstra off Rte. E6.*

Rounded, harmonious mountains distinguish Rondane National Park, as you travel north from Vinstra on Route E6. A good point of entry to the park is the resort of Høvringen, off Route E6. For thousands of years the area has given hunters their livelihood, and they've left their mark in the form of reindeer traps and burial mounds. Today Rondane is a popular recreation area, attracting hikers and skiers. Ten of the peaks rise more than 6,500 feet. Norwegian artist Harald Sohlberg (1869–1935) immortalized the Rondane mountains in his painting *Vinternatt*, which was declared Norway's national painting in 1995 and hangs in the National Gallery in Oslo.

Where to Stay & Eat

★ **$$$-$$$$** ✕ **Rondablikk Hotell.** Nestled in the mountains, near Kvam, Rondablikk has spectacular views of Rondane National Park and several lakes. Rooms are simply furnished and comfortable. Many guests spend their days cross-country skiing or mountain hiking. You can opt to order *halvpensjon* (half board), which includes the traditional Norwegian buffets at breakfast, lunch, and dinner. Rondablikk shares a lunch exchange program with Rondane SPA Hotel and Rondeslottet Mountain Hotel. Every August, Norway's best musicians play on the hotel's outdoor stage as part of the Peer Gynt Festival. ⊠ *Rte. E6, 2642 Kvam* ☎ *61–29–49–40* 🖷 *61–29–49–50* ⊕ *www.rondablikk.com* 🗐 *72 rooms* ⌂ *Restaurant, pool, exercise equipment, sauna, cross-country skiing, bar, lounge, meeting rooms* ▭ *AE, DC, MC, V.*

★ **$$$–$$$$**   ✕▣ **Rondane SPA Hotel.** This hotel is high in the mountains south of Otta. The bright, simply furnished rooms have a country charm. A full range of services, from massage to baths, is on offer at the spa. Chef Steinar Havnen changes the menu of international dishes based on Norwegian fish and game daily. To get to the hotel, turn right off Route E6 before the exit for Otto, and follow signs to Mysuseter and Rondane Spa. ⊠ *Mysuseter, 2670 Otta, off Rte. E6, 20 km (12 miles) north of Vinstra* ☎ *61–23–39–33* 🖷 *61–23–39–52* ⊕ *www.spa.no* 🗐 *52 rooms* ⌂ *Restaurant, pool, massage, sauna, spa* ▭ *AE, DC, MC, V.*

Sports & the Outdoors

BOATING   Guided canoe safaris or independent trips are possible on four mountain lakes along the Peer Gynt Road. Contact **Gålå Sommer Arena** (☎ 61–29–76–30 ⊕ www.gala.no) and **Fefor Høifjellshotell** (☎ 61–29–00–99 ⊕ www.fefor.com).

HIKING   A network of marked trails and footpaths such as those kept by the **DNT (Norwegian Mountain Touring Association)**, the **Peer Gynt Trail**, and the **Pilgrims' Track** offer varied challenges. You can pick up maps at **Vinstra Skysstasjon** (Vinstra Tourist and Transport Centre ⊠ Øvre Årdal ☎ 57–66–35–62).

HORSEBACK RIDING   **Sulseter Rideleir** (☎ 61–29–13–21) offers weeklong and weekend treks in Rondane National Park.

SKIING   Considered one of the best resorts for cross-country skiing (there are 630 km [391 mi] of trails), the **Peer Gynt Ski Region** (⊕ www.peergyntskiregion.com) includes the destinations Espedalen, Fefor, and Gålå. For downhill skiers there are pistes for all levels in Snowboard, Telemark, and Alpine.

Lom

❾   *62 km (38 mi) west of Otta, via Rte. 15.*

Torgeir Garmo shares his passion for geology in his geological museum and jewelry gallery in the **Fossheim Steinsenter** (Fossheim Stone Center). His collection is the largest private exhibition of Norwegian minerals and precious stones in the country. In the sales galleries you can buy jewelry, minerals, and fossils. The Collector Mania museum shows rare objects that people have collected through the ages. ⊠ *2686 Lom* ☎ *61–21–14–60* 🗐 *Free* ☉ *June–Aug., daily 9–9, otherwise by appointment.*

Glaciers, lakes, fertile valleys, and mountains make up **Jotunheimen National Park,** of which 90% lies in the municipality of Lom. One of the park's well-known landmarks is **Galdhøpiggen,** the country's highest

BEST PLACES TO HIKE

THE EXTRAORDINARY MOUNTAINS of central Norway draw hikers of every level of experience. The terrain varies from the relatively level Hardangervidda plateau to the rounded Rondane mountains to the jagged, tall peaks of the Jotunheimen range.

Trails are usually well marked, and there are cabins owned by the Norwegian Mountain Touring Association (DNT), which are kept for hikers who require overnight accommodations during their outing. The DNT local offices throughout the region can help you plan a hike, or sign you up for scheduled mountain trips organized for hikers of all levels of fitness and ability. One of Norway's classic mountain trips is hytte til hytte (cabin to cabin) in Jotunheimen National Park. You have to contact the organization before your hike to gain access to the cabins near your trail.

The Hardangervidda plateau's gentle slopes are perfect for beginners and those who aren't sufficiently fit to attempt high-altitude climbing. Experienced hikers tend to head to the tougher, steeper, Alpine trips in Hemsedal, Rondane, and Jotunheimen. Mountain guides based in towns throughout the region can design trips tailored to your level of fitness.

---

mountain, at 8,098 feet. Established in 1980, the park covers an area of 1,150 square km (444 square mi), and contains 27 of Norway's highest peaks. The rural town of Lom is distinguished by its dark-brown painted log cabins and a stave church from 1170.

At **Lom Bygdamuseum Presthaugen** (Lom Open Air Museum), a well-preserved 19th-century farm, you can see **Olavsstugu,** where Saint Olav is said to have spent the night; there are also exhibitions, including one about watering techniques and grain in Storstabburet. ⊠ *Town Center* ☎ *61–21–19–33* 🖼 *NKr 20* ☯ *July, daily 1–4; guided tours noon–4.*

One of Norway's oldest and most beautiful stave churches, **Lom Stavkyrkje** (Lom Stave Church), dates to the 12th century and still is the principal church in Lom. Its oldest section is Romanesque; the church was enlarged in 1634. Wood-carver Jakop Sæterdalen created the choir stalls and the pulpit. The church's baroque painting collection is one of Norway's largest. ☎ *61–21–29–90* 🖼 *NKr 40* ☯ *Mid-May–mid-June and mid-Aug.–mid-Sept., daily 10–4; mid-June–mid-Aug., daily 9–9.*

A woolly mammoth looms at the entrance to **Norsk Fjellmuseum** (Norwegian Mountain Museum). The museum focuses on people's relationship with the Norwegian mountain landscape, from the primitive hunters and gatherers who lived here to modern Norwegian society, with its belief in leisure time and outdoor recreational activities. Among the most interesting of the exhibitions is one dealing with early mountaineering and mountain road building. You can read the late-19th-century journals of W. C. Slingsby, the British father of Norwegian mountaineering, and see a reconstructed campsite. ☒ *Town Center* 🕾 *61–21–16–00* ⊕ *www.fjell.museum.no* ☒ *NKr 60* ☉ *May and mid-Sept., daily 9–4, weekends 10–5; early June and late Aug, weekdays 9–6, weekends 10–5; mid-June–mid-Aug., weekdays 9–9, weekends 10–8; late Sept.–Apr., weekdays 9–4, weekends by appointment.*

Where to Stay & Eat

$$$$
Fodor'sChoice
★

✕☒ **Røisheim Hotel.** Formerly a farm and coaching inn, this beautiful property is made up of 12 well-preserved buildings, most from the 18th century and one dating back to the 16th century. Rooms with hardwood floors and antique furniture retain the traditional look and feel of the original interior. The restaurant is renowned for its excellent cuisine, which revolves around local and seasonal ingredients, and vast wine cellar. But perhaps Røisheim's greatest asset is its location in a high-mountain pass near the road to Sognefjell, about 12 km (7½ miles) outside Lom. Walking trails in the area will leave you speechless at the beauty of the Jotunheimen range's peaks and glaciers. ☒ *2687 Bøverdalen* 🕾 *47–61–21–20–31* 🖷 *47–61–21–21–51* ⊕ *www.roisheim.no* ⤦ *24 rooms* ⚇ *Restaurant, bar, meeting rooms* ▤ *AE, DC, MC, V.*

★ $$$

✕☒ **Fossheim Turisthotell.** Svein Garmo and his family have run this mountain hotel since it began as a staging post in 1897. Solid-timber walls and antique furnishings give it a cozy look. Chef Kristofer Hovland and his dishes based on local ingredients have made the restaurant popular. Among the best-known dishes is the succulent fillet of reindeer. In summer take a seat in the aromatic outdoor café Urtehagen, surrounded by herbs and flowers. ☒ *Off Rte. E6, 2686 Lom* 🕾 *61–21–95–00* 🖷 *61–21–95–01* ⊕ *www.fossheimhotel.no* ⤦ *54 rooms, 4 apartments* ⚇ *Restaurant, café, bar, meeting room* ▤ *AE, DC, MC, V.*

Sports & the Outdoors

FISHING
Lom Fiskeguiding DA (🕾 61–21–10–24) rents fishing boats and organizes fishing trips.

HIKING &
GLACIER
WALKING
Go glacier walking and climb Galdhøpiggen or other mountains. Call **Juvasshytta** (🕾 61–21–15–50) or **Natur Opplevingar** (🕾 61–21–11–55 ⊕ www.naturopplevingar.no).

HORSEBACK
RIDING
Jotunheimen Hestesenter (Jotunheimen Equestrian Center; ☒ Raubergstulen 🕾 61–21–18–00) has mountain riding tours for all ages, beginner to advanced, on Icelandic horses.

RAFTING
Several local outfitters cater to your Sjoa River rafting needs, including **Lom Rafting** (🕾 90–80–90–90 ⊕ www.lomrafting.no) and **Villmarken** (🕾 61–23–39–57 ⊕ www.villmarken.net).

SUMMER SKIING
You can go summer skiing at **Galdhøpiggen Sommerskisenter** (☒ Lom 🕾 61–21–17–50) on a glacier 6,068 feet above sea level.

Røros

10 *317 km (197 mi) east of Lesja, 157 km (97 mi) south of Trondheim.*

At the northern end of the Østerdal, the long valley to the east of Gudbrandsdalen, lies Røros, one of Norway's great mining towns. For more than 300 years practically everyone who lived in this one-company town was connected with the copper mines. In 1980 Røros was named a UNESCO World Heritage Site. Norwegian artist Harald Sohlberg's paintings of Røros made the town famous. His statue now stands in Harald Sohlberg's plass, looking down the stretch of road that he immortalized.

The **Bergstadens Ziir** (Røros Church) towers over the wooden houses of the town. The eight-sided stone structure dates from 1784. On the tower you can see the symbol of the mines. Called "the mountain's cathedral," it can seat 1,600, quite surprising in a town with a population of only about 3,500. The pulpit looms above the center of the altar, and seats encircle the top perimeter. ☎ *72–41–95–05* *NKr 25* ⏲ *Mid–late June, Mon.–Sat. 11–1; late June–late Aug., Mon.–Sat. 10–5, Sun. 2–4; late Aug.–mid-Sept, Mon.–Sat. 11–1; mid-Sept.–May, Sat. 11–1.*

off the beaten path

OLAVSGRUVA MINE – This is the only Norwegian copper mine that was saved for posterity (in 1977 the copper works went bankrupt). Known as Olavsgruva, it consists of Nyberget (1650) and Crown Prince Olav's Mine (1936). A museum has been built over the mine shaft. Visitors can walk 164 feet underground and approximately 1,640 feet into the Miners' Hall, complete with sound and light effects. Bring warm clothing and good shoes, as the temperature below ground is about 5°C (41°F). ✉ *Near Rte. 31* ☎ *72–40–61–70* *NKr 60* ⏲ *Guided tours early June and late Aug.–early Sept., Mon.–Sat. at 1 and 3, Sun. at noon; late June–mid-Aug., daily at 10:30, noon, 1:30, 3, 4:30, and 6; early Sept.–May, Sat. at 3.*

★ Røros's main attraction is the **Old Town,** with its 250-year-old workers' cottages, slag dumps, and managers' houses, one of which is now City Hall. Descendants of the man who discovered copper ore in Røros live in the oldest of the nearly 100 protected heritage buildings. A 75-minute tour starts at the information office and ends at the church. ✉ *Peder Hiorts gt. 2* ☎ *72–41–00–50* *NKr 50* ⏲ *Tours June and late Aug.–mid-Sept., Mon.–Sat. at 11; July–mid-Aug., Mon.–Sat. at 10, noon, 1, 2, and 3, Sun. at 1; mid-Sept.–May, Sat. at 11.*

Røros Museum is in an old smelting plant, opened in 1646. In 1953 a fire destroyed the smelting works in Røros; the plant was closed and the machines were moved to Sweden. "Smelthytta," the smelting house, has been reconstructed using drawings of the workshop from 1888. Exhibitions show models of waterwheels, lift mechanisms, horse-driven capstans, mine galleries, and 19th-century clothing. ✉ *Off Rte. 30* ☎ *72–40–61–70* *NKr 65* ⏲ *Late July–mid-Aug., weekdays 10:30–6, weekends 10:30–4; mid-Aug.–late July, weekdays 11–3, weekends 11–2.*

Where to Stay & Eat

If you want to explore the green, pastured mountains just south of Røros, more than a dozen farmhouses take overnight visitors. Some are *hytter* (cabins), but others, such as the **Vingelsgaard Gjestgiveri** (☎ 62–49–45–43), have entire wings devoted to guest rooms. Rates at Vingelsgaard are around 480 NKr per person. Contact **Vingelen Turistinformasjon** (☎ 62–49–46–65 or 62–49–46–83 ⊕ www.vingelen. com) for more information.

$$–$$$ ✕⌂ **Bergstadens Hotel.** An elegant, country-style hotel, this is a Røros landmark. The staff is warm and friendly, creating a personal and intimate mood. The restaurant has a changing menu of traditional Norwegian fare. ☒ *Oslovn. 2, 7361* ☎ *72–40–60–80* 🖶 *72–41–60–81* ⊕ *www.bergstaden.no* ↝ *90 rooms, 4 suites* ♨ *2 restaurants, 2 bars, pub, nightclub, meeting room* ▤ *AE, DC, MC, V.*

Sports & the Outdoors

BOATING   Femunden and Hodal lakes make great starting points for day trips or longer tours. A canoeing trip on your own or accompanied by a guide can be memorable. **Hodalen Fjellstue** (☎ 62–49–60–72) has boat and fishnet rentals and fishing permits.

CYCLING   Easy terrain in the Røros region makes it ideal for cyclists. The Røros tourist office offers bicycling package tours, which include maps and accommodation. Contact **Heimly Huskies Adventure** (☎ 72–41–47–93 ⊕ www.heimly-huskies.com) for mountain-bike tours of three to four hours (600 NKr) or seven to eight hours (980 NKr), or dogsled tours with authentic Siberian huskies lasting from one hour to one week.

FISHING   Fishing is possible in the Gaula, one of Norway's finest salmon rivers, or in the Glåma, Norway's longest river, recommended for grayling and trout. An angling guidebook and fishing licenses are sold at the tourist office, in shops and gas stations, and at the rangers' office in Holtålen. Skilled guides can show you the area and advise you on where and how to fish, preserving and cooking your catch. Contact **Ålen Fjellstyre** (☎ 72–41–55–77).

Central Norway A to Z

To research prices, get advice from other travelers, and book travel arrangements, visit www.fodors.com.

AIR TRAVEL

Coast Air operates flight routes between Stavanger on the southern coast and Fagernes several times weekly.

🛫 **Coast Air** ☒ Haugesund Lufthavn, Postboks 163 ☎ 815–44–442 ⊕ www.coastair.no

BUS TRAVEL

Several bus companies operate in the region. Nor-Way Bussekspress and Nettbuss both have services connecting most interior cities, including Geilo, Gol, Ål, and Hemsedal. Hallingdal Billag has service between Oslo and Geilo. Sogn Billag has service from Sogn to Hemsedal, Gol, Oslo, and Bergen. JVB TUR serves Serving Jotunheimen and Valdres. Contact the local tourist office regarding special seasonal ski buses

🎵 **Hallingdal Billag** ☎ 32-08-60-60 ⊕ www.hallingdalbillag.no. **JVB TUR** ☎ 61-36-59-00 ⊕ www.jvb.no. **Nettbuss** ☎ 815-00-184 or 177. **Nor-Way Busseks-press** ☎ 815-44-444 ⊕ www.nor-way.no. **Sogn Billag** ☎ 177 or 57-65-95-12 ⊕ www.sognbillag.no.

CAR TRAVEL

The wide, two-lane Route E6 north from Oslo passes through Lillehammer. Route 3 follows Østerdalen (the eastern valley) from Oslo. Route 30 at Tynset leads to Røros and E6 on to Trondheim, 156 km (97 mi) farther north.

Roads in the north become increasingly hilly and twisty as the terrain roughens into the central mountains. The northern end of the region is threaded by E16, E6, and Routes 51 and 3. High-tech markers at the roadside, particularly prevalent in the area of Vinstra and Otta, are cameras. Exceed the speed limit, and you may receive a ticket in the mail.

For the Hallindal Valley, follow Route 7 between Oslo–Hønefoss and Bergen. Your trip will probably involve some mountain driving. In summer, road conditions are good, but in winter there can be avalanches and other obstacles.

LODGING

For information on the region's top ski resorts, check out Scandinavia's online ski booking Web site, **Skistar** (⊕ www.skistar.com).

TOUR OPERATORS

🎵 **Fjell og Fjord Ferie AS** ✉ Gamlevegen 6, Gol ☎ 32-02-99-26 ⊕ www.eventyrveien.com.

TRAIN TRAVEL

This region is served by the Oslo–Bergen line of the Norwegian State Railway (the whole run takes nearly seven hours). Between late June and mid-September, a bicycle train, which stops at Finse, runs between Oslo and Voss.

🎵 **NSB (Norwegian State Railway)** ☎ 815-00-888 ⊕ www.nsb.no.

VISITOR INFORMATION

🎵 **Hallingdal Valley to Hardangerfjord** Ål ☎ 32-08-10-60 ⊕ www.aal.as. **Geilo** ☎ 32-09-59-00 ⊕ www.geilo.no. **Gol** ☎ 32-02-97-00 ⊕ www.golinfo.no. **Hallingdal (Nesbyen)** ☎ 32-07-01-70 ⊕ www.nesbyen.no. **Hemsedal** ☎ 32-05-50-30 ⊕ www.hemsedal.com.

🎵 **Lillehammer to Røros** **Dovre/Dovrefjell/Rondane Tourist Office** ☎ 61-24-14-44 ⊕ www.dovrenett.no. **Lillehammer** ✉ Skysstasjon ☎ 61-28-98-00 ⊕ www.lillehammerturist.no. **Lom/Jotunheimen Reiseliv** ☎ 61-21-29-90 ⊕ www.visitlom.com. **Røros** ☎ 72-41-00-00 ⊕ www.rorosinfo.com. **Vågå/Jotunheimen** ✉ Vågå 37 ☎ 61-23-78-80 ⊕ www.jotunheimen-turist.com.

TRONDHEIM TO THE NORTH CAPE

Revised by
Daniel Cash

Wild and beautiful, northern Norway is known for its fast-changing weather and vast distances, and is famous as the land of the northern lights, midnight sun, and polar night. It's a land marked by high mountains, glaciers, fjords, islands, and rocky shores. The Gulf Stream warms the coast, making it the longest ice-free coast in the polar regions. Basking in the midnight sun is one of Norway's most popular attractions; every year, thousands of people flock to Nordkapp (the North Cape) for it. To cater to the large number of visitors, northern Norway has well-run tourist offices which stock excellent maps and travel literature on the area.

Numbers in the margin correspond to points of interest on the Trondheim and the North map.

Trondheim

 494 km (307 mi) north of Oslo, 657 km (408 mi) northeast of Bergen.

One of Scandinavia's oldest cities, Trondheim is Norway's third largest, with a population of 150,000. Founded in 997 by Viking king Olav Tryggvason, it was first named Nidaros (still the name of the cathedral), a composite word referring to the city's location at the mouth of the Nid River. The city was also the first capital of Norway, from AD 997 to 1380. Today Trondheim is a university town as well as a center for maritime and medical research, but the wide streets of the historic city center are still lined with brightly painted wood houses and striking warehouses.

King Olav formulated a Christian religious code for Norway in 1024, during his reign. It was on his grave that **Nidaros Domkirke** (Nidaros Cathedral) was built. The town became a pilgrimage site for the Christians of northern Europe, and Olav was canonized in 1164.

Although construction began in 1070, the oldest existing parts of the cathedral date from around 1150. It has been ravaged on several occasions by fire and rebuilt each time, generally in a Gothic style. Since the Middle Ages, Norway's kings have been crowned and blessed in the cathedral. The crown jewels are on display here. Forty-five minute guided tours are offered in English from mid-June to mid-August, weekdays at 11 and 4. ⊠ *Kongsgårdsgt. 2* ☎ *73–53–91–60* ⊕ *www.nidarosdomen.no* ⊠ *NKr 40. Ticket also permits entry to Erkebispegården* ⊙ *Call for hrs.*

The **Erkebispegården** (Archbishop's Palace) is the oldest secular building in Scandinavia, dating from around 1160. It was the residence of the archbishop until the Reformation in 1537; after that it was a residence for Danish governors, and later a military headquarters. The oldest parts of the palace, which face the cathedral, are used for government functions.

The **Archbishop's Palace Museum** (⊠ Kongsgårdsgt. ☎ 73–53–91–60 ⊠ NKr 35) has original sculptures from Nidaros Cathedral and archaeological pieces from throughout its history.

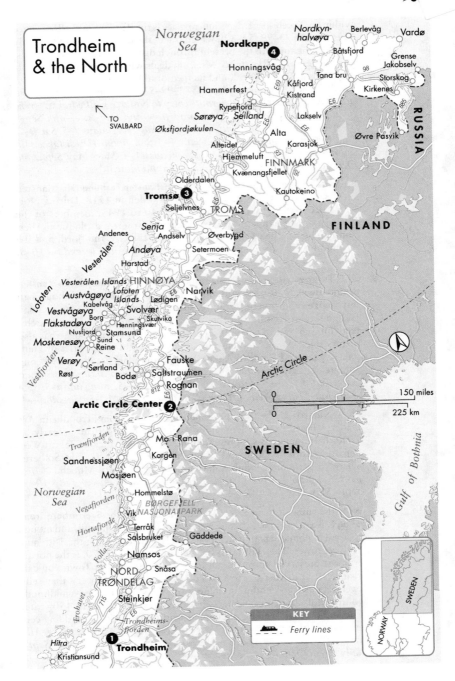

Within the Erkebispegården's inner palace is the **Rustkammeret/Resistance Museum** (☎ 73–99–52–80), which traces the development of the army from Viking times to the present through displays of uniforms, swords, and daggers. The Resistance Museum deals with events in central Norway during World War II, and its memorial hall remembers those who lost their lives. ⊠ *Kongsgårdsgt.* ☎ *73–99–52–80* ⊕ *www.nidarosdomen. no* ⊠ *NKr 40. Ticket also permits entry to Nidaros Cathedral* ☉ *Archbishop's Palace Museum: May–mid-June and mid-Aug.–mid-Sept., Mon.–Sat. 9–3, Sun. 1–4; mid-June–mid-Aug., weekdays 9–5, Sat. 9–2, Sun. 1–4; mid-Sept.–Apr., Mon.–Sat. 11–3, Sun. noon–4. Resistance Museum: June–Aug., weekdays 9–3, weekends 11–4; Mar.–May, Sept., and Oct., weekends 11–4; guided tours by appointment.*

Built after the great fire of 1681, the **Kristiansten Festning** (Kristiansten Fort) saved the city from conquest by Sweden in 1718. During Norway's occupation by Germany, from 1940 to 1945, members of the Norwegian Resistance were executed here; there's a plaque in their honor. The fort has a spectacular view of the city, the fjord, and the mountains. ☎ *73–99–52–80* ⊠ *Free* ☉ *June–Aug., weekdays 10–3, weekends 11–4.*

★ The Tiffany windows are magnificent at the **Nordenfjeldske Kunstindustrimuseum** (National Museum of Decorative Arts), which houses an impressive collection of furniture, silver, and textiles. The Scandinavian Design section features a room interior designed by the Danish architect Finn Juhl in 1952. The 1690 bridal crown by Adrian Bogarth is also memorable. "Three Women–Three Artists" features tapestries by Hannah Ryggen and Synnøve Anker Aurdal, and glass creations by Benny Motzfeldt. ⊠ *Munkegt. 5* ☎ *73–80–89–50* ⊕ *www.nkim.museum.no* ⊠ *NKr 50* ☉ *June–late Aug., Mon.–Sat. 10–5, Sun. noon–5; late Aug.–May, Tues., Wed., Fri., and Sat. 10–3, Thurs. 10–5, Sun. noon–4.*

Near Nidaros Cathedral, the **Trondheim Kunstmuseum** (Trondheim Art Gallery) houses more than 2,700 paintings dating from as early as 1800. Regional artists represented include Håkon Bleken, Jakob Weidemann, Adolph Tidemand, Christian Krohg, and Harald Solberg. There's a permanent exhibition of graphics by Edvard Munch. ⊠ *Bispegt. 7B* ☎ *73–53–81–80* ⊠ *NKr 40* ☉ *June–Aug., daily 10–5; Sept.–May, Tues.–Sat. 11–4.*

Near the ruins of King Sverre's medieval castle is the **Sverresborg Trøndelag Folkemuseum,** which has re-creations of coastal, inland, and mountain-village buildings that depict life in Trøndelag during the 18th and 19th centuries. The Haltdalen stave church, built in 1170, is the northernmost preserved stave church in Norway. In the Old Town you can visit a 1900 dentist's office and an old-fashioned grocery that sells sweets. A special exhibit examines how the stages of life—childhood, youth, adulthood, and old age—have changed over the past 150 years. The audiovisual **Trønderbua** depicts traditional regional wedding ceremonies with artifacts and a 360-degree film. ⊠ *Sverresborg Allé* ☎ *73–89–01–00* ⊕ *www.sverresborg.no* ⊠ *NKr 80* ☉ *June–Sept., daily 11–6; Oct.–May, weekdays 11–3, weekends noon–4.*

off the beaten path

MUNKHOLMEN (Monks' Island) – Now a swimming and recreation area, Monk's Island was Trondheim's execution grounds in ancient times. In the 11th century, Benedictine monks built a monastery on the island, likely one of the first monasteries in Scandinavia. In 1658 the monastery was converted into a prison and fort and, later, a customs house. There is a display of handicrafts in what was once the caretaker's house. Boats to the island depart from the fish market. ☎ 73–80–63–00 ⊕ *www.lilletorget.no* ✉ *NKr 50* ⊙ *Mid-May–late Aug., boats depart daily on the hr 10–6.*

Norway's oldest institution of science, the **NTNU Vitenskapsmuseet** (NTNU Science Museum) covers flora and fauna, minerals and rocks, church history, southern Sami culture, and archaeological finds. The eclectic exhibits have relics from the Bronze Age as well as ecclesiastical articles from the 13th to 18th century. ⊠ *Erling Skakkes gt. 47* ☎ *73–59–21–45* ⊕ *www.ntnu.no/vmuseet* ✉ *Free* ⊙ *May–mid-Sept., weekdays 9–4, weekends 11–4; mid-Sept.–Apr., Tues.–Fri. 9–2, weekends noon–4.*

Fodor'sChoice
★ Scandinavia's largest wooden palace, **Stiftsgården,** was built between 1774 and 1778 as the home of a prominent widow. Sold to the state in 1800, it's now the official royal residence in Trondheim. The architecture and interior are late baroque and highly representative of 18th-century high society's taste. Tours offer insight into the festivities marking the coronations of the kings in Nidaros Domkirke. ⊠ *Munkegt. 23* ☎ *73–80–89–50* ✉ *NKr 50* ⊙ *June 1–19, Mon.–Sat. 10–3, Sun. noon–5; June 20–Aug. 20, Mon.–Sat. 10–5, Sun. noon–5. Tours on the hr.*

Off Munkegata near the water you can see an immense variety of seafood at **Ravnklohallen Fiskehall** (Fish Market; ☎ 73–52–55–21 ⊕ www. ravnkloa.no). A former 1725 prison now houses the little **Trondhjems Sjøfartsmuseum** (Maritime Museum). Models of sailing ships, figureheads, marine instruments, and photographs of local ships make up the exhibits. Standouts include a harpoon gun from a whaler and recovered cargo from *The Pearl,* a frigate that was wrecked in 1781. ⊠ *Fjordgt. 6A* ☎ *73–89–01–00* ✉ *NKr 30* ⊙ *June–Sept., daily 10–3.*

Where to Stay & Eat

Trondheim is known for the traditional dish *surlaks* (marinated salmon served with sour cream). A sweet specialty is *tekake* (tea cake), which looks like a thick-crust pizza topped with a lattice pattern of cinnamon and sugar. The city's restaurant scene is vibrant and evolving, with more and more international restaurants serving Continental food, and bars and cafés where the city's considerable student population gathers.

★ **$$$–$$$$** ✕ **Bryggen Restaurant.** One of the city's most popular restaurants is on the bank of the Nid River. The 250-year-old warehouse exudes elegant country style, with blond woods and earthy tones. Most diners choose one of the prix-fixe menus, which are often based on traditional Norwegian ingredients such as fish and reindeer. The wine list is extensive, with many French and Italian choices. ⊠ *Øvre Bakklandet 66* ☎ *73–87–42–42* ⌘ *Reservations essential* ▤ *AE, DC, MC, V* ⊙ *Closed Sun. No lunch.*

★ **$$$–$$$$**   ✕ **Havfruen Fiskerestaurant.** "The Mermaid" is Trondheim's foremost and most stylish fish restaurant. Taking its cues from France, the restaurant excels at bouillabaisse as well as many other fish dishes, which change seasonally. The warm decor uses orange, greens, and reds accented by wood. The wine list includes a wide range of whites, highlighting dry French varieties. ✉ *Kjøpmannsgt. 7* ☎ *73–87–40–70* ▤ *AE, DC, MC, V* ⊘ *Closed Sun. No lunch.*

$$–$$$$ ✕ **Vertshuset Tavern.** Housed in what was once a 1739 tavern in downtown Trondheim, this restaurant is now part of the Trøndelag Folk Museum. The traditional menu includes homemade fish cakes; *rømmegrøt* (sour-cream porridge); *spekemat* (cured meat); and *Trøndelag klubb,* the local variation on potato dumplings. ✉ *Sverresborg Allé 7* ☎ *73–87–80–70* ▤ *AE, DC, MC, V.*

$$–$$$ ✕ **Grønn Pepper.** Tex-Mex is extremely popular throughout Norway, and this Trondheim restaurant serves a good rendition. Striped, vibrant Mexican blankets brighten up the hardwood floors and dark-wood furniture. Mexican beer and tequila go well with the fiery food on offer, which includes some Cajun and creole dishes. ✉ *Søndregt. 17 and Fjordgt. 7* ☎ *73–53–26–30* ▤ *AE, DC, MC, V.*

$$$–$$$$ ✕▥ **Britannia Hotel.** One of the Rica hotels, this classic in the heart of Trondheim opened in 1897. Luxurious rooms have regal yellow walls, gold accents, and dark-wood furniture. The elegant Palmehaven Restaurant ($$) is popular for special occasions and serves breakfast, lunch, and dinner. You can dance here in the evening. The Jonathan Restaurant is more rustic and laid-back, and the Hjørnet Bar & Brasserie is ideal for steak tartare or a quick cup of coffee. ✉ *Dronningensgt. 5, 7401* ☎ *73–800–800* ⊟ *73–800–801* ⊕ *www.britannia.no* ⇌ *247 rooms* ♻ *3 restaurants, cable TV, in-room data ports, 2 bars, pub, meeting room* ▤ *AE, DC, MC, V.*

★ **$$$–$$$$**   ✕▥ **Radisson SAS Royal Garden Hotel.** This extravaganza of glass on the Nid River is Trondheim's largest hotel. Superb service and beautiful decor make a stay here memorable. The marble-accented atrium is full of thriving plants. Sun-kissed yellow rooms are subtly accented with deep blues and reds. Prins Olav Grill ($$$) is the hotel's main restaurant. The breakfast room Bakkus Mat & Vin is also ideal for lunch or a casual dinner overlooking the river. The Galleriet Bar is a popular meeting place for drinks. Musicians perform several nights a week in the Blue Garden bar. ✉ *Kjøpmannsgt. 73, 7410* ☎ *73–80–30–00* ⊟ *73–80–30–50* ⊕ *www. radissonsas.com* ⇌ *298 rooms, 9 suites* ♻ *Restaurant, café, cable TV, in-room data ports, indoor pool, gym, sauna, bar* ▤ *AE, DC, MC, V.*

$$–$$$$ ▥ **Clarion Hotel Grand Olav.** This reasonably priced hotel is in the same building as Trondheim's large concert hall. The interior is decorated with vibrant paintings and rich, bold colors. ✉ *Kjøpmannsgt. 48, 7010* ☎ *73–80–80–80* ⊟ *73–80–80–81* ⊕ *www.choicehotels.no* ⇌ *106 rooms* ♻ *Cable TV, in-room data ports, bar, meeting rooms* ▤ *AE, DC, MC, V.*

Nightlife

Olavskvartalet is the center of much of the city's nightlife, with dance clubs, live music, bars, and cafés. The bustling **Mojo** (✉ *Nordregt. 24* ☎ *73–53–40-4–0)* is a funky tapas restaurant and bar open until 3:30

AM on weekends. **Monte Cristo** (✉ Prinsensgt. 38–40 ☎ 73–60–60–80) has a restaurant, bar, and dance club. Young people in search of cheap drinks, music, and dancing gravitate toward **Strossa** (✉ Elgesetergt. 1 ☎ 73–89–95–10). **Café Remis** (✉ Kjøpmannsgt. 12 ☎ 73–52–05–52) is one of the most popular gay clubs in Trondheim.

Downtown, in the area known as Solsiden (the Sunny Side), are several bars and clubs. **Blæst, Bar muda, and Luna Lounge** (✉ TMV-Kaia 5, Nedre Elvehavn ☎ 73–60–06–10), are especially popular summer spots, partly because of their outdoor terraces. **Choco Boco** (✉ Verfts gt. 2E ☎ 73–80–79–90) is a chocolate-obsessed café.

Sports & the Outdoors

CYCLING Some 300 **Trondheim Bysykkel City Bikes** can be borrowed in the city center. Parked in easy-to-see stands at central locations, the distinctive green bikes have shopping baskets. You'll need a 20-kroner piece to release the bike (your money's refunded when you return the bike to a parking rack).

The Trampe elevator ascends the steep Brubakken Hill near Gamle Bybro and takes cyclists nearly to Kristiansten Festning (Kristiansten Fort). Contact the tourist office to get the card you need in order to use the Trampe.

FISHING The Nid River is one of Norway's best salmon and trout rivers, famous for its large salmon (the record is 70 pounds). You can fish right in the city, but you need a license. For further information and fishing licenses, contact **TOFA (Trondheim og Omland Jakt-og Fiskeadministrasjon)** (✉ Leirfossvn. 76 ☎ 73–96–55–80 ⊕ www.tofa.org).

HIKING &   **Bymarka,** a wooded area on Trondheim's outskirts, has a varied and well-
WALKING   developed network of trails—60 km (37 mi) of gravel paths, 80 km (50 mi) of ordinary paths, 250 km (155 mi) of ski tracks. The **Ladestien** (Lade Trail) is a 14-km (9-mi) trail that goes along the edge of the Lade Peninsula and offers great views of Trondheimsfjord. The **Nidelvstien Trail** runs along the river from Tempe to the Leirfossene waterfalls.

SKIING **Bymarka** and **Estenstadmarka,** wooded areas on the periphery of Trondheim, are popular with cross-country skiers. Bymarka's Skistua (ski lodge) also has downhill runs.

Vassfjellet Skisenter (☎ 72/83–02–00 ⊕ www.vassfjellet.com), 8 km (5 mi) south of Trondheim's city limits, has six tow lifts and 10 runs. There are facilities for downhill and telemark skiing as well as snowboarding and tobogganing. In season (roughly mid-October through Easter), the center is open daily, and ski buses run every evening and weekend.

Shopping

Trondheim's **Mercur Centre** (✉ Nordregt. ⊕ www.mercursenteret.no) and **Trondheim Torg** shopping centers have helpful staffs and interesting shops.

Arne Ronning (✉ Nordregt. 10 ☎ 73–53–13–30) carries fine sweaters by Dale of Norway. Trondheim has a branch of the handicraft store **Husfliden** (✉ Olav Tryggvasongt. 18 ☎ 73–83–32–30). For knitted sweaters by such makers as Oleana and Oda, try **Jens Hoff Garn & Ide** (✉ Olav

Tryggvasongt. 20 ☎ 73–53–15–27). Founded in 1770 and Norway's oldest extant goldsmith, **Møllers Gullsmedforretning** (✉ Munkegt. 3) sells versions of the Trondheim Rose, the city symbol since the 1700s.

Arctic Circle Center

❷ *80 km (50 mi) north of Mo i Rana.*

A bleak stretch of treeless countryside marks the beginning of the Arctic Crcle. The ★ **Arctic Circle Center** (Polarsirkelsenteret) is right on the line in the Saltfjellet Mountains. Here you can build a small cairn as evidence you passed the circle. You can also get an Arctic Circle certificate to show the folks back home. ✉ *Rte. E6, Rognan* ☎ *75–12–96–96 or 75–69–02–40* ⊕ *www.polarsirkelsenteret.no* ✑ *NKr 50* ☉ *May and Sept., daily 9–6; June–Aug., daily 8 AM–10 PM.*

Tromsø

❸ *318 km (197 mi) northeast of Harstad.*

Tromsø surprised visitors in the 1800s: they thought it very sophisticated and cultured for being so close to the North Pole. It looks the way a polar town should—with ice-capped mountain ridges and jagged architecture that is an echo of the peaks. The midnight sun shines from May 21 to July 21, and it is said that the northern lights decorate the night skies over Tromsø more than over any other city in Norway. Tromsø is about the same size as Luxembourg, but home to only 58,000 people. The city's total area—2,558 square km (987 square mi)—is actually the most expansive in Norway. The downtown area is on a small, hilly island connected to the mainland by a slender bridge. The 13,000 students at the world's northernmost university are one reason the nightlife here is uncommonly lively for a northern city.

The **Ishavskatedralen** (Arctic Cathedral) is the city's signature structure. Designed by Jan Inge Hovig, it's meant to evoke the shape of a Sámi tent as well as the iciness of a glacier. Opened in 1964, it represents northern Norwegian nature, culture, and faith. The immense stained-glass window depicts the Second Coming. ✉ *Tromsdalen* ☎ *77–75–34–40* ✑ *NKr 22* ☉ *June–mid-Aug., Mon.-Sat. 9–7, Sun. 1–7; mid-Aug.–May, daily 4–6.*

☾ The **Tromsø Museum, Universitetsmuseet,** northern Norway's largest museum, is dedicated to the nature and culture of the region. Learn about the northern lights, wildlife, fossils and dinosaurs, minerals and rocks, and church art from 1300 to 1800. Outdoors you can visit a Sami *gamme* (turf hut), and a replica of a Viking longhouse. ✉ *Universitetet, Lars Thørings v. 10* ☎ *77–64–50–00* ⊕ *www.imv.uit.no* ✑ *NKr 30* ☉ *Mid-Sept.–mid-May, weekdays 9–3:30, weekends 11–5; mid-May–mid-June, daily 9–6; mid-June–mid-Aug., daily 9–8; mid-Aug.–mid-Sept., daily 9–6.*

In an 1830s former customs warehouse, the **Polarmuseet i Tromsø** (Polar Museum) documents the history of the polar region, focusing on Norway's explorers and hunters. ✉ *Søndre Tollbugt. 11B* ☎ *77–68–43–73*

⊕ *www.polarmuseum.no* ▧ *NKr 43* ⊗ *Mar.–mid-June, daily 11–5; mid-June–mid-Aug., daily 10–7; mid-Aug.–Sept., daily 11–5; Oct.–Feb., daily 11–3.*

Ludvik Mack founded **Macks Ølbryggeri** (Mack's Brewery) in 1877 and it is still family-owned. You can take a guided tour, at the end of which you're given a beer stein, pin, and a pint of your choice in the Ølhallen pub. Call ahead to reserve a place on the tour. ⊠ *Storgt. 5–13* ☎ *77–62–45–00* ⊕ *www.mack.no* ▧ *NKr 100* ⊗ *Guided tours June–Aug., Mon.–Thurs. at 1 and 3:30; Sept.–May, Mon.–Thurs. at 1.*

� The adventure center **Polaria** examines life in and around the polar and Barents regions with exhibits on polar travel and arctic research, and a panoramic film from Svalbard. The aquarium has sea mammals, including seals. ⊠ *Hjarmar Johansens gt. 12* ☎ *77–75–01–00* ⊕ *www.polaria. no* ▧ *NKr 80* ⊗ *Mid-May–mid-Aug., daily 10–7; mid-Aug.–mid-May, daily noon–5.*

★ **Tromsø Botaniske Hage** (Tromsø Botanic Garden) has plants from the antarctic and arctic as well as mountain plants from all over the world. Encompassing 4 acres, the garden has been designed as a natural landscape, with terraces, slopes, a stream, and a pond. Guides are available by advance arrangement. ⊠ *Tromsø University, Breivika* ☎ *77–64–50–78* ⊕ *www.uit.no/botanisk* ▧ *Free* ⊗ *Daily 24 hrs.*

☺ To get a sense of Tromsø's immensity and solitude, take the **Fjellheisen** (cable car) from behind the cathedral up to the mountains, just a few minutes out of the city center. **Storsteinen** (Big Rock), 1,386 feet above sea level, has a great city view. In summer a restaurant is open at the top of the lift. ⊠ *Sollivn. 12* ☎ *77–63–87–37* ▧ *NKr 80* ⊗ *Apr.–Aug., daily 10–5; Sept.–Mar., weekends 10–5.*

Where to Stay & Eat

$$ ✕**Vertshuset Skarven.** Whitewashing recalls the Greek Islands at this landmark restaurant known for its fish. Sample the fish soup, beef stew, or seal lasagna. The lunch buffet for only NKr 85 is good value. The Skarvens Biffhus and Sjømatrestauranten Arctandria restaurants are in the same building. ⊠ *Strandtorget 1* ☎ *77–60–07–20* ☖ *Reservations essential* ⊟ *AE, DC, MC, V.*

★ $$–$$$$ ⊞ **Rica Ishavshotel.** Shaped like a ship, Tromsø's snazziest hotel is right at the harbor and stretches over the sound toward Ishavskatedralen. Inside, polished wood furnishings with brass trim evoke the life of the sea. The breakfast buffet is one of the best in Norway, and even includes vitamins. Guests represent a mixture of business executives, tourists, and participants at scientific conferences. ⊠ *Fr. Langesgt. 2, Box 196, 9252* ☎ *77–66–64–00* 🖷 *77–66–64–44* ⊕ *www.rica.no* ↩ *180 rooms* ☖ *Restaurant, cable TV, in-room data ports, 2 bars, convention center, meeting rooms* ⊟ *AE, DC, MC, V.*

$$$ ⊞ **Comfort Home Hotel With.** This comfortable hotel on the waterfront has a great location. Breakfast and dinner are included in the room price. The ever-popular top-floor lounge has skylights. ⊠ *Sjøgt. 35–37, 9257* ☎ *77–66–42–00* 🖷 *77–68–96–16* ⊕ *www.with.no* ↩ *76 rooms* ☖ *Din-*

ing room, cable TV, in-room data ports, sauna, Turkish bath, lounge, meeting room ⊟ *AE, DC, MC, V* ⍩⎮ *MAP.*

$$–$$$ ⊞ **Comfort Hotel Saga.** Centrally located on a pretty town square, this hotel has basic rooms that are loaded with blond wood and warm colors. The hotel serves a free buffet-style dinner for all guests. ⊠ *Richard Withs pl. 2, 9008* ☎ *77–68–11–80* 🖷 *77–60–70–00* ⊕ *www.sagahotel. no* ⇝ *67 rooms* ♻ *Dining room, cable TV, in-room data ports* ⊟ *AE, DC, MC, V.*

$$–$$$ ⊞ **Radisson SAS Hotel Tromsø.** You can see splendid views over the Tromsø shoreline at this modern hotel. Rooms are tiny but stylish, and the service is professional and efficient. ⊠ *Sjøgt. 7, 9008* ☎ *77–60–00–00* 🖷 *77–68–54–74* ⊕ *www.radissonsas.com* ⇝ *195 rooms, 2 suites* ♻ *Restaurant, pizzeria, cable TV, in-room data ports, sauna, 2 bars* ⊟ *AE, DC, MC, V.*

Nightlife

Rock music and the city's largest selection of beer are at the **Blå Rock Café** (⊠ Strandgt. 14–16 ☎ 77–61–00–20), which has live concerts and DJs on weekends. The university's café and cultural center **DRIV** (⊠ Søndre Tollbod gt. 3 ☎ 77–60–07–76) is in a 1902 quayside building. Concerts, theater, and other cultural events are staged here. One of the city's largest cafés, **Meieriet Café & Storpub** (⊠ Grønnegt. 37/39 ☎ 77–61–36–39) has soups and wok dishes, billiards, backgammon, newspapers, and DJs on weekends. Since 1928, polar explorers, arctic skippers, hunters, whalers, and sealers have been meeting at Mack Brewery's **Ølhallen** (⊠ Storgt. 5 ☎ 77–62–45–80). At **Rica Ishavshotel** (⊠ Fr. Langesgt. 2 ☎ 77–66–64–00) you can see some of the best views in the city from the fifth-floor Skibsbroen Bar. **Victoria Fun Pub/Subsirkus/ Amtmandens Datter** (⊠ Grønnegt. 81 ☎ 77–68–49–06), a lively evening entertainment complex, has something for everyone. Subsirkus has bands and attracts a young crowd, while a broader range of ages is found at the English-style Victoria. The smoky Amtmandens Datter is a mellow Continental café.

Sports & the Outdoors

DOGSLEDDING Some 20 km (12 mi) outside the city, **Tromsø Villmarkssenter** (☎ 77–69–60–02 ⊕ www.villmarkssenter.no) organizes winter dogsledding trips, glacier walking, kayaking, summit tours, and Sami-style dinners, which take place around a campfire inside a *lavvu* (a Sami tent).

HIKING & WALKING Tromsø has more than 100 km (62 mi) of walking and hiking trails in the mountains above the city. They're reachable by funicular. Stay overnight in the middle of the Lyngen Alps, then set out for guided mountain and glacier walking with **Bo-med-oss** (☎ 77–71–06–92 ⊕ www.bo-med-oss.no). **Svensby Tursenter** (☎ 77–71–22–25) offers accommodation in small, self-serviced huts at the foot of the Lyngen Alps and arranges dogsledding, northern lights–viewing safaris, and fishing tours. **TROMSO Troms Turlag-DNT** (☎ 77–68–51–75 ⊕ www.turistforeningen.no) organizes tours and courses and has overnight cabins.

HORSEBACK RIDING **Holmeslet Gård** (☎ 77–61–9974) has horseback riding, carriage tours, northern lights–viewing adventures, and sleigh rides.

Nordkapp

④ *34 km (21 mi) north of Honningsvåg.*

On your journey to the Nordkapp (North Cape), you'll see an incredible treeless tundra, with crumbling mountains and sparse dwarf plants. The subarctic environment is very vulnerable, so don't disturb the plants. Walk only on marked trails and don't remove stones, leave car marks, or make campfires. Because the roads are closed in winter, the only access is from the tiny fishing village of Skarsvåg via Sno-Cat, a thump-and-bump ride that's as unforgettable as the desolate view.

The contrast between this near-barren territory and **Nordkapphallen** (North Cape Hall), the tourist center, is striking. Blasted into the interior of the plateau, the building is housed in a cave and includes an ecumenical chapel, a souvenir shop, and a post office. Exhibits trace the history of the cape, from Richard Chancellor, an Englishman who drifted around it and named it in 1533, to Oscar II, king of Norway and Sweden, who climbed to the top of the plateau in 1873. Celebrate your pilgrimage to the Nordkapp at Café Kompasset, Restaurant Kompasset, or at the Grotten Bar coffee shop. ⊠ *Nordkapplatået* ☎ *78–47–68–60* 🖷 *78–47–68–61* ⊕ *www.visitnorthcape.no* ✉ *NKr 190* ☉ *Call for hrs.*

Sports & the Outdoors

BIRD SAFARIS **Gjesvær Turistsenter** (☎ 78–47–57–73 ⊕ www.birdsafari.com) organizes bird safaris and deep-sea fishing. **Nordkapp Reiseliv** (☎ 78–47–70–30 ⊕ www.northcape.no) books adventures and activities including bird safaris, deep-sea fishing, boat excursions, and winter expeditions.

DIVING Scuba-dive at the top of Europe with **North Cape Adventures** (☎ 78–47–22–22 ⊕ www.northcapeadventures.com), which also provides deep-sea rafting, kayaking, ski and guided tours, and bike rentals.

RAFTING Deep-sea rafting is as exhilarating as it is beautiful. Among the tours offered is a three-hour trip to the North Cape. Call **Nordkapp Safari** (☎ 78–47–52–33).

Trondheim & the North Cape A to Z

To research prices, get advice from other travelers, and book travel arrangements, visit www.fodors.com.

AIR TRAVEL

CARRIERS SAS Braathens, Norwegian, Widerøe, and Arctic Air are the major carriers offering extensive connections throughout northern Norway. Widerøe flies to 19 destinations in the region, including Honningsvåg, the airport closest to the North Cape.

🛪 **Arctic Air** ☎ 78–98–77–01 ⊕ www.arctic.no. **Finnair** ☎ 810–01–100 in Oslo ⊕ www.finnair.com. **Norwegian** ☎ 815–21–815 ⊕ www.norwegian.no. **SAS Braathens** ☎ 815–20–400 ⊕ www.sasbraathens.no. **Widerøe** ☎ 810–01–200.

AIRPORTS

Trondheim's Værnes Airport is 32 km (21 mi) northeast of the city. With the exception of Harstad, all other cities in northern Norway are served

by airports less than 5 km (3 mi) from the center of town. Tromsø is a crossroads for air traffic between northern and southern Norway and is served by SAS Braathens and Widerøe. Honningsvåg is served by Widerøe.
📶 **Honningsvåg** ☎ 78-47-29-92. **Tromsø Airport** ☎ 77-64-84-00. **Trondheim Værnes Airport** ☎ 74-84-33-00.

BOAT & FERRY TRAVEL

Hurtigruten (the coastal express boat, which goes to 35 ports from Bergen to Kirkenes) stops at Trondheim, southbound at St. Olav's Pier, Quay 16, northbound at Pier 1, Quay 7. Other stops between Trondheim and the North Cape include Bodø, Stamsund and Svolvær (Lofotens), Sortland (Vesterålen), Harstad, Tromsø, Hammerfest, and Honningsvåg.

For travel on the *Hurtigruten* between any harbors, it is possible to buy tickets on the boats. OVDS (Ofotens og Vesterålens Dampskibsselskap), in partnership with TFDS (Troms Fylkes Dampskibsselskap), operates the Coastal Express ferries and express boats that serve many towns in the region.
📶 *Hurtigruten* ☎ 810-30-000 ⊕ www.hurtigruten.com. **OVDS** ☎ 76-96-76-00. **TFDS** ✉ Tromsø ☎ 77-64-81-00 ✉ Trondheim ☎ 73-51-51-20.

BUS TRAVEL

Bus 135 (Østerdalsekspress) runs overnight from Oslo to Trondheim via Røros. Buses also connect Bergen and Ålesund with Trondheim.

Nor-Way Bussekspress can help you put together a bus journey to destinations in the North. The Ekspress 2000 travels regularly between Oslo, Trondheim, Kautokeino, Alta, Nordkapp, and Hammerfest.

All local Trondheim buses stop at the Munkegata–Dronningens Gate intersection. Some routes end at the bus terminal at Trondheim Sentralstasjon.

North of Bodø and Narvik (a five-hour bus ride from Bodø), buses go virtually everywhere, but they don't go often. Get a comprehensive bus schedule from a tourist office or travel agent before making plans. Local bus companies include Saltens Bilruter, Ofotens Bilruter, Tromsbuss, Midttuns Busser, Finnmark Fylkesrederi og Ruteselskap, and Ekspress 2000.
📶 **Ekspress 2000** ✉ Alta ☎ 78-44-40-90. **Finnmark Fylkesrederi og Ruteselskap** ☎ 78-40-70-00 ⊕ www.ffr.no. **Lofoten (Connex)** ☎ 76-11-11-11. **Midttuns Busser** ☎ 77-67-27-87 Tromsø. **Nor-Way Bussekspress** ☎ 815-44-444. **Ofotens Bilruter** ✉ Narvik ☎ 76-92-35-00. **Saltens Bilruter** ✉ Bodø ☎ 75-55-22-10 ⊕ www.saltensbil.no. **Tromsbuss** ☎ 77-67-75-00 Tromsø ⊕ www.tromsbuss.no. **Trondheim Sentralstasjon** ☎ 73-52-14-30.

CAR RENTALS

Book a rental car as far in advance as possible. There's no better way to see the Lofoten and Vesterålen Islands than by car. Nordkapp (take the plane to Honningsvåg) is another excursion best made by car.
📶 Local Agencies **Avis Bilutleie** ☎ 77-61-58-50. **Budget Bilutleie** ☎ 73-94-10-25.

CAR TRAVEL

Trondheim is about 494 km (308 mi) from Oslo: a seven- to eight-hour drive. Speed limits are 80 kph (50 mph) or 100 kph (60 mph) much of the way. The two alternatives are the E6 through Gudbrandsdalen or Route 3 through Østerdalen. It's 723 km (448 mi) from Trondheim to Bodø on Route E6, which goes all the way to Kirkenes. There's an NKr 30 toll on E6 just east of Trondheim. The highway toll also covers the NKr 11 toll (6 AM–10 PM) for cars entering the downtown area. Anyone who makes it to the North Cape sans tour bus will be congratulated with a NKr 150 toll.

ROAD
CONDITIONS
Most roads in northern Norway are quite good, although there are always narrow and winding stretches, especially along fjords. Distances are formidable. Route 17—the **Kystriksvegen** (Coastal Highway) from Namsos to Bodø—is an excellent alternative to E6. Getting to Tromsø and the North Cape involves additional driving on narrower roads off E6. In winter, near-blizzard conditions and icy roads sometimes make it necessary to drive in a convoy. You must also drive with special studded winter tires.

EMERGENCIES
In Tromsø, Svaneapoteket pharmacy is open daily from 8:30 to 4:30 and 6 to 9. In Trondheim, Svaneapoteket pharmacy is open weekdays from 8:30 to 3 and Saturday from 9 to 3.

🔲 For medical emergencies, call 113. **St. Olavs Hospital** ⊠ Olav Kyrres gt. 17, Trondheim ☎ 73 86 80 00. **Svaneapoteket** ⊠ Kongensgt. 14B, Tromsø ☎ 73-99-03-70 ⊠ Fr. Langesgt. 9, Trondheim ☎ 73-99-03-70.

TAXIS
🔲 **Bodø Taxi** ☎ 075-500. **Nordland Taxi, Narvik** ☎ 075-500. **Tromsø** ☎ 77-60-30-00. **Trøndertaxi** ⊠ Trondheim ☎ 73-92-49-04.

TRAIN TRAVEL
The Dovrebanen has frequent departures daily on the Oslo–Trondheim route. Trains leave from Oslo S Station for the 7- to 8-hour journey. Trondheim is the gateway to the north, and two trains run daily in each direction on the 11-hour Trondheim–Bodø route. The Nordlandsbanen has three departures daily in each direction on the Bodø–Trondheim route, an 11-hour journey. The *Ofotbanen* has two departures daily in each direction on the Stockholm–Narvik route, a 21-hour journey.

VISITOR INFORMATION
Bodø-based Nordland Reiseliv publishes a helpful holiday guide and a guide to interesting tours of the region. Their "Footprints in the North" pamphlet is a cultural history of northern Norway and Namdalen, listing 103 sites. Finnmark Reiseliv publishes a detailed annual guide to Finnmark.

🔲 **Bodø (Destinasjon Bodø)** ⊠ Sjøgt. 3, 8001 ☎ 75-54-80-00 ⊕ www.visitbodo.com. **Finnmark Reiseliv** ☎ 78-44-00-20 ⊕ www.visitnorthcape.com. **Hamarøy (Kingdom of Hamsun)** ☎ 75-77-18-90 ⊕ www.hamsuns-rike.no. **Narvik (Narvik Aktiv)** ☎ 76-96-56-00 ⊕ www.narvikinfo.no. **Nordkapp** ⊠ Fiskerivn. 4, Honningsvåg ☎ 78-47-70-30 ⊕ www.northcape.no. **Nordland Reiseliv** ☎ 75-54-52-00 ⊕ www. visitnordland.no. **Tromsø** ⊠ Storgt. 61-63, 9253 ☎ 77-61-00-00 ⊕ www. destinasjontromso.no. **Trondheim** ⊠ Munkegt. 19, Torget, 7001 ☎ 73-80-76-60 ⊕ www.visit-trondheim.com. **Vesterålen** ⊠ Kjøpmannsgt. 2, 8401 Sortland ☎ 76-11-14-80 ⊕ www.visitvesteralen.com.

NORWAY A TO Z

To research prices, get advice from other travelers, and book travel arrangements, visit www.fodors.com.

AIR TRAVEL

CARRIERS From North America to Oslo Gardermoen, Air Canada has flights via London and Frankfurt; American Airlines has flights via London and Brussels; Continental has direct flights; Finnair has flights with connections through Helsinki; Iceland Air has flights with connections through Reykjavík, Amsterdam, Copenhagen, and Stockholm; Lufthansa has flights with connections through Frankfurt and Munich; and Scandinavian Airlines System (SAS), partnering with United, has flights via Copenhagen and Stockholm.

From the United Kingdom, British Airways and British Midland have direct flights to Oslo; Norwegian flies to Oslo, Bergen, and Trondheim; Ryan Air has direct flights to Oslo Torp Sandefjord and Haugesund; and SAS has direct flights to Oslo, Bergen, and Stavanger.

Within Norway, Braathens, Norwegian, and SAS connect many of the cities by regular flights, and Widerøe connects smaller towns and cities that are usually along the coast.

◪ To & From Norway **Air Canada** ☎ 888/247-2262 in Canada and the U.S. ⊕ www.aircanada.ca. **American** ☎ 800/433-7300 ⊕ www.aa.com. **British Airways** ☎ 0870/850-9850 ⊕ www.british-airways.com. **British Midland** ☎ 0870/607-0222. **Continental** ☎ 800/523-3273 ⊕ www.continental.com. **Finnair** ☎ 800/950-5000 ⊕ www.finnair.com. **Iceland Air** ☎ 800/223-5500 ⊕ www.icelandair.com. **Lufthansa** ☎ 800/645-3880, 86-90-98-00, Ext. 2 in Sweden ⊕ www.lufthansa.com ☎ 800/399-5838, 23-35-54-00 in Norway. **Ryan Air** ☎ 0871/246-0000 in the U.K. ⊕ www.ryanair.com. **SAS** ☎ 800/221-2350 ⊕ www.scandinavian.net. **United** ☎ 800/241-6522 ⊕ www.united.com.
◪ Within Norway **Braathens** ☎ 91-50-54-00 in Norway ⊕ www.sasbraathens.no. **Norwegian** ☎ 815-21-815 in Norway ⊕ www.norwegian.no. **SAS** ☎ 800/221-2350 in the U.S. ⊕ www.scandinavian.net. **Widerøe** ☎ 810-01-200 in Norway ⊕ www.wideroe.com.

CUTTING COSTS The SAS Visit Scandinavia/Europe Air Pass offers up to eight flight coupons for one-way travel between Scandinavian cities (and participating European countries). Most one-way tickets for domestic travel within each Scandinavian country cost $69; one-way fares between the Scandinavian countries usually cost $80, unless you are venturing into the far north, Lapland, Iceland, or Greenland (these flights range from $122 to $200); and fares to other European destinations range from $65 to $165. These passes can be bought only in conjunction with a round-trip ticket between North America and Europe on SAS and must be used within three months of arrival. SAS also provides family fares—a spouse and children ages 2 to 17 can each get 50% off the full fare of business-class tickets with the purchase of one full-fare business-class ticket. Contact SAS for information.

Widerøe Airline offers two types of bargain fare plans. The Fly Norway plan, available year-round, offers standard-rate tickets at either NKr 58 or NKr 82 and, for extra-short flights, NKr 47 or NKr 69. The Explore Norway by Plane plan, available between late June and mid-August, divides Norway into three parts with boundaries at Trondheim and Tromsø, and you can fly as much as you like within a 14-day period. This costs €480 for the whole country, €329 for one zone, and €414 for two zones. An extra week costs €220.

FLYING TIMES A flight from New York to Oslo takes about 8 hours. From London, a nonstop flight gets to Oslo in 1¾ hours; it's about 1½ hours to Stavanger. From Sydney and major cities in New Zealand, the flight to Oslo will be over 20 hours, and will require at least one transfer.

AIRPORTS

Gardermoen Airport, about 53 km (33 mi) northeast of Oslo, is the major entry point for most visitors to Norway. Other international airports are in Bergen, Kristiansand, Sandefjord, Stavanger, and Trondheim.

🛈 Airport Information **Gardermoen Airport** ☎ 815-50-250 or 64-81-20-00 ⊕ www.osl.no/english. **Oslo Torp** ✉ Sandefjord ☎ 33-42-70-02 ⊕ www.torp.no.

BOAT & FERRY TRAVEL

Taking a ferry isn't only fun, it's often necessary in Norway, as they remain an important means of transportation along the west coast. More specialized boat service includes hydrofoil (catamaran) trips between Stavanger, Haugesund, and Bergen. There are also fjord cruises out of these cities and others in the north. Møre og Romsdals Fylkesbåter (MRF) and Hardanger Sunnhordalandske Dampskipselskap (HSD) are two of the most important ferry companies, and Route Information Norway is a company that has comprehensive links to all forms of transport within Norway.

The famous Norwegian Coastal Voyage *Hurtigruten* sailings are covered in more detail under the Cruise Travel heading.

From the United Kingdom, DFDS Seaways has services departing from Newcastle at 3 PM and arriving in Kristiansand, southern Norway, at 9:15 AM. Fjord Line sails from Newcastle to Stavanger, Haugesund, and Bergen, with crossings taking about 22 hours. Smyril Line operates between Bergen, Tórshavn (Faroe Islands), and Lerwick (Shetland) on Monday from mid-May to mid-September.

🛈 Boat & Ferry Information **DFDS Seaways** ✉ DFDS Seaways Travel Centre, Scandinavia House, Parkeston, Harwich, Essex CO12 4QG ☎ 8705/333-111 ⊕ www.dfdsseaways.co.uk. **Fjord Line** ✉ Norway House, Royal Quays, near Newcastle, NE29 6EG North Shields ☎ 0870/143-9669 ⊕ www.fjordline.co.uk. **Hardanger Sunnhordalandske Dampskipselskap (HSD)** ✉ Sundtsgt. 36, 5817 Bergen ☎ 55-23-87-00 ⊕ www.hsd.no. **Møre og Romsdals Fylkesbåter (MRF)** ✉ Gotfred Lies Plas 2, Molde ☎ 71-21-95-00 ⊕ www.mrf.no. **Route Information Norway** ⊕ www.ruteinfo.no. **Smyril Line** ✉]. Broncks gøta 37, FO-110 Torshavn ☎ 298/34-59-00 ⊕ www.smyril-line.com.

BUS TRAVEL

Bus tours can be effective for smaller regions within Norway, but the train system is excellent and offers much greater coverage in less time. Buses do, however, tend to be less expensive.

Every end station of the railroad is supported by a number of bus routes, some of which are operated by the Norwegian State Railway (NSB), others by local companies. Long-distance buses usually take longer than the railroad, and fares are only slightly lower. Virtually every settlement on the mainland is served by bus, and for anyone with a desire to get off the beaten track, a pay-as-you-go, open-ended bus trip is the best way to see Norway.

Most long-distance buses leave from Bussterminalen close to Oslo Central Station. Nor-Way Bussekspress, a chain of 50 Norwegian bus companies serving 500 destinations, can arrange any journey. They offer a bus pass that provides 10 consecutive days of unlimited travel on all domestic lines for NKr 1,300, and another that provides 21 consecutive days for NKr 2,400.

CUTTING COSTS 🚍 Bus Information **Ruteinformasjonen** ☎ 177; for timetables and fares for the area you are situated in [except Finnmark and Svalbard]. **Bussterminalen** ✉ Galleriet Oslo, Schweigaardsgt. 10 ☎ 23-00-24-00 bus information. **Nor-Way Bussekspress** ✉ Bussterminalen ☎ 820-21-300 ⊕ www.nbe.no. **Norwegian State Railway (NSB)** ☎ 815-00-888 ⊕ www.nsb.no.

CAR TRAVEL

You can drive in Norway with your valid U.S., Canadian, U.K., Australian, or New Zealand driver's license. Excellent, well-marked roads make driving a great way to explore Norway, but it can be an expensive choice. Ferry costs can be steep, and reservations are vital. Tolls on some major roads add to the expense, as do the high fees for city parking. Tickets for illegal parking are painfully costly.

If you're planning to drive around Norway, call or check the Web site of Vegmeldingsentralen, an information center for the Statens Vegvesen (Public Roads Administration). The center monitors and provides information about roads and road conditions, distances, and ferry timetables. Phones are open 24 hours a day.

The southern part of Norway is fairly compact—all major cities are about a day's drive from each other. The distances are felt on the way north, where Norway becomes narrower as it inches up to and beyond the Arctic Circle and hooks over Sweden and Finland to touch Russia. It's virtually impossible to visit the entire country from one base.

In a few remote areas, especially in northern Norway, road conditions can be unpredictable, so plan carefully for safety's sake. Should your road trip take you over the mountains in autumn, winter, or spring, make sure that the mountain pass you're heading to is actually open. Some high mountain roads are closed as early as October due to snow, and do not open again until June. When driving in remote areas, especially in winter, let someone know your travel plans, **use a four-wheel-drive vehicle,** and **travel with at least one other car.**

There are toll charges to enter Oslo, Bergen, Trondheim, Stavanger, and Kristiansand. Costs range from NKr 10 to NKr 20, and full details of all tolls for roads and tunnels can be found at the Vegmeldingsentralen Web site listed below.

🚍 **Vegmeldingsentralen (Road Information Center)** ☎ 175 in Norway, 815-48-991 from abroad ⊕ www.vegvesen.no.

EMERGENCY SERVICES
Norsk Automobil-Forbund (NAF) offers roadside assistance. They patrol major roads and mountain passes from mid-June to mid-August. Another roadside assistance agency is Falken.

🚗 **Falken** ✉ Maridalsv. 300, 0872 Oslo ☏ 02468, 02222 for 24-hr service ⊕ www.falken. no. **Norsk Automobil-Forbund (NAF)** (Norwegian Automobile Association) ✉ Storgt. 2, Box 494, Sentrum, 0155 Oslo ☏ 22–34–14–00, 810–00–505 for 24-hr service ⊕ www. naf.no.

GASOLINE
Gas stations are plentiful, and *blyfri bensin* (unleaded gasoline) and diesel fuel are sold everywhere from self-service pumps. Those marked *kort* are 24-hour pumps, which take oil-company credit cards or bank cards, either of which is inserted directly into the pump. Gas costs approximately NKr 11.08 per liter (that's around US$4.50 per gallon). Don't wait until your tank is empty before looking for a gas station; hours vary greatly, especially outside the major cities.

INSURANCE
All vehicles registered abroad are required to carry international liability insurance and an international accident report form, which can be obtained from automobile clubs. Collision insurance is recommended.

ROAD CONDITIONS
Four-lane highways are the exception and are found only around major cities. Outside main routes, roads tend to be narrow and twisting, with only token guardrails. In summer, roads are always crowded. Along the west coast, waits for ferries and passage through tunnels can be significant. Don't expect to cover more than 240 km (150 mi) in a day, especially in fjord country.

Norwegian roads are well marked with directional, distance, and informational signs. Some roads, particularly those over mountains, can close for all or part of the winter. If you drive anywhere but on major roads in winter, make sure the car is equipped with proper snow tires. Roads are generally not salted but are left with a hard-packed layer of snow on top of the asphalt. If you're renting, choose a small car with front-wheel drive. Bring an ice scraper, snow brush, small shovel, and heavy clothes for emergencies. In remote areas, or when roads are icy or steep, consider bringing along a set of tire chains. Although the weather along the coast is sunny, a few hours inland temperatures may be about -9°C (15°F) colder, and snowfall is the rule rather than the exception.

RULES OF THE ROAD
Driving is on the right. Yield to vehicles approaching from the right. Make sure you have an up-to-date map before you venture out, because some highway numbers have changed in the past few years, particularly routes beginning with "E."

The maximum speed limit is 90 kph (55 mph) on major highways. On other highways the limit is 80 kph (50 mph) or 70 kph (43 mph). The speed limit in cities and towns is 50 kph (30 mph), and 30 kph (18 mph) in residential areas.

Keep your headlights on at all times; this is required by law. By Norwegian law, everyone, including infants, must **wear seat belts.** Children under four years of age must ride in a car seat, and children over four years must ride in the back. All cars must carry red reflective warning triangles, to be placed a safe distance from a disabled vehicle.

Norway has strict drinking-and-driving laws, and there are routine roadside checks. The legal limit is a blood-alcohol level of 0.02%, which effectively means that you should not drink any amount of alcohol before driving. If you are stopped, you may be required to take a breath test. If it is positive, you must submit to a blood test. No exceptions are made for foreigners, who can lose their licenses on the spot. Other penalties include fines and imprisonment. An accident involving a driver with an illegal blood-alcohol level usually voids all insurance agreements, so the driver becomes responsible for his own medical bills and damage to the cars.

Speeding is also punished severely. Most roads are monitored by radar and cameras in gray metal boxes. Signs warning of *Automatisk Trafikkontroll* (Automatic Traffic Monitoring) are posted periodically along many roads.

CRUISE TRAVEL

Norway's most renowned boat is *Hurtigruten,* which literally means "Rapid Route." Also known as the Coastal Steamer, the boat departs from Bergen and stops at 36 ports along the coast in six days, ending with Kirkenes, near the Russian border, before turning back. Tickets, which can be purchased for the entire journey or for individual legs, are available through Norwegian Coastal Voyage and Hurtigruten Coastal Express Bookings. Special discounts are available for AARP members. Alternatively, you can contact one of the companies that run the service: FFR in Hammerfest, OVDS in Narvik, Hurtigruten in Bergen, and TFDS in Tromsø.

🖪 Cruise Lines **Bentours–For Australia and NZ** ⊠ Level 7, 189 Kent St., Sydney, NSW 2000 Australia ☎ 612/9247–3381 ⊕ www.bentours.com.au. **FFR** ⊠ Box 308, 9615 Hammerfest ☎ 78–40–70–51 ⊕ www.ffr.no. *Hurtigruten* ⊠ Coastal Express, Veiten 2B, 5012 Bergen ☎ 810–30–300. **Hurtigruten Coastal Express Bookings** ☎ 810–30–000, 78–54–17–41 timetables ⊕ www.hurtigruten.no. **Norwegian Coastal Voyage Inc.** ⊠ 405 Park Ave., New York, NY 10022 ☎ 212/319–1300 ⊕ www.norwegiancoastalvoyage.us. **Norwegian Coastal Voyage Ltd.** ⊠ 3 Shortlands., London, U.K. W68NE ☎ 020/8846–2600 ⊕ www.norwegiancoastalvoyage.com. **OVDS** ⊠ Box 43, 8501 Narvik ☎ 76–96–76–76 ⊕ www.ovds.no. **TFDS** ⊠ 9291 Tromsø ☎ 77–64–82–00 ⊕ www.tfds.no.

DISABILITIES & ACCESSIBILITY

Facilities for travelers with disabilities are generally good, and most major tourist offices offer booklets and brochures on travel and accommodations. The Norwegian Association of the Disabled (NHF) gives advice on public transportation, sights and museums, hotels, and special-interest tours. You should get public transportation passes and make hotel reservations in advance of your visit to ensure a smooth trip.

🖪 Local Resources **Norwegian Association of the Disabled (NHF)** ⊠ Schweigaardsgt. 12, Box 9217 Gronland, N-0134 Oslo ☎ 24–10–24–00 🖶 24–10–24–99 ⊕ www.nhf.no.

LODGING Best Western has properties with wheelchair-accessible rooms in Oslo. If wheelchair-accessible rooms on other floors are not available, ground-floor rooms are provided.

🖪 Wheelchair-Accessible Chain **Best Western** ☎ 800/528–1234.

EMERGENCIES

Ambulance, fire, and police assistance is available 24 hours.

☎ **Ambulance** ☎ 113. **Fire** ☎ 110. **Police** ☎ 112.

LANGUAGE

Despite the fact that Norwegian is in the Germanic family of languages, it is a myth that someone who speaks German can understand it. Fortunately, English is widely spoken. German is the most common third language. English becomes rarer outside major cities, and it's a good idea to **take along a dictionary or phrase book.** Even here, however, anyone under the age of 50 is likely to have studied English in school. Fluent Swedish speakers can generally understand Norwegian.

Norwegian has three additional vowels: æ, ø, and å. Æ is pronounced as a short "a." The ø, sometimes printed as *oe,* is the same as ö in German and Swedish, pronounced very much like a short "u." The å is a contraction of the archaic "aa" and sounds like long "o." These three letters appear at the end of alphabetical listings, such as those in the phone book.

There are two officially sanctioned Norwegian languages, Bokmål and Nynorsk. Bokmål is used by 84% of the population and is the main written form of Norwegian and the language of books, as the first half of its name indicates. Nynorsk, which translates as "new Norwegian," is actually a compilation of older dialect forms from rural Norway. Every Norwegian also receives at least seven years of English instruction, starting in the second grade. The Sami (or Lapps), who inhabit the northernmost parts of Norway, have their own language, which is distantly related to Finnish.

MONEY MATTERS

Prices throughout this guide are given for adults. Substantially reduced fees are almost always available for children, students, and senior citizens. For information on taxes, *see* Taxes.

Costs are high in Norway. Here are some sample prices: cup of coffee, from NKr 14 in a cafeteria to NKr 25 or more in a restaurant; a 20-pack of cigarettes, NKr 60; a half liter of beer, NKr 40–NKr 50; the smallest hot dog (with bun plus *lompe*—a flat Norwegian potato bread—mustard, ketchup, and fried onions) at a convenience store, NKr 20; cheapest bottle of wine from a government store, NKr 60; the same bottle at a restaurant, NKr 120–NKr 200; urban transit fare in Oslo, NKr 20; soft drink, from NKr 20 in a cafeteria to NKr 35 in a better restaurant; sandwich at a cafeteria, NKr 40–NKr 50; 1½-km (1-mi) taxi ride, NKr 40–NKr 60 depending on time of day.

Be aware that sales taxes can be very high, but foreigners can get some refunds by shopping at tax-free stores (⇨ Taxes). City Cards can save you transportation and entrance fees in larger cities.

Liquor and strong beer (over 3% alcohol) can be purchased only in state-owned shops, at very high prices, during weekday business hours, usually 9:30 to 6 and in some areas on Saturday until mid-afternoon. (When you visit friends or relatives in Norway, a bottle of liquor or fine wine bought duty-free on the trip over is often much appreciated.) Weaker beers and ciders are usually available in grocery stores, except in certain rural areas, especially along the coast of western Norway.

CURRENCY Norway is a non-EU country, and has opted to keep its currency while its neighbors convert to the euro. The Norwegian *krone* (plural: *kroner*) translates as "crown," written officially as NOK. Price tags are seldom marked this way, but instead read "Kr" followed by the amount, such as Kr 10. (In this book, the Norwegian krone is abbreviated NKr.) One krone is divided into 100 *øre,* and coins of 50 øre and 1, 5, 10, and 20 kroner are in circulation. Bills are issued in denominations of 50, 100, 200, 500, and 1,000 kroner.

CURRENCY EXCHANGE At this writing, the rate of exchange was NKr 6 to the U.S. dollar, NKr 8 to the euro, NKr 5 to the Canadian dollar, NKr 11 to the pound sterling, NKr 5 to the Australian dollar, NKr 4 to the New Zealand dollar, and NKr 1 to the South African rand. Exchange rates fluctuate, so be sure to check them when planning a trip.

SPORTS & OUTDOORS

BIKING Norway has many cycling paths, some of them old roads that are in the mountains and along the western fjords. The Rallarvegen, from Haugastøl in the Hardangervidda National Park to Flåm, is very popular among cyclists. The southern counties of Vestfold and Rogaland have a well-developed network of cycling paths. Most routes outside large cities are hilly and can be physically demanding. **Wear a protective helmet and use lights at night.**

Many counties have produced brochures that have touring suggestions and maps. Syklistenes Landsforening has maps and general information, as well as the latest weather conditions. Several companies, including Lillehammer's Trollcycling, organize cycling tours. Den Norske Turistforening provides inexpensive lodging for cyclists planning overnight trips.

If you want to travel with your bike on an NSB long-distance train, you must make a reservation and pay an additional NKr 90. On local or InterCity trains, bikes are transported if space is available.
🏁 Resources **Syklistenes Landsforening** ✉ Storgt. 23C, 0028 Oslo ☎ 22-47-30-30 🖨 22-47-30-31 ⊕ www.slf.no.
🏁 Cycling Tour Companies **Cycle Tourism** ✉ Fylkeshuset, 3706 Skien ☎ 35-52-99-55 ⊕ www.bike-norway.com. **erik & reidar** ✉ Kirkegt. 34A, 0153 Oslo ☎ 22-41-23-80 🖨 22-41-23-90. **PedalNor** ✉ Kløvervn. 10, 4326 Sandnes ☎ 51-66-40-60 or 51-66-48-70. **Trollcycling** ✉ Box 373, 2601 Lillehammer ☎ 61-28-99-70 🖨 61-26-92-50.

CANOEING & RAFTING There are plenty of lakes and streams for canoeing and kayaking in Norway. Popular spots include Aust-Agder, in the Sørlandet; Telemark; and suburban Oslo. Norges Padlerforbund (Norwegian Canoe Association) maintains a list of rental companies and regional canoeing centers.

Rafting excursions are offered throughout Norway. For more information, contact Norwegian Wildlife and Rafting, which operates guided two-day expeditions with accommodation and transport provided. The minimum age for white-water rafting is 18 (15 with parental guidance).

🔁 Resources **Norges Padlerforbund** ⊠ Service Boks 1, Ullevål Stadion, 0840 Oslo ☎ 21-02-98-35 ⊕ www.padling.no. **Norwegian Wildlife and Rafting** ⊠ 2680 Våg ☎ 61-23-87-27 ⊕ www.nwr.no.

FISHING   Norway's fjords, lakes, and rivers make it a fisherman's paradise. Check with fly shops or the local tourist office to see what licenses you may need.

Using live fish as bait is prohibited, and imported tackle must be disinfected before use. Infectious parasites that are harmless to humans have decimated salmon populations in certain rivers in Norway. To avoid spreading parasites, make sure you dry and clean your gear before moving to another river.

GLACIER   Glacier walking is an exhilarating way to experience the mountains of
WALKING   Norway. This sport requires the right equipment and training: only try it when accompanied by an experienced local guide. Since glaciers are always moving over new land, the ice and snow may just be a thin covering for a deep crevice. Glacier centers or local tourist offices can recommend guides and tours.

🔁 Resources **Breheimsenteret** ⊠ Jostedalen National Park Visitor's Center, Rte. 604, 6871 Breheimsenteret ☎ 57-68-32-50 ⊕ www.jostedal.com. **Jostedalsbreen Nasjonalparksenter** ⊠ Rte. 15, 6799 Oppstryn ☎ 57-87-72-00 ⊕ www.jostedalsbre.no. **Norsk Bremuseum** (Norwegian Glacier Museum) ⊠ Rte. 5, 6848 Fjærland ☎ 57-69-32-88 ⊕ www.bre.museum.no.

HIKING &   Naturally, hiking and mountaineering are popular pastimes in a land
MOUNTAINEERING of mountain ranges and high plains. Well-known hiking areas include the Jotunheim Mountain Range; the Rondane and Dovrefjell mountains; the Hardangervidda (Hardanger plateau); the Trollheimen District; and Finnmarksvidda. On multiday hikes you can stay in hostels, camp out in your own tent, or head to one the DNT's cabins. Throughout the country, DNT organizes guided hiking tours as well as mountaineering courses year-round.

🔁 Resources **Den Norske Turistforening** (DNT; The Norwegian Mountain Touring Association) ⊠ Box 7, Sentrum, 0101 Oslo 1 ☎ 22-82-28-22 🖷 22-82-28-23.

SNOW SPORTS The Skiforeningen provides national snow-condition reports; tips on trails; and information on courses for cross-country and downhill skiing, telemarking, and snowboarding. If you can't make it to Norway in winter, Stryn Sommerskisenter, in the west, has a summer ski season that runs June–September.

🔁 Resources **Skiforeningen** ⊠ Kongevn. 5, 0390 Oslo 3 ☎ 22-92-32-00 ⊕ www.skiforeningen.no. **Stryn Sommerskisenter** ⊠ 6782 Stryn ☎ 57-87-40-40.

TAXES

VALUE-ADDED   Value-added tax, V.A.T. for short but called *moms* all over Scandinavia,
TAX   is a hefty 25% on all purchases except books; it is included in the prices of goods. All purchases of consumer goods totaling more than NKr 308 for export by nonresidents are eligible for V.A.T. refunds. Carry your passport when shopping to prove you are a nonresident.

Global Refund is a Europe-wide V.A.T. refund processing service with 210,000 affiliated stores (some 3,000 shops subscribe to the service in Norway, where it is called "Norway Tax-Free Shopping"). In participating stores, **ask for the Global Refund form** (called a Shopping Cheque). Have it stamped like any customs form by customs officials when you leave the country (be ready to show customs officials what you've bought). Then take the form to one of the more than 700 Global Refund counters—conveniently located at every major airport and border crossing—and 11%–18% of the tax will be refunded on the spot in the form of cash, check, or a refund to your credit-card account (minus a small percentage for processing).

Shops that do not subscribe to this program have slightly more detailed forms, which must be presented to the Norwegian Customs Office along with the goods to obtain a refund by mail. This refund is closer to the actual amount of the tax.

One way to beat high prices is to **take advantage of tax-free shopping.** You can make major purchases free of tax if you have a foreign passport. Ask about tax-free shopping when you make a purchase for $50 (about NKr 320) or more. When your purchases exceed a specified limit (which varies from country to country), you receive a special export receipt. Keep the parcels intact and take them out of the country within 30 days of purchase.

Directorate of Customs and Excise ☒ Schweigaards gt. 15, Box 8122, 0032 Oslo ☎ 22-86-03-00 ⊕ www.toll.no. **Global Refund Canada** ⌂ Box 2020, Station Main, Brampton, Ontario L6T 3S3 ☎ 800/993-4313 🖷 905/791-9078 ⊕ www.globalrefund. com. **Global Refund Norge** ☎ 67/15-60-10.

TAXIS

Even the smallest villages have some form of taxi service. Towns on the railroad normally have taxi stands just outside the station. All city taxis are connected with a central dispatching office, so there is only one main telephone number for calling a cab. Look in the telephone book under "Taxi" or "Drosje."

Never use an unmarked, or pirate, taxi, since their drivers are unlicensed and in some cases may be dangerous.

TELEPHONES

The telephone system in Norway is modern and efficient; international direct service is available throughout the country. Phone numbers consist of eight digits.

AREA & COUNTRY CODES The country code for Norway is 47. There are no area codes—you must dial all eight digits of any phone number wherever you are. Telephone numbers that start with a 9 or 4 are usually mobile phones, and are considerably more expensive to call. Telephone numbers starting with the prefix 82 cost extra. Toll-free numbers begin with 800 or 810. Numbers beginning with 815 cost NKr 1 per call. In this book, area codes precede telephone numbers.

DIRECTORY & Dial 1881 for information in Norway, 1882 for international telephone
OPERATOR numbers. To place a collect or an operator-assisted call to a number in
ASSISTANCE Norway, dial 115. Dial 117 for collect or operator-assisted calls out-
side of Norway.

INTERNATIONAL If you are able to dial directly, dial the international access code, 00,
CALLS then the country code and the number. All telephone books list coun-
try code numbers, including those for the United States and Canada (1),
Great Britain (44), Australia (61), and New Zealand (64). All interna-
tional operators speak English.
⚅ Access Codes AT&T Direct ☎ 800/CALL-ATT. **MCI WorldPhone** ☎ 800/19912.
Sprint International Access ☎ 800/19877.

MOBILE PHONES Scandinavia has been one of the world leaders in mobile phone development; almost 90% of the population owns a mobile phone. Although
standard North American cellular phones will not work in Norway, some
companies rent cellular phones to visitors. Contact the Norwegian
Tourist Board for details.

PHONE CARDS You can purchase Tellerskritt (phone cards) at Narvesen and Norsk Tipping shops and kiosks. Cards cost NKr 40 to NKr 140 and can be used
in the 8,000 green-card telephones. About half of these public phones
also take major credit cards.

PUBLIC PHONES Public telephones are of two types. Push-button phones—which accept
NKr 1, 5, and 10 coins (some also accept NKr 20 coins)—are easy to
use: lift the receiver, listen for the dial tone, insert the coins, dial the number, and wait for a connection. The digital screen at the top of the box
indicates the amount of money in your "account." Green-card telephones
only accept phone cards or credit cards.

Local calls cost NKr 3 or NKr 5 from a pay phone. If you hear a short
tone, it means that your purchased time is almost up.

TIME
Norway is one hour ahead of Greenwich Mean Time (GMT) and six
hours ahead of Eastern Standard Time (EST).

TIPPING
Tipping is kept to a minimum in Norway because service charges are
added to most bills. It is, however, handy to have a supply of NKr 5 or
NKr 10 coins for less formal service. Tip only in local currency.

Room service usually includes a service charge in the bill, so tipping is
discretionary. Round up a taxi fare to the next round digit, or tip anywhere from NKr 5 to NKr 10, a little more if the driver has been helpful. All restaurants include a service charge, ranging from 12% to 15%,
in the bill. It is customary to add up to 10% for exceptional service, but
it is not obligatory. Maître d's are not tipped, and coat checks have flat
rates, usually NKr 10 per person.

TRAIN TRAVEL
NSB, the Norwegian State Railway System, has five main lines originating from the Oslo S Station. Its 4,000 km (2,500 mi) of track con-

nect all main cities. Train tickets can be purchased in railway stations or from travel agencies. NSB has its own travel agency in Oslo.

Norway's longest rail route runs north to Trondheim, then extends onward as far as Fauske and Bodø. The southern line hugs the coast to Stavanger, while the stunning western line crosses Hardangervidda, the scenic plateau that lies between Oslo and Bergen. An eastern line to Stockholm links Norway with Sweden, while another southern line through Göteborg, Sweden, is the main connection with Continental Europe. Narvik, north of Bodø, is the last stop on Sweden's Ofot line, the world's northernmost rail system, which runs from Stockholm via Kiruna.

If you are traveling from south to north in Norway, flying is often a necessity: Stavanger is as close to Rome as it is to the northern tip of Norway.

NSB trains are clean, comfortable, and punctual. Most have special compartments for travelers with disabilities and for families with children younger than age two. First- and second-class tickets are available.

Seat reservations are required on some European trains, particularly high-speed trains, and are a good idea on trains that may be crowded. In summer reserve your seats at least five days ahead; during major holidays, reserve several weeks or a month ahead for Friday and Sunday travel. You will also need a reservation if you purchase sleeping accommodations.

Many travelers assume that rail passes guarantee them seats on the trains they wish to ride. Not so. You need to book seats ahead even if you are using a rail pass.

FROM BRITAIN Traveling from Britain to Norway by train is not difficult and takes 20 to 24 hours. The best connection leaves London's Victoria Station and connects at Dover with a boat to Oostende, Belgium. From Oostende there are overnight connections to Copenhagen, where there are express and overnight connections to Oslo. Call Rail Europe for further information.

⊞ **NSB** ⊠ Skolen Tomtekaia 21, 0048 Oslo ☎ 81–50–08–88. **ScanAm World Tours** ⊠ N. Main St. 108, Cranberry, NJ 08512 ☎ 800/545-2204. **Victoria Station** ⊠ Terminus Pl., London ☎ 0845/748-4950 in the U.K.

CUTTING COSTS A number of special discount passes are available, including the Inter-Rail Pass, which is available for European residents of all ages, and the EurailPass, sold in the United States only. Norway participates in the following rail programs: EurailPass (and its FlexiPass variations), Scan-Rail Pass, ScanRail 'n Drive, InterRail, and Nordturist Card. A Norway Rail Pass is available for three, four, and five days of unlimited rail travel for nonresidents within Norway. The ticket is sold in the United States through ScanAm. First-class rail passes are about 30% higher.

Low-season prices are offered from October through April. Discounted fares also include family, student, senior-citizen (including their not-yet-senior spouses), and off-peak "mini" fares, which must be purchased a day in advance. NSB gives student discounts only to foreigners studying at Norwegian institutions.

Whichever pass you choose, remember that you must **purchase your pass before you leave** for Europe.

🚊Rail Passes **Rail Europe** ☎877/257-2887 in the U.S., 800/361-RAIL in Canada ⊕www.raileurope.com ☎ 0870/837-1371 in the U.K. ⊕ www.raileurope.co.uk.

VISITOR INFORMATION

🚊 Tourist Information **Norwegian Tourist Board** ⊠ Charles House, 5 Lower Regent St., London SW1Y 4LR, U.K. ☎ 44/207-839-6255 🖷 44/207-839-6014 ⊠ Stortorvet 10, 0105 Oslo, Norway ☎ 47/2414-4600 🖷 47/2414-4601 ⊕ www.visitnorway.com ⊕ www.norway.com. **Oslo Visitors and Convention Bureau** ⊕ www.oslopro.no. **Royal Norwegian Embassy in the United States** ⊕www.norway.org. **Scandinavian Tourist Board** ⊠ 655 3rd Ave., New York, NY 10017 ☎ 212/885-9700 🖷 212/855-9710 ⊕ www.goscandinavia.com. **U.S. Department of State** ⊠ Overseas Citizens Services Office, Room 4811 N.S., 2201 C St. NW, Washington, DC 20520 ☎ 202/647-5225 ⊕ travel.state.gov/travel/html.

Sweden

WORD OF MOUTH

"Stockholm is truly one of the world's most beautiful capital cities. It's here that we fully appreciated the midnight sun. I took pictures from our hotel room at 11:30 PM that look like they were taken at three in the afternoon."

—kflodin

"My favorite place in all of Sweden is the walled village of Visby on Gotland Island. It has everything: cobblestone lanes, medieval architecture, the walls, great cafés, shops, restaurants, a fun harbor scene, and the views of the sea. Biking around the island is great fun."

—joegri

Updated by
Rob Hinks

SWEDEN REQUIRES THE VISITOR to travel far, in both distance and attitude. Approximately the size of California, Sweden reaches as far north as the arctic fringes of Europe, where glacier-top mountains and thousands of acres of pine, spruce, and birch forests are broken here and there by wild rivers, pristine lakes, and desolate moorland. In the more populous south, roads meander through miles of softly undulating countryside, skirting lakes and passing small villages with sharp-pointed church spires. Here the lush forests that dominate Sweden's northern landscape have largely fallen to the plow.

Once the dominant power of the region, Sweden has traditionally looked inward to find its own Nordic solutions. During the cold war it tried with considerable success to steer its famous "middle way" between the two superpowers, both economically and politically. Its citizens were in effect subjected to a giant social experiment aimed at creating a perfectly just society, one that adopted the best aspects of both socialism and capitalism.

In the late 1980s, as it slipped into the worst economic recession since the 1930s, Sweden made adjustments that lessened the role of its all-embracing welfare state in the lives of its citizens. Although fragile, the conservative coalition, which defeated the long-incumbent Social Democrats in the fall of 1991, attempted to make further cutbacks in welfare spending as the country faced one of the largest budget deficits in Europe. In a nostalgic backlash of sorts, the Social Democrats were voted back into power in 1994. Although Sweden appeared to be crawling toward stability in the mid-1990s, the struggle to balance the budget intensified again by the end of the decade. The Social Democrats won again in 2002, but the social safety net once so heavily relied upon by Swedes remains somewhat incomplete; a reflection perhaps of modern economics rather than any temporary budgetary hiccup.

Sweden took off with the rest of the globe with the explosion of the Internet and new technology and watched with it as the bubble burst at the start of the new millennium. It continues to be one of the world's dominant players in the information-based economy. New technology is widely used throughout Sweden; if there's an expensive new gadget, chances are you'll see a stylish Stockholmer using it.

On the social front, an influx of immigrants is reshaping what was once a homogeneous society. Sweden continues to face political and social difficulties in the areas of immigration and integration, although the tension appears to be fading slightly as more artists, musicians, actors, directors, and writers with immigrant backgrounds receive national recognition for their work.

Another sign that Swedes seem more willing than ever to refashion their image was Sweden's decision to join the European Union (EU) in 1995, a move that represented a radical break with its traditional independent stance on international issues. Thus far, the benefits of EU membership are still debated heavily.

As for the creative side of life, the skills of the wood-carver, the weaver, the leather worker, and the glassblower are highly prized. Despite the praise lavished abroad on introspective and dramatic Swedish artists such as August Strindberg and Ingmar Bergman, it is often slapstick humor that will get Swedes booming with laughter.

Sweden is an arresting mixture of ancient and modern. The countryside is dotted with runic stones recalling its Viking past: trade beginning in the 8th century went as far east as Kiev and as far south as Constantinople and the Mediterranean; it later expanded to the British Isles and then settled in Normandy in the 10th century. Small timbered farmhouses and maypoles—around which villagers still dance at midsummer in traditional costumes—evoke both their pagan early history and more recent agrarian culture. Venture to the country's cities, however, and you'll find them to be sci-fi modern, their shop windows filled with the latest in consumer goods and fashions.

Swedes are reluctant urbanites: their hearts and souls are in the forests and the archipelagoes, and to there they faithfully retreat in the summer and on weekends to pick berries and to enjoy the silence and breathtakingly beautiful scenery. The country possesses stunning natural assets. In the forests, moose, deer, bears, and lynx roam, coexisting with the whine of power saws and the rumble of automatic logging machines. Logging remains the country's economic backbone. Environmental awareness, however, is high. Fish abound in sparkling lakes and tumbling rivers, and eagles and ospreys soar over pine-clad islands in the archipelagoes off the east and west coasts.

Exploring Sweden

Sweden consists of 21 counties. In the southeast is Stockholm county, which includes the capital of the same name. The industrial seaport city of Göteborg and the neighboring west coastal counties of Bohuslän and Halland (the so-called Swedish Riviera) form another region, along with Värmland and Dalsland on the Norwegian border. The southernmost part of Sweden, a lovely mix of farmland, forests, and châteaus, includes Skåne, Småland ("The Kingdom of Glass"), Blekinge, Västergötland, Östergötland, and the island of Öland. Dalarna, the country's heartland, is centered on Lake Siljan and the town of Mora; this is where Swedish folklore and traditions are most visible. To the north of Stockholm is the Bothnian Coast, a land of dramatic cliffs, fjords, and port towns. The northern half of Sweden, called Norrland and including the counties of Lappland and Norrbotten, is a great expanse consisting mostly of mountains and wilderness; here the hardy Sami (also known as Lapps) herd reindeer. This is where most visitors venture to experience the midnight sun.

About the Restaurants

Sweden's major cities offer a full range of dining choices, from traditional to international restaurants. Outside the cities, restaurants are usually more local in influence. Investments in training and successes in international competitions have spurred restaurant quality to fantastic heights in Sweden. It is worth remembering, though, that for many years eating out was prohibitively expensive for many Swedes, giving rise to a home-socializing culture that still exists today. For this rea-

Sampling all of Sweden's far-flung variety is best suited to a traveler with either no time constraints or an exceedingly generous purse. The few representative stops below, however, can make even a short visit worthwhile.

If you have 3 days

Spend two days in the capital city, **Stockholm**; one of these days may be spent on a boat trip in the archipelago or on Lake Mälaren. A night at the opera will set the scene, or, for the more budget-conscious traveler, some people-watching over a beer or two downtown. On the third day either visit **Göteborg**—a port town since the Viking era, marked with attractive boulevards, canals, and important museums—by high-speed train, or fly to **Mora,** in the heart of Sweden's folklore country, Dalarna. A summertime dip in Lake Siljan will bring freshness and clarity to your travel-worn senses. You could also fly to **Gotland** for a quick island adventure. The warm climate, golden, cliff-lined beaches, and delicious local lamb specialties make it difficult to leave.

If you have 5 days

Start with two days in **Stockholm**; add a third day if you want to make a side trip to **Uppsala,** Sweden's principal university town, along the banks of the Fyris River. You can take a long boat journey out into the archipelago, sleeping in a small waterside cabin. On Day 4 fly to **Mora** and rent a car for a drive around Lake Siljan. On Day 5 head to **Göteborg.**

If you have 10 days

You can tackle this itinerary using public transportation. Start with three days in **Stockholm.** On Day 4 take the high-speed train to **Göteborg** and stay two nights and perhaps take the chance to sail out in the west-coast archipelago. It's not as big as Stockholm's archipelago, but the locals will tell you it is much more beautiful. On Day 6 take the train to **Kalmar,** with Sweden's best-preserved Renaissance castle, via **Växjö,** the starting place for many of Sweden's 1 million immigrants to America in the 19th century, now the finishing place for many family-tree-tracing pilgrimages. From Kalmar catch the ferry to **Gotland.** On Day 8 return to Stockholm. Spend Day 9 flying to either **Mora** or **Kiruna,** the northernmost city in Sweden. Alternatively, from **Gotland** you could spend a couple of days taking the train up the **Bothnian Coast** to experience wild seas, pine-clad islands, tiny fishing villages, and grand towns built on 19th-century industrial fortunes. Return to Stockholm on Day 10.

---

son many smaller towns are bereft of anything approaching a varied restaurant scene.

Restaurant meals are big-ticket items throughout Scandinavia, but there are ways to keep the cost of eating down. Take full advantage of the large buffet breakfast often included in the cost of a hotel room. At lunch look for a "menu" that offers a set two- or three-course meal for a set price, often including bread and salad, or limit yourself to a hearty appetizer. Some restaurants now include a trip to the salad bar in the dinner price. At dinner pay careful attention to the price of wine and drinks, since the high tax on alcohol raises these costs considerably.

About the Hotels

Sweden offers a variety of accommodations, from simple bed-and-breakfasts, campsites, and hostels to hotels of the highest international standard. In the larger cities lodging ranges from first-class business hotels run by SAS, Sheraton, and Scandic to good-quality tourist-class hotels, such as RESO, Best Western, Scandic Budget, and Sweden Hotels, to a wide variety of single-entrepreneur hotels. In the countryside look for independently run inns and motels, known as guesthouses. In addition, farm holidays increasingly have become available to tourists, and Sweden has organizations that can help plan stays in the countryside.

Before you leave home, ask your travel agent about discounts, including summer hotel checks for Best Western, Scandic, and Inter Nor hotels, and enormous year-round rebates at SAS hotels for travelers over 65. All EuroClass (business-class) passengers can get discounts of at least 10% at SAS hotels when they book through SAS.

Ask about high and low seasons when making reservations since different countries define their tourist seasons differently. Some hotels lower prices during tourist season, whereas others raise them during the same period. In Sweden many hotels offer lower prices on weekends and during the summer months, some by as much as 50%.

Two things about hotels usually surprise North Americans: the relatively limited dimensions of Scandinavian beds and the generous size of Scandinavian breakfasts. Scandinavian double beds are often about 60 inches wide or slightly less, close in size to the U.S. queen size. King-size beds (72 inches wide) are difficult to find and, if available, require special reservations.

Many older hotels, particularly the country inns and independently run smaller hotels in the cities, do not have private bathrooms. Inquire about this ahead of time if this is important to you.

Make reservations whenever possible. Even countryside inns, which usually have space, are sometimes packed with vacationing Europeans.

Timing

The official tourist season—when hotel rates generally go down and museum and castle doors open—runs from mid-May through mid-September. This is Sweden's balmiest time of year; summer days are sunny and warm, nights refreshingly cool. (Summer is also mosquito season, especially in the north, but also as far south as Stockholm.) The whole country goes mad for Midsummer Day, in the middle of June. Many attractions close in late August, when the schools reopen at the end of the Swedish vacation season. The colors of autumn fade out as early as September, when the rainy season begins. The weather can be bright and fresh in the spring and fall (although spring can bring lots of rain), and many visitors prefer sightseeing when there are fewer people around. Winter comes in November and stays through March, sometimes longer.

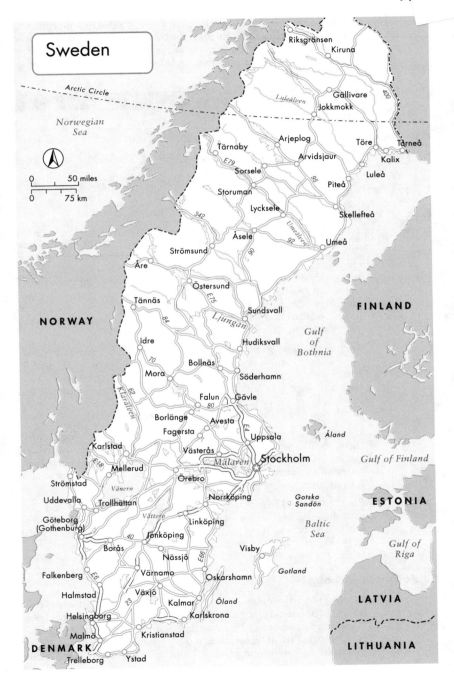

In Sweden this season is an Alpine affair, with subzero temperatures. The days can be magnificent when the snow is fresh and the sky a brilliant Nordic blue. Although many of the more traditional attractions are closed, there is skiing, skating, ice fishing, and sleigh riding on offer throughout the country.

	WHAT IT COSTS In Swedish Kronor				
	$$$$	$$$	$$	$	¢
RESTAURANTS	over 420	250–420	150–250	100–150	under 100
HOTELS	over 2,900	2,300–2,900	1,500–2,300	1,000–1,500	under 1,000

Restaurant prices are for a main course at dinner. Hotel prices are for two people in a standard double room in high season.

STOCKHOLM

Stockholm is a city in the flush of its second youth. In the last 10 years Sweden's capital has emerged from its cold, Nordic shadow to take the stage as a truly international city. What started with entry into the European Union in 1995, and continued with the extraordinary IT boom of the late 1990s, is still happening today as Stockholm gains even more global confidence. Stockholm's 1 million or so inhabitants have, almost as one, realized that their city is one to rival Paris, London, New York, or any other great metropolis.

With this realization comes change. Stockholm has become a city of design, fashion, innovation, technology, and world-class food, pairing homegrown talent with international standard. The streets are flowing with a young and confident population keen to drink in everything the city has to offer. The glittering feeling of optimism, success, and living in the "here and now" is rampant in Stockholm.

Of course, not everyone is looking to live so much in the present; for them, luckily, Stockholm also has plenty of history. Positioned where the waters of Lake Mälaren rush into the Baltic, Stockholm has been an important Baltic trading site and an international city of some wealth for centuries.

Built on 14 small islands joined by bridges crossing open bays and narrow channels, Stockholm boasts the story of its history in its glorious medieval old town, grand palaces, ancient churches, sturdy edifices, public parks, and 19th-century museums—its history is soaked into the very fabric of its airy boulevards, built as a public display of trading glory.

Exploring Stockholm

Much of Stockholm's beauty comes from its water. In the same way that Venice is unquestionably defined by its lagoon, so too is Stockholm mapped and interpreted by its archipelago landscape. For the inhabitants there's a tribal status to each of the islands. Residents of Södermalm are fiercely proud of their rather bohemian settlement, while those who call Gamla Stan home will tell you that there is nowhere else like it. But for the visitor, Stockholm's islands have a more practical, less passionate meaning: they help to dissect the city, both in terms of history and in terms of Stockholm's different characteristics, conveniently packaging the capital into easily handled, ultimately digestible, areas.

The central island of Gamla Stan wows visitors with its medieval beauty, winding, narrow lanes, cellar bars, and small café-lined squares. Directly to the east is the small island of Skeppsholmen. To the south, Södermalm challenges with contemporary boutiques, hip hangouts, and left-of-center sensibilities. North of Gamla Stan is Norrmalm, the financial and business heart of the city, and a reliable, solid, international face of Stockholm. Travel west and you'll find Kungsholmen, site of the Stadshuset (City Hall), where you'll find the first signs of residential leafiness and one of Stockholm's newly hip enclaves. Turn east from Norrmalm and Östermalm awaits, an old residential neighborhood with the most money, the most glamorous people, the most tantalizing shops, and the most expensive street on the Swedish Monopoly board. Finally, between Östermalm and Södermalm lies the island of Djurgården, once a royal game preserve, now the site of lovely parks and museums; it's a place to come to recharge and regroup before you hit the more lively parts of town again.

Modern Stockholm

The area bounded by Stadshuset, Hötorget, Stureplan, and the Kungliga Dramatiska Teatern (nicknamed Dramaten) is essentially Stockholm's downtown, where the city comes closest to feeling like a bustling metropolis. Shopping, nightlife, business, traffic, dining, festivals—all are at their most intense in this part of town. Much of this area was razed to the ground in the 1960s as part of a social experiment to move people to the new suburbs. What came in its place, a series of modernist buildings, concrete public spaces, and pedestrianized walkways, garners support and derision in equal measure. Whatever your reaction, it is part of Stockholm's unique personality and should not be missed.

a good walk

Stockholm's symbol of power, **Stadshuset** ❶ ▶, is a perfect place to begin your walk. Cross the bridge to Klara Mälarstrand and follow the waterfront to Drottninggatan. Take a left and continue north along this crowded pedestrian street, a purposeful shop-lined artery that cuts right through the center of the city. It is broken only once, by modern Stockholm's heart, **Sergels Torg** ❷. The **Kulturhuset** ❸ is in the imposing glass building on the southern side of Sergels Torg. Continue along Drottninggatan, stopping at the market-filled **Hötorget** ❹. The intersection of Kungsgatan and Sveavägen, where the Konserthuset (Concert Hall) stands, is one of the busiest pedestrian crossroads in town.

Head north on Sveavägen for a brief detour to see the spot where Prime Minister Olof Palme was assassinated in 1986. A plaque has been laid on the right-hand side of the street, just before the intersection with Olof Palmes Gata; his grave is in Adolf Fredrik's Kyrkogård, a few blocks farther on. This is the perfect place to cut back to Drottninggatan, heading southwest along Kammakargatan. Drottninggatan changes

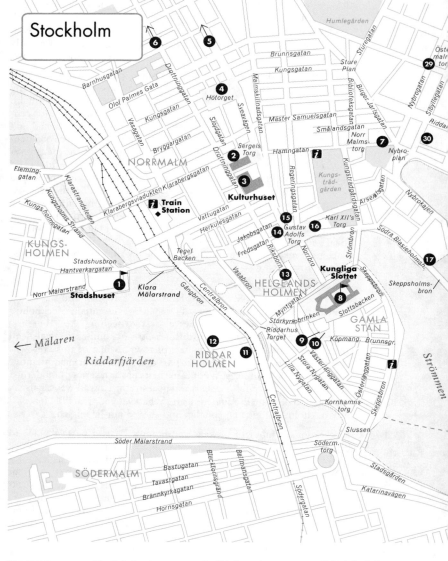

Stockholm

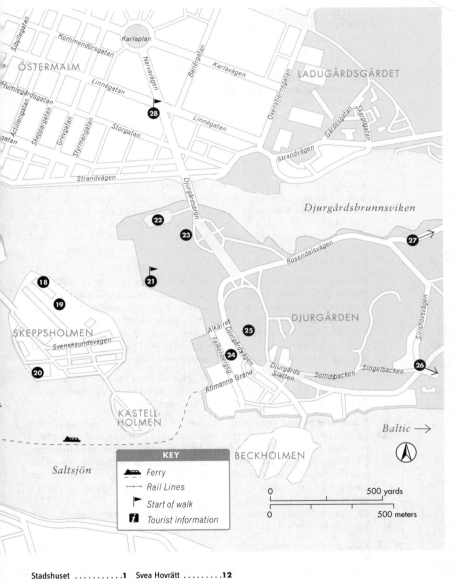

here; the crowds thin, as do the more touristy shops. Instead, the area's locals go about their business, dropping off dry cleaning, chatting in cafés, and popping into bookshops. Eventually you will reach Odengatan. On your right will be the magnificent **Stockholms Stadsbiblioteket ❺**. Find your way (from Odengatan to Sveavägen) onto Döbelnsgatan, a peaceful and pleasant residential street and head south. Turn right up Tegnérgatan to find **Strindbergsmuseet Blå Tornet ❻**, where playwright August Strindberg lived from 1908 to 1912. Return to Hötorget by way of Sveavägen, a riot of sound and activity after the head-clearing peace of Döbelnsgatan.

Next, walk east along Kungsgatan, one of Stockholm's main shopping streets, to Stureplan. On this street is Sturegallerian, an elegant mall. In front of Sturegallerian is Svampen (the mushroom), a little piece of Stockholm's social history. The fungus-shape pay-phone shelter has been a meeting point for years: "I'll see you by Svampen at eight o'clock." Here countless first dates have met, lifelong friendships have formed, and likely more than a few hearts have been broken. Head southeast along Birger Jarlsgatan—named for the nobleman generally credited with founding Stockholm around 1252—where there are still more interesting shops and restaurants.

Heading west up Hamngatan from Nybroplan, stop in at **Hallwylska Museet ❼** for a tour of the private collection of Countess von Hallwyl's treasures. Continue along Hamngatan to Kungsträdgården, a park since 1562. Outdoor cafés and restaurants are clustered by this leafy spot, a summer venue for public concerts and events. Across from the northwest corner of the park, on the opposite side of Hamngatan, is the NK department store, a paradise for shoppers of all persuasions.

TIMING Allow about 4½ hours for the walk, plus an hour each for guided tours of Stadshuset and Hallwylska Museet (September–June, Sunday only). The Strindbergsmuseet Blå Tornet is closed Monday.

WHAT TO SEE **Hallwylska Museet** (Hallwyl Museum). This private late-19th-century
❼ palace, one of the first in Stockholm to have electricity and a telephone installed, has imposing wood-panel rooms and a collection of furniture, paintings, and musical instruments that can be best described as eclectic. The palace is decked out in a bewildering mélange of styles assembled by the apparently spendaholic Countess von Hallwyl, who left it to the state on her death. ✉ *Hamng. 4, Norrmalm* ☎ *08/51955599* ⊕ *www.hallwylskamuseet.se* ✆ *SKr 40* ☉ *Guided tours only. Tours in English July and Aug., Tues.–Sun. at 1; Sept.–June, Sun. at 1.*

★ ❹ **Hötorget** (Hay Market). Once the city's hay market, this is now a popular gathering place where you're more likely to find apples and pears. Crowds come here to meet, gossip, hang out, or pick up goodies from the excellent outdoor fruit-and-vegetable market. Also lining the square are the Konserthuset (Concert Hall), fronted by a magnificent statue by Swedish-American sculptor Carl Milles, the PUB department store, and a multiscreen cinema Filmstaden Sergel. ✉ *On the corner of Kungsgatan and Sveaväg, Norrmalm.*

🐾 ❸ **Kulturhuset** (Culture House). Since it opened in 1974, architect Peter Celsing's cultural center, a glass-and-stone monolith on the south side of Sergels Torg, has become a symbol of modernism in Sweden. Stockholmers are divided on the aesthetics of this building—most either love it or hate it. Here there are exhibitions for children and adults, a library, a theater, a youth center, an exhibition center, and a restaurant. Head to Café Panorama, on the top floor, to savor traditional Swedish cuisine and a great view of Sergels Torg down below. ⊠ *Sergels Torg 3, City* ☎ *08/50831508* ⊕ *www.kulturhuset.se.*

❷ **Sergels Torg.** Named after Johan Tobias Sergel (1740–1814), one of Sweden's greatest sculptors, this busy junction in Stockholm's center is dominated by modern, functional buildings and a sunken pedestrian square with subterranean connections to the rest of the neighborhood. Visitors are often put off by its darkened covered walkways and youths in hooded tops, but it is relatively safe and a great place to witness some real Stockholm street life.

▶ ❶ **Stadshuset** (City Hall). The architect Ragnar Östberg, one of the founders
Fodor'sChoice   of the National Romantic movement, completed Stockholm's city hall
★   in 1923. Headquarters of the city council, the building is functional but ornate: its immense **Blå Hallen** (Blue Hall) is the venue for the annual Nobel Prize dinner, Stockholm's principal social event. Take a trip to the top of the 348-foot tower, most of which can be achieved by elevator, to enjoy a breathtaking panorama of the city and Riddarfjärden. ⊠ *Hantverkarg. 1, Kungsholmen* ☎ *08/50829058* ⊕ *www.stockholm. se* ⊠ *SKr 60, tower SKr 20* ☉ *Guided tours only. Tours in English, June–Aug., daily 10, 11, noon, 2, and 3; Sept., daily 10, noon and 2; Oct.–May, daily 10 and noon. Tower open May–Sept., daily 10–4.30.*

❺ **Stockholms Stadsbiblioteket** (Stockholm City Library). Libraries aren't always a top sightseeing priority, but the Stockholm City Library is among the most captivating buildings in town. Designed by the famous Swedish architect E. G. Asplund and completed in 1928, the building's cylindrical, galleried main hall gives it the appearance of a large birthday cake. Inside is an excellent "information technology" center with free Internet access—and lots of books too. ⊠ *Sveav. 73, Vasastan* ☎ *08/50831100* ⊕ *www.ssb.stockholm.se* ☉ *Mon.–Thurs. 9–9, Fri. 9–7, and weekends noon–4.*

★ ❻ **Strindbergsmuseet Blå Tornet** (Strindberg Museum, Blue Tower). Hidden away over a grocery store, this museum is dedicated to Sweden's most important author and dramatist, August Strindberg (1849–1912), who resided here from 1908 until his death four years later. The interior has been expertly reconstructed with authentic furnishings and other objects, including one of his pens. The museum also houses a library, printing press, and picture archives, and it is the setting for literary, musical, and theatrical events. ⊠ *Drottningg. 85, Norrmalm* ☎ *08/4115354* ⊕ *www. strindbergsmuseet.se* ⊠ *SKr 40* ☉ *Tues.–Sun. noon–4.*

Gamla Stan & Skeppsholmen

Gamla Stan (Old Town) sits between two of Stockholm's main islands, and is the site of the medieval city. Just east of Gamla Stan is the island

CloseUp

STOCKHOLM'S ARCHITECTURAL PROCESSION

AS IN MANY OTHER SWEDISH CITIES, a single afternoon walk in Stockholm offers a journey through centuries of architectural change and innovation. There are, of course, the classics. Take Kungliga Slottet (Royal Palace) on Gamla Stan. Designed by Nicodemus Tessin the Younger and built between 1690 and 1704, it's a rather austere palace—no domes, no great towers—and yet it commands a certain respect sitting so regally over the water. Nearby, on Riddarholmen, observe the gorgeous, medieval Riddarholmskyrkan (Riddarholm Church), with its lattice spire pointed toward the heavens. And let's not forget Drottningholms Slott, just west of the city, a 17th-century châteauesque structure— designed by Tessin the Elder and finished by his son—that has been the home of the royal family since 1981. Also at Drottningholm is the Court Theater (1766), which, remarkably, still contains its original interior and fully functional stage machinery.

Stadshuset (City Hall) is also a must-see. Completed in 1923, the building contains more than 8 million bricks and 19 million gilded mosaic tiles. Each year the Nobel Prize ceremony is held in the building's Blå Hallen (Blue Hall). Built a few years later is Stadsbiblioteket (City Library), designed by Eric Gunnar Asplund—one of Sweden's most renowned architects. The library's eye-pleasing yet simple design foreshadows the funkis (functionalist) movement that Gunnar helped spearhead in the 1920s and '30s.

Skattehuset (Tax House), also known as Skatteskrapan (a play on the word "skyscraper"), is hard to miss, looming mercilessly as it does over Södermalm. Completed in the early 1950s as part of an attempt to consolidate the nation's tax offices, the singularly dull, gray, 25-story building is often criticized for having ruined the southern skyline of Stockholm.

Farther south, another architectural oddity plagues—or enhances, depending on whom you ask—the skyline. Globen (the Globe), the world's largest spherical building, looks something like a colossal golf ball. Unveiled in 1988, it's the main arena in Stockholm for indoor sporting events and rock concerts. Despite debates concerning its aesthetics (or lack thereof), a look at the cables and beams inside reveals Globen's architecture marvel.

Another much-debated architectural undertaking is Hötorgscity, across from the highly influential Kulturhuset at Sergels Torg. Constructed in the mid-'50s, Hötorgscity was built to house retail stores and offices to bring more commerce to downtown Stockholm. The project failed, and a significant chunk of historic Stockholm was lost. The buildings were shut down in the '70s, but today there is a renewed interest in the top floors of the buildings, especially among young business owners.

What is most striking about the buildings that make up Stockholm's architectural portfolio is their diversity. Centuries of history involving both failures and successes are reflected in the styles that make up the city's skyline. Every building in Stockholm, new or old, tells a story.

of Skeppsholmen, whose twisting cobble streets are lined with superbly preserved old buildings. As the site of the original Stockholm, this area is rich in history and, understandably, a magnet for tourists. Consequently there are plenty of substandard shops and restaurants ready to take your money in return for shoddy goods and bad food. Because of this, locals often make a big show of dismissing the area as a tourist trap, but don't believe them. Secretly they love Gamla Stan and Skeppsholmen. And who wouldn't? With its divine hideaway alleys and bars, gorgeous architecture, specialty shops, and great restaurants, it's impossible to resist.

a good walk

Start at the waterfront edge of Kungsträdgården. Stand for a moment with the park behind you and look out. This is one of the most beautiful views of Stockholm, especially if the sun is shining. Walk across Strömsbron to the magnificent **Kungliga Slottet** ⑧ ⌐, where you can see the changing of the guard at noon every day—a spectacle which, although formal, lacks the cold stiffness of London's changing of the guard, reflecting the relaxed formality that pervades much of Swedish life. Walk up the sloping cobblestone drive called Slottsbacken and bear right past the Obelisk (which was built by King Gustav III in honor of the people of Stockholm) to find the main entrance to the palace.

Following Källargränd from the Obelisk, you will reach the small square called **Stortorget** ⑨, marvelously atmospheric amid magnificent old merchants' houses. Stockholm's Börshuset (Stock Exchange), which currently houses the **Nobelmuseet** ⑩, fronts the square. You are right in the heart of old Stockholm now. Prepare for an onslaught to the senses, as history, culture, and a dash of old Europe come thick and fast around here.

Walk past Svartmangatan's many ancient buildings, including the Tyska Kyrkan, or German Church, with its resplendent oxidized copper spire and airy interior. Continue along Svartmangatan and take a right on Tyska Stallplan to Prästgatan, and just to your left will be Mårten Trotzigs Gränd; this lamplit alley stairway leads downhill to Järntorget. From here, take Västerlånggatan back north across Gamla Stan, checking out the pricey fashion boutiques, galleries, and souvenir shops along the way.

Cut down Storkyrkobrinken to Myntgatan. A short walk takes you over Riddarholmsbron to Riddarholmen—Island of Knights—on which stands **Riddarholmskyrkan** ⑪. Also on Riddarholmen is the white 17th-century palace that houses the **Svea Hovrätt** ⑫. Returning across Riddarholmsbron, take Myntgatan back toward Kungliga Slottet and turn left onto Stallbron and cross the bridge. You'll then pass through the refurbished stone **Riksdagshuset** ⑬ on Helgeandsholmen, Holy Ghost Island. Another short bridge returns you to the mainland and Drottninggatan; take a right onto Fredsgatan and walk until you reach **Medelhavsmuseet** ⑭, on the left, just before Gustav Adolfs Torg. Right there on the square is the **Dansmuseet** ⑮.

The **Operan** ⑯ occupies the waterfront between Gustav Adolfs Torg and Karl XII's Torg (part of Kungsträdgården). A little farther along, on Södra Blasieholmshamn, a host of tour boats dock in front of the stately Grand Hotel. Pass the Grand and visit the **Nationalmuseum** ⑰. Cross the footbridge to the island of Skeppsholmen, a hot spot for museum lovers. Here you will find the **Östasiatiska Museet** ⑱, with a fine collection of Buddhist art, the **Moderna Museet** ⑲, which is in the same complex that houses the **Arkitekturmuseet.** and, to the southwest, **Svensk Form** ⑳, a design museum. The adjoining island, Kastellholmen, is a pleasant place for a stroll, especially on a summer evening, when views of the Baltic harbor and the lights of Djurgården's parks are served up with a warm, salty breeze and the promise of another fine day tomorrow.

TIMING Allow three hours for the walk, double that if you want to tour the various parts of the palace. The Nationalmuseum and Östasiatiska Museet will take up to an hour each to view. Note that Kungliga Slottet is closed Monday off-season, and Arkitekturmuseet, Dansmuseet, Medelhavsmuseet, Moderna Museet, Nationalmuseum, Svensk Form, and Östasiatiska Museet are always closed Monday. The Riddarhuset is open weekdays only; off-season, hit the Riddarholmskyrkan on a Wednesday or weekend.

WHAT TO SEE **Arkitekturmuseet.** The Museum of Architecture uses models, photos, and drawings to tell the long and interesting story of Swedish architecture. Certain buildings shed light on specific periods, including the Stockholm Town Hall, Vadstena Castle, and the Helsingborg Concert House. The museum also hosts lectures, debates, and architectural tours of the city. ⊠ *Skeppsholmen* ☎ *08/58727000* ⊕ *www.arkitekturmuseet. se* ⊑ *Free* ☉ *Tues. and Wed. 10–8, Thurs.–Sun. 10–6.*

⑮ **Dansmuseet** (Museum of Dance). Close to the Royal Opera House, the Museum of Dance has a permanent collection that examines dance, theater, and art from Asia, Africa, and Europe. Such artists as Fernand Léger, Francis Picabia, Giorgio de Chirico, and Jean Cocteau are represented in the exhibitions. The Rolf de Maré Study Centre has a vast collection of dance reference materials, including about 4,000 books and 3,000 videos. ⊠ *Gustav Adolfs Torg 22–24, City* ☎ *08/4417650* ⊕ *www. dansmuseet.nu* ⊑ *SKr 50* ☉ *Tues.–Fri. 11–4, weekends noon–4.*

▶ ⑧ **Kungliga Slottet** (Royal Palace). Designed by Nicodemus Tessin, the
Fodor'sChoice Royal Palace was completed in 1760 and replaced the previous palace
★ that had burned here in 1697. The four facades of the palace each have a distinct style: the west is the king's, the east the queen's, the south belongs to the nation, and the north represents royalty in general. Watch the changing of the guard in the curved terrace entrance, and view the palace's fine furnishings and Gobelin tapestries on a tour of the **Representationsvän** (State Apartments). To survey the crown jewels, which are no longer used in this self-consciously egalitarian country, head to the **Skattkammaren** (Treasury). The **Livrustkammaren** (Royal Armory) has an outstanding collection of weaponry, coaches, and royal regalia. Entrances to the Treasury and Armory are on the Slottsbacken side of the palace. ⊠ *Gamla Stan* ☎ *08/4026130* ⊕ *www.royalcourt.se* ⊑ *State Apartments SKr 80, Treasury SKr 80, Royal Armory SKr 80, combined ticket for all areas SKr 120* ☉ *State Apartments and Treasury May–Aug., daily 10–4; Sept.–Apr., Tues.–Sun. noon–3. Armory May–Aug., daily 11–4; Sept.–Apr., Tues.–Sun. 11–4.*

⓮ Medelhavsmuseet (Mediterranean Museum). During the 1700s this building housed the Royal Courts. Then, in the early 1900s, the vast interior of the building was redesigned to resemble the Palazzo Bevilaqua in Bologna, Italy. The collection has a good selection of art from Asia as well as from ancient Egypt, Greece, and Rome. In the Gold Room you can see fine gold, silver, and bronze jewelry from the Far East, Greece, and Rome. ⊠ *Fredsg. 2, City* ☎ *08/51955380* ⊕ *www.medelhavsmuseet. se* ▨*Free* ☻ *Tues. and Wed. 11–8, Thurs. and Fri. 11–4, weekends noon–5.*

★ ⓳ Moderna Museet (Museum of Modern Art). Reopened in its original venue on Skeppsholmen following extensive treatment for moisture problems, the museum's excellent collection includes works by Picasso, Kandinsky, Dalí, Brancusi, and other international artists. You can also view examples of significant Swedish painters and sculptors and an extensive section on photography. The building itself is striking. Designed by the well-regarded Spanish architect Rafael Moneo, it has seemingly endless hallways of blond wood and walls of glass. ⊠ *Skeppsholmen, City* ☎ *08/51955200* ⊕ *www.modernamuseet.se* ▨ *Free* ☻ *Tues. and Wed. 10–8, Thurs.–Sun. 10–6.*

⓱ Nationalmuseum. The museum's collection of paintings and sculptures is made up of about 12,500 works. The emphasis is on Swedish and Nordic art, but other areas are well represented. Look especially for some fine works by Rembrandt. The print and drawing department is also impressive, with a nearly complete collection of Edouard Manet prints. ⊠ *Södra Blasieholmshamnen, City* ☎ *08/51954428* ⊕ *www. nationalmuseum.se* ▨ *Free* ☻ *Jan.–Aug., Tues. 11–8, Wed.–Sun. 11–5; Sept.–Dec., Tues. and Thurs. 11–8, Wed., Fri., and weekends 11–5.*

FodorśChoice ★

⓾ Nobelmuseet. The Swedish Academy meets at Börshuset (the Stock Exchange) every year to decide the winner of the Nobel Prize for literature. The building is also the home of the Nobel Museum. Along with exhibits on creativity's many forms, the museum displays scientific models, shows films, and has a full explanation of the process of choosing prizewinners. The museum does a good job covering the controversial selections made over the years. It's a must for Nobel Prize hopefuls and others. ⊠ *Börshuset, Stortorget, Gamla Stan* ☎ *08/232506* ⊕ *www.nobelprize.org/ nobelmuseum* ▨ *SKr 50* ☻ *Wed.–Mon. 10–5, Tues. 10–8.*

⓰ Operan (Opera House). Stockholm's baroque Opera House is almost more famous for its restaurants and bars than for its opera and ballet productions, but that doesn't mean an evening performance should be missed. There's not a bad seat in the house. For just SKr 35 you can even get a listening-only seat (with no view). Still, its food and drink status can't be denied. It has been one of Stockholm's artistic and literary watering holes since the first Operakällaren restaurant opened on the site in 1787. ⊠ *Gustav Adolfs Torg, City* ☎ *08/248240* ⊕ *www. operan.se.*

⓲ Östasiatiska Museet (Museum of Far Eastern Antiquities). If you have an affinity for Asian art and culture, don't miss this impressive collection of Chinese and Japanese Buddhist sculptures and artifacts. Although some exhibits are displayed with little creativity, the pieces themselves are always worthwhile. The more than 100,000 pieces that make up the holdings here include many from China's Neolithic and Bronze ages. ✉ *Skeppsholmen, City* ☎ *08/51955750* ⊕ *www.mfea.se* ✉ *Free* ⊙ *Tues. 11–8, Wed.–Sun. 11–5.*

⑪ Riddarholmskyrkan (Riddarholm Church). Dating from 1270, the Grey Friars monastery is the second-oldest structure in Stockholm, and has been the burial place for Swedish kings for more than 400 years. The redbrick structure, distinguished by its delicate iron-fretwork spire, is rarely used for services: it's more like a museum now. The most famous figures interred within are King Gustavus Adolphus, hero of the Thirty Years' War, and the warrior King Karl XII, renowned for his daring invasion of Russia, who died in Norway in 1718. The most recent of the 17 Swedish kings to be put to rest here was Gustav V, in 1950. The different rulers' sarcophagi, usually embellished with their monograms, are visible in the small chapels dedicated to the various dynasties. ✉ *Riddarholmen* ☎ *08/4026130* ✉ *SKr 20* ⊙ *May–Aug., daily 10–4; Sept., weekends noon–3.*

⑬ Riksdagshuset (Parliament Building). When in session, the Swedish Parliament meets in this 1904 building. Above the entrance, the architect placed sculptures of a peasant, a burgher, a clergyman, and a nobleman. Take a tour of the building not only to learn about Swedish government but also to see the art within. In the former First Chamber are murals by Otte Sköld illustrating different periods in the history of Stockholm, and in the current First Chamber a massive tapestry by Elisabet Hasselberg Olsson, *Memory of a Landscape*, hangs above the podium. ✉ *Riksg. 3A, Gamla Stan* ☎ *08/7864000* ⊕ *www.riksdagen.se* ✉ *Free* ⊙ *Tours in English late June–late Aug., weekdays 12:30 and 2; late Aug.–late June, weekends 1:30. Call ahead for reservations.*

⑨ Stortorget (Great Square). Here in 1520 the Danish king Christian II ordered a massacre of Swedish noblemen. The slaughter paved the way for a national revolt against foreign rule and the founding of Sweden as a sovereign state under King Gustav Vasa, who ruled from 1523 to 1560. One legend holds that if it rains heavily enough on the anniversary of the massacre, the old stones still run red. ✉ *Near Kungliga Slottet, Gamla Stan.*

⑫ Svea Hovrätt (Swedish High Court). The Swedish High Court commands a prime site on the island of Riddarholmen, on a quiet and restful quayside. Though it's closed to the public, you can sit on the water's edge nearby and watch the boats on Riddarfjärden (Bay of Knights) and, beyond it, Lake Mälaren. From here you can see the stately arches of Västerbron (West Bridge) in the distance, the southern heights, and above all, the imposing profile of City Hall, which appears almost to be floating on the water. At the quay you may see one of the Göta Canal ships.

⑳ Svensk Form (Swedish Form). This museum emphasizes the importance of Swedish form and design, although international works and trends are also covered. Exhibits include everything from chairs to light fixtures to cups, bowls, and silverware. Find out why Sweden is considered a world leader in industrial design. Every year the museum gives out a prestigious and highly coveted design award called Utmärkt Sven-skt Form (Outstanding Swedish Design). The winning objects are then exhibited in fall. ⊠ *Holmamiralens väg 2, Skeppsholmen, City* ☎ *08/ 4633130* ⊕ *www.svenskform.se* 🖾 *SKr 20* ⊙ *Tues.–Sun. noon–5.*

Djurgården & Skansen

Throughout history, Djurgården has been Stockholm's pleasure island. There was time when only the king could enjoy this enormous green space, and enjoy it he did. Today Stockholmers of all persuasions come here to breathe some fresh air, visit the island's many museums, stroll through the forests and glades, get their pulses racing at the Gröna Lund amusement park, or just relax by the water and watch the boats sail by.

a good walk

You can approach Djurgården from the water aboard the small ferries that leave from Slussen at the southern end of Gamla Stan. In summer, ferries also leave from Nybrokajen, or New Bridge Quay, in front of the Kungliga Dramatiska Teatern. Alternatively, starting at the theater, stroll down the grandiose residential strip of Strandvägen—taking in the magnificent old sailing ships, the fine views over the harbor and the or-nately luxurious apartment buildings—and cross Djurgårdsbron, or Djurgården Bridge, to the island. Your first port of call should be the **Vasamuseet** ㉑ ⮕, with its dramatic display of splendid 17th-century warships. If you have children in tow, be sure to visit **Junibacken** ㉒, just off Djurgårdsbron. Return to Djurgårdsvägen to find the entrance to the **Nordiska Museet** ㉓, worth a visit for insight into Swedish folklore.

Continue on Djurgårdsvägen to the amusement park **Gröna Lund Tivoli** ㉔, where Stockholmers of all ages come to play. Beyond the park, cross Djurgårdsvägen to **Skansen** ㉕.

From Skansen continue on Djurgårdsvägen to Prins Eugens Väg and fol-low the signs to the beautiful late-19th-century **Waldemarsudde** ㉖. On the way back to Djurgårdsbron, take a right on Rosendalsvägen. Signs on this street lead to **Rosendals Trädgården** ㉗, which has beautiful gar-dens and a delightful café. From here you can stroll back along the water toward the city.

TIMING This is one part of Stockholm you won't want to rush through. Allow half a day for this tour, unless you're planning to turn it into a full-day event with lengthy visits to Skansen, Junibacken, and Gröna Lund Tivoli, plus a bit more time for treating yourself to some tempting ice-cream breaks on the grass or a snooze in the shade of a tree. The Vasamuseet warrants two hours, the Nordiska needs an hour, and the Biologiska museum and Waldemarsudde require about an hour. Gröna Lund Tivoli is closed from mid-September to late April. The Biologiska Museet and Waldemarsudde are closed Monday.

WHAT TO SEE **Gröna Lund Tivoli.** Smaller than Copenhagen's Tivoli or Göteborg's Lise-berg, this amusement park has managed to retain much of its histori-cal charm, while making room for some modern, hair-raising rides among the pleasure gardens, amusement arcades, and restaurants. If you're feeling especially daring, try the Power Tower. At 350 feet, it's Europe's tallest free-fall amusement-park ride and one of the best ways to see Stockholm, albeit for about three seconds, before you plummet. There isn't an adult who grew up in Stockholm who can't remember the annual excitement of Gröna Lund's April opening. Go and you will see why. ☒ *Allmänna Gränd 9, Djurgården* ☎ *08/58750100* ⊕ *www.tivoli.se* ☒ *SKr 60, not including tickets or passes for rides* ☉ *Late Apr.–mid-Sept., daily. Hrs vary but are generally noon–11 PM. Call ahead for specific information.*

★ ☾ ㉒ **Junibacken.** In this storybook house you travel in small carriages through the world of children's book writer Astrid Lindgren, creator of the irrepressible character Pippi Longstocking, among others. Lindgren's tales come alive as various scenes are revealed. Parents can enjoy a welcome moment of rest after the mini-train ride as the children lose themselves in the near-life-size model of Pippi Longstocking's house. It's perfect for children ages five and up. ☒ *Galärvarsv., Djurgården* ☎ *08/58723000* ⊕ *www.junibacken.se* ☒ *SKr 95* ☉ *Jan.–May and Sept.–Dec., Tues. to Fri. 10–5, weekends 9–6; June and Aug. daily 10–5; July daily 9–6.*

☾ ㉓ **Nordiska Museet** (Nordic Museum). An imposing late-Victorian structure housing peasant costumes from every region of the country and exhibits on the Sami (pronounced *sah*-mee)—Lapps, the formerly seminomadic reindeer herders who inhabit the far north—and many other aspects of Swedish life. Families with children should visit the delightful "village life" play area on the ground floor. ☒ *Djurgårdsv. 6–16, Djurgården* ☎ *08/51954600* ⊕ *www.nordiskamuseet.se* ☒ *SKr 60* ☉ *Weekdays 10–4, weekends 11–5.*

㉗ **Rosendals Trädgården** (Rosendal's Garden). This gorgeous slice of greenery is a perfect place to spend a few hours on a late summer afternoon. When the weather's nice, people flock to the garden café, which is in one of the greenhouses, to enjoy tasty pastries and salads made from the locally grown vegetables. Pick your own flowers from the vast flower beds (paying by weight), stroll through the creative garden displays, or take away produce from the farm shop. ☒ *Rosendalsterrassen 12, Djurgården* ☎ *08/54581270* ☒ *Free* ☉ *May–Sept., weekdays 11–5, weekends 11–6; Oct.–Apr. call ahead for specific information.*

FodorśChoice
★

★ ☾ ㉕ **Skansen.** The world's first open-air museum, Skansen was founded in 1891 by philologist and ethnographer Artur Hazelius, who is buried here. He preserved examples of traditional Swedish architecture brought from all parts of the country, including farmhouses, windmills, barns, a working glassblower's hut, and churches. Not only is Skansen a delightful trip out of time in the center of a modern city, but it also provides insight into the life and culture of Sweden's various regions. In addition, the park has a zoo, carnival area, aquarium, theater, and cafés. ☒ *Djurgårdsslätten 4951, Djurgården* ☎ *08/4428000* ⊕ *www. skansen.se* ☒ *Park and zoo: Sept.–Apr. SKr 50; May–Aug. SKr 70. Aquarium SKr 60* ☉ *Oct.–Apr., daily 10–4; May, daily 10–8; June–Aug., daily 10–10; Sept., daily 10–5.*

★ � ㉑ **Vasamuseet** (Vasa Museum). The warship *Vasa* sank 10 minutes into its maiden voyage in 1628, consigned to a watery grave until it was raised from the seabed in 1961. Its hull was preserved by the Baltic mud, free of the worms that can eat through ships' timbers. Now largely restored to her former glory (however short-lived it may have been), the man-of-war resides in a handsome museum. The sheer size of this cannon-laden hulk inspires awe and fear in equal measure. The political history of the world may have been different had she made it out of harbor. Daily tours are available year-round. ⊠ *Galärvarsv., Djurgården* ☎ *08/51954800* ⊕ *www.vasamuseet.se* ✉ *SKr 80* ☉ *Thurs.–Tues. 10–5, Wed. 10–8.*

26 **Waldemarsudde.** This estate, Djurgården's gem, was bequeathed to the Swedish people by Prince Eugen upon his death, in 1947. It maintains an important collection of Nordic paintings from 1880 to 1940, in addition to the prince's own works. The rather grand stone terrace, situated above the entrance to Stockholm's harbor, is the perfect spot to perch and watch passing boats. ⊠ *Prins Eugens väg 6, Djurgården* ☎ *08/54583700* ⊕ *www.waldemarsudde.com* ✉ *SKr 80* ☉ *May–Aug., Tues., Wed., and Fri.–Sun. 11–5, Thurs. 11–8; Sept.–Apr., Tues., Wed., and Fri. 11–4, Thurs. 11–8, weekends 11–4.*

Östermalm & Kaknästornet

Marked by waterfront rows of Renaissance buildings with palatial rooftops and ornamentation, Östermalm is a quietly regal residential section of central Stockholm. History and money are steeped into the very bricks and mortar of its elegant streets, which are lined with museums, fine shopping, and exclusive restaurants. On Strandvägen, or Beach Way, the boulevard that follows the harbor's edge from the busy downtown area to the staid diplomatic quarter, you can choose one of three routes. The waterside walk, with its splendid views of the city harbor, bustles with tour boats and sailboats. Parallel to the walk (away from the water) is a tree-shaded walking and bike path. Walk, rollerblade, or ride a bike down the middle, and you just might meet the occasional horseback rider, properly attired in helmet, jacket, and high polished boots. Take the route farthest from the water, and you will walk past upscale shops and expensive restaurants.

a good walk

Walk east from the Kungliga Dramatiska Teatern, in Nybroplan, along Strandvägen until you get to Djurgårdsbron, the ornate little bridge that leads to the island of Djurgården. Resist going to the park, and instead turn left up Narvavägen and walk along the right-hand side until you reach Oscars Kyrka. Cross the street and continue up the left side until you reach the **Historiska Museet** 28 ▶. From here it's only a short walk farther up Narvavägen to Karlaplan, a pleasant circular park with a fountain. Go across or around the park to find Karlavägen. Heading northwest along this long boulevard, you'll pass by many small shops and galleries. At Nybrogatan turn left (this intersection is beyond the limits of the Stockholm map). Be sure to take some time to check out the exclusive furniture stores on your way down to **Östermalmstorg** 29, where there's an excellent indoor food market. Cut across the square and take a right down Sibyllegatan to the **Musik Museet** 30, installed in the city's oldest industrial building.

TIMING This tour requires a little more than a half day. You'll want to spend about an hour in each of the museums. Check ahead for Monday closings in the off-season.

㉘ ✕ **Historiska Museet** (Museum of National Antiquities). Viking treasures and the Gold Room are the main draw, but well-presented temporary exhibitions also cover various periods of Swedish history. The gift shop here is excellent. ⊠ *Narvav. 13–17, Östermalm* ☎ *08/51955600* ⊕ *www. historiska.se* ⌨ *Free* ☉ *Daily 10–5*

off the
beaten
path

MILLESGÅRDEN – This gallery and sculpture garden north of the city is dedicated to the property's former owner, American-Swedish sculptor Carl Milles (1875–1955) and is one of the most magical places in Stockholm. On display throughout the property are Milles's own unique works, and inside the main building, once his house, is his private collection. Millesgården can be easily reached via subway to Ropsten, where you catch the Lidingö train and get off at Herserud, the second stop. The trip takes about 30 minutes. ⊠ *Carl Milles väg 2, Lidingö* ☎ *08/4467580* ⊕ *www.millesgarden.se* ⌨ *SKr 80* ☉ *May–Sept., daily 11–5; Oct.–Apr., Tues.–Fri. noon–4, weekends 11–5.*

㉚ **Musik Museet.** Inside what was the military's bread bakery from the 17th century to the mid-1900s, the Music Museum has more than 6,000 instruments in its collection, with the focus on pieces from 1600 to 1850. Its 18th-century woodwind collection is internationally renowned. The museum also holds jazz, folk, and world-music concerts. Children are allowed to touch and play some of the instruments, and the motion-sensitive "Sound Room" lets you produce musical effects simply by gesturing and moving around. ⊠ *Sibylleg. 2, Östermalm* ☎ *08/51955490* ⊕ *www.musikmuseet.se* ⌨ *Free* ☉ *Tues.–Sun. 11–4.*

㉙ **Östermalmstorg.** The market square and its neighboring streets represent old, established Stockholm. **Saluhall** is more a collection of boutiques than an indoor food market; the fish displays can be especially intriguing. At the other end of the square, **Hedvig Eleonora Kyrka,** a church with characteristically Swedish faux-marble painting throughout its wooden interior, is the site of frequent lunchtime concerts in spring and summer. ⊠ *Nybrog. at Humlegårdsg., Östermalm.*

Outside the City

There are a number of excellent sites only a short bus or subway ride from the city center, many of which can be combined. Stockholm's city environs very quickly become greener as you leave the bustling center. Trips to nearly all these places could be done in a morning or afternoon and even added on to the other walks. Most are excellent ways to experience Sweden's delightful countryside.

WHAT TO SEE
Fodor'sChoice
★

Bergianska Trädgården. The beautiful Bergianska Botanical Gardens, on a peninsula extending out into the small bay of Brunnsvik, are a welcome respite from the city. They are only a short subway ride away. Paths weave along the water in the open park area. Visit Edvard Anderson's modern Växthus (Greenhouse) for its impressive Mediterranean and tropical environments. The century-old Victoriahuset (Victoria House) contains tropical plants as well, and has one of the best collections of water plants in the world. ⊠ *Frescativ. near university, Universitet* ☎ *08/*

54591700 ⊕ *www.bergianska.se* ✉ *Park free, Greenhouse SKr 40, Victoria House SKr 10* ☉ *Park daily yr-round; Victoria House May–Sept., daily 11–4, weekends 11–5; Greenhouse daily 11–5.*

Fjärilshuset (Butterfly and Bird House). After a short bus ride and a walk through the magnificent Haga Park, you could be in a room filled with hundreds of tropical butterflies. In the bird room, hundreds of birds of 40 species fly freely. The Haga Park itself is impressive and worth a lengthy stroll, but be sure to combine it with a trip to this oasis. ✉ *Take Bus 515 from the Odenplan subway stop. Haga* ☏ *08/7303981* ⊕ *www. fjarilshuset.se* ✉ *SKr 70* ☉ *Apr.–Sept., Tues.–Fri. 10–4, weekends 11–5:30; Oct.–Mar., Tues.–Fri. 10–3, weekends 11–4.*

Tyresö Slott (Tyresö Castle). After a 20-minute bus ride from southern Stockholm, you'll find yourself in the gorgeous, romantic gardens that surround this castle, built in the 1660s. The Nordic Museum led the renovations that restored the grounds to their late-1800s glory. The main building is filled with elaborate salons, libraries, and studies, and the west wing has a nice café and restaurant. Be sure to leave time for both the castle and gardens. ✉ *Take Bus 805 from Gullmarsplan to Tyresö Slott Tyresö* ☏ *08/7700178* ⊕ *www.nordiskamuseet.se/slott* ✉ *SKr 80* ☉ *Sept. and Oct., daily 11–3; June 22–Aug. 19, Tues.–Sun. 11–4. Tours at noon, 1, and 2.*

Where to Eat

Stockholm's restaurant scene rivals that of any major European capital, with upscale restaurants offering creative menus at trendy, modern locations. The best combine foreign innovations with Sweden's high-quality raw ingredients. The city's top restaurants will charge accordingly, but you aren't likely to leave disappointed. Of course, there are also plenty of less-expensive restaurants with traditional Swedish cooking. Among Swedish dishes, the best bets are wild game and fish, particularly salmon, and the smorgasbord buffet, which usually offers a good variety at an inexpensive price. Reservations are often necessary on weekends.

Downtown Stockholm & Beyond

$$$–$$$$ ✗ **Edsbacka Krog.** Chef Christer Lindström is the hot ticket behind the stoves of this ancient coaching inn just outside town; he produces rarefied feasts, classically French in technique, using fresh local ingredients. Critics bemoan the formality and the hush of this place, while fans focus on the exceptional food and faultless service. Don't expect anything too contemporary (inside you'll find old-style luster and exposed beams), but do expect near-perfection. ✉ *Sollentunav. 220, Sollentuna* ☏ *08/ 963300* ▭ *AE, DC, MC, V* ☉ *Closed Sun. and Mon.*

$$$–$$$$ ✗ **Restaurangen.** Flavor is the driving force behind this hip restaurant. It's also great fun to eat here. You build three-, five-, or seven-course meals from 20 flavors, 15 of which are salty and 5 of which are sweet. Each flavor has a letter next to it that corresponds to a list of wines by the glass that are recommended to best complement it. A large box of cutlery appears, to cover all your choices, and the wine is lined up with an identifying label on each glass. The food is considered contemporary

Asian, but French, Spanish, and Swedish all appear too. The achingly cool interior was created by three students from Stockholm's prestigious Beckman's School of Design. ✉ *Oxtorgsg. 14, City* ☎ *08/220952* ⊟ *AE, DC, MC, V* ⊘ *Closed Sun.*

★ **$$$–$$$$** ✕ **Wedholms Fisk.** Noted for its fresh seafood dishes, Wedholms Fisk is appropriately set by a bay in Stockholm's center. High ceilings, large windows, and tasteful modern paintings from the owner's personal collection create a spacious, sophisticated space. The traditional Swedish cuisine, which consists almost exclusively of seafood, is simple but outstanding. The menu is divided by fish type, with a number of dish options for each type of fish, such as monkfish with a porcini cream sauce and a warm bean salad. ✉ *Nybrokajen 17, City* ☎ *08/6117874* ⊟ *AE, DC, MC, V* ⊘ *Closed Sun. and July.*

$$$ ✕ **Bon Lloc.** With an elegant and spacious dining area and a creative

Fodor's Choice Mediterranean-influenced menu, Bon Lloc has established itself as one

★ of the hottest restaurants in town. The menu uses common ingredients like ham and cod to create dishes that recall Catalonia as much as Sweden. The extensive wine list offers an excellent selection of European wines. The interior's light-brown wood and mosaic tiles allude to Mediterranean styles while still evoking Swedish simplicity, much as the food does. ✉ *Regeringsg. 111, Norrmalm* ☎ *08/6606060* ⌖ *Reservations essential* ⊟ *AE, DC, MC, V* ⊘ *Closed Sun. No lunch.*

$$$ ✕ **Fredsgatan 12.** The government crowd files into this funky restaurant

Fodor's Choice at lunch; a more casual yet stylish crowd arrives at night. All come here

★ to enjoy what is some of the best food in town. The young chef, Melker Andersson, works his magic, creating Swedish-, Asian-, and European-inspired dishes that defy convention and positively demand enjoyment. The menu offers creative combinations, such as chicken with eucalyptus or lamb with dill, licorice, and carrots. ✉ *Fredsg. 12, City* ☎ *08/248052* ⊟ *AE, DC, MC, V* ⊘ *Closed Sun. No lunch.*

$$$ ✕ **Ulriksdals Wärdshus.** The weekend lunchtime smorgasbord at this country inn can't be beat. Built in the park of an 18th-century palace in 1868, the beautiful glassed-in dining room, accented with light floral patterns and mint-green seat covers, overlooks orchards and a peaceful lake. It's an expensive restaurant, but the impeccable service and outstanding cuisine make the splurge worthwhile. Menu highlights include terrine of foie gras with rhubarb and cardamom or halibut with asparagus and sorrel. The restaurant's cellar is listed in Guinness world records as the most complete in the world. ✉ *Ulriksdals Slottspark, Solna* ☎ *08/850815* ⌖ *Reservations essential* ⊟ *AE, DC, MC, V* ⊘ *No dinner Sun.*

★ **$$$** ✕ **Vasa Eggen.** An exquisite dining room offering the real feeling of being hidden away makes this haunt a top choice among Stockholmers. Vasa Eggen is less talked about than Stockholm's other great restaurants, but no less fabulous. The food is strikingly modern, blending French and Asian techniques with top-quality local ingredients. Fans of the visual will love the clean, simple lines and the natural tones of the restaurant, which are perfectly juxtaposed by a statement-making stained-glass ceiling dome. ✉ *Birger Jarlsg. 29, Östermalm* ☎ *08/216169* ⌖ *Reservations essential* ⊟ *AE, DC, MC, V* ⊘ *Closed Sun. No lunch Sat.*

★ **$$–$$$** ✕ **Lux.** The former Electrolux household appliance factory is now an industrial-chic restaurant; hence the name. Simple wood furniture and white-cloth tables contrast nicely with the exposed brick and wrought iron of the former work space. Light floods the restaurant through enormous windows during the day. At night the space is more subdued. Young chefs Henrik Norström and Peter Johansson work the stoves here, producing fresh, light, and innovative modern European food, using excellent local ingredients. ✉ *Primusg. 116, Lilla Essingen* ☎ *08/6190190* ⌦ *Reservations essential* ☰ *AE, DC, MC, V* ☉ *Closed Mon. No lunch weekends.*

$$–$$$ ✕ **Ulla Winbladh.** Since 1897 this fine old inn on the island paradise of Djurgården has been serving classic Swedish dishes to its happy customers. The restaurant is a maze of several small dining rooms, some with exposed brick walls and scrubbed wood tables, others with softly upholstered chairs, Swedish linen on the tables, and every inch of wall space taken up by pictures. As for the food, there are plenty of native classics, but you can get delicious modern Italian cuisine, as well. ✉ *Rosendalsv. 8, Djurgården* ☎ *08/6630571* ⌦ *Reservations essential* ☰ *AE, DC, MC, V.*

$–$$$ ✕ **Storstad.** A lighter and less-expensive menu is served in the bar area of this popular hangout, which looks out on the street through wide arching windows. In the sparse but inviting dining room in the back you might try the sweet-corn soup with truffle pasta and Parmesan cheese before moving on to meat specialties such as fried duck breast with honey-baked beets, mushroom spring rolls, and port syrup. The wine list is excellent and especially strong on French and Californian wines. ✉ *Odeng. 41, Vasastan* ☎ *08/6733800* ⌦ *Reservations essential* ☰ *AE, DC, MC, V* ☉ *Closed Sun. No lunch.*

¢–$$$ ✕ **Tranan.** There's something about Tranan that makes you want to go back. The food is Swedish with a touch of French and is consistently very good. The stark walls covered with old movie posters and the red-and-white-checked tablecloths are reminders of the days when it was a workingman's beer parlor. Try the *biff rydberg,* a fillet of beef, fried potatoes, horseradish, and egg yolk—it's a Swedish classic. ✉ *Karlbergsv. 14, Vasastan* ☎ *08/52728100* ☰ *AE, DC, MC, V* ☉ *No lunch weekends.*

$$ ✕ **Lisa På Udden.** Fish is the order of the day at this light and airy waterside restaurant on Stockholm's beautiful Djurgården island. The spacious modern interior is decked out in very Scandinavian style: wood floors, simple wood furniture, and primary colors. The main draw, though, is the view across the water, through the restaurant's glass facade. The tables fill up, especially on weekends, so turn up early or late to secure one for yourself. ✉ *Biskopsv. 9, Djurgården* ☎ *08/6609475* ☰ *MC, V.*

★ **$$** ✕ **Prinsen.** Still in the same location as when it opened in 1897, the Prince serves both traditional and modern Swedish cuisine, but it is for the traditional that most people go. The interior is rich with mellow, warm lighting; dark-wood paneling; and leather chairs and booths. The restaurant is rightly known for its scampi salad and *Wallenbergare,* a classic dish of veal, cream, and peas. Downstairs are a bar and a space for larger parties. ✉ *Mäster Samuelsg. 4, City* ☎ *08/6111331* ☰ *AE, DC, MC, V* ☉ *No lunch weekends.*

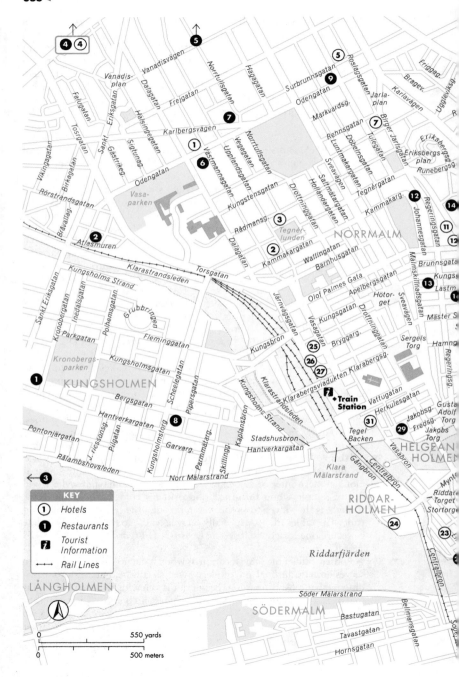

Where to Stay & Eat in Northern Stockholm

Restaurants ▼	
Bon Lloc	12
Den Gyldene Freden	22
East	17
Edsbacka Krog	10
Eriks Bakficka	11
Franska Matsalen	28
Fredsgatan 12	28
Grill Ruby	23
Halv trappa plus gård	16
Il Forno	2
India Curry House	8
Källaren Movitz	25
Kjellsons	14
Lisa På Udden	21
Lux	3
Mistral	26
Pontus in the Green House	24
Prinsen	18
Restaurangen	13
Roppongi	1
Stockholms Matvarufabriken	5
Storstad	9
Sturehof	19
Tranan	7
Ulla Winbladh	20
Ulriksdals Wärdshus	4
Vasa Eggen	15
Wasahof	6
Wedholms Fisk	27

Hotels ▼	
af Chapman	19
Arcadia	6
Bema	2
Berns	28
Birger Jarl	7
Claes på Hörnet	5
Central Hotel	25
Crystal Plaza Hotel	11
Diplomat	14
Grand Hotel	30
Hotel Esplanade	15
Hotel Gustav Wasa	1
Hotel Riddargatan	18
Lady Hamilton	21
Lydmar Hotel	13
Mornington	16
Mälardrottningen	24
Nordic Hotel	26
Örnsköld	17
Pärlan	9
Radisson SAS Strand Hotel	29
Reisen	20
Rica Hotel Gamla Stan	22
Royal Viking Radisson SAS Hotel	27
Sheraton Hotel and Towers	31
Stallmästaregården	4
Stockholm Plaza Hotel	12
Tegnérlunden	3
Victory	23
Villa Källhagen	10
Wellington	8

$$ ✕ **Stockholms Matvarufabriken.** Although it's a bit hard to find, tucked away as it is on a side street, Stockholm's Food Factory is well worth seeking out. The popular bistro restaurant, serving French, Italian, and Swedish cuisine, is packed full on the weekends as young and old come to enjoy the exposed-brick, candlelight-infused dining room and the varied menu. Here omelets are taken to new levels with ingredients such as truffles and asparagus; the choices when it comes to fresh seafood are excellent. Brown-paper tablecloths and kitchen cloths used as napkins set the informal tone. ✉ *Idung. 12, Vasastan* ☎ *08/320704* ▤ *AE, DC, MC, V* ☉ *No lunch.*

$$ ✕ **Sturehof.** This massive complex of a restaurant with two huge bars is a complete social, architectural, and dining experience amid wood paneling, leather chairs and sofas, and distinctive lighting fixtures. There's a bar directly facing Stureplan where you can sit on a summer night and watch Stockholmers gather at the nearby Svampen (the mushroomlike concrete structure that has been the city's meeting point for years). In the elegant dining room fine Swedish cuisine is offered. Upstairs is the O-Bar, a dark and smoky lounge filled well into the night with young people and loud music. ✉ *Stureplan 2, City* ☎ *08/4405730* ▤ *AE, DC, MC, V.*

$$ ✕ **Wasahof.** Across the street from Vasaparken, and just a short walk from Odenplan, Wasahof feels like an authentic bistro, but the cooking actually mixes Swedish, French, and Italian recipes. The pleasantly rustic space and good food have attracted all kinds of culturati—actors, writers, journalists—for some time. Seafood is a specialty here—this is the place in Stockholm to get oysters. ✉ *Dalag. 46, Vasastan* ☎ *08/323440* ▤ *AE, DC, MC, V* ☉ *Closed Sun.*

$–$$ ✕ **East.** Just off Stureplan, East is one of the city's culinary hot spots, offering enticing contemporary pan-Asian fare from Thailand, Japan, Korea, and Vietnam. Order a selection of appetizers to get a sampling of this cross-cultural cooking. East is a perfect spot to have dinner before a night on the town. Try the Luxor: chicken, tiger shrimp, and egg noodles with peanuts, mint leaves, and coconut sauce. The bar area at this vibrant restaurant turns into a miniclub at night, with soul and hip-hop on the turntables. ✉ *Stureplan 13, Norrmalm* ☎ *08/6114959* ▤ *AE, DC, MC, V* ☉ *No lunch weekends.*

$–$$ ✕ **Halv trappa plus gård.** This hip restaurant is exactly what its name suggests: two half floors plus a pleasant courtyard. The retro vibe here harks back to the '70s. The menu emphasizes fish, most of it done with a Mediterranean flair. The staff is good-hearted and professional. When possible, eat in the courtyard, but book a table, since there are only 10 out there. ✉ *Lästmakarg. 3, City* ☎ *08/6781050* ▤ *AE, DC, MC, V* ☉ *Closed Sun. No lunch.*

$–$$ ✕ **Kjellsons.** This pleasant hub is a bar first and a restaurant second, but this doesn't mean the menu is short on high-caliber dishes (to say nothing of fine drinks). Appetizers include an excellent pea soup (a Swedish tradition) and a delicious avocado-and-smoked-ham salad—most of the fare is traditional Swedish. And be sure to ask for a basket of cracker bread—it comes with a tube of the famous caviar. In summer there's outdoor seating. ✉ *Birger Jarlsg. 36, City* ☎ *08/6110045* ▤ *AE, DC, MC, V.*

¢–$$ ✕ **Roppongi.** Although far from downtown and not exactly in the most happening area, Roppongi's adventurous, creative menu and quality fish make it the best sushi place in Stockholm. This means it's almost always packed, so be ready to share the stripped-down space with other sushi lovers. The shrimp tempura rolls will leave you drooling for more, and the *tamaki* cones are plump and bursting with flavor. ⊠ *Hantverkarg. 76, Kungsholmen* ☎ *08/6501772* ▭ *MC, V* ⊘ *No lunch weekends.*

$ ✕ **India Curry House.** The name pretty much says it all: you will find the best Indian food in Stockholm here, but if you are searching for more than that, don't come. The decor is a nondescript hodgepodge (more tacky-mess than shabby-chic). The waiters are not rude, but neither are they superfriendly or efficient. But none of this matters if you have a hankering for great Indian food—you'll find searingly spicy vindaloo, mildly aromatic korma, and everything else in between. Delicious. ⊠ *Scheeleg. 6, Kungsholmen* ☎ *08/6502024* ▭ *MC, V* ⊘ *Closed weekends.*

¢–$ ✕ **Il Forno.** You might not expect to find brick-oven pizza in Sweden, but Il Forno serves some of the best you'll find north of the Mediterranean. Choose from more than 25 combinations, all of which use only the freshest ingredients and a tasty, crunchy crust. The kitchen also churns out a number of pasta dishes and sells many varieties of Italian olives, olive oil, and other fine foods. Sit outside when possible—the interior can feel a bit stuffy. ⊠ *Atlasg. 9, Vasastan* ☎ *08/319049* ▭ *MC, V.*

Fodor's Choice ★

Gamla Stan, Skeppsholmen & Södermalm

★ $$$–$$$$ ✕ **Franska Matsalen.** This classic French restaurant in the Grand Hotel serves the best true French cuisine in the city—plus, you can enjoy an inspiring view of Gamla Stan and the Royal Palace across the inner harbor waters. The menu changes five times a year, but the emphasis is always on Swedish ingredients. Expect such dishes as pike perch with oxtail and truffles. The lofty measure of opulence here is commensurate with the bill. ⊠ *Grand Hotel, Södra Blasieholmsh. 8, City* ☎ *08/6793584* ⌲ *Reservations essential* ⌂ *Jacket required* ▭ *AE, DC, MC, V* ⊘ *Closed Sun. No lunch weekends.*

★ $$$–$$$$ ✕ **Pontus in the Green House.** The Green House oozes class: opulent but tasteful interiors, soft lighting, wood panels, and crisp table linen. The menu has both traditional Swedish and contemporary international cuisines. Everything is delicious, and expensive. For a calmer dining experience, choose a corner table upstairs; the ground floor always bustles. You'll be dining among Sweden's rich and famous. For a cheaper menu of traditional Swedish dishes, and slightly less fanfare, sit at the bar downstairs. ⊠ *Österlångg. 17, Gamla Stan* ☎ *08/54521300* ⌲ *Reservations essential* ▭ *AE, DC, MC, V* ⊘ *Closed Sun. No lunch Sat.*

$$$ ✕ **Den Gyldene Freden.** Sweden's most famous old tavern has been open for business since 1722. The haunt of bards and barristers, artists and ad people, Freden could probably serve sawdust and still be popular, but the food and staff are worthy of the restaurant's hallowed reputation. The cuisine has a Swedish orientation, but Continental influences spice up the menu. Season permitting, try the oven-baked fillets of turbot served with chanterelles and crepes; the gray hen fried with spruce twigs

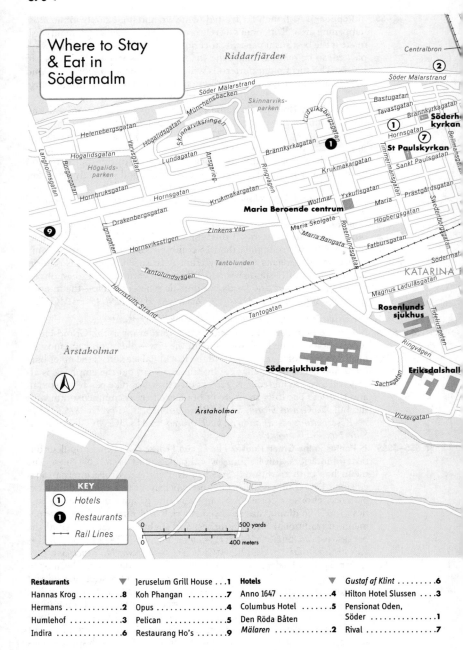

Where to Stay & Eat in Södermalm

Riddarfjärden

Centralbron

Söder Mälarstrand

Skinnarviks-parken

Söderh kyrkan

St Paulskyrkan

Maria Beroende centrum

KATARINA

Tantolunden

Rosenlunds sjukhus

Årstaholmar

Södersjukhuset

Eriksdalshall

Årstaholmar

KEY
① *Hotels*
❶ *Restaurants*
←→ *Rail Lines*

0 _____ 500 yards
0 _____ 400 meters

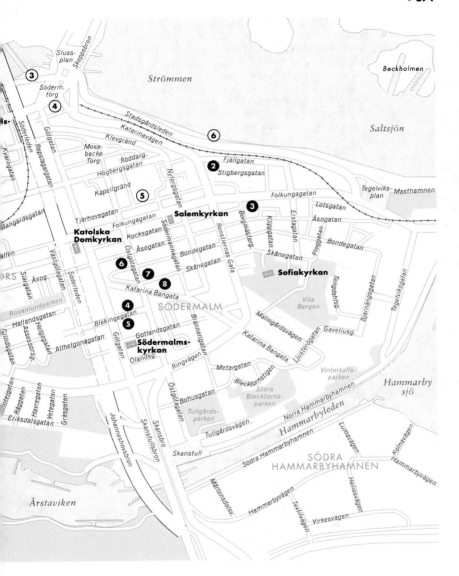

Beckholmen

Strömmen

Saltsjön

Sluss-
plan

Söderm.
torg

③

④

Stadsgårdsleden

Katarinavägen

Klevgränd

Mose-
backe
Torg

Roddarg.

Högbergsgatan

Kapellgränd

⑤

Fjällgatan ❷

Stigbergsgatan

Tegelviks-
plan

Masthamnen

Folkungagatan

Lotsgatan

Tjärhovsgatan

Folkungagatan

Salemkyrkan

❸

Borgmästarg.

Klippgatan

Erstagatan

Åsogatan

**Katolska
Domkyrkan**

Kocksgatan

Åsogatan

Bondegatan

Skånegatan

Renstiernas Gata

Skånegatan

Plogatan

Bondegatan

⑥

⑦

❽

Katarina Bangata

Sofiakyrkan

Tengdahlsg.

Bjärnångsgatan

Tegelviksgatan

❹

Blekingegatan

❺

SÖDERMALM

Vita
Bergen

Malmgårdsvägen

Gaveliusg.

Rosenlundparken

Hallandsgatan

Gotlandsgatan

**Södermalms-
kyrkan**

Ölandsg.

Brännerigatan

Ringvägen

Katarina Bangata

Ljusterögatan

Allhelgonagatan

Metargatan

Blecktornsstigen

Vintertulls-
parken

**Hammarby
sjö**

Östgötagatan

Bohusgatan

Stora
Blecktorns-
parken

Tullgårds-
parken

Johanneshovsbron

Skansbro

Skanstullsbron

Tullgårdsvägen

Norra Hammarbyhamnen

Hammarbyleden

Skanstull

Södra Hammarbyhamnen

SÖDRA
HAMMARBYHAMNEN

Lunavägen

Kölnavägen

Hammarbyvägen

Årstaviken

Mårtensdalsv.

Hammarbyvägen

Textilvägen

Heliosvägen

Virkesvägen

and dried fruit is another good selection. ⊠ *Österlångg. 51, Gamla Stan* ☎ *08/249760* ▤ *AE, DC, MC, V* ⊗ *Closed Sun. No lunch.*

$$$ ✕ **Mistral.** Mistral's chief attraction seems to be that it is near impossi-
Fodor's Choice   ble to get in; as with all things unobtainable, everyone wants it. If you
★   do manage to get yourself one of the 18 "dinner only, no weekend" ta-
bles, you will quickly realize that Mistral has a great deal of bite to back
up its considerable bark. The food here is modern and creative, relay-
ing heavily on very local ingredients; witness the smelt, line-caught
from the waters just a few hundred feet from the restaurant's front door.
Book a long, long time in advance. ⊠ *Lilla Nyg. 21, Gamla Stan* ☎ *08/
101224* ⊲ *Reservations essential* ▤ *AE, DC, MC, V* ⊗ *Closed week-
ends, Mon., and July. No lunch.*

$$–$$$ ✕ **Eriks Bakficka.** A favorite among Östermalm locals, Eriks Bakficka is
a block from the elegant waterside, a few steps down from street level.
Inside, the black-and-white tile floor, white-painted stone walls, wood
tables strewn with candles, and green-glass lamps give the place a re-
laxed and approachable ambience. Owned by the well-known Swedish
chef Erik Lallerstedt, the restaurant serves Swedish dishes, including a
delicious baked pike fish with mussels and saffron. A lower-priced menu
is served in the pub section. ⊠ *Fredrikshovsg. 4, Östermalm* ☎ *08/
6601599* ▤ *AE, DC, MC, V* ⊗ *Closed July. No lunch weekends.*

$–$$ ✕ **Grill Ruby.** This American-style barbecue joint (at least as American
as it is possible to be in Gamla Stan) is just a cobblestone's throw away
from the statue of St. George slaying the dragon. Next door to its
French cousin, Bistro Ruby, Grill Ruby skips the escargots and instead
focuses on grilled meats and fish. The steak with french fries and béarnaise sauce is delicious. On Sunday an American-style brunch is served,
where you can enjoy huevos rancheros and a big Bloody Mary while
blues and country music drift from the speakers. ⊠ *Österlångg. 14, Gamla
Stan* ☎ *08/206015* ▤ *AE, DC, MC, V.*

$–$$ ✕ **Hannas Krog.** This bohemian neighborhood restaurant is almost al-
ways filled with locals. Although it may not be as supertrendy as it was
a decade ago, it remains a Södermalm hot spot. Diners are serenaded
at 10 minutes to the hour by a mooing cow that emerges from the cuckoo
clock just inside the door. The dishes—from Caribbean shrimp to
Provençal lamb—are all flavorful. The bar in the basement is loud but
pleasant. Local bands play there on occasion. ⊠ *Skåneg. 80, Södermalm*
☎ *08/6438225* ▤ *AE, DC, MC, V* ⊗ *No lunch weekends and July.*

$–$$ ✕ **Källaren Movitz.** At first glance Movitz looks like nothing more than
a typical European pub, which is exactly what it is upstairs. But downstairs it's a restaurant serving Swedish cuisine with French and Italian
influences. The refined table settings and abundant candlelight reflecting off the curves of the light yellow walls of what used to be a potato
cellar in the 1600s make this an elegant place to dine. Dishes are simple affairs with a real dinner-party-at-home feel; expect menu choices
such as game, pasta, salmon, and plenty of rich sauces. ⊠ *Tyska Brinken
34, Gamla Stan* ☎ *08/209979* ▤ *AE, DC, MC, V* ⊗ *Closed Sun.*

★ **$–$$**   ✕ **Koh Phangan.** Creative food is served until midnight at this lively Thai
restaurant, where you'll be seated in individual "huts," each with a special name and style. The entire restaurant is decked out in colored lights,

fake palm fronds, and trinkets from Thailand. Sign up for a table on the chalkboard next to the bar when you arrive. Although you can expect at least an hour-long wait on weekends, the food is well worth it. Grilled fish and seafood with extravagant, spicy sauces are the specialty. ⊠ *Skåneg. 57, Södermalm* ☎ *08/6425040* ⌲ *Reservations not accepted* ⊟ *AE, DC, MC, V.*

$–$$ ✕ **Opus.** Don't let the stripped-down, albeit charming, small space fool you—Opus's food packs a big-time punch and has earned it a reputation as a top French restaurant in town. Everything is prepared with intense care by the French-born and -trained cook. Together they own this popular little restaurant, where the sauces are unbeatable. Try the pork fillet with chanterelle sauce or the perch fillet with avocado sauce to find out for yourself. As the restaurant has only 10 tables, be sure to call ahead. ⊠ *Blekingeg. 63, Södermalm* ☎ *08/6446080* ⌲ *Reservations essential* ⊟ *AE, DC, MC, V* ⊘ *Closed Sun. No dinner Mon.*

¢–$$ ✕ **Humlehof.** If you're feeling extrahungry and a bit tight on funds, go straight to this Bavarian restaurant serving traditional Swedish and eastern European dishes. Start by ordering an ice-cold Czech or Austrian draft beer, a bowl of what has to be the best goulash in Stockholm, and the *schweizer* (Swiss-style) schnitzel, which is as big as your face and served with salad and fried potatoes. If schnitzel's not your thing, try the panfried Haloumi cheese with sun-dried tomatoes, summer salad, and garlic bread. ⊠ *Folkungag. 128, Södermalm* ☎ *08/6410302* ⊟ *MC, V.*

¢–$$ ✕ **Pelican.** Beer, beer, and more beer is the order of the day at Pelican,
Fodor'sChoice a traditional working-class drinking hall, a relic of the days when Sö-
★ dermalm was the dwelling place of the city's blue-collar brigade. Today's more bohemian residents find it just as enticing, with the unvarnished wood-paneled walls, faded murals, and glass globe lights fulfilling all their down-at-the-heel pretensions. The food here is some of the best traditional Swedish fare in the city. The herring, meatballs, and salted bacon with onion sauce are not to be missed. ⊠ *Blekingeg. 40, Södermalm* ☎ *08/55609090* ⌲ *Reservations not accepted* ⊟ *MC, V* ⊘ *Closed Sun.*

$ ✕ **Restaurang Ho's.** Walk into this hidden gem of a Chinese restaurant and something about it just feels right. Nothing fancy—Ho's lets its authentic, intensely flavored food speak for itself. With more than 100 choices, the menu seems never-ending and includes Chinese takes on duck, squid, scallops, pork, chicken, beef, and tofu. The stir-fried squid with green and red peppers in black-bean sauce packs a serious punch. Finish with a classic fried banana and ice cream. ⊠ *Hornsg. 151, Södermalm* ☎ *08/844420* ⊟ *MC, V* ⊘ *Closed Mon.*

¢–$ ✕ **Hermans.** Hermans is a haven for vegetarians out to get the most bang
Fodor'sChoice for their kronor. The glassed-in back deck and open garden both pro-
★ vide breathtaking vistas across the water of Stockholm harbor, Gamla Stan, and the island of Djurgården. The food is always served buffet style and includes various vegetable and pasta salads, warm casseroles, and such entrées as Indonesian stew with peanut sauce and vegetarian lasagna. The fruit pies, chocolate cakes, and cookies are delicious. ⊠ *Fjällg. 23A, Södermalm* ☎ *08/6439480* ⊟ *MC, V.*

¢–$ ✕ **Indira.** This busy Indian restaurant about a block off Götgatan has an overwhelming 60 meal choices. The food is cheap and delicious and the service fast. Order as soon as you enter and find a seat at one of the mosaic-coated tables. There are a number of tables in the basement as well, so don't leave right away if it looks packed on the first floor. The chicken korma, with raisins and cashews, is fantastic, and the honey-saffron ice cream is a perfect end to a meal. ⊠ *Bondeg. 3B, Södermalm* ☎ *08/6414046* ☐ *MC, V.*

¢ ✕ **Jerusalem Grill House.** Enter this wild grill and it may be hard to believe you're still in Stockholm. The men behind the counter sing along to music blaring from the sound system, and the menu is in both Swedish and Arabic. On the walls are surreal landscape paintings, odd sculptures, and loads of hookahs—in fact, there are five or six pipes that the regulars use to smoke their tobacco. Falafel, chicken kebabs, gyros, fried-vegetable plates, lamb fillets—they've got it all, as well as authentic Arabic tea and coffee. ⊠ *Hornsg. 92, Södermalm* ☎ *08/6684131* ☐ *No credit cards.*

Where to Stay

Although Stockholm has a reputation for prohibitively expensive hotels, great deals can be found in summer, when prices are substantially lower and numerous discounts are available. More than 50 hotels offer the "Stockholm Package," which includes accommodations for one night, breakfast, and the Stockholmskortet, or Stockholm Card, which entitles the cardholder to free admission to museums and travel on public transport. Details are available from travel agents, tourist bureaus, and the **Stockholm Information Service** (🖰 Box 7542, 103 93 Stockholm ☎08/7892400 🖷08/7892450). Also try **Hotellcentralen** (⊠ Centralstation, 111 20 Stockholm ☎ 08/7892425 🖷 08/7918666); the service is free if you go in person, but a fee applies if you call.

All rooms in the hotels reviewed below are equipped with shower or bath unless otherwise noted. Unless otherwise stated, hotels do not have air-conditioning. Some hotels close during the winter holidays; call ahead if you expect to travel during that time.

Downtown Stockholm & Beyond

$$$$ 🏨 **Sheraton Hotel and Towers.** Popular with business executives, the Sheraton is also an ideal hotel for the tourist on a generous budget looking for comfort and luxury. English is the main language at the restaurant and bar, which fill up at night once the piano player arrives. The lobby is a vast steel-and-glass affair with huge vases of fresh cut flowers, adding a dash of color. There's a gift shop selling Swedish crystal and international newspapers. Rooms have hardwood floors, leather chairs, thick rugs, and sturdy, cherrywood furniture. ⊠ *Tegelbacken 6, City, 101 23* ☎ *08/4123400* 🖷 *08/4123409* ⊕ *www.sheratonstockholm. com* 🛏 *462 rooms, 30 suites, ₺ 2 restaurants, room service, a/c, room TVs with movies, in-room broadband, in-room data ports, Wi-Fi, gym, sauna, piano bar, casino, convention center, parking (fee), no-smoking rooms* ☐ *AE, DC, MC, V* 🍽 *BP.*

★ $$$–$$$$ 🏨 **Berns Hotel.** This subtly ultramodern hotel was a hot spot when it opened its doors in the late 19th century, and it retains that status today. Rooms here have hardwood floors, white walls, feather-stuffed white quilts and fabrics in cobalt blue, chocolate brown, moss green, and stone—a lesson in comfortable modernism. All feature a rotating wooden tower containing TV, CD player, and minibar. The restaurant/ bar is a joint venture with restaurant entrepreneur and designer Terence Conran. Hotel rates include the use of a nearby fitness center with a pool. ⊠ *Näckströmsg. 8, City, 111 47* ☎ *08/56632000* 🖨 *08/56632201* ⊕ *www.berns.se* 🛏 *65 rooms, 3 suites* ⚐ *Restaurant, room service, a/c, minibars, in-room broadband, Wi-Fi, bar, meeting room, no-smoking rooms* ⊟ *AE, DC, MC, V* ⁑⦿⁑ *BP.*

$$$–$$$$ 🖳 **Nordic Hotel.** Next to the central station, this modern center for the business traveler is actually two hotels—Nordic Light and Nordic Sea— in one. Nordic Light focuses on simplicity, and, not surprisingly, light plays an important role, with responsive sound-and-movement systems in the lobby and multiple light settings, including light-therapy treat-ment, in the rooms. Rooms are a mix of dark wood, gray flannel, and black-and-white tile, with adjustable spotlights in the ceiling. Nordic Sea uses lighter wood with lots of blue fabric and mosaic tiles to create a Mediterranean touch. ⊠ *Vasaplan, City, 101 37* ☎ *08/50563000* 🖨 *08/ 50563060* ⊕ *www.nordichotels.se* 🛏 *542 rooms, 28 suites* ⚐ *2 restau-rants, room service, a/c, room TVs with movies, in-room broadband, in-room data ports, Wi-Fi, 2 bars, 2 lounges, meeting rooms, parking (fee), no-smoking rooms* ⊟ *AE, DC, MC, V* ⁑⦿⁑ *BP.*

$$$ 🖳 **Royal Viking (Radisson SAS).** For the weary traveler, the Royal Viking's location right next to the central station is a gift; fall off the airport train and into one of the comfortable beds. When you awake, enjoy the at-tractive natural textiles and artwork, sturdy writing desks, separate seating areas, and plush robes in the large bathrooms. Triple-glazed win-dows and plenty of insulation keep traffic noise to a minimum. At night the excellent bar can get extremely busy. ⊠ *Vasag. 1, City, 101 24* ☎ *08/50654000* 🖨 *08/50654001* ⊕ *www.radissonsas.com* 🛏 *459 rooms, 21 suites* ⚐ *Restaurant, room service, a/c, minibars, room TVs with movies, in-room broadband, Wi-Fi, indoor pool, sauna, bar, con-vention center, no-smoking rooms* ⊟ *AE, MC, V.*

$$$ 🖳 **Stallmästaregården.** Romance is the loose theme at this hotel, with light-filled rooms stuffed with 18th-century Swedish antiques and Chi-nese artifacts. Despite the goods, rooms seem to retain an air of sim-plicity that befits a Scandinavian-designed hotel. Each room is different in design, but all share the pleasing trait of not really feeling like hotel rooms. Add to this the delightful parkland setting. Downtown Stock-holm a mere 10 minutes away by car. ⊠ *Nortull, Haga, 113 47* ☎ *08/ 6101300* 🖨 *08/6103140* ⊕ *www.stallmastaregarden.se* 🛏 *49 rooms, 4 suites* ⚐ *Restaurant, in-room broadband, bar, meeting rooms, free park-ing, no-smoking rooms* ⊟ *AE, DC, MC, V* ⁑⦿⁑ *BP.*

$$–$$$ 🖳 **Birger Jarl.** At this high-design hotel the lobby doubles as a modern-art gallery, with frequently changing exhibitions. Some rooms have been individually designed by several of the country's top designers: it costs extra to stay in these. Most rooms are not large, but all are well furnished and have nice touches, such as heated towel racks in the bath-rooms; all double rooms have bathtubs. ⊠ *Tuleg. 8, Vasastan, 104 32*

☎ *08/6741800* 🖷 *08/6737366* ⊕ *www.birgerjarl.se* ⤵ *225 rooms* ᐧᐧ *Coffee shop, room service, in-room broadband, in-room data ports, sauna, meeting room, no-smoking rooms* ▭ *AE, DC, MC, V* ⭦ *BP.*

$$–$$$ 🖵 **Crystal Plaza Hotel.** Housed in one of Stockholm's oldest hotel buildings (1895), the Crystal Plaza, with a circular tower and peach walls, is sure to catch the eye of anyone walking down Birger Jarlsgatan. Most rooms have a mix of birch-wood furniture, hardwood floors with small rugs, and the requisite hotel artwork on the walls. Rooms facing the inner courtyard can be a bit quieter than those on the street. The hotel's location, close to the hip bars of Stureplan and downtown shopping, makes it an ideal place for folks looking to have quick access to a good time in the city. ⊠ *Birger Jarlsg. 35, City, 111 45* ☎ *08/4068800* 🖷 *08/241511* ⊕ *www.crystalplazahotel.se* ⤵ *111 rooms, 1 suite* ᐧᐧ *Restaurant, minibars, in-room broadband, bar, no-smoking rooms* ▭ *AE, DC, MC, V* ⭦ *BP.*

★ **$$–$$$** 🖵 **Lydmar Hotel.** Favored by black-clad music- and film-industry types, the Lydmar appeals to the more aesthetically conscious traveler. Only a 10-minute walk from the downtown hub of Sergels Torg and right on the doorstep of Stureplan, the epicenter of Stockholm's nightlife, the Lydmar is more than just a hotel—it's also one of the trendiest bars in town. Rooms here are ultramodern with such features as sunken beds, wall-mounted light panels, polished concrete walls, plasma-screen TVs, Italian sofas, asymmetric coffee tables and super-soft bed quilts. ⊠ *Stureg. 10, City, 114 36* ☎ *08/56611300* 🖷 *08/56611301* ⊕ *www.lydmar.se* ⤵ *61 rooms, 5 suites* ᐧᐧ *Restaurant, room service, a/c, minibars, in-room DVD, in-room broadband, Wi-Fi, sauna, bar, meeting room, no-smoking rooms* ▭ *AE, DC, MC, V* ⭦ *BP.*

$$–$$$ ✕🖵 **Villa Källhagen.** The changing seasons are on display in this beautiful country hotel, reflected through the huge windows, glass walls, and **Fodor'sChoice** bedroom skylights. Rooms are spacious and furnished in light woods ★ and beautifully colored fabrics. It's only a few minutes from the city center, but its woodland surroundings can put you a million miles away. The restaurant also relies heavily on the seasons, serving a delicious blend of fresh Swedish ingredients cooked with a French influence. ⊠ *Djurgårdsbrunnsv. 10, N. Djurgården, 115 27* ☎ *08/6650300* 🖷 *08/6650399* ⊕ *www.kallhagen.se* ⤵ *20 rooms* ᐧᐧ *Restaurant, bar, meeting room, no-smoking rooms* ▭ *AE, DC, MC, V* ⭦ *BP.*

$$ 🖵 **Central Hotel.** Less than 300 yards from the central station, this practical hotel lives up to its name. The reception area is white, with a skylight, giving an immediate freshness and simplicity to the hotel. Rooms follow suit, with only the burgundy curtains and chairs interrupting the otherwise pleasing minimalism. Thanks to extra sound insulation, the chaos of Vasagatan remains outside the room. Bathrooms have showers only. ⊠ *Vasag. 38, City, 101 20* ☎ *08/56620800* 🖷 *08/247573* ⊕ *www.centralhotel.se* ⤵ *93 rooms, 1 suite* ᐧᐧ *In-room broadband, in-room data ports, meeting room, no-smoking rooms* ▭ *AE, DC, MC, V* ⭦ *BP.*

★ **$$** ✕🖵 **Claes på Hörnet.** This may be the most exclusive—and smallest—hotel in town, with only 10 rooms in a former 1739 inn. The rooms, comfortably furnished with period antiques, go quickly (book three or so months in advance, especially around Christmas). The restaurant ($$) is worth visiting even if you don't spend the night: its old-fashioned dining room serves Swedish and Continental dishes such as outstanding *strömming* (Baltic herring) and cloudberry mousse cake. ☒ *Surbrunnsg. 20, Vasastan, 113 48* ☎ *08/165130* 🖶 *08/6125315* 🛏 *10 rooms* ⅋ *Restaurant* ▤ *AE, DC, MC, V* ⍓ *BP.*

$$ ✗🖼 **Stockholm Plaza Hotel.** On one of Stockholm's foremost streets for shopping and entertainment, and only a short walk from the city's nightlife and business center, this hotel is ideal if you want to be in a central location. The building was built in 1884, and the Elite hotel chain took over in 1984. Rooms are furnished in an elegant, traditional manner, and many include the original stuccowork on the ceilings. ☒ *Birger Jarlsg. 29, Downtown, 103 95* ☎ *08/56622000* 🖶 *08/56622020* ⊕ *www.elite.se* 🛏 *151 rooms, 18 suites* ⅋ *Restaurant, room service, minibars, room TVs with movies, in room broadband, Wi-Fi, bar, meeting rooms, parking (fee), no-smoking rooms* ▤ *AE, DC, MC, V* ⍓ *BP.*

★ $-$$ 🖼 **Tegnérlunden.** A quiet city park fronts this modern hotel, a 10-minute walk along shop-lined Sveavägen from the downtown hub of Sergels Torg. Rooms here are unusually stylish for a hotel in this price range and have the added appeal of not feeling at all like hotel rooms. The modern furniture, oak tables and desks, comfortable armchairs, and potted plants will all remind you of an urban apartment. ☒ *Tegnérlunden 8, Downtown, 113 59* ☎*08/54545550* 🖶*08/54545551* ⊕*www.hoteltegnerlunden. se* 🛏 *102 rooms, 2 suites* ⅋ *Room TVs with movies, Wi-Fi, sauna, meeting room, no-smoking rooms* ▤ *AE, DC, MC, V* ⍓ *BP.*

$ 🖼 **Arcadia.** On a hilltop near a large waterfront nature preserve, this converted dormitory is within 15 minutes of downtown by bus or subway or 30 minutes on foot along pleasant shopping streets. Rooms are furnished in a spare, neutral style, with plenty of natural light. The adjoining restaurant serves meals on the terrace in summer. To get here, take Bus 43 to Körsbärsvägen. ☒ *Körsbärsv. 1, 114 89* ☎ *08/56621500* 🖶 *08/56621501* ⊕ *www.arcadia.elite.se* 🛏 *84 rooms* ⅋ *Restaurant* ▤ *AE, DC, MC, V* ⍓ *BP.*

¢–$ 🖼 **Hotel Gustav Wasa.** The Gustav Wasa is in a 19th-century residential building and has fairly large, bright rooms with herringbone hardwood floors, original trim and details along the ceilings, and a funky blend of antiques and furniture that's more modern. Some rooms have wonderful original tiled fireplaces. Ask for a room with a window out to the street in order to get a direct view of the grand Gustav Wasa Church and the Odenplan. The other available view, of the inner courtyard, is much less exciting. The downtown location and lower prices make this an excellent place for budget travelers who prefer a friendly hotel. ☒ *Västmannag. 61, Vasastan, 113 25* ☎ *08/343801* 🖶 *08/307372* ⊕ *www.gustavvasahotel.se* 🛏 *41 rooms* ▤ *AE, DC, MC, V* ⍓ *BP.*

FodorŚChoice
★

¢ 🖼 **Bema.** This small hotel is relatively central, on the ground floor of an apartment block near Tegnérlunden park. Rooms have a modern Swedish style, with beech-wood furniture. One four-bed family room is available. Breakfast is served in your room. Given the price, it's difficult to beat. ☒ *Upplandsg. 13, Vasastan, 111 23* ☎ *08/232675* 🖶 *08/ 205338* 🛏 *12 rooms* ▤ *MC, V.*

Gamla Stan & Skeppsholmen

$$$$ ▣ **Grand Hotel.** At first glance the Grand seems like any other world-
Fodor's Choice class international hotel, and in many ways it is. Its location is one of
★ the best in the city, on the quayside just across the water from the Royal
Palace. It boasts an impressive guest list. The service is slick, professional,
and predicts your every need. The large rooms are sumptuous and decadent, with robes so fluffy, beds so soft, and antiques so lovely you may
never want to leave. But the Grand offers something else: a touch of the
uniquely Scandinavian. You can feel it in the relaxed atmosphere that
pervades the hotel, you can smell it in the fresh, salt-tinged air that wafts
through the open windows, and you can see it in the purity of the light
that penetrates all corners of the hotel. If there is a more exquisite hotel
anywhere in town, it is yet to be found. ⊠ *Södra Blasieholmshamnen
8, Box 16424, City, 103 27* ☎ *08/6793500* 🖷 *08/6118686* ⊕ *www.
grandhotel.se* 🛏 *310 rooms, 21 suites* ☖ *2 restaurants, room service,
a/c, minibars, room TVs with movies, in-room broadband, in-room data
ports, Wi-Fi, gym, sauna, bar, shops, concierge, meeting room, no-
smoking rooms* ▭ *AE, DC, MC, V* ❙⊙❙ *BP.*

$$-$$$$ ▣ **Radisson SAS Strand Hotel.** An art-nouveau monolith, built in 1912 for
the Stockholm Olympics, this hotel has been completely and tastefully
modernized. It's on the water across from the Royal Dramatic Theater,
only a short walk from the Old Town and the museums on Skeppshol-
men. No two rooms are alike, but all are furnished with simple and el-
egant furniture, offset by white woodwork and hues of moss green and
cocoa brown. The Strand restaurant has a sharp, urban feel, with a cool
color scheme of stone, earth-brown, and natural greens. ⊠ *Nybrokajen
9, Box 16396, City, 103 27* ☎ *08/50664000* 🖷 *08/6112436* ⊕ *www.
radissonsas.com* 🛏 *152 rooms* ☖ *Restaurant, room service, a/c, mini-
bars, room TVs with movies, in-room broadband, in-room data ports,
Wi-Fi, sauna, meeting room, no-smoking rooms* ▭ *AE, DC, MC, V* ❙⊙❙ *BP.*

$$-$$$ ▣ **Lady Hamilton.** As charming as its namesake, Lord Nelson's mistress,
the Lady Hamilton is a modern hotel inside a typical Gamla Stan rus-
set-red 15th-century building. Swedish antiques fill the guest rooms
and common areas, including such obscure objects as old spirit cabi-
nets, complete with original bottles. The breakfast room, furnished
with captain's chairs, looks out onto the lively cobblestone street, and
the subterranean sauna rooms, in whitewashed stone, provide a se-
cluded fireplace and a chance to take a dip in the building's original,
medieval well. ⊠ *Storkyrkobrinken 5, Gamla Stan, 111 28* ☎ *08/
50640100* 🖷 *08/50640110* ⊕ *www.lady-hamilton.se* 🛏 *34 rooms*
☖ *Minibars, room TVs with movies, in-room broadband, sauna, bar,
meeting room, no-smoking rooms* ▭ *AE, DC, MC, V* ❙⊙❙ *BP.*

★ **$$-$$$**   ▣ **Reisen.** On the waterfront in Gamla Stan, this hotel opened in 1819.
The rooms looking out over the water are fantastic, and for a small sup-
plement you can get a room with a private sauna and Jacuzzi. A mix of
nautical-inspired antiques and simple, modern furniture fill the rooms,
many of which have original exposed brick and wood ceiling beams.
There is a fine Italian restaurant with a grill, tea and coffee service in
the library, and what is reputed to be the best piano bar in town.
⊠ *Skeppsbron 12–14, Gamla Stan, 111 30* ☎ *08/223260* 🖷 *08/201559*

⊕ *www.firsthotels.com* ↪ *144 rooms, 7 suites ♧ Restaurant, room service, in-room broadband, indoor pool, sauna, piano bar, meeting room, no-smoking floor ⊟ AE, DC, MC, V.*

$$ ▦ **Rica Hotel Gamla Stan.** The feel of historical Stockholm living is rarely more prevalent than in this quiet hotel tucked away on a narrow street in one of the Gamla Stan's 17th-century houses. All rooms are decorated in the Gustavian style, with hardwood floors, Oriental rugs, and antique furniture. A short walk from the Gamla Stan metro stop, it's a perfect home base for later exploring. ⊠ *Lilla Nyg. 25, Gamla Stan 111 28* ☎ *08/7237250* 🖷 *08/7237259* ⊕ *www.rica.se* ↪ *51 rooms ♧ Minibars, meeting room, no-smoking floor ⊟ AE, DC, MC, V* ▧ *BP.*

$$ ▦ **Victory.** Slightly larger than its brother and sister hotels, the Lord Nelson and Lady Hamilton, this extremely atmospheric Gamla Stan building dates from 1640. History defines the Victory: in the cellar you can see part of a medieval fortress wall, and, in the 1930s construction workers stumbled across Sweden's biggest silver treasure ever found, just beneath the hotel. The theme is nautical, with artifacts from the HMS *Victory,* as well as Swedish antiques. Each room is named after a 19th-century sea captain. ⊠ *Lilla Nyg. 5, Gamla Stan, 111 28* ☎ *08/50640000* 🖷 *08/50640010* ⊕ *www.victory-hotel.se* ↪ *48 rooms ♧ Restaurant, minibars, room TVs with movies, in-room broadband, Wi-Fi, 2 saunas, bar, meeting room, no-smoking floor ⊟ AE, DC, MC, V* ▧ *BP.*

$–$$ ▦ **Mälardrottningen.** One of the more unusual establishments in Stockholm, Mälardrottningen was once Barbara Hutton's yacht. Since 1982 it has been a hotel, with a crew as service conscious as any in Stockholm. Tied up on the freshwater side of Gamla Stan, it is minutes from everything. Not surprisingly, the theme is nautical, with endless mahogany and polished brass, groups of maritime pictures on the walls, and rooms that are a riot of navy-blue, maroon, and white. Some of the below-deck cabins are a bit stuffy, but in summer you can take your meals out on deck. ⊠ *Riddarholmen 4, Riddarholmen, 111 28* ☎ *08/54518780* 🖷 *08/243676* ⊕ *www.malardrottningen.se* ↪ *59 cabins ♧ Restaurant, BBQ, in-room broadband, sauna, bar, meeting room, no-smoking rooms ⊟ AE, DC, MC, V* ▧ *BP.*

Östermalm

$$$–$$$$ ▦ **Diplomat.** Within easy walking distance of Djurgården, this elegant
Fodor's Choice hotel is less flashy than most in its price range, but oozes a certain Eu-
★ ropean chic, evident in its subtle, tasteful designs and efficient staff. The building is a turn-of-the-20th-century town house; rooms are all individual but have fresh colors, clean lines, and subtle hints of floral prints in common, and those in the front, facing the water, have magnificent views over Stockholm Harbor. The T-Bar, formerly a rather staid tearoom and restaurant, is now one of the trendiest bars among the city's upper crust. ⊠ *Strandv. 7C, Östermalm, 104 40* ☎ *08/4596800* 🖷 *08/4596820* ⊕ *www.diplomathotel.com* ↪ *128 rooms ♧ Restaurant, room service, a/c, minibars, room TVs with movies, in-room broadband, in-room data ports, Wi-Fi, sauna, 2 bars, meeting room, no-smoking room ⊟ AE, DC, MC, V* ▧ *BP.*

$$$ ▦ **Hotel Esplanade.** Right on the water and only a few buildings down from Stockholm's Royal Dramatic Theater, Hotel Esplanade is a beautiful hotel with a real touch of old Stockholm. Somewhere between a family home, a guesthouse, and a hotel, Esplanade is a resplendent work of art nouveau. From the confection of external architecture to the oiled-wood floors and classic period furnishings, this is a real museum piece of a hotel. The rooms with a view of the water are worth the little extra money. Be sure to call well ahead to book a room, since many regulars return every year. ⊠ *Strandv. 7A, Östermalm, 114 56* ☎ *08/6630740* 🖷 *08/6625992* ⊕ *www.hotelesplanade.se* ➲ *34 rooms* ⚘ *In-room broadband, sauna, lobby lounge* ⊟ *AE, DC, MC, V* �"O" *BP.*

$$–$$$ ⊞ **Mornington.** Just off the main square of Östermalm, the Mornington is close to both the nightlife of Stureplan and the downtown business district. The lobby, bar, and restaurant area are hip places to hang out, and there's a lovely library of more than 4,000 books (mostly in Swedish) spread throughout the lobby; you can borrow them during your stay. All rooms are elegantly modern with cherrywood headboards and charcoal-gray chairs and sofas setting an urban tone. ⊠ *Nybrog. 53, Östermalm, 102 44* ☎ *08/50733000* 🖷 *08/50733039* ⊕ *www.mornington.se* ➲ *140 rooms* ⚘ *Restaurant, in-room DVD, in-room broadband, sauna, steam room, bar, meeting room, no-smoking rooms* ⊟ *AE, DC, MC, V* �"O" *BP.*

$$ ⊞ **Hotel Riddargatan.** On its way to being a fully fledged design hotel, the Riddargatan may not be truly cutting edge quite yet, but at these prices it's a great alternative for travelers who are conscious of style and budget in equal measure. The lobby pleases with its simplicity, the clean space broken only by the beech-wood wall panels and chocolate-brown leather sofas. The bedrooms are a calming blue, with pleasing curtains and accessories. Furnishings are modern and simple, making for a restful space away from the city. ⊠ *Riddarg. 14, Östermalm, 114 35* ☎ *08/55573000* 🖷 *08/55573011* ⊕ *www.profilhotels.se* ➲ *58 rooms, 2 suites* ⚘ *In-room broadband, in-room data ports, Wi-Fi, bar, meeting room* ⊟ *AE, DC, MC, V* �"O" *BP.*

★ $$ ⊞ **Wellington.** From the outside the building resembles the Industrihuset (Industry House) across the street, but inside is a delightful hotel with polite, professional staff and quality service. In a quiet residential area in Östermalm near the Hedvig Eleonora Church and cemetery, the hotel is a calm home base from which to enjoy the city. Rooms have hardwood floors and a hint of Britishness about them in the tweeds, checks, and tartans used in chair covers, rugs, and bedspreads. Rooms facing the inner courtyard have balconies. Ask for a room on the top floor for a great view of the neighborhood's rooftops. ⊠ *Storg. 6, Östermalm, 114 51* ☎ *08/6670910* 🖷 *08/6671254* ⊕ *www.wellington. se* ➲ *60 rooms* ⚘ *In-room data ports, sauna, bar, business services, meeting rooms, parking (fee)* ⊟ *AE, MC, V* �"O" *BP.*

★ $–$$ ⊞ **Örnsköld.** Right in the heart of the city, this hidden gem feels like an old private club, from its brass-and-leather lobby to the Victorian-style furniture in the moderately spacious, high-ceiling rooms. Rooms overlooking the courtyard are quieter, but those facing the street—not a particularly busy one—are sunnier. All the rooms are becoming a little faded, but somehow that seems to add to the charm. ⊠ *Nybrog. 6, Östermalm, 114 34* ☎ *08/6670285* 🖷 *08/6676991* ⊕ *www.hotelornskold.se* ➲ *33 rooms* ⊟ *AE, MC, V* ⚘ *BP.*

$　🖾 **Pärlan.** The name of this hotel means the "Pearl" and that's exactly
Fodor'sChoice　what it is. On the second floor of an early-19th-century building on a
★　quiet street, the Pärlan is a friendly alternative to the city's bigger hotels. Furniture throughout is a mix of fine antiques and flea-market bargains, making it quirky and homey. A balcony looking out over the inner
courtyard is a perfect spot for eating breakfast, which is served buffet
style in the kitchen every morning. If you want to get a feel for what
it's like to really live in this neighborhood, this is your best bet. Book
far in advance because the rooms are almost always full. ⊠ *Skepparg.
27, Östermalm, 114 52* ☎ *08/6635070* 🖷 *08/6677145* ⊕ *www.
parlanhotell.com* ⤴ *9 rooms* ▭ *AE, MC, V.*

Södermalm

$$$　🖾 **Hilton Hotel Slussen.** Working with what appears to be a dubious lo-
cation (atop a tunnel above a six-lane highway), the Hilton has pulled
a rabbit out of a hat. Built on special noise- and shock-absorbing cush-
ions, the hotel almost lets you forget about the highway. The intrigu-
ing labyrinth of levels, separate buildings, and corridors is filled with
such unique details as a rounded stairway lighted from between the steps.
The guest rooms are exquisitely designed and modern, with plenty of
stainless steel and polished-wood inlay to accent the maroon color
scheme. The hotel is at Slussen, easily accessible from downtown.
⊠ *Guldgränd 8, Södermalm, 104 65* ☎ *08/51735300* 🖷 *08/51735311*
⊕ *www.hilton.com* ⤴ *264 rooms, 28 suites* ♨ *2 restaurants, room ser-
vice, a/c, room TVs with movies, in-room broadband, Wi-Fi, indoor pool,
gym, hair salon, sauna, piano bar, meeting room, no-smoking rooms*
▭ *AE, DC, MC, V* ⦿ *BP.*

$$$　🖾 **Rival.** One of Stockholm's funkiest hotels burst onto the scene in
Fodor'sChoice　2003, causing as much of a stir among locals as its owner, pop group
★　ABBA's Benny Andersson, did when he broke into fame in the early
1970s. Rival is cool, but never to the point of being cold. Rooms here
are full of delightful ideas—such as the glass bathroom walls that let
you watch the bedroom television from the tub—and have a stylish
comfort about them. Overstuffed duvets compete with plump armchairs
for your attention, while modern art and photographs on the wall and
stylish lamps and fixtures delight the eye. If you can tear yourself away
from your room, downstairs you'll find a very cool bar, a restaurant,
a bakery, and a cinema. ⊠ *Mariatorget 3, Södermalm, 118 91* ☎ *08/
54578900* 🖷 *08/54578924* ⊕ *www.rival.se* ⤴ *99 rooms, 2 suites*
♨ *Restaurant, room service, a/c, minibars, in-room DVD, in-room
broadband, Wi-Fi, bar, cinema, meeting rooms, no-smoking rooms*
▭ *AE, DC, MC, V* ⦿ *BP.*

★ **$$**　🖾 **Anno 1647.** Named for the date the building was erected, this small,
pleasant hotel is a piece of Stockholm history. Rooms vary in shape, but
all have original, well-worn pine floors with 17th-century-style furni-
ture. There's no elevator in this four-story building. The bar and café
are a popular hangout. The menu is international. Guest DJs con-
trol the sound waves. ⊠ *Mariagränd 3, Södermalm, 116 41* ☎ *08/
4421680* 🖷 *08/4421647* ⊕ *www.anno1647.se* ⤴ *42 rooms, 2 suites*
♨ *Snack bar, some in-room broadband* ▭ *MC, V* ⦿ *BP.*

¢–$$ 🏨 **Columbus Hotel.** Just a few blocks from busy Götgatan, the Colum-
Fodor's Choice   bus is an oasis of calm in the busy urban streets of Södermalm. Built in
★   1780, it was originally a brewery, then a jail, then a hospital, then a tem-
porary housing area. Since 1976 the beautiful building, with its large,
tranquil inner courtyard, has been a hotel. Rooms have wide beams, pol-
ished hardwood floors, antique furniture, and bright wallpaper and fab-
rics. Many look out over the courtyard, others on the nearby church.
In summer breakfast is served outside. The peace and quiet this hotel
provides, even though it's close to all the action, makes it ideal for a va-
cation. ✉ *Tjärhovsg. 11, Södermalm, 116 21* ☎ *08/50311200* 🖷 *08/*
50311201 ⊕ *www.columbus.se* ❧ *64 rooms, 3 suites* ♿ *Café, bar,*
parking (fee) ⊟ *AE, MC, V* ⊠ *BP.*

¢–$ 🏨 **Pensionat Oden, Söder.** Inexpensive and centrally located, this bed-
and-breakfast is on the second floor of a 19th-century building. Horns-
gatan, the street it's on, is busy and filled with pubs, restaurants, and
shops. Rooms have hardwood floors, Oriental rugs, and an odd blend
of new and old furniture. A kitchen is available for use. The hotel is pop-
ular with parents visiting their children in college, academics traveling
on a budget, and backpackers. Book rooms well in advance, especially
during the holidays. ✉ *Hornsg. 66B, Södermalm 111 60* ☎ *08/7969600*
🖷 *08/6124501* ⊕ *www.pensionat.nu* ❧ *35 rooms, 8 with bath* ♿ *No-*
smoking rooms ⊟ *MC, V.*

Youth Hostels

Don't be put off by the "youth" bit: there's actually no age limit. The
standards of cleanliness, comfort, and facilities offered are usually ex-
tremely high.

¢–$ 🏨 **Den Röda Båten Mälaren** (The Red Boat). Built in 1914, the *Mälaren*
originally traveled the waters of the Göta Canal under the name of *Sätra.*
Today she has to settle for sitting still in Stockholm as a youth hostel.
The hostel cabins are small but clean and have bunk beds. Many have
fantastic views of the town hall across the water. There are also four
"hotel" rooms, which have private baths and nicer furniture and de-
tails. In summer the restaurant offers great views of Stockholm along
with basic, traditional Swedish food. Breakfast costs an additional Skr
55, but sheets are included in your rate. ✉ *Södermälarstrand kajplats*
6, Södermalm 117 20 ☎ *08/6444385* 🖷 *08/6413733* ⊕ *www.theredboat.*
com ❧ *35 rooms, 4 with bath* ⊟ *MC, V.*

¢   🏨 **af Chapman.** This circa-1888 sailing ship, permanently moored in Stock-
holm Harbor just across from the Royal Palace, is a landmark in its own
right. Book early—the place is so popular in summer that finding a bed
may prove difficult. Breakfast (SKr 45) is not included in the room rate;
there are no kitchen facilities. ✉ *Flaggmansv. 8, Skeppsholmen, 111 49*
☎ *08/4632266* 🖷 *08/6117155* ⊕ *www.stfchapman.com* ❧ *293 beds,*
2- to 6-bed cabins ♿ *Café* ⊟ *DC, MC, V* ☉ *Closed mid-Dec.–mid-Jan.*

¢   🏨 **Gustaf af Klint.** A "hotel ship" moored at Stadsgården quay, near the
Slussen subway station, the *Gustaf af Klint* harbors 120 beds in its two
sections: a hotel and a hostel. The hostel section has 18 four-bunk cab-
ins and 10 two-bunk cabins; a 14-bunk dormitory is also available from
May through mid-September. The hotel section has 4 single-bunk and

3 two-bunk cabins with bedsheets and breakfast included. The hostel rates are SKr 120 per person in a 4-bunk room and SKr 140 per person in a 2-bunk room; these prices do not include bedsheets or breakfast, which are available at an extra charge. All guests share common bathrooms and showers. There are a cafeteria and a restaurant, and you can dine on deck in summer with stunning views across to Gamla Stan. ⊠ *Stadsgårdskajen 153, Södermalm 116 45* ☎ *08/6404077* 🖨 *08/6406416* ⊕ *www.gustafafklint.se* 🛏 *7 hotel cabins, 28 hostel cabins, 28 dormitory beds, all without bath* 🍴 *Restaurant, cafeteria* 🖃 *AE, MC, V.*

Camping

You can camp in the Stockholm area for SKr 80–SKr 130 per night. **Bredäng Camping** (⊠ 127 31 Skärholmen ☎ 08/977071) has camping and a youth hostel. Its facilities are excellent and include a restaurant and bar. At **Rösjöbaden Camping** (⊠ 192 56 Sollentuna ☎ 08/962184), a short drive north of town, you can fish, swim, and play minigolf and volleyball. Fifteen kilometers (9 mi) from Stockholm, in Huddinge, is **Stockholm SweCamp Flottsbro** (⊠ 141 25 Huddinge ☎ 08/4499580), where you can camp, play golf, rent canoes and bikes, and hang out on a beach.

Nightlife & the Arts

Stockholm's nightlife can be broken up into two general groups based on geography. First, there's Birger Jarlsgatan, Stureplan, and the city end of Kungsträdgården, which are more upscale and trendy, and thus more expensive. At the bars and clubs in this area it's not unusual to wait in line with people who look like they just stepped off the pages of af glossy magazine. To the south, in Södermalm, things are a bit looser and wilder, but that doesn't mean the bars are any less hip. At night Söder can get pretty crazy—it's louder and more bohemian, and partygoers often walk the streets.

Many establishments will post and enforce a minimum age requirement, which could be anywhere from 18 to 30, depending on the clientele they wish to serve, and they may frown on jeans and sneakers. Your safest bet is to wear black clothes, Stockholm's shade of choice. Most places are open until around 3 AM. Wherever you end up, a night of bar-hopping in Stockholm has fresher air now, served with a tinge of desperation: in the summer of 2005 smoking was banned in all bars, clubs, and restaurants in the country.

The tourist guide *What's On* (⊕ www.stockholmtown.com) is available free of charge at most hotels, tourist centers, and some restaurants. It lists the month's events in both English and Swedish. The Thursday editions of the daily newspapers *Dagens Nyheter* (⊕ www.dn.se) and *Svenska Dagbladet* (⊕ www.svd.se) carry current listings of events, films, restaurants, and museums in Swedish. There's also a monthly guide called *Nöjesguiden* (the Entertainment Guide; ⊕ www.nojesguiden.se), which has listings and reviews in Swedish.

Nightlife

Go to Stureplan (at one end of Birger Jarlsgatan) on any given weekend night, and you'll see crowds of people gathering around Svampen (the Mushroom), *the* meeting place for people getting ready to go out in this area.

★ **Berns Salonger** (⊠ Berns Hotel, Berzelii Park, City ☎ 08/56632000) has three bars—one in 19th-century style and two modern rooms—plus a huge veranda that's spectacular in summer. Music here gets so thump-
★ ing you can hear it down the street. Glamour is on the menu at **Brasserie Godot** (⊠ Grev Tureg. 36, Östermalm ☎ 08/6600614), a toned-down, chic bar and restaurant known for its excellent cocktail list and hip crowd. The red and gold interiors of nearby **Buddha Bar** (⊠ Biblioteksg. 9, Östermalm ☎ 08/54518500) are, not surprisingly, inspired by the lounges and opium dens of the Orient. No opium here, but an equally decadent night is guaranteed. **Folkhemmet** (⊠ Renstiernas Gata 30, Södermalm ☎ 08/6405595), marked by a blue F imitating the T for the subway, is a longtime favorite of the artsy locals. It's friendly and inviting, but be prepared for a crowded bar. Don't let the name of **Hotellet** (⊠ Linneg. 18, Östermalm ☎ 08/4428900) fool you. Although originally designed as a hotel, it is now a very chic bar that has managed to retain that open lobby feel for its hot crowd. Close to the Mushroom is the casually hip **Lydmar Bar** (⊠ Stureg. 10, Östermalm ☎ 08/56611300), with black-leather couches and chairs and a small stage for bands and DJs. Many people who frequent the bar are in the music business. **Mosebacke Etablissement** (⊠ Mosebacke Torg 3, Södermalm ☎ 08/6419020) is a combined indoor theater, comedy club, and outdoor café with a spectacular view of the city. The crowd here leans toward over-30 hipsters. The **O-bar** (⊠ Stureplan 2, Östermalm ☎ 08/4405730), located upstairs through the restaurant Sturehof, is where the downtown crowd gathers for late-night drinks and music ranging from bass-heavy hip-hop to hard rock. The **Sturehof** itself is a prime location for evening people-watching. The outdoor tables are smack dab in the middle of
★ Stureplan. Lovers of the late-night cocktail should head north to **Olssons Video** (⊠ Odeng. 14, Vasastan ☎ 08/6733800), where the darkened lounge caters to a slick clientele of cool urbanites thirsty for some of the best mixes in town. For what has to be Stockholm's biggest rum collection (more than 64 varieties), slide into **Sjögräs** (Sea Grass; ⊠ Timmermansg. 24, Södermalm ☎ 08/841200), where the drinks go down smoothly to the sounds of reggae. **Sophie's Bar** (⊠ Biblioteksg. 5, City ☎ 08/6118408) is one of Stockholm's major celebrity hangouts. It can be a bit elitist and uptight, probably the reason Madonna checked it out when she was in town. From Sophie's Bar it's a short walk to **Spy Bar** (⊠ Birger Jarlsg. 20, City ☎ 08/6118408), one of Stockholm's most exclusive clubs. It's often filled with local celebrities and lots of glitz and glamour. At Odenplan the basement bar of **Tranan** (⊠ Karlbergsv. 14, Vasastan ☎ 08/52728100) is a fun place to party in semidarkness to anything from ambient music to hard rock. Lots of candles, magazines, and art are inside. A trendy youngish crowd props up the long bar at **WC** (⊠ Skåneg. 51, Södermalm ☎ 08/7022963), with ladies' drink specials on Sunday. Luckily, the only things that'll remind you of the name

(which stands for "water closet," or bathroom) are the holes in the middle of the bar stools.

Stockholm can also appease your need for pub-style intimacy. Guinness, ale, and cider enthusiasts rally in the tartan-clad **Bagpiper's Inn** (⊠ Rörstrandsg. 21, Vasastan ☎ 08/311855), where you can get a large selection of bar food. Those longing for a great whiskey travel a long way to the **Bishops Arms** (⊠ St. Eriksg. 115, Vasastan ☎ 08/56621788) where more than 150 are offered, not to mention more than 30 types of beer. **The Dubliner** (⊠ Smålandsg. 8, City ☎ 08/6797707), probably Stockholm's most popular Irish pub, serves up pub food, shows major sporting events on its big screen, and hosts live folk music on stage. It's not unusual to see people dancing on the tables. The very British **Tudor Arms** (⊠ Grevg. 31, Östermalm ☎ 08/6602712) is just as popular as when it opened in 1969. Brits who are missing home cooking will be relieved when they see the menu. **Wirströms Pub** (⊠ Stora Nyg. 13, Gamla Stan ☎ 08/212874) is in labyrinthine 17th-century cellars. Expect live acoustic music, mostly anglophone patrons, and lots of beer. There are also 130 whiskeys available.

DANCE CLUBS **Blue Moon** (⊠ Kungsg. 18, City ☎ 08/244700) is a multifloor club with a range of music and a restaurant for refueling between numbers. Music veers from dance and hip-hop to live rock and European easy listening, depending on the night you are there. **Café Opera** (⊠ Operahuset, City ☎ 08/6765807), at the waterfront end of Kungsträdgården, is a popular meeting place for young and old alike. It has the longest bar in town, fantastic 19th-century ceilings and details, plus dining and roulette, and major dancing after midnight. The kitchen offers a night menu until 2:30 AM. **Debaser** (⊠ Karl Johans torg 1, Södermalm ☎ 08/4629860) is the perfect place for those who like their dancing a bit wilder. The epicenter of Stockholm's rock music scene, this is where denim-clad legions come to shake their stuff. **Mälarsalen** (⊠ Torkel Knutssonsg. 2, Södermalm ☎ 08/6581300) caters to the nondrinking jitterbug and fox-trot crowd in Södermalm. Down on Stureplan is **Sturecompagniet** (⊠ Stureg. 4, Östermalm ☎ 08/6117800), a galleried, multifloor club where the crowd is young, the dance music is loud, and the lines are long.

GAY BARS Hidden down behind the statue of St. George and the dragon on Gamla Stan, **Mandus Bar och Kök** (⊠ Österlångg. 7, Gamla Stan ☎ 08/206055) is a warm and friendly restaurant and bar perfect for drinking and talking late into the night. **Patricia** (⊠ Stadsgården, Berth 25, Södermalm ☎ 08/7430570) is a floating restaurant, disco, and bar right next to Slussen. And don't worry—the boat doesn't rock enough to make you sick. All are welcome at **TipTop** (⊠ Sveav. 57, Norrmalm ☎ 08/329800), but most of the clientele is gay. Men and women dance nightly to '70s disco and modern techno.

JAZZ CLUBS The best and most popular jazz venue is **Fasching** (⊠ Kungsg. 63, City ☎ 08/53482964), where international and local bands play year-round. The classic club **Nalens** (⊠ Regeringsg. 74, City ☎ 08/50522200), which was popular back in the '50s and '60s, is back on the scene with major performances throughout the year; it has three stages. **Stampen**

(✉ Stora Nyg. 5, Gamla Stan ☎ 08/205793) is an overpriced but atmospheric club in Gamla Stan with traditional jazz nightly. Get there early for a seat.

PIANO BARS The **Anglais Bar** (✉ Humlegårdsg. 23, City ☎ 08/51734000), at the Hotel Anglais, is popular on weekends. Most people there are English-speaking international travelers staying at the hotel. The **Clipper Club** (✉ Skeppsbron 1214, Gamla Stan ☎ 08/223260), at the Hotel Reisen, is a pleasant, dark-wood, dimly lighted bar on Gamla Stan.

ROCK CLUBS **Pub Anchor** (✉ Sveav. 90, Norrmalm ☎ 08/152000), on Sveavägen's main drag, is the city's downtown hard-rock bar. **Krogen Tre Backar** (✉ Tegnérg. 1214, Norrmalm ☎ 08/6734400) is as popular among hard-rock fans as Pub Anchor is. It's just off Sveavägen. International rock acts often play at **Klubben** (✉ Hammarby Frabriksv. 13, Södermalm ☎ 08/4622200), a small bar and club in the Fryshuset community center south of town.

The Arts

Stockholm's theater and opera season runs from September through May. Both Dramaten (the National Theater) and Operan (the Royal Opera) shut down in the summer months. When it comes to popular music, big-name acts such as Neil Young, U2, Eminem, and even the Backstreet Boys frequently come to Stockholm in summer while on their European tours. Artists of this type always play at Globen sports arena. For a list of events pick up the free booklet *What's On,* available from hotels and tourist information offices. For tickets to theaters and shows try **Biljettdirekt** (☎ 0771/707070).

CLASSICAL MUSIC International orchestras perform at **Konserthuset** (✉ Hötorget 8, City ☎ 08/102110), the main concert hall. The **Music at the Palace series** (☎ 08/102247) runs June through August. After Konserthuset, the best place for classical music is **Nybrokajen 11** (✉ Nybrokajen 11, City ☎ 08/4071700), where top international musicians perform in relatively small halls. Off-season there are weekly concerts by Sweden's Radio Symphony Orchestra at **Berwaldhallen** (Berwald Concert Hall; ✉ Strandv. 69, Östermalm ☎ 08/7845000).

DANCE When it comes to high-quality international dance in Stockholm, there's really only one place to go. **Dansenshus** (✉ Barnhusg. 12–14, Vasastan ☎ 08/50899090) hosts the best Swedish and international acts, with shows ranging from traditional Japanese dance to street dance and modern ballet. You can also see ballet at the Royal Opera house.

FILM Stockholm has an abundance of cinemas, all listed in the *Yellow Pages* under "Biografer." Current billings are listed in evening papers, normally with Swedish titles; call ahead if you're unsure. Foreign movies are subtitled, not dubbed. Most, if not all, movie theaters take reservations over the phone: popular showings can sell out ahead of time. Cinemas are either part of the **SF** chain or of **Sandrew Metronome.** Listings for each can be found on the wall at the theater or in the back of the culture pages of the daily newspapers. If you are interested in smaller theaters with character, try the **Grand** (✉ Sveav. 45, Norrmalm ☎ 08/4112400), a nice little theater with two small screens and not a bad seat in the house. **Röda Kvarn** (✉ Biblioteksg. 5, City ☎ 08/7896073) is a beautiful old movie theater right near Stureplan. **Zita** (✉ Birger Jarlsg. 37, Norrmalm ☎ 08/232020) is a one-screen theater that shows foreign films. A small restaurant is in the back.

OPERA It is said that Queen Lovisa Ulrika began introducing opera to her subjects in 1755. Since then Sweden has become an opera center of standing, a launchpad for such names as Jenny Lind, Jussi Björling, and

★ Birgit Nilsson. **Operan** (Royal Opera House; ✉ Jakobs torg 2, City ☎ 08/7914300), dating from 1898, is now the de facto home of Sweden's operatic tradition. **Folkoperan** (✉ Hornsg. 72, Södermalm ☎ 08/6160750) is a modern company with its headquarters in Södermalm. Casting traditional presentation and interpretation of the classics to the wind, the company stages productions that are refreshingly new.

THEATER The exquisite **Drottningholms Slottsteater** (Drottningholm Court Theater; ✉ Drottningholm, Drottningholm ☎ 08/6608225) presents opera, ballet, and orchestral music from May to early September; the original 18th-century stage machinery is still used in these productions. Drottningholm, the royal residence, is reached by subway and bus or by a special theater-bus (which leaves from the Grand Hotel or opposite the central train station). Boat tours run here in summer.

Sports & the Outdoors

Like all Swedes, Stockholmers love the outdoors and spend a great deal of time enjoying outdoor sports and activities. Because the city is spread out on a number of islands, you are almost always close to the water. The many large parks, including Djurgården and Haga Park, allow people to quickly escape the hustle and bustle of downtown.

The most popular summertime activities in Stockholm are golf, biking, rollerblading, tennis, and sailing. In winter people like to ski and ice-skate.

Beaches

The best bathing places in central Stockholm are on the island of Långholmen and at Rålambshov, at the end of Norr Mälarstrand. Both are grassy or rocky lakeside hideaways. Topless sunbathing is virtually de rigueur.

Biking & Rollerblading

Stockholm is laced with bike paths, and bicycles can be taken on the commuter trains (except during peak traveling times) for excursions to the suburbs. The bike paths are also ideal for rollerblading. You can rent a bike for between SKr 160 and SKr 260 per day. Rollerblades cost between Skr 90 and SKr 120. Most places require a deposit of a couple thousand kronor. **Cykelfrämjandet** (✉ Thuleg. 43, 113 53 ☎ 08/54591030 ⊕ www.cykelframjandet.a.se), a local bicyclists' association, publishes an English-language guide to cycling trips. City and mountain bikes can be rented from **Cykel & Mopeduthyrning** (✉ Strandv. at Kajplats 24, City ☎ 08/6607959) for SKr 170.

Boating

Boating in Stockholm's archipelago is an exquisite summertime activity. From May to September sailboats large and small and gorgeous restored wooden boats cruise from island to island. Both types of boats are available for rental. Walk along the water on Strandvägen, where many large power yachts and sailboats (available for charter) are docked. Sea kayaking has also become increasingly popular and is a delightful way to explore the islands.

Contact **Svenska Seglarförbundet** (Swedish Sailing Association; ✉ Af Pontins väg 6, Djurgården 115 21 ☎ 08/4590990 ⊕ www.ssf.se) for information on sailing. **Svenska Kanotförbundet** (Swedish Canoeing Association; ✉ Rosvalla, Nyköping ☎ 0155/209080 ⊕ www.kanot.com) has information on canoeing and kayaking. **Capella Skärgårdscatering** (✉ Flaxenviks Bryggv. 14, Åkersberga ☎ 08/54443390) has a large power yacht available for afternoon and overnight charters for groups of up to 40 people. At the end of Strandvägen, before the bridge to Djurgården, is **Tvillingarnas Båtuthyrning** (✉ Strandvägskajen 27, City ☎ 08/6603714), which has large and small motorboats and small sailboats. **Point 65 N** (✉ Styrmansg. 23, Östermalm ☎ 08/6630106), a short walk up from Strandvägen, has high-quality sea kayaks for rent. Its staff will help you get them down and back from the water if it's a two- or three-day rental.

Golf

There are numerous golf courses around Stockholm. Greens fees run from about SKr 450 to SKr 650, depending on the club. Contact **Sveriges Golfförbund** (✉ Kevingestrand 20, Box 84, 182 11 Danderyd ☎ 08/6221500 ⊕ www.golf.se), which is just outside Stockholm, for information.

Tennis

With stars such as Björn Borg, Stefan Edberg, and Joachim "Pim Pim" Johansson, it's impossible for tennis not to be huge in Stockholm. Contact **Svenska Tennisförbundet** (✉ Lidingöv. 75, Box 27915, 115 94 Stockholm ☎ 08/4504310 ⊕ www.tennis.se) for information. Borg once played at **Kungliga Tennishallen** (Royal Tennis Hall; ✉ Lidingöv. 75, Norra Djurgården ☎ 08/4591500), which hosts the Stockholm Open every year. **Tennisstadion** (✉ Fiskartorpsv. 20, Norra Djurgården ☎ 08/54525254) has well-maintained courts.

Shopping

If you like to shop till you drop, then charge on down to any one of the three main department stores in the central city area, all of which carry top-name brands from Sweden and abroad for both men and women. For souvenirs and crafts peruse the boutiques and galleries in Västerlånggatan, the main street of Gamla Stan. For jewelry, crafts, and fine art, hit the shops that line the raised sidewalk at the start of Hornsgatan on Södermalm. Drottninggatan, Birger Jarlsgatan, Biblioteksgatan, Götgatan, and Hamngatan also offer some of the city's best shopping.

Department Stores & Malls

Fodor'sChoice   Sweden's leading department store is the unmissable **NK** (✉ Hamng.
★   18–20, across the street from Kungsträdgården, City ☎ 08/7628000);

the initials, pronounced enn-*koh,* stand for Nordiska Kompaniet. You pay for the high quality here. **Åhléns City** (⊠ Klarabergsg. 50, City ☎ 08/6766000) has a selection similar to NK, with slightly better prices. Before becoming a famous actress, Greta Garbo used to work at **PUB** (⊠ Drottningg. 63 and Hötorget, City ☎ 08/4021611), which has 42 independent boutiques. Garbo fans will appreciate the small exhibit on level H2—a collection of photographs begins with her employee ID card.

★ **Bruno Galleria** (⊠ Götg. 36, Södermalm ☎ 08/6412751) is a delightful glassed-in courtyard filled with cool clothing shops and interior-design stores; it's small, but perfectly appointed. **Gallerian** (⊠ Hamng. 37, City ☎ 08/7912445), in the city center just down the road from Sergels Torg, is a large indoor mall closely resembling those found in the United States. It underwent a serious revamp in 2004, and is now the last word in designer-mall chic, with everything from toys to fashion, all in beautiful surroundings. **Sturegallerian** (⊠ Grev Tureg. 9, Östermalm ☎ 08/6114606) is a midsize mall on superposh Stureplan that mostly carries exclusive clothes, bags, and accessories; it's mostly populated by rich, beautiful young shoppers.

Markets

For a good indoor market hit **Hötorgshallen** (⊠ Hötorget, City), directly under Filmstaden. The market is filled with butcher shops, coffee and tea shops, and fresh-fish markets. It's also open daily and closes at 6 PM. **Street** (⊠ Hornstulls Strand 1, Södermalm) is a waterside, weekend-only street market with stalls selling fashionable clothing, design, books, and other artsy and creative wares. If you're interested in high-quality Swedish food, try the classic European indoor market **Östermalms Saluhall** (⊠ Östermalmstorg, Östermalm), where you can buy superb fish, game, bread, vegetables, and other foodstuffs—or just have a glass of wine at one of the bars and watch the world go by.

Fodor'sChoice
★

Specialty Stores

AUCTION HOUSES   Perhaps the finest auction house in town is **Lilla Bukowski** (⊠ Strandv. 7, Östermalm ☎ 08/6140800), whose elegant quarters are on the waterfront. **Auktions Kompaniet** (⊠ Regeringsg. 47, City ☎ 08/235700) is downtown next to NK. **Stockholms Auktionsverk** (⊠ Jakobsg. 10, City ☎ 08/4536700) is under the Gallerian shopping center.

GLASS   Kosta Boda and Orrefors produce the most popular and well-regarded lines of glassware. The **Crystal Art Center** (⊠ Tegelbacken 4, City ☎ 08/217169), near the central station, has a great selection of smaller glass items. **Duka** (⊠ Sveav. 24–26, City ☎ 08/104530) specializes in crystal and porcelain at reasonable prices. **NK** carries a wide representative line of Swedish glasswork in its Swedish Shop, downstairs. **Nordiska Kristall** (⊠ Kungsg. 9, City ☎ 08/104372), near Sturegallerian, has a small gallery of one-of-a-kind art-glass sculptures as well as plates, vases, glasses, bowls, ashtrays, and decanters. **Svenskt Glas** (⊠ Birger Jarlsg. 8, City ☎ 08/7684024), near the Royal Dramatic Theater, carries a decent selection of quality Swedish glass, including bowls from Orrefors.

INTERIOR DESIGN   Sweden is recognized globally for its unique design sense and has contributed significantly to what is commonly referred to as Scandinavian design. All of this makes Stockholm one of the best cities in the world for shopping for furniture and home and office accessories.

On the corner of Östermalmstorg, in the same building as the marketplace, is **Bruka** (⊠ Humlegårdsg. 1, Östermalm ☎ 08/6601480), which has a wide selection of creative kitchen items as well as wicker baskets and chairs. Inside stylish mall Bruno Galleria, **David Design** (⊠ Gotg. 36, Södermalm ☎ 08/6947575) sells fine furniture, rugs, mirrors, and decorative items for the house. **DIS** (⊠Humlegårdsg. 19, Östermalm ☎08/ 6112907) sells heavy dark-wood furniture that has an Asian flair. The rugs and pillowcases are also stunning.

★ For high-minded, trendy furniture that blends dark woods, stainless steel, and colorfully dyed wools, head to **House** (⊠ Humlegårdsg. 14, Östermalm ☎08/54585340). There's also a nice assortment of vases and glassware. For something little more classic, you can't do better than **Modernity** (⊠ Sibylleg. 6, Östermalm ☎ 08/208025). This is *the* place for ultimate 20th-century Scandinavian design, with names like Arne Jacobsen, Alvar Aalto, and Poul Henningsen represented in full force. If you're after the *best* of Scandinavian design (and the most expensive), try **Nordiska Galleriet** (⊠ Nybrog. 11, Östermalm ☎ 08/4428360). It has everything from couches and chairs to tables and vases. Slightly out of the way, in the Fridhemsplan neighborhood in western Stockholm,

★ **R.O.O.M.** (⊠ Alströmerg. 20, Kungsholmen ☎ 08/6925000) has an impressive assortment of Swedish and international tables, chairs, rugs, pillows, beds—the list goes on. It also has a great book selection, lots of nice ceramic bowls and plates, and many decorations and utensils for the kitchen and bathroom. Not just a clever play on words, **Stockhome** (⊠ Kungsg. 25, City ☎ 08/4111300) has a great selection of things with which, well, to stock your home, including china, towels, glass, books, linen, even bicycles and patterned bandages. For elegant home furnishings, affluent Stockholmers tend to favor **Svenskt Tenn** (⊠ Strandv. 5A, Östermalm ☎08/6701600), best known for its selection of designer Josef Franck's furniture and fabrics.

MEN'S CLOTHING Men in search of a little "street cred" can head for **Beneath** (⊠ Kronobergsg. 37, Kungsholmen ☎08/6431250), purveyor of ultrahip urban street wear and limited-edition labels. **Brothers** (⊠ Drottningg. 53, City ☎ 08/4111201) sells relatively inexpensive Swedish clothes that are often inspired by the more expensive international brands. For suits and evening suits for both sale and rental, **Hans Allde** (⊠ Birger Jarlsg. 58, City ☎08/207191) provides good old-fashioned service. **J. Lindeberg** (⊠ Grev Tureg. 9, Östermalm ☎ 08/6786165) has brightly colored and highly fashionable clothes in many styles. The golf line has been made famous by Swedish golfer Jesper Parnevik. Top men's fashions can be found on the second floor of **NK** (⊠ Hamng. 18–20, City ☎ 08/7628000), which stocks everything from outdoor gear and evening wear to swimsuits and workout clothes. The Swedish label **Tiger** (☎ 08/7628772), with a section inside NK, sells fine suits, shoes, and casual wear.

PAPER PRODUCTS For unique Swedish stationery and office supplies in fun colors and styles,
Fodor'sChoice go to **Ordning & Reda** (⊠ NK, Hamng. 18–20, City ☎ 08/7282060).
★

WOMEN'S Swedish designer **Anna Holtblad** (⊠ Grev Tureg. 13, Östermalm ☎ 08/
CLOTHING 54502220) sells her elegant designs at her own boutique. She specializes in knitted clothes. **Champaigne** (⊠ Biblioteksg. 2, City ☎ 08/
6118803) has European and Swedish designs that are often discounted.
★ **Filippa K** (⊠ Grev Tureg. 18, Östermalm ☎ 08/54588888) has quickly
become one of Sweden's hottest designers. Her stores are filled with young
★ women grabbing the latest fashions. **Hennes & Mauritz** (H&M; ⊠ Hamng.
22, City ⊠ Drottningg. 53 and 56, City ⊠ Sergelg. 1 and 22, City
⊠ Sergels torg 12, City ☎ 08/7965500) is one of the few Swedish-owned
clothing stores to have achieved international success. Here you can find
updated designs at rock-bottom prices. The clothes at **Indiska** (⊠ Drottningg. 53 and elsewhere, City ☎ 08/109193) are inspired by the bright
colors of India.

Kookai (⊠ Biblioteksg. 5, City ☎ 08/6119730) carries trendy, colorful
European designs for young women. **Neu** (⊠ Nytorgsg. 36, Södermalm
☎ 08/6422004) is great for creations by up-and-coming designers that
few have heard of, but, hopefully, many will know soon. One department store with almost every style and type of clothing and apparel is
NK (⊠ Hamng. 18–20, City ☎ 08/7628000). **Polarn & Pyret** (⊠ Hamng.
10, Gallerian, Drottningg. 29, City ☎ 08/6709500) carries high-quality Swedish children's and women's clothing. For the modern rebel
look, go to **Replay** (⊠ Kungsg. 6, City ☎ 08/231416), where the collection covers everything from jeans to underwear. For lingerie and
fashionable clothing at a decent price, go to **Twilfit** (⊠ Nybrog. 11,
Östermalm ☎ 08/6637505 ⊠ Sturegallerian 16, Östermalm ☎ 08/
6110455 ⊠ Gamla Brog. 3638, Norrmalm ☎ 08/201954).

Stockholm A to Z

AIRPORTS & TRANSFERS
Stockholm's Arlanda International Airport is 42 km (26 mi) from the
city center; a freeway links the city and airport. The airport is run by
Luftfartsverket, a state-owned company.

🖪 **Arlanda International Airport** ⊠ 190 45 Stockholm-Arlanda ☎ 08/7976000 🖷 08/
7978600 ⊕ www.arlanda.lfv.se.

AIRPORT Travel between Arlanda International Airport and Stockholm has been
TRANSFERS greatly improved with the completion of the Arlanda Express, a high-
speed train service. The yellow-nose train leaves every 15 minutes (and
every 10 minutes during peak hours), travels at a speed of 200 kph (125
mph), and completes the trip from the airport to Stockholm's central
station in just 20 minutes; single tickets cost SKr 190.

Flygbussarna (airport buses) leave both the international and domestic
terminals every 10–15 minutes from 6:30 AM to 11 PM, and make a number of stops on the way to their final destination at the Cityterminalen

at Klarabergsviadukten, next to the central railway station. The trip costs SKr 89 and takes about 40 minutes.

A bus-taxi combination package is available. The bus lets you off by the taxi stand at Haga Forum, Järva Krog, or Cityterminalen and you present your receipt to the taxi driver, who takes you to your final destination. A trip will cost between SKr 190 and SKr 260, depending on your destination.

For taxis be sure to ask about a *fast pris* (fixed price) between Arlanda and the city. It should be between SKr 400 and SKr 450, depending on the final destination. The best bets for cabs are Taxi Stockholm, Taxi 020, and Taxi Kurir. All major taxi companies accept credit cards. Watch out for unregistered cabs, which charge high rates and won't provide the same service.

Arlanda Express ✉ Vasag. 11, Box 130, City ☎ 020/222224 or 08/58889000 ⊕ www.arlandaexpress.com. **Flygbussarna** ☎ 08/6001000 ⊕ www.flygbussarna.com. **Taxi 020** ☎ 020/202020. **Taxi Kurir** ☎ 08/300000. **Taxi Stockholm** ☎ 08/150000.

BIKE TRAVEL

One of the best ways to explore Stockholm is by bike. There are bike paths and special bike lanes throughout the city, making it safe and enjoyable. Bike rentals will be about SKr 120 per day. One of the best places to ride is on Djurgården. Cykel & Mopeduthyrning service that area.

Cykel & Mopeduthyrning (Bike and Moped Rentals) ✉ Standv. kajplats 24, City ☎ 08/6607959.

BOAT & FERRY TRAVEL

Waxholmsbolaget (Waxholm Ferries) offers the Båtluffarkortet (Inter Skerries Card), a discount pass for its extensive commuter network of archipelago boats; the price is SKr 300 for five days of unlimited travel. The Strömma Kanalbolaget operates a fleet of archipelago boats that provide excellent sightseeing tours and excursions.

Strömma Kanalbolaget ☎ 08/58714000 ⊕ www.strommakanalbolaget.com. **Waxholmsbolaget** ☎ 08/6795830 ⊕ www.waxholmsbolaget.se.

BUS TRAVEL TO & FROM STOCKHOLM

All the major bus services, including Flygbussarna, Swebus Express, Svenska Buss, and Interbus, arrive at Cityterminalen (City Terminal), next to the central railway station. Reservations to destinations all over Sweden can be made by calling Swebus.

Cityterminalen ✉ Karabergsviadukten 72, City ☎ 08/7625997. **Flygbussarna** ☎ 08/6001000 ⊕ www.flygbussarna.com. **Interbus** ☎ 08/7279000 ⊕ www.interbus.se. **Svenska Buss** ☎ 0771/676767 ⊕ www.svenskabuss.se. **Swebus Express** ☎ 0200/218218 ⊕ www.swebusexpress.se.

BUS TRAVEL WITHIN STOCKHOLM

Late-night bus service connects certain stations when trains stop running. The comprehensive bus network serves the entire city, including out-of-town points of interest, such as Vaxholm and Gustavsberg.

Stockholms Lokaltrafik (SL) ☎ 08/6001000 ⊕ www.sl.se.

CAR RENTAL

Rental cars are readily available in Sweden and are relatively inexpensive. Because of the availability and efficiency of public transport, there is little point in using a car within the city limits. If you are traveling elsewhere in Sweden, you'll find that roads are uncongested and well marked but that gasoline is expensive (about SKr 10 per liter, which is equivalent to SKr 40 per gallon). All major car-rental firms are represented, including Avis, Hertz, and Sixt. Statoil gas stations also rent out cars, as do local Swedish companies such as Berras and Auto, which can sometimes have better prices than the major companies.

🚗 Major Agencies **Auto** ✉ Östgötg. 75, Södermalm ☎ 08/6428040. **Avis** ✉ Ringv. 90, Södermalm ☎ 08/6449980. **Berras** ✉ Skepperg. 74, City ☎ 08/6611919. **Hertz** ✉ Vasag. 26, City ☎ 08/240720. **Sixt** ✉ Karlav. 2, City ☎ 08/4111522. **Statoil** ✉ Vasag. 16, City ☎ 020/252525 throughout Sweden, 08/202064 ✉ Birger Jarlsg. 68, Norrmalm ☎ 08/211593.

CAR TRAVEL

Approach the city by either the E20 or E18 highway from the west, or the E4 from the north or south. The roads are clearly marked and well sanded and plowed in winter. Signs for downtown read CENTRUM.

Driving in Stockholm is often deliberately frustrated by city planners, who have imposed many restrictions to keep traffic down. Keep an eye out for bus lanes, marked with BUSS on the pavement. Driving in that lane can result in a ticket. Get a good city map, called a Trafikkarta, available at most service stations for around SKr 75.

EMERGENCIES

Dial 112 for emergencies—this covers police, fire, ambulance, and medical help, as well as sea and air rescue services. Private care is available via CityAkuten. A hospital is called a *sjukhus*, which is Swedish for "sick house," and regular doctors' offices are called *Läkerhuset*. Dentists are listed under *tandläkare*, or *tandvård*. There is a 24-hour national health service via the emergency number listed below.

🚑 Doctors & Dentists **Folktandvården** (national dental service) ☎ 020/6875500. **Läkerhuset Hötorgscity** ✉ Sveav. 13–15, City ☎ 08/243800. **Läkerhuset Riddargatan 12** ✉ Riddarg. 12, Östermalm ☎ 08/6797900.

🚑 Emergency Services **CityAkuten** (Emergency Medical Care) ✉ Apelbergsg. 48, City ☎ 08/4122960. **CityAkuten Tandvården** (Emergency Dental Care) ✉ Olof Palmesg. 13A, Norrmalm ☎ 08/4122900.

🚑 Hospitals **Ersta Sjukhus** ✉ Fjällg. 44, Södermalm ☎ 08/7146100. **Karolinska Sjukhuset** ✉ Solna (just north of Stockholm), Solna ☎ 08/51770000. **Södersjukhuset** ✉ Ringv. 52, Södermalm ☎ 08/6161000. **St. Görans Sjukhus** ✉ Sankt Göransplan 1, Kungsholmen ☎ 08/58701000.

🚑 Police **Polisen** (Stockholm Police Headquarters) ✉ Norra Agneg. 33–37, Kungsholmen ☎ 08/4010000.

🚑 24-Hour Pharmacy **C. W. Scheele** ✉ Klarabergsg. 64, City ☎ 08/4548130.

SUBWAY TRAVEL

The subway system, known as T-banan (Tunnelbanan, with stations marked by a blue-on-white T), is the easiest and fastest way to get around. Servicing more than 100 stations and covering more than 96 km (60 mi) of track, trains run frequently between 5 AM and 3 AM.

TAXIS

Stockholm's taxi service is efficient but overpriced. If you call a cab, ask the dispatcher to quote you a *fast pris* (fixed price), which is usually lower than the metered fare. Reputable cab companies are Taxi 020, Taxi Stockholm, and Taxi Kurir. Taxi Stockholm has an immediate charge of SKr 25 whether you hail a cab or order one by telephone. A trip of 10 km (6 mi) should cost about SKr 97 between 6 AM and 7 PM, SKr 107 at night, and SKr 114 on weekends.

📞 **Taxi 020** ☎ 020/202020. **Taxi Kurir** ☎ 08/300000. **Taxi Stockholm** ☎ 08/150000.

TOURS

BOAT TOURS   Strömma Kanalbolaget runs sightseeing tours of Stockholm. Boats leave from the quays outside the Royal Dramatic Theater, Grand Hotel, and City Hall. Stockholm Sightseeing, which leaves from Skeppsbron in front of the Grand, has four tours, including the "Under the Bridges" and "Historical Canal" tours. Trips last from one to four hours and cost from SKr 100 to SKr 280.

📞 **City Hall** late May–early Sept. ✉ Hantverkarg. 1, Kungsholmen ☎ 08/50829000. **Stockholm Sightseeing** ✉ Skeppsbron 22, Gamla Stan ☎ 08/57814000 ⊕ www.stockholmsightseeing.com. **Strömma Kanalbolaget** ✉ Skeppsbron 22, Gamla Stan ☎ 08/58714000.

BUS TOURS   Comprehensive tours of much of Stockholm, taking in museums, Gamla Stan, and City Hall, are available through City Sightseeing.

📞 **City Sightseeing** ✉ Skeppsbron 11, Gamla Stan ☎ 08/58714000 ⊕ www.citysightseeing.com.

PRIVATE GUIDES   You can hire your own guide from Guide Centralen. In summer be sure to book guides well in advance.

📞 **Guide Centralen** ✉ Sweden House, Hamng. 27, Box 7542, City ☎ 08/58714030.

WALKING TOURS   City Sightseeing runs several tours, including the "Romantic Stockholm" tour of the cathedral and City Hall; the "Royal Stockholm" tour, which includes visits to the Royal Palace and the Treasury; and the "Old Town Walkabout," which strolls through Gamla Stan in just over one hour.

📞 **City Sightseeing** ☎ 08/58714000 ⊕ www.citysightseeing.com.

TRAIN TRAVEL

Both long-distance and commuter trains arrive at the central station in Stockholm on Vasagatan, a main boulevard in the heart of the city. For train information and ticket reservations 6 AM–11 PM, call the SJ number below. There is a ticket and information office at the station where you can make reservations. Automated ticket-vending machines are also available.

📞 **Citypendeln** (Commuter Train) ☎ 08/6001000 ⊕ www.citypendeln.se. **SJ** (State Railway Company) ✉ central station, City ☎ 0771/757575 ⊕ www.sj.se.

TRANSPORTATION AROUND STOCKHOLM

The cheapest way to travel around the city by public transport is to purchase the Stockholmskortet (Stockholm Card). In addition to unlimited transportation on city subway, bus, and rail services, it offers free admission to more than 60 museums and several sightseeing trips. The card costs SKr 220 for 24 hours, SKr 450 for two days, and SKr 640 for three days; you can purchase the card from the tourist center at Sweden House on Hamngatan, from the Hotellcentralen accommodations bureau at the central station, and from the tourist center at Kaknäs Tower.

Stockholm has an excellent bus system, which is operated by SL (Stockholm Local Traffic). In 2000 the subway system was bought from SL by Connex, the same company that runs the subways in Paris and London. Tickets for Stockholm subways and buses are interchangeable. Maps and timetables for all city transportation networks are available from the SL information desks at Sergels Torg, the central station, Slussen, and online.

Bus and subway fares are based on zones. All trips in downtown will be SKr 30. As you travel farther out of downtown, zones are added to the fare in increments of SKr 10. Each ticket is good for one hour on both the bus system and the subway. Single tickets are available at station ticket counters and on buses, but it's cheaper to buy an SL Tourist Card from one of the many Pressbyrån newsstands. There's also a pass called a Rabattkupong, valid for both subway and buses; it costs SKr 80 and is good for 10 trips downtown (fewer if you travel in more zones) within the greater Stockholm area. There is no time limit within which the 10 trips must be used. If you plan to travel within the greater Stockholm area extensively during a 24-hour period, you can purchase a 24-hour pass for SKr 95 and a 72-hour pass for SKr 180. The 24-hour pass includes transportation on the ferries between Djurgården, Nybroplan, and Slussen. The 72-hour pass also entitles you to admission to Skansen, Gröna Lund Tivoli, and Kaknäs Tower. Those under 18 or over 65 pay SKr 50 for a one-day pass and SKr 90 for a two-day pass.

🏠 **Connex** ☎ 08/6295000 ⊕ www.connex.nu. **SL** ☎ 08/6001000 ⊕ www.sl.se.

VISITOR INFORMATION

🏠 Tourist Information **Stockholm Central Station** ✉ Vasag., City ☎ 0771/757575. **Stockholm Information Service** Sweden House ✉ Hamng. 27, Box 7542, 103 93 Stockholm ☎ 08/50828508. **Swedish Travel and Tourism Council** ✉ Box 3030, Kungsg. 36, 103 61 Stockholm ☎ 08/7891000 🖨 08/7891038 ⊕ www.visit-sweden.com.

SIDE TRIPS FROM STOCKHOLM

Stockholm is a green, lively, and pleasant city—that cannot be denied. But travel a little farther from town and you will see why even Stockholmers make a regular and even hurried exit from their city on summer weekends. Immediately outside of Stockholm is the archipelago, meaning paradise on earth to a Swede with a boat and some time to kill. You can get lost among the many thousands of islands and skerries. As you'll see, pleasures here are simple: sunbathing on a rock, dipping in the chilly Baltic, enjoying a simple meal in a local bistro, and lazily watching the sun sink below the horizon.

Farther afield (south of Stockholm, in the Baltic) is the island of Gotland, a settlement whose medieval walls whisper of pirates and hidden

Side Trips
from
Stockholm

Tärnsjö

Heby 72 **Uppsala** 6   Norrtälje

Sala 55   276

Skokloster   *Åland*
Slott 3 **Sigtuna**

Västerås   Enköping   E18

                Drottningholm 1   **Vaxholm & the Archipelago** 4
Strängnäs   Gustavsberg

Eskilstuna **Gripsholm**   Södertälje   **Stockholm**
            Slott 2
            Mariefred   E3   *Ornö*

                                Utö

Katrineholm   Nynäshamn

                                Baltic Sea

            Nyköping

Kolmården Zoo   Öxelösund
and Safari Park
Bråviken
Norrköping

KEY
Ferry Line
Rail Line

5 **Gotland**

Visby

Gotland

NORWAY SWEDEN FINLAND

ESTONIA

LATVIA
LITHUANIA

0   20 miles
0   30 km

treasure. For most people, though, it is the warm climate, stunning nature reserves, and legendary nightlife that bring them here year after year.

Uppsala, north of Stockholm, is one of Europe's oldest and most respected seats of learning. The town is full of medieval and Gothic buildings that are a testament to its long history and former position of power as capital of the country. But there's always the chance to let loose; this is a student town, after all.

Drottningholm

★ ❶ *1 km (½ mi) west of Stockholm.*

Fodor'sChoice ★

Occupying an island in Mälaren (Sweden's third-largest lake) some 45 minutes from Stockholm's center, **Drottningholms Slott** (Queen's Island Castle) is a miniature Versailles dating from the 17th century. The royal family once used this property only as a summer residence, but, tiring of the Royal Palace back in town, they moved permanently to one wing of Drottningholm in the 1980s. Today it remains one of the most delightful of European palaces, reflecting the sense of style practiced by mid-18th-century royalty. The interiors, dating from the 17th, 18th, and 19th centuries, are a rococo riot of decoration with much gilding and trompe l'oeil. Most sections are open to the public. ☎ *08/ 4026280* ⊕ *www.royalcourt.se* ✉ *SKr 60* ☽ *May–Aug., daily 10–4:30; Sept., daily noon–3:30; Oct.–Apr., weekends noon–3:30; guided tours in summer only.*

The lakeside gardens of Drottningholms Slott are its most beautiful asset, containing **Drottningholms Slottsteater**, the only complete theater to survive from the 18th century anywhere in the world. Built by Queen Lovisa Ulrika in 1766 as a wedding present for her son Gustav III, the Court Theater fell into disuse after his assassination at a masked ball in 1792 (dramatized in Verdi's opera *Un Ballo in Maschera*). You can sign up for a backstage tour and see the original backdrops and stage machinery and some amazing 18th-century tools used to produce such special effects as wind and thunder. To get performance tickets, book well in advance at the box office; the season runs from late May to early September. A word of caution: the seats are extremely hard—take a cushion. ☎ *08/7590406, 08/6608225 box office* ⊕ *www. drottningholmsslottsteater.dtm.se* ✉ *SKr 60* ☽ *May, daily noon–4:30; June–Aug., daily 11–4:30; Sept., daily 1–3:30. Guided tours in English at 12:30, 1:30, 2:30, 3:30, and 4:30.*

Arriving & Departing

Boats bound for Drottningholms Slott leave from Klara Mälarstrand, a quay close to Stadshuset (City Hall). Call **Strömma Kanalbolaget** (✉ Skeppsbron 22, 111 30 ☎ 08/58714000 ⊕ www. strommakanalbolaget.com) for schedules and fares. Alternatively, you can take the T-bana (subway) to Brommaplan, and any of Buses 177, 301–323, or 336 from there. Call **Stockholms Lokal Trafik** (☎ 08/6001000) for details.

Mariefred

❷ *63 km (39 mi) southwest of Stockholm.*

The most delightful way to experience the true vastness of Mälaren is the trip to Mariefred—an idyllic little town of mostly timber houses—aboard the coal-fired steamer of the same name, built in 1903 and still going strong. The town's winding narrow streets, ancient squares, and wooded lakeside paths are all perfect for walking. The **Mariefred Tourist Office** has maps and information about tours.

Mariefred's principal attraction is **Gripsholm Slott**. Built in the 1530s by Bo Johansson Grip, the Swedish high chancellor, the castle contains fine Renaissance interiors, a superbly atmospheric theater commissioned in 1781 by the ill-fated Gustav III, and Sweden's royal portrait collection. ☎ *0159/10194* ⊕ *www.royalcourt.se* 🗺 *SKr 60* ⊘ *Mid-May–mid-Sept., daily 10–4. Mid-Sept.–mid-May, weekends noon–3; guided tours only.*

An old converted barn across from Gripsholm Slott (formerly the royal stables and a farm store) now houses **Grafikens Hus** (Graphic House), a center for contemporary graphic art and printmaking. Visitors can view exhibitions or take part in workshops covering all aspects of graphic art. The building is primarily used by working artists, giving visitors a genuine and interesting insight into printmaking as it happens. There are also a good coffee shop and a gift shop that sells artwork. ☎ *0159/23160* ⊕ *www.grafikenshus.se* 🗺 *SKr 70* ⊘ *May–Aug., daily 11–5; Sept.–Apr., Tues. 11–8, Wed.–Sun. 11–5.*

★ For more than 100 years the beautiful steamship **SS Mariefred** has slowly and regularly made her way from Stockholm to Mariefred and back—the same route, still with the original engines, making her unique in the world. The interior of the ship is museum-like, with many of the original fittings unchanged. Even the captain, Claes Insulander, although not original, has been at the helm for over a quarter century. SS *Mariefred* departs from Klara Mälarstrand, near Stadshuset, Stockholm's city hall. The journey takes 3½ hours each way, and there is a restaurant on board. ☎ *08/6698850* 🗺 *SKr 180 round-trip* ⊘ *Departures at 10: May, weekends; mid-June–late Aug., Tues.–Sun. Return trip departs from Mariefred at 4:30.*

Where to Stay & Eat

★ **$$** ✕🏨 **Gripsholms Värdshus & Hotel.** At the oldest inn in the country, guests get a sense of the real Sweden. Lovingly restored and luxuriously appointed, this yellow-wood hotel stands on the site of an old monastery. Rooms are large and airy, with wooden floors and highlights of bright yellow and sky-blue. The whole hotel is full of art and artifacts, including some old Swedish-tile fireplaces and many of the original floral-painted ceilings. In an elegant wood-paneled dining room, the restaurant serves local dishes with an international twist, such as pike-perch with steamed scallops, bell pepper sauce, and olives. ✉ *Kykog. 1, 647 23* ☎ *0159/34750* 🖷 *0159/34777* ⊕ *www.gripsholms-vardshus.se* ⤴ *45 rooms, 10 suites* ⚹ *Restaurant, room service, in-room data ports, sauna, bar, meeting rooms, no-smoking rooms* ▤ *AE, DC, MC, V* ⑩❘ *BP.*

¢–$ ▦ **In My Garden.** This could possibly be one of the loveliest bed-and-
Fodor'sChoice breakfasts in Sweden. Housed in a turn-of-the-20th-century villa with
★ a glassed-in veranda, this spot boasts stunning views across the lake.
There are only three rooms here, all of them with a delightfully personal
and tasteful touch, such as stuffed cushions, artwork, photographs,
and antiques. ⊠ *Strandv. 17, 647 30* ☎ *0159/13353* ⊕ *www.inmygarden.
se* ⇨ *3 rooms* ♨ *Lounge* ⊟ *MC, V* ⍑ *BP.*

Visitor Information
The **Mariefred Tourist Office** (☎ 0159/29799 ⊕ www.strangnas.se) is
open year-round.

Sigtuna

❸ *48 km (30 mi) northwest of Stockholm.*

An idyllic town on a northern arm of Lake Mälaren, Sigtuna was the principal trading post of the Svea, the tribe that settled Sweden after the last
Ice Age; its Viking history is still apparent in the many runic stones preserved all over town. Founded in 980, Sigtuna is Sweden's oldest town,
and as such it's not surprising that it has Sweden's oldest street, Stora Gatan.
After it was ransacked by Estonian pirates, its merchants went on to found
Stockholm sometime in the 13th century. Little remains of Sigtuna's former glory, beyond parts of the principal church. The town hall dates from
the 18th century, and the main part of the town dates from the early 1800s.
There are two houses said to date from the 15th century.

About 20 km (12 mi) northwest of Sigtuna and accessible by the same
ferryboat from Stockholm is **Skokloster Slott,** an exquisite baroque castle with equally exquisite grounds. Commissioned in 1654 by a celebrated
Swedish soldier, Field Marshal Carl Gustav Wrangel, the castle is furnished with the spoils of Wrangel's successful campaigns. Those with
more of an enthusiasm for old machines than for old houses can visit
the **Skokloster Motormuseum** on the castle grounds. The museum boasts
a very fine collection of old cars, planes, motorbikes, and engines. The
museum keeps the same hours as the castle and requires a SKr 50 entrance fee. ⊠ *Bålsta* ☎ *018/386077* ⊕ *www.lsh.se/skokloster/info.htm*
🎫 *SKr 40* ⊙ *Daily 11–5.*

Where to Stay & Eat
$$–$$$ ✕▦ **Sigtuna Stadshotell.** Near the lakeshore, this beautiful hotel was built
Fodor'sChoice in 1909, and soon after became a central gathering place among locals—
★ despite at the time being considered one of the ugliest buildings in all
of Sigtuna. In its early days the hotel had Sigtuna's first cinema, and in
the cellar the state liquor store operated an inn. Today it has been carefully restored and tastefully furnished. The emphasis is on a clean and
natural interior, where oak, sandstone, and white cotton are the focus.
The restaurant is a fine-dining treat, serving up modern Swedish food
and great views of the lake. ⊠ *Stora Nyg. 3, 193 30* ☎ *08/59250100*
🖷 *08/59251587* ⊕ *www.sigtunastadshotell.se* ⇨ *24 rooms* ♨ *Restaurant, room service, minibars, cable TV, in-room broadband, in-room data
ports, Wi-Fi, sauna, spa, meeting rooms, no-smoking rooms* ⊟ *AE, DC,
MC, V* ⍑ *BP.*

Sigtuna can be reached by driving on E4 North to 263 or by taking a commuter train from Stockholm's central station to Märsta, where you change to Bus 570 or 575.

Vaxholm & the Archipelago

❹ *32 km (20 mi) northeast of Stockholm.*

Skärgården (the archipelago) is Stockholm's greatest natural asset: more than 25,000 islands and skerries, many uninhabited, spread across an almost tideless sea of clean, clear water. The islands closer to Stockholm are larger and more lush, with pine tree–covered rock faces and forests. There are also more year-round residents on these islands. As you move away from the mainland, the islands become smaller and more remote, turning into rugged, rocky islets. To sail lazily among these islands aboard an old steamboat on a summer's night is a timeless delight, and throughout the warmer months Swedes flee the chaos of the city for quiet weekends on the waters.

For the tourist with limited time, one of the simplest ways to get a taste of the archipelago is the one-hour ferry trip to Vaxholm, an extremely pleasant, though sometimes crowded, mainland seaside town of small, red-painted wooden houses.

An even quicker trip into the archipelago is the 20-minute ferry ride to ⓒ **Fjäderholmarna** (the Feather Islands), a group of four secluded islands. In the 19th-century the islands were the last chance for a refreshment stop for archipelago residents rowing into Stockholm to sell their produce. After 50 years as a military zone, the islands were opened to the public in the early 1980s. Today they are crammed with arts-and-crafts studios, shops, an aquarium, a small petting farm, a boat museum, a large cafeteria, an ingenious "shipwreck" playground, and even a smoked-fish shop.

If you are interested in a longer voyage out into the islands, there are several possibilities. Contact the Sweden House and ask for the "Destination Stockholm Archipelago" catalog, which lists more than 350 holiday homes for rent. For booking accommodations, contact **Hotellcentralen** (☎ 08/7892425) in Stockholm's central station.

One of the most popular excursions is to **Sandhamn,** the main town on the island of Sandön, which is home to about 100 permanent residents. The journey takes about three hours by steamship, but there are faster boats available. The Royal Swedish Yacht Club was founded here at the turn of the 20th century, and sailing continues to be a popular sport. Its fine-sand beaches also make it an ideal spot for swimming. Another option is to try scuba diving—introductory lessons are available; ask at the Sweden House for details. Explore the village of Sandhamn and its narrow alleys and wooden houses, or stroll out to the graveyard outside the village, where tombstones bear the names of sailors from around the world.

A little closer to Stockholm is the island of **Grinda,** long a popular recreation spot among Stockholmers. Rental cabins from the '40s have been restored to their original condition; there are about 30 of these available through **Grinda Stugby** (☎ 08/54249072). The **Grinda Wärdshus** (☎ 08/54249491), a still-functioning inn from the turn of the 20th century, is one of the largest stone buildings in the archipelago. Since a number of walking paths cut through the woods and open fields, it takes just 15 minutes to walk from one end of Grinda to the other, and exploring is easy. The trip to the island takes about two hours.

At the far southern tip of Stockholm's archipelago lies **Trosa**, a town full of wooden houses that's right on the Baltic Sea. The tiny river that runs through the middle of the town is flanked by beautiful villas painted white, red, yellow, and mint green—a reflection of Trosa's heritage as a seaside retreat for stressed, wealthy Stockholmers. Around the small, cobbled town square are arts-and-crafts shops and market stalls selling fish, fruit, and vegetables.

★ Five kilometers (3 mi) to the north of Trosa is the impressive **Tullgarns Slott.** Built in the early 1700s, the palace was turned into a playful summer retreat in 1772 by King Gustaf's younger brother, Fredrik Adolf. The grounds include sculptured parks and gardens, an orangery, and a theater. The palace's interiors are full of ornate plasterwork, paintings of royals and landscapes, and many of the original French-influenced furnishings. ⊠ *Trosa* ☎ *08/55172011* ⊕ *www.royalcourt.se* 🏷 *SKr 50* ☉ *May–Sept., daily 11–4.*

off the
beaten
path

Fodor'sChoice
★

OAXEN SKÄRGÅRDSKROG – Thirty kilometers (20 mi) northwest of Trosa, on the little island of Oaxen (accessible by bridge), is something of a culinary happening. *Oaxen Skärgårdskrog* can be described, almost without argument, as the very best restaurant in Sweden. Set in an old wooden waterside manor house, Oaxen's interior is sleek and modern, with stunning Danish furniture, dark brown walls, crisp white linens, and oiled oak floors. The pricey-but-worth-it food is a breathtaking collection of modern-European-inspired culinary works of art. (✛ *Drive E4 south from Stockholm for about 40 minutes; take the Hölö/Mörkö exit and follow signs to the restaurant* ☎ *08/54249072* ⊕ *www.oaxenkrog.se)*

If you'd prefer to stay on board a boat and simply cruise around the islands, seek out the **Blidösund.** A coal-fired steamboat built in 1911 that has remained in almost continuous service, the *Blidösund* is now run by a small group of enthusiasts who take parties of around 250 on evening music-and-dinner cruises. The cruises depart from a berth close to the Royal Palace in Stockholm. ⊠ *Skeppsbron 11, Stockholm* ☎ *08/ 4117113* 🏷 *SKr 160* ☉ *Departures early May–late Sept., Mon.–Thurs. 6:30 PM (returns at 10:15 PM).*

Among the finest of the archipelago steamboats is the **Saltsjön,** which leaves from Nybrokajen, close to the Strand Hotel. You can take a jazz-and-dinner cruise for SKr 150 from late June to mid-August. Call for details. To go to Utö, the attractive island known for its bike paths, bakery, and restaurant, will cost you SKr 190. In December there are three daily Julbord cruises, all of which serve a Christmas smorgasbord.

✉ *Strömma Kanalbolaget, Skeppsbron 22, Stockholm* ☎ *08/58714000* ⊘ *Departures July–mid-Aug. and Dec.*

Where to Eat

★ **$$–$$$** ✕ **Fjäderholmarnas Krog.** A crackling fire on the hearth in the bar area welcomes the sailors who frequent this laid-back restaurant. In case you don't travel with your own sailboat, you can time your dinner to end before the last ferry returns to the mainland. The food here is self-consciously Swedish: fresh, light, and beautifully presented. The service is professional; it's a great choice for a special night out. ✉ *Fjäderholmarna* ☎ *08/7183355* ▤ *AE, DC, MC, V* ⊘ *Closed Oct.–Apr.*

$$ ✕ **Dykarbaren.** The idea for this old wooden harborside restaurant came from similar cafés in Brittany, France. Simple local dishes, mostly of fish, are served up in an informal wooden-table dining area. Originally just catering to local divers, Dykarbaren now serves everyone. ✉ *Strand-promenaden, Sandhamn* ☎ *08/57153554* ▤ *AE, DC, MC, V.*

¢–$ ✕ **Café Lena Linderholm.** Lena is the wife of folk singer and cookbook writer Gösta Linderholm. She runs a very pleasant interior-design shop on the first floor of this old town house and a café on the second floor. Those with a passion for great coffee, overstuffed sandwiches, and delicious Swedish vanilla buns should make a beeline for this charming spot. ✉ *Rådhusg. 19, Vaxholm* ☎ *08/54132165* ▤ *No credit cards.*

¢ ✕ **Tre Små Rum.** The old mint-green, red-roof house that contains "Three
FodorsChoice Small Rooms" is a fitting place for simple light lunches. The sandwiches
★ (made from freshly baked bread) are delicious at this lunch-only café. There are also delicious cakes and pastries—at least 40 types daily. If you don't want to sit inside in one of the rooms, there is a small outside seating area. ✉ *Östra Långg., Trosa* ☎ *0156/12151* ▤ *MC, V* ⊘ *No dinner.*

Where to Stay

Lodging options in the archipelago vary from island to island. The larger, more inhabited islands often have at least one decent hotel, if not a few, whereas some of the smaller, more deserted islands have only an inn or two or camping facilities.

$$$ ▥ **Grand Hotel Saltsjöbaden.** Many say that this is the only reason to come
FodorsChoice to the beautiful but quiet town of Saltsjöbaden. Next to the sea and the
★ surrounding countryside, the hotel is one of the most breathtaking in the whole archipelago. Built in 1893, it's a castlelike concoction of white stone, arched windows, and towers. The huge rooms are filled with colorful period furniture that is set off perfectly against the plain stone fireplaces and pastel walls. The restaurant ($$$) is a grand gilt, pillared, and mirrored affair with crisp linens, fine crystal, and a classic French menu. ✉ *113 83 Saltsjöbaden* ☎ *08/50617000* ▤ *08/ 50617025* ⊕ *www.grandsaltsjobaden.se* ⇌ *121 rooms, 10 suites* ⌂ *Restaurant, room service, minibars, cable TV, in-room broadband, Wi-Fi, miniature golf, 2 tennis courts, saltwater pool, sauna, spa, ice-skating, bar, no-smoking rooms* ▤ *AE, DC, MC, V* ⦿ *BP.*

¢–$$ ▥ **Utö Värdshus.** The rooms are large and well laid out here, with traditional furniture resembling that found in a Swedish farmhouse—lots of old pine and comfy, plump cushioning. Choose between a room in the sprawling white main hotel or one of the 30 that are in a cabin on the grounds. The restaurant ($$) has a grand wooden ceiling lighted with chandeliers. The food is eclectic, ranging from salmon with dill to Cajun chicken. ⊠ *Gruvbryggan, 130 56 Utö* ☎ 08/50420300 🖷 08/50420301 ⊕ *www.uto-vardshus.se* ⤳ *34 rooms* ⟑ *Restaurant, sauna, bar, no-smoking rooms* ⊟ *AE, DC, MC, V* ❄ *BP.*

★ $ 🏨 **Bomans.** Right on the water and brimming with history, this family-run hotel dates from the early 20th century. The bedrooms are stuffed with floral patterns, iron bedsteads, feather quilts, lace, and linen. Downstairs there is a small bar. Lace tablecloths, chandeliers, and tangerine linens and fabrics help create a warm mood in the very good restaurant ($$), where you can also dine outside in summer. The menu is unashamedly Swedish, with high-quality versions of such classic dishes as meatballs, salmon, and elk with lingonberries. ⊠ *Hamnen, 619 30 Trosa* ☎ *0156/52500* 🖷 *0156/52510* ⊕ *www.bomans.se* ⤳ *32 rooms, 2 suites* ⟑ *Restaurant, in-room data ports, sauna, spa, bar, meeting rooms, no-smoking rooms* ⊟ *AE, DC, MC, V* ❄ *BP.*

$ 🏨 **Grinda Wärdshus.** Housed in one of the archipelago's largest stone buildings, this 19th-century villa has homey rooms and bright, comfortable public areas. Since the hotel is right on the water, you may wish to take a refreshing dip in the sea before tackling the sumptuous breakfast buffet of Scandinavian classics. ⊠ *Södra Bryggan, 100 05 Grinda* ☎ *08/54249491* 🖷 *08/54249497* ⊕ *www.grindawardshus.se* ⤳ *28 rooms, 2 suites* ⟑ *Restaurant* ⊟ *AE, DC, MC, V* ❄ *BP.*

Vaxholm & the Archipelago A to Z

BOAT & FERRY TRAVEL
Regular ferry services to the archipelago depart from Strömkajen, the quayside in front of Stockholm's Grand Hotel. Boat cruises leave from the harbor in front of the Royal Palace or from Nybrokajen, across the street from the Royal Dramatic Theater. Ferries to the Feather Islands run almost constantly all day long in summer (April 29–September 17), from Slussen, Strömkajen, and Nybroplan. Contact Strömma Kanalbolaget, Waxholmsbolaget, or Fjäderholmarna.

An excellent way to see the archipelago is to purchase an **Inter Skerries Card,** which costs SKr 300 and allows unlimited boat travel throughout the islands for five days. Use the card for day trips from Stockholm, or go out for longer excursions and bounce around from island to island. The card is available at the Stockholm Tourist Center.

📱 **Fjäderholmarna** ☎ 08/7180100. **Stockholm Tourist Center** ⊠ Sweden House, Hamng. 27, Box 7542, 103 93 Stockholm ☎ 08/50828508. **Strömma Kanalbolaget** ☎ 08/58714000. **Waxholmsbolaget** ☎ 08/6795830.

TOURS
A great way to discover the remote, less-visited parts of the archipelago is to go out with Sandhamnsguiderna, a tour group that operates out of Sandhamn. Experienced guides will take you on tailor-made excursions, in small or large groups, to explore the outer reaches of the deserted archipelago. A tour price depends on how many people go and for how long.

📱 **Sandhamnsguiderna** ☎ 08/6408040 ⊕ www.sandhamnsguiderna.com.

TRAIN TRAVEL
There are regular train services to Saltsjöbaden from Stockholm's Slussen station, on Södermalm and operated by SL (Stockholm Local Traffic).

The journey takes about 20 minutes. To get to Trosa, take a one-hour train ride from Stockholm to Vagnhärad, where there is a bus waiting to take the 10-minute trip to Trosa.

🔁 **SJ** ☎ 0771/757575 ⊕ www.sj.se. **SL** ☎ 08/6001000 ⊕ www.sl.se.

VISITOR
INFORMATION The Vaxholms Turistbyrå (Vaxholm Tourist Office) is in a large kiosk at the bus terminal, adjacent to the marina and ferry landing. Hours are daily 10–5. The Utö Turistbyrå (Utö Tourist Bureau) is near the ferry landing. More information on Grinda is available from the Stockholm Tourist Center at Sweden House.

🔁 **Sweden House** ⊠ Hamng. 27, Box 7542, 103 93 Stockholm ☎ 08/50828508. **Trosa Turistbyrå** ☎ 0156/52222 ⊕ www.trosa.com. **Utö Turistbyrå** ☎ 08/50157410. **Vaxholms Turistbyrå** ⊠ Söderhamnen, 185 83 Vaxholm ☎ 08/54131480 ⊕ www.visitvaxholm.se.

Gotland

❺ *85 km (53 mi) south of Stockholm.*

Gotland is Sweden's main holiday island, a place of ancient history, a relaxed summer-party vibe, wide sandy beaches, and wild cliff formations called *raukar*. Measuring 125 km (78 mi) long and 52 km (32 mi) at its widest point, Gotland is where Swedish sheep farming has its home. In its charming glades, 35 varieties of wild orchids thrive, attracting botanists from all over the world.

Gotland's capital, **Visby,** is a delightful hilly town of about 20,000 people. Medieval houses, ruined fortifications, churches, and cottage-lined cobbled lanes make Visby look like a fairy-tale place. Thanks to a very gentle climate, the roses that grow along many of the town's facades bloom even in November.

In its heyday Visby was protected by a wall, of which 3 km (2 mi) survive today, along with 44 towers and numerous gateways. It is considered the best-preserved medieval city wall in Europe after that of Carcassonne, in southern France. Take a stroll to the north gate for an unsurpassed view of the wall.

Visby's cathedral, **St. Maria Kyrka,** is the only one of the town's 13 medieval churches that is still intact and in use. Built between 1190 and 1225 as a place of worship for the town's German parishioners, the church has few of its original fittings because of the extensive and sometimes clumsy restoration work done over the years. That said, the sandstone font and the unusually ugly angels decorating the pulpit are both original features worth a look.

The **Länsmuseet på Gotland,** Gotland's county museum, contains examples of medieval artwork, prehistoric gravestones and skeletons, and silver hoards from Viking times. Be sure to also check out the ornate "picture stones" from AD 400–600, which depict ships, people, houses, and animals. ⊠ *Strandg. 14* ☎ *0498/292700* ⊕ *www.lansmuseetgotland.se* 🎫 *SKr 40* ☉ *Mid-May–Sept., daily 11–5; Oct.–mid-May, Tues.–Sun. noon–4.*

The **Visby Art Museum** has some innovative exhibitions of contemporary painting and sculpture. On the first floor is the permanent display,

THE SWEDISH BALANCING ACT

WHEN THE WORLD THINKS OF SWEDEN *and the Swedes, blond-haired beauties are never far from mind. The truth is, if you plotted a map of global sales of blond hair dye, there would be a lot of pins in Sweden. When Swedish women talk about their roots, it's not only their Viking ancestors they refer to.*

It's almost impossible to say what constitutes being a typical Swede today. Long ago the nation realized that it had become a mix of people and influences from across the globe, and that the country is even better for it. That's not to say that there isn't a national identity, because there is—a strong one. Those searching for clues to this identity should simply examine the Swedish State.

The State plays a very important role in Swedish life. It controls and sells all alcohol, owns and runs every drugstore in the land, and keeps an eagle eye on levels of decadence, taxing accordingly.

Living in a fairly controlled, clean, well-operating environment may consequently lead to the relaxation and comfort that is source of Sweden's famed liberal attitude. People here live in clean towns and cities with excellent infrastructures; everyone has access to public transportation and affordable sports facilities; and families have unbeatable parental-leave benefits and subsidized day care.

The delicate balance of old and new; of fierce tradition and enterprising modernity; of booming capitalism and an extensive welfare system; of swimming nude whenever possible while maintaining a stiff and formal attitude; and of freedom and control is a uniquely Swedish phenomenon—and an interesting one to experience firsthand.

–Rob Hincks

which is mostly uninspiring, save for a beautiful 1917 watercolor by local artist Axel Lindman showing Visby from the beach in all its splendid medieval glory. ⊠ *St. Hansg. 21* ☎ *0498/292775* ⊠ *SKr 40* ☉ *May–Sept., daily 10–5.*

The 4 km (2½ mi) of stalactite caves at **Lummelunda,** about 18 km (11 mi) north of Visby on the coastal road, are unique in this part of the world and are worth visiting. ⊠ *Lummelunds Bruk* ☎ *0498/273050* ⊕ *www.lummelundagrottan.se* ⊠ *SKr 70* ☉ *May–Sept., daily 9–5.*

Curious rock formations dot the coasts of Gotland, remnants of reefs formed more than 400 million years ago, and two **bird sanctuaries, Stora** and **Lilla Karlsö,** stand off the coast south of Visby. The bird population consists mainly of guillemots, which look like penguins. Visits to these sanctuaries are permitted only in the company of a recognized guide. ☎ *0498/240500 for Stora, 0498/485248 for Lilla* ⊠ *SKr 225 for Stora, SKr 200 for Lilla.* ☉ *May–Aug., daily.*

Where to Eat

★ **$$** ✕ **Donners Brunn.** In a beautiful orange-brick house on a small square in Visby, the chef proprietor of this restaurant, Bo Nilsson, was once chef at the renowned Operakällaren in Stockholm. The menu uses excellent local ingredients to make French-influenced dishes that are reasonably priced, given their quality. The house specialty of Gotland lamb with fresh asparagus and hollandaise sauce is delicious. ☒ *Donners Plats 3* ☎ *0498/271090* ⌂ *Reservations essential* ⊟ *AE, DC, MC, V.*

$–$$ ✕ **Krusmyntagården.** This marvelous little garden-café opened in the late '70s and has been passed down through several owners. The garden now has more than 200 organic herbs and plants, many of which are used in the evening BBQ feasts. ☒ *Brissund* ☎ *0498/296900* ⊟ *AE, DC, MC, V.*

¢–$$ ✕ **Konstnärsgården.** Hans and Birgitta Belin run a wonderful establishment in the tiny village of Ala. He is an artist, she a chef. As you eat your lovingly prepared food in this old manor-house restaurant, you can view and buy works by Hans and other artists. The venison that's often on the menu comes from deer raised on the premises, and in the summer months whole lambs are spit-roasted outdoors in the orchard gardens. ☒ *30 km (19 mi) southeast of Visby, Ala* ☎ *0498/55055* ⊟ *MC, V.*

¢–$ ✕ **Björklunda Värdshuset.** This small restaurant in an old stone farmhouse is run by a husband-and-wife team. You can have an aperitif in the apple orchard before tucking into the menu of local salmon, lamb, and pork dishes, all of which come in ample proportions. ☒ *Björklunda, Burgsvik* ☎ *0498/497190* ⊟ *AE, DC, MC, V.*

Where to Stay

$–$$ 🏨 **Strand Hotel.** An environmentally friendly hotel with efficient heating and cooling systems, the Strand may ease your conscience with its approach. In any case, the lap pool, sauna, and bright, comfortable rooms will ease your spirit. The clubby, relaxing bar has large leather sofas in an adjoining library. ☒ *Strandg. 34, 621 56* ☎ *0498/258800* 🖷 *0498/258811* ⊕ *www.strandhotel.net* ⮑ *110 rooms, 6 suites* ⌂ *Restaurant, indoor pool, sauna, bar, no-smoking rooms* ⊟ *AE, DC, MC, V* ⎨⊙⎬ *BP.*

$–$$ 🏨 **Wisby Hotell.** The tall, thin building that's now the Wisby dates from the 1200s and is at the junction of two narrow streets. A hotel since 1855, the ocher-color walls, light floral-patterned fabrics, dark wood, and vaulted ceilings give it old European grandeur. There are two excellent bars in the hotel, one a glassed-in courtyard that serves cocktails and the other a cozy pub with a good beer selection. ☒ *Strandg. 6, 621 24* ☎ *0498/257500* 🖷 *0498/257550* ⊕ *www.wisbyhotell.se* ⮑ *134 rooms, 94 with bath; 10 suites* ⌂ *Restaurant, in-room broadband, Wi-Fi, 2 bars, no-smoking rooms* ⊟ *AE, DC, MC, V* ⎨⊙⎬ *BP.*

¢–$ 🏨 **Toftagården.** Near the Gotland coast about 20 km (12 mi) from Visby, the placid verdant grounds here are ideal for strolling, lazing about, and reading in the shade. The long sandy beach in Tofta is also nearby, as is the Kronholmen Golf Course. Most of the brightly furnished rooms, all on the ground floor, have their own terrace. There are also a number of cottages with kitchens—a two-night minimum stay is required for these. If the seawater at the beach is too cold, take a dip in the heated outdoor pool. The restaurant serves very good regional fare. ☒ *Toftagården, 621 98* ☎ *0498/297000* 🖷 *0498/265666* ⊕ *www.toftagarden.se* ⮑ *50 rooms, 15 cottages* ⌂ *Restaurant, some kitchenettes, pool, sauna* ⊟ *AE, DC, MC, V* ⎨⊙⎬ *BP.*

¢ ▦ **Hotel St. Clemens.** Four buildings make up the St. Clemens, in Visby's Old Town. They range in age from a relatively young sixtysomething years to about four centuries, dating from the 1600s. Rooms are simple and a little clumsily furnished with mismatched materials, but they are comfortable, most with an armchair or sofa; some have small kitchens. There are two gardens on the property, one of which is shared with St. Clemens Church, one of Visby's oldest. ✉ *Smedjeg. 3, 621 55* ☎ *0498/219000* 🖷 *0498/279443* ⊕ *www.clemenshotell.se* ⮑ *32 rooms* ⚘ *Some kitchenettes, cable TV, sauna, free parking* ▭ *AE, DC, MC, V* ⦿ *CP.*

★ ¢ ▦ **Villa Alskog.** A short drive from the sandy beaches in the south of Gotland, Villa Alskog is a delightful inn surrounded by beautiful open spaces, stone fences, and small groves of trees. The building dates from 1840 and was originally a residence for the local priest. Its 15 guest rooms are bright and simply furnished, with hardwood floors. Most have a private bath; when you reserve a room, verify that it's one that has its own bath. The location is ideal for swimming, hiking, and horseback riding. ✉ *620 16 Alskog* ☎ *0498/491188* 🖷 *0498/491120* ⊕ *www.villa-alskog.se* ⮑ *15 rooms* ⚘ *Restaurant, café, hot tub, sauna, meeting room* ▭ *AE, DC, MC, V* ⦿ *BP.*

Nightlife & the Arts

Medeltidsveckan (Medieval Week), celebrated in early August, is a city-wide festival marking the invasion of the prosperous island by Danish king Valdemar on July 22, 1361. Celebrations begin with Valdemar's grand entrance parade and continue with jousts, an open-air market on Strandgatan, and street-theater performances re-creating the period.

In the ruins of **St. Nicolai,** the old dilapidated church in Visby, regular concerts are held throughout the summer months. Everything from folk to rock to classical is available. The tourist office has details.

There are many bars and drinking establishments on Gotland, but the best are in Visby. The town comes alive on summer nights; the best way to experience it is simply to wander the streets, follow the loudest noise, and go with the flow.

Sports & the Outdoors

Bicycles, tents, and camping equipment can be rented from **Gotlands Cyke-luthyrning** (✉ Skeppsbron 2 ☎ 0498/214133 ⊕ www.gotlandscykeluthyrning.com). **Gotlandsleden** is a 200-km (120-mi) bicycle route around the island; contact the tourist office for details.

For an aquatic adventure, **Gotlands Upplevelser** (✉Visby ☎0730/751678) will rent you a canoe and a life jacket or windsurfing equipment. They also offer rock-climbing courses. Call for prices and locations.

Gotland A to Z

BOAT & FERRY TRAVEL
Regular and high-speed car ferries sail from Nynäshamn, a small port on the Baltic an hour by car or rail from Stockholm; commuter trains leave regularly from Stockholm's central station for Nynäshamn. Timetables change frequently, so it is best to consult the operating company, Gotland City Travel, before departure. The regular ferry takes about

5 hours; the fast ferry takes 2½ hours. Boats also leave from Oskarshamn, farther down the Swedish coast and closer to Gotland by about an hour. Call Gotland City Travel for more information.

🏛 **Gotland City Travel** ⊠ Kungsg. 57 ☎ 08/4061500 ⊕ www.destinationgotland.se.

CAR RENTAL   🏛 **Biltjänst** ⊠ Endrev. 45, Visby ☎ 0498/218790. **MABI Rental Cars** ⊠ Visby ☎ 0498/279396.

EMERGENCIES   🏛 **Visby Hospital** ☎ 0498/269000.

VISITOR
INFORMATION   The main tourist office is Gotlands Turistförening (Gotland Tourist Association) in Visby. You can also contact Gotland City Travel in Stockholm for lodging or ferry reservations.

🏛 **Gotland City Travel** ☎ 08/4061500. **Gotlands Turistförening & Visby Turistbyrå** ⊠ Hamng. 4, Visby ☎ 0498/201700 ⊕ www.gotland.info. **Gotlands Turistservice** ⊠ Österv. 3A, Visby ☎ 0498/203300 ⊕ www.gotlandsturistservice.com.

Uppsala

❻ *67 km (41 mi) north of Stockholm.*

For the title of "Sweden's principal university town," Uppsala has only one rival: Lund, to the south. August Strindberg, the nation's leading dramatist, studied here—and by all accounts hated the place. Ingmar Bergman, his modern heir, was born in town. It is also a historic site where pagan (and extremely gory) Viking ceremonies persisted into the 11th century. Uppsala University, one of the oldest institutions in Europe, was established in 1477 by Archbishop Jakob Ulfson. As late as the 16th century, nationwide *tings* (early parliaments) were convened here. Today it is a quiet home for about 170,000 people. Built along the banks of the Fyris River, the town has a pleasant jumble of old buildings that is dominated by its cathedral, which dates from the early 13th century.

In recent years Uppsala has shaken off the shadow of nearby Stockholm and is emerging as a destination in its own right. The town has established itself as something of a center for medical research and pharmaceuticals. Add to the mix the student population, and Uppsala has become a thriving place, with housing and office developments springing up in equal numbers to restaurants, bars, cultural venues, and shops.

The last day of April never fails to make the town become one big carnival—the Feast of Valborg. To celebrate the arrival of spring (and the end of the school year), students of the university don sailorlike hats and charge down the hill from the university library (try not to get in their way). The university chorus then sings traditional spring songs on the steps of the main building. And finally the whole town slips into mayhem. Thousands descend on the city as the streets are awash in champagne and celebrations. It's an age-old custom worth seeing, but it's not for the fainthearted.

Ideally you should start your visit with a trip to **Gamla Uppsala** (Old Uppsala), 5 km (3 mi) north of the town. Here under three huge mounds lie the graves of the first Swedish kings—Aun, Egil, and Adils—of the 6th-century Ynglinga dynasty. Close by in pagan times was a sacred grove containing a legendary oak from whose branches animal and human sacrifices were hung. By the 10th century Christianity had eliminated such practices. A small church, which was the seat of Sweden's first archbishop, was built on the site of a former pagan temple.

The **Gamla Uppsala Museum** contains exhibits and archaeological findings from the Viking burial mounds that dominate the local area. The museum distinguishes between the myth and legends about the area and what is actually known about its history. ☎ *018/239300* ☒ *SKr 50* ⊙ *May–Aug., daily 11–5; Sept.–Apr., Wed. and weekends noon–3.*

★ Back in Uppsala, your first visit should be to **Uppsala Domkyrka** (Uppsala Cathedral). Its 362-foot twin towers—whose height equals the length of the nave—dominate the city. Work on the cathedral began in the early 13th century; it was consecrated in 1435 and restored between 1885 and 1893. Still the seat of Sweden's archbishop, the cathedral is also the site of the tomb of Gustav Vasa, the king who established Sweden's independence in the 16th century. Inside is a silver casket containing the relics of St. Erik. ☎ *018/187177* ⊕ *www.uppsalacathedral.com* ☒ *Free* ⊙ *Daily 8–6.*

Gustav Vasa began work on **Uppsala Slott** (Uppsala Castle) in the 1540s. He intended the building to symbolize the dominance of the monarchy over the church. It was completed under Queen Christina nearly a century later. Students gather here every April 30 to celebrate the Feast of Valborg and optimistically greet the arrival of spring. Call the tourist center for more information. ☒ *Ingång C, 753 10 Uppsala* ☒ *Castle SKr 60* ⊙ *English guided tours of castle mid-Apr.–Sept., daily at 1 and 3; Oct.–mid-Apr., weekdays at 11 and 2, weekends at 10, 11, 2, and 3.*

One of Uppsala's most famous sons, Carl von Linné, also known as Linnaeus, was a professor of botany at the university during the 1740s. He created the Latin nomenclature system for plants and animals. The botanical treasures of Linnaeus's old garden have been re-created and are now on view in **Linnéträdgården.** The garden's orangery houses a pleasant cafeteria and is used for concerts and cultural events. ☒ *Svartbäcksg. 27* ☎ *018/4712576* ⊕ *www.linnaeus.uu.se* ☒ *SKr 30* ⊙ *May–Aug., daily 9–9; Sept.–Apr., daily 9–7.*

Uppsala Universitetet (Uppsala University; ☎ *018/4710000* ⊕ www.uu. se), founded in 1477, is known for the **Carolina Rediviva** university library, which contains a copy of every book published in Sweden, in addition to a large collection of foreign works. Two of its most interesting exhibits are the *Codex Argentus,* a Bible written in the 6th century, and Mozart's original manuscript for his 1791 opera *The Magic Flute.*

Completed in 1625, the **Gustavianum,** which served as the university's main building for two centuries, is easy to spot by its remarkable copper cupola, now green with age. The building houses the ancient anatomical theater—one of only seven in the world to function on natural light—where human anatomy lectures and public dissections took place. The Victoria Museum of Egyptian Antiquities is in the same building. ☒ *Akademig. 3* ☎ *018/4717571* ⊕ *www.gustavianum.uu.se* ☒ *SKr 40* ⊙ *June–Aug., daily 11–3; Anatomical Theater June–Aug., daily 10–4; Sept.–May, weekends 11–4.*

Where to Stay & Eat

★ **$$–$$$** ✕ **Guldkanten.** When Uppsala's grand old food hall burned down in 2002, Guldkanten burned with it. Now it's back with chef Anders Ericsson at the stoves, producing ambitious, modern, and delicious food inspired by Swedish ingredients and flavors from the Mediterranean and eastern Europe. Delightful dishes, such as tortellini of crab with fennel puree or pigeon with blinis, cabbage, and figs, are deftly presented and full of flavor. The restaurant is fronted by a sweeping semicircular window overlooking the river, and the interior is a subtle blend of dark wood and cream furnishings. ⊠ *St. Eriks torg 8* ☎ *018/150151* ⚱ *Reservations essential* ▤ *AE, DC, MC, V.*

$–$$$ ✕ **Wermlandskällaren.** A beautiful vaulted cellar is the venue for this tightly packed and welcoming little restaurant. The look—exposed brick walls, well-worn stone floors, dark-wood furniture, flickering candles—suggests that traditional food is on offer here. Think again. Salim Chowdhury works hard on his menu, presenting artistic and delicious contemporary food, gathering flavors from across the globe. Dishes such as smoked ostrich with Parmesan, nuts, and dates, or langoustines with spiced Swedish cheese and vanilla champagne sauce defy classification and wow the palate. ⊠ *Nedre Slottsg. 2* ☎ *018/132200* ▤ *AE, DC, MC, V.*

$ ✕ **Hyllan.** Suspended on a half floor above the rebuilt food hall, Hyllan is a dim, cozy place—some would even say it's romantic. Dark woods and cream and red sofas and chairs set the mood in the bar; the dining area follows suit. The food here consists of well-prepared bistro staples. Think steaks, salads, mussels, cod with horseradish, and the like. It's a busy, friendly place, especially at the bar, and makes for a great one-stop night out. ⊠ *St. Eriks torg 8* ☎ *018/150150* ▤ *AE, DC, MC, V.*

¢–$ ✕ **Günthers.** This classic old café has stood by the river for more than 100 years. On the wall as you enter is proof of royal appointment as cake makers to the king—still valid today. Inside, the dark-wood paneling, the thick carpet, and the solid wooden chairs and tables look as though they just might outlast the royal warrant. One side of the main room is taken up by huge glass cabinets containing exquisite cakes, delicate pastries, crusty well-filled sandwiches, and hot dishes like lasagna. Lunch here, ending with a few pieces of cake, should see you through until breakfast. ⊠ *Östra Åg. 31* ☎ *018/130757* ▤ *MC, V* ☽ *No dinner.*

$–$$$ ▦ **Gillet.** Operated by the Radisson SAS group, Uppsala's largest hotel first opened in 1971. Rooms are bright and large, with pleasant watercolors, soft furnishings, and hardwood floors. The hotel is only a short walk from Uppsala's most famous buildings. The public areas are a little bland and standardized, but very comfortable. ⊠ *Dragarbrunnsg. 23, 751 42* ☎ *018/681800* 📠 *018/681818* ⊕ *www.radissonsas.com* ↵ *160 rooms, 1 suite* ♿ *2 restaurants, room service, minibars, room TVs with movies, in-room broadband, in-room data ports, Wi-Fi, pool, gym, sauna, meeting rooms, parking (fee), no-smoking rooms* ▤ *AE, DC, MC, V* ⏐◯⏐ *BP.*

$–$$ ▦ **Grand Hotel Hörnan.** A mansionlike creation from 1906, the Hörnan's city-center location means that it's near the train station and has views of both the castle and the cathedral. The rooms are spacious and have antique furnishings and soft lighting. Once the grandest hotel in town,

Hörnan has faded a bit these days, but still keeps its head up, retaining a noble air of its former self. ✉ *Bandgårdsg. 1, 753 20* ☎ *018/139380* 🖨 *018/120311* 🌐 *www.grandhotellhornan.com* 🛏 *37 rooms* ⚑ *Bar, meeting rooms* ☰ *AE, DC, MC, V* 🍽 *BP.*

$ 🏨 **Scandic Uplandia.** This branch of the giant Nordic chain has the usual modern comforts and high-tech amenities expected of an international business hotel. There's also the pleasing design that's found in the best Scandinavian hotels. Blond wood accented with moss-green and aqua-marine fabrics gives the decor a sophisticated edge. ✉ *Dragarbrunnsg. 32, 751 40* ☎ *018/4952600* 🖨 *018/4952611* 🌐 *www.scandic-hotels. se* 🛏 *133 rooms, 2 suites* ⚑ *Restaurant, room service, room TVs with movies, in-room broadband, in-room data ports, Wi-Fi, sauna, bar, meeting rooms, no-smoking rooms* ☰ *AE, DC, MC, V* 🍽 *BP.*

¢ 🏨 **First Hotel Linné.** The namesake of this white-stone town-house hotel with lush gardens is the botanist Linnaeus (Carl von Linné). The hotel's interior is in harmony with the gardens outside: soft floral prints and warm colors dominate. In winter, enjoy the huge open fireplace. Rooms are done in a bright, modern Scandinavian design, with earth and red tones. ✉ *Skolg. 45, 750 02* ☎ *018/102000* 🖨 *018/137597* 🌐 *www.firsthotels. com* 🛏 *116 rooms, 6 suites* ⚑ *Restaurant, minibars, in-room broadband, Wi-Fi, sauna, bar, no-smoking rooms* ☰ *AE, DC, MC, V* 🍽 *BP.*

Nightlife

Bowlaget (✉ Skolg. 6 ☎ 018/553310) is Uppsala's newest and coolest meeting spot. In this huge venue you can move between a modern bar and restaurant, a neon-blue bowling alley, a sports bar with plasma-screen TVs, and a very loud, very bumpin' nightclub. Enter for dinner, leave at dawn. For a relaxed evening, head to **Katalin** (✉ Östra Station ☎ 018/140680), a former goods shed behind the railway station, now a funky bar and restaurant. The emphasis here is on the music, with live jazz, rock, and Swedish pop making most people forget about dinner.

Shopping

Jaber (✉ Fyris torg 6 ☎ 018/135050) is something of a draw for the area's wealthy elite. It is a family-run clothes shop with a line of gorgeous international designs, matched only by the personal service it provides. **Öster om Ån** (✉ Svartbäcksg. 18 ☎ 018/711545) is a handicraft cooperative that was formed many years ago. The co-op is still hugely popular today, offering a unique and beautiful range of ceramics, knitted goods, wood-work, and jewelry. **Trolltyg** (✉ Östra Åg. 25 ☎ 018/146304) has an exclusive selection of the sort of clean-line clothes and household furnishings for which Scandinavian design is known. The shop is wonderfully laid out and is a joy to explore, especially the fabrics section.

Uppsala A to Z

SIGHTSEEING TOURS You can explore Uppsala easily on your own, but English-language guided group tours can be arranged through the Uppsala Guide Service. 🚩 **Uppsala Guide Service** ☎ 018/7274818.

TRAIN TRAVEL Trains between Stockholm and Uppsala run twice hourly throughout the day year-round. The cost of a one-way trip is SKr 75. For timetables and train information, contact SJ.

🚩 **SJ** ☎ 0771/757575 🌐 www.sj.se.

VISITOR
INFORMATION The main tourist office run by the Uppsala Convention and Visitors Bureau is in the town center; in summer a small tourist information office is also open at Uppsala Castle.

🏛 **Main Tourist Office** ✉ Fyris torg 8 ☎ 018/7274800 ⊕ www.uppland.nu.

THE BOTHNIAN COAST

Indented with shimmering fjords, peppered with pine-clad islands, and lined with sheer cliffs, the Bothnian Coast is a dramatic sliver of land on Sweden's east coast.

Its history and prosperity come from the sea and the forest. This is as true of the grand 19th-century stone houses built from the profits of international sea trading and the paper industry as it is of the ancient fishing villages, which are now used mainly as holiday homes for urban Swedes.

Traveling up the Bothnian Coast is a simple task, mostly involving a single road or railway track. All the major towns are on the coast and are relatively evenly spread, making it easier for you to plan your rests. The coastline is rocky and rugged in places and is bordered by the beautiful forests and lakes of Hälsingland. By car, the E4 highway quickly eats up the miles, and takes in all the major sights. By train, the coastal line that links Stockholm to the north of Sweden does the same.

The city of Gävle is considered by many Swedes to be a gateway to the northern wildernesses and may be a convenient place to start, as there is frequent bus service there. But the mix of grand 19th-century boulevards and parks and modern, bland shopping centers that make up much of the small downtown area, probably won't be enough to keep you there for long.

Like much of coastal Sweden, the Bothnian Coast is a harsh place to be in the winter months. This leaves the high season of mid-May to mid-September as the best time to visit. This is the time of year when most of the attractions in the region are open and when the Baltic Sea becomes approachable for boat traffic.

Söderhamn

❶ *75 km (47 mi) north of Gävle (via E4).*

Söderhamn is a town with a lot of space. Besides the extensive open countryside that borders the town, the center is awash with parks, gardens, and wide boulevards. In summer Swedes come from all over to enjoy the pretty public spaces. The many trees help to remove air pollution, making sitting in an open-air café here exceptionally pleasing. The town's architecture is a mix of monumental 18th-century buildings, erected with fortunes made by fishing, and modern shopping precincts built to replace areas devastated by numerous fires. This coastal town is also close to one of the finest archipelagoes in the region: more than 500 islands, islets, and skerries are near.

For stunning panoramic views of the town and the surrounding forest and sea, climb **Oscarborg**, a 75-foot tower at the edge of town. Built in

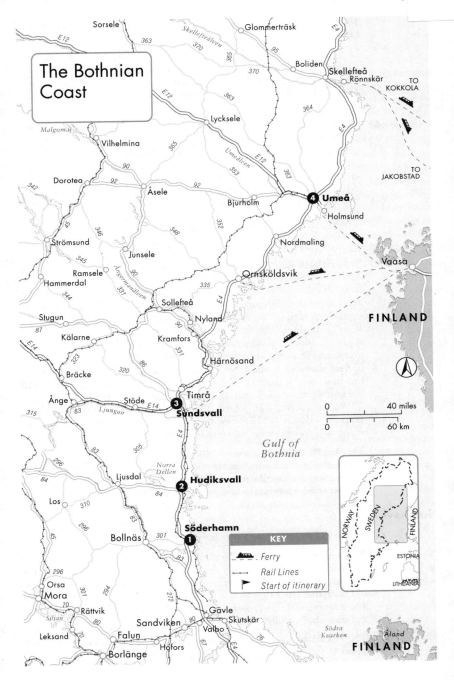

The Bothnian Coast

Sorsele
Glommerträsk
Boliden
Skellefteå
Rönnskär
TO KOKKOLA
Lycksele
Vilhelmina
TO JAKOBSTAD
Dorotea
Åsele
Bjurholm
④ Umeå
Holmsund
Strömsund
Junsele
Nordmaling
Ramsele
Hammerdal
Sollefteå
Örnsköldsvik
Vaasa
Stugun
Nyland
Kälarne
Kramfors
Härnösand
FINLAND
Bräcke
Ånge
Stöde
Timrå
③ Sundsvall
Gulf of Bothnia
Ljusdal
② Hudiksvall
Los
Bollnäs
① Söderhamn
Norra Dellen
Orsa
Mora
Rättvik
Sandviken
Gävle
Skutskär
Södra Kvarken
Åland
Leksand
Falun
Valbo
Hofors
Borlänge
FINLAND

0 ___ 40 miles
0 ___ 60 km

KEY
🚢 Ferry
⊢ Rail Lines
▷ Start of itinerary

NORWAY
SWEDEN
FINLAND
ESTONIA
LATVIA
LITHUANIA

1895, the white tower and attached building resemble a Disney-esque fairy-tale castle.

Dating to the 1600s, **Smedjan** (Blacksmiths) is a living, working museum where you can watch craftsmen use traditional methods to make horseshoes and other items. ⊠ *Kungsgården* ☎ *0270/35031* ☑ *Free* ☉ *July, Mon. 2–4, Thurs. 6–8. All other times by appointment.*

Where to Stay & Eat

$–$$$ ✕ **Restaurang Albertina.** This converted red wooden barn is on the water's edge, just north of Söderhamn, in the old fishing village of Skärså. Inside, scrubbed wooden walls and beamed ceilings blend with the crisp, white table linens. Fish is the specialty here. The locally caught salmon that they serve here is among the best in the region. ⊠ *Skärså* ☎ *0270/732010* ⊟ *AE, DC, MC, V.*

¢–$ ✕ **Rådhus Konditoriet.** Inside an uninspiring building is a restaurant that doubles as one of the few photography galleries in the north of Sweden. The gallery and the excellent selection of sandwiches, specialty teas, and light meals make it worth the trip. ⊠ *Kykog. 10* ☎ *0270/12457* ⊟ *AE, MC, V* ☉ *Closed Sun.*

$–$$ ⌷ **First Hotell Statt.** The oldest hotel in town is also the most luxurious. All the rooms are individually furnished and have wooden floors and a comfortable mix of blond wood and pastel furnishings. The public areas have their original chandeliers, stuccowork ceilings, and large open fireplaces, giving the hotel a feel of old luxury. ⊠ *Oxtorgsg. 17, 826 22* ☎ *0270/73570* ☐ *0270/13524* ⊕ *www.firsthotels.se* ⌁ *78 rooms, 1 suite* △ *Restaurant, in-room broadband, Wi-Fi, sauna, bar, nightclub, convention center* ⊟ *AE, DC, MC, V.*

¢ ⌷ **Centralhotellet.** As the name suggests, it's the central location that makes this hotel worth the stay. The rooms were all refurbished in 2004, and are much improved, featuring simple spaces and plenty of light wood. ⊠ *Rådhustorget, 826 32* ☎ *0270/70000* ☐ *0270/16060* ⊕ *www. centralhotellet.se* ⌁ *27 rooms* △ *Restaurant, in-room broadband, bar, nightclub, free parking, no-smoking rooms* ⊟ *AE, DC, MC, V.*

The Outdoors

For an energetic inland-water adventure, there are myriad lakes and rivers around Söderhamn that are perfect for canoeing. For more information contact **Fritidskontoret** (leisure office; ☎ *0270/60000*).

Hudiksvall

❷ *60 km (37 mi) north of Söderhamn (via E4).*

Granted its town charter in 1582, Hudiksvall's history is bound up with the sea. Having been partially destroyed by fire 10 times, Hudiksvall is now an interesting mix of architectural styles. The small section of the old town that remains is built around a central harbor and contains some fine examples of flower-strewn courtyards and traditional wood-panel buildings built along narrow, cobbled streets.

The **Fiskarstan** (Fishertown; ☎ *0650/19100* tourist office) neighborhood is tightly packed with striking streets of fishermen's huts and houses and boardwalks of wooden fish stores that hang precariously over the water. Lilla Kyrkogatan, the oldest street in town, leads to Hudiksvall's Church, which is still marked by cannonballs from a Russian invasion in 1721. Guided tours, maps, and information can be arranged through the town's tourist office.

Where to Stay & Eat

¢–$$ ╳ **Gretas Krog.** Built right by the fishing docks, this restaurant is rarely empty and seldom disappoints. The interior trades predictably on fishing history through sepia photographs of weather-beaten fishermen and old nets strung from the ceiling, but there is something undeniably cozy about it all. The menu is packed with good local specialties and traditional Swedish cuisine. ⊠ *Västra Tväkajen* ☎ *0650/96600* ▤ *AE, DC, MC, V* ⌲ *Reservations essential* ⊘ *No lunch.*

¢–$ ╳ **Jambo Cafe.** This is a lunch-only hot spot where Hudiksvall's young couples come to pass the summer days. On offer are a huge and varied hot-sandwich selection, fresh salads, and classic Swedish café dishes. ⊠ *Svallertorget* ☎ *0650/13025* ▤ *MC, V.*

¢–$$ ▦ **First Hotell Statt.** The grand 19th-century yellow-stone facade of this hotel, with its pillars and arches, looks like that of a typical Swedish town hall. Once you've gone inside, the more familiar marble floor and pastel shades confirm that you have arrived at your hotel. Rooms here are nothing special; most are in need of redecoration. All the bathrooms were refurbished in 2005, so the hotel has started working on it. ⊠ *Storg. 36, SE-824 22* ☎ *0650/15060* ☎ *0650/96095* ⊕ *www.firsthotels.se* ⊷ *106 rooms, 8 suites* ⌂ *Restaurant, pool, gym, sauna, pub, nightclub, convention center* ▤ *AE, DC, MC, V* ▮◯▮ *BP.*

Sports & the Outdoors

Hudiksvall's archipelago is centered around the peninsula of **Hornslandet,** just north of the town. As well as the usual fishing, swimming, and boating, the peninsula has Europe's second-largest system of mountain caves, which can be explored by experts and beginners alike. Call **Alf Siden** (☎ 0650/70492), who arranges and conducts official tours of the caves. His English is almost nonexistent, but his knowledge of the caves is quite the opposite, so bear with him.

Shopping

Slöjd i Sjöboden (⊠ Möljen ☎ 0650/12041) is a series of old fishing huts now housing stalls where 15 local craftspeople sell their wares. Locally inspired textiles, jewelry, ceramics, and glassware can all be bought at very good prices.

Sundsvall

❸ *80 km (50 mi) north of Hudiksvall (via E4).*

Sundsvall also goes by the name of Stenstan (Stone Town), and rightly so. When the town was razed by fire in 1888, it was rebuilt entirely out of stone, which is atypical for this part of Sweden. The reconstruction added more parks and widened roads to prevent later fires from spreading. Add to these Sundsvall's impressive limestone and brick buildings, and it begins to resemble Sweden's largest cities, Stockholm and Göteborg.

Gustav Adolfs kyrka, at the far end of Storgatan, is Sundsvall's main church. In keeping with much of the city, it's a grand 19th-century affair that's built of red brick. There is a pleasing order about the interior, its vaults and pillars all constructed from smooth square stones that look like children's building blocks.

The best place to get a feel for the city and its history is at the **Kulturmagasinet** (Culture Warehouse), a series of four 19th-century waterfront warehouses that now include a museum, library, archives, a children's culture center, art exhibitions, and street music. The museum, which traces the town's history, is built over an old street, where tram tracks and cobblestones are still in place. It gives a good sense of what Sundsvall was like when it was still a busy trading port. ⊠ *Packhusg. 4* ☎ *060/191000* June–Aug. SKr 20, Sept.–May free ☉ *Mon.–Thurs. 10–7, Fri. 10–6, Sat. 11–4.*

Sundsvall is a good city to walk around in, as most of the points of interest are woven into the streets, boulevards, and squares of **Storgatan and Stora Torget.** History comes to life here with churches, the town hall, and grand porticoed stone buildings all flexing their architectural muscles. Guided tours and maps can be arranged through the **tourist office** (☎ 060/610450).

Where to Stay & Eat

★ **$$–$$$** ✕ **Restaurang Grankotten.** The food here, described as modern Swedish with a French influence, has won praise from all over. Dishes such as veal with truffles and anything that uses the delicious local elk are worth traveling for. The views of Sundsvall from the turn-of-the-19th-century building are stunning, especially if you dine outside in summer. ⊠ *Norra Stadsberget* ☎ *060/614222* ⚑ *Reservations essential* ☰ *AE, DC, MC, V* ☉ *Closed Sun.*

$–$$ ✕ **Skeppsbrokällaren.** Classic Swedish design and furnishings and good Scandinavian cuisine are the main attractions at this quiet basement restaurant on the site of the original boat entrance to the city. For a more calming dining experience book a table in the Röda Rummet (Red Room), a smaller, darkened dining area at the back of the restaurant. ⊠ *Sjög. 4* ☎ *060/173660* ⚑ *Reservations essential* ☰ *AE, DC, MC, V.*

★ **$–$$** 🏨 **Elite Hotel Knaust.** The Knaust family opened this art nouveau hotel in 1860, and it has lost none of its original glory. The sweeping marble staircase and black-and-white-tile lobby is extraordinary and worth a look even if you are not staying. Comfort and luxury are watchwords in the rooms, which have warm, lush fabrics and artwork. The hotel is downtown, conveniently near Sundsvall's shops and other attractions. ⊠ *Storg. 13, 851 05* ☎ *060/6080000* 🖷 *060/6080010* ⊕ *www.elite. se* ⤢ *94 rooms, 9 suites* ⚐ *Restaurant, minibars, cable TV, room TVs with movies, in-room broadband, in-room data ports, Wi-Fi, gym, sauna, bar, business services, convention center* ☰ *AE, DC, MC, V* ❍|BP.

$ 🏨 **Comfort Hotel Sundsvall.** Grand stone arches and portals give an impression of stately luxury to this central hotel. The interior doesn't quite live up to the grand facade, but the rooms are large, comfortable, and individually furnished in earth and red tones and have wooden floors. ⊠ *Sjög. 11, 852 34* ☎ *060/150720* 🖷 *060/123456* ⊕ *www.choicehotels.*

se ⇔ 52 rooms ♨ Restaurant, cable TV, in-room broadband, in-room data ports, Wi-Fi, pool, sauna, bar, free parking ▤ *AE, DC, MC, V.*

Sports & the Outdoors

The nearby Ljungan Riveris an excellent spot for rafting. Tours include one hour of white-water rafting, beautiful scenery, and lunch on a small island. Contact the tourist office (☏ 060/610450) for more information.

Shopping

Northern Sweden's largest shopping mall, **Ikano Huset**, is 8 km (5 mi) north of Sundsvall, along Route E4. All the major Swedish shopping brands are here, like IKEA for home furnishings and H&M for clothes, plus many, many others. **Handelsgården** (✉ Norra Stadsberget ☏ 060/154000) is the place for local handicrafts made from iron and wood, as well as jams and other homemade goodies.

Umeå

❹ *225 km (140 mi) north of Härnösand (via E4).*

Built on the River Ume, Umeå is the largest city in northern Sweden. Because it's a university town with an active student population, there are many bars, restaurants, festivals, and cultural events.

Aside from taking a walk around the city's open squares and wide boulevards, the best way to get to know Umeå is by visiting **Gammlia**, a series of museums that focus on the city and surrounding area. The open-air museum has a living village made up of farmhouses and working buildings. Actors in period costumes demonstrate how people lived hundreds of years ago. You can wander around amid farm animals of all kinds and learn about baking bread, preserving meat, and harvesting grain. There are also a church and historic gardens. The indoor museums, which have exhibitions on Umeå's history, consist of the fishing and maritime museum, the Swedish ski museum, and a modern art museum that shows works from major Swedish and international artists. A sort of intellectual theme park, it can take the better part of a day to see everything in Gammlia. ✉ *Gammliav.* ☏ *090/171800* ⊕ *www.vasterbottensmuseum.se* ☑ *Free* ☉ *Daily 10–5.*

Where to Stay & Eat

$$–$$$ ✕ **Viktor.** Viktor is a restaurant outside the three big cities of Stockholm,
Fodor'sChoice Göteborg, and Malmö that can easily compete with the best they have
★ to offer. The dining room here is simple and elegant, with touches of old Swedish (such as antique brass candlesticks) mixed with 1950s Scandinavian design. The food is best described as new Scandinavian, using uniquely Nordic ingredients spiced with flavors from around the globe. ✉ *Vasag. 11* ☏ *090/711115* ▤ *AE, DC, MC, V.*

$–$$ ✕ **Lottas Krog.** On the site of a former Italian bistro, this Swedish eating house has kept some of its Mediterranean feel. The food, though, is unashamedly local, with Swedish classics filling the menu, especially at lunchtime. ✉ *Nyg. 22* ☏ *090/129551* ▤ *AE, DC, MC, V.*

$–$$ ▥ **Scandic Hotel Plaza.** A clean, modern glass-and-brick structure that dominates the city skyline, the Scandic is one of the most stylish hotels in the region. The huge open lobby has a staircase of marble and steel, copper-tone pillars, and tile floors. A lounge, restaurant, bistro, and bar all lead off from the lobby. Rooms are large, well equipped, and decorated in pastel shades. ⊠ *Storg. 40, 903 04* ☎ *090/2056300* 🖷 *090/ 2056311* ⊕ *www.scandic-hotels.se* ⤴ *196 rooms, 1 suite* ⟶ *2 restaurants, minibars, room TVs with movies, in-room broadband, Wi-Fi, sauna, bar, lounge, convention center, no-smoking rooms* ☰ *AE, DC, MC, V.*

$ 🖫 **Hotel Winn.** The beautiful powder-blue clapboard exterior of this hotel encloses a modern, officelike reception area, but one that is comfortable and welcoming nonetheless. Rooms are very stylishly furnished with paintings and lots of dark wood and asymmetrical fittings. The Mucky Duck, a classic English-style pub on the premises, serves roughly 40 types of beer and is always busy in the evening. ⊠ *Vasaplan, 901 06* ☎ *090/ 711100* 🖷 *090/711150* ⊕ *www.winnhotel.se* ⤴ *87 rooms, 4 suites* ⟶ *Restaurant, in-room broadband, Wi-Fi, sauna, bar, pub, meeting rooms, no-smoking rooms* ☰ *AE, DC, MC, V.*

¢–$ 🖫 **Royal Hotel.** The entrance to this hotel hints at its former life as a cinema, but the exterior is otherwise unremarkable. Inside, though, the Royal is very comfortable, if a little basic. They say good things come in threes, and this hotel has three that make the stay here worthwhile: 24-hour room service (rare in these parts); an excellent in-house restaurant called Gretas ($$; specialty is grilled meat); and, in a nod to its past, a small cinema showing three films nightly. ⊠ *Skolg. 62, 903 29* ☎ *090/100730* 🖷 *090/100739* ⊕ *www.rica.se* ⤴ *68 rooms, 2 suites* ⟶ *Restaurant, minibars, room TVs with movies, in-room broadband, Wi-Fi, sauna, bar, cinema, meeting rooms, no-smoking rooms* ☰ *AE, DC, MC, V.*

Nightlife & the Arts

Being a student town, Umeå is never short of a good night out. The nightlife scene here, as in many Swedish towns, revolves around bars and pubs. The **Bishops Arms** (⊠ Renmarkstorget 8 ☎ 090/100990) is a classic English-style pub. The owners even contracted English builders to ensure authenticity. There are 25 beers of tap, more by the bottle, and a staggering 240 different whiskeys. For an informal night out try **Rex** (⊠ Rådhustorget ☎ 090/126050), a friendly and popular haunt that attracts a young crowd. For those who prefer something a little more sedate and traditional, **Äpplet** (⊠ Vasaplan ☎ 090/ 156200) puts on fox-trot, cha-cha, and tango for all comers. It also serves good food.

Shopping

Inredarna (⊠ Rådhusesplanaden 10 ☎ 090/141228) sells the latest in Scandinavian and European interior design, from furniture to little plastic coat hooks.

The Bothnian Coast A to Z

AIR TRAVEL

CARRIERS The only carrier to Sundsvall Airport is SAS, which operates seven flights a day from Stockholm. To Umeå from Stockholm, there are eight flights a day with SAS, five with Malmö Aviation, and three with Fly Nordic.

Fly Nordic ☎ 08/52806820 ⊕ www.flynordic.com. **Malmö Aviation** ☎ 0771/550010 ⊕ www.malmoaviation.com. **SAS** ☎ 0770/727727 ⊕ www.scandinavian.net.

AIRPORTS

Sundsvall Airport (20 km [12 mi] west of Sundsvall) is the area's main airport. A bus service to Sundsvall and Härnösand runs in connection with arriving and departing SAS flights and costs SKr 65 to Sundsvall and SKr 90 to Härnösand. A taxi will cost SKr 225 and up.

Umeå airport (4 km [2½ mi] from town) has regular connecting flights from Stockholm. A bus service into the city center runs every 10 minutes and costs SKr 35. A taxi will cost SKr 120 and up.

Sundsvall Airport ☎ 060/197600. **Taxi Sundsvall** ☎ 060/199000.
Umeå Airport ☎ 090/716190. **Flygtaxi** ☎ 020/979797.

BUS TRAVEL

Swebus operates a twice-daily service from Stockholm to Gävle. Y-Buss operates daily from Stockholm to Hudiksvall, Sundsvall, and Umeå.

Swebus Express ☎ 0200/218218 ⊕ www.swebusexpress.se. **Y-Buss** ☎ 0771/334444 ⊕ www.ybuss.se.

CAR RENTAL

Avis and Hertz have offices in Gävle, Sundsvall, and Umeå. Europcar has offices in Gävle and Sundsvall.

Avis ✉ Gävle ☎ 026/186880 ✉ Sundsvall ☎ 060/570210 ✉ Umeå ☎ 090/131111.
Europcar ✉ Gävle ☎ 026/621095 ✉ Sundsvall ☎ 060/570120. **Hertz** ✉ Gävle ☎ 026/644938 ✉ Sundsvall ☎ 060/669080 ✉ Umeå ☎ 090/177140.

CAR TRAVEL

From Stockholm take E4 directly north 180 km (111 mi) to Gävle. From Göteborg take E20 284 km (177 mi) to Örebro, Route 60 north 164 km (102 mi) to Borlänge, and Route 80 west 70 km (43 mi) to Gävle. From Gävle the E4 runs the entire length of the Bothnian Coast through every major town north to Skellefteå.

EMERGENCIES

For emergencies dial 112. There are several hospitals in the area and emergency dental care is available at Sundsvall and Umeå. There are late-night pharmacies in Sundsvall and Umeå.

Gävle Hospital ☎ 026/154000. **Hudiksvall Hospital** ☎ 065/092000. **Söderhamn Hospital** ☎ 0270/77000. **Sundsvall Hospital** ☎ 060/181000. **Umeå Hospital** ☎ 090/7850000.
Late-Night Pharmacies ✉ Sundsvall and Umeå ☎ 0771/450450.

TOURS

The Bothnian Coast covers many miles, and tours of the entire area are not available. Individual towns and cities usually offer their own tours, either of the town or of points of interest in the surrounding area. The Umeleden Way is a waterside cycling path with many stops, including

Europe's largest hydroelectric power station. Details of tours can be obtained from an individual town's tourist information offices.

🚌 **Gävle City Tour** ☎ 026/147430. **Hudiksvall Town Walk** ☎ 0650/19100. **Skellefteå Countryside Tours** ☎ 0910/736020. **Umeleden Way** ☎ 090/161616.

TRAIN TRAVEL

SJ operates seven train services daily from Stockholm to Gävle, Söderhamn, Hudiksvall, and Sundsvall. Tågkompaniet operates a night train from Stockholm to Umeå.

🚆 **SJ** ☎ 0771/757575. **Tågkompaniet** ☎ 0771/444111.

VISITOR INFORMATION

🛈 **Gävle** ✉ Drottningg. 37 ☎ 026/147430. **Hudiksvall** ✉ Storg. 33 ☎ 0650/19100 ⊕ www. hudiksvall.se. **Söderhamn** ✉ Resecentrum ☎ 0270/75353 ⊕ www.turism.soderhamn. se. **Sundsvall** ✉ Stora Torget ☎ 060/610450 ⊕ www.sundsvallturism.com. **Umeå** ✉ Renmarksторget 15 ☎ 090/161616 ⊕ www.umea.se.

GÖTEBORG (GOTHENBURG)

Don't tell the residents of Göteborg that they live in Sweden's "second city," but not because they will get upset. People here are known for their amiability and good humor. They just may not understand what you are talking about. People who call Göteborg (pronounced YOO-teh-bor; most visitors stick with the simpler "Gothenburg") home seem to forget that the city is diminutive in size and status compared to Stockholm.

Spend a couple of days here and you'll forget, too. You'll find it's easier to ask what Göteborg hasn't got to offer rather than what it has. Culturally it is superb, boasting a fine opera house and theater, one of the country's best art museums, as well as a fantastic applied-arts museum. There's plenty of history to soak up, from the ancient port that gave the city its start to the 19th-century factory buildings and workers' houses that helped put it on the commercial map. For those looking for nature, the wild west coast and tame green fields are both within striking distance. And don't forget the food. From 1995 to 2005, 8 of the 10 "Swedish Chef of the Year" winners were cooking in Göteborg.

Exploring Göteborg

Göteborg begs to be explored by foot. A small, neat package of a city, it can be divided up into three main areas, all of which are closely interlinked. If your feet need a rest, though, there is an excellent streetcar network that runs to all parts of town. The main artery of Göteborg is Kungsportsavenyn (more commonly referred to as Avenyn, "the Avenue"), a 60-foot-wide tree-lined boulevard that bisects the city along a northwest–southeast axis. Avenyn starts at Göteborg's cultural heart, Götaplatsen, home to the city's oldest cultural institutions, where ornate carved-stone buildings keep watch over shady boulevards lined with exclusive restaurants and bars. Follow Avenyn north and you'll find the main commercial area, now dominated by the modern Nordstan shopping center. Beyond is the waterfront, busy with all the traffic of the port,

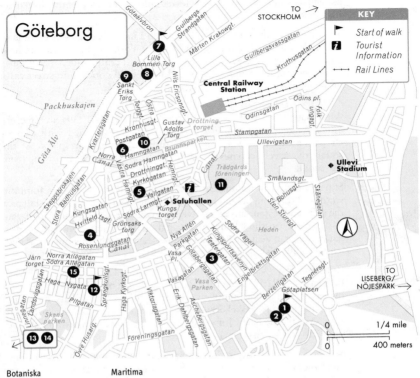

Göteborg

as well as some of Göteborg's newer cultural developments, in particular its magnificent opera house.

To the west of the city are the Haga and Linné districts. Once home to the city's dockyard, shipping, and factory workers, these areas are now chic, bohemian enclaves alive with arts-and-crafts galleries, antiques shops, boutiques selling clothes and household goods, and street cafés and restaurants.

Cultural Göteborg

A pleasant stroll will take you from Götaplatsen's 1930s architecture along Avenyn—the boulevard Kungsportsavenyn lined with elegant shops, cafés, and restaurants—to finish at Kungsportsplats. At the square the street becomes Östra Hamngatan and slopes gently up from the canal.

a good walk

Start your tour in **Götaplatsen** ➊ ▶, a square dominated by a fountain statue of Poseidon; behind him is the **Konstmuseet** ➋. Stroll downhill past the cafés and restaurants along Avenyn to the intersection with Vasagatan. A short way to the left down Vasagatan, at the junction with Teatergatan, you can visit the **Röhsska Museet** ➌, one of the few museums dedicated to Swedish design.

Continue down Vasagatan. If the weather's good, take a look at the Vasa Parken (Vasa Park). Then turn right to go north on Viktoriagatan, cross the canal, and make an immediate left to visit one of the city's most peculiar attractions, **Feskekörkan** ➍, whose name is an archaic spelling of *Fisk Kyrkan,* the Fish Church. It resembles a place of worship but is actually an indoor fish market.

You may now feel inspired to visit the city's principal place of worship, **Domkyrkan** ➎. Follow the canal eastward from Feskekörkan and turn left onto Västra Hamngatan; walk about four blocks to the church. Continue northward on Västra Hamngatan and cross the canal to get to Norra Hamngatan, where you'll find the **Stadsmuseet** ➏, housed in the 18th-century Swedish East India Company.

TIMING   Depending on how much time you want to spend in each museum, this walk may take anywhere from a couple of hours to the better part of a day. Note that many sites close Monday off-season.

WHAT TO SEE   **Domkyrkan** (Göteborg Cathedral). The cathedral, in neoclassic yellow
➎   brick, dates from 1802, the two previous cathedrals on this spot having been destroyed by fire. Though disappointingly plain on the outside, the interior is impressive. Two glassed-in verandas originally used for the bishop's private conversations run the length of each side of the cathedral. The altar is impressively ornate and gilt. ⊠ *Kyrkog. 28, Centrum* ☎ *031/7316130* 💷 *Free* ☾ *Weekdays 8–6, Sat. 9–4, Sun. 10–3.*

➍   **Feskekörkan** (Fish Church). Built in 1872, this fish market gets its nickname from its Gothic-style architectural details. The beautiful arched and vaulted wooden ceiling covers rows and rows of stalls, each offering silvery, slippery goods to the shoppers who congregate in this vast hall. ⊠ *Fisktorget, Rosenlundsg, Centrum.*

▶ **FodorśCh** **Götaplatsen** (Göta Place). This square was built in 1923 in celebration
oice of the city's 300th anniversary. In the center is the Swedish-American
★❶ sculptor Carl Milles's fountain statue of Poseidon choking a codfish.
Behind the statue stands the Konstmuseet, flanked by the **Konserthuset**
(Concert Hall) and the **Stadsteatern** (Municipal Theater), contemporary
buildings in which the city celebrates its important contribution to
Swedish cultural life.

❷ **Konstmuseet** (Art Museum). This impressive collection of the works of
leading Scandinavian painters and sculptors encapsulates some of the
moody introspection of the artistic community in this part of the
world. The museum's Hasselblad Center devotes itself to showing the
progress in the art of photography. The Konstmuseet's holdings include works by Swedes such as Carl Milles, Johan Tobias Sergel, impressionist Anders Zorn, Victorian idealist Carl Larsson, and Prince
Eugen. The 19th- and 20th-century French art collection is the best
in Sweden, and there's also a small collection of old masters. ⊠ *Götaplatsen* ☎ *031/612980* ⊠ *SKr 40* ⊙ *Tues. and Thurs. 11–6, Wed.
11–9, Fri.–Sun. 11–5.*

❸ **Röhsska Museet** (Museum of Arts and Crafts). This museum's fine collections of furniture, books and manuscripts, tapestries, and pottery are
on view. Artifacts date back as far as 1,000 years, but it's the 20th-cen-
tury gallery, with its collection of many familiar household objects, that
seems to provide the most enjoyment. ⊠ *Vasag. 37–39, Vasastan* ☎ *031/
613850* ⊕ *www.designmuseum.se* ⊠ *SKr 40* ⊙ *Tues. noon–8, Wed.–Fri.
noon–5, weekends 10–5.*

❻ **Stadsmuseet** (City Museum). Once the warehouse and auction rooms of
the Swedish East India Company, a major trading firm founded in 1731,
this palatial structure dates from 1750. Today it contains exhibits on
the Swedish west coast, with a focus on Göteborg's nautical and trading past. One interesting exhibit deals with the East India Company and
its ship the *Göteborg*. On its 1745 return from China, she sank just outside the city, while crowds there to greet the returning ship watched from
shore in horror. ⊠ *Norra Hamng. 12, Centrum* ☎ *031/612770* ⊠ *SKr
40* ⊙ *Daily 10–5.*

Commercial Göteborg

Explore Göteborg's port-side character, both historic and modern, at
the waterfront development near the town center, where the markets and
boutiques can keep you busy for hours.

**a good
walk**

Begin at the harborside square known as Lilla Bommen Torg, where the
Utkiken ❼ ▶ offers a bird's-eye view of the city and harbor. The water-
front development here includes the ship-turned-restaurant **Viking,** the
Maritima Centrum ❽, and the **Göteborgs Operan (Opera House)** ❾.

From Lilla Bommen Torg take the pedestrian bridge across the highway
to Nordstan, Sweden's largest indoor shopping mall. Leave the mall at
the opposite end, which puts you at Brunnsparken, the hub of the city's
streetcar network. Turn right and cross the street to Gustav Adolfs
Torg, the city's official center, dominated by **Rådhuset** ❿.

Head north from the square along Östra Hamngatan and turn left onto Postgatan to visit Kronhuset, the city's oldest secular building, dating from 1643. Surrounding the entrance to Kronhuset are the **Kronhusbodarna,** carefully restored turn-of-the-20th-century shops and arts-and-crafts boutiques.

Return to Gustav Adolfs Torg and follow Östra Hamngatan south over the Stora Hamnkanal to Kungsportsplats, where the Saluhall (Market Hall) has stood since 1888. A number of pedestrians-only shopping streets branch out through this neighborhood on either side of Östra Hamngatan. Crossing the bridge over Vallgraven from Kungsportsplats brings you onto Kungsportsavenyn and the entrance to **Trädgårdsföreningens Park** ⑪.

TIMING   The walk itself will take about two hours; allow extra time to explore the sites and to shop. Note that the Kronhusbodarna is closed Sunday.

WHAT TO SEE   **Göteborgs Operan** (Gothenburg's Opera). A statement in steel and glass,
★ ❾   the opera house opened in 1994, immediately dominating this section of the waterfront with its bold lines and shape. Set against a backdrop of the old docks, it makes for a striking image. The productions here are world-class and well worth seeing if you get the chance. ⊠ *Christina Nilssonsg., Nordstan* ☎ *031/108000 for bookings.*

❽ **Maritima Centrum** (Marine Center). In the world's largest floating maritime museum you'll find modern naval vessels, including a destroyer, submarines, lightship, cargo vessel, and various tugboats, providing insight into Göteborg's historic role as a major port. The main attraction is a huge naval destroyer, complete with a medical room in which a leg amputation operation is graphically re-created, with mannequins standing in for medical personnel. ⊠ *Packhuskajen 8, Nordstan* ☎ *031/ 105950* ☒ *SKr 60* ☉ *May–July, daily 10–6; Aug.–Apr., daily 10–4.*

❿ **Rådhuset.** Though the town hall dates from 1672, when it was designed by Nicodemus Tessin the Elder, its controversial modern extension by Swedish architect Gunnar Asplund is from 1937. The building therefore offers two architectural extremes. One section has the original grand chandeliers and trompe-l'oeil ceilings; the other has glass elevators, mussel-shape drinking fountains, and vast expanses of laminated aspen wood. Together they make a fascinating mix. ⊠ *Gustav Adolfs torg 1, Nordstan.*

⑪ **Trädgårdsföreningens Park** (Horticultural Society Park). Beautiful open
FodorśChoice   green spaces, manicured gardens, and tree-lined paths are the perfect
★   place to escape for some peace and rest. Rose fanciers can head for the magnificent rose garden with 5,000 roses of 2,500 varieties. Also worth a visit is the Palm House, whose late-19th-century design echoes that of London's Crystal Palace. ⊠ *Just off Kungsportsavenyn, Centrum* ☎ *031/3655858* ☒ *Park SKr 15, Palm House SKr 20* ☉ *Park May–Aug., daily 7 AM–9 PM; Sept.–Apr., daily 7 AM–7:30 PM. Palm House May–Aug., daily 10–5; Sept.–Apr., daily 10–4.*

▶ ❼ **Utkiken** (Lookout Tower). This red-and-white-stripe skyscraper towers 282 feet above the waterfront, offering an unparalleled view of the city, its green spaces, and the contrasting industrial landscape of the port—

so don't miss out on a visit to the viewing platform at the top. ⊠ *Lilla Bommen 1, Lilla Bommen* ☎ *031/3655858.*

Haga & Linné Districts

Just west of the main city, the Haga and Linné districts are at the forefront of the new cosmopolitan Göteborg. These areas once housed the city's poor, and were so run-down that they were scheduled for demolition. They now make up some of the city's most attractive areas. The older of the two neighborhoods, the Haga district, is full of cozy cafés, secondhand stores, and artists' shops along cobbled streets. The Linné district is the trendiest neighborhood in Göteborg, and real-estate prices have shot up accordingly. Corner restaurants, expensive boutiques, and stylish cafés cater to neighborhood residents and to Göteborg's wealthy young elite, there to see and be seen.

a good walk

Set off from the east end of **Haga Nygatan** ⑫ ▐ and stroll west past the busy cafés and boutiques selling art-deco light fixtures and antique kitchenware. Turn left onto Landsvägsgatan and walk up to join Linnégatan, the Dutch-inspired street that's now considered Göteborg's "Second Avenyn." There is an air of quiet sophistication about Linnégatan, with small antiques and jewelry shops competing for attention against secluded street cafés and high-end design and crafts shops.

Walk south along Linnégatan for five minutes to get to **Slottsskogen** ⑬. If relaxing is your thing, you can spend some time lounging in this huge, tranquil expanse of parkland. Alternatively, you can visit the **Botaniska Trädgården** ⑭, on the south side of the park.

Leave the park the same way you came in, and wind your way north up Nordenhemsgatan. At the end of this street turn right onto Första Långgatan and then onto Södra Allégatan. Here you can find the beautiful and tranquil oasis of the **Hagabadet** ⑮, a superbly renovated bathhouse.

TIMING At a gentle pace the walk alone will take about one hour. If you allow yourself to be tempted by the great shopping, superb cafés, and both museums, you could spend almost a whole day in this part of the city.

WHAT TO SEE **Botaniska Trädgården** (Botanical Gardens). With 1,200 plant species, this ⑭ is Sweden's largest botanical garden. Herb gardens, bamboo groves, a Japanese valley, forest plants, and tropical greenhouses are all on display. Once you've captured some inspiration, you can pick up all you need to create your own botanical garden from the on-site shop. ⊠ *Carl Skottsbergsg. 22A, Slottsskogen* ☎ *031/7411101* 🏷 *Greenhouses SKr 20, park free* ☉ *Park daily 9–sunset; greenhouses May–Aug., daily 10–5; Sept.–Apr., daily 10–4.*

⑮ **Hagabadet.** This stunning bathhouse was built at the end of the 19th century by the Swedish philanthropist Sven Renström. Originally used by local dock- and factory workers, it now plays host to Göteborg's leisure-hungry elite. It's well worth a visit. The pretty pool is art nouveau, with wall paintings, an arched ceiling, and lamps with a diving-lady motif. The Roman baths and the massage and spa area all exude relaxation, but the architecture alone is worth a visit, even if you don't intend to take the plunge. ⊠ *Södra Allég. 3, Haga* ☎ *031/600600* 🏷 *SKr 360*

Fodor'sChoice ★

for a 1-day pass to use facilities; otherwise free ☉ *Mon.–Thurs. 7 AM–9:30 PM, Fri. 7 AM–8:30 PM, Sat. 9–6, Sun. 10–6.*

▶ **⑫ Haga Nygatan.** The redbrick buildings that line this street were originally poorhouses donated by the Dickson family, the city's British industrialist forefathers. ROBERT DICKSON can still be seen carved into the facades of these buildings. Like most buildings in Haga, the buildings' ground floors were made of stone in order to prevent the spread of fire (the upper floors are wood). The Dickson family's impact on the architecture of the west of Sweden can also be seen in the impressive, fanciful mansion that belonged to Robert's grandson James, in Tjolöholm, to the south of Göteborg. ⊠ *Haga Nyg. Haga.*

☺ **⑬ Slottsskogen.** Spend some time in this stunning area of parkland containing cafés, farm animals, a seal pond, Sweden's oldest children's zoo, and many birds—in summer even pink flamingos. Slottsskogen is one of the best parts of the city for relaxing. ⊠ *South of Linnég., Slottsskogen* ☉ *Daily dawn–dusk.*

Where to Eat

Göteborg is filled with people who love to eat and cook, so you've come to the right place if you're interested in food. The fish and seafood here are some of the best in the world, owing to the clean, cold waters off Sweden's west coast. And Göteborg's chefs are some of the best in Sweden, as a glance at the list of recent "Swedish Chef of the Year" winners will confirm. Call ahead to be sure restaurants are open, as many close for a month in summer.

$$$–$$$$ ✕**Sjömagasinet.** Since 1994 Leif Mannerström has headed up what is probably the best seafood restaurant in Sweden. Mannerström, a gray-bearded Fodor'sChoice kitchen maestro, is something of a godfather on the Göteborg food scene ★ and has for many years been the leading champion of west-coast fish. In the delightful oak-beamed dining room (a 200-year-old renovated shipping warehouse), you can eat carefully presented, delicious fish dishes with a classical French touch. An outdoor terrace opens up in summer, complete with authentic sea air. ⊠ *Klippans Kulturreservat, Kiel-terminalen* ☎ *031/7755920* ⚑ *Reservations essential* ▤ *AE, DC, MC, V.*

$$$ ✕**Linnéa.** Chef Bengt Sjöström is an artist. His food is so beautifully presented it seems a shame to eat it. He works with Swedish glass and ceramic companies who design unique plates and glasses for him to show off his food to full effect. A lobster dish comes with a tiny glass of champagne on the side, the cheese on a stylish miniature wooden cutting board. But eat it you must, because Sjöström's culinary art is equally accomplished, using local seafood and classic European cooking techniques. ⊠ *Södrav. 32, Vasastan* ☎ *031/161183* ⚑ *Reservations essential* ▤ *AE, DC, MC, V* ☉ *Closed Sun.*

★ **$$$** ✕**28+.** Step down from the street into this former wine-and-cheese cellar to find an elegant restaurant owned by two of the best chefs in Göteborg. Finely set tables, flickering candles, and country-style artwork evoke the mood of a rustic French bistro. Italian and American flavors blend their way into the impeccable French dishes; choose a five- or seven-course

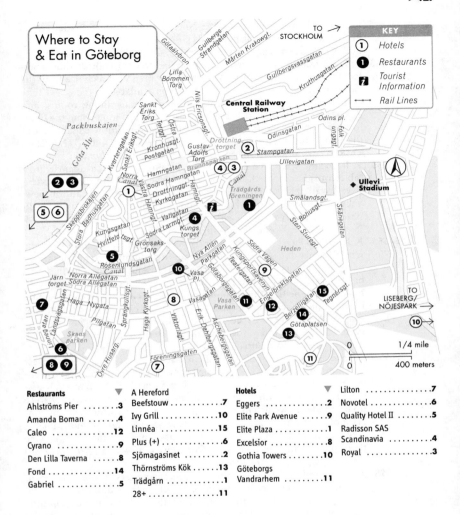

Where to Stay & Eat in Göteborg

Restaurants ▼

Ahlströms Pier 3
Amanda Boman 4
Caleo 12
Cyrano 9
Den Lilla Taverna 8
Fond 14
Gabriel 5
A Hereford Beefstouw 7
Ivy Grill 10
Linnéa 15
Plus (+) 6
Sjömagasinet 2
Thörnströms Kök 13
Trädgårn 1
28+ 11

Hotels ▼

Eggers 2
Elite Park Avenue 9
Elite Plaza 1
Excelsior 8
Gothia Towers 10
Göteborgs Vandrarhem 11
Lilton 7
Novotel 6
Quality Hotel II 5
Radisson SAS Scandinavia 4
Royal 3

meal, or take your pick à la carte. Note that one of the best wine cellars in Sweden is at your disposal. ✉ *Götaborgsg. 28, Centrum* ☎ *031/202161* ⚐ *Reservations essential* ▭ *AE, DC, MC, V* ◷ *Closed Sun.*

★ $$$ ✕ **Thörnströms Kök.** The steep climb up the street to Thörnströms is perfect for working up a thirst. Why not start then with a choice from the excellent wine list, on which every wine is available by the glass. Take your table in one of the three small and elegant dining rooms, and enjoy a series of small dishes of modern European food using the finest local ingredients. Staff here are friendly and very knowledgable about the wines and the menu. ✉ *Teknologg. 3, Vasastan* ☎ *031/182066* ⚐ *Reservations essential* ▭ *AE, DC, MC, V* ◷ *No lunch.*

$$$ ✕ **Trädgårn.** Spicy, Asian-influenced cuisine stands out against linen tablecloths in this earth-tone restaurant; the vegetarian menu is extensive. A wall of glass in the two-story dining hall affords a beautiful view; another wall is covered in blond-wood paneling, a contrast to the black-slate floor. ✉ *Nya Allén, Centrum* ☎ *031/102080* ▭ *AE, DC, MC, V* ◷ *Closed Sun. No lunch fall–spring.*

$$–$$$ ✕ **Ahlströms Pier.** Across the river from central Göteborg lies Eriksberg, where former dockyards mix with modern buildings. Perched at the end of a pier that juts out into the harbor, this restaurant has a main dining hall in an elegant triangular room on the second floor and a less-expensive brasserie on the first floor; contemporary French-inspired Swedish fare is on the menu at both. Finding the pier by car can prove difficult; consider taking a ferry from the city side of the river. ✉ *Dockepiren, Eriksberg* ☎ *031/519555* ⚐ *Reservations essential* ▭ *AE, DC, MC, V* ◷ *Main dining hall closed Sun.*

★ $$–$$$ ✕ **Fond.** Stefan Karlsson's fantastic restaurant can boast one of the best locations in Göteborg, right on the beautiful Götaplatsen. All the herbs and vegetables are grown by a farmer just 5 km (3 mi) from town. Karlsson loves to travel; the flavors he has picked up as a globe-trotter spice up his modern Swedish menu. From the semicircular dining room, diners looks out onto the square. Almost-bare wooden tables and primary-color linens make an interesting informal contrast to the haute cuisine that emerges from the kitchen. ✉ *Götaplatsen, Vasastan* ☎ *031/812580* ▭ *AE, DC, MC, V* ◷ *Closed Sun.*

$$–$$$ ✕ **A Hereford Beefstouw.** At this, an American steak house in Sweden, the chefs grill beef selections in the center of the three dining rooms. The restaurant is popular in a town otherwise dominated by fish restaurants. Thick wooden tables, pine floors, and landscape paintings give the place a rustic touch. ✉ *Linnég. 5, Linnéstaden* ☎ *031/7750441* ▭ *AE, DC, MC, V* ◷ *No lunch weekends and July.*

$$ ✕ **Ivy Grill.** Stepping inside the Ivy is like stepping into a traditional Ivy League university clubhouse. The elegant stone town house is filled with American university pennants, Latin inscriptions on the walls, shelves full of tomes, chocolate-brown leather chairs, and lots of dark wood. The menu, though, is anything but traditional, with dishes like deep-fried scallops with sweet-and-sour salad and wasabi yogurt—such delicacies appear amusingly at odds with their surroundings. In summer you'll find a tented terrace bar, perfect for predinner drinks. ✉ *Vasaplatsen 2, Vasastan* ☎ *031/7114404* ▭ *AE, DC, MC, V* ◷ *Closed Sun.*

$–$$ ✕ **Caleo.** The name means *to be warmed* in Latin; certainly a suitable moniker for this place. The natural shades throughout the restaurant and the ever-smiling staff are enough to thaw even the most frozen of spirits. And the food, with all the warming, delicious flavors of the Mediterranean, is enough to make you want to get up and dance—something you won't be able to do in the slightly cramped dining room. ⊠ *Engelbrektsg. 39, Vasastan* ☎ *031/7089340* ▤ *AE, DC, MC, V.*

$–$$ ✕ **Cyrano.** A little piece of southern France in Sweden, this superb, au-
FodorsChoice thentically Provençal bistro is an absolute must. Inside, the tables are
★ crammed close together, art hangs on the walls, and French touches extend throughout. Highlights include a sumptuously creamy fish soup, sardines with garlic, and grass-fed lamb with tomatoes and sweet peppers. Laid back and friendly, with helpful service, Cyrano continues to draw in the trendier citizens of Göteborg. ⊠ *Prinsg. 7, Linnéstaden* ☎ *031/143110* ▤ *AE, DC, MC, V.*

$–$$ ✕ **Plus (+).** This atmospheric and relaxing restaurant recalls the Sweden of the past. It's inside a beautiful early-1900s ramshackle wooden house whose foundations are attached to the original rock on which the city was built. Eat well-prepared fish and meat dishes with a varied international flavor at polished wood tables, all the while sitting beneath antique chandeliers. There's a superb selection of malt whiskeys and grappas here, the perfect way to end the evening. ⊠ *Linnég. 32, Linnéstaden* ☎ *031/240890* ▤ *AE, DC, MC, V.*

$ ✕ **Den Lilla Taverna.** A very good, lively, and popular place, this Greek restaurant has paper tablecloths and Greek mythological scenes painted on the walls. Live bouzouki music on Wednesday and Saturday evenings gives the place an authentic feel. ⊠ *Oliver Dahlsg. 17, Linnéstaden* ☎ *031/128805* ▤ *AE, MC, V.*

$ ✕ **Gabriel.** A buffet of fresh shellfish and the fish dish of the day draw crowds to this restaurant on a balcony above the fish hall. You can watch all the trading as you eat lunch. The butter-fried herring with mashed potatoes is highly recommended. ⊠ *Feskekörkan, Centrum* ☎ *031/139051* ▤ *AE, DC, MC, V* ⊘ *Closed Sun. and Mon. No dinner.*

★ **¢–$** ✕ **Amanda Boman.** This little restaurant in one corner of the market hall at Kungsportsplats keeps early hours, so unless you eat an afternoon dinner, plan on lunch instead. The cuisine is primarily Swedish and is simply presented. A big white-china bowl of fish soup and a glass of white wine here is hard to beat, and you can watch the bustling market activity through the rising steam from your bowl. ⊠ *Saluhallen, Centrum* ☎ *031/137676* ▤ *AE, MC, V* ⊘ *Closed Sun. No dinner.*

Where to Stay

Some hotels close during the winter holidays; call ahead if you expect to travel during that time. All rooms in the hotels reviewed below are equipped with shower or bath unless otherwise noted. Göteborg also has some fine camping sites if you want an alternative to staying in a hotel.

$$$ ▥ **Elite Plaza.** A five-minute walk from the central station, the Plaza is
FodorsChoice one of the smartest hotels in the city. The palatial building, an architec-
★ tural attraction itself, dates from 1889, and has been modernized with

care to give it an air of grandeur, quality, and restfulness. All original features have been retained, from the stucco ceilings to the English mosaic floors, and are tastefully matched with modern art and up-to-date guest facilities. Rooms are comfortable and luxurious, with earth tones, dark-wood furnishings, and beautiful marble-and-tile bathrooms. The only complaint is that they can be a little on the small side. ⊠ *Västra Hamng. 3, Box 110 65, Centrum, 404 22* ☎ *031/7204000* 🖷 *031/7204010* ⇗ *143 rooms, 5 suites* ⌂ *Restaurant, room service, a/c, in-room safes, minibars, in-room broadband, in-room data ports, Wi-Fi, gym, sauna, bar, pub, convention center, no-smoking rooms* ⊟ *AE, DC, MC, V* ⅼⓄⅼ *BP.*

★ **$$$** 🏨 **Gothia Towers.** A striking modern hotel with more than 700 rooms in two 23-story glass towers, this is the place to stay for great views over Göteborg, especially from the top-floor sky bar. Rooms here are sleek and urban with clean lines, dark wood, natural stone, and shades of brown and cream. The huge, bright lobby is a great place to watch the world go by. ⊠ *Mässansg. 24, Liseberg, 402 26* ☎ *031/7508800* 🖷 *031/ 7508882* ⊕ *www.gothiatowers.com* ⇗ *704 rooms, 8 suites* ⌂ *3 restaurants, room service, a/c, minibars, room TVs with movies, in-room broadband, Wi-Fi, 2 bars, convention center, meeting rooms, parking (fee), no-smoking rooms* ⊟ *AE, DC, MC, V* ⅼⓄⅼ *BP.*

$$$ 🏨 **Radisson SAS Scandinavia.** Across Drottningtorget from the central train station, the Radisson SAS is a modern and spectacular international hotel. The attractive atrium lobby has two restaurants: Frascati, which serves international cuisine, and the Atrium piano bar, with a lighter menu. Rooms are large and luxurious and decorated in pastel shades. Hotel guests receive a discount at the health club on the premises. ⊠ *Södra Hamng. 5965, Centrum, 401 24* ☎ *031/7585000* 🖷 *031/7585001* ⊕ *www. radisson.com* ⇗ *349 rooms* ⌂ *Restaurant, room service, a/c, minibars, cable TV, room TVs with movies, in-room broadband, in-room data ports, indoor pool, health club, hair salon, piano bar, casino, shops, convention center, travel services, no-smoking rooms* ⊟ *AE, DC, MC, V* ⅼⓄⅼ *BP.*

$$–$$$ 🏨 **Elite Park Avenue.** Now part of the ever-expanding Elite chain of hotels, Elite Park Avenue, a Göteborg institution, has had a thorough upgrade. It still has all the character of a hotel that has played host to everyone from the Beatles and Michael Jackson to George Bush (as confirmed by the brass plaque in the reception), but now it has a more up-to-date quality to brag about. The rooms have a pure, modern simplicity about them, with light fabrics and stylish Scandinavian furniture. ⊠ *Kungsportsavenyn 3638, Box 53233, Götaplatsen, 400 16* ☎ *031/7271000* 🖷 *031/7271010* ⊕ *www.elite.se* ⇗ *318 rooms, 10 suites* ⌂ *2 restaurants, room service, a/c, minibars, cable TV, room TVs with movies, in-room broadband, in-room data ports, gym, bar, meeting room, no-smoking floors* ⊟ *AE, DC, MC, V* ⅼⓄⅼ *BP.*

★ **$$** 🏨 **Eggers.** Dating from 1859, Best Western's Eggers may have more character and charm than any other hotel in the city. It is a minute's walk from the train station and was probably the last port of call in Sweden for many emigrants to the United States. Rooms vary in size, and all are beautifully decorated, often with antiques. A complimentary buffet breakfast is the only meal served. ⊠ *Drottningtorget, Box 323, Centrum, 401 25* ☎ *031/806070* 🖷 *031/154243* ⊕ *www.bestwestern.com*

🛏 *65 rooms* ♨ *Cable TV, meeting room, no-smoking rooms* 🖃 *AE, DC, MC, V* ¶ *BP.*

$$ 🖼 **Novotel.** The redbrick industrial-age architecture of this old brewery belies a mishmash of architectural styles inside. As it is situated just west of the city on the Göta Älv, the top floors afford spectacular views of Göteborg. Rooms are plain with deep-red curtains and wood floors. There's a large central atrium, complete with obligatory fake foliage, with a restaurant, Carnegie Kay, attached. ⊠ *Klippan 1, Majorna, 414 51* 🕾 *031/149000* 🖷 *031/422232* ⊕ *www.novotel.se* 🛏 *148 rooms, 5 suites* ♨ *Restaurant, cable TV, in-room data ports, sauna, bar, free parking, no-smoking rooms* 🖃 *AE, DC, MC, V* ¶ *BP.*

$$ 🖼 **Quality Hotel 11.** On the water's edge in Eriksberg, Hotel 11 combines the warehouse style of the old waterfront with a modern interior of multitier terraces. Commonly used by large companies for business conferences, the hotel also welcomes families that want to stay across the harbor from downtown Göteborg. The rooms are clean, bright, and modern; some offer panoramic views of the harbor. ⊠ *Masking. 11, 417 64 Eriksberg, (from city follow signs to Norra Älvstranden)* 🕾 *031/ 7791111* 🖷 *031/7791110* ⊕ *www.hotel11.se* 🛏 *184 rooms, 8 suites* ♨ *Restaurant, in-room data ports, Wi-Fi, sauna, bar, meeting room, no-smoking rooms* 🖃 *AE, DC, MC, V* ¶ *BP.*

$ 🖼 **Excelsior.** Although a little worn around the edges, this stylish 1880 building on a street of classic Göteborg houses is the place to stay to get some character and history. The Excelsior has been in operation since 1930, and its guest rooms are full of homey comfort and faded grandeur. They tend to a be little dark, though, not helped by the heavy, dark fabrics that pervade throughout. Greta Garbo and Ingrid Bergman both stayed here. Classic suites—Garbo's was number 535—with splendid 19th-century style cost no more than ordinary rooms. ⊠ *Karl Gustavsg. 7, Vasastan, 411 25* 🕾 *031/ 175435* 🖷 *031/175439* ⊕ *www.hotelexcelsior.nu* 🛏 *64 rooms, 3 suites* ♨ *Restaurant, cable TV, bar, no-smoking room* 🖃 *AE, DC, MC, V* ¶ *BP.*

★ $ 🖼 **Royal.** Göteborg's oldest hotel, built in 1852, is small, family-owned, and traditional. Make a stop in the entrance hall to admire the intricate, original ceiling paintings. Rooms, most with parquet floors and their original stuccowork, are individually decorated with reproductions of elegant Swedish traditional furniture. The Royal is in the city center a few blocks from the central train station. ⊠ *Drottningg. 67, Centrum, 411 07* 🕾 *031/7001170* 🖷 *031/7001179* ⊕ *www.hotel-royal.com* 🛏 *84 rooms* ♨ *Cable TV, no-smoking floor* 🖃 *AE, DC, MC, V* ¶ *BP.*

¢ 🖼 **Göteborgs Vandrarhem.** This hostel is 5 km (3 mi) from the train station in a modern apartment block. Rooms are very basic, with Swedish-designed furnishings. Breakfast (SKr 55) is not included in the rates, which are per person in a shared apartment. ⊠ *Mölndalsv. 23, Liseberg, 412 63* 🕾 *031/401050* 🖷 *031/401151* ⊕ *www.goteborgsvandrarhem.se* 🛏 *150 beds, 4- to 6-bed apartments* 🖃 *MC, V.*

¢ 🖼 **Lilton.** This unobtrusive bed-and-breakfast-style hotel is inside a small, ivy-covered brick building. Rooms are simple and comfortable, the service friendly and unfussy. ⊠ *Föreningsg. 9, Vasastan, 411 27* 🕾 *031/ 828808* 🖷 *031/822184* ⊕ *www.lilton.se* 🛏 *14 rooms* ♨ *No room TVs, no smoking* 🖃 *AE, MC, V* ¶ *CP.*

Nightlife & the Arts

Nightlife

BARS Hipsters should head to **Barsiden** (✉ Kungsportsavenyn 5, Centrum ☎ 031/7111541), a painfully chic, minimalist bar where the city's beautiful ones pull up designer stools. Go to **Bitter** (✉ Linnëg. 59, Linnë ☎ 031/ 249120) and you will leave with a taste that is anything but. The cocktails in this mirror-lined, darkened bar are superb. Big spenders can splash on the whiskey cocktail Bigg Mamma, a bargain at SKr 600. As its name implies, **The Dubliner** (✉ Östra Hamng. 50, Inom Vallgraven ☎ 031/ 139020) is a brave attempt at re-creating what the locals imagine to be old Irish charm. It's the perfect place for a relaxed pint and a chat with the locals. **Napoleon** (✉ Vasag. 11, Vasastan ☎ 031/137550) is a dark, mellow hangout crowded with oddities. Even the exterior walls are covered in paintings. If you're looking for an urbane bar, try **Nivå** (✉ Kungsportsavenyn 9, Centrum ☎ 031/7018090), a popular bar with a stylish tile interior and a crowd to match. **Uppåt Framåt** (✉ Magasingatan 3, Centrum ☎ 031/138755) has no pretensions to be anything other than a stylish, welcoming, superfriendly bar serving excellent cocktails in a cushion-filled lounge—something it achieves very well.

DANCE CLUBS & CABARET The **Cabaret Lorensberg** (✉ Elite Park Avenue Hotel, Kungsportsavenyn 36, Centrum ☎ 031/206058) plays traditional and contemporary music and has song and dance performances by gifted artists. **Deep** (✉ Kungsportsavenyn 15, Centrum ☎ No phone) is a hot and bustling club packed with thirtysomethings. The roof bar offers an often-welcome fresh-air break. At **Rondo** (✉ Örgrytev. 5, Liseberg ☎ 031/400200) you can dance the night away on Sweden's largest dance floor while surrounded by people of all ages. The crowd is always friendly, and there's a live band. One of the city's liveliest haunts is **Trädgårn** (✉ Nya Allén, Centrum ☎ 031/102080), a complex of five bars, a disco, and show bands housed in a strange building resembling a half-built sauna.

JAZZ CLUBS Performers at **Jazzhuset** (✉ Eric Dahlbergsg. 3, Vasastan ☎ 031/133544) tend to play traditional, swing, and Dixieland jazz. Modern jazz enthusiasts usually head for **Nefertiti** (✉ Hvitfeldtsplatsen 6, Centrum ☎ 031/ 7111533), the trendy, shadowy club where the line to get in is always long.

The Arts

FILM Like all Swedish cinemas, the ones in Göteborg show mostly English-language films. The films are subtitled, never dubbed. The strangest movie theater in town is **Bio Palatset** (✉ Kungstorget, Centrum ☎ 031/174500), a converted meat market turned into a 10-screen cinema. The walls are in various clashing fruit colors, and the floodlighted foyer has sections scooped out to reveal Göteborg's natural rock. **Hagabion** (✉ Linnég. 21, Linnéstaden ☎ 031/428810) is a good art-house cinema housed in an old ivy-covered school.

MUSIC, OPERA & THEATER Home of the highly acclaimed Göteborg Symphony Orchestra, **Konserthuset** (✉ Götaplatsen ☎ 031/7265300) has a mural by Sweden's Prince Eugen in the lobby, original decor, and Swedish-designed furniture from 1935. **Operan** (✉ Christina Nilssons gata, Packhuskajen ☎ 031/108000), where Göteborg's opera company performs, incorporates a 1,250-seat auditorium with a glassed-in dining area overlooking the harbor.

Sports & the Outdoors

Beaches
There are several excellent local beaches. The two most popular—though they're rarely crowded—are Askim and Näset. To reach Askim, take the Express Blå bus from the central station bus terminal. It's a 10-km (6-mi) journey south of the city center. For Näset, catch Bus 19 from Brunnsparken for the 11-km (7-mi) journey southwest of Göteborg.

Fishing
Mackerel fishing is popular here. The **MS Daisy** (☎ 031/963018), which leaves from Hjuvik on the Hisingen side of the Göta River, takes expeditions into the archipelago. If you are in town from the first Monday after the third Sunday in September through to May, you are there during lobster season. The *Daisy* also runs lobster fishing trips; this is your chance to catch the sweetest-tasting lobster in the world. With plenty of salmon, perch, and pike, the rivers and lakes in the area have much to offer. For details call Göteborg's **Sportfiskarnas Fishing Information Line** (☎ 031/7730700).

Golf
Chalmers Golfklubb (✉ Härrydav. 50, Landvetter ☎ 031/918430) was initially a golf club for Göteborg's Technical University, but is now open to the public. It has an 18-hole course, one of the area's best. All players are welcome, but as with all Swedish courses, you must have a handicap certificate to play. Among the many golf courses surrounding Göteborg, **Göteborgs Golfklubb** (✉ Golfbanev. 17, Hovås ☎ 031/282444) is Sweden's oldest golf club. It has an 18-hole course.

Indoor Swimming
Hagabadet (✉ Södra Allég. 3, Haga ☎ 031/600600) is a calming sanctuary with a stunning art-nouveau pool, as well as a relaxing sauna and steam area. For something a little more lively, **Vatten Palatset** (✉ Häradsv. 3, Lerum ☎ 0302/17020) is a decent indoor pool. As well as regular swimming, this huge complex offers indoor and outdoor adventure pools, waterslides, water jets, wave pools, bubble pools, and saunas.

Shopping

Department Stores
Åhléns (☎ 031/3334000), a national chain of mid-priced department stores, is in the Nordstan mall. For something much more upmarket (and more expensive), try the local branch of **NK** (✉ Östra Hamng. 42, Centrum ☎ 031/7101000) for men's and women's fashions and excellent household goods.

Specialty Stores
ANTIQUES **Antikhallarna** (Antiques Halls; ✉ Västra Hamng. 6, Centrum ☎ 031/7741525) has one of Scandinavia's largest antiques selections. Sweden's leading auction house, **Bukowskis** (✉ Kungsportsavenyn 43, Cen-

trum ☎ 031/200360), is on Avenyn. For a memorable antiques-buying experience, check out **Göteborgs Auktionsverk** (✉ Tredje Långg. 9, Linnéstaden ☎ 031/7047700). There's a large amount of very good silver, porcelain, and jewelry hidden among the more trashy items. Viewings on Friday 10–2, Saturday 10–noon, and Sunday 11–noon precede the auctions on Saturday and Sunday starting at noon.

CRAFTS   Excellent examples of local arts and crafts can be bought at **Bohusslöjden** (✉ Kungsportsavenyn 25, Centrum ☎ 031/160072). If you are looking to buy Swedish arts and crafts and glassware, visit the various shops in **Kronhusbodarna** (✉ Kronhusg. 1D, Nordstan ☎ 031/7110832). They have been selling traditional, handcrafted quality goods, including silver and gold jewelry, watches, and handblown glass, since the 18th century.

INTERIOR DESIGN   If you love the cool, sleek Scandinavian interiors you see on your trav-
★ els, head to **Room** (✉ Magasing. 3, Centrum ☎031/606630), whose rooms are tastefully stuffed with furniture, fabrics, soft furnishings, ornaments, and kitchen gadgets—all of it divine.

MEN'S CLOTHING   **Ströms** (✉ Kungsg. 2729, Centrum ☎ 031/177100) has occupied its street-corner location for two generations, offering clothing of high quality and good taste. **STUK** (✉ Södra Larmg. 16, Centrum ☎ 031/130842) sells what they describe as tailored denim, which means jeans, jackets, and trousers in denim and cotton for the semiformal but fashion-conscious shopper.

WOMEN'S   **H & M** (Hennes & Mauritz; ✉ Kungsg. 5557, Centrum ☎ 031/
CLOTHING   3399555) sells clothes roughly comparable to the choices at flashier Old Navy or Marks & Spencer. **Moms** (✉ Vasag. 15, Vasastan ☎ 031/7113280) is a must for trendy street wear, with an excellent range of Nudie Jeans, the cool label born in Göteborg. **Ströms** (✉ Kungsg. 27–29, Centrum ☎ 031/177100) offers clothing of high quality and mildly conservative style.

Food Markets

There are several large food markets in the city area, but the most impressive is **Saluhallen** (✉ Kungsgtorget, Centrum ☎ 031/7117878). Built in 1889, the barrel-roof, wrought-iron, glass, and brick building stands like a monument to industrial architecture. Everything is available here, from fish, meat, and bakery products to deli foods, herbs and spices, coffee, cheese, and even just people-watching.

Göteborg A to Z

AIR TRAVEL TO & FROM GÖTEBORG

CARRIERS   Among the airlines operating to and from Göteborg are Air France, British Airways, City Airline, Finnair, Fly Nordic, KLM, Malmö Aviation, SAS, and SN Brussels Airlines.
🛪 **Air France** ☎ 08/51999990. **British Airways** ☎ 0770/110020. **City Airline** ☎ 0200/250500. **Finnair** ☎ 0771/781100. **Fly Nordic** ☎ 08/52806820. **KLM** ☎ 08/58799757. **Malmö Aviation** ☎ 020/550010. **SAS** ☎ 0770/727727. **SN Brussels Airlines** ☎ 08/58536547.

AIRPORTS & TRANSFERS

Landvetter Airport is approximately 26 km (16 mi) from the city.
🛪 **Landvetter Airport** ☎ 031/941100 ⊕ www.lfv.se.

AIRPORT
TRANSFERS Landvetter is linked to Göteborg by freeway. Buses leave Landvetter every 15–30 minutes and arrive 30 minutes later at Nils Ericsonsplatsen by the central train station, with stops at Lisebergsstationen, Korsvägen, the Elite Park Avenue, and Kungsportsplatsen; weekend schedules include some nonstop departures. The price of the trip is SKr 70. For more information, call Flygbussarna.

The taxi ride to the city center should cost no more than SKr 325.

🚌 **Flygbussarna** ☎ 0771/414300. **Scandinavian Limousine** ☎ 031/7942424. **Taxi Göteborg** ☎ 031/650000.

BOAT & FERRY TRAVEL

Traveling the entire length of the Göta Canal by passenger boat to Stockholm takes between four and six days. For details contact the Göta Kanalbolaget or Rederi AB Göta Kanal.

🚌 **AB Göta Kanalbolaget** ☎ 0141/202050 ⊕ www.gotakanal.se. **Rederi AB Göta Kanal** ✉ Pusterviksg. 13, 413 01 ☎ 031/806315 ⊕ www.gotacanal.se.

BUS TRAVEL TO & FROM GÖTEBORG

All buses arrive in the central city area, in the bus station next to the central train station. The principal bus company is Swebus, the national company based in Stockholm.

🚌 **Swebus Express** ☎ 0200/218218 ⊕ www.swebusexpress.se.

CAR RENTAL

Avis, Hertz, and Europcar have offices at the airport and the central railway station.

🚌 **Avis** ☎ 031/946030 at airport, 031/805780 at central railway station. **Europcar** ☎ 031/947100. **Hertz** ☎ 031/946020.

CAR TRAVEL

Göteborg is reached by car either via the E20 or the E4 highway from Stockholm (495 km [307 mi]) from the east, or on the E6/E20 coastal highway from the south (Malmö is 290 km [180 mi] away). Markings are excellent, and roads are well sanded and plowed in winter.

EMERGENCIES

Dial 112 for emergencies anywhere in the country, or dial the emergency services number listed below day or night for information on medical services. Emergencies are handled by the Mölndalssjukhuset, Östra Sjukhuset, and Sahlgrenska hospitals. There is a private medical service at CityAkuten weekdays 8–6. There is a 24-hour children's emergency service at Östra Sjukhuset as well.

The national dental-service emergency number and the private dental-service number are listed below. The national service is available 8–8 on weekdays, and the private service weekdays between 8 and 5; for after-hours emergencies contact a hospital.

🚌 **Folktandvården Dental-Service Emergencies** ☎ 031/807800. **Tandakuten Private Dental Services** ☎ 031/800500.

🚌 **Medical Services Information (SOS Alarm)** ☎ 031/7031500.

🚌 **After-hours Emergencies** ☎ 08/4073000. **CityAkuten** ✉ Drottningg. 45, Centrum ☎ 031/101010. **Mölndalssjukhuset** ☎ 031/3431000. **Östra Sjukhuset** ☎ 031/3434000. **Sahlgrenska Hospital** ☎ 031/3421000.

📄 24-Hour Pharmacy **Vasen** ⊠ Götg. 12, in Nordstan shopping mall, Nordstan ☎ 0771/450450.

TAXIS

Taxi Göteborg is the main local taxi company.

📄 **Taxi Göteborg** ☎ 031/650000.

TOURS

BOAT TOURS For a view of the city from the water and an expert commentary on its sights and history in English and German, take one of the Paddan sightseeing boats. *Paddan* is Swedish for "toad," an apt commentary on the vessels' squat appearance. The boats pass under 20 bridges and take in both the canals and part of the Göta River.

📄 **Paddan** ⊠ Kungsportsplatsen, Centrum ☎ 031/609670 🚢 SKr 95.

BUS TOURS A 90-minute bus tour and a two-hour combination boat-and-bus tour of the chief points of interest leave from outside the main tourist office at Kungsportsplatsen every day from mid-May through August and on Saturday in April, September, and October. Call the tourist office for schedules.

TRAIN TRAVEL

There is regular service from Stockholm to Göteborg, which takes a little over 4½ hours, as well as frequent high-speed (X2000) train service, which takes about 3 hours. All trains arrive at the central train station in Drottningtorget, downtown Göteborg. For schedules call SJ, the Swedish national rail company. Streetcars and buses leave from here for the suburbs, but the hub for all streetcar traffic is a block down Norra Hamngatan, at Brunnsparken.

📄 **SJ** ☎ 0771/757575 🌐 www.sj.se.

TRANSPORTATION AROUND GÖTEBORG

Stadstrafiken is the name of Göteborg's excellent transit service. Transit brochures, which are available in English, explain the various discount passes and procedures; you can pick one up at a TidPunkten office.

The best bet for the tourist is the Göteborg Pass, which covers free use of public transport, various sightseeing trips, and admission to Liseberg and local museums, among other benefits. The card costs SKr 175 for one day and SKr 295 for two days; there are lower rates for children younger than 18. You can buy the Göteborg Pass as well as regular tram and bus passes at Pressbyrån shops, camping sites, and the tourist information offices.

📄 **TidPunkten** ⊠ Drottningtorget, Brunnsparken, and Nils Ericsonsplatsen, Centrum ☎ 0771/414300.

VISITOR INFORMATION

The main tourist office is Göteborg's Turistbyrå in Kungsportsplatsen. There are also offices at the Nordstan shopping center and in front of the central train station at Drottningtorget.

A free English-language newspaper with listings called *Metro* is available in summer; you can pick it up at tourist offices, shopping centers, and some restaurants, as well as on streetcars.

Göteborg's Turistbyrå's Web site has a good events calendar.

The Göteborg Pass, available from the Göteborg tourist office, and on their Web site, offers discounts and savings for sights, restaurants, hotels, and other services around the city.

🔲 **Göteborg's Turistbyrå** ✉ Kungsportsplatsen 2, 411 10 ☎ 031/612500 🖶 031/612501 ⊕ www.goteborg.com. **Nordstan shopping center** ✉ Nordstadstorget, 411 05 ☎ 031/612500.

BOHUSLÄN

It was from the rocky, rugged shores of Bohuslän that the 9th- and 10th-century Vikings sailed southward on their epic voyages. This coastal region north of Göteborg provides a foretaste of Norway's fjords farther north. Small towns and lovely fishing villages nestle among the distinctively rounded granite rocks and the thousands of skerries (rocky isles or reefs) and larger islands that form Sweden's western archipelago. The ideal way to explore the area is by drifting slowly north of Göteborg, taking full advantage of the uncluttered beaches and small rustic fishing villages. Painters and sailors haunt the region in summer.

Marstrand

❶ *17 km (11 mi) west of Kungälv (via Rte. 168).*

Unusually high stocks of herring used to swim in the waters around Marstrand, which is on an island of the same name. The fish made the town extremely rich. But after the money came greed and corruption: in the 16th century Marstrand became known as the most immoral town in Scandinavia, a reputation that reached its lowest point with the murder of a town cleric in 1586. Soon after this the town burned down and the fish disappeared. As Göteborg and Kungälv became major trade centers, in the early 19th century Marstrand turned to tourism. By 1820 all the town's wooden herring-salting houses had been turned into fashionable and lucrative bathhouses, and people still come to dip into the clear, blue waters and swim, sail, and fish.

Marstrand's main draw is **Carlstens Fästning,** the huge stone-wall castle that stands on the rock above the town. Tours of Carlstens Fortress are not completely in English, but most guides are more than willing to translate. The tours include a morbidly fascinating look at the castle's prison cells, where you can see drawings done in blood and hear tales of Carlstens's most famous prisoner, Lasse-Maja—he dressed up as a woman to seduce and then rob local farmers. ☎ *0303/60265* 💳 *SKr 60* ⊙ *June–mid-Aug., daily 11–6; mid-Aug.–end of Aug., daily noon–4; Sept.–May, weekends 11–4.*

Where to Stay & Eat

$$ ✕🏨 **Grand Hotell Marstrand.** History and luxury abound in this tile-roof hotel, which resembles a French château. Large balconies and verandas open onto a small park, beyond which lies the North Sea. Inside, the hotel is stylishly simple, with bold colors and clean Scandinavian furniture. The rooms are equally light and airy, and the bathrooms have white tiles and brass fittings. A windowed sauna in one of the towers looks out over the harbor. The traditional restaurant ($$) serves excellent local seafood specialties: the garlic-marinated langoustine is a standout. ⊠ *Rådhusg. 2, 440 30* ☏ *0303/60322* 🖷 *0303/60053* ⊕ *www. grandmarstrand.se* ↪ *22 rooms, 6 suites* ⚴ *Restaurant, in-room data ports, sauna, bar, convention center* ⊟ *AE, DC, MC, V* ⫶◎⫶ *BP.*

$ 🏨 **Hotell Nautic.** This basic but good hotel is right on the harbor. The rooms are quite plain but functional, with wood floors and a small desk and chair. The building is a classic white-clapboard construction. ⊠ *Långg. 6, 440 35* ☏ *0303/61030* 🖷 *0303/61200* ⊕ *www.hotellnautic. com* ↪ *29 rooms* ⊟ *AE, DC, MC, V* ⫶◎⫶ *BP.*

Sports & the Outdoors
The coastline around Marstrand looks most beautiful from the water. **Franckes Marina** (⊠ Södra Strandg. ☏ 0303/61584 ⊕ www.franckes.se) will rent you a boat, complete with captain, for cocktails, sightseeing, and fishing. It costs about SKr 1,500 for a two-hour excursion and SKr 650 for each additional hour. Fishing equipment is available for SKr 75 per person.

Shopping
The center of Marstrand is full of ancient cobbled streets, pastel-painted wooden houses, and arts-and-crafts shops selling locally inspired paintings, handicrafts, and ceramics. Else Langkilde of **Konstnärsateljé Langkilde** (⊠ Myren 71 ☏ 0703/965131) paints intriguingly with vivid colors. Worth a visit is **Mary Carlsson** (⊠ Kungsg. 2–4 ☏ 0303/60507), who does a fine line of ceramics and gift items.

Lysekil

❷ *30 km (19 mi) west of Uddevalla via E6 and Rte. 161.*

Perched on a peninsula at the head of Gullmarn Fjord, Lysekil has been one of Sweden's most popular summer resorts since the 19th century, when the wealthiest citizens of Sweden would come to take the therapeutic waters. Back then, the small resort was made up mainly of fancy villas painted mustard and brown. Today you can still see the original houses, but among them now are amusement arcades and cotton-candy stalls.

The surrounding coastline has great, rugged walking trails. These trails offer stunning views of the undulating skerries and islets that dot the water below. Guided botanical and marine walks can be organized by the **tourist office** (☏ 0523/13050).

Havets Hus (House of the Sea) concentrates on the fish and other sea life found in local waters. The giant aquariums contain everything from near-microscopic life-forms to giant cod and even a small but menacing shark. The tour ends with a walk with a stunning view of the fish through a 26-foot glass tunnel. ⊠ *Strandv.* ☏ *0523/19671* ⊕ *www. havetshus.lysekil.se* 🎟 *SKr 75* ◷ *Daily 10–4 (mid-June–mid-Aug., daily 10–6).*

Take any of the many flights of steps that start from Lysekil's main seafront road to get to **Lysekils Kyrka** (Lysekil Church). Probably the town's most impressive landmark, Lysekil Church was carved from the pink granite of the area and has beaten-copper doors. Its windows were painted by Albert Eldh, the early-20th-century artist. ⊠ *Stora Kyrkog.*

Twenty minutes north of Lysekil on Route 162 is **Nordens Ark.** A cut above the usual safari parks, Nordens Ark is a sanctuary for endangered animals. This haven of tranquillity is home to red pandas, lynxes, snow leopards, and arctic foxes. The best way to see the elusive wild animals is to follow the small truck that delivers their food at feeding times. ⊠ *Åby Säteri, Hunnebostrand* ☎ *0523/79590* ⊕ *www.nordensark.se* ⊠ *SKr 120* ⊙ *Mar.–mid-June, daily 10–5; mid-June–mid-Aug., daily 10–7; mid-Aug.–Oct., daily 10–5; Nov.–Feb., daily 10–4.*

off the beaten path

SMÖGEN – At the very tip of a westerly outcrop of land, Smögen is an ideal point for a quick stopover. To get here, head north on Route 162 and then west on Route 171 until it stops. The small village's red fishing huts, crystal-blue water, and pretty scrubbed boardwalks appear on many postcards of Bohuslän.

Where to Stay & Eat

$–$$
Fodor's Choice
★
✕ **Brygghuset.** A short boat ride and a walk through a breathtaking hilltop fishing village on the island of Fiskebäckskil will bring you to this lovely little restaurant. The interior is rustic, with wooden beams and plain wooden tables. Watch the chefs in the open kitchen as they prepare excellent local fish dishes. The ferry *Carl Wilhemsson* leaves from outside the tourist office in Lysekil every half hour, bringing you to the restaurant 20 minutes later. ⊠ *Lyckans Slip, Fiskebäckskil* ☎ *0523/22222* ⌣ *Reservations essential* ▤ *AE, DC, MC, V.*

$–$$
✕ **Pråmen.** This modern-looking restaurant has large windows and is propped on legs that allow it to jut out over the water. The view is great; with the windows open you can smell the sea. You can feast on good portions of simply cooked local fish and wash it down with cold beer. ⊠ *Södra Hamng.* ☎ *0523/13452* ▤ *AE, DC, MC, V.*

¢–$
▦ **Lysekil Havshotell.** This tall, narrow hotel has great views from atop a cliff. Stripped-wood floors and a miscellany of furnishings and fabrics create relaxed surroundings. Many rooms have sofas and provide bathrobes. Only breakfast is served, and there's a stocked bar (done on the honor system) in each room. For the best view across the water, reserve Room 18, which costs SKr 200 extra. ⊠ *Turistg. 13, 453 30* ☎ *0523/79750* 🖷 *0523/14204* ⊕ *www.strandflickorna.se* ⇥ *15 rooms, 2 suites* ⊘ *In-room broadband, in-room data ports, meeting room* ▤ *AE, MC, V* ⦿ *BP.*

¢
▦ **Strand Vandrarhem.** This hostel on the seafront offers simple, friendly accommodations. Unless you stipulate otherwise and pay an additional fee, you may find yourself sharing the room with another guest (the rooms are outfitted with bunk beds). The welcome here is warm, and the breakfast (SKr 50 extra) is excellent. ⊠ *Strandv. 1, 453 30* ☎ *0523/79751* 🖷 *0523/12202* ⊕ *www.strandflickorna.se* ⇥ *20 rooms* ▤ *MC, V.*

Nightlife & the Arts

In July Lysekil comes alive to the sounds of the annual **Lysekil Jazz Festival**. Big-name Swedish, and some international, jazz musicians play in open-air concerts and in bars and restaurants. Contact **Lysekils Turistbyrå** (tourist office; ☎ 0523/13050) for details of events.

Sports & the Outdoors

For a taste of the sea air and a great look at some local nature, take one of the regular seal safaris. Boat trips to view these fascinating, wallowing, slippery mammals leave from the main harbor three times daily between June and August, cost SKr 130, and take about two hours. Details and times are available from **Lysekils Turistbyrå** (☎ 0523/13050).

Strömstad

❸ *90 km (56 mi) northwest of Uddevalla, 169 km (105 mi) north of Göteborg.*

This popular Swedish resort claims to have more summer sunshine than any other town north of the Alps. Formerly Norwegian, it has been the site of many battles between warring Danes, Norwegians, and Swedes. A short trip over the Norwegian border takes you to Halden, where Sweden's warrior king, Karl XII, died in 1718.

Although it is of no particular historical importance, **Strömstads Kyrka** is well worth a visit just to marvel at its interior design. The Strömstad Church's seemingly free-form decoration policy throws together wonderfully detailed, crowded frescoes; overly ornate gilt chandeliers; brass lamps from the 1970s; and model ships hanging from the roof. ⊠ *S. Kyrkog. 10* ☎ *0526/10029.*

Where to Stay & Eat

$–$$$ ✕ **Göstases.** Somewhat resembling the interior of a wooden boat, this restaurant on the quayside specializes in locally caught fish and seafood. Knots, ropes, life preservers, stuffed fish, and similar paraphernalia abound. But it all pales when you see the low prices for fresh lobster, crab, prawns, and fish, all of which can be washed down with equally affordable cold beer. Sit outside in summer and watch the fishing boats bring in your catch and the pleasure boats float by. ⊠ *Strandpromenaden* ☎ *0526/10812* ▤ *MC, V.*

$ ✕▦ **Laholmen.** This huge, sprawling hotel and restaurant offers good-quality food and excellent accommodations on a grand scale. The rooms are a bit garish, with overly vivid color schemes, but they are large and well equipped. The restaurant ($) has a good buffet and an interesting menu of local dishes, including exquisite prawn sandwiches at lunch. The restaurant as well as most guest rooms have views across the pretty harbor and the water beyond, which is scattered with skerries. ⊠ *Laholmen, 452 30* ☎ *0526/19700* ☎ *0526/10036* ⊕ *www.laholmen.se* ⌐⊅ *152 rooms, 4 suites* ⌂ *Restaurant, sauna, bar, lounge, convention center* ▤ *AE, DC, MC, V* ⦿|*BP.*

Bohuslän A to Z

BUS TRAVEL
Buses to the region leave from behind the central train station in Göteborg; the main bus company is Västtrafik. The trip to Strömstad takes between two and three hours.

🚍 **Västtrafik** ☎ 0771/414300.

CAR TRAVEL
The best way to explore Bohuslän is by car. The E6 highway runs the length of the coast from Göteborg north to Strömstad, close to the Norwegian border, and for campers there are numerous well-equipped and uncluttered camping sites along the coast's entire length.

TRAIN TRAVEL
Regular service along the coast connects all the major towns of Bohuslän. The trip from Göteborg to Strömstad takes about two hours, and there are several trains each day. For schedules call SJ.

🚆 **SJ** ✉ Göteborg ☎ 0771/757575.

VISITOR INFORMATION
🚍 **Göteborg Turistbyrå** ✉ Kungsportsplatsen 2, 411 10 Göteborg ☎ 031/612500 🖨 031/612501 ⊕ www.goteborg.com. **Lysekil** ✉ Södra Hamng. 6 ☎ 0523/13050. **Marstrand** ✉ Hamng. ☎ 0303/60087. **Strömstad** ✉ Torget, Norra Hamnen ☎ 0526/62330 ⊕ www.stromstadtourist.se.

SWEDISH RIVIERA

The coastal region south of Göteborg, Halland—locally dubbed the Swedish Riviera—is the closest that mainland Sweden comes to having a resort area. Fine beaches abound, and there are plenty of sporting activities. But Halland's history is dark, since it was the front line in the fighting between Swedes and Danes. Evidence of such conflicts can be found in its many medieval villages and fortifications. The region stretches down to Båstad, in the country's southernmost province, Skåne.

Kungsbacka

④ *25 km (15 mi) south of Göteborg.*

This bedroom community for Göteborg holds a market for all sorts of goods on the first Thursday of every month—a 600-year-old tradition.

A break in a high ridge to the west, the **Fjärås Crack,** offers a fine view of the coast. Formed by melting ice 13,000 years ago, the ridge made a perfect transport route for nomadic tribes of 10,000 years ago, who used it to track the retreating ice northward to settle their new communities. Some important archaeological discoveries have been made here, and much of the information learned is on display on signs dotted along the ridge. The signs act as a sort of self-guided outdoor museum, dealing with the geological and anthropological history of the ridge.

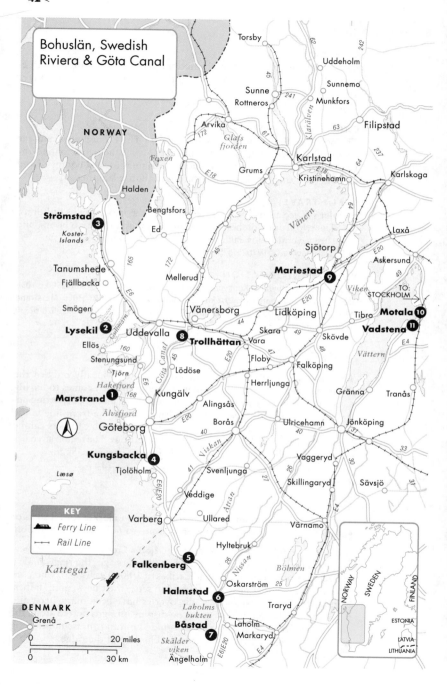

Bohuslän, Swedish
Riviera & Göta Canal

NORWAY

Torsby

Uddeholm

Sunne
Rottneros
Sunnemo
Munkfors

Arvika
Glafs
fjorden
Filipstad

Foxen
Halden
Karlstad
Grums
Kristinehamn
Karlskoga

Bengtsfors

Strömstad ❸
Koster
Islands
Ed

Vänern

Laxå

Sjötorp

Tanumshede
Fjällbacka
Mellerud

Mariestad ❾

Askersund

Smögen
Vänersborg
Lidköping
Viken
TO:
STOCKHOLM

Lysekil ❷
Uddevalla
Trollhättan ❽
Skara
Vara
Skövde
Tibro
Motala ❿

Vadstena ⓫

Vättern

Ellös
Stenungsund
Tjörn
Lödöse
Floby
Falköping

Hakefjord
Kungälv
Herrljunga
Gränna
Tranås

Marstrand ❶
Älvsfjord
Göteborg
Alingsås
Borås
Ulricehamn
Jönköping

Kungsbacka ❹
Tjolöholm
Svenljunga
Vaggeryd
Skillingaryd
Sävsjö

Læsø
Veddige
Varberg
Ullared
Värnamo

Hyltebruk

Falkenberg ❺

Bölmen

NORWAY
SWEDEN
FINLAND

Halmstad ❻

KEY
Ferry Line
Rail Line

Kattegat

DENMARK
Grenå

Laholms
bukten
Båstad ❼
Skälder
viken
Ängelholm
Oskarström
Laholm
Markaryd
Traryd

ESTONIA

LATVIA
LITHUANIA

0 ——— 20 miles
0 ——— 30 km

At Tjolöholm, 12 km (7 mi) down the E6/E20 highway from Kungsbacka, is **Tjolöholms Slott** (Tjolöholm Castle), a manor house built by James
Dickson, a Scottish merchant and horse breeder. The English Tudor–style
house, constructed at the beginning of the 20th century, contains many
fascinating elements. By and large, they have become a tribute to Dickson's passion for all things modern, including an early version of a pres-
surized shower and a horse-drawn vacuum cleaner with a very long hose
to reach up through the house windows. Dickson died of lead poison-
ing before the house was completed—he cut his finger while opening a
bottle of champagne and wrapped the lead-foil wrapper around the cut.
The house he left behind offers much insight into one man's dream.
⊠ *Fjärås* ☎ *0300/544200* 🖼 *SKr 60* ☉ *Apr.–mid-June, weekends
11–4; mid-June–Aug., daily 11–4; Sept., weekends 11–4; Oct., Sun. 11–4.*

Near Tjolöholm is the tiny 18th-century village of Äskhult, the site of
an open-air museum, the **Äskhults 1700-tals by** (Äskhult's 18th-Century
Village). When land reforms forced farmers to combine patches of land
into large estates, the four farmers living in Äskhult refused and kept
their land separate. This refusal left the village unable to expand while
both of the neighboring areas became towns. And so it stayed that way,
until the last inhabitants moved away in the mid-19th century. Today
you can wander through the houses and farm buildings to get a glimpse
of what life was like for 18th-century peasant farmers. ☎ *0300/542159*
🖼 *SKr 25* ☉ *May–Aug., daily 10–6; Sept., weekends 10–6.*

Falkenberg

❺ *30 km (20 mi) south of Varberg, 100 km (60 mi) south of Göteborg.*

With its attractive beaches and the plentiful salmon that swim in the
Ätran River, Falkenberg is one of Sweden's most attractive resorts. Its
Gamla Stan (Old Town) is full of narrow cobblestone streets and quaint,
old wooden houses.

Doktorspromenaden, on the south side of the river in the town center, is
a beautiful walk set against a backdrop of heathland and shade trees.
The walk was set up in 1861 by a local doctor in an effort to encourage the townsfolk to get more fresh air. ⊠ *Doktorspromenaden.*

Although it does have the usual archaeological and historical artifacts
depicting its town's growth and development, the **Falkenberg Museum** also
has an unusual and refreshing obsession with the 1950s. The curator here
thinks that is the most interesting period of history, and you can make
up your own mind once you've learned about the local dance-band
scene, visited the interior of a shoe-repair shop, and seen a collection of
old jukeboxes. ⊠*Skepparesträtet 2* ☎*0346/886125* 🖼*Free* ☉*June–Aug.,
Tues.–Sun. noon–4; Sept.–May, Tues.–Fri. and Sun. noon–4.*

Falkenberg's first movie theater is now home to **Fotomuseum Olympia,**
a fascinating display of cameras, camera equipment, and photographs
dating back to the 1840s. ⊠ *Sandg. 13* ☎ *0346/87928* 🖼 *SKr 35*
☉ *Mid-June–Aug., Tues.–Thurs. 1–7, Sun. 1–6; Sept.–May, Tues.–Thurs.
5–7, Sun. 2–6.*

Where to Stay & Eat

$–$$ ✕ **Restaurant Hertigen.** This beautiful white villa sits on wooded grounds on an island just outside the center of town. Dining takes place on a large veranda and garden in summer. The classic French dishes are prepared with a nod in the direction of local cooking styles. ⊠ *Hertings Gård* ☎ *0346/10018* ⌂ *Reservations essential* 🝙 *AE, DC, MC, V.*

$–$$ 🏨 **Elite Hotel Strandbaden.** A sprawling, white wood-and-glass building, Elite Hotel Strandbaden sits right on the beach at the south end of town. The rooms here are quite small but well equipped, with amenities and modern, comfortable furnishings. Most have a view of the sea. There is a state-of-the-art spa and health club in the hotel, and a very good restaurant decked out in startling blue and orange. ⊠ *Havsbadsallén, 311 42* ☎ *0346/714900* 🖶 *0346/16111* ⊕ *www.elite.se* 🛏 *135 rooms, 5 suites* ⌂ *Restaurant, minibars, cable TV, in-room data ports, health club, sauna, bar* 🝙 *AE, DC, MC, V* 🍴 *BP.*

$ 🏨 **Grand Hotel Falkenberg.** Not as imposing as the name suggests, this pretty, yellow, 19th-century hotel is comfortable and friendly, with very large rooms. The interior is a jumble of furnishings from the last 30 years, with the odd antique thrown in for good measure. Cherrywood and rich fabrics are used throughout. ⊠ *Hotellg. 1, 311 31* ☎ *0346/14450* 🖶 *0346/14459* ⊕ *www.grandhotelfalkenberg.se* 🛏 *70 rooms, 3 suites* ⌂ *2 restaurants, sauna, 2 bars, lounge* 🝙 *AE, DC, MC, V* 🍴 *BP.*

Sports & the Outdoors

BEACHES A 15-minute walk south from the town center is **Skrea Strand,** a 3-km (2-mi) stretch of sandy beach. At the northern end of the beach is the huge swimming complex **Klitterbadet** (⊠ Klitterv. ☎ 0346/886330 🏷 SKr 35 ⊙ June–Aug., Sun. and Mon. 9–4, Tues. and Thurs. 6 AM–7 PM, Wed. and Fri. 9–7, Sat. 9–5; Sept.–May, Mon. 4 PM–8 PM, Tues. and Thurs. 6 AM–8 AM and noon–8, Wed. noon–8, Fri. noon–7, Sat. 9–5, Sun. 9–3), with pools (including one just for children), waterslides, a sauna, a whirlpool, a 50-meter-long pool with heated seawater, and steam rooms. Farther south the beach opens out onto some secluded coves and grasslands.

FISHING In the 1800s Falkenberg had some of the best fly-fishing in Europe. This prompted a frenzy of fishermen, including many English aristocrats, to plunder its waters. But despite the overfishing, the Ätran is one of few remaining rivers in Europe inhabited by wild salmon. Fishing permits and rod rentals can be arranged through the local **tourist office** (☎0346/886100).

Shopping

Törngrens (⊠ Krukmakareg. 4 ☎ 0346/10354 ⊙ Weekdays 9–5) is probably the oldest pottery shop in Scandinavia, and is now owned by the seventh generation of the founding family. Call ahead to make sure the shop is open.

Halmstad

❻ *40 km (25 mi) south of Falkenberg, 143 km (89 mi) south of Göteborg.*

With a population of 55,000, Halmstad is the largest seaside resort on the west coast. The Norre Port town gate, all that remains of the town's original fortifications, dates from 1605. The modern town hall has in-

"SKÅL!"

MANY PEOPLE who have never seen Sweden have nonetheless conjured an often nearsighted image of what they think it is like: Nordic woodlands, crystalline-featured women, Greta Garbo, sexual freedom, and yet lives lived within rigid, formal constraints. There's some truth to the latter image of Swedish formality. So let's take a look at it.

Please take a seat as an invited guest at the dining table. It is set with a crisp white tablecloth, perfectly polished silver, a candelabra, napkins, and crystal glasses. The wine is chilled, and nothing is out of place. Your hostess is the shimmering image of Swedish household perfection.

Nowhere more than at the dining table will you encounter the unspoken truths of Swedish formality, especially in the toast. In Australia or New Zealand it is scarcely de rigueur and may be accompanied by a drawling "G'day, mate." In Britain it is all stiff upper lip and chivalry. In the United States the rules are as diverse as the cultures that populate it. But in Sweden there is only one way to toast, and its protocol is very specific and universally followed. So, do not touch your glass yet, even though it is full and you are nervous. Never touch the glass first; you must wait until one of the hosts, usually the man, lifts his glass to all. Do not drink. Everyone must reply to the proffered "skål" (meaning "cheers" and pronounced skohl) with a collective "skål." Then you will all tilt your glasses to the host and hostess. Delayed eye contact is imperative before, during, and after the measured sip of appreciation. Don't empty the glass. The meal has commenced.

From here on in during the dinner, toasting will still play a role, but the procedure is individualized and personal. Guests will toast each other. You are free to toast anyone but the hostess. She can toast anyone she pleases. This is a safeguard against hostess inebriation. The temptation, of course, is for everyone to intermittently toast her in thanks.

The roots of this alcohol-related tradition may lie with the Vikings. They always lived in peril, and no one could be trusted. The rule was to toast your "friend" with full eye contact and an arm behind the back to prevent a quick slitting of the throat. Later, state control would become big in Sweden; alcohol was once banned to stop the poor from brewing their potatoes into freedom-inducing alcohol. Even later alcohol was limited to stave off social and health problems. Today you can buy wine and spirits only in government-controlled liquor stores, called Systembolagett. Caution is part of the Swedish nature, and the alcohol rituals show it.

Back at the dinner table, most of the rules will be somewhat familiar to you, simply practiced in a more accentuated form.

We leave you with your Swedish hosts now. You can surely find your way from here. As a foreigner you will be granted some leeway in strictly adhering to the customs. But whatever you do, do not take the bottle as you leave. From that transgression there is certainly no way back.

terior decorations by the so-called Halmstad Group of painters, which formed here in 1929.

Most of Halmstad's architectural highlights are in and around **Stora Torget,** the large town square. In the middle is the fountain *Europa and the Bull,* by the sculptor Carl Milles. Around the square are many buildings and merchants' houses dating from Halmstad's more prosperous days in the last half of the 19th century.

At the top of Stora Torget is the grand **St. Nikolai Kyrka,** a huge church from the 14th century containing fragments of medieval murals and a 17th-century pulpit.

★ The bizarre **Martin Luther Kyrka** is unique among churches. Built entirely out of steel in the 1970s, its exterior resembles that of a shiny tin can. The interior is just as striking, as the gleaming outside gives way to rust-orange steel and art-deco furnishings that contrast with the outside. To some, Martin Luther Church may seem more like a temple to design, not deity. ⊠ *Långg.* 🕾 *035/151961* ⊗ *Weekdays 9–3, Sun. services at 10.*

In the 1930s the Halmstad Group, made up of six local artists, caused some consternation with their surrealist and cubist painting styles, influenced strongly by such artists as René Magritte and Salvador Dalí. The **Mjellby Konstgård** (Mjellby Arts Center) contains some of the most important works created over the group's 50-year alliance. ⊠ *Mjellby, (4 km [2½ mi] from Halmstad)* 🕾 *035/137195* 🎫 *SKr 50* ⊗ *Mar.–Oct., daily 1–5; July, daily 11–5.*

Where to Stay & Eat

$$–$$$ ✕ **Pio & Co.** Half informal bar and half bistro, this restaurant offers something for all. It's a bright and airy place with good service and excellent Swedish classics on the menu—the steak and mashed potatoes is wonderful. The list of drinks is extensive. ⊠ *Storg. 37* 🕾 *035/210669* 🖃 *AE, DC, MC, V.*

$$ 🏨 **Scandic Hallandia.** A shiny white-tile floor, white ceiling tiles, and a circular podlike lobby create a strange first impression. But don't be alarmed. Rooms here come with all the space, comfort, modernity, and up-to-date technology you would expect from a Scandinavian hotel. ⊠ *Rådhusg. 4, 302 43* 🕾 *035/2958600* 🖷 *035/2958611* ⊕ *www.scandic-hotels.se* ↩ *130 rooms, 1 suite* ↻ *Restaurant, in-room data ports, sauna, spa, bar, convention center* 🖃 *AE, DC, MC, V* ⦿⦿ *BP.*

$ 🏨 **Hotel Continental.** Built in 1904 in the national romantic style, the interior of this hotel has been nicely preserved. The sophisticated design includes exposed-brick walls, subtle spotlighting, and light wood fittings. The rooms are bright, modern, and spacious. Five rooms have whirlpool baths. ⊠ *Kungsg. 5, 302 45* 🕾 *035/176300* 🖷 *035/128604* ⊕ *www.continental-halmstad.se* ↩ *46 rooms, 3 suites* ↻ *In-room broadband, in-room data ports, sauna, spa, bar, meeting rooms, parking (fee)* 🖃 *AE, DC, MC, V* ⦿⦿ *BP.*

Sports & the Outdoors

There are many good beaches around Halmstad. **Tjuvahålan,** extending west of Halmstad, has an interesting old smugglers' cove that provides pleasant walking. For details, contact the **tourist office** (🕾 035/132320).

Båstad

7 *35 km (22 mi) south of Halmstad, 178 km (111 mi) south of Göteborg.*

In the southernmost province of Skåne, Båstad is regarded by locals as Sweden's most fashionable resort, where ambassadors and local captains of industry have their summerhouses. Aside from this, it is best known for its tennis. In addition to the **Båstad Open**, a grand prix tournament in late summer, there is the annual **Donald Duck Cup** in July, for children from ages 11 to 15; it was the very first trophy won by Björn Borg, who later took the Wimbledon men's singles title an unprecedented five times in a row. Spurred on by Borg and other Swedish champions, such as Stefan Edberg and Mats Wilander, thousands of youngsters take part in the Donald Duck Cup each year. For details, contact the **Svenska Tennisförbundet** (Swedish Tennis Association; ⊠ Lidingöv. 75, Stockholm ☎ 08/4504310).

The low-rise shuttered buildings in the center of Båstad give it an almost French provincial feel. In the main square is **St. Maria Kyrka** (St. Maria's Church), which looks much more solidly Swedish. Dating from the 15th century, the plain exterior hides a haven of tranquillity within the cool thick walls. The unusual altar painting depicts Christ on the cross with human skulls and bones strewn beneath him.

Norrviken Gardens, 3 km (2 mi) northwest of Båstad, are beautifully laid out in different styles, including a Japanese garden and a lovely walkway lined with rhododendrons. The creator of the gardens, Rudolf Abelin, is buried on the grounds. A restaurant, shop, and pottery studio are also on the premises. ☎ *0431/369040* ⊕ *www.norrvikenstradgardar. net* ⊠ *May–Aug. SKr 90; Sept.–Apr. free* ☉ *May–Sept., daily 10–5 (July–mid-Aug., daily 10–8); Oct.–Apr., daily dawn–dusk.*

Where to Stay & Eat

$$ ✕ **Swenson's Krog.** Well worth the 3-km (2-mi) journey out of Båstad, this harbor-front restaurant was originally a fisherman's hut and has been converted into a magnificent dining room with cornflower-blue walls, wooden floors, and a glass roof. The menu is full of Swedish classics such as white asparagus with lemon-butter sauce and delicious homemade meatballs. The service is friendly, with the family atmosphere really shining through. ⊠ *Pål Romaresg. 2, Torekov* ☎ *0431/364590* ⌲ *Reservations essential* ▤ *AE, DC, MC, V.*

¢ ✕ **Wooden Hut.** Actually, this restaurant has no name: it's just a wooden hut on the harbor side. It has no tables either. What this restaurant does have is simple and delicious smoked mackerel with potato salad, which will magically take you away from all the pomp and wealth that sometimes bogs Båstad down. Walk past all the hotels and restaurants, smell the fresh sea air, and get ready for a great meal. ⊠ *Strandpromenaden* ☎ *No phone* ⌲ *Reservations not accepted* ▤ *No credit cards.*

$$ ✕▦ **Hotel Skansen.** Set in a century-old bathhouse, Skansen's interior reflects the best of modern design. Wonderfully simple earth, cream, and moss-green tones create a sense of comfort, simplicity, and relaxation. The lovely rooms, many with a glass roof or wall, are all decorated with furniture from Stockholm's cool interior shop R.O.O.M. Restaurant Sand ($–$$), with a sea view, serves stylish and well-prepared Swedish fare, with fish as a specialty. The bar is well stocked, but the nightclub is nothing special. ✉ *Kyrkog. 2, 269 21* ☎ *0431/558100* 🖨 *0431/558110* 🌐 *www. hotelskansen.se* ⇨ *138 rooms, 1 suite* ⚓ *Restaurant, in-room data ports, sauna, spa, steam room, bar, nightclub* 🚭 *AE, DC, MC, V* ❚⊙❙ *BP.*

¢–$ ▦ **Hjortens Pensionat.** A classic summer resort hotel, Hjortens Pensionat is Båstad's oldest inn. The antiques-filled rooms are light and the common areas are comfortably cluttered with ornaments and deep armchairs. Right in the center of Båstad, the hotel is close to shops, beaches, and tennis courts. ✉ *Roxmansv. 23, 269 36* ☎ *0431/70109* 🖨 *0431/70180* 🌐 *www.hjorten.net* ⇨ *42 rooms, 37 with bath* ⚓ *Restaurant, bar* 🚭 *DC, MC, V* ❚⊙❙ *BP.*

Swedish Riviera A to Z

BUS TRAVEL

Buses to Kungsbacka, Falkenberg, Halmstad, and Båstad leave from behind Göteborg's central train station.

🚍 **Hallandstrafiken** ☎ 0771/331030. **Västtrafik** ☎ 0771/414300.

CAR TRAVEL

Simply follow the E6/E20 highway south from Göteborg toward Malmö. The highway runs parallel to the coast.

TRAIN TRAVEL

Regular train services connect Göteborg's central station with Kungsbacka, Falkenberg, Halmstad, and Båstad.

🚍 **SJ** ✉ Göteborg ☎ 0771/757575.

VISITOR INFORMATION

🚍 **Båstad** ✉ Stortorget 1 ☎ 0431/75045. **Falkenberg** ✉ Holgersg. 9 ☎ 0346/886100. **Halmstad** ✉ Halmstad Slott ☎ 035/132320.

GÖTA CANAL

Stretching 614 km (382 mi) between Stockholm and Göteborg, the Göta Canal is actually a series of interconnected canals, rivers, lakes, and even a stretch of sea. The building of the canal took 22 years and involved 58,000 men. Linking the various stretches of water required 87 km (54 mi) of man-made cuts through soil and rock and building 58 locks, 47 bridges, 27 culverts, and three dry docks. Unfortunately, the canal never achieved the financial success that its builders sought. The linking of Göteborg with Stockholm by rail in the late 19th century effectively ended the canal's commercial potential. The canal has nevertheless come into its own as a modern-day tourist attraction.

You may have trouble conceiving of the canal's industrial origins as your boat drifts lazily down this lovely series of waterways; across the enormous lakes, Vänern and Vättern; and through a microcosm of all that is best about Sweden: abundant fresh air; clear, clean water; pristine nature; and well-tended farmland. A bicycle path runs parallel to the canal, offering another means of touring the country. You can bike faster than the boats travel, so it's easy to jump off and on as you please.

Trollhättan

8 *70 km (43 mi) north of Göteborg.*

In this pleasant industrial town of about 53,000 inhabitants, a spectacular waterfall was rechanneled in 1906 to become Sweden's first hydroelectric plant. On specific days in summer the waters are allowed to follow their natural course, a fall of 106 feet in six torrents. This sight is well worth seeing. The other main point of interest is the 82-km-long (51-mi-long) Trollhätte Canal, of which a 10-km (6-mi) stretch runs through the city. The canal's six locks date from 1916. Along the canal are also disused locks from 1800 and 1844, beautiful walking trails, and the King's Cave, a rock formation on which visiting monarchs have carved their names since 1754. Trollhättan also has a fine, wide marketplace and water-side parks. The city has become somewhat of a center of the Swedish film industry, earning it the nickname "Trollywood." Lukas Moodyson (*Show Me Love, Together,* and *Lilja 4-Ever*) is just one of the directors who have chosen Trollhättan production studios.

In the summer months the **Trollhättans Turistbyrå** (Tourist Office; ✉ Åkerssjöv. 10 ☎ 0520/488472 ⊕ www.visittrollhattan.se) offers the Sommarkort (Summer Pass), with free entrance to the Innovatum, the Innovatum Cableway, Saab Bilmuseum, and the Canal Museum. It costs SKr 100 per day, and accompanying children under 16 are free.

The best way to see the town's spectacular waterfalls and locks is on the **walking trail** that winds its way through the massive system. The walk takes in the hydroelectric power station and the canal museum. Part of the walk is atop wooded cliffs that overlook the spectacular cascades of water. The falls flow freely in May and June, weekends at 3, and July and August, Wednesday and weekends at 3. In July the falls are also illuminated at 11 PM on Wednesday, Saturday, and Sunday. Details and directions can be found at the tourist office, which will also tell you the best places to watch the waterfall when the waters are allowed to follow their natural course.

Culture abounds at **Folkets Hus** (People's House), in the pedestrianized downtown area. Part of the building is given over to dramatic, ever-changing displays of contemporary art and art installations. ✉ *Kungsg. 25* ☎ *0520/422500* ✍ *Free* ☉ *Kulturhallen (Culture Hall) at Folkets Hus, Sun. and Mon. noon–4, Tues.–Thurs. noon–7, Sat. 11–2.*

The **Innovatum Cableway** will take you 1,312 feet across the canal at a height of nearly 98 feet, with spectacular views of the canal, the town, and the waterfall area. ✉ *Åkerssjöv. 10* ☎ *0520/488480* ✍ *SKr 40* ☉ *June–Aug., daily 10–6.*

☾ Kids visiting the **Innovatum–Kunskapens Hus** (Innovatum–Technology Center) get to touch, examine, and poke at objects illustrating technology, energy, media, design, and industrial history. In the film studio you can edit yourself into contemporary Swedish movies. A big hit are the two robots, Max and Gerda, that spend their days vacuum-cleaning their futuristic apartment. As a reward for their hard work, the staff at Innovatum feeds the robots trash at set times. ⊠ *Åkerssjöv. 10* ☏ *0520/ 488480* ⊕ *www.innovatum.se* ⊠ *SKr 60* ⊘ *Tues.–Sun. 10–6.*

The canal and the locks gave Trollhättan its life, and a visit to the **Kanal-museet** (Canal Museum) tells as full a history of this as you can find. Housed in a redbrick 1893 waterside building, the museum covers the history of the canal and the locks and displays model ships, old tools, and fishing gear. ⊠ *Åkersbergsv., Övre Slussen* ☏ *0520/472206* ⊠ *SKr 15* ⊘ *May, weekends noon–5; June–Aug., daily 10–7.*

Where to Stay & Eat

¢–$ ✕ **Shangri La.** The large, elegant dining room is decorated in deep brown and gold shades to go along with the restaurant's mixed Asian theme. In summer you can sup on the outdoor terrace against a backdrop of humming waterfalls. ⊠ *Storg. 36* ☏ *0520/10222* ☰ *AE, MC, V.*

¢–$ ✕ **Strandgatan.** This popular, relaxed café is in an 1867 building that once housed canal workers. There's always a good crowd, especially in summer. Locals come to while away the hours over coffee, bagels, home-cooked international cuisine, and beer and wine. ⊠ *Föerningsg. 1* ☏ *0520/83717* ☰ *AE, DC, MC, V.*

$ ▥ **Scandic Swania.** Stunning views over the waterfalls and locks to the hills above town are what distinguish this comfortable hotel near Troll-hättan's center. Ask for a top-floor room at the front of the hotel and enjoy the sights. If you're up for a party, one of Trollhättan's few clubs is in the basement. ⊠ *Storg. 49, 461 23* ☏ *0520/89000* ᛘ *0520/89001* ⊕ *www.scandic-hotels.se* ⟿ *196 rooms, 13 suites* ⌕ *Restaurant, in-room broadband, in-room data ports, bar, lounge, nightclub, no-smoking rooms* ☰ *AE, DC, MC, V* ⫯ *BP.*

Mariestad

⑨ *40 km (25 mi) northeast of Lidköping.*

This town on the eastern shore of Lake Vänern is an architectural gem and an excellent base for some aquatic exploring. The town's center has a fine medieval quarter, a pretty harbor, and houses built in styles ranging from Gustavian (a baroque style named after King Gustav Vasa of the 1500s) to art nouveau. Others resemble Swiss chalets.

Domkyrkan, the late-Gothic cathedral on the edge of the old part of town, stands as a monument to one man's competitiveness. Commissioned at the end of the 16th century by Duke Karl—who named the town after his wife, Maria—it was built to resemble and rival Klara Kyrka in Stockholm, the church of his brother King Johan III, of whom he was insanely jealous. Karl made sure the church was endowed with some wonderfully excessive features, which can still be seen today. The stained-glass windows have real insects (bees, dragonflies, etc.) sandwiched within them, and the silver-and-gold cherubs are especially roly-poly and cute.

Where to Stay & Eat

$–$$ ✕ **St. Michel.** The outdoor patio of this old-style restaurant shoots out into Lake Vänern on stilts. Both the indoor and outdoor seating options offer beautiful views of the lake. The traditional Swedish dishes are heavily meat-based, and most come with a side of *rösti* (hash potatoes mixed with grated cheese and chopped onions and shaped to a pancake). ⊠ *Kungsg. 1* ☏ *0501/19900* ⊟ *MC, V* ☻ *Closed Sun. No lunch Sat.*

$ ⊞ **Stadtshotellet.** This is the best choice in a town full of below-average hotels. The building is unobtrusive, but the rooms are comfortable, if a little bland in their furnishings. ⊠ *Nyg. 10, 542 30* ☏ *0501/13800* ⊞ *0501/77640* ⊕ *www.stadtshotelletmariestad.com* ⇌ *29 rooms* ♨ *Restaurant, in-room broadband, in-room data ports, bar, no-smoking rooms* ⊟ *AE, MC, V* �†⊙† *BP.*

Motala

⑩ *13 km (8 mi) north of Vadstena, 262 km (163 mi) northeast of Göteborg.*

Before reaching Stockholm, the canal passes through Motala, where Baltzar von Platen is buried. He had hoped that four new towns would be established along the waterway, but only Motala rose according to plan. He designed the town himself, and his statue is in the main square. Motala itself is not an essential sight. Instead, it's the activities along the canal and lake, along with a few very good museums, that make Motala worth a stop.

★ Stop at the **Motala Motormuseum** even if you are not in the slightest bit interested in cars. All the cars and motorcycles on display—from 1920s Rolls-Royces to 1950s Cadillacs and modern racing cars—are presented in their appropriate context, with music of the day playing on contemporary radios; mannequins dressed in fashions of the time; and newspapers, magazines, televisions, and everyday household objects all helping to set the stage. More a museum of 20th-century technology and life than one solely of cars, it makes for a fascinating look back at the last century. ⊠ *Hamnen* ☏ *0141/58888* ⊕ *www.motala-motormuseum.se* ⇌ *SKr 50* ☻ *June–Aug., daily 10–8; May and Sept., daily 10–6; Oct.–Apr., weekdays 8–5, weekends 11–5.*

Where to Stay

$ ⊞ **Ramada Palace Hotel.** Ship models decorate the lobby windows of this hotel with a nautical theme. The rooms are designed to look like cabins, though fortunately larger and more comfortable. Paintings of sea motifs and round windows in the bathrooms add to the charm. Just a five-minute walk from the train station, this hotel is close to most of Motala's sights. ⊠ *Kungsg. 1, 591 30* ☏ *0141/216660* ⊞ *0141/57221* ⊕ *www.ramadapalace.se* ⇌ *55 rooms, 1 suite* ♨ *Sauna, bar, free parking* ⊟ *AE, MC, V* �†⊙† *BP.*

Vadstena

⑪ *249 km (155 mi) northeast of Göteborg (via Jönköping).*

This little-known gem of a town grew up around the monastery founded by St. Birgitta, or Bridget (1303–73), who wrote in her *Revelations* that she had a vision of Christ in which he revealed the rules of the religious order she went on to establish. These rules seem to have been a precursor for the Swedish ideal of sexual equality, with both nuns and monks sharing a common church. Her order spread rapidly after her death, and at one time there were 80 Bridgetine monasteries in Europe. Little remains of the Vadstena monastery; in 1545 King Gustav Vasa ordered its demolition, and its stones were used to build **Vadstena Slott** (Vadstena Castle), a huge fortress created to defend against Danish attack. It was later refurbished and used as a home for Gustav's mentally ill son. Many of the original decorations were lost in a fire in the early 1600s. Unable to afford replacement decorations, the royal family had decorations and fittings painted with three-dimensional effect directly onto the walls. Swedish royalty held court at Vadstena Slott until 1715. Today it houses part of the National Archives, the tourist bureau, and is also the site of an annual summer opera festival. ☎ *0143/31570* ✉ *SKr 50 (in winter SKr 30)* ☉ *Mid-May–end of May, daily 11–4; June and Aug., daily 10–6; July, daily 10–7; Sept. 1–Sept. 15, daily 10–4; Sept. 16–mid-May, daily 11–2; guided tours on the hr June–Aug.*

Where to Stay

$–$$ 🏨 **Vadstena Klosterhotel.** Sweden's oldest secular building, parts of which date from the 13th century, is now a hotel. Rooms are modern and well appointed, and there are three comfortable lounges. You can choose a view of either Lake Vättern or the hotel's courtyard. The former is infinitely more preferable and only SKr 100 extra. ✉ *Klosterområdet off Lasarettsg., 592 24* ☎ *0143/31530* 🖨 *0143/13648* ⊕ *www.klosterhotel. se* ⮑ *65 rooms, 3 suites* ⚘ *Restaurant, lounge, meeting room, no-smoking rooms* ▤ *AE, DC, MC, V* ⦿ *BP.*

$ 🏨 **Starby Kungsgård.** This functional guesthouse, reached via Route 50, is next to a renovated manor house and restaurant. The rooms use light wood throughout and have earth-tone carpets and green, blue, and brown color schemes. The complex is surrounded by a park on the outskirts of town. ✉ *Ödeshögsv., 592 21* ☎ *0143/75100* 🖨 *0143/75170* ⮑ *61 rooms* ⚘ *Restaurant, indoor pool, hot tub, sauna, spa, meeting room, free parking* ▤ *AE, DC, MC, V* ⦿ *CP.*

Göta Canal A to Z

BIKE TOURS

For two-day bike tours along the canal from Sjötorp (27 km [17 mi] northeast of Mariestad), contact Resespecialisten utmed Göta Kanal. The price is SKr 1,000 for adults and SKr 500 for children under 13. The price includes lodging in a youth hostel in Töreboda, a breakfast, lunch, and dinner, as well as a bike rental for an adult. The same company also has four-day combined bike and boat tours along the canal for SKr 2,500 (all inclusive) for adults.

🚩 **Resespecialisten utmed Göta Kanal** ✉ Kungsg. 10, 545 30 Töreboda ☎ 0506/12500 ⊕ www.gotakanalturer.com.

CAR TRAVEL

From Stockholm follow E20 west; from Göteborg take Route 45 north to E20. For much of the route the canal is actually Lake Vänern, Sweden's largest lake, which cuts the canal in two. From Trollhättan to Sjötorp, you hug the lake shore. The canal proper is mostly surrounded by meadows, so gas-driven waterside transport is out of the question.

CRUISE TRAVEL
Rederi Göta Canal has cruises along the canal from one to six days, originating in Göteborg (with bus service to the canal). Prices vary.
🚢 **Rederi Göta Canal** ✉ Pusterviksg. 13, Göteborg ☎ 031/806315 🌐 www.stromma.se.

TRAIN TRAVEL
Call SJ for information about service. All towns along the canal are either on a main rail line, or have good bus connections to the nearest train stop.
🚢 **SJ** ✉ Göteborg ☎ 0771/757575.

VISITOR INFORMATION
🚢 **Mariestad** ✉ Hamnplan ☎ 0501/10001 🌐 www.turism.mariestad.se. **Motala** ✉ Göta Kanalbolagsmuseet, Hamnen ☎ 0141/225254. **Vadstena** ✉ Slottet ☎ 0143/31570.

THE SOUTH & THE KINGDOM OF GLASS

Southern Sweden is considered, even by many Swedes, to be a world of its own, clearly distinguished from the rest of the country by its geography, culture, and history. Skåne (pronounced *skoh*-neh), is a comparatively small province of beautifully fertile plains, sand beaches, thriving farms, bustling historic towns and villages, medieval churches, and summer resorts. These gently rolling hills, extensive forests, and fields are broken every few miles by lovely castles, chronologically and architecturally diverse, that have given this part of Sweden the name Château Country.

The two other southern provinces, Blekinge and Halland, are also fertile and rolling and edged by seashores. Historically, these three provinces are distinct from the rest of Sweden: they were the last to be incorporated into the country, having been ruled by Denmark until 1658. They retain the influences of the Continental culture in their architecture, language, and cuisine, viewing the rest of Sweden—especially Stockholm—with some disdain.

Småland, to the north, is larger than the other provinces, with a harsh countryside of stone and woods. The area has many small glassblowing firms, and it is these glassworks, such as the world-renowned Kosta Boda and Orrefors, that have given the area the nickname the Kingdom of Glass.

Since it covers a fairly large area of the country, this region is best explored by car. The coastal road is a pleasure to travel on, with scenic views of long, sandy beaches and the welcoming blue sea. Inland, the hills, fertile plains, and thickly wooded forests are interconnected by winding country roads. The southern peninsula around the province of Skåne has the most urban settlements and, thanks to the spectacular Øresund Bridge, fast connections to Denmark and mainland Europe.

Mölle

★ *35 km (21 mi) northwest of Helsingborg, 220 km (132 mi) south of Göteborg, 235 km (141 mi) southwest of Växjö, 95 km (57 mi) northwest of Malmö.*

Mölle, in the far northwest of Skåne, is a small town set in spectacular isolation on the dramatic headland of the Kulla Peninsula. It is an old fishing village with a beautiful harbor that sweeps up to the Kullaberg Range. You will find beech forests, stupefying views, and rugged shores and beaches, surrounded on three sides by sea.

For those who love nature or want a break from cities and touring, Mölle is perfect. Not only is it a good base from which to explore, but the town itself has a charm that has never been tarnished by an overabundance of tourists or a relentless drive to modernize at all costs.

Today it is a relatively wealthy place, as the elaborate residences and the upmarket cars crowding the narrow streets show. Much of this wealth supposedly arrived when the more fortunate men of the sea returned to build mansions.

The **Villa Italienborg** (✉ Harastolsv. 6) was completed in 1910 by a scrap dealer inspired by a trip to the Italian Riviera. The exterior is covered in striking red and white tiles that form a checked pattern, which was quite stylish at the time.

The verandas, balconies, and sliding windows all make the two-story **Villa Africa** (✉ N. Brunnsv.) stand out. It was built in a South African colonial style by a local captain to please his South African wife.

The **Kullaberg nature reserve** is just outside Mölle and covers more than 35 square km (13½ square mi). You can walk, bike, or drive in. This natural playground includes excellent trails through beech forests and along coastal routes. There's a lighthouse here set in stark land that resembles that of the Scottish Highlands—it even has long-haired Highland cattle. The park contains cafés, a restaurant, safe swimming beaches, and a golf course that's one of Sweden's most spectacular. ▦ *SKr 30 per car.*

Krapperup Castle was built in 1570 over the ruins of a medieval stronghold dating from the 13th century. The present building was extensively renovated in the late 18th century, although remnants of the stronghold still exist. The garden is among Sweden's best-preserved parks. There's an art gallery and museum inside, and concerts and performance theater are held here in summer. It is 4 km (2½ mi) from Mölle on the main road to Helsingborg. ☎ *042/344190* ▦ *Castle tours for groups of 10 minimum: SKr 75 gallery, museum SKr 35* ☽ *Call to book castle tour for group; gallery and museum May and Sept., weekends 1–6; June–Aug., daily 1–6.*

The haunting **Nimis and Arx** artworks are built of scrap wood and stone and stand on a rugged beach that can be reached only on foot. The artist Lars Vilks has been working on the weird, highly controversial structures since the 1970s. They are the most visited sight in Kullaberg. ✉ *Head 2 km (1 mi) east out of Mölle to a road sign directing you to*

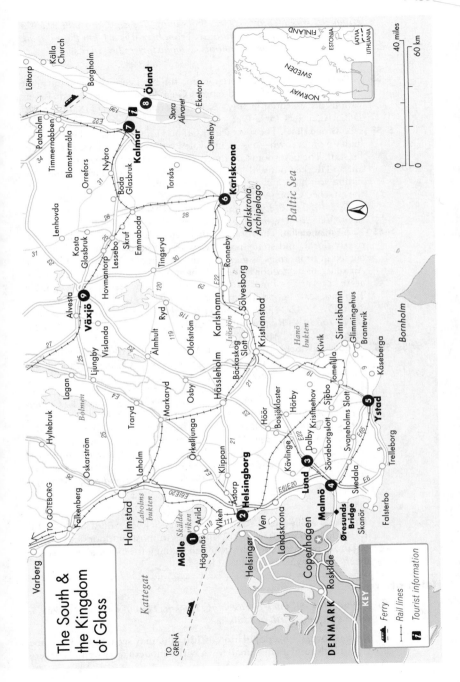

The South & the Kingdom of Glass

KEY

⛴ Ferry

╬ Rail lines

🛈 Tourist Information

Kattegat

TO GRENÅ

TO GÖTEBORG

Varberg

Falkenberg

Halmstad

Laholms bukten

Mölle ①

Höganäs

Arild

Vikén

Skälder vikén

111

112

Helsingborg ②

Ven

Landskrona

Helsingør

Copenhagen

Roskilde

DENMARK

Øresunds Bridge

Skanör

Falsterbo

Malmö ④

Lund ③

Dalby

Kävlinge

Trelleborg

Skedala

Svaneholms Slott

Sövdeborgslott

Ystad ⑤

Köpingebro

Löderup

Kåseberga

Bornholm

Baltic Sea

Varberg

Oskarström

Hyltebruk

Lagan

Ljungby

Vislanda

Bolmen

Traryd

Markaryd

Osby

Hässleholm

Höör

Hörby

Bosjökloster

Sjöbo

Tomelilla

Simrishamn

Glimmingehus

Brantevik

Kivik

Hanö bukten

Kristianstad

Bäckaskog Slott

Ivösjön

Sölvesborg

Karlshamn

Ronneby

Karlskrona ⑥

Karlskrona Arkipelago

Tingsryd

Emmaboda

Skruf

Lessebo

Kosta Glasbruk

Boda Glasbruk

Orrefors

Nybro

Torsås

Kalmar ⑦🛈

Blomstermåla

Timmernabben

Pataholm

Läötorp

Källa Church

Borgholm

Öland ⑧🛈

Stora Alvaret

Eketorp

Ottenby

Växjö ⑨🛈

Alvesta

Lenhovda

Hovmantorp

Ryd

Almhult

Olofström

Ljungby

Lagan

Laholm

Åstorp

Örkelljunga

Klippan

Ängelholm

FINLAND

ESTONIA

LATVIA

LITHUANIA

SWEDEN

NORWAY

0 ___ 40 miles

0 ___ 60 km

Himmelstorps Hembygdsgård. Following this sign you will reach a parking lot and an old farmhouse. From here it is a 1-km (½-mi) walk marked by small blue N symbols ⊕ *www.turism.hoganas.se.*

Where to Stay & Eat

$$ ✕ **Gula Boden.** With a local reputation for excellent fish meals and great views of the boat harbor and sunsets, Gula Boden is quite popular. Reservations are essential in July. ✉ *Vikens Hamn* ☎ *042/238300* ▤ *AE, DC, MC, V* ⊗ *Closed Oct.–Apr.*

$–$$ ✕▦ **Grand Hôtel.** The spectacular Grand Hôtel—a turreted building set high up on in town—has an unrivaled setting, great views, and a helpful staff. The best rooms are those with a sea view, but they are all pleasant and decked out with fresh white, blue, and aquamarine prints. For dining you have a choice of two restaurants, the one in the hotel and the attached Captain's Room. ✉ *Bökebolsv. 11, 260 42* ☎ *042/362230* 🖶 *042/362231* ⊕ *www.grand-molle.se* ⇥ *42 rooms* ⌕ *2 restaurants, sauna, bar, library, meeting rooms* ▤ *AE, D, MC, V* ⎮◎⎮ *BP.*

$–$$ ✕▦ **Turisthotellet.** The rooms at this hotel are well appointed, if a little overly floral, and some have a view of the harbor. The breakfast, included in room rates, is generous and could see you through to dinner. An annex to next-door Hotel Kullaberg, this is nonetheless run as a separate hotel and is a more affordable option. The restaurant ($$), Gran Turismo, serves good Italian food. ✉ *Kullabergsv. 32, 260 42* ☎ *042/ 347000* 🖶 *042/347100 to Hotel Kullaberg* ⊕ *www.hotelkullaberg.se* ⇥ *14 rooms* ⌕ *Restaurant, bar* ▤ *AE, DC, MC, V* ⎮◎⎮ *BP* ⊗ *Restaurant closed Sept.–May.*

★ **$$–$$$** ▦ **Hotel Kullaberg.** At this luxurious hotel all the rooms are plush and decorated in themes. One room suggests *Out of Africa,* and another has a large biplane hanging from the ceiling. You may or may not love it, depending on your feelings about kitsch. But the Kullaberg is lush, with views of the sea and the harbor and ornate reading rooms. ✉ *Gyllenstiernas Allé 16, 260 42* ☎ *042/347000* 🖶 *042/347100* ⊕ *www. hotelkullaberg.se* ⇥ *18 rooms* ⌕ *Library* ▤ *AE, DC, MC, V* ⎮◎⎮ *BP.*

$ ▦ **Pensionat Solgården.** Run by an artistic woman who spends six months of each year at a bed-and-breakfast in Tonga in the South Pacific, this quaint pension hosts poetry readings outside in summer. ✉ *Byav. 102 Lerberget* ☎ *042/330430* ⊗ *Closed mid-Sept.–mid-Apr.* ⎮◎⎮ *BP.*

Sports

The **Skola Mölle Hamn** (✉ Special Sports School, Södra Strandv. 6B ☎ 042/347705 or 070/3771210) caters to most outdoor activities. It organizes trips and provides gear and training for mountaineers, scuba divers, and kayakers of all skill levels.

Helsingborg

➋ *221 km (137 mi) south of Göteborg, 186 km (116 mi) southwest of Växjö, 64 km (40 mi) north of Malmö.*

Helsingborg, with a population of 120,000, may seem to the first-time visitor little more than a small town with a modern ferry terminal (there are about 125 daily ferry connections to Denmark and one a day to Norway). But the town has a fairly illustrious history—together with its twin town, Helsingør (Elsinore in William Shakespeare's *Hamlet*), across the Øresund, it controlled shipping traffic in and out of the Baltic for centuries—and there are a few interesting sights, as well as quite a few dining and lodging options.

All that remains of Helsingborg's castle is **Kärnan** (the Keep), which was built in the late 14th century. It has walls 15 feet thick. This surviving center tower, built to provide living quarters and defend the medieval castle, is one of the most remarkable relics of its kind in the north. The interior is divided into several floors, which contain a chapel, an exhibition of kitchen implements, old castle fittings, and some weaponry. ⊠ *Slottshagen* ☎ *042/105991* 🖃 *SKr 20* 🕙 *Jan.–Mar., Tues.–Sun. 11–3; Apr. and May, Tues.–Fri. 9–4, weekends 11–4; June–Aug., daily 11–7; Sept., Tues.–Fri. 9–4, weekends 11–4; Oct.–Dec., Tues.–Sun. 11–3.*

Maria Kyrkan (St. Mary's), begun in the early 14th century and finished 100 years later, is a fine example of Danish Gothic architecture. St. Mary's has several highlights: the 15th-century reredos, the silver treasure in the sacristy, and a memorial plaque to Dietrich Buxtehude (1637–1707), a prominent German composer as well as the church's organist. ⊠ *Mariatorget, Södra Storg. 20* ☎ *042/372830* 🕙 *Aug.–June, daily 8–4; July, daily 8–6.*

Helsingborg's refurbished harborside area, **Norra Hamnen** (Northern Harbor), has a pleasant marina with a string of architecturally impressive cafés and restaurants.

In 1865 **Sofiero Slott** (Sofiero Palace) was built in Dutch Renaissance style by Prince Oscar and his wife, Sofia, as a summer home. Half a century later Oscar II gave the palace to his grandson, Gustav Adolf, and his wife, Margareta, as a wedding gift. Since the estate is now owned by the city of Helsingborg, you can gain access to Sofiero's park, a haven for more than 10,000 samples of 300 kinds of rhododendron, various statues donated by international artists, and a large English garden; nearby greenhouses have plant exhibits. A café and fine restaurant are on the grounds. ⊠ *Sofierov. (on road to Laröd)* ☎ *042/137400* 🖃 *SKr 80* 🕙 *Mid-Apr.–Sept., daily 11–5; guided tours only. Park, restaurant, and café open year-round.*

Where to Eat

$–$$$ ✕ **Restaurang La Petite.** If you are yearning for the delicacy of French cuisine and the genuine look and feel of a French restaurant, then look no further. La Petite has been here since 1975, suggesting success, and can also indulge the diner in Spanish and international meals. ⊠ *Bruksg. 19* ☎ *042/219727* 🖃 *AE, DC, MC, V* 🕙 *Closed Sun.*

★ $$ ✕ **Pålsjö Krog.** Beside the pier that leads out to the Pålsjö Bath House, this restaurant offers a beautiful view of the Øresund. The owners have partially restored the restaurant to its original 1930s style—note the antique sofa in the lounge and the art on the walls. Seafood is the specialty in summer months, game in winter. Reservations are essential in summer. ⊠ *Drottningg. 151* ☎ *042/149730* 🖃 *AE, DC, MC, V.*

$$ ✕ **SS** *Swea.* Those with a nautical bent or nostalgia for past traveling days will be well served at this restaurant ship modeled after cruise liners of old. The docked boat specializes in fresh seafood and international menus. Enjoy the wide-ranging menu but don't forget to disembark— there are no cabin bunks here. ✉ *Kungstorget* ☎ *042/131516* ⊟ *AE, DC, MC, V.*

Where to Stay

$–$$ 🏨 **Elite Hotel Mollberg.** Only a short walk from the central station, the Mollberg has spacious rooms with hardwood floors and large windows. Corner rooms have balconies that overlook a cobblestone square. The restaurant offers dining at reasonable prices. ✉ *Stortorget 18, 251 14* ☎ *042/373700* 🖷 *042/373737* ⤴ *104 rooms, 7 suites* ⚓ *Restaurant, minibars, room TVs with movies, in-room broadband, sauna, bar, meeting room, parking (fee), no-smoking rooms* ⊟ *AE, DC, MC, V* ¶⊙¶ *BP.*

$–$$ 🏨 **Radisson SAS Grand Hotel.** One of Sweden's oldest hotels has been completely renovated, maintaining its long-standing reputation for excellence. Public areas here are, as the name suggests, grand, with dark-wood paneling, chandeliers, and a mix of contemporary furniture and antiques. The smell of fresh flowers fills the hotel. Rooms are very well equipped to offer relaxed decadence; floors are rich, dark wood and fabrics, chairs, and cushions are lush brown and soft beige. Sleeping comfortably here is no problem. ✉ *Stortorget 8–12, 251 11* ☎ *042/380400* 🖷 *042/380404* ⤴ *164 rooms, 8 suites* ⚓ *Restaurant, room service, minibars, room TVs with movies, in-room broadband, Wi-Fi, gym, sauna, bar, lounge, meeting rooms, no-smoking rooms* ⊟ *AE, DC, MC, V* ¶⊙¶ *BP.*

FodorśChoice
★

¢–$ 🏨 **Villa Thalassa.** This youth hostel 3 km (2 mi) from the city center has fine views over Øresund. In the main building and in bungalow-style buildings, all with private patios, there are 172 bunks in two-, four-, and six-bunk rooms. The SKr 45 breakfast is not included. ✉ *Dag Hammarskjölds väg, 254 33* ☎ *042/380660* 🖷 *042/128792* ⤴ *172 beds in 64 rooms (24 rooms with bath)* ⚓ *Meeting rooms* ⊟ *No credit cards.*

Nightlife & the Arts

The plush culture and art center, **Dunkers Kulturhus** (✉ Kungsg. 11 ☎ 042/107400), stages an array of events in the fields of music, drama, visual arts, and cultural heritage.

Jazz in Helsingborg stages some of its events at a cozy club on Nedre Långvinkelsgatan and some in the culture and arts center Dunkers Kulturhus. If you strike on the right night, you may well find yourself in jazz heaven, since the organizers attract jazz musicians from all over. Admission varies and goes as high as SKr 225. ✉ *Nedre Långvinkelsg. 22* ☎ *042/184900* ✉ *Dunkers Kulturhus, Kungsg. 11, Sundstorget* ☎ *042/107400.*

Sports & the Outdoors

If your bones are weary, visit **Øresundsmassage.** The professionally trained staff offers various massage services and can deal with problems such as cramping or poor blood circulation. ✉ *Roskildeg. 4* ☎ *042/127042* ⊕ *www.oresundsmassage.se* ⧆ *20 mins SKr 240; 40 mins SKr*

400; 60 mins SKr 500 ☉ *Mon. and Wed. noon–7, Tues. and Thurs. 10–6.*
Consider taking a relaxing dip in the sound at the late-19th-century
Pålsjöbaden (Pålsjö Bath House) just north of town. It's a Helsingborg
tradition to sweat in a sauna and then jump into the cool waters of the
channel—even in winter. After an evening sauna, nearby Pålsjö Krog
is a good dinner option. ⊠ *Drottningg. 151* ☏ *042/149730* 🖅 *Single visit SKr 30.*

Lund

❸ *34 km (21 mi) southeast of Landskrona via E6/E20 and Rte. 16, 25 km
(15 mi) northeast of Malmö, 183 km (113 mi) southwest of Växjö.*

One of the oldest towns in Europe, Lund was founded in 990. In 1103
Lund became the religious capital of Scandinavia, and at one time had
27 churches and eight monasteries—until King Christian III of Denmark ordered most of them razed to use their stones for the construction of Malmöhus Castle. Lund lost its importance until 1666, when
its university was established—the second-oldest university in Sweden
after Uppsala.

FodorśChoice
★
Lund's **Domkyrkan** (Cathedral), consecrated in 1145, is a monumental
gray-stone Romanesque cathedral, the oldest in Scandinavia. Since the
Reformation it has been Lutheran. Its crypt has 23 finely carved pillars,
but its main attraction is an astrological clock, Horologum Mirabile Lun-
dense, dating from 1380 and restored in 1923. The "Miraculous Clock
of Lund" depicts an amazing pageant of knights jousting on horseback,
trumpets blowing a medieval fanfare, and the Magi walking in proces-
sion past the Virgin and Child as the organ plays *In Dulci Jubilo.* The
clock plays at noon and at 3 Monday–Saturday and at 1 and 3 on Sunday. The oldest parts of the cathedral are considered the finest Romanesque constructions in Sweden. English and Swedish tours are
available, and there are concerts at 10 AM on Sunday. ☏ *046/358700*
🖅 *Free* ☉ *Weekdays 8–6, Sat. 9:30–5, Sun. 9:30–6.*

One block east of the cathedral is the **Botaniska Trädgården** (Botanical
Garden), which contains more than 7,000 specimens of plants from all
over the world, including such exotics as the paper mulberry tree, from
the islands of the South Pacific. ⊠ *Östra Vallg. 20* ☏ *046/2227320* 🖅 *Free*
☉ *Daily 6 AM–8 PM, greenhouses daily noon–3.*

Right next to the Lund Art Gallery is **Krognoshuset,** Lund's best-preserved
medieval residence, and a small but well-presented art gallery. The
building itself is worth a look, but most days you will get the added bonus
of a contemporary art exhibition showcasing anything from industrial
design to video installations. ⊠ *Mårtenstorget 3* ☏ *046/126248* 🖅 *Free*
☉ *Daily, year-round 11–5. Call ahead for exhibition details.*

☹ **Kulturen** (Museum of Cultural History) is both an outdoor and an indoor museum; it includes 20 old cottages, farms, and manor houses from
southern Sweden, plus an excellent collection of ceramics, textiles,
weapons, and furniture. ⊠ *Tegnérsplatsen* ☏ *046/350400* 🖅 *SKr 50*
☉ *Mid-Apr.–Sept., Thurs.–Tues. 11–5, Wed. 11–9; Oct.–mid-Apr.,
Tues.–Sun. noon–4.*

The all-brick **Lund Konsthall** (Lund Art Gallery) may have a rather forbidding iron entrance and few windows, but skylights allow ample sunlight into the large exhibit room full of contemporary art by Swedish painters and sculptors, as well as some European artists. ⊠ *Mårtenstorget 3* ☎ *046/355395* ▣ *Free* ☉ *Mon.–Wed. and Fri. noon–5, Thurs. noon–8, Sat. 10–5, Sun. noon–6.*

Fodor'sChoice
★

The **Heligkorskyrkan i Dalby** (Holy Cross Church of Dalby) was founded in 1060, making it the oldest stone church in Scandinavia. It was for a short time the archbishop's seat until this was moved into town. Among the hidden treasures is a renowned baptismal font, brought here in 1150. The exposed brick within the church is original, and many figures and icons date from medieval times, including a wooden relief at the front of the church of Veronica's Veil, which shows the face of Jesus. The church is on a hill less than 10 km (6 mi) from Lund. ⊠ *Head east on Rte. 16 and follow signs* ☎ *046/208600* ▣ *Free* ☉ *May–Aug., daily 9–6; Sept.–Apr., daily 9–4.*

Where to Eat

★ $$ ✕ **Restaurang Café Finn.** Connected to the Lund Konsthallen, Café Finn is an excellent option for lunch or dinner. The creamy lobster soup with mussels is perfect if you're not overly hungry, but for a more substantial meal go for the veal fillet with creamy red-onion sauce and grape jelly. The walls have an extensive collection of museum exhibit posters from the '60s, '70s, and '80s. Just outside is the Krognoshuset. ⊠ *Mårtenstorget 3* ☎ *046/130565* ▣ *AE, DC, MC, V.*

★ $–$$ ✕ **Bantorget 9.** The restaurant-bar inside this 18th-century building is true to the past, with restored woodwork and paintings on the ceilings, antique flowerpots and candleholders, and classical statues in the corners of the room. The menu offers traditional Swedish dishes plus some more intriguing entrées such as duck breast with pickled red cabbage in apple honey. Bantorget 9 is a short walk from Lund's central train station. ⊠ *Bantorget 9* ☎ *046/320200* ▣ *AE, DC, MC, V* ☉ *Closed Sun.*

$–$$ ✕ **Godset.** Inside an old railroad warehouse right on the tracks near central station, Godset's modern tables and chairs stand on rustic wooden floors between brick walls. On one wall hangs a large 1950s clock taken from Mariakyrkan (Maria Church) in nearby Ystad. The menu is mostly seafood and meat dishes. Try the roasted venison poached in a cream sauce with raspberry vinaigrette. ⊠ *Bang. 3* ☎ *046/121610* ▣ *AE, DC, MC, V* ☉ *Closed Sun.*

¢–$$ ✕ **Dalby Gästgiveri.** This is one of Skåne's oldest inns and a gastronomic delight. The many red-meat dishes on the menu follow a tradition of history and quality, but innovative Swedish fare is served, too. Entrées such as the rich, somewhat gamey deer fillet with mushroom spring rolls and cranberry sauce are not for the faint of heart. Be sure to make reservations in summer. ⊠ *Tengsg. 6* ☎ *046/200006* ▣ *AE, MC, V.*

Where to Stay

★ $$ ⊞ **Grand Hotel.** This elegant red-stone hotel is in the heart of the city on a pleasant square close to the railway station. All the rooms are furnished differently, but most have a turn-of-the-20th-century decor and charm in common. The fine restaurant serves an alternative vegetarian menu. ✉ *Bantorget 1, 221 04* ☎ *046/2806100* 🖷 *046/2806150* ⊕ *www. grandilund.se* ⤵ *84 rooms, 1 suite* ⚿ *Restaurant, hot tub, sauna, meeting room, no-smoking rooms* ▭ *AE, DC, MC, V* ⦿❙ *BP.*

$$ 🏨 **Hotel Lundia.** Only a few hundred feet from the train station, Hotel Lundia is ideal for those who want to be near the city center. Built in 1968, the modern, four-story square building has transparent glass walls on the ground floor. Rooms are decorated in a combination of Scandinavian and Japanese styles. ✉ *Knut den Stores torg 2, 221 04* ☎ *046/ 2806500* 🖷 *046/2806510* ⊕ *www.lundia.se* ⤵ *97 rooms, 1 suite* ⚿ *Restaurant, Wi-Fi, lounge, nightclub, meeting room, no-smoking rooms* ▭ *AE, DC, MC, V* ⦿❙ *BP.*

$–$$ 🏨 **Oskar.** A charming boutique-style hotel made up of two 19th-century town houses, the hotel offers spacious, modern, and bright rooms with white walls, colorful art, and oiled oak floors. All rooms are individually furnished with designer touches like chairs from Gunilla Allard and lamps by the legendary Arne Jacobsen. Downstairs is a café and a beautiful garden where you can enjoy breakfast in the morning and coffee throughout the day. ✉ *Bytareg. 3, 222 21* ☎ *046/188085* 🖷 *046/373030* ⊕ *www.hotelloskar.se* ⤵ *6 rooms* ⚿ *Café, cable TV, in-room DVD, in-room data ports; no smoking* ▭ *AE, DC, MC, V* ⦿❙ *BP.*

Nightlife & the Arts

★ **Basilika** (✉ Stora Söderg. 13 ☎ 046/2116660) has a smallish dance floor and also hosts live bands. On Friday and Saturday things don't get going until 11 and rage on until 3. Basilika draws young hipsters and will cost at least SKr 50 to get in.

The hot spot in town, **Stortorget** (✉ Stortorget 1 ☎ 046/139290), has live music as well as a DJ night and is popular with students. You won't get in here unless you are over 22.

Shopping

Saluhallen (✉ Corner of Mårtenstorget and Botulfsg.), known as Foodhall, is an adventure in itself, an excellent example of the traditional Swedish food house but also one that stocks delicacies from Italy, Japan, and beyond. Cheese, meats, fresh and pickled fish, and pastries are all in great supply. It is the perfect place to get some food for a picnic in one of Lund's many squares and parks.

Skånekraft (✉ Östra Mårtensg. 5 ☎ 046/144777) carries a wide range of ceramics, crafts, and designer goods.

Malmö

❹ *25 km (15 mi) southwest of Lund (via E22), 198 km (123 mi) southwest of Växjö.*

Capital of the province of Skåne, with a population of about 265,000, Malmö is Sweden's third-largest city. It was founded at the end of the 13th century. The remarkable 8-km (5-mi) bridge and tunnel from Malmö to Copenhagen has transformed travel and trade in the area, cutting both time and costs, and replacing the ferries that used to shuttle between the two towns.

The city's castle, **Malmöhus,** completed in 1542, was for many years used as a prison (James Bothwell, husband of Mary, Queen of Scots, was one of its notable inmates). Today Malmöhus houses a variety of **museums,** including the City Museum, the Museum of Natural History, and the Art Museum, which has a collection of Nordic art. Across the street are the Science and Technology Museum, the Maritime Museum, and a toy museum. ⊠ *Malmöhusv.* ☎ *040/344437* ☜ *SKr 40 for all museums* ⊙ *June–Aug., daily 10–4; Sept.–May, daily noon–4.*

In the same park as Malmöhus is the **Malmö Stadsbibliotek** (Malmö City Library), designed by the famous Danish architect Henning Larsen. Take a walk through the colossal main room—there's a four-story wall of glass that brings seasonal changes of colors inside. ⊠ *Kung Oscars väg* ☎ *040/6608500.*

The houses and business buildings designed and erected for the 2001 **European Housing Expo** show 58 different types of housing. Wander around the development surrounding the Ribersborgsstranden waterfront, where the expo was held, in order to see the exteriors of more than 500 homes. They were sold as residences after the expo was over. ⊠ *Ribersborgsstranden waterfront.*

★ You can learn about Scandinavian art and design at the **Form/Design Center.** The center is run by SvenskForm, a nonprofit association that promotes top-quality design in Sweden; Swedish and other Scandinavian artworks are on display throughout the center. ⊠ *9 Lilla Torg* ☎ *040/ 6645150* ⊕ *www.formdesigncenter.com* ☜ *Free admission.* ⊙ *Tues.–Fri. 11–5, Thurs. 11–6, weekends 11–4.*

Lilla Torg is a cobblestone square with some of the city's oldest buildings, which date from the 17th and 18th centuries. It is clustered with cafés, restaurants, and bars and is a great place to wander or watch the world go by. Walk into the side streets and see the traditional buildings, which were originally used mainly to store grain and produce. Check out the Saluhallen (food hall), which contains **Kryddboden,** one of Sweden's best coffee purveyors.

The **Rådhuset** (Town Hall), dating from 1546, dominates Stortorget, a huge, cobbled market square in Gamla Staden, and makes an impressive spectacle when illuminated at night.

Fodor'sChoice One of Sweden's most outstanding art museums, **Rooseum,** is in a turn-
★ of-the-20th-century brick building that was once a power plant. It has exhibitions of contemporary art and a quality selection of Nordic art. ⊠ *Gasverksg. 22* ☎ *040/121716* ⊕ *www.rooseum.se* ☜ *SKr 40* ⊙ *Wed. 2–8, Thurs.–Sun. noon–6. Guided tours in Swedish and English weekends at 2, Thurs. and Fri. at 6:30, Wed. at 6.*

★ In Gamla Staden, the Old Town, look for the **St. Petri Church,** on Kalendegatan; dating from the 14th century, it is an impressive example of the Baltic Gothic style, with distinctive stepped gables. Inside there is a fine Renaissance altar.

Where to Eat

★ **$$–$$$** ✕ **Årstiderna i Kockska Huset.** Formed by merging two discrete restaurants that were in different locations, the combination is housed in a 16th-century building with beautiful interiors. Several of the dining areas are in an underground cellar. Traditional Swedish dishes, often centered on beef, game, and seafood, are given a contemporary twist. The fried halibut, for example, is served with a crab mousse and a rich shellfish sauce flavored with curry. Like the food, the wine list is excellent. ✉ *Frans Suellsg. 3* ☎ *040/230910* ▣ *AE, DC, MC, V.*

$$–$$$ ✕ **Johan P.** This extremely popular restaurant specializes in seafood and shellfish prepared in Swedish and Continental styles. White walls and crisp white tablecloths give it an elegant air, which contrasts with the generally casual dress of the customers. An outdoor section is open in summer. ✉ *Saluhallen, Lilla Torg* ☎ *040/971818* ▣ *AE, DC, MC, V* ☾ *Closed Sun.*

$–$$ ✕ **Salt & Brygga.** The traditional Swedish kitchen has found some inspiration in the Mediterranean at this quayside restaurant. Endive and Gorgonzola toast, and smoked *saithe* (coalfish) and horseradish *fromage* appetizers are followed by rich shellfish casseroles. The restaurant not only uses only organic produce, but also uses ecologically friendly alternatives for everything from the wall paint to the table linens and the staff's clothes. The restaurant's selection of organic wines and beers is unique for the region. ✉ *Sundspromenaden 7* ☎ *040/6115940* ▣ *AE, DC, MC, V.*

Fodor'sChoice ★

¢–$ ✕ **B & B.** It stands for *Butik och Bar* (Shop and Bar) and is named as such because of its location in the food hall in central Malmö. There's always good home cooking, with dishes like grilled salmon and beef fillet with potatoes. Sometimes there's even entertainment at the piano. ✉ *Saluhallen, Lilla Torg* ☎ *040/127120* ▣ *AE, DC, MC, V.*

Where to Stay

★ **$$** ▦ **Mäster Johan Hotel.** The plain exterior of this Best Western hotel disguises a plush and meticulously crafted interior. A top-to-bottom redesign of a 19th-century building, with the focal point an Italianate atrium breakfast room, the Mäster Johan is unusually personal for a chain hotel. The rooms are impressive, with exposed plaster-and-stone walls, recessed lighting, luxurious beds, Bang & Olufsen televisions, marble bathrooms oak floors, Oriental carpets, and French cherrywood furnishings. ✉ *Mäster Johansg. 13, 211 21* ☎ *040/6646400* ⎙ *040/6646401* ⊕ *www.masterjohan.se* ⇆ *69 rooms* ♻ *Room service, room TVs with movies, in-room broadband, in-room data ports, Wi-Fi, sauna, meeting room, no-smoking rooms* ▣ *AE, DC, MC, V* ⎮◎⎮ *BP.*

$$ ▦ **Radisson SAS Hotel.** Only a five-minute walk from the train station, this modern luxury hotel has rooms decorated in several styles: Asian, maritime, and ecological—the latter being mostly furnished in recycled or biodegradable materials, although you would never know it. The restaurant serves Scandinavian and Continental cuisine, and there's a cafeteria. ✉ *Österg. 10, 211 25* ☎ *040/6984000* ⎙ *040/6984001* ⊕ *www.radissonsas.com* ⇆ *229 rooms, 4 suites* ♻ *Restaurant, cafeteria, room* *service, minibars, room TVs with movies, in-room broadband, Wi-Fi, gym, sauna, spa, meeting room, parking (fee), no-smoking rooms ⊟ AE, DC, MC, V ⦶ BP.*

★ **$–$$** ⊞ **Baltzar.** This turn-of-the-20th-century house in central Malmö makes a small, comfortable hotel. Rooms have the original hardwood floors and pleasing antique furniture, minichandeliers, and rich swathes of fabric hung at the tall windows. ⊠ *Söderg. 20, 211 34* ☎ *040/6655710* 🖷 *040/236375* ⊕ *www.baltzarhotel.se* ⇆ *41 rooms* ⚭ *Restaurant, room service, minibars, cable TV, meeting rooms, no-smoking rooms* ⊟ *AE, DC, MC, V* ⦶ *BP.*

Nightlife & the Arts

Étage (⊠ Stortorget 6 ☎ 040/232060 ⛁ SKr 50 or more ☉ Mon., Thurs., Fri., and Sat. 11 PM–5 AM) is a centrally located nightclub for hipsters, with two dance floors. It also has a piano bar for relaxing, as well as a restaurant. Dancing begins late under psychedelic lights Monday, Thursday, Friday, and Saturday. Karaoke, roulette, and blackjack tables are available.

Five rooms of an old patrician apartment make up **Klubb Plysch** (⊠ Lilla Torg 1 ☎ 040/127670 ⛁ SKr 70 ☉ Sat. 10 PM–3 AM). Lounge about in the superb velvet chairs with champagne and cigars in the early evening, and join the dance floor around 11.

The **Malmö Symfoni Orkester** (☎ 040/343500 ⊕ www.mso.se) is a symphony orchestra that has a reputation across Europe as a class act. Each concert is a finely tuned event. Performances are held at many venues, including outdoors; some are at the impressive Malmö Konserthus.

Shopping

Malmö has many quality housewares and design stores. **Cervera** (⊠ Södra Förstadsg. 24 ☎ 040/971230) carries big-name glassware brands such as Kosta and Orrefors. There's an excellent selection of glass art as well as porcelain and china—and almost everything you might need in housewares. **Duka** (⊠ Hansacompagniet Centre, Malmborgsg. 6 ☎ 040/121141) is a high-quality housewares shop specializing in glass, crockery, and glass art.

Formargruppen (⊠ Engelbrektsg. 8 ☎ 040/78060) is an arts-and-crafts cooperative owned and operated by its 22 members. It sells high-quality woodwork, including cabinets. Quality ceramics, textiles, metalwork, and jewelry are also for sale. The **Form/Design Centre** (⊠ Lilla Torg 9 ☎ 040/6645150) sells products related to its changing exhibitions on everything from ceramics to books. Also look here for the very latest in Scandinavian interior design.

At the summer market called **Möllevångstorget,** on the square of the same name, there is usually a wonderful array of flowers, fruit, and vegetables. It is an old working-class area and a nice place to stroll. The market is open Monday–Saturday. An arts-and-crafts shop with a Nordic twist, **Älgamark** (⊠ Östra Rönneholmsv. 4 ☎ 040/974960) sells many antiques dating from Viking and medieval times up to the 1600s. The shop also sells gold, silver, and bronze jewelry, much of which is also quite old.

Ystad

5 *64 km (40 mi) southeast of Malmö (via E65), 205 km (127 mi) south-west of Växjö.*

A smuggling center during the Napoleonic Wars, Ystad has preserved its medieval character with winding narrow streets and hundreds of half-timber houses built over a span of five centuries. A good place to begin exploring is the main square, Stortorget.

The Franciscan monastery **Gråbrödraklostret** adjoins St. Peter's church and is one of the best-preserved cloisters in Sweden. The oldest parts date to 1267. Together, the church and monastery are considered the most important historical site in Ystad. ⊠ *Sankt Petri Kyrkoplan* ☎ *0411/577286* ✎ *SKr 20* ☉ *Weekdays noon–5, weekends noon–4.*

The principal ancient monument, **St. Maria Kyrka** (St. Mary's Church; ⊠ Lilla Norregatan) was built shortly after 1220 as a basilica in the Romanesque style, though there have been later additions. The watchman's copper horn sounds from the church tower beginning at 9:15 PM and repeating every 15 minutes until 1 AM. It's to proclaim that "all is well." The church lies behind Stortorget on Lilla Norregatan.

Ystads Konstmuseum houses a collection of important Swedish and Danish 20th-century art, as well as a photographic collection that includes a daguerreotype from 1845. ⊠ *St. Knuts torg* ☎ *0411/577285* ⊕ *www.konstmuseet.ystad.se* ✎ *SKr 30* ☉ *Tues.–Fri. noon–5, weekends noon–4.*

Sweden's best-preserved theater from the late 1800s, **Ystads Teater** (⊠ Sjömansg. 13 ☎ 0411/577199) is a beautiful, ornate building. The dramatic interior adds a great deal to any performance seen here.

Where to Stay & Eat

$–$$ ✕ **Bryggeriet.** A lovely cross-timbered inn, this restaurant brews its own beer—there are two large copper boilers near the bar. It has a pleasant garden, and the brick vaulting of the dimly lighted interior gives it the appearance of an underground cavern. Hearty traditional fare, including reindeer and other game, is Bryggeriet's specialty. ⊠ *Långg. 20* ☎ *0411/69999.*

¢–$$ ✕ **Lottas.** In an interesting two-story building on the main square in the heart of town, Lottas offers several lighter fish dishes, including scallops in season. As is typical in Sweden, there are many red-meat options; the steaks are cooked and presented with care. ⊠ *Stortorget 11* ☎ *0411/ 78800.*

$ ✕🏠 **Hotel Continental.** The Continental opened in 1829, and is a truly stunning building, both inside and out. Take a good look at the lobby with its marble stairs, crystal chandelier, stained-glass windows, and marble pillars. No two guest rooms are alike, but are all presented in a style leaning towards Gustavian, with all its requisite carved wood and lace trim. The restaurant ($$) gives each dish its own flair. The meat dishes are served with a selection of root vegetables, including fresh potatoes, carrots, and what the British call *swedes* (rutabagas), when they're in season. ⊠ *Hamng. 13, 271 43* ☎ *0411/13700* 🖷 *0411/12570* ⊕ *www.*

FodorŚChoice ★

hotelcontinental-ystad.se 🖃 *52 rooms* ⛄ *Restaurant, meeting rooms, free parking, no-smoking rooms* 🖃 *AE, MC, V* ⏏️ *BP.*

¢–$ 🖫 **Anno 1793 Sekelgården Hotell.** Centered around a cobblestone court-yard, this small and comfortable family-owned hotel is in the heart of Ystad, a short walk from St. Maria's Church and the main square. The half-timber buildings that make up the hotel date from the late 18th cen-tury, and in the summer breakfast is served in the courtyard. All the rooms are named and all are different. Most have a rural mix of scrubbed, flower-painted desks and chairs, typical of the Dalarna region. ✉️ *Långg. 18 271 23* ☎ *0411/73900* 🖷 *0411/18997* ⊕ *www.sekelgarden.se* 🖃 *18 rooms, 2 suites* ⛄ *Restaurant, sauna, meeting room* 🖃 *AE, DC, MC, V* ⏏️ *BP.*

en route — About 41 km (25 mi) north of Ystad via Route 9 is Simrishamn, a fishing village of 20,000 that swells to many times that number in the summer. For most, Simrishamn doesn't warrant an overnight stay, but you might want to stop here to break up the drive. About 20 km (12 mi) north of Simrishamn is the tiny village of Kivik. You are now firmly in the heart of Sweden's apple country, a spectacular place to be when the trees are blooming in early to late May. If you have time,

Fodor'sChoice ★ stay a night at Vitemölle Badhotell (✉️ Lejeg. 60 ☎ 0414/70000), a stunning white weatherboard building from the early 1900s, with a glassed-in veranda right on the sand dunes of Kivik. It is the best preserved and best located of the string of original bath hotels that dot this coast. Inside, the rooms have been beautifully decorated in a simple Shaker style. The veranda restaurant offers simple, delicious local food and stunning views of the dunes and the sea beyond.

Karlskrona

❻ *111 km (69 mi) east of Kristianstad via E22, 201 km (125 mi) north-east of Malmö, 107 km (66 mi) southeast of Växjö.*

A small city built on the mainland and on 33 nearby islands, Karlskrona achieved great notoriety in 1981, when a Soviet submarine ran aground a short distance from its naval base. The town dates from 1680, when it was laid out in baroque style on the orders of Karl XI. Because of the excellent state of preservation of the naval museum and other buildings in town, Karlskrona has been designated a World Heritage Site by UNESCO.

Although the archipelago is not as large or as full of dramatic scenery as Stockholm's islands, Karlskrona is still worth the boat trip. One can be arranged through **Skärgårdstrafiken** (☎ 0455/78330).

★ The **Admiralitetskyrkan** (Admiralty Church) is Sweden's oldest wooden church, built in 1685. It is an unusual variant of the Swedish church ar-chitecture. Although it was supposed to be temporary, the stone re-placement was never built. The church is on Bastionsgatan on the naval island. Walk east a few minutes from Stortorget, the main square, to get to the bridge.

★ The **Marinmuseum** (Naval Museum), in a building dating from 1752, is one of the oldest museums in Sweden and has a superb collection perfect for those with a nautical bent. The shed for making rope is ancient (1692) and huge—nearly 1,000 feet long. The museum can also provide you with brochures of the port area, perfect for a pleasant walk. ⊠ *Stumholmen* ☎ *0455/359302* 🖅 *SKr 55* ⊙ *June–Aug., daily 10–6; Sept.–May, daily noon–5.*

Stunning **Kungsholm Fort,** on the island of Kungsholmen, was built in 1680 to defend the town's important naval port. Perhaps the most impressive aspect of the fort is the round harbor, built into the fort itself with only a narrow exit to the sea. The fort is accessible only by a boat booked through the **tourist office** (⊠ Stortorget ☎ 0455/303490) on the main island of Trossö.

The **archipelago** is made up of dozens of islands scattered off the coast of Karlskrona's mainland. They are stunning low-lying islands that make excellent places to walk and picnic. Although some are accessible by road, the best way to take it all in is to go by ferry. The cruises take half a day. Contact **Affärsverken Båttrafik** (⊠ N. Kungsg. 36 ☎ 0455/78300 🖅 SKr 40–SKr 120), the ferry operators, with offices at the ferry terminal.

Where to Stay & Eat

¢–$$ ✕ **Lisas Sjökrog.** Floating on the sea, this docked ship is a great place to see a sunset and look out over the archipelago. The emphasis here is on seafood, including herring, halibut, and shellfish in season. You can also try well-prepared meat dishes and the popular summer salads. ⊠ *Fisktorget* ☎ *0455/23465* ▤ *AE, MC, V* ⊙ *Closed Sept.–Apr.*

$ ✕ **Lokpalatset.** Formerly an art and design shop with a restaurant inside, the restaurant has taken over completely. The "Lok" part of the name refers to the building's even earlier life as a repair shop for railway locomotives. The restaurant's interior has a creative mix of Scandinavian and Japanese design. The menu is equally creative with Swedish, French, and Italian influences. ⊠ *Bleklingeg. 3, Lokstallarna* ☎ *0455/333331* ▤ *AE, DC, MC, V.*

$ ▦ **First Hotel Statt.** The rooms are well appointed, the decor classic, and the style Swedish traditional. Built around 1900, this immaculate hotel with an ornate stairwell and candelabras in the lobby is in the heart of the city and is fully renovated. ⊠ *Ronnebyg. 37–39, 371 33* ☎ *0455/ 55550* 🖷 *0455/16909* ⊕ *www.firsthotels.com* 🗨 *107 rooms* ⌂ *Restaurant, in-room data ports, Wi-Fi, hot tub, sauna, bar, nightclub, meeting rooms, no-smoking rooms* ▤ *AE, DC, MC, V* ⑩ *BP.*

¢ ▦ **Hotel Conrad.** For simple but functional accommodations at a reasonable price, the Hotel Conrad is a good choice. Rooms are colored with very tasteful hues of chocolate brown and beige. It is a short walk from shopping, restaurants, and entertainment. ⊠ *V. Köpmansg. 12, 371 34* ☎ *0455/363200* 🖷 *0455/363205* ⊕ *www.hotelconrad.se* 🗨 *58 rooms* ⌂ *Sauna, meeting rooms, free parking, no-smoking rooms* ▤ *AE, MC, V* ⑩ *BP.*

Kalmar

❼ *91 km (57 mi) northeast of Karlskrona via E22, 292 km (181 mi) northeast of Malmö, 109 km (68 mi) southeast of Växjö.*

FodorśChoice
★

The attractive coastal town of Kalmar, opposite the Baltic island of Öland, is dominated by the imposing **Kalmar Slott**, Sweden's best-preserved Renaissance castle. Part of it dates from the 12th century. The living rooms, chapel, and dungeon can be visited. ⊠ *Slottsv.* ☎ *0480/451490* ✉ *SKr 80* ☉ *Apr., May, and Sept., daily 10–4; June and Aug., daily 10–5; July, daily 10–6; Oct.–Mar., 2nd weekend of every month 11–3:30.*

Kalmar Domkyrkan is a highly impressive building designed by Nicodemus Tessin the Elder in 1660 in the Italian baroque style. Inside, the massive open spaces create stunning light effects. Music is played at noon during the week. ⊠ *Stortorget* ☎ *0480/12300* ✉ *Free* ☉ *Daily 10–6.*

The **Kalmar Läns Museum** (Kalmar District Museum), with good archaeological and ethnographic collections, contains the remains of the royal ship *Kronan*, which sank in 1676. ⊠ *Skeppsbrog. 51* ☎ *0480/451300* ✉ *SKr 50* ☉ *Mid-June–mid-Aug., daily 10–6; mid-Aug.–mid-June, Tues.–Fri. 10–4, weekends 11–4.*

Where to Stay & Eat

$$ ✕ **Källaren Kronan.** Given the quality of the eclectic international dishes here, the meals are surprisingly cheap. Try the pheasant breast with Calvados sauce or the fillet of venison with black currant sauce. The building dates from the 1660s and has been preserved as a cultural heritage site. ⊠ *Ölandsg. 7* ☎ *0480/411400* ▤ *AE, DC, MC, V.*

★ $–$$ ✕ **Byttan.** In fine weather this restaurant's large outdoor eating area and beautiful gardens are the perfect place for a leisurely meal. Served with a vast range of freshly baked breads, the summer salads, especially the chicken salad with limes, are terrific. You can also choose a heartier entrée of traditional herring with mashed potatoes. ⊠ *Slottsallén* ☎ *0480/16360* ▤ *MC, V* ☉ *Closed Oct.–Apr.*

$$ 🏨 **Calmar Stadshotell.** In the city center, Stadshotellet is a fairly large hotel with modern, fresh interiors. The main building, dating from 1907, is a beautiful art-nouveau centerpiece for the town. Guest rooms are simply decorated in cream, white, and wood, with touches of moss-green and light brown; all have hair dryers and radios, among other amenities. There's also a fine restaurant. ⊠ *Stortorget 14, 392 32* ☎ *0480/496900* 🖨 *0480/496910* ⊕ *www.profilhotels.se* ⇨ *126 rooms* ᗕ *Restaurant, cable TV, hot tub, sauna, bar, meeting room, no-smoking rooms* ▤ *AE, DC, MC, V.*

$$ 🏨 **Slottshotellet.** On a quiet street, this gracious old house faces a waterfront park that's a few minutes' walk from both the train station and Kalmar Castle. Guest rooms are charmingly individual, with carved-wood bedsteads, old-fashioned chandeliers, pretty wallpaper, wooden floors, and antique furniture. The bathrooms are spotlessly clean. Breakfast is served year-round, and full restaurant service is available in summer. ⊠ *Slottsv. 7, 392 33* ☎ *0480/88260* 🖨 *0480/88266* ⊕ *www.slottshotellet. se* ⇨ *44 rooms* ᗕ *Restaurant, sauna, meeting room, no-smoking rooms* ▤ *AE, DC, V* ⦿ *BP.*

FOR SWEDISH ROYALS, CENTURIES OF BATTLES

THEY'RE YOUNG, THEY'RE BEAUTIFUL, and they've got blue blood running through their veins. What more could a tabloid wish for?

Swedish paparazzi, and their European colleagues, can't get enough of Sweden's Crown Princess Victoria (born 1977), Prince Carl Philip (born 1979), and Princess Madeleine (born 1982). The princesses, especially, are closely monitored, with reports on their workouts and diets, favorite designers, love affairs—even updates on the progress of Princess Madeleine's summer tan. Princess "Madde" was even voted the most beautiful woman in the world by Spanish gossip magazine Hola.

It seems like a charmed life, but such constant scrutiny can be too much, even for a princess trained for a life in the public eye. When the crown princess was 20, the royal court revealed that she suffered from bulimia, an illness that is said to have plagued many European princesses, from the late Princess Diana to Princess Mary of Denmark. The crown princess interrupted her studies in Stockholm and spent two years at Yale, where she could live in relative anonymity.

The royal family may be dealing with distinctly 21st-century struggles these days, but Swedish royal history is rife with battles. Viking kings battled for power over the land around Lake Mälaren in the first millennium. The first king to reign over a unified Sweden, Gustav Vasa, claimed the throne in 1523 after a bloody rebellion against Kristian II of Denmark. His sons then spent their lives battling each other: King Erik XIV, the snubbed suitor of Elizabeth I of England, created a scandal by marrying a commoner, then jailing his brother Johan, who he felt was

getting dangerously popular. Johan and third brother Karl then joined forces to overthrow Erik, who died in jail, poisoned by arsenic-laced split-pea soup.

The glory days of Sweden's military began in 1611, when Gustav II Adolf became king. He led Sweden through the Thirty Years' War until his death at the Battle of Lützen in 1632. Swedish expansionism continued after his death; by 1718 all of Finland and Estonia, parts of Russia, and patches of the German coast were under Swedish rule.

The current royal family, the Bernadotte family, came from France in the 19th century. Then-king Karl XIII was old and had no heirs. Seeking to approach France and stave off Russia, Sweden invited one of Napoleon's marshals, Jean Baptiste Bernadotte, to become king of Sweden. He accepted and assumed the more Swedish-sounding name Karl XIV Johan.

Though debate has raged in Sweden for years whether to abolish the monarchy, it seems only a small percentage of the Swedish people would like to see the country without the royal family. Sweden's expansionist dreams have long been abandoned; Sweden hasn't been in a war for close to 200 years. And yet it seems the Swedish royal family is still looking for peace.

–Karin Palmquis

¢–$ ⊡ **Frimurare.** Set inside a spacious park, the attractive Frimurare radiates calm and peacefulness. Both the rooms and the hotel itself have old-time touches. It's a short walk from here to the castle.   ⊠ *Larmtorget 2 393 32* ☎ *0480/15230* 🖶 *0480/85887* ⊕ *www.frimurarehotellet.gs2. com* ☜ *34 rooms, 31 with bath* ♿ *Meeting rooms* ▤ MC, V.

Öland

★ ❽   *8 km (5 mi) east of Kalmar via the Ölandsbron (Öland Bridge).*

The island of Öland is a magical and ancient place—and the smallest province in Sweden. The area was first settled some 4,000 years ago and is fringed with fine sandy beaches and dotted with old windmills, churches, and archaeological remains.

The island also has spectacular bird life—swallows, cranes, geese, and birds of prey. Many migrate to Öland from Siberia. The southern part of the island, known as **Stora Alvaret**, is a UNESCO World Heritage Site due partly to its stark beauty and unique flora and fauna. Private car travel is prohibited, so let the public bus shuttle you around the island.

To get to Öland, take the 6-km (4-mi) bridge from Kalmar. Be sure to pick up a tourist information map (follow the signs as soon as you get on the island). Most of the scattered sights have no address. Close to the bridge is the popular **Historium**, where slide shows, wax figures, and constructed dioramas illustrate what Öland was like 10,000 years ago.

Head clockwise around the island. **Borgholms Slott**, the largest castle ruin in northern Europe, is just outside the island's principal town, Borgholm (25 km [15 mi] north of the bridge).

Heading farther north brings you to Löttorp. From here, drive west to **Horns Kungsgård**, a nature preserve on a lake that has a bird-watching tower and walking trails.

Some 5 km (3 mi) north along the coast from Horns Kungsgård is **Byrum**, a nature preserve with striking, wind-carved limestone cliffs. Just a few more kilometers on is **Skäftekärr**, which has a culture museum, a café, an Iron Age farm with an arboretum, and walking trails.

Turning back you will find one of the island's three nature centers, **Trollskogen**. On its trails are some majestic old oaks, prehistoric barrow graves, and pines. A little to the south is northern Europe's longest beach, a great swimming spot with sparkling white sand.

Pass back through **Löttorp**, heading south. Keep an eye out for the signs leading east off the main road for the intriguing **Källa** church ruins, some of the best on the island. Return to the main road and head south to **Kappelludden**, one of the island's best year-round bird sites. A medieval chapel's ruins and a lighthouse make this coastal spot very scenic.

Gråborg, a 6th-century fortress with massive stone walls 625 feet in diameter, is a must-see. To get here, head south from Långlöt and turn right at Norra Möckleby.

Return to Norra Möckleby and head south. About 2 km (1 mi) north of Seby are some strings of **rune stones:** engraved gravestones dating from 500 BC to AD 1050, stone circles, and cists and cairns. Continue south to come to the southeastern edge of Stora Alvaret.

Just before you reach the 5th-century fortified village of **Eketorp,** you'll reach a turnoff for the **Gräsgård,** an important fishing village. Eketorp's castle is partially renovated; the area includes small tenants' fields from the Iron and Middle ages. Admission to the castle and its grounds is SKr 50.

Now drive north up the west coastal road. Shortly after **Södra Möckleby** you'll come across the impressive burial grounds of **Gettlinge.** The site was in use from the time of Christ into the Viking era, which lasted until 1050. Beginning in late spring, the land north of here blooms with many different wild orchids.

Farther on is **Mysinge Tunukus,** a Bronze Age site. A group of rune stones here is placed in a shape resembling a ship: it's beautiful at sunset. From here, continue on back the remaining 20 km (12 mi) to the bridge and mainland Sweden.

Where to Stay & Eat

$ ✕🏠 **Halltorps Gästgiveri.** This 17th-century manor house has modernized duplex rooms decorated in Swedish landscape tones and an excellent restaurant. Driving north from Ölandsbron, it's on the left side of the road. ⊠ 387 92 Borgholm 🕾 0485/85000 🖷 0485/85001 ⊕ www.halltorpsgastgiveri.se ⟳ 36 rooms ♨ Restaurant, 2 saunas, meeting room, free parking, no-smoking rooms 🖃 AE, DC, MC, V.

¢ ✕🏠 **Guntorps Herrgård.** Spacious parkland surrounds this manor house, which is 2,500 feet from the center of Borgholm. Outside, there's a heated pool. The restaurant has hardwood floors, a grandfather clock on one wall, and copper pots hanging on another. ⊠ 387 36 Borgholm 🕾 0485/13000 🖷 0485/13319 ⊕ www.guntorpsherrgard.se ⟳ 32 rooms ♨ Restaurant, sauna, no-smoking rooms 🖃 AE, DC, MC, V.

¢ 🏠 **Värdshuset Briggen Tre Liljor.** Large trees stand alongside this lovely, old stone-clad hotel, which is 25 km (15 mi) north of Borgholm. The rooms are spacious and old-fashioned, making you feel as if you've stepped into the past. The restaurant serves good traditional food. ⊠ Lofta, 387 91 Borgholm 🕾 0485/26400 🖷 0485/26420 ⊕ www.briggentreliljor.com ⟳ 20 rooms ♨ Restaurant, meeting room 🖃 AE, MC, V.

The Kingdom of Glass

Stretching roughly 109 km (68 mi) between Kalmar and Växjö.

Småland is home to the world-famous Swedish glass industry. Scattered among the rocky woodlands of Småland province are isolated villages whose names are synonymous with high-quality crystal glassware. This spectacular creative art was at its height in the late 19th century. The conditions were perfect: large quantities of wood to fuel the furnaces and plenty of water from the streams and rivers. At the time, demand was such that the furnaces burned 24 hours a day.

The region is still home to 16 major glassworks, many of them created through the merging of the smaller firms. You can still see glass being blown and crystal being etched by craftspeople. Most glassworks also have shops selling quality firsts and not-so-perfect seconds at a discount.

Though the glass factories generally prospered before and during the 1900s, this wealth didn't filter down to many of their workers or to Småland's other inhabitants. Poverty became so widespread that the area lost vast numbers of people to the United States from the late 19th through the 20th century. If you're an American with Swedish roots, chances are your ancestors are from this area. The Utvandrarnas Hus (Emigrants' House) in Växjö tells the story of this exodus.

The Kingdom of Glass's oldest works is **Kosta Glasbruk.** Dating from 1742, it was named for the two former generals who founded it, Anders Koskull and Georg Bogislaus Stael von Holstein. Faced with a dearth of local talent, they initially imported glassblowers from Bohemia. The Kosta works pioneered the production of crystal (to qualify for that label, glass must contain at least 24% lead oxide). You can see glassblowing off-season (mid-August–early June) between 9 and 3. To get to the village of Kosta from Kalmar, drive 49 km (30 mi) west on Route 25, then 14 km (9 mi) north on Route 28. ⊠ *Kosta* ☎ *0478/34529* ⊕ *www.kostaboda.se* ⊙ *May, June, and Aug–mid-Sept., weekdays 9–10 and 11–3, Sat. 10–3; July, daily 10–4; mid-Sept–Apr., weekdays 9–10 and 11–3.*

Orrefors is one of the best-known glass companies in Sweden. Orrefors arrived on the scene late—in 1898—but set particularly high artistic standards. The skilled workers in Orrefors dance a slow, delicate minuet as they carry the pieces of red-hot glass back and forth, passing them on rods from hand to hand, blowing and shaping them. The basic procedures and tools are ancient, and the finished product is the result of unusual teamwork, from designer to craftsman to finisher. From early June to mid-August you can watch glass being blown. ⊠ *On Rte. 31, about 18 km (11 mi) east of Kosta Glasbruk* ☎ *0481/34000* ⊕ *www.orrefors.se* ⊙ *July, weekdays and Sat. 10–4, Sun. noon–4; Aug.–June, weekdays 9–3.*

Mystical animal reliefs and female figures play a big role in the work at **Målerås,** which was founded in 1890. The glassworkers are great to watch; they use classic techniques with names such as "the grail." Overlooking the factory is a pleasant restaurant with panoramic views. ⊠ *12 km (7 mi) north of Orrefors* ☎ *0481/31400* ⊙ *June–Aug., weekdays 9–6, Sat. 10–5, Sun. 11–5; Sept.–May, weekdays 10–6, Sat. 10–4, Sun. 11–4.*

Boda Glasbruk, part of the Kosta Boda Company, is the second-oldest glassworks, founded in 1864. The work here has an ethereal theme, with the designers drawing on cosmic bodies such as the sun and the moon. Much of the work has veils of violet and blue suspended in the crystal. ⊠ *Just off Rte. 25, 42 km (26 mi) west of Kalmar* ☎ *0481/42410* ⊙ *July–mid-Aug., weekdays 9–6, Sat. 10–5, Sun. 11–5; mid-Aug.–June, weekdays 9–6, Sat. 10–4, Sun. noon–4.*

Continue west from Boda Glasbruk for 20 km (12 mi) to the town of Lessebo. From mid-June to mid-August you can visit the 300-year-old **Lessebo Handpappersbruk,** which is the only handmade-paper factory in

Sweden. Since the 18th century the craftsmen have been using much the same techniques to produce fine paper, which is available from the shop. Guided tours take place on weekdays. ⊠ *Storg., Lessebo* ☎ *0478/47691* ⊕ *www.lessebo.se* ◻ *Tours free* ◷ *Weekdays 7–4; June–Aug., guided tours at 9:30, 10:30, 1, and 2:15.*

Skruf Glasbruk began in 1896. Today it's a purveyor to the king of Sweden. The royal family, the ministry of foreign affairs, and the parliament have all commissioned work from Skruf. Local farmers encouraged the development of the glassworks because they wanted a market for their wood. The factory specializes in lead-free crystal, which has a unique iridescence and form. ⊠ *10 km (6 mi) south of Lessebo. Turn left at Åkerby* ☎ *0478/20133* ⊕ *www.skruf-bergdala.se* ◷ *Weekdays 9–6, weekends 10–4. Glassblowing demonstrations weekdays 7–4.*

★ ♺ Founded in 1889, **Bergadala Glasbruk** is one of the most traditional glassworks. Alongside the main road are the former workers' homes, now used mainly as long-term rentals. Note the impressive circular furnace that stands in the middle of the wooden floor. Bergadala is often called the blue glassworks, since many of its pieces have a rich cobalt hue. A stone's throw from the smelter is a children's playground and a glass-painting workshop that will keep them occupied for hours. From here you are 10 km (6 mi) from Växjö. ⊠ *About 15 km (9 mi) northwest of Lessebo, toward Växjö* ☎ *0478/31650* ◷ *Weekdays 9–6, weekends 10–4. Glassblowing demonstrations weekdays 7–4.*

Where to Stay

¢ ▥ **Hotell Björkäng.** Set in a park that will give you plenty of opportunity to take evening strolls, the Björkäng has well-kept rooms. They have some rustic decorations, such as traditional ornaments, wood carved by nature, and glass pieces. You also have the opportunity to spend an evening in the glassblowing room. The dining room offers a range of good traditional Swedish food. ⊠ *Stora Vägen 2, Kosta* ☎ *0478/50000* 🖷 *0478/50437* ⟿ *26 rooms* ♨ *Dining room, sauna, billiards, meeting rooms, free parking* ▭ *MC, V* ⊠ *BP.*

¢ ▥ **Orrefors.** Simplicity and affordability are this small hotel's selling points. Set in a gray-color house from the 1930s, just a three-minute walk from the old Orrefors factory, rooms here are straightforward and very pleasant, with minimal furnishings. The staff is extremely friendly, the atmosphere is cozy, and the hotel is set in the authentic center of the Kingdom of Glass. The restaurant and bar are both pleasant. ⊠ *Kantav. 29, Orrefors* ☎ *0481/30035* 🖷 *0481/30035* ⟿ *10 rooms* ♨ *Restaurant, bar, meeting room, no smoking* ▭ *MC, V* ⊠ *BP.*

Växjö

❾ *109 km (68 mi) northwest of Kalmar via Rte. 25, 198 km (123 mi) northeast of Malmö, 228 km (142 mi) southeast of Göteborg, 446 km (277 mi) southwest of Stockholm.*

Some 10,000 Americans visit this town every year, for it was from this area that their Swedish ancestors departed in the 19th century. A large proportion of those emigrants went to Minnesota, attracted by the af-

AQUAVIT: A LOVE STORY

THE ORIGINS OF SWEDISH AQUAVIT (akvavit) are as muddled as the drink is crystal-clear. Most historians have it down as a drink of the common people, distilled in backyards and backwoods, using homegrown potatoes or grain. For many hundreds of years, it served as a useful elixir for keeping winter's perpetual cold at bay. Many a dark Swedish night was illuminated with a little spiced, home-distilled aquavit: mother danced to father's accordion, and grandfather's tales were as spicy as the herbal spirits.

This is a romantic image and one with a certain amount of truth in it. The full truth, though, is a lot harsher. By the late 1800s, Sweden's love affair with the home-distilled spirit reached epidemic proportions, particularly in poor rural areas—drunkenness and ill health combined to incapacitate a good percentage of the population.

The State stepped in, taking control of the production, sale, and import of all alcohol, a practice that still stands today. As with gin in England, only when production was controlled did aquavit become a more quality, drinkable spirit.

Fine spirits with an alcohol content of 40% to 50%, and with complex flavors of dill, caraway, aniseed, coriander, fennel, and saffron, became the norm. The restriction of availability and increased price, along with a vast improvement in quality, saw aquavit promoted from a daily sustenance to a toasting beverage for festivals and special occasions.

Aquavit is taken when tradition dictates. Not until midsummer's crayfish table, Christmas, or perhaps a wedding, will the sweet and bitter tones of ice-cold aquavit pass through Swedish lips. When it does, though, it is with such ferocity that you wonder why the Swedes don't drink it more often, such is their love for it.

Despite the growing global fascination for all things Swedish—think Absolut vodka, H&M, and IKEA—you would be hard-pressed to find a hip, urban Swede propping up a bar with an aquavit. Unlike other global cities, where aquavit is becoming the order of the day, metropolitan Swedes still look to whiskey, vodka, or tequila as their weekend accessory.

A Swedish party with aquavit is guaranteed to exude many songs, far too many toasts for its own good, and a general collective promise the next morning never to drink again. Whether drinking in memory of ancestors or simply to enjoy a Swedish tradition, when Swedes bring on the aquavit, very little gets done the following day.

–Rob Hincks

fordable farmland and a geography reminiscent of parts of Sweden. On the second Sunday of every August, Växjö celebrates Minnesota Day: Swedes and Swedish-Americans come together to commemorate their common heritage with American-style square dancing and other festivities. Beyond this, the city is really just a stopover.

★ The **Smålands Museum** is famous for its presentation of the development of glass and has the largest glass collection in northern Europe. Its excellent display puts the area's unique industry into perspective and explains the different styles of the various glass companies. ⊠ *Södra Järnvägsg. 2* ☎ *0470/704200* ⊕ *www.smalandsmuseum.se* ⊠ *SKr 40* ⊙ *June–Aug., weekdays 10–5, weekends 11–5; Sept.–May, Tues.–Fri. 10–5, weekends 11–5.*

The **Utvandrarnas Hus** (Emigrants' House), in the town center, tells the story of the migration, when more than a million Swedes—one quarter of the population—departed for the United States. The museum exhibits provide a vivid sense of the rigorous journey, and an archive room and a research center allow Americans with Swedish blood to trace their ancestry. The archives are open for genealogy research on weekdays. ⊠ *Vilhelm Mobergsg. 4* ☎ *0470/20120* ⊕ *www.swemi.se* ⊠ *SKr 40* ⊙ *May–Aug., weekdays 9–5, Sat. 11–4; Sept.–Apr., weekdays 9–4, weekends 11–4.*

Where to Stay

$–$$ 🏨 **Hotel Statt.** Now a Best Western hotel, the Statt is popular with tourist groups. It has a convenient, central location. The building dates from 1853, but the rooms are up to modern standards. The hotel has a cozy pub, bistro, and café. ⊠ *Kungsg. 6, 351 04* ☎ *0470/13400* 🖷 *0470/ 44837* ⟲ *124 rooms* ♻ *Restaurant, café, gym, sauna, pub, meeting room, no-smoking rooms* ⊟ *AE, DC, MC, V.*

¢–$ 🏨 **Esplanad.** In the town center, the Esplanad is a small family-run hotel with basic amenities. The rooms are sparse, to say the least, with brown plastic flooring and more brown furnishings besides. But the location and the friendly welcome from the owner make it worthwhile. ⊠ *Norra Esplanaden 21A, 352 31* ☎ *0470/22580* 🖷 *0470/26226* ⊕ *www.hotell-esplanad.com* ⟲ *23 rooms* ♻ *Free parking, no-smoking rooms* ⊟ *MC, V* ⊙*l BP.*

The South & the Kingdom of Glass A to Z

AIR TRAVEL

CARRIERS Four airlines serve the Malmö airport (Sturup).

🔷 **Direktflyg** ☎ 0243/444700. **Malmö Aviation** ☎ 0771/550010. **RyanAir** ☎ 0900/ 2020240 in Sweden ⊕ www.ryanair.com; use Web when booking from abroad. **SAS** ☎ 0770-727727.

AIRPORTS

Malmö's airport, Sturup (MMX), is approximately 30 km (19 mi) from Malmö and 25 km (15 mi) from Lund. Buses for Malmö and Lund meet all flights at Sturup Airport. The price of the trip is SKr 90 to either destination. A taxi from the airport to Malmö or Lund costs about SKr 470.

🔷 **Bus Information** ☎ 040/6696290. **Sturup** ☎ 040/6131100. **Taxi and Limousine Service** ☎ 040/70000.

BOAT & FERRY TRAVEL

Since the inauguration of the Øresund Bridge between Malmö and Copenhagen, it is no longer possible to travel by ferry between the two cities, but there is still regular ferry service between Helsingborg in Sweden and Helsingør in Denmark (by Scandlines, HH-Ferries, and Sundsbussarna). From Ystad there is ferry service to Swinoujscie in Poland (by Polferries), and from Trelleborg ferries run to Sassnitz and Rostock in Germany (by Scandlines). Stena Line ferries run between Karlskrona and Gdynia in Poland. ⚡ **HH-Ferries** ☎ 042/198000 ⊕ www.hhferries.se. **Polferries** ☎ 040121700 ⊕ www.polferries.se. **Scandlines** ☎ 0410/65000 ⊕ www.scandlines.se. **Stena Line** ✉ Danmarksterminalen, Masthuggskajen, Göteborg ☎ 031-7040000 in Göteborg, 0455366300 in Karlskrona ⊕ www.stenaline.se. **Sundsbussarna** ☎ 042/385880 ⊕ www.sundsbussarna.se.

CAR RENTAL

If you are coming from Denmark and want to rent a car as soon as you arrive, several rental companies have locations at Malmö Harbor, including Avis, Hertz, and Europcar. Hertz car rentals are available for less than SKr 600 a day on weekends (less in summer) if you book an SAS flight. ⚡ **Avis** ☎ 040/77830. **Europcar** ☎ 040/71640. **Hertz** ☎ 040/330770.

CAR TRAVEL

Copenhagen and Malmö are connected by the Øresund Bridge. It costs SKR 285 one-way.

Malmö is 620 km (386 mi) from Stockholm. Take the E4 Highway to Helsingborg, then the E6/E20 to Malmö and Lund. From Göteborg take the E6/E20.

Roads are well marked and well maintained. Traveling around the coast counterclockwise from Helsingborg, you take the E6/E20 to Landskrona, Malmö, and Lund, then the E6/E22 to Trelleborg; Route 9 goes along the south coast from there all the way to Simrishamn and then heads north until just before Kristianstad. It's there that you can pick up E22 all the way through Karlshamn, Ronneby, Karlskrona, and on across the east coast to Kalmar. From Kalmar, Route 25 goes almost directly west through Växjö to Halmstad, on the west coast between Helsingborg and Göteborg.

EMERGENCIES

As elsewhere in Sweden, call 112 for emergencies.

TRAIN TRAVEL

The major towns of the south are all connected by rail.

There is regular service from Stockholm to Helsingborg, Lund, and Malmö. Each trip takes about 6½ hours, and about 4½ hours by high-speed (X2000) train. All three railway stations are centrally located in their respective towns.

Trains between Malmö and Copenhagen take 35 minutes and run three times an hour during the day and once an hour at night. A one-way ticket is SKr 90. ⚡ **SJ** ☎ 0771/757575 ⊕ www.sj.se.

TRANSPORTATION AROUND THE SOUTH
A special 48-hour Øresund Runt (Around Øresund) pass is available from the Malmö Tourist Office or any train station in Skåne. Costing between SKr 199 and SKr 249, depending on where you start your trip, the ticket covers a train ticket from the Skåne province to Malmö, a train from Malmö to Helsingborg, a ferry to Helsingør, a train to Copenhagen, and a ferry back to Malmö (or if you so prefer, the same trip clockwise).

VISITOR INFORMATION
Helsingborg ⊠ Södra Storg. 1 ☎ 042/104350 ⊕ www.helsingborgsguiden.com. **Kalmar** ⊠ Ölandskajen 9 ☎ 0480/417700 ⊕ www.kalmar.se/turism/index2.html. **Karlskrona** ⊠ Stortorget 2 ☎ 0455/303490. **Landskrona** ⊠ Storg. 36 ☎ 0418/473000 ⊕ www.tourism.landskrona.se. **Lund** ⊠ Kyrkog. 11 ☎ 046/355040 ⊕ www.lund.se. **Malmö** ⊠ Centralstationen [central train station]) ☎ 040/341200 ⊕ www.malmo.se. **Öland** ⊠ Träffpunkt Öland, Färjestaden ☎ 0485/560600. **Simrishamn** ⊠ Tullhusg. 2 ☎ 0414/819800. **Växjö** ⊠ Stationen, Norra Järnvägsg. 3 ☎ 0470/41410. **Ystad** ⊠ St. Knuts Torg ☎ 0411/577681 ⊕ www.visitystad.com.

DALARNA: THE FOLKLORE DISTRICT

A place of forests, mountains, and red-painted wooden farmhouses and cottages by pristine, sun-dappled lakes, Dalarna is considered the most traditional of all the country's 24 provinces. It is the favorite center for celebrations on Midsummer Day, when Swedes don folk costumes and dance to fiddle and accordion music around maypoles covered with wildflower garlands.

Dalarna played a key role in the history of the nation. It was from here that Gustav Vasa recruited the army that freed the country from Danish domination during the 16th century. The region is also important artistically, both for its tradition of naive religious decoration and for producing two of the nation's best-loved painters, Anders Zorn (1860–1920) and Carl Larsson (1853–1915), and one of its favorite poets, the melancholy, mystical Dan Andersson (1888–1920). He sought inspiration in the remote forest camps of the old charcoal burners.

Dalarna is a gloriously compact region, mostly consisting of a single road that rings Lake Siljan, the area's main attraction. A drive round the lake will take in most of the highlights, leaving you only to decide whether to travel clockwise or counterclockwise.

Dalarna is truly a region for all seasons. In June and July it is where every Swede wants to be, an idyllic reflection of everything that is good about Swedish summer. In the winter months, Dalarna offers some very fine skiing, skating, and winter sports. And spring and autumn bring changing colors and fine fishing in Lake Siljan.

Falun

❶ *230 km (143 mi) northwest of Stockholm via E18 and Rte. 70.*

Falun is the traditional capital of Dalarna, though the adjacent non-descript railway town of Borlänge has grown in importance as a busi-

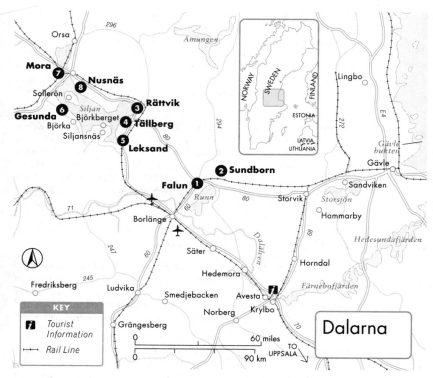

ness center. Falun's history has always been very much bound to its copper mine, worked since 1230 by Stora Kopparbergs Bergslags AB (today just Stora). During its great period of prosperity in the 17th century, it financed Sweden's "Age of Greatness," when the country became the dominant Baltic power. In 1650 Stora produced a record amount of copper; probably as a result of such rapid extraction, 37 years later its mine shafts caved in. The collapse was on Midsummer Day, when most miners were off duty, and as a result no one was killed. The mine eventually closed in 1992.

★ Today the major part of the mine is an enormous hole in the ground that, in combination with the adjoining **Stora Museum,** has become Falun's principal tourist attraction. The one-hour tour through a network of old shafts and tunnels begins with a hair-raising 150-foot descent in an old elevator. Wear old shoes and warm clothing, since the copper-tinged mud can stain footwear and it's cold down there. ☎ 023/ 782030 ⊕ www.kopparberget.com ☒ Mine SKr 90, museum free with mine tour ☉ Mine May–Aug., daily 10–5; Sept.–mid-Nov., Mar., and Apr., weekdays 11–5, weekends 11–4. Museum May–Aug., daily 10–5; Sept.–Apr., weekdays 11–5, weekends 11–4.

The folk art, folklore, clothing, and music of the area are all well covered at **Dalarnasmuseet** (Dalarna Museum). There is also a grand reconstruction of the study in which Selma Lagerlöf (1858–1940), the celebrated Swedish author, worked after she moved to Falun in 1897. ⊠ *Stigareg.* 2–4 ☎ *023/765500* ☒ *SKr 40* ☉ *Weekdays 10–5, weekends noon–5.*

Where to Stay & Eat

$$ ✕ **MS *Slussbruden.*** This restaurant on a boat offers "prawn cruises." For a set price you can feast on as many prawns as you can shell during the 3½-hour cruise. If you're not inclined to eat seafood, you can preorder either a chicken or a Greek salad. Live music acts serenade you all the while. Limitless bread and butter, cheese, fruits, and coffee are included. Combined with the beautiful scenery, the dinner cruise is a great hit. The cruise departs at 7 PM. ⊠ *Strandv.* ☎ *070/6385005* ⚓ *Reservations essential* ▤ *AE, DC, MC, V* ☉ *Closed Nov.–Apr.*

$–$$ ✕ **Blå Apelsinen.** The Blue Orange serves up Swedish food with a French twist. Simple, pork, beef, and fish dishes are all offered in a dining room decked out in the white, blue, and terra-cotta shades of the Mediterranean. The rather strange moniker is taken from a restaurant chain of the same name in the Mediterranean, which is one of the owner's favorites. ⊠ *Bergskolegränd 8A* ☎ *023/29111* ▤ *AE, MC, V*

$$ 🏨 **Scandic.** Outside Falun, the ultramodern Scandic was built for the 1993 World Skiing Championships that took place in the Lungnet sports and recreation center. The building itself looks like a giant ski jump made of Legos. The comfortable rooms have good views of the giant ski jump that's still used for competitions. ⊠ *Svärdsjög.* 51, 791 31 Falun ☎ 023/ 6692200 🖷023/669211 ⊕www.scandic-hotels.se ⤺153 rooms ⚴Restaurant, room TV with movies, in-room broadband, Wi-Fi, indoor pool, sauna, pub, meeting room, no-smoking rooms ▤ AE, DC, MC, V.

$ 🏨 **First Grand Hotel.** Part of the First Hotel chain, this conventional modern hotel is close to the town center. The bright rooms are decorated with Chippendale-style furniture. ⊠ *Trotzg.* 9–11, 791 71 ☎ 023/ 794880 🖷 023/14143 ⊕ www.firsthotels.se ⤺ 151 rooms 1 suite ⚴ Restaurant, in-room data ports, indoor pool, gym, sauna, bar, convention center, no-smoking rooms ▤ AE, DC, MC, V.

$ 🏨 **Park Inn Bermästaren.** This small, cozy hotel in the town center is built in rustic Dalarna style, but decorated in a modern way, with primary colors, wooden floors, simple desks, and asymmetric chairs in the rooms. There is a pleasant relaxation area where the hot tub and sauna will let you unwind from the day's stresses. ⊠ *Bergskolegränd* 7, 791 12 ☎ 023/701700 🖷 023/701709 ⊕ www.falun.parkinn.se ⤺ 88 rooms, 84 with bath ⚴ Restaurant, in-room data ports, Wi-Fi, hot tub, sauna, meeting room, no-smoking rooms ▤ AE, DC, MC, V.

Sports & the Outdoors

At the **Bjursås Ski Center** (☎ 023/774177 ⊕ www.bjursas-ski.se), 25 km (15 mi) northwest of Falun on Route 80, you can make use of the resort's seven lift systems and 18 varied pistes. It's open between December and April and has numerous hotels, restaurants, and cafés.

Sundborn

➋ *10 km (6 mi) northeast of Falun off Rte. 80.*

★ In this small village you can visit **Carl Larsson Gården,** the lakeside home of the Swedish artist (1853–1915). Larsson was an excellent textile designer and draftsman who painted scenes from his family's busy domestic life. The house itself was creatively painted and decorated by Larsson's wife, Karin, also trained as an artist. Waits for guided tours in summer can take two hours. You'll receive a timed ticket and can visit the café or stroll around the garden or lake while you wait. ☎ *023/60053* ⊕ *www.clg.se* ✉ *Guided tours only, SKr 90* ⊙ *May–Sept., daily 10–5; Jan.–Apr., 1 guided tour daily, weekdays at 11 in English.*

Rättvik

➌ *48 km (30 mi) northwest of Falun via Rte. 80.*

On the eastern tip of Lake Siljan, Rättvik is a pleasant town of timbered houses surrounded by wooded slopes. A center for local folklore, the town has several shops that sell handmade articles and local produce.

Every year in June, dozens of people wearing traditional costumes arrive in longboats to attend midsummer services at the town's 13th-century church, **Rättviks Kyrka,** which stands on a promontory stretching into the lake. Its interior contains some fine examples of local religious art.

The open-air museum **Rättviks Gammelgård,** a 20-minute walk along the banks of the lake north of Rättvik, reconstructs peasant life of bygone days. More than 3,500 pieces of art, clothing, ceramics, tools, and furniture are on display in the old buildings. Tours in English can be arranged through the Rättvik tourist office. ☎ *0248/797210* ✉ *Free; guided tour SKr 20* ⊙ *Mid-June–mid-Aug., daily 11–6; tours at 1 and 2:30.*

Just to the west of Rättvik in the forest is **Vidablick.** The top of this tall wooden tower, more than 100 years old, will give you some of the most stunning views across Lake Siljan that you can find.

★ Once a lucrative open chalk mine, the huge multitier quarry left at **Dalhalla** (7 km [4½] mi north of Rättvik) has become one of the world's most beautiful outdoor stages. Opera, rock concerts, and amazing light shows are all presented here, where the sound is enhanced by the quarry's incredible acoustics. Guided tours of the more remote parts of the quarry can be booked year-round. ✉ *Stationshuset, Rättvik* ☎ *0248/ 797950* ✉ *SKr 50 for exhibition and tour* ⊙ *Exhibition mid-May–Sept., daily 11–3 (July, daily 10–6).*

Where to Stay & Eat

¢–$ ✕ **Strandrestaurangen.** A family-style restaurant with a huge outdoor seating area by the lake, Strandrestaurangen serves such standard Swedish fare as meatballs, sausages, and pork chops. It's all well prepared and filling. Kids enjoy the beach, miniature golf, ice-cream bar, and swimming pool. For adults, there's a pub attached, which has live music in the evening. ✉ *Rättvik* ☎ *0248/13400* ▭ *AE, MC, V* ⊙ *Mid-June–mid-Aug.*

¢ ⊡ **Hotell Vidablick.** Set on its own grounds, with a pleasant view of the lake from the veranda, this small hotel makes a welcome, relaxing stop. Rooms are modern and sparsely furnished, and there's a small private beach where you can take to the water, if it's warm enough. ⊠ *Hantverks-byn, 795 36* ☎ *0248/30250* 🖷 *0248/30660* ⊕ *www.hantverksbyn.se* 🛏 *37 rooms* ♨ *Beach, bar* ⊟ *AE, DC, MC, V* ⦿⃝ *BP.*

Tällberg

❹ *9 km (5½ mi) south of Rättvik via Rte. 70, 57 km (35 mi) northwest of Falun via Rte. 80.*

Tällberg is considered by many to be the real Dalarna. It was a sleepy town that few knew about, but an 1850 visit from Hans Christian Andersen put an end to all that. He extolled its virtues—tiny flower-strewn cottages, sweet-smelling grass meadows, stunning lake views—to such an extent that Tällberg quickly became a major tourist stop. This tiny village, one of the smallest in the region with only about 200 permanent residents, is packed with crowds in summer.

The farm buildings that make up **Klockargården** have become a living museum of handicrafts and local industry. Artists and craftsmen work in the old buildings, performing such skills as blacksmithing, baking flat bread, making lace, and weaving textiles. ⊠ *Tällberg* ☎ *0247/50265* 🎟 *Free* ⊙ *June–Aug., daily 10–7.*

Where to Stay & Eat

★ $ ✕⊡ **Åkerblads.** A sprawling, low-built hotel, with parts dating from the 1400s, Åkerblads is known primarily for its gourmet achievements. The restaurant ($$) serves an interesting blend of Swedish and French cuisine, including such dishes as pork roasted with eggplants and blueberries, and salmon with asparagus, truffle, and burgundy wine sauce. The hotel rooms are comfortable, and most have very good views of Lake Siljan. ⊠ *Sjögattu 2, 793 70* ☎ *0247/50800* 🖷 *0247/50652* ⊕ *www. akerblads-tallberg.se* 🛏 *69 rooms, 3 suites* ♨ *Restaurant, in-room data ports, pool, sauna, spa, bar, free parking* ⊟ *AE, DC, MC, V* ⦿⃝ *BP.*

¢ ✕⊡ **Hotel Dalecarlia.** There's a homey feel to this first-class hotel, which has exacting standards and good lake views. The lobby's comfy sofas and darkened corners are welcoming spots to sink into. Rooms are large and done in soft colors, and there is a spa and fitness center with pool, sauna, and beauty treatments. The restaurant ($$) is candlelighted and reminiscent of a farmhouse. It has oak beams, crisp white linen, and a large open fireplace perfect for an after-dinner brandy. ⊠ *793 70 Täll-berg* ☎ *0247/89100* 🖷 *0247/50240* ⊕ *www.dalecarlia.se* 🛏 *80 rooms, 5 suites* ♨ *Restaurant, in-room data ports, Wi-Fi, pool, gym, sauna, spa, bar, convention center, free parking* ⊟ *AE, DC, MC, V* ⦿⃝ *BP.*

FodorśChoice
★

Leksand

❺ *9 km (5½ mi) south of Tällberg via Rte. 70, 66 km (41 mi) northwest of Falun via Rättvik.*

Thousands of tourists converge on Leksand every June for the midsummer celebrations; they also come in July for *Himlaspelet (The Play of the*

Way that Leads to Heaven), a traditional musical with a local cast that is staged outdoors near the town's church. It is easy to get seats; ask the local tourist office for details.

Leksand is also an excellent vantage point from which to watch the "church-boat" races on Siljan. These vessels are supposedly the successors to the Viking longboats. They were used in the 13th and 14th centuries to take peasants from outlying regions to church on Sunday. On midsummer eve the longboats, crewed by people in folk costumes, skim the lake once more.

Leksand is the perfect base for a bike ride around Lake Siljan. There are many paths and tracks to choose from, and maps and rental bikes are available from the **tourist office** (☎ 0247/796130).

Fodor'sChoice ★ The oldest parts of **Leksands Kyrka** date from the 13th century, and the current exterior dates from 1715. The Leksand Church's interior contains some interesting touches: a German font from the 1500s, a crucifix from 1400, and Dalarna's oldest organ. But what makes this church really shine is its location, perhaps one of the prettiest in the country. The peaceful tree-lined churchyard and the view across the entire lake are both breathtaking. ⊠ *Kyrkudden* ☎ 0247/80700.

At the **Leksands Hembygdsgårdar,** the site of the oldest farm buildings in Dalarna, you can learn more about the famous red structures that dot the region's landscape. ⊠ *Kyrkallén* ☎ 0247/80245 🎫 *SKr 20* ☉ *June–Aug., daily noon–4.*

Famous local doctor and author Axel Munthe (1857–1949) built **Munthes Hildasholm** as a present for his English wife in 1910. The house and gardens, filled with exquisite antiques, paintings, and furniture from across Europe, can now be visited and seen exactly as they were left. ⊠ *Klockareg. 5, Kyrkudden* ☎ 0247/10062 ⊕ *www.hildasholm.org* 🎫 *SKr 70* ☉ *June–Sept., Mon.–Sat. 11–6, Sun. 1–6.*

Where to Stay & Eat

¢–$$ ✕ **Bosporen Restaurang.** The large terrace outside this restaurant is a great place to dine in summer. The menu is long and interesting, with some great Swedish classics. The best bet is the selection of pizzas, which make use of such ingredients as arugula, pine nuts, Gorgonzola, and pears. Wine by the glass is of good quality, and the beers are wide-ranging and cheap. ⊠ *Stortorget 1* ☎ 0247/13280 🟰 *AE, MC, V.*

¢ ▦ **Hotell Korstäppan.** The beautiful rooms, many with traditional tile fireplaces and all with wooden floors, are the main attraction at this large, yellow-wood hotel. All the rooms are spacious and simply furnished with stylish antiques and beautiful old rugs. ⊠ *Hjortnäsv. 33, 793 31* ☎ 0247/ 12310 🖷 0247/14178 ⊕ *www.korstappan.se* ⇌ 30 *rooms* ⌂ *Restaurant, in-room data ports, meeting rooms, free parking* 🟰 *AE, MC, V* ◎| *BP.*

★ ¢ ▦ **Leksands Gästhem.** Simplicity bordering on minimalism is the theme at this converted old school near a farmyard just outside Leksand. The bedrooms have plain, scrubbed wooden floors, large windows, and pale-blue chairs. Each bathroom is shared by several rooms. In the hallway—where you can still see the low coat hooks for the schoolchildren—is a sweeping wood staircase that leads to a TV and lounge area. Wonderful breakfasts are included in the rate; nearly everything is homemade. ✉ *Krökbacken 5, 793 90* ☎ *0247/13700* 🖷 *0247/13737* ⊕ *www.leksandsguesth.nu* ⇨ *13 rooms* ♿ *Lounge* ▭ *AE, DC, MC, V* ⦿ *BP.*

Gesunda

❻ *38 km (24 mi) northwest of Leksand.*

A chairlift from Gesunda, a pleasant little village, will take you to the top of a mountain for unbeatable views over the lake. The large island of **Sollerön** is connected to the mainland by a bridge at Gesunda. The island has fine views of the mountains surrounding Siljan. Several excellent beaches and an interesting Viking grave site are also here. The church dates from 1775.

Mora

❼ *50 km (31 mi) northwest of Leksand, 40 km (25 mi) northwest of Rättvik via Rte. 70.*

To get to this relaxed lakeside town of 20,000, you can follow the northern shore of Lake Siljan (there is a bridge at Färnäs), or follow the lake's southern shore through Leksand and Gesunda to get a good sense of Dalarna.

Mora is best known as the finishing point for the world's longest cross-country ski race, the Vasalopp, which begins in March 90 km (56 mi) away at Sälen, a ski resort close to the Norwegian border. The race commemorates a fundamental piece of Swedish history: the successful attempt by Gustav Vasa in 1521 to rally local peasants to the cause of ridding Sweden of Danish occupation. The race attracts thousands of competitors from all over the world, including the Swedish king. There is a spectacular mass start at Sälen before the field thins out. The finish is eagerly awaited in Mora, though since the start of live television broadcasts, the number of spectators has fallen.

Mora is also known as the home of Anders Zorn (1860–1920), Sweden's leading impressionist painter, who lived in Stockholm and Paris before returning to his roots here and painting the local scenes for which he is now known. His former private residence—**Zorngården**— a large, sumptuous house designed with great originality and taste by the painter himself, has retained the same exquisite furnishings, paintings, and decor it had when he lived there with his wife. Next door, the

★ **Zorn Museet** (Zorn Museum), built 19 years after the painter's death, contains many of his best works. ✉ *Vasag. 36* ☎ *0250/592310* ⊕ *www. zorn.se* 🖾 *Museum SKr 40, home SKr 50* ☉ *Museum mid-May–mid-Sept., Mon.–Sat. 9–5, Sun. 11–5; mid-Sept.–mid-May, Mon.–Sat. noon–5, Sun. 1–5. Home (guided tours only) mid-May–mid-Sept., Mon.–Sat. 10–4, Sun. 11–4; mid-Sept.–mid-May, Mon.–Sat. noon–4, Sun. 1–4.*

On the south side of town is **Zorns Gammelgård,** a fine collection of old wooden houses from local farms, brought here and donated to Mora by Anders Zorn. One of them holds the **Textilkammare** (Textile Chamber), a collection of textiles and period clothing. ⊠ *Yvradsv.* ☎ *0250/ 16560 (June–Aug. only)* 🎫 *SKr 30* ☉ *June–Aug., daily noon–5.*

If you're in Mora in July, head 15 km (9 mi) north on Route 45 to Orsa, a small, sleepy town that gets very noisy every Wednesday when the **Orsa Spelmän,** groups of traditional folklore music players, take part in what's called the Orsayran (Orsa Rush). The musicians take over the streets of the town, wandering and playing their instruments. It's great fun.

Where to Stay & Eat

$$ ✕ **Lilla Krogen.** In one of Mora's oldest industrial buildings (1879), Lilla Krogen serves high-quality, classic Swedish home cooking and international dishes. The tables are bare antique oak, the wooden chairs are of a traditional Leksand style, and the linen napkins are woven locally. In the bar area, furnished in birch and stainless steel, the large windows allow for great views over the lake. ⊠ *Strandg. 6* ☎ *0250/15020* ▤ *AE, DC, MC, V.*

$ 🏨 **First Hotel Mora.** Part of the First Hotel group, this pleasant little hotel is in the town center, 5 km (3 mi) from the airport. Its comfortable rooms are brightly decorated. ⊠ *Strandg. 12, 792 30* ☎ *0250/592650* 🖷 *0250/ 18981* ⊕ *www.firsthotels.se* 🛏 *141 rooms* ♿ *Restaurant, in-room data ports, indoor pool, sauna, spa, bar, meeting room, free parking, no-smoking rooms* ▤ *AE, DC, MC, V* ꭥ *BP.*

$ 🏨 **Siljan.** Aside from the uninterrupted views over the lake, there's nothing to write home about here (unless the idea of having a radio is worthy of a postcard), but the small, modern hotel's central location is unbeatable. There is an excellent and lively pub, as well as a restaurant specializing in game. ⊠ *Morag. 6, 792 22* ☎ *0250/13000* 🖷 *0250/13098* ⊕ *www.swedenhotels.se* 🛏 *44 rooms* ♿ *Restaurant, room service, Wi-Fi, sauna, bar, meeting room, free parking, no-smoking floor* ▤ *AE, DC, MC, V* ꭥ *BP.*

Sports & the Outdoors

SKIING Dalarna's principal ski resort is **Sälen,** starting point for the Vasalopp, about 90 km (56 mi) west of Mora. Snow here is pretty much guaranteed from November to May, and there are more than 100 pistes to choose from, from simple slopes for the beginner to challenging black runs that weave through tightly forested slopes. For more information contact any of the tourist offices in Dalarna.

WALKING For the energetic traveler it's possible to walk the 90-km (56-mi) **track from Sälen to Mora** that's used for the Vasalopp ski race in March. Along the way you may very well see some elk wandering through the forest. Day shelters, basic night shelters, fireplaces, tables, signposts, and restrooms are set up along the trail. Facilities are free, but a donation of SKr 25 is suggested for the night shelters. Maps and other details can be obtained from the **Mora tourist office** (⊠ *Stationsv.* ☎ *0250/592020*).

Nusnäs

❽ *6 km (4 mi) southeast of Mora via Rte. 70, 28 km (17 mi) northwest of Falun.*

The lakeside village of Nusnäs is where the small, bright red–painted, wooden Dala horses are made. These were originally carved by the peasants of Dalarna as toys for their children, but their popularity rapidly spread in the 20th century. In 1939 they achieved international popularity after being shown at the New York World's Fair, and since then they have become a Swedish symbol.

Shops in the area are generally open every day except Sunday. The best place to buy painted horses is **Nils Olsson** (✉ Edåkersv. 17 ☎ 0250/37200).

Dalarna A to Z

AIRPORTS

There are six flights daily from Stockholm to Dala Airport, which is 8 km (5 mi) south of Borlänge. Flights also arrive from Göteborg and Malmö. Bus 601 runs every half hour from Dala Airport to Borlänge; the trip costs SKr 15. From Borlänge there are connecting buses to Falun and other parts of the region. Mora Airport has three Skyways flights daily from Stockholm on weekdays, fewer on weekends. The airport is 6 km (4 mi) from Mora; no buses serve the airport.

A taxi from Dala Airport to Borlänge costs around SKr 125, to Falun approximately SKr 275. A taxi into Mora from Mora Airport costs SKr 100. Order taxis in advance through your travel agent or when you make an airline reservation. Book a cab by calling the Borlänge taxi service.
🛈 **Dala Airport** ☎ 0243/64500 ⊕ www.dalaairport.se. **Borlänge Taxi** ☎ 0243/13100. **Mora Airport** ☎ 0250/30175.

BUS TRAVEL

Swebus runs tour buses to the area from Stockholm on weekends. The trip takes about four hours one-way.
🛈 **Swebus Express** ☎ 0200/218218 ⊕ www.swebusexpress.se.

CAR RENTAL

Avis has offices in Borlänge and Mora. Europcar has an office in Borlänge. Hertz has an office in Falun, and independent company Bilkompaniet, formerly a part of Hertz, rents cars in Mora.
🛈 **Avis** ✉ Borlänge ☎ 0243/87080 ✉ Mora ☎ 0250/16711. **Bilkompaniet** ✉ Mora ☎ 0250/28800. **Europcar** ✉ Borlänge ☎ 0243/19050. **Hertz** ✉ Falun ☎ 023/58872.

CAR TRAVEL

From Stockholm take E18 to Enköping and follow Route 70 northwest. From Göteborg take E20 to Örebro and Route 60 north from there. Villages are well signposted.

EMERGENCIES

For emergencies dial 112. There are no late-night pharmacies in the area. Vasen Pharmacy, in Falun, is open 9–7 weekdays and 9–noon on Saturday.

🏥 **Falun Hospital** ☎ 023/492000. **Mora Hospital** ☎ 0250/493000. **24-hour medical advisory service** ☎ 023/492900. **Vasen Pharmacy** ✉ Åsg. 25, Falun ☎ 0771/450450.

TOURS

Call the Falun tourist office for English-speaking guides to Falun and the region around Lake Siljan; guides cost about SKr 900 per day.

BOAT TOURS Just next to the Mora train station, on the quay in the center of town, is the MS *Gustaf Wasa*, a beautiful old steamship that's used for sightseeing tours of Lake Siljan. Trips can take from two to four hours and range in price from SKr 80 to SKr 120. It's a good way to see the stunning countryside from another perspective.

🚢 **MS *Gustaf Wasa*** ☎ 070/5421025.

TRAIN TRAVEL

There is regular daily train service from Stockholm to both Mora and Falun.

🚆 **SJ** ⊕ www.sj.se.

VISITOR INFORMATION

On the approach to the area from the south via Route 70, a 43-foot, bright orange-red Dala horse marks a rest stop just south of Avesta. It has a spacious cafeteria and a helpful tourist information center.

ℹ️ **Tourist Information Falun** ✉ Trotzg. 10-12 ☎ 023/83050 ⊕ www.visitfalun.se. **Leksand** ✉ Stationsg. 14 ☎ 0247/796130. **Ludvika** ✉ Fredsg. 10 ☎ 0240/86050. **Mora** ✉ Stationsv. ☎ 0250/592020 ⊕ www.siljan.se. **Rättvik** ✉ Riksv. 40 ☎ 0248/797210. **Sälen** ✉ Sälen Centrum ☎ 0280/18700.

NORRLAND & NORRBOTTEN

The north of Sweden is a mysterious region of wide-open spaces where the silence is almost audible. Golden eagles soar above snowcapped crags; huge salmon fight their way up wild, tumbling rivers; rare orchids bloom in arctic heathland; and wild rhododendrons splash the land with color.

In summer the sun shines at midnight above the Arctic Circle. In winter it hardly shines at all. The weather can change with bewildering speed: a June day can dawn sunny and bright; then the skies may darken and the temperature may drop to around zero as a snow squall blows in.

Here live the once-nomadic Lapps, or Sami, as they prefer to be known. They carefully guard what remains of their identity while doing their best to inform the public of their culture. Many of the 17,000 Sami who live in Sweden still earn their living herding reindeer, but as open space shrinks the younger generation is turning in greater numbers toward the allure of the cities. Nowadays many Sami depend on the tourist industry for their living, selling their crafts, such as expertly carved bone-handle knives, wooden cups and bowls, bark bags, silver jewelry, and leather straps embroidered with pewter thread.

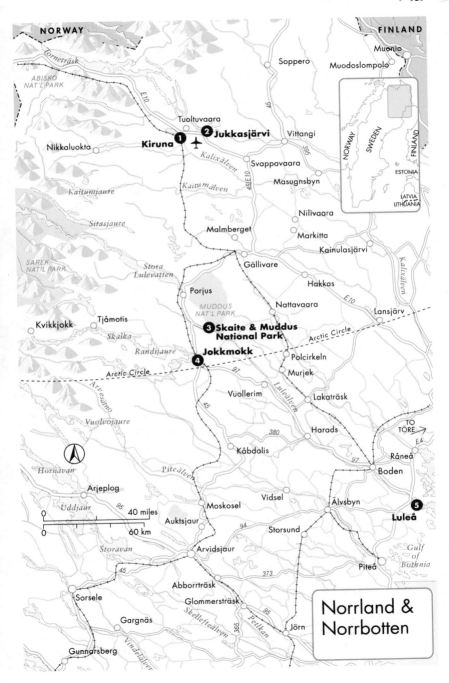

NORWAY

FINLAND

Muonio
Muodoslompolo
Soppero

Torneträsk
ABISKO
NAT'L PARK

E10

Tuoltuvaara
❷ Jukkasjärvi
Vittangi

Nikkaluokta
Kiruna ❶
Kalixälven
Svappavaara
Masugnsbyn

Kaitumjaure
Kaitumälven

Sitasjaure
Nilivaara
Malmberget
Markitta
Kainulasjärvi

SAREK
NAT'L PARK
Stora
Lulevatten
Gällivare
Hakkas

Porjus
MUDDUS
NAT'L PARK
Nattavaara
E10
Lansjärv

Kvikkjokk
Tjåmotis
Skalka
❸ Skaite & Muddus
National Park
Arctic Circle

Randijaure
Jokkmokk
❹
Polcirkeln
Murjek

Arvesund
Arctic Circle
97
Vuollerim
Luleälven
Lakaträsk

Vuolvojaure
380
Harads
TO
TÖRE

Hornavan
45
Kåbdalis
97
Råneå

Arjeplog
Boden

Uddjaur
95
40 miles
Moskosel
Vidsel
Älvsbyn
❺
Luleå

60 km
Auktsjaur
94
Storsund

Storavan
Arvidsjaur
373
Piteå
Gulf
of
Bothnia

45
Sorsele
Abborrträsk
Glommersträsk
95

Gargnäs
365
Petikån
Jörn
**Norrland &
Norrbotten**

Gunnarsberg
Skellefteälven
Vindelälven

Norrland's towns are often little more than a group of houses along a street, built around a local industry such as a mine, a lumber company, or a hydroelectric facility. Thanks to Sweden's excellent transportation infrastructure, however, Norrland and the northernmost region of Norrbotten are no longer inaccessible. Even travelers with limited time can get at least a taste of the area. Hiking, climbing, canoeing, river rafting, and fishing are all popular in summer; skiing, ice-skating, and dogsledding are winter activities. A word of warning: in summer mosquitoes are a constant nuisance, so bring plenty of repellent. Fall is perhaps the best season to visit Norrland.

Kiruna

❶ *1,352 km (840 mi) north of Stockholm.*

About 250 km (155 mi) north of the Arctic Circle, and 1,804 feet above sea level, Kiruna is Sweden's northernmost municipality. Although its inhabitants number only around 26,000, Kiruna is Sweden's largest city geographically—it spreads over the equivalent of half the area of Switzerland. It's the most logical base for exploring the area.

Kiruna lies at the eastern end of Lake Luossajärvi, spread over a wide area between two mountains, Luossavaara and Kirunavaara, that are largely composed of iron ore—Kiruna's raison d'être. Here is the world's largest underground iron mine, with reserves estimated at 420 million tons. Like most of Norrland, Kiruna is full of remarkable contrasts, from the long, pitch-black winters to the bright summers, when the sun doesn't set for 50 days at a stretch. Here, too, the ancient Sami culture persists side by side with the high-tech culture of cutting-edge satellite research. Since the 1960s the city has supported the Esrange Space Range, about 40 km (24 mi) east, which sends sounding rockets and stratospheric balloons to probe the upper reaches of earth's atmosphere, and the Swedish Institute of Space Physics, which has pioneered the investigation of the phenomenon of **the northern lights.**

One of Kiruna's few buildings of interest is **Kiruna Kyrka** (Kiruna Church; ⊠ Gruvv.), near the center of the city. It was built in 1921, its inspiration a blending of a Sami *kåta* (a Lapp wigwam) with a Swedish stave church.

Where to Stay & Eat

$ ✕⊞ **Kebne och Kaisa.** These twin modern hotels—named after the local mountain, Kebnekaise—are close to the railway station and the airport bus stop. Rooms are bland but modern and comfortable. The restaurant is one of the best in Kiruna; it's open for breakfast and dinner and serves excellent local and national specialties, particularly, when in season, very good elk. ⊠ *Konduktörsg. 3, 981 34* ☎ *0980/12380* 🖨 *0980/ 68181* ⊕ *www.hotellkebne.com* 📞 *54 rooms* ⚭ *Restaurant, 2 saunas, no-smoking rooms* ▤ *AE, DC, MC, V.*

$$ ⊞ **Ferrum.** Part of the Scandic Hotels chain, this late-1960s-vintage hotel is near the railway station. Rooms have wood floors and standard modern furniture. The hotel's best feature are its three saunas, located on the sixth floor, from which you have magnificent views across the

mountains while you sweat away. ⊠ *Lars Janssonsg. 15, 981 31* ☎ *0980/ 398600* 🖷 *0980/398600* ⊕ *www.scandic-hotels.com* ➟ *171 rooms* ♨ *3 restaurants, in-room data ports, gym, saunas, 2 bars, dance club, meeting room, no-smoking rooms* ⊟ *AE, DC, MC, V.*

¢ 🖭 **Järnvägshotellet.** Dating from 1903, this small hotel has the advantage of being close to the railway station. The entire building was refurbished in 2002, and the previously tired rooms received a much-needed update. Still, at these prices, don't expect luxury. ⊠ *Bangårdsv. 7, 981 34* ☎ *0980/84444* ⊕ *www.jarnvagshotellet.com* ➟ *20 rooms* ♨ *Restaurant, sauna, meeting room, no-smoking rooms* ⊟ *MC, V* ⧖ *BP.*

Jukkasjärvi

❷ *16 km (10 mi) east of Kiruna.*

The history of Jukkasjärvi, a Sami village by the shores of the fast-flowing Torneälven (Torne River), goes back to the early 16th century, when there was already a market here. It has a wooden church from the 17th century and a small open-air museum that evokes a sense of Sami life in times gone by.

If you are gastronomically adventuresome, you may want to sample one of the most unusual of all Sami delicacies: a cup of thick black coffee with *kaffeost*, small lumps of goat cheese. After the cheese sits in the coffee for a bit, you fish it out with a spoon and eat it, then drink the coffee.

Where to Stay & Eat

★ ¢ ✕🖭 **Icehotel Restaurang.** The restaurant specializes in Norrland cuisine—featuring reindeer, wild berries, dried and smoked meats, salted fish, fermented herring, and rich sauces using thick creams—and is the life's work of its manager, Yngve Bergqvist, who is still here, even after the place was taken over by the adjacent Icehotel. There are 45 cabins around the main building, 30 with bathroom, kitchen, and two bedrooms with bunk beds. Breakfast is not included. River-rafting and canoeing trips can be arranged. ⊠ *Marknadsv. 63, 981 91* ☎ *0980/ 66800* 🖷 *0980/66890* ⊕ *www.icehotel.com* ➟ *45 cabins* ♨ *Restaurant, sauna, meeting room* ⊟ *AE, DC, MC, V.*

$$$ 🖭 **Icehotel.** At the peak of winter, tourists are drawn by the annual construction of the world's largest igloo, which opens for business as a hotel in mid-December through April, after which it melts away, until being revised and built again nine months later. Made of snow, ice, and sheet metal, the Icehotel accommodates guests, who spend the night in specially insulated sleeping bags on top of layers of reindeer skins and spruce boughs. At the Absolut Icebar, colored electric lights liven up the solid-ice walls. Breakfast is served in the sauna, with a view of the (nonelectric) northern lights. ⊠ *Marknadsv. 63, 981 91* ☎ *0980/66800* 🖷 *0980/ 66800* ⊕ *www.icehotel.com* ➟ *120 beds without bath, 18 suites* ♨ *Restaurant, sauna, cross-country skiing, snowmobiling, bar, meeting room; no smoking* ⊟ *AE, DC, MC, V* ⊘ *Closed May–Nov.*

FodorśChoice
★

Skaite & Muddus National Park

❸ *225 km (140 mi) south of Kiruna via E10 and Rte. 45.*

Muddus National Park is less mountainous and spectacular than Sarek, but easier to explore. Its 121,770 acres are mainly taken up by virgin coniferous forest, some of whose trees may be as much as 600 years old. The park's 3,680 acres of water are composed primarily of two huge lakes at the center of the park and the Muddusjåkkå River, which tumbles spectacularly through a gorge with 330-foot-high sheer rock walls and includes a waterfall crashing 140 feet down. From Skaite, where you enter the park, a series of well-marked trails begins. There are four well-equipped, overnight communal rest huts and two tourist cabins. The park is home to bears, lynx, wolverines, moose, ermines, weasels, otters, and many bird species. A popular pastime is picking cloudberries (a member of the raspberry family) in autumn.

Jokkmokk

❹ *225 km (140 mi) south of Kiruna via E10 and Rte. 45.*

Jokkmokk is an important center of Sami culture. Every February it is the scene of the region's largest market, where everything from frozen reindeer meat to Sami handcrafted wooden utensils is sold. If you're an outdoor enthusiast, Jokkmokk may be the best base in Norrland for you. The village has good campsites and is surrounded by wilderness. The local tourist office sells fishing permits and can also supply lists of camping and housekeeping cabins.

Where to Stay

$ 🏨 **Hotel Jokkmokk.** A modern hotel this luxurious seems incongruous
Fodor'sChoice in this remote region, but is welcome nevertheless. The hotel is in the
★ town center, but the staff can arrange dogsled rides and helicopter trips to the Sarek and Muddus national parks; there is excellent fishing nearby. ✉ *Solg. 45, 962 23* ☎ *0971/77700* 🖷 *0971/77790* ⊕ *www. hoteljokkmokk.se* ↪ *75 rooms* ⚬ *Restaurant, sauna, meeting room, no-smoking rooms* ▭ *AE, DC, MC, V.*

¢ 🏨 **Jokkmokks Turistcenter.** This complex is in a pleasant forest area near Luleälven, 3 km (2 mi) from the railway station. ✉ *Nortudden, Box 75, 962 22* ☎ *0971/12370* 🖷 *0971/12476* ↪ *59 cabins* ⚬ *4 pools, sauna, meeting room* ▭ *MC, V.*

Luleå

❺ *340 km (211 mi) southeast of Kiruna via E10 and E4.*

The northernmost major town in Sweden, Luleå is an important port at the top of the Gulf of Bothnia, at the mouth of the Luleälv (Lule River). **Gammelstad Church Town,** the site of the original settlement, is now protected by the UNESCO World Heritage list. The development of Kiruna and the iron trade is linked, literally, by a railway, with the fortunes of Luleå, where a steelworks was set up in the 1940s. Like its fellow port towns farther south—Piteå, Skellefteå, Umeå, and Sundsvall—Luleå is a very modern and nondescript city, but it has some reasonable hotels. A beautiful archipelago of hundreds of islands hugs the coastline. Many of these islands can be reached by car in the wintertime through a 250-km (166-mi) network of roads on the frozen sea. Wintertime visitors with kids shouldn't miss the ice slide in the city park: each year it's in the shape of a different indigenous animal.

Where to Stay & Eat

★ $–$$ ✕🏨 **Arctic.** The imposing redbrick building that houses this hotel may at first seem a little oppressive. Step inside, though, and you are struck by the family-run feeling. Rooms are light and simple, with white walls, plump blue sofas and chairs, and burgundy curtains. The restaurant is perfect for those wanting to sample the excellent local ingredients, such as salmon and game. All in all, for the price, this is a magical place. ⊠ *Sandviksg. 80, 972 34* ☎ *0920/10980* 📠 *0920/60787* ⊕ *www. arctichotel.se* 🛏 *94 rooms* ⚒ *Restaurant, hot tub, sauna, meeting room, no-smoking rooms* ⊟ *AE, DC, MC, V.*

$ 🏨 **Aveny.** Certainly the welcome and the service here are as friendly as you could wish. As for charm, you need look no further than the randomly furnished rooms, seemingly made up of a collection of furniture picked up over many years in many places. It's Aveny's location that is the real seller, right across from the main railway station. ⊠ *Hermelinsg. 10, 973 46* ☎ *0920/221820* 📠 *0920/220122* ⊕ *www.hotellaveny.com* 🛏 *24 rooms* ⚒ *No-smoking rooms* ⊟ *AE, DC, MC, V.*

Norrland & Norrbotten A to Z

AIR TRAVEL

CARRIERS There are two nonstop SAS flights a day from Stockholm to Kiruna Airport and two additional flights via Umeå. Check SAS for specific times. 📱 **SAS** ☎ 0770/727727, 8/7972688 from outside Sweden.

AIRPORTS

In summer, buses connect Kiruna Airport, which is 5 km (3 mi) from Kiruna, to the city center; the fare is about SKr 50. A taxi from the airport to the center of Kiruna costs SKr 200 and up; book through the airline or call the taxi directly. 📱 **Kiruna Airport** ☎ 0980/68001 ⊕ www.lfv.se. **Taxi Kiruna** ☎ 020/979797.

CAR RENTAL

📱 **Major Agencies Avis** ⊠ Kiruna Airport, Kiruna ☎ 0980/13080. **Europcar** ⊠ Forv. 33, Kiruna ☎ 0980/80759. **Hertz** ⊠ Industriv. 5, Kiruna ☎ 0980/19000.

CAR TRAVEL

Since public transportation is nonexistent in this part of the country, having a car is essential. The few roads are well built and maintained, although spring thaws can present potholes. Keep in mind that habitations are few and far between in this wilderness region.

EMERGENCIES

For emergencies dial 112. A medical advisory service in Luleå is available 24 hours a day.

There are no late-night pharmacies in Norrbotten. The pharmacy at the Gallerian shopping center in Kiruna is open weekdays 9:30–6 and Saturday 9:30–1.

🄵 **Gallerian Pharmacy** ✉ Föreningsg. 6, Kiruna ☎ 0771/450450. **Jokkmokk Health Center** ✉ Lappstav. 9, Jokkmokk ☎ 0971/44455. **Kiruna Hospital** ✉ Thuleg. 29, Kiruna ☎ 0980/73000. **Sunderby Hospital Luleå** ✉ Luleå ☎ 0920/282000.

TOURS

Local tourist offices have information on guided tours involving dogsledding, snowmobiling, and ice fishing. Samelands Resor arranges tours to points of interest. Call the Swedish Sami Association for Sami tours.

🄵 **Samelands Resor** ✉ Hermelinsg. 20, 962 33 Jokkmokk ☎ 0971/10606 ⊕ www. samelandsresor.com. **Swedish Sami Association** ✉ Brog. 5, 903 25 Umeå ☎ 090/ 141180.

TRAIN TRAVEL

The best and cheapest way to get to Kiruna is to take the evening sleeper from Stockholm. There are two trains a day, seven days per week. Fares range from SKr 800 per person for simple bunks to SKr 1000 per person for beds. You'll arrive at around lunchtime the next day. To book a train, call Connex, the rail company that handles this route.

🄵 **Connex** ☎ 0771/260000 ⊕ www.connex.se.

VISITOR INFORMATION

Norrbottens Turistråd is the regional tourist office. Local tourist offices are listed below by town.

🄵 **Jokkmokk** ✉ Stortorget 4 ☎ 0971/22250. **Kiruna** ✉ Folkets Hus ☎ 0980/18880. **Luleå** ✉ Storg. 43B ☎ 0920/293500. **Norrbottens Turistråd** ☎ 0920/94070.

SWEDEN A TO Z

AIR TRAVEL

CARRIERS 🄵 To & From Sweden From North America to Stockholm Arlanda Airport, Air Canada has flights with connections through London or Frankfurt; American Airlines has direct flights; Continental has direct flights from Newark, New Jersey; Delta has flights with connections through Paris; Finnair has flights with connections through Helsinki; Icelandair has flights with connections through Reykjavík and Oslo; Lufthansa has flights with connections through Frankfurt; Scandinavian Airlines System (SAS) has direct flights, as well as additional flights with connections through London or Copenhagen (United co-shares with SAS-operated flights).

From the United Kingdom, British Airways has direct flights to Stockholm Arlanda; BMI has direct flights to Stockholm Arlanda and Göteborg Landvetter; Fly Snowflake (an SAS group) has direct flights to Stockholm Arlanda; Ryan Air has direct flights to Stockholm Vasteras and Skavska airports as well as Göteborg City airport, and Scandinavian Airlines System has direct flights to Stockholm Arlanda and Göteborg Landvetter.

🄵 Within Sweden Inside Sweden, Fly Me and Fly Nordic have direct flights from Stockholm Arlanda to Göteborg Landvetter; Malmö Aviation has direct flights from Stockholm City Airport Bromma to Göteborg Landvetter; Malmö Aviation and Scandinavian Airlines System connects all major cities by regular flights.

🛈 Airlines & Contacts **Air Canada** ☎ 888/247-2262 in Canada and the U.S. ⊕ www.aircanada.ca. **American** ☎ 800/433-7300 ⊕ www.aa.com. **British Airways** ☎ 020/88974000 ⊕ www.british-airways.com. **British Midland** ☎ 01332/854000 in the U.K ⊕ www.flybmi.com. **Continental** ☎ 800/231-0856 ⊕ www.continental.com. **Delta** ☎ 800/221-1212 ⊕ www.delta.com. **Finnair** ☎ 800/950-5000 ⊕ www.finnair.com. **Fly Me** ☎ 0313011000 ⊕ www.flyme.com. **Fly Nordic** ☎ 08/52806820 ⊕ www.flynordic.com. **Iceland Air** ☎ 800/223-5500 ⊕ www.icelandair.com. **Lufthansa** ☎ 800/399-5838 ⊕ www.lufthansa.com. **Malmö Aviation** ☎ 406602900 ⊕ www.malmoaviation.se. **Ryan Air** ☎ 0871/246-0000 in the U.K., 0155/202240 in Sweden ⊕ www.ryanair.com. **SAS** ☎ 0770/727727 in Sweden, 020/77344020 in the U.K., 800/345-9684 in the U.S. ⊕ www.scandinavian.net. **United** ☎ 800/241-6522 ⊕ www.united.com.

BIKE TRAVEL

Cycling is a very popular sport in Sweden, and the south of the country, with its low-lying, flat landscape, is perfect for the more genteel cyclist. All major towns and cities have cycle paths and designated cycle lanes. Bike-rental costs average around SKr 100 per day. Tourist offices and the Swedish Touring Association have information about cycling package holidays. The Swedish bicycling organization, Cykelfrämjandet (National Cycle Association), publishes a free English-language guide to cycling trips. Various companies, including Cycling Sweden, offer a variety of cycling tours around the country.

🛈 **Cycling Sweden** ✉ Tranmog. 10, 641 50 Katrineholm ☎ 15055091 ⊕ www.cyclingsweden.se. **Cykelfrämjandet** ✉ Thuleg. 43, 113 53 Stockholm ☎ 08/54591030 Mon.-Thurs. 9-noon 🖷 08/54591039 ⊕ www.cykelframjandet.a.se. **Swedish Touring Association** (STF) 🖅 Box 25, 101 20 Stockholm ☎ 08/4632200 🖷 08/6781938 ⊕ www.meravsverige.se.

BOAT & FERRY TRAVEL

Taking a ferry is not only fun, it is often necessary in Scandinavia. Many companies arrange package trips, some offering a rental car and hotel accommodations as part of the deal. The word *ferry* can be deceptive; generally, those vessels so named are more like small-scale cruise ships, with several dining rooms, sleeping quarters, shopping, pool and sauna, and entertainment.

Silja Line operates massive ferries between Stockholm and Helsinki, departing from Stockholm at 5 PM, with a stop at Mariehamn at 11:55 PM, and arriving at Helsinki at 9:30 AM. Fares range from SKr 50 to SKr 63 without a cabin, depending upon the day, and SKr 120 to SKr 760, depending upon the class of cabin and day. Viking Line also operates large ferries to Helsinki, departing from Stockholm at 4:45 PM with a brief stop at Mariehamn before arriving in Helsinki at 9:55 AM. Fares, without cabins, range from € 32 to € 56, depending upon the day. Unity Line operates a ferry service departing from Ystad at 10 PM and arriving at 7 AM in Świnoujście, Poland, where a minibus will be waiting to take you to the historic city of Szczecin, Poland. The fares range from SKr 550 to SKr 860, depending upon the season. ScandLines operates a frequent ferry service on the 20-minute sail between Helsingborg and Helsingør, Denmark. Single fares cost SKr 22 for a foot passenger, and SKr 290 for a car and passengers.

A rewarding way to see Sweden is from the many ferryboats that ply the archipelagoes and main lakes. In Stockholm, visitors can buy a special *Båtluffarkortet* (Inter Skerries Card, SKr 300) from Waxholmsbolaget. This card allows you five days of unlimited travel on the archipelago ferryboats. (⇨ Boat & Ferry Travel *in* Stockholm A to Z.)

⚑ Major Operators DFDS Seaways ✉ DFDS Seaways Travel Centre, Scandinavia House, Parkeston, Harwich, Essex CO12 4QG ☎ 44/8705-333-111 ⊕ www.dfdsseaways. co.uk. **DFDS Tor Line** ✉ Nordic House, Western Access Rd., Immingham Dock, Immingham, DN402LZ North East Lincolnshire ☎ 44/1469-575231. **ScandLines** ⌂ Dampfærgevej, 10, DK-2100 Copenhagen, Denmark ☎ 45/33-15-15-15 ✉ Knutpunkten 43, 252 78 Helsingborg, Sweden ☎ 46/42186100 🖷 46/42186000 ⊕ www. scandlines.com. **Silja Line** ✉ Mannerheimintie 2, 00100 Helsinki, Finland ☎ 358/9-18041 🖷 358/9-1804279 ✉ Kungsg. 2, 111 43 Stockholm, Sweden ☎ 46/86663512 🖷 46/86119162 ⊕ www.silja.com/english. **Unity Line** ✉ Färjeterminalen, 271 39 Ystad ☎ 46/0411556900 🖷 46/0411556953 ⊕ www.unityline.pl. **Viking Line** ✉ Mannerheimintie 14, 00100 Helsinki ☎ 358/9-12351 🖷 358/9-647075 ⊕ www.vikingline.fi.

BUS TRAVEL

There is excellent bus service between all major towns and cities. Consult the *Yellow Pages* under "Bussresearrangörer" for the telephone numbers of the companies concerned. Recommended are the services offered to different parts of Sweden from Stockholm by Swebus. When buying a single ticket for local bus journeys, it is usual to pay the driver on boarding. Coupons or multiple tickets for longer journeys should be purchased before your journey from the relevant bus company.

⚑ Svenska Buss ☎ 0771/676767 ⊕ www.svenskabuss.se. **Swebus Express** ☎ 0200/ 218218 ⊕ www.swebusexpress.se.

BUSINESS HOURS

BANKS & OFFICES Banks are officially open weekdays 9:30–3, but many stay open until 5 on most weekdays and until 6 on Thursday. The bank at Arlanda International Airport is open every day with extended hours, and the Forex and Valuta Specialisten currency-exchange offices also have extended hours. Most banks operate a numbered-ticket system for lining up: take a number and wait your turn. Ticket machines are always near a bank's doors. Make exchanging money your first task to avoid a frustratingly long wait. Many Swedes use Internet banking; it is not uncommon to come across cashless bank branches. These are more often found in smaller towns, so it is worth checking before traveling.

CAR RENTAL

Major car-rental companies such as Avis, Budget, Europcar, and Hertz have facilities in all major towns and cities as well as at airports. Various service stations also offer car rentals, including Q8, Shell, Statoil, and Texaco. See the *Yellow Pages* under "Biluthyrning" for telephone numbers and addresses. Renting a car is a speedy business in Sweden, with none of the usual lengthy documentation and vehicle checks; show your passport, license, and credit card, pick up the key, and away you go.

Rates in Stockholm begin at $75 a day and $190 a week for a manual-drive economy car without air-conditioning and with unlimited mileage. This does not include tax on car rentals, which is 25% in Sweden. A service charge also is usually added, which ranges from $15 to $25.

CAR TRAVEL

The Øresundsbron, the new 8-km (5-mi) bridge between Malmö and Copenhagen, simplifies car travel and makes train connections possible between the two countries. Ferry service is cheaper but slower—it takes 45 minutes to make the crossing.

Sweden has an excellent highway network of more than 80,000 km (50,000 mi). The fastest routes are those with numbers prefixed with an *E* (for "European"), some of which are the equivalent of American highways or British motorways. The size of the country compared to its population means that most roads are relatively traffic free. Rush hour in major cities can bring frustrating traffic jams.

Also be aware that there are relatively low legal blood-alcohol limits and tough penalties for driving while intoxicated in Scandinavia; Sweden, Iceland, and Finland have zero-tolerance laws. Penalties include license suspension and fines or imprisonment, and the laws are sometimes enforced by random police roadblocks in urban areas on weekends. An accident involving a driver who has an illegal blood-alcohol level usually voids all insurance agreements, making the driver responsible for all medical and car-damage bills.

EMERGENCY SERVICES The emergency number for the European Union is 112. The Sweden-specific emergency number is 90000. The Larmtjänst organization, run by a confederation of Swedish insurance companies, provides a 24-hour breakdown service. Its phone number is 41116270.

GASOLINE Sweden has some of the highest gasoline rates in Europe, about SKr 10.74 per liter (about SKr 40 per gallon). Lead-free gasoline is readily available. Gas stations are self-service: pumps marked SEDEL are automatic and accept SKr 20 and SKr 100 bills; pumps marked KASSA are paid for at the cashier; the KONTO pumps are for customers with credit cards.

PARKING Parking meters and, increasingly, timed ticket machines operate in larger towns, usually between 8 AM and 6 PM. The fee varies from about SKr 6 to SKr 35 per hour. Parking garages in urban areas are mostly automated, often with machines that accept credit cards; LEDIGT on a garage sign means space is available. Many streets in urban areas are cleaned weekly at a designated time on a designated day, during which time parking is not allowed, not even at meters. Times are marked on a yellow sign at each end of the street. Try to avoid getting a parking ticket, which can come with fines of SKr 300–SKr 700.

ROAD MAPS If you plan on extensive road touring, consider buying the *Vägatlas över Sverige,* a detailed road atlas published by the Mötormännens Riksförbund, available at bookstores for around SKr 300.

RULES OF THE ROAD Drive on the right, and—no matter where you sit in a car—seat belts are mandatory. You must also have at least low-beam headlights on at all times. Cars rented or bought in Sweden will have automatic head-lights, which are activated every time the engine is switched on. Signs indicate five basic speed limits, ranging from 30 kph (19 mph) in school or playground areas to 110 kph (68 mph) on long stretches of E roads.

CRUISE TRAVEL

You can go on one of the highly popular cruises of the Göta Canal, which traverse rivers, lakes, and, on the last lap, the Baltic Sea. A lovely wa-terway, the Göta Canal with its 65 locks links Göteborg, on the west coast, with Stockholm, on the east. Cruise participants travel on fine old steamers, some of which date back almost to the canal's opening, in 1832. The oldest and most desirable is the *Juno*, built in 1874. Prices start at SKr 6,100 for a bed in a double cabin. For more information contact the Göta Canal Steamship Company.

🔲 **Göta Canal Steamship Company** ✑ Pusterviksgatan 13, SE413-01 Göteborg ☎ 03/1806315 🖷 03/1158311 ⊕ www.gotacanal.se.

CUSTOMS & DUTIES

Travelers 21 or older entering Sweden from non-EU countries may im-port duty-free 1 liter of liquor and 2 liters of fortified wine; 2 liters of wine or 15 liters of beer; 200 cigarettes or 100 grams of cigarillos or 50 cigars or 250 grams of tobacco; 50 grams of perfume; ¼ liter of aftershave; and other goods whose total value does not exceed SKr 1,700. Travelers from the United Kingdom or other EU countries may import duty-free 1 liter of liquor or 3 liters of fortified wine; 5 liters of wine; 15 liters of beer; 300 cigarettes or 150 cigarillos or 75 cigars or 400 grams of tobacco; and other goods, including perfume and aftershave, of any value.

EMBASSIES

🔲 Australia ⊠ Sergels torg 12 ☎ 08/6132900 ⊕ www.sweden.embassy.gov.au.
🔲 Canada ⊠ Tegelbacken 4, Box 16129, 103 23 Stockholm ☎ 08/4533000.
🔲 New Zealand ⊠ Sturplan 2, Stockholm ☎ 08/6112625.
🔲 U.K. ⊠ Skarpög. 68, 115 93 Stockholm ☎ 08/6713000 ⊕ www.britishembassy.se.
🔲 U.S. ⊠ Strandv. 101, Dag Hammarskjölds väg 31, 115 89 Stockholm ☎ 08/7835300 ⊕ stockholm.usembassy.gov.

EMERGENCIES

Anywhere in Sweden, dial 112 for emergency assistance.

LANGUAGE

Swedish is closely related to Danish and Norwegian. After *z*, the Swedish alphabet has three extra letters, *å*, *ä*, and *ö*, something to bear in mind when using the phone book. Another phone-book alphabetical oddity is that *v* and *w* are interchangeable; Wittström, for example, comes be-fore Vittviks, not after. And after all that, you'll be happy to know that most Swedes are happy to speak English.

LODGING

APARTMENT & VILLA RENTALS With 250 chalet villages with high standards, Sweden enjoys popular-ity with its chalet accommodations, often arranged on the spot at tourist offices. Many are organized under the auspices of the Swedish Touring Association (STF). DFDS Seaways in Göteborg arranges package deals that combine a ferry trip from Britain across the North Sea and a stay in a chalet village.

◪ Rental Contacts **DFDS Seaways** ☎ 08705/333–111 within the U.K. **Swedish Touring Association** ☎ 08/4632100 🖷 08/6781938 ⊕ www.meravsverige.se.

CAMPING There are 760 registered campsites nationwide, many close to uncrowded swimming places and with fishing, boating, or canoeing; they may also offer bicycle rentals. Prices range from SKr 70 to SKr 130 per 24-hour period. Many campsites also offer accommodations in log cabins at various prices, depending on the facilities offered. Most are open between June and September, but about 200 remain open in winter for skiing and skating enthusiasts. Sveriges Campingvårdernas Riksförbund (Swedish Campsite Owners' Association or SCR) publishes, in English, an abbreviated list of sites; contact the office for a free copy.

◪ **Sveriges Campingvårdernas Riksförbund** ⌂ Box 255, 451 17 Uddevalla ☎ 0522/642440 🖷 0522/642430 ⊕ www.camping.se.

FARM & COTTAGE HOLIDAYS The old-fashioned farm or countryside holiday is becoming increasingly available to tourists. You can choose to stay on the farm itself and even participate in daily activities, or you can opt to rent a private housekeeping cottage. Contact the local tourist board or Swedish Farm Holidays for details.

◪ **Swedish Farm Holidays** ⌂ Box 8, 668 21 Ed, Sweden ☎ 46/53412075 🖷 46/53461011 ⊕ www.bopalantgard.org. **Upplev Landet** ⌂ 105 33 Stockholm, Sweden ☎ 771/573–573 ⊕ www.upplevlandet.se ⊕ www.stugguiden.se.

HOTELS Major hotels in larger cities often cater to business clientele and can be expensive; weekend rates are more reasonable and can even be as low as half the normal price. Prices are normally on a per-room basis and include all taxes and service charges and usually breakfast. Apart from the more modest inns and the cheapest budget establishments, private baths and showers are standard.

Whatever their size, almost all Swedish hotels provide scrupulously clean accommodations and courteous service. Since many Swedes go on vacation in July and through early August, make your hotel reservations in advance, especially if staying outside the city areas during that time. Some hotels close during the winter holidays as well; call ahead for information.

An official annual guide, *Hotels in Sweden,* published by and available free from the Swedish Travel and Tourism Council, gives comprehensive information about hotel facilities and prices. Countryside Hotels comprises 35 select resort hotels, some of them restored manor houses or centuries-old inns. Hotellcentralen is an independent agency that makes advance telephone reservations for any Swedish hotel at no cost. The Sweden Hotels group has about 100 independently owned hotels and its own classification scheme—with a letter assigned according to a hotel's facilities.

Major hotel groups like Best Western, Radisson SAS, RESO, Scandic, and Sweden Hotels also have their own central reservations services.

◪ **Countryside Hotels** ⌂ Store Wäsby, 194 37 Upplands Väsby ☎ 8590/32732 🖷 8590/340 59 ⊕ www.countrysidehotels.se. **Hotellcentralen** ✉ Centralstation, 111 20 ☎ 08/50828508 🖷 08/7918666.

MAIL & SHIPPING

POSTAL RATES Postcards and letters up to 20 grams can be mailed for SKr 8 within Sweden, SKr 10 to destinations within Europe, and SKr 10 to the United States and all other countries.

MONEY MATTERS

Here is an idea what you'll pay for food and drink in Sweden: a cup of coffee, SKr 25–SKr 35; a beer, SKr 40–SKr 55; a mineral water, SKr 12–SKr 25; a cheese roll, SKr 25–SKr 50; pepper steak à la carte, SKr 120–SKr 190; a cheeseburger, SKr 60; and pizza, starting at SKr 40.

Be aware that sales taxes can be very high, but foreigners can get some refunds by shopping at tax-free stores (⇨ Taxes). City Cards can save you transportation and entrance fees in many of the larger cities.

You can reduce the cost of food by planning. Opt for a restaurant lunch instead of dinner, since the latter tends to be significantly more expensive. Instead of beer or wine, drink tap water—liquor can cost four times the price of the same brand in a store—but do specify tap water, as the term *water* can refer to soft drinks and bottled water, which are also expensive.

ATMS The 1,200 or so blue Bankomat cash dispensers nationwide have been adapted to take some foreign cards, including MasterCard, Visa, and bank cards linked to the Cirrus network. You may encounter some complications on remote machines. It's best to use those that are next to major bank offices. For more information contact Bankomatcentralen in Stockholm or your local bank. American Express has cash and traveler's check dispensers; there's also an office at Stockholm's Arlanda Airport.
🔲 **American Express** ⊠ Birger Jarlsg. 1 ☎ 020/793211 toll-free. **Bankomatcentralen/ CEK AB** ☎ 08/7255700.

CURRENCY The unit of currency is the krona (plural kronor), which is divided into 100 öre and is written as SKr or SEK. Coins come in SKr 1, SKr 5, and SKr 10. Bank notes come in denominations of SKr 20, SKr 50, SKr 100, SKr 500, and SKr 1,000. At press time the exchange rates for the krona were SKr 7.9 to the U.S. dollar, SKr 6.7 to the Canadian dollar, SKr 13.8 to the British pound sterling, SKr 9.4 to the euro, SKr 5.9 to the Australian dollar, SKr 5.5 to the New Zealand dollar, and SKr 1.2 to the South African rand.

CURRENCY EXCHANGE Traveler's checks and foreign currency can be exchanged at banks all over Sweden and at post offices displaying the NB EXCHANGE sign. Be sure to have your passport with you when exchanging money at a bank.

TAXES

VALUE-ADDED TAX All hotel, restaurant, and departure taxes and the value-added tax (V. A.T., called *moms* all over Scandinavia) are automatically included in prices. The V.A.T. is 25%; non-EU residents can obtain a 15% refund on goods of SKr 200 or more. To receive your refund at any of the 15,000 stores that participate in the tax-free program, you'll be asked to fill out a form and show your passport. The form can then be turned in at any airport or ferry customs desk. Keep all your receipts and tags; occasionally, customs authorities ask to see your purchases, so pack them where they will be accessible.

TELEPHONES
Post offices do not have telephone facilities, but there are plenty of pay phones. Long-distance calls can be made from special telegraph offices called Telebutik, marked TELE.

AREA & COUNTRY CODES
The country code for Sweden is 46. Swedish phone numbers vary in their number of digits. When dialing a Sweden number from abroad, drop the initial "0" from the local area code.

DIRECTORY & OPERATOR ASSISTANCE
Directory Assistance ☎ 118118, 118119 for international calls. **Operator Assistance** ☎ 90200, 0018 for international calls.

INTERNATIONAL CALLS
To make an international call, dial 00, followed by the country code and then your number.

LOCAL CALLS
A local call costs a minimum of SKr 2. For calls outside the locality, dial the area code (see telephone directory). Public phones are of three types: one takes SKr 1 and SKr 5 coins (newer public phones also accept SKr 10 coins); another takes only credit cards; and the last takes only the prepaid Telefonkort (telephone card).

PHONE CARDS
A Telefonkort, available at Telebutik, Pressbyrån (large blue-and-yellow newsstands), or hospitals, costs SKr 35, SKr 60, or SKr 100. If you're making numerous domestic calls, the card saves money. Many pay phones in downtown Stockholm and Göteborg take only these cards, so it's a good idea to carry one.

TIPPING
In addition to the 12% value-added tax, most hotels usually include a service charge of 15%; it is not necessary to tip unless you have received extra services. Similarly, a service charge of 13% is usually included in restaurant bills. It is a custom, however, to leave small change when buying drinks. Taxi drivers and hairdressers expect a tip of about 10%.

TRAIN TRAVEL
From London the British Rail European Travel Center can be helpful in arranging connections to Sweden's SJ (Statens Järnvägar, ⊕ www.sj. se), the state railway.

SJ has a highly efficient network of comfortable electric trains. On nearly all long-distance routes there are buffet cars and, on overnight trips, sleeping cars and couchettes in both first- and second class. Seat reservations are advisable, and on some trains—indicated with *R, IN,* or *IC* on the timetable—they are compulsory. An extra fee of SKr 15 is charged to reserve a seat on a trip of less than 150 km (93 mi); on longer trips there is no extra charge. Reservations can be made right up to departure time. The high-speed X2000 train has been introduced on several routes; the Stockholm–Göteborg run takes just under three hours. Travelers younger than 19 years travel at half fare. Up to two children younger than 12 years may travel free if accompanied by an adult.

CUTTING COSTS SJ cooperates with a number of local traffic systems, allowing you to buy one ticket, called a Tågplusbiljett, that works on trains, buses, and subways. Speak with the reservations people about what kind of combination you are interested in and where you'd like to travel. The Eurail and InterRail passes are both valid in Sweden. SJ also organizes reduced-cost package trips in conjunction with local tourist offices. Details are available at any railway station or from SJ.

🎵 Where to Buy Rail Passes **Rail Europe** ☎ 877/257-2887 in the U.S., 800/361-RAIL in Canada ⊕ www.raileurope.com ☎ 08708/371371 in the U.K. ⊕ www.raileurope.co. uk.

VISITOR INFORMATION

🎵 **Swedish Travel and Tourism Council** ✉ 5 Upper Montague St., London W1H2AG ☎ 020/71086168 in the U.K. 🖨 020/77245872 ✉ 655 3rd Ave., 18th fl. New York, NY 10017 ☎ 212/885-9700 🖨 212/885-9710 ✉ Box 3030, Kungsg. 36, 103 61 Stockholm ☎ 08/7255500 or 08/7891000 🖨 08/7891031.

Finland

4

Updated by
Joan Lofgren

If you like majestic open spaces, fine architecture, and the Nordic quality of life, Finland is for you. Nature dictates life in this Nordic land, where winter brings perpetual darkness, and summer, perpetual light. Crystal-clear streams run through vast forests lighted by the midnight sun, and reindeer roam free. Even the arts mimic nature: witness the music of Jean Sibelius, Finland's most famous son, which can swing from a somber nocturne of midwinter darkness to the tremolo of sunlight slanting through pine and birch, or from the crescendo of a blazing sunset to the pianissimo of the next day's dawn. The architecture of Alvar Aalto and the Saarinens—Eliel and son Eero, visible in many U.S. cities, also bespeaks the Finnish affinity with nature, with soaring spaces evocative of Finland's moss-floored forests. Eliel and his family moved to the United States in 1923 and became U.S. citizens—but it was to a lonely Finnish seashore that Saarinen had his ashes returned.

Until 1917, Finland was under the domination of its nearest neighbors, Sweden and Russia, who fought over it for centuries. After more than 600 years under the Swedish crown and 100 under the Russian czars, the country inevitably bears many traces of the two cultures, including a small (just under 6%) but influential Swedish-speaking population and a scattering of Orthodox churches.

The Finns themselves are neither Scandinavian nor Slavic. They are descended from wandering tribes who probably migrated from the south and southwest to settle on the swampy shores of the Gulf of Finland before the Christian era. The Finnish tongue belongs to the Finno-Ugric language group; it is related to Estonian and, very distantly, Hungarian.

There is a tough, resilient quality to the Finns. Finland is one of the very few countries that shared a border with the Soviet Union in 1939 and retained its independence. Indeed, no country fought the Soviets to a standstill as the Finns did in the grueling 105-day Winter War of 1939–40. This resilience stems from the turbulence of the country's past and from the people's determination to work the land and survive the long, dark winters. Finns are stubborn, patriotic, and self-sufficient, yet not aggressively nationalistic. On the contrary, rather than boasting of past battles, Finns are proud of finding ways to live in peace with their neighbors.

As evidenced by the role of Finnish leaders in international diplomacy and Finland's contributions to peacekeeping and humanitarian aid worldwide, the country's neutrality has provided the basis for its steadfast role in the international political landscape. It has not shied away from other alliances, however, and plays an active role in EU affairs, particularly promoting eastern enlargement.

The country's role as a crossroads between East and West is vibrantly reflected in Helsinki, from which it has become increasingly convenient to arrange brief tours to Tallinn (the capital of Estonia), and St. Petersburg, Russia. The architectural echoes of St. Petersburg in Helsinki are par-

Keep in mind that Finland is a large country, and though train service between towns is quite good, some trips can take an entire day. To make the most of your time, take advantage of Finnair's efficient domestic air service between Helsinki and destinations farther afield, such as Savonlinna and Rovaniemi.

If you have
2 days

You'll have plenty of time to take in all the sites of ▣ **Helsinki**, but not enough to venture outside the capital city area. Since Helsinki is fairly small and its major attractions are within walking distance of one another, in one day you can see the architectural highlights and at least one important museum. On the second day, you might take a harbor tour and visit the island fortress **Suomenlinna**, or take a side trip to **Espoo, Porvoo,** or **Vantaa,** or to the **Gallen-Kallela Estate** in Tarvaspää. The museum in the former studio home of the architects Saarinen, Gesellius, and Lindgren at **Hvitträsk** is another must.

4

If you have
5 days

After spending one or two nights in ▣ **Helsinki**, head to the destination of your choice: ▣ **Lapland,** the ▣ **Southwestern Coast and the Åland Islands,** or the ▣ **Lakelands.** Another option is to spend four nights in Helsinki, venturing out for easy, fun day trips to nearby towns: the cultural center **Turku**; **Tampere**, with its amusement park; and the castle town **Hämeenlinna** all take two hours or less by train.

If you have
10 days

Ten days allows the tireless traveler time to explore much of Finland. If your goal is to see all of the regions, one option is to spend your first night in ▣ **Helsinki**, then take a train to ▣ **Turku**, on the southwest coast, the following day. Using Turku as a base, take a side trip to see the fancy homes and beaches of **Hanko**, the historic wooden town of **Rauma**, or the medieval pilgrimage village, **Naantali**. From Turku you can fly to ▣ **Rovaniemi**, the gateway to Finnish Lapland. From Rovaniemi, go as deep into the Lapland wilderness as you desire. Take a train or a plane back down south to ▣ **Savonlinna** in eastern Finland, home of Finland's greatest castle. Take a scenic boat ride through the heart of Finland from Savonlinna to ▣ **Kuopio**, site of the Ortodoksinen Kirkkomuseo (Orthodox Church Museum) and within reach of Uusi Valamo (the New Valamo Monastery). From Kuopio, you can fly back to Helsinki.

---

ticularly striking in the "white night" light of June. Tallinn, with its medieval Old Town and bargain shopping, is a popular trip that can be done in a day. Traveling there takes an hour and a half by hydrofoil, three and a half by ferry.

"The strength of a small nation lies in its culture," noted Finland's leading 19th-century statesman and philosopher, Johan Vilhelm Snellman. As though inspired by this thought, Finns—who are among the world's top readers—continue to nurture a rich cultural climate, as is illustrated by its 900 museums and the festivals throughout Finland that continue to attract the top performers, in jazz (Pori), big bands

(Imatra), opera (Savonlinna), folk music (Kaustinen), and rock (Ruis-rock in Turku).

The average Finn volunteers little information, but that's a result of re-serve, not indifference. Make the first approach and you may have a friend for life. Finns like their silent spaces, though, and won't appre-ciate backslapping familiarity—least of all in the sauna, still regarded by many as a spiritual as well as a cleansing experience.

Exploring Finland

Finland's capital, Helsinki, commands the southern coast and shelters more than one-tenth of the country's population. Towns were first set-tled in the southwest, where the culture of the South Coast and the Åland Islands has a decidedly Swedish influence. Northern Finland— Finnish Lapland—straddles the Arctic Circle and is populated by few. Finland's central region is dominated by the Lakelands, the country's vacation belt.

Numbers in the text correspond to numbers in the margin and on the maps.

About the Restaurants

Finnish food emphasizes freshness rather than variety, although in keep-ing with larger European trends, restaurants are getting more and more innovative with their cooking, and expanding on classic Finnish ingre-dients—from forest, lake, and sea. If you get tired of fish or reindeer, then pizza, Tex-Mex, Chinese, and Thai food can also easily be found in larger cities. Jacket and tie are required in most restaurants in the $$$$ category. Alcohol is expensive here, but beer lovers should not miss the well-made Finnish brews.

That more coffee is consumed per capita in Finland than in any other country is evidenced by the staggering number of cafés and coffee bars throughout the country. Particularly in Helsinki, patrons of cafés down-town and around the waterfront spill outside onto the streets. In addi-tion to coffee, Finnish cafés serve a large selection of baked goods: *munkki* (doughnuts), *pulla* (sweet bread), and other confections are con-sumed with vigor by both young and old.

About the Hotels

Every class of lodging exists in Finland, from luxurious urban hotels to rustic cabins on lake shores and in the forest. Expect private baths in rooms unless otherwise noted. Prices almost always include a generous breakfast and sauna privileges.

The price categories below are based on weekday rates. Greater discounts are available on weekends and in summer months, especially between *Juhannus* (Midsummer, the summer solstice holiday in late June) and July 31, when prices are usually 30% to 50% lower.

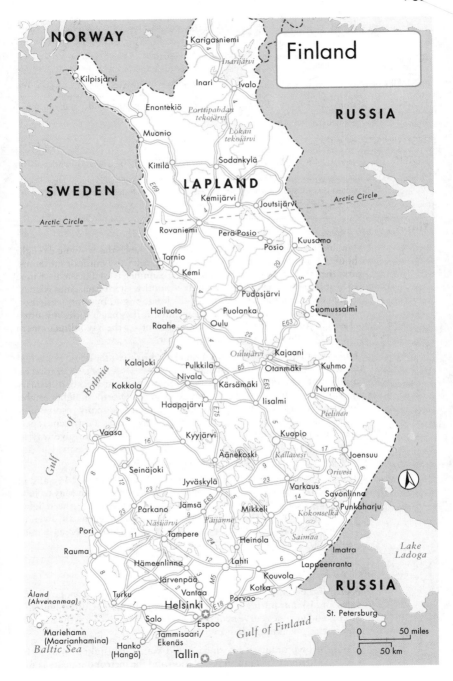

5

Finland

NORWAY

Kilpisjärvi

Karigasniemi

Inarijärvi

Inari   Ivalo

Enontekiö   *Porttipahdan tekojärvi*

RUSSIA

Muonio

Lokan tekojärvi

Kittilä   Sodankylä

SWEDEN

LAPLAND

Kemijärvi   Joutsijärvi

Arctic Circle

Arctic Circle

Rovaniemi   Perä-Posio

Posio   Kuusamo

Tornio

Kemi

Pudasjärvi

Hailuoto   Puolanka   Suomussalmi

Raahe   Oulu

Oulujärvi   Kajaani

Kalajoki   Pulkkila   Otanmäki   Kuhmo

Nivala   Kärsämäki

Kokkola   Nurmes

Haapajärvi   Iisalmi

Pielinen

Vaasa   Kyyjärvi   Kuopio

Äänekoski   *Kallavesi*   Joensuu

Seinäjoki   *Orivesi*

Jyväskylä   Varkaus

Parkano   Jämsä   Mikkeli   Savonlinna

Näsijärvi   *Päijänne*   Punkaharju

Pori   Tampere   *Kokonselkä*

Saimaa

Rauma   Heinola

Hämeenlinna   Lahti   Imatra   *Lake Ladoga*

Järvenpää   Lappeenranta

Vantaa   Kouvola

Åland (Ahvenanmaa)   Turku   Kotka   **RUSSIA**

Helsinki   Porvoo

Salo   Espoo   St. Petersburg

Mariehamn (Maarianhamina)   Tammisaari/ Ekenäs   *Gulf of Finland*   0   50 miles

Baltic Sea   Hanko (Hangö)   **Tallin**   0   50 km

Gulf   of   Bothnia

WHAT IT COSTS In Euros				
$$$$	$$$	$$	$	¢
Main Cities				
RESTAURANTS over €29	€23–€29	€17–€23	€10–€17	under €10
HOTELS over €240	€190–€240	€140–€190	€80–€140	under €80
Elsewhere				
RESTAURANTS over €22	€18–€22	€14–€18	€10–€14	under €10
HOTELS over €175	€140–€175	€105–€140	€70–€105	under €70

Restaurant prices are per person, for a main course at dinner, excluding tip. Hotel prices are for two people in a standard double room in high season, including service charge and taxes.

Timing

Finland's tourist season commences in June, when the growing daylight hours herald the opening of summer restaurants and outdoor museums, and the start of boat tours and cruises. Summer is by far the best time to visit Helsinki, the Lakelands, and the Southwestern Coast and Ålands, which come out of hibernation for the long, bright, but not overly hot, summer days. Take note that restaurants in the bigger cities are often closed in July. A special draw in the Lakelands is the Savonlinna Opera Festival, held in late July or early August.

Finland can also be exhilarating on clear, brisk winter days. For a real treat, visit Lapland—home of Santa Claus—in December. Operating on a different schedule altogether, the tourist season in the north focuses on winter events, when the snow is deep and the northern lights bright. Ski trips in Lapland in early spring are popular and many resorts offer tourist packages. Summer weather in Lapland offers a different repertoire to the traveler, when the snow and ice of the north give way to flowing rivers and greenery. The Midnight Sun Film Festival in Sodankylä offers round-the-clock screenings in tents.

You can expect warm (not hot) days in Helsinki from mid-May, and in Lapland from mid-June. The midnight sun can be seen from May to July, depending on the region. For a period in midwinter, the northern lights almost make up for the fact that the sun does not rise at all. Even in Helsinki, summer nights are brief and never really dark, whereas in midwinter daylight lasts only a few hours.

HELSINKI

A city of the sea, Helsinki was built along a series of odd-shape peninsulas and islands jutting into the Baltic coast along the Gulf of Finland. Streets and avenues curve around bays, bridges reach to nearby islands, and ferries ply among offshore islands.

Having grown dramatically since World War II, Helsinki now absorbs over one-tenth of the Finnish population and the metropolitan area covers a total of 764 square km (474 square mi) and 315 islands. Most sights, hotels, and restaurants cluster on one peninsula, forming a compact central hub. The greater Helsinki metropolitan area, which includes Espoo and Vantaa, has a total population of more than a million people.

Helsinki is a relatively young city compared with other European capitals. In the 16th century, King Gustav Vasa of Sweden decided to woo trade from the Estonian city of Tallinn and thus challenge the Hanseatic League's monopoly on Baltic trade. Accordingly, he commanded the people of four Finnish towns to pack up their belongings and relocate at the rapids on the River Vantaa. The new town, founded on June 12, 1550, was named Helsinki.

For three centuries, Helsinki (Helsingfors in Swedish) had its ups and downs as a trading town. Turku, to the west, remained Finland's capital and intellectual center. Ironically, Helsinki's fortunes improved when Finland fell under Russian rule as an autonomous grand duchy. Czar Alexander I wanted Finland's political center closer to Russia and, in 1812, selected Helsinki as the new capital. Shortly afterward, Turku suffered a disastrous fire, forcing the university to move to Helsinki. The town's future was secure.

Just before the czar's proclamation, a fire destroyed many of Helsinki's traditional wooden structures, precipitating the construction of new buildings suitable for a nation's capital. The German-born architect Carl Ludvig Engel was commissioned to rebuild the city, and as a result, Helsinki has some of the purest neoclassical architecture in the world. Add to this foundation the influence of Stockholm and St. Petersburg with the local inspiration of 20th-century Finnish design, and the result is a European capital city that is as architecturally eye-catching as it is distinct from other Scandinavian capitals. You are bound to discover endless delightful details—a grimacing gargoyle; a foursome of males supporting the weight of a balcony on their shoulders; a building painted in striking colors, with contrasting flowers in the windows. The city's 400 or so parks make it particularly inviting in summer.

Today, Helsinki is still a meeting point of eastern and western Europe, which is reflected in its cosmopolitan image, the influx of Russians and Estonians, and generally multilingual population. Outdoor summer bars ("terrassit" as the locals call them) and cafés in the city center are perfect for people-watching on a summer afternoon.

Exploring Helsinki

The city center is densely packed and easily explored on foot, the main tourist sites grouped in several clusters; nearby islands are easily accessible by ferry. Just west of Katajanokka, Senaatintori and its Tuomiokirkko mark the beginning of the city center, which extends westward along Aleksanterinkatu.

Museums & Markets

The orange tents of the Kauppatori market brighten even the coldest snowy winter months with fresh flowers, fish, crafts, and produce. In

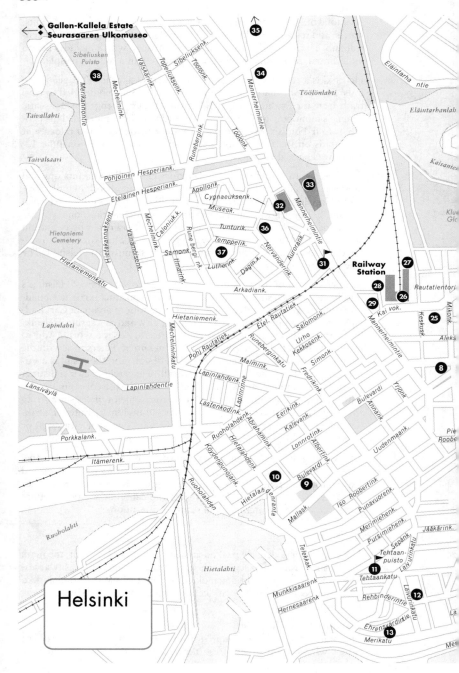

◆ **Gallen-Kallela Estate**
◆ **Seurasaaren Ulkomuseo**

Helsinki

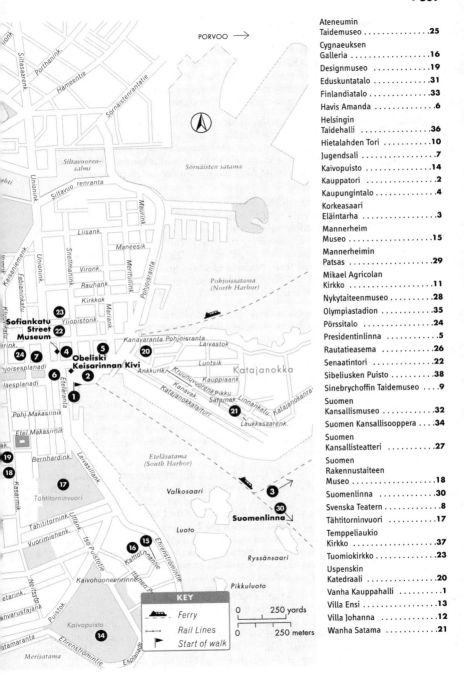

PORVOO →

KEY

🛳 *Ferry*

⊢——⊣ *Rail Lines*

▶ *Start of walk*

0   250 yards

0   250 meters

warm weather, the bazaar fills with shoppers and browsers who stop for the ubiquitous coffee and munkki, the seaborne traffic in Eteläsatama, or South Harbor, a backdrop. From here you can take the local ferry service to Suomenlinna (Finland's Castle), Korkeasaari (Korkea Island), home of the zoo, or take a walk through the neighborhoods of Helsinki, encompassing the harbor; city center shopping district; tree-lined Bulevardi; and the indoor Hietalahden Tori, another marketplace.

a good walk

Begin your walk at the indoor redbrick market hall, **Vanha Kauppahalli** ► ❶, along the South Harbor. From here you can see the orange tents of the outdoor market, the **Kauppatori** ❷. If you are with children and want to take a jaunt, Helsinki's zoo, **Korkeasaari Eläintarha** ❸, is accessible by metro or daily ferry from the South Harbor, just east of the market.

Helsinki's oldest public monument, the Obeliski Keisarinnan kivi, stands in Kauppatori along Pohjoisesplanadi. The series of beautiful old buildings along Pohjoisesplanadi includes the pale-blue **Kaupungintalo** ❹ and, at the easternmost end of the street, the well-guarded **Presidentinlinna** ❺. Walk back west along Pohjoisesplanadi and cross the street to the square with the **Havis Amanda** ❻ statue and fountain. You can stop at the City Tourist Office at Pohjoisesplanadi 19. To your left is the Esplanadi, a tree-lined boulevard park that starts at the harbor.

A few yards west of the City Tourist Office, you'll see the art nouveau **Jugendsali** ❼. After walking past the Arabian ceramics and the Marimekko clothing stores, you'll see the elephantine Gröngvistin Talo, or Grönqvist's block, on your right: designed by architect Theodor Höijer and built in 1883, this was Scandinavia's largest apartment building in its day. Continue west, and you will pass another ornate building, also by Grönqvist, which is the site of the luxurious Kämp Hotel, renowned in Scandinavia at the end of the 19th century and now beautifully restored. Before hitting Mannerheimintie, you'll pass Akateeminen Kirjakauppa and Stockmann's, respectively Finland's largest bookstore and department store. The bookstore was designed by Alvar Aalto, Finland's most famous architect.

At the intersection of Pohjoisesplanadi and Mannerheimintie, the distinctive round **Svenska Teatern** ❽ is sure to catch your eye. Turn left on Mannerheimintie, cross the street, and take a right onto tree-shaded Bulevardi, passing Vanha Kirkkopuisto, or Old Church Park, usually called Ruttopuisto, or Plague Park, for the 18th-century plague victims buried there. Continue southwest on Bulevardi until you reach the **Sinebrychoffin Taidemuseo** ❾, a former mansion surrounded by a beautiful park. The **Hietalahden Tori** ❿ is just across the street and slightly southeast of the museum, with an indoor food market and a flea market outside.

TIMING It will take about 45 minutes to walk this route from Kauppatori to Hietalahden Tori, stops not included. Head out early if you want to see both markets in action, as they close around 2 PM. In summer the Kauppatori by the South Harbor reopens at 3:30 PM, when the fruit and berry vendors do a brisk trade and local crafts stalls set up shop. Hours can vary, depending on the weather or on how busy the market is. The Sinebrychoffin Taidemuseo is closed on Monday. For a side trip to the zoo, the ferry to Korkeasaari Island takes less than a half hour, but allow time to wait for the ferry coming and going.

WHAT TO SEE

⑥ Havis Amanda. This fountain's brass centerpiece, a young woman perched on rocks surrounded by dolphins, was commissioned by the city fathers to embody Helsinki. Sculptor Ville Vallgren completed her in 1908 using a Parisian girl as his model. Partying university students annually crown the Havis Amanda with their white caps on the eve of Vappu, the May 1 holiday. ⊠ *Eteläespl. and Eteläranta, Keskusta/Kauppatori.*

⑩ Hietalahden Tori (Hietalahti Market). The brick market hall is crammed with vendors selling fish, flowers, produce, and meat. You can also find antiques, collectibles, and art. A simultaneous outdoor flea market has tables piled with the detritus of countless Helsinki attics and cellars. Shoppers can stop amid the action for coffee, doughnuts, and meat pies. This market is especially popular with Helsinki's Russian community. ⊠ *Bulevardi and Hietalahdenk., Hietalahti* ☉ *Regular market weekdays 6:30–2, Sat. 6:30–3; flea market weekdays 8–2, Sat. 8–3; market hall weekdays 10–5, weekends 10–3; summer evening flea market weekdays 3:30–8, Sun. 10–4.*

⑦ Jugendsali. Originally designed as a bank in 1906, this now serves as a cultural information office and a temporary exhibition hall for Finnish art. ⊠ *Pohjoisespl. 19, Keskusta* ☎ *09/169–2278* ☉ *Aug.–June, weekdays 9–5, Sun. 11–5; July, weekdays 9–4.*

② Kauppatori (Market Square). At this Helsinki institution, open year-round, wooden stands with orange and gold awnings bustle in the mornings when everyone—tourists and locals alike—comes to shop, browse, or sit and enjoy coffee and conversation. You can buy a freshly caught perch for the evening's dinner, a bouquet of bright flowers for a friend, or a fur pelt or hat. In summer the fruit and vegetable stalls are supplemented by an evening arts-and-crafts market. ⊠ *Eteläranta and Pohjoisespl., Keskusta/Kauppatori* ☉ *Sept.–May, weekdays 6:30–2, Sat. 6:30–3; June–Aug., weekdays 6:30–2 and 3:30–8, Sat. 6:30–3, Sun. 10–4; hrs can vary.*

④ Kaupungintalo (City Hall). The light blue building on Pohjoisesplanadi (North Esplanade), the political center of Finland, is the home of city government offices. ⊠ *Pohjoisespl. 11–13, Keskusta/Kauppatori* ☎ *09/169–2598* ☉ *Guided tours on Thurs. by appointment.*

③ Korkeasaari Eläintarha (Helsinki Zoo). Snow leopards and reindeer like the cold climate at one of the world's most northern zoos. Entirely within the limits of this small island, the winding paths make the zoo seem much larger than it actually is. Children love the outdoor play equipment. Between May and September the ferry departs approximately every 30 minutes from the Market Square and the cost of the ferry ticket (€8) includes entrance to the zoo. The trip takes 15 minutes; arrival and departure times are posted at the harbor. Alternatively, you can take the metro to the Kulosaari stop, cross under the tracks, and follow the signs for a 20-minute walk to the zoo. Bus connections are from Erottaja or Hertoniemi (weekends). ✉ *Korkeasaari (Korkea Island), Korkeasaari* ☎ *09/ 169–5969* ⊕ *www.korkeasaari.fi* 🎟 *€5* ⊙ *Mar. and Apr., daily 10–6; May–Sept., daily 10–8; Oct.–Feb., daily 10–4.*

Obeliski Keisarinnan kivi (Czarina's Stone). This obelisk with a double-headed golden eagle, the symbol of Imperial Russia, was erected in 1835, toppled during the Russian Revolution in 1917, and fully restored in 1972. ✉ *Kauppatori along Pohjoisespl., Keskusta/Kauppatori.*

❺ Presidentinlinna (President's Palace). The long history of this edifice mirrors the history of Finland itself: built between 1813 and 1820 as a private residence for a German businessman, it was redesigned in 1843 as a palace for the czars; then it served as the official residence of Finland's presidents from 1919 to 1993. Today it houses the offices of Finland's first female president, Tarja Halonen, and is the venue for official receptions. The best part of the house is said to be its hall of mirrors. It is closed to the public except for prearranged group tours organized by Helsinki Expert, the Helsinki Tourist Association, on Wednesday and Saturday from 11–4. ✉ *Pohjoisespl. 1, Keskusta/Kauppatori* ☎ *09/ 2288–1222.*

❾ Sinebrychoffin Taidemuseo (Sinebrychoff Museum of Foreign Art). The wealthy Russian Sinebrychoffs owned a brewing company and lived in this splendid yellow-and-white 1840 neo-Renaissance mansion filled with wildly opulent furniture. The family's home and foreign art collection are now a public museum; you'll find a staid collection of Dutch and Swedish 17th- and 18th-century portraits, a lively collection of landscapes, miniatures, and porcelain, and the mansion's original decorative furniture. Concerts are occasionally held in the museum's main salon. ✉ *Bulevardi 40, Hietalahti* ☎ *09/1733–6460* ⊕ *www.fng.fi* 🎟 *€7* ⊙ *Tues. and Fri. 10–6, Wed. and Thurs. 10–8, weekends 11–5.*

❽ Svenska Teatern (Swedish Theater). Dating from 1827, the first wooden theater on this site was considered too vulnerable to fire and was replaced by a stone building in 1866. Ironically, the stone building was itself nearly destroyed by a fire. In 1936, a team of architects—Eero Saarinen and Jarl Eklundhe among them—renovated it. The whitewashed round theater today displays an attractive shape and dignified simplicity of design. The Swedish Theater's own company performs plays in Swedish year-round. ✉ *Pohjoisespl. 2, Esplanadi/Erottaja* ☎ *09/ 6162–1411* ⊕ *www.svenskateatern.fi* ⊙ *Box office daily noon–performance time; closed May–Aug.*

> **need a break?**
>
> The **Café Aalto** (✉ Pohjoisespl. 39, Esplanadi ☎ 09/121–4446), on the Academic Bookstore's mezzanine, is pleasant for lunch or a snack. Choose one of the sandwiches, which usually include cold-smoked salmon, herring, tuna, mozzarella, and vegetarian options, or a fresh soup or salad, which change daily. It's a good place for a traditional afternoon *pulla* (Finnish sweet bread) and coffee.

▶ **❶ Vanha Kauppahalli** (Old Market Hall). From piles of colorful fish roe to marinated Greek olives, the old brick market hall on the waterfront is a treasury of delicacies. The vendors set up permanent stalls with decorative carved woodwork. ✉ *Eteläranta, along the South Harbor, Kauppatori* ⊙ *Weekdays 8–6, Sat. 8–4.*

Residential & Seaside Helsinki

Bordered by the sea, the south side of Helsinki is resplendent with elegant 20th-century residences and parks with winding paths. The waterfront Kaivopuisto leads into the upscale embassy neighborhood.

a good walk

Begin at the sharp-spired **Mikael Agricolan Kirkko** ▶ ⑪ in the small park, Tehtaanpuisto. Cross Tehtaankatu and walk south down Laivurinkatu past Eiran Sairaala, or Eira Hospital, with its witch-hat towers and triangular garret windows. Continue south on Laivurinkatu, passing the art nouveau **Villa Johanna** ⑫ on your left. An open view of the Baltic will be just ahead. At the end of the street, turn right on Merikatu. After passing the beautiful **Villa Ensi** ⑬, you'll arrive at the eternal flame of the Merenkulkijoiden Muistomerkki, or Seafarers' Torch, commissioned by the city as a tribute to Finnish sailors and a symbol of hope for their safe return.

Turn east to walk along Merisatamaranta, the seaside promenade. Out at sea is a handful of the thousands of islands that make up the **Gulf of Finland Archipelago.** Turn away from the water and walk south on Iso Puistotie to the shady **Kaivopuisto** ⑭ bordered by opulent estates and embassies; plan on spending half an hour wandering along its pleasant paths. From the park, follow the eastward loop of Kalliolinnantie through the embassy district to the **Mannerheim Museo** ⑮. On the same street is the tiny **Cygnaeuksen Galleria** ⑯. Follow Itäinen Puistotie north to Tehtaankatu 1, where you'll see the enormous fenced-in Russian Embassy complex; then walk up Ullankatu to the park **Tähtitorninvuori** ⑰. For those seriously interested in architecture, the **Suomen Rakennustaiteen Museo** ⑱ is just west of the observatory; follow any of the small streets that go west, and turn right on Kasarmikatu. Just north is the **Designmuseo** ⑲.

TIMING It takes a little more than one hour to walk this route, not counting time to relax in the parks and see art collections. Although the Seafarers' Torch is best seen at night, you might choose to make the walk during the day to take in the subtle beauty of the elegant residences in the area. Note some of the sites below are closed Monday and Tuesday; Monday to Thursday the Mannerheim Museo requires an appointment; the Mikael Agricolan Kirkko is usually open only during Sunday services.

WHAT TO SEE

⑯ **Cygnaeuksen Galleria** (Cygnaeus Gallery). This diminutive gallery, in a cottage with a tower overlooking the harbor, is the perfect setting for works by various Finnish painters, sculptors, and folk artists. This was once the summer home of Fredrik Cygnaeus (1807–81), a poet and historian who generously left his cottage and all the art inside to the Finnish public. ✉ *Kalliolinnantie 8, Kaivopuisto* ☎ *09/4050–9828* 💶 *€3* ⊙ *Wed. 11–7, Thurs.–Sun. 11–4.*

⑲ **Designmuseo** (Design Museum). The best of Finnish design can be seen here in displays of furnishings, jewelry, ceramics, and more. ✉ *Korkeavuorenk. 23, Keskusta* ☎ *09/622–0540* ⊕ *www.designmuseum.fi* 💶 *€7* ⊙ *Sept.–May, Tues. 11–8, Wed.–Sun. 11–6; June–Aug., daily 11–6.*

Gulf of Finland Archipelago. In winter Finns walk across the frozen sea with dogs and even baby buggies to the nearby islands. On the land side, the facades of the Eira and Kaivopuisto districts' grandest buildings form a parade of architectural splendor. One tradition that remains, even in this upscale neighborhood, is rug-washing in the sea—an incredibly arduous task. You may be astounded to see people leave their rugs to dry in the sea air without fear of theft. ⊠ *South of Merisatamaranta, Merisatama.*

⓮ **Kaivopuisto** (Well Park). This large, shady, path-filled park was once the site of a popular spa that drew people from St. Petersburg, Tallinn, and all of Scandinavia until its popularity faded during the Crimean War. All the spa structures were eventually destroyed (the main spa building was destroyed during WWII) except one, the **Kaivohuone,** now a popular bar-restaurant. Across from the entrance of Kaivohuone, take Kaivohuoneenrinne through the park past a grand Empire-style villa built by Albert Edelfelt, father of the famous Finnish painter who bore the same name. Built in 1839, it is the oldest preserved villa in the park. ⊠ *South of Puistok. on water, Kaivopuisto.*

⓯ **Mannerheim Museo** (Mannerheim Museum). Marshal Karl Gustaf Mannerheim (1867–1951) was a complex character sporting a varied résumé: he served as a high-level official in the Russian czar's guard, was a trained anthropologist who explored Asia, and is revered as a great general who fought for Finland's freedom and later became the country's president. The Mannerheim Museo is inside the great Finnish military leader's well-preserved family home and exhibits his letters and personal effects. European furniture, Asian art, and military medals and weaponry are on display. ⊠ *Kalliolinnantie 14, Kaivopuisto* ☎ *09/635–443* ⊕ *www.mannerheim-museo.fi* ⊠ *€7 includes guided tour* ☉ *Fri.–Sun. 11–4; Mon.–Thurs. by appointment.*

▶ ⓫ **Mikael Agricolan Kirkko** (Mikael Agricola Church). Built in 1935 by Lars Sonck, this church is named for the Finnish religious reformer considered to be the father of written Finnish. Mikael Agricola (circa 1510–57) wrote the first Finnish children's speller, the *Abckirja* (published around 1543), and translated the New Testament into Finnish (published in 1548). The church's sharp spire and tall brick steeple are visible amid **Tehtaanpuisto,** a small neighboring park. The inside of the church is quite bare, and no visitors are allowed except during Sunday services. ⊠ *Tehtaank. 23A, Eira* ☎ *09/709–2255* ☉ *Open only during Sun. services.*

⓲ **Suomen Rakennustaiteen Museo** (Museum of Finnish Architecture). Stop in to buy an architectural map of Helsinki that includes locations of several buildings by Alvar Aalto, the most famous being Finlandiatalo in Töölö. The permanent exhibits of this museum are far from comprehensive, and specialists will want to visit the extensive library and bookstore. ⊠ *Kasarmik. 24, Keskusta* ☎ *09/8567–5100* ⊕ *www.mfa.fi* ⊠ *€3.50* ☉ *Tues. and Thurs.–Sun. 10–4, Wed. 10–8.*

⓱ **Tähtitorninvuori** (Observatory Tower Hill). Named for the astronomical observatory within its borders, this park has sculptures, winding walkways, and a great view of the South Harbor. The observatory belongs to the astronomy department of Helsinki University and is closed to the public. ⊠ *West of Laivasillank. and South Harbor, Kaivopuisto.*

need a break? **Café Ursula** (⊠ Ehrenströmintie. 3, Kaivopuisto ☎ 09/652–817) by the sea, with views across to Suomenlinna, is a favorite among locals for coffee, ice cream, pastries, and light lunches that include soups and salads made with traditional Finnish ingredients. The lunch menu, which changes daily, includes fresh fish specialties, fish or root-vegetable soups, and a steak dish; the changing prix fixe menu often includes such delicacies as a cold-smoked fish buffet, elk, and forest-berry cheesecake.

⓭ **Villa Ensi.** This pale ocher art nouveau villa, now a private apartment building, was designed by Selim A. Lindqvist and named after his daughter, Ensi. The two bronze statues in front—*Au Revoir* and *La Joie de la Maternité* by J. Sören-Ring—date from 1910. ⊠ *Merik. 23, Kaivopuisto* ⊗ *Closed to the public.*

⓬ **Villa Johanna.** Although this stunning art nouveau villa (circa 1906) is now privately owned by a bank, which uses the villa for corporate dinners and events, it's still worth a visit for its facade. Look for the carved roaring serpent above the front door. ⊠ *Laivurink. 25, Eira* ⊗ *Closed to the public.*

Katajanokka & Senaatintori

Katajanokka is separated from the mainland by a canal and begins just east of Kauppatori. A charming residential quarter as well as a cargo- and passenger-ship port, this area also has one of the city's main landmarks, the dazzling Orthodox Uspenskin Katedraali, one of the biggest cathedrals in Europe. Not far from Katajanokka is the elegant Lutheran Cathedral that dominates Senaatintori. The Ateneumin Taidemuseo is also nearby.

a good walk The first sight on Katajanokka is the onion-dome **Uspenskin Katedraali** ⓴ on Kanavakatu. From the cathedral, walk down Kanavakatu, turn left on Ankkurikatu, and then right on Laukkasaarenkatu, where a sign will point out the **Wanha Satama** ㉑, a cleverly converted complex of brick warehouses now sheltering an exhibition center and restaurants. From there, head back southwest a short distance to the seafront and cross one of the two short bridges back over to Kauppatori.

From Kauppatori, walk along Sofiankatu (the Street Museum) and step through various periods of the city's history. The Kaupunginmuseo (Helsinki City Museum) is on the same street and has exhibits tracing Helsinki's growth from a rural village into the nation's capital. Nearby is **Senaatintori** ㉒. The north side of the square is dominated by the **Tuomiokirkko** ㉓; the Valtionneuvosto, or Council of State; and the main building of Helsingin Yliopisto, or Helsinki University, flank the east and west sides, respectively. The main university library is just north of the main building on Unioninkatu. At the south end of the square, old merchants' homes are currently occupied by stores, restaurants, and the Kiseleff Bazaar Hall.

Walk one block west to Fabianinkatu; just south is **Pörssitalo** ㉔, on the west side of the street. Head back north on Fabianinkatu 1½ blocks; then turn left on Yliopistonkatu. You'll run into the side of the **Ateneumin Taidemuseo** ㉕, one of the Finnish National Gallery museums; to enter the museum, turn right on Mikonkatu and then immediately left on Kaivokatu. Just west on Kaivokatu is the **Rautatieasema** ㉖, and on the north side of Rautatientori (Railway Square) is the **Suomen Kansallisteatteri** ㉗, which stages Finnish theater. Walk west around the train station and up Postikatu; just past the main post office you'll see the **Nykytaiteenmuseo** ㉘ on your right, a controversial backdrop to the **Mannerheimin Patsas** ㉙, standing sentinel over Mannerheimintie.

TIMING   Allow 45 minutes to an hour to walk this route. Be sure to check the opening hours of both cathedrals before you leave; both close on religious holidays, and the Uspenskin Katedraali is always closed Monday, and also Saturday off-season. The Pörssitalo closes weekends and the Ateneumin Taidemuseo closes Monday; plan accordingly.

WHAT TO SEE   **Ateneumin Taidemuseo** (Atheneum Art Museum of the Finnish National
★ ㉕   Gallery). The best traditional Finnish art is housed in this splendid neoclassical complex, one of three museums organized under the Finnish National Gallery umbrella. The gallery holds major European works, but the outstanding attraction is the Finnish art, particularly the works of Akseli Gallen-Kallela, inspired by the national epic *Kalevala*. The rustic portraits by Albert Edelfelt are enchanting, and many contemporary Finnish artists are well represented. The two other museums that make up the National Gallery are **Kiasma** and **Synebrychoff**. ✉ *Kaivok. 2–4, Keskusta* ☎ *09/ 1733–6401* ⊕ *www.fng.fi* ✍ *€5.50, additional charge for special exhibits* ⊘ *Tues. and Fri. 9–6, Wed. and Thurs. 9–8, weekends 11–5.*

㉙   **Mannerheimin Patsas** (Statue of Marshal Karl Gustaf Mannerheim). The equestrian gazes down Mannerheimintie, the major thoroughfare named in his honor. ✉ *Mannerheimintie, in front of the main post office and Museum of Contemporary Art, west of the station, Keskusta/Pääposti.*

> **off the beaten path**
>
> **LINNANMÄKI –** Helsinki's amusement park to the north of the city can be reached by Trams 3B and 3T from in front of the railway station. ✉ *Tivolikuja 1, Linnanmäki* ☎ *09/773–991* ⊕ *www. linnanmaki.fi* ✍ *Free entrance to the park, €4 for individual rides, day pass €26* ⊘ *May–late Aug., daily, hrs vary, call ahead or visit the Web site.*

★ ㉘   **Nykytaiteenmuseo (Kiasma)** (Museum of Contemporary Art). Praised for the boldness of its curved steel shell but condemned for its encroachment on the territory of the Mannerheim statue, this striking museum displays a wealth of Finnish and foreign art from the 1960s to the present. Look for the "butterfly" windows, and don't miss the view of Töölönlahti from the north side of the fifth floor gallery. ✉ *Mannerheiminaukio 2, Keskusta/Pääposti* ☎ *09/1733–6501* ⊕ *www.kiasma. fi* ✍ *€5.50* ⊘ *Tues. 9–5, Wed.–Sun. 10–8:30.*

24 **Pörssitalo** (Stock Exchange). Although the trading is fully automated, the beautiful interior of the Stock Exchange, with its bullet-shape chandeliers, is worth seeing. The Pörssitalo was designed by Lars Sonck and built in 1911. ⊠ *Fabianink. 14, Keskusta* ⊘ *Weekdays 8–5.*

26 **Rautatieasema** (train station). This outdoor square and the adjoining train station are the city's bustling commuter hub. The station's huge granite figures are by Emil Wikström; the solid building they adorn was designed by Eliel Saarinen, one of the founders of the early-20th-century National Romantic style. ⊠ *Kaivok., Rautatientori, Keskusta* ☎ *0600/41–902 for information in English (a €1 charge applies), 0307/23703 international fares* ⊕ *www.vr.fi.*

★ **22** **Senaatintori** (Senate Square). You've hit the heart of neoclassical Helsinki. The harmony of the three buildings flanking Senaatintori exemplifies one of the purest styles of European architecture, as envisioned and designed by German architect Carl Ludvig Engel. On the square's west side is one of the main buildings of **Helsingin Yliopisto** (Helsinki University), and up the hill is the university library. On the east side is the pale yellow **Valtionneuvosto** (Council of State), completed in 1822 and once the seat of the Autonomous Grand Duchy of Finland's Imperial Senate. At the lower end of the square, stores and restaurants now occupy former merchants' homes. ⊠ *Bounded by Aleksanterink. to the south and Yliopistonk. to the north, Senaatintori.*

27 **Suomen Kansallisteatteri** (National Theater). Productions in the three theaters inside are in Finnish. The elegant granite facade overlooking the railway station square is decorated with quirky relief typical of the Finnish National Romantic style. In front is a statue of writer Aleksis Kivi. ⊠ *North side of Rautatientori, Keskusta/Rautatieasema* ☎ *09/1733–1331* ⊕ *www.nationaltheatre.fi.*

23 **Tuomiokirkko** (Lutheran Cathedral of Finland). The steep steps and green domes of the church dominate Senaatintori. Completed in 1852, it is the work of famous architect Carl Ludvig Engel, who also designed parts of Tallinn and St. Petersburg. Wander through the tasteful blue-gray interior, with its white moldings and the statues of German reformers Martin Luther and Philipp Melancthon, as well as the famous Finnish bishop Mikael Agricola. Concerts are frequently held inside the church. The crypt at the rear is the site of frequent historic and architectural exhibitions and bazaars. ⊠ *Yliopistonk. 7, Senaatintori* ☎ *09/709–2455* ⊘ *June–Aug., Mon.–Sat. 9–midnight, Sun. noon (or when worship service ends)–midnight, other times Mon.–Sat. 9–6, Sun. noon (or when worship service ends)–6.*

need a break? **Café Engel** (⊠ Aleksanterink. 26, Senaatintori ☎ 09/652–776), named for the architect Carl Ludvig Engel, serves traditional lunch fare right on Senaatintori. Portions are hearty—you can fill up on a huge bowl of the tomato-basil soup or the cold smoked salmon sandwich; for a lighter snack, try a savory *karjalanpiiraka* (egg or potato pie) or one of the smaller open-faced cold-cut sandwiches. Locals stop in for coffee, wine and desserts, which include lingonberry cheesecake, fruit tarts, and an excellent Sacher torte.

★ ⓴ **Uspenskin Katedraali** (Uspenski Cathedral). Perched atop a small rocky cliff over the North Harbor in Katajanokka is the main cathedral of the Orthodox church in Finland. Its brilliant gold onion domes are its hallmark, but its imposing redbrick edifice, decorated by 19th-century Russian artists, is no less distinctive. The cathedral was built and dedicated in 1868 in the Byzantine-Slavonic style and remains the biggest Orthodox church in Scandinavia. *⊠ Kanavak. 1, Katajanokka* ☎ *09/634–267* ⊘ *May–Sept., Wed.–Fri. 9:30–4, Tues. 9:30–6, Sat. 9:30–3, Sun. noon–3; Oct.–Apr., Tues.–Fri. 9:30–4, Mon. and Sat. 9:30–3, Sun. noon–3; closed for weddings and other special events.*

need a break? On the north flank of Katajanokka, near the end of Katajanokan Pohjoisranta, you'll see the **Katajanokan Casino** (⊠ Laivastok. 1, Katajanokka ☎ 09/622–2722). It was built in 1911 as a warehouse, later became a naval officers' casino, and today is a seaside restaurant. Set on its own headland, the casino has a summer terrace from which you can gaze across the North Harbor to the Kruunuhaka district while sipping a cold beer.

⓴ **Wanha Satama** (Old Harbor). Despite its old-brick-warehouse appearance, this is actually a small shopping center with several food stores, restaurants, and cafés. There's even an exhibition hall in the left-hand (north) wing. The "W" in Wanha is pronounced "V." *⊠ Kanavak and Pikku Satamak, Katajanokka.*

Suomenlinna

ⓨ A former island fortress, **Suomenlinna** (Finland's Castle) is a perennially popular collection of museums, parks, and gardens, which has been designated a UNESCO World Heritage Site. In 1748 the Finnish army helped build the impregnable fortress, long referred to as the Gibraltar of the North; since then it has expanded into a series of interlinked islands. Although Suomenlinna has never been taken by assault, its occupants surrendered once to the Russians in 1808 and came under fire from British ships in 1855 during the Crimean War. Today Suomenlinna makes a lovely excursion from Helsinki, particularly in early summer when the island is engulfed in a mauve-and-purple mist of lilacs, introduced from Versailles by the Finnish architect Ehrensvärd.

Fodor's Choice ★

There are no street names on the island, so get a map for about €2 from the Helsinki City Tourist Office before you go, or buy one at the visitor center on the island. From June 1 to August 31, guided English-language tours leave daily at 11 AM and 2 PM from the **Suomenlinna Visitor Centre** (⊠ Suomenlinna ☎ 09/684–1880, 09/684–1850 tours ⊕ www. suomenlinna.fi); call to arrange tours at other times. The center, which is in the same building as the Suomenlinna Museum, is on the shore of Tykistölahti Bay, about 400 yards south of the main ferry terminal.

a good walk Suomenlinna is easily reached by public ferry (€2 one-way, €3.60 round-trip) or private boat (€3.50 one-way, €5.50 round-trip), both of which leave from Helsinki's Kauppatori. Although its fortification occupied six islands, its main attractions are now concentrated on three: Iso MustaSaari, Susisaari, and Kustaanmiekka. When you land at

Suomenlinna, go through the archway and proceed uphill to the **Suomenlinna Kirkko,** the local church-lighthouse. Walk south past the church and the pastel-color wooden homes toward Tykistölahti Bay. Here you'll find the Suomenlinna Visitor Centre and **Suomenlinna Museo.** Cross the bridge to Susisaari and visit **Ehrensvärd Museo,** a historical museum. Walk along the eastern coast of Susisaari until you reach the submarine *Vesikko.* From there, walk south and cross over to Kustaanmiekka, where you can visit the **Rannikkotykistömuseo** and learn everything you ever wanted to know about arms and artillery. Take the trail south of the museum to see the walls, ramparts, and cannons of Kustaanmeikka; then loop toward the eastern edge of the island to the historic King's Gate.

TIMING The ferry ride from South Harbor to Suomenlinna takes about 15 minutes. Plan to spend an afternoon on the islands; you'll need about four hours to explore the fortress and museums. Note that days open and hours of sites are limited off-season.

WHAT TO SEE **Ehrensvärd Museo** (Ehrensvärd Museum). Augustin Ehrensvärd directed the fortification of the islands of Suomenlinna from 1748 until 1772, the year of his death. This museum named for the military architect exhibits a model-ship collection and officers' quarters dating from the 18th century. Ehrensvärd's tomb is in the adjacent castle courtyard. ⊠ *Susisaari, Suomenlinna* ☎ *09/684–1850* 🖅 *€3* ☉ *Apr., weekends 11–4; early May–Aug., daily 10–5; Sept., daily 11–5; Oct., weekends 11–5.*

Rannikkotykistömuseo (Coastal Artillery Museum). Part of the Manege Military Museum, Rannikkotykistömuseo displays arms from World Wars I and II in a vaulted arsenal. Jump aboard the *Vesikko* **submarine** (☉ Early May–Aug., daily 11–4; Sept., daily 11–3), which was built in Turku in 1931–33 and served in World War II. ⊠ *Kustaanmiekka, Suomenlinna* ☎ *09/181–45295* 🖅 *€4 for museum, €4 for submarine, €6 for joint ticket to Manege Museum, Coastal Artillery Museum, and the* Vesikko ☉ *May–Aug., daily 10–6; Sept., daily 11–3.*

Suomenlinna Kirkko (Suomenlinna Church). This dual-function church-lighthouse was built in 1854 as an Orthodox church and has since become Lutheran. Call for opening hours and schedule of services. ☎ *09/ 709–2665.*

Suomenlinna Museo (Suomenlinna Museum). Open year-round and housed in the same building as the visitor center, the exhibits cover the building of the fortress and the fleet and early life on islands; the ticket price includes the *Suomenlinna Experience* multimedia show. ⊠ *Iso Mustasaari, Suomenlinna* ☎ *09/4050–9691* 🖅 *€5* ☉ *May–Aug., daily 10–6; Oct.–Apr., daily 10–4.*

Töölö

Most of Helsinki's major cultural buildings—the opera house, concert hall, and national museum—are within a short distance of each other around the perimeter of the inlet from the sea called Töölönlahti. The inlet itself is lovely in all seasons, and the walking and biking paths are well trodden by locals. The winding streets just east of Mannerheimintie enfold the Temppeliaukio Kirkko (Temple Square Church), whose unexceptional facade gives way to an amazing cavernous interior. Also nearby, the Sibelius park cuts a large swath out of the neighborhood and borders the sea.

Begin on Mannerheimintie by the equestrian statue of Gustaf Mannerheim, directly behind the main post office and next to the Museum of Contemporary Art (Kiasma). Walk northwest on Mannerheimintie, passing the red-granite **Eduskuntatalo** ▶ ③① on your way to the **Suomen Kansallismuseo** ③②, Finland's national museum, on the left. When you leave the museum, cross Mannerheimintie then follow the road a short distance north to the **Finlandiatalo** ③③, the Alvar Aalto–designed concert and congress hall. Behind the hall lies the inlet bay of Töölönlahti. If you walk along the well-used paths that follow the contour of the lake, you'll soon come to the **Suomen Kansallisooppera** ③④, Helsinki's opera house. From here, you can take the lengthy walk to the Seurasaaren Ulkomuseo.

From the opera house, walk southeast on Mannerheimintie until you see the white tower of the **Olympiastadion** ③⑤ on your left. Return to Mannerheimintie, crossing over to Cygnaeuksenkatu; take a left on Nervanderinkatu, where you'll reach the **Helsingin Taidehalli** ③⑥, with its fine collection of Finnish art. Go a few steps farther and take the small street directly across from the art hall to the modern **Temppeliaukio Kirkko** ③⑦, a church carved into rock outcrops. If you still have energy, cross Runeberginkatu and walk west on Simonkatu until you reach Mechelininkatu. Walk a ways north on Mechelininkatu, and **Sibeliusken Puisto** ③⑧ will appear on your left. Here you'll find the reason you came: the magnificent Sibelius-Monumentti.

TIMING   Allow 45 minutes to follow this tour as far as the Temppeliaukio Kirkko, adding half an hour for each museum if you decide to venture inside; from the church, it's a 20-minute walk to the Sibelius Puisto. Be sure to check the Temppeliaukio Kirkko's hours, which are slightly irregular. Note that the Suomen Kansallismuseo is closed Monday.

WHAT TO SEE   **Eduskuntatalo** (Parliament House). The imposing, colonnaded, Eduskun-
▶ ③①   tatalo stands near Mannerheim's statue on Mannerheimintie. The legislature has one of the world's highest proportions of women. ⊠ *Mannerheimintie 30, Keskusta* ☎ *09/432–2027* ⊕ *www.eduskunta.fi.*

③③ **Finlandiatalo** (Finlandia Hall). This white, winged concert hall was one of Alvar Aalto's last creations. It's especially impressive on foggy days or at night. If you can't make it to a concert here, try to take a guided tour. ⊠ *Karamzininkatu 4, Keskusta* ☎ *09/402–41* ⊕ *www.finlandia.* *hel.fi* ☉ *Symphony concerts usually held Wed. and Thurs. nights.*

③⑥ **Helsingin Taidehalli** (Helsinki Art Gallery). Here you'll see the best of contemporary Finnish art, including painting, sculpture, architecture, and industrial art and design. ⊠ *Nervanderink. 3, Keskusta* ☎ *09/454–2060* ▭ *€ 7, can vary for special exhibitions* ☉ *Tues., Thurs., and Fri. 11–6; Wed. 11–8; weekends noon–5.*

③⑤ **Olympiastadion** (Olympic Stadium). At this stadium built for the 1952 Games, take a lift to the top of the tower for sprawling city views. ⊠ *East* *of Mannerheim, Olympiastadion ⊕ www.stadion.fi ≊ €2 ⊙ weekdays 9–8, weekends 9–6.*

<table>
<tr><td>

off the beaten path

</td><td>

SEURASAAREN ULKOMESEO – On an island about 3 km (2 mi) northwest of city center, the Seurasaari Outdoor Museum was founded in 1909 to preserve rural Finnish architecture. The old farmhouses and barns that were brought to Seurasaari come from all over Finland. Many are rough-hewn log buildings dating from the 17th century, of primary inspiration to the late 19th-century architects of the national revivalist movement in Finland. All exhibits are marked by signposts along the trails; don't miss the church boat and the gabled church. Seurasaari Island is connected to land by a pedestrian bridge and is a restful place for walking throughout the year, with its forest trails and ocean views. You can walk there in about 40 minutes from the opera house; follow Mannerheimintie northeast, then turn left onto Linnankoskenkatu and follow signs along the coast. Alternatively, take Bus 24 from city center, in front of the Swedish Theater at the west end of Pohjoisesplanadi; its last stop is by the bridge to the island. Plan on spending at least three hours exploring and getting to the museum. ⊠ *Seurasaari* ☎ *09/ 4050–9660 in summer, 09/4050–9574 in winter* ⊕ *www.nba.fi* ≊ *€5. Guided tours in English available mid-June–mid-Aug., at 3, starting at ticket kiosk.* ⊙ *Mid-May–late May and early Sept.–mid-Sept., weekdays 9–3, weekends 11–5; June–Aug., Thurs.–Tues. 11–5, Wed. 11–7; closed mid-Sept.–mid-May.*

</td></tr>
</table>

㊳ Sibeliuksen Puisto. The **Sibelius-Monumentti** (Sibelius Monument) itself is worth the walk to this lakeside park. What could be a better tribute to Finland's great composer than this soaring silver sculpture of organ pipes? ⊠ *West of Mechelinin, Töölö.*

㉜ Suomen Kansallismuseo (National Museum of Finland). Architect Eliel Saarinen and his partners combined the language of Finnish medieval church architecture with elements of art nouveau to create this vintage example of the National Romantic style. The museum's collection of archaeological, cultural, and ethnological artifacts gives you an insight into Finland's past. ⊠ *Mannerheimintie 34, Keskusta* ☎ *09/40501* ⊕ *www.nba.fi* ≊ *€5.50* ⊙ *Tues. and Wed. 11–8, Thurs.–Sun. 11–6.*

㉞ Suomen Kansallisooppera (Finnish National Opera). Grand gilded operas, classical ballets, and booming concerts all take place in Helsinki's splendid opera house, a striking example of modern Scandinavian architecture. All events at the opera house draw crowds, so buy your tickets early. ⊠ *Helsinginkatu 58, Keskusta* ☎ *09/4030–2210 house tours, 09/ 4030–2211 box office* ⊕ *www.operafin.fi* ⊙ *Tues.–Fri. 10–5; house tours, in English, in summer Tues. and Thurs. at 3, also by appointment.*

★ **㊲ Temppeliaukio Kirkko** (Temple Square Church). Topped with a copper dome, the church looks like a half-buried spaceship from the outside. In truth, it's really a modern Lutheran church carved into the rock outcrops below. The sun shines in from above, illuminating the stunning interior with its birch pews, modern pipe organ, and cavernous walls.

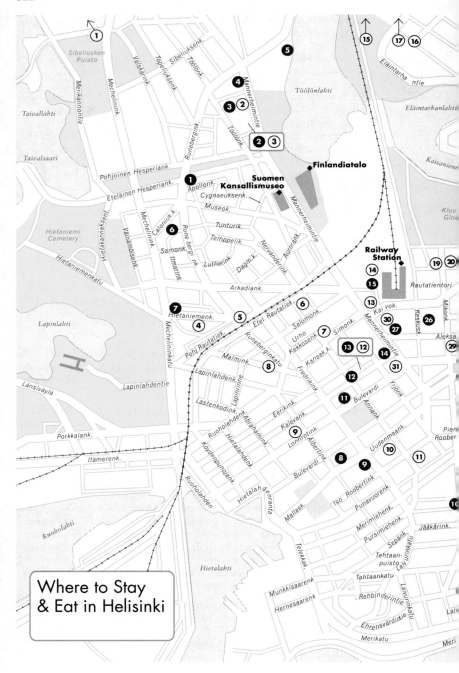

Where to Stay
& Eat in Helisinki

Restaurants ▼
Bellevue **19**
Bridges **16**
China **12**
Elite **1**
GW Sundmans **21**
Havis **20**
Kosmos **14**
Kuu **3**
Kynsilaukka **9**
Lyon **4**
Maxill **10**
Olivo **2**
Namaskaar and
Wok it **15**
Nokka **18**
Palace Gourmet **22**
Raffaello **25**
Ravintola Lautanen . . .**11**
Ravintola Perho **7**
Ravintola Torni **13**
Ristorante
Papá Giovanni **26**
Savoy **24**
Sipuli **17**
Töölönranta **5**
Troikka **6**
Villa Thai **8**
Zetor **27**
Zucchini **23**

Hotels ▼
Anna **11**
Arthur **25**
Aurora **16**
Comfort Hotel Pilotti . . .**17**
Crowne Plaza Helsinki . .**2**
Cumulus Airport **15**
Cumulus Olympia **24**
Cumulus Seurahuone . .**30**
Fenno **21**
Hilton Helsinki
Kalastajatorppa **1**
Hilton Helsinki Strand . .**18**
Holiday Inn Helsinki
City Centre **14**
Holiday Inn Helsinki,
Congress Center **22**
Hostel Academica **4**
Hotel Helka **5**
Hotel Kämp **29**
Marttahotelli **10**
Omapohja **19**
Palace **27**
Palace Hotel Linna **9**
Radisson SAS Plaza
Hotel Helsinki **20**
Radisson SAS Royal
Hotel Helsinki **8**

Rivoli Jardin **28**
Scandic Continental
Helsinki **3**
Scandic Gateway
Helsinki Airport **23**
Scandic Grand
Marina Helsinki **26**
Scandic Marski
Helsinki **31**
Scandic Simonkenttä
Helsinki **7**
Sokos Hotel Presidentti . .**6**
Sokos Hotel Torni **12**
Sokos Hotel Vaakuna . .**13**

Ecumenical and Lutheran services in various languages are held through-out the week. ⊠ *Lutherinkatu 3, Töölö* ☎ *09/494–698* ☉ *Weekdays 10–7:45, Sat. 10–6, Sun. noon–1:45 and 3:15–5:45; closed Tues. 1–2 and during weddings, concerts, and services.*

Where to Eat

Helsinki has some of Finland's best restaurants. Although Russian cui-sine is the star attraction, try to seek out Finnish specialties such as game—pheasant, reindeer, hare, and grouse—accompanied by wild-berry compotes and exotic mushroom sauces.

Most restaurants close on major national holidays—only a few hotel restaurants stay open for Christmas. Many of the more expensive es-tablishments close on weekends.

Around Kauppatori & Katajanokka

$$$$ ✕ **GW Sundmans.** This elegant restaurant by the harbor was formerly the home of Captain G. W. Sundman. The building was designed by C. L. Engel, architect of the historical center of Helsinki under Czar Alexan-der I. The grand main restaurant, with molded ceilings and chandeliers, serves modern international cuisine. Sundmans Krog on the ground floor has a nautical theme and vaulted ceilings, as well as an excellent herring buffet. ⊠ *Eteläranta 16, Kauppatori* ☎ *09/622–6410* ▤ *AE, DC, MC, V* ☉ *Closed Sun. No lunch Sat. and July.*

$$$$ ✕ **Palace Gourmet.** This outstanding hotel restaurant has a magnificent
Fodor'sChoice view of the South Harbor. Its specialties are French and Finnish fare,
★ including such creations as warm artichoke salad with smoked white-fish and basil sauce, and fillet of lamb with tarragon, tomatoes, and gar-lic sauce. Call ahead for the "Menu Surprise," a seven-course meal that changes daily. ⊠ *Palace Hotel, Eteläranta 10, Kauppatori* ☎ *09/ 1345–6715* ▤ *AE, DC, MC, V* ☉ *Closed weekends and July.*

$$$$ ✕ **Savoy.** With its airy, Alvar Aalto–designed, functionalist dining room
Fodor'sChoice overlooking the Esplanade Gardens, the Savoy is a frequent choice for
★ business lunches and was also Finnish statesman Marshal Karl Gustaf Mannerheim's favorite; he is rumored to have introduced the *vorschmack* (minced lamb and anchovies) recipe. Savoy's menu includes the ubiq-uitous reindeer fillet and a changing menu of inventive fresh fish dishes like fried whitefish with new potatoes, smoked salmon roe, and vermouth sauce. ⊠ *Eteläespl. 14, Esplanadi* ☎ *09/684–4020* ☉ *Closed weekends.*

$$$–$$$$ ✕ **Havis.** Across the street from the Market Square and the South Har-
Fodor'sChoice bor, this restaurant specializes in traditional Scandinavian fish dishes with
★ contemporary twists. Begin with the savory blue-mussel soup, and move on to specialties like the slow-fried *lavaret* (whitefish). Vegetarians will appreciate the mushroom crepes with glazed vegetables and the daily vegetarian special. The dessert menu includes old-time Finnish standards like strawberry milk and doughnuts with coffee pudding. ⊠ *Eteläran-tatie 16, Kauppatori* ☎ *09/6869–5660* ▤ *AE, DC, MC, V* ☉ *Closed Sun. mid-Sept.–Apr.*

$$$–$$$$ ✕ **Sipuli.** Sipuli stands at the foot of the Russian Orthodox Uspenski Cathe-dral and gets its name—meaning onion—from the church's golden

FINNISH CUISINE

THE BETTER FINNISH RESTAURANTS *offer some of the country's most stunning game—pheasant, reindeer, hare, and grouse—accompanied by wild-berry compotes and exotic mushroom sauces. The chanterelle grows wild in Finland, as do dozens of other edible mushrooms, the tasty morel among them. Fish wears many hats in Finland, and is especially savored smoked. Come July 21, crayfish season kicks in.*

Other specialties are poronkäristys (sautéed reindeer), lihapullat (meatballs in sauce), uunijuusto (light, crispy baked cheese), and hiilillä paistetut silakat (charcoal-grilled Baltic herring). Seisova pöytä, the Finnish version of the smorgasbord, is a cold and hot buffet available at breakfast, lunch, or dinner, and is particularly popular on cruise ships. To stretch a tight travel budget, eat a hearty breakfast in your hotel (always

included in the price unless stated otherwise) and grab a snack for lunch.

Local yogurt and dairy products are extremely good and ice cream is popular; an increasing number of places sell low-fat flavors or frozen yogurts, although the fat-free craze hasn't completely taken over. Finnish desserts and baked goods are renowned. Mämmi, a dessert made of wheat flour, malt, and orange zest and served with cream and sugar, is a treat during Easter. More filling are karjalan piirakka, thin, oval rye-bread pirogi filled with rice or mashed potatoes and served warm with munavoi, a mixture of egg and butter.

---

onionlike cupolas. The restaurant is in a 19th-century warehouse building, with redbrick walls and dark-wood panels, and a skylight with a spectacular view of the cathedral. Classic French-Finnish combinations may include fennel soup with forest mushroom ravioli, smoked fillet of pike perch with salmon mousse, and roasted fillet of veal with port sauce. ✉ *Kanavaranta 3, Katajanokka* ☎ *09/622–9280* ▤ *AE, DC, MC, V* ☉ *Closed weekends, except for group dinners, and July.*

$$–$$$ ✕ **Bellevue.** The spare lines of Bellevue belie its real age—it's been around since 1917, serving dishes inspired by Russian and Finnish cuisine. Try the *shashlik* (cubed lamb kebab served with mushroom rice) or the ox fillet à la Novgorod. The plush interior of this elegant town house has many shining samovars, but only some of them are functional; each table has lighted candles. ✉ *Rahapajank. 3, Keskusta* ☎ *09/179–560* ▤ *AE, DC, MC, V* ☉ *Closed weekends in July. No lunch weekends.*

$$–$$$ ✕ **Nokka.** In a historical building on the Katanajanokka quay and downstairs from the Helsinki Culinary Institute, this innovative restaurant specializes in seasonal fare with fresh Finnish ingredients. Try the rose-fried snow grouse from Lapland, or the fried perch fillet. ✉ *Kanavaranta 7, Katajanokka* ☎ *09/687–7330* ▤ *AE, DC, MC, V* ☉ *Closed Sun. No lunch Sat. and July and Aug.*

$-$$ ✕ **Raffaello.** In the heart of Helsinki's financial district, this cozy Italian restaurant with redbrick walls, parquet floors, and decorative frescoes has a reputation for friendly service, reasonable prices, and tasty pasta, salad, and meat dishes. Try the steak gratinated wth Gorgonzola, basil potatoes, ratatouille, and red wine sauce, or the grilled breast of pheasant with pesto duchesse potatoes. ⊠ *Aleksanterink. 46, Keskusta* ☎ *09/8568–5730* ⊟ *AE, DC, MC, V.*

$-$$ ✕ **Ristorante Papá Giovanni.** Don't let the whimsical interior with Venetian gondolas fool you. This cozy restaurant serves up sophisticated Italian fare, such as fillet of beef with garlic stewed potatoes, croutons, and Parmesan, or grilled tuna with mint sauce and lemon risotto. Wine suggestions are included on the menu and the service is excellent. ⊠ *Keskuskatu 7, Keskusta* ☎ *09/622–6010* ⊟ *AE, DC, MC, V.*

¢–$$ ✕ **Zetor.** Known as the tractor restaurant, Zetor is a haven for the weary traveler in need of some homey high-cholesterol cooking—choose from meatballs, Karelian stew, sausage, or schnitzel, washed down with the house brew. Wooden tables, farm equipment, and a witty menu make for an entertaining evening. Late nights the restaurant transforms into a hipster bar and rock club. ⊠ *Kaivopiha, Mannerheimintie 3–5 Keskusta/Kaivopiha* ☎ *09/666–966* ⊟ *AE, DC, MC, V* ☉ *No lunch Sun.–Fri.*

¢–$ ✕ **Namaskaar and Wok it.** Try generous portions of Thai, Indian, and Japanese food served in simple and elegant surroundings at this Nordic-Asian dining room. The grilled duck with espresso-Szechuan pepper sauce and the charcoal-roasted salmon with black-mustard-seed gravy are unusual and delicious. Seats on the balcony overlook the modern atrium of the Sanomatalo building and Töölönlahti Bay. ⊠ *Sanomatalo, Postikuja 2, Rautatieasema* ☎ *09/6812–1450* ⊟ *AE, DC, MC, V* ☉ *Closed Sun.*

West of Mannerheimintie

$-$$$ ✕ **Ravintola Torni.** A 1930s functional design interior provides the backdrop to the innovative contemporary cooking at this establishment, the
Fodor'sChoice main restaurant of the central Sokos Hotel Torni. Interesting combinations on the menu include smoked char with sea buckthorn berry sauce, breast of snow grouse with morel sauce, and chocolate terrine with kumquat cake. ⊠ *Hotel Torni, Kalevank. 5, Keskusta* ☎ *09/1311–3448* ⊟ *AE, DC, MC, V* ☉ *Closed Sun. and July.*

¢–$$$ ✕ **Ravintola Lautanen.** This sleek and popular restaurant offers an Asian-inspired take on Finnish dishes. For dinner, try the tandoor-marinated salmon with crayfish sauce, the tomato–goat cheese tagliatelle, or the beef fillet in a wasabi-béarnaise sauce; there's also sushi. The changing lunch menu is more traditional—on it you'll find classics like creamy salmon or cheese soup, oven sausage with potatoes, and meat casserole. ⊠ *Lönnrötinkatu13, Keskusta* ☎ *09/680–3780* ⊟ *AE, DC, MC, V* ☉ *Closed Sun. Closed weekends and nights in July.*

$-$$ ✕ **Kosmos.** Just a short walk from Stockmann's department store, this
Fodor'sChoice cozy restaurant has become a lunchtime favorite among businesspeople working nearby. Come evening, it's given over to artists and journalists. Its high ceilings and understated interior give it a Scandinavian air of simplicity and efficiency. Menu highlights include reindeer fillet

in a sauce of spruce shoots and rosemary served with roasted potatoes and vorschmack with duchesse potatoes, pickles, and beets. ⊠ *Kalevank. 3, Keskusta* ☎ *09/647–255* ▭ *AE, DC, MC, V* ⊗ *Closed Sun. and in July. No lunch Sat.*

$–$$ ✕ **Maxill.** Helsinki's café boom and an increasing demand for Continental-style bars have inspired this hybrid on a lively street just south of the city center. The trendy menu includes salad with goat-cheese croutons. ⊠ *Korkeavuorenk. 4, Keskusta* ☎ *09/638–873* ▭ *AE, DC, MC, V.*

$–$$ ✕ **Villa Thai.** Near Helsinki's shopping district, this restaurant has authentic Thai food served in traditional surroundings. The prawn curry with coconut milk and pineapple is a house specialty, as is the roast duck breast "Villa Thai." Finish with homemade coconut, banana, or mango ice cream. ⊠ *Bulevardi 28, Bulevardi* ☎ *09/680–2778, 040/828–4456 reservations* ▭ *AE, DC, MC, V* ⊗ *Closed Sun.*

¢–$$ ✕ **Kynsilaukka.** This cozy yet sophisticated restaurant appeals to the senses
Fodor'sChoice with fresh, beautifully prepared food. It's also a garlic lover's dream.
★ Stellar dishes include the garlic cream soup and bouillabaise; for dessert try the classic crepes with cloudberry sauce. A reasonably priced lunch menu and the fact it's open on holidays help make it a local favorite. All portions are served in two sizes. ⊠ *Fredrikink. 22, Keskusta* ☎ *09/ 651–939* ▭ *AE, DC, MC, V.*

$ ✕ **China.** One of the city's oldest Chinese restaurants, this place specializes in Cantonese fare. Apart from beef, pork, and chicken dishes, there's an unusual pike perch with sweet-and-sour sauce. The Peking duck is a specialty, and must be ordered two days in advance. ⊠ *Annank. 25, Keskusta* ☎ *09/640–258* ▭ *AE, DC, MC, V.*

¢–$ ✕ **Ravintola Perho.** Helsinki's catering school operates this brasserie-style restaurant decorated in pine. The emphasis is on Finnish food, particularly salmon and reindeer. Its reasonable prices, central location (just west of Mannherheimintie), and own microbrew make it a favorite. ⊠ *Mechelinkatu 7, Töölö* ☎ *09/5807–8649* ▭ *AE, DC, MC, V* ⊗ *Closed weekends June-mid Aug.*

¢ ✕ **Zucchini.** For a vegetarian lunch or just coffee and dessert, Zucchini is a cozy hideaway with quiet music, magazines, and a few sidewalk tables. Pizzas, soups, and salads are all tasty here. ⊠ *Fabianinkatu 4, Keskusta* ☎ *09/622–2907* ▭ *DC, MC, V* ⊗ *Closed weekends. No dinner.*

North of City Center

$–$$ ✕ **Bridges.** This atrium restaurant in the Hilton Helsinki Strand serves
Fodor'sChoice steak, burgers and pasta alongside Finnish classics like slightly smoked
★ arctic char in a black-currant butter sauce. ⊠ *John Stenbergin Ranta 4, Hakaniemi* ☎ *09/39351* ▭ *AE, DC, MC, V.*

Keskusta & Töölö

$$$–$$$$ ✕ **Lyon.** As you might expect from its name, French cuisine is the specialty in this eatery across Mannerheimintie from the opera. Lyon is small and unpretentious but consistent in high quality and service. The menu changes yearly and can include Finnish ingredients like *lavaret* (whitefish), dill potatoes, and arctic char prepared with French-inspired hollandaise, truffle, and oyster sauces. ⊠ *Mannerheim. 56, Töölö* ☎ *09/ 408–131* ▭ *AE, DC, MC, V* ⊗ *Closed Sun. and July. No lunch.*

★ **$–$$$** ✕ **Elite.** A short distance from the town center, but a welcome oasis after excursions to the Temppeliaukio Kirkko and the Sibelius monument, Elite's simple art deco interior and spacious layout are popular with artists and writers. Traditional Finnish dishes to sample are fried Baltic herring, salmon soup with rye bread, and select game. If you want more contemporary dishes, try the smoked salmon with morel sauce, or the reindeer pastrami with celery puree and walnut vinaigrette. The outdoor seating in summer is very popular. ✉ *Etelä Hesperiank. 22, Töölö* 🕾 *09/434–2200* 🖃 *AE, DC, MC.*

$–$$$ ✕ **Olivo.** This trendy restaurant in the Scandic Hotel Continental Helsinki serves creative French-Mediterranean dishes, including tuna fillet, chateaubriand, and beef Gorgonzola; for dessert, try the pistachio gelato. ✉ *Mannerheim. 46, Scandic Hotel Continental Helsinki, Töölö* 🕾 *09/4737–2207* 🖃 *AE, DC, MC, V* ☉ *Closed Sun. No lunch Sat.*

★ **$–$$$** ✕ **Troikka.** The Troikka takes you back to czarist times with its samovars, icons, and portraits of Russian writers—as well as the exceptionally good Russian food and friendly service. Try the *zakusky,* an assortment of Russian appetizers including such delicacies as Baltic herring, homemade poultry pâté, wild mushrooms, and marinated garlic. ✉ *Caloniuksenk. 3, Keskusta* 🕾 *09/445–229* 🖃 *AE, DC, MC, V* ☉ *Closed Sun. and July No lunch.*

$–$$ ✕ **Töölönranta.** The upscale Töölönranta packs in plenty of operagoers,
FodorśChoice since it's right behind the National Opera House overlooking the bay.
★ An innovative water-cooled wok on display in the wide-open kitchen turns out stir-fried specials. Other favorites include arctic char, wild duck, and game dishes. In summer, when the patio catches the evening sun, this is a superb place to savor a beer. ✉ *Helsinginkatu 56, Töölö* 🕾 *09/454–2100* 🖃 *AE, MC, V.*

$ ✕ **Kuu.** If you thrive on getting to the true character of a city and enjoy local color, try looking in simple, friendly restaurants such as Kuu, literally Moon. The menu combines Finnish specialties such as Baltic herring, salmon, and reindeer with imaginative international fare. It's especially convenient for nights at the opera, and the delightful terrace is open in summer. ✉ *Töölönk. 27, Töölö* 🕾 *09/2709–0973* 🖃 *AE, DC, MC, V.*

Where to Stay

Helsinki's top hotels are notoriously expensive, generally have small rooms, and mostly cater to the business traveler. Standards are high, and the level of service usually corresponds to the price. Rates are almost always less expensive on weekends, and most include a generous breakfast and sauna privileges.

City Center

$$$$ 🖳 **Sokos Hotel Vaakuna.** The quirky 1950s architecture and interior design of the Vaakuna dates back to the 1952 Helsinki Olympics. Rooms are spacious, with simple but stylish furnishings. The rooftop terrace restaurants are favorite haunts of members of parliament. The hotel is above the Sokos department store, opposite the train station. ✉ *Asemaaukio 2, Rautatieasema 00100* 🕾 *020/1234–610* 🖴 *09/4337–7100*

⊕ *www.sokoshotels.fi* ✈ *270 rooms, 12 suites* ♨ *2 restaurants, 3 saunas, meeting room, no-smoking rooms* ▤ *AE, DC, MC, V.*

$$$–$$$$ 🔲 **Cumulus Seurahuone.** Built in 1914, this Viennese-style town-house hotel across from the train station has a loyal clientele won over by its ageless charm and cosmopolitan interiors. A patina of well-worn elegance pervades all areas, from the grand main stairway and the chandeliered art nouveau café to the ornate, skylighted pub. Rooms come in many styles, from traditionally furnished ones with brass beds and high ceilings in the old section, to the newer ones with a sleek, modern design. ⊠ *Kaivokatu 12, Rautatieasema 00100* 🕾 *09/69141* 🖷 *09/691–4010* ⊕ *www.cumulus. fi* ✈ *113 rooms, 5 suites* ♨ *Restaurant, room service, minibars, bar, pub, laundry service, no-smoking rooms* ▤ *AE, DC, MC, V.*

$$ 🔲 **Holiday Inn Helsinki City Centre.** Some of the comfortable rooms in this central hotel overlook Töölönlahti, and the sleek lobby is decked out in bright colors. It's popular with business travelers. ⊠ *Elielinaukio 5, Keskusta 00100* 🕾 *09/5425–5000* 🖷 *09/5425–5299* ⊕ *www.hi-helsinkicity. com* ✈ *174 rooms, 12 executive rooms* ♨ *Restaurant, room service, minibars, cable TV, in-room data ports, gym, 2 saunas, bar, laundry service, business services, no-smoking rooms* ▤ *AE, DC, MC, V.*

¢ 🔲 **Omapohja.** Dating from 1906, this inn, which occupies a mint-green Jugendstil building, used to be a base for actors performing at the state theater next door. The rooms, named after Finnish actors, are cozily old-fashioned, with wood-paneled walls and handwoven bedspreads; they also have tremendous windows. Extra beds cost only €20, making it a good buy for families or small groups. ⊠ *Itäinen Teatterikuja 3, Rautatieasema 00100* 🕾 *09/666–211* 🖷 *09/6228–0053* ✈ *15 rooms, 4 with shower* ▤ *MC, V.*

Around Kauppatori & Katajanokka

$$$$ 🔲 **Palace.** Built for the 1952 Olympic games, this clublike hotel is on the 9th and 10th floors of a waterfront commercial building with splendid views of the South Harbor. Its faithful clientele—largely British, Swedish, and American—appreciates the personal service, such as daily afternoon tea, that comes with its small size. The hotel's restaurants, especially the Palace Gourmet, are among Helsinki's best. ⊠ *Eteläranta 10, Kauppatori 00130* 🕾 *09/1345–6656* 🖷 *09/654–786* ⊕ *www.palacehotel.fi* ✈ *37 rooms, 2 suites* ♨ *2 restaurants, café, room service, minibars, sauna, bar, business services, meeting rooms* ▤ *AE, DC, MC, V.*

$$$ 🔲 **Rivoli Jardin.** This high-class town house is tucked into the heart of
Fodor'sChoice Helsinki's shopping and business center. All rooms face the inner court-
★ yard, and are free of traffic noise. They have simple yet elegant furnishings. ⊠ *Kasarmikatu 40, Keskusta 00130* 🕾 *09/681–500* 🖷 *09/656–988* ⊕ *www.rivoli.fi* ✈ *54 rooms, 1 suite* ♨ *Minibars, in-room broadband, sauna, bar, business services, no-smoking rooms* ▤ *AE, DC, MC, V.*

$$$ 🔲 **Scandic Grand Marina Helsinki.** Housed inside an early-19th-century customs warehouse in the posh Katajanokka island neighborhood, the Grand Marina has one of the best convention centers in Finland. Its good location, friendly service, ample modern facilities, and reasonable prices have made this hotel a favorite. Ask for a room with a view of South Harbor. ⊠ *Katajanokanlaituri 7, Katajanokka 00160* 🕾 *09/16661*

🕿 09/664–764 ⊕ *www.scandic-hotels.com* ⤢ *442 rooms, 20 suites* ⚸ *Restaurant, minibars, gym, sauna, 2 bars, business services, meeting rooms, no-smoking rooms* ⊟ *AE, DC, MC, V.*

Near Mannerheimintie

$$$$ 🏨 **Hotel Kämp.** Opposite the Esplanade Park stands this splendid, luxurious, late-19th-century cultural landmark. In the past the hotel was the site of a theater and was the meeting point for Finland's most prominent politicians, artists, and celebrities, including Mannerheim, Saarinen, Gallen-Kallela, and former president Paasikivi, who became one of the hotel owners. Sibelius himself often visited the hotel and dedicated a song to it. Take the beautiful, sweeping staircase up to the grand ballroom, known as the mirror room. ✉ *Pohjoisesplanadi 29, Keskusta 00100* 🕿 *09/ 576–1111* 🖷 *09/576–1122* ⊕ *www.hotelkamp.fi or www.luxurycollection. com* ⤢ *164 rooms, 15 suites* ⚸ *2 restaurants, room service, in-room data ports, health club, sauna, bar, wine bar, laundry service, concierge, business services, parking (fee), no-smoking rooms* ⊟ *AE, DC, MC, V.*

$$$$ 🏨 **Radisson SAS Plaza Hotel Helsinki.** This Renaissance-style former of-
Fodor'sChoice fice building in the heart of the city has been adapted into a first-class
★ hotel by renowned Finnish architects Ilmo Valjakka and Pervin Imaditdin. Rooms and suites come in three styles: Nordic, with light wood furnishings; classic, with darker wood furnishings; and Italian, with sunny bright colors and bold designs. The courtyardlike main restaurant, the Pääkonttori (headquarters), is brightened by a large skylight. The sophisticated Lasibaari bar has beautiful stained-glass windows. Rates drop considerably on weekends. ✉ *Mikonkatu 23, Keskusta 00100* 🕿 *09/ 77590* 🖷 *09/7759–7100* ⊕ *www.radissonsas.com* ⤢ *195 rooms, 6 suites* ⚸ *2 restaurants, in-room data ports, Wi-Fi, 4 saunas, 2 bars, nightclub, business services, meeting room* ⊟ *AE, DC, MC, V.*

$$$$ 🏨 **Radisson SAS Royal Hotel Helsinki.** Conceived for business travelers, this hotel is in a residential section of the central city, right on the metro line. Two floors are made up of business-class rooms, including several suites and conference areas. Rooms have been renovated in an elegant Scandinavian (light colors and wood) design. If you want more space and privacy, try the art deco rooms on the top floor. ✉ *Runebergink. 2, Keskusta 00100* 🕿 *020/1234–701* 🖷 *020/1234–702* ⊕ *www. radissonsas.com* ⤢ *262 rooms, 9 suites* ⚸ *2 restaurants, room service, Wi-Fi, sauna, bar, business services, meeting room* ⊟ *AE, DC, MC, V.*

$$$$ 🏨 **Sokos Hotel Torni.** The original part of this hotel was built in 1903, and its towers and internal details still reflect some of the more fanciful touches of Helsinki's Jugendstil period an art deco–style section was added in 1931, and another renovation was completed in 2005. The higher floors of the original section, especially the Atelier Bar, have striking views of Helsinki. The bar also has monthly art exhibits. Old-section rooms on the courtyard are best; some have high ceilings with original carved-wood details and wooden writing desks; many also have little alcoves and other pleasing design oddities. The rooms on the top floors are modern, with glass bathrooms. ✉ *Yrjönkatu 26, Keskusta 00100* 🕿 *020/ 1234–604* 🖷 *09/4336–7100* ⊕ *www.sokoshotels.fi* ⤢ *152 rooms, 14 suites* ⚸ *Restaurant, room service, 2 saunas, 3 bars, pub, meeting rooms, no-smoking rooms* ⊟ *AE, DC, MC, V.*

$$$–$$$$ 🏨 **Scandic Marski Helsinki.** The Marski is favored for its absolutely central location, on the main Mannerheimintie artery and dead opposite Stockmann's department store. The suites are the last word in modern luxury, and all rooms are soundproof, shutting out the traffic. The Marski Bar and Restaurant is easygoing, with good views of the heart of the city. ⊠ *Mannerheim. 10, Keskusta 00100* ☎ *09/68061* 📠 *09/ 642–377* ⊕ *www.scandic-hotels.com* 🛏 *289 rooms, 6 suites* ♨ *Restaurant, coffee shop, minibars, health club, 3 saunas, 2 bars, business services, meeting rooms, free parking* ▭ *AE, DC, MC, V.*

$$$–$$$$ 🏨 **Scandic Simonkenttä Helsinki.** Located next to the bus station and the Forum shopping center, this hotel was specially designed to be environmentally friendly and to fulfill hypoallergenic standards. The rooms have blue, green, or red color schemes, wood floors, and cherrywood and leather furnishings. Rooms on the upper floors have good views of the city. ⊠ *Simonkatu 9, Keskusta 00100* ☎ *09/683–80* 📠 *09/683–8111* ⊕ *www.scandic-hotels.com* 🛏 *360 rooms, 3 suites* ♨ *Restaurant, cafés, minibars, in-room data ports, 3 saunas, bar, business services, meeting rooms, no-smoking rooms* ▭ *AE, DC, MC, V.*

$$$ 🏨 **Sokos Hotel Presidentti.** In the heart of Helsinki, this hotel is spacious and quiet, with well-lighted rooms. The hotel has extensive facilities and services; these include a Spanish restaurant, a breakfast banquet, and a pub. ⊠ *Eteläinen Rautatiek. 4, Keskusta 00100* ☎ *09/6911* 📠 *09/ 694–7886* ⊕ *www.sokoshotels.fi* 🛏 *494 rooms, 5 suites* ♨ *3 restaurants, Wi-Fi, indoor pool, massage, 3 saunas, pub, meeting room, no-smoking rooms* ▭ *AE, DC, MC, V.*

$$ 🏨 **Anna.** Pleasantly situated in a central, residential neighborhood, the Anna is in a seven-story apartment building dating from the 1920s. Room fittings are modern, with light, comfortable furniture. The room price includes a buffet breakfast. ⊠ *Annank. 1, Keskusta 00120* ☎ *09/616– 621* 📠 *09/602–664* ⊕ *www.hotelanna.fi* 🛏 *61 rooms, 3 suites* ♨ *Sauna, parking (fee), meeting room, no-smoking floors* ▭ *AE, DC, MC, V.*

$$ 🏨 **Palace Hotel Linna.** On a quiet side street, this small luxury hotel distinguishes itself with a rare combination of character, consistency, and
Fodor'sChoice service. The front section is a handsome 1903 stone castle with wood-
★ beam, medieval-style restaurants, lounges, conference rooms, a cavernous banquet hall, and more. A walkway across an inner court brings you to the modern building housing the guest rooms, which have comfortable, contemporary furnishings. ⊠ *Lönnrotink. 29, Hietalahti 00180* ☎ *10/344–4100* 📠 *10/344–4101* ⊕ *www.palace.fi* 🛏 *48 rooms* ♨ *Sauna, bar, meeting room, parking (fee)* ▭ *AE, DC, MC, V.*

$ 🏨 **Hotel Helka.** Privately owned by the Finnish YWCA, this is a pleasant, affordable alternative to the higher-price chain hotels in Helsinki. Although in the heart of the city, the Helka is surprisingly quiet, thanks to its double-paned windows. Furnishings are in light wood and mixed pastels. The Aurinko restaurant has a bright interior and an open kitchen, where international dishes are prepared at reasonable prices; choose from the very good wine selection. ⊠ *Pohjoinen Rautatiekatu 23, Keskusta 00100* ☎ *09/613–580* 📠 *09/441–087* ⊕ *www.helka.fi* 🛏 *147 rooms, 3 suites* ♨ *Restaurant, minibars, hot tub, sauna, meeting room* ▭ *AE, DC, MC, V.*

$ ⊞ **Marttahotelli.** Run by a century-old women's association, this convenient establishment is small and cozy, with simply decorated rooms. ⊠ *Uudenmaank. 24, Keskusta 00120* ☎ *09/618–7400* 🖷 *09/618–7401* ⊕ *www.marttahotelli.fi* 🖙 *43 rooms, 1 suite* ⟁ *Restaurant, sauna parking* ▤ *AE, DC, MC, V* ⊘ *Closed during Midsummer's weekend in June.*

¢ ⊞ **Hostel Academica.** This summer hostel is made up of what are, during the rest of the year, university students' apartments. You can choose between rooms in the old or new sections; the latter have higher rates. Each floor has a small lounge; the rooms are functional, modern, and have their own small kitchens. Family rooms and extra beds are also available, and there are special family rates. The central location is good for shopping and transport. ⊠ *Hietaniemenk. 14, Hietaniemi 00100* ☎ *09/1311–4334* 🖷 *09/441–201* ⊕ *www.hostelacademica.fi* 🖙 *260 rooms* ⟁ *Kitchenettes, pool, sauna, no-smoking rooms* ▤ *AE, DC, MC, V* ⊘ *Closed Sept.–May.*

North of City Center

$$$$ ⊞ **Hilton Helsinki Strand.** From the tastefully furnished rooftop saunas
Fodor'sChoice and the large, crisply decorated rooms, to the bathrooms with heated
★ floors and the car-wash service in the basement garage, this hotel pampers you for a price. The distinctive use of granite and Finnish marble in the central lobby is accentuated by a soaring atrium, where the Bridges restaurant is also located. The waterfront vistas are a pleasure. An entire floor is reserved for nonsmokers, and some of the suites have panoramic views of the sea. ⊠ *John Stenbergin Ranta 4, Hakaniemi 00530* ☎ *09/39351* 🖷 *09/393–53255* ⊕ *www.interconti.com* 🖙 *192 rooms, 8 suites* ⟁ *2 restaurants, room service, in-room data ports, indoor pool, sauna, bar, laundry service, business services, no-smoking rooms* ▤ *AE, DC, MC, V.*

$$ ⊞ **Comfort Hotel Pilotti.** In a quiet suburb, within a five-minute drive of the airport, the Pilotti is also about 5 km (3 mi) from Heureka, the Finnish Science Center. It is modern inside and out; each compact room has a large, round porthole-style window. ⊠ *Veromäentie 1, Airport, 01510 Vantaa* ☎ *09/3294–800* 🖷 *09/3294–8100* ⊕ *www.choicehotels.fi* 🖙 *109 rooms, 2 suites* ⟁ *Restaurant, sauna, pub, meeting room* ▤ *AE, DC, MC, V.*

★ $$ ⊞ **Cumulus Airport.** This fully equipped, modern accommodation satisfies Helsinki's need for an airport hotel that meets the highest international standards. Convenient for layovers, the hotel borders the airport commercial zone and has the best conference facilities in the area. A standard room includes a comfy armchair and queen-size bed and has such soft touches as paisley bedspreads. All rooms are soundproofed. ⊠ *Robert Huberintie 4, Airport, 01510 Vantaa* ☎ *09/4157–7100* 🖷 *09/4157–7101* ⊕ *www.cumulus.fi* 🖙 *260 rooms, 4 suites* ⟁ *Restaurant, minibars, indoor pool, 4 saunas, convention center, no-smoking rooms* ▤ *AE, DC, MC, V.*

$$ ⊞ **Cumulus Olympia.** The elegant public areas of this hotel have stone floors, wood-panel walls, and sturdy furniture. By contrast, the rooms have a bright Scandinavian touch, with textiles in blues, oranges, and reds and cherrywood furniture. There's a gym around the corner from

the hotel, which costs extra. ⊠ *Läntinen Brahenk. 2, Kallio 00510*
☎ *09/69151* 🖷 *09/691–5219* ⊕ *www.cumulus.fi* ⟿ *96 rooms, 5 family rooms* ⚏ *2 restaurants, sauna, nightclub, laundry service, no-smoking rooms* ⊟ *AE, DC, MC, V.*

$$ 🏨 **Holiday Inn Helsinki, Congress Center.** This hotel caters mainly to people attending events at the Helsinki Fair and Congress Center, which lies just on its doorstep. Transport to downtown Helsinki, 3¹/₂ km (2 mi) away, is by local train (the Pasila station is a three-minute walk away) or by tram. Select rooms are for the allergy-sensitive, and some for people with disabilities. There's even a ballroom for 2,000. ⊠ *Messuaukio 1, Pasila 00520* ☎ *09/150–900, 0800/113113 reservations* 🖷 *09/150–901* ⊕ *www.holiday-inn.com* ⟿ *239 rooms, 5 suites* ⚏ *Sauna, bar, business services, meeting room* ⊟ *AE, DC, MC, V.*

$$ 🏨 **Scandic Gateway Helsinki Airport.** At the heart of the Helsinki-Vantaa Airport, this hotel is ideal for early morning regrouping or quick overnights before connecting flights. The clean, modern design is typical of newer Finnish hotels. Some rooms are "air-side," for transit passengers who have no need or wish to leave the airport. Personal computer connections are available and there's a 24-hour breakfast service. ⊠ *Helsinki-Vantaa Airport, 01530 Vantaa* ☎ *09/818–3600* 🖷 *09/818–3609* ⊕ *www.scandic-hotels.com* ⟿ *35 rooms* ⚏ *Sauna, bar, meeting room* ⊟ *AE, DC, MC, V.*

$ 🏨 **Arthur.** Owned by the Helsinki YMCA, the Arthur is centrally located, unpretentious, and comfortable. ⊠ *Vuorikatu 19, Keskusta 00100* ☎ *09/173–441* 🖷 *09/626–880* ⊕ *www.hotelarthur.fi* ⟿ *144 rooms* ⚏ *Restaurant, 2 saunas* ⊟ *AE, DC, MC, V.*

$ 🏨 **Aurora.** This redbrick hotel has small modern rooms decorated in pale blues, greens, and peach; larger rooms have brown wood paneling. A 10-minute bus ride from the city center, it's also just across from the Linnanmäki Amusement Park and is therefore popular with families. Some rooms have a kitchenette. ⊠ *Helsinginkatu 50, Alppila 00530* ☎ *09/770–100* 🖷 *09/7701–0200* ⊕ *www.hotelaurorahelsinki.com* ⟿ *51 rooms* ⚏ *Restaurant, pool, sauna, squash* ⊟ *AE, DC, MC, V.*

¢ 🏨 **Fenno.** Ten minutes from the city center by tram (3B), in the Kallio neighborhood, this apartment hotel has simple, reasonably priced rooms. You can opt to stay in a private studio apartment with kitchenette and bathroom; an even less expensive choice is an unpretentious, light-color economy room, which includes shared bath and kitchen facilities with other guests on the same floor. ⊠ *Kaarlenkatu 7, Kallio 00530* ☎ *09/774–980* 🖷 *09/701–6889* ⊕ *www.hotelfenno.fi* ⟿ *68 apartments for 1–2 persons, 32 economy single rooms with shared facilities* ⚏ *Café, sauna, laundry facilities, parking (fee)* ⊟ *AE, DC, MC, V.*

Töölö & Munkkiniemi

$$$–$$$$ 🏨 **Scandic Continental Helsinki.** One of the most popular hotels in Helsinki,
Fodor's Choice this local institution is modern and central and particularly popular with
★ business travelers from the United States. It has hosted superpower summits and various diplomatic guests, and has a comprehensive range of business services. The hotel is close to Finlandia Hall and the Finnish National Opera. Olivo, the hotel's excellent restaurant, serves Mediterranean dishes and there's a separate wine bar. ⊠ *Mannerheim. 46,*

Töölö 00260 ☎ *09/47371* 🖨 *09/4737–2211* ⊕ *www.scandic-hotels.com* 🛏 *500 rooms, 12 suites* ♲ *Restaurant, in-room data ports, pool, gym, 3 saunas, gym, Turkish bath, bar, dry cleaning, laundry service, business services, meeting room* ⊟ *AE, DC, MC, V.*

$$$ 🏨 **Crowne Plaza Helsinki.** On Helsinki's main avenue, facing Hesperia Park and across the street from the Opera House, this upscale property has relatively spacious rooms with a modern Finnish flair; business-class rooms and suites are also available. The light and airy breakfast room has a large buffet. ⊠ *Mannerheimintie. 50, Töölö 00260* ☎ *09/ 2521–0000* 🖨 *09/2521–9999* ⊕ *www.crowneplaza-helsinki.fi* 🛏 *340 rooms, 9 suites* ♲ *Restaurant, room service, minibars, in-room data ports, indoor pool, gym, sauna, bar, pub, laundry services, concierge, business services, meeting rooms, no-smoking rooms* ⊟ *AE, DC, MC, V.*

$$$ 🏨 **Hilton Helsinki Kalastajatorppa.** In the plush western Munkkiniemi neigh-
Fodor's Choice borhood a 15- to 25-minute taxi ride from city center, this hotel rou-
★ tinely hosts statesmen and celebrities. The best rooms are in the seaside annex, but all are large and airy with clear pine and birch-wood paneling. Rooms in the main building may either be equipped with bath and terrace or with showers only; prices vary accordingly. ⊠ *Kalasta-jatorpantie 1, Munkkiniemi 00330* ☎ *09/45811* 🖨 *09/4581–2211* ⊕ *www.hilton.com* 🛏 *235 rooms, 8 suites* ♲ *Restaurant, room service, indoor pool, sauna, beach, 2 bars, business services, meeting room, no-smoking rooms* ⊟ *AE, DC, MC, V.*

Nightlife & the Arts

Nightlife

Helsinki nightlife has perked up considerably in recent years, and your choice extends from noisy bars and late-night clubs to more intimate cafés. The relatively small size of the central area makes it possible to visit several places in one night, but after around 9 on weekends expect lines at the popular hangouts. Cover charges, when required, average €5 to €10.

The Helsinki City Tourist Office has a *Clubs and Music Bars* listing of music nights and cover charges for various venues.

BARS & LOUNGES **Angleterre** (⊠ Fredrikinkatu 47, Keskusta ☎ 09/647–371) is a cozy English ale house run by a well-known Helsinki cellar master; it's frequented by an upwardly mobile, professional crowd. **Baker's** (⊠ Mannerheim. 12, Keskusta ☎ 09/612–6330) is a popular central café, with a lively restaurant/nightclub upstairs. **Cantina West** (⊠ Kasarmikatu 23, Keskusta ☎ 020/742–4210) is a lively spot with imported country and country-rock music and Tex-Mex food. **Kappeli** (⊠ Eteläespl. 1, Esplanadi ☎ 09/ 681–2440) has a huge outdoor terrace, perfect for summer nights, and an à la carte menu. Its leaded windows offer an excellent view of the Havis Amanda statue. The **Lady Moon** (⊠ Kaivok. 12, Keskusta ☎ 09/ 6843–7370) at the Seurahuone has its own DJ. **Molly Malone's** (⊠ Kaisaniemenkatu 1C, Keskusta ☎ 09/171–272) is a popular Irish pub, with nightly live music. **O'Malley's** (⊠ Sokos Hotel Torni, Yr-jönkatu 26, Keskusta ☎ 09/1311–3459) is the first Irish pub in Helsinki.

Raffaello (✉ Aleksanterink. 46, Keskusta ☎ 09/8568–5730) attracts a young crowd of professionals from the Helsinki financial district. **Vanha Ylioppilastalo** (✉ Mannerheim. 3, Keskusta ☎ 09/1311–4368 ⊕ www. vanha.fi) has a large selection of beers and attracts students with live music and DJs in three spaces—everything from blues, folk, and jazz to funk, hip-hop, and Latin. The **William K** (✉ Annankatu 3, Keskusta ☎ 09/ 680–2562 ✉ Mannerheim. 72, Töölö ☎ 09/409–484 ✉ Fleminginkatu 6, Töölö ☎ 09/821–816 ✉ Fredrikinkatu 65 [Tennispalatsi], Keskusta ☎ 09/693–1427) bars offer an excellent selection of European ales.

CASINOS **Grand Casino Helsinki** (✉ Mikonkatu 19, Keskusta ☎ 09/680–800 ⊕ www.grandcasinohelsinki.fi) has roulette, blackjack, and slot machines, as well as dinner shows and restaurants.

GAY & LESBIAN For up-to-date details of the gay scene, contact the gay rights organi-
BARS zation **SETA** (☎ 09/681–2580 ⊕ www.seta.fi). **Con Hombres** (✉ Eerikink. 14, Keskusta ☎ 09/608–826) is a popular gay bar. **dtm** (✉ Iso Roobertink. 28, Keskusta ☎ 09/676–314,) short for "Don't Tell Mama," is one of the largest gay clubs in Finland. **Lost and Found** (✉ Annank. 6, Keskusta ☎ 09/680–1010) is a bar as well as full-scale restaurant and is known for being straight-friendly. **Mann's Street** (✉ Mannerheim. 12A, 2nd fl., Keskusta ☎ 09/612–1103) is popular among older gay men and has danc-ing on weekends.

JAZZ CLUBS Helsinki's most popular jazz club, **Storyville** (✉ Museok. 8, Keskusta ☎ 09/408–007 ⊕ www.storyville.fi), has live jazz and dancing every night. The **UMO Jazz House** (✉ Pursimeihenk. 6 ☎ 09/6122–1914 ⊕ www.umo. fi) is home to the UMO Jazz Orchestra, Finland's only touring big-band orchestra.

NIGHTCLUBS For an upscale evening of cocktails, dinner, and a live show, head over to Grand Casino Helsinki's **Fennia Salon** (✉ Mikonkatu 19, Keskusta ☎ 09/680–800). Legendary Finnish film directors Aki and Mika Kau-rismäki's **Kafe Moskova/Dubrovnik Lounge** (✉ Eerikink. 11, Keskusta ☎ 09/ 611–200) offers Soviet-era nostalgia upstairs, with hipster clubbing in the basement. **Kaivohuone** (✉ Kaivohuone Kaivopuisto, Kaivopuisto ☎ 09/621–2160) is an old spa structure in beautiful Kaivopuisto; its dance floor is often packed weekends. **Tenth Floor** (✉ Sokos Hotel Vaakuna, Asemaaukio 2, Keskusta ☎ 09/1311–8225) is one of Helsinki's main hot spots.

On weekends, late night at **Manala** (✉ Dagmarinkatu 2, Töölö ☎ 09/ 5807–7707) is an extraordinary cocktail of elegant tango, bebop, and swing in the main hall and frenetic disco on the top floor. The first-floor restaurant in open until 4 AM. The university-owned **Tavastia Club** (✉ Urho Kekkosenk. 4–6, Keskusta ☎ 09/7746–7423) is one of the best rock clubs for top Finnish talent and some solid imports.

The Arts
For a list of events, pick up *Helsinki This Week,* available in hotels and tourist offices. For tickets, contact **Lippupalvelu** (✉ Ticket outlets through-out Finland ☎ 0600/10800 €1.30 per min plus a local call charge ⊕ www.lippupalvelu.fi). Call **Tiketti** (✉ Forum shopping mall, 3rd fl.,

Yrjönkatu 29C, Kukontori Keskusta ☎ 0600/11616 €.66 per min plus a local call charge ⊕ www.tiketti.fi) for the goods on pop concerts, theaters, and student and film clubs. There's also a service point on the seventh floor of Stockmann's department store.

In summer, plays and music are performed at many outdoor theaters, including Keskuspuisto, Suomenlinna, Mustikkamaa, and the Seurasaari Islands, and also at the Rowing Stadium. **Helsinki Festival** (☎ 09/6126–5100 for information ⊕ www.helsinkifestival.fi), a performance and visual-arts celebration that goes on around the city, including a specially erected tent near the City Theater, is held yearly in late August–early September. The Festival includes the **Night of the Arts,** during which much of the population is outdoors watching street performances, while galleries and theaters are open late and free of charge.

An important part of Helsinki's cultural and artistic life is the **Kaapeli Tehdas** (Cable Factory; ✉ Tallbergink. 1, Ruoholahti ☎ 09/4763–8330 ⊕ www.kaapelitehdas.fi). This huge converted industrial building houses a restaurant, the Cable Gallery, which doubles as a vast theater as well as various small but worthy museums, including the **Suomen Valokuvataiteen Museo** (Finnish Museum of Photography). The complex also has radio stations and artists' studios. It's a short bus or metro ride (Ruoholahti station) to the west of the town center.

CONCERTS **Finlandiatalo** (Finlandia Hall; ✉ Karamzinkatu 4, Keskusta ☎ 09/402–41 ⊕ www.finlandia.fi), the home of the Helsinki Philharmonic, hosts visiting world-class orchestras. Finland has produced numerous fine conductors, and because many of them are based abroad—Esa-Pekka Salonen, Jukka-Pekka Saraste, and Paavo Berglund, for example—their homecomings are lavishly fîted, as are performances by opera diva Karita Mattila. The **Sibelius Academy** (✉ Pohjoinen Rautatienkatu 9, Töölö ☎ 02/075–390) hosts frequent performances, usually by students. The splendid **Suomen Kansallisooppera** (Finnish National Opera; ✉ Helsinginkatu 58, Keskusta ☎ 09/4030–2211), is in a waterside park by Töölönlahti. Original Finnish opera is often performed here, in addition to international favorites. The rock-hewn **Temppeliaukio Kirkko** (✉ Lutherinkatu 3, Töölö ☎ 09/494–698) is a favorite venue for choral and chamber music.

THEATER Private support of the arts in Finland continues to be strong—especially for the theaters, the best-known of which are the **National Theater, City Theater, Swedish Theater,** and **Lilla Teatern.** However, unless you are fluent in Finnish or Swedish, you'll have a difficult time understanding the performances. Check *Helsinki This Week* for a listing of the latest performances.

Sports & the Outdoors

Biking
Helsinki and environs make for excellent biking through a decent network of trails, many traversing the downtown area and running through parks, forests, and fields. The free area sporting map ("Ulkoilukartta") gives details of all trails; pick up a copy at the tourist office. Daily rentals,

SAUNAS

An authentic Finnish sauna is an obligatory experience, and not hard to find: there are 1.6 million saunas in this country of just over 5 million people—even the parliament has its own sauna. The traditional Finnish sauna—which involves relaxing on wooden benches, pouring water onto hot coals, and swatting your neighbor's back with birch branches—is an integral part of cabin life and now city life, as apartments are outfitted with small saunas in their bathrooms. Almost every hotel has at least one sauna available free of charge, usually at standard times in the morning or evening for men and women to use separately. Larger hotels offer a private sauna in the higher-class rooms and suites. Public saunas (with swimsuits required) are becoming increasingly popular, even in winter, when sauna goers jump into the water through a large hole in the ice (called avantouinti). Public swimming pools are also equipped with saunas that can be used at no extra charge. For information, contact the Finnish Sauna Society.

including mountain bikes, are available from **Green Bike** (⊠ Manner-heim. 13, 00100 Keskusta, Helsinki ☎ 09/8502–2850). The shop can be difficult to find (it's not marked), but it's right across the street from the Parliament House. The city also has bikes with fluorescent wheels for free—drop a coin in the slot as a deposit, take a ride, and drop it off at any of 26 sites around the city.

Swimming

The best beaches in Helsinki are Pihlajasaari, Mustikkamaa, and Uunisaari. The beach at **Hietaniemi** is especially popular with young people. ⊠ *Hietaniemi.* Among Helsinki's indoor pools and saunas, the oldest and one of the most famous is **Yrjönkatu Uimahalli** (⊠ Yrjönk. 21B, Keskusta ☎ 09/3108–7400), which allows swimming and taking a sauna in the nude. The hall periodically closes during the summer months.

Tennis

There are some six tennis centers and 31 clubs in Helsinki. It's best to bring your own equipment, although rentals are available. For information and details about playing tennis in Helsinki, contact the **Finnish Tennis Association** (⊠ Myllypuro Tennis Center, Varikkotie 4, 00900 Myllypuro/Itäkeskus Helsinki ☎ 09/341–7151 ⊕ www.tennis.fi).

Shopping

Helsinki's shopping facilities are constantly improving. Although the signs in Finnish may be a mystery, most sales staff in the main shopping areas speak English and can help guide you. Smaller stores are generally open weekdays 9–6 and Saturday 9–1 and larger department stores are open until 9 weekdays and until 6 on Saturday. Small grocery stores are often open on Sunday year-round; other stores are often open on Sundays from June through August and December. The Forum complex and Stockmann's department store are open weekdays 9–9, Saturday 9–6, and (in summer and Christmastime) Sunday noon–6. An ever-expanding network of pedestrian tunnels connects the Forum, Stockmann's, and the train-station tunnel.

Kiosks remain open late and on weekends; they sell such basics as milk, juice, camera film, and tissues. Stores in Asematunneli, the train-station tunnel, are open weekdays 10–10 and weekends noon–10.

Department Stores

Stockmann's (✉ Aleksanterink. 52B, Keskusta ☎ 09/1211 ⊕ www. stockmann.fi) is Helsinki's premier department store. The 1950s showpiece landmark near the train station, **Sokos** (✉ Asema-aukio 2C, Rautatieasema ☎010/765–000) is a high-quality alternative to Stockmann's.

Shopping Districts

Pohjoisesplanadi (✉ Esplanadi), on the north side of the Esplanade, packs in most of Helsinki's trademark design stores. The southern part of **Senaatintori** has a host of souvenir and crafts stores, with several antiques shops and secondhand bookstores on the adjoining streets. Next to Senaatintori is the **Kiseleff Bazaar Hall** (✉ Aleksanterinkatu 22–28, Senaatintori), an attractive shopping gallery.

You'll find many smaller boutiques in the streets **west of Mannerheimintie**, Fredrikinkatu and Annankatu, for example. There is one pedestrian shopping street a few blocks south of the Esplanade, on **Iso Roobertinkatu**; stores here are conventional, and are more relaxed than around Mannerheimintie and the Esplanade. ✉ *Keskusta.*

Shopping Malls

All of Helsinki's shopping malls have a good mix of stores plus several cafés and restaurants. **Forum** (✉ Mannerheim. 20, Keskusta) is the largest shopping complex in Helsinki, with 120 stores. **Kaivopiha** (✉ Kaivok. 10, Keskusta) is across from the train station. **Kluuvi** (✉ Aleksanterink. 9–Kluuvik. 5, Keskusta) is a major shopping mall. The large **Itäkeskus** shopping complex in east Helsinki, perhaps the biggest indoor mall in Scandinavia, with 190 stores, restaurants, and other services, can be reached by metro. The **Kämp Galleria** (✉ Pohjoisesplanadi 33 Keskusta), bounded by Kluuvikatu, Pohjoisesplanadi, Mikonkatu, and Aleksanterinkatu, has 50 stores, including Finnish and international design shops.

Specialty Stores

ANTIQUES Many shops sell china, furniture, and art. Cut glass and old farm furniture are other popular products; the latter is harder to find. The **Kruunuhaka** area north of Senaatintori is the best bet if you're shopping for antiques. Try **Antik Oskar** (✉ Rauhank. 7, Kruunuhaka ☎ 09/135–7410) for a selection of furniture from the 19th century, silver, glass, and some porcelain. **Antiikkiliike Karl Fredrik** (✉ Mariank. 13, Kruunuhaka ☎ 09/630–014) stocks high-class 19th-century antiques, ranging from furniture, chandeliers, and other light fixtures, to glass and paintings, as well as a good selection of Russian objects. The **Punavuori district**, between Eerikinkatu and Tehtaankatu, has many shops that sell secondhand books (there's usually a small selection in English). **Punavuoren**

Antiikki (✉ Korkeavuorenk. 5, Punavuori ☎ 09/662–682) sells jewelry, lamps, dolls, and various machines and technical objects. Some date as far back as the 18th century. ✉ *Punavuori.*

CERAMICS & ACCESSORIES

Aarikka (✉ Pohjoisesplanadi 27, Esplanadi ☎ 09/652–277 ✉ Mannerheimintie 20, Keskusta ☎ 09/694–9846) sells wooden jewelry, toys, and gifts. **Arabian Tehtaanmyymälä** (Arabia Factory Shop); (✉ Hämeentie 135, Arabia ☎ 0204/393–507) has Arabia, Hackman, and Iittala and Rörstrand tableware, glassware, cutlery, and cookware for outlet prices. The **Iittala Concept Store** (✉ Pohjoisesplanadi 25, Esplanadi ☎ 0204/393–501) sells the crisp, functional glass and tableware designs of Iittala and Arabia. **Pentik** (✉ Mannerheimintie 5, Keskusta ☎ 09/6124–0795) is known for its classy but homey style of ceramic dishes and other housewares. Inventive gift items and cards are also on sale.

CLOTHING

At its four locations in central Helsinki, **Marimekko** (✉ Pohjoisespl. 2, Esplanadi ☎ 09/622–2317 ✉ Pohjoisespl. 31 [Kämp Galleria], Esplanadi ☎ 09/6860–2411 ✉ Eteläespl. 14, Esplanadi ☎ 09/170–704 ✉ Mannerheim. 20 [Forum shopping center], Keskusta ☎ 09/694–1498) sells bright, unusual clothes for men, women, and children in quality fabrics. Though the products are costly, they're worth a look even if you don't plan to buy.

JEWELRY

Kalevala Koru (✉ Unionink. 25, Keskusta ☎ 09/686–0400) bases its designs on traditional motifs dating back as far as the Iron Age. Its designs are also available at most jewelry shops around Finland, and at Stockmann's and Sokos, at reasonable prices. **Union Design** (✉ Eteläranta 14, inner courtyard Kauppatori ☎ 09/6220–0333) is an atelier workshop of goldsmiths, silversmiths, and jewelers emphasizing limited series and unique pieces, displaying top-notch talent in Finnish design.

SAUNA SUPPLIES

For genuine Finnish sauna supplies such as wooden buckets, bath brushes, and birch-scented soap, visit the **Sauna Shop** (✉ Aleksanterink. 28, Keskusta) in the Kiseleff Bazaar. The fourth floor of **Stockmann's** (✉ Aleksanterink. 52, Keskusta ☎ 09/1211) stocks accessories and supplies for the sauna.

Street Markets

Helsinki's main street markets and market halls specialize in food, but all have some clothing (new and used) and household products. **Hakaniemi Street Market and Market Hall** (✉ North of town center, off Unionink., Hakaniemi ⊙ Indoor Market Hall: weekdays 8–6, Sat. 8–4; street market: weekdays 6:30–3) has everything from Eastern spices to used clothing and ceramics. Visit **Kauppatori** (⇨ Exploring Helsinki), Helsinki's Market Square, to browse among the colorful stalls or just relax with a coffee. At the **Old Market Hall** (⊙ Weekdays 8–7, Sat. 8–4), almost adjacent to Kauppatori, you can browse and shop for anything from flowers to vegetables, meat, and fish. **Hietalahden Tori,** at Bulevardi and Hietalahdenkatu, is open weekdays 6:30–2 and Saturday 6:30–3 (with extended summer hours). At the outdoor flea market (open weekdays 8–2, Saturday 8–3) you can get an ever-changing assortment of used items; the indoor market is brimming with food, flowers, fish, and more.

Helsinki A to Z

AIR TRAVEL TO & FROM HELSINKI

CARRIERS Helsinki is served by most major European airlines, as well as several East European carriers. North American service is available with Finnair in cooperation with American Airlines. European airlines include SAS, Lufthansa, Swiss International Airlines, British Airways, Austrian Air, and Air France. Check the Finnair Web site for its One World partners in order to maximize frequent flyer miles.

🛪 **Air France** ⊠ Helsinki-Vantaa airport, Airport 🕾 09/856-80500 ⊕ www.airfrance. fi. **British Airways** 🕾 09/6937-9538 ⊕ www.britishairways.fi. **Finnair** ⊠ City Terminal, Elielin aukio 3, Rautatieasema 🕾 09/818-7750, 0600/140-140 24-hr contact center, €1.64 plus local charges. Note phone line schedules may be cut back in late June–early Aug. to weekdays only. Check the Finnair Web site for up-to-date information ⊕ www.finnair.fi. **Lufthansa, SAS, and Austrian Air** ⊠ Helsinki-Vantaa airport, Airport 🕾 020/585-3500 airport ticket counter, 020/386-000 reservations and customer service ⊕ www.scandinavian.net, www.lufthansa.com, or www.aua.com. **Swiss International Air lines** ⊠ Helsinki-Vantaa airport, Airport 🕾 09/6937-9034 ⊕ www. swiss.com.

AIRPORTS & TRANSFERS

All domestic and international flights to Helsinki use Helsinki-Vantaa International Airport, 20 km (12 mi) north of the city center.

🛪 **Helsinki-Vantaa Airport** 🕾 0200/14636 costs €.57 per min plus a local call charge for 24-hr information, 09/82771 for airport ⊕ www.ilmailulaitos.fi

AIRPORT
TRANSFERS Two local buses, 615 and 617, run between the airport and the main railway station downtown from 6 AM to 1 PM. The fare is €3 and the trip takes about 40 minutes. Finnair buses carry travelers to and from the railway station (Finnair's City Terminal) two to four times an hour, with a stop behind the Scandic Hotel Continental Helsinki. Stops requested along the route from the airport to the city are also made. Travel time from the Scandic Hotel Continental to the airport is about 30 minutes, 35 minutes from the main railway station; the fare is €5.30.

A limousine ride into central Helsinki will cost €142–€166, depending on size and make of vehicle. Contact Limousine Service if ordering from abroad.

There is a taxi stop at the arrivals building. A cab ride into central Helsinki costs about €30. Driving time is 20 to 35 minutes, depending on the time of day. Check to see if your hotel has a shuttle service, although this is not common here. Airport Taxi costs €20–€22 for one to four passengers, and operates shuttles between the city and the airport. If you are going to the airport, you must reserve by 7 PM the day before departure. Leaving from the airport, you do not need a reservation—just look for the Airport Taxi stands in the arrivals halls. The yellow line taxi stand at the airport also offers fixed-rate trips into the city.

🛪 **Airport Taxi** 🕾 0600/555-555. **Limousine Service** ⊠ Kääpätie 4A, Heikinlaakso 00760 Helsinki 🕾 09/2797-800 🖷 09/2797-8027 ⊕ www.limousineservice.fi.

BOAT & FERRY TRAVEL

A ferry to the Suomenlinna fortress island runs about twice an hour, depending on the time of day, and costs €2 one-way and €3.60 round-trip. Ten-trip tickets issued for city public transport can be used on the ferry, too. From June to August, private water buses run from Kauppatori to Suomenlinna, charging €3.50 one-way and €5.50 round-trip.

🚢 **Suomenlinna Ferry** ☎ 0100-111.

BUSINESS HOURS

BANKS & OFFICES Banks are open weekdays 9 or 9:15 to 4 or 5. Many offices and embassies close at 3 June to August.

SHOPS Stores are open weekdays 9 to 6 and Saturday 9 to 1 or 2 and are closed Sunday, but several of the larger stores stay open until 8 or 9 weekdays. Big stores in the town center are open Sunday, June to August, December, and five other Sundays throughout the year from noon to 6 or 9. Some stores in malls stay open until 9 on weekdays and until 5 on Saturday. In the Asematunneli (train station tunnel), stores are open weekdays 10 to 10 and weekends noon to 10.

CAR TRAVEL

Ring Roads One and Three are the two major highways that circle the city. Mannerheimintie and Hämeentie are the major trunk roads out of Helsinki. Mannerheimintie feeds into Highway E12, which travels north and takes you to the ring roads. Hämeentie leads you to Highway E75 as well as Roads 4 and 7. From either route, you will find directions for Highway 45 to the airport or, from the eastern edge of the city, you can take Mäkelänkatu, which merges into 45. For specific route information, contact the Automobile and Touring Club of Finland or the City Tourist Office.

🚗 **Automobile and Touring Club of Finland** ⊠ Autoliitto ry, Hämeentie 105 A, PL 35, 00550 Arabia Helsinki ☎ 09/7258-4400, 0200/8080 24-hr road service ⊕ www.autoliitto.fi. **Finnish Motor Insurers' Centre** ⊠ Bulevardi 28 00120 Helsinki ☎ 09/680-401 ⊕ www.vakes.fi/lvk.

EMBASSIES

🏳 Australia ⊠ Museokatu 25B, Keskusta 00100 ☎ 09/4777-6640
🏳 Canada ⊠ Pohjoisespl. 25B, Esplanadi 00100 ☎ 09/228-530.
🏳 U.K. ⊠ Itäinen Puistotie 17, Kaivopuisto 00140 ☎ 09/2286-5100.
🏳 U.S. ⊠ Itäinen Puistotie 14A, Kaivopuisto 00140 ☎ 09/616-250.

EMERGENCIES

The general emergency number is 112; call it for any emergency situation. Coins are not needed to make this call on pay phones. If you summon an ambulance, specify whether the situation seems life-threatening so medical attendants can prepare for immediate treatment in the ambulance.

Töölön Sairaala is about 2 km (1 mi) from the city center, with a 24-hour emergency room and first-aid service. Mehiläinen is a private health-care chain that offers 24-hour service in the Helsinki area. You can call their number or get a walk-in appointment at their medical center on Runeberginkatu. The company also has medical centers in Turku and Kuopio.

🚩 Emergency Services **General Emergency** ☎ 112. **Police** ✉ Central precinct: Pieni Roobertinkatu 1-3 ☎ 1022, 1891 for central precinct.

🚩 Doctors & Dentists **Doctor and Dentist Referrals** ☎ 09/10023. **Mehiläinen** ✉ Runeberginkatu 47A, 2nd fl. ☎ 010/414-4444.

🚩 Hospitals **Meilahden Sairaala** ✉ Haartmaninkatu 4, Meilahti ☎ 09/4711. **Töölön Sairaala** ✉ Töölönk. 40, Töölö ☎ 09/4711.

🚩 24-Hour Pharmacies **Yliopiston Apteekki** ✉ Mannerheim. 96, Töölö ☎ 0203/20200.

ENGLISH-LANGUAGE MEDIA

BOOKS Akateeminen Kirjakauppa (Academic Bookstore) is the largest English-language bookstore; it's also the most expensive. Like the Academic Bookstore, Suomalainen Kirjakauppa (The Finnish Bookstore) sells English-language books, newspapers, and magazines. English-language newspapers are also on sale at the kiosks in the main train station.

🚩 Bookstores **Akateeminen Kirjakauppa** ✉ Keskuskatu 1, Keskusta ☎ 09/12141. **Suomalainen Kirjakauppa** ✉ Aleksanterink. 23, Keskusta ☎ 010/405-4203.

INTERNET 🚩 Internet Cafés **Mbar** ✉ Mannherheim. 22-24, Keskusta ☎ 09/6124-5420 ⊕ www. meteori.com/netcafe. **NetCup** ✉ Stockmann's Department Store Aleksanterinkatu 52, Keskusta ☎ 09/121-3759.

TAXIS

There are numerous taxi stands; central stands are at Rautatientori at the station, the main bus station, Linja-autoasema, and in the Esplanade. Taxis can also be flagged, but this can be difficult, as many are on radio call and are often on their way to stands, where late-night lines may be very long. An average taxi ride in Helsinki can cost around €10; a taxi from the airport can cost €30 or more. All taxis in Helsinki go through the Taxi Center, or you can call Kovanen, a private company, for taxis, vans, luxury minibuses, and limousine services.

🚩 **Kovanen** ☎ 0200/6060 €.95 plus local charge (open 24 hrs) ⊕ www.kovanen.com. **Taxi Center** ☎ 0100/0700 €.99 plus 8 cents per 10 seconds plus local charge, 0100/ 06000 €.99 plus 8 cents per 10 seconds plus local charge for advance bookings ⊕ www. taksihelsinki.fi.

TOURS

BOAT TOURS Most major boat tours depart from Kauppatori Market Square. The easiest way to choose one is to go to the square in the morning and read the information boards describing the tours. Most tours run in summer only. You can go as far afield as Porvoo or take a short jaunt to the Helsinki Zoo on Korkeasaari.

BUS TOURS Bus tours are a good way to get oriented in Helsinki. The Helsinki Expert 1½-hour Audio City Tour of central Helsinki sites is €8 with the Helsinki Card; otherwise the cost is €20. The recorded commentary, which you listen to on a headset as you traverse the city, is available in 11 languages. Tours leave from Esplanade Park and the Katajanoka Terminal. Guided city tours, with live commentary in English and Swedish, are also available; they depart from the Katajanokka and Olympia

Ferry terminals and last approximately 1 hour and 45 minutes. For more information, contact Helsinki Expert.

Helsinki Expert ☎ 09/2288-1600 ⊕ www.helsinkiexpert.fi.

WALKING TOURS The Helsinki City Tourist Office employs "Helsinki Helpers," dressed in green and white. Daily, June to August, 8 to 8, they walk the streets in the city center and harbor area, freely answering questions and giving directions. Helsinki Expert is a multipurpose travel agent and guide-booking center that will arrange personal tour guides. The City Tourist Office also has an excellent brochure, *Helsinki on Foot,* with six walks covering most points of interest.

TRAIN TRAVEL

Helsinki's suburbs and most of the rest of southern, western, and central Finland are well served by trains. Travel on trains within the city limits costs the same as all public transport, €2 or less if you use a Travel Card (which carries an initial fee of €7 but reduces the cost of each trip; you can buy the card for specific amounts or time periods). A single regional ticket costs €3.40 and is good for 80 minutes, including transfers. Regional tourist tickets are available for one day (€9), three days (€18), and five days (€27).

TRANSPORTATION AROUND HELSINKI

Helsinki center is compact and best explored on foot. The City Tourist Office provides a free Helsinki route map detailing all public transportation. The Helsinki Kortti (Helsinki Card) allows unlimited travel on city public transportation, free entry to many museums, a free sightseeing tour, and other discounts. It's available for one, two, or three days (€25, €35, or €45, respectively). You can buy it at more than 70 places, including the airport (information desks), ferry terminals, some hotels and travel agencies, Stockmann's department store, the Hotel Booking Centre, the Helsinki City Tourist office, or online through Helsinki Expert; contact them for more information.

The bus and tram networks are compact but extensive, and service is frequent, with more infrequent service nights and on Sunday. Be sure to pick up a route map at the tourist office—many stops do not have them. Tickets bought from the driver cost €2 for buses and €1.80 for trams. You can also buy a tourist ticket for unlimited travel on public transportation within the city (€5.40 one day, €10.80 three days, €16.20 five days), or purchase the Travel Card, loaded with an amount or for a time period. Extensive information on routes, fares, and timetables is available from the Helsinki City Transport Web site.

Helsinki City Transport ⊕ www.hel.fi/HKL.

TRAVEL AGENCIES

Try Helsinki Expert for tour (or sightseeing) information. Suomen Matkatoimisto (Finland Travel Bureau) is the country's main travel agency.

Local Agent Referrals Helsinki Expert ✉ Lönnrotink. 7B, Keskusta ☎ 09/2288-1600. **Suomen Matkatoimisto** ✉ Kaivok. 10 A, PL 319, 00101 Keskusta Helsinki ☎ 09/18261 ⊕ www.ftb.net.

VISITOR INFORMATION

The Helsinki City Tourist office is open May to September, weekdays 9 to 8 and weekends 9 to 6; October to April, weekdays 9 to 6 and weekends 10 to 4. The Finnish Tourist Board's Information Office, covering all of Finland, is open May to September, weekdays 9 to 5 and weekends 11–3; October to April, weekdays 9 to 5.

🖪 Tourist Information **Finnish Tourist Board's Information Office** ⊠ Eteläespl. 4, 00130 Esplanadi Helsinki ☎ 09/4176-9300 ⊕ www.mek.fi or www.visitfinland.com. **Helsinki City Tourist and Convention Bureau** ⊠ Pohjoisespl. 19, 00100 Esplanadi Helsinki ☎ 09/169-3757 ⊕ www.hel.fi/tourism. **Helsinki Expert** ⊠ Lönnrotink. 7B, Keskusta 00120 ☎ 09/2288-1200 ⊕ www.helsinkiexpert.fi.

SIDE TRIPS FROM HELSINKI

Helsinki's outskirts are full of attractions, most of them no more than a half-hour bus or train ride from the city center. From the idyllic former home of Finland's national artist to the utopian garden city of Tapiola in Espoo, options abound.

Gallen-Kallela Estate

10 km (6 mi) northwest of Helsinki.

Set at the edge of the sea and surrounded by towering, wind-bent pines, the turreted brick-and-stucco Gallen-Kallela Estate was the self-designed studio and home of the Finnish Romantic painter Akseli Gallen-Kallela. Gallen-Kallela (1865–1931) lived in the mansion on and off from its completion in 1913 until his death. Inside, the open rooms of the painter's former work spaces make the perfect exhibition hall for his paintings. Also displayed are some of his posters and sketches of the ceiling murals he made for the Paris Art Exhibition at the turn of the 20th century. To get to the estate, take Tram 4 from in front of the Sokos department store on Mannerheimintie. From the Munkkiniemi stop walk 2 km (1 mi) through Munkinpuisto Park. ⊠ *Gallen-Kallelantie 27, Tarvaspää* ☎ *09/541-3388* ⊕ *www.gallen-kallela.fi* 🎫 *€8* ☉ *Mid-May–Aug., daily 10–6; Sept.–mid-May, Tues.–Sat. 10–4, Sun. 10–5.*

Espoo

20 km (13 mi) west of Helsinki.

Tapiola Garden City, an architectural showpiece in its day, is in the city of Espoo, west of Helsinki. Designed by top Helsinki artists of the 1950s— Ervi, Blomstedt, and Rewell among them—the urban landscape of alternating high and low residential buildings, fountains, gardens, and swimming pools blends into the natural surroundings. Guides and sightseeing tours of Tapiola for architecture enthusiasts and professionals are available from Helsinki Expert (Helsinki A to Z, Visitor Information) or the **Espoo Convention and Marketing** (⊠ Keskustorni, 10th fl., 02100 Espoo ☎ 09/8164-7230 🖷 09/8164-7238 ⊕ www.espootravel.com). The Helsinki Card provides discount fares to Espoo.

Hvitträsk

40 km (25 mi) west of Helsinki.

On the northwest edge of the Espoo area is Hvitträsk, the studio home of architects Herman Gesellius, Armas Lindgren, and Eliel Saarinen. In an idyllic position at the top of a wooded slope, the property dates back to the turn of the 20th century, and is now a charming museum. The whimsical main house reveals the national art nouveau style, with its rustic detail and paintings by Akseli Gallen-Kallela; Saarinen lived here, and his grave is nearby. A café and restaurant are set up in one of the architects' houses. Hvitträsk can be reached in 45 minutes by Bus 166 (last stop) from Helsinki's main bus station, Linja-autoasema, platform 55. ⊠ *Hvitträskintie 166, Kirkkonummi, Hvitträsk, Luoma* ☎ *09/ 4050–9630* ⊕ *www.nba.fi* ☜ *€4* ☉ *Museum Apr.–Oct., daily 11–6; Nov.–Mar., Tues.–Sun. 11–5.*

Ainola

50 km (31 mi) north of Helsinki.

The former home of Finland's most famous son, composer Jean Sibelius, was designed by Lars Sonck in 1904 and takes its name from his wife, Aino. From late spring through summer, the intimate wooden house set in secluded woodland is open to the public as a museum. Take a bus from the Helsinki Linja-autoasema (bus station) or a local train first to the town of Järvenpää; Ainola is 2 km (1 mi) farther by bus or taxi. ⊠ *Ainolantie, 04400 Järvenpää* ☎ *09/287–322* ⊕ *www.ainola.fi* ☜ *€5* ☉ *Early May–Sept., Tues.–Sun. 10–5.*

Porvoo

50 km (31 mi) east of Helsinki.

Porvoo is a living record of the past, with its old stone streets and painted wooden houses lining the riverbank. Artisan boutiques around the old Town Hall Square invite exploration. Take a stroll into the Old Quarter to see the multicolor wooden houses. Visit the 15th-century stone-and-wood cathedral, **Porvoon Tuomiokirkko**, where the diet of the first duchy of Finland was held in the 1800s. The **Walter Runebergin Veistoskokoelma** (Walter Runeberg Sculpture Collection; ⊠ Aleksanterink 5 ☎ 019/582–186) has some wonderful pieces and is well worth a visit. The **Porvoo Museo** (⊠ Välik. 11 ☎ 019/574–7500 or 019/574–7589 ⊕ www.porvoonmuseo.fi), inside the historic town hall built in 1764, captures the region's social and cultural history through exhibits on daily life and household objects. Next door to the Porvoo Museo, the **Edelfelt-Vallgren Museo** (⊠ Välik. 11 ☎ 019/574–7500 or 019/574–7589) exhibits Edelfelt's art, as well as paintings, sculpture, glass, and ceramics by other artists. The Edelfelt-Vallgren Museum will be closed for restoration until 2007, but many of its permanent collections can be seen at the Porvoo Museum in the meantime.

Near Porvoo in Haikko, you can visit the **Albert Edelfeltin Atelje** (☎ 019/ 577–414), the painter's studio of Albert Edelfelt. Contact the **Porvoo City Tourist Office** (✉ Rihkamakatu 4, 06100 Porvoo ☎ 019/520–2316 ⊕ www.porvoo.fi) for details about all local sights.

Part of the fun of visiting Porvoo is the journey you take to get there. On summer Saturdays (July through the end of August, except Midsummer) there is a train connection along the historical museum rail between Helsinki and Porvoo, on board the old trains from the 1950s and 1960s. Prices are €12 one-way, €20 round-trip. Once in Porvoo, you can take a historic ride on a steam train to Hinthaara and back. Contact the **Porvoo Museum Railway Society** (☎ 0400/700–717 ⊕ helsinkiww. net/pmr) for details. Far more regular than the historic train journey is the boat service. May through September, cruises depart from Helsinki's South Harbor regularly (check the Web site for exact dates and times): the *J. L. Runeberg* takes 3½ hours, and the round-trip costs €31. The *King* takes 3 hours each way and costs €32 for a round-trip. You will be taken westward through dozens of islands before landing at Porvoo, which is small enough to be covered on foot. For more information, contact the boat companies or **Porvoo City Tourist Office** (☎ 019/520–2316 tourist office, 019/524–3331 *J. L. Runeberg*, 09/612–2950 M/S *King* (Royal Line) ⊕ www.msjlruneberg.fi or www.royalline.fi). There are also bus and road connections.

Vantaa

20 km (13 mi) north of Helsinki.

Though not remarkable, Vantaa—the municipality north of Helsinki proper and the home of the international airport—has a few notable attractions. A welcome surplus of open green space and trails for biking, hiking, and running create an oasis for outdoor enthusiasts. Don't miss the 15th-century **Helsingin Pitajan Kirkko** (Parish Church).

Consider using Vantaa as home base if your trip to Helsinki coincides with a convention and you can't find accommodations there: the airport is within the city's municipal boundaries and easily reached by public transport. The Helsinki Card also works in Vantaa.

The **Heureka Suomalainen Tiedekeskus** (Heureka Finnish Science Center) has interactive exhibits on topics as diverse as energy, language, and papermaking. There is also a cafeteria, a park, and a planetarium with taped commentary in English as well as the Verne IMAX-type theater. ✉ *Tiedepuisto 1, Tikkurila* ☎ *09/85799* ⊕ *www.heureka.fi* 🎟 *€13.50 exhibitions only, €8 for the Verne theater only, €18 for both* ⊙ *Mid-Aug.–June, Mon., Wed., and Fri. 10–5, Thurs. 10–8, weekends 10–6; July–mid-Aug., weekdays 10–7, weekends 10–6.*

The peaceful **Viherpaja Japanese and Cactus gardens** in Vantaa include an exhibition of carnivorous plants. ✉ *Meiramitie 1* ☎ *09/822–628* ⊕ *www.viherpaja.fi* 🎟 *Japanese Garden and carnivorous plants €1, other gardens free* ⊙ *June–Aug., weekdays 8–6, weekends 9–4; Sept.–May, weekdays 8–7, weekends 9–5.*

The **Suomen Ilmailumuseo** (Finnish Aviation Museum) has more than 60 military and civilian aircraft on display. ✉ *Tietotie 3* ☎ *09/870–0870* ⊕ *www.suomenilmailumuseo.fi* ✇ *€6* ☼ *Daily 11–6.*

Contact the **Vantaa Travel Center** (✉ Ratatie 7, Tikkurila, 01300 ☎ 09/8392–2133 🖷 09/8392–2371 ⊕ www.vantaa.fi) for more information.

SOUTHWESTERN COAST & THE ÅLANDS

A magical world of islands stretches along Finland's coastline. In the Gulf of Finland and the Baltic, more than 30,000 islands form a magnificent archipelago. The rugged and fascinating Åland Islands group lies westward from Turku, forming an autonomous province of its own. Turku, the former capital, was the main gateway through which cultural influences reached Finland over the centuries.

A trip to Turku via Hanko and Tammisaari will give you a taste of Finland at its most historic and scenic. Many of Finland's oldest towns lie in this southwest region of the country, having been chartered by Swedish kings—hence the predominance of the Swedish language here.

The southwest is a region of flat, often mist-soaked rural farmlands, and villages peppered with traditional wooden houses. At other times pastoral and quiet, the region's culture comes alive in summer.

GETTING
AROUND
It's easy to explore this region by rail, bus, or car, then to hop on a ferry bound for the Ålands, halfway between Finland and Sweden. Drive along the southern coast toward Turku, the regional capital, stopping at the charming coastal towns along the way. Or take a train from Helsinki to Turku, catching buses from Turku to other parts of the region.

Snappertuna

39 *124 km (77 mi) southeast of Turku, 75 km (47 mi) southwest of Helsinki.*

Snappertuna is a small farming town with a proud hilltop church, a charming homestead museum, and the handsome restored ruins of **Raaseporin Linna** (Raseborg Castle), set in a small dale. The castle is believed to date from the 14th century. One 16th-century siege left the castle damaged, but restorations have given it a new face. In summer, concerts and plays are staged here, and there are old-fashioned market fairs. Call for information on guided tours. ☎ *019/234–015* ✇ *€1* ☼ *May and mid–late Aug., daily 10–5; June, daily 10–6; July–mid-Aug., daily 10–7; Sept., weekends 10–5; Oct.–Apr., call ahead to arrange tour (groups only).*

Tammisaari

40 *16 km (10 mi) west of Snappertuna, 109 km (68 mi) southeast of Turku.*

Tammisaari (or Ekenäs) has a colorful Old Quarter, 18th- and 19th-century buildings, and a lively marina. The scenery is dazzling in summer, when the sun glints off the water and marine traffic is at its peak. The **Tammisaaren Museo** (Tammisaari Museum) is the provincial museum of western Uusimaa, providing a taste of the region's culture and history.

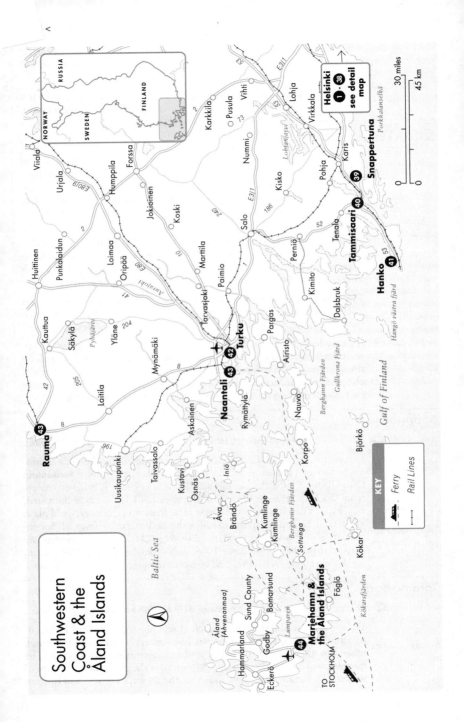

Southwestern Coast & the Åland Islands

KEY

Ferry
Rail Lines

Baltic Sea

Gulf of Finland

Helsinki
1 - 38
see detail map

39 Snappertuna
40 Tammisaari
41 Hanko
42 Turku
43 Naantali
43 Rauma
44 Mariehamn & the Åland Islands

TO STOCKHOLM

Åland (Ahvenanmaa)

Hango västra fjärd
Bergshann Fjärden
Gullkrona Fjärd
Kökarsfjärden
Lohjanjärvi
Porkkalanselkä
Pyhäjärvi

Hammarland, Eckerö, Godby, Bomarsund, Sund County, Föglö, Kökar, Sottunga, Kumlinge, Brändö, Åva, Osnäs, Kustavi, Taivassalo, Uusikaupunki, Laitila, Kauttua, Säkylä, Yläne, Rauma, Huittinen, Punkalaidun, Loimaa, Oripää, Mynämäki, Askainen, Rymättylä, Nauvo, Korpo, Björkö, Airisto, Pargas, Dalsbruk, Kimito, Perniö, Tenala, Hanko, Tammisaari, Karis, Pohja, Kisko, Salo, Kari, Martila, Paimio, Tarvasjoki, Turku, Naantali, Koski, Jokioinen, Forssa, Humppila, Urjala, Viiala, Viala, Karkkila, Pusula, Nummi, Vihti, Lohja, Virkkala, Kimito, Perniö

30 miles
45 km

NORWAY, SWEDEN, FINLAND, RUSSIA

✉ *Kustaa Vaasank. 11* ☎ *020/775–3165* ⊕ *www.tammisaari.fi* ⬚ *€2, guided tour €20 weekdays, €30 weekends* ⊙ *Mid-May–mid-Aug., daily 11–5; Sept.–May, Tues.–Thurs. 4–7, Fri.–Sun. noon–4.*

Where to Stay

$ ▦ **Ekenäs Stadshotell.** This modern, airy hotel is in the heart of Tammisaari, amid fine lawns and gardens and near the sea and Old Quarter. Some of the rooms have their own balconies; all have wide picture windows and comfortable modern furnishings in pale and neutral colors. ✉ *Pohjoinen Rantakatu 1, 10600 Tammisaari* ☎ *019/241–3131* 🖷 *019/ 246–1550* ⊕ *www.stadshotell.nu* ⇜ *18 rooms, 1 suite* ⌂ *Room service, indoor pool, 2 bars* ▭ *AE, DC, MC, V.*

Hanko

④ *37 km (23 mi) southwest of Tammisaari, 141 km (88 mi) southeast of Turku.*

In the coastal town of Hanko (Hangö), you'll find long stretches of beach—about 30 km (19 mi) of it—some sandy and some with sea-smoothed boulders. Sailing abounds here, thanks to Finland's largest guest harbor. A sampling of the grandest and most fanciful private homes in Finland dot the seacoast, their porches edged with gingerbread iron detail and woodwork, and crazy towers sprouting from their roofs. Favorite pastimes here are beachside strolls; bike rides along well-kept paths; and, best of all, long walks along the main avenue past the great wooden houses with their wraparound porches.

This customs port has a rich history. Fortified in the 18th century, Hanko defenses were destroyed by the Russians in 1854, during the Crimean War. Later it became a popular spa town for Russians, then the port from which more than 300,000 Finns emigrated to North America between 1880 and 1930.

↻ Through the telescope of **Vesitorni** (Hanko's Water Tower), you can follow the comings and goings of the town's marine traffic and get a grand view of some of the very small islands sprinkled around the peninsula's edges. ✉ *Vartiovuori* ☎ *019/220–3411 tourist office* ⬚ *€1* ⊙ *Early June–July, daily noon–6; Aug., daily 1–3.*

Where to Stay

$ ▦ **Hotel Regatta.** This historic seaside hotel in the center of town near the eastern harbor dates from the turn of the 20th century, although a modern annex was added in the 1960s. Some of the older rooms share baths and are thus less costly. ✉ *Merikatu 1, 10900 Hanko* ☎ *019/248– 6491* 🖷 *019/248–5535* ⊕ *www.surfnet.fi/regatta* ⇜ *38 rooms, 1 suite* ⌂ *Sauna, beach, meeting room.*

$ ⛺ **Camping Silversand.** There are various facilities at this large campground near the water, including eight-person cabins and full hookups for trailers, as well as trailers and tents for rent. ✉ *Hopeahietikko, 10960 Hanko* ☎ *019/248–5500, 09/6138–3210 off-season* 🖷 *09/713–713* ⊕ *www.lomaliitto.fi* ⌂ *Cafeteria, sauna, shop* ⊙ *Closed Sept.–May.*

The Outdoors

BOATING   Boats can be rented at the guest harbor Info-Point in Hanko, or through the local tourist office. Young people and families race in and attend the annual **Hanko Regatta,** setting sail during a weekend at the end of June or beginning of July.

Turku

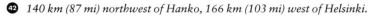 *140 km (87 mi) northwest of Hanko, 166 km (103 mi) west of Helsinki.*

Founded at the beginning of the 13th century, Turku is the nation's oldest and fourth-largest city and was the original capital of newborn Finland. Its early importance in the history of Finland has earned Turku the title of "the cradle of Finnish culture." Turku has a long history as a commercial and intellectual center (the city's name means trading post); once the site of the first Finnish university, it has two major universities, the Finnish University of Turku and the Swedish-speaking Åbo Akademi. Turku has a population of about 200,000, and a busy, year-round harbor. In summer the banks of the river come alive with boat and ship cafés and the city hosts various festivals, including Baltic Jazz and Medieval Turku festivals in July.

The 700-year-old **Turun Tuomiokirkko** (Turku Cathedral) remains the seat of the archbishop of Finland. It was partially gutted by fire in 1827 but has subsequently been completely restored. In the choir are R. W. Ekman's frescoes portraying Bishop Henry (an Englishman) baptizing the then-heathen Finns, and Mikael Agricola offering the Finnish translation of the New Testament to Gustav Vasa of Sweden. The cathedral also houses a museum, which displays medieval church vestments, silver chalices, and wooden sculptures. ⊠ *Turun Tuomiokirkko, Tuomiokirkkotori 20, Keskusta* ☎ *02/251–7100* ➩ *€2 for the Cathedral Museum* ⊕ *www.turunsrk.fi* ⊙ *Mid-Apr.–mid-Sept., daily 9–8; mid-Sept.–mid-Apr., daily 9–7.*

Where the Aura flows into the sea stands **Turun Linna** (Turku Castle), one of the city's most important historical monuments. The oldest part of the fortress was built at the end of the 13th century, and the newer part dates from the 16th century. The castle was damaged by bombing in 1941, and its restoration was completed in 1961. Many of its seemingly infinite rooms hold rather incongruous exhibits: next to a display on medieval life (featuring a dead rat to illustrate the Black Death) is a roomful of 1920s flapper costumes. The vaulted chambers themselves give you a sense of the domestic lives of the Swedish royals. A good gift shop and a pleasant café are on the castle grounds. ⊠ *Linnank. 80, Keskusta* ☎ *02/262–0300* ⊕ *www.nba.fi/en/turku_castle* ➩ *€6.50 without a guide, €8 with a guide* ⊙ *Mid-Apr.–mid-Sept., daily 10–6; mid-Sept.–mid-Apr., Tues.–Fri. and Sun. 10–3, Sat. 10–5.*

The **Luostarinmäki Handicrafts Museum** is an authentic collection of wooden houses and buildings that escaped fire in the 19th century, containing shops and workshops where traditional crafts are demonstrated and sold. Ask staff about the history of a particular workshop or call ahead for schedule of guided tours, offered several times daily in summer. ⊠ *Vartiovuorenk. 4, Keskusta* ☎ *02/262–0350* ⊕ *www.turunmuseot.fi* ▭ *€3.40 without a guide, €4.80 with a guide* ☉ *Mid-Apr.–mid-Sept., daily 10–6; mid-Sept.–mid-Apr., Tues.–Sun 10–3.*

The **Aboa Vetus/Ars Nova** museum displays a unique combination of history and art. Begun as a straightforward extension of the Villa von Rettig collection, the museum's concept changed when workers discovered archaeological remains, which were excavated and incorporated into the museum. Modern art in the old villa includes works by Auguste Herbin (1882–1960) and Max Ernst (1891–1976), as well as Picasso's *The Swordsman*. The preserved excavations in the Aboa Vetus section date to the 15th century. ⊠ *Itäinen Rantakatu 4–6, Keskusta* ☎ *02/250–0552* ⊕ *www.aboavetusarsnova.fi* ▭ *€8* ☉ *Apr.–late Sept., daily 11–7; mid-Sept.–Mar., Tues.–Sun., 11–7.*

The **Turun Taidemuseo** (Turku Art Museum) holds some of Finland's most famous paintings, including works by Akseli Gallen-Kallela, and a broad selection of turn-of-the-20th-century Finnish art and contemporary works. The impressive granite building, situated along Puolala Park, was completed in 1904 and in itself is worth the visit. Call ahead for information on guided tours. ⊠ *Aurakatu 26, 20100 Keskusta* ☎ *02/262–7100* ⊕ *www.turuntaidemuseo.fi* ▭ *€6* ☉ *Tues.–Fri. 11–7, weekends 11–5.*

Where to Stay & Eat

\$\$–\$\$\$\$ ✕ **Suomalainen Pohja.** This classic Finnish restaurant is decorated in dark wood with large windows offering a splendid view of an adjacent park. Seafood, poultry, and game dishes have earned a good reputation here. Try the fillet of reindeer with sautéed potatoes or the cold smoked rainbow trout with asparagus. ⊠ *Aurak. 24, Keskusta* ☎ *02/251–2000* ▭ *AE, DC, MC, V* ☉ *Closed weekends and July.*

\$–\$\$\$\$ ✕ **Brahen Kellari.** This cellar restaurant near the market square is named for one of Turku's most famous historical figures. It combines coziness with clean Scandinavian lines and contemporary cuisine. Classic Finnish ingredients are prepared with international accents, such as the grilled salmon with goat cheese or the whitefish with wok-fried spinach and mushrooms. Traditional game such as reindeer and pheasant are also specialties. Take a break from sightseeing with the generous lunch buffet in quiet surroundings. ⊠ *Puolankatu 1, Kauppatori* ☎ *02/232–5400* ▭ *AE, DC, MC, V* ☉ *Closed Sun.*

\$\$\$\$ ▦ **Sokos Hotel Hamburger Börs.** This is one of Turku's best-known and finest hotels. Guest rooms have modern amenities. The German-style tavern is great for drinks; the main restaurant serves Continental cuisine and Finnish specialties such as fillet of reindeer with bacon. There's often live music in the nightclub. ⊠ *Kauppiask. 6, 20100 Turku* ☎ *02/337–381* 🖶 *02/2231–1010* ⊕ *www.sokoshotels.fi* ⇲ *340 rooms, 6 suites* ⚍ *3 restaurants, café, minibars, indoor pool, sauna, bar, nightclub, parking (fee), no-smoking rooms* ▭ *AE, DC, MC, V.*

\$\$\$–\$\$\$\$ ▦ **Park Hotel.** Built in 1904 in the art nouveau style for a British executive who ran the local shipyard, the castlelike Park Hotel is one of Finland's most unusual lodgings. Rooms have high ceilings and antique furniture but offer all the comforts of a modern hotel. It's in the heart of Turku, two blocks from the main market square. ⊠ *Rauhank. 1, 20100 Turku* ☎ *02/273–2555* ☐ *02/251–9696* ⊕ *www.parkhotelturku.fi* ⇝ *20 rooms, 1 suite* ⌂ *Restaurant, bar, sauna, meeting rooms, free parking, no-smoking rooms* ⊟ *AE, DC, MC, V.*

Nightlife & the Arts

A lively artistic community thrives in Turku, and like most Finnish towns, it comes into its own in the summer. It is most active in July during the **Ruisrock Festival** (⊕ www.ruisrock.fi), drawing international acts to the seaside park 5 km (3 mi) west of the city. August's **Turku Music Festival** (⊕ www.turkumusicfestival.fi) features baroque and contemporary performances. The highlight of the festival is the well-attended, outdoor **Down by the Laituri,** with stages set up along the city's waterfront.

BARS & LOUNGES **Koulu (School)** (⊠ Eerikinkatu 18, Keskusta ☎ 02/274–5757) is a brewery restaurant in what used to be a school for girls built in the 1880s. Turku has several distinctive bars in historic buildings. **Old Bank** (⊠ Aurakatu 3, Keskusta ☎ 02/274–5700), near the market square, is one of the most popular bars in Turku, housed in a former bank and offering 150 brands of beer from all over the world. **Puutorin Vessa (Toilet)** (⊠ Puutori [Puu Square], Keskusta ☎ 02/233–8123) is decidedly Turku's most unusual pub, in a functionalist building once serving as a public restroom but now housing what the owners call a "nice-smelling bar" and restaurant. The **Uusi Apteekki (New Pharmacy)** (⊠ Kaskenkatu 1, Keskusta ☎ 02/250–2595) has a wide selection of beers on tap, served in an old apothecary.

Naantali

 17 km (10½ mi) west of Turku.

Built around a convent of the Order of Saint Birgitta in the 15th century, the coastal village of Naantali is an aging medieval town, former pilgrimage destination, artists' colony, and modern resort all rolled into one. Many of its buildings date from the 17th century, following a massive rebuilding after the Great Fire of 1628. You'll also see a number of 18th- and 19th-century buildings, which form the basis of the Old Town—a settlement by the water's edge. These shingled wooden buildings were originally built as private residences, and many remain so, although a few now house small galleries.

Naantali's extremely narrow cobblestone lanes gave rise to a very odd law. During periods when economic conditions were poor, Naantalians earned their keep by knitting socks and exporting them by the tens of thousands. Men, women, and children all knitted so feverishly that the town council forbade groups of more than six from meeting in narrow lanes with their knitting—and causing road obstructions.

A major attraction in the village is **Kultaranta,** the summer residence for Finland's presidents, with its more than 3,500 rosebushes. During the winter, the area is only open on Friday evening; call ahead to arrange tours. ⊠ *Luonnonmaasaari, Kultaranta* ☎ *02/435–9800* ⊕ *www.*

naantalinmatkailu.fi ⊙ *Guided tours late June–mid-Aug., Tues.–Sun.;* *call Naantali tourist office or check Web site for times; mid-Aug.–mid-June, Fri. 6–8.*

The convent **Naantalin Luostarikirkko** (Naantali's Vallis Gratiae) was founded in 1443 and completed in 1462. It housed both monks and nuns, and operated under the aegis of the Catholic church until it was dissolved by the Reformation in the 16th century. Buildings fell into disrepair, then were restored from 1963 to 1965. The church is all that remains of the convent. ⊠ *Nunnak, Keskusta* ☎ *02/437–5432, 02/437–5413 to check current schedules* 🖃 *Free* ⊙ *May, daily 10–6; June–Aug., daily 10–8; Sept.–Apr., Wed. noon–2, Sun. noon (or after worship service ends)–3 or by arrangement.*

Near Naantali's marina, a footbridge leads to **Kailo Island**, in summer abuzz with theater, beach, sports, picnic facilities, and a snack bar. The **Moomin World** theme park brings to life all the famous characters of the beloved children's stories written by the Finnish woman Tove Jansson. The stories emphasize family, respect for the environment, and new adventures. ⊠ *Kailo Island, PL 48, Kailo* ☎ *02/511–1111* ⊕ *www. muumimaailma.fi* 🖃 *€16, €25 for a 2-day ticket, which includes Adventure Väski Island* ⊙ *Mid-June–mid-Aug., daily 10–6.*

Where to Stay

$$$ 🏨 **Naantali Kylpylä Spa.** The emphasis here is on pampering, with foot massages, shiatsu physical therapy, mud packs, spa water, and algae baths and a recreation program that includes yoga, tai chi, gymnastics, and water aerobics. All kinds of health packages can be arranged, including health-rehabilitation programs. It is set on a peninsula in several buildings. You can also choose to stay aboard the yacht hotel, which is attached to the spa by an indoor corridor. ⊠ *Matkailijantie 2, 21100* ☎ *02/44550* 🖶 *02/445-5621* ⊕ *www.naantalispa.fi* ➷ *80 rooms, 130 suites, 140 suites in yacht* ⚐ *5 restaurants, minibars, 5 pools, hair salon, spa, Turkish bath, 2 bars, nightclub* 🖃 *AE, DC, MC, V.*

Nightlife & the Arts

The **Naantali Music Festival** (☎ 02/434–5363 ⊕ www. naantalinmusiikkijuhlat.fi) features chamber music performances and takes place in June.

Mariehamn & the Åland Islands

④④ *155 km (93 mi) west of Turku.*

The Ålands are composed of more than 6,500 small rocky islands and skerries, inhabited in large part by families that fish or run small farms. Virtually all of the more than 25,000 locals are Swedish speaking and very proud of their largely autonomous status, which includes having their own flag and stamps. Their connection with the sea is indelible, their seafaring traditions revered. Åland is demilitarized and has special privileges within the EU that allow duty-free sales on ferries between Finland and Sweden.

Mariehamn (Maariahamina), on the main island, is the capital (population more than 10,000) and hub of Åland life. At its important port, some of the greatest grain ships sailing the seas were built by the Gustav Eriksson family.

The **Museifartyget Pommern** (*Pommern* Museum Ship), in Mariehamn West Harbor at town center, is one of the last existing grain ships in the world. Once owned by the sailing fleet of the Mariehamn shipping magnate Gustaf Erikson, the ship carried wheat between Australia and England from 1923 to 1939. ✉ *Mariehamn* ☎ *018/531–421* ⊕ *www.pommern. aland.fi* ▧ *€5* ☉ *May–June and Aug., daily 9–5; July, daily 9–7; Sept., daily 10–4.*

In prehistoric times the islands were, relatively speaking, heavily populated, as is shown by traces of no fewer than 10,000 ancient settlements, graves, and strongholds. A visit to **Sund County** will take you back to the earliest days of life on the islands, with its remains from prehistoric times and the Middle Ages. **Kastelholm** is a medieval castle built by the Swedes to strengthen their presence on Åland. ✉ *Kastelholm* ☎ *018/ 432–150* ▧ *€5* ☉ *Guided tours May–June and early–mid-Aug., daily 10–5; July, daily 10–6; mid-Aug.–Oct. daily 10–4.*

Jan Karlsgården Friluftsmuseum (Jan Karlsgården Open-air Museum) is a popular open-air museum, with buildings and sheds from the 18th century that portray farming life on the island 200 years ago. ✉ *Kastelholm* ☎ *018/432–150* ▧ *Free* ☉ *May–Sept., daily 10–5.*

About 8 km (5 mi) from the village of Kastelholm in Sund are the scattered ruins of **Bomarsund Fortress,** a huge naval fortress built by the Russians in the early 19th century. It was only half finished when it was destroyed by Anglo-French forces during the Crimean War. ☎ *018/44032* ☉ *June and early Aug.–mid-Aug., weekdays 10–4; July, daily 10–4; call ahead, as times can vary.*

Where to Stay & Eat

$$–$$$ ✕▦ **Arkipelag.** In the heart of Mariehamn, the bayside Arkipelag Hotel is known for its fine marina and lively disco-bar. Rooms are modern and comfortable, with huge picture windows and balconies. Ask for a seaside room. The restaurants, set in long, wood-panel rooms with wide windows overlooking an ocean inlet, serve fresh Åland seafood. Try the crayfish when it's in season. In the terrace restaurant, the skewered fresh shrimp are a treat. ✉ *Strandgatan 31, 22100 Mariehamn* ☎ *018/24020* 🖷 *018/24384* ⊕ *www.hotellarkipelag.com* ⇥ *78 rooms, 8 suites* ⚘ *2 restaurants, indoor-outdoor pool, sauna, bar, casino, nightclub, meeting room* ▤ *DC, MC, V.*

$$ ▦ **Björklidens Stugby.** The cabins are small, but the draw here is really the outdoors. You can take out one of the free rowboats, or relax on the lawns and the tree swings. It is 25 km (16 mi) north of Mariehamn. There are outdoor grills and washing machines for guests to use. ✉ *22240 Hammarland* ☎ *018/37800* 🖷 *018/37801* ⊕ *www.bjorkliden. aland.fi* ⇥ *14 cabins, 5 apartments* ⚘ *Refrigerators, beach, fishing, playground* ▤ *MC, V* ☉ *Closed late Nov.–Mar.*

The Outdoors

BIKING Most towns have bikes for rent from about €10 per day (€50 per week). The fine scenery and the terrain, alternately dead flat and gently rolling, make for ideal cycling. The roads are not busy once you leave the highway. **Suomen Retkeilymajajärjestö** (Finnish Youth Hostel Association; ⊠ Yrjönk. 38B 15, 00100 Helsinki ☎ 09/565–7150 ⎙ 09/565–71510 ⊕ www.srmnet.org) has reasonably priced bicycle rental–hostel packages for one to two weeks starting in Helsinki. For Åland bicycle routes and tour packages, contact **Ålandsresor Ab** (⊠ PB 62, 22101 Mariehamn ☎ 018/28040 ⎙ 018/28380 ⊕ www.alandsresor.fi). **Viking Line** (⊠ Storagatan 2, 22100 Mariehamn ☎ 018/26211 ⎙ 018/26116) is a bike-friendly outfit that also offers cottage rentals in Åland.

BOATING These are great sailing waters for experienced mariners. Boats can be rented through the Åland tourist office.

FISHING Try **Ålandsresor** (⊠ Torggatan 2, 22100 Mariehamn ☎ 018/28040) for fishing packages in the Ålands. **Viking Line** (⊠ Storagatan 2, 22100 Mariehamn ☎ 018/26211) also offers packages for anglers.

Southwestern Coast & the Ålands A to Z

AIR TRAVEL
🚩 **Finnair** ☎ 018/634–500 Mariehamn ⎙ 018/634–506 ⊕ www.finnair.fi.

AIRPORTS
The region's airports are at Mariehamn and Turku. Both have connections to Helsinki and Stockholm, with service by Finnair.

BOAT & FERRY TRAVEL
Åland is most cheaply reached by boat from Turku and Naantali. Call Silja Line in Turku, Mariehamn, Tampere, or Helsinki. Or call Viking Line in Turku, Mariehamn, Tampere, or Helsinki. Tickets can also be purchased at the harbor.
🚩 **Silja Line** ☎ 02/335–6244 Turku, 018/16711 Mariehamn, 03/216–2000 Tampere, 09/18041 Helsinki ⊕ www.silja.fi. **Viking Line** ☎ 02/333–1331 Turku, 018/26011 Mariehamn, 03/249–0111 Tampere, 09/12351 in Helsinki ⊕ www.vikingline.fi.

BUS TRAVEL
Good bus service connects the capital to the southwest from Helsinki's long-distance bus station at the Kamppi, west of the train station off Mannerheimintie.
🚩 **Matkahuolto** ⊠ Narinkka 3 00100 Helsinki ☎ 0200/4000 €1.64 per call plus local charge ⎙ 09/6136–8426 ⊕ www.matkahuolto.com.

CAR TRAVEL
The Helsinki–Turku trip is 166 km (103 mi) on E18. Signs on E18 will tell you where to turn off for the south-coast towns of Tammisaari and Hanko. Most of southwestern Finland is well served by public transport, so a car is not necessary.

EMERGENCIES

A major medical center in the region is the Turun Yliopistollinen Keskusairaala (University of Turku Central Hospital). For a dentist, call the Turun Hammaslääkärikeskus (Turku Dental Center).

🚑 **Police, ambulance** ☎ 112. **Turun Hammaslääkärikeskus** ✉ Hämeenk. 2, Turku ☎ 02/233-3778. **Turun Yliopistollinen Keskusairaala** ✉ Kiinamyllynk. 4-8, Turku ☎ 02/313-0000.

TOURS

Turku TouRing is the main regional tourist organization, offering various theme trips and package tours. Between late June and early August, the six-hour Manor Tour visits three manors in the area: Louhisaari, Nuhjala, and Jäärppilä. A three-hour tour of Turku's main sights, including the cathedral and castle, is available throughout summer, as are special tours for children.

The Tammisaari tourist office has information on boat tours run by Archipelago Tours. You can board a restaurant boat and visit the national park and several coastal cities, or simply cruise through the islands. Costs range from €12 to €24 per person, depending on the length of the cruise. See the city tourism Web site, ⊕ www.ekenas.fi/english or ⊕ www.surfnet.fi/saaristoristeilyt. You can take a 3½- to 4-hour steamship cruise between Turku and Naantali, which includes a smorgasbord lunch, or dinner, while drifting around the archipelago (€13–€20 not including meals); cruises run from mid-June to mid-August. Contact the Naantali tourist office or the Steamship Company SS *Ukkopekka*.

🚢 **Steamship Company SS** *Ukkopekka* ✉ Linnank. 38, 20100 Turku ☎ 02/515-3300 ⊕ www.ukkopekka.fi. **Turku TouRing** ✉ Aurakatu 4, 20100 Turku ☎ 02/262-7444 ⊕ www.turkutouring.fi.

TRAIN TRAVEL

Trains leave Helsinki and other cities for Turku several times a day, and some go directly to the harbor within a short walk of the ferries. For most smaller towns, you must stop at stations along the Helsinki–Turku route and change to a local bus. Bus fares are usually a bit cheaper than train fares.

VISITOR INFORMATION

🛈 Tourist Information **Åland** ✉ Storagatan 8, 22100 Mariehamn ☎ 018/24000 🖷 018/24265 ⊕ www.visitaland.com. **Hanko** ✉ Raatihuoneentori 5, Box 14, 10901 ☎ 019/220-3411 🖷 019/220-3261 ⊕ www.hanko.fi. **Naantali** ✉ Kaivotori 2, 21100 ☎ 02/435-9800 🖷 02/435-0852 ⊕ www.naantali.fi. **Rauma** ✉ Valtak. 2, 26100 ☎ 02/834-4551 🖷 02/837-87741 ⊕ www.rauma.fi. **Tammisaari** Ekenäs ✉ Raatihuoneentori, 10600 ☎ 020/775-2100 🖷 020/775-2212 ⊕ www.tammisaari.fi. **Turku TouRing** ✉ Aurak. 4, 20100 Turku ☎ 02/262-7444 🖷 02/233-7673 ⊕ www.turkutouring.fi.

THE LAKELANDS

Finland is perhaps best known for its lakes, numbering about 188,000, and you don't need to travel far in this region to appreciate their beauty, whether in winter or summer. Almost every lake, big or small, is fringed

with tiny cabins. The lake cabin is a Finnish institution, and until the advent of cheap package tours abroad, nearly every Finnish family vacationed in the same way—in its cabin on a lake.

The towns in this region, while traditionally drawing fewer tourists, have much to offer, especially during summer music and theater festivals. Savonlinna stands out among the towns, not only for its stunning, water-bound views—it is hugged by gigantic Lake Saimaa—but for its cultural life. The monthlong Savonlinna Opera Festival in July is one of Finland's—and Europe's—greatest. The quality of the opera, ballet, drama, and instrumental performance here during the annual festival weeks is world-class. Most events are staged at the 14th-century Olavinlinna Castle, splendidly positioned just offshore. To the west, the smaller Hämeenlinna has its own lakeside castle. North of Hämeenlinna, high-tech Tampere has the cultural variety of a city and is nestled between two large lakes. There are small medieval churches scattered through the Lakelands, the most famous of which is the stone church in Hattula, its interior a gallery of medieval painted scenes.

For centuries the lakeland region was a much-contested buffer zone between the warring empires of Sweden and Russia. After visiting the people of the Lakelands, you should have a basic understanding of the Finnish word *sisu* (guts), a quality that has kept Finns independent.

Savonlinna is the best-placed town in the Lakelands and can make a convenient base from which to begin exploring the region. Savonlinna, Tampere, and Hämeenlinna are only short train rides from Helsinki; all three make good daylong excursions from the capital city. The Land of a Thousand Lakes is also perfect for a long or short boat cruise. Travel from one town to the next by boat, take a lake cruise with dinner on board, or simply take a sightseeing cruise.

Savonlinna

45 *335 km (208 mi) northeast of Helsinki.*

One of the larger Lakelands towns, Savonlinna is best known for having the finest castle in all of Finland. The town takes advantage of this stunning attraction by holding major events, such as the annual opera festival, in the castle courtyard. The islands that make up Savonlinna center are linked by bridges. First, stop in at the tourist office for information; then cross the bridge east to the open-air market that flourishes alongside the main passenger quay. From here you can catch the boat to Kuopio and Lappeenranta. In days when waterborne traffic was the major form of transportation, Savonlinna was the central hub of the passenger fleet serving Saimaa, the largest lake system in Europe. Now the lake traffic is dominated by cruise and sightseeing boats, but the quayside still bustles with arrivals and departures every summer morning and evening.

A 10-minute stroll from the quay to the southeast brings you to Savonlinna's most famous site, the castle **Olavinlinna**. First built in 1475 to protect Finland's eastern border, the castle retains its medieval character and is one of Scandinavia's best-preserved historic monuments. Still surrounded by water that once bolstered its defensive strength, the fortress rises majestically out of the lake. Every July the **Savonlinna Opera Festival** (✉ Olavinkatu 27, 57130 ☎ 015/476–750 ⊟ 015/476–7540 ⊕ www.operafestival.fi) is held in the castle's courtyard, which creates a spellbinding combination of music and surroundings. The festival is a showcase for Finnish opera but it also hosts foreign companies such as the Los Angeles Opera and the Royal Opera. You will need to make reservations well in advance for both tickets and hotel rooms (note higher hotel rates during the festival), as Savonlinna draws many music lovers. The festival also includes arts and crafts exhibits around town. ✉ *Olavinlinna* ☎ *015/531–164* ⊕ *www.nba.fi/en/olavinlinna_castle* ⊠ *€5 entrance to Olavinlinna* ☉ *June–mid-Aug., daily 10–5; mid-Aug.–May, daily 10–3. Guided tours daily on the hr.*

For a glimpse into the history of lake traffic, including the fascinating floating timber trains still a common sight on Saimaa today, visit the **Savonlinnan maakunta museo** (Savonlinna Provincial Museum), to which belong the 19th-century steam schooners, the SS *Salama*, the SS *Mikko*, and the SS *Savonlinna*. ✉ *Riihisaari island, near Olavinlinna, Riihisaari*

☎ *015/571–4712* ⊕ *www.savonlinna.fi/museo* ⊠ *€5* ⊙ *Sept.–June, Tues.–Sun. 11–5; July–mid-Aug., daily 11–5. Boats: mid-May–mid-Aug. during museum hrs.*

Where to Stay & Eat

$–$$$ ✕ **Majakka.** The centrally located Majakka feels intimate due to its booths, two aquariums, and many plants. Some tables offer nice views of the adjacent park and the Haukivesi Lake harbor. The menu changes twice a year, although there are some standards—try the steak topped with a pepper-and-cream sauce. Reservations are essential during festival season. ⊠ *Satamak. 11, Keskusta* ☎ *015/531–456* ▤ *AE, DC, MC, V.*

¢–$$$ ✕ **Paviljonki.** Just 1 km (½ mi) from the city center is Paviljonki, the restaurant of the Savonlinna restaurant school. The menu is short but sweet; try the fried vendace (the tiny, tasty fish abundant in the lakes) with herb-spiced potato salad or the classic pepper steak. The restaurant closes early (7 PM) and has a lunch buffet. ⊠ *Rajalahdenk. 4, Nojanmaa* ☎ *015/550–6303* ▤ *DC, MC, V.*

$–$$$ ▦ **Seurahuone.** This hotel in a 1950s town house is near the market and passenger harbor. Rooms are small but comfortable and have modern fittings; be sure to ask for one that overlooks the picturesque harbor. ⊠ *Kauppatori 4–6, 57130* ☎ *015/5731* 🖷 *015/273–918* ⊕ *www. savonhotellit.fi* ⇝ *84 rooms* ⚐ *Restaurant, sauna, bar, dance club, nightclub, meeting rooms* ▤ *AE, DC, MC, V.*

$$ ▦ **Spa Hotel Casino.** A 1960s relic, the Spa Hotel Casino has a restful lakeside location on an island linked to the town by a pedestrian bridge. Rooms are basic with brown cork floors, white walls, and simple furnishings; all except one have a balcony. ⊠ *Kylpylaitoksentie, Kasinonsaari, 57130* ☎ *015/73950* 🖷 *015/272–524* ⇝ *80 rooms* ⚐ *2 restaurants, minibars, pool, sauna, spa, boating, pub, no-smoking rooms* ▤ *AE, DC, MC, V.*

$–$$ ▦ **Family Hotel Hospitz.** In the heart of Savonlinna overlooking Saimaa Lake, this charming YMCA hotel is in a 1930s brick building on historic Linnankatu. It has small, unpretentious rooms, all individually decorated in period styles. ⊠ *Linnank. 20, 57130* ☎ *015/515–661* 🖷 *015/515–120* ⊕ *www.hospitz.com* ⇝ *21 rooms* ⚐ *Sauna, meeting rooms* ▤ *AE, DC, MC, V.*

$ ▦ **Summer Hotel Vuorilinna.** The simple white rooms of this modern student dorm become hotel rooms in summer. Guests may use the facilities, including the restaurant, of the nearby Spa Hotel Casino. ⊠ *Kasinonsaari, 57130* ☎ *015/739–5495* 🖷 *015/272–524* ⇝ *220 rooms* ▤ *AE, DC, MC, V* ⊙ *Closed Sept.–May.*

The Outdoors

BOATING **Saimaa Sailing Oy** (⊠ Mäntyk. 9, 53100 Lappeenranta ☎ 0400/485317 ⊕ www.saimaasailing.fi) is the biggest boat-rental firm in the Lakeland region. Sailboats and motorboats can be rented on a weekly basis. The base is the handsome, historic coastal town of Lappeenranta, 155 km (96 mi) southeast of Savonlinna. For information on the Saimaa canal, visit the Finnish Maritime Administration's Web site, ⊕ www.fma.fi.

> **off the beaten path**
>
> **OLD MINE OF OUTUKUMPU** – This child-friendly complex 187 km (116 mi) north of Savonlinna consists of a mining museum and activities that include a trip on a mining train and a mineral exhibition. ⊠ *Kaivosmiehenpolku 2, 83500* ☎ *013/554–795* ⊕ *www.vanhakaivos.fi* 🎫 *€9* ⊙ *June–Aug., daily 10–6.*

Punkaharju

46 *35 km (22 mi) east of Savonlinna.*

Rising out of the water and separating the Puruvesi and Pihlajavesi lakes, the 8-km (5-mi) ridge of Punkaharju is a geographic wonder that predates the Ice Age. At times the pine-covered rocks narrow to only 25 feet, yet the ridge still manages to accommodate a road and train tracks.

★ Just south of Punkaharju is the **Taidekeskus Retretti** (Retretti Art Center). One of the most popular excursions from Savonlinna, Retretti is accessible via a two-hour boat ride or a 30-minute, 29-km (18-mi) bus trip. It consists of a modern art complex of unique design and has a cavern section built into the Punkaharju ridge. It's also a magnificent setting for concerts in summer and the site of more than 40 different indoor and outdoor scheduled summertime activities. ☎ *015/775–2200* ⊕ *www. retretti.fi* 🎫 *€15* ⊙ *June and Aug., daily 10–5; July, daily 10–6.*

★ Combine your trip to Retretti with a visit to the nearby **Lusto Finnish Forest Museum.** Every kind of forestry—from the industrial to the artistic— and every aspect of Finland's close relationship with its most abundant natural resource are examined here in imaginative and absorbing displays. ⊠ *Lustontie 1, 58450 Punkaharju* ☎ *015/345–1030* ⊕ *www.lusto. fi* 🎫 *€7* ⊙ *Jan.–Apr., Tues.–Sun. 10–5; May and Sept., daily 10–5; June–Aug., daily 10–7; Oct.–Dec., Tues.–Sun. 10–5; closed last 2 wks in Jan.*

Where to Stay & Eat

$–$$ ✕🏠 **Punkaharju Valtion Hotelli.** Near Retretti, the Punkaharju National Hotel was constructed as a gamekeeper's lodge for Czar Nicholas I in 1845. Enlarged and restored, it is now a restful spot for a meal or an overnight visit. The manor house with small rooms is decorated in the old Finnish country style. The restaurant serves simple local dishes such as fried vendace. It's a half-hour drive from Savonlinna. ⊠ *Punkaharju 2, 58450* ☎ *015/739–611* 🖷 *015/441–784* ⊕ *www.lomaliitto.fi* 🛏 *18 rooms, 3 suites, 3 with shared baths; 15 summer cottages* ⟨ *Restaurant, 2 tennis courts, sauna, beach, meeting rooms* ⊟ *DC, MC, V.*

Kuopio

47 *220 km (137 mi) northwest of Punkaharju, 185 km (115 mi) northwest of Savonlinna.*

You'll get a deeper understanding of the meaning of Finland's proximity to Russia and the East in Kuopio, with its Russian Orthodox monastery and museum. The boat from Savonlinna arrives at Kuopio's passenger harbor, where a small evening market holds forth daily from 3 to 10.

Kuopio's tourist office is close to the **Tori** (marketplace). Coined *maailman napa*—the belly button of the world—Kuopio's market square should be one of your first stops, for it is one of the most colorful outdoor markets in Finland. Try the famous *kalakukko pie* (fish and bacon in a rye crust). ☉ *May–Sept., weekdays 7–5, Sat. 7–3; Oct.–Apr., Mon.–Sat. 7–3.*

★ The **Ortodoksinen Kirkkomuseo** (Orthodox Church Museum) possesses one of the most interesting and unusual collections of its kind. When Karelia (the eastern province of Finland) was ceded to the Soviet Union after World War II, religious art was taken out of the monasteries and brought to Kuopio. The collection is eclectic, and includes one of the most beautiful icon collections in the world, as well as embroidered church textiles. ✉ *Karjalank. 1, Kuopio* ☎ *017/287–2244* 🎫 *€5* ☉ *May–Aug., Tues.–Sun. 10–4; Sept.–Apr., weekdays noon–3, weekends noon–5.*

If you were fascinated by the treasures in the Orthodox Church Museum, you'll want to visit the Orthodox convent of Lintula and the **Valamon Luostari** (Valamo Monastery) in Heinävesi, between Varkaus and Joensuu. As a major center for Russian Orthodox religious and cultural life in Finland, the monastery hosts daily services. Precious 18th-century icons and sacred objects are housed in the main church and in the icon conservation center. The Orthodox library is the most extensive in Finland and is open to visitors. A café-restaurant is on the grounds, and very modest hotel and hostel accommodations are available at the monastery. ✉ *Uusi Valamo, Valamontie 42* ☎ *017/570–111, 017/570–1504 hotel reservations* ⊕ *www.valamo.fi* 🎫 *€3.50 for guided tour* ☉ *Mar.–Sept., daily 8 AM–9 PM; Oct.–Feb., daily 8–8; guided tours daily June–Aug., other times by appointment.*

The **Lintulan Luostari** (Lintula Convent) can be reached by boat from Valamo, or you can visit both the convent and the monastery by boat on scenic day excursions from Kuopio. Boat tours from Kuopio are available mid-June to mid-August from Kuopio Roll Cruises Ltd. Tours depart from Kuopio's main pier; upon arrival at Palokin pier, taxi transport is arranged to Lintulan Luostari and Valamo, and the return trip to Kuopio is made by bus. The trip can be made in reverse, going by bus and returning by boat to the harbor, to Valamo only. ☎ *017/266–2466 Kuopio Roll Cruises* 🎫 *Tours approximately €60 including boat and ground transportation* ☉ *Convent June–Aug.*

The slender **Puijon Näkötorni** (Puijo Tower), 3 km (2 mi) northwest of Kuopio, is best visited at sunset, when the lakes shimmer with reflected light. It has two observation decks and is crowned by a revolving restaurant with marvelous views. ☎ *017/255–5250* ⊕ *www.puijo.com* 🎫 *€3* ☉ *May–June, Mon.–Sat. 9 AM–10 PM, Sun. noon–6; July–mid-Aug., daily 9 AM–11 PM; Sept., Mon.–Sat. 9 AM–10 PM, Sun. noon–5; check Web site for winter hrs.*

Where to Stay & Eat

$$–$$$ ✕ **Musta Lammas.** Near the passenger harbor, Musta Lammas is in the basement of a brewery founded in 1862. It has been attractively adapted from its beer-cellar days, retaining the original redbrick walls and beer barrels. The specialty here is Finnish fish and game specialties such as *muikku* (vendace), whitefish, and lamb, prepared with innovative sauces and side dishes. ⊠ *Satamak. 4, Keskusta* ☎ *017/581–0458* ⊟ *AE, DC, MC, V* ✆ *Closed Sun. No lunch.*

$–$$$ ✕ **Isä Camillo.** This popular restaurant is in a former Bank of Finland building and serves Finnish and international cuisine—steaks and pastas are particularly popular—at reasonable prices. Ask to eat in the bank vault. ⊠ *Kauppak. 25–27, Keskusta/Tori* ☎ *017/581–0450* ⊟ *AE, DC, MC, V.*

¢–$$ ✕ **Restaurant Sampo.** In the town center, Sampo was founded in 1931, and its Scandinavian furniture dates from the 1950s. High ceilings and large chandeliers impart an elegant look. Try the muikku, which comes smoked, fried, grilled, or in a stew with pork, potatoes, and onions. ⊠ *Kauppak. 13, Keskusta/Tori* ☎ *017/261–4677* ⊟ *AE, DC, MC, V.*

$$–$$$ ⊞ **Scandic Kuopio.** This is the newest and most modern of the local hotels. Rooms are spacious by European standards, with large beds and generous towels. It's on the lakefront and also close to the town. ⊠ *Satamakatu 1, 70100* ☎ *017/195–111* ⊟ *017/195–2211* ⊕ *www.scandichotels.com* ⇨ *134 rooms* ⚷ *Restaurant, in-room data ports, pool, hot tub, 3 saunas, boating, bar, meeting room* ⊟ *AE, DC, MC, V.*

$$ ⊞ **Quality Hotel Iso-Valkeinen.** On the lakeshore only 5 km (3 mi) from town center, this hotel has large, quiet rooms in four one-story buildings. Several rooms have balconies with views of the nearby lake. ⊠ *Päiväranta, 70420* ☎ *017/539–6100* ⊟ *017/539–6555* ⊕ *www.isovalkeinen.com* ⇨ *100 rooms with shower* ⚷ *2 restaurants, miniature golf, tennis court, pool, gym, sauna, beach, boating, fishing, nightclub, free parking, no-smoking rooms* ⊟ *AE, DC, MC, V.*

$$ ⊞ **Spa Hotel Rauhalahti.** About 5 km (3 mi) from town center, Rauhalahti is set near Kallavesi Lake and has no-frills rooms and apartments. A number of amenities cater to sports lovers and families. The hotel has three restaurants and has live dance music three times a week. ⊠ *Katiskaniementie 8, 70700* ☎ *017/473–473* ⊟ *017/473–470* ⊕ *www.rauhalahti.com* ⇨ *106 rooms, 40 suites, 6 apartments* ⚷ *3 restaurants, tennis court, pool, gym, hot tub, sauna, spa, boating, horseback riding, squash* ⊟ *AE, DC, MC, V.*

Tampere

48 *293 km (182 mi) southwest of Kuopio, 174 km (108 mi) northwest of Helsinki.*

Tampere is an industrial center with a difference. From about the year 1000, this was a base from which traders and hunters set out on their expeditions to northern Finland; it was not until 1779 that a Swedish king, Gustav III, founded the city itself. In 1828 a Scotsman named James Finlayson came to the infant city and established a factory for spinning cotton. This was the beginning of "big business" in Finland. The Finlayson firm is today one of the country's major industrial enterprises, but its local factory complex has been converted to house software firms, restaurants, a museum, and a multiplex cinema. Although cotton and textile manufacturers put Tampere on the map as a traditional center of industry, the city is now known for its high-tech companies and large universities. The mobile-phone giant Nokia got its start in a small city of the same name nearby; don't be surprised to see many of the locals strolling down Tampere's compact main street, Hämeenkatu, with a *kännykkä* (cell phone) in use. Tampere's more than 200,000 inhabitants also nurture an unusually sophisticated cultural environment, with the international festivals of short film (March) and theater (August) among the most popular offerings.

Artful siting is the secret of this factory town. An isthmus little more than a half mile wide at its narrowest point separates the lakes Näsijärvi and Pyhäjärvi, and at one spot the **Tammerkoski Rapids** provide an outlet for the waters of one to cascade through to the other. Called the Mother of Tampere, these rapids once provided the electrical power on which the town's livelihood depended. Their natural beauty has been preserved in spite of the factories on either bank, and the well-designed public buildings grouped around them enhance their general effect. Don't be surprised to see people fishing for salmon off a bridge in the shadow of a pulp mill, a reminder of conscious efforts since the 1970s to keep the city's environment clean.

The old workers' wooden-housing area of **Pispala,** clustered around the steep slopes of the **Pyynikki Ridge,** is one of the most picturesque urban districts in Finland. The old **observation tower** at the top of the ridge has marvelous views across both lake systems to the north and south. The café at the foot of the tower serves excellent fresh doughnuts daily.

Adding to Tampere's natural beauty is the **Hämeensilta Bridge** in the heart of town, with its four statues by the well-known Finnish sculptor Wäinö Aaltonen. Close to the bridge, near the high-rise Sokos Hotel Ilves, are some old factory buildings that have been restored as shops and boutiques. At Verkatehtaankatu 2, the city **tourist office** offers helpful services such as walking and bus tours and free bicycle rentals. You can also buy a Tourist Card for one or more days (€6 first day plus €4 each additional day), which allows unlimited travel on city buses.

A 1½-km (1-mi) walk west, then north from the heart of Tampere brings you to the **Särkänniemen Huvikeskus** (Särkänniemi Recreation Center), a major recreation complex for both children and adults. Its many attractions include an amusement park, a children's zoo, a planetarium, and a well-planned aquarium with a separate dolphinarium. Within Särkänniemi, the **Sara Hildénin Taidemuseo** (Sara Hildén Art Museum) is a striking example of Finnish architecture, with the works of modern Finnish and international artists, including Giacometti, Klee, MirÛ, and Picasso. Särkänniemi's profile is punctuated by the 550-foot **Näsinneulan Näkötorni** (Näsinneula Observatory Tower), Finland's tallest observation tower and the dominant feature of the Tampere skyline. The top of the tower holds an observatory and a revolving restaurant. The views are magnificent, commanding the lake, forest, and town—the contrast between the industrial maze of Tampere at your feet and the serenity of the lakes stretching out to meet the horizon is unforgettable. ⊠ *Särkänniemi* ☎ *03/248–8111, 020/714–3500 museum* ⊕ *www. sarkanniemi.fi* ⊠ *€5 includes admission to the adventure park, the museum, the tower, and children's zoo (when rides are in operation). Dolphinarium, aquarium, and planetarium €5 each; individual rides in the amusement park €5, 1-day Särkänniemi Adventure Key (pass to all sights and rides in the park) €29, 2-day €36* ⊙ *Museum daily 11–6; children's zoo, adventure park, rides, tower, and other attractions; check Web site or call for hrs.*

Among the most unusual structures in Tampere is the **Tampere pääkirjasto** (Tampere Central Library), nicknamed "Metso" (wood grouse) for its unusual shape. Designed by the famous Pietilä couple, it houses an exhibit celebrating the *Moomintroll* books of Finnish author Tove Jansson. ⊠ *Pirkankatu 2, Hämeenpuisto* ☎ *03/314–614* ⊕ *www.tampere. fi/kirjasto* ⊙ *Sept.–May, weekdays 9:30–8, Sat. 9:30–3; June–Aug., weekdays 9:30–7, Sat. 9:30–3.*

While in western Tampere, be sure to visit one of the city's best museums, the **Amurin Työläiskorttelimuseo** (Amuri Museum of Workers' Housing), which consists of more than 30 apartments in a collection of wooden houses, plus a sauna, a bakery, a haberdashery, and more from the 1880s to the 1970s. Its cozy café has garden seating in summer and serves fresh bread baked on the premises. ⊠ *Makasiininkatu 12, Amuri* ☎ *020/716–6690* ⊕ *www.tampere.fi/amuri* ⊠ *€4* ⊙ *Mid-May–mid-Sept., Tues.–Sun. 10–6.*

Not far from Amuri Museum, in the old Tampella factory area, is the **Museokeskus Vapriikki** (Museum Center Vapriikki), which consolidates the collections of five separate museums (700,000 pieces) to illustrate the city's role in Finnish industrial history. Housed in a former textile and turbine factory complex that dates from the 1880s, the permanent exhibit focuses on local history, while other displays cover archaeological finds and modern art. The center also includes an excellent café and gift shop. ⊠ *Veturiaukio 4, Tampella* ☎ *020/716–6966* ⊕ *www.tampere. fi/vapriikki* ⊠ *€5* ⊙ *Tues. and Thurs.–Sun. 10–6, Wed. 11–8.*

The **Lenin Museo** (Lenin Museum), the only one of its kind left in the world, occupies the hall where Lenin and Stalin first met in the historic Tampere Workers' Hall. Photos, memorabilia, and temporary exhibits document the life of Lenin and the Russian Revolution. ⊠ *Hämeenpuisto 28, 3rd fl., Hämeenpuisto* ☎ *03/276–8100* ⊕ *www.lenin.fi* ⊠ *€4* ⊙ *Weekdays 9–6, weekends 11–4.*

At the foot of the Pyynikki ridge is the **Pyynikin Kesäteatteri** (Pyynikki Summer Theater ⊠ Joselininniemi, Pyynikki ☎ 03/216–0300), with an outdoor revolving auditorium that can be moved, even with a full load of spectators, to face any one of the sets. It's open mid-June to mid-August. On the east side of town is the modern **Kalevan Kirkko** (Kaleva Church), a soaring monument to light and space designed by Reima and Reili Pietilä, the famous architect couple who also designed the Tam-

pere city library, "Metso." ✉ *Liisanpuisto 1, Kaleva* ☎ *03/219–0404*
🕓 *May–Aug., daily 10–5 Sept.–Apr., daily 11–3.*

★ Most buildings in Tampere, including the cathedral, are comparatively
modern. The **Tuomiokirkko** (Cathedral) was built in 1907 and houses some
of the best-known masterpieces of Finnish art, including Magnus Enck-
nell's fresco *The Resurrection* and Hugo Simberg's *Wounded Angel*
and *Garden of Death.* ✉ *Tuomiokirkonkatu 3, Keskusta* 🕓 *May–Aug.,*
daily 9–6; Sept.–Apr., daily 11–3.

Where to Stay & Eat

$$–$$$$ ✕ **Astor.** Here you'll find a moderately priced brasserie menu and a more
expensive selection on the main menu. In the restaurant, try the salmon,
whitefish, duck, or reindeer dishes, many prepared in red-wine or game
sauces. Brasserie favorites include salads and open-faced sandwiches (called
toasts) with smoked-reindeer, smoked salmon, and chicken. ✉ *Aleksis*
Kivenk. 26, Keskusta ☎ *03/260–5700* 🖃 *DC, MC, V.*

$$–$$$$ ✕ **Tiiliholvi.** A romantic cellar in an art nouveau building with a colorful past, Tiiliholvi serves Finnish haute cuisine and the best wine selec-
tion in town. Fresh, seasonal ingredients like mushrooms, reindeer,
partridge, and salmon are often paired with unexpected wine or liquor
sauces or fresh herb vinaigrettes. ✉ *Kauppak. 10, Keskusta* ☎ *03/272–*
0231 🖃 *AE, DC, MC, V* 🕓 *Closed Sun. and July.*

$–$$$$ ✕ **Bodega Salud.** Salud mixes Spanish specialties with classics such as
lamb chops and steaks and unconventional dishes such as alligator tail.
A salad bar with cheese and fruit is a favorite. Try the tapas prix fixe
lunch. ✉ *Tuomiokirkonkatu 19, Keskusta* ☎ *03/233–4400* 🌐 *www.salud.*
fi 🕭 *Reservations essential* 🖃 *DC, MC, V.*

$–$$$ ✕ **Harald.** The Viking details and the hearty fare make this quirky
restaurant in the heart of the city a nice change of pace. Choose from
stews and soups of fish and game at sturdy wooden tables, along with
beer served in earthenware mugs. ✉ *Hämeenkatu 23, Keskusta* ☎ *03/*
213–8380 🖃 *AE, DC, MC, V.*

$–$$$ ✕ **Teatteriaravintola Tillikka.** Long known as a hangout for leftist intel-
lectuals, Tillikka now prepares hearty meals overlooking the rapids for
a variety of political persuasions. House specialties include meatballs,
herring fillets, fried pike perch, and pepper steak; try any of them with
one of the local brews. The restaurant is housed in the same building
as the city theater. ✉ *Teatteritalo, Hämeenkatu 14, Keskusta* ☎ *03/254–*
4724 🖃 *AE, DC, MC, V.*

$–$$ ✕ **Laterna.** In a czarist-era hotel with antique bay windows and light fixtures, oil paintings, and elegant dark-wood furniture, Laterna specializes
in Russian fare with a Finnish twist. Once the haunt of artists and writers,
the scene here is still lively—occasional performances on the weekends can
include the famous Finnish tango. Classic dishes include vorschmack (a
hash of beef, lamb, and herring), blini, and borscht with sour cream. ✉ *Pu-*
utarhakatu 11, Keskusta ☎ *03/272–0241* 🖃 *AE, DC, MC, V.*

$$$$ 🏨 **Sokos Hotel Ilves.** Soaring above a gentrified area of old warehouses
near city center, this 18-story hotel is Tampere's tallest building. All rooms
above the sixth floor have spectacular views of the city and Pyhäjärvi
and Näsijärvi lakes. ✉ *Hatanpään valtatie 1, 33100* ☎ *020/1234–631*

⌂ 03/5698–6263 ⊕ *www.sokoshotels.fi* ⤴ *327 rooms, 9 suites* ⌂ *4 restaurants, pool, gym, hot tub, 3 saunas, nightclub, some free parking, no-smoking rooms* ▭ *AE, DC, MC, V.*

$$$–$$$$ ▢ **Sokos Hotel Tammer.** A beautiful historic hotel overlooking a park, the Hotel Tammer has a grand dining room. Guest rooms are individually decorated and have modern fittings. ⊠ *Satakunnankatu 13, 33100* ☎ *020/1234–632* ⌂ *03/5697–6266* ⤴ *87 rooms* ⌂ *Restaurant, sauna, no-smoking rooms* ▭ *AE, DC, V.*

$$$ ▢ **Scandic Tampere City.** This Scandic property in the heart of the city center, opposite the train station, caters to business travelers and tourists. The hotel was completely renovated in 2005. ⊠ *Hämeenkatu 1, 33100* ☎ *03/244–6111* ⌂ *03/2446–2211* ⤴ *262 rooms, 1 suite* ⌂ *Restaurant, minibars, gym, 3 saunas, bar, business services, meeting rooms, no-smoking rooms* ▭ *AE, DC, MC, V.*

¢ ▢ **Iltatähti Apartment Hotel.** This centrally located hotel has pleasant and unpretentious accommodations at budget rates. ⊠ *Tuomiokirkonkatu 19, 33100* ☎ *03/315–161* ⌂ *03/3151–6262* ⊕ *www.hoteliltatahti.fi* ⤴ *90 rooms, 33 with bath* ⌂ *Refrigerators; no smoking* ▭ *AE, DC, MC, V.*

Nightlife & the Arts

Tampere has a lively pub and beer-bar scene. Don't be surprised if you see a quiz competition going on in one of the local pubs, a popular Tampere pastime, particularly in the winter. The Irish theme is at its most popular in Tampere at **O'Connell's** (⊠ Ratatienkatu 24, Keskusta ☎ 03/222–7032) with occasional live music. Try the in-house brew at **Plevna** (⊠ Itäinenk. 8, Keskusta ☎ 03/260–1200), timing your visit to coincide with a performance by the German-style brass band. The English-style **Salhojankadun Pub** (⊠ Salhojank. 29, Keskusta ☎ 03/255–3376) is an old favorite. The converted post office is now **Wanha Posti** (⊠ Hämeenk. 13, Keskusta ☎ 03/223–3007), lauded for its wide selection of Finnish and international brews.

For live jazz music, visit **Paapan Kapakka** (⊠ Koskikatu 9, Keskusta ☎ 03/211–0037). Stroll down from Koskikeskus to Kehräsaari island, with its old brick buildings converted to shops and restaurants, to **Fall's Cafe** (⊠ Kehräsaari, Keskusta ☎ 03/223–0061), in a cozy cellar, with central European beers on tap. Tampere's most unique bar, **Telakka** (⊠ Tullikamarin aukio 3, Keskusta ☎ 03/225–0700), is in an old granary. Founded by a cooperative of actors, who also serve tables, it has live music and a theater upstairs. There's a menu of pub food and a grill on the terrace in summer. The **Ilves Night Club** (⊠ Hotel Ilves, Hatanpään valtatie 1, Keskusta ☎ 03/262–6262) is one of the most popular nightspots in Tampere, drawing a mixed crowd of professionals and students, for dancing and drinks.

off the beaten path

RUNOILIJAN TIE – One of the most popular excursions from Tampere is the Poet's Way steam boat tour along Lake Näsijärvi. The Tarjanne, built in 1908, passes through the agricultural parish of Ruovesi, where J. L. Runeberg, Finland's national poet, once lived. Shortly before the boat docks at Virrat, you'll pass through the straits of Visuvesi, where many artists and writers spend their summers.

Laukontori 10A 3, 33100 Tampere ☎ *03/212–4804* ⊕ *www. finnishsilverline.com/poetsway* ✉ *Same-day round-trip fare for boat–bus package €36 Tampere–Ruovesi* ☉ *June–Aug. 17, Tues., Thurs., and Sat.*

ÄHTÄRI – Not far north of Virrat is Ähtäri, where you will find Ähtäri Eläinpuisto (Ähtäri Animal Park), Finland's first wildlife park. In a beautiful countryside setting, it has a "holiday village," several good hotels, including the Scandic Mesikämmen, and recreation facilities. The park, home to many indigenous species, including bears, lynx, snow owls, wolves, elk, reindeer, and snow leopards, is set on 148 forested acres. Hiking, golf, swimming, skiing, and horseback riding is plentiful in this area surrounded by lakes and coniferous forests. Contact the tourist office for more information. *Karhunkierros 130, 63700 Ähtäri* ☎ *06/5393–555* ⊕ *www. ahtarinelainpuisto.fi* ✉ *€12.50* ☉ *Jan.–May and mid-Aug.–Oct., daily 10–4; June–mid-Aug., daily 10–7; Nov.–Dec., daily 10–2.*

Hämeenlinna

❹ *78 km (49 mi) southeast of Tampere, 98 km (61 mi) north of Helsinki (via Hwy. 12).*

The big castle and small museums of Hämeenlinna make this town a good place for a day trip. It's a good point from which to visit nearby gems such as the **Iittala Lasikeskus** (Iittala Glass Center), which offers museum tours and has a shop. Top designers produce the magnificent glass; the seconds in the factory shop are bargains you won't find elsewhere. ✉ *14500 Iittala* ☎ *0204/396–230* ✉ *€2* ☉ *Museum May–Aug., daily 10–6; Sept.–Apr., Thurs.–Sun., daily 10–5; shop May–Aug., daily 9–8; Sept.–Apr., daily 10–6.*

Hämeenlinna's secondary school has educated many famous Finns, among them composer Jean Sibelius (1865–1957). The only surviving timber house in the town center is the **Sibeliuksen syntymäkoti** (Sibelius birthplace), a modest dwelling built in 1834. The museum staff will play your favorite Sibelius CD as you tour the rooms, one of which contains the harmonium Sibelius played as a child. ✉ *Hallitusk. 11, Keskusta* ☎ *03/ 621–2755* ✉ *€3* ☉ *May–Aug., daily 10–4; Sept.–Apr., daily noon–4.*

Swedish crusaders began construction on **Hämeen Linna** (Häme Castle) in the 13th century to strengthen and defend the Swedish position in the region. What began as a fortified camp evolved over the centuries into a large castle of stone and brick. In modern times, the castle, one of Finland's oldest, has served as a granary and a prison, and it is now restored and open to the public for tours and exhibitions. The castle sits on the lakeshore, 1 km (½ mi) north of Hämeenlinna's town center. Tours in English take place every hour in the summer and are available every hour in winter by appointment only. ✉ *Kustaa III:n k. 6, Hämeenlinna* ☎ *03/675–6820* ⊕ *www.nba.fi/en/hame_castle* ✉ *€5 includes guided tour* ☉ *May–mid-Aug., daily 10–6; mid-Aug.–Apr., daily 10–4.*

The **Hämeenlinnan Taidemuseo** (Hämeenlinna Art Museum), housed partly in a 19th-century granary designed by Carl Ludvig Engel, exhibits Finnish art from the 19th and 20th centuries and foreign art from the 17th century; works evacuated from Vyborg in 1939 form the core of the collection. ✉ *Viipurintie 2, Keskusta* ☎ *03/621–2669* 🖾 *€6* ⊙ *Tues., Wed., and Fri.–Sun. noon–6, Thurs. noon–8.*

Where to Stay & Eat

$$–$$$ ✗ **Huviretki.** In the heart of the city, Huviretki has specialties such as garlic steak with cherry tomatoes and roasted whitefish or smoked salmon. There are many salads, pasta dishes, and pizzas on the menu. ✉ *Cumulus Hotel, Raatihuoneenk. 16–18, Keskusta* ☎ *03/648–8210* 🝥 *AE, DC, MC, V.*

$–$$$ ✗ **Piiparkakkutalo.** In a renovated old-timber building designed by famed architect Selim Lindquist, and finished in 1907, Piiparkakkutalo (Gingerbread House) specializes in meat dishes; try the pepper steak, fillet of reindeer, or wild duck. ✉ *Kirkkorinne 2, Keskusta* ☎ *03/648–040* 🝥 *AE, DC, MC, V.*

$$$ 🏨 **Rantasipi Aulanko.** One of Finland's top hotels sits on the lakeshore
Fodor'sChoice in a beautifully landscaped park 6½ km (4 mi) from town. All rooms
★   have wall-to-wall carpeting, and some overlook the golf course, park, or lake. ✉ *Aulangontie 93, 13210 Hämeenlinna* ☎ *03/658–801* 🖷 *03/658–1922* ⊕ *www.rantasipi.fi* ⇝ *241 rooms, 5 suites* ⌂ *Restaurant, 18-hole golf course, tennis court, indoor pool, sauna, spa, boating, horseback riding, nightclub, no-smoking rooms* 🝥 *AE, DC, MC, V.*

The Outdoors

SKIING   The **Finlandia Ski Race Office** (✉ Urheilukeskus, 15110 Lahti ☎ 03/816–813 ⊕ www.finlandiahiihto.fi) has details on events. In February, you can attend the **Finlandia-hiihto,** a 60-km (37-mi) ski race. The **Lahti Ski Games** (☎ 03/816–810 ⊕ www.lahtiskigames.com) take place in March.

Lakelands A to Z

AIRPORTS

Airports in the Lakelands are at Tampere, Mikkeli, Jyväskylä, Varkaus, Lappeenranta, Savonlinna, Kuopio, and Joensuu. Flight time to the Savonlinna area from Helsinki is 40 minutes. All airports are served by Finnair's domestic service.

BUS TRAVEL

Buses are the best form of public transport into the region, with frequent connections to lake destinations from most major towns. It is a six-hour ride from Helsinki to Savonlinna.

CAR TRAVEL

The region is vast, so the route you choose will depend on your destination. You can drive inland or follow the coast to the eastern lake region from the capital. A drive to Kuopio could take you either through Tampere to Jyväskyla or to the east, close to the border with Russia. Consult the Automobile and Touring Club of Finland or tourist boards for route advice.

The Joensuu–Kuopio–Lahti–Tampere road belt will transport you quickly from one major point to the next, but if you are going to be taking a lake vacation you will usually finish your journey on small roads. The last stretch to the *mökki* (cabin) may be unpaved. You will need a detailed map to find most mökkis, which tend to be tucked away in well-hidden spots.

Automobile and Touring Club of Finland ✉ Hämeentie 105A, PL 35, 00551 Helsinki ☎ 09/7258–4400, 0200/8080 24-hr road service ⊕ www.autoliitto.fi.

EMERGENCIES

The nationwide emergency number is ☎ 112; it can be used to call police and ambulance services. A major hospital is Tampere Keskussairaala (Tampere Central Hospital). For dental care, call Hammaslääkäri Päivystys. Tampereen Yliopistollinen Sairaala (TAYS) is the Tampere University hospital.

Hammaslääkäri Päivystys ☎ 0400/625–555. **Tampereen Yliopistollinen Sairaala (TAYS)** ✉ Teiskontie 35, Tampere ☎ 03/311–611.

TOURS

Avid canoeists should contact the Finnish Canoe Federation. Almost all of its 67 clubs arrange guided tours; canoes are rented at about €30 per day. Ikaalinen Tourist Service can help organize white-water trips and canoe safaris in the region; Karelia Expert organizes various theme trips, including white-water rafting, canoeing, biking, animal watching, and dogsled tours; and Wild Canoe designs tailor-made canoe tours.

A program of Friendly Finland Tours, available through travel agencies in Finland and abroad, offers escorted packages that include stops in the Lakelands. The three-day "Saimaa Lake Tour" and the seven-day "Scenic Tour" both start in Helsinki. Brochures are available from the Finland Travel Bureau in Helsinki.

There are dozens of boat-tour companies operating in the Lakelands; contact the Finnish Tourist Board or local tourist offices in the region for a complete list as well as details of routes. Kuopio Roll Cruises Ltd. offers tours to the Lintulan Luostari (Lintula Convent).

Finland Travel Bureau ✉ Kaivokatu 10A, Box 319, 00101 Helsinki ☎ 09/18261 ⊕ www.ftb.net. **Finnish Canoe Federation** ✉ Olympiastadion, 00250 Helsinki ☎ 09/494–965. **Finnish Silverline and Poets' Way Tours** ✉ Laukontori 10A 3, 33200 Tampere ☎ 03/212–4804 ⊕ www.finnishsilverline.com. **Finnish Tourist Board** ✉ Töölönk. 11, 00100 Helsinki ☎ 09/417–6911 ⊕ www.visitfinland.com. **Ikaalinen Tourist Service** ✆ Box 33, 39501 Ikaalinen ☎ 03/450–1221. **Karelia Expert** ✉ Koskik. 5, 80100 Joensuu ☎ 013/248–5319 ⊕ www.kareliaexpert.fi. **Kuopio Roll Cruises Ltd.** ✉ Matkustajasatama, 70100 Kuopio ☎ 017/266–2466 🖶 017/266–2464. **Saimaa Lakeland** ✉ Roll Cruises of Kuopio Ltd., Matkustajasatama, 70100 Kuopio ☎ 017/266–2466. **Western Lakeland and Lake Päijänne Tour** ✉ Lake Päijänne Cruises, Pellonpää, 40820 Haapaniemi ☎ 014/618–885 or 014/263–447. **Wild Canoe** ✉ Visulahti Camping, 50180 Mikkeli ☎ 0500/840–362 ⊕ www.wildcanoe.com.

TRAIN TRAVEL

Trains run from Helsinki to Lahti, Mikkeli, Imatra, Lappeenranta, Joensuu, and Jyväskylä. There is sleeping-car service to Joensuu and

Kuopio and to Savonlinna. The trip from Helsinki to Savonlinna takes 5½ hours.

VISITOR INFORMATION

🔳 Tourist Information **Ähtäri** ⊠ Ostolank. 4, 63700 ☎ 06/533-1754 ⊕ www.ahtari. fi. **Hämeenlinna** ⊠ Raatihuoneenk. 11, 13100 ☎ 03/621-3373 ⊕ www.hameenlinna. fi/english. **Heinola** ⊠ Matkailutoimisto Kauppakatu 12, 18100 ☎ 03/849-3615. **Imatra** ⊠ Lappeent. 11, 55101 ☎ 020/495-2500 ⊕ www.travel.imatra.fi. **Joensuu** ⊠ Karelia Expert Tourist Info, Koskik. 5, 80100 ☎ 013/248-5319. **Jyväskylä** ⊠ Asemak. 6, 40100 ☎ 014/624-903 ⊕ www.jyvaskyla.fi/international. **Kuopio** ⊠ Haapaniemenk. 17, 70110 ☎ 017/182-584 ⊕ www.kuopioinfo.fi. **Lahti** ⊠ Aleksanterink. 13, 15111 ☎ 03/877-677 ⊕ www.lahtitravel.fi. **Lappeenranta** ⊠ Marketplace, Lievarinkatu 1, PL 113, 53101 ☎ 05/667-788 ⊕ www.lappeenranta.fi. **Mikkeli** ⊠ Porrassalmenkatu 15, 50100 ☎ 020/370-071 ⊕ www.travel.mikkeli.fi. **Savonlinna** ⊠ Puistokatu 1, 57100 ☎ 015/517-510 ⊕ www.savonlinnatravel.com. **Tampere** ⊠ Verkatehtaank. 2, PL 487, 33100 ☎ 020/716-6800 ⊕ www.tampere.fi.

LAPLAND

Lapland is often called Europe's last wilderness, a region of endless forests, fells, and great silences. Settlers in Finnish Lapland walked gently and left the landscape almost unspoiled. Now easily accessible by plane, train, or bus, this arctic outpost offers comfortable hotels and modern amenities, yet you won't have to go very far to find yourself in an almost primordial setting.

The oldest traces of human habitation in Finland have been found in Lapland, and hordes of Danish, English, and even Arabian coins indicate the existence of trade activities many centuries ago. Until the 1930s, Lapland was still largely unexploited, and any trip to the region was an expedition. Lapland's isolation ended when the Canadian-owned Petsamo Nickel Company completed the great road connecting Rovaniemi with the Arctic Sea, now known as the Arctic Highway. Building activities increased along this route, the land was turned and sown, and a few hotels were built to cater to an increasing number of visitors.

Only about 4,000 native Sami (also sometimes known as Lapps) still live in Lapland; the remainder of the province's population of 203,000 is Finnish. The Sami population makes up a small minority in the northern regions of Finland, Norway, Sweden, and Russia. Though modern influences have changed many aspects of their traditional way of life, there is still a thriving Sami culture. Sami crafts make use of natural resources, reflected in skilled woodwork, bonework, and items made of reindeer pelts. In March, on Maria's Day, a traditional church festival takes place in Hetta, a village near Enontekiö. It is particularly colorful, attended by many Sami in their most brilliant dress, and usually has reindeer racing or lassoing competitions. Contact the Enontekiö tourist office for details.

Summer in Lapland has the blessing of round-the-clock daylight, and beautiful weather typically accompanies the nightless days. In early fall the colors are so fabulous that the Finns have a special word for it: *ruskaa*.

If you can take the intense but dry cold, winter in Lapland is full of fascinating experiences, from the northern lights to reindeer roundups. Depending on how far north of the Arctic Circle you travel, the sun might not rise for several weeks around midwinter. But it is never pitch-black; light reflects from the invisible sun below the horizon even during midday, and there is luminosity from the ever-present snow.

Finns cherish the outdoors no matter what the light. Here it is the wilderness that's the draw. For although the cities have fine facilities and cultural events, it is the lonely moors with the occasional profile of a reindeer herd crossing, the clear forest streams, and the bright trail of the midnight sun reflected on a lake's blackest waters that leave the most indelible impressions.

While you're here sample such local foods as cloudberries; lingonberries; fresh salmon; and reindeer, served smoked and sautéed, roasted, and as steaks. Restaurants serve hearty soups, crusty rye bread, delicious baked Lappish cheese, and dark brewed coffee in wooden cups with meals—you won't leave hungry.

Crafts
You'll find unique souvenirs in Lapland, and you may learn to love the traditional Sami crafts, both functional and attractive. Keep an eye out for the camping knives with beautifully carved bone or wooden handles, birch mugs, colorful weaving and embroidered mittens and gloves, felt shoes, and birch-bark baskets and rucksacks.

Summer Sports
In summer, canoeing is a popular pursuit; you can take canoe trips on Lake Inari, or, for the intrepid, forays over the rapids of the Ivalojoki River. Summer golf takes on such unusual guises as midnight-sun golf and Green Zone Tornio-Haparanda Golf—you'll play 9 holes in Finland and the other 9 in Sweden **Meri-Lapin Golfklubi** (⊠ Näräntie, 95400 Tornio ☎ 016/431–711 🖷 016/431–710 ⊕ www.golf.fi/mlgk). In the summer it is so light that you can play during the night. The course is famous for its one-hour putt.

Winter Sports
Winter sports reign here, from the quirky ice golfing to the traditional cross-country skiing. Ylläs, Levi, and Saariselkä are Lapland's leading centers for both downhill and cross-country skiing; Kiilopää is known for cross-country skiing. Other popular resorts include Pyhä, Luosto, Salla, Suomu, Pallas, and Olos. In western Lapland, the **Levi resort** (⊠ Levi Tourist Info, Levin Portti, 99130 Sirkka ☎ 016/639–3300 ⊕ www.levi.fi) has 47 slopes and 26 lifts in an extensive fell area. **Pyhä and Luosto** (⊠ Pyhä-Luosto Travel Ltd., Laukotie 1, 99555 Luosto ☎ 0207/303–020 ⊕ www.pyha-luostomatkailu.fi, www.pyha.fi, or www.luosto.fi), in the Pyhätunturi National Park in southern Lapland, have cross-country and downhill skiing, and snowboarding possibilities. In the middle of the fells near Urho Kekkonen National Park, **Saariselkä** (⊠ Pohjois-Lapin Matkailu, Kelotie, Seula, 99830 Saariselkä ☎ 016/668–402 ⊕ www.saariselka.fi) is an international tourist center with a network of well-marked hiking, skiing, and biking trails. Down-

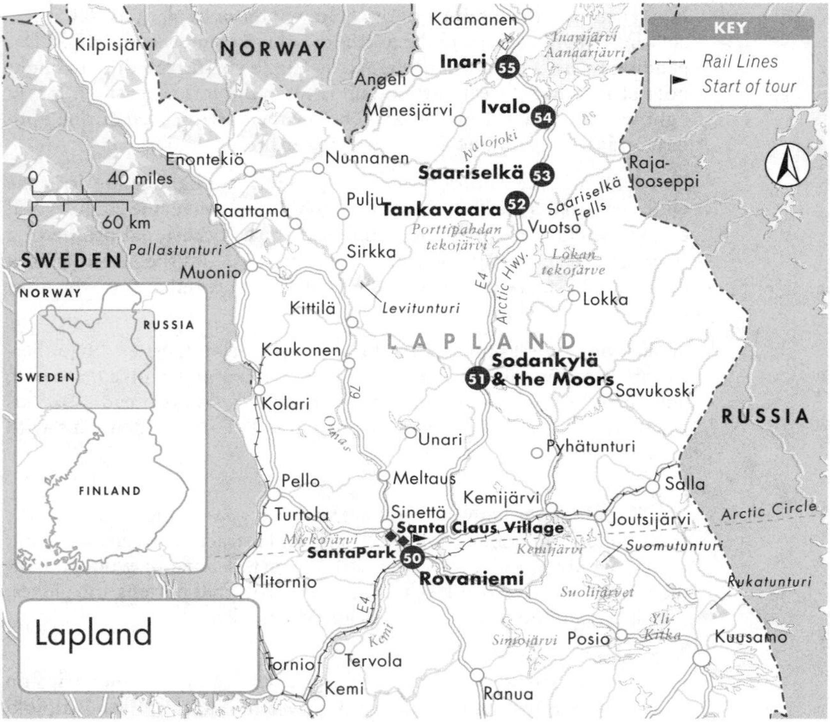

Lapland

KEY
— Rail Lines
► Start of tour

hill and cross-country skiing are popular at **Ruka** (✉ Rukakeskus, 93825 Rukatunturi ☎ 08/860–0200 ⊕ www.ruka.fi), which is also one of the most unrestricted areas in the world for snowmobiling.

Rovaniemi

► ⑤⓪ *832 km (516 mi) north of Helsinki.*

The best place to start your tour of Lapland is Rovaniemi, where the Ounas and Kemi rivers meet almost on the Arctic Circle. Often called the Gateway to Lapland, Rovaniemi is also the administrative hub and communications center of the province.

If you're expecting an Arctic shantytown, you're in for a surprise. After Rovaniemi was all but razed by the retreating German army in 1944, Alvar Aalto directed the rebuilding and devised an unusual street layout: from the air, the layout mimics the shape of reindeer antlers! During rebuilding, the population rose from 8,000 to its present-day size of around 36,000—so be prepared for a contemporary city, university town, and cultural center on the edge of the wilderness.

One of the town's architectural wonders is **Lappia-Talo** (Lappia House), the Aalto-designed concert and congress center that houses the world's northernmost professional theater. ⊠ *Hallitusk. 11, Keskusta* ☎ *016/ 322–2495 ticket office* ⊘ *Closed June–Aug.*

One of the best ways to tune in to the culture of Finland's far north is to visit the **Arktikum** (Arctic Research Center), 1 km (½ mi) north of Lappia-Talo. The Arktikum houses the Lapland Provincial Museum, whose riveting exhibit on Sami life tells the full story of their survival. ⊠ *Pohjoisranta 4, Ratantaus* ☎ *016/322–3260* ⊕ *www.arktikum.fi* ⊠ *€11* ⊘ *Early June–mid-June, daily 10–6; mid-June–mid-Aug., daily 9–7; mid–late Aug., daily 10–6; Sept.–May, Tues.–Sun. 10–6; some extended hrs in winter.*

Rovaniemi's real claim to fame is that Santa Claus lives in its suburbs, as reflected in the growing number of tourist attractions in the area. The **SantaPark** Christmas theme park is set deep inside a rocky cavern and offers a Magic Sleigh Ride, a Puppet Circus, and a Christmas Carrousel, among other attractions. Take the Santa Train from the Park to **Joulupukin Pajakylä** (Santa Claus Village) and stop along the way at the Reindeer Park to see Santa's sleigh team. Sami in native dress and reindeer hauling sleighs enhance the authenticity of the village. (This is likely to be the only place where your children will be able to pet a reindeer—the ones you'll see in the wild are shy.) Here gifts can be bought in midsummer for shipping at any time of year, and postcards can be mailed from the special Arctic Circle post office. There's also a complete souvenir shopping complex, plus the impressive mountains of mail that pour in from children all over the world. And yes, he does answer every letter. The village is closed when he is abroad, on December 25. ⊠ *96930 Arctic Circle* ☎ *016/333–0000 park, 016/356–2096 village info* ⊕ *www.santapark.com or www.santaclausvillage.info* ⊠ *Park €20, family ticket (3–6 persons) €50, village free* ⊘ *Call for hrs.*

Where to Stay & Eat

$$$ ✕ **Ounasvaaran Pirtit.** This holiday village and ski center includes two of Rovaniemi's classic restaurants, Kota and Aurora, which focus on traditional Finnish and Lapp food. At either restaurant you'll find dishes with fresh salmon and reindeer, and a dessert of soft cheese with arctic cloudberries. There's a buffet and a set menu at the Kota Restaurant and an à la carte menu at Aurora. Hours vary for both restaurants throughout the year, so call ahead. ⊠ *Antinmukka 4, Ounasvaara* ☎ *016/333–0100* ⊛ *Reservations essential* ▭ *AE, DC, MC, V.*

$–$$$ ✕ **Fransmanni.** This restaurant, with friendly service and a nice view of the Kemijoki River, specializes in different types of international, Finnish, and Lapp casserole dishes. Try the grilled beef fillet in honey-and-bacon sauce. ⊠ *Vaakuna Hotel, Koskik. 4, Keskusta* ☎ *016/332–2515* ▭ *AE, DC, MC, V.*

$$–$$$ ✕▢ **Lapland Hotels Sky Ounasvaara.** On a hilltop 3 km (2 mi) from the town, Sky Ounasvaara is the top choice in Rovaniemi for views, hiking, and skiing—both slalom and cross-country—especially for those with a car. Some rooms have bathtubs, a rarity, and 47 rooms have saunas. Larger rooms with kitchenettes are available for families. At the restaurant dine on roasted whitefish or arctic char with crayfish or fruit sauce, and try one of the desserts based on local fruits such as cloudberries.

✉ *96400 Rovaniemi* ☎ *016/335–3311* 🖶 *016/318–789* ⊕ *www. laplandhotels.com* ⬐ *70 rooms, 1 suite, 11 apartments, 10 cabins* ⬒ *Restaurant, minibars, sauna, hiking, cross-country skiing, 2 bars, meeting rooms* ▤ *AE, DC, MC, V.*

$$ 🖵 **Rantasipi Pohjanhovi.** Stretched along the shore of the Kemijoki River, this hotel combines modern amenities with quick access to the moors. Rooms are large, with low ceilings and big windows. Some are white-walled with autumn-tone upholstery and wood trim, while others have black walls with light upholstery—for those who have trouble sleeping during the days of the midnight sun. ✉ *Pohjanpuistikko 2, 96200* ☎ *016/33711* 🖶 *016/313–997* ⊕ *www.rantasipi.fi* ⬐ *212 rooms, 17 suites* ⬒ *Restaurant, room service, minibars, indoor pool, sauna, bar, casino, nightclub, laundry service, meeting rooms, no-smoking rooms* ▤ *AE, DC, MC, V.*

$$ 🖵 **Scandic Rovaniemi.** This modern hotel is in the heart of Rovaniemi, five minutes from the railway station. Guest rooms are simply furnished and comfortable. Nine rooms have individual saunas and eight have Jacuzzis. ✉ *Koskik. 23, 96200* ☎ *016/4606–000* 🖶 *016/4606–666* ⊕ *www.scandic-hotels.com* ⬐ *167 rooms* ⬒ *Restaurant, minibars, 3 saunas, bar, business services, meeting room, no-smoking rooms* ▤ *AE, DC, MC, V.*

$$ 🖵 **Sokos Hotel Vaakuna.** The Vaakuna has small but comfortable guest rooms decked in neutral shades. The lobby is dotted with armchairs and has marble floors. There are two restaurants, Fransmanni and Rosso, the latter of which turns out pastas and pizzas. ✉ *Koskikatu 4, 96200 Rovaniemi* ☎ *020/1234–695* 🖶 *016/332–2199* ⊕ *www. sokoshotels.fi* ⬐ *157 rooms, 2 suites* ⬒ *2 restaurants, 3 saunas, pub, nightclub, meeting rooms, parking (fee), no-smoking rooms* ▤ *AE, DC, MC, V.*

$ 🖵 **Hotel Oppipoika.** Modern furnishings and central location are two of the attractions of this small hotel. Rooms have pressed-birch paneling and are well lighted. ✉ *Korkalonk. 33, 96200 Rovaniemi* ☎ *016/338–8111* 🖶 *016/346–969* ⊕ *www.bestwestern.com* ⬐ *40 rooms, 1 suite* ⬒ *Restaurant, indoor pool, gym, sauna, meeting room, no-smoking rooms* ▤ *AE, DC, MC, V.*

The Outdoors

HIKING **Genimap** (✉ PL 106, 01600 Vantaa ☎ 0201/34040 🖶 0201/340449 ⊕ www.genimap.fi), provides maps of marked trails in Lapland.

Sodankylä & the Moors

🟌 *130 km (81 mi) north of Rovaniemi (via Rte. 4 or 5), 960 km (595 mi) north of Helsinki.*

The Sodankylä region is one of the oldest Sami settlements, and today it is one of the most densely populated areas of Finnish Lapland. In the town of Sodankylä is a Northern Lights Observatory (for professionals only) and an ancient wooden church. The Midnight Sun Film Festival draws crowds during the height of summer, running films in tents throughout the night. See ⊕ www.msfilmfestival.fi for more information.

Lapland is dominated by great moorlike expanses. The modern tourist center of **Luosto,** 25 km (16 mi) south of Sodankylä, is in the heart of the moor district of southern Lapland—an area of superb hiking, mountain cycling, orienteering, and skiing. If you don't have a car, a daily bus makes the 60-km (37-mi) trip from Kemijärvi to Luosto. Kemijarvi is 87 km (54 mi) north of Rovaniemi and can be reached via local train.

Where to Stay

$$ ☒ **Scandic Luosto.** Amid the plains southeast of Sodankylä, this small-scale hotel is modern and comfortable. It is built in a unique *kelo* (dead-wood) timber style. Each cabin has a fireplace, sauna, and kitchenette. If you get tired of cross-country skiing, visit the amethyst mine nearby. ☒ *Luppokeino 3, 99550 Luostotunturi* ☎ *016/624–400* 📠 *016/624–410* ⊕ *www.scandichotels.com* 🛏 *54 cabins, 5 rooms* ⟁ *3 restaurants, kitchenettes, sauna, boating, cross-country skiing, snowmobiling, meeting room, no-smoking rooms* ☰ *AE, DC, MC, V.*

Tankavaara

🔢 *105 km (65 mi) north of Sodankylä, 130 km (81 mi) north of Luosto, 225 km (140 mi) north of Rovaniemi.*

The town of Tankavaara is the most accessible and the best developed of several gold-panning areas. The **Kultamuseo** (Gold Museum) tells the century-old story of Lapland's hardy fortune seekers. Guides will show you how to pan for gold dust and tiny nuggets from the silt of an icy stream. ☒ *Kultakylä, 99695 Tankavaara* ☎ *016/626–171* ⊕ *www. tankavaara.fi* 🎫 *€7 museum, €3.50 an hr for gold panning* ☉ *June–mid-Aug., daily 9–6; mid-Aug.–Sept., daily 9–5; Oct.–May, weekdays 10–4.*

Where to Stay & Eat

$–$$ ✕ **Wanha Waskoolimies.** In the tradition of the old gold prospectors, this rustic restaurant consists of three rooms hewn from logs. Daily specials such as traditional sautéed reindeer with mashed potatoes and lingonberry sauce will give you a taste of simple but high-quality Lapland fare. ☒ *Tankavaaran Kultakylän* ☎ *016/626–158* ☰ *DC, V.*

$ ☒ **Hotel Korundi.** Just off the Arctic Highway, this hotel has quiet surroundings and cozy, contemporary rooms for two to five people; most have a fireplace. You can try your luck at panning for gold here. The restaurant is in a separate building. ☒ *99695 Tankavaara* ☎ *016/626–158* 📠 *016/626–261* 🛏 *8 rooms, 10 cabins with shared bathhouse* ⟁ *Restaurant, kitchenettes, sauna, bicycles, hiking, cross-country skiing* ☰ *AE, DC, MC, V.*

Saariselkä

🔢 *40 km (25 mi) north of Tankavaara, 135 km (84 mi) north of Sodankylä, 265 km (165 mi) north of Rovaniemi.*

You could hike and ski for days in this area without seeing another soul. Saariselkä has many hotels and is a good central base from which to set off on a trip into the true wilderness. Marked trails traverse forests and moors, where little has changed since the last Ice Age. More than 2,500 square km (962 square mi) of this magnificent area has been named the **Urhokekkosen Kansallisp isto** (Urho Kekkonen National Park). The park guide center is at Tankavaara.

Where to Stay

$$–$$$ 🏨 **Holiday Club Saariselkä.** This hotel is known for its luxurious spa center. The glass-dome swimming area is crammed with foliage, fountains, waterslides, wave machines, and a hot tub. The solarium, saunas, and Turkish baths are adjacent. Guest rooms have blond and dark-wood fittings and slate-blue carpets. Moderately priced cabin accommodations are also available. Note that the breakfast and spa facilities are included in prices. Children 4 to 14 can stay in their parents' room for the price of an extra bed, around € 25; children under 4 stay free. The bus stops at the hotel. ⊠ *99830 Saariselkä* ☎ *016/6828* 🖷 *016/682–328* ⊕ *www.holidayclub.fi* ↩ *134 rooms, 5 suites* ⚭ *Restaurant, tennis court, gym, hot tub, sauna, spa, Turkish bath, badminton, paddle tennis, squash, volleyball, bar, meeting rooms, no-smoking rooms* ☰ *AE, DC, MC, V* ❢❂❢ *BP.*

$$–$$$ 🏨 **Riekonlinna.** On the fringes of the wilderness fells, the pinewood fittings and neutral-tone textiles of this contemporary Lappish hotel go well with its natural surroundings. All rooms have a balcony, and many have a sauna. The restaurant serves fresh local specialties, including reindeer, salmon, and snow grouse. The hotel is only 30 minutes from Ivalo airport, and its location provides excellent cross-country and downhill skiing; snowmobiling and reindeer safaris are also offered. There is a children's playroom. ⊠ *Saariseläntie 13, 99830 Saariselkä* ☎ *016/679–4455* 🖷 *016/679–4456* ⊕ *www.riekkoparvi.fi* ↩ *192 rooms, 4 suites* ⚭ *Restaurant, minibars, gym, sauna, ski storage, bar, meeting rooms* ☰ *AE, DC, MC, V.*

$–$$ 🏨 **Hotelli Kieppi.** The piney comfort of the rooms and the quiet countryside make this a good Lapland retreat. Eight wood buildings with 12 to 16 rooms each make it especially popular with families. The restaurant has a cozy fireplace, pine furniture, and Sami handicrafts. Its regional and Continental menu is strong on reindeer and fish. ⊠ *Raitopolku 1, 99830 Saariselkä* ☎ *016/554–4600* 🖷 *016/554–4700* ⊕ *www. hotellikieppi.fi* ↩ *64 rooms* ⚭ *Restaurant, refrigerators, sauna, ski storage* ☰ *AE, DC, MC, V.*

Ivalo

54 *40 km (25 mi) north of Saariselkä, 193 km (116 mi) north of Rovaniemi.*

The village of Ivalo is the main center for northern Lapland. With its first-class hotel, airport, and many modern amenities, it offers little to the tourist in search of a wilderness experience, but on the huge island-studded expanses of **Inarijärvi** (Lake Inari), north of Ivalo, you can go boating, fishing, hiking, and hunting.

The Outdoors

Tunturikeskus Kiilopää (⊠ 99830 Saariselkä ☎ 016/6700–700 ⊕ www. suomenlatu.fi/kiilopaa) is a multiactivity center at the edge of Urho Kekkonen National Forest that has guided ski and snowshoe tours, accommodations, and a smoke sauna. There are summer activities, too.

BOATING A three-hour trip up the Lemmenjoki River can be arranged by **Lemmenjoen Lomamajat Oy Ahkuntupa** (✉ 99885 Lemmenjoki 🕿🕿 016/673–475 ⊙ Mar.–Sept.)

Where to Stay

$ 🏨 **Hotel Ivalo.** Modern and well equipped for business travelers and families, this hotel is 1 km (½ mi) from Ivalo, right on the Ivalojoki River. The lobby has marble floors, the lounge a brick fireplace. The rooms are spacious and modern, with oatmeal carpets and lots of blond birchwood trimming; ask for one by the river. The restaurant serves Continental fare, as well as delicious Lappi dishes. ✉ *Ivalontie 34, 99800 Ivalo* 🕿 *016/688–111* 🖷 *016/661–905* ⊕ *www.hotelivalo.fi* ⬩ *91 rooms, 3 suites ♨ Restaurant, minibars, pool, 3 saunas, boating, bar, recreation room, babysitting, meeting room, no-smoking rooms* ⊟ *AE, DC, MC, V.*

$ 🏨 **Kultahippu.** In the heart of Ivalo, along the Ivalojoki River, Kultahippu claims to have the northernmost nightclub in Finland. Guest rooms are cozy, with simple birch-wood furnishing; larger rooms with a sauna are available for families. The restaurant serves traditional Lapp meals à la carte. ✉ *Petsamontie 1, 99800 Ivalo* 🕿 *016/661–825* 🖷 *016/662–510* ⊕ *www.kultahippuhotel.fi* ⬩ *30 rooms ♨ Restaurant, hot tub, sauna, beach* ⊟ *AE, DC, MC, V.*

$ 🏨 **Tunturikeskus Kiilopää.** This "fell center" is in the midst of hiking and cross-country skiing territory in the Urho Kekkonen National Park district, 45 km (28 mi) south of Ivalo Airport. Accommodations are in beautifully crafted log cabins, apartments, or individual hotel rooms, all made of wood and stone. Apartments have picture windows and fireplaces. The restaurant serves reindeer and other game entrées. Call for rates. ✉ *99830 Saariselkä* 🕿 *016/670–0700* 🖷 *016/667–121* ⊕ *www.suomenlatu.fi/kiilopaa* ⬩ *8 cabins, 8 apartments, 34 rooms, 9 youth-hostel rooms ♨ Restaurant, cross-country skiing, ski shop, no-smoking rooms* ⊟ *AE, DC, MC, V.*

Inari

❺❺ *40 km (24 mi) northwest of Ivalo, 333 km (207 mi) north of Rovaniemi.*

It is a stunning drive northwest from Ivalo along the lakeshore to Inari, home of the *Sami Parlamenta* (Sami Parliament). The **SIIDA Center,** on the village outskirts, hosts exhibits on the Sami people and the northern seasons. The center houses the **Saamelaismuseo** (Sami Museum) and the **Ylä-Lapin luontokeskus** (Northern Lapland Nature Center). The Nature Center includes the **Metsähallitus** (Forest and Park Service; 🕿 0205/647–740 🖷 0205/647–750), which can provide camping and fishing permits along with advice on exploring the wilderness. A 17-acre open-air museum complements the indoor exhibits at the center during the summer. ✉ *Rte. 4 by Lake Inari, 99870 Inari* 🕿 *016/665–212 or 0205/647–740* 🖷 *016/665–156 or 0205/647–750* ⊕ *www.siida.fi* 🎫 *€8* ⊙ *Saamelaismuseo: June–Sept., daily 9–8; Oct.–May, Tues.–Sun. 10–5.*

off the
beaten
path

INARIN POROFARMI – At this working reindeer farm 14 km (9 mi) southeast of Inari, you can drive a reindeer sled or be pulled on skis by the magical animals. ✉ *Kaksamajärvi, 99800 Ivalo* ☎ *016/673–912* 🖷 *016/673–922* ☉ *By appointment.*

Where to Stay & Eat

$ ✕⌂ **Inarin Kultahovi.** This cozy inn is on the wooded banks of the swiftly flowing Juutuajoki Rapids. The no-frills double rooms are small, with handwoven rugs and birch-wood furniture. In summer you might need a reservation to get a table at Kultahovi's restaurant; the specialties are salmon and reindeer, but try the tasty whitefish caught from nearby Lake Inari. ✉ *99870 Inari* ☎ *016/671–221* 🖷 *016/671–250* ⇱ *29 rooms* ⌂ *Restaurant, sauna, bar* ▤ *DC, MC, V.*

The Outdoors

Many local travel agencies throughout Lapland offer different types of tours of the region. **Arctic Safaris** (✉Koskikatu 6, 96200 Rovaniemi ☎016/340–0400 🖷 016/340–0455 ⊕ www.arcticsafaris.fi) offers summer and winter tours including canoeing, hiking, and snowmobiling.

Lapland A to Z

AIR TRAVEL

There is service every day but Sunday between Rovaniemi and Ivalo. You can also fly between Oulu or Rovaniemi to Ivalo, Enontekiö, Kemi, and Sodankylä, all on Finnair domestic services. Finnair also has daily flights directly from Helsinki to Kuusamo. There are seasonal schedules.

AIRPORTS

The airports serving Lapland are at Enontekiö, Ivalo, Kemi, Kittilä, Kuusamo, Oulu, Rovaniemi, and Sodankylä. Finnair serves all these airports with flights from Helsinki, though not all flights are nonstop. You can also fly to the north from most of southwestern Finland's larger cities and from the lakes region.

BUS TRAVEL

Bus service into the region revolves around Rovaniemi; from there you can switch to local buses.

CAR TRAVEL

If you are driving north, follow Arctic Highway No. 4 (national highway) to Kuopio–Oulu–Rovaniemi, or go via the west coast to Oulu, then to Rovaniemi. From Rovaniemi, the national highway continues straight up to Lake Inari via Ivalo. Roads are generally good, but some in the extreme north may be rough.

EMERGENCIES

Lapland's leading hospital is Lapin Keskussairaala (Lapland Central Hospital). Dentists can be reached at Hammashoitola Viisaudenhammas.
🛡 **Police; emergency services** ☎ 112. **Hammashoitola Viisaudenhammas** ✉ Ukkoherrantie 15, Rovaniemi ☎ 016/334–0400. **Lapin Keskussairaala** ✉ Ounasrinteentie 22, Rovaniemi ☎ 016/3281, 016/328–2100 evenings and weekends.

TOURS

Guided tours in towns are arranged through city tourist offices. Tours to Lapland can also be purchased in Helsinki through Helsinki Expert. For adventure tours and other specialty tours that cater to both general and special interests, contact Finland Travel Bureau. For independent travelers, the Finnish Youth Hostel Association (SRM) offers a hosteling and bicycling package that can be used in Lapland.

Lapland Travel Ltd. (Lapin Matkailu OY) and Lapland Safaris offer fly-fishing and combined canoe-and-fishing trips, in addition to reindeer and snowmobile safaris and ski treks. Lake Lines Inari offer Sami tours that include a visit to SIIDA, the Sami Museum in Inari, and a cruise on Lake Inari (operated by Lake Lines Inari).

Finland Travel Bureau ✉ PL 319, Kaivokatu 10A, 00101 Helsinki ☎ 09/18261 ⊕ www.ftb.net. **Finnish Youth Hostel Association** ✉ Yrjönk. 38B 15, 00100 Helsinki ☎ 09/565-7150 🖷 09/565-71510 ⊕ www.srmnet.org. **Helsinki Expert** ✉ Lönnrotink. 7B, Keskusta ☎ 09/2288-1600. **Lake Lines Inari** ✉ Meska-Set Oy, Ruskatie 3, 99800 Inari ☎ 0400/391-017 🖷 016/663-582. **Lapland Safaris** ✉ Koskikatu 1, 96200 Rovaniemi ☎ 016/331-1200 🖷 016/331-1233 ⊕ www.lapinsafarit.fi. **Lapland Travel Ltd. (Lapin Matkailu Oy)** ✉ Koskikatu 1, 96200 Rovaniemi ☎ 016/332-3400 🖷 016/332-3411 ⊕ www.laplandtravel.fi.

TRAIN TRAVEL

Train service will get you to Rovaniemi and Kemijärvi. From there you must make connections with other forms of transport.

TRANSPORTATION AROUND LAPLAND

The best base for exploring is Rovaniemi, which connects with Helsinki and the south by road, rail, and air links; there is even a car-train from Helsinki.

The Arctic Highway will take you north from Rovaniemi at the Arctic Circle to Inari, just below the 69th parallel. If you'd rather not rent a car, however, all but the most remote towns are accessible by bus, train, or plane. Buses leave four times daily from Rovaniemi to Inari (five to six hours) and six times a day to Ivalo (four hours). You can take countryside taxis to your final destination; taxi stands are at most bus stations. Taxi drivers invariably use their meters, and specially negotiated fares—even for long distances—are unusual, but you can ask for an estimate before starting the trip.

VISITOR INFORMATION

Tourist Information **Enontekiö** ☎🖷 016/556-211 ⊕ www.enontekio.fi. **Inari** ✉ Northern Lapland Tourism Ltd., Kelotie, Seula, 99830 Saariselkä ☎ 016/668-402. **Kemijärvi** ✉ Vapaudenk. 8, 98100 ☎ 016/877-383 ⊕ www.kemijarvi.fi. **Kuusamo** ✉ Torangintaival 2, 93600 ☎ 08/850-2910. **Rovaniemi** ✉ Rovak. 21, 96200 ☎ 016/346-270 ⊕ www.rovaniemi.fi. **Saariselkä** ✉ Kelotie, Seula 99830 ☎ 016/668-402. **Salla** ✉ C/o Salla Reindeer Park-Cooperative Jotos, Hautajärventie 111, 98900 Salla ☎ 016/837-771. **Sodankylä** ✉ Jäämerentie 3, 99600 ☎ 016/618-168.

FINLAND A TO Z

To research prices, get advice from other travelers, and book travel arrangements, visit www.fodors.com.

AIR TRAVEL

CARRIERS   Finnair, British Airways, and some charter companies fly from London to Helsinki. Ask the Finnish Tourist Board for names of companies specializing in travel packages to Finland.

Finnair also runs an extensive domestic service. Domestic flights are relatively cheap, and as some planes have a set number of discount seats allotted, it's best to reserve early. There are also special fares available through the Finnair Web site.

American Airlines and British Airways are among Finnair's partners in the One World Alliance. Other European airlines include SAS, Lufthansa, Swiss International Airlines, and Air France.

🛪 **British Airways** ☎ 0870/850-9850 in the U.K., 800/247-9297 in the U.S. ⊕ www. ba.com. **Finnair** ☎ 0870/241-4411 in the U.K., 800/950-5000 in the U.S. ⊕ www. finnair.com. **Lufthansa** ☎ 800/645-3880. **SAS** ☎ 800/221-2350.

FLYING TIMES   Flying time from New York to Helsinki is about eight hours, nine hours for the return trip. Flying time from London to Helsinki is two hours, 45 minutes.

AIRPORTS

All international flights arrive at Helsinki–Vantaa International Airport, 20 km (12 mi) north of city center. Finnair offers domestic and international flights, with daily direct service from New York in summer and almost daily service at other times. For 24-hour arrival and departure information, call the phone number for the airport listed below.

🛪 **Helsinki–Vantaa International Airport** ☎ 0200/14636 costs €0.57 per min plus a local call charge for 24-hr information, 09/82771 for airport ⊕ www.ilmailulaitos.fi.

BIKE TRAVEL

Finland is a wonderful place for biking, with its easy terrain, light traffic, and a wide network of bicycle paths. You can get bike-route maps for most major cities. In Helsinki, cycling is a great way to see the main peninsula as well as some of the surrounding islands, linked by bridges. Rentals average about €7–€20 per day. Bicycles can be rented from Green Bike in Helsinki. Suomen Retkeilymajajärjestö (Finnish Youth Hostel Association) offers a hostelling by bicycle package for 7 or 14 days (regular bikes €249–€431, hybrid bikes €275–€462) that includes a rental bike from Helsinki and Finnish Hostel Cheques for accommodation in hostels. Route maps are available from local tourist offices and from the Finnish Youth Hostel Association. Look online at *Cycling in Finland*, an informative brochure available from the Finnish Tourist Board.

🛪 Bike Maps **Finnish Tourist Board** ✉ Töölönk. 11, 00100 Helsinki ☎ 09/417-6911 ⊕ www. visitfinland.com/cycling. **Suomen Retkeilymajajärjestö** (Finnish Youth Hostel Association) ✉ Yrjönk. 38B 15, 00100 Helsinki ☎ 09/565-7150 🖶 09/565-71510 ⊕ www.srmnet.org.

🛪 Bike Rentals **Green Bike** ✉ Mannerheim. 13, 00100 Helsinki ☎ 09/8502-2850.

BOAT & FERRY TRAVEL

DFDS Scandinavian Seaways sails from Newcastle to Göteborg, Sweden, with overland (bus or train) transfer to Stockholm; from there, Silja and Viking Line ships cross to the Finnish Åland Islands, Turku, and Helsinki. Traveling time is about two days.

Finland is still a major shipbuilding nation, and the ferries that cruise the Baltic to the Finnish Åland Islands and Sweden seem more like luxury liners. The boat operators make so much money selling duty-free alcohol, perfume, and chocolate that they spare no expense on facilities, which include saunas, children's playrooms, casinos, a host of bars and cafés, and often superb restaurants. With both Finland and Sweden in the EU, all ferries between them now stop at Mariehamn in order to sell duty-free alcohol on board (Åland, with its special autonomous status within Finland, has special rights within the EU).

All classes of sleeping accommodations are available on board the journeys from Stockholm to Turku (about 11 hours) and from Stockholm to Helsinki (about 15 hours). Other connections are Helsinki, Hanso, or Tallinn (Estonia) to Rostock, Travemünde, or Lübeck (Germany); Helsinki to St. Petersburg (Russia); and Helsinki to Tallinn (Estonia).

Since ferry travel is common for budget and family travelers in the region, porters are not readily available. If you need assistance with luggage, contact the information desk in the harbor and/or on the ship. There are storage boxes for luggage in the Helsinki and Stockholm terminals if you are planning a day of sightseeing in either city.

In Helsinki the Silja Line terminal for ships arriving from Stockholm is at Olympialaituri (Olympic Harbor), on the west side of the South Harbor. The Viking Line terminal for ships arriving from Stockholm is at Katajanokkanlaituri (Katajanokka Harbor), on the east side of the South Harbor. Both Silja and Viking have downtown agencies where brochures, information, and tickets are available. Ask about half-price fares for bus and train travel in conjunction with ferry trips.

🛈 **DFDS Scandinavian Seaways** ✉ Scandinavia House, Parkeston Quay, Harwich, Essex, England ☎ 0870/533-3000. **Silja Line** ✉ Mannerheim. 2, Helsinki ☎ 09/18041 ⊕ www.silja.com. **Viking Line** ✉ Mannerheim. 14, 00100 Helsinki ☎ 09/12351 ⊕ www.vikingline.fi.

BUS TRAVEL

The Finnish bus network, Matkahuolto, is extensive and the fares reasonable. You can travel the network between Finland and Norway, Sweden, or Russia.

CUTTING COSTS   For trips longer than 80 km (50 mi) one-way, full-time students and children ages 4–11 get a discount of 50%; senior citizens and teens between 12 and 16 get 30%. Adults in groups of three or more are entitled to a 25% discount. Children under 4 travel free with an adult.

🛈 **Matkahuolto** ✉ Narinkka 3, 00100 Helsinki ☎ 0200/4000 €1.64 per call plus local charge for national timetable, 09/6136-8433 🖷 09/6136-8426 ⊕ www.matkahuolto.com.

CAR RENTAL

Car rental in Finland is not cheap, but a group rental might make it worthwhile. There are package rates for three- and seven-day trips. Be on the lookout also for weekend and summer discounts. It's cheaper to rent directly from the United States before coming to Finland; most agencies allow booking through their Web sites. Some Finnish service stations also offer car rentals at reduced rates.

Regular daily rates range from about €80 to €160, and unlimited mileage rates are the norm. Car rentals are normally cheaper on weekends. Insurance is sold by the rental agencies.

🚘 **Major Agencies Avis** ✉ Hietaniemenk. 6, 00100 Helsinki ☎ 09/441-155, 09/822-833 airport office ⊕ www.avis.fi. **Budget** ✉ Malminkatu 24, 00100 Helsinki ☎ 0800/124-424, 09/870-0780 airport office ⊕ www.budget.fi. **Europcar** ✉ Hitsaajankatu 7C, 00810 Helsinki ☎ 09/7515-5300, 040/306-2444 general reservation number, 09/7515-5700 airport office ⊕ www.europcar.fi. **Hertz** ✉ Mannerheimintie, 44, 00100 Helsinki ☎ 020/555-2300, 020/112-233 general reservation number, 020/555-2100 airport office ⊕ www.hertz.fi.

CAR TRAVEL

Driving is pleasant on Finland's relatively uncongested roads.

EMERGENCY
SERVICES

Foreigners involved in road accidents should immediately notify the Finnish Motor Insurers' Center as well as the police.

🚘 **Finnish Motor Insurers' Center** ✉ Liikennevakuutuskeskus, Bulevardi 28, 00120 Helsinki ☎ 09/680-401 ⊕ www.vakes.fi/lvk.

GASOLINE

Gasoline costs about €1.30 per liter.

ROAD
CONDITIONS

Late autumn and spring are the most hazardous times to drive. Roads are often icy in autumn (*kelivaroitus* is the slippery road warning), and the spring thaw can make for *kelirikko* (heaves).

🚘 **Automobile and Touring Club of Finland** ✉ Autoliitto ry, Hämeentie 105 A, 00550 Helsinki ☎ 09/7258-4400, 0200/8080 24-hr road service 🖨 09/7258-4460 ⊕ www.autoliitto.fi.

RULES OF THE
ROAD

Driving is on the right-hand side of the road. You must use headlights at all times and seat belts are compulsory for everyone. Yield to cars coming from the right at most intersections where roads are of equal size. The use of cell phones while driving is not permitted. There are strict drinking-and-driving laws in Finland, and remember to watch out for elk and reindeer signs, placed where they are known to cross the road.

Outside urban areas, speed limits vary between 60 kph and 100 kph (37 mph and 62 mph), with a general speed limit of about 80 kph (50 mph). In towns the limit is 40 kph to 60 kph (25 mph to 37 mph) and on motorways it's 100 kph to 120 kph (62 mph to 75 mph).

CUSTOMS & DUTIES

Spirits containing over 60% alcohol by volume may not be brought into Finland. Those under 19 may not bring in spirits. Visitors to Finland may not import goods for their own use from another European Union (EU) country duty-free. If the items were purchased in a duty-free shop at an airport or harbor, or on board an airplane or ship, visitors may bring in 1 liter of spirits, 2 liters of aperitifs or sparkling wines, 2 liters of table wine, and 16 liters of beer. For more information, consult the Finnish customs Web site ⊕ www.tulli.fi.

EMBASSIES & CONSULATES

🎏 Australia ✉ Museokatu 25B, Keskusta 00100 ☎ 09/4777–6640.

🎏 Canada ✉ Pohjoisespl. 25B, 00100 Helsinki ☎ 09/228–530 ⊕ www.canada.fi.

🎏 U.K. ✉ Itäinen Puistotie 17, 00140 Helsinki ☎ 09/2286–5100 ⊕ www.ukembassy. fi.

🎏 U.S. ✉ Itäinen Puistotie 14A, 00140 Helsinki ☎ 09/616–250, 09/6162–5730 consular section inquiries weekdays 2–4 ⊕ www.usembassy.fi.

EMERGENCIES

The nationwide emergency number is 112.

Late-night pharmacies are only in large towns. Look under *Apteekki* in the phone book; listings include pharmacy hours.

LANGUAGE

Finnish, the principal language, is a Finno-Ugric tongue related to Estonian with distant links to Hungarian. The country's second official language is Swedish, although only about 6% of the population speaks it as their primary language. In the south, most towns have Finnish and Swedish names; if the Swedish name is listed first, it indicates more Swedish than Finnish speakers live in that area. A third language, Sami, is actually a group of languages spoken by the Sami, the original dwellers of Lapland in the north, and has semiofficial status in certain northern areas. English is spoken in most cities and resorts.

LODGING

CAMPING Finland's wealth of open space promises prime camping territory. If you camp outside authorized areas and in a settled area, you must get the landowner's permission, and you cannot camp closer than 300 feet to anyone's house. Camping Card Scandinavia (€6) offers discounts on campsite fees and cottages throughout Scandinavia and is available through the Finnish Campingsite Association. The *Camping in Finland* journal is a free brochure listing 160 campsites in Finland and is available from numerous city tourist offices and campgrounds.

🎏 Finnish Campingsite Association ✉ Mäntytie 7, 00270 Helsinki ☎ 09/4774–0740 🖷 09/4772–002 ⊕ www.camping.fi.

HOSTELS & DORMITORIES During the summer season (June–August) many university residence halls in Finland open their doors to visitors. Accommodation in dormitories is usually in double rooms with shared toilet, shower, and cooking facilities among two to three rooms. In addition, regular youth hostels are available to all travelers year-round regardless of age and have various types of accommodations, including single and double rooms. Prices can range from €10 to €30 per person. Meals are generally available in a coffee shop or cafeteria. Ask the Finnish Tourist Board for information on budget accommodations or contact the Finnish Youth Hostel Association.

🛈 **Finnish Tourist Board** ✉ Töölönk. 11, 00100 Helsinki ☎ 09/417-6911 ⊕ www.visitfinland.com. **Finnish Youth Hostel Association** ✉ Yrjönk. 38B 15, 00100 Helsinki ☎ 09/565-7150 🖷 09/565-71510 ⊕ www.srmnet.org.

HOTELS   The Hotel Booking Centre, run by Helsinki Expert in the Helsinki railway station, can make reservations for you in several ways: when booked in person, the charge is €5 for rooms in Helsinki and in surrounding areas and €10 for all other areas. Requests for bookings via telephone, fax, e-mail, and the Internet are free. Suomen Hotellivaraukset will make reservations anywhere in Finland at no cost by telephone, fax, and e-mail (no bookings in person). The largest hotel chains in Finland are Scandic, Sokos, Rantasipi, Cumulus, Radisson SAS, Best Western, and Ramada.

🛈 **Helsinki Expert Hotel Booking** ✉ Rautatieasema 00100 Helsinki ☎ 09/2288-1400 🖷 09/2288-1499 ⊕ www.helsinkiexpert.com. **Suomen Hotellivaraukset** ☎ 09/686-0330 🖷 09/686-03310.

RESERVING A   Lomarengas has lists of reasonably priced bed-and-breakfasts, holiday
ROOM   cottages, and farm accommodations available in Finland. It also arranges stays at different facilities, including mökki holidays.

🛈 **Lomarengas-Finnish Country Holidays** ✉ Eteläesplanadi 22 C, 3rd fl., 00130 Helsinki, Finland ☎ 358/9-5766-3350 🖷 358/9-5766-3366 ⊕ www.lomarengas.fi.

MAIL & SHIPPING

Post offices are open weekdays 9–5 (until 7, 8, or 9 and on weekends in some cities); stamps, express mail, registered mail, and insured mail service are available. There is no Saturday delivery.

POSTAL RATES   Air-mail letters and postcards (up to 50 grams) cost about €0.65 to destinations within Finland, €0.90 to other EU countries, and €1.20 to other parts of the world. For more information, visit the Finnish post Web site: ⊕ www.posti.fi.

RECEIVING MAIL   You may receive letters care of poste restante anywhere in Finland; the poste restante in the capital is at the side of the rail station. It is open weekdays 7 AM–9 PM, weekends 10–6.

🛈 **Post Restante** ✉ Elielinaukio 1F, 00100 Helsinki

MONEY MATTERS

The strength of the euro may make Finland seem somewhat expensive to travelers from non-euro countries. Some sample prices include: cup of coffee, €2.50; glass of beer, starting from €4; soft drink, €3; ham sandwich, €4.50; 2-km (1-mi) taxi ride, €6–€9 (depending on time of day).

CURRENCY   The sole unit of currency in Finland is the euro, abbreviated as EUR or the symbol €. Euro bills are divided into 5, 10, 20, 50, 100, 200, and 500. The euro is divided into 100 cents in denominations of 1-, 2-, 5-, 10-, 20-, and 50-cent coins as well as €1 and €2 coins. At this writing the exchange rate was €0.82 to the U.S. dollar, €1.45 to the pound sterling, and €0.66 to the Canadian dollar.

Finland is making advancements in the use of "smart" prepaid electronic cash cards that process even the smallest of anonymous cash transactions made at designated public pay phones, vending machines, and McDonald's—of all places. Disposable prepaid cards can be purchased at kiosks. Nokia's presence in Finland is also making itself felt; you can purchase anything from soda to tram tickets via cell phone.

CURRENCY EXCHANGE — There are exchange bureaus in all bank branches and major hotels; Forex booths in major cities; and at Helsinki–Vantaa Airport. Some large harbor terminals also have exchange bureaus, and international ferries have exchange desks. Local banks and Forex offices usually give the best rates and charge a minimal commission. You can also change back any unused currency (no coins) at no fee with the original receipt. An exchange cart moves through the trains to Russia.

SPORTS & THE OUTDOORS

For general information, contact the Finnish Sports Federation, the umbrella organization for the many specific sports associations, several of which are housed in the same building.

🚩 **Finnish Sports Federation (SLU)** ✉ Radiok. 20, Helsinki 00093 ☎ 09/348-121 ⊕ www.slu.fi.

FISHING — A fishing license is not usually needed for basic angling with a hook and line, so it is possible to angle and ice fish for free in sea areas and virtually all lakes. For other types of fishing, a management fee of €20 per year or €6 per week can be paid into a state giro account at Nordea bank. In addition to this general fishing license, a regional fishing permit must also be obtained. The Wild North travel service, operating within the Forestry and Parks Service, offers various packages including fishing. Order or download a copy of *Fishing Finland,* an informative booklet available from the Finnish Tourist Board. For more information also visit the Web site of the Federation of Finnish Fisheries Associations.

🚩 **Finnish Fisheries Association** ☎ 09/684-4590 ⊕ www.ahven.net. **Finnish Forest and Parks Service** ✉ Vernissakatu 4, PL 94, 01301 Vantaa ☎ 0205/64120 customer service, 0203/44122 Wild North, the nature travel agency of the service ⊕ www.metsa. fi or www.wildnorth.net. **Finnish Tourist Board** ✉ Töölönk. 11, 00100 Helsinki ☎ 09/417-6911 ⊕ www.visitfinland.com/fishing.

GOLF — For information on Finland's golf courses, contact the Finnish Golf Union.

🚩 **Finnish Golf Union** ✉ Radiok. 20, 00240 SLU ☎ 09/3481-2244 ⊕ www.golf.fi.

HIKING — Look at the *Hiking in Finland* guide on the Finnish Tourist Board Web site. If you want to hike on state-owned land in eastern and northern Finland, write to the Finnish Forest and Parks Service. For organized hiking tours for families with children, as well as beginners, contact Suomen Latu (Finnish Ski Track Association). Maps of marked trails throughout Finland can be ordered through Genimap Oy. Trekkers may also contact the Finnish Orienteering Federation.

🚩 **Finnish Orienteering Federation** ✉ Radiok. 20, 00093 SLU ☎ 09/348-121. **Finnish Tourist Board** ✉ Töölönk. 11, 00100 Helsinki ☎ 09/417-6911 ⊕ www.visitfinland.com/ hiking. **Genimap Oy** ✉ PL 106, 01600 Vantaa ☎ 0201/34040 🖷 0201/340-449 ⊕ www. genimap.fi. **Suomen Latu** (Finnish Ski Track Association) ✉ Fabianinkatu 7, 00130 Helsinki ☎ 09/4159-1100 ⊕ www.suomenlatu.fi.

SAUNAS   🔲 **Finnish Sauna Society** ☎ 09/686–0560 ⊕ www.sauna.fi.

SKIING   Contact Suomen Latu (Finnish Ski Track Association) for information about ski centers and resorts nationwide. The Finnish Tourist Board also has information on its Web site.
🔲 **Suomen Latu (Finnish Ski Track Association)** ⊠ Fabianink. 7, 00130 Helsinki ☎ 09/4159-1100 ⊕ www.suomenlatu.fi.

WATER SPORTS   Boating enthusiasts may contact the Finnish Yachting Association or the Finnish Boating Association. For paddling trips on Finnish waterways, contact the Finnish Canoe Federation. Some of Finland's most popular inland sailing races are the Hanko Regatta, the Helsinki Regatta, the Rauma Sea Race, and the Päijänne Regatta. Contact the Finnish Yachting Association for further information.
🔲 **Finnish Boating Association** ⊠ Hämeentie 105 A, 00550 Helsinki ☎ 09/5490-3530 ⊕ www.veneilyliitto.fi. **Finnish Canoe Federation** ⊠ Olympiastadion, 00250 Helsinki ☎ 09/494-965. **Finnish Yachting Association** ⊠ Vattuniemenk. 13, 00210 Helsinki ☎ 020/733-8888 ⊕ www.yachting.fi.

TAXES

VALUE-ADDED TAX (V.A.T.)   There is a 22% sales tax on most consumer goods. Residents of countries outside the EU can recover 10% to 16% by going through the "tax-free for tourists" procedure: when you ask for your tax rebate—and be sure to ask for it at the point of purchase—you'll get a tax-free voucher and your goods in a sealed bag. The minimum purchase required is about €32. Present the voucher and unopened bag at tax-free cashiers when leaving Finland or when departing the EU. These are located at most major airports, at the departure terminals for most long-distance ferries, and at major overland crossings into Norway and Russia. For a fee, the tax refund can also be sent to your home country.

TAXIS

Taxis travel everywhere in Finland. The meter starts at about €4.30 daytime and about €6.60 evenings and weekends. In cities people generally go to one of the numerous taxi stands and take the first one available. You can hail a cab, but most are on radio call. The taxi information number costs €0.99 per call plus 8 cents per 10 seconds. Most taxi drivers take credit cards. Tipping is unnecessary; if you want to leave something, round up to the nearest euro. A receipt is a *kuitti*.
🔲 **Taxi Center** ☎ 0100/0700 €0.99 plus 8 cents per 10 seconds plus local charge, 0100/06000 €0.99 plus 8 cents per 10 seconds plus local charge for advance bookings ⊕ www.taksihelsinki.fi.

TELEPHONES

COUNTRY CODE   The country code for Finland is 358.

DIRECTORY & OPERATOR ASSISTANCE   Dial 118 or 020202 for information in Helsinki and elsewhere in Finland; 020208 for international information (€3.49 per minute plus local charge).

INTERNATIONAL CALLS   The front of the phone book has overseas calling directions and rates. You must begin all direct overseas calls with 990, 996, 999, or 00, plus country code (1 for the United States and Canada, 44 for Great Britain).

Finnish operators can be reached by dialing ☎ 020–208 for overseas information or for placing collect calls. The long-distance services below will place collect calls at no charge.

LOCAL CALLS Remember that if you are dialing out of the immediate area you must dial 0 first; drop the 0 when calling Finland from abroad. To avoid exorbitant hotel surcharges on calls, use card pay phones; note that coin phones are becoming a rarity.

LONG-DISTANCE ⬛ Access Codes **AT&T** ☎ 9800/10010. **MCI Worldphone** ☎ 0800/110280.
SERVICES **Sprint and Global One** ☎ 0800/110284.

PHONE CARDS Major urban areas in Finland have moved to a phone-card system, and most phones only accept cards (no coins), which fortunately are usually available nearby at post offices, R-kiosks, and some grocery stores in increments such as €6, €10, €20, and €30. Public phones charge a minimum of about €0.50. Kiosks often have phones nearby. Airport and hotel phones take credit cards. Ringing tones vary but are distinguishable from busy signals, which are always rapid. Most pay phones have picture instructions illustrating how they operate. Note that regional phone companies have their own cards that don't work in telephones in other regions. The main companies include Sonera, Elisa (Helsinki), and Soon Communications (Tampere).

TIPPING

Tipping is not the norm in Finland but is becoming more of a habit, so use your own discretion. Finns normally do not tip cab drivers, but if they do they round up to the nearest euro. Give one euro to train or hotel porters. Coat-check fees are usually posted, and tips above this amount are not expected.

TRAIN TRAVEL

Passenger trains leave Helsinki twice daily for St. Petersburg (8 hours) and once daily on an overnighter to Moscow (15 hours). Travel to Russia requires a visa. To get to northern Sweden or Norway, you must combine train–bus or train–boat travel.

The Finnish State Railways, or VR, serve southern Finland well, but connections in the central and northern sections are scarcer and are supplemented by buses. Helsinki is the main junction, with Riihimäki to the north a major hub. You can get as far north as Rovaniemi and Kemijärvi by rail, but to penetrate farther into Lapland, you'll need to rely on buses, domestic flights, or local taxis.

Note that all train travelers in Finland must have a reserved seat, but it is possible to buy a seat ticket on the train. Special fast trains (Intercity and the Helsinki-Turku Pendolino) are more expensive but also more comfortable. Inquiries on train travel can be made to the Finnish State Railways at the main railroad station in Helsinki or to the Information Service.

CLASSES First- and second-class seats are available on all express trains.

CUTTING COSTS Children ages 6–16 travel half-fare. There is a 15% reduction when 3–10 people travel together and a 20% discount for groups of 11 or more.

Senior citizens (over 65) can get 50% discounts on train fares. With a Familyticket, children under 16 travel free when accompanied by an adult with a full-priced ticket.

The Finnrail Pass gives unlimited first- or second-class travel within a month's time for passengers living permanently outside Finland; the 3-day pass costs €168, the 5-day pass €222, and the 10-day pass €300 (€250, €332, and €451, respectively, for first-class). Children 6 and over and teens 13–17 pay half fare; children under 6 ride free. Passes can be purchased in the United States and Canada by calling Rail Europe; and from the Finnish Railways, or VR. TourExpert at the Helsinki City Tourist Office also sells Finnrail passes.

The ScanRail Pass allows unlimited second-class train travel throughout Denmark, Finland, Norway, and Sweden, and comes in various denominations. It is valid for 5 days of unlimited travel in any two-month period ($291); 10 days of unlimited travel in two months ($390); or 21 days of consecutive days of unlimited train travel ($453). Senior citizens, those 60 and over, and young people under 25 get discounts. Free connections or discounts on certain ferries and buses are included. The Eurailpass is good for train travel throughout all of Europe. In the United States, call Rail Europe or DER.

🚹 **DER** ☎ 800/782-2424. **Finnish Railways** (VR) ☎ 0600/41-902, €1 plus local network charge ⊕ www.vr.fi. **Rail Europe** ☎ 800/438-7245 ⊕ www.raileurope.com.

TRAVEL AGENCIES
Suomen Matkatoimisto (Finland Travel Bureau) is the country's main travel agency. The agency specializes in all kinds of travel arrangements, including special-interest tours throughout Finland, as well as Scandinavia, Russia, and the Baltic States.

🚹 Local Agent Referrals **Suomen Matkatoimisto** (Finland Travel Bureau) ✉ Kaivok. 10 A, PL 319, 00100 Helsinki ☎ 09/18261 ⊕ www.smt.fi.

VISITOR INFORMATION
🚹 Tourist Information **Finnish Tourist Board** ✉ Suomen Matkailun edistämiskeskus, Töölönk. 11, 00100 Helsinki ☎ 09/417-6911 ⊕ www.visitfinland.com ✉ Box 4649, Grand Central Station, New York, NY 10163-4649 ☎ 212/885-9700 or 800/346-4636 ⊕ www.gofinland.org ✉ Box 33213, London W6 8JX ☎ 020/7365-2512.

Iceland

WORD OF MOUTH

"Iceland's terrain was just beautiful. Waterfalls, glaciers, mountains, lava fields, geysers, rainbows . . . you never knew what would be around the corner. The Blue Lagoon was just fabulous. There is a waterfall that you can get beneath, silica mud to slather on your body, and a sauna where you can get treatments."

—dkw

"Things I learned in Iceland:
1. You will never, ever decipher the Icelandic language. 2. The best lamb in the entire world is Icelandic lamb. No lie. 3. The whole 'Fire and Ice' thing—ice-filled volcanic lava tubes pretty much sums up the concept. 4. If the road sign says '4WD,' they mean it. 5. Some of the best photos I took in Iceland are, strangely enough, of ice."

—GalavantingReprobate

Updated by
Eliza Reid

AN EERIE MOONSCAPE UNDER A MYSTICAL SUBARCTIC SKY greets you on the highway from Keflavík International Airport into Reykjavík, Iceland's capital. The low terrain is barely covered by its thin scalp of luminescent green moss. Although trees are few and far between, an occasional scrawny shrub clings to a rock outcropping. The air smells different—clean and crisp—and it's so clear that on a sunny day you can see for miles.

Welcome to Iceland, one of the most dramatic natural spectacles on this planet. It is a land of dazzling white glaciers and black sands, blue hot springs, rugged lava fields, and green, green valleys. This North Atlantic island offers insight into the ferocious powers of nature, ranging from the still-warm lava from the 1973 Vestmannaeyjar (Westman Islands) and the 2000 Mt. Hekla volcanic eruptions to the chilling splendor of the Vatnajökull Glacier. More than 80% of the island's 103,000 square km (40,000 square mi) is uninhabited. Ice caps cover 11% of the country, more than 50% is barren, 6% consists of lakes and rivers, and less than 2% of the land is cultivated. There's hardly a tree to be seen in most of the country, making the few birches, wildflowers, and delicate vegetation all the more lovely in contrast. Contrary to the country's forbidding name, the climate is surprisingly mild in winter, although in summer you're unlikely to be comfortable in just a T-shirt and shorts.

Surrounded by the sea, the Icelanders have become great fishermen, and fish remains the cornerstone of the economy. Seafood exports pay for imported foodstuffs and other goods, all of which could not be produced economically in such a small society. Because of importation needs and high value-added taxes on most goods and services, prices tend toward the steep side. Hotels and restaurants are pricey, but with a little digging you can usually find inexpensive alternatives. Tipping in restaurants is not required.

Iceland is the westernmost outpost of Europe, 800 km (500 mi) from the nearest European landfall, Scotland, and nearly 1,600 km (1,000 mi) from Copenhagen, the country's administrative capital during Danish rule from 1380 to 1918. So far north—part of the country touches the Arctic Circle—Iceland has the usual Scandinavian long hours of darkness in winter. Maybe this is why Icelanders are such good chess players (Iceland played host to the memorable Fischer–Spassky match of 1972). Such long nights may also explain why, per capita, more books are written, printed, purchased, and read in Iceland than anywhere else in the world. It's no surprise that the birthrate is unusually high for Europe, too.

History

Iceland was settled by Vikings with strong Celtic elements in the late 9th century. Tradition has it that the first Norse settlers arrived in AD 874, but there is some evidence that Irish monks landed even earlier. Icelanders today speak a language remarkably similar to the ancient Viking tongue in which the sagas were recorded in the 13th and 14th centuries. The Norse settlers brought to the island sturdy horses, robust cattle, and Celtic slaves. Perhaps Irish tales of the supernatural inspired Iceland's

5

With only a few days on your hands, you can experience a fair number of Iceland's major attractions. You can take organized day trips from Reykjavík or explore the surrounding area yourself with a rental car. Ask travel agents or tour operators about special offers within Iceland that allow you to fly one way and take a bus the other. Theoretically, you can drive the Ring Road—the most scenic route, which skirts the entire Iceland coast—in two days, but that pace qualifies as rally-race driving, and you won't see much. You should plan on at least a week to travel the Ring Road, enjoying roadside sightseeing and relaxing in the tranquil environment along the way. Side jaunts add significant time, as secondary roads are often not paved. When traveling outside Reykjavík, always allow plenty of time to make it back for departing flights. (Note: In the following itineraries, only towns that have accommodations listings are preceded by the hotel icon.)

If you have 3–4 days

Start by taking a leisurely tour of ▦ **Reykjavík.** The mix of the old and new in the capital's midtown is seen in the 19th-century **Alþingishús** and the **Ráðhús,** barely a decade old. Colorful rooftops abound, and ornate gingerbread can be spotted on the well-kept older buildings. Make sure you visit one of the seven outdoor thermal swimming pools, a great way to relax after a day of sightseeing and fun for the whole family. On Day 2 head out to the countryside for the famous **Golden Circle** tour, and take in the spectacular **Gullfoss** waterfall, the **Geysir** hot springs area, and **Þingvellir National Park.** There are many organized tours that cover this route, or you can rent a car yourself.

If you leave on Day 3, stop at the surreal **Blue Lagoon,** for a late morning–early afternoon dip that will leave you refreshed and is only 20 minutes from the airport if you have an afternoon flight connection.

If you have an extra day, wake up early and head north to the **Snæfellsnes Peninsula** on Iceland's west coast. The **Hvalfjörður tunnel** cuts travel time dramatically. On emerging from the tunnel, bypass the town of Akranes and drive north to Borgarnes. Just north of it, turn west (left) on Route 54 out on the peninsula and head to the tiny village of **Arnarstapi.** If you left the capital before 9 AM, here is a good place to have lunch and take a stroll along the shore, watch small boats come and go, and marvel at the seabirds as they dive and soar. Afterward, enter Iceland's newest national park, Snæfellsjökull, and marvel at the mystical moods of this mountain as you circle north to Ólafsvík en route to ▦ Stykkishólmur. It takes a little over two hours to drive back to Reykjavík from here.

If you have 6 days

Complete the three full days of the tour above. Then you have two options:

Option 1—Northern Journey: On the morning of Day 4 fly northeast to ▦ **Akureyri.** With a rental car visit the numerous historical houses here, such as **Matthíasarhús, Nonnahús, Laxdalshús,** and **Davíðshús.** After lunch, take some time at the **Lystigarðurinn.** Next drive east to the Lake Mývatn area, taking in **Goðafoss** and maybe even **Dettifoss** along the way. Spend a good part of Day 5 around ▦ **Mývatn,** visiting **Dimmuborgir** lava formations, **Ná-**

maskarð sulfur springs, and the shoreline birding areas. Return to Akureyri and stay the fifth night (or you can take the last flight back to Reykjavík). On Day 6, leave the north on a morning flight back to Reykjavík, and if time permits, duck in for a quick dip in the **Blue Lagoon.**

Option 2—Southern Gems: Leave Reykjavík early on Day 4 and take your rental car south along Highway 1 through the towns of Hveragerði and Selfoss and past the stunning waterfalls of Skogafoss and Seljalandsfoss, beneath the glacier Eyjafjallajökull (each is off a short spur road). The sea arch of Dyrólaey, with its beautiful black beach, is just before the town of Vík, where you can spend the night. Continue east on Day 5 over wide lava flows and broad sandy plains to Skaftafell National Park and, farther east, to the Jökulsárlón glacial lagoon, where you can take a boat trip through the chunks of glacier floating in the water. Turn around and retrace your route west, where you can spend the night near Hella. Leave early on Day 6 to head toward the airport, through the villages of Stokksheyri and Eyjarbakki, stopping for a dip in the Blue Lagoon if there's time.

---

traditional lore of the *huldufólk,* or hidden people, said to reside in splendor in rocks, crags, caves, and lava tubes.

Iceland's near-universal literacy might be attributed to its long tradition of participatory democracy, dating from AD 930, when the first parliament met at Þingvellir. Icelandic tribal chiefs decided to join the Norwegian crown in the mid-13th century, and after many centuries under Norwegian, and later Danish, rule, Iceland finally gained full independence in 1944. Today Iceland is a modern Nordic—most find the term *Scandinavian* too limited—society with a well-developed social-welfare system and one of the highest standards of living in the world.

Exploring Iceland

Iceland almost defies division into separate regions, thanks to its inlets and bays, thorough lacework of rivers, and complex coastline of fjords, all crowned by an unpopulated highland of glaciers and barrens. To divide the country into four compass directions is to oversimplify, but since the Icelandic national emblem (seen on the "tails" side of every local coin) depicts four legendary symbols—one for each corner of the country—the number is not totally arbitrary.

Reykjavík is the logical starting point for any visit to Iceland, before venturing out into the countryside, where rainbow-arched waterfalls cleave mountains with great spiked ridges and snowcapped peaks. You can climb mountains, ford rivers, watch birds, catch trout or salmon, even tend sheep and cattle at a typical Icelandic farm. The west is an expansive section of rugged fjords and lush valleys, starting just north of Reykjavík and extending all the way up to the extreme northwest. The north is a region of long, sometimes broad valleys and fingerlike peninsulas reaching toward the Arctic Circle. The east has fertile farmlands, the country's largest forest, and its share of smaller fjords. Iceland's south stretches from the lowest eastern fjords, essentially all the way west to the capital's out-

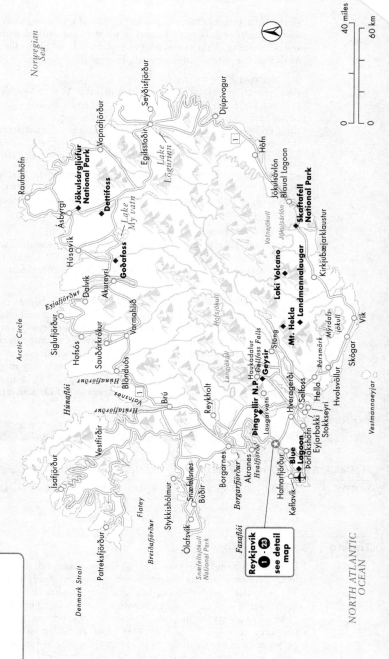

Iceland

Denmark Strait

Norwegian
Sea

Arctic Circle

NORTH ATLANTIC
OCEAN

**Reykjavík ❶ - ㉓
see detail
map**

Keflavík
Hafnarfjörður
**Blue
Lagoon**
Þorlákshöfn
Stokkseyri
Eyjarbakki
Selfoss
Hella
Hvolsvöllur
Hveragerði
Laugarvatn
Þingvellir N.P.
Geysir
Gullfoss Falls
Haukadalur
Stöng
Mt. Hekla
Landmannalaugar
Laki Volcano
Kirkjubæjarklaustur
**Skaftafell
National Park**
Bláual Lagoon
Jökulsárlón
Jökulsárlón
Vík
Skógar
Mýrdals-
jökull
Þórsmörk
Vestmannaeyjar

Borgarnes
Akranes
Hvalfjörður
Borgarfjörður
Faxaflói
Reykholt
Brú
Hvítárvatn
Hrútafjörður
Hrútafjörður
Húnaflói
Blönduós
Sauðárkrókur
Varmahlíð
Vatnsnes
Langjökull
Hofsjökull
Vatnajökull
Hofsós
Siglufjörður
Dalvík
Akureyri
Goðafoss
Húsavík
Ásbyrgi
Dettifoss
**Jökulsárgljúfur
National Park**
Lake
Mývatn
Vopnafjörður
Egilsstaðir
Lake
Lögurinn
Seyðisfjörður
Djúpivogur
Höfn

Ísafjörður
Vestfirðir
Patreksfjörður
Breiðafjörður
Flatey
Ólafsvík
Stykkishólmur
Búðir
Snæfellsnes
Snæfellsjökull
National Park

Raufarhöfn

40 miles

60 km

skirts. It encompasses rich piedmont farmland and wide, sandy coastal and glacial plains. Powerful rivers drain the area, carved with impressive waterfalls. The national parks of Skaftafell and Þingvellir are here, as well as the nation's highest peak, Hvannadalshnjúkur.

About the Restaurants

Restaurants in Iceland are small and diverse. You can expect superb seafood and lamb, and the fresh fish is not to be missed—surely some of the best you'll ever have. Besides native cuisine, eateries offer everything from Asian and Indian to French and Italian. Pizzas, hamburgers, ice cream, and a tasty local version of the hot dog, with fried onions, are widely available. Most restaurants accept major credit cards.

Perhaps the best way to save substantially on meal costs (besides choosing from the specials of the day) is to forego alcohol, the price of which essentially doubles from liquor store (where it isn't cheap to begin with) to restaurant table.

About the Hotels

Hotels in Reykjavík and larger towns usually offer standard amenities: hair dryer, trouser press, telephone, and satellite TV. Unless otherwise noted, assume rooms listed have bath or shower. Breakfast is usually included in the hotel price, but inquire to be certain.

Many travelers find simple guesthouses adequate, whereas others prefer a bed-and-breakfast in a private home. Icelandic farm holidays have been growing in popularity, even among Icelanders. On about 140 properties—half of them working farms—you can come in close contact with the country, its people, and the magnificent natural surroundings. Accommodations vary widely: you might stay in a separate cottage, in a bed in the farmhouse, or in a sleeping bag in an outbuilding. Some farms have cooking facilities; others serve full meals if requested. Make reservations well in advance.

WHAT IT COSTS In Iceland Króna					
	$$$$	$$$	$$	$	¢
RESTAURANTS	over 3,100	2,400–3,100	1,700–2,400	1,000–1,700	under 1,000
HOTELS	over 22,900	15,800–22,900	8,700–15,800	1,600–8,700	under 1,600

Restaurant prices are per person, for a main course at dinner. Hotel prices are for two people in a standard double room in high season.

Timing

Don't let its name fool you—Iceland is a year-round destination with a temperate ocean climate: cool summers and relatively mild winters. The warmest months—June, July, and August—are the most popular with visitors, but a growing number have been coming in winter for the promise of snowmobiling, snow-trekking vehicle tours, and a spectacular fireworks display on New Year's Eve. Although swimming in the perpetually frigid ocean isn't a possibility, inviting hot springs and naturally heated pools dimple the landscape. Icelanders from all walks of life—cabinet ministers on down—congregate for a soak or a swim any time of year.

In general, Iceland's weather is more unpredictable than most: in June, July, and August, sunny days alternate with spells of rain showers, crisp breezes, and occasional driving winds. From June through July, the sun barely sets. Unruly fall is beyond prediction: it can be a crisp time of berry picking and beautiful colors on the heaths, or of challenging gales, when lingering over coffee in a café may be the most appealing activity. In December the sun shines for only three hours a day. Winter temperatures can be as high as 50°F (10°C) or as low as –14°F (–10°C)—and, ironically, winter cloudiness is usually warmer than winter sun. The spellbinding northern lights are seen most often on cold, clear nights from September to March.

REYKJAVÍK

Sprawling Reykjavík, the nation's nerve center and government seat, is home to half the island's population. On a bay overlooked by proud Mt. Esja (pronounced *eh*-shyuh), with its ever-changing hues, Reykjavík presents a colorful sight, its concrete houses painted in light colors and topped by vibrant red, blue, and green roofs. In contrast to the almost treeless countryside, Reykjavík has many tall, native birches, rowans, and willows, as well as imported aspen, pines, and spruces.

Reykjavík's name comes from the Icelandic words for smoke, *reykur,* and bay, *vík.* In AD 874, Norseman Ingólfur Arnarson saw Iceland rising out of the misty sea and came ashore at a bay eerily shrouded with plumes of steam from nearby hot springs. Today most of the houses in Reykjavík are heated by near-boiling water from the hot springs. Natural heating avoids air pollution; there's no smoke around. You may notice, however, that the hot water brings a slight sulfur smell to the bathroom.

Prices are easily on a par with other major European cities. A practical option is to purchase a Reykjavík Tourist Card at the Tourist Information Center or at the Reykjavík Youth Hostel. This card permits unlimited bus usage and admission to any of the city's seven pools, the Family Park and Zoo, and city museums. The cards are valid for one (IKr 1,200), two (IKr 1,700), or three days (IKr 2,200), and they pay for themselves after three or four uses a day. Even lacking the Tourist Card, paying admission (IKr. 500 or IKr. 250 for seniors or handicapped) to one of the following city art museums gets you free same-day admission to the other two: Hafnarhús, Kjarvalsstaðir, or Ásmundarsafn.

Numbers in the text correspond to numbers in the margin and on the Reykjavík map.

Navigating Reykjavík

The best way to see Reykjavík is on foot. Many of the interesting sights are in the city center, within easy walking distance of one another. There is no subway system.

Exploring Reykjavík

Any part of town can be reached by city bus, but take a walk around to get an idea of the present and past. In the Old Town, classic wooden buildings rub shoulders with modern timber and concrete structures.

Old Town & Harbor

a good walk

What better guiding presence on a tour of historic Reykjavík than the man who started it all, one of the first settlers of Iceland and Reykjavík's founder, Ingólfur Arnarson? Overlooking the old city center and harbor is a grassy knoll known as Arnarhóll, topped by the **Ingólfur Arnarson statue** ▶ ❶. From here there's a fine panorama of midtown Reykjavík.

Behind him on his left, on Hverfisgata, the classic white Landsbókasafnið (Old National Library) has been resurrected as the **Þjóðmenningarhúsið** ❷, or National Cultural House. Outside, its crests pay tribute to giants of Icelandic literature. Inside, it includes informative cultural exhibits. Across the street and slightly east of the Þjóðmenningarhúsið is **Alþjóðahús** ❸, the Intercultural Center where there are often art exhibitions and music shows—the lively café is a good place to stop for a coffee. Walk down Hverfisgata from these buildings to Lækjargata to the **Stjórnarráðhúsið** ❹, which contains the offices of the prime minister. Across Bankastræti, continuing along the hill above Lækjargata and the oversize pavement chessboard on the same side, stands the historic mid-19th-century Bernhöftstorfan—a row of distinct two-story wooden houses, two of which are now restaurants. The building across Amtmannsstígur and closer to the pond is **Menntaskólinn í Reykjavík** ❺.

Continue south on Lækjargata to the corner of the Tjörnin Pond. Overlooking Tjörnin Pond from its northwest corner is the modern **Ráðhús** ❻, on the corner of Vonarstræti and Tjarnargata. Inside there's usually a large relief map of Iceland, which is very useful for planning any out-of-town journeys.

From the pond, follow Templarasund a little more than a block north to **Austurvöllur Square** ❼, dominated by a statue of Jón Sigurðsson (1811–79), who initiated Iceland's fight for independence from Denmark. Sigurðsson looks approvingly at the 19th-century **Alþingishús** ❽, on Kirkjustræti. Next to the Parliament is the **Dómkirkjan** ❾, on the corner of Templarasund and Kirkjustræti. From the square toward the harbor runs Pósthússtræti, taking its name from the main post office, the large red building on the corner of Austurstræti. At the northwest corner of Pósthússtræti and Tryggvagata is **Tollhúsið** ❿, which is distinguished by Iceland's largest mosaic mural, a harbor scene by Gerður Helgadóttir.

Continue west on Tryggvagata until you reach Hafnarhús, a former warehouse, now the **Listasafn Reykjavíkur** ⓫, the Reykjavík Art Museum. It's recognizable by its entrance under what looks like a wide gangplank hanging from the wall overhead. After taking in the latest exhibition, head north on Grófin and cross Geirsgata, the major street running along the harbor.

Detour: A 15-minute walk west will take you to the **Víkin-Maritime Museum** ⓬, housed in a former fish factory. Heading back east along Geirs-

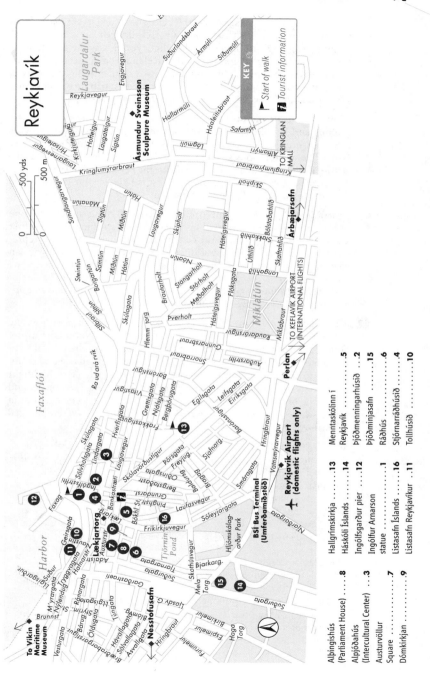

gata brings you to **Ingólfsgarður pier** 🔟, closest to Lækjartorg Plaza. Here you may spot Iceland's Coast Guard vessels docked for service. If you continue walking east along the shoreline, you'll pass the green, dual-pointed *Partnership* sculpture, a gift to Iceland from a former U.S. ambassador and his wife. A few hundred yards farther along the shore is the even more dramatic *Sólfar,* a stunning modern tribute to the Viking seafarers who first sailed into this harbor 1,100 years ago.

TIMING Allow about 90 minutes for this walk, including some time in the Ráðhús and Dómkirkja. Give yourself more time if you want to visit the Maritime Museum or exhibitions at the Listasafn Reykjavíkur. Note: The bus terminus at Lækjargata a few short blocks east of Lækjartorg Plaza is a good place to depart for the Perlan or the Árbæjarsafn, a re-created Icelandic village. Farther east is Laugardalur Park and the Ásmundur Sveinsson Sculpture Museum.

WHAT TO SEE **Alþingishús** (Parliament House). Built in 1880–81, this structure is one
★ 🔟 of the country's oldest stone buildings. Iceland's Alþingi held its first session in AD 930 and therefore can lay claim to being the oldest representative parliament in the world. From October through May you can view the parliament proceedings from the visitor's gallery here. Depending on the urgency of the agenda, any number of Iceland's 63 members of parliament, from five political parties, may be present. ⊠ *Austurvöllur Sq.* 🕾 *563–0500* ⊕ *www.althingi.is.*

🔟 **Alþjóðahús** (Intercultural Center). Look for the building with exotic gingerbreading, across from Þjóðmenningarhúsið (National Culture House), and you've found this facility dedicated to multicultural society in Iceland. An in-house support group gives legal advice and counselling to immigrants and refugees. The events held here highlight cultures from around the globe—there are art shows, live music, and films. The bistro-bar Cultura is very likely the most eclectic hangout in town, where the menu is as varied as the culture. ⊠ *Hverfisgata 18* 🕾 *530–9300* 🖷 *530–9301* ⊕ *www.ahus.is.*

off the
beaten
path **ÁRBÆJARSAFN –** At the Open-Air Municipal Museum, 18th- and 19th-century houses furnished in old-fashioned style display authentic household utensils and tools for cottage industries. You can see demonstrations of farm activities and taste piping-hot *lummur*
ᑕ (chewy pancakes) cooked over an old farmhouse stove. To get to the museum, take Bus S3 or S4 to the Mjódd station and switch to Bus 24. ⊠ *Ártúnsblettur* 🕾 *577–1111* ⊕ *www.arbaejarsafn.is* 🖭 *IKr 600* ⊙ *June–Aug., daily 10–5.*

ÁSMUNDUR SVEINSSON SCULPTURE MUSEUM – Some originals by this sculptor, depicting ordinary working people, myths, and folktale episodes, are exhibited in the museum's gallery and studio and in the surrounding garden. It's on the southwest edge of Laugardalur Park, opposite the traffic circle at its entrance. ⊠ *v/Sigtún (5-min ride from Hlemmur station on Bus S2)* 🕾 *553–2155* ⊕ *www.artmuseum.is* 🖭 *IKr 500, free Mon.* ⊙ *May–Sept., daily 10–4; Oct.–Apr., daily 1–4.*

❼ **Austurvöllur Square.** East Field is a peculiar name for a west-central square. The reason: it's just east of the presumed spot where first settler Ingólfur Arnarson built his farm, today near the corner of Aðalstræti.

★ ❾ **Dómkirkjan** (Lutheran Cathedral). A place of worship has existed on this site since AD 1200. The small, charming church, built 1788–96, represents the state religion, Lutheranism. It was here that sovereignty and independence were first blessed and endorsed by the church. It's also where Iceland's national anthem, actually a hymn, was first sung in 1874. Since 1845, members and cabinet ministers of every Alþing parliament have gathered here for a service before the annual session. Among the treasured items inside is a baptismal font carved and donated by the famous 19th-century master sculptor Bertel Thorvaldsen, who was half Icelandic. ⊠ *Austurvöllur* ☎ *520–9700* ⊕ *www.domkirkjan.is/enska. html* ☉ *Weekdays 10–5, unless in use for services.*

⓬ **Ingólfsgarður Pier.** The coast guard is the closest thing Iceland has to a national military. At the end of this pier, where the coast guard's vessels are berthed, is a distinctive yellow-beacon pylon. Today the coast guard, which tenaciously stood up to the British Navy during the cod wars, still has a handful of ships vigorously enforcing offshore fishing limits.

▶ ❶ **Ingólfur Arnarson statue.** If you look beyond Ingólfur, who faces you from his knoll, you can see the city's architectural mélange: 18th-century stone houses, 19th-century small wooden houses, and office blocks from the '30s and '40s. ⊠ *Arnarhóll.*

Lækjartorg (Brook Square). Now a focal point in Reykjavík's otherwise rambling city center, this square opens onto **Austurstræti**, a semi-pedestrian shopping street. A brook, now underground, drains Tjörnin Pond into the sea (hence the street's name). ⊠ *At Bankastræti and Lækjargata.*

off the beaten path

FodorśChoice
★
Ⓒ

LAUGARDALUR PARK – This is actually made up of several parks in one large area. Besides one of the best swimming pools in the city, the recreational expanse has picnic and barbecuing facilities. The **Húsdýragarðurinn** (Farm Animal Park; ☎ 575–7800), has reindeer, goats, cows, horses, seals, and fish; it is open daily 10–6 from mid-May through August; the rest of the year it's open daily from 10–5. The adjacent **Fjölskyldugarðurinn** (*Family Park*; ☎ 575–7800 ⊕ *www.husdyragardur.is*) has rides and games, such as Crazy Bikes—a driving school complete with miniature traffic lights—and a scale model of a Viking ship. Joint admission to both the Farm Animal Park and Family Park is IKr 350 for those aged 6–12, and IKr 450 for those over 12. The free **Grasagarður** (*Botanical Garden;* ☎ 553–8870) has an extensive outdoor collection of native and exotic plants. Coffee and baked items are sold in summer at the cozy conservatory. To get to the park, you can take Bus S2, 14, or 15 east. 🎫 *Free.*

Laugavegur. Traditionally the city's main shopping street, Laugavegur now meets stiff competition from the Kringlan and Smáralind malls. You may have to go to Paris or Vienna to find as many eateries and coffeehouses packed into such a short stretch.

⓫ Listasafn Reykjavíkur (Reykjavík Art Museum). Also known as Hafnarhús, this former warehouse of the Port of Reykjavík now houses the city's art museum. The six galleries occupy two floors, and there's a courtyard and "multipurpose" space. The museum's permanent collection includes a large number of works donated by the contemporary Icelandic artist, Erró. There are also regular temporary exhibitions. ✉ *Tryggvagata 17* ☎ *590–1200* ⊕ *www.artmuseum.is* 🎫 *IKr 500, free Mon.* ☉ *Daily 10–5.*

❺ Menntaskólinn í Reykjavík (Reykjavík Grammar School). Many graduates from the country's oldest educational institution, established in 1846, have gone on to dominate political and social life in Iceland. Former president Vigdís Finnbogadóttir and numerous cabinet ministers, including Iceland's former prime minister, Gunnlaugsson Davíð Oddsson, are graduates, as are film producer Hrafn Gunnlaugson and well-known author Þórarinn Eldjarn. ✉ *Corner of Amtmannsstígur and Lækjargata.*

> **off the beaten path**

PERLAN – On top of Öskjuhlíð, the hill overlooking Reykjavík Airport, Perlan (the Pearl) was built in 1991 as a monument to Iceland's invaluable geothermal water supplies. Among the indoor and outdoor spectacles are art exhibits, musical performances, a permanent Viking history exhibit, and fountains that spurt water like geysers. Above the six vast tanks, which held 800,000 cubic feet of hot water, the panoramic viewing platform offers telescopes and a coffee bar and ice-cream parlor. The crowning glory is a revolving restaurant under the glass dome; it's pricey, but the view is second to none. ✉ *Öskjuhlíð Hill* ☎ *562–0200* ☉ *Daily 10–9.*

❷ Þjóðmenningarhúsið (National Cultural House). Crests on the facade of the impressive former Landsbókasafnið (Old National Library) name significant Icelandic literary figures; the renovated building now houses interesting cultural exhibits, including a fixed exhibit of the precious vellum manuscripts of many of the sagas, a must-see for all interested in Norse or ancient literature. Erected between 1906 and 1908, it was primarily a library for most of the 20th century, but its book collection has been moved to the Þjóðarbókhlaðan at the National and University Library of Iceland. ✉ *North side of Hverfisgata at old midtown* ☎ *545–1400* ⊕ *www.thjodmenning.is* 🎫 *IKr 300* ☉ *Daily 11–5.*

★ ❻ Ráðhús (City Hall). Modern architecture and nature converge at this building overlooking Tjörnin Lake. Inside is a visitor information desk and coffee bar with Internet access. A three-dimensional model of Iceland, over 91 square yards in size, is usually on display in the gallery, which often hosts various temporary exhibitions. ✉ *Bounded by Fríkirkjuvegur, Vonarstræti, and Tjarnargata* ☎ *411–1000* ⊕ *www.reykjavik.is* ☉ *Weekdays 8–7, weekends noon–6.*

❹ Stjórnarráðhúsið (Government House). This low white building, constructed in the 18th century as a prison, today houses the office of the prime minister. ✉ *Lækjartorg Plaza* ☎ *545–8400* ⊕ *www.stjr.is.*

☾ Tjörnin Pond This natural pond by the City Hall attracts birds—and bird lovers—year-round and is also popular among ice-skaters in winter. Children love feeding bread to the many varieties of swans and ducks in the pond. ✉ *Next to the Raðhús* ✉ *Free.*

🔟 **Tollhúsið.** A bureaucratic necessity, especially for an island nation, the Customs House is decorated with an impressive mosaic mural. ✉ *Tryggvagata 19.*

---

off the beaten path

VÍKIN SJÓMINJASAFNIÐ Í REYKJAVÍK (VÍKIN MARITIME MUSEUM) – Housed in an old fish factory with great views of the harbor, the maritime museum opened in June 2005 and features an exhibition on trawlers in Iceland. ✉ *Grandargarði 8* ☎ *517 9400* ⊕ *www. sjominjasafn.is* ✉ *IKr 500* ⊙ *June–Sept., Tues.–Sun. 11–5; other times by arrangement.*

Museums & the University

Art lovers can keep busy in what is still called Reykjavík's "eastern" quarter—even though it is now geographically in the west and center, as the city has been expanding to the east. This tour takes you to the main museum and art gallery and, through Þingholt, to one of the most picturesque residential parts of the city.

a good walk

Start on the 210-foot stair-stepped gray tower of **Hallgrímskirkja** ☛ ⑬. The church tower offers Reykjavík's highest vantage point, with a fantastic panoramic view of the city. Take Njarðargata downhill toward the park to Sóleyjargata, turn right, and cross the street into Hljómskálagarðurinn Park. Follow the path past the Tjörnin Pond with the fountain on your right. Continue until you reach busy Hringbraut street. On your left is the main campus of the **Háskóli Íslands** ⑭, University of Iceland, founded in 1911. Next to the museum's east side, the Félagsstofnun Stúdenta, the Student Union, has an excellent international bookshop. Cross Hringbraut at the lights, and on your right you'll see the concrete **Þjóðminjasafn** ⑮, the National Museum. It houses Viking artifacts, national costumes, weaving, and more. After a stop in the museum, head north along Suðurgata, which leads from the nearby traffic circle. Just before the cemetery on your left, turn right onto Skothúsvegur and follow it over the bridge onto Fríkirkjuvegur. Bertel Thorvaldsen's rendering of *Adonis,* guards the corner of the grounds of the ornate Reykjavík Youth and Recreational Council, across Njarðargata from the president's offices. Next to the Youth and Recreational Council is the **Listasafn Íslands** ⑯, where you can find Ásgrímur Jónsson's stunningly huge *Mt. Hekla*—perhaps the best painting of an Icelandic landscape. The coffee shop inside is a pleasant place to end your walk.

TIMING It takes about an hour to complete this walk, but make sure you allocate extra time to visit the National Museum and Art Gallery.

WHAT TO SEE **Hallgrímskirkja** (Hallgrímur's Church). Completed in 1986 after more ★ ⑬ than 40 years of construction, the church is named for the 17th-century hymn writer Hallgrímur Pétursson. It has a stylized concrete facade recalling both organ pipes and the distinctive columnar basalt formations you can see around Iceland. You may luck into hearing a performance or practice on the church's huge pipe organ. In front of Hallgrímskirkja is a statue of Leifur Eiríksson, the Icelander who discovered America 500 years before Columbus. (Leif's father was Eric the Red, who discovered Greenland.) The statue, by American sculptor Alexander Calder, was presented to Iceland by the United States in 1930 to mark the millennium of the Alþing parliament. ⊠ *At the top of Skólavörðustígur* ☎ *510–1000* 🎫 *Tower IKr 350* ⊗ *Daily 9–5.*

⑭ **Háskóli Íslands** (University of Iceland). On the large crescent-shape lawn in front of the main university building is a statue of Sæmundur Fróði, a symbol of the value of book learning. Legend has it that after studying abroad, Sæmundur made a pact with the devil to get himself home, promising his soul if he arrived without getting wet. The devil changed into a seal to carry him home. Just as they arrived, Sæmundur hit the seal on the head with his Psalter, got his coattails wet, and escaped with soul intact. ⊠ *Across from Hringbraut and diagonally southwest from the park lake* ⊕ *www.hi.is.*

⑮ **Þjóðminjasafn** (National Museum). Viking treasures and artifacts, silver work, wood carvings, and some unusual whalebone carvings are on display here, as well as maritime objects, historical textiles, jewelry, and crafts. There is also a coffee shop. ⊠ *Suðurgata 41* ☎ *530-2200* ⊕ *www. natmus.is* 🎫 *IKr 600, free Wed.* ⊗ *May 1–Sept. 15, daily 10–5, Sept. 16–Apr. 30, Tues.–Sun. 11–5.*

Where to Eat

The dining scene in Reykjavík has been diversifying: traditional Icelandic restaurants now face competition from restaurants serving Asian, Italian, Mexican, Indian, and vegetarian fare.

Old Town

$$$$ ✕ **Sjávarkjallarinn (Seafood Cellar).** Reservations are strongly recommended for this excellent Asian-influenced seafood restaurant in Reykjavík's oldest cellar. Run by an award-winning chef, the "Exotic" menu features a delicious mixture of items that might include anything from kangaroo to salted cod with chili. The atmosphere is sophisticated but casual. ⊠ *Aðalstræti 2* ☎ *511–1212* ▭ *AE, DC, MC, V.*

Fodor'sChoice ★

$$$ ✕ **Argentína.** If you want to try the best steaks in Iceland, come here. Like all Icelandic meat, everything is organic, and the classy atmosphere is warm and inviting. There are also great wines to match. ⊠ *Barónstígur 11a* ☎ *551–9555* ▭ *AE, DC, MC, V* ⊗ *No lunch.*

$$$ ✕ **Lækjarbrekka.** Locals and visitors alike go to this established eatery for its excellent food at reasonable prices. On weekends, live background music emanates from a tight corner of this charming, classic restaurant. ⊠ *Bankastræti 2* ☎ *551–4430* ▭ *AE, DC, MC, V.*

$$$ ✕ **Við Tjörnina.** Enter through a classic wooden doorway and go up a flight of stairs and back in time in this early-20th-century house with a hand-carved bar and chairs, embroidered tablecloths, and crocheted drapes. The lunchtime dish of the day can be a bargain. ⊠ *Templarasund 3* ☎ *551–8666* ▭ *AE, MC, V.*

$$ ✕ **Hornið.** This welcoming bistro is light and airy, with lots of natural wood, potted plants, and cast-iron bistro tables. The emphasis is on piz-

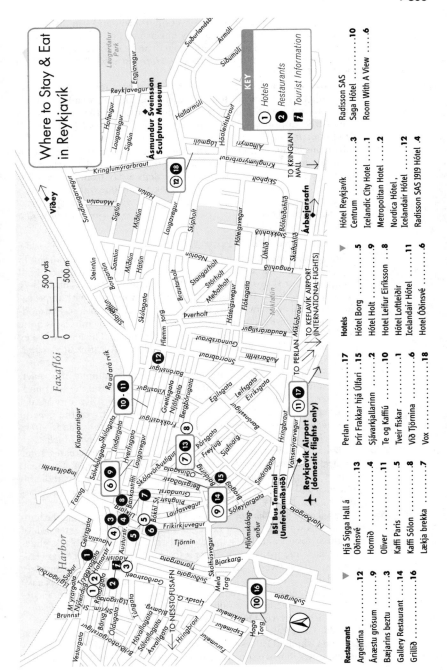

Where to Stay & Eat in Reykjavík

KEY

① Hotels
② Restaurants
ⓘ Tourist Information

Restaurants

Argentína **12**
Ánæstu grösum **9**
Bæjarins beztu **3**
Gallery Restaurant **14**
Grillið **16**

Hjá Sigga Hall á **13**
Óðinsvé **4**
Oliver **11**
Kaffi Paris **5**
Kaffi Sólon **8**
Lækja brekka **7**

Perlan **17**
Þrír Frakkar hjá Úlfari . . **15**
Sjávarkjallarinn **2**
Te og Kaffið **10**
Tveir fiskar **1**
Við Tjörnina **6**
Vox **18**

Hotels

Hótel Borg **5**
Hótel Holt **9**
Hótel Leifur Eiríksson . . . **8**
Hótel Loftleiðir **1**
Icelandair Hótel **11**
Hótel Óðinsvé **6**

Hótel Reykjavík
Centrum **3**
Icelandic City Hotel **1**
Metropolitan Hotel **2**
Nordica Hótel, ... **12**
Icelandair Hótel **12**
Radisson SAS 1919 Hótel . **4**

Radisson SAS
Saga Hótel **10**
Room With A View **6**

zas and pasta, but there's also a selection of meat and fish dishes. Try the lamb pepper steak with garlicky mushrooms or the seafood soup, a favorite for lunch. Their delicious cakes can be enjoyed with the obligatory espresso at any time of day. ⊠ *Hafnarstræti 15* ☎ *551–3340* ⊟ *DC, MC, V.*

$ ✕ **Á næstu grösum.** This cheerful restaurant serves good-value and excellent-quality vegetarian food. The all-you-can-eat bread and hummus that come with every meal are delicious, and there are always gluten-free options. ⊠ *Laugavegur 20B* ☎ *552–8410* ⊟ *MC, V* ⊘ *No lunch Sun.*

★ ¢ ✕ **Bæjarins beztu.** Facing the harbor in a parking lot, this tiny but famous fast-food hut is famous for serving the original Icelandic hot dog; one person serves about a thousand hot dogs a day from the window. Ask for *AYN-ah-med-UTL-lou*, which will get you "one with everything": mustard, tomato sauce, rémoulade (mayonnaise with finely chopped pickles), and chopped raw and fried onions. ⊠ *Tryggvagata and Pósthússtræti* ☎ *No phone* ⊟ *MC, V.*

Museums, the University & Beyond

$$$$ ✕ **Gallery Restaurant.** Icelandic art covers the walls of this restaurant in
Fodor'sChoice the Hótel Holt, within walking distance of downtown; the cocktail
★ lounge and bar showcase drawings by Jóhannes Kjarval. The Gallery has long been in the forefront of Icelandic restaurants, with impeccable service and mouthwatering wild-game and seafood dishes. The modestly priced semi-fixed lunch menu (Ikr 2,200 for two courses) is quite a good value. Favorites include gravlax and reindeer. The bar's whiskey selection is as diverse as any in Europe. ⊠ *Hótel Holt, Bergstaðastræti 37* ☎ *552–5700* ⊟ *AE, DC, MC, V.*

$$$$ ✕ **Grillið.** Atop the Saga Hotel near the university campus, this quiet, cozy restaurant has a spectacular view of the capital and the surrounding hinterlands. For less than IKr 7,000, you can try the "Discovery Meal," a four-course feast of the chef's choosing. Highlights of the general menu include seafood and reindeer (in season). ⊠ *Hagatorg* ☎ *552–5033* ⊟ *AE, DC, MC, V* ⊘ *Closed for 1 month in summer. No lunch.*

$$$$ ✕ **VOX.** Award-winning chef Hákon Máár Örvarsson creates some unique dishes at this swank restaurant, inside Hótel Nordica. The menu changes every three months, but always features the best Icelandic ingredients, and the wine list is one of the city's most impressive. ⊠ *Suðurlandsbraut 2* ☎ *444–5050* ⊟ *AE, DC, MC, V.*

★ $$$–$$$$ ✕ **Hjá Sigga Hall á Oðinsvé.** There's an air of anticipation among the hungry patrons waiting for their tables in the cozy greenhouse extension of this glossy restaurant. The sylphlike waitstaff, all dressed in black, glides swiftly back and forth. Then, there is Iceland's celebrity chef Siggi Hall, a congenial figure who visits each table, chatting easily with acquaintances old and new. The regulars know what they're in for, and first-timers have heard about the chef's adventurous fish, lamb, and game dishes, meticulously prepared and beautifully presented. ⊠ *Hotel Óðinsvé, Oðinstorg* ☎ *552–5090* ⊟ *AE, DC, MC, V* ⊘ *Closed Mon. No lunch.*

$$$–$$$$ ✕ **Perlan.** This rotating restaurant, atop Reykjavík's hot-water distribution tanks on Öskjuhlíð Hill, is the city's most glamorous, with the most spectacular views in town (one revolution takes about two hours). The international menu emphasizes fresh, quality Icelandic ingredients, such as succulent lamb and seafood. Seafood dishes, prepared with the freshest fish available, change often. ⊠ *Öskjuhlíð Hill* ☎ *562–0203* ☰ *AE, DC, MC, V* ⊘ *No lunch.*

★ **$$–$$$$** ✕ **Þrír Frakkar.** In an unassuming building in an older part of town, this restaurant serves truly traditional Icelandic food, with an emphasis on seafood. Whale-meat sushi is one of the novelties here. The bright annex overlooks a tiny, tree-filled park. ⊠ *Baldursgata 14 at Nönnugata* ☎ *552–3939* ☰ *AE, DC, MC, V.*

Harborfront

$$$ ✕ **Tveir fiskar.** Although the name means "two fish" there's plenty more on the menu here. Try the delicious shellfish soup, lobster, or the restaurant's namesake fish duo, which changes according to what is freshest in the market. Carnivores can opt for lamb or chicken. ⊠ *Geirsgata 9* ☎ *511–3474* ☰ *AE, DC, MC, V.*

Cafés

Icelanders rival the Finns for the record for per capita caffeine consumption, so it should come as no surprise that coffee bars have replaced clothing boutiques as the most common enterprise in town. Many also serve good-value meals. All cafés listed are in the Old Town or on Laugavegur.

Smoky **Kaffi Mokka** (⊠ (Skólavótígur 3A ☎ 552–1174) is Iceland's oldest café and a Reykjavík institution. **Vegamót** (⊠ (Vegamótstígur 4 ☎ 511–3040) is always buzzing with activity, whether it's over coffee, at mealtimes, or late at night when it becomes one of the city's best clubs. **Kaffi París** (⊠ Austurstræti 14 ☎ 551–1095) is a popular spot; even Hillary Clinton dropped in, on a visit to Reykjavík. At artsy **Kaffi Sólon** (⊠ Bankastræti 7A ☎ 562–3232) you can see some modern art, eat a meal (try the chicken risotto), and people-watch. Trendy **Oliver** (⊠ Laugavegur 20 ☎ 552–2300) serves terrific food. The man who started the Icelandic coffee revolution runs **Te og Kaffi** (⊠ Laugavegur 24 ☎ 562–2322).

Lodging

Lodgings range from modern, first-class Scandinavian-style hotels to inexpensive guesthouses and B&Bs offering basic amenities at relatively low prices (contact the Tourist Information Center for a register). Iceland's climate makes air-conditioning unnecessary. Most hotel rooms have televisions, though not always cable TV. Lower-price hotels sometimes have a television lounge in lieu of TV in each room. Ask if your hotel offers complimentary admission tickets to the closest swimming pool.

Old Town & East

$$$$ ▥ **Hótel Borg.** Some rooms in Reykjavík's oldest hotel, built in 1930 in **Fodor'sChoice** the art deco style, may not seem spacious, but they are elegant and combine old-fashioned quality with modern comforts. Some rooms have whirlpool baths. All rooms have fluffy down comforters, tasteful prints (some antique), coffee machines, and CD players, as well as a fax machine on request. The adjoining hotel is in the heart of the city, overlooking Austurvöllur and close to Parliament House. The Palm Court Restaurant offers a good selection of Icelandic food in a classy setting. ⊠ *Pósthússtræti*

11 IS-101 ☎ *551–1440* 🖷 *551–1420* ⊕ *www.hotelborg.is* ⇆ *51 rooms,4 junior suites, 1 tower suite* ♤ *Restaurant, cable TV, in-room VCRs, bar* ⊟ *AE, DC, MC, V.*

$$$$ ⊡ **Hótel Nordica.** This luxury hotel has been recently renovated and is primarily geared toward business travelers, although families are given priority for available larger standard rooms. Business-class rooms are spacious and include breakfast and access to the Panorama lounge, with gorgeous views of the city, where you can read newspapers and help yourself to complementary wine, coffee, tea, and hors d'oeuvres. Executive and business-class rooms include free access to the health club. ⊠ *Suðurlandsbruat 2 IS 101* ☎ *444–5000* 🖷 *444–5001* ⊕ *www. hotelnordica.is* ⇆ *258 rooms, 34 suites* ♤ *Restaurant, cable TV, health club, massage, sauna, spa, steam room, bar* ⊟ *AE, DC, MC, V.*

$$$ ⊡ **Hótel Reykjavík Centrum.** Situated downtown, this hotel opened its doors in the spring of 2005. Rooms are decorated in pastel colors, and the common areas have lots of natural light from a glass ceiling over the lobby. In the basement, there is a display of the the remains of a Viking longhouse from the 9th century that was found during construction of the hotel. ⊠ *Aðalstræti 16, IS-101* ☎ *514–6000* 🖷 *514–6030* ⊕ *www. hotelcentrum.is* ⇆ *89 rooms* ♤ *Restaurant, room service, cable TV, bar, meeting rooms.* ⊟ *AE, DC, MC, V* ⊙ *CP.*

$$$ ⊡ **Radisson SAS 1919 Hotel.** Downtown in one of Reykjavík's oldest and most famous buildings, this hotel opened its doors in the summer of 2005. The decor is reminiscent of 1919, the year the building was constructed, and great attention has been paid to everything from the light fixtures in the foyer to the artwork in the rooms. There are flat-screen TVs with video on demand in every room, and the restaurant downstairs is becoming very popular. ⊠ *Pósthússtræti 2, IS-101* ☎ *599 1000* 🖷 *599 1001* ⊕ *www.1919. reykjavik.radissonsas.com* ⇆ *70 rooms* ♤ *Restaurant, gym, bar, meeting rooms* ⊟ *AE, DC, MC, V* ⊙ *EP.*

★ $$ ⊡ **Room with a View.** Highly recommended by Fodor's readers, Room with a View offers a number of self-catering apartments in the center of town for those who prefer to cook their own meals and would like extra space. Many apartments have access to a Jacuzzi. The very friendly staff can assist you in planning the rest of your trip. ⊠ *Laugavegur 18, IS-101* ☎ *896–2559 or 552–7262* 🖷 *515-2505* ⊕ *www.roomwithaview. is* ⇆ *20 apartments* ♤ *High-speed Internet, some in-room hot tubs, kitchenettes, microwaves, refrigerators* ⊙ *EP.*

Museums, the University & Beyond

$$$$ ⊡ **Hótel Holt.** This quietly elegant member of the prestigious Relais & **Fodor's**Choice Chateau hotel group has impeccable service, an excellent restaurant, and **★** computer links in every room, all of which make it a favorite among business travelers. Though the rooms are small by modern standards, all are decorated with works by leading Icelandic artists. It's in a pleasant neighborhood close to the town center. Guests receive a complementary pass to the Laugar fitness center and pool for the duration of their stay. ⊠ *Bergstaðastræti 37 IS-101* ☎ *552–5700* 🖷 *562–3025* ⊕ *www.holt. is* ⇆ *30 rooms, 12 suites* ♤ *Restaurant, bar, lobby lounge, meeting room* ⊟ *AE, DC, MC, V* ⊙ *EP.*

$$$$ 🏨 **Hotel Óðinsvé.** Three buildings in a calm corner in an older part of town make up this hotel. No two rooms are alike, but all are cheery and efficient, some with nice views over colorful rooftops. Its many regular guests prefer its intimacy and convenience to the Old Town. ✉ *Óðinstorg IS-101* 🕾 *511–6200* 🖷 *511–6201* ⊕ *www.hotelodinsve.is* 🛏 *37 rooms* ⚴ *Restaurant, Wi-Fi, meeting rooms* ▤ *AE, DC, MC, V* ⎮⊘⎮ *CP.*

$$$ 🏨 **Hótel Loftleiðir Icelandair Hótel.** The advantage of this rather remote hotel is nearby Öskjuhlíð Hill, where you can take pleasant walks and stroll up to Perlan for ice cream. Rooms are modern, with Scandinavian pine furniture and pastel fabrics. For a little extra, guests can stay in one of the Poet rooms, which are slightly cozier and feature prints and details about the life of an Icelandic poet. There is complimentary shuttle service to the city center. ✉ *Reykjavík Airport IS-101* 🕾 *505–0900* 🖷 *505–0905* ⊕ *www.icehotels.is* 🛏 *220 rooms, 1 suite* ⚴ *Restaurant, pool, sauna, bar, convention center, travel services* ▤ *AE, DC, MC, V* ⎮⊘⎮ *CP.*

$$$ 🏨 **Radisson SAS Saga Hótel.** Just off the university campus, and near the National Musuem, this hotel is a 15-minute walk from the city center. All rooms are above the fourth floor and have spectacular views. ✉ *Hagatorg IS-107* 🕾 *525–9900* 🖷 *562–3980* ⊕ *www.radisson.com* 🛏 *209 rooms* ⚴ *Restaurant, health club, hot tub, sauna, bar, meeting room, travel services, no-smoking rooms* ▤ *AE, DC, MC, V* ⎮⊘⎮ *CP.*

$$ 🏨 **Hotel Leifur Eiríksson.** Across the street from the hilltop church of Hallgrímskirkja, this hotel is a short walk from most of Reykjavík's major attractions. Some guest rooms have balconies. ✉ *Skólavörðustígur 45 IS-101* 🕾 *562–0800* 🖷 *562–0804* ⊕ *www.hotelleifur.is* 🛏 *47 rooms* ⚴ *Café, bar* ▤ *AE, MC, V* ⎮⊘⎮ *CP.*

$$ 🏨 **Metropolitan Hotel.** This small hotel stands on a central but quiet residential street. ✉ *Ránargata 4A IS-101* 🕾 *511–1155* 🖷 *552–9040* ⊕ *www.metropolitan.is* 🛏 *31 rooms* ▤ *AE, DC, MC, V* ⎮⊘⎮ *BP.*

Nightlife & the Arts

Reykjavík has an active cultural life through most of the year, and is especially strong in the visual arts. The classical performing-arts scene tends to quiet down somewhat in summer; however, a growing number of rock and jazz concerts has been helping to fill in the lull. The Reykjavík Arts Festival is an annual event held in late spring. Past festivals have drawn Luciano Pavarotti and David Bowie, among other stars. Check out the Reykjavík Grapevine (biweekly in summer, monthly in winter) for up-to-date listings, ⊕ www.grapevine.is

Nightlife

Nightlife in Reykjavík essentially means two types of establishments: pubs and nightclubs with dancing and live music. Icelanders tend to dress up for nightspots, but visitors can get away with being a bit more casual. On weekends, unless you start before 10 PM, be prepared to wait in line, especially if summer weekend weather is good. Avoid downtown after midnight during the first weekends of summer, when excessive drinking can result in some raucous and aggressive behavior. Suffice it to say, Icelanders party en masse.

BARS **b5** (✉ Bankastræti 5 ☎ 552–9600) is a new addition to the bar scene and has a classy yet comfortable atmosphere with its huge sofa and book-lined walls. Rub elbows with reclusive celebs at **Kaffibarinn** (✉ Bergstaðastræti 1 ☎ 551–1588), which is part owned by Damon Albarn of the band Blur. **Kaffibrennslan** (✉ (Pósthússtræti 9 ☎ 561–3600) has one of the best selections of beer in town and, although always busy, is usually a little calmer than many other places. **Thorvaldsen** (✉ Austurstræti 8 ☎ 511–1413) serves great cocktails and is popular with the Reykjavík jet set. **Vínbarinn** (✉ Kirkjutorg 4 ☎ 552–4120), near the Parliament, is a great place to mingle with the country's decision makers and choose from a huge selection of wines.

DANCE CLUBS **Broadway at Hótel Ísland** (✉ Ármúli 9 ☎ 533–1100) is the largest restaurant and dance hall in Iceland and can hold more than 1,000 guests at a time. It has nightclub shows and music performances. **Pravda** (✉ Austurstræti 22 ☎ 552–9222) is more centrally located and is open late. It has jazz concerts on Thursday in summer.

LIVE MUSIC Some of Iceland's best musicians perform in intimate surroundings at **Grand Rokk** (✉ Smiðjustígur 6 ☎ 551–5522) or **Gaukur á Stöng** (✉ Tryggvagata 22 ☎ 551–1556). On weekends you'll usually find a concert at **NASA** (✉ Austurvöllur Sq. ☎ 511–1313).

The Arts

FOLKLORE You can go to **Light Nights** (✉ Iðnó 12, opposite City Hall) to watch traditional folk performances in English, based on Icelandic sagas and folktales; it takes place in July and August, and has been running for over 30 years.

MUSIC The Icelandic Opera, **Íslenska Óperan** (☎ 511–4200), a resident company, performs in winter at its home on Ingólfsstræti. The Iceland Symphony Orchestra **Sinfóníuhljómsveit Íslands** (☎ 545–2500 ⊕ www.sinfonia.is) has bloomed beautifully and won fine reviews for its tour performances at Carnegie Hall and the Kennedy Center. Regular performances are in winter and are held at the University Cinemas.

Sports & the Outdoors

Participatory Sports

FISHING The **Angling Club of Reykjavík** (✉ Háaleitisbraut 68 ☎ 568–6050) can provide information on fishing in the area. **Útivist og Veiði** (✉ Síðumúli 11 ☎ 588–6500) is a well-stocked tackle retailer. For tackle in Reykjavík, head to **Veiðihornið** (✉ Hafnarstræti 5 ☎ 551–6760).

GOLF At the southern tip of Seltjarnarnes, the westernmost part of the Reykjavík area, **Golfklúbbur Ness** (✉ Seltjarnarnes ☎ 561–1930) has a well-kept 9-hole course with a great view in all directions. **Golfklúbbur Reykjavíkur** (✉ Korpúlfsstaðir 112 Reykjavík ☎ 585–0200) is the granddaddy of them all, a challenging 18-hole course just east of Reykjavík.

HORSEBACK RIDING Two stables in the Reykjavík area rent horses by the hour or by the day. **Íshestar** (Icelandic Riding Tours; ✉ Sörlaskeiði 26, Hafnarfjörður

☎ 555–7000 ⊕ www.ishestar.is) offers one- to seven-hour rides for IKr 3,900–IKr 8,900, including guides and transportation from Reykjavík hotels. **Laxnes Horse Farm** (✉ Mosfellsdalur ☎ 566–6179 ⊕ www.laxnes.is) offers three-hour riding tours for IKr 3,500, including guides and transportation to and from Reykjavík.

SWIMMING There are 12 swimming pools in the greater Reykjavík area, all with out-
☾ door hot tubs and some with saunas. Rules of hygiene are strictly en-forced—you must shower thoroughly, without a swimsuit, before entering the pool. There is a small but popular pool in **Vesturbær** on Hofsvallagata (via Bus 11 or 13). The pool at **Laugardalur Park** (Bus 14) is also a favorite summer spot, as is **Árbæjarlaug** (Bus S5 going east) with a water-linked indoor and outdoor pool and hot tubs of varying warmths. All are open seven days a week. A locker and access to the swimming pool cost IKr 250 for adults and IKr 110 for children ages 6–15; kids under 6 swim free. A Reykjavík Tourist Card gives you free access to the seven thermal pools in the city. You can rent towels and swimsuits. Use of the sauna is extra. *Note:* Swimming pools are one of the few places in Iceland where you should be on guard against petty theft. If you are wearing snazzy running shoes, lock them up in a locker.

On the Sidelines

HANDBALL Team handball, a national obsession and a sport in which Iceland has finished as high as fourth in the Olympics, is a big draw in the winter. For information on the fast, furious, and exciting matches between Iceland's leading teams, as well as thrilling confrontations with some of the world's best handball nations, contact the **Handball Federation** (☎ 514–4200 ⊕ www.hsi.is).

SOCCER Catch an Icelandic soccer match in summer. Revved up by loyal follow-ers, the national team has stunned better-known European teams and pro-gressed further in competitions than most dared dream. A number of Icelandic soccer players are with professional soccer teams in Europe. The most important soccer matches are played at **Laugardalsvöllur Stadium** (take Bus 14 ☎ 510–2914). You can buy tickets at the box office just be-fore the game, or inquire at downtown bookstores for advance sales.

Shopping

Malls

The **Kringlan Mall** has a number of good clothing stores and a movie the-ater and is a good place to get souvenirs on a wet day. It's on the east side of town at the intersection of Miklabraut and Kringlumýrarbraut; you can get to it by taking Bus S1, S3, S4, or S5 from Hlemmur or Lækjatorg.

Iceland's second major shopping mall, **Smáralind** (pronounced *smow*-ra-lind), is in Kópavogur, a community neighboring Reykjavík to the south. Intent on rivaling Kringlan Mall, it is huge and houses, among other stores, British-based **Debenhams** as well as Iceland's own discount chain, **Hagkaup**. From Reykjavík you can take the S2 or 11 bus, but for a bit more than IKr 1,000, you can take a cab and save a lot of pre-cious shopping time.

Shopping Streets

The main shopping downtown is on and around Austurstræti, Aðalstræti, Hafnarstræti, Bankastræti, Laugavegur, and Skólavörðustígur.

Specialty Stores

ART GALLERIES   You can find crafts workshops and galleries all around town. **Gallery Fold** (✉ Rauðarárstígur 14–16 ☎ 551–0400) has a large selection of prints, drawings, paintings, and sculpture by contemporary Icelandic artists, as well as some older Icelandic art. **Listhús** (✉ Engjateigur 17–19), opposite Nordica Hótel, is a complex of art stores and ateliers selling Icelandic arts and crafts.

CRAFTS   Lava ceramics, sheepskin rugs, and Viking-inspired jewelry are popular souvenirs. An amble along **Skólavörðustígur** from Laugavegur to Hallgrímskirkja church takes you past many tempting woolen, jewelry, and crafts shops, as well as art galleries. The Handknitting Association of Iceland, **Handprjónasambandið** (✉ Skólavörðurstígur 19 ☎ 552–1890), has its own outlet, selling, of course, only hand-knit items. **Islandia** (✉ Kringlan Mall ☎ 568–9960) offers a range of woolens, giftware, and souvenirs.

Many hand- and machine-knitted woolen garments are sold at **Rammagerðin** (✉ Hafnarstræti 19 ☎ 551–1122).

JEWELRY   Laugavegur and Skólavörðustígur streets are both filled with jewelry stores that craft uniquely designed pieces, often incorporating gold or silver with materials found in Iceland, like lava rock, creating a very eye-catching effect. Try **Guðbrandur Jósef Jezorski** (✉ Laugavegur 48 ☎ 552–3485) or **Anna María design** (✉ Skólavörðustígur 3 ☎ 551–0036).

MUSIC STORES   **12 Tónar** (✉ Skólavörðustígur 15 ☎ 511 5656 ⊕ www.12tonar.is) is both a record shop and an independent record label. The staff here can tell you everything about Icelandic music while you sip a great espresso. Some popular local artists at the moment include Mugison, Trabant, Sigur Rós, Singapore Sling, and the ever famous Björk.

Reykjavík A to Z

AIR TRAVEL TO & FROM REYKJAVÍK

CARRIERS   For reservations and information in Reykjavík, contact Icelandair, or Iceland Express. For domestic reservations and information, contact either Icelandair or Flugfélag Íslands (Air Iceland).

🛈 **Flugfélag Islands** ☎ 570-3030 ⊕ www.airiceland.is. **Icelandair** ☎ 505-0300 ⊕ www.icelandair.com. **Iceland Express** ☎ 550-0600 ⊕ www.icelandexpress.com.

AIRPORTS & TRANSFERS

All international flights arrive and depart from Keflavík Airport, 50 km (31 mi) southwest of the capital. Reykjavík Airport is the central hub of domestic air travel in Iceland.

🛈 **Keflavík Airport** ☎ 505-0500 ⊕ www.keflavikairport.com. **Reykjavík Airport** ☎ 570-3030.

AIRPORT   TRANSFERS   The Reykjavík FlyBus leaves Keflavík (from directly outside the terminal building) and arrives in Reykjavík at the BSÍ bus terminal. Connections are provided from there to the larger hotels and guesthouses, or you can take a taxi to your final destination. FlyBuses are scheduled in connection with flight arrivals and departures. The FlyBus departs from BSÍ, with free pickup from some hotels (listed on its Web site). The ride takes 40–50 minutes, and the fare is IKr 1,150 per person one-way or IKr 2,100 round-trip. You can pay by credit card on the bus.

From Reykjavík Airport, the municipal Bus 15 leaves from the Icelandair terminal on the western side of the airport. Other airlines operate from the east terminal (behind the Loftleiðir Hotel), which is served by Bus 16. A taxi from the Keflavík Airport to Reykjavík is a little faster than the FlyBus and costs IKr 7,500. If you share it with others, you can split the cost. From Reykjavík Airport a taxi to your hotel costs around IKr 1,000. There are direct phones to taxi companies in the arrivals hall. Taxi companies from Keflavík include Aðalstöðin and Ökuleiðir. The taxi companies based in Reykjavík are Hreyfill and Bæjarleiðir, among others.

🚖 **Aðalstöðin** ☎ 421–1515. **Bæjarleiðir** ☎ 553–3500. **Hreyfill** ☎ 588–5522. **Ökuleiðir** ☎ 421–4141. **Reykjavík FlyBus** ☎ 562–1011 ⊕ www.flybus.is.

BUS TRAVEL WITHIN REYKJAVÍK

The municipal bus service, affectionately nicknamed Strætó (pronounced *stry*-toe), provides extensive, cheap, and reliable service throughout Reykjavík and its surrounding municipalities. Buses are yellow, with an s logo on a red circular background and run from 7 AM to midnight or 1 AM. Express buses run every 10 minutes during peak times and every half hour evenings and weekends. Route booklets are available at the main terminals of Lækjartorg, Hlemmur, Mjódd, and Ártún.

The flat fare within the sprawling capital area is IKr 220, payable to the driver in exact change on boarding. You can buy strips of tickets at a lower price from the drivers or at the main terminals. The fare allows you to travel any distance in the metro area; depending on your destination, you may have to change buses. If so, ask for *skiptimiða* (skiff-teh-mee-tha), a transfer ticket that you give the second bus driver.

If you plan an extended stay in the Reykjavík area, it may be worthwhile to spend IKr 4,500 on a monthly ticket, the Green Card, valid on all routes. For shorter stays a practical investment is the Reykjavík Tourist Card, available from the Tourist Information Center. The card permits unlimited bus usage and admission to any of the capital city's seven pools, the Family Park and Zoo, and city museums.

🚌 **Strætó** ☎ 540–2700 ⊕ www.bus.is/english.

BUSINESS HOURS

Most of the capital closes down early on weekdays, and many commercial and official establishments are closed Sunday.

GAS STATIONS | Gas stations are usually open 7:30 AM–11 PM.

MUSEUMS & SIGHTS | Museums normally open only during summer will often open in the off-season for a small group of visitors if contacted in advance.

SHOPS | Shops are open weekdays 9–6. A growing number of stores, especially food stores, are open on weekends with shorter hours. Many smaller food stores are open daily until 10 PM or 11 PM. Bakeries, souvenir shops, florists, and kiosks are open daily.

CAR RENTAL

Car-rental agencies in Reykjavík include Avis, Budget, and Hertz/Iceland. They all have offices in the Leifur Eiríksson Terminal at Keflavík Airport. ⚡ Major Agencies **Avis** ☎ 591-4000 🖨 591-4040. **Budget** ☎ 526-6060 🖨 562-6061. **Hertz/Iceland** ☎ 505-0600 🖨 505-0644.

CAR TRAVEL

The excellent bus system and quick and reasonably priced taxis make automobiles unnecessary for getting around town, doubly so considering how expensive car rentals and gasoline are. Most gas stations have self-service pumps that accept credit cards—you'll need your PIN—or you can pay with cash inside at the register.

CURRENCY EXCHANGE

⚡ Exchange Services **The Tourist Shop** ✉ Bankastræti 2 ☎ 551-7755.

EMBASSIES & CONSULATES

⚡ Canada ✉ Túngata 14 IS-101 ☎ 575-6500.
⚡ U.K. ✉ Laufásvegur 31 IS-101 ☎ 550-5100.
⚡ U.S. ✉ Laufásvegur 21 IS-101 ☎ 562-9100.

EMERGENCIES

The city branch of the national university-affiliated hospital system, Landspítali Háskólasjúkrahús, Landspítali University Hospital, deals with serious emergencies at any time and can issue prescription medication when pharmacies are closed. Many of Reykjavík's pharmacies (apótek) are open into late evening. Lyf & heilsa and Lyfja apoteks each have a late-evening location. Signs indicating other pharmacies with night hours (*næturvakt*) are posted in all pharmacies, and details are also published in newspapers.

Læknavakt (Duty Doctors) can provide general medical help during off-hours. During regular hours (8–5 weekdays), the Reykjavík Health Center, Heilsugæslan í Reykjavík, can refer you to officially appointed family doctors for general medical attention on short notice.

⚡ Doctors and Dentists **Heilsugæslan í Reykjavík (Reykjavík Health Center)** ☎ 585-1300.
⚡ Emergency Services **Ambulance, fire, police** ☎ 112.
⚡ Hospitals **Landspítali Háskólasjúkrahús (Landspítali University Hospital)** ☎ 543-1000.
⚡ Late-Night Pharmacies **Lyf & heilsa apótek** ✉ Austerver, Háaleitisbraut 68 ☎ 581-2101. **Lyfja apótek** ✉ Lágmúli 5 ☎ 533-2300.

INTERNET

There is public Internet access at libraries and tourist information offices around the country. It's usually about IKr 35 per half hour and IKr 500–600 per hour. The majority of hotels and cafés in Reykjavík have wireless Internet access for those with their own laptop. Ráðhús (City Hall) has free Internet access in the café if you buy a drink.

⚡ Internet Cafés **Ráðhús.** ✉ Bounded by Fríkirkjuvegur, Vonarstræti, and Tjarnargata ☎ 563-2000. **Tourist Information Center** ✉ Geysishús Aðalstræti 2 ☎ 590-1550. **Tourist Shop** ✉ Bankastræti 2 ☎ 510-5700.

MAIL & SHIPPING
Post offices are open weekdays 8:30–4:30 but some are open longer.
🚩 **Main Post Office** ✉ Pósthússtræti 5 IS-101 Reykjavík ☎ 580-1000.

TAXIS
Most cabs are new, fully equipped passenger sedans. They have small TAXI signs on top and can be hailed anywhere on the street; the LAUS sign indicates that the cab is available. There are taxi stands in a few locations around the city, but it is common to order a taxi by phone. Normally you have to wait only a few minutes. Most taxis accept major credit cards, but you must state that you want to pay with a credit card when requesting the taxi. Fares are regulated by meter; rides around Reykjavík run between IKr 700 and IKr 1,000. There is no tipping.
🚩 **Bæjarleiðir Taxi** ☎ 553-3500. **BSR Taxi** ☎ 561-0000. **Hreyfill Taxi** ☎ 588-5522.

TOURS
The Iceland Tour Guide Association can provide qualified guides who work in a variety of languages and have different specialties. The daily "Reykjavík City Sightseeing" tour of Reykjavík Excursions (with booking desks at the BSÍ bus terminal and at Hotels Nordica and Saga) includes museums and art galleries, shopping centers, and the like in three hours. They also operate a hop-on/hop-off bus service in the city during the summer.
🚩 **Iceland Tour Guide Association** ✉ Mörkin 6 ☎ 588-8670. **Reykjavík Excursions** ✉ BSÍ Bus Terminal ☎ 562-1011 ✉ Nordica Hótel, Suðurlandsbraut 2 ☎ 444-5080 ✉ Radisson SAS Saga Hótel, Hagatorg ☎ 562-9500 ⊕ www.re.is.

TRAVEL AGENCIES
🚩 Local Agents **Iceland Travel** ✉ Lágmúli 4 Reykjavík ☎ 585-4300 🖷 585-4390 ⊕ www.icelandtravel.is.

VISITOR INFORMATION
The Reykjavík Tourist Information Center, in the classic Geysishús at Aðalstræti 2, is open daily 8:30–7, June through August. For the rest of the year it's open weekdays 9–6, Saturday 10–4, and Sunday 10–2. The Icelandic Tourist Board is open weekdays 8–4.
🚩 Tourist Information **Icelandic Tourist Board** ✉ Lækjargata 3 ☎ 535-5500 🖷 535-5501. **Reykjavík Tourist Information Center** ✉ Geysishús; Aðalstræti 2 ☎ 590-1550 🖷 590-1501 ⊕ www.visitreykjavik.is.

SIDE TRIPS FROM REYKJAVÍK

Hafnarfjörður

10 km (6 mi) south of Reykjavík.

"Harbor fjord" had an important commercial port centuries before Reykjavík did, and today there's still healthy competition between the two. Iceland's **International Summer Solstice Viking Festival** is held here. Residents are not ashamed of their role as the butt of Icelanders' own odd ethnic humor, but they are serious about their respect for hidden folk said to live in local lava formations. As part of that respect, the local park, Hellisgerði has the world's northern-most bonsai garden. The **Tourist Information Center** (⊠ Strandgata 6 [Town Hall] ☏ 585–5500 www. hafnarfjordur.is) can give you a map of the town's sites and possible elfin homes. It is also near the Hafnarfjörður Museum (admission is IKr 300). Just off the harbor is the red-roof **Hafnarborg Art Center**. To get to the town, take Bus S1 from Lækjatorg Plaza or Hlemmur station.

Blue Lagoon

FodorśChoice
★

15 km (9 mi) from Keflavík Airport and 50 km (31 mi) from Reykjavík (turn off toward the village of Grindavík).

This world-renowned therapeutic wonder is now in a sheltered site where man-made structures blend with geologic formations. A reception area includes food concessions and boutiques where you can buy health products made from the lagoon's mineral-rich ingredients. Bathing suits are available to rent, and futuristic bracelets keep track of your locker code, any other purchases, and the length of your visit (all of which no doubt make useful marketing statistics). Buses run from the BSÍ bus terminal in Reykjavík to the Blue Lagoon twice daily and three times a day in July and August, or you can get to to the airport on your own by taking a special FlyBus. ⊠ *Bláónið, IS-240 Grindavík* ☏ *420–8800* ◷ *9–9* ⊕ *www.bluelagoon. is* ☒ *IKr 1,400 adults, IKr 700 children; under 11 years of age free.*

GOLDEN CIRCLE

If you make only one foray outside Reykjavík, take this popular trip, offered by many tour operators, to the lakes, waterfalls, and hot springs just inland from the capital. If you take the trip after the spring thaw, it will begin at Þingvellir, the ancient seat of the world's oldest continually functioning parliament, before heading on to see the original Geysir hot spring (hence the term *geyser*) and the famed Gullfoss, the "Golden Waterfall."

Þingvellir

About 50 km (31 mi) northeast of Reykjavík. Take Ring Rd. about 9 km (5½ mi) just past the town of Mosfellsbær; turn right on Rte. 36.

After an hour-long drive from Reykjavík along Route 36 across the Mosfellsheiði heath, the broad lava plain of Þingvellir suddenly opens in front of you. This has been the nation's most hallowed place since AD 930, when the settler Grímur Geitskór chose it as the first site for what is often called the world's oldest parliament, the Icelandic Alþingi (General Assembly). In July of each year delegates from all over the country camped at Þingvellir for two weeks, meeting to pass laws and render judicial sentences. Iceland remained a nation-state, ruled solely by the people without a central government, until 1262 when it came under the Norwegian crown; even then, the Alþingi continued to meet at Þingvellir until 1798, but by then it had long lost its lawmaking powers.

Þingvellir National Park, at the northern end of Þingvallavatn—Iceland's largest lake—is a potent symbol of Icelandic heritage. Many national celebrations are held here, and it was named a UNESCO World Heritage Site in 2004. Besides its historic interest, Þingvellir holds a special appeal for naturalists: it is the geologic meeting point of two continents. At Almannagjá, on the west side of the plain, is the easternmost edge of the North American tectonic plate, otherwise submerged in the Atlantic Ocean. Over on the plain's east side, at the Heiðargjá Gorge, you are at the westernmost edge of the Eurasian plate.

A path down into Almannagjá from the top of the gorge overlooking Þingvellir leads straight to the high rock wall of **Lögberg** (Law Rock), where the person chosen as guardian of the laws would recite them from memory. At the far end of the gorge is the **Öxarárfoss** (Öxará Waterfall). Beautiful, peaceful picnic spots are a bit beyond it. Just below the waterfall in a deep stretch of the river lies the forbidding **Drekkingarhylur** pool, where it is said unfaithful wives were drowned.

Across the plain from Lögberg stand the church and **Þingvallabær,** the gabled manor house of Þingvellir, where the government of Iceland often hosts visiting heads of state. The **Nikulásargjá Gorge,** reached by a footbridge, is better known these days as Peningagjá (Money Gorge) because it's customary to fling a coin into the gorge's icy-cold water and make a wish. Don't even dream about climbing down to wade here—it might look shallow, but it's more than 30 feet deep.

Haukadalur

About 35 km (22 mi) northeast of Laugarvatn via Rte. 37 and then Rte. 35.

Fodor'sChoice The geothermal field in Haukadalur, home of the Geysir and Strokkur
★   geysers, is one of Iceland's classic tourist spots.

The famous **Geysir** hot spring (the literal origin of the term, geyser) only erupts a few times a year, but the more reliable **Strokkur** spouts up boiling water as high as 100 feet at five-minute intervals. In the same area there are small natural vents from which steam rises, as well as beautiful, exotically colored pools. Don't crowd Strokkur, and always be careful when approaching hot springs or mud pots—the ground may be treacherous, suddenly giving way beneath you. Stay on formal paths or established tracks.

To get here from Laugarvatn, take Route 37 (from Lake Laugarvatn you can take the short spur, Route 364, southwest to Route 37) northeast for 25 km (16 mi) to the junction with Route 35. Take Route 35 about 10 km (6 mi) northeast to Hótel Geysir, which is next to the springs.

Gullfoss

About 6 km (4 mi) east of Geysir along Rte. 35.

Measuring 105 feet high, thundering Gullfoss (Golden Falls) is a double cascade in the Hvítá River, turning at right angles in mid-drop. Gullfoss enters a dramatic chasm, which nonetheless has its gentle sides. The modest visitor center is named in memory of Sigríður Tómasdóttir, who fought against flooding the falls for a hydroelectric reservoir scheme in the early 20th century. She is said to have threatened to throw herself into the falls; a trailside plaque further honors her.

Sports & the Outdoors

WHITE-WATER RAFTING
You can take a one-hour journey down the churning glacial Hvítá River below Gullfoss Falls; waterproof clothing and life jackets are provided. For information, contact **Icelandic Adventure** (⊠ Álftaland 17, IS-108 Reykjavík ☎ 577–5500 ⊕ www.adventure.is).

en route
The return route to Reykjavík rolls through one of the most prosperous agricultural regions in Iceland. From Gullfoss take Route 35 southbound until you reach its end at the Ring Road (Route 1). Turn right onto the Ring Road for the trip back to Reykjavík. You will pass Hveragerði on the way.

Golden Circle A to Z

BUS TRAVEL

It is possible to explore this area on your own by BSÍ bus, but you must allow plenty of time and perhaps stay overnight en route. BSÍ Travel serves Þingvellir twice daily (June to mid-September) and Gullfoss and Geysir twice daily (mid-June through August).

🚩 **BSÍ Bus Terminal** ☎ 591–1000 ⊕ www.bsi.is.

CAR RENTAL

Hertz rents several types of vehicles, including many with a CD player. For those who'd like to do the Golden Circle themselves, a self-guided CD audio tour (IKr 1,500) with a map is available.

🚩 Major Agency **Hertz** ☎ 505–0600 ⊕ www.hertz.com.

CAR TRAVEL

This circuit should take you seven or eight hours by car, if you make stops at the various sights. At the farthest point, Gullfoss, you're only 125 km (78 mi) from Reykjavík, and most of the drive is along paved main roads.

EMERGENCIES

Dial 112 for emergency assistance anywhere in Iceland.

🚩 **Emergencies** ☎ 112.

TOURS

Reykjavík Excursions provides a daily eight-hour guided Golden Circle Tour. Iceland Excursions has the same tour and also operates an evening version during the summer months.

🚩 **Iceland Excursions** ☎ 540 1313 🖨 540 1310 ⊕ www.icelandexcursions.is. **Reykjavík Excursions** ☎ 562–1011 or 562–9500 ⊕ www.re.is.

VISITOR INFORMATION

General information is available in Reykjavík at the Tourist Information Center and the Icelandic Tourist Board.

🚩 Tourist Information **South Iceland** ⊠ Breiðumörk 2, Hveragerði ☎ 483–4601 🖨 483–4604 ⊕ www.sudurland.net/info.

SNÆFELLSNES PENINSULA

If you imagine the map of Iceland as the shape of a beast, two rugged western peninsulas—Snæfellsnes and Vestfirðir (West Fjords)—would make up the jaws of a peculiar dragonlike head, opening wide around the huge bay of Breiðafjörður. The North Atlantic, just off this coast, is one of the country's prime fishing grounds.

Just north of the town of Borgarnes, the Ring Road northbound bends to the northeast. Follow Route 54, which branches northwest, leading along the southern reaches of the Snæfellsnes Peninsula, which is crowned by the majestic Snæfellsjökull (Snæfells Glacier).

Staðarsveit

As you drive farther west on the peninsula, you'll pass through the Staðarsveit district, with its beautiful mountain range. Many small lakes abound with water flowers, and there are myriad sparkling springs. At **Lýsuhóll,** a few minutes north of Route 54, you can bathe in the warm water of a naturally carbonated spring. About 10 km (6 mi) farther west is the **Búðahraun** lava field, composed of rough lava. Its surface makes walking difficult, but it's more hospitable to vegetation than are most other Icelandic landscapes; flowers, shrubs, herbs, and berries grow abundantly here.

Búðir

102 km (61 mi) northwest of Borganes.

This tiny shoreline establishment on the Snæfellsnes Peninsula has ancient origins as an inlet mooring for fishermen in the days of sails and rowing. If you look carefully, you may find centuries-old relics of the fishermen's shelters. An unpretentious church from 1850—a successor to the first chapel on this site in 1703—has retained its looks. The lava surrounding this site fosters unique flora, including a rare subspecies of the buttercup, called Goldilocks, or *Ranunculus auricomus islandicus* among scholars. The area is protected as a registered nature preserve.

Where to Stay & Eat

$$$ ✕⊡ **Hótel Búðir.** On an isolated point in the peninsula, this hotel affords
Fodor'sChoice stunning views of the sea, lava fields, mountains, and glacier. Antique
★ furnishings and art objects are part of the opulent furnishings. Popular with both tourists and Icelanders looking for a quiet weekend away, this hotel also has one of the best restaurants ($$$) in the area, with some tables facing the stunning Snæfellsjökull. Not surprisingly, all rooms are no-smoking, but you may smoke in common areas. ⊠ *Búðir, IS-355* ☎ *435–6700* 🖷 *435–6701* ⊕ *www.budir.is* ⊃ *28 rooms* ⌂ *Restaurant, bar* ⊟ *MC, V, AE* ⦿ *CP.*

en route   From Búðir, take a left turn onto coastal Route 574 for a 61-km (36-mi) drive circling the tip of the peninsula clockwise. On your right you'll see the focus of what is Iceland's newest national park, the majestic Snæfells Glacier, **Snæfellsjökull,** which, like that on

Fujiyama in Japan, caps a volcano. The glacier had a cameo in Jules Verne's novel *Journey to the Center of the Earth* as the spot where the explorers enter the depths of the world.

The coastal drive takes you past many small, beautiful villages. One such is **Arnarstapi,** where the roof of a shore cave has fallen in, leaving a high arch for cliff birds to loop through to and from their nests. **Hellnar**—with its sea-level cave, Baðstofa, which radiates blue at high tide—is also quaint. About an hour's walk from the road at the western tip of the peninsula lie the **Svörtuloft Cliffs,** where multitudes of seabirds take refuge in nesting season May to August.

Stykkishólmur

67 km (42 mi) east of Ólafsvík.

Stykkishólmur is an active fishing and port community on the peninsula's north coast with a charming, well-sheltered natural harbor. Around the harbor, classic timber houses from the 1800s, many of them beautifully restored, give glimpses of a distinguished past, when many of the now-abandoned islets of Breiðafjörður were settled.

A ferry sails twice daily from here skirting the rugged islets of Breiðafjörður, which have no permanent habitation. The tiny island **Flatey,** where the ferry stops on the way to the West Fjords, is worth a visit. The now-sleepy vacation village was an important commerce and learning hub in the 19th century; many delightful old houses, including Iceland's most miniscule library, still stand today, and the birdlife is remarkable.

Where to Stay & Eat

$–$$$ ✕ **Narfeyrarstofa.** In summer this charming little eatery in an old-time timber building serves hamburgers, coffee, light entrées, and delicious desserts from noon to late. There's a more upscale restaurant on the second floor that uses the same menu but is open only for dinner. In winter it's closed Monday and Tuesday evenings, and opens at 3 PM on weekends. ⊠ *Aðalgata 3* ☎ *438–1119* 🖷 *438–1630* ⊕ *www.narfeyrarstofa.is* ▭ *MC, V.*

$$ ✕▣ **Hótel Stykkishólmur.** This well-kept spot has a great vantage point and is a good option for overnighting in the area. Rooms are done in a crisp Scandinavian style with clean lines and parquet floors. A new wing was opened in July 2005. The restaurant ($$$) specializes in seafood dishes, including local shellfish, as well as delicious, tender lamb. Guests have free access to the 9-hole golf course behind the hotel. ⊠ *Borgarbraut 6, IS-340* ☎ *430–2100* 🖷 *430–2101* ⊕ *www.hotelstykkisholmur.is* ⤴ *80 rooms* ⟡ *Restaurant, 9-hole golf course, bar* ▭ *AE, DC, MC, V* ▮◎▮ *CP.*

Sports & the Outdoors

BOAT TOURS Cruise the islands of Breiðarfjörður and sample fresh-caught seafood, or go whale-watching off Snæfellsnes peninsula with **Seatours** (⊠ Smiðjustígur 3, IS-340 Stykkishólmur ☎ 438–1450 ⊕ www.seatours.is).

SWIMMING Parents can soak in the hot tubs or swim laps while the kids enjoy the spiral waterslide at the **Stykkishólmur pool** (☎ 438–1150).

THE ICELANDIC HORSE

THE ICELANDIC HORSE *(sometimes referred to as a pony) is a purebred descendant of its ancestors from the Viking age, in the 10th century. The horse is not native to Iceland, and its orgins are debated—they may be descendents of Germanic or Scandinavian horses, or of English and Scottish ponies. They are the only breed of horse in Iceland. Adult horses normally measure 12 to 13 hands (most North American breeds measure 16 hands or more). Small but strong, the horses are exceptionally sure-footed, intelligent, and easy to handle. This horse has a particularly interesting stepping style called the tölt, or "running walk," which yields an extraordinarily smooth ride. This gait is actually so smooth that a popular demonstration has the rider carrying a tray of drinks at full speed without spilling a drop! Horse lovers from around the world come to try these amazing five-speed steeds for themselves. A number of operators offers tours, from short 1-day trips to 12-day cross-country treks for more experienced riders.*

Snæfellsnes Peninsula A to Z

BUS TRAVEL

BSÍ Travel runs frequent daily service to most towns in the region. It's a 45-minute trip to Borgarnes, three hours to Stykkishólmur.

🚌 **BSÍ Bus Terminal** ☎ 591-1000 ⊕ www.bsi.is.

CAR TRAVEL

From Reykjavík, you reach Snæfellsnes Peninsula via the Ring Road (Route 1). The Hvalfjörður tunnel, penetrating about 6 km (about 4 mi) underwater from an entrance about 30 km (19 mi) north of Reykjavík, eases accessibility to the west from the capital. The IKr 1,000 car toll (each way) is less than what you'd pay on gas to drive around the fjord, and you'll save more than 40 minutes each way. Upon emerging from the tunnel's north end, you'll be just 10 km (6 mi) from either Akranes or Borgarnes. Heading north after Borgarnes, Route 54 branches off to the Snæfellsnes Peninsula.

EMERGENCIES

Dial 112 for emergency assistance anywhere in Iceland.

🚓 **Police Borgarnes** ☎ 437-1166. **Stykkishólmur** ☎ 430-4141.

TOURS

You can take a guided snowmobile trip to the top of the Snæfellsjökull or go in groups of six, minimum, in a Sno-Cat trailer from Snjófell at Arnarstapi. Snowmobiles rent at IKr 5,200 per person for two riders, or IKr 6,500 solo. The Sno-Cat ride is IKr 3,500 per person.

Seatours runs whale-watching and island nature tours from the village of Stykkishólmur on the Snæfellsnes peninsula.

🚌 **Tour Operators Seatours** ☎ 438-1450 at Stykkishólmur, 456-2020 at Brjánslækur ⊕ www.seatours.is. **Snjófell** ⊠ IS-311, Arnarstapi ☎ 435-6795 🖷 435-6795 ⊕ www. snjofell.is. **Iceland Travel** ☎ 585-4300.

VISITOR INFORMATION

🚩 Tourist Information **Stykkishólmur** ⊠ Íþróttamiðstöðin ☎ 438-1150 📠 438-1780. **Ólafsvík** ⊠ Gamla Pakkhúsið, IS-355 📠 436-1543 ⊕ www.snb.is/pakkhus ☯ June-Aug., daily 9-7.

THE NORTH

From the Hrútafjörður (Rams' Fjord), which gouges deeply into the western end of the coast, to Vopnafjörður in the east, Iceland's north is a land created by the interplay of fire and ice. Inland, you can find the largest lava fields on Earth, some with plants and mosses, others barren. Yet valleys sheltered by the mountains are lush with vegetation and rich in color, and the deeply indented coast offers magnificent views north toward the arctic, especially spectacular under the summer's midnight sun.

The commercial and cultural center of Akureyri is Iceland's fourth-largest town. From there it's a pleasant drive to Lake Mývatn, where bird-watchers can spot vast numbers of waterfowl and hikers can explore weird lava formations. The climate is unusually mild around Mývatn, making it a pleasant outdoor destination.

Akureyri

95 km (57 mi) east along Ring Rd. from junction with Rte. 75 south of Sauðákrókur.

Though not as cosmopolitan as Reykjavík, Akureyri—called the Capital of the North—is a lively city. Hemmed by the 64-km- (40-mi-) long Eyjafjörður, Akureyri is sheltered from the ocean winds and embraced by mountains on three sides. Late 19th-century wooden houses impart a sense of history, and the twin spires of a modern Lutheran church—rising on a green hill near the waterfront—provide a focal point.

From the church it's a short walk from the town center on Eyrarlandsvegur to the **Lystigarðurinn** (Arctic Botanical Gardens), planted with more than 400 species of flora, including rare arctic and foreign plants. **Matthíasarhús** (⊠ Eyrarlandsvegur 3 📠 462-6648 ☯ Summer, weekdays 1–3:30; by request rest of year), the house where Matthías Jochumsson once lived, is now a museum.

The **Minjasafnið** (Folk Museum) has a large collection of local relics and works of art, old farm tools, and fishing equipment. ⊠ Aðalstræti 58, IS-600 Akureyri 📠 462–4162 💷 IKr 400 ☯ Summer, daily 10–5; winter. Sat. 2–4 or by arrangement.

Dating from the 18th century, the beautifully restored **Laxdalshús** (Laxdal House) is the oldest house in Akureyri. A Lutheran priest now resides here. You can explore the grounds and see the interior if staff is present. ⊠ Hafnarstræti 11, IS-600 Akureyri.

In June and July, make a point of taking an evening drive north from Akureyri along Route 82. The midnight sun creates breathtaking views along the coast of **Eyjafjörður.** Better still, take a cruise on the fjord: a ferry plies the waters of Eyjafjörður to and from the island of **Hrísey,** home of Galloway cattle, and out to **Grímsey Island,** 40 km (25 mi) off-shore and straddling the Arctic Circle. Contact **Nonni Travel** (✉ Brekku-gata 5, IS-600 Akureyri ☎ 461–1841).

To the south of Akureyri is the pyramid-shape rhyolite mountain **Súlur.** Beyond it is **Kerling,** the highest peak in Eyjafjörður.

Where to Stay & Eat

$$$–$$$$ ✗ **Fiðlarinn.** What better name for a rooftop restaurant than Fiddler? Dine with a fabulous view overlooking Akureyri Harbor and Eyjafjörður. The food is modern Icelandic, with French and Danish influences. Based on goose and reindeer, the dishes feature seasonal ingredients. ✉ *Skip-agata 14, IS-600* ☎ *462–7100* ⊕ *www.fidlarinn.is* ▤ *AE, DC, MC, V.*

$$$ ✗ **Friðrik V.** This popular brasserie gets it name from the owner, Friðrik Valur, who has worked in five restaurants in Akureyri. It has a great view of downtown and often hosts exhibitions of local artists. ✉ *Strandgata 7 IS-600 Akureyri* ☎ *461–5775* ⊕ *www.fridrikv.is* ▤ *AE, MC, V.*

$$$ ✗☷ **Hótel KEA.** Blue and maroon hues and dark-wood trim character-ize this hotel, which is on par with many of the capital's better accom-modations. An excellent ground-level restaurant, Rósagarðurinn ($$), serves exquisite haute cuisine. ✉ *Hafnarstræti 87–89, IS-602 Akureyri* ☎ *460–2000* 🖷 *460–2060* ⊕ *www.keahotels.is* ⨠ *73 rooms, 1 suite* ⌂ *Restaurant, bar, lobby lounge, meeting room* ▤ *AE, DC, MC, V* ⫶❙❘ *CP.*

$$ ☷ **Hótel Norðurland.** All rooms here have floral prints, Danish modern furniture, and TV. On the ground floor is the separately run Pizza 67 restaurant. ✉ *Geislagata 7, IS-600 Akureyri* ☎ *462–2600* 🖷 *462–2601* ⨠ *34 rooms* ⌂ *Breakfast room, minibars* ▤ *AE, DC MC, V* ⫶❙❘ *CP.*

Sports & the Outdoors

GOLF Enjoy golf at perhaps the world's northernmost 18-hole course at the **Akureyri Golf Club** (☎ 462–2974) in Jaðar, on the outskirts of Akureyri. Golfers compete here well past midnight during the **Arctic Open Golf Tournament,** held each year around the longest day of the year (in the midnight sun, needless to say). For details, contact the Akureyri Golf Club or the **Ferðaskrifstofa Akureyrar** (✉ Ráðhústorg 3, IS-600 ☎ 460–0600).

HIKING For many different hiking choices, contact **Ferðafélag Akureyrar** (Tour-ing Club of Akureyri; ✉ Strandgata 23, IS-600 ☎ 462–2720 🖷 462–7240). **Ferðaskrifstofa Akureyrar** (✉ Ráðhústorg 3, IS-600 ☎ 460–0600) can also provide a walk on the wild side. **Nonni Travel** (✉ Brekkugata 5, IS-600 ☎ 461–1841) runs mountain hiking tours from Akureyri.

HORSEBACK RIDING For horseback trips from the Akureyri area—from hour-long to days-long—contact **Pólarhestar** (✉ Grýtubakki II, IS-600 ☎ 463–3179 🖷 463–3144 ⊕ www.nett.is/polar). It operates mid-May to mid-October.

SWIMMING Akureyri's excellent open-air **pool** is one of the best in the country, and ᨀ is very popular with kids (✉ Þingvallastræti 13 ☎ 461–4455).

CloseUp

BIRD-WATCHING

EVEN IN SETTLED AREAS, *bird-watchers are likely to find a fascinating assortment of species, among them the golden plover, a harbinger of spring; the arctic tern, a streamlined circumpolar migrator; and the colorful puffin. Of several birds of prey, two earn special status because of their rarity: the regal gyrfalcon and the majestic white-tailed eagle. A summer walk along Reykjavík's Tjörnin Pond might be accompanied by ducks of various species, swans, gulls, and the ever-present terns.*

Puffins can be spotted closest to Reykjavík at Lundey (the name means—what else?— Puffin Island). Serious bird-watchers should make a summer visit to Lake Mývatn, which has Europe's largest variety of ducks and waterbirds.

Shopping

Akureyri offers better shopping than most other towns outside Reykjavík, with many temptations along the pedestrian street Hafnarstræti. The shop **Folda-Anna** (⊠ Hafnarstræti 85, IS-600 ☎ 461–4120) sells woolens, knitting kits, sheepskin rugs, and other souvenirs.

Goðafoss

Directly from Akureyri, Goðafoss is about 50 km (30 mi) east along Ring Rd.

The name Goðafoss—Waterfall of the Gods—derives from a historic event in AD 1000 when Þorgeir Ljósvetningagoði, ordered by the Icelandic Parliament to choose between paganism and Christianity, threw his pagan icons into the waterfall. Just before you reach Goðafoss, in the Skjálfandi River, you'll pass the **Ljósavatn church** on land where Þorgeir lived a millennium ago. Although the farm is long gone, you can visit the church, which houses, among other relics, some interesting runic stones.

Mývatn

About 100 km (62 mi) along Ring Rd. east of Akureyri.

You could spend at least a day exploring this superbly natural area influenced by active geology; a fissure eruption occurred here in 1984. The area's "false craters" were formed when hot lava of ancient eruptions ran over marshland, causing steam jets to spout up, forming small cones. **Lake Mývatn** is an aqueous gem amid mountains and lava fields. Fed by cold springs in the lake bottom and warm springs in the northeastern corner, the shallow lake—42 square km (15 square mi) in area yet only 3 feet to 13 feet deep—teems with fish, birds, and insects, including the swarming midges for which the lake is named. These tiny flies are essential in the bird food chain.

Waterfowl migrate long distances to breed at Mývatn, where the duck population numbers up to 150,000 in summer. Indeed, the lake has Europe's greatest variety of nesting ducks, including some—the Harlequin duck and Barrow's goldeneye—found nowhere else in Europe. Dozens of other kinds of waders, upland birds, and birds of prey also nest here. Be sure to stay on established trails and pathways, as nests can be anywhere. During summer you might find a head net useful to protect yourself against the huge midge swarms.

Turning off the Ring Road at Route 848, you'll pass **Skútustaðir**, a tiny village on the lake's southern shore. Proceed along the eastern shore to the 1,300-foot-high **Hverfjall** ash cone, several hundred feet from the road. Many paths lead to the top. The outer walls of this volcanic crater are steep, but the ascent is easy. The walk around the top of the crater is about 4,300 feet. Southwest of Hverfjall is the **Dimmuborgir** (Dark Castles) lava field, a labyrinth of tall formations where you can choose between short and longer signposted routes through the eerie landscape. Among its mysterious arches, gates, and caves, the best-known is the **Kirkja** (church), resembling a Gothic chapel (it's marked by a sign, lest you miss it). Don't wander off the paths, as Dimmuborgir is a highly fragile environment.

Where to Stay & Eat

$$ ✕⊞ **Hótel Reynihlíð.** This popular hotel has pastel-color rooms, and staff members who provide helpful general information about surrounding attractions. The restaurant ($$) serves entrées such as fresh trout from the lake, and rhubarb pie for dessert. Another on-site though separate eatery, Gamli Bærinn, changes from a friendly daytime café to a congenial pub at night. ⊠ *Reykjahlíð, IS-660, Mývatnssveit* 🕾*464–4170* 🖷 *464–4371* ⊕ *www.reynihlid.is* ↰ *41 rooms* ♿ *Restaurant, bicycles (free for guests), horseback riding, bar* ⊟ *AE, DC, MC, V* ¶◎¶ *CP.*

$$ ⊞ **Hótel Reykjahlíð.** The small, family-run hotel has a prime lakeside location with great views. Bird-watchers can add to their lists by simply looking out their windows. ⊠ *Reykjahlíð, IS-660 Mývatnssveit* 🕾 *464–4142* 🖷 *464–4336* ↰ *9 rooms* ⊟ *MC, V* ¶◎¶ *CP.*

Sports & the Outdoors

BIKING The **Hótel Reynihlíð** (⊠ IS-660 Mývatnssveit 🕾 464–4170) in Mývatn rents bicycles (free for guests) for exploring the area around the lake.

BIRD-WATCHING Lake Mývatn is one of the best places in Iceland for bird-watching. More than 75% of all birds in the country can be found here, including the riotous harlequin duck, the barrow's goldeneye, and the elusive gyrfalcon. From the end of April to the beginning of June is the best time to go, but tours are offered year-round. **Pétur Gíslason at Hótel Reykjahlíð** offers half- or full-day bird-watching tours in the Lake Mývatn area.

BOATING At Mývatn, **Eldá Travel** (⊠Reykjahlíð, IS-660, Mývatnssveit 🕾464–4220) rents boats on Lake Mývatn.

HORSEBACK RIDING Near Hrútafjörður, **Arinbjörn Jóhannsson** (🕾 451–2938) in Brekkulækur organizes horseback rides.

LAND OF THE SAGAS

ICELAND'S LITERARY TRADITION *goes back centuries. Between the 13th and 14th centuries, dozens of sagas were written about the heroic exploits of Icelanders from the time of the settlement. They are quasi-historical texts that were passed down orally from generation to generation before being written down. The most famous sagas are the Saga of Burnt Njál, the Saga of Gréttir the Strong, and Egil's Saga. Icelandic sagas have influenced the works of many modern authors, including J.R.R. Tolkien and Philip Pullman. It is possible to visit many of the locations where sagas took place, which are scattered throughout the countryside. You can find copies of the sagas in virtually every Icelandic home, and they form an important part of the country's cultural heritage.*

SUPER JEEPS
★

At Mývatn, **Pétur Gíslason at Hótel Reykjahlíð** (✉ Reykjahlíð, IS-660, Mývatnssveit ☎ 464–4336) has Super Jeep tours to the interior, including an eerie moonscape journey to the Askja crater.

SPAS
★

Mývatn Nature Baths (✉ Jarðbaðshólar, IS-660 Mývatn ☎ 464–4411 ⊕ www.jardbodin.is ✉ IKr 1,100 ⊙ Summer, daily 9 AM–midnight; winter, weekdays 4 PM–11 PM, weekends noon–11), whose thermal pools are a bit like the Blue Lagoon of the North, opened in 2004. The water has great mineral properties, and there are wonderful steam baths.

The North A to Z

AIR TRAVEL

Air Iceland (Flugfélag Íslands) has hour-long flights from Reykjavík to Akureyri. Air Iceland also flies from Akureyri to Grímsey, Vopnafjörður and Þórshöfn, in Denmark's Faroe Islands. Landsflug flies four days a week to Sauðárkrókur. You can book through Air Iceland, which also handles bookings for Landsflug. The Mýflug air charter company flies daily charters June–August, based at the Mývatn airfield.

🛫 **Air Iceland** ✉ Akureyri ☎ 460-7000 ⊕ www.flugfelag.is ✉ Reykjavík ☎ 570-3030. **Mýflug** ☎ 464-4400 🖷 464-4401 ⊕ www.myflug.is.

BUS TRAVEL

SBA-Norðurleið has daily bus service from Reykjavík to the north. It's 4½ hours to Blönduós and 6½ hours to Akureyri. Bus service from Akureyri takes less than 1½ hours to Húsavík and 2 hours to Mývatn. The Akureyri bus terminal, Umferðamiðstöðin, handles nationwide coach service.

The Akureyri Bus Company operates scheduled trips around the region, including a tour by bus and ferry to Hrísey Island and to Grímsey Island on the Arctic Circle.

🛫 **SBA-Norðurleið** ☎ 550-0700. **Umferðamiðstöðin** ✉ Hafnarstræti 82, IS-600 Akureyri ☎ 462-4442.

CAR TRAVEL

It's a 432-km (268-mi) drive from Reykjavík to Akureyri along the Ring Road (Route 1), at least a five-hour drive. Branch off on Route 85 to Húsavík.

EMERGENCIES

Dial 🕾 112 for emergency assistance anywhere in Iceland.

🔳 **Emergencies** 🕾 112. **Police** 🕾 464-7700 in Akureyri.

TOURS

Iceland Travel operates a 12-hour day trip from Reykjavík to Akureyri and Lake Mývatn; you take a plane to Akureyri and then a bus to Mývatn. Nonni Travel runs tours from Akureyri to Mývatn, historic sites, and the islands off the north coast. Norður Sigling conducts whale-watching tours on a classic oak ship. Whale-watching and tours of Dettifoss, Kverkfjöll, and Vatnajökull are operated from Akureyri by SBA–Norðurleið.

🔳 Tour-Operator Recommendations **Iceland Travel** 🕾 585-4300. **Ferðaskrifstofa Akureyrar** ✉ Ráðhústorg 3, IS-600 Akureyri 🕾 460-0600. **Nonni Travel** ✉ Brekku-gata 5, IS-600 Akureyri 🕾 461-1841 🖷 461-1843 ⊕ www.nonnitravel.is.

VISITOR INFORMATION

🔳 Tourist Information **Akureyri** ✉ Coach Terminal, Hafnarstræti 82, IS-600 🕾 550-0720 ◷ June–Aug., daily 7:30-7; winter, weekdays 8-5.

THE SOUTH

The power of volcanoes is all too evident on this journey along the south coast. At Kirkjubæjarklaustur you can still see scars of the great Laki eruption of 1783. At Stöng you can visit excavated ruins of a farmstead buried by the 1104 eruption of Mt. Hekla, known throughout medieval Europe as the abode of the damned—and still mightily active. Other regional natural wonders include Skaftafell National Park and Þórsmörk (Thor's Wood), a popular nature reserve.

Hella

36 km (22 mi) east of Selfoss.

About 26 km (16 mi) east of Selfoss, turn left onto Route 26 and drive 40 km (25 mi) or so until you see, on your right, the tallest peak in the region. **Mt. Hekla** is also an active volcano, rightfully infamous since the Middle Ages as it has erupted 21 times in recorded history and as recently as 2000. Some 25 km (16 mi) farther, Route 26 intersects Route 32; turn left and go 15 km (9 mi) to the right turn for **Stöng,** an ancient settlement on the west bank of the Þjórsá River, Iceland's longest. The original farm here dates back almost 900 years; it was buried by Hekla's eruption in 1104, but you can visit the excavated ruins. A complete replica has been built, using the same materials the settlers used, south of Stöng at Búrfell on Route 32.

Where to Stay

$$$ 🛏 **Hotel Rangá.** Part of the Icelandair Hotel franchise, this rustic-style four-star hotel is in the countryside just east of Hella. The two outdoor Jacuzzis are great for watching the northern lights in winter. One of the

A GEOLOGIST'S DREAM

WHERE THE WARM *southern Gulf Stream confronts the icy Arctic currents from the north, Iceland straddles the mid-Atlantic ridge at the merger of the North American and European tectonic plates. Volcanic activity continues to form the island by slowly forcing the plates to separate. During the past few centuries, a volcanic eruption has occurred on average every five years. Mt. Hekla erupted in February 2000, and the cauldron that awoke under the Vatnajökull glacier in the fall of 1996 quickly melted through hundreds of feet of ice not far from Grímsvatn. Yet no one need wait for an eruption to be reminded of the fiery forces' presence, because they also heat the hot springs and geysers that gurgle, bubble, and spout in many parts of the country. The springs, in turn, provide hot water for public swimming pools and heating for most homes and buildings, helping to keep the air smog-free. Hydropower generated by harnessing some of the country's many turbulent rivers is another main energy source that helps to keep pollution and the expense of fossil fuels at a minimum.*

best rivers in the country for salmon fishing is right next door. Try the restaurant's chocolate *skyr* cake. ☒ *IS-851 Hella* ☎ *487–5700* 🖨 *487–5701* 📠 *27 rooms* ♨ *Restaurant, fishing* ▭ *AE, MC, V.*

Skógar

66 km (41 mi) east of Hella.

en route About 30 km (19 mi) along the Ring Road before Skógar or 36 km (22 mi) past Hella, follow the turnoff north to **Seljalandsfoss,** a waterfall on the left. This graceful, ribbonlike waterfall drops from an overhanging lava cliff. If you step carefully, you can walk behind it, but be prepared to get wet.

Several hundred feet west of Skógar, just off the Ring Road, is **Skógafoss,** another impressive waterfall that's more than 197 feet high and is the last in a series of huge cascades up the mountain.

The tiny settlement of Skógar has one of Iceland's best folk museums, **Byggðarsafnið Skógar.** The curator of these beautifully preserved old houses and memorabilia is highly knowledgeable and has been commended for his efforts with the Falcon Medal of Honor, Iceland's highest distinction. He may even serenade you on the antique harmonium. Among the mementos of this region's past is a tiny, frail boat local fishermen once navigated along the treacherous coast. ✉ *100 yards east of Edda Hotel* ☎ *487–8845* ⏱ *June–Aug., daily 9–4:30; Sept. and Apr, daily 10–5; Oct.–Apr, daily 11–4.*

Where to Stay

$ 🏠 **Stóramörk.** Recommended by Fodor's readers, this farm provides basic accommodations in the beautiful countryside very near Þórsmörk National Park. ✉ *Stóramörk, IS-861 Hvolsvöllur* ☎ *487–8903* ⊕ *frontpage.simnet. is/storamork/farmstoramork.htm* ⇗ *5 rooms, 2 with bath* ⌂ *Kitchen.*

The Outdoors

HIKING ★ Adventurers can take a three-day hike into the interior to visit **Landmannalaugar,** where hot and cold springs punctuate a landscape rich in yellow, brown, and red rhyolite hills carved by glacial rivers.

The **Ferðafélag Íslands touring club** (✉ Mörkin 6, IS-108 Reykjavík ☎ 568–2533 🖷 568–2535 ⊕ www.fi.is) conducts cabin and camping tours of the region. **Útivist** (✉ Laugavegur 178, IS-105 Reykjavík ☎ 562–1000 ⊕ www.utivist.is) is another option for hiking tours; it has both cabin and sleeping-bag accommodations. Both groups offer many long-distance hikes from Þórsmörk.

Skaftafell National Park

147 km east of Vík.

Bordering Vatnajökull is Skaftafell National Park, the largest of Iceland's three national reserves. Glaciers branching off Vatnajökull shelter Skaftafell from winds, creating a verdant oasis. In the park, you can walk for days on beautiful trails through a rare combination of green forest, clear water, waterfalls, sands, mountains, and glaciers. Iceland's highest peak, **Hvannadalshnjúkur,** reaching 6,950 feet, is just outside the park and provides a stunning backdrop. The famous **Svartifoss** (Black Falls) tumbles over a cliff whose sides resemble the pipes of a great organ. Don't miss **Sel,** a restored gabled farmhouse high up on the slope. Guided walks in the national park are organized daily in July and August.

Where to Stay

$$ 🏠 **Hótel Skaftafell.** Few hotels in Iceland have such a serendipitous setting—near breathtaking Skaftafell National Park. A roomy bar is upstairs over the expanded lobby of this family-run facility. A travel shop and gas station are also on the property. It's closed between November and January except for prior reservations. ✉ *Freysnes, Öræfi, IS-785* ☎ *478–1945* 🖷 *478–1846* ⊕ *www.hotelskaftafell.is* ⇗ *63 rooms* ⌂ *Restaurant, shop, bar* ☰ *AE, MC, V* ⏹ *CP.*

Jökulsárlón

50 km (31 mi) east of Skaftafell National Park along Ring Rd.

Fodor'sChoice ★ At the Glacial River Lagoon, about 50 km (31 mi) west of Höfn, you can see large chunks of the glacier tumble and float around in a spectacular ice show. So magnificent is the scenery, it has been used as a location for scenes in some James Bond movies *A View to a Kill* and *Die Another Day*, as well as *Lara Croft Tombraider*. Boat trips on the lagoon are operated throughout the summer; for details call **Einar B. Einarsson** (⊠ IS-780 Höfn ☎ 478–2122 ⊕ www.jokulsarlon.com). On the **Breiðamerkur sands,** west of the lagoon, is the largest North Atlantic colony of skua, large predatory seabirds that unhesitatingly dive-bomb intruders during nesting season.

Eyrarbakki

12 km (7 mi) southwest of Selfoss along Rte. 34.

This close-knit village right on the shore of the North Atlantic was the largest community in the south less than a century ago. A few buildings remaining from that era have been restored. The pleasant **Árnes Folk Museum** (⊠ Húsið ☎ 483–1504), an older gentry house, has interesting exhibits. Its surrounding turf walls were the most effective means of shelter from stiff onshore breezes. Another attraction is the **Eyrarbakki Maritime Museum** (⊠ Túngata 59 ☎ 483–1273 or 483–1504). Nearby tidal marshes are a bird-watcher's wonderland.

Where to Eat

$$–$$$$ ✕ **Rauða Husið.** Seafood and vegetarian dishes, along with homemade desserts and great java, are served in this popular restaurant. ⊠ *Búðarstígur 4, IS-800* ☎ *483–3330* ▭ *AE, MC, V.*

The South A to Z

BUS TRAVEL

Austurleið Bus Companý has daily service from Reykjavík, stopping in Hella, Hvolsvöllur, Selfoss, Vík, and Þorlakshöfn. The journey to Vík takes less than four hours; to Þorlakshöfn or Selfoss, one hour.

🚌 **Austurleið** ⊠ BSÍ Bus Terminal Vatnsmýrarvegur 10, Reykjavík ☎ 562-1011

EMERGENCIES

Dial ☎ 112 for emergency assistance anywhere in Iceland.

🚌 **Police: Selfoss** ☎ 480-1010. **Vík** ☎ 487-1414.

TOURS

Reykjavík Excursions Kynnisferðir and Iceland Excursions both operate trips to various places in the south and in the interior. Iceland Excursions also operates a day trip from Reykjavík to Jökulsárlón Glacial Lagoon.

VISITOR INFORMATION

🚌 **Tourist Information Selfoss** ⊠ Nesbúð Nesjavöllum, IS-800 ☎ 482-3415 ⊕ www.sudurland.inet/info

ICELAND A TO Z

To research prices, get advice from other travelers, and book travel arrangements, visit www.fodors.com.

AIR TRAVEL

Because so much of Iceland's central region is uninhabited, domestic air transport has been well developed to link the coastal towns. It isn't particularly cheap—round-trip fares for open tickets range from IKr 16,000 to IKr 25,000—but discounts are available. The longest domestic flight takes just over an hour.

CARRIERS In summer, Air Iceland (Flugfélag Íslands) schedules daily or frequent flights from Reykjavík to most of the large areas, such as Akureyri, Egilsstaðir, Höfn, Ísafjörður, and Vestmannaeyjar. Bus connections between airports outside Reykjavík and nearby towns and villages are available.

Landsflug flies five times a week from Reykjavík to Bíldudalur and four times weekly to Sauðárkrókur. You can book tickets via Air Iceland. APEX tickets are available on domestic flights if booked three days in advance. These offer savings of 40% off the full airfare. Internet offers can bring savings of 50% off the full airfare.

Icelandair operates regular direct flights—which take 5½ hours to the nearest destinations—to Boston, New York's JFK Airport, Baltimore, Orlando, and Minneapolis. The frequency of flights depends on the season. Icelandair also flies to San Francisco twice a week during summer, and it flies daily from London's Heathrow Airport and Copenhagen. It operates regular flights to and from numerous European destinations, with even more flights during summer. The flight from London takes three hours. Iceland Express, the country's low-cost carrier, flies daily to London's Stansted Airport and Copenhagen, and is expanding to other destinations.

🔁 To & From Iceland **British Airways** ⊕ www.ba.com ☎ 1-800-AIRWAYS. **Icelandair** ☎ 505-0100 in Iceland, 800/223-5500 in the U.S. ⊕ www.icelandair.com. **Iceland Express** ⊕ www.icelandexpress.is.

🔁 Around Iceland **Air Iceland** ☎ 570-3030 ⊕ www.airiceland.is.

CUTTING COSTS The Fly As You Please Holiday Ticket is valid for unlimited travel on all Air Iceland (Flugfélag Íslands) domestic routes for 12 days. The Four-Sector Air Iceland Pass is valid for a month and can be used on any four sectors flown by Icelandair and its domestic line, Air Iceland (Flugfélag Íslands); this pass must be booked before arrival in Iceland. Several other types of air passes, covering different combinations of sectors, are also available. The Mini–Air Iceland Pass is valid on two sectors.

AIRPORTS

Virtually all international flights originate from and arrive at Keflavík Airport 50 km (31 mi) south of Reykjavík. On arrival you may spot some military aircraft, for Keflavík is also a U.S. military installation.

🔁 **Keflavík Airport** ☎ 505-0500 ⊕ www.keflavikairport.com.

BOAT & FERRY TRAVEL

It is possible to sail to Iceland on the car-and-passenger ferry *Norröna*, operated by Smyril Line. The *Norröna* plies among the Faroes and Esbjerg in Denmark, Bergen in Norway, Scotland's Shetland Islands, and Seyðisfjörður on the east coast of Iceland. Depending on your point of departure and your destination, the trip may involve a stopover of some days in the Faroes. Special offers for accommodations may be available through Smyril Line, and special fly-cruise arrangements are available through Smyril Line and Icelandair.

The town of Seyðisfjörður on the eastern side of the country is the arrival port for the ferry from Europe. It's easy a short drive to join the Ring Road and drive head either to the north or south from this quaint seaside village with 18th-century buildings and Norwegian-style wooden houses, either with a car rented in town or brought on the ferry. If you need to stay the night, try the **Hótel Aldan** (⊠ Norðugata 2, IS-710 ☎ 472–1277), a classic Norse-style wooden building with newly renovated rooms, or the **Youth Hostel** (⊠ Ránargata 9, IS-710 ☎ 472–1410); it's closed in winter. There are also larger hotels in nearby Egilsstaðir.

The *Baldur* car ferry sails twice daily in summer from Stykkishólmur, on the Snæfellsnes Peninsula, across Breiðafjörður Bay to Brjánslækur, via Flatey Island. Ferries run daily between Þorlákshöfn and Vestmannaeyjar on the ferry *Herjólfur*.

🚢 *Baldur* ☎ 438–1450 for booking at Stykkishólmur, 456–2020 at Brjánslækur ⊕ www. saeferdir.is. **Seyðisfjörður Tourist Information** ⊠ Ferjuleira 1 ☎ 472–1551. **Herjólfur** ☎ 483–3413 or 481–2800 🖷 481–2991. **Egilsstaðir** Tourist Information Office at campsite ⊠ Hafnarbraut 52 ☎ 471–2320. **Smyril Line** ⊠ Passenger Dept., Box 370, FR–110 Tórshavn, Faroe Islands ☎ 298–315–950 🖷 298–315–707 ⊕ www.smyril-line.com ⊠ Sætún 8, Reykjavík Iceland ☎ 570–8600 🖷 591–9001.

BUS TRAVEL

An extensive network of buses serves most parts of Iceland. Services are intermittent in the winter season, and some routes are operated only in summer. Fares from Reykjavík range from IKr 1,600 for a one-way trip in summer to Laugarvatn near Þingvellir, to IKr 9,200 for a summer roundtrip, Reykjavík to Akureyri. The bus network is operated by Bifreiðastöð Íslands; its terminal is on the northern rim of Reykjavík Airport.

🚌 **Bifreiðastöð Íslands (BSÍ)** ⊠ Vatnsmýrarvegur 10, IS-101 ☎ 591–1000 🖷 591–1050 ⊕ www.bsi.is.

CUTTING COSTS Holders of BSÍ Passport tickets are entitled to discounts on ferries, BSÍ-rented mountain bikes, stays at campsites and Edda hotels, and other travel needs.

If you want to explore the island extensively, it's a good idea to buy the Omnibus Passport, which covers travel on all scheduled bus routes with unlimited stopovers. The Full Circle Passport is valid for a circular trip on the Ring Road mid-July to mid-September; you can take as long as you like to complete the journey but you have to keep heading in the same direction on the circuit (detours into the interior must be paid for separately). The Air/Bus Rover ticket offered by Air Iceland (Flugfélag Íslands) and BSÍ allows you to fly one-way to any domestic Air Iceland destination and travel by bus back, so you can save some time and still have a chance to explore the countryside.

BUSINESS HOURS

BANKS & OFFICES All banks in Iceland are open weekdays 9:15–4. In addition, ATMs have sprouted up like mushrooms, almost wherever there is a sizable store.

SHOPS Even outside Reykjavík, most food stores are generally open daily until at least 5, but the ones known by Icelanders as "clock" stores—because their hours are in their name (like "10–10" and "10–11")—stay open later (and not necessarily in accordance with their name).

CAR RENTAL

Renting a car in Iceland is relatively expensive; it may well be worth arranging a car in advance over the Internet or through your travel agent, who may be able to offer a better deal. A typical price for a compact car without insurance is around IKr 7,000 per day, with 100 km (62 mi) free, plus about IKr 50 per km, or about IKr 13,000 for a compact with unlimited mileage and all insurance. A four-wheel-drive vehicle for rougher roads will cost about IKr 14,800 per day, with Collision Damage Waiver (CDW) and 100 km (62 mi) included plus IKr 100 per km. There are many car-rental agencies in Iceland, so it is worth shopping around for the best buy. If you plan to explore the interior, make sure you rent a four-wheel-drive vehicle. As elsewhere in Europe, many car-rental agencies provide cars with standard transmission unless you specify automatic (which shouldn't cost extra).

Avis, Budget, and Hertz operate offices in the Leifur Eiríksson Terminal at Keflavík Airport. Hasso Car Rental is also a competitive car-rental option. SG Car Rental specializes in larger vehicles, and SS Car Rental provides a discount to members of the U.S. military who present their military ID.

🚗 Major Agencies **Avis** ☎ 591–4000. **Budget** ☎ 526–6060. **Hertz** ☎ 505–0600.
🚗 Local Agencies **Geysir Car Rental** ✉ Holtsgata 56, IS-260 Njarðvík ☎ 893–4455 ⊕ www.geysir.is. **Hasso Car Rental** ✉ Álfaskeið 115, IS-220 Hafnarfjörður ☎ 555–3330 🖷 565–3340 ⊕ www.hasso.is. **SG Car Rental** ✉ Keflavík Airport, Keflavík ☎ 421–3737 🖷 421–4737 ⊕ www.travelnet.is/sgcar/main.htm. **SS Car Rental** ✉ Iðjustígur 1, Keflavík ☎ 421–2220 🖷 421–3720 ⊕ www.travelnet.is/sscar/.

CAR TRAVEL

The Ring Road, which generally hugs the coastline, runs for 1,400 km (900 mi) around Iceland. Although 90% of the road is paved, a stretch across the Möðrudalsöræfi highlands and stretches in the east are still gravel. Much of Iceland's secondary road system is unpaved. Take great care on these roads, as driving on loose gravel surface takes some getting used to and is not for the timid motorist. Be careful of livestock that may stray onto roadways.

Caution pays off when driving in Iceland's interior, too. The terrain can be treacherous, and many roads can be traversed only in four-wheel-drive vehicles; always drive in the company of at least one other car. Unbridged rivers that must be forded constitute a real hazard and should never be crossed without the advice of an experienced Iceland highland driver. Most mountain roads are closed by snow in winter and do not open again until mid-June or early July, when the road surface has dried out after the spring thaw.

Use extra caution when approaching single-lane bridges or blind hills (*blindhæð*). Before driving any distance in rural Iceland, be sure to pick up the brochure *Driving in Iceland* from any Tourist Information Center, if your rental agency hasn't already given you one. It has informative tips and advice about driving the country's back roads.

EMERGENCY SERVICES The general emergency number, available 24 hours throughout Iceland, is ☎ 112.

GASOLINE Gas prices are high, about IKr 110 to IKr 115 per liter (¼ gallon) depending on octane rating. Service stations are spaced no more than half a day's drive apart, on both main roads and most side roads. Service stations are usually open daily until at least 10 PM; the cheaper, unmanned ÓB stations are open later and have multilingual credit-card machines. For information on the availability of gas off the beaten track, call Vegagerð Ríkisins (Public Roads Administration).

🚩 **Vegagerð Ríkisins** (Public Roads Administration) ✉ Borgartún 5–7, IS-105, Reykjavík ☎ 1777 or 522–1112 (emergency number) for 24-hr road status in English ⊕ www.vegag.is/faerd/indexe.html.

ROAD MAPS It is essential to have a good map when traveling in rural Iceland.

Don't be fooled into thinking all site names on some maps are active settlements. Many of these sites (Icelanders call them *Örnefni*) are landmarks or farm sites, and some have been abandoned. They may have historic significance but in general lack service stations or food stores.

RULES OF THE ROAD Traffic outside Reykjavík is generally light, but roads have only one lane going in each direction; stay within the speed limit: 90 kph (55 mph) in rural areas on the Ring Road, 70 kph (42 mph) on secondary open roads, and 30 kph–50 kph (about 20 mph–30 mph) in urban areas; the slower speed limits also apply near schools or in denser neighborhoods. Drivers are required by law to use headlights at all times. Seat belts are required for the driver and all passengers; child seats are mandatory.

CUSTOMS & DUTIES
Tourists can bring to Iceland 200 cigarettes and one of the following: 6 liters of beer; 1 liter of liquor with up to 60% alcohol; 3 liters of wine containing up to 21% alcohol; or 1 liter each of strong spirits and wine.

EMBASSIES
🚩 Canada ✉ Túngata 14, IS-101 Reykjavík ☎ 575–6500.
🚩 U.K. ✉ Laufásvegur 31, IS-108 Reykjavík ☎ 550–5100.
🚩 U.S. ✉ Laufásvegur 21, IS-101 Reykjavík ☎ 562–9100.

EMERGENCIES
Dial ☎ 112 in an emergency; it is a nationwide number.

LANGUAGE
The official language is Icelandic, a highly inflected Germanic tongue brought to the country by the early Viking settlers. Since it has only changed slightly over the centuries, modern Icelanders can read the ancient manuscripts of the sagas without difficulty. An official committee tries to keep the language pure by inventing new words for modern usage. Nouns may either be masculine, feminine, or neutral. English is widely spoken and understood; many Icelanders also speak Danish, other Scandinavian languages, or German.

The Icelandic alphabet contains two unique letters—þ, called "thorn" and pronounced like the *th* in thin, and ð, called "eth" and pronounced like the *th* in leather. The Scandinavian ligature, æ, is pronounced, as it is called in everyday Icelandic, as a long "i" as in "bike." Otherwise, the "j" is pronounced as "y" and whenever you see a vowel accented, it becomes long. All words have emphasis on the first syllable.

LODGING

Renting a summer house or cottage or staying on a farm are pleasant, economical alternatives for those seeking more independence. Icelandic Farm Holidays has a listing of places around the country. A double room on a farm with breakfast costs IKr 3,000–IKr 6,000 per night; sleeping-bag accommodations without breakfast cost IKr 2,000–IKr 2,800 per night.

Summer cottages can be rented by the week, with rates varying according to number of beds, location, and conveniences. For example, a six-bed cottage may run about IKr 30,000–IKr 45,000 during peak season. A number of cottages are available nationwide from Viator, with a minimum of three or four nights' rental. These should be booked well in advance during high season. Contact the local Tourist Information Center for other cottage options.

🖪 **Ferðafélag Íslands** ☒ Mörkin 6, IS-108 Reykjavík ☎ 568–2533 🖶 568–2535 ⊕ www.fi.is. **Icelandic Farm Holidays** ☒ Síðumúli 13, IS-108 Reykjavík ☎ 570–2700 🖶 570–2799 ⊕ www.farmholidays.is. **Viator Service Center** ☒ Njarðarbraut 11a, IS-260 Njarðvík ☎ 544–8990 ⊕ www.viator.is/index_en.php.

HOTELS Both Icelandair and Radisson SAS have affiliate hotels offering points in their frequent-flier associations. In addition to the Icelandair-operated Edda summer hotels, there are two other local hotel chains: FossHótels and KEA Hotels. In summer, hotels and even youth hostels may be fully booked, so make reservations well in advance.

🖪 **FossHótels** ☒ Borgartún 33, Reykjavík ☎ 562–4000 🖶 562–4001 ⊕ www.fosshotel. is. **Icelandair Hotels** ☒ Reykjavíkurflugvöllur, IS-101 Reykjavík ☎ 444–4000 ⊕ www. icehotels.is. **KEA Hotels** (Kea Hotels) ☒ Hafnarstræti 87–89, IS-600 Akureyri ☎ 460–2000 ⊕ www.keahotels.is.

INTERNET

Local libraries have Internet services for a small fee, and most hotels provide facilities for guests. Fees are about IKr 350 for 30 minutes. The majority of cafés in Reykjavík and Akureryi now have wireless Internet access for those with their own laptops.

MAIL & SHIPPING

Post offices in most towns are open weekdays only from 8:30 or 9 to 4:30 or 5.

POSTAL RATES Within Europe, postcards and airmail letters both need IKr 70 postage. Letter and postcard postage to the United States is IKr 90.

RECEIVING MAIL Mail to Iceland from northern Europe and Scandinavia usually takes two to three days; other services are slower. All post offices have fax machines.

MONEY MATTERS

Iceland is an expensive destination. However, some luxury items are actually cheaper than in other large international cities, especially after tax refunds.

Some sample prices are: a cup of coffee, IKr 290; imported German beer or Icelandic brew, IKr 600; can of soda, IKr 150; film, IKr 1,200 for 36 exposures; short taxi ride within Reykjavík, IKr 800.

CURRENCY The unit of currency in Iceland is the króna; plural krónur (IKr). Icelandic notes come in denominations of IKr 500, 1,000, 2,000, and

5,000. Coins are IKr 1, 5, 10, 50, and 100. In summer 2005 the rate of exchange was IKr 63 to the U.S. dollar, IKr 53 to the Canadian dollar, IKr 114 to the pound sterling, IKr to the euro, IKr 48 to the Australian dollar, IKr 44 to the New Zealand dollar, and IKr 10 to the South African rand. No limitations apply to the import and export of currency.

CURRENCY EXCHANGE   Don't bother trying to exchange currency before you depart, because Icelandic money is usually unavailable at foreign banks, and sometimes when it is, you'll get old banknotes, no longer accepted in Iceland. It is also highly unlikely that Icelandic money will be exchangeable back home, so exchange any last krónur at the departure terminal in Keflavík Airport.

TAXES

VALUE-ADDED TAX (V.A.T.)   A 24.5% *virðisaukaskattur* (value-added tax, or V.A.T.), commonly called VSK, applies to most goods and services. Usually the V.A.T. is included in a price; if not, that fact must be stated explicitly. Foreign visitors can claim a partial refund on the V.A.T., which accounts for 19.68% of the purchase price of most goods and services. Fifteen percent of the purchase price for goods is refunded, provided you buy a minimum of IKr 4,000 at one time. Souvenir stores issue tax-free forms that allow foreign visitors to collect the V.A.T. rebates directly in the duty-free store when departing from Keflavík Airport. To qualify, keep your purchases in tax-free packages (except woolens), and show them to customs officers at the departure gate along with a passport and the tax-free form. If you depart the country from somewhere other than Keflavík, have customs authorities stamp your tax-free form and then mail the stamped check within three months to **Iceland Tax-Free Shopping** (⌦ Box 1200, 235 Keflavík, Iceland). You will be reimbursed in U.S. dollars at the current exchange rate.

TELEPHONES

Iceland's telephone system is entirely digital, which, along with widespread introduction of the ITT phone–modem jack, greatly facilitates computer transmissions. The country is part of the Nordic Automatic Mobile Telephone System (NMT) and the GSM global mobile phone network. Coverage for phones with NMT capability includes all but the highest remote glacial areas of Iceland; the GSM system has expanded tremendously and nearly matches the NMT range. Iceland has one of the world's highest per-capita mobile phone distributions.

Iceland's country code is 354.

DIRECTORY & OPERATOR ASSISTANCE   Iceland has no area codes; within the country, simply dial the seven-digit number. Non-800 numbers starting with 8 often indicate cellular phones. For domestic directory assistance dial ☎ 118. Dial ☎ 115 for operator assistance with overseas calls, including directory assistance.

INTERNATIONAL CALLS   You can dial direct, starting with 00 then following with the country code and local number. An international calling card is a convenient mode of payment. Avoid charging overseas calls to your hotel bills, as the surcharge can double the cost of the call.

You can dial local access codes to reach U.S. operators AT&T and Sprint.

LOCAL CALLS Names are listed alphabetically in the telephone book by first name as a result of the patronymic system (for a last name, men add -*son* to their father's first name, women add -*dóttir*). Jobs or professions are often listed together with names and addresses.

Pay phones are usually indoors in post offices, hotels, or at transportation terminals. They accept IKr 5-, IKr 10-, or IKr 50-coins, which are placed in the slot before dialing. The dial tone is continuous. A 10-minute call between regions costs between IKr 50 and IKr 75. Card phones are becoming more common: 100-unit phone cards (IKr 500) can be purchased at all post offices and some other outlets, such as supermarkets, gas stations, and kiosks.

LONG-DISTANCE SERVICES

☎ Access Codes **AT&T** ☎ 800-9001. **Sprint** ☎ 800-9003. **World Phone** ☎ 800-9002.

TIPPING

Tipping is not conventional in Iceland and might even be frowned upon.

TOURS

Inclusive guided tours are offered by a number of travel agencies in Iceland, the largest of which are listed below. Most operators offer tours by bus; some itineraries include air travel. Many agencies also combine Icelandic vacations with Greenland tours.

For the fit and active, hiking, biking, or horseback-riding tours are also available. In these cases, accommodations will usually be in tents, guesthouses, or mountain huts. Guided hiking tours of the interior are organized by Ferðafélag Íslands (Iceland Touring Association). The Útivist Travel Association is another group with assorted tours of varying lengths. Smaller travel agencies also offer tours, some of them quite specialized. The Icelandic Tourist Board also has information on other agencies.

☎ Tour Operators **Ferðafélag Íslands** ✉ Mörkin 6, IS-108 Reykjavík ☎ 568-2533 🖨 568-2535. **Guðmundur Jónasson Travel** ✉ Borgartún 34, IS-105 Reykjavík ☎ 511-1515 🖨 511-1511 ⊕ www.gjtravel.is. **Iceland Excursions Allrahanda** ✉ Höfðatún 12, IS-105 Reykjavík ☎ 540-1313 🖨 540-1310 ⊕ www.icelandexcursions.is.

Reykjavík Excursions ✉ Vesturvör 6, IS-200 Kópavogur ⊕ www.re.is ✉ Sales desks ✉ Hótel Loftleiðir ☎ 444-4080 ✉ Nordica Hótel ☎ 444-5080 ✉ Iða Lækjargata 2A ☎ 580-5434 ✉ BSÍ bus terminal. ☎ 562-1011. **Útivis Travel Association** ✉ Laugavegur 178, IS-105 Reykjavík ☎ 562-1000 🖨 562-1001 ⊕ www.utivist.is.

TRAVEL AGENCIES

☎ Local Agencies **Iceland Travel** ✉ Lágmúli 4, IS-128 Reykjavík ☎ 585-4300 🖨 585-4390 ⊕ www.icelandtravel.is.

VISITOR INFORMATION

☎ Tourist Information **Icelandic Tourist Board** ✉ 655 3rd Ave., New York, NY 10017 ☎ 212/885-9700 🖨 212/885-9710 ⊕ www.IcelandTouristboard.com ✉ Lærkjargata 3, IS-101 Reykjavík ☎ 535-5500 🖨 535-5501 ⊕ www.icetourist.is. **Icelandic Travel Industry Association** ✉ Borgartún 35, IS 105 Reykjavík ☎ 511-8000 🖨 511-8008 ⊕ www.saf.is.

DANISH VOCABULARY

	English	Danish	Pronunciation
Basics			
	Yes/no	Ja/nej	yah/nie
	Thank you	Tak	tak
	You're welcome	Selv tak	**sell** tak
	Excuse me (to apologize)	Undskyld	**unsk**-ul
	Hello	Hej	hi
	Goodbye	Farvel	fa-**vel**
	Today	I dag	ee **day**
	Tomorrow	I morgen	ee **morn**
	Yesterday	I går	ee **gore**
	Morning	Morgen	**more**-n
	Afternoon	Eftermiddag	**ef-tah**-mid-day
	Night	Nat	nat
Numbers			
	1	en/et	een/eet
	2	to	toe
	3	tre	treh
	4	fire	fear
	5	fem	fem
	6	seks	sex
	7	syv	syoo
	8	otte	**oh**-te
	9	ni	nee
	10	ti	tee
Days of the Week			
	Monday	mandag	**man**-day
	Tuesday	tirsdag	**tears**-day
	Wednesday	onsdag	**ons**-day
	Thursday	torsdag	**trs**-day
	Friday	fredag	**free**-day
	Saturday	lørdag	**lore**-day
	Sunday	søndag	**soo**(n)-day
Useful Phrases			
	Do you speak English?	Taler du engelsk?	te-ler doo in-galsk
	I don't speak Danish.	Jeg taler ikke dansk.	yi tal-ler **ick** Dansk
	I don't understand.	Jeg forstår ikke.	yi fahr-store **ick**

I don't know.	Det ved jeg ikke.	deh **ved** yi ick
I am American/ British.	Jeg er amerikansk/britisk.	yi ehr a-mehr-i-**kansk**/bri-**tisk**
I am sick.	Jeg er syg.	yi ehr **syoo**
Please call a doctor.	Kan du ringe til en læge?	can **doo** rin-geh til en lay-eh
Do you have a vacant room?	Har du et værelse?	har **doo** eet va(l)r-sa
How much does it cost?	Hvad koster det?	va cos-ta **deh**
It's too expensive.	Det er for dyrt.	deh ehr **fohr** dyrt
Beautiful	Smukt	smukt
Help!	Hjælp	yelp
Stop!	Stop	stop
How do I get to . . .	Hvordan kommer jeg til . . .	vore-**dan** kom-mer yi til
...the train station?	banegården	**ban** eh-gore-en
...the post office?	postkontoret	**post**-kon-toh-raht
...the tourist office?	turistkontoret	too-**reest**-kon-tor-et
...the hospital?	hospitalet	hos-peet-**tal**-et
Does this bus go to . . . ?	Går denne bus til . . . ?	**goh** den-na boos til
Where is the bathroom ?	Hvor er toilettet?	vor **ehr** toi-le(tt)-et
On the left	Til venstre	til **ven**-strah
On the right	Til højre	til **hoy**-ah
Straight ahead	Lige ud	**lee** u(l)

Dining Out

Please bring me . . .	Må jeg få . . .	mo yi foh
menu	menu	me-**nu**
fork	gaffel	gaf-**fel**
knife	kniv	kan-**ew**
spoon	ske	skee
napkin	serviet	serv-**eet**
bread	brød	brood
butter	smør	smoor
milk	mælk	malk
pepper	peber	**pee**-wer
salt	salt	selt
sugar	sukker	**su**-kar

water/bottled water	vand/dansk vand	van/dansk van
The check, please.	Må jeg bede om regningen.	mo yi bi(d) om **ri**-ning

FINNISH VOCABULARY

English	Finnish	Pronunciation

Basics

Yes/no	Kyllä/ei	kue-leh/ay
Please	Olkaa hyvä	**ol**-kah **hue**-veh
Thank you very much.	Kiitoksia paljon.	**kee**-tohk-seeah **pahl**-yon
You're welcome.	Olkaa hyvä.	**ol**-kah **hue**-veh
Excuse me. (to get by someone)	Anteeksi suokaa	**ahn**-tehk-see **soo**-oh-kah
(to apologize)	Anteeksi	**ahn**-teek-see
Sorry.	Sori.	**sor**-ee
Hello	Hyvää päivää terve	**hue**-veh **paee**-veh **tehr**-veh
Hi	Hei	hay
Goodbye	Näkemiin	**neh**-keh-meen
Today	Tänään	**teh**-nehn
Tomorrow	Huomenna	**who**-oh-men-nah
Yesterday	Eilen	**ay**-len
Morning	Aamu	**ah**-moo
Afternoon	Iltapäivä	**ill**-tah-**pay**-va
Night	Yö	**ue**-uh

Numbers

1	yksi	uek-see
2	kaksi	**kahk**-see
3	kolme	**kohl**-meh
4	neljä	**nel**-yeh
5	viisi	**vee**-see
6	kuusi	**koo**-see
7	seitsemän	**sate**-seh-men
8	kahdeksan	**kah**-dek-sahn
9	yhdeksän	**ueh**-dek-sen
10	kymmenen	**kue**-meh-nen

Days of the Week

Monday	maanantai	**mah**-nahn-tie
Tuesday	tiistai	**tees**-tie

Wednesday	keskiviikko	**kes**-kee-veek-koh
Thursday	torstai	**tohrs**-tie
Friday	perjantai	**pehr**-yahn-tie
Saturday	lauantai	**lou**-ahn-tie
Sunday	sunnuntai	**soon**-noon-tie

Useful Phrases

Do you speak English?	Puhutteko englantia?	poo-hoot-teh-koh ehng-lahn-tee-ah
I don't speak Finnish.	En puhu suomea . . .	ehn **poo**-hoo **soo**-oh-may-ah
I don't understand.	En ymmärrä.	ehn **eum**-mehr-reh
I don't know.	En tiedä.	ehn **tee**-eh-deh
I am American/ British.	Minä olen amerikkalainen/ englantilainen.	**mee**-neh **oh**-len **ah**-mehr-ee-kah-lie-nehn/**ehn**-glahn-tee-lie-nehn
I am sick.	Olen sairas.	**oh**-len **sigh**-rahs
I need a doctor.	Tarvitsen lääkäri.	**tar**-vitt-sen **leh**-keh-rieh
Do you have a vacant room?	Onko teillä vapaata huonetta?	**ohn**-koh **tay**-leh **vah**-pah-tah **who**-oh-neht-tah?
How much does it cost?	Paljonko tämä maksaa?	**pahl**-yohn-koh **teh**-meh **mahk**-sah
It's too expensive.	Se on liian kallis.	**say** ohn **lee**-ahn **kahl**-lees
Beautiful	Kaunis	**kow**-nees
Help!	Auttakaa!	**ow**-tah-kah
Stop!	Seis!/Pysähtykää!	say(s) **peu**-seh-teu-keh
How do I get to . . .	Voitteko sanoa miten pääsen . . .	**voy**-teh-koh **sah**-noh-ah **mit**-ten **peh**-sen
...the train station?	asema (. . . pääsen asemalle?)	**ah**-seh-mah (**peh**-sen **ah**-say-mah-leh)
...the post office?	posti (. . . paasen-postiin?)	**pohs**-tee (**peh**-sen **pohs**teen)
...the tourist office?	matkatoimisto (. . . pääsen matkatoimistoon?)	**maht**-kah-**toy**- mees-toh (**peh**-sen **maht**-kah-**toy**-mees-tohn)
...the hospital? sairaalaan?)	sairaala (. . . pääsen **sigh**-rah-lahn)	**sigh**-rah-lah (**peh**-sen
Does this bus go to . . . ?	Kulkeeko tämä bussi-n . . . ?	**kool**-kay-koh **teh**-meh **boo**-see-n

Where is the bathroom?	Missä on W.C.?	**mihs**-seh ohn **ves**-sah
On the left	Vasemmalle	**vah**-say-mahl-leh
On the right	Oikealle	**ohy**-kay-ah-leh
Straight ahead	Suoraan eteenpäin	**soo**-oh-rahn **eh**-tayn-pa-een

Dining Out

Please bring me . . .	Tuokaa minulle . . .	too-oh-kah **mee**-me new-leh
menu	ruokalista	**roo**-oh-kah-lees-tah
fork	haarukka	**hahr**-oo-kah
knife	veitsi	**vayt**-see
spoon	lusikka	**loo**-see-kah
napkin	lautasliina	**lou**-tahs-lee-nah
bread	leipä	**lay**-pa
butter	voi	**voh**(ee)
milk	maito	**my**-toh
pepper	pippuri	**peep**-poor-ee
salt	suola	**soo**-oh-lah
sugar	sokeri	**soh**-ker-ee
water/bottled water	vesi/ kivennäisvesi	**veh**-see/**kee**-ven-eyes-veh-see
mineral water	Vichy	**vis**-soo
The check, please.	Lasku, olkaa hyvä/ Haluan maksaa.	**lahs**-kew, **ohl**-kah **heu**-va/**hah**-lu-ahn **mahk**-sah

ICELANDIC VOCABULARY

English	Icelandic	Pronunciation

Basics

Yes/no	Já/nei	yow/nay
Thank you very much.	Kærar Þakkir takk.	**kie**-rahr **thah**-kihr **ta**hkk
You're welcome.	Ekkert að-Þakka	**ehk**-kehrt **thah**-ka ath.
Excuse me. (to get by someone)	Afsakið	**ahf**-sah-kith(e)
(to apologize)	Fyrirgefið	**feer**-ee-geh-vith(e)
Hello	Góðan dag	goh-than **dahgh**
Goodbye	Bless	bless

Today	Í dag	ee **dahgh**
Tomorrow	Á morgun	ow **mohr**-gun
Yesterday	Í gær	ee **gah-eer**
Morning	Morgun	**mohr**-gun
Afternoon	Eftirmidagur	**ehf**-teer-mihth-dahg-ur
Night	Nótt	noht

Numbers

1	einn	ehnn
2	tveir	**tveh**-eer
3	Þrír	threer
4	fjórir	**fyohr**-eer
5	fimm	fehm
6	sex	sex
7	sjö	sy-uh
8	átta	**owt**-tah
9	níu	**nee**-uh
10	tíu	**tee**-uh

Days of the Week

Monday	mánudagur	**mown**-ah-dah-gur
Tuesday	Þriðjudagur	**thrithe**-yoo-dah-gur
Wednesday	miðvikudagur	**meethe**-veek-uh dah-gur
Thursday	fimmtudagur	**feem**-too-dah-gur
Friday	föstudagur	**fuhs**-too-dah-gur
Saturday	laugardagur	**loy**-gahr-dah-gur
Sunday	sunnudagur	**soon**-noo-dah-gur

Useful Phrases

Do you speak English?	Talar Þú ensku?	tah-lahr thoo ehn-skoo
I don't speak Icelandic.	Ég tala ekki. islensku	**yeh** tah-lah **ehk**-keh **ees**-lehn-skoo
I don't understand.	Ég skil ekki.	yeh **skeel ehk**-keh
I don't know.	Ég veit ekki.	yeh **vayt ehk**-keh
I am American/ British.	Ég er ameriskur/ breskur.	yeh ehr **ah**-mehre eskur/brehs-koor
I am sick.	Ég er veik(ur).	yeh ehr vehk(oor)
Please call a doctor.	Viltu hringja í lækni, takk.	veel-too **hreeng**-yah ee **lahk**-nee **tah**-kk
Do you have a vacant room?	Átt þú laust herbergi?	owt thoo laysht **hehr**-behr-ghee

How much does it cost?	Hvað kostar Það?	kvathe kohs-tahr thathe
It's too expensive.	Þuð er of dy´rt	thahthe ehr ohf deert
Beautiful	Fallegur/t	**fahl**-lehg-oor
Help!	Hjálp	hyalp
Stop!	Stopp	stohp
How do I get to . . .	Hvernig kemst ég . . .	**kvehr**-neeg kehmst **yehg**
...the post office?	á pósthúsið?	ow pohst-hoos-ihthe
...the tourist office?	á feramálará?	ow **fehr**-tha-mow-lahr-owthe
...the hospital?	á spitalan?	ow **spee**-tah-lahn
Does this bus go to . . . ?	Fer Þessi vagn . . . ?	fehr **thehs**-see**vakn**
Where is the bathroom?	Hvar er salerni?	kvahr ehr sahl-ehr-nihthe
On the left	Til vinstri	teel **veen**-stree
On the right	Til hægri	teel **hie**-ree
Straight ahead	Beint áfram	baynt **ow**-frahm

Dining Out

Please bring me . . .	Get ég fengið . . .	geht yehg fehn-gihthe
menu	matseðil	**maht**-seh-theel
fork	gaffal	**gah**-fahl(t)
knife	hnif	hneef
spoon	skeið	skaythe
napkin	servetta	sehr-**veht**-tah
bread	brauð	braythe
butter	smjör	smyoor
milk	mjólk	myoolk
pepper	pipar	**pay**-pahr
salt	salt	sahlt
sugar	sykur	**say**-koor
water/bottled water	vatn/bergvatn	vahtn/**behrg**-vahtn
The check, please.	takk reikninginn	takk **rehk**-nihn-ghihn

NORWEGIAN VOCABULARY

English	Norwegian	Pronunciation

Basics

English	Norwegian	Pronunciation
Yes/no	Ja/nei	yah/nay
Please	Vær så snill	**vehr** soh snihl
Thank you very much.	Tusen takk.	**tews**-sehn tahk
You're welcome.	Vær så god.	**vehr** soh goo
Excuse me.	Unnskyld.	**ewn**-shewl
Hello	God dag	goo **dahg**
Goodbye	Ha det	**ha** day
Today	I dag	ee **dahg**
Tomorrow	I morgen	ee **moh**-ern
Yesterday	I går	ee **gohr**
Morning	Morgen	**moh**-ern
Afternoon	Ettermiddag	**eh-terr**-mid-dahg
Night	Natt	naht

Numbers

1	en	ehn
2	to	too
3	tre	treh
4	fire	**feer**-eh
5	fem	fehm
6	seks	sehks
7	syv, sju	shew
8	åtte	**oh**-teh
9	ni	nee
10	ti	tee

Days of the Week

Monday	mandag	**mahn**-dahg
Tuesday	tirsdag	**teesh**-dahg
Wednesday	onsdag	**oonss**-dahg
Thursday	torsdag	**tohsh**-dahg
Friday	fredag	**fray**-dahg
Saturday	lørdag	**loor**-dahg
Sunday	søndag	**suhn**-dahg

Useful Phrases

Do you speak English?	Snakker De engelsk?	snahk-kerr dee ehng-ehlsk

I don't speak Norwegian.	Jeg snakker ikke norsk.	yay **snahk**-kerr **ik**-keh nohrshk
I don't understand.	Jeg forstår ikke.	yay fosh-**tawr ik**-keh
I don't know.	Jeg vet ikke.	yay veht **ik**-keh
I am American/ British.	Jeg er amerikansk/ engelsk.	yay ehr ah-mehr-ee-kahnsk/ehng-ehlsk
I am sick.	Jeg er dårlig.	yay ehr **dohr**-lee
Please call a doctor.	Vær så snill og ring etter en lege.	vehr soh snihl oh ring **eht**-ehrehn **lay**-geh
Do you have a vacant room?	Har du et rom som er ledig?	yay vil **yehr**-neh hah eht room
How much does it cost?	Hva koster det?	vah **koss**-terr deh
It's too expensive.	Det er for dyrt.	deh ehr for **deert**
Beautiful	Vakker	**vah**-kehr
Help!	Hjelp!	yehlp
Stop!	Stopp!	stop
How do I get to . . .	Hvor er . . .	voor ehr
...the train station?	jernbanestasjonen	yehrn-bahn-eh sta-**shoon**-ern
...the post office?	posthuset	**pohsst**-hewss
...the tourist office?	turistkontoret	tew-**reest**-koon-t oor-er
...the hospital?	sykehuset	**see**-keh-hoo-seh
Does this bus go to . . . ?	Går denne bussen til . . . ?	gohr **den**-nah boos teel
Where is the bathroom?	Hvor er toalettene?	voor ehr too-ah-**leht**-te-ne
On the left	Til venstre	teel **vehn**-streh
On the right	Til høyre	teel **hooy**-reh
Straight ahead	Rett fram	reht **frahm**

Dining Out

menu	meny	meh-new
fork	gaffel	gahff-erl
knife	kniv	kneev
spoon	skje	shay
napkin	serviett	ssehr-vyeht
bread	brød	brur
butter	smør	smurr
milk	melk	mehlk

pepper	pepper	pehp-per
salt	salt	sahlt
sugar	sukker	sook-kerr
water	vann	vahn
The check, please.	Jeg vil gjerne betale.	yay vil **yehr**-neh beh-**tah**-leh

SWEDISH VOCABULARY

English	Swedish	Pronunciation

Basics

Yes/no	Ja/nej	yah/nay
Please	Var snäll; vahr vehn-leeg	vahr snehll; Var vänlig
Thank you very much.	Tack så mycket.	tahk soh **mee**-keh
You're welcome.	Var så god.	vahr shoh **goo**
Excuse me. (to get by someone)	Ursäkta.	oor-**shehk**-tah
(to apologize)	Förlåt.	fur-**loht**
Hello	God dag	goo **dahg**
Goodbye	Hej dä	ah-**yoo**
Today	I dag	ee **dahg**
Tomorrow	I morgon	ee **mor**-ron
Yesterday	I går	ee **gohr**
Morning	Morgon	**mohr**-on
Afternoon	Eftermiddag	**ehf**-ter-meed-dahg
Night	Natt	naht

Numbers

1	ett	eht
2	två	tvoh
3	tre	tree
4	fyra	fee-rah
5	fem	fem
6	sex	sex
7	sju	shoo
8	åtta	oht-tah
9	nio	nee-ah
10	tio	tee-ah

Days of the Week

Monday	måndag	**mohn**-dahg
Tuesday	tisdag	**tees**-dahg

Wednesday	onsdag	**ohns**-dahg
Thursday	torsdag	**tohrs**-dahg
Friday	fredag	**freh**-dahg
Saturday	lördag	**luhr**-dahg
Sunday	söndag	**suhn**-dahg

Useful Phrases

Do you speak English?	Talar du engelska?	tah-lahr doo ehng-ehl-skah
I don't speak Swedish.	Jag talar inte svenska.	yah tah-lahr een-teh **sven**-skah
I don't understand.	Jag förstår inte.	yah fuhr-**stohr** een-teh
I don't know.	Jag vet inte.	yah **veht** een-teh
I am American/ British.	Jag är amerikan/ engelsman.	yah air ah-mehr-ee-**kahn ehng**-ehls-mahn
I am sick.	Jag är sjuk.	yah air **shyook**
Please call a doctor.	Jag vill skicka efter en läkare.	yah veel **shee**-kah **ehf**-tehr ehn **lay**-kah-reh
Do you have a vacant room?	Har Ni något rum ledigt?	hahr nee noh-goht **room leh**-deekt
How much does it cost?	Vad kostar det?/ Hur mycketdeh kostar det?	vah **kohs**-tahr/hor **mee**-keh **kohs**-tahr deh
It's too expensive.	Den är för dyr.	dehn ay foor **deer**
Beautiful	Vacker	**vah**-kehr
Help!	Hjälp	yehlp
Stop!	Stopp!/Stanna!	stop, **stahn**-nah
How do I get to . . .	Kan Ni visa mig vägen till	kahn nee **vee**-sah may**vay**-gehn teel
...the train station?	stationen	stah-**shoh**-nehn
...the post office?	posten	**pohs**-tehn
...the tourist office?	en resebyrå	ehn-**reh**-seh-**bee**-roh
...the hospital?	sjukhuset	**shyook**-hoo-seht
Does this bus go to . . . ?	Går den bussen här till . . . ?	gohr dehn **boo**-sehn hehr teel
Where is the bathroom?	Var är toalett?/ toaletten?	vahr ay twah-**leht** twah-**leht**-en
On the left	Till vänster	teel **vehn**-stur
On the right	Till höger	teel **huh**-gur
Straight ahead	Rakt fram	rahkt **frahm**

Dining Out

Please bring me . . .	Var snäll och hämta åt mig . . .	vahr snehl oh hehm-tah oht may
menu	matsedeln	maht-seh-dehln
fork	en gaffel	ehn gahf-fehl
knife	en kniv	ehn kneev
spoon	en sked	ehn shehd
napkin	en servett	ehn sehr-veht
bread	bröd	bruh(d)
butter	smör	smuhr
milk	mjölk	myoolk
pepper	peppar	pehp-pahr
salt	salt	sahlt
sugar	socker	soh-kehr
water	vatten	vaht-n
The check, please.	Får jag be om notan.	fohr yah beh ohm **noh**-tahn

INDEX

NOTES

NOTES

ABOUT OUR WRITERS

British journalist **Rob Hincks** primarily writes and edits for food and travel magazines in Sweden and England. Rob has lived in Stockholm since 2000, but through his Swedish wife, Mikaela, his associations with the country go back much farther. Since the birth of his two daughters, Annie and Jessie, Rob has focused his energies on getting to know Sweden even better, in an effort to impress his girls when homework time comes around.

Growing up in the north of Sweden, **Karin Palmquist** used to dread summer vacations when her parents would pack the camper with kids and pets and slowly make their way down to her grandparent's house in the south, stopping at every church and archeological site on the way. Yet, somehow, those road trips awoke in her a lifelong love for travel. Now a freelance writer for newspapers including the *Washington Times* and *Washington Post,* Karin roams the globe for six months a year. She spends the rest of her time in Washington, D.C., her adopted home.

Australian **Daniel Cash** has lived in Oslo since 2001. He resides with his family in a former wheat silo converted into a modern apartment building with a view of the city. Daniel has contributed to previous editions of *Fodor's Norway* and *Fodor's Australia,* and during another stint in Oslo in 1998 he was co-editor of *TradeWinds,* the Norwegian shipping newspaper. Besides writing and editing, he runs a company to recruit Norwegian students to Australian universities. Daniel says that the best thing about living in Oslo is the variety of activities available due to the dramatic change in seasons. "In late summer you can swim in a beautiful lake, just 10 minutes' drive from Oslo's center, and only four months later skate or ski on top of the same lake. On the other hand, the most difficult thing about living in Nor-way for an Australian is the expensive beer prices."

Norman Renouf was born in London and educated at Charlton Secondary School, Greenwich. Always interested in travel, he started writing travel guides, articles, and newspaper contributions in the early 1990s and has covered destinations throughout Europe. Norman updated the Smart Travel Tips chapter for this edition of *Fodor's Scandinavia.* Now living in Richmond, Virginia, he has also written several guides about Washington, D.C., and the mid-Atlantic region.

In the 12 years since he finished his political science degree at the University of Bergen, **Lars Ursin** has worked as a freelance journalist and translator. He has traveled extensively in Norway, partly for his journalistic assignments, but mainly to satisfy his addiction to everything mountain related, especially hiking, skiing, and snowboarding. Lars updated the Bergen and West Coast sections of the Norway chapter.

Canadian journalist **Eliza Reid** spent her first visit to Iceland nestled in a cozy summerhouse on the Snæfellsnes peninsula. She visited the country on many more occasions before making it her home in 2003. She currently lives in Reykjavík with her Icelandic husband. Eliza is a regular contributor to numerous English-language publications in Iceland.

Canadian writer **Bruce Bishop,** who was born and raised in Nova Scotia, is still awed that his home province is bigger geographically than the whole country of Denmark. His love affair with Denmark began as an impressionable 18-year-old in the late '70s, when he visited a Danish school buddy. Bruce has been a freelance travel writer since 1994 and a frequent contributor to Fodor's since 1998. He is former president of the Travel Media Association of Canada and an award-winning journalist and author. Among his many projects, he currently serves as the travel editor for *The European Reporter,* a bi-weekly tabloid from Toronto, and a media relations consultant for his company, Global Travel Communicators.

Nima Adl, a native New Jerseyan, can often be seen jetlagged from the many miles he travels in his waking hours, and the many more he travels in his dreams. His essay on Christiania, an anarchist commune in Copenhagen, was based on the former.